# The Personal Memoirs of
# Ulysses S. Grant

## THE COMPLETE ANNOTATED EDITION

## ULYSSES S. GRANT

*The Bultema-Williams Collection, Ulysses S. Grant Presidential Library,*
*Mississippi State Libraries*

# The Personal Memoirs of
# Ulysses S. Grant

## THE COMPLETE ANNOTATED EDITION

EDITED BY John F. Marszalek

WITH David S. Nolen & Louie P. Gallo

THE BELKNAP PRESS OF
HARVARD UNIVERSITY PRESS
*Cambridge, Massachusetts*
*London, England*
*2017*

First Printing

BOOK DESIGN BY ANNAMARIE MCMAHON WHY

*Library of Congress Cataloging-in-Publication Data*
Names: Grant, Ulysses S. (Ulysses Simpson), 1822–1885, author. | Marszalek, John F., editor. |
Nolen, David S., editor. | Gallo, Louie P., editor.
Title: The personal memoirs of Ulysses S. Grant : the complete annotated edition /
edited by John F. Marszalek with David S. Nolen and Louie P. Gallo.
Description: Cambridge, Massachusetts : The Belknap Press of Harvard University Press, 2017.
Identifiers: LCCN 2017012584 | ISBN 9780674976290 (hardcover : alk. paper)
Subjects: LCSH: Grant, Ulysses S. (Ulysses Simpson), 1822–1885. | Generals—United States—
Biography. | Presidents—United States—Biography. | United States. Army—Biography. |
United States—History—Civil War, 1861–1865—Campaigns. | United States—History—
Civil War, 1861–1865—Personal narratives. | Mexican War, 1846–1848—Personal narratives.
Classification: LCC E672 .A3 2017 | DDC 973.8/2092 [B]—dc23
LC record available at https://lccn.loc.gov/2017012584

In Memory of

MICHAEL B. BALLARD

# Contents

# *Preface*

Ulysses S. Grant discovered his uniqueness while serving a nation at war with itself. He told that story in his *Personal Memoirs,* composed during his final race against death in the mid-1880s. Rather than the *Memoirs* being a Greek tragedy, however, it is an American epic poem, the tale of a soldier-spouse-father who became a democratic leader and died as a citizen of the world. It was through Ulysses S. Grant that the rest of the world came to see the meaning of the new American hero.

Working side by side with Abraham Lincoln, his commander in chief, the "hero of Appomattox" saved the Union. He did not emulate the aristocratic veneer of George Washington, but instead fought in tandem with his civilian frontier president. They were two of a kind—poetic leaders and warrior writers. Like Lincoln, Grant was the no-nonsense American who could naturally separate fact from fiction, whether aiming weapons or words.

The critic and author Edmund Wilson referred to Grant's *Memoirs* as "a unique expression of the national character. . . . Perhaps never has a book so objective in form seemed so personal in every line. . . . Somehow, despite its sobriety, it communicates the spirit of the battles themselves and makes it possible to understand how Grant won them." And Grant's fellow warrior and friend William T. Sherman wrote about the *Memoirs:* "Other books of the war will be forgotten, mislaid, dismissed. Millions will read Grant's *Memoirs* and remember them."

The Ulysses S. Grant Association began in 1962 to publish thirty-two volumes of *The Papers of Ulysses S. Grant*—with all the volumes now in print, digitized, and available at www.usgrantlibrary.org. What began under the leadership of John Y. Simon and Ralph G. Newman continues under the new leadership of John F. Marszalek and Frank J. Williams. In 2012, the Ulysses S. Grant Association created the Ulysses S. Grant Presidential Library at Mississippi State University, which, in 2017, will move to a state-of-the-art facility in the Mitchell Memorial Library.

Based on this history, the Association feels an obligation to provide readers with a definitive annotated edition of Grant's *Memoirs* to renew, as it has in the past, his unique democratic legacy to our country and its unique place in the world.

We are indebted to Harvard University Press for working with us to keep this literary gem in print and understandable to both a modern reading public and the scholarly community. The Association owes, too, deep gratitude and appreciation to Mississippi State University, Interim Presidents Vance Watson and Roy Ruby and President Mark Keenum, and Mississippi State University Libraries dean Frances Coleman for welcoming us into their university home.

FRANK J. WILLIAMS, PRESIDENT, Ulysses S. Grant Association

# *Introduction*

Prior to 1885, Ulysses S. Grant was a complete unknown as a writer. It is true that he wrote exceedingly clear orders while leading the U.S. Army to victory in the Civil War, but few Americans were aware of this talent. To most people, he was a hard-driving general but one of few words, known more for his silence than for any ability with oral or written prose. Writing was the last thing anyone could imagine him doing.

Yet, after his presidency, more than a few publishers approached him about giving the public insight into his life and career. They did so not because they thought he had any particular writing skills but because they thought the public, already captivated with him, would eagerly purchase whatever he put down on paper. When *Century Magazine* editors Richard W. Gilder, Robert U. Johnson, and Roswell Smith approached him about participating in their Civil War series, he showed no interest. Similarly, when Samuel Clemens, better known as the irrepressible Mark Twain, wanted him to write his remembrances for publication, he once again said no. He insisted that he could not write, and any resultant book would simply not sell. Besides, he said repeatedly: "It's all in Badeau," referring to the three-volume book about his role in the Civil War that he had helped an aide, Adam Badeau, write.

Grant hated public speaking and, when forced to get up before a crowd or even a small group, he grew nervous and quietly stammered, his eyes cast down. Consequently, the art of writing, which contemporaries tied so closely to oratory, seemed beyond Grant's reach. Besides, he had no financial reason to take on such an onerous task; he was busy with a variety of other pastimes. He was constantly in demand to attend veterans' reunions, political meetings, family weddings, and public and private gatherings of all sorts. In 1881, he became president of the Mexican Southern Railroad Company, meant to tie Mexico to the United States and thus open a variety of economic possibilities for both nations. But it failed.

On Christmas Eve 1883, the sixty-one-year-old Grant had further bad luck. He returned home from a holiday gathering, got out of his horse-drawn coach, and began walking into his home at 3 East 66th Street in New York City. He was practically inside the door when he realized that he should give the driver a Christmas gift. He walked back down the stairs, gave the coachman some money, and suddenly slipped on the icy pavement, landing hard on his left leg. His injury was so severe that he never got over it. For the remaining two years of his life, he had to limp along with a cane.

Undeterred, Grant became interested in another endeavor, a Wall Street venture that promised untold riches to all investors. Grant's son Buck and Ferdinand Ward, the latter widely reputed to be the most successful wheeler-dealer on Wall Street, were partners in an investment business. Ward and the young Grant encouraged the former president to join them and tie the prestige of his name to the company. The firm of Grant and Ward was born. Grant invested his money and that of many others in his family, and the interest and dividends began to pour in. Grant saw himself becoming a millionaire, accumulating financial security equal to his wealthy friends. It seemed too good to be true.

It was. Ward was no financial wizard; he was a cheating scoundrel, operating what later would be known as a "Ponzi scheme." The money he paid out in purported dividends to Grant and others was actually money he was receiving from new investors. Grant did not realize what was happening; all he did was sign documents placed before him when he visited the Grant and Ward offices.

On May 4, 1884, the financial enterprise collapsed. Ward came to Grant and said that the bank he was using in his transactions was experiencing difficulties. He asked the former president to let him have $150,000 for a few days to tide the bank over. It was all just a technicality, Ward assured Grant. Unsuspecting, Grant immediately paid a visit to an old millionaire friend, William H. Vanderbilt, president of the New York Central Railroad Company, and asked for and received a check for the amount he requested. He handed over the bank draft to Ward, but, on May 6, Grant came to realize that the bank and the firm were bankrupt—and so was he. The only money he and his wife Julia had was in his pocket and in her purse, and it was not much.

Grant was shocked and embarrassed. On May 7, he went to Vanderbilt expressing his willingness to sell all the assets that he and Julia possessed to pay off the loan. He even gave Vanderbilt the many gifts and trophies that he had received during his career and world tour. Vanderbilt later excused the entire loan and donated all the collateral artifacts to the Smithsonian Institution.

Meanwhile, Grant had to look for other sources of income. In June 1884, the editors of *Century Magazine* approached him again to ask him to contribute articles to their Civil War series. He was still hesitant about his ability to write but consented to take on the task. He needed the money, and $500 an article for four articles was just too good to refuse. He agreed to write about Shiloh, Vicksburg, the Wilderness, and Appomattox. Ultimately, he wrote about Chattanooga instead of Appomattox.

The first article he sent to *Century* seemed to corroborate his insistence that he could not write. The magazine's editors were shocked at how bad the submitted article was. It read like a battle report; it was stiff and dull. Robert U. Johnson hesitatingly brought it back to Grant and suggested, as carefully as he could, that Grant retell the story of Shiloh but, this time, do so in a conversational tone, as if he were talking to friends. Grant took the carefully phrased criticism well and revised the manuscript. He improved it immensely and, even more importantly, came to realize that he enjoyed the process of writing.

But it was not to be that simple. On June 2, 1884, as if his injured leg and his bankruptcy were not enough, Grant found that he had a more formidable enemy. He was eating lunch with his family, two weeks before the *Century* editor Johnson's visit to his summer home at Long Branch, New Jersey, when he bit into a peach. He bolted straight up and said he thought something on the peach, perhaps a bee, had stung him in the back of his mouth.

Water only made his throat feel like it was on fire, so when the pain persisted for days, Julia wanted him to see a doctor. He refused. A doctor came to visit a friend next door, and when he looked at Grant's throat, he immediately advised him to see his family physician. Grant ignored that advice too. He did not return to New York until the fall, but his family doctor was traveling in Europe at the time. Finally at the end of October, about four months after the peach incident, he and his longtime doctor met, and the doctor quickly sent him to a leading throat specialist, Dr. John Hancock Douglas.

Dr. Douglas had been a leader in the Civil War's United States Sanitary Commission and had known Grant during the conflict. He looked carefully in his former general's mouth. When he finally finished, Grant inquired: "Is it cancer?" Grant had made his own diagnosis, and it was correct. He had what modern doctors call carcinoma of the right tonsillar pillar. The only treatment for such a cancer in the nineteenth century was to gargle with a mixture of permanganate, potash, and brewer's yeast or to apply codeine, morphine, brandy, or a cocaine solution. Such treatment, however, only eased the pain temporarily.

While suffering from an increasingly serious throat cancer at least four months old, he had several teeth extracted because doctors worried that these diseased molars were causing the mouth problem. As he had to deal simultaneously with his cancer, his left leg injured the previous Christmas, neuralgia for which he had to wear a skull cap, his long-recurring migraine headaches, and a bankruptcy of major proportion, Ulysses S. Grant began to seriously consider doing what he said he would never do: write his memoirs. He needed the money.

At first, he labored on the articles he had promised to *Century,* but he also began composing his memoirs. The *Century* editors had not only urged him to write such a remembrance, but they had also prepared a contract for his signature. He seemed ready to sign. On the very day that he saw Dr. Douglas for his throat pain, he visited the Century Company offices in New York and, for all intents and purposes, indicated that he wanted to publish the book with that company.

Samuel Clemens had been watching all of these developments from a distance. He knew that Grant was writing the articles for publication and that he was willing to write his memoirs, too. Shockingly to him, the Century Company was going to publish both. Clemens hurried to Grant's home. He wanted to learn: Was Grant really going to publish with Century?

He confronted Grant, whom he knew and enjoyed smoking cigars with. He was appalled when he read the contract Century had given the ailing general. It was an insult, he said. Century was offering Grant only 10 percent royalty, the same amount they would routinely offer any new writer who might sell a few thousand copies. Clemens was convinced that Grant's memoirs would sell several hundred thousand copies, so the size of his royalty should be correspondingly higher. Clemens said that his publishing firm, Charles L. Webster and Company, would do much better than Century, if only Grant would let him do the publishing.

The Century Company still thought that they had the inside track because of Grant's apparent steadfastness in wanting them to publish the memoirs. Clemens and Webster kept the pressure on the Old Hero, however, and finally, on February 27, 1885, Grant decided that he would publish with Clemens. When the author-publisher asked Grant whether he wished to be compensated 20 percent of sales or 70 percent of the profit, Grant chose the latter. He wanted to share the risk with Clemens.

Grant's writing of his memoirs proved to be a heroic venture. It was a difficult task in itself, but the increasing growth of the cancer at the rear of his mouth put horrific pressure on his already ravaged body. When Sigmund Freud later suffered from a similar cancer in the twentieth century, then called squamous cell carcinoma of the palate, he bore the pain and suffering as long as he could, over sixteen years, but then, in 1939, he had his doctor euthanize him. Grant would not allow any such treatment. No matter the pain, he had to stay alive and complete his writing in order to leave Julia and the family with the financial means to continue their lives.

To achieve what became his obsession, he maintained a disciplined regimen. Most of the text was written in his New York City home, in the library lit by one window and warmed by a single fireplace. Here he sat at his desk or in his chair, his cane nearby, and a pencil racing across the paper. While he was still able to speak, he dictated to a clerk. He also had many helpers around him: son Fred and sometimes sons Buck and Jesse, his longtime military aide Adam Badeau, and his African American servant Harrison Terrell.

His doctors were also frequently present. At first, he broke into his writing time to visit Dr. Douglas twice a day for treatment of his painful mouth. Julia was never far away, and daughters-in-law and grandchildren came to his room when they could, much to his delight. Meanwhile, homes on his street became filled with newspaper reporters filing updates on his condition. Even four-year-old Ulysses S. Grant III was accosted by these newsmen, when he stepped outside the house, for information about his grandfather.

No matter any disruption, Grant spent five to seven hours every day writing. His helpers checked facts, even though his sharp memory recalled information with amazing precision. Clemens's and Grant's helpers did none of the writing; it was all Grant. He utilized his *Century* articles and made but few alterations in them. Despite his painful illness, he kept writing and making progress on his book. Death was always hovering nearby, but he had to finish his memoirs before death conquered him.

Several times he came close to dying from overwhelming coughing and gagging caused by his cancer, and, as time passed, he grew increasingly sicker. His work became his respite, however; his determination to finish his memoirs overrode the horrible physical pain. On June 16, 1885, as the weather grew hot and humid, he was moved to a friend's summer home atop Mount McGregor, near Saratoga, New York. The hope was that the cooler weather there might make his life more bearable. Here, however, he could find little peace and quiet because complete strangers frequently gawked at him or approached when he tried to sit on the cottage porch.

But he kept writing, and by July 20, 1885, he laid down his pencil for the last time. Soon after that, he asked to be put to bed, so one was moved into the main room on the first floor of the cottage. He lay there in pain suffering stoically but resigned to his fate now that his book was finished. During his last night of life, thunder and lightning rattled the area. Surrounded by Julia, his children, some of his grandchildren, and his doctors, he died peacefully at

8:08 A.M. on July 23, 1885. Unlike the alleged last words of so many nineteenth-century Victorians, his were hardly memorable. He said simply, "I am thirsty," and then died. Sadly, although no one knew it at the time, better medical treatment might have saved his life.

Considering his many years of oratorical deficiencies, it made sense to believe that Grant's writing style would also be weak. Yet just the opposite was the case. During the Civil War, he had been a master military writer when he sent orders to his subordinates. There was no one who received a message from him who did not understand precisely what Grant wanted him to know and to do. When he wrote letters to his wife, family, and political and personal acquaintances, the prose was again clear. He avoided ornate structure and, instead, wrote in a simple, direct way, presenting to the reader an immediacy that was clarifying. Sometimes he lapsed into parenthetical phrases, but, most of the time, his sentences possessed simplicity and thus clarity.

Grant also had the ability to use words accurately and forcefully, sometimes picturesquely, usually mixing the style of the average American of his time with military connotations well known to the post–Civil War populace. When he lapsed into the passive voice or some other problematic prose, the power of his words still pushed the narrative forward.

What made the *Personal Memoirs of U. S. Grant* particularly appealing to readers was Grant's humility about himself and his infrequent criticism of others. He wrote nothing about the rumors concerning his alleged drunkenness, the difficulties of his life as a citizen just before the start of the Civil War, his relationship with his abolitionist father and slaveholding father-in-law, and his wartime expulsion of the Jews from his then Civil War military district. His *Memoirs* did not deal with his eight years as president and his personal bankruptcy. He did not even write about his world tour, a time in his life of significance and enjoyment. He only briefly mentioned his life in Ohio up to his time at West Point, but he did discuss the Mexican-American War. Most of all, he wrote about his role in the Civil War.

It could be argued that, in this way, Grant was able to talk about successes and ignore failures. In fact, he was giving his audience just what it was most interested in: the story of his successful activities in preserving the Union. He and his publisher, Samuel Clemens, realized the incredible interest in the *Century* "Battles and Leaders" Civil War series and saw clearly that interest in the reminiscences of Grant, the leading figure of that war, would only be greater.

The manufacture of the *Memoirs* was carefully done to be physically attractive, distinctive, and readily available. The *Christian Union* of May 12, 1887, indicated that, in order to manufacture over 300,000 sets of the Grant *Memoirs* (each containing two volumes), it required some 44,400 square yards of cloth, or over 25 miles of 1-yard-wide fabric. It took 276 barrels (69,000 pounds) of glue, 300,000 reams of paper weighing 1,800,000 tons, and 41 steam presses operated by 1,000 men, day and night, to produce the book. And this was just the basic edition; the deluxe leather edition required even more.

All the effort and all the material would be for naught if the public did not buy the book. In the years after the Civil War, books, like so many other products, were often sold by itinerant peddlers or traveling salesmen. In the towns and especially in the countryside, these men or, in a few instances, women, went door to door selling a variety of products that they convinced the town dweller and the farmer and their wives they could not live without. This form of selling was popular after the Civil War and into the 1890s, eventually being replaced by the Sears and Roebuck catalog, first published in 1893.

There were numerous success stories told about the agents' sale of their variety of products, but their selling of the Grant *Memoirs* is no doubt the most spectacular story of them all. Some ten thousand salesmen, often organized by supervising agents, took to the roads across the nation. Many were Union Army veterans, and they did their selling in uniform. They carried with them a sales manual of thirty-seven pages of small print, instructing them forcefully how to be successful. The advice in this *How to Introduce the Personal Memoirs of U. S. Grant* was nonflinching, definitive, and insistent. It warned salesmen that, despite the great desire of the nation to buy the memoirs, the job required hard work on their part. On the first page, the manual encapsulated all such advice into a short paragraph:

> We believe the intelligent agent will so thoroughly prepare himself before starting out on his mission that he shall not only be fortified to meet and overcome every argument and objection that will be raised against the work, but by his glowing description of its contents he will interest the people, create a desire, and make sales even where they were previously opposed to the book.

The rest of the manual was just as specific in all of its instructions. The text told the salesman the proper way to introduce himself and how to clinch an order by countering negative arguments. Then, in order to drive home the detailed argument, the manual included a section entitled "Aids and Arguments," followed by a similar section entitled "Hints and Helps." For example, the brief paragraph "Can't Subscribe for Anything To-day" states simply but forcefully: "This declaration should not bluff you in the least, for those who say so are very likely to subscribe, if the salesman does his duty."

And many salesmen did just that. They sold over 300,000 sets of the *Memoirs* at a cost of $7 a set for the standard cloth edition and $25 for the leather version. They made these sales at a time when the average carpenter made only $2.57 a day for a 6-day, 60-hour week. In February 1886, Charles L. Webster, the head of Samuel Clemens's publishing company, sent Julia, the deceased author's wife, the largest royalty check then ever written—$200,000. In all, Julia Grant received $420,000 to $450,000. In 2017 dollars this translates to over $11,000,000.

Such success was accomplished despite the fact that, as a letter to the editor of the *Chicago Tribune* in August 1885 warned, "unscrupulous agents" were tricking people into purchasing fake memoirs under such names as *The Personal History of U. S. Grant, The Life and History of U. S. Grant,* and *The Life and Times of U. S. Grant.* How many of these fake books were sold is unknown, but imposter agents were certainly hawking them. Charles L. Webster and Company, the publishing company, R. S. Peale and Company, the distributor, and Grant, before his death, were so concerned about these fraudulent editions that they wrote letters to newspapers warning the public of the scam. Peale and Company said their only concern was to "protect a mourning widow," and they wanted all newspaper editors to "aid in exposing a rascally attempt to rob Mrs. U. S. Grant."

The press was certainly willing to talk about the *Memoirs.* The major newspapers covered the publication, of course, but, more significantly, so did the smaller ones. For example, the Biddeford (Maine) *Journal* wrote: "No review of this remarkable work can do it justice; the book is its own review." The *Miami Helmet* of Piqua, Ohio, said the book was "not only for the present generation but for future generations" too. The Mobile *Register,* a southern newspaper, did not let its sectionalism distort its view and called the *Memoirs* "really and morally great."

The *Southern Historical Society Papers,* the organ of the South's Lost Cause, was not as kind. An article published there showed its pro-Confederate bias and called the memoirs "a book full of blunders and flat contradictions . . . utterly unreliable and untrustworthy." The *Spectator* of London was more even-handed, but it still curbed its enthusiasm. The *Memoirs'* "view is great," it said, "but it ought not to be exaggerated." The *British Quarterly Review* marveled at how Grant "held off the King of Terror until the last chapter was complete." The *Chatauquan* praised "its manly, straightforward, very modest style," while the *Unitarian Review and Religious Magazine* compared the book to the writings of nineteenth-century favorite Sir Walter Scott. "Grant's success, materially, and intellectually . . . was much greater than Scott's," the publication insisted.

From the time that the *Memoirs* were first published in 1885–1886, they have never been out of print. In 1895 Grant's son Frederick D. Grant published an edition that included the first, although brief, annotations of the original text. Later came other editions, including those edited by E. B. Long, James M. McPherson, Brooks D. Simpson, Michael Fellman, and perhaps the most famous edition of all, the Library of America publication prepared by William S. and Mary McFeely. They all utilized the first-edition text and added annotations, but they did not do so in any thorough manner. None clarified all the uncertainties contained within. However, most included a perceptive introduction.

Over the years, then, the Grant *Memoirs* have continued to intrigue their readers. They have attracted the interest and praise not only of the general reading public, but also of many of the leading literati of the nineteenth and twentieth centuries. Many have considered the *Memoirs* to be one of the greatest pieces of nonfiction in American literary history.

Not surprisingly, the leading praise for the *Memoirs* came from its publisher, Samuel Clemens, and from Grant's friend William T. Sherman. Leading twentieth-century historian Lloyd Lewis summarized their evaluations: "Grant's superb style of writing is what Sherman and Mark Twain thought it—the best of any general's since Caesar." Henry James found the *Memoirs* "as hard and dry as sandpaper" but then added: "Great is the name . . . when so great a bareness practically blooms." Matthew Arnold attacked Grant's grammar, but he also said that he found the Grant in his *Memoirs* to be "a man of sterling good sense as well as of the firmest resolution." William Dean Howells said that "we have heard a lot about what the American was to be in literature when he got there. What if this were he—this good form without formality, this inner dignity, this straight forward arrival, this mid-day clearness."

Early twentieth-century writers were similarly effusive about Grant and his *Memoirs*. Sherwood Anderson and Gertrude Stein wanted to write a book together about Grant, and Sinclair Lewis hoped to do so with Stein too. Anderson obsessed about the idea for years, pointing out that his father allegedly knew Grant in the army and later was a seller of his *Memoirs*. Stein even held Grant superior to Lincoln and included him in her book *Four in America*. American poet Robert Frost told a friend: "You have to concede him [Grant] rank with the greatest our rank has had."

Writers of a more modern period have agreed. Leading presidential historian Henry Graff has stated, with no equivocation, that "the best autobiographical writing by a President was done by Ulysses S. Grant." Critic Edmund Wilson compared the *Memoirs* to Henry David Thoreau's *Walden* and Walt Whitman's *Leaves of Grass,* while Gore Vidal said, "It is simply not possible to read Grant's *Memoirs* without realizing that the author is a man of first-rate intelligence. . . . His book is a classic."

Consequently, soon after its publication and throughout the history of its many republications, important writers have considered the *Memoirs* not only a major piece of war literature, but also a classic of all American literature. They place Grant at the pinnacle of American nonfiction, and they do so enthusiastically.

# *Editorial Procedure*

This edition of the *Personal Memoirs of U. S. Grant* is the first completely annotated edition ever produced. The text and punctuation are those of the first published edition from 1885–1886, but the editors correct acknowledged errata and other typographical errors. The text is presented here in one volume, although the original edition was published in two volumes, with the second volume starting at Chapter 40. The editors provide thorough annotation of the text, but they do not add any extensive explanation for data that the general reader can easily find. The purpose of the annotations is to provide details that casual readers can use to understand the context and that scholarly researchers can use to track down further information.

An excellent way to explain the editors' role is to recall the conversation between *Century Magazine* editor Robert U. Johnson and Ulysses S. Grant when the editor was trying to tell Grant how he might improve his manuscript on the Battle of Shiloh for the magazine's Battles and Leaders of the Civil War series. Johnson told Grant to write as though he were speaking to a group of friends after dinner. Consequently, if Grant is accurate in the substance of the details, or in citing a date, or is making an evaluative comment that might even be debatable, the editors do not interrupt. They only interject their own words to identify a named or unnamed individual or place not readily identifiable in Grant's narrative, or if a supplied date is not clear. If Grant makes a mistake in citing a particular fact, the editors provide an annotation to correct the misstatement.

The editors try to identify every person Grant mentions in the *Memoirs* the first time he or she appears. Such notes include full name, date of birth and death, a geographic identifier, and, if in the military, highest rank and date of rank at the moment in the narrative. When the editors rely on genealogy websites or sources that are difficult to verify, they identify birth and death dates with a "c." for "circa." A lack of dates or a question mark in a biographical entry indicates no reliable dates were found. Any special relationship to Grant is also noted, as are unusual or outstanding facts about the individual.

Named places that still exist and are readily identifiable are not annotated. On the other hand, places that no longer exist or whose names have changed or are now unknown are annotated to explain their location.

The editors present estimates of distances from place to place. Rather than trying to guess at possible routes, the editors give straight-line (as the crow flies) mileage.

The editors do not include the appendix, which is Grant's final report. In the few instances when the *Memoirs* reference a letter in the appendix, the editors cite the *Papers of Ulysses S. Grant.*

Because the original maps in the *Memoirs* are not clear and thus not helpful to the reader, the editors do not include them in the text.

Original notes from the first edition are rendered as footnotes but distinguished from the editors' annotations. Source entries are in alphabetical order by the name of the source author or title.

The thirty-two volumes of *The Papers of Ulysses S. Grant (PUSG)* provided the editors of the *Memoirs* and its readers a highly accurate base of information for annotating or further researching the annotations. *PUSG* is cited when the text of the *Memoirs* mentions or quotes Grant's correspondence, but does so without notation, or refers to communications from others that are buried in the *PUSG*'s extensive notes. However, *PUSG* is not cited when Grant gives the name / date of his own correspondence. The format as a whole follows *The Chicago Manual of Style, 16th edition.*

With this edition completed, work will proceed in earnest on a digitized version that will display, as only that medium can, the procedure that Grant followed in writing and editing his remembrances. The digital edition will allow the scholar to see clearly the various versions Grant created from his articles in *Century Magazine,* how he chose his words and sentence structure, how he organized the text, and how he used Adam Badeau, Fred Grant, and all his other assistants. In brief, clarifying the content of Grant's thoughts is the purpose of this hard copy edition; understanding how Grant wrote his manuscript is the purpose of the later digitized edition.

# Abbreviations

| | |
|---|---|
| Adjt. | Adjutant |
| AG | Adjutant General |
| AGO | Adjutant General's Office |
| Art. | Artillery |
| Asst. | Assistant |
| Brig. | Brigadier |
| Capt. | Captain |
| Cav. | Cavalry |
| Co. | Company |
| *CWHC* | John H. Eicher and David J. Eicher, *Civil War High Commands* (Stanford, CA: Stanford University Press, 2001) |
| Dept. | Department |
| Div. | Division |
| FDG | Frederick Dent Grant |
| Gen. | General |
| Inf. | Infantry |
| JDG | Julia Dent Grant |
| JRG | Jesse Root Grant (1794–1873) |
| Lt. | Lieutenant |
| Maj. | Major |
| *OR* | *The War of the Rebellion: A Compilation of the Official Records of the Union and Confederate Armies,* 128 vols. (Washington, DC: Government Printing Office, 1880–1901) |
| *ORN* | *Official Records of the Union and Confederate Navies in the War of the Rebellion,* 30 vols. (Washington, DC: Government Printing Office, 1894–1922) |
| *PUSG* | John Y. Simon and John F. Marszalek, eds., *The Papers of Ulysses S. Grant,* 32 vols. (Carbondale: Southern Illinois University Press, 1967–2012) |
| USG | Ulysses S. Grant |
| USMA | United States Military Academy, West Point, NY |

# The Personal Memoirs of
# Ulysses S. Grant

THE COMPLETE ANNOTATED EDITION

*Personal Memoirs of U. S. Grant*

These volumes are
dedicated to the American
Soldier and Sailor.

U. S. Grant.

New York City
May 23d 1885.

# Preface

"Man proposes and God disposes."[1] There are but few important events in the affairs of men brought about by their own choice.

Although frequently urged by friends to write my memoirs I had determined never to do so, nor to write anything for publication. At the age of nearly sixty-two I received an injury from a fall, which confined me closely to the house while it did not apparently affect my general health.[2] This made study a pleasant pastime. Shortly after, the rascality of a business partner developed itself by the announcement of a failure.[3] This was followed soon after by universal depression of all securities, which seemed to threaten the extinction of a good part of the income still retained, and for which I am indebted to the kindly act of friends. At this juncture the editor of the *Century Magazine* asked me to write a few articles for him.[4] I consented for the money it gave me; for at that moment I was living upon borrowed money. The work I found congenial, and I determined to continue it. The event is an important one for me, for good or evil; I hope for the former.

[1] "For man proposes, but God disposes" is a phrase that comes from the English translation of Thomas à Kempis's work *The Imitation of Christ.* See, for example, the edition translated by R. Challoner (Dublin: McGlashan and Gill, 1873), 52.

[2] On Dec. 24, 1883, USG slipped on ice, injuring his left leg. *PUSG,* 31:xxix.

[3] In May 1884, the brokerage firm of Grant and Ward collapsed (along with the Marine Bank) when it was unable to pay its creditors. It was later revealed that Ferdinand Ward (1851–1925), the business partner of USG and his son Ulysses S. Grant Jr. was using the same collateral for multiple loans. The collapse left the Grant family bankrupt. Geoffrey C. Ward, *A Disposition to Be Rich* (New York: Knopf, 2012), 5, 71, 177, 203–204, 219, 235, 361.

[4] Richard W. Gilder (1844–1809) had become the editor in chief of *Century Magazine* in 1881 and approached USG about writing for the magazine in Jan. 1884. After the collapse of Grant and Ward, Gilder and his team of editors contacted USG again and found him more interested in the offer. *Dictionary of American Biography,* 2nd ed., s.v. "Gilder, Richard Watson"; Charles Bracelen Flood, *Grant's Final Victory* (Cambridge, MA: Da Capo, 2011), 56–57.

In preparing these volumes for the public, I have entered upon the task with the sincere desire to avoid doing injustice to any one, whether on the National or Confederate side, other than the unavoidable injustice of not making mention often where special mention is due. There must be many errors of omission in this work, because the subject is too large to be treated of in two volumes in such way as to do justice to all the officers and men engaged. There were thousands of instances, during the rebellion, of individual, company, regimental and brigade deeds of heroism which deserve special mention and are not here alluded to. The troops engaged in them will have to look to the detailed reports of their individual commanders for the full history of those deeds.

The first volume, as well as a portion of the second, was written before I had reason to suppose I was in a critical condition of health. Later I was reduced almost to the point of death, and it became impossible for me to attend to anything for weeks. I have, however, somewhat regained my strength, and am able, often, to devote as many hours a day as a person should devote to such work. I would have more hope of satisfying the expectation of the public if I could have allowed myself more time. I have used my best efforts, with the aid of my eldest son, F. D. Grant, assisted by his brothers, to verify from the records every statement of fact given.[5] The comments are my own, and show how I saw the matters treated of whether others saw them in the same light or not. With these remarks I present these volumes to the public, asking no favor but hoping they will meet the approval of the reader.

U. S. GRANT.

MOUNT MACGREGOR, NEW YORK, July 1, 1885.

---

[5] FDG (1850–1912) was born in Missouri and graduated from the USMA in 1871. He served as American minister to Austria-Hungary from 1889 to 1893 and was a New York City police commissioner from 1895 to 1897. He was a brigadier general during the Spanish-American War. Ulysses S. Grant Jr. (1852–1929) was born in Ohio and was known by the nickname "Buck." He graduated from Harvard University in 1874 and studied law at Columbia University. Jesse Root Grant (1858–1934) was born in Missouri and studied at Cornell University and Columbia University. He unsuccessfully ran for the Democratic nomination for president in 1908 and authored the book *In the Days of My Father, General Grant* (New York: Harper and Brothers, 1925). *Dictionary of American Biography*, 2nd ed., s.v. "Grant, Frederick Dent"; "Jesse Grant Dead; Son of General," *New York Times*, June 9, 1934, 15; "The President's Children," *Cambridge City Tribune*, Sept. 4, 1873, 1; "Son of Soldier and Statesman Expires," *Los Angeles Times*, Sept. 27, 1929, A1.

# I

## Ancestry—Birth—Boyhood

M Y FAMILY IS American, and has been for generations, in all its branches, direct and collateral.

Mathew Grant,[1] the founder of the branch in America, of which I am a descendant, reached Dorchester, Massachusetts, in May, 1630. In 1635 he moved to what is now Windsor, Connecticut, and was the surveyor for that colony for more than forty years. He was also, for many years of the time, town clerk. He was a married man when he arrived at Dorchester, but his children were all born in this country. His eldest son, Samuel,[2] took lands on the east side of the Connecticut River, opposite Windsor, which have been held and occupied by descendants of his to this day.

I am of the eighth generation from Mathew Grant, and seventh from Samuel. Mathew Grant's first wife[3] died a few years after their settlement in Windsor, and he soon after married the widow Rockwell,[4] who, with her first husband, had been fellow-passengers with him and his first wife, on the ship *Mary and John,* from Dorchester,[5] England, in 1630. Mrs. Rockwell had

---

[1] Matthew Grant (1601–1681) arrived in Boston Harbor in May 1630 and was officially recognized as a free citizen of the town of Dorchester in May 1631. Arthur H. Grant, *The Grant Family: A Genealogical History of the Descendants of Matthew Grant of Windsor, Conn., 1601–1898* (Poughkeepsie, NY: A. V. Haight, 1898), 1.

[2] Samuel Grant (1631–1718) worked as a carpenter, constable, and surveyor in the Connecticut colony. Ibid., 2.

[3] Priscilla Grant (?–1645). Ibid., 1.

[4] Susannah Rockwell (1602–1666), widow of William Rockwell (?–1640), married Matthew Grant on May 29, 1645. Ibid.; James Savage, *A Genealogical Dictionary of the First Settlers of New England Showing Three Generations of Those Who Came before May, 1692* (Boston: Little, Brown, 1861), 558.

[5] Matthew Grant and family boarded the ship in Plymouth, England, on Mar. 20, 1630. Grant, *Grant Family,* 1.

several children by her first marriage, and others by her second. By intermarriage, two or three generations later, I am descended from both the wives of Mathew Grant.[6]

In the fifth descending generation my great grandfather, Noah Grant,[7] and his younger brother, Solomon,[8] held commissions in the English army, in 1756, in the war against the French and Indians. Both were killed that year.

My grandfather, also named Noah,[9] was then but nine years old. At the breaking out of the war of the Revolution, after the battles of Concord and Lexington, he went with a Connecticut company to join the Continental army, and was present at the battle of Bunker Hill. He served until the fall of Yorktown, or through the entire Revolutionary war. He must, however, have been on furlough part of the time—as I believe most of the soldiers of that period were—for he married in Connecticut during the war, had two children, and was a widower at the close.[10] Soon after this he emigrated to Westmoreland County, Pennsylvania, and settled near the town of Greensburg in that county. He took with him the younger of his two children, Peter Grant.[11] The elder, Solomon,[12] remained with his relatives in Connecticut until old enough to do for himself, when he emigrated to the British West Indies.

Not long after his settlement in Pennsylvania, my grandfather, Captain Noah Grant, married a Miss Kelly,[13] and in 1799 he emigrated again, this time to Ohio, and settled where the town of Deerfield now stands. He had now

[6] In 1717, Noah Grant (1693–1727), a descendant of Matthew Grant and USG's great-great grandfather, married Martha Huntington (1696–?), a descendant of William and Susannah Rockwell. Ibid., 6; Emma G. Lathrop, "General Grant's Ancestry—No. 2," *Daughters of the American Revolution Magazine* 8 (1896): 888–889.

[7] Noah Grant (1718–1756) probably died during an overland expedition to Fort William Henry. Grant, *Grant Family,* 15–16.

[8] Solomon Grant (1723–1756) died in battle against Native Americans at Williamstown, MA. Ibid., 16.

[9] Noah Grant (1748–1819) was a farmer and tanner who was the first Grant to settle in Ohio. Ibid., 33.

[10] There are no records confirming Noah Grant's military service during the Revolutionary War. He married Anna Buell Richardson (1738–1789) in 1775. Ibid.; William S. McFeely, *Grant: A Biography* (New York: Norton, 1981), 5.

[11] Peter Grant (1781–1829) died in Kentucky after a career as a tanner and coal mine owner. Grant, *Grant Family,* 65.

[12] According to family lore, Solomon Grant (c.1779–1798?) may have settled in the West Indies and left a large family or died in a shipwreck before he arrived in the Caribbean. Ibid.

[13] Noah Grant married Rachel Kelly (?–1805) on Mar. 4, 1792. Ibid., 33.

five children, including Peter, a son by his first marriage.[14] My father, Jesse R. Grant,[15] was the second child—oldest son, by the second marriage.

Peter Grant went early to Maysville, Kentucky, where he was very prosperous, married, had a family of nine children, and was drowned at the mouth of the Kanawha River, Virginia, in 1825, being at the time one of the wealthy men of the West.[16]

My grandmother Grant died in 1805, leaving seven children.[17] This broke up the family. Captain Noah Grant was not thrifty in the way of "laying up stores on earth,"[18] and, after the death of his second wife, he went, with the two youngest children, to live with his son Peter, in Maysville. The rest of the family found homes in the neighborhood of Deerfield, my father in the family of Judge Tod,[19] the father of the late Governor Tod,[20] of Ohio. His industry and independence of character were such, that I imagine his labor compensated fully for the expense of his maintenance.

There must have been a cordiality in his welcome into the Tod family, for to the day of his death he looked upon Judge Tod and his wife,[21] with all the reverence he could have felt if they had been parents instead of benefactors.

---

[14] Five children were born to Noah and Rachel Grant in Pennsylvania (not counting Noah Grant's two sons by his first marriage, Solomon and Peter): Susan A. Grant (1792–1871); Jesse R. Grant (JRG) (1794–1873); Margaret M. Grant (1795–1873); Noah B. Grant (1797–1821); and John K. Grant (1799–1832). Ibid., 66.

[15] JRG was born in Pennsylvania. He worked as a tanner, was active in local politics, and served as postmaster of Covington, KY. Ibid., 65–66.

[16] Peter Grant was living in Maysville by 1807 when he married Permelia Bean (or Bane) on Nov. 12 of that year. He died in 1829. Ibid., 65.

[17] The two children born to the Grants in Ohio were Roswell M. Grant (1802–1886 [or 1885]) and Rachel M. Grant (1804–1882). Ibid., 66.

[18] USG probably referred to Matt. 6:19, "Lay not up for yourselves treasures upon earth, where moth and rust doth corrupt, and where thieves break through and steal" (King James Version).

[19] George Tod (1773–1841) served on the Ohio Supreme Court from 1806 to 1810 and was presiding judge of the 3rd District Circuit Court of Appeals from 1816 to 1829. *Dictionary of American Biography*, 2nd ed., s.v. "Tod, George."

[20] David Tod (1805–1868) served as governor of Ohio from 1862 to 1864. Joseph P. Smith, ed., *History of the Republican Party in Ohio* (Chicago: Lewis, 1898), 2:424–427. For correspondence with USG, see *PUSG*, 18:422–423.

[21] George Tod married Sally Isaacs (1778–1847) in 1797. Joseph G. Butler, *History of Youngstown and the Mahoning Valley, Ohio* (Chicago: American Historical Society, 1921), 220; "Deaths," *Portage Sentinel*, Nov. 3, 1847, 3.

I have often heard him speak of Mrs. Tod as the most admirable woman he had ever known. He remained with the Tod family only a few years, until old enough to learn a trade. He went first, I believe, with his half-brother, Peter Grant, who, though not a tanner himself, owned a tannery in Maysville, Kentucky. Here he learned his trade, and in a few years returned to Deerfield and worked for, and lived in the family of a Mr. Brown,[22] the father of John Brown—"whose body lies mouldering in the grave, while his soul goes marching on."[23] I have often heard my father speak of John Brown, particularly since the events at Harper's Ferry. Brown was a boy when they lived in the same house, but he knew him afterwards, and regarded him as a man of great purity of character, of high moral and physical courage, but a fanatic and extremist in whatever he advocated. It was certainly the act of an insane man to attempt the invasion of the South, and the overthrow of slavery, with less than twenty men.

My father set up for himself in business, establishing a tannery at Ravenna, the county seat of Portage County. In a few years he removed from Ravenna, and set up the same business at Point Pleasant, Clermont County, Ohio.[24]

During the minority of my father, the West afforded but poor facilities for the most opulent of the youth to acquire an education, and the majority were dependent, almost exclusively, upon their own exertions for whatever learning they obtained. I have often heard him say that his time at school was limited to six months, when he was very young, too young, indeed, to learn much, or to appreciate the advantages of an education, and to a "quarter's schooling" afterwards, probably while living with Judge Tod. But his thirst for education

[22] Owen Brown (1771–1856) owned a tannery in Hudson, OH, where JRG worked as an apprentice. Stephen B. Oates, *To Purge This Land with Blood: A Biography of John Brown* (Amherst: University of Massachusetts Press, 1984), 4, 112; *Proceedings of the Worcester Society of Antiquity for the Year 1886* (Worcester, MA: Worcester Society of Antiquity, 1887), 89.

[23] John Brown (1800–1859) led the 1859 raid on Harpers Ferry, VA. USG's quoted text is a paraphrase of a line from the popular Civil War song known as "John Brown's Body" or the "John Brown Song." The actual lyric, based on early printed versions of the song, is "John Brown's body lies a mouldering in the grave, / His soul's marching on!" *Dictionary of American Biography*, 2nd ed., s.v. "Brown, John"; George Kimball, "Origin of the John Brown Song," *New England Magazine* 1, no. 4 (1889): 371–374.

[24] JRG moved to Ravenna, OH, in approximately 1817 or 1818. He moved to Point Pleasant, OH, c.1820. Edward C. Marshall, *The Ancestry of General Grant, and Their Contemporaries* (New York: Sheldon, 1869), 64; Henry Howe, *Historical Collections of Ohio in Two Volumes* (Cincinnati: Krehbiel, 1908), 2:438; Grant, *Grant Family,* 65.

was intense. He learned rapidly, and was a constant reader up to the day of his death—in his eightieth year. Books were scarce in the Western Reserve[25] during his youth, but he read every book he could borrow in the neighborhood where he lived. This scarcity gave him the early habit of studying everything he read, so that when he got through with a book, he knew everything in it. The habit continued through life. Even after reading the daily papers—which he never neglected—he could give all the important information they contained. He made himself an excellent English scholar, and before he was twenty years of age was a constant contributor to Western newspapers, and was also, from that time until he was fifty years old, an able debater in the societies for this purpose, which were common in the West at that time.[26] He always took an active part in politics, but was never a candidate for office, except, I believe, that he was the first Mayor of Georgetown.[27] He supported Jackson[28] for the Presidency; but he was a Whig, a great admirer of Henry Clay,[29] and never voted for any other democrat for high office after Jackson.

---

[25] In 1800, Connecticut ceded its western lands to the federal government. The portion of land on Lake Erie was known as the Western Reserve and eventually became the northeastern portion of the new state of Ohio. Harlan Hatcher, *The Western Reserve: The Story of New Connecticut in Ohio* (Indianapolis: Bobbs-Merrill, 1949), 20–21; Robert A. Wheeler, ed., *Visions of the Western Reserve* (Columbus: Ohio State University Press, 2000), 1.

[26] JRG was a member of the Bethel, OH, and the Georgetown, OH, debating societies. During the late 1700s and early 1800s, debating societies provided young men with opportunities to enhance important social skills (such as public speaking) and form relationships with other aspiring professionals. Carolyn Eastman, *A Nation of Speechifiers: Making an American Public after the Revolution* (Chicago: University of Chicago Press, 2009), 115–116; Byron Williams, *History of Clermont and Brown Counties, Ohio: From Earliest Times Down to the Present* (Milford, OH: Hobart, 1913), 439.

[27] In May 1823, JRG moved his family to Georgetown in Brown County to open a tannery. He was a regular contributor to the *Castigator,* an abolitionist newspaper. S. Glaze is recorded as the first mayor of Georgetown in 1832, with JRG serving as the fifth mayor of the town from 1837 to 1839. McFeely, *Grant,* 8; Marshall, *Ancestry of Grant,* 67; Josiah Morrow, *The History of Brown County, Ohio* (Chicago: W. H. Beers, 1883), 393.

[28] Andrew Jackson (1767–1845) was a candidate for president of the United States in 1824, 1828, and 1832, winning election in 1828 and 1832. *Dictionary of American Biography,* 2nd ed., s.v. "Jackson, Andrew."

[29] Henry Clay (1777–1852) was born in Virginia and moved to Kentucky in 1797. He served in the U.S. House of Representatives and U.S. Senate for many years and was known for his role in the formation of the Compromise of 1850 (among other major legislative compromises). He ran for president in 1824, and then as the Whig candidate in 1832 and 1844. John A.

My mother's family lived in Montgomery County, Pennsylvania, for several generations. I have little information about her ancestors. Her family took no interest in genealogy, so that my grandfather, who died when I was sixteen years old, knew only back to his grandfather.[30] On the other side, my father took a great interest in the subject, and in his researches, he found that there was an entailed estate in Windsor, Connecticut, belonging to the family, to which his nephew, Lawson Grant[31]—still living—was the heir. He was so much interested in the subject that he got his nephew to empower him to act in the matter, and in 1832 or 1833, when I was a boy ten or eleven years old, he went to Windsor, proved the title beyond dispute, and perfected the claim of the owners for a consideration—three thousand dollars, I think. I remember the circumstance well, and remember, too, hearing him say on his return that he found some widows living on the property, who had little or nothing beyond their homes. From these he refused to receive any recompense.

My mother's father, John Simpson, moved from Montgomery County, Pennsylvania, to Clermont County, Ohio, about the year 1819, taking with him his four children, three daughters and one son.[32] My mother, Hannah Simpson, was the third of these children, and was then over twenty years of age.[33] Her oldest sister was at that time married, and had several children. She still lives in Clermont County at this writing, October 5th, 1884, and is over ninety years of age. Until her memory failed her, a few years ago, she thought the country ruined beyond recovery when the Democratic party lost control in 1860. Her family, which was large, inherited her views, with the exception of one son who settled in Kentucky before the war. He was the

Garraty and Mark C. Carnes, eds., *American National Biography* (New York: Oxford University Press, 1999), s.v. "Clay, Henry."

[30] USG's maternal grandfather was John Simpson (c.1767–1837), whose father was also named John Simpson (1738–1804); his father (USG's maternal great-great-grandfather) was William Simpson (c.1710–1794). William W. H. Davis, *History of Bucks County Pennsylvania from the Discovery of the Delaware to the Present Time* (New York: Lewis, 1905), 3:13; Gary B. Roberts, *Ancestors of American Presidents* (Boston: New England Historical Genealogical Society, 1989), 29–30.

[31] Lawson Grant (1810–1887) was the son of USG's uncle Peter Grant and Permelia Bean. Grant, *Grant Family*, 140.

[32] Mary S. Griffith (1794–1885), Samuel (?–1887), and Sarah (c.1800–c.1823) were the siblings of USG's mother. FDG annotation, USG, *Personal Memoirs of U.S. Grant* (New York: Charles L. Webster, 1895), 6–7.

[33] Hannah Simpson Grant (1798–1883) was born in Montgomery County, PA, about twenty miles from Philadelphia. Grant, *Grant Family*, 65.

only one of the children who entered the volunteer service to suppress the rebellion.[34]

Her brother, next of age and now past eighty-eight, is also still living in Clermont County, within a few miles of the old homestead, and is as active in mind as ever. He was a supporter of the Government during the war, and remains a firm believer, that national success by the Democratic party means irretrievable ruin.

In June, 1821, my father, Jesse R. Grant, married Hannah Simpson. I was born on the 27th of April, 1822, at Point Pleasant, Clermont County, Ohio. In the fall of 1823 we moved to Georgetown, the county seat of Brown, the adjoining county east. This place remained my home, until at the age of seventeen, in 1839, I went to West Point.

The schools, at the time of which I write, were very indifferent. There were no free schools, and none in which the scholars were classified. They were all supported by subscription, and a single teacher—who was often a man or a woman incapable of teaching much, even if they imparted all they knew—would have thirty or forty scholars, male and female, from the infant learning the A B C's up to the young lady of eighteen and the boy of twenty, studying the highest branches taught—the three R's, "Reading, 'Riting, 'Rithmetic." I never saw an algebra, or other mathematical work higher than the arithmetic, in Georgetown, until after I was appointed to West Point. I then bought a work on algebra in Cincinnati; but having no teacher it was Greek to me.

My life in Georgetown was uneventful. From the age of five or six until seventeen, I attended the subscription schools of the village, except during the winters of 1836–7 and 1838–9. The former period was spent in Maysville, Kentucky, attending the school of Richardson and Rand;[35] the latter in Ripley, Ohio, at a private school.[36] I was not studious in habit, and probably did not make progress enough to compensate for the outlay for board and tuition. At all events both winters were spent in going over the same old arithmetic which I knew every word of before, and repeating: "A noun is the name of a thing," which I had also heard my Georgetown teachers repeat, until I had come to

[34] Louis Griffith. FDG annotation, *Personal Memoirs*, 6.

[35] W. W. Richeson and Jacob W. Rand (c.1799–c.1874) operated the Maysville Academy (also known as Maysville Seminary). Hamlin Garland, "The Early Life of Ulysses Grant," *McClure's Magazine* 8 (Dec. 1896): 132; Paul A. Tenkotte and James Claypool, eds., *The Encyclopedia of Northern Kentucky* (Lexington: University Press of Kentucky, 2009), 596–597.

[36] The Presbyterian Academy. Albert D. Richardson, *A Personal History of Ulysses S. Grant* (Providence, RI: Buker, 1885), 61.

believe it—but I cast no reflections upon my old teacher, Richardson. He turned out bright scholars from his school, many of whom have filled conspicuous places in the service of their States. Two of my cotemporaries there—who, I believe, never attended any other institution of learning—have held seats in Congress, and one, if not both, other high offices; these are Wadsworth and Brewster.[37]

My father was, from my earliest recollection, in comfortable circumstances, considering the times, his place of residence, and the community in which he lived. Mindful of his own lack of facilities for acquiring an education, his greatest desire in maturer years was for the education of his children. Consequently, as stated before, I never missed a quarter from school from the time I was old enough to attend till the time of leaving home. This did not exempt me from labor. In my early days, every one labored more or less, in the region where my youth was spent, and more in proportion to their private means. It was only the very poor who were exempt. While my father carried on the manufacture of leather and worked at the trade himself, he owned and tilled considerable land. I detested the trade, preferring almost any other labor; but I was fond of agriculture, and of all employment in which horses were used. We had, among other lands, fifty acres of forest within a mile of the village. In the fall of the year choppers were employed to cut enough wood to last a twelve-month. When I was seven or eight years of age, I began hauling all the wood used in the house and shops. I could not load it on the wagons, of course, at that time, but I could drive, and the choppers would load, and some one at the house unload. When about eleven years old, I was strong enough to hold a plough. From that age until seventeen I did all the work done with horses, such as breaking up the land, furrowing, ploughing corn and potatoes, bringing in the crops when harvested, hauling all the wood, besides tending two or three horses, a cow or two, and sawing wood for stoves, etc., while still attending school. For this I was compensated by the fact that there was never any scolding or punishing by my parents; no objection to rational enjoyments, such as fishing, going to the creek a mile away to swim in summer, taking a horse and visiting my grandparents in the adjoining county, fifteen

---

[37] William H. Wadsworth (1821–1893) served as U.S. representative from Kentucky from 1861 to 1865 and from 1885 to 1887. "Brewster" is probably a reference to Elijah C. Phister (1822–1887), who served as U.S. representative from Kentucky from 1879 to 1883. *Biographical Directory of the United States Congress 1774–2005* (Washington, DC: Government Printing Office, 2005), s.vv. "Wadsworth, William Henry," "Phister, Elijah Conner"; FDG annotation, *Personal Memoirs*, 8. For Wadsworth's interactions with USG, see *PUSG,* 20:3n–4n.

miles off, skating on the ice in winter, or taking a horse and sleigh when there was snow on the ground.

While still quite young I had visited Cincinnati, forty-five miles away, several times, alone; also Maysville, Kentucky, often, and once Louisville. The journey to Louisville was a big one for a boy of that day. I had also gone once with a two-horse carriage to Chilicothe, about seventy miles, with a neighbor's family, who were removing to Toledo, Ohio, and returned alone; and had gone once, in like manner, to Flat Rock, Kentucky, about seventy miles away. On this latter occasion I was fifteen years of age. While at Flat Rock, at the house of a Mr. Payne,[38] whom I was visiting with his brother, a neighbor of ours in Georgetown, I saw a very fine saddle horse, which I rather coveted, and proposed to Mr. Payne, the owner, to trade him for one of the two I was driving. Payne hesitated to trade with a boy, but asking his brother about it, the latter told him that it would be all right, that I was allowed to do as I pleased with the horses. I was seventy miles from home, with a carriage to take back, and Mr. Payne said he did not know that his horse had ever had a collar on. I asked to have him hitched to a farm wagon and we would soon see whether he would work. It was soon evident that the horse had never worn harness before; but he showed no viciousness, and I expressed a confidence that I could manage him. A trade was at once struck, I receiving ten dollars difference.

The next day Mr. Payne, of Georgetown, and I started on our return. We got along very well for a few miles, when we encountered a ferocious dog that frightened the horses and made them run. The new animal kicked at every jump he made. I got the horses stopped, however, before any damage was done, and without running into anything. After giving them a little rest, to quiet their fears, we started again. That instant the new horse kicked, and started to run once more. The road we were on, struck the turnpike within half a mile of the point where the second runaway commenced, and there was an embankment twenty or more feet deep on the opposite side of the pike. I got the horses stopped on the very brink of the precipice. My new horse was terribly frightened and trembled like an aspen; but he was not half so badly frightened as my companion, Mr. Payne, who deserted me after this last experience, and took passage on a freight wagon for Maysville. Every time I attempted to start, my new horse would commence to kick. I was in quite a dilemma for a time. Once in Maysville I could borrow a horse from an uncle who lived there;

[38] Probably William P. Payne. Jesse E. Peyton, *Reminiscences of the Past* (Philadelphia: n.p., 1893), 17.

but I was more than a day's travel from that point. Finally I took out my bandanna—the style of handkerchief in universal use then—and with this blindfolded my horse. In this way I reached Maysville safely the next day, no doubt much to the surprise of my friend. Here I borrowed a horse from my uncle, and the following day we proceeded on our journey.

About half my school-days in Georgetown were spent at the school of John D. White, a North Carolinian, and the father of Chilton White who represented the district in Congress for one term during the rebellion. Mr. White was always a Democrat in politics, and Chilton followed his father.[39] He had two older brothers—all three being school-mates of mine at their father's school—who did not go the same way. The second brother died before the rebellion began; he was a Whig, and afterwards a Republican. His oldest brother was a Republican and brave soldier during the rebellion.[40] Chilton is reported as having told of an earlier horse-trade of mine. As he told the story, there was a Mr. Ralston[41] living within a few miles of the village, who owned a colt which I very much wanted. My father had offered twenty dollars for it, but Ralston wanted twenty-five. I was so anxious to have the colt, that after the owner left, I begged to be allowed to take him at the price demanded. My father yielded, but said twenty dollars was all the horse was worth, and told me to offer that price; if it was not accepted I was to offer twenty-two and a half, and if that would not get him, to give the twenty-five. I at once mounted a horse and went for the colt. When I got to Mr. Ralston's house, I said to him: "Papa says I may offer you twenty dollars for the colt, but if you won't take that, I am to offer twenty-two and a half, and if you won't take that, to give you twenty-five." It would not require a Connecticut man to guess the price finally agreed upon.[42] This story is nearly true. I certainly showed very plainly that I had come for the colt and meant to have him. I could not have been over eight years old at the time. This transaction caused me great heart-

[39] John D. White (c.1836–1855) was the father of Chilton A. White (1826–1900), who served two terms as a Democrat in the U.S. House of Representatives from 1861 to 1865. *Biographical Directory*, s.v. "White, Chilton Allen"; Morrow, "Biographical Sketches," *History of Brown County*, 47.

[40] Carr B. White (1823–1871) served with the 12th Ohio Inf., eventually reaching the rank of brevet brigadier general. *CWHC*, 565.

[41] Probably Robert Ralston. Richardson, *Personal History*, 45.

[42] The expression regarding a "Connecticut man" may have referred to the reputation for cleverness attributed to residents of Connecticut in that day. See, for example, "Beecher's Norwood," *New Catholic World* (Dec. 1869): 396.

burning. The story got out among the boys of the village, and it was a long time before I heard the last of it. Boys enjoy the misery of their companions, at least village boys in that day did, and in later life I have found that all adults are not free from the peculiarity. I kept the horse until he was four years old, when he went blind, and I sold him for twenty dollars. When I went to Maysville to school, in 1836, at the age of fourteen, I recognized my colt as one of the blind horses working on the tread-wheel of the ferry-boat.

I have described enough of my early life to give an impression of the whole. I did not like to work; but I did as much of it, while young, as grown men can be hired to do in these days, and attended school at the same time. I had as many privileges as any boy in the village, and probably more than most of them. I have no recollection of ever having been punished at home, either by scolding or by the rod. But at school the case was different. The rod was freely used there, and I was not exempt from its influence. I can see John D. White—the school teacher—now, with his long beech switch always in his hand. It was not always the same one, either. Switches were brought in bundles, from a beech wood near the school house, by the boys for whose benefit they were intended. Often a whole bundle would be used up in a single day. I never had any hard feelings against my teacher, either while attending the school, or in later years when reflecting upon my experience. Mr. White was a kind-hearted man, and was much respected by the community in which he lived. He only followed the universal custom of the period, and that under which he had received his own education.

# 2

## West Point—Graduation

I

N THE WINTER of 1838–9 I was attending school at Ripley, only ten miles distant from Georgetown, but spent the Christmas holidays at home.[1] During this vacation my father received a letter from the Honorable Thomas Morris,[2] then United States Senator from Ohio. When he read it he said to me, "Ulysses, I believe you are going to receive the appointment." "What appointment?" I inquired. "To West Point; I have applied for it." "But I won't go," I said. He said he thought I would, *and I thought so too, if he did.* I really had no objection to going to West Point, except that I had a very exalted idea of the acquirements necessary to get through. I did not believe I possessed them, and could not bear the idea of failing. There had been four boys from our village, or its immediate neighborhood, who had been graduated from West Point, and never a failure of any one appointed from Georgetown, except in the case of the one whose place I was to take.[3] He was the son of Dr. Bailey, our nearest and most intimate neighbor.[4] Young Bailey had been appointed in 1837. Finding before the January examination following, that he could not pass, he resigned and went to a private school, and remained there until the following year, when he was reappointed. Before the next examination he was dismissed.

[1] USG attended the Presbyterian Academy in Ripley, OH, from fall 1838 to spring 1839. *PUSG,* 1:xxxvii.

[2] Thomas Morris (1776–1844) served as a U.S. senator from Ohio from 1833 to 1839. B. F. Morris, *The Life of Thomas Morris: Pioneer and Long a Legislator of Ohio, and U.S. Senator from 1833 to 1839* (Cincinnati: William Overend, 1856), 13, 404.

[3] George Bartlett Bailey (c.1821–c.1861) withdrew from the USMA as a cadet in Oct. 1838. *PUSG,* 1:3.

[4] George B. Bailey (c.1797–c.1869) ran an apothecary east of the courthouse in downtown Georgetown, OH, in 1839. Josiah Morrow, *The History of Brown County, Ohio* (Chicago: W. H. Beers, 1883), 392; *PUSG,* 1:3; Brooks D. Simpson, *Ulysses S. Grant: Triumph over Adversity, 1822–1865* (Boston: Houghton Mifflin, 2000), 9.

Dr. Bailey was a proud and sensitive man, and felt the failure of his son so keenly that he forbade his return home. There were no telegraphs in those days to disseminate news rapidly, no railroads west of the Alleghanies, and but few east; and above all, there were no reporters prying into other people's private affairs. Consequently it did not become generally known that there was a vacancy at West Point from our district until I was appointed. I presume Mrs. Bailey[5] confided to my mother the fact that Bartlett had been dismissed, and that the doctor had forbidden his son's return home.

The Honorable Thomas L. Hamer, one of the ablest men Ohio ever produced, was our member of Congress at the time, and had the right of nomination.[6] He and my father had been members of the same debating society (where they were generally pitted on opposite sides), and intimate personal friends from their early manhood up to a few years before. In politics they differed. Hamer was a life-long Democrat, while my father was a Whig. They had a warm discussion, which finally became angry—over some act of President Jackson, the removal of the deposit of public moneys, I think—after which they never spoke until after my appointment. I know both of them felt badly over this estrangement, and would have been glad at any time to come to a reconciliation; but neither would make the advance. Under these circumstances my father would not write to Hamer for the appointment, but he wrote to Thomas Morris, United States Senator from Ohio, informing him that there was a vacancy at West Point from our district, and that he would be glad if I could be appointed to fill it. This letter, I presume, was turned over to Mr. Hamer, and, as there was no other applicant, he cheerfully appointed me. This healed the breach between the two, never after reopened.

Besides the argument used by my father in favor of my going to West Point—that "he thought I would go"—there was another very strong inducement. I had always a great desire to travel. I was already the best travelled boy in Georgetown, except the sons of one man, John Walker,[7] who had emigrated

---

[5] Jane Bailey (c.1802–?) was the wife of Dr. Bailey. In 1875, six years after her husband's death, Mrs. Bailey was serving as postmaster of Georgetown. *PUSG,* 1:27–29; *Register of Officers and Agents, Civil, Military, and Naval, in the Service of the United States* (Washington, DC: Government Printing Office, 1876), 1045.

[6] Thomas L. Hamer (1800–1846) moved to Georgetown in Aug. 1821 and started a law practice. Hamer served as U.S. congressman from Ohio from 1832 to 1839. Morrow, *History of Brown County,* 343–349; *PUSG,* 1:3–4.

[7] John Walker ran a saddle- and harness-making shop that was located next to Dr. Bailey's office. Morrow, *History of Brown County,* 392.

to Texas with his family, and immigrated back as soon as he could get the means to do so. In his short stay in Texas he acquired a very different opinion of the country from what one would form going there now.

I had been east to Wheeling, Virginia, and north to the Western Reserve, in Ohio, west to Louisville, and south to Bourbon County, Kentucky, besides having driven or ridden pretty much over the whole country within fifty miles of home. Going to West Point would give me the opportunity of visiting the two great cities of the continent, Philadelphia and New York. This was enough. When these places were visited I would have been glad to have had a steamboat or railroad collision, or any other accident happen, by which I might have received a temporary injury sufficient to make me ineligible, for a time, to enter the Academy. Nothing of the kind occurred, and I had to face the music.

Georgetown has a remarkable record for a western village. It is, and has been from its earliest existence, a democratic town. There was probably no time during the rebellion when, if the opportunity could have been afforded, it would not have voted for Jefferson Davis[8] for President of the United States, over Mr. Lincoln,[9] or any other representative of his party; unless it was immediately after some of John Morgan's men, in his celebrated raid through Ohio, spent a few hours in the village.[10] The rebels helped themselves to whatever they could find, horses, boots and shoes, especially horses, and many ordered meals to be prepared for them by the families. This was no doubt a far pleasanter duty for some families than it would have been to render a like service for Union soldiers. The line between the Rebel and Union element in Georgetown was so marked that it led to divisions even in the churches. There were churches in that part of Ohio where treason was preached regularly, and

[8] Jefferson F. Davis (1808–1889) was born in Kentucky and moved to Mississippi in 1811. He graduated from the USMA in 1828 and was a colonel throughout most of the Mexican-American War. He served as a representative and senator from Mississippi in the U.S. Congress. He was U.S. secretary of war from 1853 to 1857 and president of the Confederate States of America during the Civil War. *CWHC*, 202–203.

[9] Abraham Lincoln (1809–1865) was the Republican Party nominee for president in 1860 and 1864, winning the presidency both times. *Dictionary of American Biography*, 2nd ed., s.v. "Lincoln, Abraham."

[10] John Hunt Morgan (1825–1864) was born in Alabama and moved to Kentucky c.1830. At the outbreak of the Civil War, Morgan was a captain in the Confederate Army's 2nd Kentucky Cav. In July 1863, Georgetown residents allegedly assisted Morgan and his troops during their raid through Ohio and Indiana. *CWHC*, 397; Jennifer L. Weber, *Copperheads: The Rise and Fall of Lincoln's Opponents in the North* (New York: Oxford University Press, 2006), 113.

where, to secure membership, hostility to the government, to the war and to the liberation of the slaves, was far more essential than a belief in the authenticity or credibility of the Bible. There were men in Georgetown who filled all the requirements for membership in these churches.

Yet this far-off western village, with a population, including old and young, male and female, of about one thousand—about enough for the organization of a single regiment if all had been men capable of bearing arms—furnished the Union army four general officers and one colonel, West Point graduates, and nine generals and field officers of Volunteers, that I can think of. Of the graduates from West Point, all had citizenship elsewhere at the breaking out of the rebellion, except possibly General A. V. Kautz,[11] who had remained in the army from his graduation. Two of the colonels also entered the service from other localities. The other seven, General McGroierty,[12] Colonels White,[13] Fyffe,[14] Loudon[15] and Marshall,[16] Majors King[17] and Bailey, were all residents of

[11] August V. Kautz (1828–1895) was born in Germany and moved to Georgetown when he was a child. He enlisted as a private during the Mexican-American War in 1846 and later graduated from the USMA in 1852. Kautz served on the Pacific Coast until the start of the Civil War. *The National Cyclopaedia of American Biography*, vol. 14 (New York: James T. White, 1910), 142; *PUSG*, 10:9n.

[12] Stephen J. McGroarty (1830–1870) was born in Ireland and moved to Ohio in 1833. In May 1861, he was a captain in the 10th Ohio Inf. and was brevetted brigadier general in May 1865. *CWHC*, 379.

[13] Carr B. White was colonel of the 12th Ohio Inf. at the start of the Civil War. On Mar. 13, 1865, White was brevetted brigadier general. Morrow, "Biographical Sketches" in *History of Brown County*, 47.

[14] James P. Fyffe (c.1822–1864) was born in Kentucky and was a first lieutenant in the 1st Ohio Inf. during the Mexican-American War. He was a colonel in the 59th Ohio Inf. during the Civil War. Milton Jamieson, *Journal and Notes of a Campaign in Mexico* (Cincinnati: Ben Franklin Printing, 1849), 94; Morrow, *History of Brown County*, 474; William Hugh Robarts, *Mexican War Veterans: A Complete Roster of the Regular and Volunteer Troops in the War between the United States and Mexico, from 1846 to 1848* (Washington, DC: Brentano's, 1887), 69.

[15] D. W. C. Loudon (1827–1897) served under Gen. William T. Sherman as a colonel in the Army of the Tennessee. He was discharged due to a disability, and returned to Georgetown in 1864. Morrow, "Biographical Sketches," in *History of Brown County*, 26.

[16] John G. Marshall (1823–1878), a cousin of USG, served as a colonel in the 89th Ohio Inf. during the Civil War. Ibid., 29.

[17] Silas W. King (1836–?) was born in Pleasant Township, Brown County, OH. At the start of the Civil War, he enlisted in Capt. John S. Foster's Independent Cav. After approximately one year of service, he was discharged from the military due to a disability. Ibid., 296.

Georgetown when the war broke out, and all of them, who were alive at the close, returned there. Major Bailey was the cadet who had preceded me at West Point. He was killed in West Virginia, in his first engagement. As far as I know, every boy who has entered West Point from that village since my time has been graduated.

I took passage on a steamer at Ripley, Ohio, for Pittsburg, about the middle of May, 1839. Western boats at that day did not make regular trips at stated times, but would stop anywhere, and for any length of time, for passengers or freight. I have myself been detained two or three days at a place after steam was up, the gang planks, all but one, drawn in, and after the time advertised for starting had expired. On this occasion we had no vexatious delays, and in about three days Pittsburg was reached. From Pittsburg I chose passage by the canal to Harrisburg, rather than by the more expeditious stage.[18] This gave a better opportunity of enjoying the fine scenery of Western Pennsylvania, and I had rather a dread of reaching my destination at all. At that time the canal was much patronized by travellers, and, with the comfortable packets of the period, no mode of conveyance could be more pleasant, when time was not an object. From Harrisburg to Philadelphia there was a railroad, the first I had ever seen, except the one on which I had just crossed the summit of the Alleghany Mountains, and over which canal boats were transported.[19] In travelling by the road from Harrisburg, I thought the perfection of rapid transit had been reached. We travelled at least eighteen miles an hour, when at full speed, and made the whole distance averaging probably as much as twelve miles an hour. This seemed like annihilating space. I stopped five days in Philadelphia, saw about every street in the city, attended the theatre, visited Girard College[20]

---

[18] During the 1820s, Pennsylvania began construction on a series of canals which spanned much of the state and transformed its industry and economy. USG would have traveled the Western and Juniata Divisions of the canal, which ran through the Allegheny Mountains. Ronald E. Shaw, *Canals for a Nation: The Canal Era in the United States* (Lexington: University Press of Kentucky, 1990), 75–79.

[19] USG traveled along the Columbia Railroad from Harrisburg, PA, to Philadelphia. Nathaniel Parker Willis, *American Scenery; or, Land, Lake, and River Illustrations of Transatlantic Nature* (Cambridge: Cambridge University Press, 1840), 1:viii.

[20] Stephen Girard (1750–1831), a wealthy private banker in Philadelphia, left a substantial portion of his estate to establish a grammar school for orphaned boys. The cornerstone of Girard College was laid in 1833, but the Panic of 1837 had brought construction to a near halt and the project became mired in legal troubles. The school eventually opened in 1848. Charles Dickens, *American Notes for General Circulation,* 2nd ed. (London: Chapman and Hall, 1842), 1:237; Cheesman A. Herrick, *History of Girard College* (Philadelphia: Girard College, 1927), 1–40; Henry A. Ingram, *The Life and Character of Stephen Girard* (Philadelphia, 1896), 17, 96.

(which was then in course of construction), and got reprimanded from home afterwards, for dallying by the way so long. My sojourn in New York was shorter, but long enough to enable me to see the city very well. I reported at West Point on the 30th or 31st of May, and about two weeks later passed my examination for admission, without difficulty, very much to my surprise.[21]

A military life had no charms for me, and I had not the faintest idea of staying in the army even if I should be graduated, which I did not expect. The encampment which preceded the commencement of academic studies was very wearisome and uninteresting.[22] When the 28th of August came—the date for breaking up camp and going into barracks—I felt as though I had been at West Point always, and that if I staid to graduation, I would have to remain always. I did not take hold of my studies with avidity, in fact I rarely ever read over a lesson the second time during my entire cadetship. I could not sit in my room doing nothing. There is a fine library connected with the Academy from which cadets can get books to read in their quarters.[23] I devoted more time to these, than to books relating to the course of studies. Much of the time, I am sorry to say, was devoted to novels, but not those of a trashy sort. I read all of Bulwer's[24] then published, Cooper's,[25] Marryat's,[26]

---

[21] The cadets at the USMA faced examinations in Jan. and June. The June examination occurred in the presence of the Civilian Board of Visitors. Stephen E. Ambrose, *Duty, Honor, Courage: A History of West Point* (Baltimore: Johns Hopkins University Press, 1966), 67–73.

[22] Although an 1812 law required a three-month encampment, Superintendent Alden Partridge had ignored it. In 1818, Sylvanus Thayer, the school's transformational superintendent, had abolished furloughs and vacations, except in extraordinary circumstances. In place of summer furloughs, the students encamped from July 1 until Aug. 31. Ambrose, *Duty, Honor, Courage,* 51; Francis S. Drake, ed., *Dictionary of American Biography, Including Men of the Time . . .* (Boston: Houghton, Osgood, 1879), 693; Robert H. Hall, "Early Discipline at the United States Military Academy," *Journal of the Military Service Institution of the United States* 2 (1881): 467.

[23] The library at the USMA in that time contained few literary works and cadets had very limited access to the collection. USG ordered several novels by mail in 1843, and probably exchanged novels with other cadets. *PUSG,* 1:11; Ronald C. White, *American Ulysses: A Life of Ulysses S. Grant* (New York: Random House, 2016), 34–35.

[24] British novelist and playwright Edward Bulwer-Lytton (1803–1873). Christine L. Krueger, ed., *Encyclopedia of British Writers, 19th and 20th Centuries* (New York: Facts on File, 2003), 50–51.

[25] American author James Fenimore Cooper (1789–1851). Christopher J. Murray, ed., *Encyclopedia of the Romantic Era, 1760–1850* (New York: Routledge, 2003), 218.

[26] British novelist Frederick Marryat (1792–1848). David Hannay and John P. Anderson, *The Life of Captain Frederick Marryat* (London: Walter Scott, 1889), 58.

Scott's,[27] Washington Irving's[28] works, Lever's,[29] and many others that I do not now remember. Mathematics was very easy to me, so that when January came, I passed the examination, taking a good standing in that branch. In French, the only other study at that time in the first year's course, my standing was very low. In fact, if the class had been turned the other end foremost I should have been near head. I never succeeded in getting squarely at either end of my class, in any one study, during the four years. I came near it in French, artillery, infantry and cavalry tactics, and conduct.[30]

Early in the session of the Congress which met in December, 1839, a bill was discussed abolishing the Military Academy.[31] I saw in this an honorable way to obtain a discharge, and read the debates with much interest, but with impatience at the delay in taking action, for I was selfish enough to favor the bill. It never passed, and a year later, although the time hung drearily with me, I would have been sorry to have seen it succeed. My idea then was to get through the course, secure a detail for a few years as assistant professor of mathematics at the Academy, and afterwards obtain a permanent position as professor in some respectable college; but circumstances always did shape my course different from my plans.

---

[27] British author Sir Walter Scott (1771–1832). Laura Dabundo, ed., *Encyclopedia of Romanticism: Culture in Britain, 1780s–1830s* (New York: Routledge, 2010), 514–516.

[28] American author Washington Irving (1783–1859). Murray, *Encyclopedia of the Romantic Era,* 566–567.

[29] Irish novelist Charles Lever (1806–1872). In Mar. 1843, USG wrote to Lever's publisher for copies of Lever's books *Charles O'Malley, the Irish Dragoon* and *The Confessions of Harry Lorrequer. PUSG,* 1:11.

[30] In a class of sixty, USG finished sixteenth in mathematics and forty-ninth in French in 1839–1840, his first year at the USMA. He finished his second year ranked tenth in mathematics and forty-fourth in French in a class of fifty-three. In 1842–1843, his final year, he was twenty-fifth in artillery and twenty-eighth in infantry tactics out of thirty-nine. In conduct, USG was ranked 147 out of 233 cadets in 1840; 144 out of 219 in 1841; 157 out of 217 in 1842; and 156 out of 223 in 1843. *Official Register of the Officers and Cadets of the U.S. Military Academy, West Point, New York. June, 1840* (New York: USMA Printing Office, 1840), 16, 23; *Official Register . . . June, 1841,* 13, 20; *Official Register . . . June, 1842,* 21; *Official Register . . . June, 1843,* 7, 19. For an account of USG's studies, particularly in regard to French and mathematics, see *PUSG,* 1:4–8; 32:3–6.

[31] On July 20, 1840, the U.S. House of Representatives voted on a bill to fund the USMA. Some members, including Christopher H. Williams of Tennessee, argued that the USMA should be abolished entirely, while John Pope of Kentucky defended the importance of the institution. After much debate, the funding bill was passed by the House. The Senate approved the bill the next day. *Congressional Globe,* 26th Congress, 1st Session, 544, 546 (1840).

At the end of two years the class received the usual furlough, extending from the close of the June examination to the 28th of August. This I enjoyed beyond any other period of my life. My father had sold out his business in Georgetown—where my youth had been spent, and to which my day-dreams carried me back as my future home, if I should ever be able to retire on a competency. He had moved to Bethel, only twelve miles away, in the adjoining county of Clermont,[32] and had bought a young horse that had never been in harness, for my special use under the saddle during my furlough. Most of my time was spent among my old school-mates—these ten weeks were shorter than one week at West Point.

Persons acquainted with the Academy know that the corps of cadets is divided into four companies for the purpose of military exercises. These companies are officered from the cadets, the superintendent and commandant selecting the officers for their military bearing and qualifications. The adjutant, quartermaster, four captains and twelve lieutenants are taken from the first, or Senior class; the sergeants from the second, or Junior class; and the corporals from the third, or Sophomore class. I had not been "called out" as a corporal, but when I returned from furlough I found myself the last but one—about my standing in all the tactics—of eighteen sergeants. The promotion was too much for me. That year my standing in the class— as shown by the number of demerits of the year—was about the same as it was among the sergeants, and I was dropped, and served the fourth year as a private.

During my first year's encampment General Scott visited West Point, and reviewed the cadets.[33] With his commanding figure, his quite colossal size and showy uniform, I thought him the finest specimen of manhood my eyes had ever beheld, and the most to be envied. I could never resemble him in appearance, but I believe I did have a presentiment for a moment that some day I should occupy his place on review—although I had no intention then of remaining in the army. My experience in a horse-trade ten years before, and the ridicule it caused me, were too fresh in my mind for me to communicate this

[32] By Mar. 1840, JRG had sold his company and moved from Georgetown to Bethel, OH, where he formed a partnership with fellow tanner E. A. Collins. *PUSG,* 1:8–9.

[33] Winfield Scott (1786–1866) was born in Virginia and entered the U.S. Army as a captain in 1808. He fought in the War of 1812 and was promoted to brigadier general in 1814. He attained the rank of major general in 1841 and served as commanding general of the U.S. Army from 1841 to 1861. He was the Whig Party presidential candidate in 1852. *CWHC,* 475–476.

presentiment to even my most intimate chum. The next summer Martin Van Buren, then President of the United States,[34] visited West Point and reviewed the cadets; he did not impress me with the awe which Scott had inspired.[35] In fact I regarded General Scott and Captain C. F. Smith,[36] the Commandant of Cadets, as the two men most to be envied in the nation. I retained a high regard for both up to the day of their death.

The last two years wore away more rapidly than the first two, but they still seemed about five times as long as Ohio years, to me. At last all the examinations were passed, and the members of the class were called upon to record their choice of arms of service and regiments. I was anxious to enter the cavalry, or dragoons as they were then called, but there was only one regiment of dragoons in the Army at that time, and attached to that, besides the full complement of officers, there were at least four brevet second lieutenants. I recorded therefore my first choice, dragoons; second, 4th infantry; and got the latter.[37] Again there was a furlough—or, more properly speaking, leave of absence for the class were now commissioned officers—this time to the end of September. Again I went to Ohio to spend my vacation among my old schoolmates; and again I found a fine saddle horse purchased for my special use, besides a horse and buggy that I could drive—but I was not in a physical condition to enjoy myself quite as well as on the former occasion. For six months before graduation I had had a desperate cough ("Tyler's grip"[38] it was called), and I was very much reduced, weighing but one hundred and seventeen pounds, just my weight at entrance, though I had grown six inches in

---

[34] Martin Van Buren (1782–1862) served as United States president from 1837 to 1841. *Dictionary of American Biography,* 2nd ed., s.v. "Van Buren, Martin."

[35] Pres. Martin Van Buren, Gen. Winfield Scott, and Secretary of War Joel R. Poinsett all traveled to the USMA during summer 1839. Donald C. Pfanz, *Richard S. Ewell: A Soldier's Life* (Chapel Hill: University of North Carolina Press, 1998), 25; *PUSG,* 1:6–7.

[36] Charles F. Smith (1807–1862) was born in Pennsylvania, graduated from the USMA in 1825, and served as commandant of cadets from 1838 to 1843 (while USG was a cadet). He served in the Mexican-American War and was a colonel in the U.S. 3rd Inf. in 1861. He served under USG and was promoted to major general in Mar. 1862. *CWHC,* 493; *PUSG,* 1:10n.

[37] In Nov. 1843, USG unsuccessfully attempted to secure a transfer from the 4th U.S. Inf. to the dragoons. *PUSG,* 1:23n.

[38] In the early 1840s, a severe strain of influenza spread throughout the United States. The disease, also known as "lightning catarrh," was usually referred to as "Tyler's Grip," a response to the unpopular presidency of John Tyler. C. P. Skip, "The Homoeopathic Medical Society of Allegheny Co., PA.," *Hahnemannian Monthly* 13, no. 8 (1878): 458.

stature in the mean time. There was consumption in my father's family, two of his brothers having died of that disease, which made my symptoms more alarming. The brother and sister next younger than myself died, during the rebellion, of the same disease, and I seemed the most promising subject for it of the three in 1843.[39]

Having made alternate choice of two different arms of service with different uniforms, I could not get a uniform suit until notified of my assignment. I left my measurement with a tailor, with directions not to make the uniform until I notified him whether it was to be for infantry or dragoons. Notice did not reach me for several weeks, and then it took at least a week to get the letter of instructions to the tailor and two more to make the clothes and have them sent to me. This was a time of great suspense. I was impatient to get on my uniform and see how it looked, and probably wanted my old school-mates, particularly the girls, to see me in it. The conceit was knocked out of me by two little circumstances that happened soon after the arrival of the clothes, which gave me a distaste for military uniform that I never recovered from. Soon after the arrival of the suit I donned it, and put off for Cincinnati on horseback. While I was riding along a street of that city, imagining that every one was looking at me, with a feeling akin to mine when I first saw General Scott, a little urchin, bareheaded, barefooted, with dirty and ragged pants held up by a single gallows—that's what suspenders were called then—and a shirt that had not seen a wash-tub for weeks, turned to me and cried: "Soldier! will you work? No, sir—ee; I'll sell my shirt first!!" The horse trade and its dire consequences were recalled to mind.

The other circumstance occurred at home. Opposite our house in Bethel stood the old stage tavern where "man and beast" found accommodation. The stable-man was rather dissipated, but possessed of some humor. On my return I found him parading the streets, and attending in the stable, barefooted, but in a pair of sky-blue nankeen pantaloons—just the color of my uniform trousers—with a strip of white cotton sheeting sewed down the outside seams in imitation of mine. The joke was a huge one in the

[39] USG probably referred to his uncles Noah B. Grant (1797–1821) and John K. Grant (1799–1832), his brother Samuel S. Grant (1825–1861), and his sister Clara R. Grant (1828–1865). Arthur H. Grant, *The Grant Family: A Genealogical History of the Descendants of Matthew Grant of Windsor, Conn., 1601–1898* (Poughkeepsie, NY: A. V. Haight, 1898), 66, 143; *PUSG*, 2:289–290.

mind of many of the people, and was much enjoyed by them; but I did not appreciate it so highly.

During the remainder of my leave of absence, my time was spent in visiting friends in Georgetown and Cincinnati, and occasionally other towns in that part of the State.

# 3

## Army Life—Causes of the Mexican War—Camp Salubrity

O N THE 30TH of September I reported for duty at Jefferson Barracks, St. Louis, with the 4th United States infantry. It was the largest military post in the country at that time, being garrisoned by sixteen companies of infantry, eight of the 3d regiment, the remainder of the 4th.[1] Colonel Steven Kearney,[2] one of the ablest officers of the day, commanded the post, and under him discipline was kept at a high standard, but without vexatious rules or regulations. Every drill and roll-call had to be attended, but in the intervals officers were permitted to enjoy themselves, leaving the garrison, and going where they pleased, without making written application to state where they were going for how long, etc., so that they were back for their next duty. It did seem to me, in my early army days, that too many of the older officers, when they came to command posts, made it a study to think what orders they could publish to annoy their subordinates and render them uncomfortable. I noticed, however, a few years later, when the Mexican war broke out, that most of this class of officers discovered they were possessed of disabilities which entirely incapacitated them for active field service. They had the moral courage to proclaim it, too. They were right; but they did not always give their disease the right name.

---

[1] With the arrival of the U.S. 3rd Inf. in Apr. 1843, Jefferson Barracks housed roughly 1,031 officers and enlisted men when USG arrived. USG accepted an appointment as brevet second lieutenant in a letter dated July 31, 1843. Marc E. Kollbaum, *Gateway to the West: The History of Jefferson Barracks from 1826–1894,* vol. 1 (St. Louis: Friends of Jefferson Barracks, 2001), 96–99; *PUSG,* 1:22.

[2] Stephen W. Kearny (1794–1848) was appointed commander of the 3rd Military District in 1842. Dwight L. Clarke, *Stephen Watts Kearny: Soldier of the West* (Norman: University of Oklahoma Press, 1961), 3, 83, 387.

At West Point I had a class-mate—in the last year of our studies he was room-mate also—F. T. Dent,[3] whose family resided some five miles west of Jefferson Barracks. Two of his unmarried brothers were living at home at that time, and as I had taken with me from Ohio, my horse, saddle and bridle, I soon found my way out to White Haven, the name of the Dent estate. As I found the family congenial my visits became frequent. There were at home, besides the young men, two daughters, one a school miss of fifteen, the other a girl of eight or nine. There was still an older daughter of seventeen, who had been spending several years at boarding-school in St. Louis, but who, though through school, had not yet returned home.[4] She was spending the winter in the city with connections, the family of Colonel John O'Fallon,[5] well known in St. Louis. In February she returned to her country home. After that I do not know but my visits became more frequent; they certainly did become more enjoyable. We would often take walks, or go on horseback to visit the neighbors, until I became quite well acquainted in that vicinity. Sometimes one of the brothers would accompany us, sometimes one of the younger sisters. If the 4th infantry had remained at Jefferson Barracks it is possible, even probable, that this life might have continued for some years without my finding out that there was anything serious the matter with me; but in the following May a circumstance occurred which developed my sentiment so palpably that there was no mistaking it.

[3] Frederick T. Dent (1820–1892), the brother of USG's future wife JDG and cousin of James Longstreet, had been USG's roommate during their final year at the USMA. Following graduation, Dent was assigned to the U.S. 6th Inf. at Fort Towson in Indian Territory. *CWHC,* 206; Felice F. Lewis, *Trailing Clouds of Glory: Zachary Taylor's Mexican War Campaign and His Emerging Civil War Leaders* (Tuscaloosa: University of Alabama Press, 2010), 241*n.*

[4] White Haven, owned by Frederick Dent (1786–1873), was a 950-acre plantation located near St. Louis. Members of the immediate Dent Family included Dent's wife Ellen (179?–1857); sons John (1816–1889), George (1819–1899), Frederick, and Lewis (or Louis) (1823–1874); and daughters JDG (1826–1902), Ellen (Nellie) (1828–1904), and Emily (Emma) (1836–?). In her memoirs, JDG does not mention specifically which family members were at home when USG began his courtship. The two unmarried brothers referenced by USG were likely John and Lewis; George had married in 1841. JDG, *The Personal Memoirs of Julia Dent Grant (Mrs. Ulysses S. Grant),* ed. John Y. Simon (New York: G. P. Putnam's Sons, 1975), 30, 33–35, 48–52, 337; Mark Perry, *Grant and Twain: The Story of a Friendship That Changed America* (New York: Random House, 2004), 16.

[5] John O'Fallon (1791–1865) was a former soldier and successful businessman in St. Louis who was a friend of the Dent family. In 1848, he and his wife presented JDG with a very expensive dress for her wedding. JDG, *Memoirs,* 47, 55, 63*n*; Mary E. Rowe, "A Respectable Independence: The Early Career of John O'Fallon," *Missouri Historical Review* 90 (1996): 409.

The annexation of Texas was at this time the subject of violent discussion in Congress, in the press, and by individuals. The administration of President Tyler,[6] then in power, was making the most strenuous efforts to effect the annexation, which was, indeed, the great and absorbing question of the day. During these discussions the greater part of the single rifle regiment in the army—the 2d dragoons, which had been dismounted a year or two before, and designated "Dismounted Rifles"—was stationed at Fort Jessup,[7] Louisiana, some twenty-five miles east of the Texas line, to observe the frontier. About the 1st of May the 3d infantry was ordered from Jefferson Barracks to Louisiana, to go into camp in the neighborhood of Fort Jessup, and there await further orders.[8] The troops were embarked on steamers and were on their way down the Mississippi within a few days after the receipt of this order. About the time they started I obtained a leave of absence for twenty days to go to Ohio to visit my parents.[9] I was obliged to go to St. Louis to take a steamer for Louisville or Cincinnati, or the first steamer going up the Ohio River to any point. Before I left St. Louis orders were received at Jefferson Barracks for the 4th infantry to follow the 3d. A messenger was sent after me to stop my leaving; but before he could reach me I was off, totally ignorant of these events. A day or two after my arrival at Bethel I received a letter from a classmate and fellow lieutenant in the 4th,[10] informing me of the circumstances related above, and advising me not to open any letter post marked St. Louis or Jefferson Barracks, until the expiration of my leave, and saying that he would pack up my things and take them along for me. His advice was not necessary, for no other letter was sent to me. I now discovered that I was exceedingly anxious to get back

[6] John Tyler (1790–1862) served as United States president from 1841 to 1845. Edward P. Crapol, *John Tyler: The Accidental President* (Chapel Hill: University of North Carolina Press, 2006), 3, 30, 219–220, 268.

[7] Fort Jesup was established in 1830 near the Sabine River, on the border of Louisiana and Mexico. Named for army quartermaster Gen. Thomas Jesup, it served as the primary military post in the region and became a staging area for U.S. soldiers during the Mexican-American War. Lewis, *Trailing Clouds of Glory*, 1; Lisa Kay-Wolfe, "Fort Jesup," in *The Louisiana Purchase: A Historical and Geographical Encyclopedia*, ed. Junius P. Rodriguez (Santa Barbara, CA: ABC-CLIO, 2002), 162–163; *PUSG*, 1:23–27.

[8] On Apr. 22, 1844, Asst. AG Lorenzo Thomas ordered the 4th U.S. Inf. to Fort Jesup. William Q. Force, *Army and Navy Chronicle, and Scientific Repository*, vol. 3 (Washington, DC: B. Homans, 1844), 543; *Public Documents Printed by Order of the Senate of the United States First Session of the Twenty-Eighth Congress, Begun and Held at the City of Washington*, Dec. 4, 1843, vol. 5 (Washington, DC: Gales and Seaton, 1844), 341.

[9] USG was on leave May 1–20, 1844. *PUSG*, 1:23–27.

[10] The editors of *PUSG* have not identified a letter matching this description.

to Jefferson Barracks, and I understood the reason without explanation from any one. My leave of absence required me to report for duty, at Jefferson Barracks, at the end of twenty days. I knew my regiment had gone up the Red River, but I was not disposed to break the letter of my leave; besides, if I had proceeded to Louisiana direct, I could not have reached there until after the expiration of my leave. Accordingly, at the end of the twenty days, I reported for duty to Lieutenant Ewell,[11] commanding at Jefferson Barracks, handing him at the same time my leave of absence. After noticing the phraseology of the order—leaves of absence were generally worded, "at the end of which time he will report for duty with his proper command"—he said he would give me an order to join my regiment in Louisiana. I then asked for a few days' leave before starting, which he readily granted. This was the same Ewell who acquired considerable reputation as a Confederate general during the rebellion. He was a man much esteemed, and deservedly so, in the old army, and proved himself a gallant and efficient officer in two wars—both in my estimation unholy.

I immediately procured a horse and started for the country, taking no baggage with me, of course. There is an insignificant creek—the Gravois—between Jefferson Barracks and the place to which I was going, and at that day there was not a bridge over it from its source to its mouth. There is not water enough in the creek at ordinary stages to run a coffee mill, and at low water there is none running whatever. On this occasion it had been raining heavily, and, when the creek was reached, I found the banks full to overflowing, and the current rapid. I looked at it a moment to consider what to do. One of my superstitions had always been when I started to go any where, or to do anything, not to turn back, or stop until the thing intended was accomplished. I have frequently started to go to places where I had never been and to which I did not know the way, depending upon making inquiries on the road, and if I got past the place without knowing it, instead of turning back, I would go on until a road was found turning in the right direction, take that, and come in

---

[11] Richard S. Ewell (1817–1872) was born in Maryland and his family moved to Pennsylvania when he was one year old. A USMA graduate, he became first lieutenant on Nov. 1, 1840. Ewell was assigned to Jefferson Barracks in May 1844, and during that winter he reported to Louisville, KY, for recruitment duties. Ewell would go on to become a lieutenant general in the Confederate Army and would command Gen. Thomas "Stonewall" Jackson's 2nd Corps after Jackson's death. Donald C. Pfanz, *Richard S. Ewell: A Soldier's Life* (Chapel Hill: University of North Carolina Press, 1998), 5, 38–41; Ezra J. Warner, *Generals in Gray: Lives of the Confederate Commanders* (Baton Rouge: Louisiana State University Press, 1959), 84–85.

by the other side. So I struck into the stream, and in an instant the horse was swimming and I being carried down by the current. I headed the horse towards the other bank and soon reached it, wet through and without other clothes on that side of the stream. I went on, however, to my destination and borrowed a dry suit from my—future—brother-in-law. We were not of the same size, but the clothes answered every purpose until I got more of my own.

Before I returned I mustered up courage to make known, in the most awkward manner imaginable, the discovery I had made on learning that the 4th infantry had been ordered away from Jefferson Barracks. The young lady afterwards admitted that she too, although until then she had never looked upon me other than as a visitor whose company was agreeable to her, had experienced a depression of spirits she could not account for when the regiment left. Before separating it was definitely understood that at a convenient time we would join our fortunes, and not let the removal of a regiment trouble us. This was in May, 1844. It was the 22d of August, 1848, before the fulfilment of this agreement.[12] My duties kept me on the frontier of Louisiana with the Army of Observation during the pendency of Annexation; and afterwards I was absent through the war with Mexico, provoked by the action of the army, if not by the annexation itself. During that time there was a constant correspondence between Miss Dent and myself, but we only met once in the period of four years and three months. In May, 1845, I procured a leave for twenty days, visited St. Louis, and obtained the consent of the parents for the union, which had not been asked for before.[13]

As already stated, it was never my intention to remain in the army long, but to prepare myself for a professorship in some college. Accordingly, soon after I was settled at Jefferson Barracks, I wrote a letter to Professor Church[14]— Professor of Mathematics at West Point—requesting him to ask my designation as his assistant, when next a detail had to be made. Assistant professors

[12] USG spent most of his weeklong stay in Missouri at White Haven. On an excursion to St. Louis during this trip, USG proposed marriage to JDG. JDG, *Memoirs,* 50.

[13] USG was on leave Apr. 1–May 5, 1845, when he visited the Dents at White Haven. In her memoirs, JDG stated that her father initially hesitated in giving permission for the marriage since he believed JDG unsuited for the role of a soldier's wife, but he consented to their courtship after talking with USG. JDG, *Memoirs,* 51; *PUSG,* 1:45*n.*

[14] Albert E. Church (1807–1878) was professor of mathematics at the USMA from 1828 to 1831 and from 1833 to 1878. The letter to Church may have been written in the autumn of 1843. Theodore J. Crackel, *West Point: A Bicentennial History* (Lawrence: University Press of Kansas, 2002), 126–127; *PUSG,* 1:365; 32:135.

at West Point are all officers of the army, supposed to be selected for their special fitness for the particular branch of study they are assigned to teach. The answer from Professor Church was entirely satisfactory, and no doubt I should have been detailed a year or two later but for the Mexican War coming on. Accordingly I laid out for myself a course of studies to be pursued in garrison, with regularity, if not persistency. I reviewed my West Point course of mathematics during the seven months at Jefferson Barracks, and read many valuable historical works, besides an occasional novel. To help my memory I kept a book in which I would write up, from time to time, my recollections of all I had read since last posting it. When the regiment was ordered away, I being absent at the time, my effects were packed up by Lieutenant Haslett,[15] of the 4th infantry, and taken along. I never saw my journal after, nor did I ever keep another, except for a portion of the time while travelling abroad. Often since a fear has crossed my mind lest that book might turn up yet, and fall into the hands of some malicious person who would publish it. I know its appearance would cause me as much heart-burning as my youthful horse-trade, or the later rebuke for wearing uniform clothes.

The 3d infantry had selected camping grounds on the reservation at Fort Jessup, about midway between the Red River and the Sabine. Our orders required us to go into camp in the same neighborhood, and await further instructions.[16] Those authorized to do so selected a place in the pine woods, between the old town of Natchitoches and Grand Ecore, about three miles from each, and on high ground back from the river. The place was given the name of Camp Salubrity,[17] and proved entitled to it. The camp was on a high, sandy, pine ridge, with spring branches in the valley, in front and rear. The springs furnished an abundance of cool, pure water, and the ridge was above the flight of mosquitoes, which abound in that region in great multitudes and of great voracity. In the valley they swarmed in myriads, but never came

[15] Robert Hazlitt (c.1821–1846), originally from Ohio, attended the USMA with USG and was an officer in the U.S. 4th Inf. Hazlitt was killed at the Battle of Monterey during the Mexican-American War. George W. Cullum, *Biographical Register of the Officers and Graduates of the U.S. Military Academy at West Point, N.Y.* (Boston: Houghton, Mifflin, 1891), 2:180; *PUSG*, 1:25, 26*n*.

[16] On Apr. 11, 1844, one day before Secretary of State John C. Calhoun signed the annexation treaty, the U.S. 3rd Inf. was ordered to move from Jefferson Barracks to Fort Jesup. On Apr. 22, the U.S. 4th Inf. received a similar order. *Dictionary of American Biography,* 2nd ed., s.v. "Calhoun, John Caldwell"; Lewis, *Trailing Clouds of Glory,* 1.

[17] On May 24, 1844, Camp Salubrity was established about three miles from Natchitoches, LA. *PUSG,* 1:23–27.

to the summit of the ridge. The regiment occupied this camp six months before the first death occurred, and that was caused by an accident.[18]

There was no intimation given that the removal of the 3d and 4th regiments of infantry to the western border of Louisiana was occasioned in any way by the prospective annexation of Texas, but it was generally understood that such was the case. Ostensibly we were intended to prevent filibustering into Texas, but really as a menace to Mexico in case she appeared to contemplate war. Generally the officers of the army were indifferent whether the annexation was consummated or not; but not so all of them. For myself, I was bitterly opposed to the measure, and to this day regard the war, which resulted, as one of the most unjust ever waged by a stronger against a weaker nation. It was an instance of a republic following the bad example of European monarchies, in not considering justice in their desire to acquire additional territory.

Texas was originally a state belonging to the republic of Mexico. It extended from the Sabine River on the east to the Rio Grande on the west, and from the Gulf of Mexico on the south and east to the territory of the United States and New Mexico—another Mexican state at that time—on the north and west. An empire in territory, it had but a very sparse population, until settled by Americans who had received authority from Mexico to colonize. These colonists paid very little attention to the supreme government, and introduced slavery into the state almost from the start, though the constitution of Mexico did not, nor does it now, sanction that institution.[19] Soon they set up an independent government of their own, and war existed, between Texas and Mexico, in name from that time until 1836, when active hostilities very nearly ceased upon the capture of Santa Anna, the Mexican President.[20] Before long, however, the same people—who with permission of Mexico had colonized Texas, and afterwards set up slavery there, and then seceded as soon as they felt strong enough to do so—offered themselves and the State to the United

[18] USG may be referring to the death of army paymaster Peter Muhlenberg at Grand Ecore, LA, on Aug. 21, 1844. *Official Army Register for 1845* (Washington, DC: C. Alexander, 1845), 32.

[19] Immigrants from the United States had begun settlement of Texas by Dec. 1821. Slavery was outlawed in Mexico in 1829, but slaveholding in Texas continued. Spencer Tucker, ed., *The Encyclopedia of the Mexican-American War* (Santa Barbara, CA: ABC-CLIO, 2013), s.v. "Slavery."

[20] Antonio López de Santa Anna (1794–1876) was a politician and general who from 1833 to 1855 was president eleven times. Michael S. Werner, ed., *Concise Encyclopedia of Mexico* (Chicago: Fitzroy Dearborn, 2001), 729.

States, and in 1845 their offer was accepted.[21] The occupation, separation and annexation were, from the inception of the movement to its final consummation, a conspiracy to acquire territory out of which slave states might be formed for the American Union.

Even if the annexation itself could be justified, the manner in which the subsequent war was forced upon Mexico cannot. The fact is, annexationists wanted more territory than they could possibly lay any claim to, as part of the new acquisition. Texas, as an independent State, never had exercised jurisdiction over the territory between the Nueces River and the Rio Grande. Mexico had never recognized the independence of Texas, and maintained that, even if independent, the State had no claim south of the Nueces. I am aware that a treaty, made by the Texans with Santa Anna while he was under duress, ceded all the territory between the Nueces and the Rio Grande; but he was a prisoner of war when the treaty was made, and his life was in jeopardy. He knew, too, that he deserved execution at the hands of the Texans, if they should ever capture him. The Texans, if they had taken his life, would have only followed the example set by Santa Anna himself a few years before, when he executed the entire garrison of the Alamo and the villagers of Goliad.[22]

In taking military possession of Texas after annexation, the army of occupation, under General Taylor,[23] was directed to occupy the disputed territory. The army did not stop at the Nueces and offer to negotiate for a settlement of the boundary question, but went beyond, apparently in order to force Mexico to initiate war. It is to the credit of the American nation, however, that after conquering Mexico, and while practically holding the country in our possession, so that we could have retained the whole of it, or made any terms we chose, we paid a round sum for the additional territory taken; more than it was worth, or was likely to be, to Mexico. To us it was an empire and of incalculable value; but it might have been obtained by other means. The

[21] On Dec. 29, 1845, Texas entered the Union as a state. Tucker, *Encyclopedia of the Mexican-American War,* s.v. "Texas."

[22] On Apr. 21, 1836, Texans won independence from Mexico at the Battle of Jacinto. Santa Anna signed the Treaty of Velasco while imprisoned after the battle. This treaty granted Texas its independence and was largely recognized by other countries including the United States. Mexican authorities, however, refused to honor the treaty. John S. D. Eisenhower, *So Far from God: The U.S. War with Mexico, 1846–1848* (Norman: University of Oklahoma Press, 1989), 14.

[23] Zachary Taylor (1784–1850) was a career soldier who was brevetted brigadier general in 1838. After the Mexican-American War, he won the 1848 presidential election as the Whig Party candidate. *Dictionary of American Biography,* 2nd edition, "Taylor, Zachary."

Southern rebellion was largely the outgrowth of the Mexican war. Nations, like individuals, are punished for their transgressions. We got our punishment in the most sanguinary and expensive war of modern times.

The 4th infantry went into camp at Salubrity in the month of May, 1844, with instructions, as I have said, to await further orders. At first, officers and men occupied ordinary tents. As the summer heat increased these were covered by sheds to break the rays of the sun. The summer was whiled away in social enjoyments among the officers, in visiting those stationed at, and near, Fort Jessup, twenty-five miles away, visiting the planters on the Red River, and the citizens of Natchitoches and Grand Ecore. There was much pleasant inter-course between the inhabitants and the officers of the army. I retain very agree-able recollections of my stay at Camp Salubrity, and of the acquaintances made there, and no doubt my feeling is shared by the few officers living who were there at the time. I can call to mind only two officers of the 4th infantry, be-sides myself, who were at Camp Salubrity with the regiment, who are now alive.[24]

With a war in prospect, and belonging to a regiment that had an unusual number of officers detailed on special duty away from the regiment, my hopes of being ordered to West Point as instructor vanished. At the time of which I now write, officers in the quartermaster's, commissary's and adjutant-general's departments were appointed from the line of the army, and did not vacate their regimental commissions until their regimental and staff commissions were for the same grades. Generally lieutenants were appointed to captaincies to fill vacancies in the staff corps. If they should reach a captaincy in the line before they arrived at a majority in the staff, they would elect which commis-sion they would retain. In the 4th infantry, in 1844, at least six line officers were on duty in the staff, and therefore permanently detached from the regi-ment. Under these circumstances I gave up everything like a special course of reading, and only read thereafter for my own amusement, and not very much for that, until the war was over. I kept a horse and rode, and staid out of doors most of the time by day, and entirely recovered from the cough which I had

---

[24]There were seven officers who were part of the U.S. 4th Inf. in 1844–1845 and were still alive in 1885–1886. These included Granville O. Haller (1819–1897), James Longstreet (1821–1904), Pitcairn Morrison (1795–1887), Abraham C. Myers (1811–1889), Henry Prince (1811–1892), Henry L. Scott (1814–1886), and Henry D. Wallen (1819–1886). "Col. Haller Is Dead," *Seattle Post-Intelligencer,* May 3, 1897, 8; Cullum, *Biographical Register,* 2:146; *Dictionary of American Biography,* 2nd ed., s.v. "Myers, Abraham Charles"; *CWHC,* 352, 399, 441, 552; *Official Army Register for 1845,* 20; *Seventeenth Annual Reunion of the Association of the Graduates of the United States Military Academy* (East Saginaw, MI: Evening News, 1886), 69.

carried from West Point, and from all indications of consumption. I have often thought that my life was saved, and my health restored, by exercise and exposure, enforced by an administrative act, and a war, both of which I disapproved.

As summer wore away, and cool days and colder nights came upon us, the tents we were occupying ceased to afford comfortable quarters; and "further orders" not reaching us, we began to look about to remedy the hardship. Men were put to work getting out timber to build huts, and in a very short time all were comfortably housed—privates as well as officers. The outlay by the government in accomplishing this was nothing, or nearly nothing. The winter was spent more agreeably than the summer had been. There were occasional parties given by the planters along the "coast"—as the bottom lands on the Red River were called. The climate was delightful.

Near the close of the short session of Congress of 1844–5, the bill for the annexation of Texas to the United States was passed.[25] It reached President Tyler on the 1st of March, 1845, and promptly received his approval. When the news reached us we began to look again for "further orders." They did not arrive promptly, and on the 1st of May following I asked and obtained a leave of absence for twenty days, for the purpose of visiting St. Louis. The object of this visit has been before stated.

Early in July the long expected orders were received, but they only took the regiment to New Orleans Barracks. We reached there before the middle of the month, and again waited weeks for still further orders. The yellow fever was raging in New Orleans during the time we remained there, and the streets of the city had the appearance of a continuous well-observed Sunday.[26] I recollect but one occasion when this observance seemed to be broken by the inhabitants. One morning about daylight I happened to be awake, and, hearing the discharge of a rifle not far off, I looked out to ascertain where the sound came from. I observed a couple of clusters of men near by, and learned afterwards that "it was nothing; only a couple of gentlemen deciding a difference of opinion with rifles, at twenty paces." I do not remember if either was killed, or even hurt, but no doubt the question of difference was settled satisfactorily, and "honorably," in the estimation of the parties engaged. I do not believe I ever would have the courage to fight a duel. If any man should wrong me to

[25] On Feb. 28, 1845, the U.S. House of Representatives accepted the U.S. Senate's amended version of the joint resolution on the annexation of Texas. Crapol, *John Tyler*, 220.

[26] The U.S. 4th Inf. arrived in New Orleans on July 5, 1845. USG made no reference to the yellow fever outbreak in his correspondence at the time. *PUSG*, 1:49n.

the extent of my being willing to kill him, I would not be willing to give him the choice of weapons with which it should be done, and of the time, place and distance separating us, when I executed him. If I should do another such a wrong as to justify him in killing me, I would make any reasonable atonement within my power, if convinced of the wrong done. I place my opposition to dueling on higher grounds than any here stated. No doubt a majority of the duels fought have been for want of moral courage on the part of those engaged to decline.

At Camp Salubrity, and when we went to New Orleans Barracks, the 4th infantry was commanded by Colonel Vose,[27] then an old gentleman who had not commanded on drill for a number of years. He was not a man to discover infirmity in the presence of danger. It now appeared that war was imminent, and he felt that it was his duty to brush up his tactics. Accordingly, when we got settled down at our new post, he took command of the regiment at a battalion drill. Only two or three evolutions had been gone through when he dismissed the battalion, and, turning to go to his own quarters, dropped dead. He had not been complaining of ill health, but no doubt died of heart disease. He was a most estimable man, of exemplary habits, and by no means the author of his own disease.

[27] Josiah H. Vose (c.1786–1845) was from Massachusetts and joined the army in 1812. By 1834, Vose was in charge of Fort Jesup as a lieutenant colonel in the U.S. 3rd Inf. In 1844, Vose, as commander of the 4th U.S. Inf., established the location of Camp Salubrity, but by June he had become so weak that Lt. Col. John Garland took command. Lewis, *Trailing Clouds of Glory*, 4. For USG's letter to JDG about Vose's death, see *PUSG*, 1:51–52.

# 4

## Corpus Christi—Mexican Smuggling—Spanish Rule in Mexico—Supplying Transportation

Early in september the regiment left New Orleans for Corpus Christi, now in Texas.[1] Ocean steamers were not then common, and the passage was made in sailing vessels.[2] At that time there was not more than three feet of water in the channel at the outlet of Corpus Christi Bay; the debarkation, therefore, had to take place by small steamers, and at an island in the channel called Shell Island, the ships anchoring some miles out from shore.[3] This made the work slow, and as the army was only supplied with one or two steamers, it took a number of days to effect the landing of a single regiment with its stores, camp and garrison equipage, etc. There happened to be pleasant weather while this was going on, but the land-swell was so great that when the ship and steamer were on opposite sides of the same wave they would be at considerable distance apart. The men and baggage were let down to a point higher than the lower deck of the steamer, and when ship and steamer got into the trough between the waves, and were close together, the load would be drawn over the steamer and rapidly run down until it rested on the deck.

After I had gone ashore, and had been on guard several days at Shell Island, quite six miles from the ship, I had occasion for some reason or other

---

[1] In June 1845, Andrew J. Donelson, the nephew of Andrew Jackson and chargé d'affaires in Texas, recommended to Secretary of State James Buchanan that Corpus Christi be a military camp. George L. Rives, *The United States and Mexico, 1821–1848* (New York: Charles Scribner's Sons, 1913), 2:137; *PUSG*, 1:53–56.

[2] Gen. Zachary Taylor and the U.S. 3rd Inf. traveled aboard the steamboat *Alabama* and arrived at Aransas Bay in Texas on July 25, 1845. The remaining part of the army followed on sailing vessels. John S. D. Eisenhower, *So Far from God: The U.S. War with Mexico, 1846–1848* (Norman: University of Oklahoma Press, 1989), 33.

[3] Shell Island, also called Saint Joseph's Island, was a sand barrier in the Aransas Bay located about twenty-five miles from Corpus Christi. Ibid., 31.

to return on board. While on the *Suviah*—I think that was the name of our vessel—I heard a tremendous racket at the other end of the ship, and much and excited sailor language, such as "damn your eyes," etc. In a moment or two the captain, who was an excitable little man, dying with consumption, and not weighing much over a hundred pounds, came running out, carrying a sabre nearly as large and as heavy as he was, and crying that his men had mutinied. It was necessary to sustain the captain without question, and in a few minutes all the sailors charged with mutiny were in irons. I rather felt for a time a wish that I had not gone aboard just then. As the men charged with mutiny submitted to being placed in irons without resistance, I always doubted if they knew that they had mutinied until they were told.[4]

By the time I was ready to leave the ship again I thought I had learned enough of the working of the double and single pulley, by which passengers were let down from the upper deck of the ship to the steamer below, and determined to let myself down without assistance. Without saying anything of my intentions to any one, I mounted the railing, and taking hold of the centre rope, just below the upper block, I put one foot on the hook below the lower block, and stepped off. Just as I did so some one called out "hold on." It was too late. I tried to "hold on" with all my might, but my heels went up, and my head went down so rapidly that my hold broke, and I plunged head foremost into the water, some twenty-five feet below, with such velocity that it seemed to me I never would stop. When I came to the surface again, being a fair swimmer, and not having lost my presence of mind, I swam around until a bucket was let down for me, and I was drawn up without a scratch or injury. I do not believe there was a man on board who sympathized with me in the least when they found me uninjured. I rather enjoyed the joke myself. The captain of the *Suviah* died of his disease a few months later, and I believe before the mutineers were tried. I hope they got clear, because, as before stated, I always thought the mutiny was all in the brain of a very weak and sick man.

---

[4] *Suviah* was one of the ships used as transports to Corpus Christi. The ship's captain during this time was a man named Gibbons. On Sept. 2, 1845, it was reported that three crew members from the ship had been arrested and were awaiting trial in New Orleans. Felice F. Lewis, *Trailing Clouds of Glory: Zachary Taylor's Mexican War Campaign and His Emerging Civil War Leaders* (Tuscaloosa: University of Alabama Press, 2010), 24; "Rumors of War, Movements of Troops &c," *American Republican and Baltimore Daily Clipper,* Sept. 2, 1845, 2; "Texas," *Richmond Enquirer,* Sept. 2, 1845, 2.

After reaching shore, or Shell Island, the labor of getting to Corpus Christi was slow and tedious.[5] There was, if my memory serves me, but one small steamer to transport troops and baggage when the 4th infantry arrived.[6] Others were procured later. The distance from Shell Island to Corpus Christi was some sixteen or eighteen miles. The channel to the bay was so shallow that the steamer, small as it was, had to be dragged over the bottom when loaded. Not more than one trip a day could be effected. Later this was remedied, by deepening the channel and increasing the number of vessels suitable to its navigation.[7]

Corpus Christi is near the head of the bay of the same name, formed by the entrance of the Nueces River into tide-water, and is on the west bank of that bay. At the time of its first occupancy by United States troops there was a small Mexican hamlet there, containing probably less than one hundred souls. There was, in addition, a small American trading post, at which goods were sold to Mexican smugglers.[8] All goods were put up in compact packages of about one hundred pounds each, suitable for loading on pack mules. Two of these packages made a load for an ordinary Mexican mule, and three for the larger ones. The bulk of the trade was in leaf tobacco, and domestic cotton-cloths and calicoes. The Mexicans had, before the arrival of the army, but little to offer in exchange except silver. The trade in tobacco was enormous, considering the population to be supplied. Almost every Mexican above the age of ten years, and many much younger, smoked the cigarette. Nearly

[5] Taylor and his troops took several days to land at Corpus Christi because of the rough and shallow waters in the bay. They began arriving on July 31, 1845, but USG did not reach Corpus Christi until Aug. 9. Lewis, *Trailing Clouds of Glory*, 24.

[6] On July 29, Taylor attempted to move his troops aboard the *Undine*, a smaller steamer, but it "drew more than four feet of water" and forced him to use only smaller vessels. W. A. Croffut, ed., *Fifty Years in Camp and Field: Diary of Major-General Ethan Allen Hitchcock, U.S.A.* (New York: G. P. Putnam's Sons, 1909), 194.

[7] Between 1879 and 1885, the U.S. Army Corps of Engineers built a jetty off Mustang Island just south of St. Joseph's Island, but it failed. In 1907, Aransas Pass was finally protected from drifting sediment with the construction of two more permanent jetties. Thomas T. Smith, *The U.S. Army and the Texas Frontier Economy, 1845–1900* (College Station: Texas A&M University Press, 1999), 150–151.

[8] In Aug. 1845, U.S. citizen Henry Kinney was in charge of the only well-established trading post in the Corpus Christi area. His business and wealth increased drastically with the arrival of Taylor's army and other people who were drawn to the disputed region. Mary Jo O'Rear, *Storm over the Bay: The People of Corpus Christi and Their Port* (College Station: Texas A&M University Press, 2009), 11–13.

every Mexican carried a pouch of leaf tobacco, powdered by rolling in the hands, and a roll of corn husks to make wrappers. The cigarettes were made by the smokers as they used them.

Up to the time of which I write, and for years afterwards—I think until the administration of President Juarez[9]—the cultivation, manufacture and sale of tobacco constituted a government monopoly, and paid the bulk of the revenue collected from internal sources.[10] The price was enormously high, and made successful smuggling very profitable. The difficulty of obtaining tobacco is probably the reason why everybody, male and female, used it at that time. I know from my own experience that when I was at West Point, the fact that tobacco, in every form, was prohibited, and the mere possession of the weed severely punished, made the majority of the cadets, myself included, try to acquire the habit of using it. I failed utterly at the time and for many years afterward; but the majority accomplished the object of their youthful ambition.[11]

Under Spanish rule Mexico was prohibited from producing anything that the mother-country could supply. This rule excluded the cultivation of the grape, olive and many other articles to which the soil and climate were well adapted. The country was governed for "revenue only;" and tobacco, which cannot be raised in Spain, but is indigenous to Mexico, offered a fine instrumentality for securing this prime object of government.[12] The native population had been in the habit of using "the weed" from a period, back of any recorded history of this continent. Bad habits—if not restrained by law or

---

[9] Benito Juárez (1806–1872) was born in Oaxaca, Mexico, and served as president of Mexico from 1861 to 1872. Donald C. Lee Stacy, ed., *Mexico and the United States* (New York: Marshall Cavendish, 2003), 435.

[10] Between the 1830s and 1860s, the Mexican government relinquished control of tobacco manufacturing to private entrepreneurs. Susan Deans-Smith, *Bureaucrats, Planters, and Workers: The Making of a Tobacco Monopoly in Bourbon Mexico* (Austin: University of Texas Press, 1992), xii–xiii, 258.

[11] A former Dent family slave, Mary Robinson, recounted that USG smoked a pipe as early as the 1850s. USG stated that he had been "a very light smoker" before the 1862 Battle of Fort Donelson. After the fort was captured, newspapers reported that USG smoked a cigar during the battle and, in response, citizens sent USG about 10,000 cigars. Charles Bracelen Flood, *Grant's Final Victory* (Cambridge, MA: Da Capo, 2011), 110–112.

[12] The Spanish government relied on its colonies to pay for its participation in several European conflicts. Mexico was required to provide enough revenue to pay its own administrative and defensive expenses while supplying Spain with money. Mark A. Burkholder, "An Empire beyond Compare," in *The Oxford History of Mexico*, ed. William H. Beezley and Michael C. Meyer (New York: Oxford University Press, 2000), 143–149.

public opinion—spread more rapidly and universally than good ones, and the Spanish colonists adopted the use of tobacco almost as generally as the natives. Spain, therefore, in order to secure the largest revenue from this source, prohibited the cultivation, except in specified localities—and in these places farmed out the privilege at a very high price.[13] The tobacco when raised could only be sold to the government, and the price to the consumer was limited only by the avarice of the authorities, and the capacity of the people to pay.

All laws for the government of the country were enacted in Spain, and the officers for their execution were appointed by the Crown, and sent out to the New El Dorado. The Mexicans had been brought up ignorant of how to legislate or how to rule. When they gained their independence, after many years of war, it was the most natural thing in the world that they should adopt as their own the laws then in existence. The only change was, that Mexico became her own executor of the laws and the recipient of the revenues. The tobacco tax, yielding so large a revenue under the law as it stood, was one of the last, if not the very last, of the obnoxious imposts to be repealed. Now, the citizens are allowed to cultivate any crops the soil will yield. Tobacco is cheap, and every quality can be produced. Its use is by no means so general as when I first visited the country.

Gradually the "Army of Occupation" assembled at Corpus Christi.[14] When it was all together it consisted of seven companies of the 2d regiment of dragoons, four companies of light artillery, five regiments of infantry—the 3d, 4th, 5th, 7th and 8th—and one regiment of artillery acting as infantry—not more than three thousand men in all.[15] General Zachary Taylor commanded the whole. There were troops enough in one body to establish a drill and discipline sufficient to fit men and officers for all they were capable of in case of battle. The rank and file were composed of men who had enlisted in time of peace, to serve for seven dollars a month, and were necessarily inferior as material to the average volunteers enlisted later in the war expressly to fight, and also to the volunteers in the war for the preservation of the Union. The men

---

[13] Spain allowed tobacco production only in the villas of Orizaba and Cordoba. Deans-Smith, *Bureaucrats, Planters, and Workers,* xii–xiii, 258.

[14] The forces stationed at Fort Jesup were actually called the Army of Observation because their orders were to watch for Mexican military activity. James M. McCaffrey, *Army of Manifest Destiny: The American Soldiers in the Mexican War, 1846–1848* (New York: New York University Press, 1992), 6.

[15] The U.S. Army had almost 4,000 men stationed at Corpus Christi by late Oct. 1845. K. Jack Bauer, *The Mexican War, 1846–1848* (New York: Macmillan, 1974), 32–34.

engaged in the Mexican war were brave, and the officers of the regular army, from highest to lowest, were educated in their profession. A more efficient army for its number and armament, I do not believe ever fought a battle than the one commanded by General Taylor in his first two engagements on Mexican—or Texan soil.

The presence of United States troops on the edge of the disputed territory furthest from the Mexican settlements, was not sufficient to provoke hostilities. We were sent to provoke a fight, but it was essential that Mexico should commence it. It was very doubtful whether Congress would declare war; but if Mexico should attack our troops, the Executive could announce, "Whereas, war exists by the acts of, etc.," and prosecute the contest with vigor. Once initiated there were but few public men who would have the courage to oppose it. Experience proves that the man who obstructs a war in which his nation is engaged, no matter whether right or wrong, occupies no enviable place in life or history. Better for him, individually, to advocate "war, pestilence, and famine," than to act as obstructionist to a war already begun. The history of the defeated rebel will be honorable hereafter, compared with that of the Northern man who aided him by conspiring against his government while protected by it. The most favorable posthumous history the stay-at-home traitor can hope for is—oblivion.

Mexico showing no willingness to come to the Nueces to drive the invaders from her soil, it became necessary for the "invaders" to approach to within a convenient distance to be struck. Accordingly, preparations were begun for moving the army to the Rio Grande, to a point near Matamoras.[16] It was desirable to occupy a position near the largest centre of population possible to reach, without absolutely invading territory to which we set up no claim whatever.

The distance from Corpus Christi to Matamoras is about one hundred and fifty miles. The country does not abound in fresh water, and the length of the marches had to be regulated by the distance between water supplies. Besides the streams, there were occasional pools, filled during the rainy season, some probably made by the traders, who travelled constantly between Corpus Christi and the Rio Grande, and some by the buffalo.[17] There was not at that time a

---

[16] On Mar. 8, 1846, Taylor's forces started their march toward Matamoros, Mexico (commonly spelled "Matamoras" by American troops). Eisenhower, *So Far from God*, 49–51; *PUSG*, 1:74–79.

[17] During the nearly 200-mile march, soldiers went thirty-six hours without water. Eisenhower, *So Far from God*, 52–53.

single habitation, cultivated field, or herd of domestic animals, between Corpus Christi and Matamoras. It was necessary, therefore, to have a wagon train sufficiently large to transport the camp and garrison equipage, officers' baggage, rations for the army, and part rations of grain for the artillery horses and all the animals taken from the north, where they had been accustomed to having their forage furnished them. The army was but indifferently supplied with transportation. Wagons and harness could easily be supplied from the north; but mules and horses could not so readily be brought. The American traders and Mexican smugglers came to the relief. Contracts were made for mules at from eight to eleven dollars each. The smugglers furnished the animals, and took their pay in goods of the description before mentioned. I doubt whether the Mexicans received in value from the traders five dollars per head for the animals they furnished, and still more, whether they paid anything but their own time in procuring them. Such is trade; such is war. The government paid in hard cash to the contractor the stipulated price.

Between the Rio Grande and the Nueces there was at that time a large band of wild horses feeding; as numerous, probably, as the band of buffalo roaming further north was before its rapid extermination commenced. The Mexicans used to capture these in large numbers and bring them into the American settlements and sell them. A picked animal could be purchased at from eight to twelve dollars, but taken at wholesale, they could be bought for thirty-six dollars a dozen. Some of these were purchased for the army, and answered a most useful purpose. The horses were generally very strong, formed much like the Norman horse, and with very heavy manes and tails. A number of officers supplied themselves with these, and they generally rendered as useful service as the northern animal; in fact they were much better when grazing was the only means of supplying forage.

There was no need for haste, and some months were consumed in the necessary preparations for a move. In the meantime the army was engaged in all the duties pertaining to the officer and the soldier. Twice, that I remember, small trains were sent from Corpus Christi, with cavalry escorts, to San Antonio and Austin, with paymasters and funds to pay off small detachments of troops stationed at those places. General Taylor encouraged officers to accompany these expeditions. I accompanied one of them in December, 1845.[18] The distance from Corpus Christi to San Antonio was then computed at one hundred and fifty miles. Now that roads exist it is probably less. From San Antonio to Austin we

[18] On Nov. 20, 1845, USG requested permission to accompany the paymaster's escort to San Antonio. He was granted thirty days leave and set out on Dec. 2. *PUSG,* 1:64–68.

computed the distance at one hundred and ten miles, and from the latter place back to Corpus Christi at over two hundred miles. I know the distance now from San Antonio to Austin is but little over eighty miles, so that our computation was probably too high.[19]

There was not at the time an individual living between Corpus Christi and San Antonio until within about thirty miles of the latter point, where there were a few scattering Mexican settlements along the San Antonio River. The people in at least one of these hamlets lived underground for protection against the Indians. The country abounded in game, such as deer and antelope, with abundance of wild turkeys along the streams and where there were nut-bearing woods. On the Nueces, about twenty-five miles up from Corpus Christi, were a few log cabins, the remains of a town called San Patricio, but the inhabitants had all been massacred by the Indians, or driven away.[20]

San Antonio was about equally divided in population between Americans and Mexicans.[21] From there to Austin there was not a single residence except at New Braunfels, on the Guadalupe River. At that point was a settlement of Germans who had only that year come into the State. At all events they were living in small huts, about such as soldiers would hastily construct for temporary occupation. From Austin to Corpus Christi there was only a small settlement at Bastrop, with a few farms along the Colorado River; but after leaving that, there were no settlements except the home of one man, with one female slave, at the old town of Goliad. Some of the houses were still standing. Goliad had been quite a village for the period and region, but some years before there had been a Mexican massacre, in which every inhabitant had been killed or driven away. This, with the massacre of the prisoners in the Alamo, San Antonio, about the same time, more than three hundred men in all, furnished

[19] USG returned to Corpus Christi by Jan. 2, 1846. Ibid., 1:66.

[20] San Patricio was a settlement founded by Irish immigrants in the 1830s. Although conflict with Native Americans and bandits was common, the settlement had been most recently abandoned during the raids conducted by the Mexican general Rafael Vasquez's forces in 1842. Keith Guthrie, *The History of San Patricio County* (Austin, TX: Nortex, 1986), 10–15; William H. Oberste, *Texas Irish Empresarios and Their Colonies* (Austin, TX: Von Boeckmann-Jones, 1953), 243.

[21] In 1845, the inhabitants of San Antonio were mostly Tejanos ("Texans of Spanish or Mexican descent"). USG confirms this fact in a Jan. 2, 1846, letter to JDG. *PUSG*, 1:66; Spencer Tucker, ed., *The Encyclopedia of the Mexican-American War* (Santa Barbara, CA: ABC-CLIO, 2013), s.v. "San Antonio."

the strongest justification the Texans had for carrying on the war with so much cruelty.[22] In fact, from that time until the Mexican war, the hostilities between Texans and Mexicans was so great that neither was safe in the neighborhood of the other who might be in superior numbers or possessed of superior arms. The man we found living there seemed like an old friend; he had come from near Fort Jessup, Louisiana, where the officers of the 3d and 4th infantry and the 2d dragoons had known him and his family. He had emigrated in advance of his family to build up a home for them.

[22] On Mar. 27, 1836, Mexican troops executed approximately 407 Texan prisoners at Goliad. The Battle of the Alamo had occurred on Mar. 6. Tucker, *Encyclopedia of the Mexican-American War,* s.vv. "Goliad Massacre," "Alamo, Battle of the."

# 5

## Trip to Austin—Promotion to Full Second Lieutenant—Army of Occupation

W HEN OUR PARTY left Corpus Christi[1] it was quite large, including the cavalry escort, Paymaster, Major Dix,[2] his clerk and the officers who, like myself, were simply on leave; but all the officers on leave, except Lieutenant Benjamin[3]—afterwards killed in the valley of Mexico—Lieutenant, now General, Augur,[4] and myself, concluded to spend their allotted time at San Antonio and return from there. We were all to be back at Corpus Christi by the end of the month. The paymaster was detained in Austin so long that, if we had waited for him, we would have exceeded our leave. We concluded, therefore, to start back at once with the animals we had, and having to rely principally on grass for their food, it was a good six days' journey. We had to sleep on the prairie every night, except at Goliad, and possibly one night on the Colorado, without shelter and with only such food as we carried with us, and prepared ourselves. The journey was hazardous on account of Indians,

[1] The trip began on Dec. 2, 1845. *PUSG*, 1:66–68.

[2] Roger S. Dix (c.1810–1849), of New Hampshire, graduated from the USMA in 1832. Dix served in the Quartermaster's Dept. and also at Fort Jesup. On Sept. 30, 1845, Pres. James K. Polk appointed Dix paymaster of the army. *Journal of the Executive Proceedings of the Senate of the United States of America, from December 1, 1845 to August 14, 1848, All Inclusive,* vol. 7 (Washington, DC: Government Printing Office, 1887), 4; *Niles' National Register* 69 (July 5, 1846): 179; *American Quarterly Register and Magazine* 2 (1849): 252.

[3] Calvin Benjamin (c.1818–1847) was born in New York and moved to Indiana. He graduated from the USMA in 1842. He died in the assault on the Garita Belén on Sept. 13, 1847. George W. Cullum, *Biographical Register of the Officers and Graduates of the U.S. Military Academy at West Point, N.Y.* (Boston: Houghton, Mifflin, 1891), 2:122.

[4] Christopher C. Augur (1821–1898) was born in New York and graduated from the USMA in 1843. Augur served in the army throughout the Civil War and retired as a brigadier general in 1885. *CWHC,* 109.

and there were white men in Texas whom I would not have cared to meet in a secluded place. Lieutenant Augur was taken seriously sick before we reached Goliad and at a distance from any habitation. To add to the complication, his horse—a mustang that had probably been captured from the band of wild horses before alluded to, and of undoubted longevity at his capture—gave out. It was absolutely necessary to get forward to Goliad to find a shelter for our sick companion. By dint of patience and exceedingly slow movements, Goliad was at last reached, and a shelter and bed secured for our patient. We remained over a day, hoping that Augur might recover sufficiently to resume his travels. He did not, however, and knowing that Major Dix would be along in a few days, with his wagon-train, now empty, and escort, we arranged with our Louisiana friend to take the best of care of the sick lieutenant until thus relieved, and went on.[5]

I had never been a sportsman in my life; had scarcely ever gone in search of game, and rarely seen any when looking for it. On this trip there was no minute of time while travelling between San Patricio and the settlements on the San Antonio River, from San Antonio to Austin, and again from the Colorado River back to San Patricio, when deer or antelope could not be seen in great numbers. Each officer carried a shot-gun, and every evening, after going into camp, some would go out and soon return with venison and wild turkeys enough for the entire camp.[6] I, however, never went out, and had no occasion to fire my gun; except, being detained over a day at Goliad, Benjamin and I concluded to go down to the creek—which was fringed with timber, much of it the pecan—and bring back a few turkeys. We had scarcely reached the edge of the timber when I heard the flutter of wings overhead, and in an instant I saw two or three turkeys flying away. These were soon followed by more, then more, and more, until a flock of twenty or thirty had left from just over my head. All this time I stood watching the turkeys to see where they flew—with my gun on my shoulder, and never

---

[5] Augur had only recently joined the U.S. 4th Inf., having previously served at Fort Ontario, NY, with the U.S. 2nd Inf. Ibid.; Felice F. Lewis, *Trailing Clouds of Glory: Zachary Taylor's Mexican War Campaign and His Emerging Civil War Leaders* (Tuscaloosa: University of Alabama Press, 2010), 34.

[6] The standard rations for the soldiers during this time period were meat, bread, and beans. While on the march, however, shortages forced the soldiers to catch their own wild game or barter with Mexican locals for a portion of their diets. James M. McCaffrey, *Army of Manifest Destiny: The American Soldiers in the Mexican War, 1846–1848* (New York: New York University Press, 1992), 92–97.

once thought of levelling it at the birds. When I had time to reflect upon the matter, I came to the conclusion that as a sportsman I was a failure, and went back to the house. Benjamin remained out, and got as many turkeys as he wanted to carry back.

After the second night at Goliad, Benjamin and I started to make the remainder of the journey alone. We reached Corpus Christi just in time to avoid "absence without leave."[7] We met no one—not even an Indian—during the remainder of our journey, except at San Patricio. A new settlement had been started there in our absence of three weeks, induced possibly by the fact that there were houses already built, while the proximity of troops gave protection against the Indians.[8] On the evening of the first day out from Goliad we heard the most unearthly howling of wolves, directly in our front. The prairie grass was tall and we could not see the beasts, but the sound indicated that they were near. To my ear it appeared that there must have been enough of them to devour our party, horses and all, at a single meal. The part of Ohio that I hailed from was not thickly settled, but wolves had been driven out long before I left. Benjamin was from Indiana, still less populated, where the wolf yet roamed over the prairies. He understood the nature of the animal and the capacity of a few to make believe there was an unlimited number of them. He kept on towards the noise, unmoved. I followed in his trail, lacking moral courage to turn back and join our sick companion. I have no doubt that if Benjamin had proposed returning to Goliad, I would not only have "seconded the motion" but have suggested that it was very hard-hearted in us to leave Augur sick there in the first place; but Benjamin did not propose turning back. When he did speak it was to ask: "Grant, how many wolves do you think there are in that pack?" Knowing where he was from, and suspecting that he thought I would overestimate the number, I determined to show my acquaintance with the animal by putting the estimate below what possibly could be correct, and answered: "Oh, about twenty," very indifferently. He smiled and rode on. In a minute we were close upon them, and before they saw us. There were just *two* of them. Seated upon their haunches, with their mouths close together, they had made all the noise we had been hearing for the past ten minutes. I have often thought of this incident since when I have heard the noise of a few

[7] USG returned from the trip by Jan. 2, 1846. *PUSG,* 1:66–68.

[8] Taylor based the U.S. 2nd Dragoons in San Patricio in Aug. 1845. Some of the settlers who had fled San Patricio due to conflict with Mexican troops and bandits in the early 1840s returned to their homes during that period. Keith Guthrie, *The History of San Patricio County* (Austin, TX: Nortex, 1986), 16.

disappointed politicians who had deserted their associates. There are always more of them before they are counted.

A week or two before leaving Corpus Christi on this trip, I had been promoted from brevet second-lieutenant, 4th infantry, to full second-lieutenant, 7th infantry. Frank Gardner* of the 7th, was promoted to the 4th in the same orders. We immediately made application to be transferred, so as to get back to our old regiments. On my return, I found that our application had been approved at Washington.[10] While in the 7th infantry I was in the company of Captain Holmes, afterwards a Lieutenant-general in the Confederate army.[11] I never came in contact with him in the war of the Rebellion, nor did he render any very conspicuous service in his high rank. My transfer carried me to the company of Captain McCall, who resigned from the army after the Mexican war and settled in Philadelphia. He was prompt, however, to volunteer when the rebellion broke out, and soon rose to the rank of major-general in the Union army.[12] I was not fortunate enough to meet him after he resigned. In the old army he was esteemed very highly as a soldier and gentleman. Our relations were always most pleasant.

*Afterwards General Gardner, C.S.A.[9]

[9] Franklin Gardner (1823–1873) was born in New York and moved to Iowa. He graduated from the USMA in 1843. Gardner attained the rank of major general in the Confederate Army and fought at Shiloh, during the Kentucky campaign, and at Port Hudson (where he was captured). After being exchanged, he spent the rest of the war in Mississippi. *CWHC*, 248; Ezra J. Warner, *Generals in Gray: Lives of the Confederate Commanders* (Baton Rouge: Louisiana State University Press, 1959), 97.

[10] USG was promoted to second lieutenant on Sept. 30, 1845; Frank Gardner had received his promotion on Sept. 12. On Oct. 23, Gardner requested that he and USG be able to return to their previous regiments. This request was approved: Gardner was transferred back to the U.S. 7th Inf. and USG was returned to the U.S. 4th Inf. in Dec. *PUSG*, 1:61–63, 63*n*, 80.

[11] Theophilus H. Holmes (1804–1880) was born in North Carolina and graduated from the USMA in 1829. In 1846, he was brevetted major for his involvement at Monterrey. He resigned from the U.S. Army in Apr. 1861 to serve as a colonel in the Confederate Army. He reached lieutenant general in Oct. 1862. *CWHC*, 301–302; Lewis, *Trailing Clouds of Glory*, 28.

[12] George A. McCall (1802–1868) was born in Pennsylvania and graduated from the USMA in 1822. He was promoted to captain in 1836, fought in the Mexican-American War, and resigned from the military as a colonel in 1850. He was a major general in the Pennsylvania Militia in 1861 and was wounded and captured at Glendale, VA, on June 30, 1862. He was exchanged for Confederate general Simon B. Buckner, who had been captured at Fort Donelson. *CWHC*, 152, 371.

The preparations at Corpus Christi for an advance progressed as rapidly in the absence of some twenty or more lieutenants as if we had been there. The principal business consisted in securing mules, and getting them broken to harness. The process was slow but amusing. The animals sold to the government were all young and unbroken, even to the saddle, and were quite as wild as the wild horses of the prairie. Usually a number would be brought in by a company of Mexicans, partners in the delivery. The mules were first driven into a stockade, called a *corral,* inclosing an acre or more of ground. The Mexicans,—who were all experienced in throwing the lasso,—would go into the *corral* on horseback, with their lassos attached to the pommels of their saddles. Soldiers detailed as teamsters and blacksmiths would also enter the *corral,* the former with ropes to serve as halters, the latter with branding irons and a fire to keep the irons heated. A lasso was then thrown over the neck of a mule, when he would immediately go to the length of his tether, first one end, then the other in the air. While he was thus plunging and gyrating, another lasso would be thrown by another Mexican, catching the animal by a fore-foot. This would bring the mule to the ground, when he was seized and held by the teamsters while the blacksmith put upon him, with hot irons, the initials "U. S." Ropes were then put about the neck, with a slip-noose which would tighten around the throat if pulled. With a man on each side holding these ropes, the mule was released from his other bindings and allowed to rise. With more or less difficulty he would be conducted to a picket rope outside and fastened there. The delivery of that mule was then complete. This process was gone through with every mule and wild horse with the army of occupation.

The method of breaking them was less cruel and much more amusing. It is a well-known fact that where domestic animals are used for specific purposes from generation to generation, the descendants are easily, as a rule, subdued to the same uses. At that time in Northern Mexico the mule, or his ancestors, the horse and the ass, was seldom used except for the saddle or pack. At all events the Corpus Christi mule resisted the new use to which he was being put. The treatment he was subjected to in order to overcome his prejudices was summary and effective.

The soldiers were principally foreigners who had enlisted in our large cities, and, with the exception of a chance drayman among them, it is not probable that any of the men who reported themselves as competent teamsters had ever driven a mule-team in their lives, or indeed that many had had any previous experience in driving any animal whatever to harness. Numbers together can accomplish what twice their number acting individually could not perform. Five mules were allotted to each wagon. A teamster would select at the picket rope five animals of nearly the same color and general appearance for his team. With a full corps of assistants, other teamsters, he would then proceed to get his mules together. In two's the men would approach each animal selected, avoiding as far as possible its heels. Two ropes would be put about the neck of each animal, with a slip noose, so that he could be choked if too unruly. They were then led out, harnessed by force and hitched to the wagon in the position they had to keep ever after. Two men remained on either side of the leader, with the lassos about its neck, and one man retained the same restraining influence over each of the others. All being ready, the hold would be slackened and the team started. The first motion was generally five mules in the air at one time, backs bowed, hind feet extended to the rear. After repeating this movement a few times the leaders would start to run. This would bring the breeching tight against the mules at the wheels, which these last seemed to regard as a most unwarrantable attempt at coercion and would resist by taking a seat, sometimes going so far as to lie down. In time all were broken in to do their duty submissively if not cheerfully, but there never was a time during the war when it was safe to let a Mexican mule get entirely loose. Their drivers were all teamsters by the time they got through.

I recollect one case of a mule that had worked in a team under the saddle, not only for some time at Corpus Christi, where he was broken, but all the way to the point opposite Matamoras, then to Camargo, where he got loose from his fastenings during the night. He did not run away at first, but staid in the neighborhood for a day or two, coming up sometimes to the feed trough even; but on the approach of the teamster he always got out of the way. At last, growing tired of the constant effort to catch him, he disappeared altogether. Nothing short of a Mexican with his lasso could have caught him. Regulations would not have warranted the expenditure of a dollar in hiring a man with a lasso to catch that mule; but they did allow the expenditure "of the mule," on a certificate that he had run away without any fault of the quartermaster on whose returns he was borne, and also the purchase of another to take his place. I am a competent witness, for I was regimental quartermaster at the time.

While at Corpus Christi all the officers who had a fancy for riding kept horses. The animals cost but little in the first instance, and when picketed they would get their living without any cost. I had three not long before the army moved, but a sad accident bereft me of them all at one time. A colored boy who gave them all the attention they got—besides looking after my tent and that of a class-mate and fellow-lieutenant[13] and cooking for us, all for

[13] USG probably referred to his friend Robert Hazlitt who, along with USG, had employed a young boy to care for their horses while in Louisiana. *PUSG* 1:26*n*, 41–42.

about eight dollars per month, was riding one to water and leading the other two. The led horses pulled him from his seat and all three ran away. They never were heard of afterwards. Shortly after that some one told Captain Bliss,[14] General Taylor's Adjutant-General, of my misfortune. "Yes; I heard Grant lost five or six dollars' worth of horses the other day," he replied. That was a slander; they were broken to the saddle when I got them and cost nearly twenty dollars. I never suspected the colored boy of malicious intent in letting them get away, because, if they had not escaped, he could have had one of them to ride on the long march then in prospect.

---

[14] William W. S. Bliss (1815–1853) was born in New York and graduated from the USMA in 1833. K. Jack Bauer, *Zachary Taylor: Soldier, Planter, Statesmen of the Old Southwest* (Baton Rouge: Louisiana State University Press, 1985), 243, 253–254; Thomas W. Cutrer, ed., *The Mexican War Diary and Correspondence of George B. McClellan* (Baton Rouge: Louisiana State University Press, 2009), 69*n*.

# 6

## Advance of the Army—Crossing the Colorado— The Rio Grande

AT LAST THE preparations were complete and orders were issued for the advance to begin on the 8th of March.[1] General Taylor had an army of not more than three thousand men.[2] One battery, the siege guns and all the convalescent troops were sent on by water to Brazos Santiago, at the mouth of the Rio Grande.[3] A guard was left back at Corpus Christi to look after public property and to take care of those who were too sick to be removed. The remainder of the army, probably not more than twenty five hundred men, was divided into three brigades, with the cavalry independent. Colonel Twiggs,[4] with seven companies of dragoons and a battery of light artillery, moved on the 8th. He was followed by the three infantry brigades, with a day's interval between the commands. Thus the rear brigade did not move from Corpus Christi until the 11th of March. In view of the immense bodies of men moved on the same day over narrow roads, through dense forests and across large streams, in our late war, it seems strange now that a body of less than three

---

[1] Taylor received President Polk's order to move his forces to the Rio Grande River on Jan. 13, 1846, but did not move out until Mar. 8. Spencer Tucker, ed., *Almanac of American Military History* (Santa Barbara, CA: ABC-CLIO, 2013), s.v. "March 8, 1846."

[2] Taylor's army had almost 4,000 men stationed at Corpus Christi by Oct. 1845. K. Jack Bauer, *The Mexican War, 1846–1848* (New York: Macmillan, 1974), 32–34.

[3] Brazos Santiago was a port north of the Rio Grande. It was situated on the Laguna Madre, a body of water that flowed into the Gulf of Mexico. John S. D. Eisenhower, *So Far from God: The U.S. War with Mexico, 1846–1848* (Norman: University of Oklahoma Press, 1989), 55.

[4] David E. Twiggs (1790–1862) was born in Georgia and fought in the War of 1812, the Mexican-American War, and in the Confederate Army during the Civil War. He was brevetted major general for his service in the Mexican-American War. *CWHC,* 538.

thousand men should have been broken into four columns, separated by a day's march.

General Taylor was opposed to anything like plundering by the troops, and in this instance, I doubt not, he looked upon the enemy as the aggrieved party and was not willing to injure them further than his instructions from Washington demanded. His orders to the troops enjoined scrupulous regard for the rights of all peaceable persons and the payment of the highest price for all supplies taken for the use of the army.

All officers of foot regiments who had horses were permitted to ride them on the march when it did not interfere with their military duties. As already related, having lost my "five or six dollars' worth of horses" but a short time before I determined not to get another, but to make the journey on foot. My company commander, Captain McCall, had two good American horses, of considerably more value in that country, where native horses were cheap, than they were in the States.[5] He used one himself and wanted the other for his servant. He was quite anxious to know whether I did not intend to get me another horse before the march began. I told him No; I belonged to a foot regiment. I did not understand the object of his solicitude at the time, but, when we were about to start, he said: "There, Grant, is a horse for you." I found that he could not bear the idea of his servant riding on a long march while his lieutenant went a-foot. He had found a mustang, a three-year-old colt only recently captured, which had been purchased by one of the colored servants with the regiment for the sum of three dollars. It was probably the only horse at Corpus Christi that could have been purchased just then for any reasonable price. Five dollars, sixty-six and two-thirds per cent. advance, induced the owner to part with the mustang. I was sorry to take him, because I really felt that, belonging to a foot regiment, it was my duty to march with the men. But I saw the Captain's earnestness in the matter, and accepted the horse for the trip. The day we started was the first time the horse had ever been under saddle. I had, however, but little difficulty in breaking him, though for the first day there were frequent disagreements between us as to which way we should go, and sometimes whether we should go at all. At no time during the day could I

[5] Quartermaster General Thomas Jesup believed that grass-fed western horses were inferior to ones raised in the east. However, in early 1846, a shortage of horses forced the army to purchase local horses. Thomas T. Smith, *The U.S. Army and the Texas Frontier Economy, 1845–1900* (College Station: Texas A&M University Press, 1999), 111–115.

choose exactly the part of the column I would march with; but after that, I had as tractable a horse as any with the army, and there was none that stood the trip better. He never ate a mouthful of food on the journey except the grass he could pick within the length of his picket rope.

A few days out from Corpus Christi, the immense herd of wild horses that ranged at that time between the Nueces and the Rio Grande was seen directly in advance of the head of the column and but a few miles off. It was the very band from which the horse I was riding had been captured but a few weeks before. The column was halted for a rest, and a number of officers, myself among them, rode out two or three miles to the right to see the extent of the herd. The country was a rolling prairie, and, from the higher ground, the vision was obstructed only by the earth's curvature. As far as the eye could reach to our right, the herd extended. To the left, it extended equally. There was no estimating the number of animals in it; I have no idea that they could all have been corralled in the State of Rhode Island, or Delaware, at one time. If they had been, they would have been so thick that the pasturage would have given out the first day. People who saw the Southern herd of buffalo, fifteen or twenty years ago, can appreciate the size of the Texas band of wild horses in 1846.

At the point where the army struck the Little Colorado River, the stream was quite wide and of sufficient depth for navigation. The water was brackish and the banks were fringed with timber. Here the whole army concentrated before attempting to cross. The army was not accompanied by a pontoon train, and at that time the troops were not instructed in bridge building. To add to the embarrassment of the situation, the army was here, for the first time, threatened with opposition. Buglers, concealed from our view by the brush on the opposite side, sounded the "assembly," and other military calls. Like the wolves before spoken of, they gave the impression that there was a large number of them and that, if the troops were in proportion to the noise, they were sufficient to devour General Taylor and his army. There were probably but few troops, and those engaged principally in watching the movements of the "invader." A few of our cavalry dashed in, and forded and swam the stream, and all opposition was soon dispersed. I do not remember that a single shot was fired.[6]

---

[6] Before the incident, Taylor was informed about the proclamation of Gen. Francisco Mejia, who threatened to use overwhelming force against U.S. troops marching through Mexico. Spencer Tucker, ed., *The Encyclopedia of the Mexican-American War* (Santa Barbara, CA: ABC-CLIO, 2013), s.v. "Mejia, Francisco"; *PUSG,* 1:76–79.

The troops waded the stream, which was up to their necks in the deepest part. Teams were crossed by attaching a long rope to the end of the wagon tongue, passing it between the two swing mules and by the side of the leader, hitching his bridle as well as the bridle of the mules in rear to it, and carrying the end to men on the opposite shore. The bank down to the water was steep on both sides. A rope long enough to cross the river, therefore, was attached to the back axle of the wagon, and men behind would hold the rope to prevent the wagon "beating" the mules into the water. This latter rope also served the purpose of bringing the end of the forward one back, to be used over again. The water was deep enough for a short distance to swim the little Mexican mules which the army was then using, but they, and the wagons, were pulled through so fast by the men at the end of the rope ahead, that no time was left them to show their obstinacy. In this manner the artillery and transportation of the "army of occupation" crossed the Colorado River.

About the middle of the month of March the advance of the army reached the Rio Grande and went into camp near the banks of the river, opposite the city of Matamoras and almost under the guns of a small fort at the lower end of the town. There was not at that time a single habitation from Corpus Christi until the Rio Grande was reached.[7]

The work of fortifying was commenced at once. The fort was laid out by the engineers, but the work was done by the soldiers under the supervision of their officers, the chief engineer retaining general directions.[8] The Mexicans now became so incensed at our near approach that some of their troops crossed the river above us, and made it unsafe for small bodies of men to go far beyond the limits of camp.[9] They captured two companies of dragoons, commanded by Captains Thornton[10] and Hardee. The latter figured as a general in the late war, on the Confederate side, and was author of the tactics

[7] USG's regiment had completed setting up camp near Matamoros by Mar. 29, 1846. *PUSG,* 1:76.

[8] Fort Texas was constructed under the supervision of Capt. Joseph K. F. Mansfield. Tucker, *Encyclopedia of the Mexican-American War,* s.v. "Fort Texas (Fort Brown)."

[9] Gen. Pedro de Ampudia came to Matamoros on Apr. 11, 1846, and instructed Taylor to move east of the Nueces River. Taylor had twenty-four hours to comply, or war would result. Taylor stated that only an armed force would move his men from their position. *PUSG,* 1:81–82.

[10] Seth B. Thornton (c.1818–1847) was born in Virginia and commissioned a second lieutenant in the U.S. 2nd Dragoons in 1836. On Apr. 25, 1846, Thornton and his men rode into an ambush at Rancho de Carricitos, nearly twenty miles from the American camp. In the fight,

first used by both armies.[11] Lieutenant Theodric Porter, of the 4th infantry, was killed while out with a small detachment; and Major Cross, the assistant quartermaster-general, had also been killed not far from camp.[12]

There was no base of supplies nearer than Point Isabel, on the coast, north of the mouth of the Rio Grande and twenty-five miles away. The enemy, if the Mexicans could be called such at this time when no war had been declared, hovered about in such numbers that it was not safe to send a wagon train after supplies with any escort that could be spared. I have already said that General Taylor's whole command on the Rio Grande numbered less than three thousand men. He had, however, a few more troops at Point Isabel or Brazos Santiago. The supplies brought from Corpus Christi in wagons were running short. Work was therefore pushed with great vigor on the defences, to enable the minimum number of troops to hold the fort. All the men who could be employed, were kept at work from early dawn until darkness closed the labors of the day. With all this the fort was not completed until the supplies grew so short that further delay in obtaining more could not be thought of. By the latter part of April the work was in a partially defensible condition, and the 7th infantry, Major Jacob Brown[13] commanding, was marched in to garrison it, with some few pieces of artillery. All the supplies on hand, with the exception of enough to carry the rest of the army to Point Isabel, were left with the

---

eleven Americans were killed, six were wounded, and the rest were captured. Tucker, *Encyclopedia of the Mexican-American War*, s.v. "Thornton, Seth Barton"; *PUSG*, 1:83.

[11] William J. Hardee (1815–1873) was born in Georgia and graduated from the USMA in 1838. His version of the skirmish differed from Thornton's. A court of inquiry later determined that Hardee had acted appropriately, and cleared him of any guilt. Later, he published *Hardee's Rifle and Light Infantry Tactics* (Memphis, TN: E. C. Kirk, 1861), which focused on infantry maneuvering and strategy. Tucker, *Encyclopedia of the Mexican-American War*, s.v. "Hardee, William Joseph"; Nathaniel C. Hughes, *General William Hardee: Old Reliable* (Baton Rouge: Louisiana State University Press, 1965), 25–29.

[12] Col. Trueman Cross (c.1795–1846), from Maryland, went missing on Apr. 10, 1846, and on Apr. 21 his body was found stripped of valuables. Taylor reported that bandits had likely robbed and killed him.

Theodoric H. Porter (c.1817–1846) was from Pennsylvania and was the son of U.S. Navy officer David Porter. He was killed on Apr. 19 while searching for the presumed attackers of Trueman Cross. Bauer, *Mexican War*, 46; *PUSG*, 1:83–84, 84n.

[13] Jacob Brown (1789–1846) was born in Charlton, MA. He served with the U.S. 6th Inf. from 1818 to 1825, rejoined the U.S. 6th Inf. in 1840, and was promoted to major in 1843. Tucker, *Encyclopedia of the Mexican-American War*, s.v. "Brown, Jacob."

garrison, and the march was commenced with the remainder of the command, every wagon being taken with the army. Early on the second day after starting the force reached its destination, without opposition from the Mexicans.[14] There was some delay in getting supplies ashore from vessels at anchor in the open roadstead.

[14] On May 1, 1846, Taylor and his men left Fort Texas for Point Isabel, leaving Brown and the U.S. 7th Inf. to defend the fort. They arrived at Point Isabel at noon on May 2. Bauer, *Mexican War*, 46–49; Eisenhower, *So Far from God*, 74–75.

# 7

## The Mexican War—The Battle of Palo Alto—
## The Battle of Resaca de la Palma—Army of Invasion—
## General Taylor—Movement on Camargo

W HILE GENERAL TAYLOR was away with the bulk of his army, the little garrison up the river was besieged. As we lay in our tents upon the sea-shore, the artillery at the fort on the Rio Grande could be distinctly heard.[1]

The war had begun.

There were no possible means of obtaining news from the garrison, and information from outside could not be otherwise than unfavorable. What General Taylor's feelings were during this suspense I do not know;[2] but for myself, a young second-lieutenant who had never heard a hostile gun before, I felt sorry that I had enlisted. A great many men, when they smell battle afar off, chafe to get into the fray. When they say so themselves they generally fail to convince their hearers that they are as anxious as they would like to make believe, and as they approach danger they become more subdued. This rule is not universal, for I have known a few men who were always aching for a fight

[1] After Taylor and his forces left from Point Isabel, TX, the Mexican Army commenced its attack on Fort Texas on May 3, 1846. John S. D. Eisenhower, *So Far from God: The U.S. War with Mexico, 1846–1848* (Norman: University of Oklahoma Press, 1989), 63, 73–74; *PUSG,* 1:83–84; Spencer Tucker, ed., *The Encyclopedia of the Mexican-American War* (Santa Barbara, CA: ABC-CLIO, 2013), s.v. "Fort Texas (Fort Brown)."

[2] Taylor sent Capt. Samuel H. Walker to the embattled Fort Texas urging its defense on May 3, 1846. On May 5, Walker returned to Taylor and reported that Brown, the fort's commander, believed the fort could be defended because of the Mexican artillery losses and his own troops' conservation of ammunition. K. Jack Bauer, *The Mexican War, 1846–1848* (New York: Macmillan, 1974), 49; Eisenhower, *So Far from God,* 74–76; Alexander Mendoza and Charles D. Grear, *Texans and War: New Interpretations of the State's Military History* (College Station: Texas A&M University Press, 2012), 115, 122; *PUSG,* 1:87.

when there was no enemy near, who were as good as their word when the battle did come. But the number of such men is small.

On the 7th of May the wagons were all loaded and General Taylor started on his return, with his army reinforced at Point Isabel, but still less than three thousand strong, to relieve the garrison on the Rio Grande.[3] The road from Point Isabel to Matamoras is over an open, rolling, treeless prairie, until the timber that borders the bank of the Rio Grande is reached. This river, like the Mississippi, flows through a rich alluvial valley in the most meandering manner, running towards all points of the compass at times within a few miles. Formerly the river ran by Resaca de la Palma, some four or five miles east of the present channel. The old bed of the river at Resaca had become filled at places, leaving a succession of little lakes. The timber that had formerly grown upon both banks, and for a considerable distance out, was still standing. This timber was struck six or eight miles out from the besieged garrison, at a point known as Palo Alto—"Tall trees" or "woods."

Early in the forenoon of the 8th of May as Palo Alto was approached, an army, certainly outnumbering our little force, was seen, drawn up in line of battle just in front of the timber. Their bayonets and spearheads glistened in the sunlight formidably. The force was composed largely of cavalry armed with lances. Where we were the grass was tall, reaching nearly to the shoulders of the men, very stiff, and each stock was pointed at the top, and hard and almost as sharp as a darning-needle. General Taylor halted his army before the head of column came in range of the artillery of the Mexicans. He then formed a line of battle, facing the enemy. His artillery, two batteries and two eighteen-pounder iron guns, drawn by oxen, were placed in position at intervals along the line. A battalion was thrown to the rear, commanded by Lieutenant-Colonel Childs,[4] of the artillery, as reserves. These preparations completed, orders were given for a platoon of each company to stack arms and go to a stream off to the right of the command, to fill their canteens and also those of the rest of their respective companies. When the men were all back in their places in line, the command to advance was given. As I looked down that long line of about three thousand armed men, advancing towards a larger force also armed, I thought what a fearful responsibility General Taylor must feel, commanding such a host and so far away from friends. The Mexicans immediately

---

[3] Taylor left Point Isabel with a force of 2,228 men. Bauer, *Mexican War,* 52.

[4] Thomas Childs (1796–1853) was born in Massachusetts and graduated from the USMA in 1814. He was brevetted lieutenant colonel for his service at Palo Alto. Tucker, *Encyclopedia of the Mexican-American War,* s.v. "Childs, Thomas."

opened fire upon us, first with artillery and then with infantry. At first their shots did not reach us, and the advance was continued. As we got nearer, the cannon balls commenced going through the ranks. They hurt no one, however, during this advance, because they would strike the ground long before they reached our line, and ricochetted through the tall grass so slowly that the men would see them and open ranks and let them pass. When we got to a point where the artillery could be used with effect, a halt was called, and the battle opened on both sides.

The infantry under General Taylor was armed with flint-lock muskets, and paper cartridges charged with powder, buck-shot and ball. At the distance of a few hundred yards a man might fire at you all day without your finding it out. The artillery was generally six-pounder brass guns throwing only solid shot; but General Taylor had with him three or four twelve-pounder howitzers throwing shell, besides his eighteen-pounders before spoken of, that had a long range. This made a powerful armament. The Mexicans were armed about as we were so far as their infantry was concerned, but their artillery only fired solid shot. We had greatly the advantage in this arm.[5]

The artillery was advanced a rod or two in front of the line, and opened fire. The infantry stood at order arms as spectators, watching the effect of our shots upon the enemy, and watching his shots so as to step out of their way. It could be seen that the eighteen-pounders and the howitzers did a great deal of execution. On our side there was little or no loss while we occupied this position. During the battle Major Ringgold, an accomplished and brave artillery officer, was mortally wounded,[6] and Lieutenant Luther, also of the artillery, was struck.[7] During the day several advances were made, and just at dusk it became evident that the Mexicans were falling back. We again advanced,

---

[5] Twelve-pounder howitzers had a typical range of roughly 1,000 yards. While solid shot was more accurate than shell of that day, the explosion and shards of metal from shell provided a demoralizing effect on enemy troops. Jack Coggins, *Arms and Equipment of the Civil War* (Garden City, NY: Doubleday, 1962), 31–33, 66–67.

[6] Maj. Samuel Ringgold (1796–1846) graduated first in his class from the USMA in 1818. He pioneered the use of light mobile artillery units. The U.S. Army based its revision of *Instruction for Field Artillery, Horse and Foot,* on his recommendations. Eisenhower, *So Far from God,* 80; Robert W. Johannsen, *To the Halls of Montezuma: The Mexican War in the American Imagination* (New York: Oxford University Press, 1985), 124.

[7] Roland A. Luther (c.1815–1853) was born in Rhode Island and graduated from the USMA in 1836. He was brevetted major for his actions in the Battle of Buena Vista. George W. Cullum, *Biographical Register of the Officers and Graduates of the U.S. Military Academy at West Point, N.Y.* (Boston: Houghton, Mifflin, 1891), 1:642.

and occupied at the close of the battle substantially the ground held by the enemy at the beginning. In this last move there was a brisk fire upon our troops, and some execution was done. One cannon-ball passed through our ranks, not far from me. It took off the head of an enlisted man, and the under jaw of Captain Page[8] of my regiment, while the splinters from the musket of the killed soldier, and his brains and bones, knocked down two or three others, including one officer, Lieutenant Wallen[9]—hurting them more or less. Our casualties for the day were nine killed and forty-seven wounded.[10]

At the break of day on the 9th, the army under Taylor was ready to renew the battle; but an advance showed that the enemy had entirely left our front during the night. The chaparral before us was impenetrable except where there were roads or trails, with occasionally clear or bare spots of small dimensions. A body of men penetrating it might easily be ambushed. It was better to have a few men caught in this way than the whole army, yet it was necessary that the garrison at the river should be relieved. To get to them the chaparral had to be passed. Thus I assume General Taylor reasoned. He halted the army not far in advance of the ground occupied by the Mexicans the day before, and selected Captain C. F. Smith, of the artillery, and Captain McCall, of my company, to take one hundred and fifty picked men each and find where the enemy had gone. This left me in command of the company, an honor and responsibility I thought very great.

Smith and McCall found no obstruction in the way of their advance until they came up to the succession of ponds, before described, at Resaca. The Mexicans had passed them and formed their lines on the opposite bank. This position they had strengthened a little by throwing up dead trees and brush in their front, and by placing artillery to cover the approaches and open places. Smith and McCall deployed on each side of the road as well as they could, and engaged the enemy at long range. Word was sent back, and the advance

[8] John Page (?–1846) was born in Massachusetts. He died from his wounds on July 12, 1846, near St. Louis, MO. *Official Army Register for 1847* (Washington, DC: C. Alexander, 1847), 36; *PUSG,* 1:39n, 85.

[9] Henry D. Wallen (1819–1886) was born in Florida and graduated from the USMA in 1840. He attained the rank of brevet brigadier general in the U.S. Army during the Civil War. *CWHC,* 552; *PUSG,* 1:39n.

[10] The official casualty report listed five killed, forty-three wounded, and ten dying of wounds after the battle. "Report of the Secretary of War, December 10, 1846," in *Public Documents Printed by Order of the Senate of the United States during the Second Session of the Twenty-Ninth Congress,* vol. 2, no. 4 (Washington, DC: Ritchie and Heiss, 1847), 8.

of the whole army was at once commenced. As we came up we were deployed in like manner. I was with the right wing, and led my company through the thicket wherever a penetrable place could be found, taking advantage of any clear spot that would carry me towards the enemy. At last I got pretty close up without knowing it. The balls commenced to whistle very thick overhead, cutting the limbs of the chaparral right and left. We could not see the enemy, so I ordered my men to lie down, an order that did not have to be enforced. We kept our position until it became evident that the enemy were not firing at us, and then withdrew to find better ground to advance upon.

By this time some progress had been made on our left. A section of artillery had been captured by the cavalry, and some prisoners had been taken. The Mexicans were giving way all along the line, and many of them had, no doubt, left early. I at last found a clear space separating two ponds. There seemed to be a few men in front and I charged upon them with my company. There was no resistance, and we captured a Mexican colonel, who had been wounded, and a few men.[11] Just as I was sending them to the rear with a guard of two or three men, a private came from the front bringing back one of our officers, who had been badly wounded in advance of where I was. The ground had been charged over before. My exploit was equal to that of the soldier who boasted that he had cut off the leg of one of the enemy. When asked why he did not cut off his head, he replied: "Some one had done that before." This left no doubt in my mind but that the battle of Resaca de la Palma would have been won, just as it was, if I had not been there.

There was no further resistance. The evening of the 9th the army was encamped on its old ground near the Fort, and the garrison was relieved. The siege had lasted a number of days, but the casualties were few in number. Major Jacob Brown, of the 7th infantry, the commanding officer, had been killed, and in his honor the fort was named. Since then a town of considerable importance has sprung up on the ground occupied by the fort and troops, which has also taken his name.[12]

---

[11] USG did not write of his experience in the battle in his May 11, 1846, letter to JDG, but he mentioned the capture of Gen. Rómulo Díaz de la Vega (1804–1877). There is no mention of a Mexican colonel. Tucker, *Encyclopedia of the Mexican-American War,* s.v. "Díaz de la Vega, Rómulo"; *PUSG,* 1:84–87.

[12] Brown commanded Fort Texas throughout the siege but was wounded on May 6, 1846. He died three days later. A few days after his death, Taylor issued Gen. Orders No. 62, which renamed Fort Texas as Fort Brown. The city of Brownsville, TX, subsequently grew up around Fort Brown and was also named in honor of the fort commander. Eisenhower, *So Far from*

The battles of Palo Alto and Resaca de la Palma seemed to us engaged, as pretty important affairs; but we had only a faint conception of their magnitude until they were fought over in the North by the Press and the reports came back to us. At the same time, or about the same time, we learned that war existed between the United States and Mexico, by the acts of the latter country.[13] On learning this fact General Taylor transferred our camps to the south or west bank of the river, and Matamoras was occupied. We then became the "Army of Invasion."

Up to this time Taylor had none but regular troops in his command; but now that invasion had already taken place, volunteers for one year commenced arriving.[14] The army remained at Matamoras until sufficiently reinforced to warrant a movement into the interior.[15] General Taylor was not an officer to trouble the administration much with his demands, but was inclined to do the best he could with the means given him. He felt his responsibility as going no further. If he had thought that he was sent to perform an impossibility with the means given him, he would probably have informed the authorities of his opinion and left them to determine what should be done. If the judgment was against him he would have gone on and done the best he could with the means at hand without parading his grievance before the public. No soldier could face either danger or responsibility more calmly than he. These are qualities more rarely found than genius or physical courage.

General Taylor never made any great show or parade, either of uniform or retinue. In dress he was possibly too plain, rarely wearing anything in the field to indicate his rank, or even that he was an officer; but he was known to every soldier in his army, and was respected by all. I can call to mind only one instance when I saw him in uniform, and one other when I heard of his wearing it. On both occasions he was unfortunate. The first was at Corpus Christi.

---

*God,* 84; Tucker, *Encyclopedia of the Mexican-American War,* s.vv. "Brown, Jacob," "Fort Texas (Fort Brown)."

[13] On May 11, 1846, President Polk requested that Congress declare war on Mexico. Congress approved the war declaration on May 13. Bauer, *Mexican War,* 68–69.

[14] On May 13, 1846, the same day that war was declared, Congress authorized 50,000 volunteers to serve for one year. In New Orleans, Gen. Edmund P. Gaines recruited 8,000 volunteers, and the first group of these men landed at Point Isabel on May 11. Bauer, *Mexican War,* 69; Eisenhower, *So Far from God,* 101–102; Tucker, *Encyclopedia of the Mexican-American War,* s.vv. "Gaines, Edmund Pendleton," "Marcy, William Learned."

[15] Taylor's Army of Occupation arrived in Matamoros on May 18, 1846, and remained there until Aug., when Taylor moved his headquarters to Camargo. Bauer, *Mexican War,* 82–89.

He had concluded to review his army before starting on the march and gave orders accordingly. Colonel Twiggs was then second in rank with the army, and to him was given the command of the review. Colonel and Brevet Brigadier-General Worth,[16] a far different soldier from Taylor in the use of the uniform, was next to Twiggs in rank, and claimed superiority by virtue of his brevet rank when the accidents of service threw them where one or the other had to command. Worth declined to attend the review as subordinate to Twiggs until the question was settled by the highest authority. This broke up the review, and the question was referred to Washington for final decision.

General Taylor was himself only a colonel, in real rank, at that time, and a brigadier-general by brevet. He was assigned to duty, however, by the President, with the rank which his brevet gave him.[17] Worth was not so assigned, but by virtue of commanding a division he must, under the army regulations of that day, have drawn the pay of his brevet rank. The question was submitted to Washington, and no response was received until after the army had reached the Rio Grande. It was decided against General Worth, who at once tendered his resignation and left the army, going north, no doubt, by the same vessel that carried it. This kept him out of the battles of Palo Alto and Resaca de la Palma. Either the resignation was not accepted, or General Worth withdrew it before action had been taken. At all events he returned to the army in time to command his division in the battle of Monterey, and served with it to the end of the war.[18]

The second occasion on which General Taylor was said to have donned his uniform, was in order to receive a visit from the Flag Officer of the naval squadron off the mouth of the Rio Grande. While the army was on that river the Flag Officer sent word that he would call on the General to pay his respects on a certain day. General Taylor, knowing that naval officers habitually

[16] William J. Worth (1794–1849), of New York, enlisted as a private in the army at the outbreak of the War of 1812. Edward S. Wallace, *General William Jenkins Worth, Monterey's Forgotten Hero* (Dallas: Southern Methodist University Press, 1953), 3, 14.

[17] On May 30, 1846, Polk brevetted Taylor major general for his victories at Palo Alto and Resaca de la Palma. Wayne Cutler, ed., *Correspondence of James K. Polk*, vol. 11 (Knoxville: University of Tennessee Press, 2009), 188; John S. D. Eisenhower, *Zachary Taylor* (New York: Times Books, 2008), 28.

[18] Worth resigned on Apr. 2, 1846, with the request that his resignation not be accepted if his superiors in Washington expected military action in the near future. On May 9, he requested that his resignation be withdrawn and that he be ordered back to command of troops, a request that Secretary of War William Marcy (1786–1857) approved that same day. Tucker, *Encyclopedia of the Mexican-American War*, s.v. "Marcy, William Learned"; Wallace, *General William Jenkins Worth*, 74–75.

wore all the uniform the "law allowed" on all occasions of ceremony, thought it would be only civil to receive his guest in the same style. His uniform was therefore got out, brushed up, and put on, in advance of the visit. The Flag Officer,[19] knowing General Taylor's aversion to the wearing of the uniform, and feeling that it would be regarded as a compliment should he meet him in civilian's dress, left off his uniform for this occasion. The meeting was said to have been embarrassing to both, and the conversation was principally apologetic.

The time was whiled away pleasantly enough at Matamoras, while we were waiting for volunteers. It is probable that all the most important people of the territory occupied by our army left their homes before we got there, but with those remaining the best of relations apparently existed. It was the policy of the Commanding General to allow no pillaging, no taking of private property for public or individual use without satisfactory compensation, so that a better market was afforded than the people had ever known before.

Among the troops that joined us at Matamoras was an Ohio regiment, of which Thomas L. Hamer, the Member of Congress who had given me my appointment to West Point, was major. He told me then that he could have had the colonelcy, but that as he knew he was to be appointed a brigadier-general, he preferred at first to take the lower grade.[20] I have said before that Hamer was one of the ablest men Ohio ever produced. At that time he was in the prime of life, being less than fifty years of age, and possessed an admirable physique, promising long life. But he was taken sick before Monterey, and died within a few days.[21] I have always believed that had his life been spared, he would have been President of the United States during the term filled by President Pierce.[22] Had Hamer filled that office his partiality for me was such, there is but little doubt I should have been appointed to one of the staff corps

[19] Commodore David E. Conner (1792–1856) was commander of the navy's Home Squadron. When Conner received word of a declaration of war he moved his vessels to Point Isabel. Conner assisted General Taylor along the Rio Grande, and raided port cities during the war. Edward Moseley and Paul Clark Jr., *The A to Z of the United States-Mexican War* (Lanham, MD: Scarecrow Press, 1997), 84.

[20] In July 1846, Hamer raised the 1st Ohio Brigade, to which he was elected major. Soon after, Polk commissioned him as a brigadier general. He arrived in Mexico in Aug. Josiah Morrow, *The History of Brown County, Ohio* (Chicago: W. H. Beers, 1883), 348–351.

[21] Hamer died on Dec. 2, 1846, from what was reported at the time as "congestion of the bowels." "General Thomas L. Hamer Is No More!," *Carroll Free Press* [Carrollton, OH], Jan. 8, 1847, 3; *PUSG,* 1:121 and *n.*

[22] Franklin Pierce (1804–1869) was born in New Hampshire and served as U.S. president from 1853 to 1857. *Dictionary of American Biography,* 2nd ed., s.v. "Pierce, Franklin."

of the army—the Pay Department probably—and would therefore now be preparing to retire. Neither of these speculations is unreasonable, and they are mentioned to show how little men control their own destiny.

Reinforcements having arrived, in the month of August the movement commenced from Matamoras to Camargo, the head of navigation on the Rio Grande.[23] The line of the Rio Grande was all that was necessary to hold, unless it was intended to invade Mexico from the North. In that case the most natural route to take was the one which General Taylor selected. It entered a pass in the Sierra Madre Mountains, at Monterey, through which the main road runs to the City of Mexico. Monterey itself was a good point to hold, even if the line of the Rio Grande covered all the territory we desired to occupy at that time. It is built on a plain two thousand feet above tide water, where the air is bracing and the situation healthy.

On the 19th of August the army started for Monterey, leaving a small garrison at Matamoras. The troops, with the exception of the artillery, cavalry, and the brigade to which I belonged, were moved up the river to Camargo on steamers. As there were but two or three of these, the boats had to make a number of trips before the last of the troops were up. Those who marched did so by the south side of the river. Lieutenant-Colonel Garland, of the 4th infantry,[24] was the brigade commander, and on this occasion commanded the entire marching force. One day out convinced him that marching by day in that latitude, in the month of August, was not a beneficial sanitary measure, particularly for Northern men. The order of marching was changed and night marches were substituted with the best results.[25]

When Camargo was reached, we found a city of tents outside the Mexican hamlet. I was detailed to act as quartermaster and commissary to the regiment.[26] The teams that had proven abundantly sufficient to transport all sup-

---

[23] USG left Matamoros on Aug. 5, 1846, reaching Camargo by Aug. 14. *PUSG,* 1:103–104.

[24] John Garland (1792–1861) was born in Virginia and joined the military as a first lieutenant in 1813. He was brevetted colonel after the Battles of Palo Alto and Resaca de la Palma. *CWHC,* 249.

[25] USG's company had been chosen to march to Camargo to protect a battery of artillery. In an Aug. 14, 1846, letter to JDG he described the difficult march. *PUSG,* 1:103–104.

[26] USG asked to be relieved from duty as quartermaster and commissary, objecting to any assignment "which removes me from sharing in the dangers and honors of service with my company at the front." Taylor, however, had received favorable reports of USG's work as quartermaster, so Garland denied the request. Christopher D. Dishman, *A Perfect Gibraltar: The Battle for Monterrey, Mexico, 1846* (Norman: University of Oklahoma Press, 2010), 232n; *PUSG,* 1:107 and *n.*

plies from Corpus Christi to the Rio Grande over the level prairies of Texas, were entirely inadequate to the needs of the reinforced army in a mountainous country. To obviate the deficiency, pack mules were hired, with Mexicans to pack and drive them. I had charge of the few wagons allotted to the 4th infantry and of the pack train to supplement them. There were not men enough in the army to manage that train without the help of Mexicans who had learned how. As it was the difficulty was great enough. The troops would take up their march at an early hour each day. After they had started, the tents and cooking utensils had to be made into packages, so that they could be lashed to the backs of the mules. Sheet-iron kettles, tent-poles and mess chests were inconvenient articles to transport in that way. It took several hours to get ready to start each morning, and by the time we were ready some of the mules first loaded would be tired of standing so long with their loads on their backs. Sometimes one would start to run, bowing his back and kicking up until he scattered his load; others would lie down and try to disarrange their loads by attempting to get on the top of them by rolling on them; others with tent-poles for part of their loads would manage to run a tent-pole on one side of a sapling while they would take the other. I am not aware of ever having used a profane expletive in my life; but I would have the charity to excuse those who may have done so, if they were in charge of a train of Mexican pack mules at the time.

# 8

## Advance on Monterey—The Black Fort—The Battle of Monterey—Surrender of the City

T HE ADVANCE FROM Camargo was commenced on the 5th of September. The army was divided into four columns, separated from each other by one day's march. The advance reached Cerralvo in four days and halted for the remainder of the troops to come up. By the 13th the rear-guard had arrived, and the same day the advance resumed its march, followed as before, a day separating the divisions. The forward division halted again at Marin, twenty-four miles from Monterey. Both this place and Cerralvo were nearly deserted, and men, women and children were seen running and scattered over the hills as we approached; but when the people returned they found all their abandoned property safe, which must have given them a favorable opinion of *Los Grengos*—"the Yankees." From Marin the movement was in mass. On the 19th General Taylor, with his army, was encamped at Walnut Springs, within three miles of Monterey.[1]

The town is on a small stream coming out of the mountain-pass, and is backed by a range of hills of moderate elevation.[2] To the north, between the city and Walnut Springs, stretches an extensive plain. On this plain, and entirely outside of the last houses of the city, stood a strong fort, enclosed on all sides, to which our army gave the name of "Black Fort."[3] Its guns commanded

[1]On Sept. 19, 1846, Taylor's troops camped at el Bosque de San Domingo. The troops rested in a grove of oak and pecan trees, which they named "Walnut Springs." K. Jack Bauer, *The Mexican War, 1846–1848* (New York: Macmillan, 1974), 92.

[2]The Santa Catarina, the local branch of the San Juan River, flowed east to west along the southern edge of Monterrey. The Sierra Madre Oriental Mountains ran along the southern bank of the river. Ibid.

[3]The Mexicans had strongly fortified an unfinished cathedral about 1,000 yards north of Monterrey. The old cathedral, known as the Citadel, was twenty feet high and surrounded by a moat. Over time, the walls had turned a dark color, leading the Americans to call it the "Black

the approaches to the city to the full extent of their range. There were two detached spurs of hills or mountains to the north and north-west of the city, which were also fortified. On one of these stood the Bishop's Palace. The road to Saltillo leaves the upper or western end of the city under the fire of the guns from these heights.[4] The lower or eastern end was defended by two or three small detached works, armed with artillery and infantry.[5] To the south was the mountain stream before mentioned, and back of that the range of foot-hills. The plaza in the centre of the city was the citadel, properly speaking. All the streets leading from it were swept by artillery, cannon being intrenched behind temporary parapets. The house-tops near the plaza were converted into infantry fortifications by the use of sand-bags for parapets. Such were the defences of Monterey in September, 1846. General Ampudia,[6] with a force of certainly ten thousand men, was in command.

General Taylor's force was about six thousand five hundred strong,[7] in three divisions, under Generals Butler,[8] Twiggs and Worth. The troops went into camp at Walnut Springs, while the engineer officers, under Major Mansfield[9]—a

Fort." Christopher D. Dishman, *A Perfect Gibraltar: The Battle for Monterrey, Mexico, 1846* (Norman: University of Oklahoma Press, 2010), 34.

[4] USG was describing the fortifications due west and southwest of the city. Independencia Hill stood on the western side of the city of Monterrey, with Fort Libertad on its western summit and the fortified ruins of an abandoned bishop's palace on the eastern slope. Federación Hill stood on the southwestern part of the city, hosting two small stone forts known as Fort Federación and Fort Soldado. Bauer, *Mexican War*, 93; Dishman, *Perfect Gibraltar*, 33–34.

[5] To protect the eastern portion of the town, engineers had created El Fortín del Teneria (the Tannery Fort) and El Fortín del Rincón del Diablo (the Fort of the Devil's Corner). Dishman, *Perfect Gibraltar*, 33–34.

[6] Pedro de Ampudia (1805–1868) commanded the Division of the North. Contrary to USG's assertion, Ampudia had only 7,303 men and forty-two guns to defend Monterrey. Bauer, *Mexican War*, 42, 93; Abner Doubleday, *My Life in the Old Army: The Reminiscences of Abner Doubleday*, ed. Joseph E. Chance (Fort Worth: Texas Christian University Press, 1998), 309.

[7] In mid-Aug. 1846, when Taylor's army departed for Cerralvo, a town outside of Monterrey, he had a force of 6,200 men comprised of 3,000 regulars and 3,200 volunteers. Dishman, *Perfect Gibraltar*, 75.

[8] William O. Butler (1791–1880) was a Kentucky politician who served in the War of 1812. He was appointed major general of the 1st Div. of Volunteers at the start of the Mexican-American War. Edward Moseley and Paul Clark Jr., *The A to Z of the United States-Mexican War* (Lanham, MD: Scarecrow Press, 1997), 65–66.

[9] Joseph K. F. Mansfield (1803–1862) was born in Connecticut and graduated second in his class from the USMA in 1822. In 1862, during the Civil War, he was promoted to major general

General in the late war—commenced their reconnoissance. Major Mansfield found that it would be practicable to get troops around, out of range of the Black Fort and the works on the detached hills to the north-west of the city, to the Saltillo road. With this road in our possession, the enemy would be cut off from receiving further supplies, if not from all communication with the interior. General Worth, with his division somewhat reinforced, was given the task of gaining possession of the Saltillo road, and of carrying the detached works outside the city, in that quarter.[10] He started on his march early in the afternoon of the 20th. The divisions under Generals Butler and Twiggs were drawn up to threaten the east and north sides of the city and the works on those fronts, in support of the movement under General Worth. Worth's was regarded as the main attack on Monterey, and all other operations were in support of it. His march this day was uninterrupted; but the enemy was seen to reinforce heavily about the Bishop's Palace and the other outside fortifications on their left. General Worth reached a defensible position just out of range of the enemy's guns on the heights north-west of the city, and bivouacked for the night. The engineer officers with him—Captain Sanders[11] and Lieutenant George G. Meade,[12] afterwards the commander of the victorious National army at the battle of Gettysburg—made a reconnoissance to the Saltillo road under cover of night.

During the night of the 20th General Taylor had established a battery, consisting of two twenty-four-pounder howitzers and a ten-inch mortar, at a point from which they could play upon Black Fort. A natural depression in the plain, sufficiently deep to protect men standing in it from the fire from the fort, was selected and the battery established on the crest nearest the enemy.

in the U.S. Army. In Sept. of that year, he was killed at the Battle of Antietam. *CWHC*, 363; John D. Wright, *The Routledge Encyclopedia of Civil War Era Biographies* (New York: Routledge, 2013), s.v. "Mansfield, Joseph King Fenno 1803–62."

[10] Taylor reinforced Worth's 2nd Div. with Col. John C. Hay's 1st Texas Mounted Riflemen. Bauer, *Mexican War*, 93; Dan L. Thrapp, *Encyclopedia of Frontier Biography* (Glendale, CA: Arthur H. Clark, 1988), s.v. "Hays, John Coffee (Jack)."

[11] John Sanders (1810–1858) was born in Kentucky and graduated second in his class from the USMA in 1834. Moseley and Clark, *A to Z of the United States-Mexican War*, 239; George W. Cullum, *Biographical Register of the Officers and Graduates of the U.S. Military Academy at West Point, N.Y.* (Boston: Houghton, Mifflin, 1891), 1:567–568.

[12] George G. Meade (1815–1872) was born in Spain to American parents. He graduated from the USMA in 1835 and in Sept. 1846, after the Battle of Monterrey, he was brevetted first lieutenant. He reached major general during the Civil War, and served as the commanding general, Army of the Potomac, from 1863 to 1865. *CWHC*, 384–385.

The 4th infantry, then consisting of but six reduced companies, was ordered to support the artillerists while they were intrenching themselves and their guns. I was regimental quartermaster at the time and was ordered to remain in charge of camp and the public property at Walnut Springs. It was supposed that the regiment would return to its camp in the morning.

The point for establishing the siege battery was reached and the work performed without attracting the attention of the enemy. At daylight the next morning fire was opened on both sides and continued with, what seemed to me at that day, great fury. My curiosity got the better of my judgment, and I mounted a horse and rode to the front to see what was going on. I had been there but a short time when an order to charge was given, and lacking the moral courage to return to camp—where I had been ordered to stay—I charged with the regiment. As soon as the troops were out of the depression they came under the fire of Black Fort. As they advanced they got under fire from batteries guarding the east, or lower, end of the city, and of musketry. About one-third of the men engaged in the charge were killed or wounded in the space of a few minutes. We retreated to get out of fire, not backward, but eastward and perpendicular to the direct road running into the city from Walnut Springs. I was, I believe, the only person in the 4th infantry in the charge who was on horseback. When we got to a place of safety the regiment halted and drew itself together—what was left of it. The adjutant of the regiment, Lieutenant Hoskins,[13] who was not in robust health, found himself very much fatigued from running on foot in the charge and retreat, and, seeing me on horseback, expressed a wish that he could be mounted also. I offered him my horse and he accepted the offer. A few minutes later I saw a soldier, a quartermaster's man, mounted, not far away. I ran to him, took his horse and was back with the regiment in a few minutes. In a short time we were off again; and the next place of safety from the shots of the enemy that I recollect of being in, was a field of cane or corn to the north-east of the lower batteries. The adjutant to whom I had loaned my horse was killed, and I was designated to act in his place.

This charge was ill-conceived, or badly executed. We belonged to the brigade commanded by Lieutenant-Colonel Garland, and he had received orders to charge the lower batteries of the city, and carry them if he could without too much loss, for the purpose of creating a diversion in favor of Worth, who

---

[13] Charles Hoskins (1818–1846) was born in North Carolina and graduated from the USMA in 1836. *PUSG*, 1:111*n*; William S. Powell, ed., *Dictionary of North Carolina Biography* (Chapel Hill: University of North Carolina Press, 1988), s.v. "Hoskins, Charles W."

was conducting the movement which it was intended should be decisive.[14] By a movement by the left flank Garland could have led his men beyond the range of the fire from Black Fort and advanced towards the north-east angle of the city, as well covered from fire as could be expected. There was no undue loss of life in reaching the lower end of Monterey, except that sustained by Garland's command.

Meanwhile Quitman's[15] brigade, conducted by an officer of engineers,[16] had reached the eastern end of the city, and was placed under cover of the houses without much loss. Colonel Garland's brigade also arrived at the suburbs, and, by the assistance of some of our troops that had reached house-tops from which they could fire into a little battery covering the approaches to the lower end of the city, the battery was speedily captured and its guns were turned upon another work of the enemy. An entrance into the east end of the city was now secured, and the houses protected our troops so long as they were inactive.

On the west General Worth had reached the Saltillo road after some fighting but without heavy loss. He turned from his new position and captured the forts on both heights in that quarter. This gave him possession of the upper or west end of Monterey.[17] Troops from both Twiggs's and Butler's divisions were in possession of the east end of the town, but the Black Fort to the north of the town and the plaza in the centre were still in the possession of the enemy. Our camps at Walnut Springs, three miles away, were guarded by a company from each regiment. A regiment of Kentucky volunteers guarded the mortars and howitzers engaged against Black Fort. Practically Monterey was invested.

There was nothing done on the 22d by the United States troops; but the enemy kept up a harmless fire upon us from Black Fort and the batteries still in their possession at the east end of the city. During the night they evacuated

[14] Garland attempted a diversionary assault on the eastern side of Monterrey with 800 men from the U.S. 1st and 3rd Inf. Bauer, *Mexican War*, 95–96.

[15] John A. Quitman (1798–1858) was a former governor of Mississippi and a major general in the Mississippi militia. He served as a brigadier general of volunteers during the Mexican-American War. Spencer Tucker, ed., *The Encyclopedia of the Mexican-American War* (Santa Barbara, CA: ABC-CLIO, 2013), s.v. "Quitman, John Anthony."

[16] Lt. J. M. Scarritt (c.1817–1854) was born in New Hampshire and graduated from the USMA in 1838. Cullum, *Biographical Register*, 1:699.

[17] On Sept. 21, 1846, Worth's forces had taken both Independence Hill and Federation Hill. John S. D. Eisenhower, *So Far from God: The U.S. War with Mexico, 1846–1848* (Norman: University of Oklahoma Press, 1989), 131–140.

these; so that on the morning of the 23d we held undisputed possession of the east end of Monterey.

Twiggs's division was at the lower end of the city, and well covered from the fire of the enemy. But the streets leading to the plaza—all Spanish or Spanish-American towns have near their centres a square called a plaza—were commanded from all directions by artillery. The houses were flat-roofed and but one or two stories high, and about the plaza the roofs were manned with infantry, the troops being protected from our fire by parapets made of sand-bags. All advances into the city were thus attended with much danger. While moving along streets which did not lead to the plaza, our men were protected from the fire, and from the view, of the enemy except at the crossings; but at these a volley of musketry and a discharge of grape-shot were invariably en-countered. The 3d and 4th regiments of infantry made an advance nearly to the plaza in this way and with heavy loss. The loss of the 3d infantry in com-missioned officers was especially severe. There were only five companies of the regiment and not over twelve officers present, and five of these officers were killed.[18] When within a square of the plaza this small command, ten compa-nies in all, was brought to a halt. Placing themselves under cover from the shots of the enemy, the men would watch to detect a head above the sand-bags on the neighboring houses. The exposure of a single head would bring a volley from our soldiers.

We had not occupied this position long when it was discovered that our ammunition was growing low. I volunteered to go back* to the point we had started from, report our position to General Twiggs, and ask for ammunition to be forwarded. We were at this time occupying ground off from the street, in rear of the houses. My ride back was an exposed one. Before starting I ad-justed myself on the side of my horse furthest from the enemy, and with only one foot holding to the cantle of the saddle, and an arm over the neck of the horse exposed, I started at full run. It was only at street crossings that my horse

*General Garland expressed a wish to get a message back to General Twiggs, his division commander, or General Taylor, to the effect that he was nearly out of am-munition and must have more sent to him, or otherwise be reinforced. Deeming the return dangerous he did not like to order any one to carry it, so he called for a volun-teer. Lieutenant Grant offered his services, which were accepted.—PUBLISHERS.

[18] The U.S. 3rd Inf. officers killed on Sept. 21, 1846, were Brevet Maj. Philip N. Barbour, Capt. Lewis N. Morris, Capt. George P. Field, 2nd Lt. Douglass S. Irwin, and 2nd Lt. Robert Hazlitt. *Official Army Register for 1847* (Washington, DC: C. Alexander, 1845), 36.

was under fire, but these I crossed at such a flying rate that generally I was past and under cover of the next block of houses before the enemy fired. I got out safely without a scratch.

At one place on my ride, I saw a sentry walking in front of a house, and stopped to inquire what he was doing there. Finding that the house was full of wounded American officers and soldiers, I dismounted and went in. I found there Captain Williams,[19] of the Engineer Corps, wounded in the head, probably fatally, and Lieutenant Territt,[20] also badly wounded, his bowels protruding from his wound. There were quite a number of soldiers also. Promising them to report their situation, I left, readjusted myself to my horse, recommenced the run, and was soon with the troops at the east end. Before ammunition could be collected, the two regiments I had been with were seen returning, running the same gauntlet in getting out that they had passed in going in, but with comparatively little loss. The movement was countermanded and the troops were withdrawn. The poor wounded officers and men I had found, fell into the hands of the enemy during the night, and died.

While this was going on at the east, General Worth, with a small division of troops, was advancing towards the plaza from the opposite end of the city. He resorted to a better expedient for getting to the plaza—the citadel—than we did on the east. Instead of moving by the open streets, he advanced through the houses, cutting passage-ways from one to another. Without much loss of life, he got so near the plaza during the night that before morning, Ampudia, the Mexican commander, made overtures for the surrender of the city and garrison. This stopped all further hostilities. The terms of surrender were soon agreed upon. The prisoners were paroled and permitted to take their horses and personal property with them.[21]

My pity was aroused by the sight of the Mexican garrison of Monterey marching out of town as prisoners, and no doubt the same feeling was experienced by most of our army who witnessed it. Many of the prisoners were

[19] William G. Williams (1801–1846) was born in South Carolina and graduated from the USMA in 1824. Cullum, *Biographical Register,* 1:330.

[20] John C. Terrett (1817–1846) was from Virginia and entered the army in 1839. He fought in the Seminole Wars in Florida. Terrett died on Sept. 21, 1846. Frank B. Hough, *American Biographical Notes* (Albany, NY: Joel Munsell, 1875), 390; *PUSG,* 1:111*n.*

[21] On Sept. 24, 1846, American forces received the first flag of truce from Ampudia's army. In the afternoon, both sides agreed to the "Terms of Capitulation." Felice F. Lewis, *Trailing Clouds of Glory: Zachary Taylor's Mexican War Campaign and His Emerging Civil War Leaders* (Tuscaloosa: University of Alabama Press, 2010), 156–157.

cavalry, armed with lances, and mounted on miserable little half-starved horses that did not look as if they could carry their riders out of town. The men looked in but little better condition. I thought how little interest the men before me had in the results of the war, and how little knowledge they had of "what it was all about."

After the surrender of the garrison of Monterey a quiet camp life was led until midwinter.[22] As had been the case on the Rio Grande, the people who remained at their homes fraternized with the "Yankees" in the pleasantest manner. In fact, under the humane policy of our commander, I question whether the great majority of the Mexican people did not regret our departure as much as they had regretted our coming. Property and person were thoroughly protected, and a market was afforded for all the products of the country such as the people had never enjoyed before. The educated and wealthy portion of the population here, as elsewhere, abandoned their homes and remained away from them as long as they were in the possession of the invaders; but this class formed a very small percentage of the whole population.[23]

---

[22] American forces remained at Monterrey until leaving for Saltillo in Nov. 1846. Eisenhower, *So Far from God,* 166–168; Justin H. Smith, *The War with Mexico* (New York: Macmillan, 1919), 1:264–266.

[23] U.S. soldiers and Mexican civilians were frequently in conflict. Taylor, concerned with maintaining order, appealed to Secretary of War William L. Marcy to establish a code that would punish any criminal activity between soldiers and civilians. Marcy offered little guidance. In response to the murder of a civilian by a U.S. soldier, Taylor eventually mustered out of service the entire mounted Texas volunteers. By mid-Nov. 1846, Mexican citizens were still complaining of criminal actions by U.S. troops. Bauer, *Mexican War,* 101–102; Tucker, *Encyclopedia of the Mexican-American War,* s.v. "Marcy, William Learned."

# 9

## Political Intrigue—Buena Vista—Movement against Vera Cruz—Siege and Capture of Vera Cruz

THE MEXICAN WAR was a political war, and the administration conducting it desired to make party capital out of it. General Scott was at the head of the army, and, being a soldier of acknowledged professional capacity, his claim to the command of the forces in the field was almost indisputable and does not seem to have been denied by President Polk,[1] or Marcy,[2] his Secretary of War. Scott was a Whig and the administration was democratic. General Scott was also known to have political aspirations, and nothing so popularizes a candidate for high civil positions as military victories. It would not do therefore to give him command of the "army of conquest." The plans submitted by Scott for a campaign in Mexico were disapproved by the administration, and he replied, in a tone possibly a little disrespectful, to the effect that, if a soldier's plans were not to be supported by the administration, success could not be expected. This was on the 27th of May, 1846. Four days later General Scott was notified that he need not go to Mexico.[3] General

[1] James K. Polk (1795–1849) was born in North Carolina and served as U.S. representative from Tennessee and governor before serving as president from 1845 to 1849. *Dictionary of American Biography*, 2nd ed., s.v. "Polk, James Knox."

[2] William L. Marcy (1786–1857) was born in Massachusetts and served as a senator and governor for New York before becoming Polk's secretary of war. Spencer Tucker, ed., *The Encyclopedia of the Mexican-American War* (Santa Barbara, CA: ABC-CLIO, 2013), s.v. "Marcy, William Learned."

[3] On May 25, 1846, Scott received word (via Secretary Marcy) that Polk had removed him from field command in the Mexican-American War and that he was to remain in Washington. Timothy D. Johnson, *Winfield Scott: The Quest for Military Glory* (Lawrence: University Press of Kansas, 1998), 151–155.

Gaines[4] was next in rank, but he was too old and feeble to take the field. Colonel Zachary Taylor—a brigadier-general by brevet—was therefore left in command. He, too, was a Whig, but was not supposed to entertain any political ambitions; nor did he; but after the fall of Monterey, his third battle and third complete victory, the Whig papers at home began to speak of him as the candidate of their party for the Presidency. Something had to be done to neutralize his growing popularity. He could not be relieved from duty in the field where all his battles had been victories: the design would have been too transparent. It was finally decided to send General Scott to Mexico in chief command, and to authorize him to carry out his own original plan: that is, capture Vera Cruz and march upon the capital of the country.[5] It was no doubt supposed that Scott's ambition would lead him to slaughter Taylor or destroy his chances for the Presidency, and yet it was hoped that he would not make sufficient capital himself to secure the prize.

The administration had indeed a most embarrassing problem to solve. It was engaged in a war of conquest which must be carried to a successful issue, or the political object would be unattained. Yet all the capable officers of the requisite rank belonged to the opposition, and the man selected for his lack of political ambition had himself become a prominent candidate for the Presidency. It was necessary to destroy his chances promptly. The problem was to do this without the loss of conquest and without permitting another general of the same political party to acquire like popularity. The fact is, the administration of Mr. Polk made every preparation to disgrace Scott, or, to speak more correctly, to drive him to such desperation that he would disgrace himself.

General Scott had opposed conquest by the way of the Rio Grande, Matamoras and Saltillo from the first. Now that he was in command of all the forces in Mexico, he withdrew from Taylor most of his regular troops and left him only enough volunteers, as he thought, to hold the line then in possession of the invading army.[6] Indeed Scott did not deem it important to hold anything beyond the Rio Grande, and authorized Taylor to fall back to that

---

[4] Edmund P. Gaines (1777–1849) was an American military officer who served in the War of 1812 and the Seminole Wars. He was brevetted major general in 1814. Tucker, *Encyclopedia of the Mexican-American War,* s.v. "Gaines, Edmund Pendleton."

[5] Polk appointed Scott to command the Veracruz expedition on Nov. 19, 1846. K. Jack Bauer, *The Mexican War, 1846–1848* (New York: Macmillan, 1974), 235.

[6] In Nov. 1846, Scott informed Taylor of his plan to transfer Worth's division of 4,000 men, 2 batteries of artillery, 1,000 cavalry, and several volunteer units to his own command in preparation for the invasion. Upon arriving in Camargo on Jan. 3, 1847, Scott issued orders for the

line if he chose. General Taylor protested against the depletion of his army, and his subsequent movement upon Buena Vista would indicate that he did not share the views of his chief in regard to the unimportance of conquest beyond the Rio Grande.[7]

Scott had estimated the men and material that would be required to capture Vera Cruz and to march on the capital of the country, two hundred and sixty miles in the interior. He was promised all he asked and seemed to have not only the confidence of the President, but his sincere good wishes. The promises were all broken. Only about half the troops were furnished that had been pledged, other war material was withheld and Scott had scarcely started for Mexico before the President undertook to supersede him by the appointment of Senator Thomas H. Benton as lieutenant-general.[8] This being refused by Congress, the President asked legislative authority to place a junior over a senior of the same grade, with the view of appointing Benton to the rank of major-general and then placing him in command of the army, but Congress failed to accede to this proposition as well, and Scott remained in command: but every general appointed to serve under him was politically opposed to the chief, and several were personally hostile.[9]

transfer. John S. D. Eisenhower, *Agent of Destiny: The Life and Times of General Winfield Scott* (New York: Free Press, 1997), 229–230; Johnson, *Winfield Scott*, 160–161, 164; *PUSG*, 1:125n.

[7] Taylor focused his defensive preparations farther south than the Rio Grande. Santa Anna, having intercepted U.S. military communications, set out to overwhelm Taylor's reduced forces, resulting in the Battle of Buena Vista on Feb. 22–23, 1847. K. Jack Bauer, *Zachary Taylor: Soldier, Planter, Statesmen of the Old Southwest* (Baton Rouge: Louisiana State University Press, 1985), 193–200.

[8] Thomas Hart Benton (1782–1858) was born in North Carolina. He served as a lieutenant colonel in the War of 1812 and was elected U.S. senator from Missouri in 1820. In Nov. 1846 Benton, who had been advising the president on military strategy, suggested that he himself command the proposed Veracruz campaign. Polk offered him a command as a major general, but Benton would only accept the rank of lieutenant general and remained a civilian. Paul H. Bergeron, *The Presidency of James K. Polk* (Norwalk, CT: Easton, 1991), 92–94; William M. Meigs, *The Life of Thomas Hart Benton* (Philadelphia: J. B. Lippincott, 1904), 16–17, 121, 517; John C. Pinheiro, *Manifest Ambition: James K. Polk and Civil-Military Relations during the Mexican War* (Westport, CT: Praeger, 2007), 67–70.

[9] Polk appointed thirteen generals for the volunteer troops who were longtime Democratic loyalists: William O. Butler (1791–1880), George Cadwalader (1806–1879), Caleb Cushing (1800–1879), Thomas L. Hamer (1800–1846), Enos D. Hopping (1805–1847), Joseph Lane (1801–1881), Thomas Marshall (1793–1853), Robert Patterson (1792–1881), Franklin Pierce (1804–1869), Gideon J. Pillow (1806–1878), Sterling Price (1809–1867), John A. Quitman (1798–1858), and

General Scott reached Brazos Santiago or Point Isabel, at the mouth of the Rio Grande, late in December, 1846, and proceeded at once up the river to Camargo, where he had written General Taylor to meet him. Taylor, however, had gone to, or towards Tampico, for the purpose of establishing a post there. He had started on this march before he was aware of General Scott being in the country. Under these circumstances Scott had to issue his orders designating the troops to be withdrawn from Taylor, without the personal consultation he had expected to hold with his subordinate.

General Taylor's victory at Buena Vista, February 22d, 23d, and 24th, 1847, with an army composed almost entirely of volunteers who had not been in battle before, and over a vastly superior force numerically, made his nomination for the Presidency by the Whigs a foregone conclusion. He was nominated and elected in 1848.[10] I believe that he sincerely regretted this turn in his fortunes, preferring the peace afforded by a quiet life free from abuse to the honor of filling the highest office in the gift of any people, the Presidency of the United States.

When General Scott assumed command of the army of invasion, I was in the division of General David Twiggs, in Taylor's command; but under the new orders my regiment was transferred to the division of General William Worth, in which I served to the close of the war. The troops withdrawn from Taylor to form part of the forces to operate against Vera Cruz, were assembled at the mouth of the Rio Grande preparatory to embarkation for their destination. I found General Worth a different man from any I had before served directly under. He was nervous, impatient and restless on the march, or when important or responsible duty confronted him. There was not the least reason for haste on the march, for it was known that it would take weeks

James Shields (1806–1879). Tucker, *Encyclopedia of the Mexican-American War,* s.vv. "Butler, William Orlando," "Cadwalader, George," "Cushing, Caleb," "Hamer, Thomas Lyon," "Lane, Joseph," "Marshall, Thomas," "Patterson, Robert," "Pierce, Franklin," "Pillow, Gideon Johnson," "Price, Sterling," "Quitman, John Anthony," "Shields, James"; James K. Polk, *The Diary of James K. Polk during His Presidency, 1845–1849,* ed. Milo M. Quaife (Chicago: A. C. McClurg, 1910), 2:402n; Richard B. Winders, *Mr. Polk's Army: The American Military Experience in the Mexican War* (College Station: Texas A&M University Press, 1997), 35–42.

[10] Taylor's army fought Santa Anna's army near Hacienda San Juan de la Buena Vista on Feb. 22–24, 1847. Taylor's forces were 90 percent volunteers, and only 700 out of 4,800 troops had previous experience in battle. After the victory, Taylor's candidacy for president in 1848 gained steady support among members of the Whig Party. Bauer, *Mexican War,* 209–218; Bauer, *Zachary Taylor,* 230, 232; John S. D. Eisenhower, *So Far from God: The U.S. War with Mexico, 1846–1848* (Norman: University of Oklahoma Press, 1989), 183.

to assemble shipping enough at the point of our embarkation to carry the army, but General Worth moved his division with a rapidity that would have been commendable had he been going to the relief of a beleaguered garrison. The length of the marches was regulated by the distances between places affording a supply of water for the troops, and these distances were sometimes long and sometimes short. General Worth on one occasion at least, after having made the full distance intended for the day, and after the troops were in camp and preparing their food, ordered tents struck and made the march that night which had been intended for the next day.[11] Some commanders can move troops so as to get the maximum distance out of them without fatigue, while others can wear them out in a few days without accomplishing so much. General Worth belonged to this latter class. He enjoyed, however, a fine reputation for his fighting qualities, and thus attached his officers and men to him.

The army lay in camp upon the sand-beach in the neighborhood of the mouth of the Rio Grande for several weeks, awaiting the arrival of transports to carry it to its new field of operations. The transports were all sailing vessels. The passage was a tedious one, and many of the troops were on shipboard over thirty days from the embarkation at the mouth of the Rio Grande to the time of debarkation south of Vera Cruz. The trip was a comfortless one for officers and men. The transports used were built for carrying freight and possessed but limited accommodations for passengers, and the climate added to the discomfort of all.[12]

The transports with troops were assembled in the harbor of Anton Lizardo, some sixteen miles south of Vera Cruz, as they arrived, and there awaited the remainder of the fleet, bringing artillery, ammunition and supplies of all kinds from the North. With the fleet there was a little steam propeller dispatch-boat—the first vessel of the kind I had ever seen, and probably the first of its kind ever seen by any one then with the army. At that day ocean steamers were rare, and what there were were sidewheelers. This little vessel, going through

[11] Worth's division left Saltillo and arrived at Camargo on Jan. 18, 1847. They reached Matamoros on Jan. 22. Edward Wallace, *General William Jenkins Worth: Monterey's Forgotten Hero* (Dallas: Southern Methodist University Press, 1953), 112–113.

[12] All of the commands gathered at Tampico as they waited to join Scott's army. From Tampico, the troops sailed sixty-five miles to Lobos Island. Scott selected the island to prepare his troops for the landing at Veracruz. Bauer, *Mexican War,* 237–240; Thomas W. Cutrer, ed., *The Mexican War Diary and Correspondence of George B. McClellan* (Baton Rouge: Louisiana State University Press, 2009), 68; Eisenhower, *So Far from God,* 256–257.

the fleet so fast, so noiselessly and with its propeller under water out of view, attracted a great deal of attention.[13] I recollect that Lieutenant Sidney Smith,[14] of the 4th infantry, by whom I happened to be standing on the deck of a vessel when this propeller was passing, exclaimed, "Why, the thing looks as if it was propelled by the force of circumstances."

Finally on the 7th of March, 1847, the little army of ten or twelve thousand men, given Scott to invade a country with a population of seven or eight millions, a mountainous country affording the greatest possible natural advantages for defence, was all assembled and ready to commence the perilous task of landing from vessels lying in the open sea.[15]

The debarkation took place inside of the little island of Sacrificios, some three miles south of Vera Cruz.[16] The vessels could not get anywhere near shore, so that everything had to be landed in lighters or surf-boats; General Scott had provided these before leaving the North.[17] The breakers were sometimes high, so that the landing was tedious. The men were got ashore rapidly, because they could wade when they came to shallow water; but the camp and garrison equipage, provisions, ammunition and all stores had to be protected from the salt water, and therefore their landing took several days. The Mexicans were very kind to us, however, and threw no obstacles in the way of our landing except an occasional shot from their nearest fort.[18] During the debarkation one shot took off the head of Major Albertis.[19] No

[13] Steam propeller ships used by the United States in the Mexican-American War that match USG's description include *Legare* (364 tons), *Princeton* (672 tons), *Scourge* (230 tons), and *Spencer* (398 tons). K. Jack Bauer, *Surfboats and Horse Marines: U.S. Naval Operations in the Mexican War, 1846–48* (Annapolis, MD: United States Naval Institute, 1969), 255–258.

[14] Sidney Smith (c.1819–1847) was born in Virginia. He was killed during the Mexico City campaign. *PUSG*, 1:148n.

[15] In Mar. 1847, Scott landed near Vera Cruz with only 9,000 men. Johnson, *Winfield Scott*, 171.

[16] The debarkation occurred on Mar. 9, 1847. Bauer, *Mexican War*, 241–246.

[17] The surfboats used for the landing at Collado Beach near the Isla de Sacrificios were flat-bottomed wooden boats between thirty-five and forty feet long, built specifically for landing troops on the Mexican coast. Bauer, *Mexican War*, 241; Bauer, *Surfboats and Horse Marines*, 66.

[18] Mexican forces did not contest the beach landing because they did not want to risk significant casualties that would diminish their capabilities to man the city's defenses. Bauer, *Mexican War*, 244; Timothy D. Johnson, *A Gallant Little Army: The Mexico City Campaign* (Lawrence: University Press of Kansas, 2007), 22.

[19] William Alburtis (c.1815–1847) was born in Virginia. Although USG refers to him as a major, Alburtis was a first lieutenant in the U.S. 2nd Inf. brevetted to captain for his actions in

other, I believe, reached anywhere near the same distance. On the 9th of March the troops were landed and the investment of Vera Cruz, from the Gulf of Mexico south of the city to the Gulf again on the north, was soon and easily effected. The landing of stores was continued until everything was got ashore.

Vera Cruz, at the time of which I write and up to 1880, was a walled city. The wall extended from the water's edge south of the town to the water again on the north. There were fortifications at intervals along the line and at the angles. In front of the city, and on an island half a mile out in the Gulf, stands San Juan de Ulloa, an enclosed fortification of large dimensions and great strength for that period.[20] Against artillery of the present day the land forts and walls would prove elements of weakness rather than strength. After the invading army had established their camps out of range of the fire from the city, batteries were established, under cover of night, far to the front of the line where the troops lay. These batteries were intrenched and the approaches sufficiently protected. If a sortie had been made at any time by the Mexicans, the men serving the batteries could have been quickly reinforced without great exposure to the fire from the enemy's main line. No serious attempt was made to capture the batteries or to drive our troops away.

The siege continued with brisk firing on our side till the 27th of March, by which time a considerable breach had been made in the wall surrounding the city.[21] Upon this General Morales,[22] who was Governor of both the city and of San Juan de Ulloa, commenced a correspondence with General Scott looking to the surrender of the town, forts and garrison. On the 29th Vera Cruz and

the Seminole War. Daniel H. Hill, *A Fighter from Way Back: The Mexican War Diary of Lt. Daniel Harvey Hill, 4th Artillery, USA,* ed. Nathaniel Cheairs Hughes Jr. and Timothy D. Johnson (Kent, OH: Kent State University Press, 2002), 203*n;* William H. Robarts, *Mexican War Veterans: A Complete Roster of the Regular and Volunteer Troops in the War between the United States and Mexico, from 1846 to 1848* (Washington, DC: Brentano's, 1887), 19.

[20] Fort Concepción stood at the northwest corner of Veracruz while Fort Santiago stood on the southwest corner. The heavily fortified San Juan de Ulúa stood across the gulf. Bauer, *Mexican War,* 107, 245; Eisenhower, *So Far from God,* 259–261; Johnson, *Gallant Little Army,* 23.

[21] The siege of Veracruz began on Monday, Mar. 22, 1847, and ended on Friday morning, Mar. 27. Johnson, *Gallant Little Army,* 38–39, 48.

[22] Brig. Gen. Juan Morales (1802–1847) commanded the defenses at Veracruz. Morales fled the city and died from unknown causes in Atlixco, Puebla, Mexico. José Juan de Landero assumed command of the city and oversaw the surrender to U.S. forces. Bauer, *Mexican War,* 244; Tucker, *Encyclopedia of the Mexican-American War,* s.v. "Morales, Juan."

San Juan de Ulloa were occupied by Scott's army. About five thousand prisoners and four hundred pieces of artillery, besides large amounts of small arms and ammunition, fell into the hands of the victorious force. The casualties on our side during the siege amounted to sixty-four officers and men, killed and wounded.[23]

[23] At the surrender, the Mexican Army marched out with full military honors before being paroled. The terms allowed the approximately 5,000 Mexican troops to keep their guns, horses, and other personal items. The U.S. forces took possession of over 350 cannons. A recent estimate of U.S. casualties is thirteen killed and fifty-five wounded. Johnson, *Gallant Little Army,* 48–49, 51.

# 10

## March to Jalapa—Battle of Cerro Gordo—Perote—
## Puebla—Scott and Taylor

GENERAL SCOTT HAD less than twelve thousand men at Vera Cruz. He had been promised by the administration a very much larger force, or claimed that he had, and he was a man of veracity.[1] Twelve thousand was a very small army with which to penetrate two hundred and sixty miles into an enemy's country, and to besiege the capital; a city, at that time, of largely over one hundred thousand inhabitants. Then, too, any line of march that could be selected led through mountain passes easily defended. In fact, there were at that time but two roads from Vera Cruz to the City of Mexico that could be taken by an army; one by Jalapa and Perote, the other by Cordova and Orizaba, the two coming together on the great plain which extends to the City of Mexico after the range of mountains is passed.[2]

It was very important to get the army away from Vera Cruz as soon as possible, in order to avoid the yellow fever, or vomito, which usually visits that city early in the year, and is very fatal to persons not acclimated; but transportation, which was expected from the North, was arriving very slowly. It was absolutely necessary to have enough to supply the army to Jalapa, sixty-five

[1] During a May 14, 1846, meeting with President Polk and Secretary of War Marcy, Scott insisted that he needed 20,000 volunteers for the war effort. Polk disagreed, believing Scott to have overestimated the number of troops needed. In Mar. 1847, Scott landed at Vera Cruz with 9,000 men. Timothy D. Johnson, *Winfield Scott: The Quest for Military Glory* (Lawrence: University Press of Kansas, 1998), 151, 171.

[2] Scott opted to take the National Road, which passed Jalapa and Perote, because it was in better condition than the road to Cordova and Orizaba. John S. D. Eisenhower, *So Far from God: The U.S. War with Mexico, 1846–1848* (Norman: University of Oklahoma Press, 1989), 267; Allan Peskin, *Winfield Scott and the Profession of Arms* (Kent, OH: Kent State University Press, 2003), 162.

miles in the interior and above the fevers of the coast.[3] At that point the country is fertile, and an army of the size of General Scott's could subsist there for an indefinite period. Not counting the sick, the weak and the garrisons for the captured city and fort, the moving column was now less than ten thousand strong. This force was composed of three divisions, under Generals Twiggs, Patterson,[4] and Worth. The importance of escaping the vomito was so great that as soon as transportation enough could be got together to move a division the advance was commenced. On the 8th of April, Twiggs's division started for Jalapa. He was followed very soon by Patterson, with his division.[5] General Worth was to bring up the rear with his command as soon as transportation enough was assembled to carry six days' rations for his troops with the necessary ammunition and camp and garrison equipage. It was the 13th of April before this division left Vera Cruz.

The leading division ran against the enemy at Cerro Gordo, some fifty miles west, on the road to Jalapa, and went into camp at Plan del Rio, about three miles from the fortifications. General Patterson reached Plan del Rio with his division soon after Twiggs arrived.[6] The two were then secure against an attack from Santa Anna, who commanded the Mexican forces.[7] At all events they confronted the enemy without reinforcements and without molestation, until the 18th of April. General Scott had remained at Vera Cruz to hasten preparations for the field; but on the 12th, learning the situation at the front,

[3] In the 1840s, people understood that staying in close proximity to low-lying stagnant pools of water, specifically near coastal regions, caused yellow fever outbreaks. However, they did not realize that mosquitoes were responsible for spreading the disease. Timothy D. Johnson, *A Gallant Little Army: The Mexico City Campaign* (Lawrence: University Press of Kansas, 2007), 61.

[4] Robert Patterson (1792–1881) was born in Ireland and immigrated to the United States in 1799. After serving in the U.S. military from 1812 to 1815, he reentered the army at the rank of major general in 1846. He commanded the 2nd Div. of Volunteers during the Mexican-American War and was commanding general, Army of the Shenandoah, in 1861. *CWHC,* 418–419; Spencer Tucker, ed., *The Encyclopedia of the Mexican-American War* (Santa Barbara, CA: ABC-CLIO, 2013), s.v. "Patterson, Robert."

[5] Patterson's division departed Veracruz on Apr. 9, 1847. K. Jack Bauer, *The Mexican War, 1846–1848* (New York: Macmillan, 1974), 261.

[6] Twiggs arrived at Plan del Rio on Apr. 11, 1847, and Patterson arrived the following day. Eisenhower, *So Far from God,* 275.

[7] After his defeat at the Battle of Buena Vista, Santa Anna returned to Mexico City to quell the rising political turmoil. His focus then shifted toward organizing a new army to counter Scott's invasion. Will Fowler, *Santa Anna of Mexico* (Lincoln: University of Nebraska Press, 2007), 265–267.

he hastened on to take personal supervision.[8] He at once commenced his preparations for the capture of the position held by Santa Anna and of the troops holding it.

Cerro Gordo is one of the higher spurs of the mountains some twelve to fifteen miles east of Jalapa, and Santa Anna had selected this point as the easiest to defend against an invading army.[9] The road, said to have been built by Cortez, zigzags around the mountain-side and was defended at every turn by artillery.[10] On either side were deep chasms or mountain walls. A direct attack along the road was an impossibility. A flank movement seemed equally impossible. After the arrival of the commanding-general upon the scene, reconnoissances were sent out to find, or to make, a road by which the rear of the enemy's works might be reached without a front attack.[11] These reconnoissances were made under the supervision of Captain Robert E. Lee,[12] assisted by Lieutenants P. G. T. Beauregard,[13] Isaac I. Stevens,[14] Z. B. Tower,[15]

[8] On Apr. 14, 1847, Scott arrived at Plan del Rio. He prepared his troops to confront Santa Anna's army at Cerro Gordo. Worth's division arrived at Plan del Rio by Apr. 17, just in time for the attack. Eisenhower, *So Far from God*, 277–278.

[9] Santa Anna stationed 9,000 men at Cerro Gordo. The hill known as Cerro Gordo, and also called El Telégrafo, towered over the Mexican fortifications. Fowler, *Santa Anna of Mexico*, 266–267.

[10] In 1519, during an attack on the Aztec capital, Tenochtitlan, Spanish conquistador Hernán Cortés (1485–1547) took a route that later became the National Road. Eisenhower, *So Far from God*, 267; Paul Legassé, ed., *The Columbia Encyclopedia* (New York: Columbia University Press, 2000), s.v. "Cortés, Hernán."

[11] Before Scott's arrival on Apr. 14, 1847, Capt. Joseph E. Johnston and Lt. Zealous B. Tower were sent out to discern the enemy's position. Johnson, *Gallant Little Army*, 69.

[12] Robert E. Lee (1807–1870) was born in Virginia and graduated from the USMA in 1829. As a Confederate general, Lee commanded the Army of Northern Virginia from 1862 to 1865. *CWHC*, 344.

[13] P. G. T. Beauregard (1818–1893) was born in Louisiana and graduated from the USMA in 1838. He resigned from the U.S. Army in 1861 to join the Confederate Army as a brigadier general. He held numerous command positions during the Civil War. Ibid., 123–124.

[14] Isaac I. Stevens (1818–1862) was born in Massachusetts and graduated first in his class from the USMA in 1839. During the Civil War, Stevens served as a brigadier general in the U.S. Army. In Sept. 1862, he was killed in combat at Chantilly, VA. Ibid., 510.

[15] Zealous B. Tower (1819–1900) was born in Massachusetts and graduated first in his class from the USMA in 1841. In 1865, near the end of the Civil War, Tower was brevetted major general. Ibid., 534.

G. W. Smith,[16] George B. McClellan,[17] and J. G. Foster,[18] of the corps of engineers, all officers who attained rank and fame, on one side or the other, in the great conflict for the preservation of the unity of the nation. The reconnoissance was completed, and the labor of cutting out and making roads by the flank of the enemy was effected by the 17th of the month. This was accomplished without the knowledge of Santa Anna or his army, and over ground where he supposed it impossible. On the same day General Scott issued his order for the attack on the 18th.

The attack was made as ordered, and perhaps there was not a battle of the Mexican war, or of any other, where orders issued before an engagement were nearer being a correct report of what afterwards took place. Under the supervision of the engineers, roadways had been opened over chasms to the right where the walls were so steep that men could barely climb them. Animals could not. These had been opened under cover of night, without attracting the notice of the enemy. The engineers, who had directed the opening, led the way and the troops followed. Artillery was let down the steep slopes by hand, the men engaged attaching a strong rope to the rear axle and letting the guns down, a piece at a time, while the men at the ropes kept their ground on top, paying out gradually, while a few at the front directed the course of the piece. In like manner the guns were drawn by hand up the opposite slopes. In this way Scott's troops reached their assigned position in rear of most of the intrenchments of the enemy, unobserved. The attack was made, the Mexican reserves behind the works beat a hasty retreat, and those occupying them surrendered. On the left General Pillow's command made a formidable demonstration, which doubtless held a part of the enemy in his front and contributed to the victory. I am not pretending to give full details of all the battles fought, but of the portion that I saw. There were troops engaged on both sides at other points in which both sustained losses; but the battle was won as here narrated.

[16] Gustavus W. Smith (1821–1896) was born in Kentucky and graduated from the USMA in 1842. He served as a major general with the Confederate Army of Northern Virginia during the Civil War. Ibid., 495.

[17] George B. McClellan (1826–1885) was born in Pennsylvania and graduated from the USMA in 1846. McClellan was general-in-chief of the U.S. Army from Nov. 1861 to Mar. 1862. Ibid., 371–372.

[18] John G. Foster (1823–1874) was born in New Hampshire and graduated from the USMA in 1846. Foster served as commanding general, U.S. Army of the Ohio, from Dec. 1863 to Feb. 1864. Ibid., 241.

The surprise of the enemy was complete, the victory overwhelming; some three thousand prisoners fell into Scott's hands, also a large amount of ordnance and ordnance stores. The prisoners were paroled, the artillery parked and the small arms and ammunition destroyed.[19] The battle of Buena Vista was probably very important to the success of General Scott at Cerro Gordo and in his entire campaign from Vera Cruz to the great plains reaching to the City of Mexico. The only army Santa Anna had to protect his capital and the mountain passes west of Vera Cruz, was the one he had with him confronting General Taylor. It is not likely that he would have gone as far north as Monterey to attack the United States troops when he knew his country was threatened with invasion further south. When Taylor moved to Saltillo and then advanced on to Buena Vista, Santa Anna crossed the desert confronting the invading army, hoping no doubt to crush it and get back in time to meet General Scott in the mountain passes west of Vera Cruz. His attack on Taylor was disastrous to the Mexican army, but, notwithstanding this, he marched his army to Cerro Gordo, a distance not much short of one thousand miles by the line he had to travel, in time to intrench himself well before Scott got there. If he had been successful at Buena Vista his troops would no doubt have made a more stubborn resistance at Cerro Gordo. Had the battle of Buena Vista not been fought Santa Anna would have had time to move leisurely to meet the invader further south and with an army not demoralized nor depleted by defeat.

After the battle the victorious army moved on to Jalapa, where it was in a beautiful, productive and healthy country, far above the fevers of the coast. Jalapa, however, is still in the mountains, and between there and the great plain the whole line of the road is easy of defence. It was important, therefore, to get possession of the great highway between the sea-coast and the capital up to the point where it leaves the mountains, before the enemy could have time to re-organize and fortify in our front. Worth's division was selected to go forward to secure this result. The division marched to Perote on the great plain, not far from where the road debouches from the mountains. There is a low, strong fort on the plain in front of the town, known as the Castle of Perote. This, however, offered no resistance and fell into our hands, with its armament.[20]

---

[19] Because of the difficulty in caring for prisoners and captured weaponry, Scott paroled the Mexican prisoners, destroyed approximately 4,000 muskets, and sent 6 of the 40 cannons captured to the United States. He ordered the remaining cannons spiked and rendered useless. Johnson, *Gallant Little Army,* 100–101.

[20] On Apr. 22, 1847, troops from Worth's division (including USG) occupied Fort San Carlos de Perote on the road to Jalapa. When U.S. troops arrived there, they found the fort

General Scott having now only nine or ten thousand men west of Vera Cruz, and the time of some four thousand of them being about to expire, a long delay was the consequence. The troops were in a healthy climate, and where they could subsist for an indefinite period even if their line back to Vera Cruz should be cut off. It being ascertained that the men whose time would expire before the City of Mexico could possibly fall into the hands of the American army, would not remain beyond the term for which they had volunteered, the commanding-general determined to discharge them at once, for a delay until the expiration of their time would have compelled them to pass through Vera Cruz during the season of the vomito. This reduced Scott's force in the field to about five thousand men.[21]

Early in May, Worth, with his division, left Perote and marched on to Puebla. The roads were wide and the country open except through one pass in a spur of mountains coming up from the south, through which the road runs. Notwithstanding this the small column was divided into two bodies, moving a day apart. Nothing occurred on the march of special note, except that while lying at the town of Amozoque—an easy day's march east of Puebla—a body of the enemy's cavalry, two or three thousand strong, was seen to our right, not more than a mile away. A battery or two, with two or three infantry regiments, was sent against them and they soon disappeared. On the 15th of May we entered the city of Puebla.[22]

General Worth was in command at Puebla until the latter end of May, when General Scott arrived. Here, as well as on the march up, his restlessness, particularly under responsibilities, showed itself. During his brief command he had the enemy hovering around near the city, in vastly superior numbers to his own. The brigade to which I was attached changed quarters three different times in about a week, occupying at first quarters near the plaza, in the heart

deserted and subsequently converted it into a hospital. Bauer, *Mexican War*, 268–269; Johnson, *Gallant Little Army*, 121; *PUSG*, 1:131–132.

[21] When Scott reached Jalapa in May 1847, he sent seven volunteer regiments, whose enlistments were about to expire, back toward Veracruz. This left him approximately 7,000 soldiers, with whom he pressed forward to Perote and then Puebla. John S. D. Eisenhower, *Agent of Destiny: The Life and Times of General Winfield Scott* (New York: Free Press, 1997), 260; Johnson, *Gallant Little Army*, 130.

[22] Worth and his troops began marching the eight-mile journey for Puebla on May 10, 1847. Early on May 14, Mexican cavalry tried to attack Worth's army near Amozoc de Mota but failed. Santa Anna retreated to Mexico City from Puebla with approximately 4,000 troops. Johnson, *Gallant Little Army*, 122–123; *PUSG*, 1:138.

of the city; then at the western entrance; then at the extreme east. On one occasion General Worth had the troops in line, under arms, all day, with three days' cooked rations in their haversacks. He galloped from one command to another proclaiming the near proximity of Santa Anna with an army vastly superior to his own. General Scott arrived upon the scene the latter part of the month, and nothing more was heard of Santa Anna and his myriads.[23] There were, of course, bodies of mounted Mexicans hovering around to watch our movements and to pick up stragglers, or small bodies of troops, if they ventured too far out. These always withdrew on the approach of any considerable number of our soldiers. After the arrival of General Scott I was sent, as quartermaster, with a large train of wagons, back two days' march at least, to procure forage. We had less than a thousand men as escort, and never thought of danger. We procured full loads for our entire train at two plantations, which could easily have furnished as much more.

There had been great delay in obtaining the authority of Congress for the raising of the troops asked for by the administration. A bill was before the National Legislature from early in the session of 1846–7, authorizing the creation of ten additional regiments for the war to be attached to the regular army, but it was the middle of February before it became a law. Appointments of commissioned officers had then to be made; men had to be enlisted, the regiments equipped and the whole transported to Mexico.[24] It was August before General Scott received reinforcement sufficient to warrant an advance. His moving column, not even now more than ten thousand strong, was in four divisions, commanded by Generals Twiggs, Worth, Pillow and Quitman.[25] There was also a cavalry corps under General Harney,[26] composed of detachments of the

---

[23] Scott arrived in Puebla on May 28, 1847. Johnson, *Gallant Little Army*, 125.

[24] On Dec. 29, 1846, a bill authorizing ten regiments of regular army troops had been introduced in the U.S. House of Representatives. The bill was proposed in response to Secretary of War Marcy's call for additional troops. News that American troops were nearly outnumbered by Mexican forces at Saltillo ensured passage of the bill, and Polk signed it into law on Feb. 11, 1847. John C. Pinheiro, *Manifest Ambition: James K. Polk and Civil-Military Relations during the Mexican War* (Westport, CT: Praeger, 2007), 51–55.

[25] By Aug. 1847, Scott received reinforcements of 6,900 men, bringing the total number of troops to 14,000. Of those 14,000, 3,000 were ill, and an additional 600 were recovering from illness. Eisenhower, *Agent of Destiny*, 269.

[26] William S. Harney (1800–1889) was born in Tennessee and joined the U.S. 1st Inf. as a second lieutenant in 1818. After the Battle of Cerro Gordo, Harney was brevetted brigadier general. Tucker, *Encyclopedia of the Mexican-American War*, s.v. "Harney, William Selby."

1st, 2d, and 3d dragoons. The advance commenced on the 7th of August with Twiggs's division in front. The remaining three divisions followed, with an interval of a day between. The marches were short, to make concentration easier in case of attack.[27]

I had now been in battle with the two leading commanders conducting armies in a foreign land. The contrast between the two was very marked. General Taylor never wore uniform, but dressed himself entirely for comfort. He moved about the field in which he was operating to see through his own eyes the situation. Often he would be without staff officers, and when he was accompanied by them there was no prescribed order in which they followed. He was very much given to sit his horse side-ways—with both feet on one side—particularly on the battle-field. General Scott was the reverse in all these particulars. He always wore all the uniform prescribed or allowed by law when he inspected his lines; word would be sent to all division and brigade commanders in advance, notifying them of the hour when the commanding general might be expected. This was done so that all the army might be under arms to salute their chief as he passed. On these occasions he wore his dress uniform, cocked hat, aiguillettes, sabre and spurs. His staff proper, besides all officers constructively on his staff—engineers, inspectors, quartermasters, etc., that could be spared—followed, also in uniform and in prescribed order. Orders were prepared with great care and evidently with the view that they should be a history of what followed.

In their modes of expressing thought, these two generals contrasted quite as strongly as in their other characteristics. General Scott was precise in language, cultivated a style peculiarly his own; was proud of his rhetoric; not averse to speaking of himself, often in the third person, and he could bestow praise upon the person he was talking about without the least embarrassment. Taylor was not a conversationalist, but on paper he could put his meaning so plainly that there could be no mistaking it. He knew how to express what he wanted to say in the fewest well-chosen words, but would not sacrifice meaning to the construction of high-sounding sentences. But with their opposite characteristics both were great and successful soldiers; both were true, patriotic and upright in all their dealings. Both were pleasant to

[27] On Aug. 7, 1847, Harney's two cavalry battalions, which were part of Quitman's division, led the march toward Mexico City, followed by Twiggs's 2nd Div. On Aug. 8, Quitman's men started their march, followed by Worth's division the next day. Maj. Gen. Gideon Pillow's men were the last to leave. Eisenhower, *Agent of Destiny,* 269.

serve under—Taylor was pleasant to serve with. Scott saw more through the eyes of his staff officers than through his own. His plans were deliberately prepared, and fully expressed in orders. Taylor saw for himself, and gave orders to meet the emergency without reference to how they would read in history.

# II

Advance on the City of Mexico—Battle of Contreras—
Assault at Churubusco—Negotiations for Peace—
Battle of Molino del Rey—Storming of
Chapultepec—San Cosme—Evacuation of the City—
Halls of the Montezumas

T HE ROUTE FOLLOWED by the army from Puebla to the City of Mexico
was over Rio Frio mountain, the road leading over which, at the highest point,
is about eleven thousand feet above tide water.[1] The pass through this mountain
might have been easily defended, but it was not; and the advanced division
reached the summit in three days after leaving Puebla. The City of Mexico lies
west of Rio Frio mountain, on a plain backed by another mountain six miles
farther west, with others still nearer on the north and south. Between the
western base of Rio Frio and the City of Mexico there are three lakes, Chalco
and Xochimilco on the left and Texcoco on the right, extending to the east
end of the City of Mexico. Chalco and Texcoco are divided by a narrow strip of
land over which the direct road to the city runs. Xochimilco is also to the left
of the road, but at a considerable distance south of it, and is connected
with Lake Chalco by a narrow channel. There is a high rocky mound, called El
Peñon, on the right of the road, springing up from the low flat ground dividing the lakes. This mound was strengthened by intrenchments at its base
and summit and rendered a direct attack impracticable.[2]

Scott's army was rapidly concentrated about Ayotla and other points near
the eastern end of Lake Chalco. Reconnoissances were made up to within

---

[1] USG and his fellow soldiers left Puebla on Aug. 5, 1847. *PUSG*, 1:142–143.

[2] Santa Anna made his headquarters at El Peñón and posted 7,000 men there. John S. D.
Eisenhower, *So Far from God: The U.S. War with Mexico, 1846–1848* (Norman: University of
Oklahoma Press, 1989), 309.

gun-shot of El Peñon, while engineers were seeking a route by the south side of Lake Chalco to flank the city, and come upon it from the south and south-west. A way was found around the lake, and by the 18th of August troops were in St. Augustin Tlalpam, a town about eleven miles due south from the plaza of the capital.[3] Between St. Augustin Tlalpam and the city lie the hacienda of San Antonio and the village of Churubusco, and south-west of them is Contreras. All these points, except St. Augustin Tlalpam, were intrenched and strongly garrisoned. Contreras is situated on the side of a mountain, near its base, where volcanic rocks are piled in great confusion, reaching nearly to San Antonio. This made the approach to the city from the south very difficult.

The brigade to which I was attached—Garland's, of Worth's division—was sent to confront San Antonio, two or three miles from St. Augustin Tlalpam, on the road to Churubusco and the City of Mexico.[4] The ground on which San Antonio stands is completely in the valley, and the surface of the land is only a little above the level of the lakes, and, except to the south-west, it was cut up by deep ditches filled with water. To the south-west is the Pedregal—the volcanic rock before spoken of—over which cavalry or artillery could not be passed, and infantry would make but poor progress if confronted by an enemy.[5] From the position occupied by Garland's brigade, therefore, no movement could be made against the defences of San Antonio except to the front, and by a narrow causeway, over perfectly level ground, every inch of which was commanded by the enemy's artillery and infantry. If Contreras, some three miles west and south, should fall into our hands, troops from there could move to the right flank of all the positions held by the enemy between us and the city. Under these circumstances General Scott directed the holding of the front of the enemy without making an attack until further orders.

[3] The village of Tlalpam was called San Agustín de las Cuevas during the colonial era and is now known as Tlalpan. Salvador Padilla Aguilar, *San Agustín Tlalpan: Historias y tradiciones de un Viejo pueblo (25–1999 d.C.)* (Mexico City: Comité Editorial del Gobierno del Distrito Federal, 1999), 25.

[4] After U.S. forces avoided El Peñón, Santa Anna shifted the bulk of his forces to the south-west. Establishing his command at Churubusco, he placed troops at several fortified posts between Contreras and Churubusco. Will Fowler, *Santa Anna of Mexico* (Lincoln: University of Nebraska Press, 2007), 273–274; Timothy D. Johnson, *Winfield Scott: The Quest for Military Glory* (Lawrence: University Press of Kansas, 1998), 199.

[5] The jagged black lava formations of the Pedregal stretched for three miles west of San Antonio. Timothy D. Johnson, *A Gallant Little Army: The Mexico City Campaign* (Lawrence: University Press of Kansas, 2007), 158.

On the 18th of August, the day of reaching San Augustin Tlalpam, Garland's brigade secured a position within easy range of the advanced intrenchments of San Antonio, but where his troops were protected by an artificial embankment that had been thrown up for some other purpose than defence. General Scott at once set his engineers reconnoitring the works about Contreras, and on the 19th movements were commenced to get troops into positions from which an assault could be made upon the force occupying that place. The Pedregal on the north and north-east, and the mountain on the south, made the passage by either flank of the enemy's defences difficult, for their work stood exactly between those natural bulwarks; but a road was completed during the day and night of the 19th, and troops were got to the north and west of the enemy.

This affair, like that of Cerro Gordo, was an engagement in which the officers of the engineer corps won special distinction. In fact, in both cases, tasks which seemed difficult at first sight were made easier for the troops that had to execute them than they would have been on an ordinary field. The very strength of each of these positions was, by the skill of the engineers, converted into a defence for the assaulting parties while securing their positions for final attack. All the troops with General Scott in the valley of Mexico, except a part of the division of General Quitman at San Augustin Tlalpam and the brigade of Garland (Worth's division) at San Antonio, were engaged at the battle of Contreras, or were on their way, in obedience to the orders of their chief, to reinforce those who were engaged.[6] The assault was made on the morning of the 20th, and in less than half an hour from the sound of the advance the position was in our hands, with many prisoners and large quantities of ordnance and other stores. The brigade commanded by General Riley[7] was from

---

[6]The battle took place near the ranch called Padierna and the village known as Contreras. The U.S. forces sometimes mistakenly called the ranch Contreras, and this became the name for the battle used by U.S. troops. It was referred to as the Battle of Padierna by Mexican forces. George L. Rives, *The United States and Mexico, 1821–1848: A History of the Relations between the Two Countries from the Independence of Mexico to the Close of the War with the United States* (New York: C. Scribner's Sons, 1913), 2:461.

[7]Bennett Riley (c.1790–1853) earned the rank of lieutenant colonel before the outbreak of the Mexican-American War. During the war, he was brevetted major general. Charles J. Peterson, *The Military Heroes of the War with Mexico with a Narrative of the War,* 10th ed. (Philadelphia: William A. Leary, 1858), 253; William H. Powell, *List of Officers of the Army of the United States from 1779 to 1900* (New York: R. Hamersly, 1900), 554.

its position the most conspicuous in the final assault, but all did well, volunteers and regulars.[8]

From the point occupied by Garland's brigade we could see the progress made at Contreras and the movement of troops toward the flank and rear of the enemy opposing us. The Mexicans all the way back to the city could see the same thing, and their conduct showed plainly that they did not enjoy the sight. We moved out at once, and found them gone from our immediate front. Clarke's[9] brigade of Worth's division now moved west over the point of the Pedregal, and after having passed to the north sufficiently to clear San Antonio, turned east and got on the causeway leading to Churubusco and the City of Mexico. When he approached Churubusco his left, under Colonel Hoffman,[10] attacked a tête-de-pont at that place and brought on an engagement. About an hour after, Garland was ordered to advance directly along the causeway, and got up in time to take part in the engagement. San Antonio was found evacuated, the evacuation having probably taken place immediately upon the enemy seeing the stars and stripes waving over Contreras.

The troops that had been engaged at Contreras, and even then on their way to that battle-field, were moved by a causeway west of, and parallel to the one by way of San Antonio and Churubusco. It was expected by the commanding general that these troops would move north sufficiently far to flank the enemy out of his position at Churubusco, before turning east to reach the San Antonio road, but they did not succeed in this, and Churubusco proved to be about the severest battle fought in the valley of Mexico. General Scott coming upon the battle-field about this juncture, ordered two brigades, under Shields,[11] to move north and turn the right of the enemy. This Shields did, but not

[8] Just after 6:00 A.M. on Aug. 20, 1847, Riley led his brigade in a surprise attack on Gen. Gabriel Valencia's (1799–1848) troops, routing them in a brief but intense seventeen-minute battle. John S. D. Eisenhower, *Agent of Destiny: The Life and Times of General Winfield Scott* (New York: Free Press, 1997), 278–282; Johnson, *Winfield Scott*, 199; Robert L. Scheina, *Latin America's Wars: The Age of the Caudillo, 1791–1899* (Washington, DC: Brassey's, 2003), 471n.

[9] Col. Newman S. Clarke (?–1860) was a career military officer who was brevetted brigadier general for gallantry at the siege of Veracruz. Thomas H. S. Hamersly, *Complete Regular Army Register of the United States: For One Hundred Years (1779 to 1879) . . .* (Washington, DC: T. H. S. Hamersly, 1880), 361.

[10] William Hoffman (1807–1884) was born in New York and graduated from the USMA in 1829. Hoffman was brevetted major for his involvement at Contreras and Churubusco. He reached the rank of brevet major general in Mar. 1865. *CWHC,* 300.

[11] James Shields (1810–1879) immigrated to Illinois from Ireland in 1823. He was appointed brigadier general on July 1, 1846. After being wounded in the left arm at Chapultepec, Shields

without hard fighting and heavy loss. The enemy finally gave way, leaving in our hands prisoners, artillery and small arms. The balance of the causeway held by the enemy, up to the very gates of the city, fell in like manner. I recollect at this place that some of the gunners who had stood their ground, were deserters from General Taylor's army on the Rio Grande.[12]

Both the strategy and tactics displayed by General Scott in these various engagements of the 20th of August, 1847, were faultless as I look upon them now, after the lapse of so many years. As before stated, the work of the engineer officers who made the reconnoissances and led the different commands to their destinations, was so perfect that the chief was able to give his orders to his various subordinates with all the precision he could use on an ordinary march. I mean, up to the points from which the attack was to commence. After that point is reached the enemy often induces a change of orders not before contemplated. The enemy outside the city outnumbered our soldiery quite three to one, but they had become so demoralized by the succession of defeats this day, that the City of Mexico could have been entered without much further bloodshed. In fact, Captain Philip Kearney—afterwards a general in the war of the rebellion—rode with a squadron of cavalry to the very gates of the city, and would no doubt have entered with his little force, only at that point he was badly wounded, as were several of his officers. He had not heard the call for a halt.[13]

General Franklin Pierce had joined the army in Mexico, at Puebla, a short time before the advance upon the capital commenced. He had consequently not been in any of the engagements of the war up to the battle of Contreras.

was honorably mustered out of the volunteers. He went on to serve in the U.S. Army during the Civil War, attaining the rank of major general. Ibid., 486.

[12] At the Battle of Churubusco, the battalion known as the San Patricios defended a convent against U.S. forces. The San Patricios, a battalion of largely Irish and Catholic troops, had deserted from Taylor's Army of Occupation. The Mexican government had appealed to them as Catholics while offering them better pay to encourage their desertion. Most of them were captured at Churubusco and fifty of them were hanged in Sept. 1847. John C. Pinheiro, *Missionaries of Republicanism: A Religious History of the Mexican-American War* (New York: Oxford University Press, 2014), 102–106.

[13] Philip W. Kearny (1815–1862) was born in New York. As the Mexican troops retreated from Churubusco, Kearny and the U.S. 1st Dragoons pursued them toward Mexico City. While Scott ordered a halt to the pursuit, Kearny and others continued toward the Garita San Antonio, the fortified southern gate into Mexico City. As they rode into enemy fire, grapeshot struck Kearny's left arm, which had to be amputated near the shoulder. He served as a brigadier general in the U.S. Army during the Civil War and died from wounds received at Chantilly, VA. *CWHC,* 328; Johnson, *Gallant Little Army,* 190.

By an unfortunate fall of his horse on the afternoon of the 19th he was pain-
fully injured. The next day, when his brigade, with the other troops engaged
on the same field, was ordered against the flank and rear of the enemy guarding
the different points of the road from San Augustin Tlalpam to the city, General
Pierce attempted to accompany them. He was not sufficiently recovered to
do so, and fainted. This circumstance gave rise to exceedingly unfair and unjust criticisms of him when he became a candidate for the Presidency. Whatever General Pierce's qualifications may have been for the Presidency, he was
a gentleman and a man of courage. I was not a supporter of him politically, but
I knew him more intimately than I did any other of the volunteer generals.[14]

General Scott abstained from entering the city at this time, because
Mr. Nicholas P. Trist,[15] the commissioner on the part of the United States to
negotiate a treaty of peace with Mexico, was with the army, and either he or
General Scott thought—probably both of them—that a treaty would be more
possible while the Mexican government was in possession of the capital than
if it was scattered and the capital in the hands of an invader.[16] Be this as it
may, we did not enter at that time. The army took up positions along the slopes
of the mountains south of the city, as far west as Tacubaya.[17] Negotiations were

---

[14] On Aug. 19, 1847, Pierce injured his knee and his groin when his horse fell during battle.
The pain from his injuries caused him to lose consciousness. He returned to action the next
day at Churubusco, but twisted his already injured knee and collapsed from the pain. He was
thus branded the "fainting General" by Whig opponents in the election of 1852. Larry Gara,
*The Presidency of Franklin Pierce* (Lawrence: University Press of Kansas, 1991), 38; Roy F.
Nichols, *Franklin Pierce: Young Hickory of the Granite Hills,* 2nd ed. (Philadelphia: University
of Pennsylvania Press, 1969), 161–163.

[15] Nicholas P. Trist (1800–1874) was born in Virginia and was the chief clerk of the U.S.
State Dept., its highest-ranking officer. He was fluent in Spanish, had served as American consul
in Havana, and was well versed in Latin American customs. Paul H. Bergeron, *The Presidency of
James K. Polk* (Norwalk, CT: Easton, 1991), 99; Wallace Ohrt, *Defiant Peacemaker: Nicholas
Trist in the Mexican War* (College Station: Texas A&M University Press, 1997), 102, 131–132.

[16] Polk and the cabinet drafted a proposed treaty that demanded the Rio Grande boundary
as the southern border of Texas and the cession by Mexico of all of California. Polk also authorized Trist to pay the Mexican government up to $30,000,000. The treaty was sealed and Trist
was instructed not to divulge the contents to anyone, including Scott. K. Jack Bauer, *The
Mexican War, 1846–1848* (New York: Macmillan, 1974), 282; Bergeron, *Presidency of James K.
Polk,* 99; Ohrt, *Defiant Peacemaker,* 102, 131–132.

[17] On Aug. 21, 1847, the day after the Battle of Churubusco, Scott ordered artillery to the
front as he prepared for a siege. Bauer, *Mexican War,* 306; Johnson, *Gallant Little Army,* 194–
197; Johnson, *Winfield Scott,* 200–201.

at once entered into with Santa Anna, who was then practically *the Government* and the immediate commander of all the troops engaged in defence of the country.[18] A truce was signed which denied to either party the right to strengthen its position, or to receive reinforcements during the continuance of the armistices, but authorized General Scott to draw supplies for his army from the city in the meantime.[19]

Negotiations were commenced at once and were kept up vigorously, between Mr. Trist and the commissioners appointed on the part of Mexico, until the 2d of September. At that time Mr. Trist handed in his ultimatum. Texas was to be given up absolutely by Mexico, and New Mexico and California ceded to the United States for a stipulated sum to be afterwards determined. I do not suppose Mr. Trist had any discretion whatever in regard to boundaries. The war was one of conquest, in the interest of an institution, and the probabilities are that private instructions were for the acquisition of territory out of which new States might be carved. At all events the Mexicans felt so outraged at the terms proposed that they commenced preparations for defence, without giving notice of the termination of the armistice. The terms of the truce had been violated before, when teams had been sent into the city to bring out supplies for the army. The first train entering the city was very severely threatened by a mob. This, however, was apologized for by the authorities and all responsibility for it denied; and thereafter, to avoid exciting the Mexican people and soldiery, our teams with their escorts were sent in at night, when the troops were in barracks and the citizens in bed. The circumstance was overlooked and negotiations continued. As soon as the news reached General Scott of the second violation of the armistice, about the 4th of September, he wrote a vigorous note to President Santa Anna, calling his attention to it, and, receiving an unsatisfactory reply, declared the armistice at an end.[20]

---

[18] Trist actually negotiated with ex-president José Joaquín de Herrera, José B. Couto, Gen. Ignacio Mora y Villamil, and Miguel Atristain. Ohrt, *Defiant Peacemaker,* 131.

[19] On Aug. 22, 1847, Mexican and U.S. forces agreed to a truce. In addition to the terms described by USG, other provisions covered such issues as respect for the civil rights of Mexicans living in areas under U.S. control; the treatment of the wounded; the exchange of prisoners; and the stipulation that the truce could only be ended by either side following a forty-eight-hour notice of intent. Eisenhower, *So Far from God,* 329–331.

[20] Although the armistice prevented Santa Anna from procuring supplies for the army, Mexican forces had been strengthening the city's defenses and fortifying strategic points. By the first week of Sept. 1847, Mexico City's defenses had been renewed and forces repositioned for an attack from the south. On Sept. 6, after numerous warnings to Santa Anna, Scott notified

General Scott, with Worth's division, was now occupying Tacubaya, a village some four miles south-west of the City of Mexico, and extending from the base up the mountain-side for the distance of half a mile.[21] More than a mile west, and also a little above the plain, stands Molino del Rey.[22] The mill is a long stone structure, one story high and several hundred feet in length. At the period of which I speak General Scott supposed a portion of the mill to be used as a foundry for the casting of guns. This, however, proved to be a mistake. It was valuable to the Mexicans because of the quantity of grain it contained. The building is flat roofed, and a line of sand-bags over the outer walls rendered the top quite a formidable defence for infantry. Chapultepec is a mound springing up from the plain to the height of probably three hundred feet, and almost in a direct line between Molino del Rey and the western part of the city. It was fortified both on the top and on the rocky and precipitous sides.[23]

The City of Mexico is supplied with water by two aqueducts, resting on strong stone arches. One of these aqueducts draws its supply of water from a mountain stream coming into it at or near Molino del Rey, and runs north close to the west base of Chapultepec; thence along the centre of a wide road, until it reaches the road running east into the city by the Garita San Cosme; from which point the aqueduct and road both run east to the city. The second aqueduct starts from the east base of Chapultepec, where it is fed by a spring, and runs north-east to the city. This aqueduct, like the other, runs in the middle of a broad road-way, thus leaving a space on each side. The arches supporting the aqueduct afforded protection for advancing troops as well as to those engaged defensively.[24] At points on the San Cosme road parapets were thrown

him that the armistice would end. Bauer, *Mexican War*, 306–308; Johnson, *Gallant Little Army*, 199–202; Johnson, *Winfield Scott*, 200–201.

[21] During the ceasefire, Scott's men occupied Tacubaya and surrounding towns but after the ceasefire ended, the camp was within range of Mexican artillery. Eisenhower, *Agent of Destiny*, 288–289; Justin H. Smith, *The War with Mexico* (New York: Macmillan, 1919), 2:140–143.

[22] The cluster of buildings known as Molino del Rey (literally "King's Mill") had at one time been a cannon foundry. The stone buildings were a part of the walled portion of the Chapultepec Park. Molino del Rey stood only 3,000 feet from Chapultepec Castle. Bauer, *Mexican War*, 308; Eisenhower, *Agent of Destiny*, 289.

[23] The entire Chapultepec site was a strategic position west of Mexico City. It consisted of a rectangular walled complex three-quarters of a mile long and one-quarter of a mile wide containing both Chapultepec Castle and Molino del Rey. Chapultepec Castle stood at the top of a 200-foot hill. Eisenhower, *Agent of Destiny*, 292–293; Johnson, *Gallant Little Army*, 213.

[24] Mexican forces had bricked in the arches of the aqueduct to create a solid wall. Johnson, *Gallant Little Army*, 213.

across, with an embrasure for a single piece of artillery in each. At the point where both road and aqueduct turn at right angles from north to east, there was not only one of these parapets supplied by one gun and infantry supports, but the houses to the north of the San Cosme road, facing south and commanding a view of the road back to Chapultepec, were covered with infantry, protected by parapets made of sand-bags. The roads leading to garitas (the gates) San Cosme and Belen, by which these aqueducts enter the city, were strongly intrenched. Deep, wide ditches, filled with water, lined the sides of both roads.[25] Such were the defences of the City of Mexico in September, 1847, on the routes over which General Scott entered.

Prior to the Mexican war General Scott had been very partial to General Worth—indeed he continued so up to the close of hostilities—but, for some reason, Worth had become estranged from his chief.[26] Scott evidently took this coldness somewhat to heart. He did not retaliate, however, but on the contrary showed every disposition to appease his subordinate. It was understood at the time that he gave Worth authority to plan and execute the battle of Molino del Rey without dictation or interference from any one, for the very purpose of restoring their former relations. The effort failed, and the two generals remained ever after cold and indifferent towards each other, if not actually hostile.

The battle of Molino del Rey was fought on the 8th of September. The night of the 7th, Worth sent for his brigade and regimental commanders, with their staffs, to come to his quarters to receive instructions for the morrow. These orders contemplated a movement up to within striking distance of the Mills before daylight. The engineers had reconnoitred the ground as well as possible, and had acquired all the information necessary to base proper orders both for approach and attack.[27]

---

[25] The Garita San Cosme was a fortified customs station that controlled the western entrance to Mexico City. At the Garita Belén, in the southwest corner of the town, two roads intersected: one from the west, one from the south. Bauer, *Mexican War*, 314–315.

[26] The rift between Scott and Worth began with the occupation of Puebla in May 1847. Scott disapproved of Worth's decision to allow Mexican citizens to be tried in local Mexican courts for crimes against U.S. soldiers. This decision contradicted Scott's martial law order, which declared that those Mexicans accused of crimes against soldiers would be tried in military courts. This disagreement led to further incidents of conflict between the two. Johnson, *Gallant Little Army*, 128–130; Johnson, *Winfield Scott*, 191–192.

[27] Maj. James L. Mason (1817–1853), Worth's division engineer, and Lt. Col. James Duncan (1814–1849) led a scouting expedition in preparation for the battle. Mason was born in Rhode Island and graduated from the USMA in 1836. Duncan was born in New York and graduated

By daylight on the morning of the 8th, the troops to be engaged at Molino were all at the places designated. The ground in front of the Mills, to the south, was commanded by the artillery from the summit of Chapultepec as well as by the lighter batteries at hand; but a charge was made, and soon all was over. Worth's troops entered the Mills by every door, and the enemy beat a hasty retreat back to Chapultepec.[28] Had this victory been followed up promptly, no doubt Americans and Mexicans would have gone over the defences of Chapultepec so near together that the place would have fallen into our hands without further loss. The defenders of the works could not have fired upon us without endangering their own men. This was not done, and five days later more valuable lives were sacrificed to carry works which had been so nearly in our possession on the 8th. I do not criticise the failure to capture Chapultepec at this time. The result that followed the first assault could not possibly have been foreseen, and to profit by the unexpected advantage, the commanding general must have been on the spot and given the necessary instructions at the moment, or the troops must have kept on without orders. It is always, however, in order to follow a retreating foe, unless stopped or otherwise directed. The loss on our side at Molino del Rey was severe for the numbers engaged. It was especially so among commissioned officers.[29]

I was with the earliest of the troops to enter the Mills. In passing through to the north side, looking towards Chapultepec, I happened to notice that there were armed Mexicans still on top of the building, only a few feet from many of our men. Not seeing any stairway or ladder reaching to the top of the building, I took a few soldiers, and had a cart that happened to be standing near brought up, and, placing the shafts against the wall and chocking the wheels so that the cart could not back, used the shafts as a sort of ladder extending to within three or four feet of the top. By this I climbed to the roof of the building, followed by a few men, but found a private soldier had preceded me by some other way. There were still quite a number of Mexicans on the roof, among them a major and five or six officers of lower grades, who had

from the USMA in 1834. George W. Cullum, *Biographical Register of the Officers and Graduates of the U.S. Military Academy at West Point, N.Y.* (Boston: Houghton, Mifflin, 1891), 1:569, 629; Eisenhower, *So Far from God*, 313, 334–335; Charles K. Gardner, *A Dictionary of All Officers* (New York: D. Van Nostrand, 1860), 157.

[28] Mexican forces drove back the initial assaults by U.S. forces on Molino del Rey. Johnson, *Gallant Little Army*, 204–208.

[29] Out of Worth's force of approximately 3,450 men, there were 116 killed and 671 wounded. Eleven of fourteen officers leading the 500-man storming party were killed or wounded. Eisenhower, *So Far from God*, 335–336; Johnson, *Gallant Little Army*, 203, 205.

not succeeded in getting away before our troops occupied the building. They still had their arms, while the soldier before mentioned was walking as sentry, guarding the prisoners he had *surrounded,* all by himself. I halted the sentinel, received the swords from the commissioned officers, and proceeded, with the assistance of the soldiers now with me, to disable the muskets by striking them against the edge of the wall, and throw them to the ground below.

Molino del Rey was now captured, and the troops engaged, with the exception of an appropriate guard over the captured position and property, were marched back to their quarters in Tacubaya. The engagement did not last many minutes, but the killed and wounded were numerous for the number of troops engaged.[30]

During the night of the 11th batteries were established which could play upon the fortifications of Chapultepec. The bombardment commenced early on the morning of the 12th, but there was no further engagement during this day than that of the artillery. General Scott assigned the capture of Chapultepec to General Pillow,[31] but did not leave the details to his judgment. Two assaulting columns, two hundred and fifty men each, composed of volunteers for the occasion, were formed. They were commanded by Captains McKinzie[32] and Casey[33] respectively. The assault was successful, but bloody.[34]

In later years, if not at the time, the battles of Molino del Rey and Chapultepec have seemed to me to have been wholly unnecessary.[35] When the assaults upon the garitas of San Cosme and Belen were determined upon, the road running east to the former gate could have been reached easily,

---

[30] Although it is unclear exactly how many Mexican troops were engaged in the battle, approximately 2,000 were either killed or wounded. Bauer, *Mexican War,* 308–309, 311.

[31] Gideon Pillow (1806–1878) was born in Tennessee. He was ordered by Scott to occupy the captured buildings of Molino del Rey and to prepare for an attack on Chapultepec up the western slope. *CWHC,* 430; Johnson, *Gallant Little Army,* 216.

[32] Samuel Mackenzie (?–1847) was born in North Carolina and graduated from the USMA in 1818. He served in the U.S. 2nd Art. in the Mexican-American War. He died a noncombat death in Mexico City in Oct. 1847. Cullum, *Biographical Register,* 1:197; *Official Army Register for 1848* (Washington, DC: C. Alexander, 1848), 51.

[33] Silas Casey (1807–1882) was born in Rhode Island and graduated from the USMA in 1826. After the Battle of Chapultepec, Casey was promoted to lieutenant colonel. He served as a general in the U.S. Army during the Civil War. *CWHC,* 167.

[34] This assault began on Sept. 13, 1847, and continued until noon on Sept. 14. Eisenhower, *So Far from God,* 334–336.

[35] In USG's letters from the time, he lamented the loss of lives in battle and commented that the strongest fortifications could have been avoided if the army had maneuvered to attack the city from the northwest. *PUSG,* 1:145–148.

without an engagement, by moving along south of the Mills until west of them sufficiently far to be out of range, thence north to the road above mentioned; or, if desirable to keep the two attacking columns nearer together, the troops could have been turned east so as to come on the aqueduct road out of range of the guns from Chapultepec. In like manner, the troops designated to act against Belen could have kept east of Chapultepec, out of range, and come on to the aqueduct, also out of range of Chapultepec. Molino del Rey and Chapultepec would both have been necessarily evacuated if this course had been pursued, for they would have been turned.

General Quitman, a volunteer from the State of Mississippi, who stood well with the army both as a soldier and as a man, commanded the column acting against Belen. General Worth commanded the column against San Cosme. When Chapultepec fell the advance commenced along the two aqueduct roads.[36] I was on the road to San Cosme, and witnessed most that took place on that route. When opposition was encountered our troops sheltered themselves by keeping under the arches supporting the aqueduct, advancing an arch at a time. We encountered no serious obstruction until within gun-shot of the point where the road we were on intersects that running east to the city, the point where the aqueduct turns at a right angle. I have described the defences of this position before. There were but three commissioned officers besides myself, that I can now call to mind, with the advance when the above position was reached. One of these officers was a Lieutenant Semmes,[37] of the Marine Corps. I think Captain Gore,[38] and Lieutenant Judah,[39] of the 4th infantry,

[36] Scott had ordered Quitman to hold back on the attack of the Garita Belén and allow Worth to attack the Garita San Cosme in order to present a unified assault. Quitman ignored the messages and his men fought their way into the city in a bloody battle with the Mexican troops. Robert E. May, *John A. Quitman: Old South Crusader* (Baton Rouge: Louisiana State University Press, 1985), 192–193.

[37] Raphael Semmes (1809–1877) was born in Maryland and joined the U.S. Navy as a midshipman in 1826. At the start of the war, Semmes served as the lieutenant commanding the *Somers* in the Gulf of Mexico. In Dec. 1846, the *Somers* sank, and Semmes joined Scott's invasion of Veracruz. He later served in the Confederate Navy and commanded the *Alabama*. *CWHC,* 478; Warren F. Spencer, *Raphael Semmes: The Philosophical Mariner* (Tuscaloosa: University of Alabama Press, 1997), 33–36.

[38] John Gore (?–1852) was born in Maryland and brevetted captain for his service at the battles of Contreras and Churubusco. He was brevetted major at Molino del Rey. William H. Powell, *A History of the Organization and Movements of the Fourth Regiment of Infantry . . .* (Washington, DC: M'Gill and Witherow, 1871), 125.

[39] Henry M. Judah (1821–1866) was born in Maryland and graduated from the USMA in 1843. He served in the U.S. Army during the Civil War. *CWHC,* 326.

were the others. Our progress was stopped for the time by the single pie(
artillery at the angle of the roads and the infantry occupying the house
back from it.

West of the road from where we were, stood a house occupying the south-
west angle made by the San Cosme road and the road we were moving upon.
A stone wall ran from the house along each of these roads for a considerable
distance and thence back until it joined, enclosing quite a yard about the
house. I watched my opportunity and skipped across the road and behind
the south wall. Proceeding cautiously to the west corner of the enclosure, I
peeped around and seeing nobody, continued, still cautiously, until the road
running east and west was reached. I then returned to the troops, and called
for volunteers. All that were close to me, or that heard me, about a dozen,
offered their services. Commanding them to carry their arms at a trail, I
watched our opportunity and got them across the road and under cover of
the wall beyond, before the enemy had a shot at us. Our men under cover
of the arches kept a close watch on the intrenchments that crossed our path
and the house-tops beyond, and whenever a head showed itself above the
parapets they would fire at it. Our crossing was thus made practicable
without loss.

When we reached a safe position I instructed my little command again to
carry their arms at a trail, not to fire at the enemy until they were ordered,
and to move very cautiously following me until the San Cosme road was
reached; we would then be on the flank of the men serving the gun on the
road, and with no obstruction between us and them. When we reached the
south-west corner of the enclosure before described, I saw some United States
troops pushing north through a shallow ditch near by, who had come up since
my reconnaissance. This was the company of Captain Horace Brooks,[40] of the
artillery, acting as infantry. I explained to Brooks briefly what I had discovered
and what I was about to do. He said, as I knew the ground and he did not, I
might go on and he would follow. As soon as we got on the road leading to the
city the troops serving the gun on the parapet retreated, and those on the house-
tops near by followed; our men went after them in such close pursuit—the
troops we had left under the arches joining—that a second line across the road,
about half-way between the first and the garita, was carried. No reinforcements
had yet come up except Brooks's company, and the position we had taken was

---

[40] Horace Brooks (1814–1894) was born in Massachusetts and graduated from the USMA in
1835. Brooks was promoted to lieutenant colonel for his actions at Molino del Rey. He reached
the rank of brevet major general in Mar. 1865. Ibid., 145.

too advanced to be held by so small a force. It was given up, but retaken later in the day, with some loss.

Worth's command gradually advanced to the front now open to it. Later in the day in reconnoitring I found a church off to the south of the road, which looked to me as if the belfry would command the ground back of the garita San Cosme. I got an officer of the voltigeurs,[41] with a mountain howitzer and men to work it, to go with me. The road being in possession of the enemy, we had to take the field to the south to reach the church. This took us over several ditches breast deep in water and grown up with water plants. These ditches, however, were not over eight or ten feet in width. The howitzer was taken to pieces and carried by the men to its destination. When I knocked for admission a priest came to the door, who, while extremely polite, declined to admit us. With the little Spanish then at my command, I explained to him that he might save property by opening the door, and he certainly would save himself from becoming a prisoner, for a time at least; and besides, I intended to go in whether he consented or not. He began to see his duty in the same light that I did, and opened the door, though he did not look as if it gave him special pleasure to do so. The gun was carried to the belfry and put together. We were not more than two or three hundred yards from San Cosme. The shots from our little gun dropped in upon the enemy and created great confusion. Why they did not send out a small party and capture us, I do not know. We had no infantry or other defences besides our one gun.

The effect of this gun upon the troops about the gate of the city was so marked that General Worth saw it from his position.* He was so pleased that he sent a staff officer, Lieutenant Pemberton—later Lieutenant-General commanding the defences of Vicksburg—to bring me to him.[42] He expressed his

*Mentioned in the reports of Major Lee, Colonel Garland and General Worth.—Publishers.

[41] The Regiment of Voltigeurs and Foot Riflemen, a special infantry unit, was established for service in the Mexican-American War. The unit was based on French military innovations and utilized more flexible tactics and formations than regular infantry, along with rapid battlefield movement. Spencer Tucker, ed., *The Encyclopedia of the Mexican-American War* (Santa Barbara, CA: ABC-CLIO, 2013), s.v. "Voltigeurs and Foot Riflemen, U.S."

[42] John C. Pemberton (1814–1881) was born in Pennsylvania and graduated from the USMA in 1837. During the Civil War, he attained the rank of lieutenant general and commanded Confederate forces at Vicksburg, MS, surrendering to USG on July 4, 1863. *CWHC,* 423; *PUSG,* 8:467–468.

gratification at the services the howitzer in the church steeple was doing, saying that every shot was effective, and ordered a captain of voltigeurs to report to me with another howitzer to be placed along with the one already rendering so much service.[43] I could not tell the General that there was not room enough in the steeple for another gun, because he probably would have looked upon such a statement as a contradiction from a second lieutenant. I took the captain with me, but did not use his gun.[44]

The night of the 13th of September was spent by the troops under General Worth in the houses near San Cosme, and in line confronting the general line of the enemy across to Belen. The troops that I was with were in the houses north of the road leading into the city, and were engaged during the night in cutting passage-ways from one house to another towards the town. During the night Santa Anna, with his army—except the deserters—left the city.[45] He liberated all the convicts confined in the town, hoping, no doubt, that they would inflict upon us some injury before daylight; but several hours after Santa Anna was out of the way, the city authorities sent a delegation to General Scott to ask—if not demand—an armistice, respecting church property, the rights of citizens and the supremacy of the city government in the management of municipal affairs. General Scott declined to trammel himself with conditions, but gave assurances that those who chose to remain within our lines would be protected so long as they behaved themselves properly.[46]

General Quitman had advanced along his line very successfully on the 13th, so that at night his command occupied nearly the same position at Belen that Worth's troops did about San Cosme. After the interview above related between General Scott and the city council, orders were issued for the cautious entry of both columns in the morning. The troops under Worth were to stop at the Alameda, a park near the west end of the city. Quitman was to go di-

---

[43] Worth commended USG and recommended him for promotion. *PUSG*, 1:376.

[44] While USG and the soldiers with him manned the howitzer in the church on the right of the road leading to the Garita San Cosme, U.S. troops under the command of Lt. Raphael Semmes placed a howitzer on the left side of the road. Bauer, *Mexican War*, 320.

[45] On Sept. 13, 1847, the U.S. forces finally breached the Garita Belén and the Garita San Cosme. During the evening Santa Anna met with his high command. They decided to abandon the capital and march to the nearby town of Guadalupe Hidalgo. On the morning of Sept. 14, Santa Anna left the city with his army of approximately 12,000 troops. The following day, the civilian government fled for Querétaro. Fowler, *Santa Anna*, 278.

[46] At 4:00 A.M. on Sept. 14, 1847, a delegation from Mexico City's local government informed Scott that Santa Anna and the Mexican army had fled. Scott refused any conditions and insisted on an unconditional surrender. Eisenhower, *Agent of Destiny*, 298–299.

rectly to the Plaza, and take possession of the Palace—a mass of buildings on the east side in which Congress has its sessions, the national courts are held, the public offices are all located, the President resides, and much room is left for museums, receptions, etc. This is the building generally designated as the "Halls of the Montezumas."[47]

[47] In recognition of Quitman and his volunteers, Scott allowed Quitman to enter the Grand Plaza and raise the U.S. flag over the National Palace. The phrase "Halls of Montezuma" (or "Halls of the Montezumas") was also used to refer to Chapultepec Castle because the site had been connected with Aztec leaders dating back to the time of Emperor Montezuma. May, *John A. Quitman,* 194; Tucker, *Encyclopedia of the Mexican-American War,* s.v. "Halls of the Montezuma, Mexico City."

# 12

## Promotion to First Lieutenant—Capture of the City of Mexico—The Army—Mexican Soldiers— Peace Negotiations

O N ENTERING THE city the troops were fired upon by the released convicts, and possibly by deserters and hostile citizens. The streets were deserted,
and the place presented the appearance of a "city of the dead," except for this
firing by unseen persons from house-tops, windows, and around corners. In
this firing the lieutenant-colonel of my regiment, Garland, was badly wounded,
Lieutenant Sidney Smith, of the 4th infantry, was also wounded mortally. He
died a few days after, and by his death I was promoted to the grade of first
lieutenant.[1] I had gone* into the battle of Palo Alto in May, 1846, a second
lieutenant, and I entered the city of Mexico sixteen months later with the same

*NOTE—It had been a favorite idea with General Scott for a great many years
before the Mexican war to have established in the United States a soldiers' home,
patterned after something of the kind abroad, particularly, I believe, in France. He
recommended this uniformly, or at least frequently, in his annual reports to the Secretary of War, but never got any hearing. Now, as he had conquered the state, he
made assessments upon the different large towns and cities occupied by our troops,
in proportion to their capacity to pay, and appointed officers to receive the money. In
addition to the sum thus realized he had derived, through capture at Cerro Gordo,
sales of captured government tobacco, etc., sums which swelled the fund to a total of
about $220,000. Portions of this fund were distributed among the rank and file,
given to the wounded in hospital, or applied in other ways, leaving a balance of
some $118,000 remaining unapplied at the close of the war. After the war was over
and the troops all home, General Scott applied to have this money, which had never

[1] Smith died on Sept. 16, 1847, two days after being shot during the battle for Mexico City.
*PUSG,* 1:147–148, 148*n*.

rank, after having been in all the engagements possible for any one man and in a regiment that lost more officers during the war than it ever had present at any one engagement. My regiment lost four commissioned officers, all senior to me, by steamboat explosions during the Mexican war. The Mexicans were not so discriminating. They sometimes picked off my juniors.[3]

General Scott soon followed the troops into the city, in state. I wonder that he was not fired upon, but I believe he was not; at all events he was not hurt. He took quarters at first in the "Halls of the Montezumas," and from there issued his wise and discreet orders for the government of a conquered city, and for suppressing the hostile acts of liberated convicts already spoken of—orders which challenge the respect of all who study them.[4] Lawlessness was

---

been turned into the Treasury of the United States, expended in establishing such homes as he had previously recommended. This fund was the foundation of the Soldiers' Home at Washington City, and also one at Harrodsburgh, Kentucky.

The latter went into disuse many years ago. In fact it never had many soldiers in it, and was, I believe, finally sold.[2]

[2] In Mar. 1851, Congress established the Military Asylum (renamed the United States Soldiers' Home in 1859) in Washington, DC, funded in part by the $118,791.19 mentioned in USG's original note. The Western Military Asylum in Harrodsburg, KY, was in operation from 1853 to 1858, the property eventually being sold in 1887. John P. Deeben, "Caring for Veterans in the Nation's Capital," *Prologue* 47 (2015): 54–62; Paul R. Goode, *The United States Soldiers' Home: A History of Its First Hundred Years* (Richmond, VA: William Byrd Press, 1957), 39–40.

[3] On Sept. 12, 1845, Lts. Benjamin A. Berry and Thaddeus Higgins were killed on the steamer *Dayton* after its boilers exploded near Corpus Christi, TX. Lt. Allen H. Norton drowned off the coast of Connecticut in Nov. 1846 after a steam chest on the *Atlantic* exploded and destroyed the wooden boat. Lt. Christopher R. Perry died at sea while returning home from the war in Oct. 1848. At least twenty-nine officers from the U.S. 4th Inf., including those lost at sea, died during combat operations in Mexico. George W. Cullum, *Biographical Register of the Officers and Graduates of the U.S. Military Academy at West Point, N.Y.* (Boston: Houghton, Mifflin, 1891), 2:47, 105, 150; Henry Ferguson, *Fishers Island, N.Y., 1614–1925* (New York: n.p., 1925), 88–89; Felice F. Lewis, *Trailing Clouds of Glory: Zachary Taylor's Mexican War Campaign and His Emerging Civil War Leaders* (Tuscaloosa: University of Alabama Press, 2010), 29–30.

[4] On Sept. 14, 1847, Scott entered the main plaza of Mexico City and occupied an apartment in the National Palace. That same day, Scott appointed General Quitman as the civil and mili-

soon suppressed, and the City of Mexico settled down into a quiet, law-abiding place. The people began to make their appearance upon the streets without fear of the invaders. Shortly afterwards the bulk of the troops were sent from the city to the villages at the foot of the mountains, four or five miles to the south and south-west.[5]

Whether General Scott approved of the Mexican war and the manner in which it was brought about, I have no means of knowing. His orders to troops indicate only a soldierly spirit, with probably a little regard for the perpetuation of his own fame. On the other hand, General Taylor's, I think, indicate that he considered the administration accountable for the war, and felt no responsibility resting on himself further than for the faithful performance of his duties. Both generals deserve the commendations of their countrymen and to live in the grateful memory of this people to the latest generation.

Earlier in this narrative I have stated that the plain, reached after passing the mountains east of Perote, extends to the cities of Puebla and Mexico. The route travelled by the army before reaching Puebla, goes over a pass in a spur of mountain coming up from the south. This pass is very susceptible of defence by a smaller against a larger force. Again, the highest point of the road-bed between Vera Cruz and the City of Mexico is over Rio Frio mountain, which also might have been successfully defended by an inferior against a superior force. But by moving north of the mountains, and about thirty miles north of Puebla, both of these passes would have been avoided. The road from Perote to the City of Mexico, by this latter route, is as level as the prairies in our West. Arriving due north from Puebla, troops could have been detached to take possession of that place, and then proceeding west with the rest of the army no mountain would have been encountered before reaching the City of Mexico. It is true this road would have brought troops in by Guadalupe—a town, church and detached spur

tary governor of the city. W. A. Croffut, ed., *Fifty Years in Camp and Field: Diary of Major-General Ethan Allen Hitchcock, U.S.A.* (New York: G. P. Putnam's Sons, 1909), 304; John S. D. Eisenhower, *Agent of Destiny: The Life and Times of General Winfield Scott* (New York: Free Press, 1997), 299.

[5] USG may be referring to Scott's plans to send troops to Toluca and Cuernavaca in Dec. 1847 and Feb. 1848. Winfield Scott, *Memoirs of Lieut.-General Scott, LL. D.* (New York: Sheldon, 1864), 2:558, 570.

of mountain about two miles north of the capital, all bearing the same general name—and at this point Lake Texcoco comes near to the mountain, which was fortified both at the base and on the sides: but troops could have passed north of the mountain and come in only a few miles to the northwest, and so flanked the position, as they actually did on the south.

It has always seemed to me that this northern route to the City of Mexico, would have been the better one to have taken. But my later experience has taught me two lessons: first, that things are seen plainer after the events have occurred; second, that the most confident critics are generally those who know the least about the matter criticised. I know just enough about the Mexican war to approve heartily of most of the generalship, but to differ with a little of it. It is natural that an important city like Puebla should not have been passed with contempt; it may be natural that the direct road to it should have been taken; but it could have been passed, its evacuation insured and possession acquired without danger of encountering the enemy in intricate mountain defiles. In this same way the City of Mexico could have been approached without any danger of opposition, except in the open field.

But General Scott's successes are an answer to all criticism. He invaded a populous country, penetrating two hundred and sixty miles into the interior, with a force at no time equal to one-half of that opposed to him; he was without a base; the enemy was always intrenched, always on the defensive; yet he won every battle, he captured the capital, and conquered the government. Credit is due to the troops engaged, it is true, but the plans and the strategy were the general's.

I had now made marches and been in battle under both General Scott and General Taylor. The former divided his force of 10,500 men into four columns, starting a day apart, in moving from Puebla to the capital of the nation, when it was known that an army more than twice as large as his own stood ready to resist his coming. The road was broad and the country open except in crossing the Rio Frio mountain. General Taylor pursued the same course in marching toward an enemy. He moved even in smaller bodies. I never thought at the time to doubt the infallibility of these two generals in all matters pertaining to their profession. I supposed they moved in small bodies because more men could not be passed over a single road on the same day with their artillery and necessary trains. Later I found the fallacy of this belief. The rebellion, which followed as a sequence to the Mexican war, never could have been suppressed if larger bodies of men could not have been moved at the same time than was the custom under Scott and Taylor.

The victories in Mexico were, in every instance, over vastly superior numbers.[6] There were two reasons for this. Both General Scott and General Taylor had such armies as are not often got together. At the battles of Palo Alto and Resaca-de-la-Palma, General Taylor had a small army, but it was composed exclusively of regular troops, under the best of drill and discipline. Every officer, from the highest to the lowest, was educated in his profession, not at West Point necessarily, but in the camp, in garrison, and many of them in Indian wars. The rank and file were probably inferior, as material out of which to make an army, to the volunteers that participated in all the later battles of the war; but they were brave men, and then drill and discipline brought out all there was in them. A better army, man for man, probably never faced an enemy than the one commanded by General Taylor in the earliest two engagements of the Mexican war. The volunteers who followed were of better material, but without drill or discipline at the start. They were associated with so many disciplined men and professionally educated officers, that when they went into engagements it was with a confidence they would not have felt otherwise. They became soldiers themselves almost at once.[7] All these conditions we would enjoy again in case of war.

The Mexican army of that day was hardly an organization. The private soldier was picked up from the lower class of the inhabitants when wanted; his consent was not asked; he was poorly clothed, worse fed, and seldom paid. He was turned adrift when no longer wanted. The officers of the lower grades were but little superior to the men. With all this I have seen as brave stands made by some of these men as I have ever seen made by soldiers. Now Mexico has a standing army larger than that of the United States. They have a military school modelled after West Point. Their officers are educated and, no doubt, generally brave. The Mexican war of 1846–8 would be an impossibility in this generation.[8]

---

[6] The U.S. Army was outnumbered in every major battle of the Mexican-American War. Spencer Tucker, ed., *The Encyclopedia of the Mexican-American War* (Santa Barbara, CA: ABC-CLIO, 2013), s.v. "Army Life, Mexican and U.S."

[7] Contrary to USG's assertion, many officers noted that the volunteers resisted discipline and were prone to insubordination. Justin H. Smith, *The War with Mexico* (New York: Macmillan, 1919), 1:207–208.

[8] In 1886, the U.S. Army consisted of over 27,000 soldiers, while the Mexican Army had approximately 22,000 troops. Ainsworth R. Spofford, *American Almanac and Treasury of Facts, Statistical, Financial, and Political for the Year 1886* (New York: American News, 1886), 120, 171.

The Mexicans have shown a patriotism which it would be well if we would imitate in part, but with more regard to truth. They celebrate the anniversaries of Chapultepec and Molino del Rey as of very great victories. The anniversaries are recognized as national holidays.[9] At these two battles, while the United States troops were victorious, it was at very great sacrifice of life compared with what the Mexicans suffered. The Mexicans, as on many other occasions, stood up as well as any troops ever did. The trouble seemed to be the lack of experience among the officers, which led them after a certain time to simply quit, without being particularly whipped, but because they had fought enough. Their authorities of the present day grow enthusiastic over their theme when telling of these victories, and speak with pride of the large sum of money they forced us to pay in the end. With us, now twenty years after the close of the most stupendous war ever known, we have writers—who profess devotion to the nation—engaged in trying to prove that the Union forces were not victorious; practically, they say, we were slashed around from Donelson to Vicksburg and to Chattanooga; and in the East from Gettysburg to Appomattox, when the physical rebellion gave out from sheer exhaustion.[10] There is no difference in the amount of romance in the two stories.

I would not have the anniversaries of our victories celebrated, nor those of our defeats made fast days and spent in humiliation and prayer; but I would like to see truthful history written. Such history will do full credit to

[9] In 1871, a group of Mexican veterans gathered in Mexico City to petition President Juárez to create two national holidays commemorating the Battles of Chapultepec and Molino del Rey. Juárez decided to make Sept. 13 a holiday honoring the Battle of Chapultepec, but he did not establish a holiday for Molino del Rey. Michael Van Wagenen, *Remembering the Forgotten War: The Enduring Legacies of the U.S./Mexican War* (Amherst: University of Massachusetts Press, 2012), 81–82.

[10] In this section, USG was commenting on the burgeoning Lost Cause movement that attempted to cast the Confederate war effort in a better light and downplay the role of slavery as the cause of the Civil War. One of the most prominent Lost Cause historians was ex-Confederate Jubal A. Early. During the mid-1870s, as president of the Southern Historical Society, Early published articles and gave speeches promoting Lost Cause perspectives. Gary W. Gallagher, "From Antebellum Unionist to Lost Cause Warrior: The Personal Journey of Jubal A. Early," in *New Perspectives on the Civil War: Myths and Realities of the National Conflict,* ed. John Y. Simon and Michael E. Stevens (Lanham, MD: Rowman and Littlefield, 2002), 107; Joan Waugh, *U.S. Grant: American Hero, American Myth* (Chapel Hill: University of North Carolina Press, 2009), 189–192.

the courage, endurance and soldierly ability of the American citizen, no matter what section of the country he hailed from, or in what ranks he fought. The justice of the cause which in the end prevailed, will, I doubt not, come to be acknowledged by every citizen of the land, in time. For the present, and so long as there are living witnesses of the great war of sections, there will be people who will not be consoled for the loss of a cause which they believed to be holy. As time passes, people, even of the South, will begin to wonder how it was possible that their ancestors ever fought for or justified institutions which acknowledged the right of property in man.

After the fall of the capital and the dispersal of the government of Mexico, it looked very much as if military occupation of the country for a long time might be necessary. General Scott at once began the preparation of orders, regulations and laws in view of this contingency. He contemplated making the country pay all the expenses of the occupation, without the army becoming a perceptible burden upon the people. His plan was to levy a direct tax upon the separate states, and collect, at the ports left open to trade, a duty on all imports. From the beginning of the war private property had not been taken, either for the use of the army or of individuals, without full compensation. This policy was to be pursued. There were not troops enough in the valley of Mexico to occupy many points, but now that there was no organized army of the enemy of any size, reinforcements could be got from the Rio Grande, and there were also new volunteers arriving from time to time, all by way of Vera Cruz. Military possession was taken of Cuernavaca, fifty miles south of the City of Mexico; of Toluca, nearly as far west, and of Pachuca, a mining town of great importance, some sixty miles to the north-east. Vera Cruz, Jalapa, Orizaba, and Puebla were already in our possession.

Meanwhile the Mexican government had departed in the person of Santa Anna, and it looked doubtful for a time whether the United States commissioner, Mr. Trist, would find anybody to negotiate with.[11] A temporary government, however, was soon established at Queretaro, and Trist began

[11] On Sept. 15, 1847, Santa Anna resigned the presidency and handed power over to Manuel de la Peña y Peña, the head of the Mexican Supreme Court, until an election for interim president could be held. On Nov. 11, Pedro María Anaya was elected, and peace talks commenced a week later. John S. D. Eisenhower, *So Far from God: The U.S. War with Mexico, 1846–1848* (Norman: University of Oklahoma Press, 1989), 347, 360.

negotiations for a conclusion of the war. Before terms were finally agreed upon he was ordered back to Washington, but General Scott prevailed upon him to remain, as an arrangement had been so nearly reached, and the administration must approve his acts if he succeeded in making such a treaty as had been contemplated in his instructions.[12] The treaty was finally signed the 2d of February, 1848, and accepted by the government at Washington. It is that known as the "Treaty of Guadalupe Hidalgo," and secured to the United States the Rio Grande as the boundary of Texas, and the whole territory then included in New Mexico and Upper California, for the sum of $15,000,000.[13]

Soon after entering the city of Mexico, the opposition of Generals Pillow, Worth and Colonel Duncan to General Scott became very marked. Scott claimed that they had demanded of the President his removal. I do not know whether this is so or not, but I do know of their unconcealed hostility to their chief.[14] At last he placed them in arrest, and preferred charges against them of insubordination and disrespect. This act brought on a crisis in the career of the general commanding. He had asserted from the beginning that the administration was hostile to him; that it had failed in its promises of men and war material; that the President himself had shown duplicity if not treachery in the endeavor to procure the appointment of Benton: and the administration now gave open evidence of its enmity. About the middle of February orders came convening a court of inquiry,

[12] In late Oct. 1847, President Polk recalled Trist after learning that he had offered the Mexican government some flexibility on the matter of the boundary dispute and the acquisition of California. When his replacement failed to arrive, Trist feared the opportunity for negotiations would end. By Dec. 4, Trist had decided to ignore the order, remain in Mexico, and negotiate the treaty. Smith, *War with Mexico,* 1:237.

[13] On Mar. 10, 1848, the U.S. Senate approved the Treaty of Guadalupe Hidalgo. Eisenhower, *So Far from God,* 367.

[14] In the aftermath of the Mexico City campaign, two letters were published in American newspapers that bestowed credit for the successful campaign on Worth and Pillow, and diminished Scott's involvement. In response, Scott issued Gen. Order No. 349, announcing that soldiers were forbidden to publish information on combat operations. Worth and Pillow wrote to Polk and accused Scott of a "gross injustice" by indirectly accusing them of wrongdoing. Eisenhower, *Agent of Destiny,* 310–314; Timothy D. Johnson, *A Gallant Little Army: The Mexico City Campaign* (Lawrence: University Press of Kansas, 2007), 259–262.

composed of Brevet Brigadier-General Towson,[15] the paymaster-general of
the army, Brigadier-General Cushing[16] and Colonel Belknap,[17] to inquire
into the conduct of the accused and the accuser, and shortly afterwards
orders were received from Washington, relieving Scott of the command of
the army in the field and assigning Major-General William O. Butler of
Kentucky to the place. This order also released Pillow, Worth and Duncan
from arrest.[18]

If a change was to be made the selection of General Butler was agreeable to
every one concerned, so far as I remember to have heard expressions on the
subject. There were many who regarded the treatment of General Scott as
harsh and unjust. It is quite possible that the vanity of the General had led
him to say and do things that afforded a plausible pretext to the administration for doing just what it did and what it had wanted to do from the start.
The court tried the accuser quite as much as the accused. It was adjourned
before completing its labors, to meet in Frederick, Maryland. General Scott
left the country, and never after had more than the nominal command of the
army until early in 1861.[19] He certainly was not sustained in his efforts to maintain discipline in high places.

---

[15] Nathan Towson (1784–1854) was born in Maryland and joined the army as a captain in
the U.S. 2nd Art. in 1812. In 1848, he was brevetted major general for his actions in the
Mexican-American War. *The National Cyclopaedia of American Biography*, vol. 7 (New York:
James T. White, 1897), 379.

[16] Caleb Cushing (1800–1879) was a lawyer and politician from Massachusetts. By 1847,
Cushing organized the 1st Massachusetts Inf., but failed to reach Mexico in time for combat.
John M. Belohlavek, *Broken Glass: Caleb Cushing and the Shattering of the Union* (Kent, OH:
Kent State University Press, 2005), 193–204; John R. Vile, ed., *Great American Lawyers: An
Encyclopedia* (Santa Barbara, CA: ABC-CLIO, 2001), s.v. "Cushing, Caleb."

[17] William G. Belknap (1794–1851) was born in New York and joined the army in 1813 as a
second lieutenant in the 23rd Inf. Contrary to USG's assertion, Belknap was not on the court
of inquiry. The court consisted of Towson, Cushing, and Col. Edward G. W. Butler (1800–
1888) of the 3rd Dragoons. Edward Moseley and Paul Clark Jr., *The A to Z of the United States-
Mexican War* (Lanham, MD: Scarecrow Press, 1997), s.v. "Butler, Edward G. W."; Eisenhower,
*Agent of Destiny*, 314; Tucker, *Encyclopedia of the Mexican-American War*, 2, s.v. "Belknap, William Goldsmith."

[18] The court of inquiry, which cleared the men of any wrongdoing, was held on Apr. 13–22,
1848, in Mexico City, and on June 5–July 6, in Frederick, MD. K. Jack Bauer, *The Mexican
War, 1846–1848* (New York: Macmillan, 1974), 373–374.

[19] Scott embarked from Veracruz on May 2, 1848. Ibid., 374.

The efforts to kill off politically the two successful generals, made them both candidates for the Presidency. General Taylor was nominated in 1848, and was elected. Four years later General Scott received the nomination but was badly beaten, and the party nominating him died with his defeat.*

*The Mexican war made three presidential candidates, Scott, Taylor and Pierce—and any number of aspirants for that high office. It made also governors of States, members of the cabinet, foreign ministers and other officers of high rank both in state and nation. The rebellion, which contained more war in a single day, at some critical periods, than the whole Mexican war in two years, has not been so fruitful of political results to those engaged on the Union side. On the other side, the side of the South, nearly every man who holds office of any sort whatever, either in the state or in the nation, was a Confederate soldier; but this is easily accounted for from the fact that the South was a military camp, and there were very few people of a suitable age to be in the army who were not in it.[20]

[20] The Whig Party was divided over the issue of slavery and the passage of the Kansas-Nebraska Act. After Pierce's defeat of Scott in 1852, the party completely dissolved, with northern Whigs joining the Republican Party and southern Whigs joining the Democratic Party. Daniel Walker Howe, *What Hath God Wrought: The Transformation of America, 1815–1848* (New York: Oxford University Press, 2007), 611; Robert McKinley Ormsby, *A History of the Whig Party or Some of Its Main Features, with a Hurried Glance at the Formation of Parties in the United States, and the Outlines of the History of the Principal Parties of the Country to the Present Time, Etc. Etc.* (Boston: Crosby, Nichols, 1859), 348–350.

# 13

## Treaty of Peace—Mexican Bull Fights—Regimental Quartermaster—Trip to Popocatapetl—Trip to the Caves of Mexico

T HE TREATY OF peace between the two countries was signed by the commissioners of each side early in February, 1848. It took a considerable time for it to reach Washington, receive the approval of the administration, and be finally ratified by the Senate.[1] It was naturally supposed by the army that there would be no more fighting, and officers and men were of course anxious to get home, but knowing there must be delay they contented themselves as best they could.[2] Every Sunday there was a bull fight for the amusement of those who would pay their fifty cents. I attended one of them—just one—not wishing to leave the country without having witnessed the national sport. The sight to me was sickening. I could not see how human beings could enjoy the sufferings of beasts, and often of men, as they seemed to do on these occasions.

At these sports there are usually from four to six bulls sacrificed. The audience occupies seats around the ring in which the exhibition is given, each seat but the foremost rising higher than the one in front, so that every one can get a full view of the sport. When all is ready a bull is turned into the ring. Three or four men come in, mounted on the merest skeletons of horses blind or blind-folded and so weak that they could not make a sudden turn with their riders without danger of falling down. The men are armed with spears having

[1] On Feb. 22, 1848, President Polk sent the Treaty of Guadalupe Hidalgo to the U.S. Senate for ratification. In spite of numerous objections to the treaty by various senators, the Senate ratified the slightly modified treaty on Mar. 10. Richard Griswold del Castillo, *The Treaty of Guadalupe Hidalgo: A Legacy of Conflict* (Norman: University of Oklahoma Press, 1990), 43–53.

[2] On May 19, 1848, the Mexican Senate also ratified the treaty. On May 30, U.S. troops began to leave Mexico City, the same day that the Mexican and U.S. governments exchanged formal notifications of the treaty ratification. Ibid., 43; *PUSG,* 1:155–157.

a point as sharp as a needle. Other men enter the arena on foot, armed with red flags and explosives about the size of a musket cartridge. To each of these explosives is fastened a barbed needle which serves the purpose of attaching them to the bull by running the needle into the skin. Before the animal is turned loose a lot of these explosives are attached to him. The pain from the pricking of the skin by the needles is exasperating; but when the explosions of the cartridges commence the animal becomes frantic. As he makes a lunge towards one horseman, another runs a spear into him. He turns towards his last tormentor when a man on foot holds out a red flag; the bull rushes for this and is allowed to take it on his horns. The flag drops and covers the eyes of the animal so that he is at a loss what to do; it is jerked from him and the torment is renewed. When the animal is worked into an uncontrollable frenzy, the horsemen withdraw, and the matadores—literally murderers—enter, armed with knives having blades twelve or eighteen inches long, and sharp. The trick is to dodge an attack from the animal and stab him to the heart as he passes. If these efforts fail the bull is finally lassoed, held fast and killed by driving a knife blade into the spinal column just back of the horns. He is then dragged out by horses or mules, another is let into the ring, and the same performance is renewed.

On the occasion when I was present one of the bulls was not turned aside by the attacks in the rear, the presentations of the red flag, etc., etc., but kept right on, and placing his horns under the flanks of a horse threw him and his rider to the ground with great force. The horse was killed and the rider lay prostrate as if dead. The bull was then lassoed and killed in the manner above described. Men came in and carried the dead man off in a litter. When the slaughtered bull and horse were dragged out, a fresh bull was turned into the ring. Conspicuous among the spectators was the man who had been carried out on a litter but a few minutes before. He was only dead so far as that performance went; but the corpse was so lively that it could not forego the chance of witnessing the discomfiture of some of his brethren who might not be so fortunate. There was a feeling of disgust manifested by the audience to find that he had come to life again. I confess that I felt sorry to see the cruelty to the bull and the horse. I did not stay for the conclusion of the performance; but while I did stay, there was not a bull killed in the prescribed way.

Bull fights are now prohibited in the Federal District—embracing a territory around the City of Mexico, somewhat larger than the District of Columbia—and they are not an institution in any part of the country.[3] During

---

[3] Mexican president Benito Juárez banned bullfighting in the Federal District on Nov. 28, 1867, and the decree remained in effect until Dec. 1886. María del Carmen Vázquez Mantecón,

one of my recent visits to Mexico, bull fights were got up in my honor at Puebla and at Pachuca. I was not notified in advance so as to be able to decline and thus prevent the performance; but in both cases I civilly declined to attend.[4]

Another amusement of the people of Mexico of that day, and one which nearly all indulged in, male and female, old and young, priest and layman, was Monte playing. Regular feast weeks were held every year at what was then known as St. Augustin Tlalpam, eleven miles out of town.[5] There were dealers to suit every class and condition of people. In many of the booths *tlacos*—the copper coin of the country, four of them making six and a quarter cents of our money—were piled up in great quantities, with some silver, to accommodate the people who could not bet more than a few pennies at a time. In other booths silver formed the bulk of the capital of the bank, with a few doubloons to be changed if there should be a run of luck against the bank. In some there was no coin except gold. Here the rich were said to bet away their entire estates in a single day. All this is stopped now.[6]

"¡Toros Sí!, ¡Toros No!: Del Tiempo Cuando Benito Juárez Prohibió las Corridas de Toros," *Historia Mexicana* 63 (2013): 171, 190.

[4] USG visited Puebla and Pachuca in Mar. 1880. A "bull-tailing entertainment" (likely a *coleadero*—a competition where horsemen bring down cattle by grabbing their tails) was scheduled for Mar. 10 in Puebla, but no references to bullfights in Puebla or Pachuca can be found in English-language reports of the visit. In 1893, Matías Romero claimed that USG attended a portion of a bullfight in Mexico City but did not stay throughout the entire event. "Gen. Grant in Mexico," *New York Times,* Mar. 12, 1880, 2; Matías Romero, "Speech of Señor Romero," in *Proceedings on the Occasion of the Banquet to Celebrate the Seventy-First Anniversary of the Birth of General U.S. Grant: at The Waldorf, on Thursday, April 27, 1893* (New York: Press of the American Bank Note Company, 1893), 18–19; Kathleen Mullen Sands, *Charrería Mexicana: An Equestrian Folk Tradition* (Tucson: University of Arizona Press, 1993), 318.

[5] The village of Tlalpan hosted an annual gambling festival during Pentecost each year. Salvador Padilla Aguilar, *San Agustín Tlalpan: Historias y tradiciones de un Viejo pueblo (25–1999 d.C.)* (Mexico City: Comité Editorial del Gobierno del Distrito Federal, 1999), 25; *Ferguson's Anecdotical Guide to Mexico, with a Map of the Railways* (New York: Lange, Little, 1876), 92.

[6] This system of currency persisted into the 1890s, but *tlacos* had mostly fallen out of common usage by the end of the nineteenth century. Efforts by the Mexican government to ban gambling were sporadically enforced and the festival described by USG enjoyed continued popularity into the twentieth century. Hubert Howe Bancroft, *History of Mexico,* vol. 6, *1861–1887* (San Francisco: History, 1888), 623; Reau Campbell, *Campbell's New Revised Complete Guide and Descriptive Book of Mexico* (City of Mexico: Sonora News, 1899), 44, 128; T. Phillip Terry, *Terry's Guide to Mexico* (Boston: Houghton Mifflin, 1923), 406–407.

For myself, I was kept somewhat busy during the winter of 1847–8. My regiment was stationed in Tacubaya. I was regimental quartermaster and commissary. General Scott had been unable to get clothing for the troops from the North. The men were becoming—well, they needed clothing. Material had to be purchased, such as could be obtained, and people employed to make it up into "Yankee uniforms." A quartermaster in the city was designated to attend to this special duty; but clothing was so much needed that it was seized as fast as made up.[7] A regiment was glad to get a dozen suits at a time. I had to look after this matter for the 4th infantry. Then our regimental fund had run down and some of the musicians in the band had been without their extra pay for a number of months.

The regimental bands at that day were kept up partly by pay from the government, and partly by pay from the regimental fund. There was authority of law for enlisting a certain number of men as musicians. So many could receive the pay of non-commissioned officers of the various grades, and the remainder the pay of privates. This would not secure a band leader, nor good players on certain instruments.[8] In garrison there are various ways of keeping up a regimental fund sufficient to give extra pay to musicians, establish libraries and ten-pin alleys, subscribe to magazines and furnish many extra comforts to the men. The best device for supplying the fund is to issue bread to the soldiers instead of flour. The ration used to be eighteen ounces per day of either flour or bread; and one hundred pounds of flour will make one hundred and forty pounds of bread. This saving was purchased by the commissary for the benefit of the fund. In the emergency the 4th infantry was laboring under, I rented a bakery in the city, hired bakers—Mexicans—bought fuel and whatever was necessary, and I also got a contract from the chief commissary of the army for baking a large amount of hard bread. In two months I made more money for the fund than my pay amounted to during the entire war. While

[7] The long supply lines had made getting uniforms to U.S. troops difficult. Scott's quartermaster, Capt. James R. Irwin, employed Mexican tailors to make the needed uniforms at great expense. Buying uniforms from Mexican merchants ended as supply lines improved. Richard Bruce Winders, *Mr. Polk's Army: The American Military Experience in the Mexican War* (College Station: Texas A&M University Press, 1997), 107–111.

[8] Since 1821, the military had paid for regimental bands. During the Mexican-American War, a sergeant served as the lead musician of the twelve-member regimental band. The band not only provided marching music but also entertainment for the men. Edward H. McKinley, "Music in the Military," in *A Companion to American Military History*, ed. James C. Bradford (Malden, MA: Wiley-Blackwell, 2009), 2:834; Winders, *Mr. Polk's Army*, 22.

stationed at Monterey I had relieved the post fund in the same way. There, however, was no profit except in the saving of flour by converting it into bread.

In the spring of 1848 a party of officers obtained leave to visit Popocatapetl, the highest volcano in America, and to take an escort.[9] I went with the party, many of whom afterwards occupied conspicuous positions before the country. Of those who "went south," and attained high rank, there was Lieutenant Richard Anderson,[10] who commanded a corps at Spottsylvania; Captain Sibley,[11] a major-general, and, after the war, for a number of years in the employ of the Khédive of Egypt;[12] Captain George Crittenden,[13] a rebel general; S. B. Buckner,[14] who surrendered Fort Donelson; and Mansfield

[9]The expedition left Mexico City on Apr. 3, 1848. Popocatépetl, at over 17,000 feet high, was considered the tallest volcanic peak in North America in the 1880s. It is actually the second tallest volcano in North America behind Pico de Orizaba (18,491 feet), also in Mexico. P. Mackinlay, *Standard Geography* (London: Chambers, 1877), 136; S. A. Alaniz-Alvarez and A. F. Nieto-Samaniego, eds., *Geology of Mexico: Celebrating the Centenary of the Geological Society of Mexico* (Boulder, CO: Geological Society of America, 2007), 200–201; Jerry Thompson, "Winfield Scott's Army of Occupation as Pioneer Alpinists: Epic Ascents of Popocatepetl and Citlaltepetl," *Southwestern Historical Quarterly* 105 (2002): 565–566.

[10]Richard H. Anderson (1821–1879) was born in South Carolina and graduated from the USMA in 1842. He reached the rank of captain by 1855, but resigned from the U.S. Army at the beginning of the Civil War and joined the Confederate Army as a colonel. Anderson attained the rank of major general in 1862 and commanded the 1st Corps, Army of Northern Virginia, at Spotsylvania. *CWHC*, 105.

[11]Henry H. Sibley (1816–1886) was born in Louisiana and graduated from the USMA in 1838. He led the expedition to Popocatépetl. In May 1861, Sibley resigned as major in the U.S. Army and joined the Confederate Army. He was soon appointed brigadier general. After the Civil War, Sibley traveled to Egypt and became general of artillery in the Egyptian Army from 1869 to 1873. Ibid., 487; Jerry Thompson, *Henry Hopkins Sibley: Confederate General of the West* (Natchitoches, LA: Northwestern State University Press, 1987), 70–73.

[12]Ismail Pasha (1830–1895) ruled Egypt from 1863 to 1879 and held the title khedive from 1866 until he was deposed by the Ottoman sultan. Paul Legassé, ed., *The Columbia Encyclopedia* (New York: Columbia University Press, 2000), s.v. "Ismail Pasha."

[13]George B. Crittenden (1812–1880) graduated from the USMA in 1832. At the outbreak of the Civil War, he resigned his U.S. Army rank as a lieutenant colonel and became a brigadier general in the Confederate Army. In Nov. 1861, Crittenden earned the rank of major general. James M. Prichard, "Maj. Gen. George Bibb Crittenden," in *Kentuckians in Gray: Confederate Generals and Field Officers of the Bluegrass State,* ed. Bruce S. Allardice and Lawrence Lee Hewitt (Lexington: University Press of Kentucky, 2008), 69–75.

[14]Simon B. Buckner (1823–1914) graduated from the USMA in 1844. When the Civil War started, he turned down offers from both the U.S. and Confederate armies. He joined the

Lovell,[15] who commanded at New Orleans before that city fell into the hands of the National troops. Of those who remained on our side there were Captain Andrew Porter,[16] Lieutenant C. P. Stone[17] and Lieutenant Z. B. Tower. There were quite a number of other officers, whose names I cannot recollect.[18]

At a little village (Ozumba) near the base of Popocatapetl, where we purposed to commence the ascent, we procured guides and two pack mules with forage for our horses. High up on the mountain there was a deserted house of one room, called the Vaqueria, which had been occupied years before by men in charge of cattle ranging on the mountain. The pasturage up there was very fine when we saw it, and there were still some cattle, descendants of the former domestic herd, which had now become wild. It was possible to go on horseback as far as the Vaqueria, though the road was somewhat hazardous in places. Sometimes it was very narrow with a yawning precipice on one side, hundreds of feet down to a roaring mountain torrent below, and almost perpendicular walls on the other side. At one of these places one of our mules loaded with two sacks of barley, one on each side, the two about as big as he was, struck his load against the mountain-side and was precipitated to the bottom. The descent was steep but not perpendicular. The mule rolled over and over until the bottom was reached, and we supposed of course the poor animal was

Confederate Army in 1861 after the invasion of Kentucky. In 1862, he surrendered Fort Donelson to USG. Buckner had a lifelong friendship with USG, being one of the last people to see him before his death in July 1885. He served as the governor of Kentucky from 1887 to 1891. He was the vice presidential candidate for the National Democrats in 1896. *CWHC*, 151–152; Jean Edward Smith, *Grant* (New York: Simon and Schuster, 2001), 163–165, 626–627.

[15] Mansfield Lovell (1822–1884) graduated from the USMA in 1842. In Sept. 1861, he resigned his job with the New York City government and, in Oct. 1861, became a major general in the Confederate Army. In Apr. 1862, Lovell unsuccessfully attempted to defend New Orleans against Union forces. *CWHC*, 355.

[16] Andrew Porter (1820–1872) studied at the USMA for six months during 1836–1837. During the Mexican-American War, he was brevetted lieutenant colonel. During the Civil War, Porter served in various capacities in the Union Army until he resigned in Apr. 1864 due to illness. Ibid., 434.

[17] Charles P. Stone (1824–1887) graduated from the USMA in 1845. In May 1861, he returned to the military as a brigadier general. Stone later served in the Dept. of the Gulf and with USG in the Army of the Potomac at the siege of Petersburg. After the Civil War, Stone served in the Egyptian Army and then was involved in the construction of the base of the Statue of Liberty. Ibid., 513–514.

[18] In total, the group included twenty-five officers, seventy dragoons, and many civilians. Thompson, "Winfield Scott's Army of Occupation," 565–566.

dashed to pieces. What was our surprise, not long after we had gone into bivouac, to see the lost mule, cargo and owner coming up the ascent. The load had
protected the animal from serious injury; and his owner had gone after him
and found a way back to the path leading up to the hut where we were to stay.

The night at the Vaqueria was one of the most unpleasant I ever knew. It was
very cold and the rain fell in torrents. A little higher up the rain ceased and
snow began. The wind blew with great velocity. The log-cabin we were in had
lost the roof entirely on one side, and on the other it was hardly better than a
sieve. There was little or no sleep that night. As soon as it was light the next
morning, we started to make the ascent to the summit. The wind continued
to blow with violence and the weather was still cloudy, but there was neither
rain nor snow. The clouds, however, concealed from our view the country
below us, except at times a momentary glimpse could be got through a clear
space between them. The wind carried the loose snow around the mountain-
sides in such volumes as to make it almost impossible to stand up against it. We
labored on and on, until it became evident that the top could not be reached
before night, if at all in such a storm, and we concluded to return. The descent
was easy and rapid, though dangerous, until we got below the snow line. At the
cabin we mounted our horses, and by night were at Ozumba.

The fatigues of the day and the loss of sleep the night before drove us to
bed early. Our beds consisted of a place on the dirt-floor with a blanket under
us. Soon all were asleep; but long before morning first one and then another
of our party began to cry out with excruciating pain in the eyes. Not one escaped it. By morning the eyes of half the party were so swollen that they were
entirely closed. The others suffered pain equally. The feeling was about what
might be expected from the prick of a sharp needle at a white heat. We remained in quarters until the afternoon bathing our eyes in cold water. This
relieved us very much, and before night the pain had entirely left. The swelling,
however, continued, and about half the party still had their eyes entirely closed;
but we concluded to make a start back, those who could see a little leading
the horses of those who could not see at all. We moved back to the village of
Ameca Ameca,[19] some six miles, and stopped again for the night. The next
morning all were entirely well and free from pain.[20] The weather was clear

[19] Ameca Ameca is now known as Amecameca de Juárez. Saul B. Cohen, ed., *The Columbia
Gazetteer of the World* (New York: Columbia University Press, 1998), s.v. "Amecameca de Juárez."

[20] The men on the expedition were likely suffering from snow blindness. Robert K. Collins
and John F. Marszalek, "164 Years Later, a Case Report: U. S. Grant, Eye Pain and Swelling in
Mexico 1848," *Journal of the Mississippi State Medical Association* 54 (2013): 11–12.

and Popocatapetl stood out in all its beauty, the top looking as if not a mile away, and inviting us to return. About half the party were anxious to try the ascent again, and concluded to do so. The remainder—I was with the remainder—concluded that we had got all the pleasure there was to be had out of mountain climbing, and that we would visit the great caves of Mexico, some ninety miles from where we then were, on the road to Acapulco.[21]

The party that ascended the mountain the second time succeeded in reaching the crater at the top, with but little of the labor they encountered in their first attempt. Three of them—Anderson, Stone and Buckner—wrote accounts of their journey, which were published at the time.[22] I made no notes of this excursion, and have read nothing about it since, but it seems to me that I can see the whole of it as vividly as if it were but yesterday. I have been back at Ameca Ameca, and the village beyond, twice in the last five years. The scene had not changed materially from my recollection of it.

The party which I was with moved south down the valley to the town of Cuantla,[23] some forty miles from Ameca Ameca. The latter stands on the plain at the foot of Popocatapetl, at an elevation of about eight thousand feet above tide water. The slope down is gradual as the traveller moves south, but one would not judge that, in going to Cuantla, descent enough had been made to occasion a material change in the climate and productions of the soil; but such is the case. In the morning we left a temperate climate where the cereals and fruits are those common to the United States; we halted in the evening in a tropical climate where the orange and banana, the coffee and the sugar-cane were flourishing. We had been travelling, apparently, on a plain all day, but in the direction of the flow of water.

Soon after the capture of the City of Mexico an armistice had been agreed to, designating the limits beyond which troops of the respective armies were not to go during its continuance.[24] Our party knew nothing about these limits.

---

[21] USG probably referred to the cave system of Cacahuamilpa in the state of Guerrero. Cohen, *Columbia Gazetteer of the World,* s.v. "Cacahuamilpa."

[22] Buckner published "A Visit to Popocatepetl" in the Apr. 1, 1853, *Putnam's Monthly.* No published accounts of the expedition by Anderson and Stone have been found, but Henry Sibley published "Ascending the Popocatepetl" in *Frank Leslie's Chimney Corner,* June 1881. Thompson, "Winfield Scott's Army of Occupation," 571–572.

[23] USG probably referred to the town of Cuautla in the Mexican state of Morelos. Cohen, *Columbia Gazetteer of the World,* s.v. "Cuautla."

[24] USG probably referred to the provisions outlined in the Second Article of the "Military Convention for the Provisional Suspension of Hostilities," which went into effect Mar. 5, 1848.

As we approached Cuantla bugles sounded the assembly, and soldiers rushed from the guard-house in the edge of the town towards us. Our party halted, and I tied a white pocket handkerchief to a stick and, using it as a flag of truce, proceeded on to the town. Captains Sibley and Porter followed a few hundred yards behind. I was detained at the guard-house until a messenger could be dispatched to the quarters of the commanding general, who authorized that I should be conducted to him. I had been with the general but a few minutes when the two officers following announced themselves. The Mexican general reminded us that it was a violation of the truce for us to be there. However, as we had no special authority from our own commanding general, and as we knew nothing about the terms of the truce, we were permitted to occupy a vacant house outside the guard for the night, with the promise of a guide to put us on the road to Cuernavaca the next morning.

Cuernavaca is a town west of Cuantla. The country through which we passed, between these two towns, is tropical in climate and productions and rich in scenery. At one point, about half-way between the two places, the road goes over a low pass in the mountains in which there is a very quaint old town, the inhabitants of which at that day were nearly all full-blooded Indians. Very few of them even spoke Spanish. The houses were built of stone and generally only one story high. The streets were narrow, and had probably been paved before Cortez visited the country. They had not been graded, but the paving had been done on the natural surface. We had with us one vehicle, a cart, which was probably the first wheeled vehicle that had ever passed through that town.

On a hill overlooking this town stands the tomb of an ancient king; and it was understood that the inhabitants venerated this tomb very highly, as well as the memory of the ruler who was supposed to be buried in it. We ascended the mountain and surveyed the tomb; but it showed no particular marks of architectural taste, mechanical skill or advanced civilization.[25] The next day we went into Cuernavaca.

After a day's rest at Cuernavaca our party set out again on the journey to the great caves of Mexico. We had proceeded but a few miles when we were stopped, as before, by a guard and notified that the terms of the existing

The armistice limited the movements of U.S. and Mexican troops to areas occupied by their respective forces. Charles I. Bevans, ed., *Treaties and Other International Agreements of the United States of America, 1776–1949*, vol. 9 (Washington, DC: Dept. of State Publications, 1972), 808.

[25] Although the exact location of the tomb is unclear, the travelers may have visited ruins in the area around Yautepec. Thompson, *Henry Hopkins Sibley*, 74.

armistice did not permit us to go further in that direction. Upon convincing the guard that we were a mere party of pleasure seekers desirous of visiting the great natural curiosities of the country which we expected soon to leave, we were conducted to a large hacienda near by, and directed to remain there until the commanding general of that department could be communicated with and his decision obtained as to whether we should be permitted to pursue our journey. The guard promised to send a messenger at once, and expected a reply by night. At night there was no response from the commanding general, but the captain of the guard was sure he would have a reply by morning. Again in the morning there was no reply. The second evening the same thing happened, and finally we learned that the guard had sent no message or messenger to the department commander. We determined therefore to go on unless stopped by a force sufficient to compel obedience.

After a few hours' travel we came to a town where a scene similar to the one at Cuantla occurred. The commanding officer sent a guide to conduct our party around the village and to put us upon our road again. This was the last interruption: that night we rested at a large coffee plantation, some eight miles from the cave we were on the way to visit. It must have been a Saturday night; the peons had been paid off, and spent part of the night in gambling away their scanty week's earnings. Their coin was principally copper, and I do not believe there was a man among them who had received as much as twenty-five cents in money. They were as much excited, however, as if they had been staking thousands. I recollect one poor fellow, who had lost his last tlaco, pulled off his shirt and, in the most excited manner, put that up on the turn of a card. Monte was the game played, the place out of doors, near the window of the room occupied by the officers of our party.

The next morning we were at the mouth of the cave at an early hour, provided with guides, candles and rockets. We explored to a distance of about three miles from the entrance, and found a succession of chambers of great dimensions and of great beauty when lit up with our rockets. Stalactites and stalagmites of all sizes were discovered. Some of the former were many feet in diameter and extended from ceiling to floor; some of the latter were but a few feet high from the floor; but the formation is going on constantly, and many centuries hence these stalagmites will extend to the ceiling and become complete columns. The stalagmites were all a little concave, and the cavities were filled with water. The water percolates through the roof, a drop at a time—often the drops several minutes apart—and more or less charged with mineral matter. Evaporation goes on slowly, leaving the mineral behind. This in time makes the immense columns, many of them thousands of tons in weight, which serve to support the roofs over the vast chambers. I recollect that at one point in the cave one of these columns is of such huge proportions that there is only a narrow passage left on either side of it. Some of our party became satisfied with their explorations before we had reached the point to which the guides were accustomed to take explorers, and started back without guides. Coming to the large column spoken of, they followed it entirely around, and commenced retracing their steps into the bowels of the mountain, without being aware of the fact. When the rest of us had completed our explorations, we started out with our guides, but had not gone far before we saw the torches of an approaching party. We could not conceive who these could be, for all of us had come in together, and there were none but ourselves at the entrance when we started in. Very soon we found it was our friends. It took them some time to conceive how they had got where they were. They were sure they had kept straight on for the mouth of the cave, and had gone about far enough to have reached it.

# 14

## Return of the Army—Marriage—Ordered to the Pacific Coast—Crossing the Isthmus— Arrival at San Francisco

My EXPERIENCE in the Mexican war was of great advantage to me afterwards. Besides the many practical lessons it taught, the war brought nearly all the officers of the regular army together so as to make them personally acquainted. It also brought them in contact with volunteers, many of whom served in the war of the rebellion afterwards. Then, in my particular case, I had been at West Point at about the right time to meet most of the graduates who were of a suitable age at the breaking out of the rebellion to be trusted with large commands. Graduating in 1843, I was at the military academy from one to four years with all cadets who graduated between 1840 and 1846—seven classes. These classes embraced more than fifty officers who afterwards became generals on one side or the other in the rebellion, many of them holding high commands. All the older officers, who became conspicuous in the rebellion, I had also served with and known in Mexico: Lee, J. E. Johnston,[1] A. S. Johnston,[2]

---

[1] Joseph E. Johnston (1807–1891) was born in Virginia and graduated from the USMA in 1829. During the Mexican-American War, he was wounded at Cerro Gordo and Chapultepec. He resigned from the U.S. Army in Apr. 1861 and immediately joined the Confederate Army as a major general. After the Civil War, he served as a U.S. representative from Virginia from 1879 to 1881. *CWHC,* 322–323.

[2] Albert Sidney Johnston (1803–1862) was born in Kentucky and graduated from the USMA in 1826. Before the Mexican-American War, he fought in the Black Hawk War, served as an aide-de-camp to Sam Houston in 1836, and was the secretary of war for the Republic of Texas from 1838 to 1840. He was a volunteer assistant inspector under Gen. William Butler from Sept. to Oct. 1846. He resigned from the U.S. Army in May 1861 and joined the Confederate Army as a general. Ibid., 322.

Holmes, Hébert[3] and a number of others on the Confederate side; McCall, Mansfield, Phil. Kearney and others on the National side. The acquaintance thus formed was of immense service to me in the war of the rebellion—I mean what I learned of the characters of those to whom I was afterwards opposed. I do not pretend to say that all movements, or even many of them, were made with special reference to the characteristics of the commander against whom they were directed. But my appreciation of my enemies was certainly affected by this knowledge. The natural disposition of most people is to clothe a commander of a large army whom they do not know, with almost superhuman abilities. A large part of the National army, for instance, and most of the press of the country, clothed General Lee with just such qualities, but I had known him personally, and knew that he was mortal; and it was just as well that I felt this.

The treaty of peace was at last ratified, and the evacuation of Mexico by United States troops was ordered. Early in June the troops in the City of Mexico began to move out.[4] Many of them, including the brigade to which I belonged, were assembled at Jalapa, above the vomito, to await the arrival of transports at Vera Cruz: but with all this precaution my regiment and others were in camp on the sand beach in a July sun, for about a week before embarking, while the fever raged with great virulence in Vera Cruz, not two miles away. I can call to mind only one person, an officer, who died of the disease. My regiment was sent to Pascagoula, Mississippi, to spend the summer. As soon as it was settled in camp I obtained a leave of absence for four months and proceeded to St. Louis. On the 22d of August, 1848, I was married to Miss Julia Dent, the lady of whom I have before spoken.[5] We visited my parents and

---

[3] Paul O. Hébert (1818–1880) was born in Louisiana and graduated first in his class from the USMA in 1840. In Sept. 1847, he was brevetted colonel for his actions at Molino del Rey and Chapultepec during the Mexican-American War. He was discharged from the U.S. Army in July 1848. He joined the Confederate Army as a colonel in Feb. 1861 and reached brigadier general in Oct. 1861. Ibid., 292.

[4] On May 30, 1848, the United States and Mexico exchanged notification of the treaty. U.S. troops began evacuating Mexico City the same day. The evacuation of the city was completed by June 12. *PUSG*, 1:157n.

[5] JDG also identified Aug. 22, 1848, as the day of the wedding in her memoirs. The marriage license records Sept. 10 (the date the license was issued) as the wedding date. *PUSG*, 1:164n; 32:8; JDG, *The Personal Memoirs of Julia Dent Grant (Mrs. Ulysses S. Grant)*, ed. John Y. Simon (New York: G. P. Putnam's Sons, 1975), 55.

relations in Ohio,[6] and, at the end of my leave, proceeded to my post at Sackett's Harbor, New York.[7] In April following I was ordered to Detroit, Michigan, where two years were spent with but few important incidents.[8]

The present constitution of the State of Michigan was ratified during this time. By the terms of one of its provisions, all citizens of the United States residing within the State at the time of the ratification became citizens of Michigan also.[9] During my stay in Detroit there was an election for city officers. Mr. Zachariah Chandler[10] was the candidate of the Whigs for the office of Mayor, and was elected, although the city was then reckoned democratic. All the officers stationed there at the time who offered their votes were permitted to cast them. I did not offer mine, however, as I did not wish to consider myself a citizen of Michigan. This was Mr. Chandler's first entry into politics, a career he followed ever after with great success, and in which he died enjoying the friendship, esteem and love of his countrymen.

In the spring of 1851 the garrison at Detroit was transferred to Sackett's Harbor,[11] and in the following spring the entire 4th infantry was ordered to the Pacific Coast.[12] It was decided that Mrs. Grant should visit my parents at first for a few months, and then remain with her own family at their St. Louis home

[6] After the Ohio visit, the Grants returned to St. Louis. On Sept. 20, 1848, Gen. Scott's Special Orders No. 6 extended USG's leave for two months. Special Orders No. 22, issued on Oct. 13, also granted the two-month leave, resulting in duplicate leave applications. JDG, *Memoirs*, 55–58; *PUSG*, 1:167n.

[7] Before arriving at Sackets Harbor, USG reported to regimental headquarters in Detroit, MI, on Nov. 17, 1848. By Dec. 2, USG had arrived at Madison Barracks, Sackets Harbor. *PUSG*, 1:168–169.

[8] In Feb. 1849, USG complained that he had been incorrectly assigned to Sackets Harbor and should have been stationed in Detroit. By Mar. 9, USG had received orders to join his regiment at Detroit. He served in Detroit from Apr. 18, 1849 to June 7, 1851. Ibid., 1:175–177, 177n–178n, 181, and n, 206.

[9] Michigan adopted its second constitution in 1850. Willis F. Dunbar, *Michigan: A History of the Wolverine State* (Grand Rapids, MI: William B. Eerdmans, 1995), 292.

[10] Zachariah Chandler (1813–1879) was born in Bedford, NH, and moved to Detroit in 1833. In 1851, he was elected mayor as a Whig. In 1857, he was elected to the U.S. Senate as a Republican. Arthur T. Pierson, *Zachariah Chandler: An Outline Sketch of His Life and Public Services* (Detroit: Post and Tribune, 1880), 37, 388; *PUSG*, 1:195n.

[11] On June 7, 1851, USG wrote to JDG that he had received orders to relocate to Sackets Harbor. *PUSG*, 1:206–207.

[12] On May 26, 1852, USG wrote that the 4th Inf. had received orders to move to Fort Columbus, NY, in preparation for deployment to the Pacific Div. *PUSG*, 1:232–233.

until an opportunity offered of sending for her.[13] In the month of April the regiment was assembled at Governor's Island, New York Harbor,[14] and on the 5th of July eight companies sailed for Aspinwall.[15] We numbered a little over seven hundred persons, including the families of officers and soldiers. Passage was secured for us on the old steamer *Ohio,* commanded at the time by Captain Schenck,[16] of the navy. It had not been determined, until a day or two before starting, that the 4th infantry should go by the *Ohio*; consequently, a complement of passengers had already been secured. The addition of over seven hundred to this list crowded the steamer most uncomfortably, especially for the tropics in July.[17]

In eight days Aspinwall was reached. At that time the streets of the town were eight or ten inches under water, and foot passengers passed from place to place on raised foot-walks. July is at the height of the wet season, on the Isthmus. At intervals the rain would pour down in streams, followed in not many minutes by a blazing, tropical summer's sun. These alternate changes, from rain to sunshine, were continuous in the afternoons. I wondered how any person could live many months in Aspinwall, and wondered still more why any one tried.

In the summer of 1852 the Panama railroad was completed only to the point where it now crosses the Chagres River.[18] From there passengers were carried by boats to Gorgona,[19] at which place they took mules for Panama, some

[13] JDG was pregnant with the couple's second child, Ulysses S. "Buck" Grant Jr. (1852–1929), when USG departed for the West Coast. JDG, *Memoirs,* 29, 71–75.

[14] USG reached Governors Island on June 17, 1852. *PUSG,* 1:237n.

[15] On Feb. 2, 1852, the town of Aspinwall (known as Colón since 1890) was established. It was named after entrepreneur William H. Aspinwall (1807–1875), who was instrumental in the construction of a road to the area. Saul B. Cohen, ed., *The Columbia Gazetteer of the World* (New York: Columbia University Press, 1998), s.v. "Colón"; J. C. Levenson et al., eds., *The Letters of Henry Adams* (Boston: Massachusetts Historical Society, 1982), 1:350n; F. N. Otis, *Isthmus of Panama: History of the Panama Railroad; and of the Pacific Mail Steamship Company* (New York: Harper and Brothers, 1867), 33.

[16] James F. Schenck (1807–1882) was born in Ohio and was promoted to commodore of the U.S. Navy in 1855. In 1868, he was promoted to rear admiral. *CWHC,* 471.

[17] USG related the conditions of the voyage in a July 15, 1852, letter to JDG. *PUSG,* 1:248.

[18] Construction on the Panama Railroad began in 1850 and was completed in 1855. William H. Aspinwall was a partner in the construction of the railroad, which was forty-seven and one-half miles long and cost $8,000,000. David McCullough, *The Path between the Seas: The Creation of the Panama Canal, 1870–1914* (New York: Simon and Schuster, 1977), 35.

[19] With the creation of the Gatun Lake portion of the Panama Canal, Gorgona was abandoned in July and Aug. 1913. Ralph E. Avery, *Picturesque Panama and the Great Canal* (n.p.: n.p., 1913), 235; "Notes of Progress—Depopulation of the Zone," *Canal Record,* May 20, 1914, 378.

twenty-five miles further. Those who travelled over the Isthmus in those days will remember that boats on the Chagres River were propelled by natives not inconveniently burdened with clothing. These boats carried thirty to forty passengers each. The crews consisted of six men to a boat, armed with long poles. There were planks wide enough for a man to walk on conveniently, running along the sides of each boat from end to end. The men would start from the bow, place one end of their poles against the river bottom, brace their shoulders against the other end, and then walk to the stern as rapidly as they could. In this way from a mile to a mile and a half an hour could be made, against the current of the river.

I, as regimental quartermaster, had charge of the public property and had also to look after the transportation. A contract had been entered into with the steamship company in New York for the transportation of the regiment to California, including the Isthmus transit.[20] A certain amount of baggage was allowed per man, and saddle animals were to be furnished to commissioned officers and to all disabled persons. The regiment, with the exception of one company left as guards to the public property—camp and garrison equipage principally—and the soldiers with families, took boats, propelled as above described, for Gorgona. From this place they marched to Panama, and were soon comfortably on the steamer anchored in the bay, some three or four miles from the town. I, with one company of troops and all the soldiers with families, all the tents, mess chests and camp kettles, was sent to Cruces,[21] a town a few miles higher up the Chagres River than Gorgona. There I found an impecunious American who had taken the contract to furnish transportation for the regiment at a stipulated price per hundred pounds for the freight and so much for each saddle animal. But when we reached Cruces there was not a mule, either for pack or saddle, in the place. The contractor promised that the animals should be on hand in the morning. In the morning he said that they were on the way from some imaginary place, and would arrive in the course of the day. This went on until I saw that he could not procure the animals at all at the price he had promised to furnish them for. The unusual number of passengers that had come over on the steamer, and the large amount of freight to pack, had created an unprecedented demand for mules. Some of

[20] The steamships *Golden Gate* and *Northerner* were used to transport the troops to California. Charles S. Tripler, "Report of the Regimental Surgeon, Fourth Infantry, U.S.A.," in "Crossing the Isthmus in 1852," *Canal Record,* July 1, 1908, 347; *PUSG,* 1:251.

[21] Like Gorgona (see note 19 above), Cruces was abandoned by May 1914 due to the creation of Gatun Lake. "Notes of Progress," 378.

the passengers paid as high as forty dollars for the use of a mule to ride twenty-five miles, when the mule would not have sold for ten dollars in that market at other times. Meanwhile the cholera had broken out, and men were dying every hour. To diminish the food for the disease, I permitted the company detailed with me to proceed to Panama. The captain and the doctors accompanied the men, and I was left alone with the sick and the soldiers who had families. The regiment at Panama was also affected with the disease; but there were better accommodations for the well on the steamer, and a hospital, for those taken with the disease, on an old hulk anchored a mile off. There were also hospital tents on shore on the island of Flamingo, which stands in the bay.

I was about a week at Cruces before transportation began to come in. About one-third of the people with me died, either at Cruces or on the way to Panama. There was no agent of the transportation company at Cruces to consult, or to take the responsibility of procuring transportation at a price which would secure it. I therefore myself dismissed the contractor and made a new contract with a native, at more than double the original price.[22] Thus we finally reached Panama. The steamer, however, could not proceed until the cholera abated, and the regiment was detained still longer. Altogether, on the Isthmus and on the Pacific side, we were delayed six weeks. About one-seventh of those who left New York harbor with the 4th infantry on the 5th of July, now lie buried on the Isthmus of Panama or on Flamingo island in Panama Bay.[23]

One amusing circumstance occurred while we were lying at anchor in Panama Bay. In the regiment there was a Lieutenant Slaughter[24] who was very liable to sea-sickness. It almost made him sick to see the wave of a table-cloth when the servants were spreading it. Soon after his graduation, Slaughter was ordered to California and took passage by a sailing vessel going around Cape Horn. The vessel was seven months making the voyage, and Slaughter was sick every moment of the time, never more so than while lying at anchor after reaching his place of destination. On landing in California he found orders which had come by the Isthmus, notifying him of a mistake in his assignment;

---

[22] On July 21, 1852, a contract was drawn up between USG and José M. Saravia, who promised to deliver the baggage of the 4th Inf. to Panama. *PUSG*, 1:249–250, 250*n*.

[23] During the cholera outbreak, approximately 150 members of the 4th Inf. traveling party died. William S. McFeely, *Grant: A Biography* (New York: Norton, 1981), 47; *PUSG*, 1:251–252.

[24] William A. Slaughter (1826–1855) was born in Kentucky and graduated from the USMA in 1844. Francis B. Heitman, *Historical Register and Dictionary of the United States Army: From Its Organization, September 29, 1789, to March 2, 1903* (Washington, DC: Government Printing Office, 1903), 1:891.

he should have been ordered to the northern lakes. He started back by the Isthmus route and was sick all the way. But when he arrived at the East he was again ordered to California, this time definitely, and at this date was making his third trip. He was as sick as ever, and had been so for more than a month while lying at anchor in the bay. I remember him well, seated with his elbows on the table in front of him, his chin between his hands, and looking the picture of despair. At last he broke out, "I wish I had taken my father's advice; he wanted me to go into the navy; if I had done so, I should not have had to go to sea so much." Poor Slaughter! it was his last sea voyage. He was killed by Indians in Oregon.[25]

By the last of August the cholera had so abated that it was deemed safe to start. The disease did not break out again on the way to California, and we reached San Francisco early in September.

---

[25] On Dec. 4, 1855, Slaughter died in combat against Native Americans at Brannan's Prairie in the White River region of the Washington Territory. Ibid.

# 15

## San Francisco—Early California Experiences— Life on the Pacific Coast—Promoted Captain— Flush Times in California

Sᴀɴ ꜰʀᴀɴᴄɪꜱᴄᴏ ᴀᴛ ᴛʜᴀᴛ ᴅᴀʏ was a lively place. Gold, or placer digging as it was called, was at its height. Steamers plied daily between San Francisco and both Stockton and Sacramento. Passengers and gold from the southern mines came by the Stockton boat; from the northern mines by Sacramento. In the evening when these boats arrived, Long Wharf—there was but one wharf in San Francisco in 1852—was alive with people crowding to meet the miners as they came down to sell their "dust" and to "have a time."[1] Of these some were runners for hotels, boarding houses or restaurants; others belonged to a class of impecunious adventurers, of good manners and good presence, who were ever on the alert to make the acquaintance of people with some ready means, in the hope of being asked to take a meal at a restaurant. Many were young men of good family, good education and gentlemanly instincts. Their parents had been able to support them during their minority, and to give them good educations, but not to maintain them afterwards. From 1849 to 1853 there was a rush of people to the Pacific coast, of the class described.[2] All thought that fortunes were to be picked up, without effort, in the gold fields on the Pacific. Some realized more than their most sanguine expectations; but for one such there were hundreds disappointed, many of whom now fill unknown

[1] There were numerous wharves in San Francisco by 1852, but the Commercial Street Wharf (known as Long Wharf) had been the first wharf to extend out to deep water to better accommodate the increased traffic of larger ships arriving with cargo in the bay area. John S. Hittell, *A History of the City of San Francisco; and Incidentally of the State of California* (San Francisco: A. L. Bancroft, 1878), 133–134, 164–165.

[2] In 1849, nearly 100,000 people had migrated to California. By 1854, the migration had brought approximately 300,000 people from around the world. David Igler and William Deverell, eds., *A Companion to California History* (Malden, MA: Wiley-Blackwell, 2008), 6.

graves; others died wrecks of their former selves, and many, without a vicious instinct, became criminals and outcasts. Many of the real scenes in early California life exceed in strangeness and interest any of the mere products of the brain of the novelist.

Those early days in California brought out character. It was a long way off then, and the journey was expensive. The fortunate could go by Cape Horn or by the Isthmus of Panama; but the mass of pioneers crossed the plains with their ox-teams. This took an entire summer. They were very lucky when they got through with a yoke of worn-out cattle. All other means were exhausted in procuring the outfit on the Missouri River. The immigrant, on arriving, found himself a stranger, in a strange land, far from friends. Time pressed, for the little means that could be realized from the sale of what was left of the outfit would not support a man long at California prices.[3] Many became discouraged. Others would take off their coats and look for a job, no matter what it might be. These succeeded as a rule. There were many young men who had studied professions before they went to California, and who had never done a day's manual labor in their lives, who took in the situation at once and went to work to make a start at anything they could get to do. Some supplied carpenters and masons with material—carrying plank, brick, or mortar, as the case might be; others drove stages, drays, or baggage wagons, until they could do better. More became discouraged early and spent their time looking up people who would "treat," or lounging about restaurants and gambling houses where free lunches were furnished daily. They were welcomed at these places because they often brought in miners who proved good customers.

My regiment spent a few weeks at Benicia barracks,[4] and then was ordered to Fort Vancouver,[5] on the Columbia River, then in Oregon Territory. During the winter of 1852–3 the territory was divided, all north of the Columbia River being taken from Oregon to make Washington Territory.[6]

---

[3] Uneven supply and increasing demand led to wild fluctuations in prices. Examples of high prices in California during 1848–1849 include $50 for a pair of blankets in Dec. 1848 and $65 for a barrel of pork in Nov. 1849. Rand Richards, *Mud, Blood, and Gold: San Francisco in 1849* (San Francisco: Heritage House, 2009), 56–57.

[4] In 1849, Benecia Barracks was established at the head of Suisun Bay, near San Francisco, and soon became the primary ordnance facility on the West Coast. Durwood Ball, *Army Regulars on the Western Frontier, 1848–1861* (Norman: University of Oklahoma Press, 2001), xxvii.

[5] On Sept. 20, 1852, USG arrived at Columbia Barracks. In 1853, the barracks was renamed Fort Vancouver. Ibid., xxviii; *PUSG,* 1:264*n.*

[6] On Mar. 2, 1853, Congress created the Washington Territory by splitting the Oregon Territory in two. The division placed Columbia Barracks in the Washington Territory. *PUSG,* 1:269*n.*

Prices for all kinds of supplies were so high on the Pacific coast from 1849 until at least 1853—that it would have been impossible for officers of the army to exist upon their pay, if it had not been that authority was given them to purchase from the commissary such supplies as he kept, at New Orleans wholesale prices. A cook could not be hired for the pay of a captain. The cook could do better.[7] At Benicia, in 1852, flour was 25 cents per pound; potatoes were 16 cents; beets, turnips and cabbage, 6 cents; onions, 37 1/2 cents; meat and other articles in proportion. In 1853 at Vancouver vegetables were a little lower. I with three other officers concluded that we would raise a crop for ourselves, and by selling the surplus realize something handsome. I bought a pair of horses that had crossed the plains that summer and were very poor. They recuperated rapidly, however, and proved a good team to break up the ground with. I performed all the labor of breaking up the ground while the other officers planted the potatoes. Our crop was enormous. Luckily for us the Columbia River rose to a great height from the melting of the snow in the mountains in June, and overflowed and killed most of our crop.[8] This saved digging it up, for everybody on the Pacific coast seemed to have come to the conclusion at the same time that agriculture would be profitable. In 1853 more than three-quarters of the potatoes raised were permitted to rot in the ground, or had to be thrown away.[9] The only potatoes we sold were to our own mess.

While I was stationed on the Pacific coast we were free from Indian wars. There were quite a number of remnants of tribes in the vicinity of Portland in Oregon, and of Fort Vancouver in Washington Territory.[10] They had

[7] The pay of an infantry captain in 1853 was $79.50 per month, while USG estimated that the cook in his employ in 1853 and her husband, an enlisted man in the U.S. Army, together earned roughly $75 per month. Ball, *Army Regulars on the Western Frontier,* 60; Edward M. Coffman, *The Old Army: A Portrait of the American Army in Peacetime, 1784–1898* (New York: Oxford University Press, 1986), 153–155; *Official Army Register for 1853* (Washington, DC: C. Alexander, 1853), 36; *PUSG,* 1:279–280.

[8] In 1853, USG purchased potato seeds for $2 a bushel and planned to raise about 200 bushels, in addition to 20 acres of oats and a vegetable garden. However, he reported to JDG in July that flooding from the Columbia River had killed the oats, vegetables, and half of the potatoes. *PUSG,* 1:289, 301, 304.

[9] In other areas of the Pacific Northwest, abundant harvests (especially of grains) were reported in the fall of 1853, but the editors have found no direct confirmation of USG's assertion regarding potatoes. "Interesting from Oregon, Utah, and the Sandwich Islands," *New York Times,* Sept. 10, 1853, 3.

[10] A detailed map of Native American tribes in the Pacific Northwest is found in Robert H. Ruby and John A. Brown, *Indians of the Pacific Northwest: A History* (Norman: University of Oklahoma Press, 1981), 39.

generally acquired some of the vices of civilization, but none of the virtues, except in individual cases. The Hudson's Bay Company had held the Northwest with their trading posts for many years before the United States was represented on the Pacific coast. They still retained posts along the Columbia River and one at Fort Vancouver, when I was there. Their treatment of the Indians had brought out the better qualities of the savages. Farming had been undertaken by the company to supply the Indians with bread and vegetables; they raised some cattle and horses; and they had now taught the Indians to do the labor of the farm and herd. They always compensated them for their labor, and always gave them goods of uniform quality and at uniform price.[11]

Before the advent of the American, the medium of exchange between the Indian and the white man was pelts. Afterward it was silver coin. If an Indian received in the sale of a horse a fifty dollar gold piece, not an infrequent occurrence, the first thing he did was to exchange it for American half dollars. These he could count. He would then commence his purchases, paying for each article separately, as he got it. He would not trust any one to add up the bill and pay it all at once. At that day fifty dollar gold pieces, not the issue of the government, were common on the Pacific coast. They were called slugs.

The Indians, along the lower Columbia as far as the Cascades and on the lower Willamette, died off very fast during the year I spent in that section; for besides acquiring the vices of the white people they had acquired also their diseases.[12] The measles and the small-pox were both amazingly fatal. In their wild state, before the appearance of the white man among them, the principal complaints they were subject to were those produced by long involuntary fasting, violent exercise in pursuit of game, and over-eating. Instinct more than reason had taught them a remedy for these ills. It was the steam bath. Something like a bake-oven was built, large enough to admit a man lying down. Bushes were stuck in the ground in two rows, about six feet long

[11] Since 1821, the Hudson's Bay Company had enjoyed a monopoly of trade with Native Americans in the region. The British company actively cultivated good business relations with the Native American population through policies that offered uniform pricing and buying on credit. Charles H. Carey, *History of Oregon* (Chicago: Pioneer Historical, 1922), 1:262; Ruby and Brown, *Indians of the Pacific Northwest*, 47.

[12] A series of shipwrecks in late 1852 and early 1853 are believed to have sparked a smallpox epidemic among Native Americans in the area, who probably contracted the disease from clothing and other items scavenged from the shipwrecks. Robert Boyd, *The Coming of the Spirit of Pestilence: Introduced Infectious and Population Decline among the Northwest Coast Indians, 1774–1874* (Seattle: University of Washington Press, 1999), 160–163.

and some two or three feet apart; other bushes connected the rows at one end. The tops of the bushes were drawn together to interlace, and confined in that position; the whole was then plastered over with wet clay until every opening was filled. Just inside the open end of the oven the floor was scooped out so as to make a hole that would hold a bucket or two of water. These ovens were always built on the banks of a stream, a big spring, or pool of water. When a patient required a bath, a fire was built near the oven and a pile of stones put upon it. The cavity at the front was then filled with water. When the stones were sufficiently heated, the patient would draw himself into the oven; a blanket would be thrown over the open end, and hot stones put into the water until the patient could stand it no longer. He was then withdrawn from his steam bath and doused into the cold stream near by. This treatment may have answered with the early ailments of the Indians. With the measles or small-pox it would kill every time.

During my year on the Columbia River, the small-pox exterminated one small remnant of a band of Indians entirely, and reduced others materially.[13] I do not think there was a case of recovery among them, until the doctor with the Hudson Bay Company took the matter in hand and established a hospital.[14] Nearly every case he treated recovered. I never, myself, saw the treatment described in the preceding paragraph, but have heard it described by persons who have witnessed it. The decimation among the Indians I knew of personally, and the hospital, established for their benefit, was a Hudson's Bay building not a stone's throw from my own quarters.

The death of Colonel Bliss, of the Adjutant General's department, which occurred July 5th, 1853, promoted me to the captaincy of a company then stationed at Humboldt Bay, California. The notice reached me in September of

[13] The smallpox outbreak decimated many of the tribes in the region, including the Chinook and Klickitat. USG probably referred to the Klickitats in the area around Fort Vancouver. Ibid., 161–171; *PUSG*, 1:310.

[14] There were two hospitals at Fort Vancouver: one inside the fort that served the men of high social standing and their families, and the other outside the fort near the employees' village, which offered care to Native Americans and others. The hospital outside the fort had been constructed in the early 1830s. The doctor mentioned by USG is probably Alfred R. Benson, the surgeon assigned to Fort Vancouver during USG's time there. John A. Hussey, *Historic Structures Report: Fort Vancouver National Historic Site*, vol. 2 (Washington, DC: National Park Service, 1976), 68, 71; John A. Hussey, *The History of Fort Vancouver and Its Physical Structure* (Portland: National Park Service and Washington State Historical Society, 1957), 216, 220–221; Dorothy B. Smith, ed., *The Reminiscences of Doctor John Sebastian Helmcken* (Vancouver: University of British Columbia, 1975), 49, 108–109.

the same year, and I very soon started to join my new command.[15] There was no way of reaching Humboldt at that time except to take passage on a San Francisco sailing vessel going after lumber. Red wood, a species of cedar, which on the Pacific coast takes the place filled by white pine in the East, then abounded on the banks of Humboldt Bay. There were extensive saw-mills engaged in preparing this lumber for the San Francisco market, and sailing vessels, used in getting it to market, furnished the only means of communication between Humboldt and the balance of the world.

I was obliged to remain in San Francisco for several days before I found a vessel. This gave me a good opportunity of comparing the San Francisco of 1852 with that of 1853. As before stated, there had been but one wharf in front of the city in 1852—Long Wharf. In 1853 the town had grown out into the bay beyond what was the end of this wharf when I first saw it. Streets and houses had been built out on piles where the year before the largest vessels visiting the port lay at anchor or tied to the wharf. There was no filling under the streets or houses. San Francisco presented the same general appearance as the year before; that is, eating, drinking and gambling houses were conspicuous for their number and publicity. They were on the first floor, with doors wide open. At all hours of the day and night in walking the streets, the eye was regaled, on every block near the water front, by the sight of players at faro. Often broken places were found in the street, large enough to let a man down into the water below. I have but little doubt that many of the people who went to the Pacific coast in the early days of the gold excitement, and have never been heard from since, or who were heard from for a time and then ceased to write, found watery graves beneath the houses or streets built over San Francisco Bay.

Besides the gambling in cards there was gambling on a larger scale in city lots. These were sold "On Change," much as stocks are now sold on Wall Street. Cash, at time of purchase, was always paid by the broker; but the purchaser had only to put up his margin. He was charged at the rate of two or three per cent. a month on the difference, besides commissions. The sand hills, some of them almost inaccessible to foot-passengers, were surveyed off and mapped into fifty vara lots—a vara being a Spanish yard. These were sold at first at very low prices, but were sold and resold for higher prices until they went up to many thousands of dollars. The brokers did a fine business, and so

---

[15] William W. S. Bliss died of yellow fever on Aug. 5, 1853. Four days later, Secretary of War Jefferson Davis wrote to USG of the promotion and ordered him to join Co. F at Fort Humboldt, CA. George W. Cullum, *Biographical Register of the Officers and Graduates of the U.S. Military Academy at West Point, N.Y.* (Boston: Houghton, Mifflin, 1891), 1:544; *PUSG*, 1:312n.

did many such purchasers as were sharp enough to quit purchasing before the final crash came. As the city grew, the sand hills back of the town furnished material for filling up the bay under the houses and streets, and still further out. The temporary houses, first built over the water in the harbor, soon gave way to more solid structures. The main business part of the city now is on solid ground, made where vessels of the largest class lay at anchor in the early days. I was in San Francisco again in 1854. Gambling houses had disappeared from public view. The city had become staid and orderly.[16]

---

[16] Crime and corruption in local government continued to plague San Francisco in 1854. George H. Tinkham, *California Men and Events: Time 1769–1890* (Stockton, CA: Record, 1915), 151.

# 16

## Resignation—Private Life—Life at Galena— The Coming Crisis

M Y FAMILY, all this while, was at the East. It consisted now of a wife and two children.[1] I saw no chance of supporting them on the Pacific coast out of my pay as an army officer. I concluded, therefore, to resign, and in March applied for a leave of absence until the end of the July following, tendering my resignation to take effect at the end of that time.[2] I left the Pacific coast very much attached to it, and with the full expectation of making it my future home. That expectation and that hope remained uppermost in my mind until the Lieutenant-Generalcy bill was introduced into Congress in the winter of 1863–4. The passage of that bill, and my promotion, blasted my last hope of ever becoming a citizen of the further West.[3]

In the late summer of 1854 I rejoined my family, to find in it a son whom I had never seen, born while I was on the Isthmus of Panama.[4] I was now to commence, at the age of thirty-two, a new struggle for our support. My wife had a farm near St. Louis, to which we went, but I had no means to stock it.

---

[1] FDG (1850–1912) and Ulysses S. "Buck" Grant Jr. (1852–1929). JDG, *The Personal Memoirs of Julia Dent Grant (Mrs. Ulysses S. Grant),* ed. John Y. Simon (New York: G. P. Putnam's Sons, 1975), 29.

[2] USG's resignation was actually dated Apr. 11, 1854. Rumors that his resignation was tied to discipline for drunkenness have persisted but have never been verified. JRG attempted to have the resignation rescinded by writing to his congressman, Rep. Andrew Ellison, and Secretary of War Jefferson Davis, but was unsuccessful. *PUSG,* 1:329–331. For a summary of the rumors surrounding USG's resignation, see Lloyd Lewis, *Captain Sam Grant* (Boston: Little, Brown, 1950), 329–331, 336–338.

[3] The bill, which revived the rank of lieutenant general, passed both houses of Congress on Feb. 26, 1864. Lincoln nominated USG for the rank on Feb. 29, and on Mar. 2 he was confirmed. *PUSG,* 10:188–189, 189*n*.

[4] USG's second son, Buck, was born on July 22, 1852. Ibid., 1:249*n*.

A house had to be built also.[5] I worked very hard, never losing a day because of bad weather, and accomplished the object in a moderate way. If nothing else could be done I would load a cord of wood on a wagon and take it to the city for sale. I managed to keep along very well until 1858, when I was attacked by fever and ague. I had suffered very severely and for a long time from this disease, while a boy in Ohio. It lasted now over a year, and, while it did not keep me in the house, it did interfere greatly with the amount of work I was able to perform.[6] In the fall of 1858 I sold out my stock, crops and farming utensils at auction, and gave up farming.

In the winter I established a partnership with Harry Boggs, a cousin of Mrs. Grant, in the real estate agency business.[7] I spent that winter at St. Louis myself, but did not take my family into town until the spring. Our business might have become prosperous if I had been able to wait for it to grow. As it was, there was no more than one person could attend to, and not enough to support two families. While a citizen of St. Louis and engaged in the real estate agency business, I was a candidate for the office of county engineer, an office of respectability and emolument which would have been very acceptable to me at that time.[8] The incumbent was appointed by the county court, which consisted of five members. My opponent had the advantage of birth over me (he was a citizen by adoption) and carried off the prize.[9] I now withdrew from the co-partnership with Boggs, and, in May, 1860, removed to Galena, Illinois, and took a clerkship in my father's store.[10]

[5] In the summer of 1856, USG finished construction of a house he named "Hardscrabble." The house was located on sixty acres of land (given to JDG by her father) adjacent to the White Haven estate. Ibid., 1:334–335.

[6] In Sept. 1858, USG's family and some slaves living on the White Haven property were also sick. Ibid., 1:343.

[7] Harry Boggs (c.1814–?), JDG's cousin, was born in Pennsylvania and later moved to St. Louis. The partnership involved collecting rents and other debts as well as facilitating buying and selling property. Ibid., 1:345–346, 346n.

[8] On Aug. 15, 1859, USG applied for the county engineer position. Ibid., 1:348–349.

[9] Although USG had much support for the position, the vote came down to party lines. The Free-Soil and Republican County Commissioners voted against USG because of his support for James Buchanan in the 1856 presidential election. On Sept. 22, 1859, the board appointed Charles E. Salomon, a German immigrant and later a colonel in the U.S. Army during the Civil War. *CWHC*, 468; *PUSG*, 1:353n; Brooks D. Simpson, *Ulysses S. Grant: Triumph over Adversity, 1822–1865* (Boston: Houghton Mifflin, 2000), 72.

[10] In Mar. 1860, USG visited his family in Covington, KY, where he accepted an offer to work as a clerk in his father's leather shop in Galena, IL. *PUSG*, 1:355–356; Simpson, *Ulysses S. Grant*, 73.

While a citizen of Missouri, my first opportunity for casting a vote at a Presidential election occurred. I had been in the army from before attaining my majority and had thought but little about politics, although I was a Whig by education and a great admirer of Mr. Clay. But the Whig party had ceased to exist before I had an opportunity of exercising the privilege of casting a ballot; the Know-Nothing party had taken its place, but was on the wane;[11] and the Republican party was in a chaotic state and had not yet received a name. It had no existence in the Slave States except at points on the borders next to Free States.[12] In St. Louis City and County, what afterwards became the Republican party was known as the Free-Soil Democracy, led by the Honorable Frank P. Blair.[13] Most of my neighbors had known me as an officer of the army with Whig proclivities. They had been on the same side, and, on the death of their party, many had become Know-Nothings, or members of the American party. There was a lodge near my new home, and I was invited to join it. I accepted the invitation; was initiated; attended a meeting just one week later, and never went to another afterwards.

I have no apologies to make for having been one week a member of the American party; for I still think native-born citizens of the United States should have as much protection, as many privileges in their native country, as those who voluntarily select it for a home. But all secret, oath-bound political parties are dangerous to any nation, no matter how pure or how patriotic the motives and principles which first bring them together. No political party can or ought to exist when one of its corner-stones is opposition to freedom of thought and to the right to worship God "according to the dictate of one's own conscience," or according to the creed of any religious denomination whatever.

---

[11] The Know-Nothing Party, officially known as the American Party, espoused anti-immigrant and anti-Catholic positions and emerged in the 1850s in the wake of the dissolution of the Whig Party. Tyler Anbinder, *Nativism and Slavery: The Northern Know Nothings and the Politics of the 1850s* (New York: Oxford University Press, 1992), 104–106.

[12] In 1854, antislavery activists founded the new Republican Party in part as a response to the Kansas-Nebraska Act. The Republicans initially attracted former Whigs, Democrats, and Free-Soil Party members, and later incorporated Know-Nothings as well. Lewis L. Gould, *Grand Old Party* (New York: Oxford University Press, 2003), 14, 17–18.

[13] Francis P. Blair Jr. (1821–1875) was born in Kentucky and moved to Missouri in 1842. He won election to Congress as a Democrat in 1856. He was very involved with Free-Soil politics in Missouri and by 1858 sought broad support, running as a "Free Democrat" and eventually winning a contentious election. By 1860, he was openly affiliated with the Republican Party. *CWHC*, 133; William E. Parrish, *Frank Blair: Lincoln's Conservative* (Columbia: University of Missouri Press, 1998), 59–64, 73; *PUSG*, 1:358*n*.

Nevertheless, if a sect sets up its laws as binding above the State laws, wherever the two come in conflict this claim must be resisted and suppressed at whatever cost.

Up to the Mexican war there were a few out and out abolitionists, men who carried their hostility to slavery into all elections, from those for a justice of the peace up to the Presidency of the United States. They were noisy but not numerous. But the great majority of people at the North, where slavery did not exist, were opposed to the institution, and looked upon its existence in any part of the country as unfortunate. They did not hold the States where slavery existed responsible for it; and believed that protection should be given to the right of property in slaves until some satisfactory way could be reached to be rid of the institution. Opposition to slavery was not a creed of either political party. In some sections more anti-slavery men belonged to the Democratic party, and in others to the Whigs. But with the inauguration of the Mexican war, in fact with the annexation of Texas, "the inevitable conflict" commenced.[14]

As the time for the Presidential election of 1856—the first at which I had the opportunity of voting—approached, party feeling began to run high. The Republican party was regarded in the South and the border States not only as opposed to the extension of slavery, but as favoring the compulsory abolition of the institution without compensation to the owners. The most horrible visions seemed to present themselves to the minds of people who, one would suppose, ought to have known better. Many educated and, otherwise, sensible persons appeared to believe that emancipation meant social equality. Treason to the Government was openly advocated and was not rebuked.[15] It was evident to my mind that the election of a Republican President in 1856 meant the secession of all the Slave States, and rebellion. Under these circumstances

[14] USG used a phrase commonly applied to the Civil War. Horace Greeley said in 1856, after the passage of the Kansas-Nebraska Act, that "conflict is inevitable" between slave and free states. Lincoln famously used the phrase to describe the war in his Annual Address to Congress on Dec. 3, 1861. Roy P. Basler, ed., *The Collected Works of Abraham Lincoln,* vol. 5 (New Brunswick, NJ: Rutgers University Press, 1959), 49; Robert C. Williams, *Horace Greeley: Champion of American Freedom* (New York: New York University Press, 2006), 173.

[15] During the presidential campaign of 1856, some Southern proslavery leaders (such as Robert Toombs and James Mason) threatened secession if the Republican candidate, John C. Frémont, won the presidency, but these threats had become commonplace in the political sphere by that point. James McPherson, *Battle Cry of Freedom* (Oxford: Oxford University Press, 2003), 158; Kenneth M. Stampp, *And the War Came: The North and the Secession Crisis, 1860–1861* (Baton Rouge: Louisiana State University Press, 1950), 5–6.

I preferred the success of a candidate whose election would prevent or post-pone secession, to seeing the country plunged into a war the end of which no man could foretell. With a Democrat elected by the unanimous vote of the Slave States, there could be no pretext for secession for four years.[16] I very much hoped that the passions of the people would subside in that time, and the catastrophe be averted altogether; if it was not, I believed the country would be better prepared to receive the shock and to resist it. I therefore voted for James Buchanan[17] for President. Four years later the Republican party was successful in electing its candidate to the Presidency. The civilized world has learned the consequence. Four millions of human beings held as chattels have been liberated; the ballot has been given to them; the free schools of the country have been opened to their children. The nation still lives, and the people are just as free to avoid social intimacy with the blacks as ever they were, or as they are with white people.

While living in Galena I was nominally only a clerk supporting myself and family on a stipulated salary. In reality my position was different. My father had never lived in Galena himself, but had established my two brothers there, the one next younger than myself in charge of the business, assisted by the youngest. When I went there it was my father's intention to give up all con-nection with the business himself, and to establish his three sons in it: but the brother who had really built up the business was sinking with consumption, and it was not thought best to make any change while he was in this condi-tion. He lived until September, 1861, when he succumbed to that insidious disease which always flatters its victims into the belief that they are growing better up to the close of life.[18] A more honorable man never transacted busi-

[16] In 1856, Republican presidential candidate John C. Frémont lost to Democratic nominee James Buchanan. Frémont received 45 percent of the popular vote in Northern states but only garnered a total of 1,196 votes in all Southern states combined. William E. Gienapp, *The Origins of the Republican Party, 1852–1856* (New York: Oxford University Press, 1987), 526.

[17] James Buchanan (1791–1868) was born in Pennsylvania and graduated from Dickinson College in 1809. He served in both houses of Congress and as a diplomat in various countries. He also served as secretary of state from 1845 to 1849 and as U.S. president from 1857 to 1861. *CWHC*, 150.

[18] In 1841, JRG entered into a partnership with Eli A. Collins of Claremont County, OH, to establish a leather goods business in Galena. In 1853, he ended the partnership and began a rival shop with his son Samuel Simpson Grant (1825–1861) as manager. As Simpson Grant's health deteriorated, USG's youngest brother, Orvil L. Grant (1835–1881), took over more of the management of the business. Simpson Grant died on Sept. 13, 1861, near St. Paul, MN. John S. Collins, *Across the Plains in 64* (Omaha, NE: National Print, 1904), 139–140; JDG, *Memoirs*, 29;

ness. In September, 1861, I was engaged in an employment which required all my attention elsewhere.[19]

During the eleven months that I lived in Galena prior to the first call for volunteers, I had been strictly attentive to my business, and had made but few acquaintances other than customers and people engaged in the same line with myself. When the election took place in November, 1860, I had not been a resident of Illinois long enough to gain citizenship and could not, therefore, vote. I was really glad of this at the time, for my pledges would have compelled me to vote for Stephen A. Douglas,[20] who had no possible chance of election. The contest was really between Mr. Breckinridge[21] and Mr. Lincoln; between minority rule and rule by the majority. I wanted, as between these candidates, to see Mr. Lincoln elected. Excitement ran high during the canvass, and torch-light processions enlivened the scene in the generally quiet streets of Galena many nights during the campaign. I did not parade with either party, but occasionally met with the "wide awakes"—Republicans—in their rooms, and superintended their drill.[22] It was evident, from the time of the Chicago nomination to the close of the canvass, that the election of the Republican candidate would be the signal for some of the Southern States to secede. I still had hopes that the four years which had elapsed since the first nomination of a Presidential candidate by a party distinctly opposed to slavery

*PUSG*, 1:350–351; 2:70*n*; Edward Chauncey Marshall, *The Ancestry of General Grant and Their Contemporaries* (New York: Sheldon, 1869), 68.

[19] In Sept. 1861, as brigadier general, USG commanded the District of Southeast Missouri. *PUSG*, 2:xxxii.

[20] Stephen A. Douglas (1813–1861) was born in Vermont and moved to Illinois, where he was admitted to the bar in 1834. As a Democrat, Douglas served in the U.S. House of Representatives and U.S. Senate before running for president in 1860. His popular sovereignty stance turned Southern Democrats against him and ended up dividing the party in the presidential election of 1860. William L. Barney, *The Oxford Encyclopedia of the Civil War* (New York: Oxford University Press, 2011), s.v. "Douglas, Stephen A."

[21] John C. Breckinridge (1821–1875) was born in Kentucky and served as vice president of the United States from 1857 to 1861. In June 1860, the southern Democrats, the "Seceders," nominated Breckinridge for president. *CWHC*, 143; Frank H. Heck, *Proud Kentuckian, John C. Breckinridge, 1821–1875* (Lexington: University Press of Kentucky, 1976), 115.

[22] Members of the diminished Know-Nothing movement formed "Wide Awake" clubs to help organize and promote Lincoln's election. They usually marched in military formation. Anbinder, *Nativism and Slavery*, 268–270; Douglas R. Egerton, *Year of Meteors: Stephen Douglas, Abraham Lincoln and the Election That Brought the Civil War* (New York: Bloomsbury Press, 2010), 182–183.

extension, had given time for the extreme pro-slavery sentiment to cool down; for the Southerners to think well before they took the awful leap which they had so vehemently threatened. But I was mistaken.

The Republican candidate was elected, and solid substantial people of the North-west, and I presume the same order of people throughout the entire North, felt very serious, but determined, after this event. It was very much discussed whether the South would carry out its threat to secede and set up a separate government, the corner-stone of which should be, protection to the "Divine" institution of slavery.[23] For there were people who believed in the "divinity" of human slavery, as there are now people who believe Mormonism and Polygamy to be ordained by the Most High. We forgive them for entertaining such notions, but forbid their practice. It was generally believed that there would be a flurry; that some of the extreme Southern States would go so far as to pass ordinances of secession. But the common impression was that this step was so plainly suicidal for the South, that the movement would not spread over much of the territory and would not last long.

Doubtless the founders of our government, the majority of them at least, regarded the confederation of the colonies as an experiment. Each colony considered itself a separate government; that the confederation was for mutual protection against a foreign foe, and the prevention of strife and war among themselves. If there had been a desire on the part of any single State to withdraw from the compact at any time while the number of States was limited to the original thirteen, I do not suppose there would have been any to contest the right, no matter how much the determination might have been regretted. The problem changed on the ratification of the Constitution by all the colonies; it changed still more when amendments were added; and if the right of any one State to withdraw continued to exist at all after the ratification of the Constitution, it certainly ceased on the formation of new States, at least so far as the new States themselves were concerned. It was never possessed at all by Florida or the States west of the Mississippi, all of which were purchased by the treasury of the entire nation. Texas and the territory brought into the Union in consequence of annexation, were purchased with both blood and treasure; and Texas, with a domain greater than that of any European state except Russia, was

---

[23] USG may have referred to Confederate vice president Alexander Stephens's famous "Cornerstone Speech," which declared that the cornerstone of the Confederate government rested "upon the great truth, that the negro is not equal to the white man; that slavery—subordination to the superior race—is his natural and normal condition." Thomas E. Schott, *Alexander H. Stephens of Georgia: A Biography* (Baton Rouge: Louisiana State University Press, 1988), 334.

permitted to retain as state property all the public lands within its borders. It would have been ingratitude and injustice of the most flagrant sort for this State to withdraw from the Union after all that had been spent and done to introduce her; yet, if separation had actually occurred, Texas must necessarily have gone with the South, both on account of her institutions and her geographical position. Secession was illogical as well as impracticable; it was revolution.

Now, the right of revolution is an inherent one. When people are oppressed by their government, it is a natural right they enjoy to relieve themselves of the oppression, if they are strong enough, either by withdrawal from it, or by overthrowing it and substituting a government more acceptable. But any people or part of a people who resort to this remedy, stake their lives, their property, and every claim for protection given by citizenship—on the issue. Victory, or the conditions imposed by the conqueror—must be the result.

In the case of the war between the States it would have been the exact truth if the South had said,—"We do not want to live with you Northern people any longer; we know our institution of slavery is obnoxious to you, and, as you are growing numerically stronger than we, it may at some time in the future be endangered. So long as you permitted us to control the government, and with the aid of a few friends at the North to enact laws constituting your section a guard against the escape of our property, we were willing to live with you. You have been submissive to our rule heretofore; but it looks now as if you did not intend to continue so, and we will remain in the Union no longer." Instead of this the seceding States cried lustily,—"Let us alone; you have no constitutional power to interfere with us." Newspapers and people at the North reiterated the cry. Individuals might ignore the constitution; but the Nation itself must not only obey it, but must enforce the strictest construction of that instrument; the construction put upon it by the Southerners themselves. The fact is the constitution did not apply to any such contingency as the one existing from 1861 to 1865. Its framers never dreamed of such a contingency occurring. If they had foreseen it, the probabilities are they would have sanctioned the right of a State or States to withdraw rather than that there should be war between brothers.[24]

---

[24] The topic of secession arose during the ratification of the Constitution. The issue was debated most extensively in the New York ratification convention in 1788, where some insisted that the state should reserve the right to leave the Union. In response, Alexander Hamilton and John Jay insisted that the Union was permanent. Akhil R. Amar, *America's Constitution* (New York: Random House, 2012), 37–38.

The framers were wise in their generation and wanted to do the very best possible to secure their own liberty and independence, and that also of their descendants to the latest days. It is preposterous to suppose that the people of one generation can lay down the best and only rules of government for all who are to come after them, and under unforeseen contingencies. At the time of the framing of our constitution the only physical forces that had been subdued and made to serve man and do his labor, were the currents in the streams and in the air we breathe. Rude machinery, propelled by water power, had been invented; sails to propel ships upon the waters had been set to catch the passing breeze—but the application of steam to propel vessels against both wind and current, and machinery to do all manner of work had not been thought of. The instantaneous transmission of messages around the world by means of electricity would probably at that day have been attributed to witch-craft or a league with the Devil. Immaterial circumstances had changed as greatly as material ones. We could not and ought not to be rigidly bound by the rules laid down under circumstances so different for emergencies so utterly unanticipated. The fathers themselves would have been the first to declare that their prerogatives were not irrevocable. They would surely have resisted secession could they have lived to see the shape it assumed.

I travelled through the Northwest considerably during the winter of 1860–1. We had customers in all the little towns in south-west Wisconsin, south-east Minnesota and north-east Iowa. These generally knew I had been a captain in the regular army and had served through the Mexican war. Consequently wherever I stopped at night, some of the people would come to the public-house where I was, and sit till a late hour discussing the probabilities of the future. My own views at that time were like those officially expressed by Mr. Seward[25] at a later day, that "the war would be over in ninety days."[26] I

[25] William H. Seward (1801–1872) was born in New York and graduated from Union College in 1820. He served as governor of New York from 1839 to 1843 and as a U.S. senator from New York from 1849 to 1861. He was the favorite for the Republican nomination but lost. Lincoln appointed him secretary of state in Mar. 1861. *CWHC,* 479; Harold Holzer, *Lincoln, President-Elect: Abraham Lincoln and the Great Secession Winter, 1860–1861* (New York: Simon and Schuster, 2008), 102–103.

[26] On Nov. 30, 1861, Seward made his estimation about the war's duration in a letter to Charles F. Adams, U.S. Minister to Great Britain. *Correspondence concerning Claims against Great Britain, Transmitted to the Senate of the United States in Answer to the Resolutions of December 4 and 10, 1867, and of May 27, 1868,* vol. 1 (Washington, DC: Government Printing Office, 1869), 396.

continued to entertain these views until after the battle of Shiloh. I believe now that there would have been no more battles at the West after the capture of Fort Donelson if all the troops in that region had been under a single commander who would have followed up that victory.[27]

There is little doubt in my mind now that the prevailing sentiment of the South would have been opposed to secession in 1860 and 1861, if there had been a fair and calm expression of opinion, unbiased by threats, and if the ballot of one legal voter had counted for as much as that of any other. But there was no calm discussion of the question. Demagogues who were too old to enter the army if there should be a war, others who entertained so high an opinion of their own ability that they did not believe they could be spared from the direction of the affairs of state in such an event, declaimed vehemently and unceasingly against the North; against its aggressions upon the South; its interference with Southern rights, etc., etc. They denounced the Northerners as cowards, poltroons, negro-worshippers; claimed that one Southern man was equal to five Northern men in battle; that if the South would stand up for its rights the North would back down. Mr. Jefferson Davis said in a speech, delivered at La Grange, Mississippi, before the secession of that State, that he would agree to drink all the blood spilled south of Mason and Dixon's line if there should be a war.[28] The young men who would have the fighting to do in case of war, believed all these statements, both in regard to the aggressiveness of the North and its cowardice. They, too, cried out for a separation from such people. The great bulk of the legal voters of the South were men who owned no slaves; their homes were generally in the hills and poor country; their facilities for educating their children, even up to the point of reading and writing, were very limited; their interest in the contest was very meagre— what there was, if they had been capable of seeing it, was with the North; they too needed emancipation. Under the old régime they were looked down upon by those who controlled all the affairs in the interest of slave-owners, as

[27] The U.S. Army commander in the West in 1862 was Henry W. Halleck. Jean Edward Smith, *Grant* (New York: Simon and Schuster, 2001), 134.

[28] Davis spoke at LaGrange, GA, on Feb. 16, 1861. However, the Charleston *Daily Courier* in Oct. 1863 attributed this quotation to former U.S. senator James Chesnut, one of Davis's primary advisers and a senator in the Confederate congress. E. Merton Coulter, *The Confederate States of America, 1861–1865* (Baton Rouge: Louisiana State University Press, 1950), 15; Jefferson Davis, *The Papers of Jefferson Davis*, vol. 7, ed. Lynda L. Crist and Mary S. Dix (Baton Rouge: Louisiana State University Press, 1992), xl, 386.

poor white trash who were allowed the ballot so long as they cast it according to direction.

I am aware that this last statement may be disputed and individual testimony perhaps adduced to show that in ante-bellum days the ballot was as untrammelled in the South as in any section of the country; but in the face of any such contradiction I reassert the statement. The shot-gun was not resorted to. Masked men did not ride over the country at night intimidating voters; but there was a firm feeling that a class existed in every State with a sort of divine right to control public affairs. If they could not get this control by one means they must by another. The end justified the means. The coercion, if mild, was complete.

There were two political parties, it is true, in all the States, both strong in numbers and respectability, but both equally loyal to the institution which stood paramount in Southern eyes to all other institutions in state or nation. The slave-owners were the minority, but governed both parties. Had politics ever divided the slave-holders and the non-slave-holders, the majority would have been obliged to yield, or internecine war would have been the consequence. I do not know that the Southern people were to blame for this condition of affairs. There was a time when slavery was not profitable, and the discussion of the merits of the institution was confined almost exclusively to the territory where it existed. The States of Virginia and Kentucky came near abolishing slavery by their own acts, one State defeating the measure by a tie vote and the other only lacking one.[29] But when the institution became profitable, all talk of its abolition ceased where it existed; and naturally, as human nature is constituted, arguments were adduced in its support. The cotton-gin probably had much to do with the justification of slavery.

The winter of 1860–1 will be remembered by middle-aged people of to-day as one of great excitement. South Carolina promptly seceded after the result of the Presidential election was known. Other Southern States proposed to follow. In some of them the Union sentiment was so strong that it had to be suppressed by force.[30] Maryland, Delaware, Kentucky and Missouri, all Slave

[29] An apparent reference to a popular legend about the debate regarding emancipation that occurred in Virginia in 1832 as well as debates in Kentucky that occurred in 1792, 1799, or 1849. There is no evidence to support assertions that the emancipation measures in each state failed in close votes. USG, *Personal Memoirs of U. S. Grant*, ed. E. B. Long (New York: Da Capo, 1985), 113n; USG, *Personal Memoirs of U. S. Grant*, ed. William S. McFeely (New York: Library of America, 1990), 1175n.

[30] On Dec. 20, 1860, a convention organized by the South Carolina legislature in Charleston adopted an Ordinance of Secession. Mississippi, Florida, Alabama, Georgia, and Louisiana

States, failed to pass ordinances of secession; but they were all represented in the so-called congress of the so-called Confederate States. The Governor and Lieutenant-Governor of Missouri, in 1861, Jackson[31] and Reynolds,[32] were both supporters of the rebellion and took refuge with the enemy. The governor soon died, and the lieutenant-governor assumed his office; issued proclamations as governor of the State; was recognized as such by the Confederate Government, and continued his pretensions until the collapse of the rebellion. The South claimed the sovereignty of States, but claimed the right to coerce into their confederation such States as they wanted, that is, all the States where slavery existed. They did not seem to think this course inconsistent. The fact is, the Southern slave-owners believed that, in some way, the ownership of slaves conferred a sort of patent of nobility—a right to govern independent of the interest or wishes of those who did not hold such property. They convinced themselves, first, of the divine origin of the institution and, next, that that particular institution was not safe in the hands of any body of legislators but themselves.

Meanwhile the Administration of President Buchanan looked helplessly on and proclaimed that the general government had no power to interfere; that the Nation had no power to save its own life. Mr. Buchanan had in his cabinet two members at least, who were as earnest—to use a mild term—in the cause of secession as Mr. Davis or any Southern statesman. One of them, Floyd, the Secretary of War, scattered the army so that much of it could be captured when hostilities should commence, and distributed the cannon and small arms from Northern arsenals throughout the South so as to be on hand when treason

had seceded by the end of Jan. 1861. Specific instances of violence against pro-Union Southerners included lynchings in Mississippi and physical attacks by so-called Regulators in Florida. Coulter, *Confederate States*, 1–2; David Williams, *Bitterly Divided: The South's Inner Civil War* (New York: New Press, 2008), 11.

[31] Claiborne F. Jackson (c.1806–1862) was born in Kentucky and moved to Missouri in 1825. Jackson served as the Confederate governor of Missouri from Jan. 1861 until his death from cancer in Dec. 1862. *CWHC*, 314.

[32] Thomas C. Reynolds (1821–1887) was born in South Carolina and moved to Missouri in 1849. He served as a Missouri legislator before the Civil War and was lieutenant governor of Missouri from 1861 to 1862. Reynolds was the Confederate governor of Missouri from Dec. 1862 to May 1865 and worked with the Confederate government on matters in the Trans-Mississippi Dept. Missouri remained in Union hands, leaving Reynolds with little control over his state. Albert Castel, *General Sterling Price and the Civil War in the West* (Baton Rouge: Louisiana State University Press, 1968), 164–165; *CWHC*, 451.

wanted them.[33] The navy was scattered in like manner.[34] The President did not prevent his cabinet preparing for war upon their government, either by destroying its resources or storing them in the South until a de facto government was established with Jefferson Davis as its President, and Montgomery, Alabama, as the Capital. The secessionists had then to leave the cabinet.[35] In their own estimation they were aliens in the country which had given them birth. Loyal men were put into their places. Treason in the executive branch of the government was estopped. But the harm had already been done. The stable door was locked after the horse had been stolen.

During all of the trying winter of 1860–1, when the Southerners were so defiant that they would not allow within their borders the expression of a sentiment hostile to their views, it was a brave man indeed who could stand up and proclaim his loyalty to the Union. On the other hand men at the North—prominent men—proclaimed that the government had no power to coerce the South into submission to the laws of the land; that if the North undertook to raise armies to go south, these armies would have to march over the dead bodies of the speakers.[36] A portion of the press of the North was con-

[33] John B. Floyd (1806–1863) was born in Virginia and served as governor from 1849 to 1852. He served as U.S. secretary of war from Mar. 1857 to Dec. 1860. He resigned amid allegations of corruption and treason. No charges against him came from the investigation of the allegations, but he was widely considered a traitor in the North. He was hailed as a hero in the South and on May 23, 1861, he joined the Confederate Army as a brigadier general. However, Jefferson Davis removed him from command in 1862 after he abandoned Fort Donelson. He died from an unspecified illness. John M. Belohavek, "The Politics of Scandal: A Reassessment of John B. Floyd as Secretary of War, 1857–1861," *West Virginia History* 31 (1969–1970): 145–160; Edward S. Cooper, *Traitors: The Secession Period, November 1860–July 1861* (Madison-Teaneck, NJ: Fairleigh Dickinson University Press, 2008), 37–40; *CWHC,* 237.

[34] Isaac Toucey, Buchanan's secretary of the navy, was criticized for not taking action to enhance the readiness of the U.S. Navy for the looming conflict. He allowed U.S. naval vessels to set out on long-distance voyages instead of concentrating them in preparation for combat. He was also criticized and censured by Congress for quickly accepting resignations of Southern-sympathizing officers. During the Civil War, he returned to his native Connecticut and supported the U.S. war effort. *Congressional Globe,* 36th Congress, 2nd Session, 1095–1096 (1861); Harold D. Langley, "Isaac Toucey," in *American Secretaries of the Navy,* ed. Paolo E. Coletta (Annapolis, MD: Naval Institute Press, 1980), 1:303–318.

[35] In addition to Floyd, Howell Cobb (1815–1868), Buchanan's secretary of the treasury, resigned in Dec. 1860. He then presided as the president of the Confederate Provisional Congress and served as a brigadier general in the Confederate Army. *CWHC,* 178.

[36] Prominent Democratic leaders in the North, such as Horatio Seymour, Samuel Tilden, and George Bancroft, openly expressed support for the idea that the Southern states had the

stantly proclaiming similar views. When the time arrived for the President-
elect to go to the capital of the Nation to be sworn into office, it was deemed
unsafe for him to travel, not only as a President-elect, but as any private citizen should be allowed to do. Instead of going in a special car, receiving the
good wishes of his constituents at all the stations along the road, he was obliged
to stop on the way and to be smuggled into the capital. He disappeared from
public view on his journey, and the next the country knew, his arrival was announced at the capital. There is little doubt that he would have been assassinated if he had attempted to travel openly throughout his journey.[37]

---

right to secede and the federal government could not compel them to remain part of the Union.
Russell McClintock, *Lincoln and the Decision for War: The Northern Response to Secession* (Chapel
Hill: University of North Carolina Press, 2008), 220.

[37] After the discovery of a threat to assassinate Lincoln in Baltimore, the president-elect
boarded a train in Harrisburg, PA, on Feb. 22, 1861. The next day, Lincoln traveled through
Baltimore to Washington, DC, undetected. Holzer, *Lincoln, President-Elect,* 382, 388, 392–393.

# 17

## Outbreak of the Rebellion—Presiding at a Union Meeting—Mustering Officer of State Troops—Lyon at Camp Jackson—Services Tendered to the Government

T HE 4TH OF MARCH, 1861, came, and Abraham Lincoln was sworn to maintain the Union against all its enemies. The secession of one State after another followed, until eleven had gone out. On the 11th of April Fort Sumter, a National fort in the harbor of Charleston, South Carolina, was fired upon by the Southerners and a few days after was captured.[1] The Confederates proclaimed themselves aliens, and thereby debarred themselves of all right to claim protection under the Constitution of the United States. We did not admit the fact that they were aliens, but all the same, they debarred themselves of the right to expect better treatment than people of any other foreign state who make war upon an independent nation. Upon the firing on Sumter President Lincoln issued his first call for troops and soon after a proclamation convening Congress in extra session.[2] The call was for 75,000 volunteers for ninety days' service. If the shot fired at Fort Sumter "was heard around the world," the call of the President for 75,000 men was heard throughout the Northern States.[3] There was not a state in the North of a million of inhabit-

---

[1] On Apr. 14, 1861, Maj. Robert Anderson surrendered Fort Sumter after thirty-four hours of shelling by Confederate forces. Spencer Tucker, ed., *American Civil War: The Definitive Encyclopedia and Document Collection* (Santa Barbara, CA: ABC-CLIO, 2013), s.v. "Fort Sumter, South Carolina, Confederate Bombardment of."

[2] Lincoln issued the proclamation calling for troops on Apr. 15, 1861, and the extra session of Congress began on July 4. Chester G. Hearn, *Lincoln, the Cabinet, and the Generals* (Baton Rouge: Louisiana State University Press, 2010), 62.

[3] USG alluded to Ralph Waldo Emerson's poem "Concord Hymn: Sung at the Completion of the Battle Monument, Apr. 19, 1837," which contains the line "And fired the shot heard round the world," referring to the first shot of the American Revolution. Tiffany K. Wayne,

ants that would not have furnished the entire number faster than arms could have been supplied to them, if it had been necessary.

As soon as the news of the call for volunteers reached Galena, posters were stuck up calling for a meeting of the citizens at the court-house in the evening. Business ceased entirely; all was excitement; for a time there were no party distinctions; all were Union men, determined to avenge the insult to the national flag. In the evening the court-house was packed. Although a comparative stranger I was called upon to preside; the sole reason, possibly, was that I had been in the army and had seen service.[4] With much embarrassment and some prompting I made out to announce the object of the meeting. Speeches were in order, but it is doubtful whether it would have been safe just then to make other than patriotic ones. There was probably no one in the house, however, who felt like making any other. The two principal speeches were by B. B. Howard, the post-master and a Breckinridge Democrat at the November election the fall before,[5] and John A. Rawlins,[6] an elector on the Douglas ticket. E. B. Washburne,[7] with whom I was not acquainted at that time, came in after the meeting had been organized, and expressed, I understood afterwards, a little surprise that Galena could not furnish a presiding officer for such an occasion without taking a stranger. He came forward and was introduced, and made a speech appealing to the patriotism of the meeting.

After the speaking was over volunteers were called for to form a company. The quota of Illinois had been fixed at six regiments; and it was supposed that one company would be as much as would be accepted from Galena. The

---

ed., *Encyclopedia of Transcendentalism* (New York: Facts on File, 2006), s.v. "Concord Hymn, Ralph Waldo Emerson, 1837."

[4] The meeting occurred on Apr. 16, 1861. *PUSG,* 2:7n.

[5] Bushrod B. Howard (c.1821–1861), a veteran of the Mexican-American War and the post-master of Galena, IL, oversaw the formation of a company of the 19th Illinois Inf. He was killed in a train accident in Sept. 1861. Stephen Chicoine, *John Basil Turchin and the Fight to Free the Slaves* (Westport, CT: Praeger, 2003), 27–28.

[6] John A. Rawlins (1831–1869) was born in Galena and worked as a farmer and lawyer prior to the Civil War. He went on to serve on USG's staff throughout the war as a trusted adviser. He served as U.S. secretary of war during the first six months of USG's presidency until he died of tuberculosis in Sept. 1869. *CWHC,* 447.

[7] Elihu B. Washburne (1816–1887) was born in Maine and moved to Galena in 1840. A long-serving member of the U.S. Congress and a Radical Republican, he was a close friend and ally of both Lincoln and USG. During USG's presidency, Washburne served as U.S. secretary of state for five days before resigning to become the U.S. minister to France. Tucker, *American Civil War,* s.v. "Washburne, Elihu."

company was raised and the officers and non-commissioned officers elected before the meeting adjourned.[8] I declined the captaincy before the balloting, but announced that I would aid the company in every way I could and would be found in the service in some position if there should be a war. I never went into our leather store after that meeting, to put up a package or do other business.

The ladies of Galena were quite as patriotic as the men. They could not enlist, but they conceived the idea of sending their first company to the field uniformed. They came to me to get a description of the United States uniform for infantry; subscribed and bought the material; procured tailors to cut out the garments, and the ladies made them up.[9] In a few days the company was in uniform and ready to report at the State capital for assignment. The men all turned out the morning after their enlistment, and I took charge, divided them into squads and superintended their drill. When they were ready to go to Springfield I went with them and remained there until they were assigned to a regiment.[10]

There were so many more volunteers than had been called for that the question whom to accept was quite embarrassing to the governor, Richard Yates.[11] The legislature was in session at the time, however, and came to his relief. A law was enacted authorizing the governor to accept the services of ten additional regiments, one from each congressional district, for one month, to be paid by the State, but pledged to go into the service of the United States if there should be a further call during their term.[12] Even with this relief the governor was still very much embarrassed. Before the war was over he was like

[8]The company, known as the Jo Daviess Guards, was not actually raised until two days later during a separate meeting, when twenty-two men volunteered. By Apr. 20, 1861, the company had grown to eighty men and had elected its officers. Augustus Chetlain was elected as the company's captain. *PUSG*, 2:8n.

[9]The Galena banking firm of N. Corwith and Co. paid for the cloth used to make the uniforms. Ibid., 2:7n.

[10]On Apr. 25, 1861, USG accompanied the Jo Daviess Guards to Camp Yates, located on the perimeter of Springfield, IL. Ibid., 2:11n.

[11]Richard Yates (1818–1873) was born in Kentucky and moved to Illinois in 1831. He served as governor of Illinois from 1861 to 1865. He was informed on Apr. 29, 1861, that the state had filled its quota of six regiments and that there were an additional 2,380 volunteers waiting at Camp Yates. *CWHC*, 584; *PUSG*, 2:11n.

[12]On May 2, 1861, the Illinois legislature passed two laws: one provided the volunteers with pay, and the other authorized the governor to accept ten regiments of infantry and one battalion of light artillery. *PUSG*, 2:11n.

the President when he was taken with the varioloid: "at last he had something he could give to all who wanted it."[13]

In time the Galena company was mustered into the United States service, forming a part of the 11th Illinois volunteer infantry.[14] My duties, I thought, had ended at Springfield, and I was prepared to start home by the evening train, leaving at nine o'clock. Up to that time I do not think I had been introduced to Governor Yates, or had ever spoken to him. I knew him by sight, however, because he was living at the same hotel and I often saw him at table. The evening I was to quit the capital I left the supper room before the governor and was standing at the front door when he came out. He spoke to me, calling me by my old army title "Captain," and said he understood that I was about leaving the city. I answered that I was. He said he would be glad if I would remain over-night and call at the Executive office the next morning. I complied with his request, and was asked to go into the Adjutant-General's office and render such assistance as I could, the governor saying that my army experience would be of great service there. I accepted the proposition.[15]

My old army experience I found indeed of very great service. I was no clerk, nor had I any capacity to become one. The only place I ever found in my life to put a paper so as to find it again was either a side coat-pocket or the hands of a clerk or secretary more careful than myself. But I had been quartermaster, commissary and adjutant in the field. The army forms were familiar to me and I could direct how they should be made out. There was a clerk in the office of the Adjutant-General who supplied my deficiencies.[16] The ease with which the State of Illinois settled its accounts with the government at the close of the war is evidence of the efficiency of Mr. Loomis[17] as an accountant on a large scale. He remained in the office until that time.

[13] USG referenced a quotation attributed to Lincoln by Dr. W. C. Van Bibber while Lincoln was suffering from a mild form of smallpox in 1863. Describing how the crowds who came to seek favors from him as president would be susceptible to catching the disease, Lincoln stated, "For once in my life as President, I find myself in a position to give everybody something!" Armond S. Goldman and Frank C. Schmalstieg Jr., "Abraham Lincoln's Gettysburg Illness," *Journal of Medical Biography* 15 (2007): 106.

[14] By May 15, 1861, the Jo Daviess Guards were a part of the 12th Illinois Inf., Co. F. *PUSG*, 2:32*n*.

[15] On Apr. 29, 1861, USG became an aide to Yates and submitted a report to him on the condition of the state's armory, which Yates then provided to the legislature. Ibid., 2:12–13, 15*n*.

[16] M. A. T. McHugh, Chauncey Miller, Benjamin F. Johnson, Robert B. Nay, and John Belser were clerks working in the AGO during USG's time there. Ibid., 2:17*n*.

[17] John S. Loomis (1835–1887) was born in Indiana and served in the Illinois AGO as assistant adjutant general and aide to Yates throughout the war, reaching the rank of colonel.

As I have stated, the legislature authorized the governor to accept the services of ten additional regiments. I had charge of mustering these regiments into the State service.[18] They were assembled at the most convenient railroad centres in their respective congressional districts. I detailed officers to muster in a portion of them, but mustered three in the southern part of the State myself. One of these was to assemble at Belleville, some eighteen miles south-east of St. Louis. When I got there I found that only one or two companies had arrived. There was no probability of the regiment coming together under five days. This gave me a few idle days which I concluded to spend in St. Louis.[19]

There was a considerable force of State militia at Camp Jackson, on the outskirts of St. Louis, at the time. There is but little doubt that it was the design of Governor Claiborn Jackson to have these troops ready to seize the United States arsenal and the city of St. Louis. Why they did not do so I do not know.[20] There was but a small garrison, two companies I think, under Captain N. Lyon[21] at the arsenal, and but for the timely services of the Hon. F. P. Blair, I have little doubt that St. Louis would have gone into rebel hands, and with it the arsenal with all its arms and ammunition.

Blair was a leader among the Union men of St. Louis in 1861. There was no State government in Missouri at the time that would sanction the raising of troops or commissioned officers to protect United States property, but Blair had probably procured some form of authority from the President to raise troops in Missouri and to muster them into the service of the United States.[22] At all events, he did raise a regiment and took command himself as Colonel. With this

Elisha S. Loomis, *Descendants of Joseph Loomis in America, and His Antecedents in the Old World* (Berea, OH: E. S. Loomis, 1909), 591; *PUSG,* 2:17n.

[18] On May 8, 1861, Asst. AG J. B. Wyman of Illinois issued Gen. Orders No. 52, instructing USG to muster in companies in the 7th, 8th, and 9th Congressional Districts. *PUSG,* 2:25n.

[19] On May 9, 1861, in Mattoon, IL, soldiers from the 7th Congressional District were not ready to be mustered into service. On May 11, when USG first arrived in Belleville, troops from the 8th Congressional District were ready to be mustered into state service. Ibid., 2:25–26, 25n.

[20] On May 3, 1861, Jackson ordered troops into camps, with Camp Jackson being established on the western edge of St. Louis. He ordered Brig. Gen. Daniel M. Frost to seize the U.S. arsenal to assist in the secession of Missouri. Lawrence O. Christensen et al., eds., *Dictionary of Missouri Biography* (Columbia: University of Missouri Press, 1999), 423–425; *PUSG,* 2:29n.

[21] Nathaniel Lyon (1818–1861) was born in Connecticut and graduated from the USMA in 1841. He was promoted to captain in June 1851. He was promoted to commanding general, Army of the West, in July 1861. *CWHC,* 357.

[22] On Apr. 20, 1861, Blair had received permission from U.S. secretary of war Simon Cameron to activate the Union Home Guards. In addition, Lyon had received permission from Lincoln on Apr. 30 to enlist a maximum of 10,000 troops and declare martial law if necessary.

force he reported to Captain Lyon and placed himself and regiment under his orders. It was whispered that Lyon thus reinforced intended to break up Camp Jackson and capture the militia. I went down to the arsenal in the morning to see the troops start out. I had known Lyon for two years at West Point and in the old army afterwards. Blair I knew very well by sight. I had heard him speak in the canvass of 1858, possibly several times, but I had never spoken to him. As the troops marched out of the enclosure around the arsenal, Blair was on his horse outside forming them into line preparatory to their march. I introduced myself to him and had a few moments' conversation and expressed my sympathy with his purpose. This was my first personal acquaintance with the Honorable— afterwards Major-General F. P. Blair. Camp Jackson surrendered without a fight and the garrison was marched down to the arsenal as prisoners of war.[23]

Up to this time the enemies of the government in St. Louis had been bold and defiant, while Union men were quiet but determined. The enemies had their head-quarters in a central and public position on Pine Street, near Fifth— from which the rebel flag was flaunted boldly.[24] The Union men had a place of meeting somewhere in the city, I did not know where, and I doubt whether they dared to enrage the enemies of the government by placing the national flag outside their head-quarters.[25] As soon as the news of the capture of Camp Jackson reached the city the condition of affairs was changed. Union men became rampant, aggressive, and, if you will, intolerant. They proclaimed their sentiments boldly, and were impatient at anything like disrespect for the Union. The secessionists became quiet but were filled with suppressed rage.[26] They had been playing the bully. The Union men ordered the rebel flag taken down from the building on Pine Street. The command was given in tones of authority and it was taken down, never to be raised again in St. Louis.

I witnessed the scene. I had heard of the surrender of the camp and that the garrison was on its way to the arsenal. I had seen the troops start out in

OR, I, 1, 675; William E. Parrish, *Frank Blair: Lincoln's Conservative* (Columbia: University of Missouri Press, 1998), 96.

[23] Lyon's forces captured the Missouri militia at Camp Jackson on May 10, 1861. *PUSG,* 2:29n.

[24] Prosecession forces were headquartered at the mansion formerly owned by Bartholomew Berthold. Louis S. Gerteis, *Civil War St. Louis* (Lawrence: University Press of Kansas, 2001), 73, 87, 112.

[25] One of the most prominent groups of Union supporters was headquartered at Turner Hall on 10th and Walnut Streets. Robert J. Rombauer, *The Union Cause in St. Louis in 1861: An Historical Sketch* (St. Louis: Nixon-Jones, 1909), 192, 441.

[26] A riot broke out as the militia members were being marched to the arsenal, resulting in twenty-eight deaths. *PUSG,* 2:29n.

the morning and had wished them success. I now determined to go to the arsenal and await their arrival and congratulate them. I stepped on a car standing at the corner of 4th and Pine streets, and saw a crowd of people standing quietly in front of the head-quarters, who were there for the purpose of hauling down the flag. There were squads of other people at intervals down the street. They too were quiet but filled with suppressed rage, and muttered their resentment at the insult to, what they called, "their" flag.[27] Before the car I was in had started, a dapper little fellow—he would be called a dude at this day—stepped in. He was in a great state of excitement and used adjectives freely to express his contempt for the Union and for those who had just perpetrated such an outrage upon the rights of a free people. There was only one other passenger in the car besides myself when this young man entered. He evidently expected to find nothing but sympathy when he got away from the "mud sills" engaged in compelling a "free people" to pull down a flag they adored. He turned to me saying: "Things have come to a —— pretty pass when a free people can't choose their own flag. Where I came from if a man dares to say a word in favor of the Union we hang him to a limb of the first tree we come to." I replied that "after all we were not so intolerant in St. Louis as we might be; I had not seen a single rebel hung yet, nor heard of one; there were plenty of them who ought to be, however." The young man subsided. He was so crestfallen that I believe if I had ordered him to leave the car he would have gone quietly out, saying to himself: "More Yankee oppression."

By nightfall the late defenders of Camp Jackson were all within the walls of the St. Louis arsenal, prisoners of war. The next day I left St. Louis for Mattoon, Illinois, where I was to muster in the regiment from that congressional district. This was the 21st Illinois infantry, the regiment of which I subsequently became colonel. I mustered one regiment afterwards, when my services for the State were about closed.[28]

Brigadier-General John Pope[29] was stationed at Springfield, as United States mustering officer, all the time I was in the State service. He was a native of Illi-

[27] In reaction to the fall of Camp Jackson and growing violence between secessionists and German immigrants, many Confederate sympathizers left the city or concealed their loyalties. The influence of the secessionists sparked violence on May 11, 1861, and sporadic fighting in the days afterward. Gerteis, *Civil War St. Louis,* 73, 87, 110–120, 141.

[28] By May 15, 1861, USG was in a camp near Mattoon where he organized the 7th Congressional District troops. On June 28, they became the 21st Illinois Inf. *PUSG,* 2:30–31, 53–54.

[29] John Pope (1822–1892) graduated from the USMA in 1842 and was brevetted captain for his service at the Battle of Buena Vista during the Mexican-American War. After the firing on

nois and well acquainted with most of the prominent men in the State. I was a carpet-bagger and knew but few of them. While I was on duty at Springfield the senators, representatives in Congress, ex-governors and the State legislators were nearly all at the State capital. The only acquaintance I made among them was with the governor, whom I was serving, and, by chance, with Senator S. A. Douglas. The only members of Congress I knew were Washburne and Philip Foulk.[30] With the former, though he represented my district and we were citizens of the same town, I only became acquainted at the meeting when the first company of Galena volunteers was raised. Foulk I had known in St. Louis when I was a citizen of that city. I had been three years at West Point with Pope and had served with him a short time during the Mexican war, under General Taylor. I saw a good deal of him during my service with the State. On one occasion he said to me that I ought to go into the United States service. I told him I intended to do so if there was a war. He spoke of his acquaintance with the public men of the State, and said he could get them to recommend me for a position and that he would do all he could for me. I declined to receive endorsement for permission to fight for my country.

Going home for a day or two soon after this conversation with General Pope, I wrote from Galena the following letter to the Adjutant-General of the Army.

GALENA, ILLINOIS,
*May* 24, 1861.

COL. L. THOMAS,[31]
Adjt. Gen. U. S. A.,
Washington, D. C.
    SIR:—Having served for fifteen years in the regular army, including four years at West Point, and feeling it the duty of every one who has

Fort Sumter, Captain Pope took a leave of absence from the U.S. Army and received Lincoln's approval to go to Illinois, where Yates placed him in charge of organizing and mustering the state's volunteer forces. Peter Cozzens, *General John Pope: A Life for the Nation* (Urbana: University of Illinois Press, 2000), 31–32; *CWHC,* 433–434.

[30] Philip B. Fouke (1818–1876) served as a U.S. representative from Illinois from 1859 to 1863. He served as a colonel in the 30th Illinois Inf. and was wounded at the Battle of Belmont. John T. Hubbell et al., eds., *Biographical Dictionary of the Union: Northern Leaders of the Civil War* (Westport, CT: Greenwood Press, 1995), 183–184.

[31] Lorenzo Thomas (1804–1875) was born in Delaware and graduated from the USMA in 1823. He served as AG from 1861–1869. *CWHC,* 528.

been educated at the Government expense to offer their services for the support of that Government, I have the honor, very respectfully, to tender my services, until the close of the war, in such capacity as may be offered. I would say, in view of my present age and length of service, I feel myself competent to command a regiment, if the President, in his judgment, should see fit to intrust one to me.

Since the first call of the President I have been serving on the staff of the Governor of this State, rendering such aid as I could in the organization of our State militia, and am still engaged in that capacity. A letter addressed to me at Springfield, Illinois, will reach me.

I am very respectfully,
Your obt. svt.,
U. S. GRANT.

This letter failed to elicit an answer from the Adjutant-General of the Army. I presume it was hardly read by him, and certainly it could not have been submitted to higher authority. Subsequent to the war General Badeau[32] having heard of this letter applied to the War Department for a copy of it. The letter could not be found and no one recollected ever having seen it. I took no copy when it was written. Long after the application of General Badeau, General Townsend,[33] who had become Adjutant-General of the Army, while packing up papers preparatory to the removal of his office, found this letter in some

[32] Adam Badeau (1831–1895) was born in New York and was a writer before the outbreak of the Civil War. During the war, he served as aide-de-camp and military secretary for USG. After the war, he was president of the Relief Commission to Richmond. He went on to serve as U.S. consul general in England from 1870 to 1881 and in Cuba from 1882 to 1884. His relationship with USG dissolved during the writing of USG's *Personal Memoirs* because Badeau believed he deserved more compensation and credit for his work on the project. In 1888, after USG's death, Badeau sued JDG. He won the suit and received the original compensation he was promised, but was legally required to say that the composition of the *Personal Memoirs* "was entirely that of Gen. Grant, and to limit his claim to that of suggestion, revision, and verification." Ibid., 111–112; Charles Bracelen Flood, *Grant's Final Victory* (Cambridge, MA: Da Capo, 2011), 174.

[33] Edward D. Townsend (1817–1893) was born in Massachusetts and graduated from the USMA in 1837. After the Civil War, he served as acting U.S. secretary of war from May to June 1868. He became adjutant general of the U.S. Army in 1869. *CWHC*, 534.

out-of-the-way place. It had not been destroyed, but it had not been regularly filed away.[34]

I felt some hesitation in suggesting rank as high as the colonelcy of a regiment, feeling somewhat doubtful whether I would be equal to the position. But I had seen nearly every colonel who had been mustered in from the State of Illinois, and some from Indiana, and felt that if they could command a regiment properly, and with credit, I could also.

Having but little to do after the muster of the last of the regiments authorized by the State legislature, I asked and obtained of the governor leave of absence for a week to visit my parents in Covington, Kentucky, immediately opposite Cincinnati. General McClellan had been made a major-general and had his headquarters at Cincinnati. In reality I wanted to see him. I had known him slightly at West Point, where we served one year together, and in the Mexican war. I was in hopes that when he saw me he would offer me a position on his staff. I called on two successive days at his office but failed to see him on either occasion, and returned to Springfield.[35]

[34] On Dec. 19, 1876, Townsend made an official copy of the letter for USG. The copy here apparently came from Asst. AG Chauncey McKeever in 1884. McKeever assisted USG in the research for his *Personal Memoirs*. Ibid., 380; *PUSG*, 2:36n; 31:374n.

[35] USG arrived in Covington on June 9, 1861. In the days following, he visited McClellan's headquarters in Cincinnati. According to McClellan, he was inspecting troops in Indianapolis at the time of USG's visit, but USG claimed that he was told otherwise. The written record lacks sufficient evidence to reconcile the discrepancy between the dates of USG's visit and McClellan's absence. By June 16, Yates appointed USG to command the troops from the 7th Congressional District. USG was back in Springfield by June 17. *PUSG*, 2:xxx, 40–41, 41n–42n, 42–43, 43n.

# 18

Appointed Colonel of the 21st Illinois—Personnel of
the Regiment—General Logan—March to Missouri—
Movement against Harris at Florida, Mo.—General
Pope in Command—Stationed at Mexico, Mo.

WHILE I WAS absent from the State capital on this occasion the President's second call for troops was issued. This time it was for 300,000 men, for three years or the war.[1] This brought into the United States service all the regiments then in the State service.[2] These had elected their officers from highest to lowest and were accepted with their organizations as they were, except in two instances. A Chicago regiment, the 19th infantry, had elected a very young man to the colonelcy. When it came to taking the field the regiment asked to have another appointed colonel and the one they had previously chosen made lieutenant-colonel.[3] The 21st regiment of infantry, mustered in by me at Mattoon, refused to go into the service with the colonel of their

[1] Lincoln actually issued his second call for troops on May 3, 1861, not while USG was away from Springfield, IL, in Covington, KY, and Cincinnati, OH, in June. The call was for 42,034 volunteers for three years "unless sooner discharged," 22,714 officers and men for the regular army, and 18,000 men for the navy. Lincoln's third call for troops came in his July 4 address to Congress. In that address he called for 400,000 men; Congress responded by authorizing up to 500,000 volunteers for service of three years or the duration of the war. *OR*, III, 1, 145–146, 316, 380–381; *PUSG*, 2:xxx, 19, 40–43.

[2] Originally, the U.S. War Dept. had requested six regiments from Illinois but enlistments exceeded expectations. By Aug. 4, 1861, Illinois had twenty-two regiments. Victor Hicken, *Illinois in the Civil War* (Urbana: University of Illinois Press, 1966), 2; *Illinois Military Units in the Civil War* (Springfield: Civil War Centennial Commission of Illinois, 1962), 20–22, 39, 42.

[3] On June 17, 1861, John B. Turchin (1822–1901) replaced Joseph Scott as commander of the 19th Illinois Inf. Stephen Chicoine, *John Basil Turchin and the Fight to Free the Slaves* (Westport, CT: Praeger, 2003), 17; *CWHC*, 537.

selection in any position. While I was still absent Governor Yates appointed me colonel of this latter regiment. A few days after I was in charge of it and in camp on the fair grounds near Springfield.[4]

My regiment was composed in large part of young men of as good social position as any in their section of the State. It embraced the sons of farmers, lawyers, physicians, politicians, merchants, bankers and ministers, and some men of maturer years who had filled such positions themselves. There were also men in it who could be led astray; and the colonel, elected by the votes of the regiment, had proved to be fully capable of developing all there was in his men of recklessness. It was said that he even went so far at times as to take the guard from their posts and go with them to the village near by and make a night of it. When there came a prospect of battle the regiment wanted to have some one else to lead them. I found it very hard work for a few days to bring all the men into anything like subordination; but the great majority favored discipline, and by the application of a little regular army punishment all were reduced to as good discipline as one could ask.[5]

The ten regiments which had volunteered in the State service for thirty days, it will be remembered, had done so with a pledge to go into the National service if called upon within that time. When they volunteered the government had only called for ninety days' enlistments. Men were called now for three years or the war. They felt that this change of period released them from the obligation of re-volunteering. When I was appointed colonel, the 21st regiment was still in the State service. About the time they were to be mustered into the United States service, such of them as would go, two members of Congress from the State, McClernand[6] and Logan,[7] appeared at the capital

---

[4] On June 15, 1861, USG replaced Col. Simon S. Goode as commander of troops from the 7th Congressional District, later known as the 21st Illinois Inf. Goode had been city clerk of Decatur, IL. His behavior (which included claiming that he never slept and visiting a tavern with his men) undermined the trust of other officers and his attempts to maintain discipline of the unit. *PUSG*, 2:43*n*.

[5] USG prevented men from leaving camp without passes, punished deserters, and required officers to supervise daily drills. Ibid., 2:46–49.

[6] John A. McClernand (1812–1900) was born in Kentucky and moved to Illinois in 1816. He was U.S. representative from Illinois from 1843 to 1851 and from 1859 to 1861. On Oct. 18, 1861, he resigned from the U.S. House of Representatives after being commissioned brigadier general earlier that year. In Mar. 1862, he was promoted to major general. *CWHC*, 372.

[7] John A. Logan (1826–1886) was a U.S. representative from Illinois from 1859 to 1862 and from 1867 to 1871. In July 1861, Logan traveled with the 2nd Michigan Inf. and took part in the First Battle of Bull Run. He served as a senator from Illinois from 1871 to 1877 and from 1879

and I was introduced to them. I had never seen either of them before, but I had read a great deal about them, and particularly about Logan, in the newspapers. Both were democratic members of Congress, and Logan had been elected from the southern district of the State, where he had a majority of eighteen thousand over his Republican competitor.[8] His district had been settled originally by people from the Southern States, and at the breaking out of secession they sympathized with the South. At the first outbreak of war some of them joined the Southern army; many others were preparing to do so; others rode over the country at night denouncing the Union, and made it as necessary to guard railroad bridges over which National troops had to pass in southern Illinois, as it was in Kentucky or any of the border slave states. Logan's popularity in this district was unbounded. He knew almost enough of the people in it by their Christian names, to form an ordinary congressional district. As he went in politics, so his district was sure to go. The Republican papers had been demanding that he should announce where he stood on the questions which at that time engrossed the whole of public thought. Some were very bitter in their denunciations of his silence. Logan was not a man to be coerced into an utterance by threats. He did, however, come out in a speech before the adjournment of the special session of Congress which was convened by the President soon after his inauguration, and announced his undying loyalty and devotion to the Union.[9] But I had not happened to see that speech, so that when I first met Logan my impressions were those formed from reading denunciations of him. McClernand, on the other hand, had early taken strong grounds for the maintenance of the Union and had been praised accordingly by the Republican papers. The gentlemen who presented these two members of Congress asked me if I would have any objections to their addressing my regiment. I hesitated a little before answering. It was but a few days before the time set for mustering into the United States service such of the men as were willing to volunteer for three years or the war. I had some doubt as to the

to 1886 and was a Republican vice presidential candidate in 1884. Ibid., 351; James P. Jones, *Black Jack: John A. Logan and Southern Illinois in the Civil War Era* (Carbondale: Southern Illinois University Press, 1995), 96–97.

[8] In 1860, Logan had defeated his Republican opponent, David T. Linegar, for the seat representing the 9th Congressional District, polling 20,863 votes to Linegar's 5,207. Jones, *Black Jack*, 62.

[9] On Feb. 5, 1861, in a speech delivered before Congress, Logan suggested the adoption of a compromise between the states in order to preserve the Union. Gary Ecelbarger, *Black Jack Logan: An Extraordinary Life in Peace and War* (Guilford, CT: Lyon's Press, 2005), 65–66.

effect a speech from Logan might have; but as he was with McClernand, whose sentiments on the all-absorbing questions of the day were well known, I gave my consent.[10] McClernand spoke first; and Logan followed in a speech which he has hardly equalled since for force and eloquence. It breathed a loyalty and devotion to the Union which inspired my men to such a point that they would have volunteered to remain in the army as long as an enemy of the country continued to bear arms against it. They entered the United States service almost to a man.[11]

General Logan went to his part of the State and gave his attention to raising troops. The very men who at first made it necessary to guard the roads in southern Illinois became the defenders of the Union. Logan entered the service himself as colonel of a regiment and rapidly rose to the rank of major-general.[12] His district, which had promised at first to give much trouble to the government, filled every call made upon it for troops, without resorting to the draft. There was no call made when there were not more volunteers than were asked for. That congressional district stands credited at the War Department to-day with furnishing more men for the army than it was called on to supply.[13]

I remained in Springfield with my regiment until the 3d of July, when I was ordered to Quincy, Illinois. By that time the regiment was in a good state of discipline and the officers and men were well up in the company drill. There was direct railroad communication between Springfield and Quincy, but I thought it would be good preparation for the troops to march there. We had no transportation for our camp and garrison equipage, so wagons were hired for the occasion and on the 3d of July we started. There was no hurry, but fair marches were made every day until the Illinois River was crossed. There I was overtaken by a dispatch saying that the destination of the regiment had been changed to Ironton, Missouri, and ordering me to halt where I was and await the arrival of a steamer which had been dispatched up the Illinois River to

[10] An article in the June 20, 1861, *Illinois State Journal* indicated that Logan spoke to the troops on June 19. However, according to the June 25 reprint of McClernand's speech in the *Illinois State Journal*, both he and Logan addressed the troops on June 18.

[11] On June 28, 1861, the 7th Congressional District Regiment was mustered into U.S. service as the 21st Illinois Inf. *PUSG*, 2:52–53, 53n–54n.

[12] On Sept. 18, 1861, Logan became colonel of the 31st Illinois Inf. He was promoted to major general on Nov. 29, 1862. *CWHC*, 351.

[13] The southern region of Illinois supplied 50 percent more volunteers to the U.S. war effort than what had been requested. Arthur Charles Cole, *The Era of the Civil War, 1848–1870*, vol. 3 of *The Centennial History of Illinois* (Springfield: Illinois Centennial Commission, 1919), 279.

take the regiment to St. Louis. The boat, when it did come, grounded on a sand-bar a few miles below where we were in camp. We remained there several days waiting to have the boat get off the bar, but before this occurred news came that an Illinois regiment was surrounded by rebels at a point on the Hannibal and St. Joe Railroad some miles west of Palmyra, in Missouri, and I was ordered to proceed with all dispatch to their relief.[14] We took the cars and reached Quincy in a few hours.[15]

When I left Galena for the last time to take command of the 21st regiment I took with me my oldest son, Frederick D. Grant, then a lad of eleven years of age. On receiving the order to take rail for Quincy I wrote to Mrs. Grant, to relieve what I supposed would be her great anxiety for one so young going into danger, that I would send Fred home from Quincy by river. I received a prompt letter in reply decidedly disapproving my proposition, and urging that the lad should be allowed to accompany me. It came too late. Fred was already on his way up the Mississippi bound for Dubuque, Iowa, from which place there was a railroad to Galena.[16]

My sensations as we approached what I supposed might be "a field of battle" were anything but agreeable. I had been in all the engagements in Mexico that it was possible for one person to be in; but not in command. If some one else had been colonel and I had been lieutenant-colonel I do not think I would have felt any trepidation. Before we were prepared to cross the Mississippi River at Quincy my anxiety was relieved; for the men of the besieged regiment came straggling into town. I am inclined to think both sides got frightened and ran away.

I took my regiment to Palmyra and remained there for a few days, until relieved by the 19th Illinois infantry. From Palmyra I proceeded to Salt River, the railroad bridge over which had been destroyed by the enemy.[17] Colonel John M. Palmer[18] at that time commanded the 13th Illinois, which was acting

---

[14] On July 10, 1861, Pope changed the orders after secessionist guerrillas attacked the 16th Illinois Inf. near Monroe Station, MO. The guerrillas also destroyed property along the Hannibal and St. Joseph Railroad. *PUSG,* 2:64–65, 64n–65n.

[15] USG and the 21st Illinois Inf. reached Quincy, IL, by July 11, 1861. Ibid., 2:64.

[16] On July 12, 1861, USG put his son FDG on a steamer bound for home. Ibid., 2:67, 69n.

[17] USG and his troops moved to the area around the Salt River on July 15–16, 1861. Ibid., 2:72n.

[18] John M. Palmer (1817–1900) was born in Kentucky and entered the military in 1861 as a colonel in the 14th Illinois Inf. He rose to major general during the Civil War, was the Republican governor of Illinois from 1869 to 1873, and served as a U.S. senator from Illinois from

as a guard to workmen who were engaged in rebuilding this bridge. Palmer was my senior and commanded the two regiments as long as we remained together. The bridge was finished in about two weeks, and I received orders to move against Colonel Thomas Harris,[19] who was said to be encamped at the little town of Florida, some twenty-five miles south of where we then were.

At the time of which I now write we had no transportation and the country about Salt River was sparsely settled, so that it took some days to collect teams and drivers enough to move the camp and garrison equipage of a regiment nearly a thousand strong, together with a week's supply of provision and some ammunition. While preparations for the move were going on I felt quite comfortable; but when we got on the road and found every house deserted I was anything but easy. In the twenty-five miles we had to march we did not see a person, old or young, male or female, except two horsemen who were on a road that crossed ours. As soon as they saw us they decamped as fast as their horses could carry them. I kept my men in the ranks and forbade their entering any of the deserted houses or taking anything from them. We halted at night on the road and proceeded the next morning at an early hour. Harris had been encamped in a creek bottom for the sake of being near water. The hills on either side of the creek extend to a considerable height, possibly more than a hundred feet. As we approached the brow of the hill from which it was expected we could see Harris' camp, and possibly find his men ready formed to meet us, my heart kept getting higher and higher until it felt to me as though it was in my throat. I would have given anything then to have been back in Illinois, but I had not the moral courage to halt and consider what to do; I kept right on. When we reached a point from which the valley below was in full view I halted. The place where Harris had been encamped a few days before was still there and the marks of a recent encampment were plainly visible, but the troops were gone. My heart resumed its place. It occurred to me at once that Harris had been as much afraid of me as I had been of him. This was a view of the question I had never taken before; but it was one I never forgot afterwards. From that event to the close of the war, I never experienced trepidation upon confronting an enemy, though I always felt more or less anxiety. I never forgot that he had as much reason to fear my forces as I had his. The lesson was valuable.

1891 to 1897. In 1896, Palmer was a presidential candidate on the National Democratic ticket. *CWHC,* 415.

[19]Thomas A. Harris (1826–1895) was born in Virginia and was a brigadier general in the Confederate Missouri State Guard from June to Dec. 1861. Ibid., 282–283.

Inquiries at the village of Florida divulged the fact that Colonel Harris, learning of my intended movement, while my transportation was being collected took time by the forelock and left Florida before I had started from Salt River. He had increased the distance between us by forty miles. The next day I started back to my old camp at Salt River bridge. The citizens living on the line of our march had returned to their houses after we passed, and finding everything in good order, nothing carried away, they were at their front doors ready to greet us now. They had evidently been led to believe that the National troops carried death and devastation with them wherever they went.

In a short time after our return to Salt River bridge I was ordered with my regiment to the town of Mexico. General Pope was then commanding the district embracing all of the State of Missouri between the Mississippi and Missouri rivers, with his headquarters in the village of Mexico. I was assigned to the command of a sub-district embracing the troops in the immediate neighborhood, some three regiments of infantry and a section of artillery.[20] There was one regiment encamped by the side of mine. I assumed command of the whole and the first night sent the commander of the other regiment the parole and countersign. Not wishing to be outdone in courtesy, he immediately sent me the countersign for his regiment for the night. When he was informed that the countersign sent to him was for use with his regiment as well as mine, it was difficult to make him understand that this was not an unwarranted interference of one colonel over another. No doubt he attributed it for the time to the presumption of a graduate of West Point over a volunteer pure and simple. But the question was soon settled and we had no further trouble.

My arrival in Mexico had been preceded by that of two or three regiments in which proper discipline had not been maintained, and the men had been in the habit of visiting houses without invitation and helping themselves to food and drink, or demanding them from the occupants. They carried their muskets while out of camp and made every man they found take the oath of allegiance to the government. I at once published orders prohibiting the soldiers from going into private houses unless invited by the inhabitants, and from appropriating private property to their own or to government uses.[21] The people were

---

[20] On July 19, 1861, Gen. Stephen A. Hurlbut ordered USG's regiment to Mexico, MO. On July 24, Pope ordered USG to take command at Mexico. *PUSG*, 2:73*n*, 75*n*.

[21] USG referred to Gen. Orders No. 1, issued on July 25, 1861. Ibid., 2:74–75.

no longer molested or made afraid. I received the most marked courtesy from the citizens of Mexico as long as I remained there.

Up to this time my regiment had not been carried in the school of the soldier beyond the company drill, except that it had received some training on the march from Springfield to the Illinois River. There was now a good opportunity of exercising it in the battalion drill. While I was at West Point the tactics used in the army had been Scott's and the musket the flint lock.[22] I had never looked at a copy of tactics from the time of my graduation. My standing in that branch of studies had been near the foot of the class.[23] In the Mexican war in the summer of 1846, I had been appointed regimental quartermaster and commissary and had not been at a battalion drill since. The arms had been changed since then and Hardee's tactics had been adopted.[24] I got a copy of tactics and studied one lesson, intending to confine the exercise of the first day to the commands I had thus learned. By pursuing this course from day to day I thought I would soon get through the volume.

We were encamped just outside of town on the common, among scattering suburban houses with enclosed gardens, and when I got my regiment in line and rode to the front I soon saw that if I attempted to follow the lesson I had studied I would have to clear away some of the houses and garden fences to make room. I perceived at once, however, that Hardee's tactics—a mere translation from the French with Hardee's name attached—was nothing more than common sense and the progress of the age applied to Scott's system. The commands were abbreviated and the movement expedited. Under the old tactics almost every change in the order of march was preceded by a "halt," then

[22] The primary text on tactics used at the USMA during USG's years there was Winfield Scott's *Infantry Tactics or Rules for the Exercise of the United States Infantry*, 3 vols. (New York: George Dearborn, 1835). Paddy Griffith, *Battle Tactics of the Civil War* (New Haven, CT: Yale University Press, 1989), 99–101; *Official Register of the Officers and Cadets of the U.S. Military Academy, West Point, New York. June, 1843* (New York: USMA Printing Office, 1843), 22.

[23] In his fourth year at the USMA, USG ranked twenty-eighth out of thirty-nine cadets in "Infantry Tactics." *Official Register of the Officers and Cadets, 7*.

[24] In 1855, the U.S. Army began transitioning from the smoothbore musket to the .58 caliber rifle. During the Civil War, Lt. Col. William J. Hardee's *Rifle and Light Infantry Tactics for the Exercise and Manoeuvres of Troops When Acting as Light Infantry or Riflemen*, 2 vols. (Philadelphia: Lippincott, Grambo, 1855), became the most widely used text on military tactics. Carl L. Davis, *Arming the Union: Small Arms in the Civil War* (Port Washington, NY: Kennikat Press, 1973), 10; Griffith, *Battle Tactics of the Civil War*, 100–101.

came the change, and then the "forward march." With the new tactics all these changes could be made while in motion. I found no trouble in giving commands that would take my regiment where I wanted it to go and carry it around all obstacles. I do not believe that the officers of the regiment ever discovered that I had never studied the tactics that I used.

# 19

## Commissioned Brigadier-General—Command at Ironton, Mo.—Jefferson City—Cape Girardeau— General Prentiss—Seizure of Paducah— Headquarters at Cairo

I HAD NOT BEEN IN MEXICO many weeks when, reading a St. Louis paper, I found the President had asked the Illinois delegation in Congress to recommend some citizens of the State for the position of brigadier-general, and that they had unanimously recommended me as first on a list of seven. I was very much surprised because, as I have said, my acquaintance with the Congressmen was very limited and I did not know of anything I had done to inspire such confidence. The papers of the next day announced that my name, with three others, had been sent to the Senate, and a few days after our confirmation was announced.[1]

When appointed brigadier-general I at once thought it proper that one of my aides should come from the regiment I had been commanding, and so selected Lieutenant C. B. Lagow.[2] While living in St. Louis, I had had a desk in the law office of McClellan, Moody and Hillyer.[3] Difference in views

[1] There is no evidence that Lincoln asked for nominations for brigadier general from the Illinois congressional delegation. On July 30, 1861, Lincoln asked U.S. secretary of war Simon Cameron to send him USG's nomination as brigadier general. USG probably received word in the Aug. 3 issue of the *Missouri Democrat*. USG's commission was dated Aug. 9 but he probably first saw an official notice in AGO Gen. Orders No. 62, issued Aug. 20. *PUSG*, 2:82n, 132–133, 214n.

[2] Clark B. Lagow (1828–1867) was born in Illinois and served as USG's aide-de-camp from Aug. 1861 to Nov. 1863. *CWHC*, 337; *PUSG*, 2:99n, 116.

[3] Josiah G. McClellan (1824–1890) was born in Virginia and moved to St. Louis in 1850. James C. Moody—also spelled "Moodey"—(1816–1880) was born in Shippensburg, PA. William S. Hillyer (1830–1874) was born in Kentucky. The three men formed their law partnership in 1851, and USG and Harry Boggs used space in the firm's offices. Moody was impeached in 1867

between the members of the firm on the questions of the day, and general hard times in the border cities, had broken up this firm. Hillyer was quite a young man, then in his twenties, and very brilliant. I asked him to accept a place on my staff. I also wanted to take one man from my new home, Galena. The canvass in the Presidential campaign the fall before had brought out a young lawyer by the name of John A. Rawlins, who proved himself one of the ablest speakers in the State. He was also a candidate for elector on the Douglas ticket. When Sumter was fired upon and the integrity of the Union threatened, there was no man more ready to serve his country than he. I wrote at once asking him to accept the position of assistant adjutant-general with the rank of captain, on my staff. He was about entering the service as major of a new regiment then organizing in the north-western part of the State; but he threw this up and accepted my offer.[4]

Neither Hillyer nor Lagow proved to have any particular taste or special qualifications for the duties of the soldier, and the former resigned during the Vicksburg campaign; the latter I relieved after the battle of Chattanooga.[5] Rawlins remained with me as long as he lived, and rose to the rank of brigadier-general and chief-of-staff to the General of the Army—an office created for him—before the war closed. He was an able man, possessed of great firmness, and could say "no" so emphatically to a request which he thought should not be granted that the person he was addressing would understand at once that there was no use of pressing the matter. General Rawlins was a very useful officer in other ways than this. I became very much attached to him.

Shortly after my promotion I was ordered to Ironton, Missouri, to command a district in that part of the State, and took the 21st Illinois, my old

---

for refusing to administer Missouri's version of the "Ironclad Oath." Hillyer served as USG's aide-de-camp from Sept. 1861 until May 1863. *CWHC,* 297; Hillyer G. Norment Jr., *Descendants of John Hillyer of Windsor, Connecticut* (Baltimore: Gateway Press, 2004), 174; E. B. Parsons, *Phi Beta Kappa, Gamma of Massachusetts, Williams College* (Williamstown, MA: n.p., 1891), "Members"; *PUSG* 1:347n–348n.

[4] On Aug. 21, 1861, USG sent a request to Frémont asking for the appointment. Rawlins was appointed as assistant adjutant general on Aug. 30. *CWHC,* 243–244; *PUSG,* 2:97n, 117n, 125–126.

[5] Hillyer resigned on Apr. 27, 1863, citing the need to return to his legal and real estate business and also to attend to his wife's family's estates. USG accepted the resignation and commended him for the quality of his service. Hillyer wrote to USG on June 30 explaining that he left abruptly due to pain from "rheumatism" in his arm. On Nov. 18, amid incidents of delayed communications, erroneous reports, and late-night drinking, Lagow submitted his resignation to Brig. Gen. Lorenzo Thomas citing disability. *PUSG,* 8:219n–220n; 9:475–476.

regiment, with me. Several other regiments were ordered to the same destination about the same time.[6] Ironton is on the Iron Mountain railroad, about seventy miles south of St. Louis, and situated among hills rising almost to the dignity of mountains. When I reached there, about the 8th of August, Colonel B. Gratz Brown—afterwards Governor of Missouri and in 1872 Vice-Presidential candidate—was in command.[7] Some of his troops were ninety days' men and their time had expired some time before.[8] The men had no clothing but what they had volunteered in, and much of this was so worn that it would hardly stay on. General Hardee—the author of the tactics I did not study—was at Greenville, some twenty-five miles further south, it was said, with five thousand Confederate troops.[9] Under these circumstances Colonel Brown's command was very much demoralized. A squadron of cavalry could have ridden into the valley and captured the entire force. Brown himself was gladder to see me on that occasion than he ever has been since. I relieved him and sent all his men home, within a day or two, to be mustered out of service.

Within ten days after reaching Ironton I was prepared to take the offensive against the enemy at Greenville. I sent a column east out of the valley we were in, with orders to swing around to the south and west and come into the Greenville road ten miles south of Ironton. Another column marched on the direct road and went into camp at the point designated for the two columns to meet. I was to ride out the next morning and take personal command of the movement. My experience against Harris, in northern Missouri, had inspired me with confidence. But when the evening train came in, it brought

[6] On Aug. 6, 1861, Frémont instructed Pope to send the 14th, 15th, and 21st Inf. to Ironton. Pope had sent USG to St. Louis, where he received the instructions on Aug. 7. The following day, USG issued Gen. Orders No. 7 from Ironton assuming command. Ibid., 2:85–87.

[7] Benjamin Gratz Brown (1826–1885) served as U.S. senator from Missouri from 1863 to 1867 and governor of Missouri from 1871 to 1873. In 1872, he ran as the vice presidential candidate on the Liberal Republican ticket. Brown and Horace Greeley, the presidential candidate, were defeated by USG and Vice Pres. Henry Wilson. Lawrence O. Christensen et al., eds., *Dictionary of Missouri Biography* (Columbia: University of Missouri Press, 1999), 121–124; *Dictionary of American Biography,* 2nd ed., s.v. "Brown, Benjamin Gratz."

[8] On Aug. 8, 1861, Brown reported that his men's enlistments had expired the previous day and that they desired to return to St. Louis. When most returned to St. Louis, only three of his men remained at Ironton. *PUSG,* 2:87n.

[9] On Aug. 4, 1861, Hardee informed Maj. Gen. Leonidas Polk that he had 1,000 infantrymen, 250 cavalrymen, and a battery of artillery. He also believed that he could put as many as 1,500 Missourians in the field. Ibid., 2:95n.

General B. M. Prentiss[10] with orders to take command of the district. His orders did not relieve me, but I knew that by law I was senior, and at that time even the President did not have the authority to assign a junior to command a senior of the same grade. I therefore gave General Prentiss the situation of the troops and the general condition of affairs, and started for St. Louis the same day. The movement against the rebels at Greenville went no further.

From St. Louis I was ordered to Jefferson City, the capital of the State, to take command.[11] General Sterling Price,[12] of the Confederate army, was thought to be threatening the capital, Lexington, Chillicothe and other comparatively large towns in the central part of Missouri. I found a good many troops in Jefferson City, but in the greatest confusion, and no one person knew where they all were. Colonel Mulligan,[13] a gallant man, was in command, but he had not been educated as yet to his new profession and did not know how to maintain discipline. I found that volunteers had obtained permission from the department commander, or claimed they had, to raise, some of them, regiments; some battalions; some companies—the officers to be commissioned according to the number of men they brought into the service. There were recruiting stations all over town, with notices, rudely lettered on boards over the doors, announcing the arm of service and length of time for which recruits at that station would be received. The law required all volunteers to serve for three years or the war. But in Jefferson City in August, 1861, they were recruited for different periods and on different conditions; some were enlisted for six months, some for a year, some without any condition as to where they were to serve, others were not to be sent out of the State. The recruits were

---

[10] Benjamin M. Prentiss (1819–1901) was born in Virginia and settled in Illinois by 1841. After serving in the Mexican-American War, he reentered military service in 1861 and had reached brigadier general by May. Prentiss was in control of the Ironton-Western Dept. from Aug. 15 to Sept. 1, 1861. *CWHC*, 438.

[11] On Aug. 19, 1861, USG was transferred to Jefferson City, MO, by Frémont to command the District of Northern Missouri, where he relieved Col. James A. Mulligan. Ibid., 401; *PUSG*, 2:123*n*–124*n*.

[12] Sterling Price (1809–1867) was born in Virginia and moved to Missouri in 1831. Price was governor of Missouri from 1853 to 1857. By May 1861, he was a major general in the Missouri State Guard. *CWHC*, 440.

[13] James A. Mulligan (1829–1864) was born in New York and moved to Illinois in 1836. Mulligan commanded the 23rd Illinois Inf. at the start of the Civil War. He was wounded in action in 1864 near Winchester, VA, and died three days later. Mark M. Boatner III, *The Civil War Dictionary* (New York: David McKay, 1988), 574; *CWHC*, 401.

principally men from regiments stationed there and already in the service, bound for three years if the war lasted that long.

The city was filled with Union fugitives who had been driven by guerilla bands to take refuge with the National troops. They were in a deplorable condition and must have starved but for the support the government gave them. They had generally made their escape with a team or two, sometimes a yoke of oxen with a mule or a horse in the lead. A little bedding besides their clothing and some food had been thrown into the wagon. All else of their worldly goods were abandoned and appropriated by their former neighbors; for the Union man in Missouri who staid at home during the rebellion, if he was not immediately under the protection of the National troops, was at perpetual war with his neighbors. I stopped the recruiting service, and disposed the troops about the outskirts of the city so as to guard all approaches. Order was soon restored.

I had been at Jefferson City but a few days when I was directed from department headquarters to fit out an expedition to Lexington, Booneville and Chillicothe, in order to take from the banks in those cities all the funds they had and send them to St. Louis.[14] The western army had not yet been supplied with transportation. It became necessary therefore to press into the service teams belonging to sympathizers with the rebellion or to hire those of Union men. This afforded an opportunity of giving employment to such of the refugees within our lines as had teams suitable for our purposes. They accepted the service with alacrity. As fast as troops could be got off they were moved west some twenty miles or more. In seven or eight days from my assuming command at Jefferson City, I had all the troops, except a small garrison, at an advanced position and expected to join them myself the next day.[15]

But my campaigns had not yet begun, for while seated at my office door, with nothing further to do until it was time to start for the front, I saw an officer of rank approaching, who proved to be Colonel Jefferson C. Davis.[16]

[14] On Aug. 20, 1861, Frémont ordered USG to send detachments to Lexington, Liberty, and Paris, MO. *PUSG*, 2:136*n*.

[15] It is unclear exactly which "advanced position" and troop movements USG referred to in this passage. On Aug. 28, 1861, Col. Thomas A. Marshall, who led the Lexington expedition, wrote to USG from Tipton, MO, which is approximately thirty-five miles west of Jefferson City. USG's correspondence from this time period does not indicate plans to join the expedition; on the contrary, he advocated concentrating forces at Jefferson City. Ibid., 2:131, 135, 143, 342.

[16] Jefferson C. Davis (1828–1879) was born in Indiana and was colonel of the 22nd Indiana Inf. He served in the Union Army throughout the war and was brevetted major general in 1865. *CWHC*, 202.

I had never met him before, but he introduced himself by handing me an order for him to proceed to Jefferson City and relieve me of the command. The orders directed that I should report at department headquarters at St. Louis without delay, to receive important special instructions.[17] It was about an hour before the only regular train of the day would start. I therefore turned over to Colonel Davis my orders, and hurriedly stated to him the progress that had been made to carry out the department instructions already described. I had at that time but one staff officer,* doing myself all the detail work usually performed by an adjutant-general. In an hour after being relieved from the command I was on my way to St. Louis, leaving my single staff officer to follow the next day with our horses and baggage.

The "important special instructions" which I received the next day, assigned me to the command of the district of south-east Missouri, embracing all the territory south of St. Louis, in Missouri, as well as all southern Illinois.[18] At first I was to take personal command of a combined expedition that had been ordered for the capture of Colonel Jeff. Thompson,[19] a sort of independent or partisan commander who was disputing with us the possession of south-east Missouri. Troops had been ordered to move from Ironton to Cape Girardeau, sixty or seventy miles to the south-east, on the Mississippi River; while the forces at Cape Girardeau had been ordered to move to Jacksonville, ten miles out towards Ironton; and troops at Cairo and Bird's Point, at the junction of the Ohio and Mississippi rivers, were to hold themselves in readiness to go down the Mississippi to Belmont, eighteen miles below, to be moved west from there when an officer should come to command them. I was the officer who had been selected for this purpose. Cairo was to become my headquarters when the expedition terminated.

In pursuance of my orders I established my temporary headquarters at Cape Girardeau and sent instructions to the commanding officer at Jackson,

*C. B. Lagow, the others not yet having joined me.

[17] On Aug. 27, 1861, Frémont had ordered USG to report to headquarters at St. Louis. *PUSG,* 2:149*n*, 151*n*.

[18] On Aug. 28, 1861, Frémont ordered USG to Cape Girardeau, where he was instructed to pursue Brig. Gen. M. Jeff Thompson, who commanded the 1st Military District of the Missouri State Guard. USG assumed command of the District of Southeast Missouri on Sept. 1. Ibid., 2:151–153, 163.

[19] Meriwether Jefferson Thompson (1826–1876) was born in Virginia and moved to Missouri in 1847. On July 25, 1861, Thompson was promoted to brigadier general of the Missouri State Guard. *CWHC,* 529.

to inform me of the approach of General Prentiss from Ironton. Hired wagons were kept moving night and day to take additional rations to Jackson, to supply the troops when they started from there. Neither General Prentiss nor Colonel Marsh,[20] who commanded at Jackson, knew their destination. I drew up all the instructions for the contemplated move, and kept them in my pocket until I should hear of the junction of our troops at Jackson.[21] Two or three days after my arrival at Cape Girardeau, word came that General Prentiss was approaching that place (Jackson). I started at once to meet him there and to give him his orders. As I turned the first corner of a street after starting, I saw a column of cavalry passing the next street in front of me. I turned and rode around the block the other way, so as to meet the head of the column. I found there General Prentiss himself, with a large escort. He had halted his troops at Jackson for the night, and had come on himself to Cape Girardeau, leaving orders for his command to follow him in the morning. I gave the General his orders—which stopped him at Jackson—but he was very much aggrieved at being placed under another brigadier-general, particularly as he believed himself to be the senior. He had been a brigadier, in command at Cairo, while I was mustering officer at Springfield without any rank. But we were nominated at the same time for the United States service, and both our commissions bore date May 17th, 1861. By virtue of my former army rank I was, by law, the senior. General Prentiss failed to get orders to his troops to remain at Jackson, and the next morning early they were reported as approaching Cape Girardeau. I then ordered the General very peremptorily to countermarch his command and take it back to Jackson. He obeyed the order, but bade his command adieu when he got them to Jackson, and went to St. Louis and reported himself.[22] This broke up the expedition. But little harm was done, as Jeff. Thompson moved light and had no fixed place for even nominal headquarters. He was as much at home in Arkansas as he was in Missouri and would keep out of the way of a superior force. Prentiss was sent to another part of the State.[23]

[20] C. Carroll Marsh (1829–?) was born in New York and commanded the 20th Illinois Inf. He served in the U.S. Army until 1863. Ibid., 604; James G. Wilson, *Biographical Sketches of Illinois Officers Engaged in the War against the Rebellion of 1861* (Chicago: James Barnet, 1862), 45.

[21] USG issued his orders calling for the rendezvous of soldiers at Jackson, MO, in Gen. Orders No. 1 on Aug. 30, 1861. *PUSG,* 2:153–154.

[22] On Sept. 1, 1861, Prentiss sent his resignation to Frémont when USG refused to have the dispute over rank mediated. He later served under USG at Shiloh and resigned from the army in Oct. 1863. *CWHC,* 438; *PUSG,* 2:170n.

[23] Prentiss was sent to Mason City, MO, from Sept. 17 to Nov. 9, 1861. *CWHC,* 439.

General Prentiss made a great mistake on the above occasion, one that he would not have committed later in the war. When I came to know him better, I regretted it much. In consequence of this occurrence he was off duty in the field when the principal campaign at the West was going on, and his juniors received promotion while he was where none could be obtained. He would have been next to myself in rank in the district of south-east Missouri, by virtue of his services in the Mexican war. He was a brave and very earnest soldier. No man in the service was more sincere in his devotion to the cause for which we were battling; none more ready to make sacrifices or risk life in it.

On the 4th of September I removed my headquarters to Cairo and found Colonel Richard Oglesby[24] in command of the post. We had never met, at least not to my knowledge. After my promotion I had ordered my brigadier-general's uniform from New York, but it had not yet arrived, so that I was in citizen's dress. The Colonel had his office full of people, mostly from the neighboring States of Missouri and Kentucky, making complaints or asking favors. He evidently did not catch my name when I was presented, for on my taking a piece of paper from the table where he was seated and writing the order assuming command of the district of south-east Missouri, Colonel Richard J. Oglesby to command the post at Bird's Point, and handing it to him, he put on an expression of surprise that looked a little as if he would like to have some one identify me. But he surrendered the office without question.[25]

The day after I assumed command at Cairo a man[26] came to me who said he was a scout of General Fremont.[27] He reported that he had just come from

[24] Richard J. Oglesby (1824–1899) was born in Kentucky and moved to Illinois in 1832. In June 1846, Oglesby served as a first lieutenant of the 4th Illinois Inf. At the start of the Civil War, he was appointed colonel of the 8th Illinois Inf. and reached major general in Nov. 1862. Oglesby served as governor of Illinois from 1865 to 1869; from Jan. 13, 1873 to Jan. 23, 1873; and from 1885–1889. He also served as U.S. senator from Illinois 1873–1879. Ibid., 408.

[25] Both USG and Oglesby stated that this meeting occurred on Sept. 4, 1861, but it may have occurred earlier since USG had arrived in Cairo on Sept. 2. *PUSG*, 2:184n.

[26] USG referred to Charles De Arnaud (c.1835–1905), a civilian spy who worked for Frémont and later sought medals and financial compensation from the U.S. government for his claimed service during the war and the physical and mental injuries sustained. He was eventually awarded a Union pension, although his claims about the nature of his service to the Union cause have never been verified. James W. Harlow, " 'An Imposter If There Ever Was One': The Trials of Charles de Arnaud," *Prologue: Quarterly of the National Archives and Records Administration* 47 (2015): 6–14; *PUSG*, 2:193; 3:243n–245n.

[27] John C. Frémont (1813–1890) was born in Georgia and attended Charleston College. He entered the U.S. Army in 1838 and rose to fame as an explorer of the western United States. He

Columbus, a point on the Mississippi twenty miles below on the Kentucky side, and that troops had started from there, or were about to start, to seize Paducah, at the mouth of the Tennessee. There was no time for delay; I reported by telegraph to the department commander the information I had received, and added that I was taking steps to get off that night to be in advance of the enemy in securing that important point. There was a large number of steamers lying at Cairo and a good many boatmen were staying in the town. It was the work of only a few hours to get the boats manned, with coal aboard and steam up. Troops were also designated to go aboard. The distance from Cairo to Paducah is about forty-five miles. I did not wish to get there before daylight of the 6th, and directed therefore that the boats should lie at anchor out in the stream until the time to start. Not having received an answer to my first dispatch, I again telegraphed to department headquarters that I should start for Paducah that night unless I received further orders. Hearing nothing, we started before midnight and arrived early the following morning, anticipating the enemy by probably not over six or eight hours.[28] It proved very fortunate that the expedition against Jeff. Thompson had been broken up. Had it not been, the enemy would have seized Paducah and fortified it, to our very great annoyance.[29]

When the National troops entered the town the citizens were taken by surprise. I never after saw such consternation depicted on the faces of the people. Men, women and children came out of their doors looking pale and frightened at the presence of the invader. They were expecting rebel troops that day. In fact, nearly four thousand men from Columbus were at that time within ten or fifteen miles of Paducah on their way to occupy the place. I had but two regiments and one battery with me; but the enemy did not know this and returned to Columbus. I stationed my troops at the best points to guard the roads leading into the city, left gunboats to guard the river fronts and by

served as senator from California from 1850 to 1851 and was the Republican candidate for president in 1856. Frémont reentered the army in 1861 as a major general and was governor of the Arizona Territory from 1878 to 1881. *CWHC*, 243–244.

[28] Records from Sept. 5, 1861, indicate that Frémont had responded by letter and telegram (which had been translated into Hungarian for secrecy), but apparently neither had reached USG by the time he left. Only one of USG's telegrams to Frémont regarding his plans for Paducah has been found. *PUSG*, 2:191n–192n.

[29] In spite of the information supplied by De Arnaud, Confederate records do not indicate plans to move on Paducah, and there were no Confederate forces on their way to the city when USG arrived. William B. Feis, *Grant's Secret Service: The Intelligence War from Belmont to Appomattox* (Lincoln: University of Nebraska Press, 2002), 23; *PUSG*, 3:245n.

noon was ready to start on my return to Cairo. Before leaving, however, I addressed a short printed proclamation to the citizens of Paducah assuring them of our peaceful intentions, that we had come among them to protect them against the enemies of our country, and that all who chose could continue their usual avocations with assurance of the protection of the government.[30] This was evidently a relief to them; but the majority would have much preferred the presence of the other army. I reinforced Paducah rapidly from the troops at Cape Girardeau; and a day or two later General C. F. Smith, a most accomplished soldier, reported at Cairo and was assigned to the command of the post at the mouth of the Tennessee. In a short time it was well fortified and a detachment was sent to occupy Smithland, at the mouth of the Cumberland.[31]

The State government of Kentucky at that time was rebel in sentiment, but wanted to preserve an armed neutrality between the North and the South, and the governor really seemed to think the State had a perfect right to maintain a neutral position.[32] The rebels already occupied two towns in the State, Columbus and Hickman, on the Mississippi; and at the very moment the National troops were entering Paducah from the Ohio front, General Lloyd Tilghman[33]—a Confederate—with his staff and a small detachment of men, were getting out in the other direction, while, as I have already said, nearly four thousand Confederate troops were on Kentucky soil on their way to take possession of the town.[34] But, in the estimation of the governor and of those who thought with him, this did not justify the National authorities in invading the soil of Kentucky. I informed the legislature of the State of what I was doing, and my action was approved by the majority of that body. On my return to Cairo I found authority from department headquarters for me to take Paducah "if I felt strong enough," but very soon after I was reprimanded from the same

---

[30] For the text of the proclamation, see *PUSG*, 2:194–195.

[31] On Sept. 7, 1861, USG sent Col. Joseph Webster to Paducah to begin fortifications there. On the same day, USG relayed Frémont's instructions to Smith to occupy Smithland, KY, in order to control the Cumberland River. *CWHC*, 558; *PUSG*, 2:203–206.

[32] Beriah Magoffin (1815–1885) served as Kentucky governor from 1859 to 1862. A Confederate sympathizer, Magoffin declared Kentucky a neutral state. *CWHC*, 360; Donald Stoker, *The Grand Design: Strategy and the U.S. Civil War* (New York: Oxford University Press, 2010), 48–50.

[33] Lloyd Tilghman (1816–1863) was born in Maryland and graduated from the USMA in 1836. In Oct. 1861, Tilghman was promoted to brigadier general in the Confederate Army. *CWHC*, 531.

[34] Tilghman's force consisted of approximately 2,000 soldiers armed with Enfield rifles. *PUSG*, 2:203n.

quarters for my correspondence with the legislature and warned against a repetition of the offence.[35]

Soon after I took command at Cairo, General Fremont entered into arrangements for the exchange of the prisoners captured at Camp Jackson in the month of May. I received orders to pass them through my lines to Columbus as they presented themselves with proper credentials. Quite a number of these prisoners I had been personally acquainted with before the war. Such of them as I had so known were received at my headquarters as old acquaintances, and ordinary routine business was not disturbed by their presence. On one occasion when several were present in my office my intention to visit Cape Girardeau the next day, to inspect the troops at that point, was mentioned. Something transpired which postponed my trip; but a steamer employed by the government was passing a point some twenty or more miles above Cairo, the next day, when a section of rebel artillery with proper escort brought her to. A major, one of those who had been at my headquarters the day before, came at once aboard and after some search made a direct demand for my delivery. It was hard to persuade him that I was not there. This officer was Major Barrett,[36] of St. Louis. I had been acquainted with his family before the war.

[35] On Sept. 5, 1861, USG sent a telegram to Kentucky House of Representatives speaker Richard A. Buckner, who shared the communication with his fellow representatives. The following day Frémont informed USG that no commanders were to communicate with state authorities and that all matters should be referred to the major general. *Journal of the House of Representatives of the Commonwealth of Kentucky*, vol. 1 (Frankfort, KY: State Journal, 1861), 49; *PUSG*, 2:189.

[36] It is unclear exactly which Confederate officer USG referred to. One possibility is Confederate captain Overton W. Barret of the Missouri Militia, who was one of the Confederate prisoners exchanged at Neosho, MO, on Oct. 26, 1861. Another possibility is Col. J. Richard Barrett (also spelled Barret), who was a Confederate officer authorized to represent Maj. Gen. Sterling Price in prisoner exchanges in Springfield, MO, on Nov. 1, 1861. Prior to the Civil War, he had served as U.S. representative from Missouri from Mar. 1859 to June 1860 and Dec. 1860 to Mar. 1861. *Biographical Directory of the United States Congress 1774–2005* (Washington, DC: Government Printing Office, 2005), s.v. "Barret, John Richard"; *OR*, II, 1, 555, 559.

# 20

## General Fremont in Command—Movement against Belmont—Battle of Belmont—A Narrow Escape— After the Battle

FROM THE OCCUPATION of Paducah up to the early part of November nothing important occurred with the troops under my command. I was reinforced from time to time and the men were drilled and disciplined preparatory for the service which was sure to come. By the 1st of November I had not fewer than 20,000 men, most of them under good drill and ready to meet any equal body of men who, like themselves, had not yet been in an engagement. They were growing impatient at lying idle so long, almost in hearing of the guns of the enemy they had volunteered to fight against. I asked on one or two occasions to be allowed to move against Columbus. It could have been taken soon after the occupation of Paducah; but before November it was so strongly fortified that it would have required a large force and a long siege to capture it.[1]

In the latter part of October General Fremont took the field in person and moved from Jefferson City against General Sterling Price, who was then in the State of Missouri with a considerable command.[2] About the first of November I was directed from department headquarters to make a demon-

[1] On Sept. 10, 1861, USG hinted to Frémont about taking Columbus, KY, which sat strategically high on a bluff overlooking the Mississippi River. In Oct., the number of Confederate troops at Columbus had increased from 13,708 to 17,230. In addition, the Columbus fortifications had approximately 140 guns. James M. McPherson, *War on the Waters: The Union and Confederate Navies, 1861–1865* (Chapel Hill: University of North Carolina Press, 2012), 73; *PUSG*, 2:225; 3:11n.

[2] On Sept. 21, 1861, after failing to capture Confederate occupied Lexington, MO, Col. James Mulligan surrendered to Price. The loss prompted Frémont to take action against Price. Albert Castel, *General Sterling Price and the Civil War in the West* (Baton Rouge: Louisiana State University Press, 1996), 55–57.

stration on both sides of the Mississippi River with the view of detaining the
rebels at Columbus within their lines. Before my troops could be got off, I
was notified from the same quarter that there were some 3,000 of the enemy
on the St. Francis River about fifty miles west, or south-west, from Cairo, and
was ordered to send another force against them. I dispatched Colonel Oglesby at
once with troops sufficient to compete with the reported number of the enemy.
On the 5th word came from the same source that the rebels were about to detach a large force from Columbus to be moved by boats down the Mississippi
and up the White River, in Arkansas, in order to reinforce Price, and I was directed to prevent this movement if possible. I accordingly sent a regiment from
Bird's Point under Colonel W. H. L. Wallace[3] to overtake and reinforce Oglesby,
with orders to march to New Madrid, a point some distance below Columbus,
on the Missouri side. At the same time I directed General C. F. Smith to move
all the troops he could spare from Paducah directly against Columbus, halting
them, however, a few miles from the town to await further orders from me.
Then I gathered up all the troops at Cairo and Fort Holt, except suitable
guards, and moved them down the river on steamers convoyed by two gunboats, accompanying them myself.[4] My force consisted of a little over 3,000
men and embraced five regiments of infantry, two guns and two companies
of cavalry. We dropped down the river on the 6th to within about six miles of
Columbus, debarked a few men on the Kentucky side and established pickets
to connect with the troops from Paducah.[5]

I had no orders which contemplated an attack by the National troops, nor
did I intend anything of the kind when I started out from Cairo; but after we
started I saw that the officers and men were elated at the prospect of at last
having the opportunity of doing what they had volunteered to do—fight the
enemies of their country. I did not see how I could maintain discipline, or
retain the confidence of my command, if we should return to Cairo without
an effort to do something. Columbus, besides being strongly fortified, contained

<hr>

[3] W. H. L. Wallace (1821–1862) was born in Ohio and moved to Illinois in 1833. In 1846, he
joined the 1st Illinois Inf. as a second lieutenant. In June 1861, he was promoted to colonel in
the 11th Illinois Inf. He became a brigadier general on Mar. 21, 1862. *CWHC,* 551–552.

[4] Fort Holt, KY, was situated opposite Cairo, IL, along the Mississippi River. The steamers
were convoyed by the gunboats *Tyler* and *Lexington.* Nathaniel C. Hughes, *The Battle of Belmont: Grant Strikes South* (Chapel Hill: University of North Carolina Press, 1991), 209;
Myron J. Smith Jr., *The Timberclads in the Civil War: The Lexington, Conestoga and Tyler on the
Western Waters* (Jefferson, NC: McFarland, 2008), 181.

[5] The fleet stopped at the old Fort Jefferson site eight miles south of Cairo and eleven miles
north of Columbus. Hughes, *Battle of Belmont,* 50.

a garrison much more numerous than the force I had with me. It would not do, therefore, to attack that point. About two o'clock on the morning of the 7th, I learned that the enemy was crossing troops from Columbus to the west bank to be dispatched, presumably, after Oglesby.[6] I knew there was a small camp of Confederates at Belmont, immediately opposite Columbus, and I speedily resolved to push down the river, land on the Missouri side, capture Belmont, break up the camp and return. Accordingly, the pickets above Columbus were drawn in at once, and about daylight the boats moved out from shore. In an hour we were debarking on the west bank of the Mississippi, just out of range of the batteries at Columbus.

The ground on the west shore of the river, opposite Columbus, is low and in places marshy and cut up with sloughs. The soil is rich and the timber large and heavy. There were some small clearings between Belmont and the point where we landed, but most of the country was covered with the native forests. We landed in front of a cornfield. When the debarkation commenced, I took a regiment down the river to post it as a guard against surprise. At that time I had no staff officer who could be trusted with that duty. In the woods, at a short distance below the clearing, I found a depression, dry at the time, but which at high water became a slough or bayou. I placed the men in the hollow, gave them their instructions and ordered them to remain there until they were properly relieved. These troops, with the gunboats, were to protect our transports.

Up to this time the enemy had evidently failed to divine our intentions. From Columbus they could, of course, see our gunboats and transports loaded with troops. But the force from Paducah was threatening them from the land side, and it was hardly to be expected that if Columbus was our object we would separate our troops by a wide river. They doubtless thought we meant to draw a large force from the east bank, then embark ourselves, land on the east bank and make a sudden assault on Columbus before their divided command could be united.[7]

About eight o'clock we started from the point of debarkation, marching by the flank. After moving in this way for a mile or a mile and a half, I halted

[6] In a revised postbattle report, USG claimed that he received the message from Col. W. H. L. Wallace, who was in Charleston, MO. However, there is no documentary evidence to verify USG's claim. *OR,* I, 3, 269; *PUSG,* 3:150–151.

[7] On Nov. 6, 1861, Confederate general Gideon Pillow prepared his troops to march toward Clarksville, TN, when a message from Confederate general Leonidas Polk informed him that USG's forces had been spotted upriver and that he must return to defend Belmont. Nathaniel C. Hughes and Roy P. Stonesifer, *The Life and Wars of Gideon J. Pillow* (Chapel Hill: University of North Carolina Press, 1993), 197.

where there was marshy ground covered with a heavy growth of timber in our front, and deployed a large part of my force as skirmishers. By this time the enemy discovered that we were moving upon Belmont and sent out troops to meet us. Soon after we had started in line, his skirmishers were encountered and fighting commenced. This continued, growing fiercer and fiercer, for about four hours, the enemy being forced back gradually until he was driven into his camp. Early in this engagement my horse was shot under me, but I got another from one of my staff and kept well up with the advance until the river was reached.

The officers and men engaged at Belmont were then under fire for the first time. Veterans could not have behaved better than they did up to the moment of reaching the rebel camp.[8] At this point they became demoralized from their victory and failed to reap its full reward. The enemy had been followed so closely that when he reached the clear ground on which his camp was pitched he beat a hasty retreat over the river bank, which protected him from our shots and from view. This precipitate retreat at the last moment enabled the National forces to pick their way without hinderance through the abatis—the only artificial defence the enemy had. The moment the camp was reached our men laid down their arms and commenced rummaging the tents to pick up trophies.[9] Some of the higher officers were little better than the privates. They galloped about from one cluster of men to another and at every halt delivered a short eulogy upon the Union cause and the achievements of the command.

All this time the troops we had been engaged with for four hours, lay crouched under cover of the river bank, ready to come up and surrender if summoned to do so; but finding that they were not pursued, they worked their way up the river and came up on the bank between us and our transports. I saw at the same time two steamers coming from the Columbus side towards the west shore, above us, black—or gray—with soldiers from boiler-deck to roof.[10] Some of my men were engaged in firing from captured guns at empty steamers down the river, out of range, cheering at every shot. I tried to get them to turn their guns upon the loaded steamers above and not so far away. My efforts were in vain. At last I directed my staff officers to set fire to the

[8] USG referred to Camp Johnston. Hughes, *Battle of Belmont,* 118.

[9] In response to this trophy hunting, USG issued Gen. Orders No. 15 on Nov. 15, 1861, which reminded soldiers that captured property and horses were to be turned over to the post quartermaster. *PUSG,* 3:169 and *n.*

[10] The Confederate steamers *Prince* and *Harry W. R. Hill* were carrying reinforcements. Hughes, *Battle of Belmont,* 122.

camps.[11] This drew the fire of the enemy's guns located on the heights of Columbus. They had abstained from firing before, probably because they were afraid of hitting their own men; or they may have supposed, until the camp was on fire, that it was still in the possession of their friends. About this time, too, the men we had driven over the bank were seen in line up the river between us and our transports. The alarm "surrounded" was given. The guns of the enemy and the report of being surrounded, brought officers and men completely under control. At first some of the officers seemed to think that to be surrounded was to be placed in a hopeless position, where there was nothing to do but surrender. But when I announced that we had cut our way in and could cut our way out just as well, it seemed a new revelation to officers and soldiers. They formed line rapidly and we started back to our boats, with the men deployed as skirmishers as they had been on entering camp. The enemy was soon encountered, but his resistance this time was feeble. Again the Confederates sought shelter under the river banks. We could not stop, however, to pick them up, because the troops we had seen crossing the river had debarked by this time and were nearer our transports than we were. It would be prudent to get them behind us; but we were not again molested on our way to the boats.

From the beginning of the fighting our wounded had been carried to the houses at the rear, near the place of debarkation. I now set the troops to bringing their wounded to the boats. After this had gone on for some little time I rode down the road, without even a staff officer, to visit the guard I had stationed over the approach to our transports. I knew the enemy had crossed over from Columbus in considerable numbers and might be expected to attack us as we were embarking. This guard would be encountered first and, as they were in a natural intrenchment, would be able to hold the enemy for a considerable time. My surprise was great to find there was not a single man in the trench. Riding back to the boat I found the officer who had commanded the guard and learned that he had withdrawn his force when the main body fell back.[12] At first I ordered the guard to return, but finding that it would take some time to get the men together and march them back to their position, I countermanded the order. Then fearing that the enemy we had seen crossing the river below might be coming upon us unawares, I rode out in the field to our front,

[11] On Nov. 10, 1861, USG explained in his postbattle report that his decision to set fire to Camp Johnston was due to the lack of transportation needed to move the captured property. *PUSG*, 3:142.

[12] USG stationed Capt. John E. Dietrich and 350 men from various companies of the 22nd Illinois Inf. and the 7th Iowa Inf. to protect the transports. *OR*, I, 3, 294–295.

still entirely alone, to observe whether the enemy was passing.[13] The field was grown up with corn so tall and thick as to cut off the view of even a person on horseback, except directly along the rows. Even in that direction, owing to the overhanging blades of corn, the view was not extensive. I had not gone more than a few hundred yards when I saw a body of troops marching past me not fifty yards away. I looked at them for a moment and then turned my horse towards the river and started back, first in a walk, and when I thought myself concealed from the view of the enemy, as fast as my horse could carry me. When at the river bank I still had to ride a few hundred yards to the point where the nearest transport lay.

The cornfield in front of our transports terminated at the edge of a dense forest. Before I got back the enemy had entered this forest and had opened a brisk fire upon the boats. Our men, with the exception of details that had gone to the front after the wounded, were now either aboard the transports or very near them. Those who were not aboard soon got there, and the boats pushed off. I was the only man of the National army between the rebels and our transports. The captain of a boat that had just pushed out but had not started, recognized me and ordered the engineer not to start the engine; he then had a plank run out for me.[14] My horse seemed to take in the situation. There was no path down the bank and every one acquainted with the Mississippi River knows that its banks, in a natural state, do not vary at any great angle from the perpendicular. My horse put his fore feet over the bank without hesitation or urging, and with his hind feet well under him, slid down the bank and trotted aboard the boat, twelve or fifteen feet away, over a single gang plank. I dismounted and went at once to the upper deck.

The Mississippi River was low on the 7th of November, 1861, so that the banks were higher than the heads of men standing on the upper decks of the steamers.[15] The rebels were some distance back from the river, so that their

[13] According to other accounts of the incident, USG was accompanied by Rawlins and a slave named Bob. Albert D. Richardson, *A Personal History of Ulysses S. Grant . . . with a Portrait and Sketch of Schuyler Colfax* (Hartford, CT: American Publishing, 1868), 202–203.

[14] This was the steamer *Belle Memphis.* Hughes, *Battle of Belmont,* 171.

[15] Before the construction of the Upper Mississippi River locks and dams in the 1930s, the depth of the Mississippi River was unpredictable. In 1861, the section of the Mississippi River between the mouth of the Ohio River and the high bluffs of Columbus flowed through an alluvial region that kept it below flood level. Andrew A. Humphreys and Henry L. Abbot, *Report upon the Physics and Hydraulics of the Mississippi River* (Philadelphia: J. B. Lippincott, 1861), 95; Dorothy Zeisler-Vralsted, *Rivers, Memory, and Nation-Building: A History of the Volga and Mississippi Rivers* (New York: Berghahn Books, 2014), 126.

fire was high and did us but little harm. Our smoke-stack was riddled with bullets, but there were only three men wounded on the boats, two of whom were soldiers.[16] When I first went on deck I entered the captain's room adjoining the pilot-house, and threw myself on a sofa. I did not keep that position a moment, but rose to go out on the deck to observe what was going on. I had scarcely left when a musket ball entered the room, struck the head of the sofa, passed through it and lodged in the foot.

When the enemy opened fire on the transports our gunboats returned it with vigor. They were well out in the stream and some distance down, so that they had to give but very little elevation to their guns to clear the banks of the river. Their position very nearly enfiladed the line of the enemy while he was marching through the cornfield. The execution was very great, as we could see at the time and as I afterwards learned more positively. We were very soon out of range and went peacefully on our way to Cairo, every man feeling that Belmont was a great victory and that he had contributed his share to it.

Our loss at Belmont was 485 in killed, wounded and missing. About 125 of our wounded fell into the hands of the enemy.[17] We returned with 175 prisoners and two guns, and spiked four other pieces.[18] The loss of the enemy, as officially reported, was 642 men, killed, wounded and missing.[19] We had engaged about 2,500 men, exclusive of the guard left with the transports. The enemy had about 7,000; but this includes the troops brought over from Columbus who were not engaged in the first defence of Belmont.

The two objects for which the battle of Belmont was fought were fully accomplished. The enemy gave up all idea of detaching troops from Columbus. His losses were very heavy for that period of the war. Columbus was beset by people looking for their wounded or dead kin, to take them home for medical treatment or burial. I learned later, when I had moved further south, that Belmont had caused more mourning than almost any other battle up to that time.[20]

---

[16] The other wounded man was a deckhand. Richardson, *Personal History of Ulysses S. Grant*, 203.

[17] Estimates of U.S. casualties ranged from 500 to 600. Approximately 90 were killed, and 320 to 400 were wounded. Over 200 were captured, over 100 of whom were wounded. Hughes, *Battle of Belmont*, 184.

[18] On Nov. 8, 1861, USG reported that the U.S. Army had taken 130 prisoners at Belmont. *PUSG*, 3:133.

[19] The Confederate casualties were approximately 105 killed, 419 wounded, and 117 missing. Hughes, *Battle of Belmont*, 184.

[20] While news of the battle initially stunned Southerners, Pillow and Southern newspapers portrayed it as a Confederate victory. Ibid., 189–190.

The National troops acquired a confidence in themselves at Belmont that did not desert them through the war.

The day after the battle I met some officers from General Polk's[21] command, arranged for permission to bury our dead at Belmont and also commenced negotiations for the exchange of prisoners.[22] When our men went to bury their dead, before they were allowed to land they were conducted below the point where the enemy had engaged our transports. Some of the officers expressed a desire to see the field; but the request was refused with the statement that we had no dead there.

While on the truce-boat I mentioned to an officer, whom I had known both at West Point and in the Mexican war, that I was in the cornfield near their troops when they passed; that I had been on horseback and had worn a soldier's overcoat at the time. This officer was on General Polk's staff. He said both he and the general had seen me and that Polk had said to his men, "There is a Yankee; you may try your marksmanship on him if you wish," but nobody fired at me.[23]

Belmont was severely criticised in the North as a wholly unnecessary battle, barren of results, or the possibility of them from the beginning. If it had not been fought, Colonel Oglesby would probably have been captured or destroyed with his three thousand men. Then I should have been culpable indeed.

[21] Leonidas Polk (1806–1864) was born in North Carolina and was the third cousin of Pres. James K. Polk. He graduated from the USMA in 1827 and served in the artillery before resigning to become an Episcopal clergyman. He was bishop of Louisiana from 1841 to 1864 and was a founder of the University of the South. Polk became a major general in the Confederate Army in 1861, and was hit by an artillery shell and killed at Pine Mountain, GA. *CWHC,* 432–433.

[22] On Nov. 8, 1861, Maj. Joseph D. Webster discussed the exchange of prisoners with Capt. Edward Blake, one of Polk's staff officers, aboard the steamer *Belle Memphis.* A few wounded prisoners were exchanged that day. On Nov. 13, USG met for a larger exchange of prisoners. *PUSG,* 3:131–132; Hughes, *Battle of Belmont,* 186–187.

[23] The Confederate officer who most closely matches USG's description is John P. McCown (1815–1879), who was born in Tennessee and graduated from the USMA in 1840. He was brevetted captain for his actions at the Battle of Cerro Gordo during the Mexican-American War. He resigned from the U.S. Army in 1861 to join the Confederate Army. McCown was promoted to brigadier general in Oct. 1861 and, although not listed as a member of Polk's staff, was involved in the exchange of prisoners and present at the meeting USG mentioned. *CWHC,* 375; Hughes, *Battle of Belmont,* 187; *PUSG,* 3:10, 160*n.*

# 21

## General Halleck in Command—Commanding the District of Cairo—Movement on Fort Henry— Capture of Fort Henry

Wᴴɪʟᴇ ᴀᴛ ᴄᴀɪʀᴏ I had frequent opportunities of meeting the rebel officers of the Columbus garrison. They seemed to be very fond of coming up on
steamers under flags of truce. On two or three occasions I went down in like
manner. When one of their boats was seen coming up carrying a white flag, a
gun would be fired from the lower battery at Fort Holt, throwing a shot
across the bow as a signal to come no farther. I would then take a steamer
and, with my staff and occasionally a few other officers, go down to receive
the party. There were several officers among them whom I had known before,
both at West Point and in Mexico. Seeing these officers who had been educated for the profession of arms, both at school and in actual war, which is a
far more efficient training, impressed me with the great advantage the South
possessed over the North at the beginning of the rebellion. They had from
thirty to forty per cent. of the educated soldiers of the Nation.[1] They had no
standing army and, consequently, these trained soldiers had to find employment with the troops from their own States. In this way what there was of
military education and training was distributed throughout their whole
army. The whole loaf was leavened.

The North had a greater number of educated and trained soldiers, but the
bulk of them were still in the army and were retained, generally with their old
commands and rank, until the war had lasted many months. In the Army of
the Potomac there was what was known as the "regular brigade," in which,

---

[1] While USG's assertion is difficult to confirm, it has been established that regular army of-
ficers made up 36.7 percent of Confederate generals and 43.9 percent of U.S. generals. Wayne
We-siang Hsieh, *West Pointers in the Civil War: The Old Army in War and Peace* (Chapel Hill:
University of North Carolina Press, 2009), 200.

from the commanding officer down to the youngest second lieutenant, every one was educated to his profession. So, too, with many of the batteries; all the officers, generally four in number to each, were men educated for their profession. Some of these went into battle at the beginning under division commanders who were entirely without military training.[2] This state of affairs gave me an idea which I expressed while at Cairo; that the government ought to disband the regular army, with the exception of the staff corps, and notify the disbanded officers that they would receive no compensation while the war lasted except as volunteers. The register should be kept up, but the names of all officers who were not in the volunteer service at the close, should be stricken from it.

On the 9th of November, two days after the battle of Belmont, Major-General H. W. Halleck[3] superseded General Fremont in command of the Department of the Missouri.[4] The limits of his command took in Arkansas and west Kentucky east to the Cumberland River. From the battle of Belmont until early in February, 1862, the troops under my command did little except prepare for the long struggle which proved to be before them.

The enemy at this time occupied a line running from the Mississippi River at Columbus to Bowling Green and Mill Springs, Kentucky. Each of these positions was strongly fortified, as were also points on the Tennessee and Cumberland rivers near the Tennessee state line. The works on the Tennessee were called Fort Heiman and Fort Henry, and that on the Cumberland was Fort Donelson. At these points the two rivers approached within eleven miles of each other. The lines of rifle pits at each place extended back from the water at least two miles, so that the garrisons were in reality only seven miles apart. These positions were of immense importance to the enemy; and of course correspondingly important for us to possess ourselves of. With Fort Henry in our hands we had a navigable stream open to us up to Muscle Shoals, in

[2] In order to encourage widespread support, Lincoln appointed at the outset of the war both Republican and Democratic politicians as generals, regardless of their previous military experience. T. Harry Williams, *Lincoln and His Generals* (New York: Random House, 2011), 10–11.

[3] Henry W. Halleck (1815–1872) was born in New York and graduated from the USMA in 1839. He served as general-in-chief of the army from July 1862 to Mar. 1864. *CWHC*, 274.

[4] Unable to stop Price's military operations in Missouri, Frémont was relieved of command on Nov. 2, 1861. On Nov. 9, Halleck was appointed commander of the Dept. of the Missouri. John F. Marszalek, *Commander of All Lincoln's Armies: A Life of General Henry W. Halleck* (Cambridge, MA: Harvard University Press, 2004), 108–109; *PUSG*, 3:149n–150n.

Alabama. The Memphis and Charleston Railroad strikes the Tennessee at East-port, Mississippi, and follows close to the banks of the river up to the shoals.[5] This road, of vast importance to the enemy, would cease to be of use to them for through traffic the moment Fort Henry became ours. Fort Donelson was the gate to Nashville—a place of great military and political importance—and to a rich country extending far east in Kentucky. These two points in our pos-session the enemy would necessarily be thrown back to the Memphis and Charleston road, or to the boundary of the cotton states, and, as before stated, that road would be lost to them for through communication.

The designation of my command had been changed after Halleck's arrival, from the District of South-east Missouri to the District of Cairo, and the small district commanded by General C. F. Smith, embracing the mouths of the Tennessee and Cumberland rivers, had been added to my jurisdiction.[6] Early in January, 1862, I was directed by General McClellan, through my depart-ment commander, to make a reconnoissance in favor of Brigadier-General Don Carlos Buell,[7] who commanded the Department of the Ohio, with head-quarters at Louisville, and who was confronting General S. B. Buckner with a larger Confederate force at Bowling Green.[8] It was supposed that Buell was

---

[5] Eastport, MS, on the south side of the Tennessee River near the Alabama state line, was approximately seven miles from the Memphis and Charleston Railroad, the Confederacy's only complete east-west line. It started in Memphis, TN, and ran through Mississippi and Ala-bama to Chattanooga, TN. From there, other railroad lines connected it to several important ports in the South. With the completion of the railroad in 1857, the residents of Eastport abandoned the town and relocated to Iuka, MS, which was closer to the rail line. George B. Davis et al., *The Official Military Atlas of the Civil War* (New York: Fairfax Press, 1983), plate 149; *Mississippi: The WPA Guide to the Magnolia State* (Jackson: University Press of Mississippi, 1988), 442; *PUSG,* 4:321*n*; Timothy B. Smith, *Mississippi in the Civil War: The Home Front* (Jackson: University Press of Mississippi, 2010), 81.

[6] On Dec. 20, 1861, Capt. John C. Kelton, by order of Halleck, issued Special Orders No. 78, changing USG's command to the District of Cairo, IL. USG instituted the change with Gen. Orders No. 22. *OR,* I, 52(I), 201; *PUSG,* 3:330–331, 331*n*–332*n*.

[7] Don Carlos Buell (1818–1898) was born in Ohio and graduated from the USMA in 1841. He took command of the Dept. of the Ohio on Nov. 9, 1861. *CWHC,* 152.

[8] On Jan. 6, 1862, Halleck instructed USG to make a demonstration against Confederate forces in Kentucky. Halleck ordered that troops stationed at Fort Holt and Paducah, KY, should meet in Mayfield, KY, and threaten Camp Beauregard and Camp Murray, leading the Confederates to believe that Dover, TN, near Fort Donelson, was the object of the movement. *PUSG,* 4:3–4, 4*n*.

about to make some move against the enemy, and my demonstration was in-tended to prevent the sending of troops from Columbus, Fort Henry or Do-nelson to Buckner. I at once ordered General Smith to send a force up the west bank of the Tennessee to threaten forts Heiman and Henry; McClernand at the same time with a force of 6,000 men was sent out into west Kentucky, threatening Columbus with one column and the Tennessee River with another.[9] I went with McClernand's command. The weather was very bad; snow and rain fell; the roads, never good in that section, were intolerable. We were out more than a week splashing through the mud, snow and rain, the men suffering very much. The object of the expedition was accomplished. The enemy did not send reinforcements to Bowling Green, and General George H. Thomas fought and won the battle of Mill Springs before we returned.[10]

As a result of this expedition General Smith reported that he thought it prac-ticable to capture Fort Heiman. This fort stood on high ground, completely commanding Fort Henry on the opposite side of the river, and its possession by us, with the aid of our gunboats, would insure the capture of Fort Henry. This report of Smith's confirmed views I had previously held, that the true line of operations for us was up the Tennessee and Cumberland rivers. With us there, the enemy would be compelled to fall back on the east and west en-tirely out of the State of Kentucky. On the 6th of January, before receiving orders for this expedition, I had asked permission of the general commanding the department to go to see him at St. Louis.[11] My object was to lay this plan of campaign before him. Now that my views had been confirmed by so able a general as Smith, I renewed my request to go to St. Louis on what I deemed important military business. The leave was granted, but not graciously.[12]

---

[9] On Jan. 8, 1862, USG ordered Smith to leave Paducah and move slowly to Mayfield. The next day, USG ordered McClernand to proceed to Fort Jefferson, just north of Columbus, KY. Ibid., 4:11–12, 19–20.

[10] George H. Thomas (1816–1870) was born in Virginia and graduated from the USMA in 1840. On Jan. 19, 1862, Thomas led the U.S. troops to victory at the Battle of Mill Springs, KY. *CWHC*, 527; Brian Steel Wills, *George Henry Thomas: As True as Steel* (Lawrence: University Press of Kansas, 2012), 136–141.

[11] On Nov. 20, 1861, USG wrote to Halleck seeking permission to visit him. Halleck denied USG's request the following day, insisting that all reports would continue to be made in writing. *PUSG*, 3:202 and *n*.

[12] On Jan. 22, 1862, Halleck granted the request for USG to travel to St. Louis. USG left Cairo for St. Louis on Jan. 23 and returned to Cairo on Jan. 28. Ibid., 4:75*n*, 94, 100*n*.

I had known General Halleck but very slightly in the old army, not having met him either at West Point or during the Mexican war. I was received with so little cordiality that I perhaps stated the object of my visit with less clearness than I might have done, and I had not uttered many sentences before I was cut short as if my plan was preposterous. I returned to Cairo very much crestfallen.

Flag-officer Foote[13] commanded the little fleet of gunboats then in the neighborhood of Cairo and, though in another branch of the service, was subject to the command of General Halleck. He and I consulted freely upon military matters and he agreed with me perfectly as to the feasibility of the campaign up the Tennessee. Notwithstanding the rebuff I had received from my immediate chief, I therefore, on the 28th of January, renewed the suggestion by telegraph that "if permitted, I could take and hold Fort Henry on the Tennessee." This time I was backed by Flag-officer Foote, who sent a similar dispatch. On the 29th I wrote fully in support of the proposition. On the 1st of February I received full instructions from department headquarters to move upon Fort Henry.[14] On the 2d the expedition started.

In February, 1862, there were quite a good many steamers laid up at Cairo for want of employment, the Mississippi River being closed against navigation below that point. There were also many men in the town whose occupation had been following the river in various capacities, from captain down to deck hand. But there were not enough of either boats or men to move at one time the 17,000 men I proposed to take with me up the Tennessee. I loaded the boats with more than half the force, however, and sent General McClernand in command. I followed with one of the later boats and found McClernand had stopped, very properly, nine miles below Fort Henry. Seven gunboats under Flag-officer Foote had accompanied the advance.[15] The transports we had with us had to return to Paducah to bring up a division from there, with General C. F. Smith in command.

---

[13] Andrew H. Foote (1806–1863) was born in Connecticut and joined the U.S. Navy as a midshipman in 1822. He commanded multiple gunboats from Nov. 1861 to Mar. 1862, including *Lexington, Cincinnati, St. Louis, Conestoga,* and *Benton.* Foote died suddenly from kidney disease. *CWHC,* 238.

[14] Halleck's telegram to USG containing instructions regarding Fort Henry was dated Jan. 30, 1862. *PUSG,* 4:104*n*.

[15] The boats included under Foote's command were the flagship *Essex,* Commander William D. Porter; *Cincinnati,* Commander Roger N. Stembel; *Carondelet,* Commander Henry Walke; *St. Louis,* Lt. Commander Hiram Paulding; *Conestoga,* Lt. Commander Seth L. Phelps; *Tyler,* Lt. Commander William Gwin; *Lexington,* Lt. Commander James W. Shirk. *OR,* I, 7, 122.

Before sending the boats back I wanted to get the troops as near to the enemy as I could without coming within range of their guns. There was a stream emptying into the Tennessee on the east side, apparently at about long range distance below the fort.[16] On account of the narrow water-shed separating the Tennessee and Cumberland rivers at that point, the stream must be insignificant at ordinary stages, but when we were there, in February, it was a torrent. It would facilitate the investment of Fort Henry materially if the troops could be landed south of that stream. To test whether this could be done I boarded the gunboat *Essex* and requested Captain Wm. Porter[17] commanding it, to approach the fort to draw its fire.[18] After we had gone some distance past the mouth of the stream we drew the fire of the fort, which fell much short of us. In consequence I had made up my mind to return and bring the troops to the upper side of the creek, when the enemy opened upon us with a rifled gun that sent shot far beyond us and beyond the stream. One shot passed very near where Captain Porter and I were standing, struck the deck near the stern, penetrated and passed through the cabin and so out into the river. We immediately turned back, and the troops were debarked below the mouth of the creek.

When the landing was completed I returned with the transports to Paducah to hasten up the balance of the troops. I got back on the 5th with the advance, the remainder following as rapidly as the steamers could carry them. At ten o'clock at night, on the 5th, the whole command was not yet up. Being anxious to commence operations as soon as possible before the enemy could reinforce heavily, I issued my orders for an advance at 11 A.M. on the 6th. I felt sure that all the troops would be up by that time.

Fort Henry occupies a bend in the river which gave the guns in the water battery a direct fire down the stream. The camp outside the fort was intrenched, with rifle pits and outworks two miles back on the road to Donelson and Dover. The garrison of the fort and camp was about 2,800, with strong reinforcements from Donelson halted some miles out. There were seventeen heavy guns in the fort. The river was very high, the banks being overflowed except where the bluffs come to the water's edge. A portion of the ground on which Fort Henry stood was two feet deep in water. Below, the water extended into the woods several hundred yards back from the bank on the east side. On the west bank

[16] USG referred to Panther Creek, which emptied into the Tennessee River just north of Fort Henry. *PUSG*, 4:144 (map).

[17] William D. Porter (1809–1864) was born in Louisiana, joined the U.S. Navy as a midshipman in 1823, and was promoted to commodore in 1862. *CWHC*, 436.

[18] USG boarded *Essex* on Feb. 4, 1862. *PUSG*, 4:147.

Fort Heiman stood on high ground, completely commanding Fort Henry. The distance from Fort Henry to Donelson is but eleven miles. The two positions were so important to the enemy, *as he saw his interest,* that it was natural to suppose that reinforcements would come from every quarter from which they could be got. Prompt action on our part was imperative.

The plan was for the troops and gunboats to start at the same moment. The troops were to invest the garrison and the gunboats to attack the fort at close quarters. General Smith was to land a brigade of his division on the west bank during the night of the 5th and get it in rear of Heiman.

At the hour designated the troops and gunboats started. General Smith found Fort Heiman had been evacuated before his men arrived. The gunboats soon engaged the water batteries at very close quarters, but the troops which were to invest Fort Henry were delayed for want of roads, as well as by the dense forest and the high water in what would in dry weather have been un-important beds of streams. This delay made no difference in the result. On our first appearance Tilghman had sent his entire command, with the exception of about one hundred men left to man the guns in the fort, to the out-works on the road to Dover and Donelson, so as to have them out of range of the guns of our navy; and before any attack on the 6th he had ordered them to retreat on Donelson.[19] He stated in his subsequent report that the defence was intended solely to give his troops time to make their escape.

Tilghman was captured with his staff and ninety men, as well as the arma-ment of the fort, the ammunition and whatever stores were there.[20] Our cavalry pursued the retreating column towards Donelson and picked up two guns and a few stragglers; but the enemy had so much the start, that the pursuing force did not get in sight of any except the stragglers.

All the gunboats engaged were hit many times. The damage, however, beyond what could be repaired by a small expenditure of money, was slight, except to the *Essex.* A shell penetrated the boiler of that vessel and exploded it, killing and wounding forty-eight men, nineteen of whom were soldiers who had been detailed to act with the navy.[21] On several occasions during the

[19] Before 5 A.M. on Feb. 5, 1862, Confederate general Lloyd Tilghman transferred his troops from Fort Heiman to Fort Henry. Ibid., 4:155n.

[20] On Feb. 6, 1862, Union forces captured Tilghman, eleven officers, sixty-six enlisted men, and sixteen wounded at Fort Henry. Ibid., 4:160n.

[21] On Feb. 6, 1862, USG reported that thirty-two men were killed or wounded by the dam-aged boiler, Porter being one of the wounded. Ibid., 4:157.

war such details were made when the complement of men with the navy was insufficient for the duty before them. After the fall of Fort Henry Captain Walke,[22] commanding the iron-clad *Carondelet,* at my request ascended the Tennessee River and thoroughly destroyed the bridge of the Memphis and Ohio Railroad.[23]

[22] Henry Walke (1808–1896) was born in Virginia and moved to Ohio in 1810. He joined the U.S. Navy as a midshipman in 1827, was assigned to *Carondelet* in 1862, and was promoted to rear admiral in 1870. *CWHC,* 548.

[23] The railroad USG referred to was the Memphis, Clarksville, and Louisiana line. The bridge was approximately eleven miles upriver from Fort Henry in Danville, TN. *PUSG,* 4:169*n.*

# 22

## Investment of Fort Donelson—The Naval Operations—Attack of the Enemy—Assaulting the Works—Surrender of the Fort

I INFORMED THE DEPARTMENT commander of our success at Fort Henry and that on the 8th I would take Fort Donelson. But the rain continued to fall so heavily that the roads became impassable for artillery and wagon trains. Then, too, it would not have been prudent to proceed without the gunboats. At least it would have been leaving behind a valuable part of our available force.[1]

On the 7th, the day after the fall of Fort Henry, I took my staff and the cavalry—a part of one regiment—and made a reconnoissance to within about a mile of the outer line of works at Donelson.[2] I had known General Pillow in Mexico, and judged that with any force, no matter how small, I could march up to within gunshot of any intrenchments he was given to hold. I said this to the officers of my staff at the time. I knew that Floyd was in command, but he was no soldier, and I judged that he would yield to Pillow's pretensions. I met, as I expected, no opposition in making the reconnoissance and, besides learning the topography of the country on the way and around Fort Donelson, found that there were two roads available for marching; one leading to the village of Dover, the other to Donelson.[3]

Fort Donelson is two miles north, or down the river, from Dover. The fort, as it stood in 1861, embraced about one hundred acres of land. On the east it fronted the Cumberland; to the north it faced Hickman's creek, a small stream which at that time was deep and wide because of the back-water from the river;

---

[1] The gunboats, under the command of Capt. Seth L. Phelps, were on an expedition up the Tennessee River. They returned on Feb. 10, 1862. *PUSG*, 4:182, 183*n*.

[2] USG accompanied the reconnaissance mission on Feb. 9, 1862. The group came within four miles of Fort Donelson. Ibid., 4:180*n*.

[3] Ridge Road led to Dover, TN; Telegraph Road led to Fort Donelson. Ibid., 4:191–192.

on the south was another small stream,[4] or rather a ravine, opening into the Cumberland. This also was filled with back-water from the river. The fort stood on high ground, some of it as much as a hundred feet above the Cumberland. Strong protection to the heavy guns in the water batteries had been obtained by cutting away places for them in the bluff. To the west there was a line of rifle-pits some two miles back from the river at the farthest point. This line ran generally along the crest of high ground, but in one place crossed a ravine which opens into the river between the village and the fort. The ground inside and outside of this intrenched line was very broken and generally wooded. The trees outside of the rifle-pits had been cut down for a considerable way out, and had been felled so that their tops lay outwards from the intrenchments. The limbs had been trimmed and pointed, and thus formed an abatis in front of the greater part of the line. Outside of this intrenched line, and extending about half the entire length of it, is a ravine running north and south and opening into Hickman creek at a point north of the fort. The entire side of this ravine next to the works was one long abatis.

General Halleck commenced his efforts in all quarters to get reinforcements to forward to me immediately on my departure from Cairo. General Hunter[5] sent men freely from Kansas, and a large division under General Nelson,[6] from Buell's army, was also dispatched.[7] Orders went out from the War Department to consolidate fragments of companies that were being recruited in the Western States so as to make full companies, and to consolidate companies into regiments. General Halleck did not approve or disapprove of my going to Fort Donelson. He said nothing whatever to me on the subject. He informed Buell on the 7th that I would march against Fort Donelson the next day; but on the 10th he directed me to fortify Fort Henry strongly, particularly to the land side, saying that he forwarded me intrenching tools for that purpose. I received this dispatch in front of Fort Donelson.

[4] Indian Creek. Ibid., 4:156.

[5] David Hunter (1802–1886) was born in New Jersey and graduated from the USMA in 1822. He took command of the Dept. of Kansas in Nov. 1861. *CWHC*, 310.

[6] William "Bull" Nelson (1824–1862) was born in Kentucky and became a midshipman in Jan. 1840. In Sept. 1861, he was assigned to duty in the U.S. Army. He commanded the 4th Div., Army of the Ohio, during the attack on Fort Donelson. Ibid., 405.

[7] On Feb. 6, 1862, Buell sent a brigade and two regiments from Indiana and six regiments from Ohio to reinforce USG. Stephen D. Engle, *Don Carlos Buell: Most Promising of All* (Chapel Hill: University of North Carolina Press, 1999), 161.

I was very impatient to get to Fort Donelson because I knew the importance of the place to the enemy and supposed he would reinforce it rapidly. I felt that 15,000 men on the 8th would be more effective than 50,000 a month later. I asked Flag-officer Foote, therefore, to order his gunboats still about Cairo to proceed up the Cumberland River and not to wait for those gone to Eastport and Florence; but the others got back in time and we started on the 12th. I had moved McClernand out a few miles the night before so as to leave the road as free as possible.

Just as we were about to start the first reinforcement reached me on transports. It was a brigade composed of six full regiments commanded by Colonel Thayer, of Nebraska.[8] As the gunboats were going around to Donelson by the Tennessee, Ohio and Cumberland rivers, I directed Thayer to turn about and go under their convoy.

I started from Fort Henry with 15,000 men, including eight batteries and part of a regiment of cavalry, and, meeting with no obstruction to detain us, the advance arrived in front of the enemy by noon. That afternoon and the next day were spent in taking up ground to make the investment as complete as possible. General Smith had been directed to leave a portion of his division behind to guard forts Henry and Heiman. He left General Lew. Wallace[9] with 2,500 men. With the remainder of his division he occupied our left, extending to Hickman creek. McClernand was on the right and covered the roads running south and south-west from Dover. His right extended to the backwater up the ravine opening into the Cumberland south of the village. The troops were not intrenched, but the nature of the ground was such that they were just as well protected from the fire of the enemy as if rifle-pits had been thrown up. Our line was generally along the crest of ridges. The artillery was

---

[8] John M. Thayer (1820–1906) was born in Massachusetts and moved to the Nebraska Territory in 1854. He served as a major general in the Nebraska Militia before the Civil War and was appointed colonel of the 1st Nebraska Inf. in 1861. At the Battle of Fort Donelson, Thayer commanded the 3rd Brigade, which included the 1st Nebraska Inf. and the 58th, 68th, and 76th Ohio Inf. Additionally, the 46th, 57th, and 58th Illinois Inf. and the 20th Ohio Inf. were placed under Thayer's command. *CWHC*, 525–526; Timothy B. Smith, *Grant Invades Tennessee: The 1862 Battles for Forts Henry and Donelson* (Lawrence: University Press of Kansas, 2016), 413.

[9] Lewis Wallace (1827–1905) was born in Indiana and joined the 1st Indiana Inf. as a second lieutenant in June 1846. He left the U.S. Army in 1847. At the start of the Civil War, he reentered the military as an adjutant general in the Indiana Militia. After the war, he was governor of the New Mexico Territory from 1878 to 1881. He wrote the 1880 novel *Ben-Hur: A Tale of the Christ*. *CWHC*, 551.

protected by being sunk in the ground. The men who were not serving the guns were perfectly covered from fire on taking position a little back from the crest. The greatest suffering was from want of shelter. It was midwinter and during the siege we had rain and snow, thawing and freezing alternately. It would not do to allow camp-fires except far down the hill out of sight of the enemy, and it would not do to allow many of the troops to remain there at the same time. In the march over from Fort Henry numbers of the men had thrown away their blankets and overcoats. There was therefore much discomfort and absolute suffering.

During the 12th and 13th, and until the arrival of Wallace and Thayer on the 14th, the National forces, composed of but 15,000 men, without intrenchments, confronted an intrenched army of 21,000, without conflict further than what was brought on by ourselves.[10] Only one gunboat had arrived.[11] There was a little skirmishing each day, brought on by the movement of our troops in securing commanding positions; but there was no actual fighting during this time except once, on the 13th, in front of McClernand's command. That general had undertaken to capture a battery of the enemy which was annoying his men. Without orders or authority he sent three regiments to make the assault. The battery was in the main line of the enemy, which was defended by his whole army present. Of course the assault was a failure, and of course the loss on our side was great for the number of men engaged.[12] In this assault Colonel William Morrison[13] fell badly wounded. Up to this time the surgeons with the army had no difficulty in finding room in the houses near our line for all the sick and wounded; but now hospitals were overcrowded. Owing, however, to the energy and skill of the surgeons the suffering was not so great as it might have been. The hospital arrangements at Fort Donelson were as

[10] Many of USG's estimates of the number of troops in this chapter cannot be definitively confirmed. The estimated number of Confederate soldiers at Fort Donelson ranged from 13,000 to over 21,000. *PUSG*, 4:210n.

[11] *Carondelet* was the first gunboat to arrive at Fort Donelson. Spencer Tucker, *Unconditional Surrender: The Capture of Forts Henry and Donelson* (Abilene, TX: McWhiney Foundation, 2001), 75.

[12] The attack resulted in 142 U.S. casualties. Richard L. Kiper, *Major General John Alexander McClernand: Politician in Uniform* (Kent, OH: Kent State University Press, 1999), 76–79.

[13] William R. Morrison (1824–1909) was born in Illinois and enlisted in the U.S. Army to fight in the Mexican-American War. After being wounded at Fort Donelson, Morrison recovered and eventually served as a U.S. representative from Illinois. John T. Hubbell et al., eds., *Biographical Dictionary of the Union: Northern Leaders of the Civil War* (Westport, CT: Greenwood Press, 1995), 366.

complete as it was possible to make them, considering the inclemency of the weather and the lack of tents, in a sparsely settled country where the houses were generally of but one or two rooms.

On the return of Captain Walke to Fort Henry on the 10th, I had requested him to take the vessels that had accompanied him on his expedition up the Tennessee, and get possession of the Cumberland as far up towards Donelson as possible. He started without delay, taking, however, only his own gunboat, the *Carondelet,* towed by the steamer *Alps.* Captain Walke arrived a few miles below Donelson on the 12th, a little after noon. About the time the advance of troops reached a point within gunshot of the fort on the land side, he engaged the water batteries at long range. On the 13th I informed him of my arrival the day before and of the establishment of most of our batteries, requesting him at the same time to attack again that day so that I might take advantage of any diversion. The attack was made and many shots fell within the fort, creating some consternation, as we now know. The investment on the land side was made as complete as the number of troops engaged would admit of.

During the night of the 13th Flag-officer Foote arrived with the iron-clads *St. Louis, Louisville* and *Pittsburg* and the wooden gunboats *Tyler* and *Conestoga,* convoying Thayer's brigade.[14] On the morning of the 14th Thayer was landed. Wallace, whom I had ordered over from Fort Henry, also arrived about the same time. Up to this time he had been commanding a brigade belonging to the division of General C. F. Smith. These troops were now restored to the division they belonged to, and General Lew. Wallace was assigned to the command of a division composed of the brigade of Colonel Thayer and other reinforcements that arrived the same day. This new division was assigned to the centre, giving the two flanking divisions an opportunity to close up and form a stronger line.

The plan was for the troops to hold the enemy within his lines, while the gunboats should attack the water batteries at close quarters and silence his guns if possible. Some of the gunboats were to run the batteries, get above the fort and above the village of Dover. I had ordered a reconnoissance made with the view of getting troops to the river above Dover in case they should be needed there. That position attained by the gunboats it would have been but a question of time—and a very short time, too—when the garrison would have been compelled to surrender.

By three in the afternoon of the 14th Flag-officer Foote was ready, and advanced upon the water batteries with his entire fleet. After coming in range

[14] The ironclad *Carondelet* also accompanied the fleet. *PUSG,* 4:215*n.*

of the batteries of the enemy the advance was slow, but a constant fire was delivered from every gun that could be brought to bear upon the fort. I occupied a position on shore from which I could see the advancing navy. The leading boat got within a very short distance of the water battery, not further off I think than two hundred yards, and I soon saw one and then another of them dropping down the river, visibly disabled. Then the whole fleet followed and the engagement closed for the day. The gunboat which Flag-officer Foote was on, besides having been hit about sixty times, several of the shots passing through near the water-line, had a shot enter the pilot-house which killed the pilot, carried away the wheel and wounded the flag-officer himself. The tiller-ropes of another vessel were carried away and she, too, dropped helplessly back. Two others had their pilot-houses so injured that they scarcely formed a protection to the men at the wheel.[15]

The enemy had evidently been much demoralized by the assault, but they were jubilant when they saw the disabled vessels dropping down the river entirely out of the control of the men on board. Of course I only witnessed the falling back of our gunboats and felt sad enough at the time over the repulse. Subsequent reports, now published, show that the enemy telegraphed a great victory to Richmond. The sun went down on the night of the 14th of February, 1862, leaving the army confronting Fort Donelson anything but comforted over the prospects. The weather had turned intensely cold; the men were without tents and could not keep up fires where most of them had to stay, and, as previously stated, many had thrown away their overcoats and blankets. Two of the strongest of our gunboats had been disabled, presumably beyond the possibility of rendering any present assistance. I retired this night not knowing but that I would have to intrench my position, and bring up tents for the men or build huts under the cover of the hills.

On the morning of the 15th, before it was yet broad day, a messenger from Flag-officer Foote handed me a note, expressing a desire to see me on the flag-ship and saying that he had been injured the day before so much that he could not come himself to me. I at once made my preparations for starting. I directed my adjutant-general[16] to notify each of the division commanders

[15] Foote was wounded aboard the flagship *St. Louis*; the pilot killed was Francis A. Riley (c.1820–1862). *Louisville* lost its tiller-ropes during the exchange of fire, while *Pittsburg* and *Carondelet* also suffered severe damage. Benjamin F. Cooling, *Forts Henry and Donelson: The Key to the Confederate Heartland* (Knoxville: University of Tennessee Press, 1987), 157.

[16] John A. Rawlins was assistant adjutant general on USG's staff during the Battle of Fort Donelson. *PUSG*, 4:225.

of my absence and instruct them to do nothing to bring on an engagement until they received further orders, but to hold their positions. From the heavy rains that had fallen for days and weeks preceding and from the constant use of the roads between the troops and the landing four to seven miles below, these roads had become cut up so as to be hardly passable. The intense cold of the night of the 14th-15th had frozen the ground solid. This made travel on horseback even slower than through the mud; but I went as fast as the roads would allow.

When I reached the fleet I found the flag-ship was anchored out in the stream. A small boat, however, awaited my arrival and I was soon on board with the flag-officer. He explained to me in short the condition in which he was left by the engagement of the evening before, and suggested that I should intrench while he returned to Mound City[17] with his disabled boats, expressing at the time the belief that he could have the necessary repairs made and be back in ten days. I saw the absolute necessity of his gunboats going into hospital and did not know but I should be forced to the alternative of going through a siege. But the enemy relieved me from this necessity.

When I left the National line to visit Flag-officer Foote I had no idea that there would be any engagement on land unless I brought it on myself. The conditions for battle were much more favorable to us than they had been for the first two days of the investment. From the 12th to the 14th we had but 15,000 men of all arms and no gunboats. Now we had been reinforced by a fleet of six naval vessels, a large division of troops under General L. Wallace and 2,500 men brought over from Fort Henry belonging to the division of C. F. Smith. The enemy, however, had taken the initiative. Just as I landed I met Captain Hillyer of my staff, white with fear, not for his personal safety, but for the safety of the National troops. He said the enemy had come out of his lines in full force and attacked and scattered McClernand's division, which was in full retreat.[18] The roads, as I have said, were unfit for making fast time, but I got to my command as soon as possible. The attack had been made on the National right. I was some four or five miles north of our left. The line was about three miles long. In reaching the point where the disaster had occurred I had to pass the divisions of Smith and Wallace. I saw no sign of

---

[17] After his meeting with USG, Foote's Feb. 15, 1862, report to U.S. secretary of the navy Gideon Welles indicates that he proceeded to Cairo, IL, not Mound City, IL. *ORN*, I, 22, 585.

[18] The Confederate troops had been ordered to retreat to Nashville, which necessitated breaking through the Union lines. On the morning of Feb. 15, 1862, several Confederate brigades attacked McClernand's division in an effort to do so. Kiper, *John Alexander McClernand*, 77–78.

excitement on the portion of the line held by Smith; Wallace was nearer the scene of conflict and had taken part in it. He had, at an opportune time, sent Thayer's brigade to the support of McClernand and thereby contributed to hold the enemy within his lines.

I saw everything favorable for us along the line of our left and centre. When I came to the right appearances were different. The enemy had come out in full force to cut his way out and make his escape. McClernand's division had to bear the brunt of the attack from this combined force. His men had stood up gallantly until the ammunition in their cartridge-boxes gave out. There was abundance of ammunition near by lying on the ground in boxes, but at that stage of the war it was not all of our commanders of regiments, brigades, or even divisions, who had been educated up to the point of seeing that their men were constantly supplied with ammunition during an engagement. When the men found themselves without ammunition they could not stand up against troops who seemed to have plenty of it. The division broke and a portion fled, but most of the men, as they were not pursued, only fell back out of range of the fire of the enemy. It must have been about this time that Thayer pushed his brigade in between the enemy and those of our troops that were without ammunition. At all events the enemy fell back within his intrenchments and was there when I got on the field.

I saw the men standing in knots talking in the most excited manner. No officer seemed to be giving any directions. The soldiers had their muskets, but no ammunition, while there were tons of it close at hand. I heard some of the men say that the enemy had come out with knapsacks, and haversacks filled with rations. They seemed to think this indicated a determination on his part to stay out and fight just as long as the provisions held out. I turned to Colonel J. D. Webster,[19] of my staff, who was with me, and said: "Some of our men are pretty badly demoralized, but the enemy must be more so, for he has attempted to force his way out, but has fallen back: the one who attacks first now will be victorious and the enemy will have to be in a hurry if he gets ahead of me." I determined to make the assault at once on our left. It was clear to my mind that the enemy had started to march out with his entire force, except a few pickets, and if our attack could be made on the left before the enemy could redistribute his forces along the line, we would find but little opposition except from the intervening abatis. I directed Colonel Webster to ride with me and call out to the men as we passed: "Fill your cartridge-boxes, quick,

[19] Joseph D. Webster (1811–1876) was born in New Hampshire and later moved to Massachusetts. He was on USG's staff during the Fort Donelson campaign. *CWHC,* 558; *PUSG,* 4:225.

and get into line; the enemy is trying to escape and he must not be permitted to do so." This acted like a charm. The men only wanted some one to give them a command. We rode rapidly to Smith's quarters, when I explained the situation to him and directed him to charge the enemy's works in his front with his whole division, saying at the same time that he would find nothing but a very thin line to contend with. The general was off in an incredibly short time, going in advance himself to keep his men from firing while they were working their way through the abatis intervening between them and the enemy. The outer line of rifle-pits was passed, and the night of the 15th General Smith, with much of his division, bivouacked within the lines of the enemy. There was now no doubt but that the Confederates must surrender or be captured the next day.

There seems from subsequent accounts to have been much consternation, particularly among the officers of high rank, in Dover during the night of the 15th. General Floyd, the commanding officer, who was a man of talent enough for any civil position, was no soldier and, possibly, did not possess the elements of one. He was further unfitted for command, for the reason that his conscience must have troubled him and made him afraid. As Secretary of War he had taken a solemn oath to maintain the Constitution of the United States and to uphold the same against all its enemies. He had betrayed that trust. As Secretary of War he was reported through the northern press to have scattered the little army the country had so that the most of it could be picked up in detail when secession occurred. About a year before leaving the Cabinet he had removed arms from northern to southern arsenals. He continued in the Cabinet of President Buchanan until about the 1st of January, 1861, while he was working vigilantly for the establishment of a confederacy made out of United States territory.[20] Well may he have been afraid to fall into the hands of National troops. He would no doubt have been tried for misappropriating public property, if not for treason, had he been captured. General Pillow, next in command, was conceited, and prided himself much on his services in the Mexican war. He telegraphed to General Johnston, at Nashville, after our men were within the rebel rifle-pits, and almost on the eve of his making his escape, that the Southern troops had had great success all day. Johnston forwarded the dispatch to Richmond.[21] While the authorities at the capital were reading it Floyd and Pillow were fugitives.

[20] John B. Floyd resigned as U.S. secretary of war on Dec. 29, 1861. *CWHC,* 237.

[21] For Pillow's Feb. 14, 1862, message as relayed to Polk by Asst. AG Nathaniel Wickliffe, see *OR,* I, 7, 880. For Johnston's Feb. 14 forwarding of the same message to Confederate secretary of war Judah P. Benjamin, see *OR,* I, 7, 255.

A council of war was held by the enemy at which all agreed that it would be impossible to hold out longer. General Buckner, who was third in rank in the garrison but much the most capable soldier, seems to have regarded it a duty to hold the fort until the general commanding the department, A. S. Johnston, should get back to his headquarters at Nashville. Buckner's report shows, however, that he considered Donelson lost and that any attempt to hold the place longer would be at the sacrifice of the command. Being assured that Johnston was already in Nashville, Buckner too agreed that surrender was the proper thing. Floyd turned over the command to Pillow, who declined it. It then devolved upon Buckner, who accepted the responsibility of the position. Floyd and Pillow took possession of all the river transports at Dover and before morning both were on their way to Nashville, with the brigade formerly commanded by Floyd and some other troops, in all about 3,000.[22] Some marched up the east bank of the Cumberland; others went on the steamers. During the night Forrest[23] also, with his cavalry and some other troops, about a thousand in all, made their way out, passing between our right and the river. They had to ford or swim over the back-water in the little creek just south of Dover.[24]

Before daylight General Smith brought to me the following letter from General Buckner:

HEADQUARTERS, FORT DONELSON,
*February* 16, 1862.

SIR:—In consideration of all the circumstances governing the present situation of affairs at this station, I propose to the Commanding Officer of the Federal forces the appointment of Commissioners to agree upon terms of capitulation of the forces and fort under my command, and in that view suggest an armistice until 12 o'clock to-day.

I am, sir, very respectfully,
Your ob't se'v't,

---

[22] According to *OR,* Floyd had 2,381 men under his command in Jan. 1862, but there is no record of the number that left Fort Donelson with him. Ibid., I, 7, 852.

[23] Nathan Bedford Forrest (1821–1877) was born in Tennessee and was a planter and slave trader. He joined the Confederate Army as a private in the 7th Tennessee Cav. in June 1861 and had risen to the rank of colonel by Jan. 1862. He attained the rank of major general in 1863. He was the first grand wizard of the Ku Klux Klan (1867–1869). *CWHC,* 240.

[24] Forrest was accompanied by roughly 700 soldiers when he crossed Lick Creek to escape capture. Cooling, *Forts Henry and Donelson,* 205.

S. B. BUCKNER,
Brig. Gen. C. S. A.

To Brigadier-General U. S. GRANT,
Com'ding U. S. Forces,
Near Fort Donelson.[25]

To this I responded as follows:

HEADQUARTERS ARMY IN THE FIELD,
Camp near Donelson,
*February* 16, 1862.

General S. B. BUCKNER,
Confederate Army.

SIR:—Yours of this date, proposing armistice and appointment of
Commissioners to settle terms of capitulation, is just received. No terms
except an unconditional and immediate surrender can be accepted. I
propose to move immediately upon your works.

I am, sir, very respectfully,
Your ob't se'v't,
U. S. GRANT,
Brig. Gen.

To this I received the following reply:

HEADQUARTERS, DOVER, TENNESSEE,
*February* 16, 1862.

To Brig. Gen'l U. S. GRANT,
U. S. Army.

SIR:—The distribution of the forces under my command, incident to
an unexpected change of commanders, and the overwhelming force
under your command, compel me, notwithstanding the brilliant success
of the Confederate arms yesterday, to accept the ungenerous and
unchivalrous terms which you propose.

I am, sir,
Your very ob't se'v't,
S. B. BUCKNER,
Brig. Gen. C. S. A.[26]

---

[25] *PUSG*, 4:218*n*.
[26] Ibid.

General Buckner, as soon as he had dispatched the first of the above letters, sent word to his different commanders on the line of rifle-pits, notifying them that he had made a proposition looking to the surrender of the garrison, and directing them to notify National troops in their front so that all fighting might be prevented. White flags were stuck at intervals along the line of rifle-pits, but none over the fort. As soon as the last letter from Buckner was received I mounted my horse and rode to Dover. General Wallace, I found, had preceded me an hour or more. I presume that, seeing white flags exposed in his front, he rode up to see what they meant and, not being fired upon or halted, he kept on until he found himself at the headquarters of General Buckner.[27]

I had been at West Point three years with Buckner and afterwards served with him in the army, so that we were quite well acquainted. In the course of our conversation, which was very friendly, he said to me that if he had been in command I would not have got up to Donelson as easily as I did. I told him that if he had been in command I should not have tried in the way I did: I had invested their lines with a smaller force than they had to defend them, and at the same time had sent a brigade full 5,000 strong, around by water; I had relied very much upon their commander to allow me to come safely up to the outside of their works. I asked General Buckner about what force he had to surrender. He replied that he could not tell with any degree of accuracy; that all the sick and weak had been sent to Nashville while we were about Fort Henry; that Floyd and Pillow had left during the night, taking many men with them; and that Forrest, and probably others, had also escaped during the preceding night: the number of casualties he could not tell; but he said I would not find fewer than 12,000, nor more than 15,000.

He asked permission to send parties outside of the lines to bury his dead, who had fallen on the 15th when they tried to get out. I gave directions that his permit to pass our limits should be recognized. I have no reason to believe that this privilege was abused, but it familiarized our guards so much with the sight of Confederates passing to and fro that I have no doubt many got beyond our pickets unobserved and went on. The most of the men who went in that way no doubt thought they had had war enough, and left with the intention of remaining out of the army. Some came to me and asked permission to go, saying that they were tired of the war and would not be caught in the ranks again, and I bade them go.

[27] Wallace crossed enemy lines to see his old friend Buckner, who was headquartered at the Dover Hotel. Ibid., 4:210–211.

The actual number of Confederates at Fort Donelson can never be given with entire accuracy. The largest number admitted by any writer on the Southern side, is by Colonel Preston Johnston. He gives the number at 17,000.[28] But this must be an underestimate. The commissary general of prisoners reported having issued rations to 14,623 Fort Donelson prisoners at Cairo, as they passed that point.[29] General Pillow reported the killed and wounded at 2,000; but he had less opportunity of knowing the actual numbers than the officers of McClernand's division, for most of the killed and wounded fell outside their works, in front of that division, and were buried or cared for by Buckner after the surrender and when Pillow was a fugitive. It is known that Floyd and Pillow escaped during the night of the 15th, taking with them not less than 3,000 men. Forrest escaped with about 1,000 and others were leaving singly and in squads all night. It is probable that the Confederate force at Donelson, on the 15th of February, 1862, was 21,000 in round numbers.

On the day Fort Donelson fell I had 27,000 men to confront the Confederate lines and guard the road four or five miles to the left, over which all our supplies had to be drawn on wagons. During the 16th, after the surrender, additional reinforcements arrived.

During the siege General Sherman[30] had been sent to Smithland, at the mouth of the Cumberland River, to forward reinforcements and supplies to me. At that time he was my senior in rank and there was no authority of law to assign a junior to command a senior of the same grade. But every boat that came up with supplies or reinforcements brought a note of encouragement from Sherman, asking me to call upon him for any assistance he could render and saying that if he could be of service at the front I might send for him and he would waive rank.

---

[28] William Preston Johnston (1831–1899), son of Confederate general Albert Sidney Johnston, was born in Louisville, KY. His estimate of the number of Confederate troops at Fort Donelson was published in his book *The Life of Gen. Albert Sidney Johnston, Embracing His Services in the Armies of the United States, the Republic of Texas, and the Confederate States* (New York: D. Appleton, 1878), 443; *Dictionary of American Biography*, 2nd ed., s.v. "Johnston, William Preston."

[29] Approximately 16,500 to 17,500 prisoners passed through Cairo. *PUSG*, 4:226.

[30] William Tecumseh Sherman (1820–1891) was born in Ohio and graduated from the USMA in 1840. He reached the rank of captain before resigning in 1853. He was superintendent of the Louisiana State Seminary of Learning and Military Academy from 1859 to 1861. He reentered the U.S. Army in 1861 as a colonel in the U.S. 13th Inf. and was promoted to brigadier general in May. He was promoted to major general in May 1862. After the war, he served as USG's interim secretary of war from Sept. 8, 1869 to Oct. 18, 1869. *CWHC*, 484–485.

# 23

Promoted Major-General of Volunteers—Unoccupied
Territory—Advance upon Nashville—Situation of
the Troops—Confederate Retreat—Relieved of
the Command—Restored to the Command—
General Smith

THE NEWS OF THE FALL of Fort Donelson caused great delight all over the
North. At the South, particularly in Richmond, the effect was correspondingly depressing. I was promptly promoted to the grade of Major-General of
Volunteers, and confirmed by the Senate.[1] All three of my division commanders were promoted to the same grade and the colonels who commanded
brigades were made brigadier-generals in the volunteer service.[2] My chief,
who was in St. Louis, telegraphed his congratulations to General Hunter in
Kansas for the services he had rendered in securing the fall of Fort Donelson
by sending reinforcements so rapidly. To Washington he telegraphed that the
victory was due to General C. F. Smith; "promote him," he said, "and the whole
country will applaud."[3] On the 19th there was published at St. Louis a formal
order thanking Flag-officer Foote and myself, and the forces under our com-

[1] On Feb. 16, 1862, Lincoln signed USG's nomination as major general. The U.S. Senate
confirmed the nomination on Feb. 19. *PUSG*, 4:272*n*–273*n*.
[2] On Mar. 21, 1862, John A. McClernand, Charles F. Smith, and Lew Wallace were all promoted to major general, while six of the ten colonels (Richard J. Oglesby, William H. L. Wallace, John McArthur, John Cook, Jacob G. Lauman, and John A. Logan) were promoted to
brigadier general. *CWHC*, 183, 340, 351, 370, 372, 408, 493, 551–552.
[3] On Feb. 19, 1862, Halleck wrote to McClellan regarding Smith: "Honor him for this victory and the whole country will applaud." For Halleck's correspondence with Hunter and
McClellan, see *OR*, I, 7, 636–637.

mand, for the victories on the Tennessee and the Cumberland.[4] I received no other recognition whatever from General Halleck. But General Cullum,[5] his chief of staff, who was at Cairo, wrote me a warm congratulatory letter on his own behalf.[6] I approved of General Smith's promotion highly, as I did all the promotions that were made.

My opinion was and still is that immediately after the fall of Fort Donelson the way was opened to the National forces all over the South-west without much resistance. If one general who would have taken the responsibility had been in command of all the troops west of the Alleghanies, he could have marched to Chattanooga, Corinth, Memphis and Vicksburg with the troops we then had, and as volunteering was going on rapidly over the North there would soon have been force enough at all these centres to operate offensively against any body of the enemy that might be found near them. Rapid movements and the acquisition of rebellious territory would have promoted volunteering, so that reinforcements could have been had as fast as transportation could have been obtained to carry them to their destination. On the other hand there were tens of thousands of strong able-bodied young men still at their homes in the South-western States, who had not gone into the Confederate army in February, 1862, and who had no particular desire to go. If our lines had been extended to protect their homes, many of them never would have gone. Providence ruled differently. Time was given the enemy to collect armies and fortify his new positions; and twice afterwards he came near forcing his north-western front up to the Ohio River.

I promptly informed the department commander of our success at Fort Donelson and that the way was open now to Clarksville and Nashville; and that unless I received orders to the contrary I should take Clarksville on the 21st and Nashville about the 1st of March. Both these places are on the Cumberland River above Fort Donelson. As I heard nothing from headquarters on the subject, General C. F. Smith was sent to Clarksville at the time designated and

---

[4] On Feb. 19, 1862, Capt. Nathaniel McLean issued Gen. Orders No. 43, offering congratulations to both USG and Foote. *PUSG,* 4:273n.

[5] George W. Cullum (1809–1892) was born in New York, moved to Pennsylvania, and graduated from the USMA in 1833. He served as the chief of staff for the Dept. of the Missouri from Nov. 1861 to Mar. 1862 and attained the rank of brevet major general by the end of the war. He authored numerous books and served as editor of the *Biographical Register of the Officers and Graduates of the U.S. Military Academy. CWHC,* 193.

[6] For Cullum's Feb. 20, 1862, letter to USG, see *PUSG,* 4:235n–236n.

found the place evacuated.[7] The capture of forts Henry and Donelson had broken the line the enemy had taken from Columbus to Bowling Green, and it was known that he was falling back from the eastern point of this line and that Buell was following, or at least advancing. I should have sent troops to Nashville at the time I sent to Clarksville, but my transportation was limited and there were many prisoners to be forwarded north.

None of the reinforcements from Buell's army arrived until the 24th of February.[8] Then General Nelson came up, with orders to report to me with two brigades, he having sent one brigade to Cairo. I knew General Buell was advancing on Nashville from the north, and I was advised by scouts that the rebels were leaving that place, and trying to get out all the supplies they could. Nashville was, at that time, one of the best provisioned posts in the South. I had no use for reinforcements now, and thinking Buell would like to have his troops again, I ordered Nelson to proceed to Nashville without debarking at Fort Donelson. I sent a gunboat also as a convoy.[9] The Cumberland River was very high at the time; the railroad bridge at Nashville had been burned, and all river craft had been destroyed, or would be before the enemy left. Nashville is on the west bank of the Cumberland, and Buell was approaching from the east. I thought the steamers carrying Nelson's division would be useful in ferrying the balance of Buell's forces across. I ordered Nelson to put himself in communication with Buell as soon as possible, and if he found him more than two days off from Nashville to return below the city and await orders. Buell, however, had already arrived in person at Edgefield, opposite Nashville, and Mitchell's[10] division of his command reached there the same day. Nelson immediately took possession of the city.

After Nelson had gone and before I had learned of Buell's arrival, I sent word to department headquarters that I should go to Nashville myself on the 28th if I received no orders to the contrary. Hearing nothing, I went as I had informed my superior officer I would do. On arriving at Clarksville I saw a fleet of steamers at the shore—the same that had taken Nelson's division—and troops going aboard. I landed and called on the commanding officer,

[7] On Feb. 19, 1862, USG ordered Smith to garrison Clarksville, TN. The next day, USG visited the captured town. Ibid., 4:249, 252.

[8] Buell arrived outside Nashville, TN, on Feb. 22, 1862. Ibid., 4:279n.

[9] USG referred to the gunboat *Carondelet*. Ibid., 4:282.

[10] Gen. Ormsby M. Mitchel (c.1809–1862) was born in Kentucky and later moved to Ohio. He graduated from the USMA in 1829, and was promoted to major general on Apr. 11, 1862. Mitchel died from yellow fever in Beaufort, SC. *CWHC*, 392.

General C. F. Smith. As soon as he saw me he showed an order he had just
received from Buell in these words:

NASHVILLE, *February* 25, 1862.

GENERAL C. F. SMITH,
Commanding U. S. Forces, Clarksville.
    GENERAL:—The landing of a portion of our troops, contrary to my
intentions, on the south side of the river has compelled me to hold this
side at every hazard. If the enemy should assume the offensive, and I am
assured by reliable persons that in view of my position such is his
intention, my force present is altogether inadequate, consisting of only
15,000 men. I have to request you, therefore, to come forward with all
the available force under your command. So important do I consider
the occasion that I think it necessary to give this communication all
the force of orders, and I send four boats, the *Diana, Woodford, John
Rain,* and *Autocrat,* to bring you up. In five or six days my force will
probably be sufficient to relieve you.

Very respectfully, your ob't srv't,<br>D. C. BUELL,<br>Brigadier-General Comd'g.

    P. S.—The steamers will leave here at 12 o'clock to-night.

General Smith said this order was nonsense. But I told him it was better to
obey it. The General replied, "of course I must obey," and said his men were
embarking as fast as they could. I went on up to Nashville and inspected the
position taken by Nelson's troops. I did not see Buell during the day, and wrote
him a note saying that I had been in Nashville since early morning and had
hoped to meet him.[11] On my return to the boat we met. His troops were still
east of the river, and the steamers that had carried Nelson's division up were
mostly at Clarksville to bring Smith's division. I said to General Buell my information was that the enemy was retreating as fast as possible. General Buell
said there was fighting going on then only ten or twelve miles away. I said:
"Quite probably; Nashville contained valuable stores of arms, ammunition and
provisions, and the enemy is probably trying to carry away all he can.[12] The

---

[11] USG wrote to Buell from Nashville on Feb. 27, 1862. *PUSG,* 4:293–294.

[12] On Feb. 18, 1862, Confederate forces made an effort to clear out food and ammunition as
Gen. Albert Sidney Johnston prepared to evacuate Nashville. The onset of panic, poor weather
conditions, and transportation problems prevented them from taking most of the supplies.

fighting is doubtless with the rear-guard who are trying to protect the trains they are getting away with." Buell spoke very positively of the danger Nashville was in of an attack from the enemy. I said, in the absence of positive information, I believed my information was correct. He responded that he "knew." "Well," I said, "I do not know; but as I came by Clarksville General Smith's troops were embarking to join you."

Smith's troops were returned the same day.[13] The enemy were trying to get away from Nashville and not to return to it.

At this time General Albert Sidney Johnston commanded all the Confederate troops west of the Alleghany Mountains, with the exception of those in the extreme south. On the National side the forces confronting him were divided into, at first three, then four separate departments.[14] Johnston had greatly the advantage in having supreme command over all troops that could possibly be brought to bear upon one point, while the forces similarly situated on the National side, divided into independent commands, could not be brought into harmonious action except by orders from Washington.

At the beginning of 1862 Johnston's troops east of the Mississippi occupied a line extending from Columbus, on his left, to Mill Springs, on his right. As we have seen, Columbus, both banks of the Tennessee River, the west bank of the Cumberland and Bowling Green, all were strongly fortified. Mill Springs was intrenched. The National troops occupied no territory south of the Ohio, except three small garrisons along its bank and a force thrown out from Louisville to confront that at Bowling Green. Johnston's strength was no doubt numerically inferior to that of the National troops; but this was compensated for by the advantage of being sole commander of all the Confederate forces at the West, and of operating in a country where his friends would take care of his rear without any detail of soldiers. But when General George H. Thomas moved upon the enemy at Mill Springs and totally routed him, inflicting a loss of some 300 killed and wounded, and forts Henry and Heiman fell into the hands of the National forces, with their armaments and about 100 prisoners,

---

Thomas L. Connolly, *Army of the Heartland: The Army of Tennessee, 1861–1862* (Baton Rouge: Louisiana State University Press, 1967), 136–137.

[13] USG met with Buell on Feb. 28, 1862. Buell did not order Smith back to Clarksville until Mar. 1. *OR,* I, 7, 675; *PUSG,* 4:293–294.

[14] USG commanded the Army of the Tennessee, Buell commanded the Army of the Ohio, and eventually they were joined by the Army of the Mississippi, commanded by John Pope. Halleck commanded the Dept. of the Missouri, in addition to all Western forces. *CWHC,* 152, 264, 274, 433–434.

those losses seemed to dishearten the Confederate commander so much that he immediately commenced a retreat from Bowling Green on Nashville. He reached this latter place on the 14th of February, while Donelson was still besieged. Buell followed with a portion of the Army of the Ohio, but he had to march and did not reach the east bank of the Cumberland opposite Nashville until the 24th of the month, and then with only one division of his army.

The bridge at Nashville had been destroyed and all boats removed or disabled, so that a small garrison could have held the place against any National troops that could have been brought against it within ten days after the arrival of the force from Bowling Green. Johnston seemed to lie quietly at Nashville to await the result at Fort Donelson, on which he had staked the possession of most of the territory embraced in the States of Kentucky and Tennessee. It is true, the two generals senior in rank at Fort Donelson were sending him encouraging dispatches, even claiming great Confederate victories up to the night of the 16th when they must have been preparing for their individual escape. Johnston made a fatal mistake in intrusting so important a command to Floyd, who he must have known was no soldier even if he possessed the elements of one. Pillow's presence as second was also a mistake. If these officers had been forced upon him and designated for that particular command, then he should have left Nashville with a small garrison under a trusty officer, and with the remainder of his force gone to Donelson himself. If he had been captured the result could not have been worse than it was.

Johnston's heart failed him upon the first advance of National troops. He wrote to Richmond on the 8th of February, "I think the gunboats of the enemy will probably take Fort Donelson without the necessity of employing their land force in co-operation." After the fall of that place he abandoned Nashville and Chattanooga without an effort to save either, and fell back into northern Mississippi, where, six weeks later, he was destined to end his career.

From the time of leaving Cairo I was singularly unfortunate in not receiving dispatches from General Halleck. The order of the 10th of February directing me to fortify Fort Henry strongly, particularly to the land side, and saying that intrenching tools had been sent for that purpose, reached me after Donelson was invested.[15] I received nothing direct which indicated that the department commander knew we were in possession of Donelson. I was reporting regularly to the chief of staff, who had been sent to Cairo, soon after the troops

[15] For Halleck's Feb. 10, 1862, order, see *PUSG*, 4:193n–194n.

left there, to receive all reports from the front and to telegraph the substance to the St. Louis headquarters.[16] Cairo was at the southern end of the telegraph wire. Another line was started at once from Cairo to Paducah and Smithland, at the mouths of the Tennessee and Cumberland respectively. My dispatches were all sent to Cairo by boat, but many of those addressed to me were sent to the operator at the end of the advancing wire and he failed to forward them. This operator afterwards proved to be a rebel; he deserted his post after a short time and went south taking his dispatches with him.[17] A telegram from General McClellan to me of February 16th, the day of the surrender, directing me to report in full the situation, was not received at my headquarters until the 3d of March.[18]

On the 2d of March I received orders dated March 1st to move my command back to Fort Henry, leaving only a small garrison at Donelson. From Fort Henry expeditions were to be sent against Eastport, Mississippi, and Paris, Tennessee. We started from Donelson on the 4th, and the same day I was back on the Tennessee River. On March 4th I also received the following dispatch from General Halleck:

MAJ.-GEN. U. S. GRANT,
Fort Henry:
   You will place Maj.-Gen. C. F. Smith in command of expedition, and remain yourself at Fort Henry. Why do you not obey my orders to report strength and positions of your command?
                                                        H. W. HALLECK,
                                                        Major-General.[19]

I was surprised. This was the first intimation I had received that General Halleck had called for information as to the strength of my command. On the 6th he wrote to me again. "Your going to Nashville without authority, and when your presence with your troops was of the utmost importance, was a

[16] USG's troops left Cairo, IL, on Feb. 2, 1862, and Cullum arrived in Cairo by Feb. 7. *OR*, I, 7, 594; *PUSG*, 4:xxii, 173*n*.

[17] On Mar. 21, 1862, USG informed Halleck that the telegraph operator at Fort Henry had not sent certain communications to him, but that he was uncertain as to what had happened to that soldier. However, most of USG's communications with headquarters were by letters carried by boat. *PUSG*, 4:320*n*–321*n*, 401 and *n*.

[18] McClellan requested information from USG on Feb. 15, 1862. Ibid., 4:320*n*.

[19] Ibid., 4:319*n*.

matter of very serious complaint at Washington, so much so that I was advised to arrest you on your return."[20] This was the first I knew of his objecting to my going to Nashville. That place was not beyond the limits of my command, which, it had been expressly declared in orders, were "not defined."[21] Nashville is west of the Cumberland River, and I had sent troops that had reported to me for duty to occupy the place. I turned over the command as directed and then replied to General Halleck courteously, but asked to be relieved from further duty under him.[22]

Later I learned that General Halleck had been calling lustily for more troops, promising that he would do something important if he could only be sufficiently reinforced. McClellan asked him what force he then had. Halleck telegraphed me to supply the information so far as my command was concerned, but I received none of his dispatches. At last Halleck reported to Washington that he had repeatedly ordered me to give the strength of my force, but could get nothing out of me; that I had gone to Nashville, beyond the limits of my command, without his authority, and that my army was more demoralized by victory than the army at Bull Run had been by defeat. General McClellan, on this information, ordered that I should be relieved from duty and that an investigation should be made into any charges against me. He even authorized my arrest. Thus in less than two weeks after the victory at Donelson, the two leading generals in the army were in correspondence as to what disposition should be made of me, and in less than three weeks I was virtually in arrest and without a command.

On the 13th of March I was restored to command, and on the 17th Halleck sent me a copy of an order from the War Department which stated that accounts of my misbehavior had reached Washington and directed him to investigate and report the facts. He forwarded also a copy of a detailed dispatch from himself to Washington entirely exonerating me; but he did not inform me that it was his own reports that had created all the trouble. On the contrary, he wrote to me, "Instead of relieving you, I wish you, as soon as your new army is in the field, to assume immediate command, and lead it to new

---

[20] Ibid., 4:331*n*.

[21] USG referred to Gen. Orders No. 1, which he had issued on Feb. 17, 1862, from Fort Donelson. Ibid., 4:230.

[22] On Mar. 5, 1862, as ordered by Halleck, USG informed Smith of his promotion as commander of the expedition up the Tennessee River. Ibid., 4:321–324.

victories."[23] In consequence I felt very grateful to him, and supposed it was his interposition that had set me right with the government. I never knew the truth until General Badeau unearthed the facts in his researches for his history of my campaigns.[24]

General Halleck unquestionably deemed General C. F. Smith a much fitter officer for the command of all the forces in the military district than I was, and, to render him available for such command, desired his promotion to antedate mine and those of the other division commanders. It is probable that the general opinion was that Smith's long services in the army and distinguished deeds rendered him the more proper person for such command. Indeed I was rather inclined to this opinion myself at that time, and would have served as faithfully under Smith as he had done under me. But this did not justify the dispatches which General Halleck sent to Washington, or his subsequent concealment of them from me when pretending to explain the action of my superiors.

On receipt of the order restoring me to command I proceeded to Savannah on the Tennessee, to which point my troops had advanced. General Smith was delighted to see me and was unhesitating in his denunciation of the treatment I had received. He was on a sick bed at the time, from which he never came away alive. His death was a severe loss to our western army.[25] His personal courage was unquestioned, his judgment and professional acquirements were unsurpassed, and he had the confidence of those he commanded as well as of those over him.

[23] This is an excerpt from Halleck's Mar. 13, 1862, telegram regarding USG's Mar. 13 request to be relieved from command. Ibid., 4:354n–355n. For Halleck's Mar. 17 telegram that included the accusations against USG and Halleck's defense of him, see ibid., 4:415n–416n.

[24] Adam Badeau, *Military History of Ulysses S. Grant, from April, 1861, to April, 1865* (New York: D. Appleton, 1881), 1:64–65.

[25] On Apr. 25, 1862, Smith died from the effects of dysentery and an infection caused by an accidental leg injury. *CWHC*, 493.

# 24

The Army at Pittsburg Landing—Injured by a
Fall—The Confederate Attack at Shiloh—The First
Day's Fight at Shiloh—General Sherman—Condition
of the Army—Close of the First Day's Fight—
The Second Day's Fight—Retreat and Defeat
of the Confederates

W HEN I REASSUMED command on the 17th of March I found the army
divided, about half being on the east bank of the Tennessee at Savannah, while
one division was at Crump's landing on the west bank about four miles
higher up, and the remainder at Pittsburg landing, five miles above Crump's.[1]
The enemy was in force at Corinth, the junction of the two most important
railroads in the Mississippi valley—one connecting Memphis and the Mississippi River with the East, and the other leading south to all the cotton
states.[2] Still another railroad connects Corinth with Jackson, in west Tennessee.[3] If we obtained possession of Corinth the enemy would have no railroad
for the transportation of armies or supplies until that running east from
Vicksburg was reached. It was the great strategic position at the West between the Tennessee and the Mississippi rivers and between Nashville and
Vicksburg.

[1] Lew Wallace's division was stationed at Crump's Landing, TN, while Sherman's and Stephen A. Hurlbut's divisions were partially debarked at Pittsburg Landing. *PUSG*, 4:386.

[2] There were approximately 40,000 Confederate troops stationed at Corinth, MS. John F.
Marszalek, *Sherman: A Soldier's Passion for Order* (New York: Free Press, 1993), 174–175.

[3] The Memphis and Charleston Railroad ran east-west, and the Mobile and Ohio Railroad
ran north-south. *PUSG*, 5:10–11 (map).

I at once put all the troops at Savannah in motion for Pittsburg landing, knowing that the enemy was fortifying at Corinth and collecting an army there under Johnston. It was my expectation to march against that army as soon as Buell, who had been ordered to reinforce me with the Army of the Ohio, should arrive; and the west bank of the river was the place to start from. Pittsburg is only about twenty miles from Corinth, and Hamburg landing, four miles further up the river, is a mile or two nearer. I had not been in command long before I selected Hamburg as the place to put the Army of the Ohio when it arrived. The roads from Pittsburg and Hamburg to Corinth converge some eight miles out. This disposition of the troops would have given additional roads to march over when the advance commenced, within supporting distance of each other.

Before I arrived at Savannah, Sherman, who had joined the Army of the Tennessee and been placed in command of a division, had made an expedition on steamers convoyed by gunboats to the neighborhood of Eastport, thirty miles south, for the purpose of destroying the railroad east of Corinth.[4] The rains had been so heavy for some time before that the low-lands had become impassable swamps. Sherman debarked his troops and started out to accomplish the object of the expedition; but the river was rising so rapidly that the back-water up the small tributaries threatened to cut off the possibility of getting back to the boats, and the expedition had to return without reaching the railroad. The guns had to be hauled by hand through the water to get back to the boats.

On the 17th of March the army on the Tennessee River consisted of five divisions, commanded respectively by Generals C. F. Smith, McClernand, L. Wallace, Hurlbut[5] and Sherman. General W. H. L. Wallace was temporarily in command of Smith's division, General Smith, as I have said, being confined to his bed. Reinforcements were arriving daily and as they came up they were organized, first into brigades, then into a division, and the com-

---

[4] On Mar. 14, 1862, the gunboat *Tyler* escorted nineteen steamers up the Tennessee River. Steven E. Woodworth, *Nothing but Victory: The Army of the Tennessee, 1861–1865* (New York: Knopf, 2005), 137.

[5] Stephen A. Hurlbut (1815–1882) was born in South Carolina and moved to Illinois in 1845. After practicing law and serving as an Illinois legislator, Hurlbut joined the Union as a brigadier general in May 1861. After the war, he served as the commander in chief of the Grand Army of the Republic from 1866 to 1868. During USG's first term as president, Hurlbut served as the U.S. minister to Colombia from 1869 to 1872. He was a U.S. representative from Illinois from 1873 to 1877 and U.S. minister to Peru from 1881 to 1882. *CWHC,* 311–312.

mand given to General Prentiss, who had been ordered to report to me.[6]
General Buell was on his way from Nashville with 40,000 veterans. On the
19th of March he was at Columbia, Tennessee, eighty-five miles from Pittsburg.[7] When all reinforcements should have arrived I expected to take the
initiative by marching on Corinth, and had no expectation of needing fortifications, though this subject was taken into consideration. McPherson,[8] my
only military engineer, was directed to lay out a line to intrench. He did so,
but reported that it would have to be made in rear of the line of encampment
as it then ran. The new line, while it would be nearer the river, was yet too far
away from the Tennessee, or even from the creeks, to be easily supplied with
water, and in case of attack these creeks would be in the hands of the enemy.
The fact is, I regarded the campaign we were engaged in as an offensive one
and had no idea that the enemy would leave strong intrenchments to take the
initiative when he knew he would be attacked where he was if he remained.
This view, however, did not prevent every precaution being taken and every
effort made to keep advised of all movements of the enemy.

   Johnston's cavalry meanwhile had been well out towards our front, and occasional encounters occurred between it and our outposts. On the 1st of April this
cavalry became bold and approached our lines, showing that an advance of some
kind was contemplated. On the 2d Johnston left Corinth in force to attack my
army.[9] On the 4th his cavalry dashed down and captured a small picket guard of
six or seven men, stationed some five miles out from Pittsburg on the Corinth
road. Colonel Buckland[10] sent relief to the guard at once and soon followed in
person with an entire regiment, and General Sherman followed Buckland taking
the remainder of a brigade. The pursuit was kept up for some three miles beyond the point where the picket guard had been captured, and after nightfall
Sherman returned to camp and reported to me by letter what had occurred.

   [6] USG assigned Prentiss as commander of the newly formed 6th Div. on Mar. 26, 1862.
Woodworth, *Nothing but Victory,* 145.

   [7] On Mar. 23, 1862, Buell reported that his progress was being impeded "by high water and
the absence of bridges." *PUSG,* 4:394n.

   [8] James B. McPherson (1828–1864) was born in Ohio and graduated from the USMA in
1853. In Mar. 1862, he became an engineer in the Army of the Tennessee. Later that year, he
served as aide-de-camp to USG and was promoted to major general in Oct. *CWHC,* 383–384.

   [9] On Apr. 3, 1862, Johnston left Corinth with the Confederate Army of the Mississippi to
attack the Union lines. *PUSG,* 5:xxi.

   [10] Ralph P. Buckland (1812–1892) was an Ohio legislator before serving in the Civil War. In
Jan. 1862, he joined the 72nd Ohio Inf. as a colonel. After the war, he served as a U.S. representative from Ohio. *CWHC,* 151.

At this time a large body of the enemy was hovering to the west of us, along the line of the Mobile and Ohio railroad. My apprehension was much greater for the safety of Crump's landing than it was for Pittsburg. I had no apprehension that the enemy could really capture either place. But I feared it was possible that he might make a rapid dash upon Crump's and destroy our transports and stores, most of which were kept at that point, and then retreat before Wallace could be reinforced. Lew. Wallace's position I regarded as so well chosen that he was not removed.

At this time I generally spent the day at Pittsburg and returned to Savannah in the evening. I was intending to remove my headquarters to Pittsburg, but Buell was expected daily and would come in at Savannah. I remained at this point, therefore, a few days longer than I otherwise should have done, in order to meet him on his arrival.[11] The skirmishing in our front, however, had been so continuous from about the 3d of April that I did not leave Pittsburg each night until an hour when I felt there would be no further danger before the morning.

On Friday the 4th, the day of Buckland's advance, I was very much injured by my horse falling with me, and on me, while I was trying to get to the front where firing had been heard. The night was one of impenetrable darkness, with rain pouring down in torrents; nothing was visible to the eye except as revealed by the frequent flashes of lightning. Under these circumstances I had to trust to the horse, without guidance, to keep the road. I had not gone far, however, when I met General W. H. L. Wallace and Colonel (afterwards General) McPherson coming from the direction of the front. They said all was quiet so far as the enemy was concerned. On the way back to the boat my horse's feet slipped from under him, and he fell with my leg under his body. The extreme softness of the ground, from the excessive rains of the few preceding days, no doubt saved me from a severe injury and protracted lameness. As it was, my ankle was very much injured, so much so that my boot had to be cut off. For two or three days after I was unable to walk except with crutches.

On the 5th General Nelson, with a division of Buell's army, arrived at Savannah and I ordered him to move up the east bank of the river, to be in a position where he could be ferried over to Crump's landing or Pittsburg as occasion required.[12] I had learned that General Buell himself would be at Savannah the next day, and desired to meet me on his arrival. Affairs at Pittsburg landing had been such for several days that I did not want to be away during the day. I determined, therefore, to take a very early breakfast and ride

[11] Prior to the Battle of Shiloh, USG's headquarters were located at the home of William H. Cherry in Savannah, TN. *PUSG*, 4:407*n*.

[12] Buell was in command of the 4th Div., Army of the Ohio. *CWHC*, 405.

out to meet Buell, and thus save time. He had arrived on the evening of the 5th, but had not advised me of the fact and I was not aware of it until some time after. While I was at breakfast, however, heavy firing was heard in the direction of Pittsburg landing, and I hastened there, sending a hurried note to Buell informing him of the reason why I could not meet him at Savannah.[13] On the way up the river I directed the dispatch-boat to run in close to Crump's landing, so that I could communicate with General Lew. Wallace. I found him waiting on a boat apparently expecting to see me, and I directed him to get his troops in line ready to execute any orders he might receive. He replied that his troops were already under arms and prepared to move.

Up to that time I had felt by no means certain that Crump's landing might not be the point of attack. On reaching the front, however, about eight A.M., I found that the attack on Pittsburg was unmistakable, and that nothing more than a small guard, to protect our transports and stores, was needed at Crump's.[14] Captain Baxter,[15] a quartermaster on my staff, was accordingly directed to go back and order General Wallace to march immediately to Pittsburg by the road nearest the river. Captain Baxter made a memorandum of this order. About one P.M., not hearing from Wallace and being much in need of reinforcements, I sent two more of my staff, Colonel McPherson and Captain Rowley,[16] to bring him up with his division. They reported finding him marching towards Purdy, Bethel, or some point west from the river, and farther from Pittsburg by several miles than when he started. The road from his first position to Pittsburg landing was direct and near the river. Between the two points a bridge had been built across Snake Creek by our troops, at which Wallace's command had assisted, expressly to enable the troops at the two places to support each other in case of need. Wallace did not arrive in time to take part

---

[13] In a report dated Apr. 15, 1862, Buell did not mention receiving USG's letter. *PUSG*, 5:17*n*.

[14] Although it is not clear exactly when USG arrived, estimates generally place his arrival time around 8:15 A.M. or 8:30 A.M. and no later than 9:00 A.M. Timothy B. Smith, *Shiloh: Conquer or Perish* (Lawrence: University Press of Kansas, 2014), 146.

[15] Algernon S. Baxter (1819–1897) was born in Vermont and became acquainted with USG while working as a merchant in St. Louis. He served as assistant quartermaster from Nov. 23, 1861 to Apr. 27, 1862. After the Battle of Shiloh, he left the army because of an unspecified health problem. He subsequently moved to New York to work in the financial sector. *PUSG*, 3:358*n*; James G. Wilson, ed., *General Grant's Letters to a Friend, 1861–1880* (New York: T. Y. Crowell, 1897), 112.

[16] William R. Rowley (1824–1886) was born in New York and joined the 45th Illinois Inf. as a first lieutenant in Nov. 1861. He served as an aide-de-camp to USG throughout much of the war. *CWHC*, 464.

in the first day's fight. General Wallace has since claimed that the order delivered to him by Captain Baxter was simply to join the right of the army, and that the road over which he marched would have taken him to the road from Pittsburg to Purdy where it crosses Owl Creek on the right of Sherman; but this is not where I had ordered him nor where I wanted him to go.

I never could see and do not now see why any order was necessary further than to direct him to come to Pittsburg landing, without specifying by what route. His was one of three veteran divisions that had been in battle, and its absence was severely felt. Later in the war General Wallace would not have made the mistake that he committed on the 6th of April, 1862. I presume his idea was that by taking the route he did he would be able to come around on the flank or rear of the enemy, and thus perform an act of heroism that would redound to the credit of his command, as well as to the benefit of his country.

Some two or three miles from Pittsburg landing was a log meeting-house called Shiloh.[17] It stood on the ridge which divides the waters of Snake and Lick creeks, the former emptying into the Tennessee just north of Pittsburg landing, and the latter south. This point was the key to our position and was held by Sherman. His division was at that time wholly raw, no part of it ever having been in an engagement; but I thought this deficiency was more than made up by the superiority of the commander. McClernand was on Sherman's left, with troops that had been engaged at forts Henry and Donelson and were therefore veterans so far as western troops had become such at that stage of the war. Next to McClernand came Prentiss with a raw division, and on the extreme left, Stuart[18] with one brigade of Sherman's division. Hurlbut was in rear of Prentiss, massed, and in reserve at the time of the onset. The division of General C. F. Smith was on the right, also in reserve. General Smith was still sick in bed at Savannah, but within hearing of our guns. His services would no doubt have been of inestimable value had his health permitted his presence. The command of his division devolved upon Brigadier-General W. H. L. Wallace, a most estimable and able officer; a veteran too, for he had served a year in the Mexican war and had been with his command at Henry and Donelson. Wallace was mortally wounded in the first day's

[17] The Shiloh meetinghouse, a Methodist church built in the 1850s, was located approximately three miles southwest of Pittsburg Landing. Timothy B. Smith, *This Great Battlefield of Shiloh: History, Memory, and the Establishment of a Civil War National Military Park* (Knoxville: University of Tennessee Press, 2004), 139.

[18] David Stuart (1816–1868) was born in New York and later moved to Illinois. In July 1861, he became a colonel in the 42nd Illinois Inf. *CWHC*, 611.

engagement,[19] and with the change of commanders thus necessarily effected in the heat of battle the efficiency of his division was much weakened.

The position of our troops made a continuous line from Lick Creek on the left to Owl Creek, a branch of Snake Creek, on the right, facing nearly south and possibly a little west. The water in all these streams was very high at the time and contributed to protect our flanks. The enemy was compelled, therefore, to attack directly in front. This he did with great vigor, inflicting heavy losses on the National side, but suffering much heavier on his own.

The Confederate assaults were made with such a disregard of losses on their own side that our line of tents soon fell into their hands. The ground on which the battle was fought was undulating, heavily timbered with scattered clearings, the woods giving some protection to the troops on both sides. There was also considerable underbrush. A number of attempts were made by the enemy to turn our right flank, where Sherman was posted, but every effort was repulsed with heavy loss. But the front attack was kept up so vigorously that, to prevent the success of these attempts to get on our flanks, the National troops were compelled, several times, to take positions to the rear nearer Pittsburg landing. When the firing ceased at night the National line was all of a mile in rear of the position it had occupied in the morning.

In one of the backward moves, on the 6th, the division commanded by General Prentiss did not fall back with the others. This left his flanks exposed and enabled the enemy to capture him with about 2,200 of his officers and men. General Badeau gives four o'clock of the 6th as about the time this capture took place.[20] He may be right as to the time, but my recollection is that the hour was later. General Prentiss himself gave the hour as half-past five. I was with him, as I was with each of the division commanders that day, several times, and my recollection is that the last time I was with him was about half-past four, when his division was standing up firmly and the General was as cool as if expecting victory. But no matter whether it was four or later, the story that he and his command were surprised and captured in their camps is without any foundation whatever. If it had been true, as currently reported at the time and yet believed by thousands of people, that Prentiss and his division had been captured in their beds, there would not have been an all-day struggle, with the loss of thousands killed and wounded on the Confederate side.

With the single exception of a few minutes after the capture of Prentiss, a continuous and unbroken line was maintained all day from Snake Creek or

---

[19] Wallace died on Apr. 10, 1862. *PUSG,* 5:36*n.*

[20] Adam Badeau, *Military History of Ulysses S. Grant, from April, 1861, to April, 1865* (New York: D. Appleton, 1881), 1:83.

its tributaries on the right to Lick Creek or the Tennessee on the left above Pittsburg. There was no hour during the day when there was not heavy firing and generally hard fighting at some point on the line, but seldom at all points at the same time. It was a case of Southern dash against Northern pluck and endurance. Three of the five divisions engaged on Sunday were entirely raw, and many of the men had only received their arms on the way from their States to the field. Many of them had arrived but a day or two before and were hardly able to load their muskets according to the manual. Their officers were equally ignorant of their duties. Under these circumstances it is not astonishing that many of the regiments broke at the first fire. In two cases, as I now remember, colonels led their regiments from the field on first hearing the whistle of the enemy's bullets. In these cases the colonels were constitutional cowards, unfit for any military position; but not so the officers and men led out of danger by them. Better troops never went upon a battle-field than many of these, officers and men, afterwards proved themselves to be, who fled panic-stricken at the first whistle of bullets and shell at Shiloh.[21]

During the whole of Sunday I was continuously engaged in passing from one part of the field to another, giving directions to division commanders. In thus moving along the line, however, I never deemed it important to stay long with Sherman. Although his troops were then under fire for the first time, their commander, by his constant presence with them, inspired a confidence in officers and men that enabled them to render services on that bloody battle-field worthy of the best of veterans. McClernand was next to Sherman, and the hardest fighting was in front of these two divisions. McClernand told me on that day, the 6th, that he profited much by having so able a commander supporting him. A casualty to Sherman that would have taken him from the field that day would have been a sad one for the troops engaged at Shiloh. And how near we came to this! On the 6th Sherman was shot twice, once in the hand, once in the shoulder, the ball cutting his coat and making a slight wound, and a third ball passed through his hat. In addition to this he had several horses shot during the day.

The nature of this battle was such that cavalry could not be used in front; I therefore formed ours into line in rear, to stop stragglers—of whom there were many. When there would be enough of them to make a show, and after they had recovered from their fright, they would be sent to reinforce some part of the line which needed support, without regard to their companies, regiments or brigades.

[21] On Apr. 8, 1862, Rawlins issued Special Orders No. 48 requiring division commanders to submit field reports in order to bring charges against officers who "disgraced themselves by their cowardice." *PUSG*, 5:22n.

On one occasion during the day I rode back as far as the river and met General Buell, who had just arrived; I do not remember the hour, but at that time there probably were as many as four or five thousand stragglers lying under cover of the river bluff, panic-stricken, most of whom would have been shot where they lay, without resistance, before they would have taken muskets and marched to the front to protect themselves. This meeting between General Buell and myself was on the dispatch-boat used to run between the landing and Savannah.[22] It was brief, and related specially to his getting his troops over the river. As we left the boat together, Buell's attention was attracted by the men lying under cover of the river bank. I saw him berating them and trying to shame them into joining their regiments. He even threatened them with shells from the gunboats near by. But it was all to no effect. Most of these men afterward proved themselves as gallant as any of those who saved the battle from which they had deserted. I have no doubt that this sight impressed General Buell with the idea that a line of retreat would be a good thing just then. If he had come in by the front instead of through the stragglers in the rear, he would have thought and felt differently. Could he have come through the Confederate rear, he would have witnessed there a scene similar to that at our own. The distant rear of an army engaged in battle is not the best place from which to judge correctly what is going on in front. Later in the war, while occupying the country between the Tennessee and the Mississippi, I learned that the panic in the Confederate lines had not differed much from that within our own. Some of the country people estimated the stragglers from Johnston's army as high as 20,000. Of course this was an exaggeration.[23]

The situation at the close of Sunday was as follows: along the top of the bluff just south of the log-house which stood at Pittsburg landing, Colonel J. D. Webster, of my staff, had arranged twenty or more pieces of artillery facing south or up the river. This line of artillery was on the crest of a hill overlooking a deep ravine opening into the Tennessee. Hurlbut with his division intact was on the right of this artillery, extending west and possibly a little north. McClernand came next in the general line, looking more to the west. His division was complete in its organization and ready for any duty. Sherman came next, his right extending to Snake Creek. His command, like the other two,

---

[22] USG and Buell met aboard the *Tigress* on Apr. 6, 1862. Stephen D. Engle, *Don Carlos Buell: Most Promising of All* (Chapel Hill: University of North Carolina Press, 1999), 224.

[23] While no accurate numbers are available, at least one estimate placed the number of Confederate deserters at approximately 4,000 after the Battle of Shiloh. E. Merton Coulter, *The Confederate States of America, 1861–1865* (Baton Rouge: Louisiana State University Press, 1950), 463.

was complete in its organization and ready, like its chief, for any service it might be called upon to render. All three divisions were, as a matter of course, more or less shattered and depleted in numbers from the terrible battle of the day. The division of W. H. L. Wallace, as much from the disorder arising from changes of division and brigade commanders, under heavy fire, as from any other cause, had lost its organization and did not occupy a place in the line as a division. Prentiss' command was gone as a division, many of its members having been killed, wounded or captured; but it had rendered valiant services before its final dispersal, and had contributed a good share to the defence of Shiloh.

The right of my line rested near the bank of Snake Creek, a short distance above the bridge which had been built by the troops for the purpose of connecting Crump's landing and Pittsburg landing. Sherman had posted some troops in a log-house and out-buildings which overlooked both the bridge over which Wallace was expected and the creek above that point. In this last position Sherman was frequently attacked before night, but held the point until he voluntarily abandoned it to advance in order to make room for Lew. Wallace, who came up after dark.

There was, as I have said, a deep ravine in front of our left. The Tennessee River was very high and there was water to a considerable depth in the ravine. Here the enemy made a last desperate effort to turn our flank, but was repelled. The gunboats *Tyler* and *Lexington,* Gwin[24] and Shirk[25] commanding, with the artillery under Webster, aided the army and effectually checked their further progress. Before any of Buell's troops had reached the west bank of the Tennessee, firing had almost entirely ceased; anything like an attempt on the part of the enemy to advance had absolutely ceased. There was some artillery firing from an unseen enemy, some of his shells passing beyond us; but I do not remember that there was the whistle of a single musket-ball heard. As his troops arrived in the dusk General Buell marched several of his regiments part way down the face of the hill where they fired briskly for some minutes, but I do not think a single man engaged in this firing received an injury. The attack had spent its force.

General Lew. Wallace, with 5,000 effective men, arrived after firing had ceased for the day, and was placed on the right. Thus night came, Wallace

[24] Lt. William Gwin (1832–1863) was born in Indiana and was appointed a U.S. Navy midshipman in 1847. After commanding *Tyler* during the Battle of Fort Henry, Gwin assisted with gunboat raids up the Tennessee River. Spencer Tucker, ed., *Civil War Naval Encyclopedia* (Santa Barbara, CA: ABC-CLIO, 2011), s.v. "Gwin, William."

[25] Lt. James W. Shirk (1832–1873) was born in Pennsylvania and was appointed a U.S. Navy midshipman in 1849. During the Battle of Fort Henry, he commanded *Lexington.* Ibid., s.v. "Shirk, James W."

came, and the advance of Nelson's division came; but none—unless night—in time to be of material service to the gallant men who saved Shiloh on that first day against large odds. Buell's loss on the 6th of April was two men killed and one wounded, all members of the 36th Indiana infantry. The Army of the Tennessee lost on that day at least 7,000 men.[26] The presence of two or three regiments of Buell's army on the west bank before firing ceased had not the slightest effect in preventing the capture of Pittsburg landing.

So confident was I before firing had ceased on the 6th that the next day would bring victory to our arms if we could only take the initiative, that I visited each division commander in person before any reinforcements had reached the field. I directed them to throw out heavy lines of skirmishers in the morning as soon as they could see, and push them forward until they found the enemy, following with their entire divisions in supporting distance, and to engage the enemy as soon as found. To Sherman I told the story of the assault at Fort Donelson, and said that the same tactics would win at Shiloh. Victory was assured when Wallace arrived, even if there had been no other support. I was glad, however, to see the reinforcements of Buell and credit them with doing all there was for them to do. During the night of the 6th the remainder of Nelson's division, Buell's army, crossed the river and were ready to advance in the morning, forming the left wing. Two other divisions, Crittenden's[27] and McCook's,[28] came up the river from Savannah in the transports and were on the west bank early on the 7th. Buell commanded them in person. My command was thus nearly doubled in numbers and efficiency.

During the night rain fell in torrents and our troops were exposed to the storm without shelter. I made my headquarters under a tree a few hundred yards back from the river bank. My ankle was so much swollen from the fall of my horse the Friday night preceding, and the bruise was so painful, that I could get no rest. The drenching rain would have precluded the possibility of

---

[26] After the first day of fighting, the Confederate forces lost approximately 8,000 men, while approximately 7,000 U.S. soldiers were killed or wounded and about 3,000 captured. Earl J. Hess, *The Civil War in the West: Victory and Defeat from the Appalachians to the Mississippi* (Chapel Hill: University of North Carolina Press, 2012), 47.

[27] Thomas L. Crittenden (1819–1893) began his military service as a private in the Kentucky Mounted Volunteers in 1836. He reentered the military in 1847 and served as a lieutenant colonel in the 3rd Kentucky Inf., mustering out in 1848. In Apr. 1862, he was brigadier general of the 5th Div., Army of the Ohio. He was promoted to major general in July 1862. *CWHC*, 191.

[28] Alexander M. McCook (1831–1903) was born in Ohio and graduated from the USMA in 1852. In Apr. 1862, he was brigadier general of the 2nd Div., Army of the Ohio. After the Civil War, he attained the rank of major general, retiring in 1895. Ibid., 374.

sleep without this additional cause. Some time after midnight, growing restive under the storm and the continuous pain, I moved back to the log-house under the bank. This had been taken as a hospital, and all night wounded men were being brought in, their wounds dressed, a leg or an arm amputated as the case might require, and everything being done to save life or alleviate suffering. The sight was more unendurable than encountering the enemy's fire, and I returned to my tree in the rain.

The advance on the morning of the 7th developed the enemy in the camps occupied by our troops before the battle began, more than a mile back from the most advanced position of the Confederates on the day before. It is known now that they had not yet learned of the arrival of Buell's command. Possibly they fell back so far to get the shelter of our tents during the rain, and also to get away from the shells that were dropped upon them by the gunboats every fifteen minutes during the night.

The position of the Union troops on the morning of the 7th was as follows: General Lew. Wallace on the right; Sherman on his left; then McClernand and then Hurlbut. Nelson, of Buell's army, was on our extreme left, next to the river. Crittenden was next in line after Nelson and on his right; McCook followed and formed the extreme right of Buell's command. My old command thus formed the right wing, while the troops directly under Buell constituted the left wing of the army. These relative positions were retained during the entire day, or until the enemy was driven from the field.

In a very short time the battle became general all along the line. This day everything was favorable to the Union side. We had now become the attacking party. The enemy was driven back all day, as we had been the day before, until finally he beat a precipitate retreat. The last point held by him was near the road leading from the landing to Corinth, on the left of Sherman and right of McClernand. About three o'clock, being near that point and seeing that the enemy was giving way everywhere else, I gathered up a couple of regiments, or parts of regiments, from troops near by, formed them in line of battle and marched them forward, going in front myself to prevent premature or long-range firing.[29] At this point there was a clearing between us and the enemy favorable for charging, although exposed. I knew the enemy were ready to break and only wanted a little encouragement from us to go quickly and join their friends who had started earlier. After marching to within musket-range I

---

[29] USG ordered Col. James C. Veatch to gather reserve soldiers from Buell's and Hurlbut's divisions and attack the weakening Confederate troops. The makeshift regiment was assisted by men from Brig. Gen. Lovell Rousseau's brigade. Wiley Sword, *Shiloh: Bloody April* (New York: William Morrow, 1974), 417.

stopped and let the troops pass. The command, *Charge,* was given, and was executed with loud cheers and with a run; when the last of the enemy broke.*

*NOTE.—Since writing this chapter I have received from Mrs. W. H. L. Wallace, widow of the gallant general who was killed in the first day's fight on the field of Shiloh, a letter from General Lew. Wallace to him dated the morning of the 5th.[30] At the date of this letter it was well known that the Confederates had troops out along the Mobile & Ohio railroad west of Crump's landing and Pittsburg landing, and were also collecting near Shiloh. This letter shows that at that time General Lew. Wallace was making preparations for the emergency that might happen for the passing of reinforcements between Shiloh and his position, extending from Crump's landing westward, and he sends it over the road running from Adamsville to the Pittsburg landing and Purdy road. These two roads intersect nearly a mile west of the crossing of the latter over Owl Creek, where our right rested. In this letter General Lew. Wallace advises General W. H. L. Wallace that he will send "to-morrow" (and his letter also says "April 5th," which is the same day the letter was dated and which, therefore, must have been written on the 4th) some cavalry to report to him at his headquarters, and suggesting the propriety of General W. H. L. Wallace's sending a company back with them for the purpose of having the cavalry at the two landings familiarize themselves with the road so that they could "act promptly in case of emergency as guides to and from the different camps."

This modifies very materially what I have said, and what has been said by others, of the conduct of General Lew. Wallace at the battle of Shiloh. It shows that he naturally, with no more experience than he had at the time in the profession of arms, would take the particular road that he did start upon in the absence of orders to move by a different road.

The mistake he made, and which probably caused his apparent dilatoriness, was that of advancing some distance after he found that the firing, which would be at first directly to his front and then off to the left, had fallen back until it had got very much in rear of the position of his advance. This falling back had taken place before I sent General Wallace orders to move up to Pittsburg landing and, naturally, my order was to follow the road nearest the river. But my order was verbal, and to a staff officer who was to deliver it to General Wallace, so that I am not competent to say just what order the General actually received.

General Wallace's division was stationed, the First brigade at Crump's landing, the Second out two miles, and the Third two and a half miles out. Hearing the sounds of battle General Wallace early ordered his First and Third brigades to concentrate on the Second. If the position of our front had not changed, the road which Wallace took would have been somewhat shorter to our right than the River road.

U. S. GRANT.

MOUNT MACGREGOR, NEW YORK, *June* 21, 1885.

---

[30] Ann D. Wallace (c.1833–c.1889) was the daughter of Col. T. Lyle Dickey. She wrote the letter to USG on Jan. 5, 1885. *PUSG,* 7:397*n*; 31:261*n*.

# 25

Struck by a Bullet—Precipitate Retreat of the
Confederates—Intrenchments at Shiloh—General
Buell—General Johnston—Remarks on Shiloh

Duringこの second day of the battle I had been moving from right to left and back, to see for myself the progress made. In the early part of the afternoon, while riding with Colonel McPherson and Major Hawkins,[1] then my chief commissary, we got beyond the left of our troops. We were moving along the northern edge of a clearing, very leisurely, toward the river above the landing. There did not appear to be an enemy to our right, until suddenly a battery with musketry opened upon us from the edge of the woods on the other side of the clearing. The shells and balls whistled about our ears very fast for about a minute. I do not think it took us longer than that to get out of range and out of sight. In the sudden start we made, Major Hawkins lost his hat. He did not stop to pick it up. When we arrived at a perfectly safe position we halted to take an account of damages. McPherson's horse was panting as if ready to drop. On examination it was found that a ball had struck him forward of the flank just back of the saddle, and had gone entirely through. In a few minutes the poor beast dropped dead; he had given no sign of injury until we came to a stop. A ball had struck the metal scabbard of my sword, just below the hilt, and broken it nearly off; before the battle was over it had broken off entirely. There were three of us: one had lost a horse, killed; one a hat and one a sword-scabbard. All were thankful that it was no worse.

After the rain of the night before and the frequent and heavy rains for some days previous, the roads were almost impassable. The enemy carrying his

---

[1] John P. Hawkins (1830–1914) was born in Indiana and graduated from the USMA in 1852. He served as commissary of subsistence for the Army of the Tennessee under USG from Dec. 1862 to Apr. 1863. Hawkins attained the rank of brevet major general during the Civil War and went on to serve as commissary general of subsistence from 1892 to 1894. *CWHC*, 288.

artillery and supply trains over them in his retreat, made them still worse for troops following. I wanted to pursue, but had not the heart to order the men who had fought desperately for two days, lying in the mud and rain whenever not fighting, and I did* not feel disposed to positively order Buell, or any part of his command, to pursue. Although the senior in rank at the time I had been so only a few weeks. Buell was, and had been for some time past, a department commander, while I commanded only a district. I did not meet Buell in person until too late to get troops ready and pursue with effect; but had I seen him at the moment of the last charge I should have at least requested him to follow.

I rode forward several miles the day after the battle, and found that the enemy had dropped much, if not all, of their provisions, some ammunition

*NOTE: In an article on the battle of Shiloh which I wrote for the *Century* Magazine,[2] I stated that General A. McD. McCook, who commanded a division of Buell's army, expressed some unwillingness to pursue the enemy on Monday, April 7th, because of the condition of his troops. General Badeau, in his history, also makes the same statement, on my authority.[3] Out of justice to General McCook and his command, I must say that they left a point twenty-two miles east of Savannah on the morning of the 6th. From the heavy rains of a few days previous and the passage of trains and artillery, the roads were necessarily deep in mud, which made marching slow. The division had not only marched through this mud the day before, but it had been in the rain all night without rest. It was engaged in the battle of the second day and did as good service as its position allowed. In fact an opportunity occurred for it to perform a conspicuous act of gallantry which elicited the highest commendation from division commanders in the Army of the Tennessee. General Sherman both in his memoirs and report makes mention of this fact.[4] General McCook himself belongs to a family which furnished many volunteers to the army. I refer to these circumstances with minuteness because I did General McCook injustice in my article in the *Century,* though not to the extent one would suppose from the public press. I am not willing to do any one an injustice, and if convinced that I have done one, I am always willing to make the fullest admission.

[2] USG's article on Shiloh appeared in the Feb. 1885 issue of *Century Magazine.* Ulysses S. Grant, "The Battle of Shiloh," *Century Illustrated Monthly Magazine,* Feb. 1885, 593–613.

[3] In this note, USG referred to a passage in Adam Badeau, *Military History of Ulysses S. Grant, from April, 1861, to April, 1865* (New York: D. Appleton, 1881), 1:90.

[4] In their postbattle reports, both Sherman and Hurlbut praised McCook for his contributions on Apr. 7, 1862. *OR,* I, 10(I), 206, 252; William T. Sherman, *Memoirs of General William T. Sherman* (New York: D. Appleton, 1875), 1:267–268.

and the extra wheels of their caissons, lightening their loads to enable them to get off their guns. About five miles out we found their field hospital abandoned. An immediate pursuit must have resulted in the capture of a considerable number of prisoners and probably some guns.

Shiloh was the severest battle fought at the West during the war, and but few in the East equalled it for hard, determined fighting. I saw an open field, in our possession on the second day, over which the Confederates had made repeated charges the day before, so covered with dead that it would have been possible to walk across the clearing, in any direction, stepping on dead bodies, without a foot touching the ground. On our side National and Confederate troops were mingled together in about equal proportions; but on the remainder of the field nearly all were Confederates. On one part, which had evidently not been ploughed for several years, probably because the land was poor, bushes had grown up, some to the height of eight or ten feet. There was not one of these left standing unpierced by bullets. The smaller ones were all cut down.

Contrary to all my experience up to that time, and to the experience of the army I was then commanding, we were on the defensive. We were without intrenchments or defensive advantages of any sort, and more than half the army engaged the first day was without experience or even drill as soldiers.[5] The officers with them, except the division commanders and possibly two or three of the brigade commanders, were equally inexperienced in war. The result was a Union victory that gave the men who achieved it great confidence in themselves ever after.

The enemy fought bravely, but they had started out to defeat and destroy an army and capture a position. They failed in both, with very heavy loss in killed and wounded, and must have gone back discouraged and convinced that the "Yankee" was not an enemy to be despised.

After the battle I gave verbal instructions to division commanders to let the regiments send out parties to bury their own dead, and to detail parties, under commissioned officers from each division, to bury the Confederate dead in their respective fronts and to report the numbers so buried.[6] The latter

[5] Although many of the U.S. troops at Shiloh were inexperienced, the terrain provided some defensive advantages. Timothy B. Smith, *Shiloh: Conquer or Perish* (Lawrence: University Press of Kansas, 2014), 41–47, 53, 87–89, 96.

[6] On Apr. 8, 1862, Beauregard asked USG for permission to bury the dead Confederate soldiers. The following day, USG denied the request after having ordered his men to bury both Confederate and U.S. dead. *PUSG,* 5:30 and *n.*

part of these instructions was not carried out by all; but they were by those sent from Sherman's division, and by some of the parties sent out by Mc-Clernand. The heaviest loss sustained by the enemy was in front of these two divisions.

The criticism has often been made that the Union troops should have been intrenched at Shiloh. Up to that time the pick and spade had been but little resorted to at the West.[7] I had, however, taken this subject under consideration soon after re-assuming command in the field, and, as already stated, my only military engineer reported unfavorably.[8] Besides this, the troops with me, officers and men, needed discipline and drill more than they did experience with the pick, shovel and axe. Reinforcements were arriving almost daily, composed of troops that had been hastily thrown together into companies and regiments—fragments of incomplete organizations, the men and officers strangers to each other. Under all these circumstances I concluded that drill and discipline were worth more to our men than fortifications.

General Buell was a brave, intelligent officer, with as much professional pride and ambition of a commendable sort as I ever knew. I had been two years at West Point with him, and had served with him afterwards, in garrison and in the Mexican war, several years more. He was not given in early life or in mature years to forming intimate acquaintances. He was studious by habit, and commanded the confidence and respect of all who knew him. He was a strict disciplinarian, and perhaps did not distinguish sufficiently between the volunteer who "enlisted for the war" and the soldier who serves in time of peace. One system embraced men who risked life for a principle, and often men of social standing, competence, or wealth and independence of character. The other includes, as a rule, only men who could not do as well in any other occupation. General Buell became an object of harsh criticism later, some going so far as to challenge his loyalty. No one who knew him ever believed him capable of a dishonorable act, and nothing could be more dishonorable than to accept high rank and command in war and then betray the trust. When

[7] In regard to entrenchments at Shiloh, Gen. James M. Tuttle said that "an officer would have been laughed out of camp" had he proposed to build works for the defense of the army at that time. William W. Belknap, *History of the Fifteenth, Iowa Veteran Volunteer Infantry* (Keokuk, IA: R. B. Ogden and Son, 1887), 192.

[8] See USG's comments on McPherson's report in Chapter 24.

I came into command of the army in 1864, I requested the Secretary of War[9] to restore General Buell to duty.[10]

After the war, during the summer of 1865, I travelled considerably through the North, and was everywhere met by large numbers of people. Every one had his opinion about the manner in which the war had been conducted: who among the generals had failed, how, and why. Correspondents of the press were ever on hand to hear every word dropped, and were not always disposed to report correctly what did not confirm their preconceived notions, either about the conduct of the war or the individuals concerned in it. The opportunity frequently occurred for me to defend General Buell against what I believed to be most unjust charges. On one occasion a correspondent put in my mouth the very charge I had so often refuted—of disloyalty. This brought from General Buell a very severe retort, which I saw in the New York *World* some time before I received the letter itself. I could very well understand his grievance at seeing untrue and disgraceful charges apparently sustained by an officer who, at the time, was at the head of the army. I replied to him, but not through the press. I kept no copy of my letter, nor did I ever see it in print; neither did I receive an answer.[11]

---

[9] Edwin M. Stanton (1814–1869) was born in Ohio and was U.S. attorney general from Dec. 1860 to Mar. 1861. He served as U.S. secretary of war from 1862 to 1868. On Dec. 20, 1869, he was appointed and confirmed as associate justice of the U.S. Supreme Court, but he never served because he died four days later. *CWHC*, 505.

[10] After the Battle of Perrysville in Oct. 1862, Buell received criticism for not pursuing Confederate general Braxton Bragg into east Tennessee. On Oct. 24, Lincoln ordered Buell to turn over his command to William S. Rosecrans. Soon after, Buell requested a court of inquiry to restore his reputation and clear him of any wrongdoing. The court examined Buell's operations in Kentucky and Tennessee and attempted to determine if he had committed treason through his conciliatory stance toward Southerners. After five months of deliberation, Buell was cleared of any disloyalty. In spring 1864, at the behest of USG, Halleck, and Sherman, Stanton interviewed Buell and offered him numerous options for command. Buell refused them all, deeming them unimportant. In May 1864, Buell was mustered out of the service as a major general. Stephen D. Engle, *Don Carlos Buell: Most Promising of All* (Chapel Hill: University of North Carolina Press, 1999), 323–324, 336, 339–340; *OR*, I, 16(II), 641–642.

[11] On Aug. 3, 1865, the *New York Herald* published an article by an unidentified reporter entitled "Personal Intelligence," which contained USG's supposed assessment of Buell's generalship leading up to Shiloh. Two days later, Buell wrote to USG about the article, but USG did not respond to it until Dec. 29. Buell defended his actions before Shiloh in a letter to USG dated Apr. 3, 1866. *PUSG*, 15:447–448, 448n–449n.

General Albert Sidney Johnston, who commanded the Confederate forces at the beginning of the battle, was disabled by a wound on the afternoon of the first day. This wound, as I understood afterwards, was not necessarily fatal, or even dangerous. But he was a man who would not abandon what he deemed an important trust in the face of danger and consequently continued in the saddle, commanding, until so exhausted by the loss of blood that he had to be taken from his horse, and soon after died. The news was not long in reaching our side and I suppose was quite an encouragement to the National soldiers.

I had known Johnston slightly in the Mexican war and later as an officer in the regular army. He was a man of high character and ability. His contemporaries at West Point, and officers generally who came to know him personally later and who remained on our side, expected him to prove the most formidable man to meet that the Confederacy would produce.

I once wrote that nothing occurred in his brief command of an army to prove or disprove the high estimate that had been placed upon his military ability; but after studying the orders and dispatches of Johnston I am compelled to materially modify my views of that officer's qualifications as a soldier. My judgment now is that he was vacillating and undecided in his actions.

All the disasters in Kentucky and Tennessee were so discouraging to the authorities in Richmond that Jefferson Davis wrote an unofficial letter to Johnston expressing his own anxiety and that of the public, and saying that he had made such defence as was dictated by long friendship, but that in the absence of a report he needed facts. The letter was not a reprimand in direct terms, but it was evidently as much felt as though it had been one.[12] General Johnston raised another army as rapidly as he could, and fortified or strongly intrenched at Corinth. He knew the National troops were preparing to attack him in his chosen position. But he had evidently become so disturbed at the results of his operations that he resolved to strike out in an offensive campaign which would restore all that was lost, and if successful accomplish still more. We have the authority of his son and biographer for saying that his plan was to attack the forces at Shiloh and crush them; then to cross the Tennessee and destroy the army of Buell, and push the war across the Ohio River.[13] The de-

[12] Davis wrote the letter to Johnston on Mar. 12, 1862. Jefferson Davis, *The Papers of Jefferson Davis*, vol. 8, ed. Lynda L. Crist and Mary S. Dix (Baton Rouge: Louisiana State University Press, 1995), 92–95.

[13] W. Preston Johnston, *The Life of Gen. Albert Sidney Johnston, Embracing His Services in the Armies of the United States, the Republic of Texas, and the Confederate States* (New York: D. Appleton, 1878), 538–539, 637–638.

sign was a bold one; but we have the same authority for saying that in the execution Johnston showed vacillation and indecision. He left Corinth on the 2d of April and was not ready to attack until the 6th. The distance his army had to march was less than twenty miles. Beauregard, his second in command, was opposed to the attack for two reasons: first, he thought, if let alone the National troops would attack the Confederates in their intrenchments; second, we were in ground of our own choosing and would necessarily be intrenched. Johnston not only listened to the objection of Beauregard to an attack, but held a council of war on the subject on the morning of the 5th. On the evening of the same day he was in consultation with some of his generals on the same subject, and still again on the morning of the 6th.[14] During this last consultation, and before a decision had been reached, the battle began by the National troops opening fire on the enemy. This seemed to settle the question as to whether there was to be any battle of Shiloh. It also seems to me to settle the question as to whether there was a surprise.

I do not question the personal courage of General Johnston, or his ability. But he did not win the distinction predicted for him by many of his friends. He did prove that as a general he was over-estimated.

General Beauregard was next in rank to Johnston and succeeded to the command, which he retained to the close of the battle and during the subsequent retreat on Corinth, as well as in the siege of that place. His tactics have been severely criticised by Confederate writers, but I do not believe his fallen chief could have done any better under the circumstances.[15] Some of these critics claim that Shiloh was won when Johnston fell, and that if he had not fallen the army under me would have been annihilated or captured. *Ifs* defeated the Confederates at Shiloh. There is little doubt that we would have been disgracefully beaten *if* all the shells and bullets fired by us had passed harmlessly over the enemy and *if* all of theirs had taken effect. Commanding generals are liable to be killed during engagements; and the fact that when he was shot Johnston was leading a brigade to induce it to make a charge which had been repeatedly ordered, is evidence that there was neither the universal demoralization on our side nor the unbounded confidence on theirs which has been

[14] Gens. Leonidas Polk, Braxton Bragg, Jeremy Gilmer, and John C. Breckinridge attended the council of war held by Johnston. Ibid., 567.

[15] For a Confederate writer's critique of Beauregard, see William Allan, "A Review by Colonel Wm. Allan, Formerly Chief of Ordnance Second Corps, A.N.V." [review of *The Military Operations of General Beauregard in the War between the States* by Alfred Roman], *Southern Historical Society Papers* 12 (1884): 258–266.

claimed.[16] There was, in fact, no hour during the day when I doubted the eventual defeat of the enemy, although I was disappointed that reinforcements so near at hand did not arrive at an earlier hour.

The description of the battle of Shiloh given by Colonel Wm. Preston Johnston is very graphic and well told. The reader will imagine that he can see each blow struck, a demoralized and broken mob of Union soldiers, each blow sending the enemy more demoralized than ever towards the Tennessee River, which was a little more than two miles away at the beginning of the onset. If the reader does not stop to inquire why, with such Confederate success for more than twelve hours of hard fighting, the National troops were not all killed, captured or driven into the river, he will regard the pen picture as perfect. But I witnessed the fight from the National side from eight o'clock in the morning until night closed the contest. I see but little in the description that I can recognize. The Confederate troops fought well and deserve commendation enough for their bravery and endurance on the 6th of April, without detracting from their antagonists or claiming anything more than their just dues.

The reports of the enemy show that their condition at the end of the first day was deplorable; their losses in killed and wounded had been very heavy, and their stragglers had been quite as numerous as on the National side, with the difference that those of the enemy left the field entirely and were not brought back to their respective commands for many days.[17] On the Union side but few of the stragglers fell back further than the landing on the river, and many of these were in line for duty on the second day. The admissions of the highest Confederate officers engaged at Shiloh make the claim of a victory for them absurd. The victory was not to either party until the battle was over. It was then a Union victory, in which the Armies of the Tennessee and the Ohio both participated. But the Army of the Tennessee fought the entire rebel army on the 6th and held it at bay until near night; and night alone closed the conflict and not the three regiments of Nelson's division.[18]

---

[16] Johnston was killed while attempting to motivate a Tennessee regiment, under the command of Gen. John C. Breckinridge, to attack the U.S. lines. Charles Roland, *Albert Sidney Johnston: Soldier of Three Republics* (Lexington: University Press of Kentucky, 2001), 336.

[17] For the reports of Beauregard, Polk, Bragg, and Breckinridge, see *OR,* I, 10(I), 384–392, 405–412, 463–470, 613.

[18] According to Nelson's postbattle report, on Apr. 6, 1862, at 6:30 P.M., Col. Jacob Ammen led the 10th Brigade (consisting of the 36th Indiana, 6th Ohio, and 24th Ohio Inf.) against the Confederate troops near Pittsburg Landing. Nelson claimed that Ammen's brigade "drove back the enemy and restored the line of battle" before nightfall ended the battle. Ibid., I, 10(I), 323–324.

The Confederates fought with courage at Shiloh, but the particular skill claimed I could not and still cannot see; though there is nothing to criticise except the claims put forward for it since. But the Confederate claimants for superiority in strategy, superiority in generalship and superiority in dash and prowess are not so unjust to the Union troops engaged at Shiloh as are many Northern writers.[19] The troops on both sides were American, and united they need not fear any foreign foe. It is possible that the Southern man started in with a little more dash than his Northern brother; but he was correspondingly less enduring.

The endeavor of the enemy on the first day was simply to hurl their men against ours—first at one point, then at another, sometimes at several points at once. This they did with daring and energy, until at night the rebel troops were worn out. Our effort during the same time was to be prepared to resist assaults wherever made. The object of the Confederates on the second day was to get away with as much of their army and material as possible. Ours then was to drive them from our front, and to capture or destroy as great a part as possible of their men and material. We were successful in driving them back, but not so successful in captures as if farther pursuit could have been made. As it was, we captured or recaptured on the second day about as much artillery as we lost on the first; and, leaving out the one great capture of Prentiss, we took more prisoners on Monday than the enemy gained from us on Sunday. On the 6th Sherman lost seven pieces of artillery, McClernand six, Prentiss eight, and Hurlbut two batteries. On the 7th Sherman captured seven guns, McClernand three and the Army of the Ohio twenty.

At Shiloh the effective strength of the Union forces on the morning of the 6th was 33,000 men. Lew. Wallace brought 5,000 more after nightfall. Beauregard reported the enemy's strength at 40,955.[20] According to the custom of enumeration in the South, this number probably excluded every man enlisted as musician or detailed as guard or nurse, and all commissioned officers—everybody who did not carry a musket or serve a cannon. With us everybody in the field receiving pay from the government is counted. Excluding the troops who fled, panic-stricken, before they had fired a shot, there was not a time

---

[19] Soon after the battle, the Cincinnati *Gazette* published an article by Whitelaw Reid, under the pseudonym of "Agate," claiming that the U.S. Army was surprised and caught completely unprepared at Shiloh. The sensationalized account was picked up by multiple Northern and Southern newspapers. James G. Smart, ed., *A Radical View: The "Agate" Dispatches of Whitelaw Reid, 1861–1865* (Memphis, TN: Memphis State University Press, 1976), 2, 129–131.

[20] According to prebattle totals included in the *OR*, Beauregard reportedly had 40,335 troops at the start of the battle. *OR*, I, 10(I), 396.

during the 6th when we had more than 25,000 men in line. On the 7th Buell brought 20,000 more. Of his remaining two divisions, Thomas's did not reach the field during the engagement; Wood's[21] arrived before firing had ceased, but not in time to be of much service.[22]

Our loss in the two days' fight was 1,754 killed, 8,408 wounded and 2,885 missing. Of these, 2,103 were in the Army of the Ohio. Beauregard reported a total loss of 10,699, of whom 1,728 were killed, 8,012 wounded and 957 missing.[23] This estimate must be incorrect. We buried, by actual count, more of the enemy's dead in front of the divisions of McClernand and Sherman alone than here reported, and 4,000 was the estimate of the burial parties for the whole field. Beauregard reports the Confederate force on the 6th at over 40,000, and their total loss during the two days at 10,699; and at the same time declares that he could put only 20,000 men in battle on the morning of the 7th.

The navy gave a hearty support to the army at Shiloh, as indeed it always did both before and subsequently when I was in command. The nature of the ground was such, however, that on this occasion it could do nothing in aid of the troops until sundown on the first day. The country was broken and heavily timbered, cutting off all view of the battle from the river, so that friends would be as much in danger from fire from the gunboats as the foe. But about sundown, when the National troops were back in their last position, the right of the enemy was near the river and exposed to the fire of the two gun-boats, which was delivered with vigor and effect.[24] After nightfall, when firing had entirely ceased on land, the commander of the fleet informed himself, approximately, of the position of our troops and suggested the idea of dropping a shell within the lines of the enemy every fifteen minutes during the night. This was done with effect, as is proved by the Confederate reports.[25]

Up to the battle of Shiloh I, as well as thousands of other citizens, believed that the rebellion against the Government would collapse suddenly and soon,

[21] Thomas J. Wood (1823–1906) was born in Kentucky and graduated from the USMA in 1845. As a colonel, he commanded the 6th Div., Army of the Ohio, at the time of the Battle of Shiloh. He reached the rank of major general and served as an assistant commissioner in the Bureau of Refugees, Freedmen, and Abandoned Lands. *CWHC,* 579–580.

[22] Buell reported that Thomas's division and a part of Wood's division did not arrive in time for the battle. *OR,* I, 10(I), 296.

[23] The *OR* lists 959 missing. Ibid., I, 10(I), 396.

[24] USG referred to the gunboats *Lexington* and *Tyler. PUSG,* 5:33, 36*n.*

[25] Lt. Commander William Gwin, who commanded the gunboat *Tyler,* approached both Gen. Stephen A. Hurlbut and USG with his request to shell Confederate forces, which was granted. David D. Porter, *The Naval History of the Civil War* (New York: Sherman, 1886), 153.

if a decisive victory could be gained over any of its armies. Donelson and Henry were such victories. An army of more than 21,000 men was captured or destroyed. Bowling Green, Columbus and Hickman, Kentucky, fell in consequence, and Clarksville and Nashville, Tennessee, the last two with an immense amount of stores, also fell into our hands. The Tennessee and Cumberland rivers, from their mouths to the head of navigation, were secured. But when Confederate armies were collected which not only attempted to hold a line farther south, from Memphis to Chattanooga, Knoxville and on to the Atlantic, but assumed the offensive and made such a gallant effort to regain what had been lost, then, indeed, I gave up all idea of saving the Union except by complete conquest. Up to that time it had been the policy of our army, certainly of that portion commanded by me, to protect the property of the citizens whose territory was invaded, without regard to their sentiments, whether Union or Secession. After this, however, I regarded it as humane to both sides to protect the persons of those found at their homes, but to consume everything that could be used to support or supply armies. Protection was still continued over such supplies as were within lines held by us and which we expected to continue to hold; but such supplies within the reach of Confederate armies I regarded as much contraband as arms or ordnance stores. Their destruction was accomplished without bloodshed and tended to the same result as the destruction of armies. I continued this policy to the close of the war. Promiscuous pillaging, however, was discouraged and punished. Instructions were always given to take provisions and forage under the direction of commissioned officers who should give receipts to owners, if at home, and turn the property over to officers of the quartermaster or commissary departments to be issued as if furnished from our Northern dépôts. But much was destroyed without receipts to owners, when it could not be brought within our lines and would otherwise have gone to the support of secession and rebellion.

This policy I believe exercised a material influence in hastening the end.

The battle of Shiloh, or Pittsburg landing, has been perhaps less understood, or, to state the case more accurately, more persistently misunderstood, than any other engagement between National and Confederate troops during the entire rebellion. Correct reports of the battle have been published, notably by Sherman, Badeau and, in a speech before a meeting of veterans, by General Prentiss; but all of these appeared long subsequent to the close of the rebellion and after public opinion had been most erroneously formed.[26]

[26] In Jan. 1882, Prentiss delivered a speech entitled "The Surprise at Shiloh" at a reunion and banquet of Civil War veterans in Cincinnati, OH. *Chicago Tribune,* Jan. 14, 1882. For Badeau's

I myself made no report to General Halleck, further than was contained in a letter, written immediately after the battle informing him that an engagement had been fought and announcing the result.[27] A few days afterwards General Halleck moved his headquarters to Pittsburg landing and assumed command of the troops in the field.[28] Although next to him in rank, and nominally in command of my old district and army, I was ignored as much as if I had been at the most distant point of territory within my jurisdiction; and although I was in command of all the troops engaged at Shiloh I was not permitted to see one of the reports of General Buell or his subordinates in that battle, until they were published by the War Department long after the event.[29] For this reason I never made a full official report of this engagement.

and Sherman's postwar accounts, see Badeau, *Military History of Ulysses S. Grant,* 1:57–98; Sherman, *Memoirs,* 1:223–247.

[27] USG wrote to Halleck on Apr. 9, 1862, but his letter of the same day to McLean, adjutant general of the Dept. of the Mississippi, effectively served as his battle report. *PUSG,* 5:31–36.

[28] Halleck assumed command at Pittsburg Landing on Apr. 11, 1862. Ibid., 5:xxii.

[29] The first volume of *The War of the Rebellion: A Compilation of the Official Records of the Union and Confederate Armies* was published in 1881, and publication continued until 1901. David S. Heidler and Jeanne T. Heidler, eds., *Encyclopedia of the American Civil War* (Santa Barbara, CA: ABC-CLIO, 2000), s.v. "The War of the Rebellion (Official Records)."

# 26

## Halleck Assumes Command in the Field— The Advance upon Corinth—Occupation of Corinth—The Army Separated

$G$ENERAL HALLECK ARRIVED at Pittsburg landing on the 11th of April and immediately assumed command in the field. On the 21st General Pope arrived with an army 30,000 strong, fresh from the capture of Island Number Ten in the Mississippi River.[1] He went into camp at Hamburg landing[2] five miles above Pittsburg. Halleck had now three armies: the Army of the Ohio, Buell commanding; the Army of the Mississippi, Pope commanding; and the Army of the Tennessee. His orders divided the combined force into the right wing, reserve, centre and left wing.[3] Major-General George H. Thomas, who had been in Buell's army, was transferred with his division to the Army of the Tennessee and given command of the right wing, composed of all of that army except McClernand's and Lew. Wallace's divisions. McClernand was assigned to the command of the reserve, composed of his own and Lew. Wallace's divisions. Buell commanded the centre, the Army of the Ohio; and Pope the left wing, the Army of the Mississippi. I was named second in command of the

---

[1] On Apr. 8, 1862, one day after the Battle of Shiloh, Pope captured Island Number 10, which was located six miles downriver from New Madrid, MO. Spencer Tucker, ed., *Civil War Naval Encyclopedia* (Santa Barbara, CA: ABC-CLIO, 2011), s.v. "Island Number 10, Battle of."

[2] Hamburg Landing was located five miles southeast of the Shiloh battlefield and was approximately twenty miles from Corinth, MS. George B. Davis et al., *The Official Military Atlas of the Civil War* (New York: Fairfax Press, 1983), plate 14, map 2.

[3] After Pope's arrival, Halleck had more than 100,000 troops encamped from Pittsburg Landing southward toward Hamburg Landing. Steven E. Woodworth, *Nothing but Victory: The Army of the Tennessee, 1861–1865* (New York: Knopf, 2005), 206.

whole, and was also supposed to be in command of the right wing and reserve.[4]

Orders were given to all the commanders engaged at Shiloh to send in their reports without delay to department headquarters. Those from officers of the Army of the Tennessee were sent through me; but from the Army of the Ohio they were sent by General Buell without passing through my hands. General Halleck ordered me, verbally, to send in my report, but I positively declined on the ground that he had received the reports of a part of the army engaged at Shiloh without their coming through me. He admitted that my refusal was justifiable under the circumstances, but explained that he had wanted to get the reports off before moving the command, and as fast as a report had come to him he had forwarded it to Washington.[5]

Preparations were at once made upon the arrival of the new commander for an advance on Corinth. Owl Creek, on our right, was bridged, and expeditions were sent to the north-west and west to ascertain if our position was being threatened from those quarters; the roads towards Corinth were corduroyed and new ones made; lateral roads were also constructed, so that in case of necessity troops marching by different routes could reinforce each other. All commanders were cautioned against bringing on an engagement and informed in so many words that it would be better to retreat than to fight. By the 30th of April all preparations were complete; the country west to the Mobile and Ohio railroad had been reconnoitred, as well as the road to Corinth as far as Monterey twelve miles from Pittsburg. Everywhere small bodies of the enemy had been encountered, but they were observers and not in force to fight battles.

Corinth, Mississippi, lies in a south-westerly direction from Pittsburg landing and about nineteen miles away as the bird would fly, but probably twenty-two by the nearest wagon-road. It is about four miles south of the line dividing the States of Tennessee and Mississippi, and at the junction of the Mississippi and Chattanooga railroad with the Mobile and Ohio road which runs from Columbus to Mobile.[6] From Pittsburg to Corinth the land is

---

[4] On Apr. 30, 1862, Halleck issued Special Field Orders No. 35, reorganizing the U.S. forces stationed at Pittsburg Landing. *OR,* I, 10(II), 144–145.

[5] On Apr. 9, 1862, USG enclosed a report of the Battle of Shiloh in a letter to Asst. AG N. H. McLean. He later composed a report on Shiloh in Aug.–Sept. *PUSG,* 5:32–36, 340–342.

[6] The Memphis and Charleston Railroad, not the Mississippi and Chattanooga, met the Mobile and Ohio Railroad at Corinth, MS. Davis et al., *Official Military Atlas of the Civil War,* plate 149.

rolling, but at no point reaching an elevation that makes high hills to pass over. In 1862 the greater part of the country was covered with forest with intervening clearings and houses. Underbrush was dense in the low grounds along the creeks and ravines, but generally not so thick on the high land as to prevent men passing through with ease. There are two small creeks running from north of the town and connecting some four miles south, where they form Bridge Creek which empties into the Tuscumbia River.[7] Corinth is on the ridge between these streams and is a naturally strong defensive position. The creeks are insignificant in volume of water, but the stream to the east widens out in front of the town into a swamp, impassable in the presence of an enemy. On the crest of the west bank of this stream the enemy was strongly intrenched.

Corinth was a valuable strategic point for the enemy to hold, and consequently a valuable one for us to possess ourselves of. We ought to have seized it immediately after the fall of Donelson and Nashville, when it could have been taken without a battle, but failing then it should have been taken, without delay, on the concentration of troops at Pittsburg landing after the battle of Shiloh. In fact the arrival of Pope should not have been awaited. There was no time from the battle of Shiloh up to the evacuation of Corinth when the enemy would not have left if pushed. The demoralization among the Confederates from their defeats at Henry and Donelson; their long marches from Bowling Green, Columbus, and Nashville, and their failure at Shiloh; in fact from having been driven out of Kentucky and Tennessee, was so great that a stand for the time would have been impossible. Beauregard made strenuous efforts to reinforce himself and partially succeeded. He appealed to the people of the South-west for new regiments, and received a few. A. S. Johnston had made efforts to reinforce in the same quarter, before the battle of Shiloh, but in a different way. He had negroes sent out to him to take the place of teamsters, company cooks and laborers in every capacity, so as to put all his white men into the ranks. The people, while willing to send their sons to the field, were not willing to part with their negroes. It is only fair to state that they probably wanted their blacks to raise supplies for the army and for the families left at home.

[7] Phillips Creek ran along the east side of Corinth, and Elam Creek ran along the west side. Timothy B. Smith, *Corinth 1862: Siege, Battle, Occupation* (Lawrence: University Press of Kansas, 2012), 224.

Beauregard, however, was reinforced by Van Dorn immediately after Shiloh with 17,000 men.[8] Interior points, less exposed, were also depleted to add to the strength at Corinth. With these reinforcements and the new regiments, Beauregard had, during the month of May, 1862, a large force on paper, but probably not much over 50,000 effective men. We estimated his strength at 70,000. Our own was, in round numbers, 120,000. The defensible nature of the ground at Corinth, and the fortifications, made 50,000 then enough to maintain their position against double that number for an indefinite time but for the demoralization spoken of.

On the 30th of April the grand army commenced its advance from Shiloh upon Corinth.[9] The movement was a siege from the start to the close. The National troops were always behind intrenchments, except of course the small reconnoitring parties sent to the front to clear the way for an advance. Even the commanders of these parties were cautioned, "not to bring on an engagement." "It is better to retreat than to fight." The enemy were constantly watching our advance, but as they were simply observers there were but few engagements that even threatened to become battles. All the engagements fought ought to have served to encourage the enemy. Roads were again made in our front, and again corduroyed; a line was intrenched, and the troops were advanced to the new position. Cross roads were constructed to these new positions to enable the troops to concentrate in case of attack. The National armies were thoroughly intrenched all the way from the Tennessee River to Corinth.

For myself I was little more than an observer. Orders were sent direct to the right wing or reserve, ignoring me, and advances were made from one line of intrenchments to another without notifying me. My position was so embarrassing in fact that I made several applications during the siege to be relieved.[10]

---

[8] Earl Van Dorn (1820–1863) was born in Mississippi and graduated from the USMA in 1842. On Mar. 4, 1862, as a major general, he was named commander of the Confederate Army of the West. On Apr. 8, Van Dorn's force of more than 15,000 men left Des Arc, AR, for Corinth. The head of his column arrived in Corinth on Apr. 24, Van Dorn himself arrived on Apr. 30, and the rest of his men arrived during the first days of May. *CWHC,* 542; Smith, *Corinth,* 14–15.

[9] Apr. 29, 1862, was the date set for the start of the campaign, but individual units began movements either before or after that date. Smith, *Corinth,* 24.

[10] On May 11, 1862, USG wrote a letter of complaint to Halleck about his dissatisfaction with his responsibilities. USG suspected that the decision to diminish his command came

General Halleck kept his headquarters generally, if not all the time, with the right wing. Pope being on the extreme left did not see so much of his chief, and consequently got loose as it were at times. On the 3d of May he was at Seven Mile Creek with the main body of his command, but threw forward a division to Farmington, within four miles of Corinth. His troops had quite a little engagement at Farmington on that day, but carried the place with considerable loss to the enemy.[11] There would then have been no difficulty in advancing the centre and right so as to form a new line well up to the enemy, but Pope was ordered back to conform with the general line. On the 8th of May he moved again, taking his whole force to Farmington, and pushed out two divisions close to the rebel line.[12] Again he was ordered back. By the 4th of May the centre and right wing reached Monterey, twelve miles out. Their advance was slow from there, for they intrenched with every forward movement. The left wing moved up again on the 25th of May and intrenched itself close to the enemy. The creek, with the marsh before described, separated the two lines. Skirmishers thirty feet apart could have maintained either line at this point.

Our centre and right were, at this time, extended so that the right of the right wing was probably five miles from Corinth and four from the works in their front. The creek, which was a formidable obstacle for either side to pass on our left, became a very slight obstacle on our right. Here the enemy occupied two positions. One of them, as much as two miles out from his main line, was on a commanding elevation and defended by an intrenched battery with infantry supports. A heavy wood intervened between this work and the National forces. In rear to the south there was a clearing extending a mile or more, and south of this clearing a log-house which had been loop-holed and was occupied by infantry. Sherman's division carried these two positions with some loss to himself, but with probably greater to the enemy, on the 28th of May, and on that day the investment of Corinth was complete, or as com-

"from higher authority." He asked Halleck to relieve him from command, but Halleck refused, writing, "You have precisely the position to which your rank entitles you." *PUSG,* 5:114–115.

[11] Pope reported that thirty Confederate soldiers were killed at the skirmish near Farmington, MS, on May 3, 1862. U.S. forces lost two men, and twelve more were wounded. *OR,* I, 10(I), 801–802.

[12] Heavy rainfall May 4–7, 1862, prevented Pope from advancing on Corinth. On May 9, Pope's troops stopped an advance of 20,000 Confederate soldiers at Seven Mile Creek. Ibid., I, 10(I), 804; Smith, *Corinth,* 26–27.

plete as it was ever made.[13] Thomas' right now rested west of the Mobile and Ohio railroad. Pope's left commanded the Memphis and Charleston railroad east of Corinth.

Some days before I had suggested to the commanding general that I thought if he would move the Army of the Mississippi at night, by the rear of the centre and right, ready to advance at daylight, Pope would find no natural obstacle in his front and, I believed, no serious artificial one. The ground, or works, occupied by our left could be held by a thin picket line, owing to the stream and swamp in front. To the right the troops would have a dry ridge to march over. I was silenced so quickly that I felt that possibly I had suggested an unmilitary movement.

Later, probably on the 28th of May, General Logan, whose command was then on the Mobile and Ohio railroad, said to me that the enemy had been evacuating for several days and that if allowed he could go into Corinth with his brigade. Trains of cars were heard coming in and going out of Corinth constantly. Some of the men who had been engaged in various capacities on railroads before the war claimed that they could tell, by putting their ears to the rail, not only which way the trains were moving but which trains were loaded and which were empty. They said loaded trains had been going out for several days and empty ones coming in. Subsequent events proved the correctness of their judgment. Beauregard published his orders for the evacuation of Corinth on the 26th of May and fixed the 29th for the departure of his troops, and on the 30th of May General Halleck had his whole army drawn up prepared for battle and announced in orders that there was every indication that our left was to be attacked that morning. Corinth had already been evacuated and the National troops marched on and took possession without opposition. Everything had been destroyed or carried away. The Confederate commander had instructed his soldiers to cheer on the arrival of every train to create the impression among the Yankees that reinforcements were arriving. There was not a sick or wounded man left by the Confederates, nor stores of any kind.[14] Some ammunition had been blown up—not removed—but the

---

[13] On May 28–30, 1862, Sherman, supported by a brigade from McClernand's division and another brigade from Hurlbut's division, pushed the Confederate troops from their entrenched positions back into Corinth. Sherman's postbattle report stated that he could not definitively state the losses by his troops or the Confederate troops. *OR*, I, 10(I), 741, 744; William T. Sherman, *Memoirs of General William T. Sherman* (New York: D. Appleton, 1875), 1:251–252.

[14] By the second week of May 1862, Beauregard deemed an attack on the Union troops impossible. Withstanding a siege at Corinth would also be difficult since nearly 20,000 men had

trophies of war were a few Quaker guns, logs of about the diameter of ordinary cannon, mounted on wheels of wagons and pointed in the most threatening manner towards us.

The possession of Corinth by the National troops was of strategic importance, but the victory was barren in every other particular. It was nearly bloodless. It is a question whether the *morale* of the Confederate troops engaged at Corinth was not improved by the immunity with which they were permitted to remove all public property and then withdraw themselves. On our side I know officers and men of the Army of the Tennessee—and I presume the same is true of those of the other commands—were disappointed at the result. They could not see how the mere occupation of places was to close the war while large and effective rebel armies existed. They believed that a well-directed attack would at least have partially destroyed the army defending Corinth. For myself I am satisfied that Corinth could have been captured in a two days' campaign commenced promptly on the arrival of reinforcements after the battle of Shiloh.

General Halleck at once commenced erecting fortifications around Corinth on a scale to indicate that this one point must be held if it took the whole National army to do it. All commanding points two or three miles to the south, south-east and south-west were strongly fortified. It was expected in case of necessity to connect these forts by rifle-pits. They were laid out on a scale that would have required 100,000 men to fully man them. It was probably thought that a final battle of the war would be fought at that point. These fortifications were never used. Immediately after the occupation of Corinth by the National troops, General Pope was sent in pursuit of the retreating garrison and General Buell soon followed. Buell was the senior of the two generals and commanded the entire column. The pursuit was kept up for some thirty miles, but did not result in the capture of any material of war or prisoners, unless a few stragglers who had fallen behind and were willing captives.[15] On the 10th

---

fallen ill because of unsanitary conditions. Before Union troops encircled the town, Beauregard abandoned Corinth on May 30. Thomas L. Connolly, *Army of the Heartland: The Army of Tennessee, 1861–1862* (Baton Rouge: Louisiana State University Press, 1967), 176–177.

[15] On May 30, 1862, Pope, reinforced by one division of Buell's army, led the pursuit against the retreating Confederate forces. Pope reported to Halleck that approximately 10,000 stragglers were in the area, and would soon turn themselves over to the Union. Halleck mistakenly interpreted the report as Pope having captured the deserters. Pope received heavy criticism because of the discrepancy. John Pope, *The Military Memoirs of General John Pope* (Chapel Hill: University of North Carolina Press, 1998), 69–74.

of June the pursuing column was all back at Corinth. The Army of the Tennessee was not engaged in any of these movements.

The Confederates were now driven out of West Tennessee, and on the 6th of June, after a well-contested naval battle, the National forces took possession of Memphis and held the Mississippi river from its source to that point. The railroad from Columbus to Corinth was at once put in good condition and held by us. We had garrisons at Donelson, Clarksville and Nashville, on the Cumberland River, and held the Tennessee River from its mouth to Eastport. New Orleans and Baton Rouge had fallen into the possession of the National forces, so that now the Confederates at the west were narrowed down for all communication with Richmond to the single line of road running east from Vicksburg. To dispossess them of this, therefore, became a matter of the first importance. The possession of the Mississippi by us from Memphis to Baton Rouge was also a most important object. It would be equal to the amputation of a limb in its weakening effects upon the enemy.

After the capture of Corinth a movable force of 80,000 men, besides enough to hold all the territory acquired, could have been set in motion for the accomplishment of any great campaign for the suppression of the rebellion. In addition to this fresh troops were being raised to swell the effective force. But the work of depletion commenced. Buell with the Army of the Ohio was sent east, following the line of the Memphis and Charleston railroad. This he was ordered to repair as he advanced—only to have it destroyed by small guerilla bands or other troops as soon as he was out of the way. If he had been sent directly to Chattanooga as rapidly as he could march, leaving two or three divisions along the line of the railroad from Nashville forward, he could have arrived with but little fighting, and would have saved much of the loss of life which was afterwards incurred in gaining Chattanooga. Bragg[16] would then not have had time to raise an army to contest the possession of middle and east Tennessee and Kentucky; the battles of Stone River and Chickamauga would not necessarily have been fought; Burnside[17] would not have been be-

---

[16] Braxton Bragg (1817–1876) was born in North Carolina and graduated from the USMA in 1837. He served in the U.S. Army until 1856. He was a member of the Louisiana Militia and rose to general in the Confederate Army by 1862. *CWHC*, 140–141.

[17] Ambrose E. Burnside (1824–1881) was born in Indiana and graduated from the USMA in 1847. He was promoted to major general in the U.S. Army on Mar. 18, 1862. He commanded the Army of the Potomac from Nov. 1862 to Jan. 1863 and the Dept. of the Ohio from Mar. 1863 to Dec. 1863. After the war, he served as the governor of Rhode Island from 1866 to 1869 and as senator from 1875 to 1881. Ibid., 155.

sieged in Knoxville without the power of helping himself or escaping; the battle of Chattanooga would not have been fought. These are the negative advantages, if the term negative is applicable, which would probably have resulted from prompt movements after Corinth fell into the possession of the National forces. The positive results might have been: a bloodless advance to Atlanta, to Vicksburg, or to any other desired point south of Corinth in the interior of Mississippi.

# 27

Headquarters Moved to Memphis—On the Road to
Memphis—Escaping Jackson—Complaints and
Requests—Halleck Appointed Commander-in-Chief—
Return to Corinth—Movements of Bragg—Surrender
of Clarksville—The Advance upon Chattanooga—
Sheridan Colonel of a Michigan Regiment

M̲y position at corinth, with a nominal command and yet no command, became so unbearable that I asked permission of Halleck to remove my headquarters to Memphis.[1] I had repeatedly asked, between the fall of Donelson and the evacuation of Corinth, to be relieved from duty under Halleck; but all my applications were refused until the occupation of the town.[2] I then obtained permission to leave the department, but General Sherman happened to call on me as I was about starting and urged me so strongly not to think of going, that I concluded to remain.[3] My application to be permitted to

[1] There is no known correspondence between USG and Halleck discussing his request to be moved to Memphis, TN. USG first mentioned the possibility of being based in Memphis to JDG on May 13, 1862. *PUSG*, 5:117.

[2] USG requested to be relieved from duty at least three times in Mar. 1862 alone. Halleck ignored these requests until the occupation of Corinth, MS, on May 30. Ibid., 4:331, 334, 353; 5:134.

[3] In his memoirs, Sherman described his influence on USG's decision to stay in the department in much the same way as USG described it in this passage. However, USG did not describe his conversation with Sherman in his own correspondence at the time. He mentioned his intended leave of absence in a June 1, 1862, letter to Elihu B. Washburne, but then wrote to JDG on June 3 that his plans had changed. On June 19, he wrote to Washburne that he would not be taking leave, explaining that Halleck had informed him that he was needed with the

remove my headquarters to Memphis was, however, approved, and on the 21st of June I started for that point with my staff and a cavalry escort of only a part of one company.[4] There was a detachment of two or three companies going some twenty-five miles west to be stationed as a guard to the railroad. I went under cover of this escort to the end of their march, and the next morning proceeded to La Grange with no convoy but the few cavalry men I had with me.

From La Grange to Memphis the distance is forty-seven miles. There were no troops stationed between these two points, except a small force guarding a working party which was engaged in repairing the railroad. Not knowing where this party would be found I halted at La Grange.[5] General Hurlbut was in command there at the time and had his headquarters tents pitched on the lawn of a very commodious country house.[6] The proprietor was at home and, learning of my arrival, he invited General Hurlbut and me to dine with him. I accepted the invitation and spent a very pleasant afternoon with my host, who was a thorough Southern gentleman fully convinced of the justice of secession. After dinner, seated in the capacious porch, he entertained me with a recital of the services he was rendering the cause. He was too old to be in the ranks himself—he must have been quite seventy then—but his means enabled him to be useful in other ways. In ordinary times the homestead where he was now living produced the bread and meat to supply the slaves on his main plantation, in the low-lands of Mississippi. Now he raised food and forage on both places, and thought he would have that year a surplus sufficient to feed three hundred families of poor men who had gone into the war and left their families dependent upon the "patriotism" of those better off. The crops around me looked fine, and I had at the moment an idea that about the time they were ready to be gathered the "Yankee" troops would be in the neighborhood and harvest them for the benefit of those engaged in the suppression of the

army. Ibid., 5:137, 145; William T. Sherman, *Memoirs of General William T. Sherman* (New York: D. Appleton, 1875), 1:255–256.

[4] Rawlins issued Gen. Orders No. 55 on June 19, 1862, stating that USG's headquarters would be in Memphis from that date forward. *PUSG,* 5:143*n.*

[5] USG arrived in La Grange, TN, on June 22, 1862. Gary L. Donhardt, "On the Road to Memphis with General Ulysses S. Grant," *West Tennessee Historical Society Papers* 53 (1999): 4.

[6] Hurlbut may have been staying at the estate of Charles Michie, a wealthy local landowner. Hurlbut and his men guarded the railroad at Grand Junction, TN, approximately fifty miles east of Memphis, located at the intersection of the Mississippi Central and Memphis and Charleston Railroads. Ibid.; *PUSG,* 5:149–150, 150*n.*

rebellion instead of its support. I felt, however, the greatest respect for the candor of my host and for his zeal in a cause he thoroughly believed in, though our views were as wide apart as it is possible to conceive.

The 23d of June, 1862, on the road from La Grange to Memphis was very warm, even for that latitude and season. With my staff and small escort I started at an early hour, and before noon we arrived within twenty miles of Memphis.[7] At this point I saw a very comfortable-looking white-haired gentleman seated at the front of his house, a little distance from the road.[8] I let my staff and escort ride ahead while I halted and, for an excuse, asked for a glass of water. I was invited at once to dismount and come in. I found my host very genial and communicative, and staid longer than I had intended, until the lady of the house[9] announced dinner and asked me to join them. The host, however, was not pressing, so that I declined the invitation and, mounting my horse, rode on.

About a mile west from where I had been stopping a road comes up from the south-east,[10] joining that from La Grange to Memphis. A mile west of this junction I found my staff and escort halted and enjoying the shade of forest trees on the lawn of a house located several hundred feet back from the road, their horses hitched to the fence along the line of the road. I, too, stopped and we remained there until the cool of the afternoon, and then rode into Memphis.

The gentleman with whom I had stopped twenty miles from Memphis was a Mr. De Loche, a man loyal to the Union. He had not pressed me to tarry longer with him because in the early part of my visit a neighbor, a Dr. Smith, had called and, on being presented to me, backed off the porch as if something had hit him. Mr. De Loche knew that the rebel General Jackson[11] was

[7] USG stated that there were twelve men in his escort. *PUSG,* 5:149.

[8] Josiah Deloach (1807–1880) was a well-known opponent of secession but had several family members who fought in the Confederate Army. Pres. USG appointed him postmaster of Memphis in 1869. Donhardt, "On the Road to Memphis," 5; "The Late Josiah Deloach," *Memphis Daily Appeal,* Dec. 22, 1880, 2; "Postmaster," *Memphis Daily Appeal,* Apr. 7, 1869, 2.

[9] Olivia Bills Hill Deloach (c.1807–1883), widow of Dr. Duncan Hill, married Josiah Deloach in 1847 after the death of his first wife. "Died—Deloach," *Memphis Daily Appeal,* Sept. 8, 1883, 1; Clarene Pinkston Russell, *Collierville, Tennessee, Her People and Neighbors* (n.p.: Clarene Pinkston Russell, 1994), 345.

[10] USG possibly referred to Bailey Station Road, located approximately eight-tenths of a mile west of the Deloach house. Donhardt, "On the Road to Memphis," 13*n*.

[11] William H. Jackson (1835–1903) was born in Tennessee and graduated from the USMA in 1856. He was wounded at the Battle of Belmont. In June 1862 he was a colonel in the Confederate

in that neighborhood with a detachment of cavalry. His neighbor was as earnest in the southern cause as was Mr. De Loche in that of the Union. The exact location of Jackson was entirely unknown to Mr. De Loche; but he was sure that his neighbor would know it and would give information of my presence, and this made my stay unpleasant to him after the call of Dr. Smith.[12]

I have stated that a detachment of troops was engaged in guarding workmen who were repairing the railroad east of Memphis. On the day I entered Memphis, Jackson captured a small herd of beef cattle which had been sent east for the troops so engaged.[13] The drovers were not enlisted men and he released them. A day or two after one of these drovers came to my headquarters and, relating the circumstances of his capture, said Jackson was very much disappointed that he had not captured me; that he was six or seven miles south of the Memphis and Charleston railroad when he learned that I was stopping at the house of Mr. De Loche, and had ridden with his command to the junction of the road he was on with that from La Grange and Memphis, where he learned that I had passed three-quarters of an hour before. He thought it would be useless to pursue with jaded horses a well-mounted party with so much of a start. Had he gone three-quarters of a mile farther he would have found me with my party quietly resting under the shade of trees and without even arms in our hands with which to defend ourselves.

General Jackson of course did not communicate his disappointment at not capturing me to a prisoner, a young drover; but from the talk among the soldiers the facts related were learned. A day or two later Mr. De Loche called on me in Memphis to apologize for his apparent incivility in not insisting on my staying for dinner. He said that his wife accused him of marked discourtesy, but that, after the call of his neighbor, he had felt restless until I got away. I never met General Jackson before the war, nor during it, but have met

Army and was in command of the 1st Tennessee Cav. (later known as the 7th Tennessee Cav.). *CWHC*, 316–317.

[12] In another version of this story told by Mrs. Deloach's daughter, a family servant informed the Deloaches of Confederate troops in the area. Mr. and Mrs. Deloach then informed USG, who left quickly for Memphis. In that version of the story, there is no mention of Dr. Smith, and the editors have been unable to identify anyone by that name. Mary Frances Hill Joy, *Genealogy of the Hill Family and Personal Recollections of Mrs. Mary Frances Hill Joy* (St. Louis: n.p., 1912), 9–10.

[13] Jackson's cavalry destroyed a train during a raid near Germantown, TN, on June 25, 1862. *PUSG*, 5:159–161, 161n.

him since at his very comfortable summer home at Manitou Springs, Colorado.[14] I reminded him of the above incident, and this drew from him the response that he was thankful now he had not captured me. I certainly was very thankful too.

My occupation of Memphis as district headquarters did not last long.[15] The period, however, was marked by a few incidents which were novel to me. Up to that time I had not occupied any place in the South where the citizens were at home in any great numbers. Dover was within the fortifications at Fort Donelson, and, as far as I remember, every citizen was gone. There were no people living at Pittsburg landing, and but very few at Corinth. Memphis, however, was a populous city,[16] and there were many of the citizens remaining there who were not only thoroughly impressed with the justice of their cause, but who thought that even the "Yankee soldiery" must entertain the same views if they could only be induced to make an honest confession. It took hours of my time every day to listen to complaints and requests. The latter were generally reasonable, and if so they were granted; but the complaints were not always, or even often, well founded. Two instances will mark the general character. First: the officer who commanded at Memphis immediately after the city fell into the hands of the National troops had ordered one of the churches of the city to be opened to the soldiers. Army chaplains were authorized to occupy the pulpit.[17] Second: at the beginning of the war the Confederate Congress had passed a law confiscating all property of "alien enemies" at the South, including the debts of Southerners to Northern men. In consequence

[14] USG and JDG visited Manitou Springs, CO, during summer 1880. *PUSG*, 29:442–446.

[15] USG arrived in Memphis on June 23, 1862, and maintained his headquarters there until he was ordered to Corinth on July 11. Ibid., 5:xxiii, 206, 206n–207n.

[16] According to U.S. census records, the population of Memphis in 1860 was 22,623. Lynette B. Wrenn, *Crisis and Commission Government in Memphis: Elite Rule in a Gilded Age City* (Knoxville: University of Tennessee Press, 1998), 2.

[17] On June 6, 1862, Col. Graham N. Fitch of the 46th Indiana Inf. initially took possession of the city after its capture by U.S. Army and Navy forces. He was superseded on June 13 by Col. James R. Slack of the 47th Indiana Inf. Lew Wallace arrived in Memphis on June 17 and was the highest-ranking officer in the city at the time. Prior to USG's arrival on June 23, Wallace designated the Second Presbyterian Church as a chapel for U.S. Army troops. George M. Apperson, "Lincoln, the Churches, and Memphis Presbyterians," *American Presbyterians* 72 (1994): 102; *OR*, I, 10(I), 911; I, 17(II), 15; *PUSG*, 5:147n–148n, 149n; Lewis Wallace, *Lewis Wallace: An Autobiography* (New York: Harper and Brothers, 1906), 2:586.

of this law, when Memphis was occupied the provost-marshal had forcibly collected all the evidences he could obtain of such debts.[18]

Almost the first complaints made to me were these two outrages. The gentleman who made the complaints informed me first of his own high standing
as a lawyer, a citizen and a Christian. He was a deacon in the church which
had been defiled by the occupation of Union troops, and by a Union chaplain filling the pulpit. He did not use the word "defile," but he expressed the
idea very clearly. He asked that the church be restored to the former congregation. I told him that no order had been issued prohibiting the congregation
attending the church. He said of course the congregation could not hear a
Northern clergyman who differed so radically with them on questions of government. I told him the troops would continue to occupy that church for the
present, and that they would not be called upon to hear disloyal sentiments
proclaimed from the pulpit. This closed the argument on the first point.

Then came the second. The complainant said that he wanted the papers
restored to him which had been surrendered to the provost-marshal under protest; he was a lawyer, and before the establishment of the "Confederate States
Government" had been the attorney for a number of large business houses at
the North; that "his government" had confiscated all debts due "alien enemies,"
and appointed commissioners, or officers, to collect such debts and pay them
over to the "government": but in his case, owing to his high standing, he had
been permitted to hold these claims for collection, the responsible officials
knowing that he would account to the "government" for every dollar received.
He said that his "government," when it came in possession of all its territory,
would hold him personally responsible for the claims he had surrendered to
the provost-marshal. His impudence was so sublime that I was rather amused
than indignant. I told him, however, that if he would remain in Memphis I
did not believe the Confederate government would ever molest him. He left,

[18] The Confederate Congress had passed the Sequestration Act on Aug. 30, 1861, allowing
the Confederacy to seize Northern property in the South. Slack countered the Confederate
mandate by issuing Gen. Orders No. 3 on June 13, 1862, requiring "parties who have in their
possession notes, bills, and choses in action belonging to loyal citizens of the United States" to
return the property to its rightful owners. Daniel W. Hamilton, *The Limits of Sovereignty:
Property Confiscation in the Union and Confederacy during the Civil War* (Chicago: University
of Chicago Press, 2007), 125–127; J. M. Keating, *History of the City of Memphis and Shelby
County, Tennessee: With Illustrations and Biographical Sketches of Some of Its Prominent Citizens*
(Syracuse, NY: D. Mason, 1888), 1:514.

no doubt, as much amazed at my assurance as I was at the brazenness of his request.

On the 11th of July General Halleck received telegraphic orders appointing him to the command of all the armies, with headquarters in Washington. His instructions pressed him to proceed to his new field of duty with as little delay as was consistent with the safety and interests of his previous command. I was next in rank, and he telegraphed me the same day to report at department headquarters at Corinth. I was not informed by the dispatch that my chief had been ordered to a different field and did not know whether to move my headquarters or not. I telegraphed asking if I was to take my staff with me, and received word in reply: "This place will be your headquarters. You can judge for yourself."[19] I left Memphis for my new field without delay, and reached Corinth on the 15th of the month. General Halleck remained until the 17th of July; but he was very uncommunicative, and gave me no information as to what I had been called to Corinth for.

When General Halleck left to assume the duties of general-in-chief I remained in command of the district of West Tennessee. Practically I became a department commander, because no one was assigned to that position over me and I made my reports direct to the general-in-chief; but I was not assigned to the position of department commander until the 25th of October.[20] General Halleck while commanding the Department of the Mississippi had had control as far east as a line drawn from Chattanooga north. My district only embraced West Tennessee and Kentucky west of the Cumberland River. Buell, with the Army of the Ohio, had, as previously stated, been ordered east towards Chattanooga, with instructions to repair the Memphis and Charleston railroad as he advanced.[21] Troops had been sent north by Halleck along the line of the Mobile and Ohio railroad to put it in repair as far as Columbus. Other troops were stationed on the railroad from Jackson, Tennessee, to Grand Junction, and still others on the road west to Memphis.[22]

[19] *PUSG*, 5:206n–207n.

[20] USG was assigned to the command of the Dept. of the Tennessee on Oct. 16, 1862. However, he did not assume command until Oct. 25. Ibid., 6:186.

[21] On June 9, 1862, Halleck ordered Buell to move toward Chattanooga but he did not leave for Chattanooga until June 13. *OR*, I, 10(II), 280–281.

[22] The railroad line between Grand Junction and Jackson, TN, was part of the Tennessee and Ohio line. USG referred to that section of track as part of the Mississippi Central Railroad. George B. Davis et al., *The Official Military Atlas of the Civil War* (New York: Fairfax Press, 1983), plate 154; *PUSG*, 6:14–15 (map).

The remainder of the magnificent army of 120,000 men which entered Corinth on the 30th of May had now become so scattered that I was put entirely on the defensive in a territory whose population was hostile to the Union. One of the first things I had to do was to construct fortifications at Corinth better suited to the garrison that could be spared to man them. The structures that had been built during the months of May and June were left as monuments to the skill of the engineer, and others were constructed in a few days, plainer in design but suited to the command available to defend them.

I disposed the troops belonging to the district in conformity with the situation as rapidly as possible. The forces at Donelson, Clarksville and Nashville, with those at Corinth and along the railroad eastward, I regarded as sufficient for protection against any attack from the west. The Mobile and Ohio railroad was guarded from Rienzi, south of Corinth, to Columbus; and the Mississippi Central railroad from Jackson, Tennessee, to Bolivar. Grand Junction and La Grange on the Memphis railroad were abandoned.[23]

South of the Army of the Tennessee, and confronting it, was Van Dorn, with a sufficient force to organize a movable army of thirty-five to forty thousand men, after being reinforced by Price from Missouri.[24] This movable force could be thrown against either Corinth, Bolivar or Memphis; and the best that could be done in such event would be to weaken the points not threatened in order to reinforce the one that was. Nothing could be gained on the National side by attacking elsewhere, because the territory already occupied was as much as the force present could guard. The most anxious period of the war, to me, was during the time the Army of the Tennessee was guarding the territory acquired by the fall of Corinth and Memphis and before I was sufficiently reinforced to take the offensive. The enemy also had cavalry operating in our rear, making it necessary to guard every point of the railroad back to Columbus, on the security of which we were dependent for all our supplies. Headquarters were connected by telegraph with all points of the command except Memphis and the Mississippi below Columbus. With these points communication was had by the railroad to Columbus, then down the

[23] USG ordered U.S. forces to be withdrawn from La Grange and Grand Junction on July 15, 1862, but concerns about the safety of Union loyalists and their property in Grand Junction delayed the complete withdrawal. U.S. troops under the command of Col. Mortimer D. Leggett eventually evacuated Grand Junction on July 24, arriving in Bolivar, TN, on the morning of July 25. *OR*, I, 17(II), 116; *PUSG*, 5:209n, 212n, 244n.

[24] Price joined forces with Van Dorn on Sept. 28, 1862. Albert Castel, *General Sterling Price and the Civil War in the West* (Baton Rouge: Louisiana State University Press, 1968), 104.

river by boat. To reinforce Memphis would take three or four days, and to get an order there for troops to move elsewhere would have taken at least two days. Memphis therefore was practically isolated from the balance of the command. But it was in Sherman's hands. Then too the troops were well intrenched and the gunboats made a valuable auxiliary.

During the two months after the departure of General Halleck there was much fighting between small bodies of the contending armies, but these encounters were dwarfed by the magnitude of the main battles so as to be now almost forgotten except by those engaged in them. Some of them, however, estimated by the losses on both sides in killed and wounded, were equal in hard fighting to most of the battles of the Mexican war which attracted so much of the attention of the public when they occurred. About the 23d of July Colonel Ross,[25] commanding at Bolivar, was threatened by a large force of the enemy so that he had to be reinforced from Jackson and Corinth.[26] On the 27th there was skirmishing on the Hatchie River, eight miles from Bolivar.[27] On the 30th I learned from Colonel P. H. Sheridan,[28] who had been far to the south, that Bragg in person was at Rome, Georgia, with his troops moving by rail (by way of Mobile) to Chattanooga and his wagon train marching overland to join him at Rome. Price was at this time at Holly Springs, Mississippi, with a large force, and occupied Grand Junction as an outpost. I proposed to the general-in-chief to be permitted to drive him away, but was

[25] Leonard Ross (1823–1901) was born in Illinois and enlisted as a private in the 4th Illinois Inf. in July 1846. He was promoted to colonel in May 1861 and then brigadier general in Apr. 1862. Ross was arrested and court-martialed in Dec. 1862 for refusing to obey orders. He received an official reprimanded by USG in Jan. 1863 as his sentence. *CWHC,* 462; *PUSG,* 7:110n.

[26] Ross reported that a force of about 2,000 men had surrounded his troops at Bolivar and requested reinforcements on July 27, 1862. USG sent six infantry regiments and a battery from Corinth as well as additional reinforcements from Jackson, TN. *PUSG,* 5:243, 244n–248n.

[27] Maj. Warren Stewart's men had fought Confederate forces along the Hatchie River on July 29, 1862. Stewart was defeated by a force of 400 men and suffered considerable losses as well as having a number of men wounded or taken prisoner. Following this action, Confederate colonel William H. Jackson had moved the majority of his regiment across the Hatchie River. On Aug. 2, McClernand informed USG that he had forced the enemy to retreat from the Hatchie. Ibid., 5:251n–253n, 259n.

[28] Philip H. Sheridan (1831–1888) was probably born in New York and graduated from the USMA in 1853. He was promoted to colonel in May 1862 and to brigadier general in July. He reached the rank of major general in Nov. 1864. He commanded the Army of the Shenandoah from Aug. 1864 to Apr. 1865. He was promoted to lieutenant general during USG's first term as president in 1869. *CWHC,* 483.

informed that, while I had to judge for myself, the best use to make of my troops *was not to scatter them,* but hold them ready to reinforce Buell.[29]

The movement of Bragg himself with his wagon trains to Chattanooga across country, while his troops were transported over a long round-about road to the same destination, without need of guards except when in my immediate front, demonstrates the advantage which troops enjoy while acting in a country where the people are friendly. Buell was marching through a hostile region and had to have his communications thoroughly guarded back to a base of supplies. More men were required the farther the National troops penetrated into the enemy's country. I, with an army sufficiently powerful to have destroyed Bragg, was purely on the defensive and accomplishing no more than to hold a force far inferior to my own.

On the 2d of August I was ordered from Washington to live upon the country, on the resources of citizens hostile to the government, so far as practicable. I was also directed to "handle rebels within our lines without gloves," to imprison them, or to expel them from their homes and from our lines.[30] I do not recollect having arrested and confined a citizen (not a soldier) during the entire rebellion. I am aware that a great many were sent to northern prisons, particularly to Joliet, Illinois, by some of my subordinates with the statement that it was my order.[31] I had all such released the moment I learned of their arrest; and finally sent a staff officer north to release every prisoner who was said to be confined by my order.[32] There were many citizens at home who deserved punishment because they were soldiers when an opportunity was afforded to inflict an injury to the National cause. This class was not of the kind that were apt to get arrested, and I deemed it better that a few guilty men should escape than that a great many innocent ones should suffer.

[29] USG sent Halleck his request on July 30, 1862, and Halleck responded on July 31. *PUSG,* 5:254–255, 255*n.*

[30] Halleck issued this order, which included the following directive: "If necessary, take up all active sympathizers and either hold them as prisoners or put them beyond our lines. Handle that class without gloves and take their property for public use." Ibid., 5:244*n.*

[31] In an Oct. 30, 1862, letter to Col. Jesse Hildebrand, USG stated that some political prisoners in custody at Joliet had been arrested by his orders. Ibid., 6:228.

[32] Col. John Riggin Jr. (1835–1886) was born in Missouri. He became aide-de-camp to USG in Dec. 1861 and reached the rank of colonel in May 1862. He was eventually brevetted brigadier general in 1865. *CWHC,* 453–454; *PUSG,* 6:228, 228*n*–229*n.*

On the 14th of August I was ordered to send two more divisions to Buell. They were sent the same day by way of Decatur.[33] On the 22d Colonel Rodney Mason surrendered Clarksville with six companies of his regiment.[34]

Colonel Mason was one of the officers who had led their regiments off the field at almost the first fire of the rebels at Shiloh.[35] He was by nature and education a gentleman, and was terribly mortified at his action when the battle was over. He came to me with tears in his eyes and begged to be allowed to have another trial. I felt great sympathy for him and sent him, with his regiment, to garrison Clarksville and Donelson.[36] He selected Clarksville for his headquarters, no doubt because he regarded it as the post of danger, it being nearer the enemy. But when he was summoned to surrender by a band of guerillas, his constitutional weakness overcame him. He inquired the number of men the enemy had, and receiving a response indicating a force greater than his own he said if he could be satisfied of that fact he would surrender. Arrangements were made for him to count the guerillas, and having satisfied himself that the enemy had the greater force he surrendered and informed his subordinate[37] at Donelson of the fact, advising him to do the same.[38] The guerillas paroled their prisoners and moved upon Donelson, but the officer in command at that point marched out to meet them and drove them away.

[33] USG ordered the divisions of Jefferson C. Davis and Eleazer A. Paine to move toward Decatur, AL. *PUSG,* 5:292–293.

[34] Rodney Mason (1824–1893) was born in Ohio and graduated from Jefferson College in 1844. He was commissioned as a lieutenant colonel in Apr. 1861. He commanded a portion of the 71st Ohio Inf. when he surrendered at Clarksville, TN, on Aug. 18, 1862. Richard F. Miller, ed., *A Reference Guide for Ohio in the Civil War,* vol 5 of *States at War* (Lebanon, NH: University Press of New England, 2015), 342*n; OR,* I, 16(I), 865.

[35] Col. David Stuart's postbattle report stated that Mason and his 71st Ohio Inf. had retreated from the battlefield at the start of the Battle of Shiloh. *OR,* I, 10(I), 257–262.

[36] USG had ordered Mason and his regiment to Donelson and Clarksville on Apr. 16, 1862. *PUSG,* 5:45, 45*n*–46*n.*

[37] Maj. James H. Hart (1814–1867) was born in Ohio and joined the 71st Ohio Inf. as a first lieutenant in Oct. 1861. He was promoted to major in Jan. 1862, and was the commander at Fort Donelson in late Aug. 1862. B. Franklin Cooling, *Fort Donelson's Legacy: War and Society in Kentucky and Tennessee, 1862–1863* (Knoxville: University of Tennessee Press, 1997), 101; *CWHC,* 284; *OR,* I, 17(II), 183.

[38] On Aug. 22, 1862, Mason was dismissed from the service "for repeated acts of cowardice in the face of the enemy." Mason later challenged the ruling and was honorably mustered out of service by the U.S. War Dept. in Mar. 1866. Miller, *Reference Guide,* 5:342*n.*

Among other embarrassments, at the time of which I now write, was the fact that the government wanted to get out all the cotton possible from the South and directed me to give every facility toward that end. Pay in gold was authorized, and stations on the Mississippi River and on the railroad in our possession had to be designated where cotton would be received.[39] This opened to the enemy not only the means of converting cotton into money, which had a value all over the world and which they so much needed, but it afforded them means of obtaining accurate and intelligent information in regard to our position and strength. It was also demoralizing to the troops. Citizens obtaining permits from the treasury department had to be protected within our lines and given facilities to get out cotton by which they realized enormous profits. Men who had enlisted to fight the battles of their country did not like to be engaged in protecting a traffic which went to the support of an enemy they had to fight, and the profits of which went to men who shared none of their dangers.

On the 30th of August Colonel M. D. Leggett,[40] near Bolivar, with the 20th and 29th Ohio volunteer infantry, was attacked by a force supposed to be about 4,000 strong. The enemy was driven away with a loss of more than one hundred men.[41] On the 1st of September the bridge guard at Medon was attacked by guerillas. The guard held the position until reinforced, when the enemy were routed leaving about fifty of their number on the field dead or wounded, our loss being only two killed and fifteen wounded.[42] On the same day Colonel Dennis,[43] with a force of less than 500 infantry and two pieces of artillery, met the cavalry of the enemy in strong force, a few miles

[39] On Aug. 2, 1862, Halleck sent USG the orders to buy cotton with gold. *PUSG*, 5:244n.

[40] Mortimer D. Leggett (1821–1896) was born in New York and moved to Ohio in 1836. He began his military career by volunteering as McClellan's aide-de-camp in 1861. He was promoted to colonel in Jan. 1862, and, after being wounded at Shiloh and Corinth, was promoted to brigadier general in Nov. After the war, Leggett was promoted to major general of volunteers in Aug. 1865. Pres. USG appointed him as U.S. commissioner of patents from 1871 to 1875. *CWHC*, 346.

[41] Leggett had approximately 900 men under his command during the Battle of Bolivar. The Confederate force, under the command of Acting Brig. Gen. Frank C. Armstrong, consisted of about 3,500 men. *PUSG*, 5:338n.

[42] Armstrong, along with approximately 500 Confederate cavalry, attacked Ross's forces at Medon, TN, on Aug. 31, 1862. Ibid., 6:4n.

[43] Elias S. Dennis (1812–1894) was born in New York and moved to Illinois in 1836. He was mustered into the army as a lieutenant colonel of the 30th Illinois Inf. in Aug. 1861 and became colonel of the regiment on May 1, 1862. *CWHC*, 206; *PUSG*, 6:9n–10n.

west of Medon, and drove them away with great loss.[44] Our troops buried 179 of the enemy's dead, left upon the field. Afterwards it was found that all the houses in the vicinity of the battle-field were turned into hospitals for the wounded. Our loss, as reported at the time, was forty-five killed and wounded. On the 2d of September I was ordered to send more reinforcements to Buell. Jackson and Bolivar were yet threatened, but I sent the reinforcements. On the 4th I received direct orders to send Granger's division also to Louisville, Kentucky.[45]

General Buell had left Corinth about the 10th of June to march upon Chattanooga;[46] Bragg, who had superseded Beauregard in command, sent one division from Tupelo on the 27th of June for the same place.[47] This gave Buell about seventeen days' start. If he had not been required to repair the railroad as he advanced, the march could have been made in eighteen days at the outside, and Chattanooga must have been reached by the National forces before the rebels could have possibly got there. The road between Nashville and Chattanooga could easily have been put in repair by other troops, so that communication with the North would have been opened in a short time after the occupation of the place by the National troops. If Buell had been permitted to move in the first instance, with the whole of the Army of the Ohio and that portion of the Army of the Mississippi afterwards sent to him, he could have thrown four divisions from his own command along the line of road to repair and guard it.

Granger's division was promptly sent on the 4th of September. I was at the station at Corinth when the troops reached that point, and found General P. H.

---

[44] The Battle of Britton Lane occurred on Sept. 1, 1862, one day after the Battle of Medon Station. *PUSG,* 6:9 and *n.*

[45] Halleck first asked USG on Aug. 31, 1862 about the possibility of sending additional troops into Tennessee or Kentucky. USG responded on Sept. 1 that he could not send additional troops unless he abandoned points along the railroad east of Bear Creek in Alabama. Halleck replied on Sept. 2 that the railroad east of Corinth could be abandoned and Gen. Gordon Granger's troops could be sent to Louisville, KY, to reinforce Buell. This message was garbled and so Halleck clarified his order on Sept. 4. Granger (1822–1876) was born in New York, graduated from the USMA in 1845, and was brevetted second lieutenant in the U.S. 2nd Inf. At the start of the Civil War, he was the assistant adjutant general to McClellan. *CWHC,* 262–263; *PUSG,* 6:5, 7*n,* 12, 13*n.*

[46] Buell left Corinth on June 13, 1862. *OR,* I, 16(II), 16.

[47] Bragg replaced Beauregard as the commander of Dept. No. Two on June 17, 1862, and on June 27 ordered Gen. John P. McCown to move his division of the Army of the West to Chattanooga. *CWHC,* 123–124, 141; *OR,* I, 16(II), 710.

Sheridan with them. I expressed surprise at seeing him and said that I had not expected him to go. He showed decided disappointment at the prospect of being detained. I felt a little nettled at his desire to get away and did not detain him.

Sheridan was a first lieutenant in the regiment in which I had served eleven years, the 4th infantry, and stationed on the Pacific coast when the war broke out. He was promoted to a captaincy in May, 1861, and before the close of the year managed in some way, I do not know how, to get East. He went to Missouri. Halleck had known him as a very successful young officer in managing campaigns against the Indians on the Pacific coast, and appointed him acting-quartermaster in south-west Missouri.[48] There was no difficulty in getting supplies forward while Sheridan served in that capacity; but he got into difficulty with his immediate superiors because of his stringent rules for preventing the use of public transportation for private purposes. He asked to be relieved from further duty in the capacity in which he was engaged and his request was granted. When General Halleck took the field in April, 1862, Sheridan was assigned to duty on his staff.[49] During the advance on Corinth a vacancy occurred in the colonelcy of the 2d Michigan cavalry.[50] Governor Blair, of Michigan,[51] telegraphed General Halleck asking him to suggest the name of a professional soldier for the vacancy, saying he would appoint a good man without reference to his State. Sheridan was named; and was so conspicuously efficient that when Corinth was reached he was assigned to command a cavalry brigade in the Army of the Mississippi.[52] He was in command at Booneville on the 1st of July with two small regiments, when he was attacked

[48] In Nov. 1861, after being relieved from duty in Yamhill, OR, Sheridan traveled to Jefferson Barracks in St. Louis. He was assigned as chief quartermaster, Army of Southwest Missouri, on Dec. 26, 1861. P. H. Sheridan, *Personal Memoirs of P. H. Sheridan, General, United States Army* (New York: Charles L. Webster, 1888), 1:124–127.

[49] Halleck made Sheridan an assistant quartermaster, Army of the Mississippi, on Apr. 26, 1862. *CWHC,* 483.

[50] According to Sheridan, the 2nd Michigan Cav. was depleted due to sickness and in need of new leadership because of the growth of factions within the regiment. Sheridan, *Memoirs,* 1:140.

[51] Austin Blair (1818–1894) was born in New York and moved to Michigan in 1841. After serving as a lawyer and a Michigan legislator, he was sworn in as governor of Michigan in 1861, serving until 1865. Blair was a U.S. representative from Michigan from 1867 to 1873. *CWHC,* 133.

[52] Sheridan was promoted to colonel of the 2nd Michigan Cav. on May 25, 1862. Ibid., 483; Sheridan, *Memoirs,* 1:141.

by a force full three times as numerous as his own. By very skilful manœuvres and boldness of attack he completely routed the enemy.[53] For this he was made a brigadier-general and became a conspicuous figure in the army about Corinth. On this account I was sorry to see him leaving me. His departure was probably fortunate, for he rendered distinguished services in his new field.

Granger and Sheridan reached Louisville before Buell got there, and on the night of their arrival Sheridan with his command threw up works around the railroad station for the defence of troops as they came from the front.[54]

[53] Eight to ten Confederate regiments, under the command of Gen. James R. Chalmers, unsuccessfully attacked Sheridan's forces, which consisted of the 2nd Michigan Cav. and the 2nd Iowa Cav., near Booneville, MS, on July 1, 1862. *OR*, I, 17(I), 17. For Sheridan's report on the battle, see ibid., I, 17(I), 19–20.

[54] On Sept. 14, 1862, Sheridan reported to Gen. William "Bull" Nelson in Louisville, KY. Sheridan, *Memoirs,* 1:185.

# 28

## Advance of Van Dorn and Price—
## Price Enters Iuka—Battle of Iuka

AT THIS TIME, September 4th, I had two divisions of the Army of the Mississippi stationed at Corinth, Rienzi, Jacinto and Danville.[1] There were at Corinth also Davies'[2] division and two brigades of McArthur's,[3] besides cavalry and artillery. This force constituted my left wing, of which Rosecrans[4] was in command. General Ord[5] commanded the centre, from Bethel to Humboldt on the Mobile and Ohio railroad and from Jackson to Bolivar where the Mississippi Central is crossed by the Hatchie River. General Sherman commanded on the right at Memphis with two of his brigades back at Browns-

[1] Danville, MS, roughly nine miles southwest of Corinth, MS, was abandoned after its occupation by U.S. troops during the Civil War. *PUSG*, 5:307; Franklin L. Riley, "Extinct Towns and Villages of Mississippi," *Publications of the Mississippi Historical Society* 5 (1902): 314–315.

[2] Thomas A. Davies (1809–1899) was born in New York and graduated from the USMA in 1829. Davies was promoted to brigadier general on Mar. 7, 1862. In early Sept. 1862, he commanded the 2nd Div., Army of the Tennessee, in the District of Corinth. He was brevetted major general in July 1865. *CWHC*, 200–201.

[3] John McArthur (1826–1906) was born in Scotland and immigrated to Illinois in 1849. In 1861, he served in the Illinois Militia as a captain and then joined the 12th Illinois Inf. as a colonel. McArthur was promoted to brigadier general on Mar. 21, 1862. By early Sept. 1862, McArthur commanded the 1st Brigade, 6th Div., Army of the Tennessee, in the District of Corinth. Pres. USG nominated McArthur as postmaster of Chicago on Dec. 18, 1872, a position he held until 1877. Ibid., 370; *PUSG*, 23:469.

[4] William S. Rosecrans (1819–1898) was born in Ohio and graduated from the USMA in 1842. He was brevetted major general on Mar. 21, 1862. By early Sept. 1862, he was in command of the Army of the Mississippi. *CWHC*, 461.

[5] Edward O. C. Ord (1818–1883) was born in Maryland and moved to Washington, DC, in 1819. He graduated from the USMA in 1839. Ord was promoted to major general on May 2, 1862. Ibid., 409–410.

ville, at the crossing of the Hatchie River by the Memphis and Ohio railroad. This made the most convenient arrangement I could devise for concentrating all my spare forces upon any threatened point. All the troops of the command were within telegraphic communication of each other, except those under Sherman. By bringing a portion of his command to Brownsville, from which point there was a railroad and telegraph back to Memphis, communication could be had with that part of my command within a few hours by the use of couriers. In case it became necessary to reinforce Corinth, by this arrangement all the troops at Bolivar, except a small guard, could be sent by rail by the way of Jackson in less than twenty-four hours; while the troops from Brownsville could march up to Bolivar to take their place.

On the 7th of September I learned of the advance of Van Dorn and Price, apparently upon Corinth. One division was brought from Memphis to Bolivar to meet any emergency that might arise from this move of the enemy.[6] I was much concerned because my first duty, after holding the territory acquired within my command, was to prevent further reinforcing of Bragg in Middle Tennessee. Already the Army of Northern Virginia had defeated the army under General Pope and was invading Maryland.[7] In the Centre General Buell was on his way to Louisville and Bragg marching parallel to him with a large Confederate force for the Ohio River.

I had been constantly called upon to reinforce Buell until at this time my entire force numbered less than 50,000 men, of all arms. This included everything from Cairo south within my jurisdiction. If I too should be driven back, the Ohio River would become the line dividing the belligerents west of the Alleghanies, while at the East the line was already farther north than when hostilities commenced at the opening of the war. It is true Nashville was never given up after its first capture, but it would have been isolated and the garrison there would have been obliged to beat a hasty retreat if the troops in West Tennessee had been compelled to fall back. To say at the end of the second year of the war the line dividing the contestants at the East was pushed north of Maryland, a State that had not seceded, and at the West beyond Kentucky,

---

[6] Reports on Sept. 7, 1862, indicated that 36,000 Confederate troops were five miles below Jacinto, MS, at Twenty Mile Creek. On Sept. 11, Hurlbut received USG's command to move his forces to Bolivar, TN, in order to reinforce Corinth if necessary. *PUSG*, 6:26*n*, 30*n*.

[7] At the Second Battle of Bull Run, Aug. 28–30, 1862, the Confederate Army of Northern Virginia under the command of Robert E. Lee defeated the U.S. Army of Virginia under the command of Pope. James McPherson, *Battle Cry of Freedom* (Oxford: Oxford University Press, 2003), 526–532.

another State which had been always loyal, would have been discouraging indeed. As it was, many loyal people despaired in the fall of 1862 of ever saving the Union. The administration at Washington was much concerned for the safety of the cause it held so dear. But I believe there was never a day when the President did not think that, in some way or other, a cause so just as ours would come out triumphant.

Up to the 11th of September Rosecrans still had troops on the railroad east of Corinth, but they had all been ordered in. By the 12th all were in except a small force under Colonel Murphy[8] of the 8th Wisconsin. He had been detained to guard the remainder of the stores which had not yet been brought in to Corinth.

On the 13th of September General Sterling Price entered Iuka, a town about twenty miles east of Corinth on the Memphis and Charleston railroad. Colonel Murphy with a few men was guarding the place. He made no resistance, but evacuated the town on the approach of the enemy.[9] I was apprehensive lest the object of the rebels might be to get troops into Tennessee to reinforce Bragg, as it was afterwards ascertained to be. The authorities at Washington, including the general-in-chief of the army,[10] were very anxious, as I have said, about affairs both in East and Middle Tennessee; and my anxiety was quite as great on their account as for any danger threatening my command. I had not force enough at Corinth to attack Price even by stripping everything; and there was danger that before troops could be got from other points he might be far on his way across the Tennessee. To prevent this all spare forces at Bolivar and Jackson were ordered to Corinth, and cars were concentrated at Jackson for their transportation. Within twenty-four hours from the transmission of the order the troops were at their destination, although there had been a delay of four hours resulting from the forward train getting off the track and stopping

[8] Robert C. Murphy (c.1827–c.1888) was born in Ohio and graduated from the Partridge Military School. He was appointed as the American consul in China by Pres. Franklin Pierce. He moved to St. Croix, WI, in 1860 and was appointed colonel of the 8th Wisconsin Inf. at the outset of the Civil War. Elijah E. Edwards, ed., *Fifty Years in the Northwest* (St. Paul, MN: Pioneer Press, 1888), 108–109.

[9] On Sept. 13, 1862, Confederate brigadier general Frank C. Armstrong's cavalry attacked Murphy's command at Iuka, MS. The U.S. troops held them off. Later that day, however, Price appeared with a larger force and Murphy retreated. *PUSG*, 6:38–43.

[10] Halleck served as general-in-chief of the U.S. Army from July 23, 1862 to Mar. 9, 1864. *CWHC*, 274.

all the others.[11] This gave a reinforcement of near 8,000 men, General Ord in command. General Rosecrans commanded the district of Corinth with a movable force of about 9,000, independent of the garrison deemed necessary to be left behind. It was known that General Van Dorn was about a four days' march south of us, with a large force. It might have been part of his plan to attack at Corinth, Price coming from the east while he came up from the south. My desire was to attack Price before Van Dorn could reach Corinth or go to his relief.[12]

General Rosecrans had previously had his headquarters at Iuka, where his command was spread out along the Memphis and Charleston railroad eastward. While there he had a most excellent map prepared showing all the roads and streams in the surrounding country. He was also personally familiar with the ground, so that I deferred very much to him in my plans for the approach. We had cars enough to transport all of General Ord's command, which was to go by rail to Burnsville, a point on the road about seven miles west of Iuka. From there his troops were to march by the north side of the railroad and attack Price from the north-west, while Rosecrans was to move eastward from his position south of Corinth by way of the Jacinto road. A small force was to hold the Jacinto road where it turns to the north-east, while the main force moved on the Fulton road which comes into Iuka further east. This plan was suggested by Rosecrans.[13]

Bear Creek, a few miles to the east of the Fulton road, is a formidable obstacle to the movement of troops in the absence of bridges, all of which, in September, 1862, had been destroyed in that vicinity. The Tennessee, to the north-east, not many miles away, was also a formidable obstacle for an army followed by a pursuing force. Ord was on the north-west, and even if a rebel movement had been possible in that direction it could have brought only temporary relief, for it would have carried Price's army to the rear of the National forces and isolated it from all support. It looked to me that, if Price would remain in Iuka until we could get there, his annihilation was inevitable.

[11] On Sept. 14, 1862, USG ordered troops at Bolivar and Jackson, TN, to leave for Corinth by train. The delay USG mentioned occurred on Sept. 15. *PUSG*, 6:30n.

[12] By Sept. 12, 1862, reports indicated that Van Dorn's force of 9,000 men had reached Holly Springs, MS, approximately fifty-five miles southwest of Corinth. George B. Davis et al., *The Official Military Atlas of the Civil War* (New York: Fairfax Press, 1983), plate 154; *PUSG*, 6:48n.

[13] Rosecrans detailed his proposals in a series of telegrams to USG on Sept. 18, 1862. *PUSG*, 6:65n–66n.

On the morning of the 18th of September General Ord moved by rail to Burnsville, and there left the cars and moved out to perform his part of the programme. He was to get as near the enemy as possible during the day and intrench himself so as to hold his position until the next morning. Rosecrans was to be up by the morning of the 19th on the two roads before described, and the attack was to be from all three quarters simultaneously. Troops enough were left at Jacinto and Rienzi to detain any cavalry that Van Dorn might send out to make a sudden dash into Corinth until I could be notified. There was a telegraph wire along the railroad, so there would be no delay in communication. I detained cars and locomotives enough at Burnsville to transport the whole of Ord's command at once, and if Van Dorn had moved against Corinth instead of Iuka I could have thrown in reinforcements to the number of 7,000 or 8,000 before he could have arrived. I remained at Burnsville with a detachment of about 900 men from Ord's command and communicated with my two wings by courier. Ord met the advance of the enemy soon after leaving Burnsville. Quite a sharp engagement ensued, but he drove the rebels back with considerable loss,[14] including one general officer killed.[15] He maintained his position and was ready to attack by daylight the next morning. I was very much disappointed at receiving a dispatch from Rosecrans after midnight from Jacinto, twenty-two miles from Iuka, saying that some of his command had been delayed, and that the rear of his column was not yet up as far as Jacinto. He said, however, that he would still be at Iuka by two o'clock the next day.[16] I did not believe this possible because of the distance and the condition of the roads, which was bad; besides, troops after a forced march of twenty miles are not in a good condition for fighting the moment they get through. It might do in marching to relieve a beleaguered garrison, but not to make an assault. I immediately sent Ord a copy of Rosecrans' dispatch and ordered him to be in readiness to attack the moment he heard the sound of guns to the south or south-east.[17] He was instructed to notify his officers to be on the alert for any

[14] Ord reported that only one of his troops was wounded during the skirmish, with three Confederates wounded and eleven taken prisoner. *OR*, I, 17(I), 119.

[15] Brig. Gen. Lewis H. Little (1817–1862) was born in Maryland and became a second lieutenant, U.S. 5th Inf., in July 1839. He fought in the Mexican-American War but resigned from the U.S. Army at the outset of the Civil War to join the Confederate Army. He was promoted to major in May 1861, and eventually to brigadier general in Apr. 1862. At the time of his death, he was in command of Price's 1st Div., Army of the West. *CWHC*, 350.

[16] For Rosecrans's telegram, see *PUSG*, 6:65n.

[17] No correspondence from USG to Ord on Sept. 19, 1862, has been found. However, Ord's report included a message from Lagow on Sept. 19 that stated "I send you dispatch received from Rosencrans [*sic*] late in the night." Ibid.

indications of battle. During the 19th the wind blew in the wrong direction to transmit sound either towards the point where Ord was, or to Burnsville where I had remained.[18]

A couple of hours before dark on the 19th Rosecrans arrived with the head of his column at Barnets,[19] the point where the Jacinto road to Iuka leaves the road going east. He here turned north without sending any troops to the Fulton road. While still moving in column up the Jacinto road he met a force of the enemy and had his advance badly beaten and driven back upon the main road. In this short engagement his loss was considerable for the number engaged, and one battery was taken from him.[20] The wind was still blowing hard and in the wrong direction to transmit sound towards either Ord or me. Neither he nor I nor any one in either command heard a gun that was fired upon the battle-field. After the engagement Rosecrans sent me a dispatch announcing the result. This was brought by a courier. There was no road between Burnsville and the position then occupied by Rosecrans and the country was impassable for a man on horseback. The courier bearing the message was compelled to move west nearly to Jacinto before he found a road leading to Burnsville. This made it a late hour of the night before I learned of the battle that had taken place during the afternoon. I at once notified Ord of the fact and ordered him to attack early in the morning.[21] The next morning Rosecrans himself renewed the attack and went into Iuka with but little resistance. Ord also went in according to orders, without hearing a gun from the south of town but supposing the troops coming from the south-west must be up by that time. Rosecrans, however, had put no troops upon the Fulton road, and the enemy had taken advantage of this neglect and retreated by that road

[18] USG referred to the phenomenon known as an "acoustic shadow." Charles D. Ross, *Civil War Acoustic Shadows* (Shippensburg, PA: White Mane Books, 2001), 94–101.

[19] Barnett Knob was located approximately eight miles east of Jacinto. *PUSG*, 6:43*n*.

[20] Rosecrans reported a Union loss of 141 killed, 613 wounded, and thirty-six missing. Surgeon Archibald B. Campbell, U.S. Army medical director, reported the Confederate loss at 520 killed, 1,300 wounded, and 181 prisoners; however, the Confederates reported having far fewer casualties, with approximately 85 killed, 410 wounded, and 157 missing. *OR*, I, 17(I), 77–80, 127, 133.

[21] Shortly before 3:30 A.M. on Sept. 20, 1862, USG received a telegram from Rosecrans detailing the engagement. He immediately sent a letter to Ord with orders to attack as early as possible in the morning. See *PUSG*, 6:68–69, 69*n*–70*n*, for the text of these communications and discussion of the discrepancy with USG's official report, wherein he stated that the telegram from Rosecrans did not arrive until 8:35 A.M. on Sept. 20.

during the night.[22] Word was soon brought to me that our troops were in Iuka. I immediately rode into town and found that the enemy was not being pursued even by the cavalry. I ordered pursuit by the whole of Rosecrans' command and went on with him a few miles in person. He followed only a few miles after I left him and then went into camp, and the pursuit was continued no further.[23] I was disappointed at the result of the battle of Iuka—but I had so high an opinion of General Rosecrans that I found no fault at the time.

[22] In testimony about his Civil War campaigns given before Congress on Apr. 22, 1865, Rosecrans asserted that moving a portion of his command to the Fulton Road would have been "unsafe" because the two columns would not have been able to support one another. "Rosecrans' Campaigns," in *Report of the Joint Committee on the Conduct of the War* (Washington, DC: Government Printing Office, 1865), 3:19.

[23] Rosecrans's earliest communications to USG on the morning of Sept. 20, 1862, indicated pursuit of the retreating Confederate forces by U.S. forces under the command of Brig. Gen. Charles S. Hamilton and Brig. Gen. David S. Stanley. By 1:00 A.M. on Sept. 21, Rosecrans and his troops had pursued the Confederate Army as far as Jacinto. *PUSG*, 6:72*n*–73*n*, 76*n*.

# 29

## Van Dorn's Movements—Battle of Corinth—
## Command of the Department of the Tennessee

O<small>N THE</small> 19TH of September General Geo. H. Thomas was ordered east to reinforce Buell.[1] This threw the army at my command still more on the defensive. The Memphis and Charleston railroad was abandoned, except at Corinth, and small forces were left at Chewalla and Grand Junction. Soon afterwards the latter of these two places was given up and Bolivar became our most advanced position on the Mississippi Central railroad.[2] Our cavalry was kept well to the front and frequent expeditions were sent out to watch the movements of the enemy. We were in a country where nearly all the people, except the negroes, were hostile to us and friendly to the cause we were trying to suppress. It was easy, therefore, for the enemy to get early information of our every move. We, on the contrary, had to go after our information in force, and then often returned without it.

On the 22d Bolivar was threatened by a large force from south of Grand Junction, supposed to be twenty regiments of infantry with cavalry and artillery. I reinforced Bolivar, and went to Jackson in person to superintend the movement of troops to whatever point the attack might be made upon.[3] The

---

[1] In orders dated Sept. 23, 1862, Thomas was directed to replace Buell as commander of the Dept. of the Tennessee. He protested the assignment on Sept. 29, 1862, and the order was suspended. Brian Steel Wills, *George Henry Thomas: As True as Steel* (Lawrence: University Press of Kansas, 2012), 155–157; *OR,* I, 16(II), 539, 555.

[2] U.S. Army forces had completely withdrawn from Grand Junction, TN, by July 25, 1862 (see note 23 in Chapter 27 for additional details of the withdrawal). *OR,* I, 17(II), 116; *PUSG,* 5:244*n.*

[3] On Sept. 22, 1862, USG reported to Halleck that Confederate forces under the command of Brig. Gen. John B. Villepigue, a portion of Breckinridge's troops, and other Confederate troops planned to attack Bolivar, TN. USG traveled to Jackson, TN, on Sept. 23. *PUSG,* 6:79, 81.

troops from Corinth were brought up in time to repel the threatened movement without a battle. Our cavalry followed the enemy south of Davis' mills in Mississippi.[4]

On the 30th I found that Van Dorn was apparently endeavoring to strike the Mississippi River above Memphis.[5] At the same time other points within my command were so threatened that it was impossible to concentrate a force to drive him away. There was at this juncture a large Union force at Helena, Arkansas, which, had it been within my command, I could have ordered across the river to attack and break up the Mississippi Central railroad far to the south.[6] This would not only have called Van Dorn back, but would have compelled the retention of a large rebel force far to the south to prevent a repetition of such raids on the enemy's line of supplies. Geographical lines between the commands during the rebellion were not always well chosen, or they were too rigidly adhered to.

Van Dorn did not attempt to get upon the line above Memphis, as had apparently been his intention. He was simply covering a deeper design; one much more important to his cause. By the 1st of October it was fully apparent that Corinth was to be attacked with great force and determination, and that Van Dorn, Lovell, Price, Villepigue[7] and Rust[8] had joined their strength for this purpose. There was some skirmishing outside of Corinth with the advance of the enemy on the 3d. The rebels massed in the north-west angle of the Memphis and Charleston and the Mobile and Ohio railroads, and were thus between the troops at Corinth and all possible reinforcements. Any fresh troops for us must come by a circuitous route.

---

[4] Davis Mills, MS, was located on the Mississippi Central Railroad near the Tennessee-Mississippi state line. Ibid., 6:80n.

[5] On Sept. 29 and 30, 1862, Rosecrans and Hurlbut sent numerous messages to USG about Van Dorn's location near Memphis, TN. Ibid., 6:95n–96n.

[6] Union forces stationed at Helena, AR, during Sept. 1862 were under the command of Brig. Gen. Frederick Steele, Army of the Southwest. *CWHC*, 507; *OR*, I, 13, 272–273.

[7] Brig. Gen. John B. Villepigue (1830–1862) was born in South Carolina and graduated from the USMA in 1854. He resigned from the U.S. Army and joined the Confederate Army as a captain in Mar. 1861. He was promoted to brigadier general in Mar. 1862 and died of pneumonia at Port Hudson, LA, in Nov. *CWHC*, 545.

[8] Brig. Gen. Albert Rust (1818–1870) was born in Virginia and moved to Arkansas in 1837. He represented Arkansas in the Confederate Provisional Congress from May 1861 to Feb. 1862. He joined the Confederate Army as a colonel in July 1861 and was promoted to brigadier general in Mar. 1862. Ibid., 466.

On the night of the 3d, accordingly, I ordered General McPherson, who was at Jackson, to join Rosecrans at Corinth with reinforcements picked up along the line of the railroad equal to a brigade. Hurlbut had been ordered from Bolivar to march for the same destination; and as Van Dorn was coming upon Corinth from the north-west some of his men fell in with the advance of Hurlbut's and some skirmishing ensued on the evening of the 3d. On the 4th Van Dorn made a dashing attack, hoping, no doubt, to capture Rosecrans before his reinforcements could come up. In that case the enemy himself could have occupied the defences of Corinth and held at bay all the Union troops that arrived. In fact he could have taken the offensive against the reinforcements with three or four times their number and still left a sufficient garrison in the works about Corinth to hold them. He came near success, some of his troops penetrating the National lines at least once, but the works that were built after Halleck's departure enabled Rosecrans to hold his position until the troops of both McPherson and Hurlbut approached towards the rebel front and rear. The enemy was finally driven back with great slaughter: all their charges, made with great gallantry, were repulsed. The loss on our side was heavy, but nothing to compare with Van Dorn's. McPherson came up with the train of cars bearing his command as close to the enemy as was prudent, debarked on the rebel flank and got in to the support of Rosecrans just after the repulse. His approach, as well as that of Hurlbut, was known to the enemy and had a moral effect. General Rosecrans, however, failed to follow up the victory, although I had given specific orders in advance of the battle for him to pursue the moment the enemy was repelled. He did not do so, and I repeated the order after the battle. In the first order he was notified that the force of 4,000 men which was going to his assistance would be in great peril if the enemy was not pursued.[9]

General Ord had joined Hurlbut on the 4th and being senior took command of his troops.[10] This force encountered the head of Van Dorn's re-

---

[9] On Oct. 4, 1862, USG ordered Rosecrans to follow the Confederate Army if they fell back. On Oct. 5, USG telegraphed Rosecrans asking about his progress. Rosecrans did not begin the pursuit until the morning of Oct. 5 in order to allow his troops to rest and receive rations. *PUSG*, 6:114, 123 and *n*, 223; "Rosecrans' Campaigns," in *Report of the Joint Committee on the Conduct of the War* (Washington, DC: Government Printing Office, 1865), 3:21–22.

[10] Ord took over Hurlbut's command on Oct. 5, 1862. *OR*, I, 17(I), 302.

treating column just as it was crossing the Hatchie by a bridge some ten miles out from Corinth. The bottom land here was swampy and bad for the operations of troops, making a good place to get an enemy into. Ord attacked the troops that had crossed the bridge and drove them back in a panic. Many were killed, and others were drowned by being pushed off the bridge in their hurried retreat. Ord followed and met the main force. He was too weak in numbers to assault, but he held the bridge and compelled the enemy to resume his retreat by another bridge higher up the stream.[11] Ord was wounded in this engagement and the command devolved on Hurlbut.

Rosecrans did not start in pursuit till the morning of the 5th and then took the wrong road. Moving in the enemy's country he travelled with a wagon train to carry his provisions and munitions of war. His march was therefore slower than that of the enemy, who was moving towards his supplies. Two or three hours of pursuit on the day of battle, without anything except what the men carried on their persons, would have been worth more than any pursuit commenced the next day could have possibly been. Even when he did start, if Rosecrans had followed the route taken by the enemy, he would have come upon Van Dorn in a swamp with a stream in front and Ord holding the only bridge; but he took the road leading north and towards Chewalla instead of west, and, after having marched as far as the enemy had moved to get to the Hatchie, he was as far from battle as when he started. Hurlbut had not the numbers to meet any such force as Van Dorn's if they had been in any mood for fighting, and he might have been in great peril.

I now regarded the time to accomplish anything by pursuit as past and, after Rosecrans reached Jonesboro,[12] I ordered him to return. He kept on to Ripley, however, and was persistent in wanting to go farther. I thereupon ordered him to halt and submitted the matter to the general-in-chief, who allowed

[11]The first bridge mentioned was Davis Bridge; the second bridge, by which Confederate forces continued their retreat, was known as Crum's Bridge, six miles south of Davis Bridge. Peter Cozzens, *The Darkest Days of the War: The Battles of Iuka and Corinth* (Chapel Hill: University of North Carolina Press, 2006), 291; *PUSG*, 6:118n–119n.

[12]Jonesborough, MS, was approximately eighteen miles east of Corinth, MS. *PUSG*, 6:130n.

me to exercise my judgment in the matter, but inquired "why not pursue?" Upon this I ordered Rosecrans back.[13] Had he gone much farther he would have met a greater force than Van Dorn had at Corinth and behind intrench-ments or on chosen ground, and the probabilities are he would have lost his army.

The battle of Corinth was bloody, our loss being 315 killed, 1,812 wounded and 232 missing. The enemy lost many more. Rosecrans reported 1,423 dead and 2,225 prisoners.[14] We fought behind breastworks, which accounts in some degree for the disparity. Among the killed on our side was General Hackelman.[15] General Oglesby was badly, it was for some time supposed mortally, wounded.[16] I received a congratulatory letter from the President, which expressed also his sorrow for the losses.[17]

This battle was recognized by me as being a decided victory, though not so complete as I had hoped for, nor nearly so complete as I now think was within the easy grasp of the commanding officer at Corinth. Since the war it is known that the result, as it was, was a crushing blow to the enemy, and felt by him much more than it was appreciated at the North. The battle relieved me from any further anxiety for the safety of the territory within my jurisdiction, and soon after receiving reinforcements I suggested to the general-in-chief a for-ward movement against Vicksburg.

On the 23d of October I learned of Pemberton's being in command at Holly Springs and much reinforced by conscripts and troops from Alabama and Texas.[18] The same day General Rosecrans was relieved from duty with my

[13] After receiving this telegram sent by Halleck on Oct. 8, 1862, USG ordered Rosecrans to end the pursuit and return to Corinth. Ibid., 6:130 and *n*, 133–134, 138*n*.

[14] The Confederate Army lost 4,233 men out of approximately 22,000 during the Battle of Corinth. The U.S. Army lost 2,520 men out of 21,147. Smith, *Corinth*, 274.

[15] Pleasant A. Hackelman (1814–1862) was born in Indiana and later served as an Indiana legislator. He became colonel of the 16th Indiana Inf. in May 1861 and was promoted to brigadier general in Apr. 1862. He was mortally wounded in the neck at Corinth on Oct. 3. *CWHC*, 272.

[16] USG informed Lincoln that Oglesby had been shot in the chest and that the bullet was located near his spine. Oglesby eventually recovered from his wounds. Ibid., 408; *PUSG*, 6:143 and *n*, 144*n*–145*n*.

[17] The telegrams between USG and Lincoln after the Battle of Corinth were the beginning of their direct military correspondence. *PUSG*, 6:143*n*.

[18] On Oct. 22, 1862, Sherman wrote to USG regarding Pemberton's location and number of troops. Ibid., 6:179*n*.

command, and shortly after he succeeded Buell in the command of the army in Middle Tennessee.[19] I was delighted at the promotion of General Rosecrans to a separate command, because I still believed that when independent of an immediate superior the qualities which I, at that time, credited him with possessing, would show themselves. As a subordinate I found that I could not make him do as I wished, and had determined to relieve him from duty that very day.

At the close of the operations just described my force, in round numbers, was 48,500. Of these 4,800 were in Kentucky and Illinois, 7,000 in Memphis, 19,200 from Mound City south, and 17,500 at Corinth.[20] General McClernand had been authorized from Washington to go north and organize troops to be used in opening the Mississippi.[21] These new levies with other reinforcements now began to come in.

On the 25th of October I was placed in command of the Department of the Tennessee.[22] Reinforcements continued to come from the north and by the 2d of November I was prepared to take the initiative.[23] This was a great relief after the two and a half months of continued defence over a large district of country, and where nearly every citizen was an enemy ready to give information of our every move. I have described very imperfectly a few of the battles and skirmishes that took place during this time. To describe all would take more space than I can allot to the purpose; to make special

[19] On Oct. 24, 1862, Halleck, on Lincoln's orders, placed Rosecrans in command of the Dept. of the Cumberland and ordered him to immediately travel to Buell's headquarters to relieve him from command. *OR,* I, 16(II), 640.

[20] According to the abstract from monthly returns of the Dept. of the Tennessee, USG had an aggregate of 56,689 present for duty within his command for the month of Oct. 1862, with 5,948 in the District of Columbus, 7,814 in the District of Memphis, 19,836 in the District of Jackson, and 23,076 in the District of Corinth. Ibid., I, 17(II), 311.

[21] On Oct. 21, 1862, Stanton ordered McClernand to proceed to Indiana, Illinois, and Iowa for the "preparation of the Mississippi expedition." Ibid., I, 17(II), 332.

[22] Gen. Orders No. 159, AGO, War Dept., issued on Oct. 16, 1862, placed USG in command of the Dept. of the Tennessee. He assumed command on Oct. 25. *PUSG,* 6:186.

[23] On Nov. 2, 1862, USG notified Halleck of his movements toward Grand Junction. Ibid., 6:243 and *n.*

mention of all the officers and troops who distinguished themselves, would take a volume.*

*NOTE.—For gallantry in the various engagements, from the time I was left in command down to 26th of October and on my recommendation, Generals McPherson and C. S. Hamilton[24] were promoted to be Major-Generals, and Colonels C. C. Marsh, 20th Illinois, M. M. Crocker,[25] 13th Iowa, J. A. Mower,[26] 11th Missouri, M. D. Leggett, 78th Ohio, J. D. Stevenson,[27] 7th Missouri, and John E. Smith,[28] 45th Illinois, to be Brigadiers.

[24] Charles S. Hamilton (1822–1891) was born in New York and graduated from the USMA in July 1843. He became colonel of the 3rd Wisconsin Inf. on May 11, 1861, was promoted to brigadier general only six days later. He was promoted to major general on Sept. 19, 1862. *CWHC,* 275.

[25] Marcellus M. Crocker (1830–1865) was born in Indiana and entered the USMA in 1847. He resigned in Feb. 1849 and became a lawyer. He joined the 2nd Iowa Inf. as a captain in May 1861 and was promoted to brigadier general in Nov. 1862. He died of tuberculosis. Ibid., 191.

[26] Joseph A. Mower (1827–1870) was born in Vermont and moved to Massachusetts in 1833. He joined the U.S. Army as a private in 1847. He was discharged in 1848 and in 1855 reentered as a second lieutenant, U.S. 1st Inf. After being wounded in the neck at the Battle of Corinth in Oct. 1862, he was promoted to brigadier general in Nov. Ibid., 401.

[27] John D. Stevenson (1821–1897) was born in Virginia and later moved to Missouri, where he became a captain in the Missouri Mounted Volunteers in June 1846. He was honorably mustered out of volunteer service in June 1848. He was made colonel of the 7th Missouri Inf. in June 1861, and in Nov. 1862 he was promoted to brigadier general. Ibid., 510.

[28] John E. Smith (1816–1897) was born in Switzerland and immigrated to Pennsylvania in 1817, eventually settling in Illinois in 1836. He was aide-de-camp to Gov. Richard Yates beginning in Apr. 1861. He was promoted to colonel of the 45th Illinois Inf. in July and to brigadier general in Nov. 1862. In Jan. 1865, Smith was brevetted major general. Ibid., 497.

# 30

## The Campaign against Vicksburg—Employing the Freedmen—Occupation of Holly Springs—Sherman Ordered to Memphis—Sherman's Movements down the Mississippi—Van Dorn Captures Holly Springs—Collecting Forage and Food

Vicksburg was important to the enemy because it occupied the first high ground coming close to the river below Memphis. From there a railroad runs east, connecting with other roads leading to all points of the Southern States. A railroad also starts from the opposite side of the river, extending west as far as Shreveport, Louisiana.[1] Vicksburg was the only channel, at the time of the events of which this chapter treats, connecting the parts of the Confederacy divided by the Mississippi. So long as it was held by the enemy, the free navigation of the river was prevented. Hence its importance. Points on the river between Vicksburg and Port Hudson were held as dependencies; but their fall was sure to follow the capture of the former place.

The campaign against Vicksburg commenced on the 2d of November as indicated in a dispatch to the general-in-chief in the following words: "I have commenced a movement on Grand Junction, with three divisions from Corinth and two from Bolivar. Will leave here [Jackson, Tennessee] to-morrow, and take command in person. If found practicable, I will go to Holly Springs, and, may be, Grenada, completing railroad and telegraph as I go."[2]

---

[1] The Southern Railroad of Mississippi extended east from Vicksburg to Meridian, MS. The Vicksburg, Shreveport and Texas Railroad extended west from Vicksburg to Monroe, LA. *PUSG,* 7:30–31.

[2] The original letter concludes with the following sentence: "Bolivar has been threatened for some days but it may be a feint to cover a retreat[.]" Ibid., 6:243.

At this time my command was holding the Mobile and Ohio railroad from about twenty-five miles south of Corinth, north to Columbus, Kentucky; the Mississippi Central from Bolivar north to its junction with the Mobile and Ohio; the Memphis and Charleston from Corinth east to Bear Creek,[3] and the Mississippi River from Cairo to Memphis. My entire command was no more than was necessary to hold these lines, and hardly that if kept on the defensive. By moving against the enemy and into his unsubdued, or not yet captured, territory, driving their army before us, these lines would nearly hold themselves; thus affording a large force for field operations. My moving force at that time was about 30,000 men,[4] and I estimated the enemy confronting me, under Pemberton, at about the same number. General McPherson commanded my left wing and General C. S. Hamilton the centre, while Sherman was at Memphis with the right wing.[5] Pemberton was fortified at the Tallahatchie,[6] but occupied Holly Springs and Grand Junction on the Mississippi Central railroad. On the 8th we occupied Grand Junction and La Grange, throwing a considerable force seven or eight miles south, along the line of the railroad.[7] The road from Bolivar forward was repaired and put in running order as the troops advanced.

Up to this time it had been regarded as an axiom in war that large bodies of troops must operate from a base of supplies which they always covered and guarded in all forward movements. There was delay therefore in repairing the road back, and in gathering and forwarding supplies to the front.[8]

[3] The point where the Memphis and Charleston Railroad intersected with Bear Creek was in Alabama, near the Mississippi state line. Ibid., 5:43n.

[4] On Nov. 4, 1862, USG reported that his total force was about 31,000 men. Ibid., 6:256.

[5] On Nov. 4, 1862, USG informed Halleck that McPherson's troops would form the right wing and that Hamilton's would comprise the left. Ibid.

[6] USG probably referred to Confederate efforts to fortify the crossings along the Tallahatchie River during Nov. 1862. Ibid., 6:312n–313n.

[7] The occupation of Grand Junction, TN, and La Grange, TN, occurred on Nov. 4, 1862. Ibid., 6:xxiii.

[8] USG probably referred to a principle of military thought at the time expressed by the influential military theorist Antoine Henri Jomini's fourth maxim regarding supply depots: "In countries where the population is too sparse, and the soil little fertile, an army will lack the most essential resources; hence it will be prudent not to remove it too far from its magazines, and to carry along supplies of reserve sufficient to give it time, at need, to fall back upon the base of its grand depôts." Baron de Jomini, *Summary of the Art of War*, trans. O. F. Winship and E. E. McLean (New York: Putnam, 1854), 159.

By my orders, and in accordance with previous instructions from Washington, all the forage within reach was collected under the supervision of the chief quartermaster and the provisions under the chief commissary, receipts being given when there was any one to take them; the supplies in any event to be accounted for as government stores. The stock was bountiful, but still it gave me no idea of the possibility of supplying a moving column in an enemy's country from the country itself.[9]

It was at this point, probably, where the first idea of a "Freedman's Bureau"[10] took its origin. Orders of the government prohibited the expulsion of the negroes from the protection of the army, when they came in voluntarily. Humanity forbade allowing them to starve. With such an army of them, of all ages and both sexes, as had congregated about Grand Junction, amounting to many thousands, it was impossible to advance. There was no special authority for feeding them unless they were employed as teamsters, cooks and pioneers with the army; but only able-bodied young men were suitable for such work. This labor would support but a very limited percentage of them. The plantations were all deserted; the cotton and corn were ripe: men, women and children above ten years of age could be employed in saving these crops. To do this work with contrabands, or to have it done, organization under a competent chief was necessary. On inquiring for such a man Chaplain Eaton, now and for many years the very able United States Commissioner of Education, was suggested.[11] He proved as efficient in that field

[9] On Nov. 13, 1862, USG requested twelve additional trains from Halleck in order to supply the troops with food during the invasion into northern Mississippi. Two days later, Halleck denied the request, instead ordering USG's troops to feed "as far as possible upon the country." *PUSG*, 6:305n.

[10] The Bureau of Refugees, Freedmen, and Abandoned Lands (commonly called the Freedmen's Bureau) was created by Congress on Mar. 3, 1865, as a means to support displaced whites and formerly enslaved African Americans during the Civil War. However, faced with white opposition and inadequate resources, the bureau ceased all operations in 1872. Faustine C. Jones-Wilson et al., eds., *Encyclopedia of African American Education* (Westport, CT: Greenwood, 1996), s.v. "Bureau of Refugees, Freedmen, and Abandoned Lands."

[11] John Eaton Jr. (1829–1906) was born in New Hampshire and joined the 27th Ohio Inf. Reg. as a chaplain in Aug. 1861. On Nov. 13, 1862, USG appointed Eaton "to take charge of the Contrabands that come into Camp." On Dec. 17 Eaton was appointed as the general superintendent of contrabands for the Dept. of the Tennessee. In 1870, Pres. USG appointed him as the U.S. Commissioner of Education, where he served until 1886. Eaton wrote about his experiences with the newly freed slaves in his book *Grant, Lincoln and the Freedmen: Reminiscences of the Civil War* (New York: Longmans, Green, 1907). *CWHC*, 222; *PUSG*, 6:315n–316n.

as he has since done in his present one. I gave him all the assistants and guards he called for. We together fixed the prices to be paid for the negro labor, whether rendered to the government or to individuals. The cotton was to be picked from abandoned plantations, the laborers to receive the stipulated price (my recollection is twelve and a half cents per pound for picking and ginning) from the quartermaster, he shipping the cotton north to be sold for the benefit of the government.[12] Citizens remaining on their plantations were allowed the privilege of having their crops saved by freedmen on the same terms.

At once the freedmen became self-sustaining. The money was not paid to them directly, but was expended judiciously and for their benefit. They gave me no trouble afterwards.

Later the freedmen were engaged in cutting wood along the Mississippi River to supply the large number of steamers on that stream. A good price was paid for chopping wood used for the supply of government steamers (steamers chartered and which the government had to supply with fuel). Those supplying their own fuel paid a much higher price. In this way a fund was created not only sufficient to feed and clothe all, old and young, male and female, but to build them comfortable cabins, hospitals for the sick, and to supply them with many comforts they had never known before.

At this stage of the campaign against Vicksburg I was very much disturbed by newspaper rumors that General McClernand was to have a separate and independent command within mine, to operate against Vicksburg by way of the Mississippi River. Two commanders on the same field are always one too many, and in this case I did not think the general selected had either the experience or the qualifications to fit him for so important a position. I feared for the safety of the troops intrusted to him, especially as he was to raise new levies, raw troops, to execute so important a trust. But on the 12th I received a dispatch from General Halleck saying that I had command of all the troops sent to my department and authorizing me to fight the enemy where I pleased.[13] The next day my cavalry was in Holly Springs, and the enemy fell back south of the Tallahatchie.

---

[12] Eaton quoted this passage when commenting on his work with contrabands and did not dispute USG's numbers. Eaton, *Grant, Lincoln and the Freedmen*, 13–14.

[13] On Oct. 29, 1862, Hillyer referred to newspaper reports of McClernand's potential expedition in a letter to Sherman. On Nov. 10, USG asked Halleck about his role in the Vicksburg campaign. Halleck responded on Nov. 11, "You have command of all troops sent to your Dept, and have permission to fight the enemy when you please." *PUSG*, 6:180n, 288n.

Holly Springs I selected for my dépôt of supplies and munitions of war, all of which at that time came by rail from Columbus, Kentucky, except the few stores collected about La Grange and Grand Junction. This was a long line (increasing in length as we moved south) to maintain in an enemy's country. On the 15th of November, while I was still at Holly Springs, I sent word to Sherman to meet me at Columbus. We were but forty-seven miles apart, yet the most expeditious way for us to meet was for me to take the rail to Columbus and Sherman a steamer for the same place. At that meeting, besides talking over my general plans I gave him his orders to join me with two divisions and to march them down the Mississippi Central railroad if he could. Sherman, who was always prompt, was up by the 29th to Cottage Hill, ten miles north of Oxford. He brought three divisions with him, leaving a garrison of only four regiments of infantry, a couple of pieces of artillery and a small detachment of cavalry. Further reinforcements he knew were on their way from the north to Memphis. About this time General Halleck ordered troops from Helena, Arkansas (territory west of the Mississippi was not under my command then) to cut the road in Pemberton's rear.[14] The expedition was under Generals Hovey[15] and C. C. Washburn[16] and was successful so

[14] On Nov. 3, 1862, Halleck suggested to Maj. Gen. Samuel R. Curtis a possible move against Grenada, MS. However, the start of the expedition from Helena, AR, on Nov. 27 was actually precipitated by Sherman communicating the strategic plans from his Nov. 21 meeting with USG to Brig. Gen. Frederick Steele. *OR*, I, 13, 778; I, 17(I), 529; I, 17(II), 382, 383–384; *PUSG*, 6:xxiii, 312*n*. For detailed discussion of the confusion about who ordered the expedition, see Kenneth P. Williams, *Grant Rises in the West: From Iuka to Vicksburg, 1862–1863* (Lincoln: University of Nebraska Press, 1997), 509*n*–510*n*.

[15] Alvin P. Hovey (1821–1891) was born in Indiana and joined the 2nd Indiana Inf. as a first lieutenant in 1846. By 1864, he was brevetted major general in the Army of the Ohio. After the war, he served as U.S. minister to Peru from 1865 to 1870. He was a U.S. representative from Indiana from 1887 to 1889. He became governor of Indiana in Jan. 1889 and served in that capacity until his death in Nov. 1891. *CWHC*, 305.

[16] Cadwallader C. Washburn (1818–1882) was born in Maine and moved to Wisconsin in 1842. He was the brother of Elihu B. Washburne, who served as secretary of state and later U.S. minister to France during USG's presidency. In Feb. 1862, Washburn joined the 2nd Wisconsin Cav. as a colonel. In Nov., he was promoted to major general and commanded the 3rd Cav. Div., District of Arkansas, Dept. of the Missouri. After the war, he served as a U.S. representative from Wisconsin from 1867 to 1871 and as governor from 1872 to 1874. Gaillard Hunt, *Israel, Elihu and Cadwallader Washburn: A Chapter in American Biography* (New York: Macmillan, 1925), 5, 245, 247; *CWHC*, 555.

far as reaching the railroad was concerned, but the damage done was very slight and was soon repaired.

The Tallahatchie, which confronted me, was very high, the railroad bridge destroyed and Pemberton strongly fortified on the south side. A crossing would have been impossible in the presence of an enemy. I sent the cavalry higher up the stream and they secured a crossing. This caused the enemy to evacuate their position, which was possibly accelerated by the expedition of Hovey and Washburn.[17] The enemy was followed as far south as Oxford by the main body of troops, and some seventeen miles farther by McPherson's command. Here the pursuit was halted to repair the railroad from the Tallahatchie northward, in order to bring up supplies. The piles on which the railroad bridge rested had been left standing. The work of constructing a roadway for the troops was but a short matter, and, later, rails were laid for cars.[18]

During the delay at Oxford in repairing railroads I learned that an expedition down the Mississippi now was inevitable and, desiring to have a competent commander in charge, I ordered Sherman on the 8th of December back to Memphis to take charge. The following were his orders:

Headquarters 13th Army Corps, Department of the Tennessee.
OXFORD, MISSISSIPPI, *December* 8, 1862.

MAJOR-GENERAL W. T. SHERMAN,
Commanding Right Wing:

You will proceed, with as little delay as possible, to Memphis, Tennessee, taking with you one division of your present command. On your arrival at Memphis you will assume command of all the troops there, and that portion of General Curtis's[19] forces at present east of the Mississippi River, and organize them into brigades and divisions in your own army. As soon as possible move with them down the river to the vicinity of Vicksburg, and with the co-operation of the gunboat

[17] On Dec. 1, 1862, USG reported that his cavalry was crossing the Tallahatchie River. *PUSG*, 6:367.

[18] By Dec. 4, 1862, troops under the command of Brig. Gen. Isaac F. Quinby and McPherson completed repairs on three bridges between Coldwater, MS, and Holly Springs, MS. Ibid., 6:387*n*.

[19] Samuel R. Curtis (1805–1866) was born in New York and graduated from the USMA in 1831. Curtis was promoted to major general Mar. 21, 1862, and served first as commanding general, U.S. Army of the Southwest, and later as commanding general, U.S. Army of the Border. *CWHC*, 195–196.

fleet under command of Flag-officer Porter[20] proceed to the reduction
of that place in such manner as circumstances, and your own judgment, may dictate.

The amount of rations, forage, land transportation, etc., necessary
to take, will be left entirely with yourself. The Quartermaster at
St. Louis will be instructed to send you transportation for 30,000 men;
should you still find yourself deficient, your quartermaster will be
authorized to make up the deficiency from such transports as may
come into the port of Memphis.

On arriving in Memphis, put yourself in communication with
Admiral Porter, and arrange with him for his co-operation.

Inform me at the earliest practicable day of the time when you will
embark, and such plans as may then be matured. I will hold the forces
here in readiness to co-operate with you in such manner as the movements of the enemy may make necessary.

Leave the District of Memphis in the command of an efficient
officer, and with a garrison of four regiments of infantry, the siege
guns, and whatever cavalry may be there.

U. S. GRANT,<br>
Major-General.[21]

This idea had presented itself to my mind earlier, for on the 3d of December
I asked Halleck if it would not be well to hold the enemy south of the Yallabusha and move a force from Helena and Memphis on Vicksburg.[22] On the
5th again I suggested, from Oxford, to Halleck that if the Helena troops were
at my command I thought it would be possible to take them and the Memphis forces south of the mouth of the Yazoo River, and thus secure Vicksburg
and the State of Mississippi. Halleck on the same day, the 5th of December,
directed me not to attempt to hold the country south of the Tallahatchie, but

---

[20] David D. Porter (1813–1891) was born in Pennsylvania and began his military career as a
cadet in the Mexican Navy in 1826. In 1829, he entered the U.S. Navy as a midshipman. In
1861, he held the rank of commander. By Oct. 1862, he oversaw the Mississippi River Squadron.
Ibid., 434–435.

[21] The original letter concluded with the following paragraph: "One regiment of Infantry
and at least one section of Artillery will also be left at Friar's Point or Delta to protect the stores
of the Cavalry post that will be left there." *PUSG,* 6:407.

[22] USG's telegram was sent to Halleck on Dec. 3, 1862, but was not received until Dec. 4.
Ibid., 6:371–372, 372n.

to collect 25,000 troops at Memphis by the 20th for the Vicksburg expedition.[23] I sent Sherman with two divisions at once, informed the general-in-chief of the fact, and asked whether I should command the expedition down the river myself or send Sherman. I was authorized to do as I thought best for the accomplishment of the great object in view. I sent Sherman and so informed General Halleck.[24]

As stated, my action in sending Sherman back was expedited by a desire to get him in command of the forces separated from my direct supervision. I feared that delay might bring McClernand, who was his senior and who had authority from the President and Secretary of War to exercise that particular command,—and independently. I doubted McClernand's fitness; and I had good reason to believe that in forestalling him I was by no means giving offence to those whose authority to command was above both him and me.

Neither my orders to General Sherman, nor the correspondence between us or between General Halleck and myself, contemplated at the time my going further south than the Yallabusha.[25] Pemberton's force in my front was the main part of the garrison of Vicksburg, as the force with me was the defence of the territory held by us in West Tennessee and Kentucky. I hoped to hold Pemberton in my front while Sherman should get in his rear and into Vicksburg. The further north the enemy could be held the better.

It was understood, however, between General Sherman and myself that our movements were to be co-operative; if Pemberton could not be held away from Vicksburg I was to follow him; but at that time it was not expected to abandon the railroad north of the Yallabusha. With that point as a secondary base of supplies, the possibility of moving down the Yazoo until communications could be opened with the Mississippi was contemplated.

It was my intention, and so understood by Sherman and his command, that if the enemy should fall back I would follow him even to the gates of Vicks-

[23] For Halleck's Dec. 5, 1862, telegram to USG, see ibid., 6:372*n*.

[24] On Dec. 7, 1862, USG asked Halleck if he should command the Vicksburg expedition or whether Sherman should be sent. Halleck replied the same day, instructing USG to "move your troops as you may deem best." After consulting with Sherman, USG sent him to Memphis with one division on Dec. 8 and communicated that plan to Halleck on the same day. Ibid., 6:401, 403, 404, 406–407.

[25] The Yalobusha River, a tributary of the Yazoo River, flowed through Grenada, MS, at the intersection of the Mississippi Central and the Mississippi and Tennessee Railroads. George B. Davis et al., *The Official Military Atlas of the Civil War* (New York: Fairfax Press, 1983), plate 154.

burg. I intended in such an event to hold the road to Grenada on the Yalla-busha and cut loose from there, expecting to establish a new base of supplies on the Yazoo, or at Vicksburg itself, with Grenada to fall back upon in case of failure. It should be remembered that at the time I speak of it had not been demonstrated that an army could operate in an enemy's territory depending upon the country for supplies. A halt was called at Oxford with the advance seventeen miles south of there, to bring up the road to the latter point and to bring supplies of food, forage and munitions to the front.

On the 18th of December I received orders from Washington to divide my command into four army corps, with General McClernand to command one of them and to be assigned to that part of the army which was to operate down the Mississippi.[26] This interfered with my plans, but probably resulted in my ultimately taking the command in person. McClernand was at that time in Springfield, Illinois. The order was obeyed without any delay. Dispatches were sent to him the same day in conformity.

On the 20th General Van Dorn appeared at Holly Springs, my secondary base of supplies, captured the garrison of 1,500 men commanded by Colonel Murphy, of the 8th Wisconsin regiment, and destroyed all our munitions of war, food and forage. The capture was a disgraceful one to the officer commanding but not to the troops under him. At the same time Forrest got on our line of railroad between Jackson, Tennessee, and Columbus, Kentucky, doing much damage to it.[27] This cut me off from all communication with the north for more than a week, and it was more than two weeks before rations or forage could be issued from stores obtained in the regular way. This demonstrated the impossi-bility of maintaining so long a line of road over which to draw supplies for an army moving in an enemy's country. I determined, therefore, to abandon my campaign into the interior with Columbus as a base, and returned to La Grange and Grand Junction destroying the road to my front and repairing the road to Memphis, making the Mississippi river the line over which to draw supplies. Pemberton was falling back at the same time.

The moment I received the news of Van Dorn's success I sent the cavalry at the front back to drive him from the country. He had start enough to move north destroying the railroad in many places, and to attack several small gar-risons intrenched as guards to the railroad. All these he found warned of his coming and prepared to receive him. Van Dorn did not succeed in capturing

---

[26] See *PUSG*, 7:62*n*.

[27] On Dec. 18, 1862, Forrest defeated U.S. cavalry at Lexington, TN. Two days later, he captured both Humboldt and Trenton, TN. Ibid., 7:xxi–xxii.

a single garrison except the one at Holly Springs, which was larger than all the others attacked by him put together. Murphy was also warned of Van Dorn's approach, but made no preparations to meet him. He did not even notify his command.[28]

Colonel Murphy was the officer who, two months before, had evacuated Iuka on the approach of the enemy. General Rosecrans denounced him for the act and desired to have him tried and punished. I sustained the colonel at the time because his command was a small one compared with that of the enemy—not one-tenth as large—and I thought he had done well to get away without falling into their hands. His leaving large stores to fall into Price's possession I looked upon as an oversight and excused it on the ground of inexperience in military matters. He should, however, have destroyed them.[29] This last surrender demonstrated to my mind that Rosecrans' judgment of Murphy's conduct at Iuka was correct. The surrender of Holly Springs was most reprehensible and showed either the disloyalty of Colonel Murphy to the cause which he professed to serve, or gross cowardice.[30]

After the war was over I read from the diary of a lady who accompanied General Pemberton in his retreat from the Tallahatchie, that the retreat was almost a panic.[31] The roads were bad and it was difficult to move the artillery and trains. Why there should have been a panic I do not see. No expedition had yet started down the Mississippi River. Had I known the demoralized condition of the enemy, or the fact that central Mississippi abounded so in all army supplies, I would have been in pursuit of Pemberton while his cavalry was destroying the roads in my rear.

After sending cavalry to drive Van Dorn away, my next order was to dispatch all the wagons we had, under proper escort, to collect and bring in all supplies of forage and food from a region of fifteen miles east and west of the road from our front back to Grand Junction, leaving two months' supplies

[28] On Dec. 19, 1862, USG had telegraphed news of Confederate cavalry movements to Murphy. Ibid., 7:76 and *n*.

[29] For a summary of Murphy's actions at Iuka and subsequent court-martial, see ibid., 6:38–39, 40*n*–41*n*, 177*n*.

[30] On Dec. 28, 1862, USG ordered Murphy arrested. Rawlins issued Gen. Orders No. 4 on Jan. 8, 1863, dismissing Murphy from the army. Ibid., 7:106*n*.

[31] USG probably referred to Mary Ann Webster Loughborough's book *My Cave Life in Vicksburg: With Letters of Trial and Travel* (New York: Appleton, 1864); for a description of the retreat, see 189–196.

for the families of those whose stores were taken.[32] I was amazed at the quantity of supplies the country afforded. It showed that we could have subsisted off the country for two months instead of two weeks without going beyond the limits designated. This taught me a lesson which was taken advantage of later in the campaign when our army lived twenty days with the issue of only five days' rations by the commissary.[33] Our loss of supplies was great at Holly Springs, but it was more than compensated for by those taken from the country and by the lesson taught.

The news of the capture of Holly Springs and the destruction of our supplies caused much rejoicing among the people remaining in Oxford. They came with broad smiles on their faces, indicating intense joy, to ask what I was going to do now without anything for my soldiers to eat. I told them that I was not disturbed; that I had already sent troops and wagons to collect all the food and forage they could find for fifteen miles on each side of the road. Countenances soon changed, and so did the inquiry. The next was, "What are *we* to do?" My response was that we had endeavored to feed ourselves from our own northern resources while visiting them; but their friends in gray had been uncivil enough to destroy what we had brought along, and it could not be expected that men, with arms in their hands, would starve in the midst of plenty. I advised them to emigrate east, or west, fifteen miles and assist in eating up what we left.

[32] On Dec. 21, 1862, USG authorized "organized foraging parties" to gather provisions and distribute them. *PUSG,* 7:85.

[33] In his report on the Vicksburg campaign, USG stated that the army subsisted on five days' rations and supplies foraged from the surrounding countryside during the twenty-day period encompassing the march from Bruinsburg, MS, to Vicksburg. The troops landed at Bruinsburg on Apr. 30, 1863, set out for Vicksburg on May 4, and besieged the city on May 18. Ibid., 8:xxii, 156, 506, 521*n.*

# 31

Headquarters Moved to Holly Springs—General
McClernand in Command—Assuming Command
at Young's Point—Operations above Vicksburg—
Fortifications about Vicksburg—The Canal—Lake
Providence—Operations at Yazoo Pass

Tₕᵢₛ INTERRUPTION IN MY COMMUNICATIONS north—I was really cut
off from communication with a great part of my own command during this
time—resulted in Sherman's moving from Memphis before McClernand could
arrive, for my dispatch of the 18th did not reach McClernand.[1] Pemberton
got back to Vicksburg before Sherman got there.[2] The rebel positions were on
a bluff on the Yazoo River, some miles above its mouth.[3] The waters were high
so that the bottoms were generally overflowed, leaving only narrow causeways
of dry land between points of debarkation and the high bluffs. These were
fortified and defended at all points. The rebel position was impregnable against
any force that could be brought against its front. Sherman could not use

[1] Sherman left Memphis, TN, on Dec. 20, 1862; McClernand did not arrive in Memphis
until Dec. 28. *OR*, I, 17(II), 480; *PUSG*, 7:136n. For USG's Dec. 18 communications intended
for Sherman and McClernand, see *PUSG*, 7:61–62, 62n–63n.

[2] Sherman reached Chickasaw Bayou, directly north of Vicksburg, on Dec. 26, 1862, one
day after Pemberton arrived there to reinforce the city. *OR*, I, 17(II), 803–804; William T.
Sherman, *Memoirs of General William T. Sherman* (New York: D. Appleton, 1875), 1:289;
Brooks D. Simpson and Jean V. Berlin, eds., *Sherman's Civil War: Selected Correspondence of
William T. Sherman, 1860–1865* (Chapel Hill: University of North Carolina, 1999), 348.

[3] The Confederate troops were stationed along the bluffs of Walnut Hills, near Chickasaw
Bayou. Michael B. Ballard, *The Civil War in Mississippi: Major Campaigns and Battles* (Oxford,
MS: University Press of Mississippi, 2011), 118–119.

one-fourth of his force.[4] His efforts to capture the city, or the high ground north of it, were necessarily unavailing.[5]

Sherman's attack was very unfortunate, but I had no opportunity of communicating with him after the destruction of the road and telegraph to my rear on the 20th. He did not know but what I was in the rear of the enemy and depending on him to open a new base of supplies for the troops with me. I had, before he started from Memphis, directed him to take with him a few small steamers suitable for the navigation of the Yazoo, not knowing but that I might want them to supply me after cutting loose from my base at Grenada.[6]

On the 23d I removed my headquarters back to Holly Springs. The troops were drawn back gradually, but without haste or confusion, finding supplies abundant and no enemy following. The road was not damaged south of Holly Springs by Van Dorn, at least not to an extent to cause any delay. As I had resolved to move headquarters to Memphis, and to repair the road to that point, I remained at Holly Springs until this work was completed.

On the 10th of January, the work on the road from Holly Springs to Grand Junction and thence to Memphis being completed, I moved my headquarters to the latter place. During the campaign here described, the losses (mostly captures) were about equal, crediting the rebels with their Holly Springs capture, which they could not hold.

When Sherman started on his expedition down the river he had 20,000 men, taken from Memphis, and was reinforced by 12,000 more at Helena, Arkansas. The troops on the west bank of the river had previously been assigned to my command.[7] McClernand having received the orders for his assignment reached the mouth of the Yazoo on the 2d of January, and immediately assumed

[4] Because of the narrow approaches, only 6,000 of Sherman's roughly 33,000 troops were engaged in the bulk of the assault. Francis Vinton Greene, *The Mississippi* (New York: Scribner's Sons, 1882), 77–79; *OR*, I, 17(I), 602, 604.

[5] On Jan. 1, 1863, Sherman withdrew his forces, ending the Battle of Chickasaw Bayou and USG's plans to take Vicksburg directly. Michael B. Ballard, *Vicksburg: The Campaign That Opened the Mississippi* (Chapel Hill: University of North Carolina Press, 2004), 129, 146.

[6] In a dispatch dated Dec. 14, 1862, USG advised Sherman, "It would be well if you could have two or three small boats suitable for navigating the Yazoo. It may become necessary for me to look to that base for supplies before we get through." *PUSG*, 7:34.

[7] On Dec. 16, 1862, Sherman had a total of 20,523 men ready to embark from Memphis with an additional 9,552 men under the command of Brig. Gen. Frederick Steele at Helena, AR. *OR*, I, 17(I), 602, 604.

command of all the troops with Sherman, being a part of his own corps, the 13th, and all of Sherman's, the 15th.[8] Sherman, and Admiral Porter with the fleet, had withdrawn from the Yazoo. After consultation they decided that neither the army nor navy could render service to the cause where they were, and learning that I had withdrawn from the interior of Mississippi, they determined to return to the Arkansas River and to attack Arkansas Post, about fifty miles up that stream and garrisoned by about five or six thousand men. Sherman had learned of the existence of this force through a man who had been captured by the enemy with a steamer loaded with ammunition and other supplies intended for his command. The man had made his escape.[9] McClernand approved this move reluctantly, as Sherman says.[10] No obstacle was encountered until the gunboats and transports were within range of the fort. After three days' bombardment by the navy an assault was made by the troops and marines, resulting in the capture of the place, and in taking 5,000 prisoners and 17 guns.[11] I was at first disposed to disapprove of this move as an unnecessary side movement having no especial bearing upon the work before us; but when the result was understood I regarded it as very important.[12] Five thousand Confederate troops left in the rear might have caused us much trouble and loss of property while navigating the Mississippi.

Immediately after the reduction of Arkansas Post and the capture of the garrison, McClernand returned with his entire force to Napoleon, at the mouth of the Arkansas River.[13] From here I received messages from both Sherman

[8] McClernand assumed command on Jan. 4, 1863. Ibid., I, 17(I), 700–701.

[9] According to U.S. Army Col. N. P. Chipman's Dec. 30, 1862, letter to Maj. Gen. Samuel Curtis, Confederate troops captured the steamer *Blue Wing* between Dec. 28 and Dec. 30, 1862. Two crewmen from *Blue Wing* and two "conscript refugees" were later taken aboard the steamer *Sunshine* and reported the capture of the boat and the presence of Confederate troops at Arkansas Post. Ibid., I, 17(I), 886–887.

[10] In his *Memoirs,* Sherman stated that McClernand initially objected to any movement against Arkansas Post. However, Chipman's Dec. 31, 1862, letter to Curtis indicated that McClernand considered a movement against Arkansas Post an important endeavor. Ibid., I, 17(I), 887; Sherman, *Memoirs,* 1:296.

[11] U.S. Navy gunboats began the bombardment of Arkansas Post on Jan. 10, 1863. After a series of infantry assaults and additional fire from artillery and the gunboats on Jan. 11, 4,791 Confederate troops surrendered. Edwin Cole Bearss, *Unvexed to the Sea,* vol. 1 of *The Campaign for Vicksburg* (Dayton, OH: Morningside House, 1985), 371, 379–383, 401–405.

[12] See *PUSG*, 7:209–210, 210*n*, 211*n*, 218–219 for USG's comments on the expedition.

[13] According to the 1860 census, the region around Napoleon, AR, had a population of 992. During the Civil War, the local population largely abandoned the town, and by 1876 the area

and Admiral Porter, urging me to come and take command in person, and expressing their distrust of McClernand's ability and fitness for so important and intricate an expedition.[14]

On the 17th I visited McClernand and his command at Napoleon. It was here made evident to me that both the army and navy were so distrustful of McClernand's fitness to command that, while they would do all they could to insure success, this distrust was an element of weakness. It would have been criminal to send troops under these circumstances into such danger. By this time I had received authority to relieve McClernand, or to assign any person else to the command of the river expedition, or to assume command in person.[15] I felt great embarrassment about McClernand. He was the senior major-general after myself within the department. It would not do, with his rank and ambition, to assign a junior over him. Nothing was left, therefore, but to assume the command myself. I would have been glad to put Sherman in command, to give him an opportunity to accomplish what he had failed in the December before; but there seemed no other way out of the difficulty, for he was junior to McClernand. Sherman's failure needs no apology.

On the 20th I ordered General McClernand with the entire command, to Young's Point[16] and Milliken's Bend,[17] while I returned to Memphis to make all the necessary preparation for leaving the territory behind me secure. General Hurlbut with the 16th corps was left in command. The Memphis and Charleston railroad was held, while the Mississippi Central was given up.

---

was almost completely uninhabited, having been submerged under water due to the erratic flow of the Mississippi and Arkansas Rivers. Michael D. Hammond, "Arkansas Atlantis: The Lost Town of Napoleon," *Arkansas Historical Quarterly* 65 (2006): 201, 206, 214, 221–222.

[14] While the message from Porter to USG has not been found, he did express his contempt for McClernand in a Jan. 16, 1863, letter to Asst. Secretary of the Navy Gustavus V. Fox. In a Jan. 17 letter to USG, Sherman questioned McClernand's abilities as commander of the Vicksburg expedition. *PUSG*, 7:235, 236n, 295n.

[15] On Jan. 12, 1863, Halleck gave USG the authorization to relieve McClernand from command of the expedition against Vicksburg. Ibid., 7:210n.

[16] Young's Point, LA, was eight miles north of Vicksburg on the Mississippi River. USG first ordered a portion of McClernand's troops to Young's Point on Jan. 18, 1863. Ibid., 7:232n, 246n.

[17] Milliken's Bend, LA, was home to a busy steamboat landing before the Civil War. It ceased to exist after the war when the Mississippi River shifted course and overtook the town. It was located about fifteen miles north of Vicksburg. On Jan. 13, 1863, USG first suggested to McClernand that he move to Milliken's Bend. Marion Bragg, *Historic Names and Places on the Lower Mississippi River* (Vicksburg: Mississippi River Commission, 1977), 153–154; *PUSG*, 7:212n, 218.

Columbus was the only point between Cairo and Memphis, on the river, left
with a garrison. All the troops and guns from the posts on the abandoned railroad and river were sent to the front.

On the 29th of January I arrived at Young's Point and assumed command
the following day.[18] General McClernand took exception in a most characteristic way—for him. His correspondence with me on the subject was more in
the nature of a reprimand than a protest.[19] It was highly insubordinate, but I
overlooked it, as I believed, for the good of the service. General McClernand
was a politician of very considerable prominence in his State; he was a member
of Congress when the secession war broke out; he belonged to that political
party which furnished all the opposition there was to a vigorous prosecution
of the war for saving the Union; there was no delay in his declaring himself
for the Union at all hazards, and there was no uncertain sound in his declaration of where he stood in the contest before the country. He also gave up
his seat in Congress to take the field in defence of the principles he had
proclaimed.[20]

The real work of the campaign and siege of Vicksburg now began. The
problem was to secure a footing upon dry ground on the east side of the river
from which the troops could operate against Vicksburg. The Mississippi River,
from Cairo south, runs through a rich alluvial valley of many miles in width,
bound on the east by land running from eighty up to two or more hundred
feet above the river. On the west side the highest land, except in a few places,
is but little above the highest water. Through this valley the river meanders in
the most tortuous way, varying in direction to all points of the compass. At
places it runs to the very foot of the bluffs. After leaving Memphis, there are
no such highlands coming to the water's edge on the east shore until Vicksburg is reached.

The intervening land is cut up by bayous filled from the river in high
water—many of them navigable for steamers. All of them would be, except
for overhanging trees, narrowness and tortuous course, making it impossible
to turn the bends with vessels of any considerable length. Marching across this

[18] USG arrived at Young's Point on Jan. 28, 1863, and assumed command on Jan. 30. *PUSG,*
7:253, 265*n.*

[19] For the correspondence between USG and McClernand, see ibid., 7:265*n*–268*n.*

[20] Elected as a Democrat from Illinois to the U.S. House of Representatives in 1859,
McClernand resigned his seat on Oct. 8, 1861. *CWHC,* 372; Richard L. Kiper, *Major General
John Alexander McClernand: Politician in Uniform* (Kent, OH: Kent State University Press,
1999), 15.

country in the face of an enemy was impossible; navigating it proved equally impracticable. The strategical way according to the rule, therefore, would have been to go back to Memphis; establish that as a base of supplies; fortify it so that the storehouses could be held by a small garrison, and move from there along the line of railroad, repairing as we advanced, to the Yallabusha, or to Jackson, Mississippi. At this time the North had become very much discouraged. Many strong Union men believed that the war must prove a failure. The elections of 1862 had gone against the party which was for the prosecution of the war to save the Union if it took the last man and the last dollar.[21] Voluntary enlistments had ceased throughout the greater part of the North, and the draft had been resorted to to fill up our ranks.[22] It was my judgment at the time that to make a backward movement as long as that from Vicksburg to Memphis, would be interpreted, by many of those yet full of hope for the preservation of the Union, as a defeat, and that the draft would be resisted, desertions ensue and the power to capture and punish deserters lost. There was nothing left to be done but to *go forward to a decisive victory.* This was in my mind from the moment I took command in person at Young's Point.

The winter of 1862–3 was a noted one for continuous high water in the Mississippi and for heavy rains along the lower river. To get dry land, or rather land above the water, to encamp the troops upon, took many miles of river front. We had to occupy the levees and the ground immediately behind. This was so limited that one corps, the 17th, under General McPherson, was at Lake Providence, seventy miles above Vicksburg.[23]

It was in January the troops took their position opposite Vicksburg. The water was very high and the rains were incessant. There seemed no possibility of a land movement before the end of March or later, and it would not do to lie idle all this time. The effect would be demoralizing to the troops and

[21] The Republican Party suffered defeats throughout the North in the fall elections of 1862. The party lost thirty-two seats in the House of Representatives to Democrats, but they gained five seats in the Senate. Jennifer L. Weber, *Copperheads: The Rise and Fall of Lincoln's Opponents in the North* (New York: Oxford University Press, 2006), 68–69.

[22] Empowered by the Militia Act of 1862 (enacted July 17, 1862), on Aug. 4 Lincoln had set a quota of 300,000 men to serve in the war for nine months. On Aug. 9, Stanton had communicated to state governors the regulations for filling the quotas, which included the use of the draft. Robert W. Coakley, *The Role of Federal Military Forces in Domestic Disorders, 1789–1878* (Washington, DC: Center of Military History, 1988), 230.

[23] McPherson arrived at Lake Providence, LA, on Feb. 23, 1863. Bearss, *Unvexed to the Sea,* 470.

injurious to their health. Friends in the North would have grown more and more discouraged, and enemies in the same section more and more insolent in their gibes and denunciation of the cause and those engaged in it.

I always admired the South, as bad as I thought their cause, for the boldness with which they silenced all opposition and all croaking, by press or by individuals, within their control. War at all times, whether a civil war between sections of a common country or between nations, ought to be avoided, if possible with honor. But, once entered into, it is too much for human nature to tolerate an enemy within their ranks to give aid and comfort to the armies of the opposing section or nation.

Vicksburg, as stated before, is on the first high land coming to the river's edge, below that on which Memphis stands. The bluff, or high land, follows the left bank of the Yazoo for some distance and continues in a southerly direction to the Mississippi River, thence it runs along the Mississippi to Warrenton,[24] six miles below. The Yazoo River leaves the high land a short distance below Haines' Bluff and empties into the Mississippi nine miles above Vicksburg. Vicksburg is built on this high land where the Mississippi washes the base of the hill. Haines' Bluff, eleven miles from Vicksburg, on the Yazoo River, was strongly fortified. The whole distance from there to Vicksburg and thence to Warrenton was also intrenched, with batteries at suitable distances and rifle-pits connecting them.

From Young's Point the Mississippi turns in a north-easterly direction to a point just above the city, when it again turns and runs south-westerly, leaving vessels, which might attempt to run the blockade, exposed to the fire of batteries six miles below the city before they were in range of the upper batteries. Since then the river has made a cut-off, leaving what was the peninsula in front of the city, an island.[25] North of the Yazoo was all a marsh, heavily timbered, cut up with bayous, and much overflowed. A front attack was therefore impossible, and was never contemplated; certainly not by me. The problem then became, how to secure a landing on high ground east of the Mississippi without

[24] Founded in 1809, Warrenton, MS, steadily declined as Vicksburg grew in prominence. The town was heavily damaged by Union shelling during the Vicksburg campaign and was eventually abandoned when the Mississippi River shifted its course westward. Bragg, *Historic Names and Places,* 165–167.

[25] On Apr. 26, 1876 (one day before Pres. USG's fifty-fourth birthday), the Centennial Cutoff formed when the Mississippi River broke through the peninsula called De Soto Point, LA, creating De Soto Island and shifting the course of the river away from the Vicksburg waterfront. Ibid., 158–159.

an apparent retreat. Then commenced a series of experiments to consume time, and to divert the attention of the enemy, of my troops and of the public generally. I, myself, never felt great confidence that any of the experiments resorted to would prove successful.[26] Nevertheless I was always prepared to take advantage of them in case they did.

In 1862 General Thomas Williams[27] had come up from New Orleans and cut a ditch ten or twelve feet wide and about as deep, straight across from Young's Point to the river below. The distance across was a little over a mile. It was Williams' expectation that when the river rose it would cut a navigable channel through; but the canal started in an eddy from both ends, and, of course, it only filled up with water on the rise without doing any execution in the way of cutting.[28] Mr. Lincoln had navigated the Mississippi in his younger days and understood well its tendency to change its channel, in places, from time to time. He set much store accordingly by this canal. General McClernand had been, therefore, directed before I went to Young's Point to push the work of widening and deepening this canal.[29] After my arrival the work was diligently pushed with about 4,000 men—as many as could be used to advantage—until interrupted by a sudden rise in the river that broke a dam at the upper end, which had been put there to keep the water out until the excavation was completed. This was on the 8th of March.[30]

Even if the canal had proven a success, so far as to be navigable for steamers, it could not have been of much advantage to us. It runs in a direction almost perpendicular to the line of bluffs on the opposite side, or east bank, of the river. As soon as the enemy discovered what we were doing he established a battery commanding the canal throughout its length. This battery soon drove out our dredges, two in number, which were doing the work

[26] In fact, USG expressed optimism about the various attempts to reach Vicksburg in his correspondence during the campaign. *PUSG*, 7:252, 281, 284, 401*n*, 455–456.

[27] Thomas Williams (1815–1862) was born in New York and later moved to Michigan. He graduated from the USMA in 1837. On Sept. 28, 1861, he was promoted to brigadier general. He was killed in Aug. 1862 during the defense of Baton Rouge, LA. *CWHC*, 572; G. Mott Williams, "Letters of General Thomas Williams, 1862," *American Historical Review* 14 (1909): 305.

[28] Williams's brigade and over 1,200 contrabands began digging a canal at Young's Point in June 1862. The effort was abandoned because of low water levels and illness among those working on the canal. Bearss, *Unvexed to the Sea*, 437.

[29] On Jan. 22, 1863, USG first wrote to McClernand urging him to at least begin preparations for the canal project. USG arrived at Young's Point on Jan. 28. *PUSG*, 7:239, 253.

[30] The dam broke on the evening of Mar. 6, 1863. Ibid., 7:399.

of thousands of men.[31] Had the canal been completed it might have proven of some use in running transports through, under the cover of night, to use below; but they would yet have to run batteries, though for a much shorter distance.

While this work was progressing we were busy in other directions, trying to find an available landing on high ground on the east bank of the river, or to make water-ways to get below the city, avoiding the batteries.

On the 30th of January, the day after my arrival at the front, I ordered General McPherson, stationed with his corps at Lake Providence, to cut the levee at that point. If successful in opening a channel for navigation by this route, it would carry us to the Mississippi River through the mouth of the Red River, just above Port Hudson and four hundred miles below Vicksburg by the river.[32]

Lake Providence is a part of the old bed of the Mississippi, about a mile from the present channel. It is six miles long and has its outlet through Bayou Baxter, Bayou Macon, and the Tensas, Washita and Red Rivers. The last three are navigable streams at all seasons. Bayous Baxter and Macon are narrow and tortuous, and the banks are covered with dense forests overhanging the channel. They were also filled with fallen timber, the accumulation of years. The land along the Mississippi River, from Memphis down, is in all instances highest next to the river, except where the river washes the bluffs which form the boundary of the valley through which it winds. Bayou Baxter, as it reaches lower land, begins to spread out and disappears entirely in a cypress swamp before it reaches the Macon. There was about two feet of water in this swamp at the time. To get through it, even with vessels of the lightest draft, it was necessary to clear off a belt of heavy timber wide enough to make a passage way. As the trees would have to be cut close to the bottom—under water—it was an undertaking of great magnitude.

---

[31] On Feb. 21, 1863, Capt. Frederick E. Prime reported that Confederate batteries had been constructed across from the canal's outlet, although they were not yet active. There were three dredges at work on the canal by Mar. 7, two of which were *Samson* and *Hercules*. By Mar. 27, USG reported that Confederate forces had driven the dredges out of the canal. "The Dredging Machine, *Samson*," *Frank Leslie's Illustrated Newspaper*, Apr. 4, 1863, 23; *OR*, I, 24(I), 121; *PUSG*, 7:390n–391n, 402n, 477.

[32] On Jan. 30, 1863, USG instructed McClernand to detail a brigade to begin work on a canal at Lake Providence. On Feb. 5, USG ordered McPherson to Lake Providence. *PUSG*, 7:257–258, 261, 284–285.

On the 4th of February I visited General McPherson, and remained with him several days.[33] The work had not progressed so far as to admit the water from the river into the lake, but the troops had succeeded in drawing a small steamer, of probably not over thirty tons' capacity, from the river into the lake. With this we were able to explore the lake and bayou as far as cleared. I saw then that there was scarcely a chance of this ever becoming a practicable route for moving troops through an enemy's country. The distance from Lake Providence to the point where vessels going by that route would enter the Mississippi again, is about four hundred and seventy miles by the main river. The distance would probably be greater by the tortuous bayous through which this new route would carry us. The enemy held Port Hudson, below where the Red River debouches, and all the Mississippi above to Vicksburg. The Red River, Washita and Tensas were, as has been said, all navigable streams, on which the enemy could throw small bodies of men to obstruct our passage and pick off our troops with their sharpshooters. I let the work go on, believing employment was better than idleness for the men. Then, too, it served as a cover for other efforts which gave a better prospect of success. This work was abandoned after the canal proved a failure.[34]

Lieutenant-Colonel Wilson[35] of my staff was sent to Helena, Arkansas, to examine and open a way through Moon Lake and the Yazoo Pass if possible.[36] Formerly there was a route by way of an inlet from the Mississippi River into Moon Lake, a mile east of the river, thence east through Yazoo Pass to

[33] USG did not meet with McPherson at Lake Providence on Feb. 4, 1863. On Feb. 5, USG traveled to Lake Providence, where he sent McPherson orders to move one division of his command from Memphis to Lake Providence. On Feb. 12, USG again traveled to Lake Providence in an attempt to speak with McPherson, but McPherson did not make it from Memphis in time for the meeting due to bad roads and a lack of transportation for his troops. Ibid., 7:xxiii, 284–285, 312–313, 313n.

[34] McPherson broke the levee at Lake Providence on Mar. 17, 1863, flooding the lake and its surrounding bayous. On Mar. 30, USG wrote to McPherson and inquired about the viability of the route through Lake Providence, stating, "I do not expect to use that route but want to know if it can be used in case of necessity." Ibid., 7:423n, 489.

[35] James H. Wilson (1837–1925) was born in Illinois and graduated from the USMA in 1860. On Oct. 30, 1863, he was promoted to brigadier general and served as aide-de-camp for USG in Dec. that year. After the war, he coauthored with Charles A. Dana *The Life of Ulysses S. Grant, General of the Armies of the United States* (Springfield, MA: Gordon Bill, 1868). *CWHC*, 574–575.

[36] On Jan. 29, 1863, USG informed Halleck of Wilson's mission. *PUSG*, 7:253–254.

Coldwater,[37] along the latter to the Tallahatchie, which joins the Yallabusha about two hundred and fifty miles below Moon Lake and forms the Yazoo River. These were formerly navigated by steamers trading with the rich plantations along their banks; but the State of Mississippi had built a strong levee across the inlet some years before, leaving the only entrance for vessels into this rich region the one by way of the mouth of the Yazoo several hundreds of miles below.[38]

On the 2d of February this dam, or levee, was cut.[39] The river being high the rush of water through the cut was so great that in a very short time the entire obstruction was washed away. The bayous were soon filled and much of the country was overflowed. This pass leaves the Mississippi River but a few miles below Helena. On the 24th General Ross, with his brigade of about 4,500 men on transports, moved into this new water-way. The rebels had obstructed the navigation of Yazoo Pass and the Coldwater by felling trees into them. Much of the timber in this region being of greater specific gravity than water, and being of great size, their removal was a matter of great labor; but it was finally accomplished, and on the 11th of March Ross found himself, accompanied by two gunboats under the command of Lieutenant-Commander Watson Smith,[40] confronting a fortification at Greenwood, where the Tallahatchie and Yallabusha unite and the Yazoo begins.[41] The bends of the rivers are such at this point as to almost form an island, scarcely above water at that stage of the river. This island was fortified and manned. It was named Fort Pemberton after the commander at Vicksburg.[42] No land approach was ac-

[37] USG here referred to the Coldwater River. Ibid., 7:30.

[38] Between 1856 and 1859, more than $1,000,000 went toward construction on the levee that closed off Yazoo Pass and also toward other flood control measures in the Mississippi-Yazoo Delta. Bragg, *Historic Names and Places,* 98; "The Yazoo Pass Expedition; Moon Lake the Rendezvous of the Expedition," *New York Times,* Mar. 6, 1863, 1.

[39] On Jan. 29, 1863, USG gave the order to cut the levee leading into Yazoo Pass. The levee was cut on Feb. 3. *PUSG,* 7:xxiii, 253–254, 286n–287n.

[40] Watson Smith (c.1823–1864) was living in New Jersey before he became a midshipman in Oct. 1841. He was promoted to lieutenant commander on July 16, 1862. On Dec. 19, 1864, Smith became ill and died. Myron J. Smith Jr., *The Fight for the Yazoo, August 1862–July 1864: Swamps, Forts and Fleets on Vicksburg's Northern Flank* (London: McFarland, 2012), 403n.

[41] Smith, Ross, and Wilson were aboard the *Chillicothe,* followed by the ironclad *De Kalb* and the ram *Lioness* during the assault on Fort Pemberton near Greenwood, MS. Bearss, *Unvexed by the Sea,* 519–521.

[42] Fort Pemberton—also called Fort Greenwood—was located three miles above Greenwood. *PUSG,* 7:30, 423n, 433n.

cessible. The troops, therefore, could render no assistance towards an assault further than to establish a battery on a little piece of ground which was discovered above water. The gunboats, however, attacked on the 11th and again on the 13th of March. Both efforts were failures and were not renewed. One gunboat was disabled and we lost six men killed and twenty-five wounded. The loss of the enemy was less.[43]

Fort Pemberton was so little above the water that it was thought that a rise of two feet would drive the enemy out. In hope of enlisting the elements on our side, which had been so much against us up to this time, a second cut was made in the Mississippi levee, this time directly opposite Helena, or six miles above the former cut.[44] It did not accomplish the desired result, and Ross, with his fleet, started back. On the 22d he met Quinby[45] with a brigade at Yazoo Pass. Quinby was the senior of Ross, and assumed command. He was not satisfied with returning to his former position without seeing for himself whether anything could be accomplished. Accordingly Fort Pemberton was revisited by our troops; but an inspection was sufficient this time without an attack. Quinby, with his command, returned with but little delay. In the meantime I was much exercised for the safety of Ross, not knowing that Quinby had been able to join him. Reinforcements were of no use in a country covered with water, as they would have to remain on board of their transports. Relief had to come from another quarter. So I determined to get into the Yazoo below Fort Pemberton.

Steel's Bayou empties into the Yazoo River between Haines' Bluff and its mouth. It is narrow, very tortuous, and fringed with a very heavy growth of timber, but it is deep. It approaches to within one mile of the Mississippi at Eagle Bend, thirty miles above Young's Point. Steel's Bayou connects with Black Bayou, Black Bayou with Deer Creek, Deer Creek with Rolling Fork, Rolling Fork with the Big Sunflower River, and the Big Sunflower with the Yazoo River

[43] Both *Chillicothe* and *De Kalb* were heavily damaged by the fighting at Fort Pemberton. The Confederate troops reported three wounded and one dead. *OR,* I, 24(I), 378–379, 416.

[44] The idea to raise the water level and force the abandoning of Fort Pemberton was first suggested by Wilson in a Mar. 16, 1863, letter to Ross. Ross forwarded the suggestion to Prentiss, who, on Mar. 20, reported to USG his intent to cut the levee eighteen miles above Helena. Bearss, *Unvexed by the Sea,* 528.

[45] Isaac F. Quinby (1821–1891) was born in New Jersey and later moved to New York. He graduated from the USMA in 1843, left the military in 1852, and then reentered the army as a colonel in the 13th New York Inf. at the start of the Civil War. He was a brigadier general commanding the 7th Div., 7th Corps, Army of the Tennessee, in Mar. 1863. *CWHC,* 442–443.

about ten miles above Haines' Bluff in a right line but probably twenty or twenty-five miles by the winding of the river. All these waterways are of about the same nature so far as navigation is concerned, until the Sunflower is reached; this affords free navigation.

Admiral Porter explored this waterway as far as Deer Creek on the 14th of March, and reported it navigable. On the next day he started with five gun-boats and four mortar-boats. I went with him for some distance.[46] The heavy, overhanging timber retarded progress very much, as did also the short turns in so narrow a stream. The gunboats, however, ploughed their way through without other damage than to their appearance. The transports did not fare so well although they followed behind. The road was somewhat cleared for them by the gunboats. In the evening I returned to headquarters to hurry up reinforcements. Sherman went in person on the 16th, taking with him Stuart's division of the 15th corps. They took large river transports to Eagle Bend on the Mississippi, where they debarked and marched across to Steel's Bayou, where they re-embarked on the transports. The river steamers, with their tall smoke-stacks and light guards extending out, were so much impeded that the gunboats got far ahead. Porter, with his fleet, got within a few hundred yards of where the sailing would have been clear and free from the obstructions caused by felling trees into the water, when he encountered rebel sharp-shooters, and his progress was delayed by obstructions in his front. He could do nothing with gunboats against sharp-shooters. The rebels, learning his route, had sent in about 4,000 men—many more than there were sailors in the fleet.

Sherman went back, at the request of the admiral, to clear out Black Bayou and to hurry up reinforcements, which were far behind. On the night of the 19th he received notice from the admiral that he had been attacked by sharp-shooters and was in imminent peril. Sherman at once returned through Black Bayou in a canoe, and passed on until he met a steamer, with the last of the reinforcements he had, coming up. They tried to force their way through Black Bayou with their steamer, but, finding it slow and tedious work, debarked and pushed forward on foot. It was night when they landed, and intensely dark. There was but a narrow strip of land above water, and that was grown up with underbrush or cane. The troops lighted their way through this with candles carried in their hands for a mile and a half, when they came to an open

---

[46] Porter explored Steele's Bayou on Mar. 13, 1863. USG accompanied Porter on his subsequent exploration of Steele's Bayou on Mar. 15. *PUSG*, 7:xxiii, 420*n*.

plantation.[47] Here the troops rested until morning. They made twenty-one miles from this resting-place by noon the next day, and were in time to rescue the fleet. Porter had fully made up his mind to blow up the gunboats rather than have them fall into the hands of the enemy. More welcome visitors he probably never met than the "boys in blue" on this occasion. The vessels were backed out and returned to their rendezvous on the Mississippi; and thus ended in failure the fourth attempt to get in rear of Vicksburg.[48]

---

[47] According to Sherman, his troops stopped at "Hill's Plantation" on the night of Mar. 20, 1863. Sherman, *Memoirs,* 1:307–308.

[48] Porter ended the Steele's Bayou expedition on Mar. 22, 1863. *PUSG,* 7:xxiv.

# 32

## The Bayous West of the Mississippi—Criticisms of the Northern Press—Running the Batteries—Loss of the *Indianola*—Disposition of the Troops

THE ORIGINAL CANAL scheme was also abandoned on the 27th of March. The effort to make a waterway through Lake Providence and the connecting bayous was abandoned as wholly impracticable about the same time.[1] At Milliken's Bend, and also at Young's Point, bayous or channels start, which connecting with other bayous passing Richmond, Louisiana, enter the Mississippi at Carthage twenty-five or thirty miles above Grand Gulf.[2] The Mississippi levee cuts the supply of water off from these bayous or channels, but all the rainfall behind the levee, at these points, is carried through these same channels to the river below. In case of a crevasse in this vicinity, the water escaping would find its outlet through the same channels. The dredges and laborers from the canal having been driven out by overflow and the enemy's batteries, I determined to open these other channels, if possible. If successful the effort would afford a route, away from the enemy's batteries, for our trans- ports. There was a good road back of the levees, along these bayous, to carry the troops, artillery and wagon trains over whenever the water receded a little, and after a few days of dry weather.[3] Accordingly, with the abandonment of

[1] On Mar. 30, 1863, USG informed McPherson that he did not anticipate using the Lake Providence, LA, to Bayou Macon route. *PUSG*, 7:489.

[2] Grand Gulf, MS, was a major shipping port located in Claiborne County along the Mis- sissippi River. By the beginning of the twentieth century, Grand Gulf was stranded after the river's course shifted west. In 1907, it was a village with only 150 citizens. Dunbar Rowland, *Mississippi: Comprising Sketches of Counties, Towns, Events, Institutions, and Persons, Arranged in Cyclopedic Form* (Atlanta: Southern Historical Association, 1907), 1:794.

[3] USG probably referred to the route commonly called the Richmond Road. *OR*, I, 24(II), 458.

all the other plans for reaching a base heretofore described, this new one was undertaken.

As early as the 4th of February I had written to Halleck about this route, stating that I thought it much more practicable than the other undertaking (the Lake Providence route), and that it would have been accomplished with much less labor if commenced before the water had got all over the country.[4]

The upper end of these bayous being cut off from a water supply, further than the rainfall back of the levees, was grown up with dense timber for a distance of several miles from their source. It was necessary, therefore, to clear this out before letting in the water from the river. This work was continued until the waters of the river began to recede and the road to Richmond, Louisiana, emerged from the water. One small steamer and some barges were got through this channel, but no further use could be made of it because of the fall in the river.[5] Beyond this it was no more successful than the other experiments with which the winter was whiled away. All these failures would have been very discouraging if I had expected much from the efforts; but I had not. From the first the most I hoped to accomplish was the passage of transports, to be used below Vicksburg, without exposure to the long line of batteries defending that city.

This long, dreary and, for heavy and continuous rains and high water, unprecedented winter was one of great hardship to all engaged about Vicksburg. The river was higher than its natural banks from December, 1862, to the following April. The war had suspended peaceful pursuits in the South, further than the production of army supplies, and in consequence the levees were neglected and broken in many places and the whole country was covered with water. Troops could scarcely find dry ground on which to pitch their tents. Malarial fevers broke out among the men. Measles and small-pox also attacked them. The hospital arrangements and medical attendance were so perfect, however, that the loss of life was much less than might have been expected. Visitors to the camps went home with dismal stories to relate; Northern papers came back to the soldiers with these stories exaggerated. Because I would not divulge my ultimate plans to visitors, they pronounced me idle, incompetent and unfit to command men in an emergency, and clamored for my removal.[6] They were not to be satisfied, many of them, with

[4] For USG's Feb. 4, 1863, letter to Asst. AG John C. Kelton, see *PUSG*, 7:281.

[5] The steamboat *Victor* had traversed the channel by May 4, 1863. *OR*, I, 24(I), 125.

[6] Articles describing the dire conditions of sick soldiers in U.S. Army camps during the Vicksburg campaign appeared in the *Chicago Times* on Feb. 20 and 26, 1863, and in the *New*

my simple removal, but named who my successor should be. McClernand, Fremont, Hunter and McClellan were all mentioned in this connection. I took no steps to answer these complaints, but continued to do my duty, as I understood it, to the best of my ability. Every one has his superstitions. One of mine is that in positions of great responsibility every one should do his duty to the best of his ability where assigned by competent authority, without application or the use of influence to change his position. While at Cairo I had watched with very great interest the operations of the Army of the Potomac, looking upon that as the main field of the war. I had no idea, myself, of ever having any large command, nor did I suppose that I was equal to one; but I had the vanity to think that as a cavalry officer I might succeed very well in the command of a brigade. On one occasion, in talking about this to my staff officers, all of whom were civilians without any military education whatever, I said that I would give anything if I were commanding a brigade of cavalry in the Army of the Potomac and I believed I could do some good. Captain Hillyer spoke up and suggested that I make application to be transferred there to command the cavalry. I then told him that I would cut my right arm off first, and mentioned this superstition.

In time of war the President, being by the Constitution Commander-in-chief of the Army and Navy, is responsible for the selection of commanders. He should not be embarrassed in making his selections. I having been selected, my responsibility ended with my doing the best I knew how. If I had sought the place, or obtained it through personal or political influence, my belief is that I would have feared to undertake any plan of my own conception, and would probably have awaited direct orders from my distant superiors. Persons obtaining important commands by application or political influence are apt to keep a written record of complaints and predictions of defeat, which are shown in case of disaster. Somebody must be responsible for their failures.

With all the pressure brought to bear upon them, both President Lincoln and General Halleck stood by me to the end of the campaign. I had never met Mr. Lincoln, but his support was constant.

At last the waters began to recede; the roads crossing the peninsula behind the levees of the bayous, were emerging from the waters; the troops were all

*York Times* on Feb. 23 and Mar. 4. As one example of the criticism described by USG, see journalist Murat Halstead's Feb. 19 letter to Secretary of the Treasury Salmon P. Chase arguing for USG's removal. J. Cutler Andrews, *The North Reports the Civil War* (Pittsburgh, PA: University of Pittsburgh Press, 1983), 384, 714*n*.

concentrated from distant points at Milliken's Bend preparatory to a final move which was to crown the long, tedious and discouraging labors with success.[7]

I had had in contemplation the whole winter the movement by land to a point below Vicksburg from which to operate, subject only to the possible but not expected success of some one of the expedients resorted to for the purpose of giving us a different base. This could not be undertaken until the waters receded. I did not therefore communicate this plan, even to an officer of my staff, until it was necessary to make preparations for the start. My recollection is that Admiral Porter was the first one to whom I mentioned it.[8] The co-operation of the navy was absolutely essential to the success (even to the contemplation) of such an enterprise. I had no more authority to command Porter than he had to command me. It was necessary to have part of his fleet below Vicksburg if the troops went there. Steamers to use as ferries were also essential. The navy was the only escort and protection for these steamers, all of which in getting below had to run about fourteen miles of batteries. Porter fell into the plan at once, and suggested that he had better superintend the preparation of the steamers selected to run the batteries, as sailors would probably understand the work better than soldiers. I was glad to accept his proposition, not only because I admitted his argument, but because it would enable me to keep from the enemy a little longer our designs. Porter's fleet was on the east side of the river above the mouth of the Yazoo, entirely concealed from the enemy by the dense forests that intervened. Even spies could not get near him, on account of the undergrowth and overflowed lands. Suspicions of some mysterious movements were aroused. Our river guards discovered one day a small skiff moving quietly and mysteriously up the river near the east shore, from the direction of Vicksburg, towards the fleet. On overhauling the boat they found a small white flag, not much larger than a handkerchief, set up in the stern, no doubt intended as a flag of truce in case of discovery. The boat, crew and passengers were brought ashore to me. The chief personage aboard proved to be Jacob Thompson,[9] Secretary of the Interior under the administration of President

---

[7] On Mar. 28, 1863, USG ordered Prentiss to send divisions from the Yazoo Pass expedition to join McClernand's forces at Milliken's Bend, LA. *PUSG*, 7:482, 482n–483n.

[8] USG informed Porter of his plan on Apr. 2, 1863. Ibid., 8:3–5.

[9] Jacob Thompson (1810–1888) was born in North Carolina. He later moved to Mississippi and became a planter. He served as secretary of the interior from Mar. 6, 1857 to Jan. 8, 1861.

Buchanan. After a pleasant conversation of half an hour or more I allowed the boat and crew, passengers and all, to return to Vicksburg, without creating a suspicion that there was a doubt in my mind as to the good faith of Mr. Thompson and his flag.[10]

Admiral Porter proceeded with the preparation of the steamers for their hazardous passage of the enemy's batteries. The great essential was to protect the boilers from the enemy's shot, and to conceal the fires under the boilers from view. This he accomplished by loading the steamers, between the guards and boilers on the boiler deck up to the deck above, with bales of hay and cotton, and the deck in front of the boilers in the same way, adding sacks of grain. The hay and grain would be wanted below, and could not be transported in sufficient quantity by the muddy roads over which we expected to march.

Before this I had been collecting, from St. Louis and Chicago, yawls and barges to be used as ferries when we got below. By the 16th of April Porter was ready to start on his perilous trip. The advance, flagship *Benton*, Porter commanding, started at ten o'clock at night, followed at intervals of a few minutes by the *Lafayette* with a captured steamer, the *Price*,[11] lashed to her side, the *Louisville, Mound City, Pittsburgh* and *Carondelet*—all of these being naval vessels. Next came the transports—*Forest Queen, Silver Wave* and *Henry Clay*, each towing barges loaded with coal to be used as fuel by the naval and transport steamers when below the batteries. The gunboat *Tuscumbia* brought up the rear. Soon after the start a battery between Vicksburg and Warrenton opened fire across the intervening peninsula, followed by the upper batteries, and then by batteries all along the line. The gunboats ran up close under the bluffs, delivering their fire in return at short distances, probably without much effect. They were under fire for more than two hours and every vessel was struck many times, but with little damage to

In 1862, he served as aide-de-camp to Generals Johnston and Beauregard. Thompson was a Confederate agent in Canada from 1864 to 1865. *CWHC,* 528–529.

[10] Thompson was named an unindicted coconspirator in the murder of Lincoln. On June 26, 1867, during the trial of accused Lincoln assassination conspirator John H. Surratt, USG testified about his encounter with Thompson outside of Vicksburg in 1863. *PUSG,* 17:200–201; Edward Steers, *Blood on the Moon: The Assassination of Abraham Lincoln* (Lexington: University Press of Kentucky, 2005), 223.

[11] USG referred to the wooden gunboat *General Price*. David D. Porter, *The Naval History of the Civil War* (New York: Sherman, 1886), 310.

the gunboats. The transports did not fare so well. The *Henry Clay* was disabled and deserted by her crew. Soon after a shell burst in the cotton packed about the boilers, set the vessel on fire and burned her to the water's edge. The burning mass, however, floated down to Carthage before grounding, as did also one of the barges in tow.

The enemy were evidently expecting our fleet, for they were ready to light up the river by means of bonfires on the east side and by firing houses on the point of land opposite the city on the Louisiana side. The sight was magnificent, but terrible. I witnessed it from the deck of a river transport, run out into the middle of the river and as low down as it was prudent to go. My mind was much relieved when I learned that no one on the transports had been killed and but few, if any, wounded.[12] During the running of the batteries men were stationed in the holds of the transports to partially stop with cotton shot-holes that might be made in the hulls. All damage was afterwards soon repaired under the direction of Admiral Porter.

The experiment of passing batteries had been tried before this, however, during the war. Admiral Farragut[13] had run the batteries at Port Hudson with the flagship *Hartford* and one iron-clad and visited me from below Vicksburg.[14] The 13th of February Admiral Porter had sent the gunboat *Indianola*, Lieutenant-Commander George Brown[15] commanding, below. She met Colonel Ellet

[12] Porter's Apr. 19, 1863, report listed twelve wounded. *ORN,* I, 24, 554.

[13] David G. Farragut (1801–1870) was born in Tennessee and moved to Louisiana in 1807. He was the foster brother of David Dixon Porter. At the age of nine, he joined the U.S. Navy as a midshipman. In July 1862, he was promoted to rear admiral after being wounded near Vicksburg the previous month. *CWHC,* 231–232.

[14] In mid-Mar. 1863, Farragut had led a flotilla from New Orleans up the Mississippi River. Although Confederate fire had disabled three of his vessels at Port Hudson, two more made it upriver to Warrenton. This had effectively shut off Confederate supply from the Red River and allowed Union troops to be transported between Vicksburg, Port Hudson, and Grand Gulf. Michael B. Ballard, *Vicksburg: The Campaign That Opened the Mississippi* (Chapel Hill: University of North Carolina Press, 2004), 188.

[15] George W. Brown (1835–c.1913) was born in Indiana and joined the U.S. Navy in 1849 at the rank of midshipman. He was promoted to rear admiral in 1893. D. C. Gilman, H. T. Peck, and F. M. Colby, eds., *New International Encyclopedia* (New York: Dodd, Mead, 1905), s.v. "Brown, George."

of the Marine brigade[16] below Natchez on a captured steamer. Two of the Colonel's fleet had previously run the batteries, producing the greatest consternation among the people along the Mississippi from Vicksburg* to the Red River.

The *Indianola* remained about the mouth of the Red River some days, and then started up the Mississippi. The Confederates soon raised the *Queen of the West*,[†] and repaired her. With this vessel and the ram *Webb*, which they had had for some time in the Red River, and two other steamers, they followed the *Indianola*. The latter was encumbered with barges of coal in tow, and consequently could make but little speed against the rapid current of the Mississippi. The Confederate fleet overtook her just above Grand Gulf, and attacked her after dark on the 24th of February. The *Indianola* was superior to all the others in armament, and probably would have destroyed them or driven them away, but for her encumbrance. As it was she fought them for an hour and a half, but, in the dark, was struck seven or eight times by the ram

---

*Colonel Ellet reported having attacked a Confederate battery on the Red River two days before with one of his boats, the De Soto. Running aground, he was obliged to abandon his vessel. However, he reported that he set fire to her and blew her up. Twenty of his men fell into the hands of the enemy. With the balance he escaped on the small captured steamer, the New Era, and succeeded in passing the batteries at Grand Gulf and reaching the vicinity of Vicksburg.[17]

†One of Colonel Ellet's vessels which had run the blockade on February the 2d and been sunk in the Red River.[18]

---

[16] In order to combat Confederate guerillas along waterways, the War Dept. organized a group of soldiers and boats known as the Marine Brigade. Several members of the Ellet family served in the brigade, including Charles R. Ellet (1841–1863), who was born in Pennsylvania. He was an assistant surgeon in a military hospital at the start of the Civil War and served in the Marine Brigade until his death from an unspecified illness in 1863. Francis S. Drake, ed., *Dictionary of American Biography, Including Men of the Time* . . . (Boston: Houghton, Osgood, 1879), 301; Porter, *Naval History of the Civil War*, 333.

[17] On Feb. 14, 1863, Ellet attempted to attack a Confederate battery near Gordon's Landing, LA, on the Red River. In this encounter, Ellet was forced to abandon *Queen of the West* when the pilot intentionally ran the vessel aground. Ellet scuttled and set fire to *De Soto* after she lost her rudder, making his escape from the area aboard the captured vessel *Era No. 5. ORN*, I, 24, 384–385.

[18] *Queen of the West* had been captured by Confederate forces on Feb. 14, 1863. Ibid., I, 24, 385.

and other vessels, and was finally disabled and reduced to a sinking condition. The armament was thrown overboard and the vessel run ashore. Officers and crew then surrendered.[19]

I had started McClernand with his corps of four divisions on the 29th of March, by way of Richmond, Louisiana, to New Carthage,[20] hoping that he might capture Grand Gulf before the balance of the troops could get there; but the roads were very bad, scarcely above water yet. Some miles from New Carthage the levee to Bayou Vidal was broken in several places, overflowing the roads for the distance of two miles. Boats were collected from the surrounding bayous, and some constructed on the spot from such material as could be collected, to transport the troops across the overflowed interval. By the 6th of April McClernand had reached New Carthage with one division and its artillery, the latter ferried through the woods by these boats. On the 17th I visited New Carthage in person, and saw that the process of getting troops through in the way we were doing was so tedious that a better method must be devised. The water was falling, and in a few days there would not be depth enough to use boats; nor would the land be dry enough to march over. McClernand had already found a new route from Smith's plantation[21] where the crevasse occurred, to Perkins' plantation,[22] eight to twelve miles below New Carthage. This increased the march from Milliken's Bend from twenty-seven to nearly forty miles.[23] Four bridges had to be built across bayous, two of them each over six hundred feet long, making about two thousand feet of bridging in all. The river falling made the current in these bayous very rapid, increasing the difficulty of building and permanently fastening these bridges; but the ingenuity of the "Yankee soldier" was equal to any emergency. The bridges were soon built of such material as could be found near by, and so

[19] The Confederates captured *Indianola* on Feb. 24, 1863, and destroyed the vessel two nights later when they sighted a dummy gunboat that U.S. forces had floated down the river. *PUSG*, 7:355n.

[20] New Carthage, LA, was approximately twenty miles downriver from Vicksburg. Ibid., 7:269n.

[21] Smith's plantation was approximately two miles from New Carthage. Ibid., 8:20n, 57n.

[22] Somerset, the plantation owned by Confederate senator John Perkins, was about six miles south of New Carthage. Edwin Cole Bearss, *Grant Strikes a Blow*, vol. 2 of *The Campaign for Vicksburg* (Dayton, OH: Morningside House, 1985), 291 and n; *PUSG*, 8:97n.

[23] USG's July 6, 1863, report indicated the route's distance was thirty-five miles. *PUSG*, 8:511n.

substantial were they that not a single mishap occurred in crossing all the army with artillery, cavalry and wagon trains, except the loss of one siege gun (a thirty-two pounder). This, if my memory serves me correctly, broke through the only pontoon bridge we had in all our march across the peninsula. These bridges were built by McClernand's command, under the supervision of Lieutenant Hains[24] of the Engineer Corps.[25]

I returned to Milliken's Bend on the 18th or 19th,[26] and on the 20th issued the following final order for the movement of troops:

> HEADQUARTERS DEPARTMENT OF THE TENNESSEE,
> MILLIKEN'S BEND, LOUISIANA,
> *April* 20, 1863.

Special Orders, No. 110.

     \*      \*      \*      \*      \*      \*      \*

VIII. The following orders are published for the information and guidance of the "Army in the Field," in its present movement to obtain a foothold on the east bank of the Mississippi River, from which Vicksburg can be approached by practicable roads.

*First.*—The Thirteenth army corps, Major-General John A. McClernand commanding, will constitute the right wing.

*Second.*—The Fifteenth army corps, Major-General W. T. Sherman commanding, will constitute the left wing.

*Third.*—The Seventeenth army corps, Major-General James B. McPherson commanding, will constitute the centre.

*Fourth.*—The order of march to New Carthage will be from right to left.

*Fifth.*—Reserves will be formed by divisions from each army corps; or, an entire army corps will be held as a reserve, as necessity

---

[24] Peter C. Hains (1840–1921) was born in Pennsylvania and graduated from the USMA in 1861. He entered the Corps of Topographical Engineers in July 1862. During the Vicksburg campaign, Hains was the chief engineer of the 13th Army Corps. William H. Powell and Edward Shippen, eds., *Officers of the Army and the Navy Who Served in the Civil War* (Philadelphia: L. R. Hamersly, 1892), s.v. "Lieutenant-Colonel Peter C. Hains, U.S.A."

[25] On Apr. 18, 1863, USG informed McClernand that he was sending him a pontoon train for the purpose of building bridges across the levee crevasse near New Carthage. Work on the bridges was completed by Apr. 26. Bearss, *Grant Strikes a Blow*, 275; *PUSG*, 8:88.

[26] USG returned to Milliken's Bend on the night of Apr. 18, 1863. *PUSG*, 8:90.

may require. When the reserve is formed by divisions, each division will remain under the immediate command of its respective corps commander, unless otherwise specially ordered for a particular emergency.

*Sixth.*—Troops will be required to bivouac, until proper facilities can be afforded for the transportation of camp equipage.

*Seventh.*—In the present movement, one tent will be allowed to each company for the protection of rations from rain; one wall tent for each regimental headquarters; one wall tent for each brigade headquarters; and one wall tent for each division headquarters; corps commanders having the books and blanks of their respective commands to provide for, are authorized to take such tents as are absolutely necessary, but not to exceed the number allowed by General Orders No. 160, A. G. O., series of 1862.[27]

*Eighth.*—All the teams of the three army corps, under the immediate charge of the quartermasters bearing them on their returns, will constitute a train for carrying supplies and ordnance and the authorized camp equipage of the army.

*Ninth.*—As fast as the Thirteenth army corps advances, the Seventeenth army corps will take its place; and it, in turn, will be followed in like manner by the Fifteenth army corps.

*Tenth.*—Two regiments from each army corps will be detailed by corps commanders, to guard the lines from Richmond to New Carthage.

*Eleventh.*—General hospitals will be established by the medical director, between Duckport[28] and Milliken's Bend. All sick and disabled soldiers will be left in these hospitals. Surgeons in charge of hospitals will report convalescents as fast as they become fit for duty. Each corps commander will detail an intelligent and good drill officer, to remain behind and take charge of the convalescents of their respective

[27] On Oct. 18, 1862, AG Lorenzo Thomas had issued Gen. Orders No. 160, establishing regulations for army trains and baggage. Thomas M. O'Brien and Oliver Diefendorf, eds., *General Orders of the War Department, Embracing the Years 1861, 1862 and 1863* (New York: Derby and Miller, 1864), 1:409.

[28] Duckport, LA, was approximately ten miles east of Tallulah, LA, on the Mississippi River. Alcée Fortier, ed., *Louisiana: Comprising Sketches of Parishes, Towns, Events, Institutions, and Persons, Arranged in Cyclopedic Form* (Madison, WI: Century Historical Association, 1914), s.v. "Duck Port."

corps; officers so detailed will organize the men under their charge into squads and companies, without regard to the regiments they belong to; and in the absence of convalescent commissioned officers to command them, will appoint non-commissioned officers or privates. The force so organized will constitute the guard of the line from Duckport to Milliken's Bend. They will furnish all the guards and details required for general hospitals, and with the contrabands that may be about the camps, will furnish all the details for loading and unloading boats.

*Twelfth.*—The movement of troops from Milliken's Bend to New Carthage will be so conducted as to allow the transportation of ten days' supply of rations, and one-half the allowance of ordnance, required by previous orders.

*Thirteenth.*—Commanders are authorized and enjoined to collect all the beef cattle, corn and other necessary supplies on the line of march; but wanton destruction of property, taking of articles useless for military purposes, insulting citizens, going into and searching houses without proper orders from division commanders, are positively prohibited. All such irregularities must be summarily punished.

*Fourteenth.*—Brigadier-General J. C. Sullivan[29] is appointed to the command of all the forces detailed for the protection of the line from here to New Carthage. His particular attention is called to General Orders, No. 69, from Adjutant-General's Office, Washington, of date March 20, 1863.[30]

By order of<br>Major-General U. S. Grant.[31]

McClernand was already below on the Mississippi. Two of McPherson's divisions were put upon the march immediately. The third had not yet arrived

---

[29] Jeremiah C. Sullivan (1830–1890) was born in Indiana and served in the U.S. Navy from 1848 to 1854. He entered the U.S. Army in 1861 as a captain in the 6th Indiana Inf. and was promoted to brigadier general in Apr. 1862. *CWHC*, 518.

[30] Gen. Orders No. 69 outlined the procedures for organizing "Invalid Detachments" for limited duty until those wounded or otherwise disabled were fit for field duty again. O'Brien and Diefendorf, *General Orders of the War Department*, 2:68; *PUSG*, 8:99n.

[31] *PUSG*, 8:98n–99n.

from Lake Providence; it was on its way to Milliken's Bend and was to follow on arrival.[32]

Sherman was to follow McPherson. Two of his divisions were at Duckport and Young's Point, and the third under Steele[33] was under orders to return from Greenville, Mississippi, where it had been sent to expel a rebel battery that had been annoying our transports.[34]

It had now become evident that the army could not be rationed by a wagon train over the single narrow and almost impassable road between Milliken's Bend and Perkins' plantation. Accordingly six more steamers were protected as before, to run the batteries, and were loaded with supplies.[35] They took twelve barges in tow, loaded also with rations. On the night of the 22d of April they ran the batteries, five getting through more or less disabled while one was sunk.[36] About half the barges got through with their needed freight.

When it was first proposed to run the blockade at Vicksburg with river steamers there were but two captains or masters who were willing to accompany their vessels, and but one crew. Volunteers were called for from the army, men who had had experience in any capacity in navigating the western rivers. Captains, pilots, mates, engineers and deck-hands enough presented themselves to take five times the number of vessels we were moving through this dangerous ordeal. Most of them were from Logan's division, composed generally of men from the southern part of Illinois and from Missouri. All but two of the steamers were commanded by volunteers from the army, and all but one

---

[32] Portions of Quinby's division (commanded by Col. John B. Sanborn due to Quinby's illness) had arrived via transport at Milliken's Bend on Apr. 15, 1863. Logan's division had arrived via transport on Apr. 18. Most of McArthur's division began moving from Lake Providence to Milliken's Bend on Apr. 21. Bearss, *Grant Strikes a Blow*, 271–272, 297.

[33] Frederick Steele (1819–1868) was born in New York and graduated from the USMA in 1843. In Nov. 1862, he was promoted to major general. He commanded the 1st Div., 15th Corps, Army of the Tennessee, from Jan. to July 1863. *CWHC*, 507–508.

[34] On Mar. 31, 1863, Sherman had ordered Steele to conduct an expedition to Greenville, MS, and the area around Deer Creek in response to Confederate attacks on U.S. boats in the vicinity. On Apr. 22, Steele was ordered to return to Young's Point, LA. *OR*, I, 24(III), 158, 221.

[35] The six boats were *Tigress, Empire City, Moderator, J. W. Cheeseman, Anglo-Saxon,* and *Horizon*. Ibid., I, 24(I), 567.

[36] On Apr. 23, 1863, USG reported to Halleck that *Tigress* had been sunk. *PUSG*, 8:111.

so manned.[37] In this instance, as in all others during the war, I found that volunteers could be found in the ranks and among the commissioned officers to meet every call for aid whether mechanical or professional. Colonel W. S. Oliver[38] was master of transportation on this occasion by special detail.

[37] The following officers commanded steamboats on the night of Apr. 22, 1863: Lt. Col. William S. Oliver *(Tigress)*, Capt. Monroe Harrison *(J. W. Cheeseman)*, Capt. Leander B. Fisk *(Anglo-Saxon)*, Capt. George W. Kennard *(Horizon)*, and Col. Clark B. Lagow, aide-de-camp to USG, commanded the fleet. The civilian captains of *Empire City* and *Moderator* are not named in the *OR*. Bearss, *Grant Strikes a Blow*, 76n; *OR*, I, 24(I), 564–569.

[38] William S. Oliver (1836–1896) was born in Alabama and was living in St. Louis at the outbreak of the Civil War. He was a lieutenant colonel in the 7th Missouri Inf. during the Vicksburg campaign. *OR*, I, 24(I), 567; *Report of the Proceedings of the Society of the Army of the Tennessee at the Twenty-Eighth Meeting, Held at St. Louis, MO., November 18–19, 1896* (Cincinnati: F. W. Freeman, 1897), 211.

# 33

## Attack on Grand Gulf—Operations below Vicksburg

O<small>N THE 24TH</small> my headquarters were with the advance at Perkins' plantation.[1] Reconnoissances were made in boats to ascertain whether there was high land on the east shore of the river where we might land above Grand Gulf. There was none practicable. Accordingly the troops were set in motion for Hard Times,[2] twenty-two miles farther down the river and nearly opposite Grand Gulf. The loss of two steamers and six barges reduced our transportation so that only 10,000 men could be moved by water. Some of the steamers that had got below were injured in their machinery, so that they were only useful as barges towed by those less severely injured. All the troops, therefore, except what could be transported in one trip, had to march. The road lay west of Lake St. Joseph.[3] Three large bayous had to be crossed.[4] They were rapidly bridged in the same manner as those previously encountered.*

*N<small>OTE</small>.—On this occasion Governor Richard Yates, of Illinois, happened to be on a visit to the army, and accompanied me to Carthage.[5] I furnished an ambulance for his use and that of some of the State officers who accompanied him.

[1] On Apr. 24, 1863, USG's headquarters were at Smith's plantation. *PUSG,* 8:117.

[2] The Hard Times plantation was located three miles above Grand Gulf, MS, on the Louisiana side of the Mississippi River. Ibid., 8:128*n*.

[3] Col. James Keigwin of the 49th Indiana Inf. called this road simply "the Lake Saint Joseph road" in his May 30, 1863, report. *OR,* I, 24(I), 571.

[4] On the march that began on Apr. 25, 1863, U.S. Army troops had to cross Holt, Durossette, and Phelps Bayous. Ibid.

[5] On Apr. 26, 1863, Yates attended a review of Illinois troops under the command of McClernand at New Carthage, LA. Richard L. Kiper, *Major General John Alexander McClernand: Politician in Uniform* (Kent, OH: Kent State University Press, 1999), 216.

On the 27th McClernand's corps was all at Hard Times, and McPherson's was following closely.[6] I had determined to make the attempt to effect a landing on the east side of the river as soon as possible. Accordingly, on the morning of the 29th, McClernand was directed to embark all the troops from his corps that our transports and barges could carry. About 10,000 men were so embarked.[7] The plan was to have the navy silence the guns at Grand Gulf, and to have as many men as possible ready to debark in the shortest possible time under cover of the fire of the navy and carry the works by storm. The following order was issued:

PERKINS' PLANTATION, LA.,
*April* 27, 1863.

MAJOR-GENERAL J. A. McCLERNAND,
Commanding 13th A. C.

Commence immediately the embarkation of your corps, or so much of it as there is transportation for. Have put aboard the artillery and every article authorized in orders limiting baggage, except the men, and hold them in readiness, with their places assigned, to be moved at a moment's warning.

All the troops you may have, except those ordered to remain behind, send to a point nearly opposite Grand Gulf, where you see, by special orders of this date, General McPherson is ordered to send one division.

The plan of the attack will be for the navy to attack and silence all the batteries commanding the river. Your corps will be on the river, ready to run to and debark on the nearest eligible land below the promontory first brought to view passing down the river. Once on shore, have each commander instructed beforehand to form his men the best the ground will admit of, and take possession of the most commanding points, but avoid separating your command so that it cannot support itself. The first object is to get a foothold where our troops can maintain themselves until such time as preparations can be made and troops collected for a forward movement.

---

[6] McClernand's corps arrived at the Hard Times plantation on Apr. 28, 1863. *OR*, I, 24(I), 142.

[7] On Apr. 29, 1863, McClernand's 9th, 10th, and 12th Divs. were aboard transports near Grand Gulf. Ibid.

Admiral Porter has proposed to place his boats in the position indicated to you a few days ago, and to bring over with them such troops as may be below the city after the guns of the enemy are silenced.

It may be that the enemy will occupy positions back from the city, out of range of the gunboats, so as to make it desirable to run past Grand Gulf and land at Rodney.[8] In case this should prove the plan, a signal will be arranged and you duly informed, when the transports are to start with this view. Or, it may be expedient for the boats to run past, but not the men. In this case, then, the transports would have to be brought back to where the men could land and move by forced marches to below Grand Gulf, re-embark rapidly and proceed to the latter place. There will be required, then, three signals; one, to indicate that the transports can run down and debark the troops at Grand Gulf; one, that the transports can run by without the troops; and the last, that the transports can run by with the troops on board.

Should the men have to march, all baggage and artillery will be left to run the blockade.

If not already directed, require your men to keep three days' rations in their haversacks, not to be touched until a movement commences.

U. S. GRANT,
Major-General.

At 8 o'clock A.M., 29th, Porter made the attack with his entire strength present, eight gunboats.[9] For nearly five and a half hours the attack was kept up without silencing a single gun of the enemy. All this time McClernand's 10,000 men were huddled together on the transports in the stream ready to attempt a landing if signalled. I occupied a tug from which I could see the effect of the battle on both sides, within range of the enemy's guns; but a small tug, without armament, was not calculated to attract the fire of batteries while they were being assailed themselves. About half-past one the fleet withdrew, seeing their efforts were entirely unavailing. The enemy ceased firing as soon

[8] Rodney, MS, was an established village by 1834. After the Civil War, the town became landlocked after the Mississippi River began to shift westward and was nearly deserted by 1935. Marion Bragg, *Historic Names and Places on the Lower Mississippi River* (Vicksburg: Mississippi River Commission, 1977), 178–179.

[9] The gunboats used by Porter were *Pittsburg, Louisville, Mound City, Carondelet, Tuscumbia, Benton, Lafayette,* and *General Price.* David D. Porter, *The Naval History of the Civil War* (New York: Sherman, 1886), 313–314.

as we withdrew. I immediately signalled the Admiral and went aboard his ship. The navy lost in this engagement eighteen killed and fifty-six wounded.[10] A large proportion of these were of the crew of the flagship,[11] and most of those from a single shell which penetrated the ship's side and exploded between decks where the men were working their guns. The sight of the mangled and dying men which met my eye as I boarded the ship was sickening.

Grand Gulf is on a high bluff where the river runs at the very foot of it. It is as defensible upon its front as Vicksburg and, at that time, would have been just as impossible to capture by a front attack. I therefore requested Porter to run the batteries with his fleet that night, and to take charge of the transports, all of which would be wanted below.

There is a long tongue of land from the Louisiana side extending towards Grand Gulf, made by the river running nearly east from about three miles above and nearly in the opposite direction from that point for about the same distance below. The land was so low and wet that it would not have been practicable to march an army across but for a levee. I had had this explored before, as well as the east bank below to ascertain if there was a possible point of debarkation north of Rodney. It was found that the top of the levee afforded a good road to march upon.

Porter, as was always the case with him, not only acquiesced in the plan, but volunteered to use his entire fleet as transports. I had intended to make this request, but he anticipated me. At dusk, when concealed from the view of the enemy at Grand Gulf, McClernand landed his command on the west bank. The navy and transports ran the batteries successfully. The troops marched across the point of land under cover of night, unobserved. By the time it was light the enemy saw our whole fleet, iron-clads, gunboats, river steamers and barges, quietly moving down the river three miles below them, black, or rather blue, with National troops.

When the troops debarked, the evening of the 29th, it was expected that we would have to go to Rodney, about nine miles below, to find a landing; but that night a colored man came in who informed me that a good landing would be found at Bruinsburg,[12] a few miles above Rodney, from which point

[10] Porter's Apr. 29, 1863, report indicated twenty-four killed and fifty-six wounded. *ORN,* I, 24, 610.

[11] Porter's flagship was *Benton.* Ibid.

[12] Bruinsburg, MS, named for the Bruin family of Virginia, was established in 1788. It was located at Bayou Pierre, a tributary of the Mississippi River. Bragg, *Historic Names and Places,* 176–177.

there was a good road leading to Port Gibson some twelve miles in the interior. The information was found correct, and our landing was effected without opposition.[13]

Sherman had not left his position above Vicksburg yet. On the morning of the 27th I ordered him to create a diversion by moving his corps up the Yazoo and threatening an attack on Haines' Bluff.[14]

My object was to compel Pemberton to keep as much force about Vicksburg as I could, until I could secure a good footing on high land east of the river. The move was eminently successful and, as we afterwards learned, created great confusion about Vicksburg and doubts about our real design.[15] Sherman moved the day of our attack on Grand Gulf, the 29th, with ten regiments of his command and eight gunboats which Porter had left above Vicksburg.

He debarked his troops and apparently made every preparation to attack the enemy while the navy bombarded the main forts at Haines' Bluff. This move was made without a single casualty in either branch of the service. On the first of May Sherman received orders from me (sent from Hard Times the evening of the 29th of April) to withdraw from the front of Haines' Bluff and follow McPherson with two divisions as fast as he could.

I had established a depot of supplies at Perkins' plantation. Now that all our gunboats were below Grand Gulf it was possible that the enemy might fit out boats in the Big Black[16] with improvised armament and attempt to destroy these supplies. McPherson was at Hard Times with a portion of his corps, and the depot was protected by a part of his command. The night of the 29th I directed him to arm one of the transports with artillery and send it up to

[13] The troops landed on the morning of Apr. 30, 1863. *PUSG,* 8:512*n.*

[14] USG suggested the demonstration to Sherman, but allowed him to make the final determination as to the course of action. Sherman, in spite of concerns about how a demonstration would be perceived by the troops and the press, followed through with the maneuver. Ibid., 8:130 and *n,* 131*n.*

[15] On Apr. 28, 1863, Gen. Carter L. Stevenson, who was in command of the Confederate forces near Haines' Bluff, MS, suggested to Pemberton that the U.S. forces opposite Grand Gulf were being used as a feint to open an attack upon Vicksburg. As a result, Pemberton did not order Stevenson to send reinforcements to Grand Gulf until the afternoon of Apr. 29. Edwin Cole Bearss, *Grant Strikes a Blow,* vol. 2 of *The Campaign for Vicksburg* (Dayton, OH: Morningside House, 1985), 259; *OR,* I, 24(III), 800.

[16] Big Black River, MS. George B. Davis et al., *The Official Military Atlas of the Civil War* (New York: Fairfax Press, 1983), plate 155.

Perkins' plantation as a guard; and also to have the siege guns we had brought along moved there and put in position.[17]

The embarkation below Grand Gulf took place at De Shroon's,[18] Louisiana, six miles above Bruinsburg, Mississippi. Early on the morning of 30th of April McClernand's corps and one division of McPherson's corps were speedily landed.[19]

When this was effected I felt a degree of relief scarcely ever equalled since. Vicksburg was not yet taken it is true, nor were its defenders demoralized by any of our previous moves. I was now in the enemy's country, with a vast river and the stronghold of Vicksburg between me and my base of supplies. But I was on dry ground on the same side of the river with the enemy. All the campaigns, labors, hardships and exposures from the month of December previous to this time that had been made and endured, were for the accomplishment of this one object.

I had with me the 13th corps, General McClernand commanding, and two brigades of Logan's division of the 17th corps, General McPherson commanding—in all not more than twenty thousand men to commence the campaign with. These were soon reinforced by the remaining brigade of Logan's division and Crocker's division of the 17th corps. On the 7th of May I was further reinforced by Sherman with two divisions of his, the 15th corps. My total force was then about thirty-three thousand men.[20]

The enemy occupied Grand Gulf, Haines' Bluff and Jackson with a force of nearly sixty thousand men.[21] Jackson is fifty miles east of Vicksburg and is connected with it by a railroad. My first problem was to capture Grand Gulf to use as a base.

Bruinsburg is two miles from high ground. The bottom at that point is higher than most of the low land in the valley of the Mississippi, and a good road leads to the bluff. It was natural to expect the garrison from Grand Gulf to come out to meet us and prevent, if they could, our reaching this solid base.

[17] USG identified *Empire City* as the transport to be used as an improvised gunboat. *PUSG,* 8:134.

[18] This plantation's name was also spelled D'Schron or Disharoon in documents from the era. *ORN,* I, 24, 699.

[19] Approximately 22,000 U.S. Army troops crossed the Mississippi River on Apr. 30, 1863. Bearss, *Grant Strikes a Blow,* 346.

[20] For the number of troops in the individual corps and divisions as of Apr. 30, 1863, see *OR,* I, 24(III), 249.

[21] Pemberton had a total of 61,495 men on Mar. 31, 1863. Ibid., I, 24(III), 702.

Bayou Pierre enters the Mississippi just above Bruinsburg and, as it is a navigable stream and was high at the time, in order to intercept us they had to go by Port Gibson, the nearest point where there was a bridge to cross upon. This more than doubled the distance from Grand Gulf to the high land back of Bruinsburg. No time was to be lost in securing this foothold. Our transportation was not sufficient to move all the army across the river at one trip, or even two; but the landing of the 13th corps and one division of the 17th was effected during the day, April 30th, and early evening. McClernand was advanced as soon as ammunition and two days' rations (to last five) could be issued to his men. The bluffs were reached an hour before sunset and McClernand was pushed on, hoping to reach Port Gibson and save the bridge spanning the Bayou Pierre before the enemy could get there; for crossing a stream in the presence of an enemy is always difficult. Port Gibson, too, is the starting point of roads to Grand Gulf, Vicksburg and Jackson.

McClernand's advance met the enemy about five miles west of Port Gibson at Thompson's plantation.[22] There was some firing during the night, but nothing rising to the dignity of a battle until daylight. The enemy had taken a strong natural position with most of the Grand Gulf garrison, numbering about seven or eight thousand men, under General Bowen.[23] His hope was to hold me in check until reinforcements under Loring could reach him from Vicksburg; but Loring did not come in time to render much assistance south of Port Gibson.[24] Two brigades of McPherson's corps followed McClernand

[22] On May 1, 1863, U.S. forces encountered Confederate troops near the plantation owned by A. K. Shaifer. Although most commonly called the Battle of Port Gibson, the engagement that followed was also known as the Battle of Thompson's Hill. H. G. Hawkins, "History of Port Gibson, Mississippi," *Publications of the Mississippi Historical Society* 10 (1909): 291–292; *The Union Army: Cyclopedia of Battles* (Madison, WI: Federal Publishing, 1908), s.v. "Port Gibson, Miss."; *OR,* I, 24(I), 143.

[23] John S. Bowen (1830–1863) was born in Georgia and graduated from the USMA in 1853. He moved to Missouri in 1857 and joined the Missouri State Guard in 1861. He became a colonel in the Confederate Army in June and was promoted to brigadier general in Mar. 1862. Bowen died of dysentery. *CWHC,* 138.

[24] William W. Loring (1818–1886) was born in North Carolina and later moved to Florida. He fought in the Mexican-American War, in which he lost his left arm during the Battle of Chapultepec in Sept. 1847. He joined the Confederate Army as a colonel in Mar. 1861 but did not officially resign from the U.S. Army until May. By 1862, Loring had risen to the rank of major general. During the fighting around Port Gibson, he did not arrive at Bowen's headquarters until late evening of May 2, 1863. Loring served in the Egyptian Army 1869–1879, rising to major general. Ibid., 353–354; *OR,* I, 24(I), 666.

as fast as rations and ammunition could be issued, and were ready to take position upon the battle-field whenever the 13th corps could be got out of the way.

The country in this part of Mississippi stands on edge, as it were, the roads running along the ridges except when they occasionally pass from one ridge to another. Where there are no clearings the sides of the hills are covered with a very heavy growth of timber and with undergrowth, and the ravines are filled with vines and canebrakes, almost impenetrable. This makes it easy for an inferior force to delay, if not defeat, a far superior one.

Near the point selected by Bowen to defend, the road to Port Gibson divides, taking two ridges which do not diverge more than a mile or two at the widest point. These roads unite just outside the town. This made it necessary for McClernand to divide his force. It was not only divided, but it was separated by a deep ravine of the character above described. One flank could not reinforce the other except by marching back to the junction of the roads. McClernand put the divisions of Hovey, Carr[25] and A. J. Smith[26] upon the right-hand branch and Osterhaus[27] on the left. I was on the field by ten A.M., and inspected both flanks in person. On the right the enemy, if not being pressed back, was at least not repulsing our advance. On the left, however, Osterhaus was not faring so well. He had been repulsed with some loss. As soon as the road could be cleared of McClernand's troops I ordered up McPherson, who was close upon the rear of the 13th corps, with two brigades of Logan's division. This was about noon. I ordered him to send one brigade (General John E. Smith's was selected) to support Osterhaus, and to move to the left and flank the enemy out of his position. This movement carried the

[25] Eugene A. Carr (1830–1910) was born in New York and graduated from the USMA in 1850. He was stationed at Fort Washita, Indian Territory, in Jan. 1861 and was promoted to brigadier general in Mar. 1862. For his service during the Battle of Pea Ridge on Mar. 7, 1862, Carr was awarded the Medal of Honor on Jan. 16, 1894. *CWHC,* 164.

[26] Andrew J. Smith (1815–1897) was born in Pennsylvania and graduated from the USMA in 1838. At the start of the Civil War, he was stationed at Fort Walla-Walla, Washington Territory. He was promoted to brigadier general in Mar. 1862. During the Vicksburg campaign, he commanded the 1st Div., 13th Corps. Smith served as postmaster of St. Louis during USG's presidency (1869–1877). Ibid., 492–493.

[27] Peter J. Osterhaus (1823–1917) was born in Prussia, graduated from the Berlin Military Academy, and served in the Prussian Army. In 1849, he immigrated to Illinois, where he served as a bookkeeper and clerk. He moved to Missouri in 1851 and became a major in the 2nd Missouri Inf. in Apr. 1861. He was promoted to brigadier general in June 1862. Osterhaus served as the U.S. consul in Lyons, France, from 1866 to 1877. Ibid., 411.

brigade over a deep ravine to a third ridge and, when Smith's troops were seen well through the ravine, Osterhaus was directed to renew his front attack. It was successful and unattended by heavy loss.[28] The enemy was sent in full retreat on their right, and their left followed before sunset. While the movement to our left was going on, McClernand, who was with his right flank, sent me frequent requests for reinforcements, although the force with him was not being pressed.[29] I had been upon the ground and knew it did not admit of his engaging all the men he had. We followed up our victory until night overtook us about two miles from Port Gibson; then the troops went into bivouac for the night.

---

[28] While casualty reports vary, Confederate forces lost approximately 60 killed, 340 wounded, and 387 missing. U.S. forces lost approximately 131 killed, 719 wounded, and 25 missing. *PUSG*, 8:139*n*.

[29] USG referred to his order regarding John E. Smith and McClernand's messages in his report on the Battle of Port Gibson, but the specific texts of those communications have not survived. Ibid., 8:513*n*.

# 34

## Capture of Port Gibson—Grierson's Raid—
## Occupation of Grand Gulf—Movement up the
## Big Black—Battle of Raymond

W E STARTED NEXT morning for Port Gibson as soon as it was light
enough to see the road. We were soon in the town, and I was delighted to
find that the enemy had not stopped to contest our crossing further at the
bridge, which he had burned. The troops were set to work at once to construct a bridge across the South Fork of the Bayou Pierre. At this time the
water was high and the current rapid. What might be called a raft-bridge was
soon constructed from material obtained from wooden buildings, stables,
fences, etc., which sufficed for carrying the whole army over safely. Colonel J. H. Wilson, a member of my staff, planned and superintended the
construction of this bridge, going into the water and working as hard as any
one engaged.[1] Officers and men generally joined in this work. When it was
finished the army crossed and marched eight miles beyond to the North
Fork that day. One brigade of Logan's division was sent down the stream to
occupy the attention of a rebel battery, which had been left behind with infantry supports to prevent our repairing the burnt railroad bridge. Two of
his brigades were sent up the bayou to find a crossing and reach the North
Fork to repair the bridge there. The enemy soon left when he found we were
building a bridge elsewhere. Before leaving Port Gibson we were reinforced
by Crocker's division, McPherson's corps, which had crossed the Mississippi
at Bruinsburg and come up without stopping except to get two days' rations.
McPherson still had one division west of the Mississippi River, guarding the

---

[1] On May 2, 1863, Capt. Stewart R. Tresilian, under the orders of Wilson, led the construction of a 166-foot raft bridge over the south fork of Bayou Pierre, which was completed in only
four hours. *OR,* I, 24(II), 204.

road from Milliken's Bend to the river below until Sherman's command should relieve it.

On leaving Bruinsburg for the front I left my son Frederick, who had joined me a few weeks before,[2] on board one of the gunboats asleep, and hoped to get away without him until after Grand Gulf should fall into our hands; but on waking up he learned that I had gone, and being guided by the sound of the battle raging at Thompson's Hill—called the Battle of Port Gibson—found his way to where I was.[3] He had no horse to ride at the time, and I had no facilities for even preparing a meal. He, therefore, foraged around the best he could until we reached Grand Gulf. Mr. C. A. Dana,[4] then an officer of the War Department, accompanied me on the Vicksburg campaign and through a portion of the siege. He was in the same situation as Fred so far as transportation and mess arrangements were concerned. The first time I call to mind seeing either of them, after the battle, they were mounted on two enormous horses, grown white from age, each equipped with dilapidated saddles and bridles.

Our trains arrived a few days later, after which we were all perfectly equipped.

My son accompanied me throughout the campaign and siege, and caused no anxiety either to me or to his mother, who was at home. He looked out for himself and was in every battle of the campaign. His age, then not quite thirteen, enabled him to take in all he saw, and to retain a recollection of it that would not be possible in more mature years.

When the movement from Bruinsburg commenced we were without a wagon train. The train still west of the Mississippi was carried around with proper escort, by a circuitous route from Milliken's Bend to Hard Times seventy or more miles below, and did not get up for some days after the battle of Port Gibson. My own horses, headquarters' transportation, servants, mess chest, and everything except what I had on, was with this train. General A. J. Smith happened to have an extra horse at Bruinsburg which I borrowed, with

[2] USG's oldest son, FDG, who was twelve years old at that time, joined his father on Mar. 29, 1863. *PUSG*, 7:xxiv.

[3] On the night of Apr. 30, 1863, USG left Bruinsburg, MS, for Port Gibson, MS. FDG, "With Grant at Vicksburg," *Outlook* 59 (1898): 534.

[4] Charles A. Dana (1819–1897) was born in New Hampshire and served on the editorial staff of the *New York Tribune* from 1847 to 1861. In 1863, he was appointed assistant secretary of war and served in that capacity until the end of the Civil War. *The National Cyclopaedia of American Biography,* vol. 1 (New York: James T. White, 1898), 307–309.

a saddle-tree without upholstering further than stirrups. I had no other for nearly a week.

It was necessary to have transportation for ammunition. Provisions could be taken from the country; but all the ammunition that can be carried on the person is soon exhausted when there is much fighting. I directed, therefore, immediately on landing that all the vehicles and draft animals, whether horses, mules, or oxen, in the vicinity should be collected and loaded to their capacity with ammunition. Quite a train was collected during the 30th, and a motley train it was. In it could be found fine carriages, loaded nearly to the top with boxes of cartridges that had been pitched in promiscuously, drawn by mules with plough-harness, straw collars, rope-lines, etc.; long-coupled wagons, with racks for carrying cotton bales, drawn by oxen, and everything that could be found in the way of transportation on a plantation, either for use or pleasure. The making out of provision returns was stopped for the time. No formalities were to retard our progress until a position was secured when the time could be spared to observe them.

It was at Port Gibson I first heard through a Southern paper of the complete success of Colonel Grierson,[5] who was making a raid through central Mississippi. He had started from La Grange April 17th with three regiments of about 1,700 men. On the 21st he had detached Colonel Hatch[6] with one regiment to destroy the railroad between Columbus and Macon and then return to La Grange. Hatch had a sharp fight with the enemy at Columbus and retreated along the railroad, destroying it at Okalona and Tupelo, and arriving in La Grange April 26.[7] Grierson continued his movement with about 1,000 men, breaking the Vicksburg and Meridian railroad and the New Orleans and

[5] Benjamin H. Grierson (1826–1911) was born in Pennsylvania and later moved to Illinois, where he worked as a shopkeeper. During the Civil War, he served as a volunteer aide-de-camp to Prentiss from May 1861 to Sept. 1862 and was promoted to colonel in Apr. 1862. In June 1863, he was promoted to brigadier general. *CWHC*, 268.

[6] Edward Hatch (1832–1889) was born in Maine and graduated from the Norwich Military Academy in 1852. He was commissioned a captain in the 2nd Iowa Cav. in Aug. 1861 and promoted to colonel in June 1862. *The National Cyclopaedia of American Biography*, vol. 12 (New York: James T. White, 1904), 343.

[7] Based on Hatch's report, his detachment never reached Columbus, MS, because of a shortage of ammunition. On Apr. 21, 1863, Hatch's men were attacked by Confederate forces at Palo Alto, MS. The next day, Hatch moved his men north along the Mobile and Ohio Railroad to Okolona, MS, where he forced out the Confederates and destroyed their stores and ammunition. Hatch did not mention destroying the railroad during his retreat to La Grange, TN. *OR*, I, 24(I), 529–531.

Jackson railroad, arriving at Baton Rouge May 2d. This raid was of great importance, for Grierson had attracted the attention of the enemy from the main movement against Vicksburg.

During the night of the 2d of May the bridge over the North Fork was repaired, and the troops commenced crossing at five the next morning. Before the leading brigade was over it was fired upon by the enemy from a commanding position; but they were soon driven off. It was evident that the enemy was covering a retreat from Grand Gulf to Vicksburg. Every commanding position from this (Grindstone) crossing[8] to Hankinson's ferry[9] over the Big Black was occupied by the retreating foe to delay our progress. McPherson, however, reached Hankinson's ferry before night, seized the ferry boat, and sent a detachment of his command across and several miles north on the road to Vicksburg. When the junction of the road going to Vicksburg with the road from Grand Gulf to Raymond and Jackson was reached, Logan with his division was turned to the left towards Grand Gulf. I went with him a short distance from this junction. McPherson had encountered the largest force yet met since the battle of Port Gibson and had a skirmish nearly approaching a battle; but the road Logan had taken enabled him to come up on the enemy's right flank, and they soon gave way. McPherson was ordered to hold Hankinson's ferry and the road back to Willow Springs[10] with one division; McClernand, who was now in the rear, was to join in this as well as to guard the line back down the bayou. I did not want to take the chances of having an enemy lurking in our rear.

On the way from the junction to Grand Gulf, where the road comes into the one from Vicksburg to the same place six or seven miles out, I learned that the last of the enemy had retreated past that place on their way to Vicksburg. I left Logan to make the proper disposition of his troops for the night, while I rode into the town with an escort of about twenty cavalry. Admiral Porter had already arrived with his fleet. The enemy had abandoned his heavy guns and evacuated the place.

When I reached Grand Gulf May 3d I had not been with my baggage since the 27th of April and consequently had had no change of underclothing, no meal except such as I could pick up sometimes at other headquarters, and no

[8] Grindstone Ford was about eight miles northeast of Port Gibson, MS. *PUSG*, 8:148n.

[9] Hankinson's ferry was approximately ten miles north of Grindstone Ford. George B. Davis et al., *The Official Military Atlas of the Civil War* (New York: Fairfax Press, 1983), plate 36, map 1.

[10] Willow Springs, MS, was approximately five miles north of Grindstone Ford. Ibid.

tent to cover me. The first thing I did was to get a bath, borrow some fresh underclothing from one of the naval officers and get a good meal on the flagship. Then I wrote letters to the general-in-chief informing him of our present position, dispatches to be telegraphed from Cairo, orders to General Sullivan commanding above Vicksburg, and gave orders to all my corps commanders. About twelve o'clock at night I was through my work and started for Hankinson's ferry, arriving there before daylight. While at Grand Gulf I heard from Banks,[11] who was on the Red River, and who said that he could not be at Port Hudson before the 10th of May and then with only 15,000 men.[12] Up to this time my intention had been to secure Grand Gulf, as a base of supplies, detach McClernand's corps to Banks and co-operate with him in the reduction of Port Hudson.

The news from Banks forced upon me a different plan of campaign from the one intended. To wait for his co-operation would have detained me at least a month. The reinforcements would not have reached ten thousand men after deducting casualties and necessary river guards at all high points close to the river for over three hundred miles. The enemy would have strengthened his position and been reinforced by more men than Banks could have brought. I therefore determined to move independently of Banks, cut loose from my base, destroy the rebel force in rear of Vicksburg and invest or capture the city.

Grand Gulf was accordingly given up as a base and the authorities at Washington were notified.[13] I knew well that Halleck's caution would lead him to disapprove of this course; but it was the only one that gave any chance of success. The time it would take to communicate with Washington and get a reply would be so great that I could not be interfered with until it was demonstrated whether my plan was practicable. Even Sherman, who afterwards ignored bases of supplies other than what were afforded by the country while marching through four States of the Confederacy with an army more than twice as large as mine at this time, wrote me from Hankinson's ferry, advising

[11] Nathaniel P. Banks (1816–1894) was the governor of Massachusetts from 1853 to 1861 and joined the U.S. Army as a major general in May 1861. During the Vicksburg campaign, he commanded the Dept. of the Gulf. *CWHC,* 115.

[12] On Apr. 10, 1863, Banks informed USG that he had 15,000 troops that could be sent to Port Hudson, LA, by May 10. On May 8, Banks said that his troops would not be able to make it to Port Hudson until May 25 or June 1. *PUSG,* 7:447*n*; 8:93*n*.

[13] On May 11, 1863, USG wrote to Halleck and revealed his decision to stop using Grand Gulf, MS, as a supply base. The message did not reach Washington, DC, until May 18. Ibid., 8:196 and *n*.

me of the impossibility of supplying our army over a single road. He urged me to "stop all troops till your army is partially supplied with wagons, and then act as quick as possible; for this road will be jammed, as sure as life." To this I replied: "I do not calculate upon the possibility of supplying the army with full rations from Grand Gulf. I know it will be impossible without constructing additional roads. What I do expect is to get up what rations of hard bread, coffee and salt we can, and make the country furnish the balance."[14] We started from Bruinsburg with an average of about two days' rations, and received no more from our own supplies for some days; abundance was found in the mean time. A delay would give the enemy time to reinforce and fortify.

McClernand's and McPherson's commands were kept substantially as they were on the night of the 2d, awaiting supplies sufficient to give them three days' rations in haversacks. Beef, mutton, poultry and forage were found in abundance. Quite a quantity of bacon and molasses was also secured from the country, but bread and coffee could not be obtained in quantity sufficient for all the men. Every plantation, however, had a run of stone, propelled by mule power, to grind corn for the owners and their slaves. All these were kept running while we were stopping, day and night, and when we were marching, during the night, at all plantations covered by the troops. But the product was taken by the troops nearest by, so that the majority of the command was destined to go without bread until a new base was established on the Yazoo above Vicksburg.

While the troops were awaiting the arrival of rations I ordered reconnoissances made by McClernand and McPherson, with the view of leading the enemy to believe that we intended to cross the Big Black and attack the city at once.[15]

On the 6th Sherman arrived at Grand Gulf and crossed his command that night and the next day. Three days' rations had been brought up from Grand Gulf for the advanced troops and were issued. Orders were given for a forward movement the next day. Sherman was directed to order up Blair, who had been left behind to guard the road from Milliken's Bend to Hard Times with two brigades.[16]

---

[14] For Sherman's May 9, 1863, letter to USG, see ibid., 8:178n–179n. For USG's May 9 reply, see ibid., 8:183–184.

[15] For USG's May 4, 1863, orders to McClernand and to McPherson, see ibid., 8:156, 158.

[16] On May 6, 1863, Sherman informed Blair of Special Orders No. 98, ordering him to guard the road from Milliken's Bend to Hard Times plantation in Louisiana. Sherman advised

The quartermaster[17] at Young's Point was ordered to send two hundred wagons with Blair, and the commissary[18] was to load them with hard bread, coffee, sugar, salt and one hundred thousand pounds of salt meat.[19]

On the 3d Hurlbut, who had been left at Memphis, was ordered to send four regiments from his command to Milliken's Bend to relieve Blair's division,[20] and on the 5th he was ordered to send Lauman's[21] division in addition, the latter to join the army in the field. The four regiments were to be taken from troops near the river so that there would be no delay.

During the night of the 6th McPherson drew in his troops north of the Big Black and was off at an early hour on the road to Jackson, viâ Rocky Springs,[22] Utica and Raymond. That night he and McClernand were both at Rocky Springs ten miles from Hankinson's ferry. McPherson remained there during the 8th, while McClernand moved to Big Sandy[23] and Sherman marched from Grand Gulf to Hankinson's ferry. The 9th, McPherson moved to a point within a few miles west of Utica; McClernand and Sherman remained where

Blair to send Gen. Jeremiah C. Sullivan, the commanding officer at Milliken's Bend, to guard the road. *OR*, I, 24(III), 273, 277.

[17] Judson Bingham (1831–1909) was born in New York and graduated from the USMA in 1854. In Jan. 1863, he was promoted to lieutenant colonel, quartermaster of the 17th Corps, Army of the Tennessee. In May, he was stationed near Milliken's Bend on the Mississippi River. *CWHC*, 131; *PUSG*, 8:166n.

[18] Robert MacFeely (1826–1901) was born in Pennsylvania and graduated from the USMA in 1850. In May 1861, he was promoted to captain in the U.S. Army Commissary of Subsistence. In 1863, he was promoted to major in the Commissary of Subsistence, Army of the Tennessee. *CWHC*, 358.

[19] On Apr. 30, 1863, Rawlins issued Special Orders No. 120, which gave USG's then aide-de-camp Hillyer command over the transportation of supplies to the army below Grand Gulf. *PUSG*, 8:137n.

[20] On May 4, 1863, Rawlins ordered Hurlbut to send four regiments to Milliken's Bend. Ibid., 8:162n.

[21] Jacob G. Lauman (1813–1867) was born in Maryland and by 1844 had settled in Iowa. He entered the U.S. Army as a colonel in the 7th Iowa Inf. in 1861 and was promoted to brigadier general in 1862. He commanded the 4th Div., 16th Corps, from Jan. to June 1863. *CWHC*, 340.

[22] Rocky Springs, MS, was two miles south of the Big Black River between Big Sandy Creek and Little Sandy Creek. *PUSG*, 8:27 (map).

[23] Big Sandy Creek (later called Big Sand Creek) connects to the Big Black River and flows near the site of the abandoned town of Rocky Springs. Edwin Cole Bearss, *Grant Strikes a Blow*, vol. 2 of *The Campaign for Vicksburg* (Dayton, OH: Morningside House, 1985), 445; *PUSG*, 8:27 (map).

they were. On the 10th McPherson moved to Utica, Sherman to Big Sandy; McClernand was still at Big Sandy. The 11th, McClernand was at Five Mile Creek; Sherman at Auburn; McPherson five miles advanced from Utica. May 12th, McClernand was at Fourteen Mile Creek; Sherman at Fourteen Mile Creek; McPherson at Raymond after a battle.

After McPherson crossed the Big Black at Hankinson's ferry Vicksburg could have been approached and besieged by the south side. It is not probable, however, that Pemberton would have permitted a close besiegement. The broken nature of the ground would have enabled him to hold a strong defensible line from the river south of the city to the Big Black, retaining possession of the railroad back to that point. It was my plan, therefore, to get to the railroad[24] east of Vicksburg, and approach from that direction. Accordingly, McPherson's troops that had crossed the Big Black were withdrawn and the movement east to Jackson commenced.

As has been stated before, the country is very much broken and the roads generally confined to the tops of the hills. The troops were moved one (sometimes two) corps at a time to reach designated points out parallel to the railroad and only from six to ten miles from it. McClernand's corps was kept with its left flank on the Big Black guarding all the crossings. Fourteen Mile Creek, a stream substantially parallel with the railroad, was reached and crossings effected by McClernand and Sherman with slight loss.[25] McPherson was to the right of Sherman, extending to Raymond. The cavalry was used in this advance in reconnoitring to find the roads: to cover our advances and to find the most practicable routes from one command to another so they could support each other in case of an attack. In making this move I estimated Pemberton's movable force at Vicksburg at about eighteen thousand men, with smaller forces at Haines' Bluff and Jackson.[26] It would not be possible for Pemberton to attack me with all his troops at one place, and I determined to throw my army between his and fight him in detail. This was

[24] USG referred to the Vicksburg and Jackson Railroad. *PUSG*, 8:27 (map).

[25] Total U.S. losses were six killed and twenty-four wounded during the crossing. *OR*, I, 24(II), 167.

[26] Pemberton commanded over 30,000 men between his forces at Haines' Bluff, in the field between Vicksburg and USG's army, and Vicksburg, but it is unclear exactly how many were in Vicksburg itself. James R. Arnold, *Grant Wins the War: Decision at Vicksburg* (New York: John Wiley and Sons, 1997), 94, 125.

done with success, but I found afterwards that I had entirely under-estimated Pemberton's strength.

Up to this point our movements had been made without serious opposition. My line was now nearly parallel with the Jackson and Vicksburg railroad and about seven miles south of it. The right was at Raymond eighteen miles from Jackson, McPherson commanding; Sherman in the centre on Fourteen Mile Creek, his advance thrown across; McClernand to the left, also on Fourteen Mile Creek, advance across, and his pickets within two miles of Edward's station,[27] where the enemy had concentrated a considerable force and where they undoubtedly expected us to attack. McClernand's left was on the Big Black. In all our moves, up to this time, the left had hugged the Big Black closely, and all the ferries had been guarded to prevent the enemy throwing a force on our rear.

McPherson encountered the enemy, five thousand strong with two batteries under General Gregg,[28] about two miles out of Raymond.[29] This was about two P.M. Logan was in advance with one of his brigades. He deployed and moved up to engage the enemy. McPherson ordered the road in rear to be cleared of wagons, and the balance of Logan's division, and Crocker's, which was still farther in rear, to come forward with all dispatch. The order was obeyed with alacrity. Logan got his division in position for assault before Crocker could get up, and attacked with vigor, carrying the enemy's position easily, sending Gregg flying from the field not to appear against our front again until we met at Jackson.

In this battle McPherson lost 66 killed, 339 wounded, and 37 missing— nearly or quite all from Logan's division. The enemy's loss was 100 killed, 305 wounded, besides 415 taken prisoners.[30]

---

[27] Edward's Station was situated on the Vicksburg and Jackson Railroad approximately twenty-five miles west of Jackson, MS. Davis et al., *Official Military Atlas of the Civil War,* plate 36, map 1.

[28] John Gregg (1828–1864) was born in Alabama and graduated from LaGrange College in 1847. In 1852, he moved to Texas where he served as a judge. In Sept. 1861, he joined the Confederate Army as a colonel, 7th Texas Inf. By the time of the Vicksburg campaign, he had been promoted to brigadier general. On Oct. 7, 1864, Gregg was killed in action near Richmond, VA. *CWHC,* 267.

[29] On May 12, 1863, McPherson engaged the Confederate troops two and one-half miles outside of Raymond, MS. *PUSG,* 8:206n–207n.

[30] Confederate losses were reported as seventy-three killed and 251 wounded. *OR,* I, 24(I), 739.

I regarded Logan and Crocker as being as competent division commanders as could be found in or out of the army and both equal to a much higher command. Crocker, however, was dying of consumption when he volunteered. His weak condition never put him on the sick report when there was a battle in prospect, as long as he could keep on his feet. He died not long after the close of the rebellion.[31]

[31] Crocker died of tuberculosis on Aug. 26, 1865, four months after the Confederate surrender. *CWHC,* 191.

# 35

## Movement against Jackson—Fall of Jackson— Intercepting the Enemy—Battle of Champion's Hill

W HEN THE NEWS reached me of McPherson's victory at Raymond about sundown my position was with Sherman. I decided at once to turn the whole column towards Jackson and capture that place without delay.[1]

Pemberton was now on my left, with, as I supposed, about 18,000 men; in fact, as I learned afterwards, with nearly 50,000.[2] A force was also collecting on my right, at Jackson, the point where all the railroads communicating with Vicksburg connect.[3] All the enemy's supplies of men and stores would come by that point. As I hoped in the end to besiege Vicksburg I must first destroy all possibility of aid.[4] I therefore determined to move swiftly towards Jackson, destroy or drive any force in that direction and then turn upon Pemberton. But by moving against Jackson, I uncovered my own communication. So I finally decided to have none—to cut loose altogether from my base and move my whole force eastward.[5] I then had no fears for my communications, and

---

[1] On May 12, 1863, USG was at Dillon's plantation and ordered his generals to redirect his forces toward Jackson, MS. Edwin Cole Bearss, *Grant Strikes a Blow*, vol. 2 of *The Campaign for Vicksburg* (Dayton, OH: Morningside House, 1985), 512; *PUSG*, 8:204–205.

[2] By the end of Mar. 1863, the Confederacy reportedly had 61,495 troops in the Dept. of Mississippi and Eastern Louisiana. *OR*, I, 24(III), 702.

[3] The Confederate forces in Jackson were under the command of Brig. Gen. John Gregg until Johnston arrived on the night of May 13, 1863. Bearss, *Grant Strikes a Blow*, 529; *OR*, I, 24(I), 239.

[4] USG's orders and messages from this time period indicate that he hoped to take Vicksburg quickly and avoid a prolonged siege. See, for example, USG's May 17, 1863, letter to Sherman. *PUSG*, 8:232–233.

[5] Although USG claimed that he abandoned his supply base here and elsewhere in this chapter, he did not completely disregard supply lines during this movement. Supplies were transported along the river and wagon trains from Grand Gulf, MS, and Milliken's Bend, LA,

if I moved quickly enough could turn upon Pemberton before he could attack me in the rear.

Accordingly, all previous orders given during the day for movements on the 13th were annulled by new ones. McPherson was ordered at daylight to move on Clinton, ten miles from Jackson; Sherman was notified of my determination to capture Jackson and work from there westward. He was ordered to start at four in the morning and march to Raymond. McClernand was ordered[6] to march with three divisions by Dillon's[7] to Raymond. One was left to guard the crossing of the Big Black.

On the 10th I had received a letter from Banks, on the Red River, asking reinforcements. Porter had gone to his assistance with a part of his fleet on the 3d, and I now wrote to him describing my position and declining to send any troops.[8] I looked upon side movements as long as the enemy held Port Hudson and Vicksburg as a waste of time and material.

General Joseph E. Johnston arrived at Jackson in the night of the 13th from Tennessee, and immediately assumed command of all the Confederate troops in Mississippi. I knew he was expecting reinforcements from the south and east. On the 6th I had written to General Halleck: "Information from the other side leaves me to believe the enemy are bringing forces from Tullahoma."

Up to this time my troops had been kept in supporting distances of each other, as far as the nature of the country would admit. Reconnoissances were constantly made from each corps to enable them to acquaint themselves with the most practicable routes from one to another in case a union became necessary.

McPherson reached Clinton with the advance early on the 13th and immediately set to work destroying the railroad. Sherman's advance reached Raymond before the last of McPherson's command had got out of the town. McClernand withdrew from the front of the enemy, at Edward's station, with much skill

followed the movement toward Jackson. Michael B. Ballard, *Vicksburg: The Campaign That Opened the Mississippi* (Chapel Hill: University of North Carolina Press, 2004), 248.

[6] For USG's May 12, 1863, instructions to McPherson, Sherman, and McClernand, see *PUSG*, 8:204–208.

[7] Dillon's plantation was approximately seven miles west of Raymond. Bearss, *Grant Strikes a Blow*, 512. McClernand ordered the 10th Div., commanded by Gen. Andrew J. Smith, to Baldwin's Ferry on the Big Black River in an attempt to prevent the enemy from crossing. *OR*, I, 24(III), 294–295.

[8] In a letter dated May 3, 1863, Banks asked USG for reinforcements. On May 10, USG denied Banks's request. *PUSG*, 8:92n, 190.

and without loss, and reached his position for the night in good order. On the night of the 13th, McPherson was ordered to march at early dawn upon Jackson, only fifteen miles away. Sherman was given the same order; but he was to move by the direct road from Raymond to Jackson, which is south of the road McPherson was on and does not approach within two miles of it at the point where it crossed the line of intrenchments which, at that time, defended the city.[9] McClernand was ordered to move one division of his command to Clinton, one division a few miles beyond Mississippi Springs[10] following Sherman's line, and a third to Raymond. He was also directed to send his siege guns, four in number with the troops going by Mississippi Springs. McClernand's position was an advantageous one in any event. With one division at Clinton he was in position to reinforce McPherson, at Jackson, rapidly if it became necessary; the division beyond Mississippi Springs was equally available to reinforce Sherman; the one at Raymond could take either road. He still had two other divisions farther back now that Blair had come up, available within a day at Jackson. If this last command should not be wanted at Jackson, they were already one day's march from there on their way to Vicksburg and on three different roads leading to the latter city. But the most important consideration in my mind was to have a force confronting Pemberton if he should come out to attack my rear. This I expected him to do; as shown further on, he was directed by Johnston to make this very move.[11]

I notified General Halleck that I should attack the State capital on the 14th. A courier carried the dispatch to Grand Gulf through an unprotected country.

Sherman and McPherson communicated with each other during the night and arranged to reach Jackson at about the same hour. It rained in torrents during the night of the 13th and the fore part of the day of the 14th. The roads were intolerable, and in some places on Sherman's line, where the land was low,

---

[9] The "direct road from Raymond to Jackson" that Sherman moved along was known simply as the Raymond Road. McPherson took the Clinton Road. Timothy B. Smith, *Champion Hill: Decisive Battle for Vicksburg* (New York: Savas Beatie, 2006), 94; George B. Davis et al., *The Official Military Atlas of the Civil War* (New York: Fairfax Press, 1983), plate 37, map 2; *PUSG*, 8:210–211.

[10] Mississippi Springs, formerly known as Bankston's, was located approximately ten miles west of Jackson. Davis et al., *Official Military Atlas of the Civil War*, plate 36, map 1; B. L. C. Wailes, *Report on the Agriculture and Geology of Mississippi: Embracing a Sketch of the Social and Natural History of the State* (Jackson, MS: E. Barksdale, 1854), 258.

[11] On May 14, 1863, Johnston instructed Pemberton to attack Sherman's rear "if practicable." *OR*, I, 24(III), 870.

they were covered more than a foot deep with water. But the troops never murmured. By nine o'clock Crocker, of McPherson's corps, who was now in advance, came upon the enemy's pickets and speedily drove them in upon the main body. They were outside of the intrenchments in a strong position, and proved to be the troops that had been driven out of Raymond. Johnston had been reinforced during the night by Georgia and South Carolina regiments, so that his force amounted to eleven thousand men, and he was expecting still more.[12]

Sherman also came upon the rebel pickets some distance out from the town, but speedily drove them in. He was now on the south and south-west of Jackson confronting the Confederates behind their breastworks, while McPherson's right was nearly two miles north, occupying a line running north and south across the Vicksburg railroad. Artillery was brought up and reconnoissances made preparatory to an assault. McPherson brought up Logan's division while he deployed Crocker's for the assault. Sherman made similar dispositions on the right. By eleven A.M. both were ready to attack. Crocker moved his division forward, preceded by a strong skirmish line. These troops at once encountered the enemy's advance and drove it back on the main body, when they returned to their proper regiment and the whole division charged, routing the enemy completely and driving him into this main line. This stand by the enemy was made more than two miles outside of his main fortifications. McPherson followed up with his command until within range of the guns of the enemy from their intrenchments, when he halted to bring his troops into line and reconnoitre to determine the next move. It was now about noon.

While this was going on Sherman was confronting a rebel battery which enfiladed the road on which he was marching—the Mississippi Springs road—and commanded a bridge spanning a stream[13] over which he had to pass. By detaching right and left the stream was forced and the enemy flanked and speedily driven within the main line. This brought our whole line in front of the enemy's line of works, which was continuous on the north, west and south sides from the Pearl River north of the city to the same river south. I was with Sherman. He was confronted by a force sufficient to hold us back. Appearances did not justify an assault where we were. I had directed Sherman to send a force to the right, and to reconnoitre as far as to the Pearl River.[14] This

[12] On May 13, 1863, a Georgia brigade commanded by W. H. T. Walker and a South Carolina brigade commanded by States Rights Gist reinforced Johnston. Ballard, *Vicksburg*, 273.

[13] USG referred to Lynch Creek. Bearss, *Grant Strikes a Blow*, 536.

[14] The editors were unable to find a written copy of these orders.

force, Tuttle's[15] division, not returning I rode to the right with my staff, and soon found that the enemy had left that part of the line. Tuttle's movement or McPherson's pressure had no doubt led Johnston to order a retreat, leaving only the men at the guns to retard us while he was getting away. Tuttle had seen this and, passing through the lines without resistance, came up in the rear of the artillerists confronting Sherman and captured them with ten pieces of artillery. I rode immediately to the State House, where I was soon followed by Sherman. About the same time McPherson discovered that the enemy was leaving his front, and advanced Crocker, who was so close upon the enemy that they could not move their guns or destroy them. He captured seven guns and, moving on, hoisted the National flag over the rebel capital of Mississippi.[16] Stevenson's brigade was sent to cut off the rebel retreat, but was too late or not expeditious enough.

Our loss in this engagement was: McPherson, 37 killed, 228 wounded; Sherman, 4 killed and 21 wounded and missing. The enemy lost 845 killed, wounded and captured.[17] Seventeen guns fell into our hands, and the enemy destroyed by fire their store-houses, containing a large amount of commissary stores.

On this day Blair reached New Auburn[18] and joined McClernand's 4th division. He had with him two hundred wagons loaded with rations, the only commissary supplies received during the entire campaign.

I slept that night in the room that Johnston was said to have occupied the night before.[19]

---

[15] James M. Tuttle (1823–1892) was born in Ohio and moved to Iowa in 1846. On May 31, 1861, he joined the 2nd Iowa Inf. as a lieutenant colonel. He was promoted to colonel in Sept. and to brigadier general in June 1862. *CWHC*, 538.

[16] On May 14, 1863, U.S. forces captured Jackson at 3:00 P.M. *PUSG*, 8:213.

[17] The return of casualties from May 14, 1863, listed forty-two U.S. troops killed and 251 wounded during the Battle of Jackson. Confederate casualty reports indicated 200 killed, wounded, or missing during the battle. *OR*, I, 24(I), 751, 786.

[18] New Auburn, MS, was approximately thirty miles west of Jackson and about ten miles south of Edward's Station, MS. Davis et al., *Official Military Atlas of the Civil War*, plate 36, map 1.

[19] USG stayed in the Bowman House on the night of May 14, 1863. The Bowman House was built in 1857 and used as a hotel until it burned down less than a month after USG's stay. The cause of the fire was never determined. Mary C. Miller, *Lost Landmarks of Mississippi* (Jackson: University Press of Mississippi, 2002), 47; Timothy B. Smith, *Mississippi in the Civil War: The Home Front* (Jackson: University Press of Mississippi, 2010), 39–40, 195.

About four in the afternoon I sent for the corps commanders and directed the dispositions to be made of their troops. Sherman was to remain in Jackson until he destroyed that place as a railroad centre, and manufacturing city of military supplies. He did the work most effectually. Sherman and I went together into a manufactory which had not ceased work on account of the battle nor for the entrance of Yankee troops. Our presence did not seem to attract the attention of either the manager or the operatives, most of whom were girls. We looked on for a while to see the tent cloth which they were making roll out of the looms, with "C. S. A." woven in each bolt. There was an immense amount of cotton, in bales, stacked outside. Finally I told Sherman I thought they had done work enough. The operatives were told they could leave and take with them what cloth they could carry. In a few minutes cotton and factory were in a blaze.[20] The proprietor visited Washington while I was President to get his pay for this property, claiming that it was private. He asked me to give him a statement of the fact that his property had been destroyed by National troops, so that he might use it with Congress where he was pressing, or proposed to press, his claim. I declined.[21]

On the night of the 13th Johnston sent the following dispatch to Pemberton at Edward's station: "I have lately arrived, and learn that Major-General Sherman is between us with four divisions at Clinton. It is important to establish communication, that you may be reinforced. If practicable, come up in his rear at once. To beat such a detachment would be of immense value. All the troops you can quickly assemble should be brought. Time is all-important."[22] This dispatch was sent in triplicate, by different messengers. One of the messengers happened to be a loyal man who had been expelled from Memphis some months before by Hurlbut for uttering disloyal and threatening sentiments. There was a good deal of parade about his expulsion, ostensibly as a warning to those who entertained the sentiments he expressed; but Hurlbut and the expelled man understood each other. He delivered his copy of Johnston's dispatch to McPherson who forwarded it to me.[23]

[20] The cotton mill was owned by Joshua and Thomas Green. *OR*, I, 24(I), 754; *PUSG*, 15:608–609.

[21] On Dec. 9, 1873, the Green brothers unsuccessfully petitioned the U.S. Congress to reimburse them for the destruction of their cotton mill after the Battle of Jackson. *PUSG*, 15:609.

[22] For the full text of Johnston's May 13, 1863, dispatch to Pemberton, see ibid., 8:214n.

[23] This man was most likely Charles S. Bell. He was born in New York in 1843, and moved to Illinois before the start of the Civil War. In June 1861, he enlisted in the 19th Illinois Inf., Co. B. After being discharged for medical reasons, he was hired by Hurlbut as a scout and performed

Receiving this dispatch on the 14th I ordered McPherson to move promptly in the morning back to Bolton, the nearest point where Johnston could reach the road.[24] Bolton is about twenty miles west of Jackson. I also informed McClernand of the capture of Jackson and sent him the following order: "It is evidently the design of the enemy to get north of us and cross the Big Black, and beat us into Vicksburg. We must not allow them to do this. Turn all your forces towards Bolton station, and make all dispatch in getting there. Move troops by the most direct road from wherever they may be on the receipt of this order."

And to Blair I wrote: "Their design is evidently to cross the Big Black and pass down the peninsula between the Big Black and Yazoo rivers. We must beat them. Turn your troops immediately to Bolton; take all the trains with you. Smith's division, and any other troops now with you, will go to the same place. If practicable, take parallel roads, so as to divide your troops and train."

Johnston stopped on the Canton road only six miles north of Jackson, the night of the 14th. He sent from there to Pemberton dispatches announcing the loss of Jackson, and the following order:

"As soon as the reinforcements are all up, they must be united to the rest of the army. I am anxious to see a force assembled that may be able to inflict a heavy blow upon the enemy. Can Grant supply himself from the Mississippi? Can you not cut him off from it, and above all, should he be compelled to fall back for want of supplies, beat him."[25]

The concentration of my troops was easy, considering the character of the country. McPherson moved along the road parallel with and near the railroad.[26] McClernand's command was, one division (Hovey's) on the road McPherson had to take, but with a start of four miles. One (Osterhaus) was at Raymond, on a converging road that intersected the other near Champion's Hill; one (Carr's) had to pass over the same road with Osterhaus, but being back at Mississippi Springs, would not be detained by it; the fourth (Smith's)

---

at least thirty-seven missions during the war. William B. Feis, "Charles S. Bell: Union Scout," *North and South* 4 (2001): 26–37.

[24] On May 13, 1863, USG informed McClernand that he planned for McPherson to move toward Bolton, MS. However, the editors have not found a copy of his specific orders to McPherson. *PUSG,* 8:208.

[25] For the full text of Johnston's May 14, 1863, letter to Pemberton, see *OR,* I, 24(III), 877.

[26] McPherson was on the Clinton Road, which ran parallel to the Vicksburg and Jackson Railroad. Davis et al., *Official Military Atlas of the Civil War,* plate 36, map 1.

with Blair's division, was near Auburn with a different road to pass over.[27] McClernand faced about and moved promptly. His cavalry from Raymond seized Bolton by half-past nine in the morning, driving out the enemy's pickets and capturing several men.

The night of the 15th Hovey was at Bolton; Carr and Osterhaus were about three miles south, but abreast, facing west; Smith was north of Raymond with Blair in his rear.

McPherson's command, with Logan in front, had marched at seven o'clock, and by four reached Hovey and went into camp; Crocker bivouacked just in Hovey's rear on the Clinton road. Sherman with two divisions, was in Jackson, completing the destruction of roads, bridges and military factories. I rode in person out to Clinton. On my arrival I ordered McClernand to move early in the morning on Edward's station, cautioning him to watch for the enemy and not bring on an engagement unless he felt very certain of success.[28]

I naturally expected that Pemberton would endeavor to obey the orders of his superior, which I have shown were to attack us at Clinton. This, indeed, I knew he could not do; but I felt sure he would make the attempt to reach that point. It turned out, however, that he had decided his superior's plans were impracticable, and consequently determined to move south from Edward's station and get between me and my base. I, however, had no base, having abandoned it more than a week before. On the 15th Pemberton had actually marched south from Edward's station, but the rains had swollen Baker's Creek, which he had to cross, so much that he could not ford it, and the bridges were washed away. This brought him back to the Jackson road, on which there was a good bridge over Baker's Creek. Some of his troops were marching until midnight to get there.[29] Receiving here early on the 16th a repetition of his order to join Johnston at Clinton, he concluded to obey, and sent a

---

[27] For the relative positions of these troops, see ibid., plates 36–37.

[28] For USG's May 15, 1863, orders to McClernand, see *PUSG*, 8:216n.

[29] Bakers Creek flowed into Fourteen Mile Creek south of Edward's Station. Leading up to the battle, the lower bridge over Bakers Creek, which was on the Raymond-Edwards Road, had washed out. The Upper Bakers Creek Bridge on the Jackson Road was passable. Alexander W. Reynolds's brigade, which was marching at the rear with the wagon train, did not stop until daylight on May 16, 1863. Ballard, *Vicksburg,* 288; Edwin C. Bearss, *Receding Tide: Vicksburg and Gettysburg: The Campaigns That Changed the Civil War* (Washington, DC: National Geographic Society, 2010), 205.

dispatch to his chief, informing him of the route by which he might be expected.[30]

About five o'clock in the morning (16th) two men, who had been employed on the Jackson and Vicksburg railroad, were brought to me.[31] They reported that they had passed through Pemberton's army in the night, and that it was still marching east. They reported him to have eighty regiments of infantry and ten batteries; in all, about twenty-five thousand men.[32]

I had expected to leave Sherman at Jackson another day in order to complete his work; but getting the above information I sent him orders to move with all dispatch to Bolton, and to put one division with an ammunition train on the road at once, with directions to its commander to march with all possible speed until he came up to our rear. Within an hour after receiving this order Steele's division was on the road. At the same time I dispatched to Blair, who was near Auburn, to move with all speed to Edward's station. McClernand was directed to embrace Blair in his command for the present. Blair's division was a part of the 15th army corps (Sherman's); but as it was on its way to join its corps, it naturally struck our left first, now that we had faced about and were moving west. The 15th corps, when it got up, would be on our extreme right. McPherson was directed to get his trains out of the way of the troops, and to follow Hovey's division as closely as possible. McClernand had two roads about three miles apart, converging at Edward's station, over which to march his troops. Hovey's division of his corps had the advance on a third road (the Clinton) still farther north. McClernand was directed to move Blair's and A. J. Smith's divisions by the southernmost of these roads, and Osterhaus and Carr by the middle road. Orders were to move cautiously with skirmishers to the front to feel for the enemy.

Smith's division on the most southern road was the first to encounter the enemy's pickets, who were speedily driven in. Osterhaus, on the middle road, hearing the firing, pushed his skirmishers forward, found the enemy's pickets and forced them back to the main line. About the same time Hovey encountered the enemy on the northern or direct wagon road from Jackson to Vicksburg. McPherson was hastening up to join Hovey, but was embarrassed by

---

[30] In a dispatch dated May 15, 1863, Johnston suggested to Pemberton that he move his forces to Clinton, MS. On May 16 Pemberton responded to the order when he was four miles south of Edward's Station. *OR*, I, 24(III), 882, 884.

[31] Peter McCardle and William Hennessey. Bearss, *Grant Strikes a Blow*, 579.

[32] Pemberton had 49 regiments, 15 batteries, and approximately 23,000 men. Smith, *Champion Hill*, 134–135.

Hovey's trains occupying the roads. I was still back at Clinton. McPherson sent me word of the situation, and expressed the wish that I was up.[33] By half-past seven I was on the road and proceeded rapidly to the front, ordering all trains that were in front of troops off the road. When I arrived Hovey's skirmishing amounted almost to a battle.

McClernand was in person on the middle road and had a shorter distance to march to reach the enemy's position than McPherson. I sent him word by a staff officer to push forward and attack. These orders were repeated several times without apparently expediting McClernand's advance.[34]

Champion's Hill, where Pemberton had chosen his position to receive us, whether taken by accident or design, was well selected. It is one of the highest points in that section, and commanded all the ground in range. On the east side of the ridge, which is quite precipitous, is a ravine running first north, then westerly, terminating at Baker's Creek. It was grown up thickly with large trees and undergrowth, making it difficult to penetrate with troops, even when not defended. The ridge occupied by the enemy terminated abruptly where the ravine turns westerly. The left of the enemy occupied the north end of this ridge. The Bolton and Edward's station wagon-road turns almost due south at this point and ascends the ridge, which it follows for about a mile; then turning west, descends by a gentle declivity to Baker's Creek, nearly a mile away. On the west side the slope of the ridge is gradual and is cultivated from near the summit to the creek. There was, when we were there, a narrow belt of timber near the summit west of the road.

From Raymond there is a direct road to Edward's station, some three miles west of Champion's Hill. There is one also to Bolton. From this latter road there is still another, leaving it about three and a half miles before reaching Bolton and leads direct to the same station. It was along these two roads that three divisions of McClernand's corps, and Blair of Sherman's, temporarily under McClernand, were moving. Hovey of McClernand's command was with McPherson, farther north on the road from Bolton direct to Edward's station.

[33] On May 16, 1863, at 6 A.M., McPherson sent this dispatch from Jones's plantation. *PUSG,* 8:227n.

[34] USG's letters to McClernand on the morning of May 16, 1863, urged him to advance cautiously. In his letter written at 12:35 P.M. that day, USG directed McClernand to attack the enemy in force if an opportunity occurred. McClernand may not have received that message to attack with full force until midafternoon. Richard L. Kiper, *Major General John Alexander McClernand: Politician in Uniform* (Kent, OH: Kent State University Press, 1999), 245–247; *PUSG,* 8:224–225, 225n–226n.

The middle road comes into the northern road at the point where the latter turns to the west and descends to Baker's Creek; the southern road is still several miles south and does not intersect the others until it reaches Edward's station. Pemberton's lines covered all these roads, and faced east.[35] Hovey's line, when it first drove in the enemy's pickets, was formed parallel to that of the enemy and confronted his left.

By eleven o'clock the skirmishing had grown into a hard-contested battle. Hovey alone, before other troops could be got to assist him, had captured a battery of the enemy. But he was not able to hold his position and had to abandon the artillery.[36] McPherson brought up his troops as fast as possible, Logan in front, and posted them on the right of Hovey and across the flank of the enemy. Logan reinforced Hovey with one brigade from his division; with his other two he moved farther west to make room for Crocker, who was coming up as rapidly as the roads would admit. Hovey was still being heavily pressed, and was calling on me for more reinforcements. I ordered Crocker, who was now coming up, to send one brigade from his division. McPherson ordered two batteries to be stationed where they nearly enfiladed the enemy's line, and they did good execution.

From Logan's position now a direct forward movement carried him over open fields, in rear of the enemy and in a line parallel with them. He did make exactly this move, attacking, however, the enemy through the belt of woods covering the west slope of the hill for a short distance. Up to this time I had kept my position near Hovey where we were the most heavily pressed; but about noon I moved with a part of my staff by our right around, until I came up with Logan himself. I found him near the road leading down to Baker's Creek. He was actually in command of the only road over which the enemy could retreat;[37] Hovey, reinforced by two brigades from McPherson's command, confronted the enemy's left; Crocker, with two brigades, covered their

[35] The three east-west roads USG mentioned here are the Jackson Road, farthest north; the Middle Road, connecting with the Jackson road at the famous Crossroads; and the Raymond Road to the south. William L. Shea and Terrence J. Winschel, *Vicksburg Is the Key: The Struggle for the Mississippi River* (Lincoln: University of Nebraska Press, 2003), 131, 134.

[36] Hovey had pushed back a portion of Confederate general Stevenson's division just north of the Jackson Road. Bowen and his division were able to launch a strong counterattack against Hovey. Michael B. Ballard, *The Civil War in Mississippi: Major Campaigns and Battles* (Oxford: University Press of Mississippi, 2011), 160.

[37] Pemberton's engineers had rebuilt the bridge over Baker's Creek at the Raymond Road. Ballard, *Vicksburg*, 304–305.

left flank; McClernand two hours before, had been within two miles and a half of their centre with two divisions, and the two divisions, Blair's and A. J. Smith's, were confronting the rebel right; Ransom,[38] with a brigade of McArthur's division of the 17th corps (McPherson's), had crossed the river at Grand Gulf a few days before, and was coming up on their right flank. Neither Logan nor I knew that we had cut off the retreat of the enemy. Just at this juncture a messenger came from Hovey, asking for more reinforcements. There were none to spare. I then gave an order to move McPherson's command by the left flank around to Hovey. This uncovered the rebel line of retreat, which was soon taken advantage of by the enemy.

During all this time, Hovey, reinforced as he was by a brigade from Logan and another from Crocker, and by Crocker gallantly coming up with two other brigades on his right, had made several assaults, the last one about the time the road was opened to the rear. The enemy fled precipitately. This was between three and four o'clock. I rode forward, or rather back, to where the middle road intersects the north road, and found the skirmishers of Carr's division just coming in. Osterhaus was farther south and soon after came up with skirmishers advanced in like manner. Hovey's division, and McPherson's two divisions with him, had marched and fought from early dawn, and were not in the best condition to follow the retreating foe. I sent orders to Osterhaus to pursue the enemy, and to Carr, whom I saw personally, I explained the situation and directed him to pursue vigorously as far as the Big Black, and to cross it if he could; Osterhaus to follow him. The pursuit was continued until after dark.

The battle of Champion's Hill lasted about four hours, hard fighting, preceded by two or three hours of skirmishing, some of which almost rose to the dignity of battle. Every man of Hovey's division and of McPherson's two divisions was engaged during the battle. No other part of my command was engaged at all, except that as described before. Osterhaus's and A. J. Smith's divisions had encountered the rebel advanced pickets as early as half-past seven. Their positions were admirable for advancing upon the enemy's line. McClernand, with two divisions, was within a few miles of the battle-field long before noon and in easy hearing. I sent him repeated orders by staff

[38] Thomas E. G. Ransom (1834–1864) was born in Vermont and graduated from Norwich University in 1851. He moved to Illinois later that year. On Apr. 24, 1861, he became a captain in the 11th Illinois Inf., was promoted to major in June and to brigadier general in Nov. 1862. Ransom was wounded in combat in Apr. 1864. He died in Oct. and was posthumously brevetted major general shortly after. *CWHC,* 446.

officers fully competent to explain to him the situation. These traversed the wood separating us, without escort, and directed him to push forward; but he did not come. It is true, in front of McClernand there was a small force of the enemy and posted in a good position behind a ravine obstructing his advance; but if he had moved to the right by the road my staff officers had followed the enemy must either have fallen back or been cut off. Instead of this he sent orders to Hovey, who belonged to his corps, to join on to his right flank.[39] Hovey was bearing the brunt of the battle at the time. To obey the order he would have had to pull out from the front of the enemy and march back as far as McClernand had to advance to get into battle, and substantially over the same ground. Of course I did not permit Hovey to obey the order of his intermediate superior.

We had in this battle about 15,000 men absolutely engaged.[40] This excludes those that did not get up, all of McClernand's command except Hovey. Our loss was 410 killed, 1,844 wounded and 187 missing. Hovey alone lost 1,200 killed, wounded and missing—more than one-third of his division.[41]

Had McClernand come up with reasonable promptness, or had I known the ground as I did afterwards, I cannot see how Pemberton could have escaped with any organized force. As it was he lost over three thousand killed and wounded and about three thousand captured in battle and in pursuit.[42] Loring's division, which was the right of Pemberton's line, was cut off from the retreating army and never got back into Vicksburg. Pemberton himself fell back that night to the Big Black River. His troops did not stop before midnight and many of them left before the general retreat commenced, and no doubt a good part of them returned to their homes. Logan alone captured 1,300 prisoners and eleven guns. Hovey captured 300 under fire and about 700 in all, exclusive of 500 sick and wounded whom he paroled, thus making 1,200.[43]

McPherson joined in the advance as soon as his men could fill their cartridge-boxes, leaving one brigade to guard our wounded. The pursuit was continued

[39] For McClernand's May 16, 1863, order to Hovey, see *OR,* I, 24(III), 316.

[40] USG had approximately 29,000 men on the field of battle, but Hovey's, Logan's, and Crocker's divisions, totaling 15,380 men, accounted for 92.6 percent of the U.S. Army casualties. Smith, *Champion Hill,* 372.

[41] Hovey reported 211 killed, 872 wounded, and 119 missing or captured. *OR,* I, 24(II), 8.

[42] The Confederates reported 381 killed, 1,018 wounded, and 2,441 captured. Ballard, *Vicksburg,* 308.

[43] Hovey reported that he had paroled 569 nurses and sick and wounded Confederate troops. *OR,* I, 24(II), 46.

as long as it was light enough to see the road. The night of the 16th of May found McPherson's command bivouacked from two to six miles west of the battle-field, along the line of the road to Vicksburg. Carr and Osterhaus were at Edward's station, and Blair was about three miles south-east; Hovey remained on the field where his troops had fought so bravely and bled so freely. Much war material abandoned by the enemy was picked up on the battle-field, among it thirty pieces of artillery. I pushed through the advancing column with my staff and kept in advance until after night. Finding ourselves alone we stopped and took possession of a vacant house. As no troops came up we moved back a mile or more until we met the head of the column just going into bivouac on the road. We had no tents, so we occupied the porch of a house which had been taken for a rebel hospital and which was filled with wounded and dying who had been brought from the battle-field we had just left.[44]

While a battle is raging one can see his enemy mowed down by the thousand, or the ten thousand, with great composure; but after the battle these scenes are distressing, and one is naturally disposed to do as much to alleviate the suffering of an enemy as a friend.

[44] On the night of May 16, 1863, USG stayed at the home of Isaac Roberts. The house was Pemberton's former headquarters and had been converted into a Confederate field hospital. Smith, *Champion Hill*, 369.

# 36

## Battle of Black River Bridge—Crossing the Big Black—
## Investment of Vicksburg—Assaulting the Works

W E WERE NOW assured of our position between Johnston and Pemberton, without a possibility of a junction of their forces. Pemberton might have made a night march to the Big Black, crossed the bridge there and, by moving north on the west side, have eluded us and finally returned to Johnston. But this would have given us Vicksburg. It would have been his proper move, however, and the one Johnston would have made had he been in Pemberton's place. In fact it would have been in conformity with Johnston's orders to Pemberton.

Sherman left Jackson with the last of his troops about noon on the 16th and reached Bolton, twenty miles west, before halting. His rear guard did not get in until two A.M. the 17th, but renewed their march by daylight. He paroled his prisoners at Jackson, and was forced to leave his own wounded in care of surgeons and attendants.[1] At Bolton he was informed of our victory. He was directed to commence the march early next day, and to diverge from the road he was on to Bridgeport on the Big Black River, some eleven miles above the point where we expected to find the enemy. Blair was ordered to join him there with the pontoon train as early as possible.

This movement brought Sherman's corps together, and at a point where I hoped a crossing of the Big Black might be effected and Sherman's corps used to flank the enemy out of his position in our front, thus opening a crossing for the remainder of the army. I informed him that I would endeavor to hold the enemy in my front while he crossed the river.

The advance division, Carr's (McClernand's corps), resumed the pursuit at half-past three A.M. on the 17th, followed closely by Osterhaus, McPherson bringing up the rear with his corps. As I expected, the enemy was found in

---

[1] On May 16, 1863, Sherman ordered Mower to parole the prisoners of war and evacuate Jackson, MS, once Tuttle's division left at noon. *OR,* I, 24(I), 754–755.

position on the Big Black. The point was only six miles from that where my advance had rested for the night, and was reached at an early hour. Here the river makes a turn to the west, and has washed close up to the high land; the east side is a low bottom, sometimes overflowed at very high water, but was cleared and in cultivation. A bayou runs irregularly across this low land, the bottom of which, however, is above the surface of the Big Black at ordinary stages. When the river is full water runs through it, converting the point of land into an island. The bayou was grown up with timber, which the enemy had felled into the ditch. At this time there was a foot or two of water in it. The rebels had constructed a parapet along the inner bank of this bayou by using cotton bales from the plantation close by and throwing dirt over them. The whole was thoroughly commanded from the height west of the river. At the upper end of the bayou there was a strip of uncleared land which afforded a cover for a portion of our men. Carr's division was deployed on our right, Lawler's[2] brigade forming his extreme right and reaching through these woods to the river above. Osterhaus' division was deployed to the left of Carr and covered the enemy's entire front. McPherson was in column on the road, the head close by, ready to come in wherever he could be of assistance.

While the troops were standing as here described an officer from Banks' staff came up and presented me with a letter from General Halleck, dated the 11th of May.[3] It had been sent by the way of New Orleans to Banks to be forwarded to me. It ordered me to return to Grand Gulf and to co-operate from there with Banks against Port Hudson, and then to return with our combined forces to besiege Vicksburg. I told the officer that the order came too late, and that Halleck would not give it now if he knew our position. The bearer of the dispatch insisted that I ought to obey the order, and was giving arguments to support his position when I heard great cheering to the right of our line and, looking in that direction, saw Lawler in his shirt sleeves leading a charge upon the enemy. I immediately mounted my horse and rode in the direction

---

[2] Michael K. Lawler (1814–1882) was born in Ireland and immigrated to New York in 1816. He moved to Illinois, where he became a captain in the 3rd Illinois Inf. in 1846. He reentered the military in 1861 as a colonel in the 18th Illinois Inf. He was promoted to brigadier general in 1862. *CWHC,* 341.

[3] The officer who probably delivered the letter was William Dwight (1831–1888). Dwight was born in Massachusetts and joined the 70th New York Inf. as a captain in May 1861. In Nov. 1862, he was promoted to brigadier general. Bruce Catton, *Grant Moves South* (Boston: Little, Brown, 1960), 447; *CWHC,* 220.

of the charge, and saw no more of the officer who delivered the dispatch; I think not even to this day.[4]

The assault was successful. But little resistance was made. The enemy fled from the west bank of the river, burning the bridge behind him and leaving the men and guns on the east side to fall into our hands.[5] Many tried to escape by swimming the river. Some succeeded and some were drowned in the attempt. Eighteen guns were captured and 1,751 prisoners. Our loss was 39 killed, 237 wounded and 3 missing. The enemy probably lost but few men except those captured and drowned. But for the successful and complete destruction of the bridge, I have but little doubt that we should have followed the enemy so closely as to prevent his occupying his defences around Vicksburg.

As the bridge was destroyed and the river was high, new bridges had to be built. It was but little after nine o'clock A.M. when the capture took place. As soon as work could be commenced, orders were given for the construction of three bridges. One was taken charge of by Lieutenant Hains, of the Engineer Corps, one by General McPherson himself and one by General Ransom, a most gallant and intelligent volunteer officer. My recollection is that Hains built a raft bridge; McPherson a pontoon, using cotton bales in large numbers, for pontoons; and that Ransom felled trees on opposite banks of the river, cutting only on one side of the tree, so that they would fall with their tops interlacing in the river, without the trees being entirely severed from their stumps. A bridge was then made with these trees to support the roadway. Lumber was taken from buildings, cotton gins and wherever found, for this purpose. By eight o'clock in the morning of the 18th all three bridges were complete and the troops were crossing.[6]

---

[4] On May 11, 1863, in a letter to Banks and in a telegram to USG, Halleck urged both men to unite their forces and attack Port Hudson and then Vicksburg. No surviving order from Halleck matches the one described by USG here. *PUSG,* 8:221n. For a detailed discussion of the discrepancies between USG's description of the incident and the documentary record, see Catton, *Grant Moves South,* 447–448, 533–534.

[5] The Big Black River Bridge carried the Vicksburg and Jackson Railroad across the Big Black River. Michael B. Ballard, *Vicksburg: The Campaign That Opened the Mississippi* (Chapel Hill: University of North Carolina Press, 2004), 311 (map); George B. Davis et al., *The Official Military Atlas of the Civil War* (New York: Fairfax Press, 1983), plate 36.

[6] McClernand reported that members of the Pioneer Corps under the direction of Capt. William F. Patterson constructed a bridge on the night of May 17, 1863. McPherson reported that by the evening of May 18, Ransom's brigade had constructed a raft bridge made of timber, and Quinby's division had built a bridge that was made of timber and cotton bales. *OR,* I, 24(I), 153, 641.

Sherman reached Bridgeport about noon of the 17th and found Blair with the pontoon train already there. A few of the enemy were intrenched on the west bank, but they made little resistance and soon surrendered. Two divisions were crossed that night and the third the following morning.

On the 18th I moved along the Vicksburg road in advance of the troops and as soon as possible joined Sherman. My first anxiety was to secure a base of supplies on the Yazoo River above Vicksburg. Sherman's line of march led him to the very point on Walnut Hills occupied by the enemy the December before when he was repulsed. Sherman was equally anxious with myself. Our impatience led us to move in advance of the column and well up with the advanced skirmishers. There were some detached works along the crest of the hill. These were still occupied by the enemy, or else the garrison from Haines' Bluff had not all got past on their way to Vicksburg. At all events the bullets of the enemy whistled by thick and fast for a short time. In a few minutes Sherman had the pleasure of looking down from the spot coveted so much by him the December before on the ground where his command had lain so helpless for offensive action. He turned to me, saying that up to this minute he had felt no positive assurance of success. This, however, he said was the end of one of the greatest campaigns in history and I ought to make a report of it at once. Vicksburg was not yet captured, and there was no telling what might happen before it was taken; but whether captured or not, this was a complete and successful campaign. I do not claim to quote Sherman's language; but the substance only. My reason for mentioning this incident will appear further on.

McPherson, after crossing the Big Black, came into the Jackson and Vicksburg road which Sherman was on, but to his rear. He arrived at night near the lines of the enemy, and went into camp. McClernand moved by the direct road near the railroad to Mount Albans,[7] and then turned to the left and put his troops on the road from Baldwin's ferry[8] to Vicksburg. This brought him south of McPherson. I now had my three corps up to the works built for the defence of Vicksburg, on three roads—one to the north, one to the east and one to the south-east of the city.[9] By the morning of the 19th the investment was as complete as my limited number of troops would allow. Sherman

[7] Mount Alban Station, MS, was approximately five miles east of Vicksburg on the Vicksburg and Jackson Railroad. Davis et al., *Official Military Atlas of the Civil War,* plate 36, map 1.

[8] Baldwin's Ferry was about nine miles southeast of Vicksburg on the Big Black River. Ibid.

[9] USG probably referred to Sherman's corps approaching the city on the north by Graveyard Road; McPherson's corps approaching via the Jackson Road and taking up positions to the northeast of the city; and McClernand's corps approaching the city on the southeast via

was on the right, and covered the high ground from where it overlooked the Yazoo as far south-east as his troops would extend. McPherson joined on to his left, and occupied ground on both sides of the Jackson road. McClernand took up the ground to his left and extended as far towards Warrenton as he could, keeping a continuous line.

On the 19th there was constant skirmishing with the enemy while we were getting into better position. The enemy had been much demoralized by his defeats at Champion's Hill and the Big Black, and I believed he would not make much effort to hold Vicksburg. Accordingly, at two o'clock I ordered an assault. It resulted in securing more advanced positions for all our troops where they were fully covered from the fire of the enemy.[10]

The 20th and 21st were spent in strengthening our position and in making roads in rear of the army, from Yazoo River or Chickasaw Bayou. Most of the army had now been for three weeks with only five days' rations issued by the commissary. They had an abundance of food, however, but began to feel the want of bread. I remember that in passing around to the left of the line on the 21st, a soldier, recognizing me, said in rather a low voice, but yet so that I heard him, "Hard tack." In a moment the cry was taken up all along the line, "Hard tack! Hard tack!" I told the men nearest to me that we had been engaged ever since the arrival of the troops in building a road over which to supply them with everything they needed. The cry was instantly changed to cheers. By the night of the 21st all the troops had full rations issued to them. The bread and coffee were highly appreciated.

I now determined on a second assault. Johnston was in my rear, only fifty miles away, with an army not much inferior in numbers to the one I had with me, and I knew he was being reinforced.[11] There was danger of his coming to the assistance of Pemberton, and after all he might defeat my anticipations of capturing the garrison if, indeed, he did not prevent the capture of the city.

---

Baldwin's Ferry Road. Edwin Cole Bearss, *Vicksburg Is the Key*, vol. 3 of *Campaign for Vicksburg* (Dayton, OH: Morningside House, 1986), 743–746, 749, 760 (map); *PUSG*, 8:236–237.

[10] U.S. troops were able to get within 400 yards of the Confederate lines but were unable to take their works. U.S. losses were 157 killed, 777 wounded, and 8 missing, while estimates of Confederate casualties place their losses at approximately 200. Bearss, *Vicksburg Is the Key*, 772–773.

[11] Johnston had approximately 23,000–30,000 troops by the end of May 1863. U.S. forces in Mississippi numbered 50,000–56,000 by the end of May / early June. Bearss, *Vicksburg Is the Key*, 1071; *OR*, I, 24(I), 192–193; Timothy B. Smith, *Champion Hill: Decisive Battle for Vicksburg* (New York: Savas Beatie, 2006), 397.

The immediate capture of Vicksburg would save sending me the reinforcements which were so much wanted elsewhere, and would set free the army under me to drive Johnston from the State. But the first consideration of all was—the troops believed they could carry the works in their front, and would not have worked so patiently in the trenches if they had not been allowed to try.

The attack was ordered to commence on all parts of the line at ten o'clock A.M. on the 22d with a furious cannonade from every battery in position. All the corps commanders set their time by mine so that all might open the engagement at the same minute. The attack was gallant, and portions of each of the three corps succeeded in getting up to the very parapets of the enemy and in planting their battle flags upon them; but at no place were we able to enter. General McClernand reported that he had gained the enemy's intrenchments at several points, and wanted reinforcements. I occupied a position from which I believed I could see as well as he what took place in his front, and I did not see the success he reported. But his request for reinforcements being repeated I could not ignore it, and sent him Quinby's division of the 17th corps. Sherman and McPherson were both ordered to renew their assaults as a diversion in favor of McClernand. This last attack only served to increase our casualties without giving any benefit whatever.[12] As soon as it was dark our troops that had reached the enemy's line and been obliged to remain there for security all day, were withdrawn; and thus ended the last assault upon Vicksburg.

[12] During the assault, 502 U.S. soldiers were killed, 2,550 were wounded, and 147 were captured or missing. *OR*, I, 24(II), 165.

# 37

## Siege of Vicksburg

I NOW DETERMINED UPON a regular siege—to "out-camp the enemy," as it were, and to incur no more losses. The experience of the 22d convinced officers and men that this was best, and they went to work on the defences and approaches with a will. With the navy holding the river, the investment of Vicksburg was complete. As long as we could hold our position the enemy was limited in supplies of food, men and munitions of war to what they had on hand. These could not last always.

The crossing of troops at Bruinsburg commenced April 30th. On the 18th of May the army was in rear of Vicksburg. On the 19th, just twenty days after the crossing, the city was completely invested and an assault had been made: five distinct battles (besides continuous skirmishing) had been fought and won by the Union forces; the capital of the State had fallen and its arsenals, military manufactories and everything useful for military purposes had been destroyed; an average of about one hundred and eighty miles had been marched by the troops engaged; but five days' rations had been issued, and no forage; over six thousand prisoners had been captured, and as many more of the enemy had been killed or wounded; twenty-seven heavy cannon and sixty-one field-pieces had fallen into our hands; and four hundred miles of the river, from Vicksburg to Port Hudson, had become ours.[1] The Union force that had crossed the Mississippi River up to this time was less than forty-three thousand men.[2] One division of these, Blair's, only arrived in time to take part in the battle of Champion's Hill, but was not engaged there; and one brigade, Ransom's of McPherson's corps, reached the field after the battle. The enemy had

[1] In a May 24, 1863, letter to Halleck, USG stated that his forces had captured "74 guns besides what was found at Hain's Bluffs" during the Vicksburg campaign. *PUSG*, 8:261–262.

[2] On May 22, 1863, USG had 45,556 troops present for duty near Vicksburg. Thomas L. Livermore, *Numbers and Losses in the Civil War in America, 1861–65* (Boston: Houghton, Mifflin, 1900), 100.

at Vicksburg, Grand Gulf, Jackson, and on the roads between these places, over sixty thousand men.[3] They were in their own country, where no rear guards were necessary. The country is admirable for defence, but difficult for the conduct of an offensive campaign. All their troops had to be met. We were fortunate, to say the least, in meeting them in detail: at Port Gibson seven or eight thousand; at Raymond, five thousand; at Jackson, from eight to eleven thousand; at Champion's Hill, twenty-five thousand; at the Big Black, four thousand.[4] A part of those met at Jackson were all that was left of those encountered at Raymond. They were beaten in detail by a force smaller than their own, upon their own ground. Our loss up to this time was:

| AT | KILLED. | WOUNDED. | MISSING. |
|---|---|---|---|
| Port Gibson | 131 | 719 | 25 |
| South Fork Bayou Pierre | | 1 | |
| Skirmishes, May 3 | 1 | 9 | |
| Fourteen Mile Creek | 6 | 24 | |
| Raymond | 66 | 339 | 37 |
| Jackson | 42 | 251 | 7 |
| Champion's Hill | 410 | 1,844 | 187 |
| Big Black | 39 | 237 | 3 |
| Bridgeport | | 1 | |
| Total | 695 | 3,425 | 259 |

Of the wounded many were but slightly so, and continued on duty. Not half of them were disabled for any length of time.

After the unsuccessful assault of the 22d the work of the regular siege began. Sherman occupied the right starting from the river above Vicksburg, McPherson the centre (McArthur's division now with him) and McClernand the left,

[3] By the end of Mar. 1863, the Confederacy reportedly had 61,495 troops in the Dept. of Mississippi and Eastern Louisiana. *OR*, I, 24(III), 702.

[4] Bowen reported on May 2, 1863, that he had 5,500 men under his command at the Battle of Port Gibson. However, on May 6, Loring reported that Bowen had informed him that he had 7,000 men. Gregg reported on May 20 that 2,500 Confederate troops engaged in the Battle of Raymond. Johnston reported 6,000 troops at Jackson on May 13, with expected reinforcements of 5,000 troops to arrive on May 14. At the Battle of Champion Hill, Pemberton had about 24,000 troops available, with 16,313 primarily engaged in the battle. At the Battle of Big Black River Bridge on May 17, there were not more than 5,000 Confederate troops. Francis Vinton Greene, *The Mississippi* (New York: Scribner's Sons, 1882), 163–164; *OR*, I, 24(I), 239, 655, 662, 739; Timothy B. Smith, *Champion Hill: Decisive Battle for Vicksburg* (New York: Savas Beatie, 2006), 372.

holding the road south to Warrenton. Lauman's division arrived at this time and was placed on the extreme left of the line.

In the interval between the assaults of the 19th and 22d, roads had been completed from the Yazoo River and Chickasaw Bayou, around the rear of the army, to enable us to bring up supplies of food and ammunition; ground had been selected and cleared on which the troops were to be encamped, and tents and cooking utensils were brought up.[5] The troops had been without these from the time of crossing the Mississippi up to this time. All was now ready for the pick and spade. Prentiss and Hurlbut were ordered to send forward every man that could be spared.[6] Cavalry especially was wanted to watch the fords along the Big Black, and to observe Johnston. I knew that Johnston was receiving reinforcements from Bragg, who was confronting Rosecrans in Tennessee.[7] Vicksburg was so important to the enemy that I believed he would make the most strenuous efforts to raise the siege, even at the risk of losing ground elsewhere.

My line was more than fifteen miles long, extending from Haines' Bluff to Vicksburg, thence to Warrenton. The line of the enemy was about seven. In addition to this, having an enemy at Canton and Jackson, in our rear, who was being constantly reinforced, we required a second line of defence facing the other way. I had not troops enough under my command to man these. General Halleck appreciated the situation and, without being asked, forwarded reinforcements with all possible dispatch.[8]

The ground about Vicksburg is admirable for defence. On the north it is about two hundred feet above the Mississippi River at the highest point and very much cut up by the washing rains; the ravines were grown up with cane and underbrush, while the sides and tops were covered with a dense forest. Farther south the ground flattens out somewhat, and was in cultivation. But here, too, it was cut up by ravines and small streams. The enemy's line of defence followed the crest of a ridge from the river north of the city east-

[5] On May 19, 1863, USG informed McClernand that he had ordered "forage and supplies to be sent to Lake's Landing at the mouth of Chickasaw Bayou." *PUSG*, 8:241.

[6] Ibid., 8:272, 273*n*.

[7] On May 30, 1863, Hurlbut informed USG that Bragg was sending troops from Tennessee to reinforce Johnston's army, in addition to reinforcements being sent from Mobile, AL, and Port Hudson, LA. Ibid., 8:274*n*.

[8] Halleck promised to reinforce USG in a June 2, 1863, telegram. On June 3, Halleck ordered Burnside to send 8,000 troops to USG. On June 11, USG reported that reinforcements had begun to arrive. *OR*, I, 23(II), 384; *PUSG*, 8:283*n*–284*n*, 344–345.

ward, then southerly around to the Jackson road, full three miles back of the city; thence in a southwesterly direction to the river. Deep ravines of the description given lay in front of these defences. As there is a succession of gullies, cut out by rains along the side of the ridge, the line was necessarily very irregular. To follow each of these spurs with intrenchments, so as to command the slopes on either side, would have lengthened their line very much. Generally therefore, or in many places, their line would run from near the head of one gully nearly straight to the head of another, and an outer work triangular in shape, generally open in the rear, was thrown up on the point; with a few men in this outer work they commanded the approaches to the main line completely.

The work to be done, to make our position as strong against the enemy as his was against us, was very great. The problem was also complicated by our wanting our line as near that of the enemy as possible. We had but four engineer officers with us. Captain Prime, of the Engineer Corps, was the chief, and the work at the beginning was mainly directed by him. His health soon gave out,[9] when he was succeeded by Captain Comstock,[10] also of the Engineer Corps. To provide assistants on such a long line I directed that all officers who had graduated at West Point, where they had necessarily to study military engineering, should in addition to their other duties assist in the work.[11]

The chief quartermaster and the chief commissary were graduates. The chief commissary, now the Commissary-General of the Army, begged off, however, saying that there was nothing in engineering that he was good for unless he would do for a sap-roller.[12] As soldiers require rations while working in the

[9] Frederick E. Prime (1829–1900) was born in Italy and graduated from the USMA in 1850. On Aug. 6, 1861, he was promoted to captain. He joined the Army of the Tennessee on June 18, 1862, as an engineer and was promoted to major on June 1, 1863. Prime was chief engineer of the Army of Tennessee until June 28, when he was forced to take sick leave. *CWHC,* 441; *OR,* I, 24(II), 177–178.

[10] Cyrus B. Comstock (1831–1910) was born in Massachusetts, graduated from the USMA in 1855, and entered the U.S. Army Engineers. He was promoted to captain in Mar. 1863. He served as USG's senior aide-de-camp from Mar. 1864 to July 1866. *CWHC,* 181.

[11] According to Prime's postbattle report, a few officers "had been detailed, either from a list of additional aides-de-camp or from the line, for engineer duty; these were assigned to the headquarters of corps or divisions." *OR,* I, 24(II), 171.

[12] At the time of the Vicksburg campaign, Judson D. Bingham served as the chief quartermaster for the Army of the Tennessee; Robert MacFeely was the chief commissary of subsistence

ditches as well as when marching and fighting, and as we would be sure to lose him if he was used as a sap-roller, I let him off. The general is a large man; weighs two hundred and twenty pounds, and is not tall.

We had no siege guns except six thirty-two pounders, and there were none at the West to draw from. Admiral Porter, however, supplied us with a battery of navy-guns of large calibre, and with these, and the field artillery used in the campaign, the siege began. The first thing to do was to get the artillery in batteries where they would occupy commanding positions; then establish the camps, under cover from the fire of the enemy but as near up as possible; and then construct rifle-pits and covered ways, to connect the entire command by the shortest route. The enemy did not harass us much while we were constructing our batteries. Probably their artillery ammunition was short; and their infantry was kept down by our sharpshooters, who were always on the alert and ready to fire at a head whenever it showed itself above the rebel works.

In no place were our lines more than six hundred yards from the enemy. It was necessary, therefore, to cover our men by something more than the ordinary parapet. To give additional protection sand bags, bullet-proof, were placed along the tops of the parapets far enough apart to make loop-holes for musketry. On top of these, logs were put. By these means the men were enabled to walk about erect when off duty, without fear of annoyance from sharpshooters. The enemy used in their defence explosive musket-balls, no doubt thinking that, bursting over our men in the trenches, they would do some execution; but I do not remember a single case where a man was injured by a piece of one of these shells. When they were hit and the ball exploded, the wound was terrible. In these cases a solid ball would have hit as well. Their use is barbarous, because they produce increased suffering without any corresponding advantage to those using them.[13]

and later served as U.S. Army commissary general of subsistence from 1875 to 1890. Sap rollers were large, cylindrical baskets used by soldiers constructing trenches for shelter from enemy fire. Mark M. Boatner III, *The Civil War Dictionary* (New York: David McKay, 1988), 721; *CWHC*, 131, 358.

[13] After the Civil War, some Confederate soldiers condemned the use of exploding musket rounds and claimed that Confederate troops never used them. However, exploding rounds were available to and used by both sides in limited numbers. Some evidence indicates limited usage by Confederate troops during the siege of Vicksburg. Earl J. Hess, *The Rifle Musket in Civil War Combat: Reality and Myth* (Lawrence: University Press of Kansas, 2008), 76–78.

The enemy could not resort to our method to protect their men, because we had an inexhaustible supply of ammunition to draw upon and used it freely. Splinters from the timber would have made havoc among the men behind.

There were no mortars with the besiegers, except what the navy had in front of the city; but wooden ones were made by taking logs of the toughest wood that could be found, boring them out for six or twelve pound shells and binding them with strong iron bands. These answered as coehorns, and shells were successfully thrown from them into the trenches of the enemy.

The labor of building the batteries and intrenching was largely done by the pioneers, assisted by negroes who came within our lines and who were paid for their work; but details from the troops had often to be made. The work was pushed forward as rapidly as possible, and when an advanced position was secured and covered from the fire of the enemy the batteries were advanced. By the 30th of June there were two hundred and twenty guns in position, mostly light field-pieces, besides a battery of heavy guns belonging to, manned and commanded by the navy. We were now as strong for defence against the garrison of Vicksburg as they were against us; but I knew that Johnston was in our rear, and was receiving constant reinforcements from the east. He had at this time a larger force than I had had at any time prior to the battle of Champion's Hill.

As soon as the news of the arrival of the Union army behind Vicksburg reached the North, floods of visitors began to pour in. Some came to gratify curiosity; some to see sons or brothers who had passed through the terrible ordeal; members of the Christian and Sanitary Associations came to minister to the wants of the sick and the wounded. Often those coming to see a son or brother would bring a dozen or two of poultry. They did not know how little the gift would be appreciated. Many of the soldiers had lived so much on chickens, ducks and turkeys without bread during the march, that the sight of poultry, if they could get bacon, almost took away their appetite. But the intention was good.

Among the earliest arrivals was the Governor of Illinois,[14] with most of the State officers. I naturally wanted to show them what there was of most interest. In Sherman's front the ground was the most broken and most wooded,

[14] Gov. Richard Yates visited the area around Vicksburg in Apr. 1863. "Gov. Yates," *Illinois State Journal*, Apr. 8, 1863, 3; *PUSG*, 8:254n–255n.

and more was to be seen without exposure. I therefore took them to Sherman's headquarters and presented them. Before starting out to look at the lines—possibly while Sherman's horse was being saddled—there were many questions asked about the late campaign, about which the North had been so imperfectly informed. There was a little knot around Sherman and another around me, and I heard Sherman repeating, in the most animated manner, what he had said to me when we first looked down from Walnut Hills upon the land below on the 18th of May, adding: "Grant is entitled to every bit of the credit for the campaign; I opposed it. I wrote him a letter about it." But for this speech it is not likely that Sherman's opposition would have ever been heard of. His untiring energy and great efficiency during the campaign entitle him to a full share of all the credit due for its success. He could not have done more if the plan had been his own.*

*NOTE.—When General Sherman first learned of the move I proposed to make, he called to see me about it. I recollect that I had transferred my headquarters from a boat in the river to a house a short distance back from the levee. I was seated on the piazza engaged in conversation with my staff when Sherman came up.[15] After a few moments' conversation he said that he would like to see me alone. We passed into the house together and shut the door after us. Sherman then expressed his alarm at the move I had ordered, saying that I was putting myself in a position voluntarily which an enemy would be glad to manœuvre a year—or a long time—to get me in. I was going into the enemy's country, with a large river behind me and the enemy holding points strongly fortified above and below. He said that it was an axiom in war that when any great body of troops moved against an enemy they should do so from a base of supplies, which they would guard as they would the apple of the eye, etc. He pointed out all the difficulties that might be encountered in the campaign proposed, and stated in turn what would be the true campaign to make. This was, in substance, to go back until high ground could be reached on the east bank of the river; fortify there and establish a depot of supplies, and move from there, being always prepared to fall back upon it in case of disaster. I said this would take us back to Memphis. Sherman

[15] Sherman visited USG at his headquarters on Apr. 1, 1863, but it is unclear if USG referred to that visit or another in this passage. The editors have been unable to identify the house USG used as his headquarters. USG used both the boats *Magnolia* and *Henry Von Phul* as headquarters during the spring of 1863. Edwin Cole Bearss, *Grant Strikes a Blow*, vol. 2 of *The Campaign for Vicksburg* (Dayton, OH: Morningside House, 1985), 71; Mary A. Livermore, *My Story of the War: A Woman's Narrative of Four Years Personal Experience as Nurse in the Union Army, and in Relief Work at Home, in Hospitals, Camps, and at the Front, during the War of the Rebellion* (Hartford, CT: A. D. Worthington, 1889), 307–308; *PUSG*, 8:5n.

On the 26th of May I sent Blair's division up the Yazoo to drive out a force of the enemy supposed to be between the Big Black and the Yazoo. The country was rich and full of supplies of both food and forage. Blair was instructed to take all of it. The cattle were to be driven in for the use of our army, and the food and forage to be consumed by our troops or destroyed by fire; all bridges were to be destroyed, and the roads rendered as nearly impassable as possible. Blair went forty-five miles and was gone almost a week.

------------

then said that was the very place he would go to, and would move by railroad from Memphis to Grenada, repairing the road as we advanced. To this I replied, the country is already disheartened over the lack of success on the part of our armies; the last election went against the vigorous prosecution of the war, voluntary enlistments had ceased throughout most of the North and conscription was already resorted to, and if we went back so far as Memphis it would discourage the people so much that bases of supplies would be of no use: neither men to hold them nor supplies to put in them would be furnished. The problem for us was to move forward to a decisive victory, or our cause was lost. No progress was being made in any other field, and we had to go on.

Sherman wrote to my adjutant general, Colonel J. A. Rawlins, embodying his views of the campaign that should be made, and asking him to advise me to at least get the views of my generals upon the subject. Colonel Rawlins showed me the letter, but I did not see any reason for changing my plans. The letter was not answered and the subject was not subsequently mentioned between Sherman and myself to the end of the war, that I remember of. I did not regard the letter as official, and consequently did not preserve it. General Sherman furnished a copy himself to General Badeau, who printed it in his history of my campaigns.[16] I did not regard either the conversation between us or the letter to my adjutant-general as protests, but simply friendly advice which the relations between us fully justified. Sherman gave the same energy to make the campaign a success that he would or could have done if it had been ordered by himself. I make this statement here to correct an impression which was circulated at the close of the war to Sherman's prejudice, and for which there was no fair foundation.[17]

[16] For Sherman's Apr. 8, 1863, letter to Rawlins, see *PUSG*, 8:13*n*. For Badeau's reprint of the letter, see Adam Badeau, *Military History of Ulysses S. Grant, from April, 1861, to April, 1865* (New York: D. Appleton, 1881), 1:616–617.

[17] USG may have referred to an account of Sherman's letter that appeared in an article titled "A Scrap of History" on p. 4 of the May 29, 1865, *New York Times*, which described it as a letter of protest.

His work was effectually done. I requested Porter at this time to send the marine brigade, a floating nondescript force which had been assigned to his command and which proved very useful, up to Haines' Bluff to hold it until reinforcements could be sent.[18]

On the 26th I also received a letter from Banks, asking me to reinforce him with ten thousand men at Port Hudson. Of course I could not comply with his request, nor did I think he needed them. He was in no danger of an attack by the garrison in his front, and there was no army organizing in his rear to raise the siege.[19]

On the 3d of June a brigade from Hurlbut's command arrived, General Kimball[20] commanding. It was sent to Mechanicsburg, some miles northeast of Haines' Bluff and about midway between the Big Black and the Yazoo. A brigade of Blair's division and twelve hundred cavalry had already, on Blair's return from the Yazoo, been sent to the same place with instructions to watch the crossings of the Big Black River, to destroy the roads in his (Blair's) front, and to gather or destroy all supplies.

On the 7th of June our little force of colored and white troops across the Mississippi, at Milliken's Bend, were attacked by about 3,000 men from Richard Taylor's[21] trans-Mississippi command. With the aid of the gunboats they were speedily repelled. I sent Mower's brigade over with instructions to drive the enemy beyond the Tensas Bayou; and we had no further trouble in that quarter during the siege. This was the first important engagement of the

[18] On May 29, 1863, USG requested that Porter send the Marine Brigade to Haines' Bluff. Brig. Gen. Alfred Ellet of the Marine Brigade reported its arrival the following day. *PUSG*, 8:284, 285*n*.

[19] On May 28, 1863, Banks wrote to USG requesting reinforcements of "at least one Brigade of four or five thousand men." USG denied the request on May 31. *PUSG*, 8:270*n*, 294–295.

[20] Nathan Kimball (1822–1898) was born in Indiana and joined the 2nd Indiana Inf. as a captain in June 1846. He was mustered out in 1847 and joined the 14th Indiana Inf. in 1861 as a captain. He was promoted to colonel in June that year, to brigadier general in Apr. 1862, and was brevetted major general in Feb. 1865. After the war, Kimball was appointed by Pres. USG as the surveyor general of the Utah territory in 1873. *CWHC*, 332–333.

[21] Richard Taylor (1826–1879) was born in Kentucky and graduated from Yale in 1845. He was the son of Pres. Zachary Taylor, and served as a military secretary to him during the Mexican-American War. In 1861, he entered the Confederate Army as a colonel in the 9th Louisiana Inf. He was promoted to major general in 1862. Ibid., 523.

war in which colored troops were under fire. These men were very raw, having all been enlisted since the beginning of the siege, but they behaved well.[22]

On the 8th of June a full division arrived from Hurlbut's command, under General Sooy Smith.[23] It was sent immediately to Haines' Bluff, and General C. C. Washburn was assigned to the general command at that point.

On the 11th a strong division arrived from the Department of the Missouri under General Herron,[24] which was placed on our left. This cut off the last possible chance of communication between Pemberton and Johnston, as it enabled Lauman to close up on McClernand's left while Herron intrenched from Lauman to the water's edge. At this point the water recedes a few hundred yards from the high land. Through this opening no doubt the Confederate commanders had been able to get messengers under cover of night.[25]

On the 14th General Parke[26] arrived with two divisions of Burnside's corps, and was immediately dispatched to Haines' Bluff.[27] These latter troops—

[22] The 11th Louisiana Inf. (African descent) fought at the Battle of Milliken's Bend on June 7, 1863. However, the Battle of Island Mound on Oct. 29, 1862, was the first time an African American regiment (1st Kansas Inf.) fought against the Confederates in the Civil War. Diane M. Burke, *On Slavery's Border: Missouri's Small Slaveholding Households, 1815–1865* (Athens: University of Georgia Press, 2010), 292; John David Smith, ed., *Black Soldiers in Blue: African American Troops in the Civil War Era* (Chapel Hill: University of North Carolina Press, 2002), 110.

[23] William Sooy Smith (1830–1916) was born in Ohio and graduated from the USMA in 1853. He resigned from the U.S. Army in June 1854. He reentered the army in the 13th Ohio Inf. as a colonel in June 1861, and was promoted to brigadier general in Apr. 1862. He commanded the 1st Div., 16th Corps, Army of the Tennessee, during the Vicksburg campaign. *CWHC,* 500.

[24] Francis J. Herron (1837–1902) was born in Pennsylvania and moved to Iowa in 1855. He became a captain in the Iowa Militia in 1861. In July 1862 he was promoted to brigadier general and in Nov. to major general. He commanded a division in the 13th Corps, Army of the Tennessee, in June 1863. Herron's division arrived at Young's Point, LA, on June 13 and got into position at Vicksburg on June 15. After the war, Herron served as Louisiana secretary of state from 1872 to 1873. Ibid., 294–295; *OR,* I, 24(II), 319.

[25] The editors found no indication that Confederate couriers used this route or that the arrival of Herron's troops disrupted Confederate communications during this time. *OR,* I, 24(III), 958, 965–966.

[26] John G. Parke (1827–1900) was born in Pennsylvania and graduated from the USMA in 1849. He was promoted to second lieutenant in Apr. 1854 and to major general in July 1862. *CWHC,* 416.

[27] On June 15, 1863, USG ordered Parke to move his troops to Haines' Bluff. *PUSG,* 8:372n.

Herron's and Parke's—were the reinforcements already spoken of sent by Halleck in anticipation of their being needed. They arrived none too soon.

I now had about seventy-one thousand men. More than half were disposed across the peninsula, between the Yazoo at Haines' Bluff and the Big Black, with the division of Osterhaus watching the crossings of the latter river farther south and west from the crossing of the Jackson road to Baldwin's ferry and below.

There were eight roads leading into Vicksburg,[28] along which and their immediate sides, our work was specially pushed and batteries advanced; but no commanding point within range of the enemy was neglected.

On the 17th I received a letter from General Sherman and one on the 18th from General McPherson, saying that their respective commands had complained to them of a fulsome, congratulatory order published by General McClernand to the 13th corps, which did great injustice to the other troops engaged in the campaign. This order had been sent North and published, and now papers containing it had reached our camps. The order had not been heard of by me, and certainly not by troops outside of McClernand's command until brought in this way. I at once wrote to McClernand, directing him to send me a copy of this order. He did so, and I at once relieved him from the command of the 13th army corps and ordered him back to Springfield, Illinois. The publication of his order in the press was in violation of War Department orders and also of mine.[29]

---

[28] While it is unclear which eight roads USG referred to, the six main roads leading into the city were the Yazoo City Road, Graveyard Road, the Jackson Road, Baldwin's Ferry Road, Hall's Ferry Road, and the Warrenton Road. William L. Shea and Terrence J. Winschel, *Vicksburg Is the Key* (Lincoln: University of Nebraska Press, 2003), 144–145 (map).

[29] On May 30, 1863, McClernand issued Gen. Orders No. 72, praising the 13th Corps for their fighting during the Vicksburg campaign. *OR*, I, 24(I), 159–161. For a copy of Sherman's and McPherson's letters to USG, see *PUSG*, 8:429n–431n.

# 38

Johnston's Movements—Fortifications at Haines'
Bluff—Explosion of the Mine—Explosion of the
Second Mine—Preparing for the Assault—The Flag of
Truce—Meeting with Pemberton—Negotiations for
Surrender—Accepting the Terms—
Surrender of Vicksburg

O N THE 22D OF JUNE positive information was received that Johnston
had crossed the Big Black River for the purpose of attacking our rear, to raise
the siege and release Pemberton. The correspondence between Johnston and
Pemberton shows that all expectation of holding Vicksburg had by this time
passed from Johnston's mind.[1] I immediately ordered Sherman to the command of all the forces from Haines' Bluff to the Big Black River. This amounted
now to quite half the troops about Vicksburg. Besides these, Herron and A. J.
Smith's divisions were ordered to hold themselves in readiness to reinforce
Sherman. Haines' Bluff had been strongly fortified on the land side, and on all
commanding points from there to the Big Black at the railroad crossing batteries had been constructed. The work of connecting by rifle-pits where this
was not already done, was an easy task for the troops that were to defend them.

We were now looking west, besieging Pemberton, while we were also looking
east to defend ourselves against an expected siege by Johnston. But as against
the garrison of Vicksburg we were as substantially protected as they were against
us. Where we were looking east and north we were strongly fortified, and on
the defensive. Johnston evidently took in the situation and wisely, I think, abstained from making an assault on us because it would simply have inflicted
loss on both sides without accomplishing any result. We were strong enough

[1] See *OR*, I, 24(III), 963–965, 967, 969, 971, 974.

to have taken the offensive against him; but I did not feel disposed to take any risk of losing our hold upon Pemberton's army, while I would have rejoiced at the opportunity of defending ourselves against an attack by Johnston.

From the 23d of May the work of fortifying and pushing forward our position nearer to the enemy had been steadily progressing. At three points on the Jackson road, in front of Leggett's brigade, a sap was run up to the enemy's parapet, and by the 25th of June we had it undermined and the mine charged. The enemy had countermined, but did not succeed in reaching our mine. At this particular point the hill on which the rebel work stands rises abruptly. Our sap ran close up to the outside of the enemy's parapet. In fact this parapet was also our protection. The soldiers of the two sides occasionally conversed pleasantly across this barrier; sometimes they exchanged the hard bread of the Union soldiers for the tobacco of the Confederates; at other times the enemy threw over hand-grenades, and often our men, catching them in their hands, returned them.

Our mine had been started some distance back down the hill; consequently when it had extended as far as the parapet it was many feet below it. This caused the failure of the enemy in his search to find and destroy it. On the 25th of June at three o'clock, all being ready, the mine was exploded. A heavy artillery fire all along the line had been ordered to open with the explosion.[2] The effect was to blow the top of the hill off and make a crater where it stood. The breach was not sufficient to enable us to pass a column of attack through. In fact, the enemy having failed to reach our mine had thrown up a line farther back, where most of the men guarding that point were placed. There were a few men, however, left at the advance line, and others working in the countermine, which was still being pushed to find ours. All that were there were thrown into the air, some of them coming down on our side, still alive. I remember one colored man, who had been under ground at work when the explosion took place, who was thrown to our side. He was not much hurt, but terribly frightened. Some one asked him how high he had gone up. "Dun no, massa, but t'ink 'bout t'ree mile," was his reply. General Logan commanded at this point and took this colored man to his quarters, where he did service to the end of the siege.[3]

---

[2] USG ordered McPherson to detonate the explosives and penetrate the Confederate fort known as Fort Hill. Herron was directed to fire on the enemy with artillery for "fifteen or twenty minutes" after the explosion occurred. Ibid., I, 24(II), 294; *PUSG*, 8:415*n*.

[3] The enslaved man known only as "Abraham" was reportedly thrown high into the air during the second mine explosion on July 1, 1863. After working for Logan, Abraham became

As soon as the explosion took place the crater was seized by two regiments of our troops who were near by, under cover, where they had been placed for the express purpose.[4] The enemy made a desperate effort to expel them, but failed, and soon retired behind the new line. From here, however, they threw hand-grenades, which did some execution. The compliment was returned by our men, but not with so much effect. The enemy could lay their grenades on the parapet, which alone divided the contestants, and roll them down upon us; while from our side they had to be thrown over the parapet, which was at considerable elevation. During the night we made efforts to secure our position in the crater against the missiles of the enemy, so as to run trenches along the outer base of their parapet, right and left; but the enemy continued throwing their grenades, and brought boxes of field ammunition (shells), the fuses of which they would light with port-fires, and throw them by hand into our ranks. We found it impossible to continue this work. Another mine was consequently started which was exploded on the 1st of July, destroying an entire rebel redan, killing and wounding a considerable number of its occupants and leaving an immense chasm where it stood.[5] No attempt to charge was made this time, the experience of the 25th admonishing us. Our loss in the first affair was about thirty killed and wounded. The enemy must have lost more in the two explosions than we did in the first. We lost none in the second.[6]

From this time forward the work of mining and pushing our position nearer to the enemy was prosecuted with vigor, and I determined to explode no more mines until we were ready to explode a number at different points and assault immediately after. We were up now at three different points, one in front of each corps, to where only the parapet of the enemy divided us.

a part of P. T. Barnum's traveling American Museum. Gary Ecelbarger, *Black Jack Logan: An Extraordinary Life in Peace and War* (Guilford, CT: Lyon's Press, 2005), 148.

[4] The 45th Illinois Inf. was the first regiment to enter the crater. They were relieved by the 20th Illinois Inf. and then followed by other regiments from Illinois, Indiana, and Iowa. *OR*, I, 24(II), 294.

[5] Captain Andrew Hickenlooper, chief engineer of the 17th Army Corps, reported that an explosive under the "left curtain" of Fort Hill was detonated at 1:00 P.M. He wrote that seven or eight Confederates countermining toward U.S. lines were killed by the blast. Ibid., I, 24(II), 203.

[6] During the June 25–26, 1863, assault, thirty-four U.S. troops were killed and 209 wounded. Twenty-one Confederates were killed and seventy-three wounded. Confederate casualties from the July 1 explosion included at least three killed and twenty-five wounded. Edwin Cole Bearss, *Vicksburg Is the Key*, vol. 3 of *Campaign for Vicksburg* (Dayton, OH: Morningside House, 1986), 924, 928n.

At this time an intercepted dispatch from Johnston to Pemberton informed me that Johnston intended to make a determined attack upon us in order to relieve the garrison at Vicksburg.[7] I knew the garrison would make no formidable effort to relieve itself. The picket lines were so close to each other—where there was space enough between the lines to post pickets—that the men could converse. On the 21st of June I was informed, through this means, that Pemberton was preparing to escape, by crossing to the Louisiana side under cover of night; that he had employed workmen in making boats for that purpose; that the men had been canvassed to ascertain if they would make an assault on the "Yankees" to cut their way out; that they had refused, and almost mutinied, because their commander would not surrender and relieve their sufferings, and had only been pacified by the assurance that boats enough would be finished in a week to carry them all over. The rebel pickets also said that houses in the city had been pulled down to get material to build these boats with. Afterwards this story was verified: on entering the city we found a large number of very rudely constructed boats.[8]

All necessary steps were at once taken to render such an attempt abortive. Our pickets were doubled; Admiral Porter was notified, so that the river might be more closely watched; material was collected on the west bank of the river to be set on fire and light up the river if the attempt was made; and batteries were established along the levee crossing the peninsula on the Louisiana side. Had the attempt been made the garrison of Vicksburg would have been drowned, or made prisoners on the Louisiana side. General Richard Taylor was expected on the west bank to co-operate in this movement, I believe, but he did not come, nor could he have done so with a force sufficient to be of service.[9] The Mississippi was now in our possession from its source to its mouth,

---

[7] In his known correspondence, USG did not reference any letter from Johnston to Pemberton that was intercepted in late June 1863. However, on June 24, Col. James H. Blood of the 6th Missouri Inf. captured a Confederate mail courier leaving Vicksburg. USG reported that some of the letters Blood took expressed confidence that Johnston would reinforce Vicksburg. In a June 27 letter that Pemberton never received, Johnston expressed his hope of relieving the defenders of Vicksburg while also acknowledging that Pemberton may have had to enter into surrender negotiations with USG. *OR,* I, 24(III), 980; *PUSG,* 8:423, 424n.

[8] On June 22, 1863, Johnston advised Pemberton to attempt an escape by crossing the river. However, no surviving Confederate sources document a plan to construct boats, and no other eyewitnesses to the end of the siege indicate the discovery of large numbers of boats at Vicksburg in their reports. Michael B. Ballard, *Grant at Vicksburg: The General and the Siege* (Carbondale: Southern Illinois University Press, 2013), 123; *OR,* I, 24(III), 971–972.

[9] Instead of reinforcing Vicksburg, Taylor attacked and captured Brashear City, LA, on June 23, 1863, to try to interfere with Banks's assault on Port Hudson, LA. *OR,* I, 26(I), 210.

except in the immediate front of Vicksburg and of Port Hudson. We had nearly exhausted the country, along a line drawn from Lake Providence to opposite Bruinsburg. The roads west were not of a character to draw supplies over for any considerable force.

By the 1st of July our approaches had reached the enemy's ditch at a number of places. At ten points we could move under cover to within from five to one hundred yards of the enemy. Orders were given to make all preparations for assault on the 6th of July. The debouches were ordered widened to afford easy egress, while the approaches were also to be widened to admit the troops to pass through four abreast. Plank, and bags filled with cotton packed in tightly, were ordered prepared, to enable the troops to cross the ditches.

On the night of the 1st of July Johnston was between Brownsville and the Big Black, and wrote Pemberton from there that about the 7th of the month an attempt would be made to create a diversion to enable him to cut his way out.[10] Pemberton was a prisoner before this message reached him.

On July 1st Pemberton, seeing no hope of outside relief, addressed the following letter to each of his four division commanders:[11]

"Unless the siege of Vicksburg is raised, or supplies are thrown in, it will become necessary very shortly to evacuate the place. I see no prospect of the former, and there are many great, if not insuperable obstacles in the way of the latter. You are, therefore, requested to inform me with as little delay as possible, as to the condition of your troops and their ability to make the marches and undergo the fatigues necessary to accomplish a successful evacuation."

Two of his generals suggested surrender, and the other two practically did the same. They expressed the opinion that an attempt to evacuate would fail. Pemberton had previously got a message to Johnston suggesting that he should try to negotiate with me for a release of the garrison with their arms. Johnston replied that it would be a confession of weakness for him to do so; but he authorized Pemberton to use his name in making such an arrangement.[12]

---

[10] Johnston wrote to Pemberton on July 3, 1863, from a camp near Birdsong Ferry on the Big Black River. Ibid., I, 24(III), 987; *PUSG,* 8:259n.

[11] Pemberton sent the letter to Maj. Gen. Carter L. Stevenson, Maj. Gen. John H. Forney, Maj. Gen. Martin L. Smith, and Maj. Gen. John S. Bowen. OR, I, 24(I), 281–283.

[12] See ibid. for the response of each general and the exchange between Pemberton and Johnston.

On the 3d about ten o'clock A.M. white flags appeared on a portion of the rebel works. Hostilities along that part of the line ceased at once. Soon two persons were seen coming towards our lines bearing a white flag. They proved to be General Bowen, a division commander, and Colonel Montgomery,[13] aide-de-camp to Pemberton, bearing the following letter to me:

> "I have the honor to propose an armistice for——hours, with the view to arranging terms for the capitulation of Vicksburg. To this end, if agreeable to you, I will appoint three commissioners, to meet a like number to be named by yourself, at such place and hour to-day as you may find convenient. I make this proposition to save the further effusion of blood, which must otherwise be shed to a frightful extent, feeling myself fully able to maintain my position for a yet indefinite period. This communication will be handed you under a flag of truce, by Major-General John S. Bowen."[14]

It was a glorious sight to officers and soldiers on the line where these white flags were visible, and the news soon spread to all parts of the command. The troops felt that their long and weary marches, hard fighting, ceaseless watching by night and day, in a hot climate, exposure to all sorts of weather, to diseases and, worst of all, to the gibes of many Northern papers that came to them saying all their suffering was in vain, that Vicksburg would never be taken, were at last at an end and the Union sure to be saved.

Bowen was received by General A. J. Smith, and asked to see me. I had been a neighbor of Bowen's in Missouri, and knew him well and favorably before the war; but his request was refused. He then suggested that I should meet Pemberton. To this I sent a verbal message saying that, if Pemberton desired it, I would meet him in front of McPherson's corps at three o'clock that afternoon. I also sent the following written reply to Pemberton's letter:

---

[13] Louis M. Montgomery was assigned to Lt. Gen. E. Kirby Smith's staff in the Trans-Mississippi Dept. but was unable to travel there and instead volunteered as an aide-de-camp to Pemberton. He was present at the conference between Pemberton and USG on July 3, 1863. Pemberton listed Montgomery's rank as captain in his Vicksburg report but referred to him as lieutenant colonel when describing that he had been assigned to Smith's staff. Ibid., I, 24(I), 267, 284, 294.

[14] See *PUSG*, 8:455*n*.

"Your note of this date is just received, proposing an armistice for several hours, for the purpose of arranging terms of capitulation through commissioners, to be appointed, etc. The useless effusion of blood you propose stopping by this course can be ended at any time you may choose, by the unconditional surrender of the city and garrison. Men who have shown so much endurance and courage as those now in Vicksburg, will always challenge the respect of an adversary, and I can assure you will be treated with all the respect due to prisoners of war. I do not favor the proposition of appointing commissioners to arrange the terms of capitulation, because I have no terms other than those indicated above."

At three o'clock Pemberton appeared at the point suggested in my verbal message, accompanied by the same officers who had borne his letter of the morning. Generals Ord, McPherson, Logan and A. J. Smith, and several officers of my staff, accompanied me. Our place of meeting was on a hillside within a few hundred feet of the rebel lines. Near by stood a stunted oak-tree, which was made historical by the event. It was but a short time before the last vestige of its body, root and limb had disappeared, the fragments taken as trophies. Since then the same tree has furnished as many cords of wood, in the shape of trophies, as "The True Cross."

Pemberton and I had served in the same division during part of the Mexican War.[15] I knew him very well therefore, and greeted him as an old acquaintance. He soon asked what terms I proposed to give his army if it surrendered. My answer was the same as proposed in my reply to his letter. Pemberton then said, rather snappishly, "The conference might as well end," and turned abruptly as if to leave. I said, "Very well." General Bowen, I saw, was very anxious that the surrender should be consummated. His manner and remarks while Pemberton and I were talking, showed this. He now proposed that he and one of our generals should have a conference.[16] I had no objection to this, as nothing could be made binding upon me that they might propose. Smith and Bowen

[15] Pemberton was in the U.S. 4th Art. during the Mexican-American War while USG was in the U.S. 4th Inf. John C. Pemberton, *Pemberton: Defender of Vicksburg* (Chapel Hill: University of North Carolina Press, 2002), 15.

[16] Pemberton stated in his Vicksburg report that USG proposed a conference between A. J. Smith, McPherson, Bowen, and Montgomery. Bowen may have told USG and Pemberton that the other desired a meeting in order to bring them together. Michael B. Ballard, *Vicksburg: The Campaign That Opened the Mississippi* (Chapel Hill: University of North Carolina Press, 2004), 397; *OR*, I, 24(I), 284.

accordingly had a conference, during which Pemberton and I, moving a short distance away towards the enemy's lines were in conversation. After a while Bowen suggested that the Confederate army should be allowed to march out with the honors of war, carrying their small arms and field artillery. This was promptly and unceremoniously rejected. The interview here ended, I agreeing, however, to send a letter giving final terms by ten o'clock that night.

Word was sent to Admiral Porter soon after the correspondence with Pemberton commenced, so that hostilities might be stopped on the part of both army and navy. It was agreed on my parting with Pemberton that they should not be renewed until our correspondence ceased.

When I returned to my headquarters I sent for all the corps and division commanders with the army immediately confronting Vicksburg. Half the army was from eight to twelve miles off, waiting for Johnston.[17] I informed them of the contents of Pemberton's letters, of my reply and the substance of the interview, and that I was ready to hear any suggestion; but would hold the power of deciding entirely in my own hands. This was the nearest approach to a "council of war" I ever held. Against the general, and almost unanimous judgment of the council I sent the following letter:

"In conformity with agreement of this afternoon, I will submit the following proposition for the surrender of the City of Vicksburg, public stores, etc. On your accepting the terms proposed, I will march in one division as a guard, and take possession at eight A.M. to-morrow. As soon as rolls can be made out, and paroles be signed by officers and men, you will be allowed to march out of our lines, the officers taking with them their side-arms and clothing, and the field, staff and cavalry officers one horse each. The rank and file will be allowed all their clothing, but no other property. If these conditions are accepted, any amount of rations you may deem necessary can be taken from the stores you now have, and also the necessary cooking utensils for preparing them. Thirty wagons also, counting two two-horse or mule teams as one, will be allowed to transport such articles as cannot be carried along. The same conditions will be allowed to all sick and wounded officers and soldiers as fast as they

[17] On June 22, 1863, USG had placed Sherman in command of the troops watching for Johnston. Sherman's forces, consisting of a division from each army corps involved at Vicksburg, were stationed from Haines' Bluff to the Big Black River. *PUSG,* 8:408; William T. Sherman, *Memoirs of General William T. Sherman* (New York: D. Appleton, 1875), 1:328–329.

become able to travel. The paroles for these latter must be signed, however, whilst officers present are authorized to sign the roll of prisoners."

By the terms of the cartel then in force, prisoners captured by either army
were required to be forwarded as soon as possible to either Aiken's landing
below Dutch Gap on the James River, or to Vicksburg, there to be exchanged,
or paroled until they could be exchanged.[18] There was a Confederate commissioner at Vicksburg, authorized to make the exchange. I did not propose to take
him a prisoner, but to leave him free to perform the functions of his office.[19] Had
I insisted upon an unconditional surrender there would have been over thirty
thousand men to transport to Cairo, very much to the inconvenience of the
army on the Mississippi. Thence the prisoners would have had to be transported
by rail to Washington or Baltimore; thence again by steamer to Aiken's—all at
very great expense. At Aiken's they would have had to be paroled, because the
Confederates did not have Union prisoners to give in exchange. Then again
Pemberton's army was largely composed of men whose homes were in the
South-west; I knew many of them were tired of the war and would get home
just as soon as they could. A large number of them had voluntarily come into
our lines during the siege, and requested to be sent north where they could get
employment until the war was over and they could go to their homes.

Late at night I received the following reply to my last letter:

"I have the honor to acknowledge the receipt of your communication of
this date, proposing terms of capitulation for this garrison and post. In the
main your terms are accepted; but, in justice both to the honor and spirit
of my troops, manifested in the defence of Vicksburg, I have to submit
the following amendments, which, if acceded to by you, will perfect the

[18] The agreement negotiated on July 22, 1862, by Gen. John A. Dix (U.S. Army) and Gen.
D. H. Hill (Confederate Army) established Aiken's Landing, VA, and Vicksburg as points for
exchanging and delivering prisoners of war. John Martin Davis Jr. and George B. Tremmel,
*Parole, Pardon, Pass and Amnesty Documents of the Civil War: An Illustrated History* (Jefferson,
NC: McFarland, 2014), 22; *OR*, II, 4, 266–268.

[19] Nathan G. Watts (c.1815–?) was a deputy U.S. marshal and served as a quartermaster in
the Confederate Army. In Apr. 1863, he was a Confederate agent for the exchange of prisoners
at Vicksburg. By Oct., he had been promoted to lieutenant colonel and was stationed at Mobile,
AL. Jefferson Davis, *The Papers of Jefferson Davis*, vol. 10, ed. Lynda Laswell Crist, Kenneth
H. Williams, and Peggy L. Dillard (Baton Rouge: Louisiana State University Press, 1999),
218; *OR*, II, 5, 476; II, 6, 601.

agreement between us. At ten o'clock A.M. to-morrow, I propose to evacuate the works in and around Vicksburg, and to surrender the city and garrison under my command, by marching out with my colors and arms, stacking them in front of my present lines. After which you will take possession. Officers to retain their side-arms and personal property, and the rights and property of citizens to be respected."[20]

This was received after midnight. My reply was as follows:

"I have the honor to acknowledge the receipt of your communication of 3d July. The amendment proposed by you cannot be acceded to in full. It will be necessary to furnish every officer and man with a parole signed by himself, which, with the completion of the roll of prisoners, will necessarily take some time. Again, I can make no stipulations with regard to the treatment of citizens and their private property. While I do not propose to cause them any undue annoyance or loss, I cannot consent to leave myself under any restraint by stipulations. The property which officers will be allowed to take with them will be as stated in my proposition of last evening; that is, officers will be allowed their private baggage and side-arms, and mounted officers one horse each. If you mean by your proposition for each brigade to march to the front of the lines now occupied by it, and stack arms at ten o'clock A.M., and then return to the inside and there remain as prisoners until properly paroled, I will make no objection to it. Should no notification be received of your acceptance of my terms by nine o'clock A.M. I shall regard them as having been rejected, and shall act accordingly. Should these terms be accepted, white flags should be displayed along your lines to prevent such of my troops as may not have been notified, from firing upon your men."

Pemberton promptly accepted these terms.

During the siege there had been a good deal of friendly sparring between the soldiers of the two armies, on picket and where the lines were close together. All rebels were known as "Johnnies," all Union troops as "Yanks." Often "Johnny" would call: "Well, Yank, when are you coming into town?" The reply was sometimes: "We propose to celebrate the 4th of July there." Sometimes it would be: "We always treat our prisoners with kindness and do not want to hurt them;" or, "We are holding you as prisoners of war while you are feeding

[20] See *PUSG*, 8:458*n*.

yourselves." The garrison, from the commanding general down, undoubtedly expected an assault on the fourth. They knew from the temper of their men it would be successful when made; and that would be a greater humiliation than to surrender. Besides it would be attended with severe loss to them.

The Vicksburg paper, which we received regularly through the courtesy of the rebel pickets, said prior to the fourth, in speaking of the "Yankee" boast that they would take dinner in Vicksburg that day, that the best receipt for cooking a rabbit was "First ketch your rabbit." The paper at this time and for some time previous was printed on the plain side of wall paper. The last number was issued on the fourth and announced that we had "caught our rabbit."[21]

I have no doubt that Pemberton commenced his correspondence on the third with a two-fold purpose: first, to avoid an assault, which he knew would be successful, and second, to prevent the capture taking place on the great national holiday, the anniversary of the Declaration of American Independence. Holding out for better terms as he did he defeated his aim in the latter particular.

At the appointed hour the garrison of Vicksburg marched out of their works and formed line in front, stacked arms and marched back in good order. Our whole army present witnessed this scene without cheering. Logan's division, which had approached nearest the rebel works, was the first to march in; and the flag of one of the regiments of his division was soon floating over the courthouse.[22] Our soldiers were no sooner inside the lines than the two armies began to fraternize. Our men had had full rations from the time the siege commenced, to the close. The enemy had been suffering, particularly towards the last. I myself saw our men taking bread from their haversacks and giving it to the enemy they had so recently been engaged in starving out. It was accepted with avidity and with thanks.

Pemberton says in his report:

[21] The July 2, 1863, *Vicksburg Daily Citizen* included the comment that if USG wanted to celebrate July 4 with dinner in Vicksburg as reported, he first "must get into the city before he dines in it. The way to cook a rabbit is 'first catch the rabbit.'" U.S. troops who entered the city on July 4 found the July 2 edition ready to be printed and added a message that "Gen. Grant has 'caught the rabbit.'" Bearss, *Vicksburg Is the Key,* 1299; "Note" and "On Dit," Vicksburg *Daily Citizen,* July 4, 1863; M. M. Quaife, "Historical Fragments: Some Light on Two Historical Hoaxes," *Wisconsin Magazine of History* 2 (1918): 78.

[22] Soldiers from both the 45th Illinois Inf. and the 4th Minnesota Inf. claimed that their regimental flag flew over the courthouse at the surrender. Bearss, *Vicksburg Is the Key,* 1294–1295.

"If it should be asked why the 4th of July was selected as the day for surrender, the answer is obvious. I believed that upon that day I should obtain better terms. Well aware of the vanity of our foe, I knew they would attach vast importance to the entrance on the 4th of July into the stronghold of the great river, and that, to gratify their national vanity, they would yield then what could not be extorted from them at any other time."[23]

This does not support my view of his reasons for selecting the day he did for surrendering. But it must be recollected that his first letter asking terms was received about 10 o'clock A.M., July 3d. It then could hardly be expected that it would take twenty-four hours to effect a surrender. He knew that Johnston was in our rear for the purpose of raising the siege, and he naturally would want to hold out as long as he could. He knew his men would not resist an assault, and one was expected on the fourth. In our interview he told me he had rations enough to hold out for some time—my recollection is two weeks.[24] It was this statement that induced me to insert in the terms that he was to draw rations for his men from his own supplies.

On the 4th of July General Holmes, with an army of eight or nine thousand men belonging to the trans-Mississippi department, made an attack upon Helena, Arkansas. He was totally defeated by General Prentiss, who was holding Helena with less than forty-two hundred soldiers. Holmes reported his loss at 1,636, of which 173 were killed; but as Prentiss buried 400, Holmes evidently understated his losses. The Union loss was 57 killed, 127 wounded, and between 30 and 40 missing. This was the last effort on the part of the Confederacy to raise the siege of Vicksburg.[25]

On the third, as soon as negotiations were commenced, I notified Sherman and directed him to be ready to take the offensive against Johnston, drive him out of the State and destroy his army if he could. Steele and Ord were directed at the same time to be in readiness to join Sherman as soon as the surrender took place. Of this Sherman was notified.

[23] See *OR*, I, 24(I), 285.

[24] In a July 6, 1863, letter to his father USG stated that the Confederates at Vicksburg had about four days of rations left when they surrendered the city. *PUSG*, 8:524.

[25] Prentiss estimated that the Confederate forces numbered at least 15,000, but Holmes reported that he had 7,646 troops. Prentiss reported that he had 4,129 men engaged in the defense of Helena, AR. In addition to the numbers of killed and wounded cited by USG, Prentiss reported thirty-six U.S. troops missing. *OR*, I, 22(I), 389, 411.

I rode into Vicksburg with the troops, and went to the river to exchange congratulations with the navy upon our joint victory. At that time I found that many of the citizens had been living under ground. The ridges upon which Vicksburg is built, and those back to the Big Black, are composed of a deep yellow clay of great tenacity. Where roads and streets are cut through, perpendicular banks are left and stand as well as if composed of stone. The magazines of the enemy were made by running passage-ways into this clay at places where there were deep cuts. Many citizens secured places of safety for their families by carving out rooms in these embankments. A door-way in these cases would be cut in a high bank, starting from the level of the road or street, and after running in a few feet a room of the size required was carved out of the clay, the dirt being removed by the door-way. In some instances I saw where two rooms were cut out, for a single family, with a door-way in the clay wall separating them. Some of these were carpeted and furnished with considerable elaboration. In these the occupants were fully secure from the shells of the navy, which were dropped into the city night and day without intermission.

I returned to my old headquarters outside in the afternoon, and did not move into the town until the sixth. On the afternoon of the fourth I sent Captain Wm. M. Dunn[26] of my staff to Cairo, the nearest point where the telegraph could be reached, with a dispatch to the general-in-chief. It was as follows:

"The enemy surrendered this morning. The only terms allowed is their parole as prisoners of war. This I regard as a great advantage to us at this moment. It saves, probably, several days in the capture, and leaves troops and transports ready for immediate service. Sherman, with a large force, moves immediately on Johnston, to drive him from the State. I will send troops to the relief of Banks, and return the 9th army corps to Burnside."

This news, with the victory at Gettysburg won the same day, lifted a great load of anxiety from the minds of the President, his Cabinet and the loyal people all over the North. The fate of the Confederacy was sealed when Vicksburg fell. Much hard fighting was to be done afterwards and many precious lives were to be sacrificed; but the *morale* was with the supporters of the Union ever after.

---

[26] William M. Dunn Jr. (c.1843–c.1891) enlisted in the 6th Indiana Inf. as a private in Apr. 1861 and was promoted to first lieutenant while serving in the 83rd Indiana Inf. During the siege of Vicksburg, he started his service as acting aide to USG. *PUSG,* 9:576*n.*

I at the same time wrote to General Banks informing him of the fall and sending him a copy of the terms; also saying I would send him all the troops he wanted to insure the capture of the only foothold the enemy now had on the Mississippi River. General Banks had a number of copies of this letter printed, or at least a synopsis of it, and very soon a copy fell into the hands of General Gardner, who was then in command of Port Hudson. Gardner at once sent a letter to the commander of the National forces saying that he had been informed of the surrender of Vicksburg and telling how the information reached him. He added that if this was true, it was useless for him to hold out longer. General Banks gave him assurances that Vicksburg had been surrendered, and General Gardner surrendered unconditionally on the 9th of July.[27] Port Hudson with nearly 6,000 prisoners, 51 guns, 5,000 small-arms and other stores fell into the hands of the Union forces: from that day to the close of the rebellion the Mississippi River, from its source to its mouth, remained in the control of the National troops.

Pemberton and his army were kept in Vicksburg until the whole could be paroled. The paroles were in duplicate, by organization (one copy for each, Federals and Confederates), and signed by the commanding officers of the companies or regiments. Duplicates were also made for each soldier and signed by each individually, one to be retained by the soldier signing and one to be retained by us. Several hundred refused to sign their paroles, preferring to be sent to the North as prisoners to being sent back to fight again. Others again kept out of the way, hoping to escape either alternative.

Pemberton appealed to me in person to compel these men to sign their paroles, but I declined.[28] It also leaked out that many of the men who had signed their paroles, intended to desert and go to their homes as soon as they got out of our lines. Pemberton hearing this, again appealed to me to assist him. He wanted arms for a battalion, to act as guards in keeping his men together while being marched to a camp of instruction, where he expected to keep them until exchanged. This request was also declined. It was precisely what I expected and hoped that they would do. I told him, however, that I would see that they marched beyond our lines in good order. By the eleventh, just one week after the surrender, the paroles were completed and the Confederate garrison

[27] Gardner wrote to Banks from Port Hudson on July 7, 1863, and Banks responded the next day. *OR,* I, 26(I), 52–53.

[28] On July 8, 1863, USG directed McPherson to inform Confederate prisoners that they would be confined aboard steamers until they signed their paroles or sent to prisoner-of-war camps in the North if they still refused. *PUSG,* 9:4.

marched out. Many deserted, and fewer of them were ever returned to the ranks to fight again than would have been the case had the surrender been unconditional and the prisoners sent to the James River to be paroled.

As soon as our troops took possession of the city guards were established along the whole line of parapet, from the river above to the river below. The prisoners were allowed to occupy their old camps behind the intrenchments. No restraint was put upon them, except by their own commanders. They were rationed about as our own men, and from our supplies. The men of the two armies fraternized as if they had been fighting for the same cause. When they passed out of the works they had so long and so gallantly defended, between lines of their late antagonists, not a cheer went up, not a remark was made that would give pain. Really, I believe there was a feeling of sadness just then in the breasts of most of the Union soldiers at seeing the dejection of their late antagonists.

The day before the departure the following order was issued:

"Paroled prisoners will be sent out of here to-morrow. They will be authorized to cross at the railroad bridge, and move from there to Edward's Ferry,* and on by way of Raymond. Instruct the commands to be orderly and quiet as these prisoners pass, to make no offensive remarks, and not to harbor any who fall out of ranks after they have passed."[29]

*Meant Edward's Station.[30]

[29] USG issued this order on July 8, 1863. The paroled prisoners marched out of Vicksburg on July 11. Ibid., and 9:8*n*.

[30] The version of the order from July 8, 1863, identified the place as "Edward's station." Ibid., 9:8.

# 39

Retrospect of the Campaign—Sherman's Movements—
Proposed Movement upon Mobile—A Painful
Accident—Ordered to Report at Cairo

T HE CAPTURE OF Vicksburg, with its garrison, ordnance and ordnance stores, and the successful battles fought in reaching them, gave new spirit to the loyal people of the North. New hopes for the final success of the cause of the Union were inspired. The victory gained at Gettysburg, upon the same day, added to their hopes. Now the Mississippi River was entirely in the possession of the National troops; for the fall of Vicksburg gave us Port Hudson at once. The army of northern Virginia was driven out of Pennsylvania and forced back to about the same ground it occupied in 1861. The Army of the Tennessee united with the Army of the Gulf, dividing the Confederate States completely.

The first dispatch I received from the government after the fall of Vicksburg was in these words:

> "I fear your paroling the prisoners at Vicksburg, without actual delivery to a proper agent as required by the seventh article of the cartel, may be construed into an absolute release, and that the men will immediately be placed in the ranks of the enemy. Such has been the case elsewhere. If these prisoners have not been allowed to depart, you will detain them until further orders."[1]

Halleck did not know that they had already been delivered into the hands of Major Watts, Confederate commissioner for the exchange of prisoners.

[1] Halleck's original telegram erroneously mentioned the nonexistent fourteenth article of the Dix-Hill Cartel. For Halleck's July 8, 1863, telegram to USG, see *PUSG*, 8:470n. For the text of the cartel, see *OR*, II, 4, 266–268.

At Vicksburg 31,600 prisoners were surrendered, together with 172 cannon, about 60,000 muskets and a large amount of ammunition.[2] The small-arms of the enemy were far superior to the bulk of ours. Up to this time our troops at the West had been limited to the old United States flint-lock muskets changed into percussion, or the Belgian musket imported early in the war—almost as dangerous to the person firing it as to the one aimed at—and a few new and improved arms. These were of many different calibers, a fact that caused much trouble in distributing ammunition during an engagement.[3] The enemy had generally new arms which had run the blockade and were of uniform caliber.[4] After the surrender I authorized all colonels whose regiments were armed with inferior muskets, to place them in the stack of captured arms and replace them with the latter. A large number of arms turned in to the Ordnance Department as captured, were thus arms that had really been used by the Union army in the capture of Vicksburg.

In this narrative I have not made the mention I should like of officers, dead and alive, whose services entitle them to special mention. Neither have I made that mention of the navy which its services deserve. Suffice it to say, the close of the siege of Vicksburg found us with an army unsurpassed, in proportion to its numbers, taken as a whole of officers and men. A military education was acquired which no other school could have given. Men who thought a company was quite enough for them to command properly at the beginning, would have made good regimental or brigade commanders; most of the brigade commanders were equal to the command of a division, and one, Ransom,

[2] The numbers recorded in the *OR* reflect 29,491 Confederate prisoners, along with the surrender of over 50,000 small arms and 600,000 rounds of ammunition. Edwin Cole Bearss, *Vicksburg Is the Key*, vol. 3 of *Campaign for Vicksburg* (Dayton, OH: Morningside House, 1986), 1301; *OR*, I, 24(I), 62.

[3] Most of USG's troops carried .577-caliber British 1853 Enfield rifle-muskets, .58-caliber Springfield rifle-muskets, or other similar weapons classed as "first class." The remainder carried mostly "second class" weapons, which included older-model rifled muskets in a wide variety of calibers. Some were rifled muskets of varying quality manufactured in Liege, Belgium. Only the 101st Illinois Inf. used weapons designated "third class," which would have included smoothbore muskets in various calibers. Joseph D. Bilby, *Civil War Firearms: Their Historical Background, Tactical Use and Modern Collecting and Shooting* (Conshohocken, PA: Combined Books, 1996), 20–23, 69; Christopher R. Gabel, *Staff Ride Handbook for the Vicksburg Campaign, December 1862–July 1863* (Fort Leavenworth, KS: Combat Studies Institute, 2001), 32.

[4] Many of the arms used by Confederates at Vicksburg, MS, were 1853 Enfields, but they used many other models and calibers as well. Gabel, *Staff Ride Handbook*, 32–33.

would have been equal to the command of a corps at least. Logan and Crocker ended the campaign fitted to command independent armies.

General F. P. Blair joined me at Milliken's Bend a full-fledged general, without having served in a lower grade. He commanded a division in the campaign. I had known Blair in Missouri, where I had voted against him in 1858 when he ran for Congress. I knew him as a frank, positive and generous man, true to his friends even to a fault, but always a leader. I dreaded his coming; I knew from experience that it was more difficult to command two generals desiring to be leaders than it was to command one army officered intelligently and with subordination. It affords me the greatest pleasure to record now my agreeable disappointment in respect to his character. There was no man braver than he, nor was there any who obeyed all orders of his superior in rank with more unquestioning alacrity. He was one man as a soldier, another as a politician.

The navy under Porter was all it could be, during the entire campaign. Without its assistance the campaign could not have been successfully made with twice the number of men engaged. It could not have been made at all, in the way it was, with any number of men without such assistance. The most perfect harmony reigned between the two arms of the service. There never was a request made, that I am aware of, either of the flag-officer or any of his subordinates, that was not promptly complied with.

The campaign of Vicksburg was suggested and developed by circumstances. The elections of 1862 had gone against the prosecution of the war. Voluntary enlistments had nearly ceased and the draft had been resorted to; this was resisted, and a defeat or backward movement would have made its execution impossible. A forward movement to a decisive victory was necessary. Accordingly I resolved to get below Vicksburg, unite with Banks against Port Hudson, make New Orleans a base and, with that base and Grand Gulf as a starting point, move our combined forces against Vicksburg. Upon reaching Grand Gulf, after running its batteries and fighting a battle, I received a letter from Banks informing me that he could not be at Port Hudson under ten days, and then with only fifteen thousand men.[5] The time was worth more than the reinforcements; I therefore determined to push into the interior of the enemy's country.

With a large river behind us, held above and below by the enemy, rapid movements were essential to success. Jackson was captured the day after a new

[5] On May 13, 1863, Banks informed USG that he could only send 12,000 troops in "10 or 12" days. USG was in the Raymond, MS, area on May 13. *PUSG,* 8:191*n,* 208–212.

commander had arrived, and only a few days before large reinforcements were expected.[6] A rapid movement west was made; the garrison of Vicksburg was met in two engagements and badly defeated, and driven back into its stronghold and there successfully besieged. It looks now as though Providence had directed the course of the campaign while the Army of the Tennessee executed the decree.

Upon the surrender of the garrison of Vicksburg there were three things that required immediate attention. The first was to send a force to drive the enemy from our rear, and out of the State. The second was to send reinforcements to Banks near Port Hudson, if necessary, to complete the triumph of opening the Mississippi from its source to its mouth to the free navigation of vessels bearing the Stars and Stripes. The third was to inform the authorities at Washington and the North of the good news, to relieve their long suspense and strengthen their confidence in the ultimate success of the cause they had so much at heart.

Soon after negotiations were opened with General Pemberton for the surrender of the city, I notified Sherman, whose troops extended from Haines' Bluff on the left to the crossing of the Vicksburg and Jackson road over the Big Black on the right, and directed him to hold his command in readiness to advance and drive the enemy from the State as soon as Vicksburg surrendered. Steele and Ord were directed to be in readiness to join Sherman in his move against General Johnston, and Sherman was advised of this also. Sherman moved promptly, crossing the Big Black at three different points with as many columns, all concentrating at Bolton, twenty miles west of Jackson.[7]

Johnston heard of the surrender of Vicksburg almost as soon as it occurred, and immediately fell back on Jackson. On the 8th of July Sherman was within ten miles of Jackson and on the 11th was close up to the defences of the city and shelling the town. The siege was kept up until the morning of the 17th, when it was found that the enemy had evacuated during the night. The weather was very hot, the roads dusty and the water bad. Johnston destroyed the roads as he passed and had so much the start that pursuit was useless; but Sherman sent one division, Steele's, to Brandon, fourteen miles east of Jackson.

The National loss in the second capture of Jackson was less than one thousand men, killed, wounded and missing. The Confederate loss was

[6] On May 13, 1863 (the night before the Battle of Jackson), Johnston took command of Confederate troops in Jackson, MS. *OR,* I, 24(I), 239.

[7] On July 3, 1863, after the siege of Vicksburg was lifted, USG informed Sherman, Steele, and Ord of his proposed movements. *PUSG,* 8:461.

probably less, except in captured. More than this number fell into our hands as prisoners.[8]

Medicines and food were left for the Confederate wounded and sick who had to be left behind. A large amount of rations was issued to the families that remained in Jackson. Medicine and food were also sent to Raymond for the destitute families as well as the sick and wounded, as I thought it only fair that we should return to these people some of the articles we had taken while marching through the country. I wrote to Sherman: "Impress upon the men the importance of going through the State in an orderly manner, abstaining from taking anything not absolutely necessary for their subsistence while travelling. They should try to create as favorable an impression as possible upon the people."[9] Provisions and forage, when called for by them, were issued to all the people, from Bruinsburg to Jackson and back to Vicksburg, whose resources had been taken for the supply of our army. Very large quantities of groceries and provisions were so issued.

Sherman was ordered back to Vicksburg, and his troops took much the same position they had occupied before—from the Big Black to Haines' Bluff.[10]

Having cleaned up about Vicksburg and captured or routed all regular Confederate forces for more than a hundred miles in all directions, I felt that the troops that had done so much should be allowed to do more before the enemy could recover from the blow he had received, and while important points might be captured without bloodshed. I suggested to the General-in-chief the idea of a campaign against Mobile, starting from Lake Pontchartrain.[11] Halleck preferred another course. The possession of the trans-Mississippi by the Union forces seemed to possess more importance in his mind than almost any campaign east of the Mississippi. I am well aware that the President was very

[8] During the Second Battle of Jackson, the U.S. Army lost 1,122 troops, with 129 killed, 762 wounded, and 231 captured or missing. The Confederate Army reported 71 killed, 504 wounded, and 25 captured or missing. The Confederate totals are inaccurate because most of the Confederate commanders failed to submit casualty reports. Edwin C. Bearss, *The Battle of Jackson, May 14, 1863; The Siege of Jackson, July 10–17, 1863; Three Other Post-Vicksburg Actions* (Baltimore: Gateway Press, 1981), 124, 129.

[9] USG wrote this letter from Vicksburg on Aug. 6, 1863. *PUSG*, 9:155.

[10] On July 17, 1863, USG ordered Sherman back to Vicksburg once he deemed the pursuit of Confederate forces no longer valuable. On July 20, he told Sherman he could place his forces along the Big Black River or in their previous position just north of Vicksburg. Ibid., 9:66n, 67, 83.

[11] USG first wrote to Halleck on July 18, 1863, about his idea to capture Mobile, AL. Ibid., 9:70.

anxious to have a foothold in Texas, to stop the clamor of some of the foreign governments which seemed to be seeking a pretext to interfere in the war, at least so far as to recognize belligerent rights to the Confederate States.[12] This, however, could have been easily done without wasting troops in western Louisiana and eastern Texas, by sending a garrison at once to Brownsville on the Rio Grande.

Halleck disapproved of my proposition to go against Mobile, so that I was obliged to settle down and see myself put again on the defensive as I had been a year before in west Tennessee. It would have been an easy thing to capture Mobile at the time I proposed to go there. Having that as a base of operations, troops could have been thrown into the interior to operate against General Bragg's army.[13] This would necessarily have compelled Bragg to detach in order to meet this fire in his rear. If he had not done this the troops from Mobile could have inflicted inestimable damage upon much of the country from which his army and Lee's were yet receiving their supplies. I was so much impressed with this idea that I renewed my request later in July and again about the 1st of August, and proposed sending all the troops necessary, asking only the assistance of the navy to protect the debarkation of troops at or near Mobile. I also asked for a leave of absence to visit New Orleans, particularly if my suggestion to move against Mobile should be approved. Both requests were refused.[14] So far as my experience with General Halleck went it was very much easier for him to refuse a favor than to grant one. But I did not regard this as a favor.[15] It was simply in line of duty, though out of my department.

The General-in-chief having decided against me, the depletion of an army, which had won a succession of great victories, commenced, as had been the case the year before after the fall of Corinth when the army was sent where it

[12] In an Aug. 9, 1863, letter, Lincoln explained to USG his desire to send troops to western Texas in response to the French occupation of Mexico. Dean B. Mahin, *One War at a Time: The International Dimensions of the American Civil War* (Washington, DC: Brassey's, 1999), 224–225; *PUSG*, 9:197n.

[13] On July 4, 1863, Bragg's Army of Tennessee retreated from Middle Tennessee into Chattanooga, TN. Judith L. Hallock, *Braxton Bragg and Confederate Defeat*, vol. 2 (Tuscaloosa: University of Alabama Press, 1991), 21–22.

[14] USG wrote to Halleck about the proposed capture of Mobile on July 24 and Aug. 1, 1863. His Aug. 1 request to visit New Orleans, LA, was approved by Halleck on Aug. 9. *PUSG*, 9:109, 137–138, 138n.

[15] Halleck believed he was deferring to the wishes of the Lincoln administration by sending troops to Texas instead of attacking Mobile. *OR*, I, 26(I), 675; *PUSG*, 9:160n.

would do the least good. By orders, I sent to Banks a force of 4,000 men; returned the 9th corps to Kentucky and, when transportation had been collected, started a division of 5,000 men to Schofield[16] in Missouri where Price was raiding the State.[17] I also detached a brigade under Ransom to Natchez, to garrison that place permanently. This latter move was quite fortunate as to the time when Ransom arrived there. The enemy happened to have a large number, about 5,000 head, of beef cattle there on the way from Texas to feed the Eastern armies, and also a large amount of munitions of war which had probably come through Texas from the Rio Grande and which were on the way to Lee's and other armies in the East.[18]

The troops that were left with me around Vicksburg were very busily and unpleasantly employed in making expeditions against guerilla bands and small detachments of cavalry which infested the interior, and in destroying mills, bridges and rolling stock on the railroads. The guerillas and cavalry were not there to fight but to annoy, and therefore disappeared on the first approach of our troops.

The country back of Vicksburg was filled with deserters from Pemberton's army and, it was reported, many from Johnston's also. The men determined not to fight again while the war lasted. Those who lived beyond the reach of the Confederate army wanted to get to their homes. Those who did not, wanted to get North where they could work for their support till the war was over. Besides all this there was quite a peace feeling, for the time being, among the citizens of that part of Mississippi, but this feeling soon subsided. It is not probable that Pemberton got off with over 4,000 of his army to the camp where he proposed taking them, and these were in a demoralized condition.[19]

[16] John M. Schofield (1831–1906) was born in New York and graduated from the USMA in 1853. In Mar. 1855, he was promoted to first lieutenant and served as aide-de-camp to Nathaniel Lyon in 1861. Schofield was promoted to major general during the Civil War and served as U.S. secretary of war from July 1868 to Mar. 1869. *CWHC*, 472–473.

[17] On July 22, 1863, Halleck instructed USG to reinforce Banks and to send the 9th Corps, Army of the Tennessee, to reinforce Rosecrans if circumstances dictated. On July 27, Halleck placed Schofield in command of the troops in Helena, AR, who were to counter Price's movements in Missouri. *PUSG*, 9:71n, 115n.

[18] On July 13, 1863, Ransom and his forces arrived at Natchez, MS, and on July 14 he sent out an expedition that captured 5,000 Texas cattle approximately four miles outside the city. *OR*, I, 24(II), 680–681.

[19] On July 17, 1863, Pemberton reported that troops from areas in Mississippi and westward had already deserted and that he expected those from Georgia, Alabama, and Tennessee to

On the 7th of August I further depleted my army by sending the 13th corps, General Ord commanding, to Banks. Besides this I received orders to co-operate with the latter general in movements west of the Mississippi. Having received this order I went to New Orleans to confer with Banks about the proposed movement. All these movements came to naught.[20]

During this visit I reviewed Banks' army a short distance above Carrollton. The horse I rode was vicious and but little used, and on my return to New Orleans ran away and, shying at a locomotive in the street, fell, probably on me. I was rendered insensible, and when I regained consciousness I found myself in a hotel near by with several doctors attending me.[21] My leg was swollen from the knee to the thigh, and the swelling, almost to the point of bursting, extended along the body up to the arm-pit. The pain was almost beyond endurance. I lay at the hotel something over a week without being able to turn myself in bed. I had a steamer stop at the nearest point possible, and was carried to it on a litter. I was then taken to Vicksburg, where I remained unable to move for some time afterwards.[22]

While I was absent General Sherman declined to assume command because, he said, it would confuse the records; but he let all the orders be made in my name, and was glad to render any assistance he could. No orders were issued by my staff, certainly no important orders, except upon consultation with and approval of Sherman.

On the 13th of September, while I was still in New Orleans, Halleck telegraphed to me to send all available forces to Memphis and thence to Tuscumbia, to co-operate with Rosecrans for the relief of Chattanooga. On the 15th he telegraphed again for all available forces to go to Rosecrans. This was received

desert soon. However, he did not provide a definite number of those who remained. Ibid., I, 24(III), 1010.

[20] On July 30, 1863, Halleck ordered USG to send a corps to reinforce Banks. On Aug. 6, he ordered USG to send a special messenger to Banks in New Orleans with instructions to gain a foothold in Texas. USG arrived in New Orleans to meet with Banks on Sept. 2. *PUSG*, 9:159n–160n, 222n.

[21] After the accident on Sept. 4, 1863, Grant was taken to the Carrollton Hotel. Some people, including Banks and Rawlins, accused him of being drunk when the incident occurred, but there was no proof of this. Bruce Catton, *Grant Takes Command* (Boston: Little, Brown, 1969), 26–27; *PUSG*, 9:xxii, 222n–223n, 475n.

[22] USG arrived at Vicksburg on Sept. 16, 1863, aboard the steamboat *Ben Franklin*. He established his headquarters at the Lum House, a twenty-six-room mansion. Catton, *Grant Takes Command*, 27; *PUSG*, 9:222n.

on the 27th.[23] I was still confined to my bed, unable to rise from it without assistance; but I at once ordered Sherman to send one division to Memphis as fast as transports could be provided. The division of McPherson's corps, which had got off and was on the way to join Steele in Arkansas, was recalled and sent, likewise, to report to Hurlbut at Memphis. Hurlbut was directed to forward these two divisions with two others from his own corps at once, and also to send any other troops that might be returning there.[24] Halleck suggested that some good man, like Sherman or McPherson, should be sent to Memphis to take charge of the troops going east. On this I sent Sherman, as being, I thought, the most suitable person for an independent command, and besides he was entitled to it if it had to be given to any one. He was directed to take with him another division of his corps. This left one back, but having one of McPherson's divisions he had still the equivalent.

Before the receipt by me of these orders the battle of Chickamauga had been fought and Rosecrans forced back into Chattanooga.[25] The administration as well as the General-in-chief was nearly frantic at the situation of affairs there. Mr. Charles A. Dana, an officer of the War Department, was sent to Rosecrans' headquarters. I do not know what his instructions were, but he was still in Chattanooga when I arrived there at a later period.[26]

It seems that Halleck suggested that I should go to Nashville as soon as able to move and take general direction of the troops moving from the west.[27] I received the following dispatch dated October 3d: "It is the wish of the Secretary of War that as soon as General Grant is able he will come to Cairo and

[23] On Sept. 22, 1863, USG acknowledged receipt of Halleck's Sept. 15 letter pertaining to the reinforcement of Rosecrans. *PUSG,* 9:229.

[24] On Sept. 22, 1863, Rawlins telegraphed Halleck's orders to Sherman, issued orders for Brig. Gen. John E. Smith's division of McPherson's 17th Corps to report to Hurlbut at Memphis, TN, and wrote to Hurlbut. Ibid., 9:229*n*–231*n*.

[25] The Battle of Chickamauga and Rosecrans's movement to Chattanooga occurred on Sept. 19 and 20, 1863. Ibid., 9:xxii.

[26] Dana arrived at Rosecrans's headquarters in Chattanooga on Sept. 11, 1863. He gave Rosecrans an Aug. 30 letter from Stanton that indicated Dana's visit was "for the purpose of conferring with you upon any subject which you may desire to have brought to the notice of the department." USG arrived in Chattanooga on Oct. 23, 1863. Charles A. Dana, *Recollections of the Civil War: With the Leaders at Washington and in the Field in the Sixties* (New York: D. Appleton, 1898), 104, 107; *PUSG,* 9:308.

[27] Because of a telegrapher's error, Halleck's Sept. 28, 1863, telegram to USG suggested that he go to Nashville (instead of Memphis) to take command of the effort to reinforce Rosecrans. *PUSG,* 9:273, 276*n*.

report by telegraph."[28] I was still very lame, but started without delay. Arriving at Columbus on the 16th I reported by telegraph: "Your dispatch from Cairo of the 3d directing me to report from Cairo was received at 11.30 on the 10th. Left the same day with staff and headquarters and am here en route for Cairo."[29]

END OF VOL. I

[28] On Oct. 10, 1863, Wilson delivered this message to USG. Ibid., 9:276*n*–277*n*.

[29] USG sent this telegram from Columbus, KY, on Oct. 15, 1863. His original text mistakenly indicated that he received Halleck's Oct. 3 message on Oct. 9. The letterbook copies indicate USG received the telegram on Oct. 10. Ibid., 9:284*n*.

# 40

### First Meeting with Secretary Stanton—General Rosecrans—Commanding Military Division of Mississippi—Andrew Johnson's Address— Arrival at Chattanooga

T HE REPLY (to my telegram of October 16, 1863, from Cairo, announcing my arrival at that point) came on the morning of the 17th, directing me to proceed immediately to the Galt House, Louisville, where I would meet an officer of the War Department with my instructions.[1] I left Cairo within an hour or two after the receipt of this dispatch, going by rail via Indianapolis. Just as the train I was on was starting out of the depot at Indianapolis a messenger came running up to stop it, saying the Secretary of War was coming into the station and wanted to see me.

I had never met Mr. Stanton up to that time, though we had held frequent conversations over the wires the year before, when I was in Tennessee. Occasionally at night he would order the wires between the War Department and my headquarters to be connected, and we would hold a conversation for an hour or two. On this occasion the Secretary was accompanied by Governor Brough of Ohio, whom I had never met, though he and my father had been old acquaintances.[2] Mr. Stanton dismissed the special train that had brought him to Indianapolis, and accompanied me to Louisville.

Up to this time no hint had been given me of what was wanted after I left Vicksburg, except the suggestion in one of Halleck's dispatches that I had better go to Nashville and superintend the operation of troops sent to relieve Rose-

---

[1] For Halleck's Oct. 16, 1863, telegram to USG, see *PUSG*, 9:296*n*.

[2] John Brough (1811–1865) was born in Ohio and served as governor from Jan. 1864 to Aug. 1865. He died from an infection that resulted from an injury to his ankle. *CWHC*, 146.

crans.[3] Soon after we started the Secretary handed me two orders, saying that I might take my choice of them. The two were identical in all but one particular. Both created the "Military Division of the Mississippi," (giving me the command) composed of the Departments of the Ohio, the Cumberland, and the Tennessee, and all the territory from the Alleghanies to the Mississippi River north of Banks's command in the south-west. One order left the department commanders as they were, while the other relieved Rosecrans and assigned Thomas to his place. I accepted the latter.[4] We reached Louisville after night and, if I remember rightly, in a cold, drizzling rain. The Secretary of War told me afterwards that he caught a cold on that occasion from which he never expected to recover. He never did.[5]

A day was spent in Louisville, the Secretary giving me the military news at the capital and talking about the disappointment at the results of some of the campaigns. By the evening of the day after our arrival all matters of discussion seemed exhausted, and I left the hotel to spend the evening away, both Mrs. Grant (who was with me) and myself having relatives living in Louisville.[6] In the course of the evening Mr. Stanton received a dispatch from Mr. C. A. Dana, then in Chattanooga, informing him that unless prevented Rosecrans would retreat, and advising peremptory orders against his doing so.[7]

As stated before, after the fall of Vicksburg I urged strongly upon the government the propriety of a movement against Mobile. General Rosecrans had

[3] On Sept. 28, 1863, Halleck wrote to USG about reinforcing Rosecrans. He suggested that USG should go to Memphis, TN, but the telegraph operator transmitted the city as "Nashville." *PUSG*, 9:273, 276n.

[4] Based on the conversation between Stanton and USG while aboard the train, War Dept. Gen. Orders No. 337, dated Oct. 16, 1863, were issued on Oct. 18. Ibid., 9:297n.

[5] Stanton suffered from asthma, and the condition took such a heavy toll on his respiratory system and heart that it eventually killed him in 1869, shortly after Pres. USG nominated him to the U.S. Supreme Court. William Marvel, *Lincoln's Autocrat: The Life of Edwin Stanton* (Chapel Hill: University of North Carolina Press, 2015), 457, 461–462.

[6] USG probably referred to JDG's aunt and uncle, Emily Wrenshall Page and Samuel K. Page. Mrs. Page was the younger sister of JDG's mother, Ellen Bray Wrenshall Dent. A number of descendants of USG's uncle Peter Grant lived in the Louisville area in the mid-nineteenth century, but it is unclear if any of them were still living there at the time of USG's visit to Louisville. Arthur H. Grant, *The Grant Family: A Genealogical History of the Descendants of Matthew Grant of Windsor, Conn., 1601–1898* (Poughkeepsie, NY: A. V. Haight, 1898), 279–280; *PUSG*, 5:8n; 9:397n.

[7] See Dana's Oct. 18, 1863, message to Stanton, *OR*, I, 30(I), 221.

been at Murfreesboro', Tennessee, with a large and well-equipped army from early in the year 1863, with Bragg confronting him with a force quite equal to his own at first, considering it was on the defensive. But after the investment of Vicksburg Bragg's army was largely depleted to strengthen Johnston, in Mississippi, who was being reinforced to raise the siege. I frequently wrote General Halleck suggesting that Rosecrans should move against Bragg.[8] By so doing he would either detain the latter's troops where they were or lay Chattanooga open to capture. General Halleck strongly approved the suggestion, and finally wrote me that he had repeatedly ordered Rosecrans to advance, but that the latter had constantly failed to comply with the order, and at last, after having held a council of war, had replied in effect that it was a military maxim "not to fight two decisive battles at the same time."[9] If true, the maxim was not applicable in this case. It would be bad to be defeated in two decisive battles fought the same day, but it would not be bad to win them. I, however, was fighting no battle, and the siege of Vicksburg had drawn from Rosecrans' front so many of the enemy that his chances of victory were much greater than they would be if he waited until the siege was over, when these troops could be returned. Rosecrans was ordered to move against the army that was detaching troops to raise the siege.[10] Finally he did move, on the 24th of June, but ten days afterwards Vicksburg surrendered, and the troops sent from Bragg were free to return.[11]

It was at this time that I recommended to the general-in-chief the movement against Mobile.[12] I knew the peril the Army of the Cumberland was in, being depleted continually, not only by ordinary casualties, but also by having to detach troops to hold its constantly extending line over which to draw supplies, while the enemy in front was as constantly being strengthened. Mobile was important to the enemy, and in the absence of a threatening force

[8] See, for example, USG's May 6, 1863, telegram to Halleck, *PUSG*, 8:169.

[9] In his June 11 and June 21, 1863, letters to Halleck, Rosecrans may have been paraphrasing Antoine Henri Jomini's assertion of "the danger of undertaking two wars at once." Baron de Jomini, *Summary of the Art of War*, trans. O. F. Winship and E. E. McLean (New York: Putnam, 1854), 48; *OR*, I, 23(I), 8–9.

[10] For Halleck's June 1863 correspondence with Rosecrans pertaining to the issue of troop movements, see *OR*, I, 23(I), 8–10.

[11] Halleck's Nov. 15, 1863, report identified June 25 as the date of Rosecrans's move. Ibid., I, 23(I), 9.

[12] USG suggested an expedition against Mobile, AL, in letters to Halleck on July 24 and Aug. 1, 1863. *PUSG*, 9:109, 137–138.

was guarded by little else than artillery. If threatened by land and from the water at the same time the prize would fall easily, or troops would have to be sent to its defence. Those troops would necessarily come from Bragg. My judgment was overruled, and the troops under my command were dissipated over other parts of the country where it was thought they could render the most service.[13]

Soon it was discovered in Washington that Rosecrans was in trouble and required assistance. The emergency was now too immediate to allow us to give this assistance by making an attack in rear of Bragg upon Mobile. It was therefore necessary to reinforce directly, and troops were sent from every available point.[14]

Rosecrans had very skilfully manœuvred Bragg south of the Tennessee River, and through and beyond Chattanooga. If he had stopped and intrenched, and made himself strong there, all would have been right and the mistake of not moving earlier partially compensated. But he pushed on, with his forces very much scattered, until Bragg's troops from Mississippi began to join him. Then Bragg took the initiative. Rosecrans had to fall back in turn, and was able to get his army together at Chickamauga, some miles south-east of Chattanooga,[15] before the main battle was brought on. The battle was fought on the 19th and 20th of September, and Rosecrans was badly defeated, with a heavy loss in artillery and some sixteen thousand men killed, wounded and captured.[16] The corps under Major-General George H. Thomas stood its ground, while Rosecrans, with Crittenden and McCook, returned to Chattanooga. Thomas returned also, but later, and with his troops in good order. Bragg followed and took possession of Missionary Ridge, overlooking Chattanooga. He also occupied Lookout Mountain, west of the town, which Rosecrans had abandoned, and with it his control of the river and the river road as far back as Bridgeport. The National troops were now strongly intrenched in Chattanooga Valley, with the Tennessee River behind them and the enemy occupying

[13] On Aug. 6, 1863, Halleck informed USG of the decision to send troops to Texas instead. Ibid., 9:159n–160n.

[14] On Sept. 13, 1863, Halleck began ordering reinforcements to be sent to Rosecrans. *OR*, I, 30(I), 35–36; *PUSG*, 9:233n.

[15] The distance between the Chickamauga, GA, area and Chattanooga, TN, was approximately eleven miles in 1863. George B. Davis et al., *The Official Military Atlas of the Civil War* (New York: Fairfax Press, 1983), plate 149.

[16] U.S. Army casualties totaled approximately 16,170. David J. Eicher, *The Longest Night: A Military History of the Civil War* (New York: Simon and Schuster, 2001), 590.

commanding heights to the east and west, with a strong line across the valley from mountain to mountain, and with Chattanooga Creek, for a large part of the way, in front of their line.

On the 29th Halleck telegraphed me the above results, and directed all the forces that could be spared from my department to be sent to Rosecrans.[17] Long before this dispatch was received Sherman was on his way, and McPherson was moving east with most of the garrison of Vicksburg.[18]

A retreat at that time would have been a terrible disaster. It would not only have been the loss of a most important strategic position to us, but it would have been attended with the loss of all the artillery still left with the Army of the Cumberland and the annihilation of that army itself, either by capture or demoralization.

All supplies for Rosecrans had to be brought from Nashville. The railroad between this base and the army was in possession of the government up to Bridgeport, the point at which the road crosses to the south side of the Tennessee River;[19] but Bragg, holding Lookout and Raccoon mountains west of Chattanooga, commanded the railroad, the river and the shortest and best wagon-roads, both south and north of the Tennessee, between Chattanooga and Bridgeport. The distance between these two places is but twenty-six miles by rail; but owing to the position of Bragg, all supplies for Rosecrans had to be hauled by a circuitous route north of the river and over a mountainous country, increasing the distance to over sixty miles.

This country afforded but little food for his animals, nearly ten thousand of which had already starved, and not enough were left to draw a single piece of artillery or even the ambulances to convey the sick. The men had been on half rations of hard bread for a considerable time, with but few other supplies except beef driven from Nashville across the country. The region along the road became so exhausted of food for the cattle that by the time they reached Chattanooga they were much in the condition of the few animals left alive

[17] For Halleck's Sept. 29, 1863, telegram to USG, see *PUSG,* 9:273, 275n–276n.

[18] On Sept. 22, 1863, USG received a Sept. 15 dispatch from Halleck requesting reinforcements for Rosecrans. That same day USG ordered one division from Sherman's U.S. 15th Army Corps and one division from McPherson's U.S. 17th Army Corps to report to Rosecrans. USG ordered additional troops to reinforce Rosecrans on Sept. 25. Ibid., 9:229, 229n–230n, 233, 233n–237n.

[19] The Nashville and Chattanooga Railroad crossed the Tennessee River from west to east at Bridgeport, AL. Davis et al, *Official Military Atlas of the Civil War,* plate 48, map 1.

there—"on the lift."[20] Indeed, the beef was so poor that the soldiers were in the habit of saying, with a faint facetiousness, that they were living on "half rations of hard bread and *beef dried on the hoof.*"

Nothing could be transported but food, and the troops were without sufficient shoes or other clothing suitable for the advancing season. What they had was well worn. The fuel within the Federal lines was exhausted, even to the stumps of trees. There were no teams to draw it from the opposite bank, where it was abundant. The only way of supplying fuel, for some time before my arrival, had been to cut trees on the north bank of the river at a considerable distance up the stream, form rafts of it and float it down with the current, effecting a landing on the south side within our lines by the use of paddles or poles. It would then be carried on the shoulders of the men to their camps.

If a retreat had occurred at this time it is not probable that any of the army would have reached the railroad as an organized body, if followed by the enemy.

On the receipt of Mr. Dana's dispatch Mr. Stanton sent for me. Finding that I was out he became nervous and excited, inquiring of every person he met, including guests of the house, whether they knew where I was, and bidding them find me and send me to him at once. About eleven o'clock I returned to the hotel, and on my way, when near the house, every person met was a messenger from the Secretary, apparently partaking of his impatience to see me. I hastened to the room of the Secretary and found him pacing the floor rapidly in his dressing-gown. Saying that the retreat must be prevented, he showed me the dispatch. I immediately wrote an order assuming command of the Military Division of the Mississippi, and telegraphed it to General Rosecrans.[21] I then telegraphed to him the order from Washington assigning Thomas to the command of the Army of the Cumberland; and to Thomas that he must hold Chattanooga at all hazards, informing him at the same time that I would be at the front as soon as possible. A prompt reply was received from Thomas, saying, "We will hold the town till we starve."[22] I appreciated the force of this dispatch later when I witnessed the condition of affairs which prompted it. It looked, indeed, as if but two courses were open: one to starve, the other to surrender or be captured.

[20] The phrase "on the lift" meant "on the move" or "ready to depart." John S. Farmer and W. E. Henley, eds., *Slang and Its Analogues, Past and Present,* vol. 4 (n.p.: n.p., 1896), 193.

[21] For the text of USG's Oct. 18, 1863, Gen. Orders No. 1, see *PUSG,* 9:296–297.

[22] For Thomas's Oct. 19, 1863, telegram to USG, see ibid., 9:302*n.*

On the morning of the 20th of October I started, with my staff, and proceeded as far as Nashville. At that time it was not prudent to travel beyond
that point by night, so I remained in Nashville until the next morning. Here
I met for the first time Andrew Johnson, Military Governor of Tennessee.[23]
He delivered a speech of welcome. His composure showed that it was by no
means his maiden effort. It was long, and I was in torture while he was delivering it, fearing something would be expected from me in response. I was relieved, however, the people assembled having apparently heard enough. At all
events they commenced a general hand-shaking, which, although trying where
there is so much of it, was a great relief to me in this emergency.[24]

From Nashville I telegraphed to Burnside, who was then at Knoxville, that
important points in his department ought to be fortified, so that they could
be held with the least number of men; to Admiral Porter at Cairo, that Sherman's advance had passed Eastport, Mississippi, that rations were probably
on their way from St. Louis by boat for supplying his army, and requesting
him to send a gunboat to convoy them; and to Thomas, suggesting that
large parties should be put at work on the wagon-road then in use back to
Bridgeport.[25]

On the morning of the 21st we took the train for the front, reaching Stevenson, Alabama, after dark. Rosecrans was there on his way north. He came
into my car and we held a brief interview, in which he described very clearly
the situation at Chattanooga, and made some excellent suggestions as to what
should be done. My only wonder was that he had not carried them out. We
then proceeded to Bridgeport, where we stopped for the night. From here
we took horses and made our way by Jasper and over Waldron's Ridge[26] to
Chattanooga. There had been much rain, and the roads were almost impass-

---

[23] Andrew Johnson (1808–1875) was born in North Carolina and moved to Tennessee in
1825. He served as the military governor of the state from 1862 to 1865. On Mar. 4, 1865, he
became U.S. vice president and assumed the presidency after Lincoln was assassinated on
Apr. 15. *CWHC*, 319.

[24] During the evening of Oct. 20, 1863, in front of the St. Cloud Hotel in Nashville, USG
reportedly remarked to the assembled crowd that he had "never made a speech in his life, and
was too old to learn now." Instead, Johnson delivered a speech to the crowd. *PUSG*, 9:304n.

[25] For USG's Oct. 20, 1863, telegrams to Burnside, Porter, and Thomas, see ibid., 9:304–
305, 308.

[26] This elevation is actually called Walden's Ridge. Peter Cozzens, *The Shipwreck of Their
Hopes: The Battles for Chattanooga* (Urbana: University of Illinois Press, 1994), 14.

able from mud, knee-deep in places, and from wash-outs on the mountain sides. I had been on crutches since the time of my fall in New Orleans, and had to be carried over places where it was not safe to cross on horseback. The roads were strewn with the *débris* of broken wagons and the carcasses of thousands of starved mules and horses. At Jasper, some ten or twelve miles from Bridgeport, there was a halt. General O. O. Howard[27] had his headquarters there. From this point I telegraphed Burnside to make every effort to secure five hundred rounds of ammunition for his artillery and small-arms.[28] We stopped for the night at a little hamlet some ten or twelve miles farther on.[29] The next day we reached Chattanooga a little before dark. I went directly to General Thomas's headquarters, and remaining there a few days, until I could establish my own.

During the evening most of the general officers called in to pay their respects and to talk about the condition of affairs. They pointed out on the map the line, marked with a red or blue pencil, which Rosecrans had contemplated falling back upon. If any of them had approved the move they did not say so to me. I found General W. F. Smith occupying the position of chief engineer of the Army of the Cumberland.[30] I had known Smith as a cadet at West Point, but had no recollection of having met him after my graduation, in 1843, up to this time. He explained the situation of the two armies and the topography of the country so plainly that I could see it without an inspection. I found that he had established a saw-mill on the banks of the river, by utilizing an old engine found in the neighborhood; and, by rafting logs from the north side of the river above, had got out the lumber and completed pontoons and

[27] Oliver Otis Howard (1830–1909) was born in Maine and graduated from the USMA in 1854. He taught at the USMA, resigning in 1861 to join a Maine regiment. He participated in a variety of battles and was awarded the Medal of Honor for his actions at Fair Oaks, VA. Howard headed the Freedmen's Bureau after the war and founded Howard University. *CWHC*, 305–306.

[28] For USG's Oct. 22, 1863, telegram to Burnside, see *PUSG*, 9:305*n*.

[29] USG was in Jasper, TN, on Oct. 22, 1863, and arrived in Chattanooga on Oct. 23. The precise location of the "little hamlet" is unclear. Ibid., 9:305*n*, 308.

[30] William F. "Baldy" Smith (1824–1903) was born in Vermont and graduated from the USMA in 1845. He was promoted to brigadier general of volunteers in 1861. Smith served as chief engineer of the Army of the Cumberland and of the Military Div. of the Mississippi from 1863 to 1864, resigning from the military in 1867. George W. Cullum, *Biographical Register of the Officers and Graduates of the U.S. Military Academy at West Point, N.Y.* (Boston: Houghton, Mifflin, 1891), 2:210–211; *CWHC*, 499–500.

roadway plank for a second bridge, one flying bridge[31] being there already. He was also rapidly getting out the materials and constructing the boats for a third bridge. In addition to this he had far under way a steamer for plying between Chattanooga and Bridgeport whenever we might get possession of the river. This boat consisted of a scow, made of the plank sawed out at the mill, housed in, and a stern wheel attached which was propelled by a second engine taken from some shop or factory.[32]

I telegraphed to Washington this night, notifying General Halleck of my arrival, and asking to have General Sherman assigned to the command of the Army of the Tennessee, headquarters in the field. The request was at once complied with.[33]

[31] The flying bridge used at Chattanooga consisted of a barge that was able to carry "four 6-mule teams and wagons besides infantry and cavalry. The cable was attached to an island above and was supported upon three floats." *Engineer Field Manual: Professional Papers of the Corps of Engineers, U.S. Army, No. 29* (Washington, DC: Government Printing Office, 1907), 214–215.

[32] The boat was given the name *Chattanooga.* Francis Trevelyan Miller, *The Photographic History of the Civil War in Ten Volumes* (New York: Review of Reviews, 1911), 2:297.

[33] USG telegraphed Halleck on Oct. 23, 1863, and Sherman took command of the Army of the Tennessee on Oct. 24. *PUSG,* 9:308, 309*n.*

# 41

## Assuming the Command at Chattanooga—Opening a Line of Supplies—Battle of Wauhatchie—On the Picket Line

THE NEXT DAY, the 24th, I started out to make a personal inspection, taking Thomas and Smith with me, besides most of the members of my personal staff.[1] We crossed to the north side of the river, and, moving to the north of detached spurs of hills, reached the Tennessee at Brown's Ferry,[2] some three miles below Lookout Mountain, unobserved by the enemy. Here we left our horses back from the river and approached the water on foot. There was a picket station of the enemy on the opposite side, of about twenty men, in full view, and we were within easy range. They did not fire upon us nor seem to be disturbed by our presence. They must have seen that we were all commissioned officers. But, I suppose, they looked upon the garrison of Chattanooga as prisoners of war, feeding or starving themselves, and thought it would be inhuman to kill any of them except in self-defence.[3]

That night I issued orders for opening the route to Bridgeport—*a cracker line,* as the soldiers appropriately termed it. They had been so long on short

---

[1] In his postbattle report on Chattanooga, USG stated that his staff at that time consisted of Brig. Gens. John A. Rawlins, John H. Wilson, and William F. Smith, Lt. Col. William L. Duff, Maj. William R. Rowley, and Capts. Orlando H. Ross and Peter T. Hudson. *PUSG,* 9:566.

[2] Brown's Ferry was a crossing on the Tennessee River approximately two and one-half miles north of Lookout Mountain and one mile south of Williams Island. George B. Davis et al., *The Official Military Atlas of the Civil War* (New York: Fairfax Press, 1983), plate 50, map 1.

[3] W. F. Smith reported that there had been an agreement between the U.S. and Confederate troops on picket duty to not fire upon one another. William Farrar Smith, "Comments on General Grant's 'Chattanooga,'" in *Battles and Leaders of the Civil War,* vol. 3, ed. Robert Underwood Johnson and Clarence Clough Buel (New York: Century, 1888), 714.

rations that my first thought was the establishment of a line over which food might reach them.[4]

Chattanooga is on the south bank of the Tennessee, where that river runs nearly due west. It is at the northern end of a valley five or six miles in width, through which Chattanooga Creek runs. To the east of the valley is Missionary Ridge, rising from five to eight hundred feet above the creek and terminating somewhat abruptly a half mile or more before reaching the Tennessee. On the west of the valley is Lookout Mountain, twenty-two hundred feet above-tide water.[5] Just below the town the Tennessee makes a turn to the south and runs to the base of Lookout Mountain, leaving no level ground between the mountain and river. The Memphis and Charleston Railroad passes this point, where the mountain stands nearly perpendicular. East of Missionary Ridge flows the South Chickamauga River; west of Lookout Mountain is Lookout Creek; and west of that, Raccoon Mountains. Lookout Mountain, at its northern end, rises almost perpendicularly for some distance, then breaks off in a gentle slope of cultivated fields to near the summit, where it ends in a palisade thirty or more feet in height. On the gently sloping ground, between the upper and lower palisades, there is a single farm-house, which is reached by a wagon-road from the valley east.[6]

The intrenched line of the enemy commenced on the north end of Missionary Ridge and extended along the crest for some distance south, thence across Chattanooga valley to Lookout Mountain. Lookout Mountain was also fortified and held by the enemy, who also kept troops in Lookout valley west, and on Raccoon Mountain, with pickets extending down the river so as to command the road on the north bank and render it useless to us. In addition to this there was an intrenched line in Chattanooga valley extending from the

---

[4] The editors have not been able to locate any written orders from USG regarding opening the route to Bridgeport, AL.

[5] Modern measurements of the elevation of Lookout Mountain place the highest point along the ridge at 2,393 feet above sea level, with the northern point roughly 1,986 feet above sea level. The northern point of the ridge near Chattanooga, TN, towers 1,300–1,800 feet above the surrounding valley. Peter Cozzens, *The Shipwreck of Their Hopes: The Battles for Chattanooga* (Urbana: University of Illinois Press, 1994), 15; William F. Hull, *Images of America: Lookout Mountain* (Charleston, SC: Arcadia, 2009), 29.

[6] Robert Cravens owned a farmhouse about 3,000 feet south of the Tennessee River and about halfway up the north end of Lookout Mountain. The house was on the level ground between the ledge known as the "bench" and the steep rock cliffs known as the "palisades." Cozzens, *Shipwreck of Their Hopes,* 16; James L. McDonough, *Chattanooga: A Death Grip on the Confederacy* (Knoxville: University of Tennessee Press, 1989), 131.

river east of the town to Lookout Mountain, to make the investment complete. Besides the fortifications on Mission Ridge,[7] there was a line at the base of the hill, with occasional spurs of rifle-pits half-way up the front. The enemy's pickets extended out into the valley towards the town, so far that the pickets of the two armies could converse. At one point they were separated only by the narrow creek which gives its name to the valley and town, and from which both sides drew water. The Union lines were shorter than those of the enemy.

Thus the enemy, with a vastly superior force, was strongly fortified to the east, south, and west, and commanded the river below.[8] Practically, the Army of the Cumberland was besieged. The enemy had stopped with his cavalry north of the river the passing of a train loaded with ammunition and medical supplies.[9] The Union army was short of both, not having ammunition enough for a day's fighting.

General Halleck had, long before my coming into this new field, ordered parts of the 11th and 12th corps, commanded respectively by Generals Howard and Slocum,[10] Hooker[11] in command of the whole, from the Army of the Potomac to reinforce Rosecrans. It would have been folly to send them to Chattanooga to help eat up the few rations left there. They were consequently

[7] Both "Mission Ridge" and "Missionary Ridge" were used to refer to the same geographic feature. Zella Armstrong, *The History of Hamilton County and Chattanooga, Tennessee* (1931; repr. Johnson City, TN: Overmountain Press, 1993), 1:285; *PUSG,* 9:448n.

[8] Prior to the Battle of Chickamauga in Sept. 1863, the U.S. Army of the Cumberland had an estimated 58,222 men, with 16,170 becoming casualties in that engagement. By Nov., U.S. forces in the Chattanooga area numbered approximately 72,808. On Oct. 31, 1863, Bragg had approximately 46,496 men available for duty. McDonough, *Chattanooga,* 15; *OR,* I, 31(II), 12–13, 656. For troop distribution on Oct. 25, 1863, see Cozzens, *Shipwreck of Their Hopes,* 54–55 (map).

[9] USG probably referred to an incident in late Aug. 1863 when Confederate general Joseph Wheeler's cavalry captured two train cars and destroyed telegraph lines, railroads, and bridges between Chattanooga and Nashville, TN. Michael B. Cavender, *The First Georgia Cavalry in the Civil War: A History and Roster* (Jefferson, NC: McFarland, 2016), 127.

[10] Henry W. Slocum (1827–1894) was born in New York and graduated from the USMA in 1852. In Oct. 1856, he resigned from the military and pursued a career as a lawyer and a legislator. On May 21, 1861, he was appointed colonel of the 27th New York Inf., and by Oct. 1863, he was a major general in the 12th Corps, Army of the Potomac. *CWHC,* 491.

[11] Joseph Hooker (1814–1879) was born in Massachusetts and graduated from the USMA in 1837. He fought in the Mexican-American War and later as a colonel in the California Militia from 1859 to 1861. In May 1861, he was promoted to brigadier general in the U.S. Army. On May 5, 1862, Hooker was promoted to major general. Ibid., 303–304.

left on the railroad, where supplies could be brought to them. Before my arrival, Thomas ordered their concentration at Bridgeport.[12]

General W. F. Smith had been so instrumental in preparing for the move which I was now about to make, and so clear in his judgment about the manner of making it, that I deemed it but just to him that he should have command of the troops detailed to execute the design, although he was then acting as a staff officer and was not in command of troops.[13]

On the 24th of October, after my return to Chattanooga, the following details were made: General Hooker, who was now at Bridgeport, was ordered to cross to the south side of the Tennessee and march up by Whitesides and Wauhatchie[14] to Brown's Ferry. General Palmer, with a division of the 14th corps, Army of the Cumberland, was ordered to move down the river on the north side, by a back road, until opposite Whitesides, then cross and hold the road in Hooker's rear after he had passed.[15] Four thousand men were at the same time detailed to act under General Smith directly from Chattanooga. Eighteen hundred of them, under General Hazen,[16] were to take sixty pontoon boats, and under cover of night float by the pickets of the enemy at the north base of Lookout, down to Brown's Ferry, then land on the south side and capture or drive away the pickets at that point. Smith was to march with the remainder of the detail, also under cover of night, by the north bank of the river to Brown's Ferry, taking with him all the material for laying the bridge as soon as the crossing was secured.

---

[12] On Sept. 24, 1863, Rosecrans informed Halleck that any reinforcements should be sent to Stevenson, AL, and Bridgeport. That same day Stanton placed Hooker in command of the reinforcements being sent from the 11th and 12th Corps, Army of the Potomac. On Sept. 27, Rosecrans ordered Hooker to go directly to Bridgeport. On Oct. 23 and 24, Thomas ordered Hooker to concentrate his forces at Stevenson and Bridgeport in preparation for the movement against Brown's Ferry. *OR*, I, 29(I), 151; I, 30(III), 904; I, 31(I), 43–44.

[13] W. F. Smith was placed in command of the expedition on Oct. 25, 1863. In USG's Oct. 26 and Oct. 28 communications with Halleck, he credited Thomas with the successful planning and preparation for the operation. Ibid., I, 31(I), 77; *PUSG*, 9:320, 335.

[14] The railroad station at Wauhatchie, TN, was approximately six miles west of Chattanooga on the Nashville and Chattanooga Railroad. Davis et al., *Official Military Atlas of the Civil War*, plate 50, map 1.

[15] On Oct. 24, 1863, Thomas ordered Hooker and Palmer to move forward with the operation. *OR*, I, 31(I), 43–44.

[16] William B. Hazen (1830–1887) was born in Vermont and moved to Ohio in 1833. He graduated from the USMA in 1855. In Nov. 1862, Hazen was promoted to brigadier general. *CWHC*, 291.

On the 26th, Hooker crossed the river at Bridgeport and commenced his eastward march. At three o'clock on the morning of the 27th, Hazen moved into the stream with his sixty pontoons and eighteen hundred brave and well-equipped men.[17] Smith started enough in advance to be near the river when Hazen should arrive. There are a number of detached spurs of hills north of the river at Chattanooga, back of which is a good road parallel to the stream, sheltered from the view from the top of Lookout. It was over this road Smith marched. At five o'clock Hazen landed at Brown's Ferry, surprised the picket guard, and captured most of it. By seven o'clock the whole of Smith's force was ferried over and in possession of a height commanding the ferry. This was speedily fortified, while a detail was laying the pontoon bridge. By ten o'clock the bridge was laid, and our extreme right, now in Lookout valley, was fortified and connected with the rest of the army. The two bridges over the Tennessee River—a flying one at Chattanooga and the new one at Brown's Ferry—with the road north of the river, covered from both the fire and the view of the enemy, made the connection complete. Hooker found but slight obstacles in his way, and on the afternoon of the 28th emerged into Lookout valley at Wauhatchie. Howard marched on to Brown's Ferry, while Geary,[18] who commanded a division in the 12th corps, stopped three miles south.[19] The pickets of the enemy on the river below were now cut off, and soon came in and surrendered.

The river was now opened to us from Lookout valley to Bridgeport. Between Brown's Ferry and Kelly's Ferry[20] the Tennessee runs through a narrow gorge in the mountains, which contracts the stream so much as to increase the current beyond the capacity of an ordinary steamer to stem it. To get up these rapids, steamers must be cordelled; that is, pulled up by ropes from the shore. But there is no difficulty in navigating the stream from Bridgeport to Kelly's Ferry. The latter point is only eight miles from Chattanooga and connected with it by a good wagon-road, which runs through a low pass in the

---

[17] Hazen had 1,500 men when he moved on Brown's Ferry. *OR*, I, 31(I), 77.

[18] John W. Geary (1819–1873) was born in Pennsylvania and attained the rank of colonel during the Mexican-American War. He was mayor of San Francisco, CA, from 1850 to 1851 and governor of the Kansas Territory from 1856 to 1857. In Apr. 1862, he was promoted to brigadier general. Geary served as governor of Pennsylvania from 1867 to 1873. *CWHC*, 251–252.

[19] Beginning on Sept. 25, 1863, Geary commanded the 2nd Div. of the 12th Corps, Army of the Cumberland. Ibid., 252.

[20] Kelly's Ferry was a boat landing on the Tennessee River approximately six miles west of Chattanooga. Davis et al., *Official Military Atlas of the Civil War*, plate 50, map 1.

Raccoon Mountains on the south side of the river to Brown's Ferry, thence on the north side to the river opposite Chattanooga. There were several steamers at Bridgeport, and abundance of forage, clothing and provisions.

On the way to Chattanooga I had telegraphed back to Nashville for a good supply of vegetables and small rations, which the troops had been so long deprived of.[21] Hooker had brought with him from the east a full supply of land transportation. His animals had not been subjected to hard work on bad roads without forage, but were in good condition. In five days from my arrival in Chattanooga the way was open to Bridgeport and, with the aid of steamers and Hooker's teams, in a week the troops were receiving full rations. It is hard for any one not an eye-witness to realize the relief this brought. The men were soon reclothed and also well fed; an abundance of ammunition was brought up, and a cheerfulness prevailed not before enjoyed in many weeks. Neither officers nor men looked upon themselves any longer as doomed. The weak and languid appearance of the troops, so visible before, disappeared at once. I do not know what the effect was on the other side, but assume it must have been correspondingly depressing. Mr. Davis had visited Bragg but a short time before, and must have perceived our condition to be about as Bragg described it in his subsequent report.[22] "These dispositions," he said, "faithfully sustained, insured the enemy's speedy evacuation of Chattanooga for want of food and forage. Possessed of the shortest route to his depot, and the one by which reinforcements must reach him, we held him at our mercy, and his destruction was only a question of time."[23] But the dispositions were not "faithfully sustained," and I doubt not but thousands of men engaged in trying to "sustain" them now rejoice that they were not. There was no time during the rebellion when I did not think, and often say, that the South was more to be benefited by its defeat than the North. The latter had the people, the institutions, and the territory to make a great and prosperous nation. The former was burdened with an institution abhorrent to all civilized people not brought up under it, and one which degraded labor, kept it in ignorance, and enervated the governing class. With the outside world at war with this institution, they could not have extended their territory. The labor of the country was not

---

[21] See Theodore S. Bowers's Oct. 22, 1863, letter to Samuel J. Little, *PUSG*, 9:328*n*.

[22] On Oct. 9, 1863, Confederate president Jefferson Davis visited Bragg's headquarters atop Missionary Ridge. Jefferson Davis, *The Papers of Jefferson Davis*, vol. 10, ed. Lynda Laswell Crist, Kenneth H. Williams, and Peggy L. Dillard (Baton Rouge: Louisiana State University Press, 1999), 20.

[23] For Bragg's report, see *OR*, I, 30(II), 36–37.

skilled, nor allowed to become so. The whites could not toil without becoming degraded, and those who did were denominated "poor white trash." The system of labor would have soon exhausted the soil and left the people poor. The non-slaveholders would have left the country, and the small slaveholder must have sold out to his more fortunate neighbor. Soon the slaves would have outnumbered the masters, and, not being in sympathy with them, would have risen in their might and exterminated them. The war was expensive to the South as well as to the North, both in blood and treasure, but it was worth all it cost.

The enemy was surprised by the movements which secured to us a line of supplies. He appreciated its importance, and hastened to try to recover the line from us. His strength on Lookout Mountain was not equal to Hooker's command in the valley below.[24] From Missionary Ridge he had to march twice the distance we had from Chattanooga, in order to reach Lookout Valley; but on the night of the 28th and 29th an attack was made on Geary at Wauhatchie by Longstreet's corps.[25] When the battle commenced, Hooker ordered Howard up from Brown's Ferry. He had three miles to march to reach Geary. On his way he was fired upon by rebel troops from a foot-hill to the left of the road and from which the road was commanded. Howard turned to the left, charged up the hill and captured it before the enemy had time to intrench, taking many prisoners. Leaving sufficient men to hold this height, he pushed on to reinforce Geary. Before he got up, Geary had been engaged for about three hours against a vastly superior force. The night was so dark that the men could not distinguish one from another except by the light of the flashes of their muskets. In the darkness and uproar, Hooker's teamsters became frightened and deserted their teams. The mules also became frightened, and breaking

[24] When Hooker assumed command of the U.S. 11th and 12th Army Corps on Sept. 24, 1863, he had between 14,000 and 17,615 troops. Dana reported that there were about 25,000 U.S. troops in Lookout Valley by Oct. 29. In Oct. 27 correspondence, Longstreet lobbied for an entire division of Confederate troops to be stationed on Lookout Mountain. He stated in his Mar. 25, 1864, report that he had only "a small picket upon the summit of the mountain" on Oct. 9, 1863. Daniel Butterfield, *Major-General Joseph Hooker and the Troops from the Army of the Potomac at Wauhatchie, Lookout Mountain and Chattanooga* (New York: Exchange Printing, 1896), 28; *OR,* I, 29(I), 151; I, 31(I), 72–73, 216, 221.

[25] James Longstreet (1821–1904), USG's cousin-in-law, was born in South Carolina and moved to Georgia. He moved to Alabama in 1833 and graduated from the USMA in 1842. In Mar. 1861, he joined the Confederate Army as a lieutenant colonel. By Oct. he had attained the rank of major general. On Oct. 28, 1863, Longstreet sent a Confederate brigade under the command of Col. John Bratton against U.S. forces at Wauhatchie. Cozzens, *Shipwreck of Their Hopes,* 79, 81–83; *CWHC,* 352–353.

loose from their fastenings stampeded directly towards the enemy. The latter, no doubt, took this for a charge, and stampeded in turn.[26] By four o'clock in the morning the battle had entirely ceased, and our "cracker line" was never afterward disturbed.

In securing possession of Lookout Valley, Smith lost one man killed and four or five wounded. The enemy lost most of his pickets at the ferry, captured. In the night engagement of the 28th–9th Hooker lost 416 killed and wounded. I never knew the loss of the enemy, but our troops buried over one hundred and fifty of his dead and captured more than a hundred.[27]

After we had secured the opening of a line over which to bring our supplies to the army, I made a personal inspection to see the situation of the pickets of the two armies. As I have stated, Chattanooga Creek comes down the centre of the valley to within a mile or such a matter of the town of Chattanooga, then bears off westerly, then north-westerly, and enters the Tennessee River at the foot of Lookout Mountain. This creek, from its mouth up to where it bears off west, lay between the two lines of pickets, and the guards of both armies drew their water from the same stream. As I would be under short-range fire and in an open country, I took nobody with me, except, I believe, a bugler, who stayed some distance to the rear. I rode from our right around to our left. When I came to the camp of the picket guard of our side, I heard the call, "Turn out the guard for the commanding general." I replied, "Never mind the guard," and they were dismissed and went back to their tents. Just back of these, and about equally distant from the creek, were the guards of the Confederate pickets. The sentinel on their post called out in like manner, "Turn out the guard for the commanding general," and, I believe, added, "General Grant." Their line in a moment front-faced to the north, facing me, and gave a salute, which I returned.

The most friendly relations seemed to exist between the pickets of the two armies. At one place there was a tree which had fallen across the stream, and

[26] U.S. veterans published several versions of the story of the mule charge. Confederate veteran John L. Coker, who was present for the battle, wrote a letter in 1887 that disputed the version told by USG. Coker claimed that Howard's advance upon Bratton's rear halted the attack, not the mule stampede. Gene C. Armistead, *Horses and Mules in the Civil War: A Complete History with a Roster of More than 700 War Horses* (Jefferson, NC: McFarland, 2013), 69–71; McDonough, *Chattanooga*, 92.

[27] The *New York Times* reported that the Confederate Army suffered 654 casualties. Special Correspondent, "The Battle of Wauhatchie," *New York Times*, Nov. 9, 1863, 1. For Hooker's report on the battle, see *OR*, I, 31(I), 92–95.

which was used by the soldiers of both armies in drawing water for their camps. General Longstreet's corps was stationed there at the time, and wore blue of a little different shade from our uniform. Seeing a soldier in blue on this log, I rode up to him, commenced conversing with him, and asked whose corps he belonged to. He was very polite, and, touching his hat to me, said he belonged to General Longstreet's corps. I asked him a few questions—but not with a view of gaining any particular information—all of which he answered, and I rode off.

# 42

Condition of the Army—Rebuilding the Railroad—
General Burnside's Situation—Orders for Battle—
Plans for the Attack—Hooker's Position—
Sherman's Movements

Having got the Army of the Cumberland in a comfortable position, I now began to look after the remainder of my new command. Burnside was in about as desperate a condition as the Army of the Cumberland had been, only he was not yet besieged. He was a hundred miles from the nearest possible base, Big South Fork of the Cumberland River, and much farther from any railroad we had possession of. The roads back were over mountains, and all supplies along the line had long since been exhausted. His animals, too, had been starved, and their carcasses lined the road from Cumberland Gap, and far back towards Lexington, Ky. East Tennessee still furnished supplies of beef, bread and forage, but it did not supply ammunition, clothing, medical supplies, or small rations, such as coffee, sugar, salt and rice.

Sherman had started from Memphis for Corinth on the 11th of October. His instructions required him to repair the road in his rear in order to bring up supplies.[1] The distance was about three hundred and thirty miles through a hostile country. His entire command could not have maintained the road if it had been completed. The bridges had all been destroyed by the enemy, and much other damage done. A hostile community lived along the road; guerilla bands infested the country, and more or less of the cavalry of the enemy was still in the West. Often Sherman's work was destroyed as soon as completed, and he only a short distance away.

The Memphis and Charleston Railroad strikes the Tennessee River at Eastport, Mississippi. Knowing the difficulty Sherman would have to supply

[1] See USG's Oct. 8, 1863, letter to Sherman, *PUSG,* 9:273.

himself from Memphis, I had previously ordered supplies sent from St. Louis on small steamers, to be convoyed by the navy, to meet him at Eastport.[2] These he got. I now ordered him to discontinue his work of repairing roads and to move on with his whole force to Stevenson, Alabama, without delay. This order was borne to Sherman by a messenger, who paddled down the Tennessee in a canoe and floated over Muscle Shoals; it was delivered at Iuka on the 27th. In this Sherman was notified that the rebels were moving a force towards Cleveland, East Tennessee, and might be going to Nashville, in which event his troops were in the best position to beat them there.[3] Sherman, with his characteristic promptness, abandoned the work he was engaged upon and pushed on at once. On the 1st of November he crossed the Tennessee at Eastport, and that day was in Florence, Alabama, with the head of column, while his troops were still crossing at Eastport, with Blair bringing up the rear.[4]

Sherman's force made an additional army, with cavalry, artillery, and trains, all to be supplied by the single track road from Nashville. All indications pointed also to the probable necessity of supplying Burnside's command in East Tennessee, twenty-five thousand more, by the same route. A single track could not do this. I gave, therefore, an order to Sherman to halt General G. M. Dodge's[5] command, of about eight thousand men, at Athens, and subsequently directed the latter to arrange his troops along the railroad from Decatur north towards Nashville, and to rebuild that road.[6] The road from Nashville to Decatur passes over a broken country, cut up with innumerable streams, many of them of considerable width, and with valleys

---

[2] By Oct. 7, 1863, Chief Commissary of Subsistence Col. Thomas J. Haines had begun preparations for supplies to be sent to Eastport, MS. *OR,* I, 31(I), 688.

[3] For USG's Oct. 24, 1863, telegram to Sherman regarding the movement toward Stevenson, AL, see *PUSG,* 9:311–312.

[4] Blair had joined Sherman in the march toward Chattanooga, TN, on Oct. 4, 1863. Ibid., 9:200*n.*

[5] Grenville M. Dodge (1831–1916) was born in Massachusetts and moved to Iowa where he became a civil engineer and captain in the Iowa Militia. In 1861 he became a colonel in the 4th Iowa Inf., rising to the rank of brigadier general in 1862. In 1866 he was chief civil engineer for the Union-Pacific Railroad. Dodge served as U.S. representative from Iowa from 1867 to 1869. He authored several works, including *Personal Recollections of President Abraham Lincoln, General Ulysses S. Grant, and General William T. Sherman* (Council Bluffs, IA: Monarch Printing, 1914). *CWHC,* 211–212.

[6] See USG's Nov. 5, 1863, telegram to Sherman, *PUSG,* 9:360; and Sherman's Nov. 9 message to Dodge, *OR,* I, 31(III), 100.

far below the road-bed. All the bridges over these had been destroyed, and the rails taken up and twisted by the enemy. All the cars and locomotives not carried off had been destroyed as effectually as they knew how to destroy them. All bridges and culverts had been destroyed between Nashville and Decatur, and thence to Stevenson, where the Memphis and Charleston and the Nashville and Chattanooga roads unite. The rebuilding of this road would give us two roads as far as Stevenson over which to supply the army. From Bridgeport, a short distance farther east, the river supplements the road.

General Dodge, besides being a most capable soldier, was an experienced railroad builder. He had no tools to work with except those of the pioneers— axes, picks, and spades. With these he was able to intrench his men and protect them against surprises by small parties of the enemy. As he had no base of supplies until the road could be completed back to Nashville, the first matter to consider after protecting his men was the getting in of food and forage from the surrounding country. He had his men and teams bring in all the grain they could find, or all they needed, and all the cattle for beef, and such other food as could be found. Millers were detailed from the ranks to run the mills along the line of the army. When these were not near enough to the troops for protection they were taken down and moved up to the line of the road. Blacksmith shops, with all the iron and steel found in them, were moved up in like manner. Blacksmiths were detailed and set to work making the tools necessary in railroad and bridge building. Axemen were put to work getting out timber for bridges and cutting fuel for locomotives when the road should be completed. Car-builders were set to work repairing the locomotives and cars. Thus every branch of railroad building, making tools to work with, and supplying the workmen with food, was all going on at once, and without the aid of a mechanic or laborer except what the command itself furnished. But rails and cars the men could not make without material, and there was not enough rolling stock to keep the road we already had worked to its full capacity. There were no rails except those in use. To supply these deficiencies I ordered eight of the ten engines General McPherson had at Vicksburg to be sent to Nashville, and all the cars he had except ten.[7] I also ordered the troops in West Tennessee to points on the river and on the Memphis and Charleston road, and ordered the cars, locomotives and rails from all the railroads except the Memphis and Charleston

---

[7] See USG's Nov. 3, 1863, telegram to McPherson, *PUSG*, 9:357*n*.

to Nashville.[8] The military manager of railroads also was directed to furnish more rolling stock and, as far as he could, bridge material.[9] General Dodge had the work assigned him finished within forty days after receiving his orders. The number of bridges to rebuild was one hundred and eighty-two, many of them over deep and wide chasms; the length of road repaired was one hundred and two miles.

The enemy's troops, which it was thought were either moving against Burnside or were going to Nashville, went no farther than Cleveland. Their presence there, however, alarmed the authorities at Washington, and, on account of our helpless condition at Chattanooga, caused me much uneasiness. Dispatches were constantly coming, urging me to do something for Burnside's relief; calling attention to the importance of holding East Tennessee; saying the President was much concerned for the protection of the loyal people in that section, etc.[10] We had not at Chattanooga animals to pull a single piece of artillery, much less a supply train. Reinforcements could not help Burnside, because he had neither supplies nor ammunition sufficient for them; hardly, indeed, bread and meat for the men he had. There was no relief possible for him except by expelling the enemy from Missionary Ridge and about Chattanooga.

On the 4th of November Longstreet left our front with about fifteen thousand troops, besides Wheeler's[11] cavalry, five thousand more, to go against Burnside. The situation seemed desperate, and was more aggravating because nothing could be done until Sherman should get up. The authorities at

[8] For troop movements in western Tennessee, see Halleck's Sept. 15, 1863, message to Hurlbut, and USG's Sept. 22 response to Halleck. It is unclear what order USG referred to regarding moving railroad cars to Nashville, TN. Ibid., 9:229 and *n.*

[9] John B. Anderson (1817–c.1897) was superintendent of military railroads. He was born in Pennsylvania and graduated from Washington and Jefferson College. Anderson was superintendent of transportation on the Louisville and Nashville Railroad at the outbreak of the Civil War. On Nov. 1, 1863, USG directed him to provide railroad cars loaded with supplies to Stevenson and Bridgeport, AL. On Nov. 4, Anderson suggested to USG the idea of sending supplies to build bridges. *Portrait and Biographical Album of Washington, Clay, and Riley Counties, Kansas* (Chicago: Chapman Brothers, 1890), s.v. "John Byers Anderson"; *PUSG,* 9:346–347, 356, 356*n*–357*n.*

[10] See, for example, Halleck's Nov. 16, 1863, telegram to USG, *PUSG,* 9:404*n.*

[11] Joseph Wheeler (1836–1906) was born in Georgia and graduated from the USMA in 1859. He resigned from the U.S. Army in 1861 to join the Confederate Army, where he rose to the rank of major general by 1863. After the war, he became a U.S. representative from Alabama. He served in the U.S. Army as a major general during the Spanish-American War. *CWHC,* 563.

Washington were now more than ever anxious for the safety of Burnside's army, and plied me with dispatches faster than ever, urging that something should be done for his relief. On the 7th, before Longstreet could possibly have reached Knoxville, I ordered Thomas peremptorily to attack the enemy's right, so as to force the return of the troops that had gone up the valley. I directed him to take mules, officers' horses, or animals wherever he could get them to move the necessary artillery. But he persisted in the declaration that he could not move a single piece of artillery, and could not see how he could possibly comply with the order.[12] Nothing was left to be done but to answer Washington dispatches as best I could; urge Sherman forward, although he was making every effort to get forward, and encourage Burnside to hold on, assuring him that in a short time he should be relieved. All of Burnside's dispatches showed the greatest confidence in his ability to hold his position as long as his ammunition held out. He even suggested the propriety of abandoning the territory he held south and west of Knoxville, so as to draw the enemy farther from his base and make it more difficult for him to get back to Chattanooga when the battle should begin.[13]

Longstreet had a railroad as far as Loudon; but from there to Knoxville he had to rely on wagon trains. Burnside's suggestion, therefore, was a good one, and it was adopted. On the 14th I telegraphed him:

"Sherman's advance has reached Bridgeport. His whole force will be ready to move from there by Tuesday at farthest. If you can hold Longstreet in check until he gets up, or by skirmishing and falling back can avoid serious loss to yourself and gain time, I will be able to force the enemy back from here and place a force between Longstreet and Bragg that must inevitably make the former take to the mountain-passes by every available road, to get to his supplies. Sherman would have been here before this but for high water in Elk River driving him some thirty miles up that river to cross."

And again later in the day, indicating my plans for his relief, as follows:

"Your dispatch and Dana's just received. Being there, you can tell better how to resist Longstreet's attack than I can direct. With your showing

---

[12] USG communicated to Halleck on the morning of Nov. 8, 1863, that Thomas could not comply with the order, but Thomas's message to USG has not been found. *PUSG*, 9:376*n*.

[13] See Burnside's Nov. 13, 1863, telegram to USG, ibid., 9:392*n*.

you had better give up Kingston at the last moment and save the most productive part of your possessions. Every arrangement is now made to throw Sherman's force across the river, just at and below the mouth of Chickamauga Creek, as soon as it arrives. Thomas will attack on his left at the same time, and together it is expected to carry Missionary Ridge, and from there push a force on to the railroad between Cleveland and Dalton. Hooker will at the same time attack, and, if he can, carry Lookout Mountain. The enemy now seems to be looking for an attack on his left flank. This favors us. To further confirm this, Sherman's advance division will march direct from Whiteside to Trenton. The remainder of his force will pass over a new road just made from Whiteside to Kelly's Ferry, thus being concealed from the enemy, and leave him to suppose the whole force is going up Lookout Valley. Sherman's advance has only just reached Bridgeport. The rear will only reach there on the 16th. This will bring it to the 19th as the earliest day for making the combined movement as desired. Inform me if you think you can sustain yourself until this time. I can hardly conceive of the enemy breaking through at Kingston and pushing for Kentucky. If they should, however, a new problem would be left for solution. Thomas has ordered a division of cavalry to the vicinity of Sparta. I will ascertain if they have started, and inform you. It will be entirely out of the question to send you ten thousand men, not because they cannot be spared, but how would they be fed after they got even one day east from here?"

Longstreet, for some reason or other, stopped at Loudon until the 13th. That being the terminus of his railroad communications, it is probable he was directed to remain there awaiting orders.[14] He was in a position threatening Knoxville, and at the same time where he could be brought back speedily to Chattanooga. The day after Longstreet left Loudon, Sherman reached Bridgeport in person and proceeded on to see me that evening, the 14th, and reached Chattanooga the next day.

[14] A shortage of supplies and transportation caused considerable delay. Longstreet reached Loudon, TN, on Nov. 13, 1863, nearly two weeks after he set out. Thomas Lawrence Connelly, *Autumn of Glory: The Army of Tennessee, 1862–1865* (Baton Rouge: Louisiana State University Press, 1971), 265.

My orders for battle were all prepared in advance of Sherman's arrival,*
except the dates, which could not be fixed while troops to be engaged were so
far away. The possession of Lookout Mountain was of no special advantage to

*CHATTANOOGA, *November* 18, 1863.

MAJOR-GENERAL W. T. SHERMAN:

Enclosed herewith I send you copy of instructions to Major-General
Thomas. You having been over the ground in person, and having heard the
whole matter discussed, further instructions will not be necessary for you. It
is particularly desirable that a force should be got through to the railroad
between Cleveland and Dalton, and Longstreet thus cut off from communication with the South; but being confronted by a large force here, strongly
located, it is not easy to tell how this is to be effected until the result of our
first effort is known.

I will add, however, what is not shown in my instructions to Thomas, that
a brigade of cavalry has been ordered here which, if it arrives in time, will be
thrown across the Tennessee above Chickamauga, and may be able to make
the trip to Cleveland or thereabouts.

U. S. GRANT,
Maj.-Gen'l.

CHATTANOOGA, *November* 18, 1863.

MAJOR-GENERAL GEO. H. THOMAS,

Chattanooga:

All preparations should be made for attacking the enemy's position on
Missionary Ridge by Saturday at daylight. Not being provided with a map
giving names of roads, spurs of the mountains, and other places, such definite
instructions cannot be given as might be desirable. However, the general plan,
you understand, is for Sherman, with the force brought with him strengthened by a division from your command, to effect a crossing of the Tennessee
River just below the mouth of Chickamauga; his crossing to be protected by
artillery from the heights on the north bank of the river (to be located by your
chief of artillery), and to secure the heights on the northern extremity to
about the railroad tunnel before the enemy can concentrate against him. You
will co-operate with Sherman. The troops in Chattanooga Valley should be
well concentrated on your left flank, leaving only the necessary force to defend
fortifications on the right and centre, and a movable column of one division
in readiness to move wherever ordered. This division should show itself as
threateningly as possible on the most practicable line for making an attack up

us now. Hooker was instructed to send Howard's corps to the north side of the Tennessee, thence up behind the hills on the north side, and to go into camp opposite Chattanooga; with the remainder of the command, Hooker was, at a time to be afterwards appointed, to ascend the western slope between the upper and lower palisades, and so get into Chattanooga valley.[15]

The plan of battle was for Sherman to attack the enemy's right flank, form a line across it, extend our left over South Chickamauga River so as to threaten or hold the railroad in Bragg's rear, and thus force him either to weaken his lines elsewhere or lose his connection with his base at Chickamauga Station.[16] Hooker was to perform like service on our right. His problem was to get from Lookout Valley to Chattanooga Valley in the most expeditious way possible; cross the latter valley rapidly to Rossville, south of Bragg's line on Missionary Ridge, form line there across the ridge facing north, with

---

the valley. Your effort then will be to form a junction with Sherman, making your advance well towards the northern end of Missionary Ridge, and moving as near simultaneously with him as possible. The junction once formed and the ridge carried, communications will be at once established between the two armies by roads on the south bank of the river. Further movements will then depend on those of the enemy. Lookout Valley, I think, will be easily held by Geary's division and what troops you may still have there belonging to the old Army of the Cumberland. Howard's corps can then be held in readiness to act either with you at Chattanooga or with Sherman. It should be marched on Friday night to a position on the north side of the river, not lower down than the first pontoon-bridge, and there held in readiness for such orders as may become necessary. All these troops will be provided with two days' cooked rations in haversacks, and one hundred rounds of ammunition on the person of each infantry soldier. Special care should be taken by all officers to see that ammunition is not wasted or unnecessarily fired away. You will call on the engineer department for such preparations as you may deem necessary for carrying your infantry and artillery over the creek.

U. S. GRANT,
Major-General.

---

[15] On Nov. 15, 1863, USG informed Halleck that his initial plan for Hooker's troops was to attack Confederate forces on Lookout Mountain. In his Nov. 18 letter to Thomas, USG suggested the movement of Howard's troops. *PUSG*, 9:399–400, 411.

[16] Chickamauga Station was approximately five miles east of Chattanooga. George B. Davis et al., *The Official Military Atlas of the Civil War* (New York: Fairfax Press, 1983), plate 50, map 5.

his right flank extended to Chickamauga Valley east of the ridge, thus threatening the enemy's rear on that flank and compelling him to reinforce this also. Thomas, with the Army of the Cumberland, occupied the centre, and was to assault while the enemy was engaged with most of his forces on his two flanks.

To carry out this plan, Sherman was to cross the Tennessee at Brown's Ferry and move east of Chattanooga to a point opposite the north end of Mission Ridge, and to place his command back of the foot-hills out of sight of the enemy on the ridge. There are two streams called Chickamauga emptying into the Tennessee River east of Chattanooga—North Chickamauga, taking its rise in Tennessee, flowing south, and emptying into the river some seven or eight miles east; while the South Chickamauga, which takes its rise in Georgia, flows northward, and empties into the Tennessee some three or four miles above the town. There were now one hundred and sixteen pontoons in the North Chickamauga River, their presence there being unknown to the enemy.

At night a division was to be marched up to that point, and at two o'clock in the morning moved down with the current, thirty men in each boat. A few were to land east of the mouth of the South Chickamauga, capture the pickets there, and then lay a bridge connecting the two banks of the river. The rest were to land on the south side of the Tennessee, where Missionary Ridge would strike it if prolonged, and a sufficient number of men to man the boats were to push to the north side to ferry over the main body of Sherman's command while those left on the south side intrenched themselves. Thomas was to move out from his lines facing the ridge, leaving enough of Palmer's[17] corps to guard against an attack down the valley. Lookout Valley being of no present value to us, and being untenable by the enemy if we should secure Missionary Ridge, Hooker's orders were changed. His revised orders brought him to Chattanooga by the established route north of the Tennessee. He was then to move out to the right to Rossville.[18]

Hooker's position in Lookout Valley was absolutely essential to us so long as Chattanooga was besieged. It was the key to our line for supplying the army. But it was not essential after the enemy was dispersed from our front, or even after the battle for this purpose was begun. Hooker's orders, there-

---

[17] Palmer commanded the 14th Corps, Army of the Cumberland, from Oct. 1863 to Aug. 1864. *CWHC*, 415.

[18] The editors have been unable to locate a copy of these revised orders. For Hooker's description of the orders, see *OR*, I, 31(II), 314.

fore, were designed to get his force past Lookout Mountain and Chattanooga Valley, and up to Missionary Ridge. By crossing the north face of Lookout the troops would come into Chattanooga Valley in rear of the line held by the enemy across the valley, and would necessarily force its evacuation. Orders were accordingly given to march by this route. But days before the battle began the advantages as well as the disadvantages of this plan of action were all considered. The passage over the mountain was a difficult one to make in the face of an enemy. It might consume so much time as to lose us the use of the troops engaged in it at other points where they were more wanted. After reaching Chattanooga Valley, the creek of the same name, quite a formidable stream to get an army over, had to be crossed. I was perfectly willing that the enemy should keep Lookout Mountain until we got through with the troops on Missionary Ridge. By marching Hooker to the north side of the river, thence up the stream, and recrossing at the town, he could be got in position at any named time; when in this new position, he would have Chattanooga Creek behind him, and the attack on Missionary Ridge would unquestionably cause the evacuation by the enemy of his line across the valley and on Lookout Mountain. Hooker's order was changed accordingly. As explained elsewhere, the original order had to be reverted to, because of a flood in the river rendering the bridge at Brown's Ferry unsafe for the passage of troops at the exact juncture when it was wanted to bring all the troops together against Missionary Ridge.[19]

The next day after Sherman's arrival I took him, with Generals Thomas and Smith and other officers, to the north side of the river, and showed them the ground over which Sherman had to march, and pointed out generally what he was expected to do.[20] I, as well as the authorities in Washington, was still in a great state of anxiety for Burnside's safety. Burnside himself, I believe, was the only one who did not share in this anxiety. Nothing could be done for him, however, until Sherman's troops were up. As soon, therefore, as the inspection was over, Sherman started for Bridgeport to hasten matters, rowing a boat himself, I believe, from Kelly's Ferry. Sherman had left Bridgeport

[19] For Thomas's Nov. 23–24, 1863, orders to Hooker (issued by Maj. Gen. Joseph J. Reynolds, Thomas's chief of staff) regarding the assault of Lookout Mountain, see ibid., I, 31(II), 105–106.

[20] On Nov. 16, 1863, USG, Sherman, Thomas, W. F. Smith, Brig. Gen. John M. Brannan and others went to the west bank of the Tennessee River with maps of the area to discuss the battle plan. *PUSG*, 9:390n; William T. Sherman, *Memoirs of General William T. Sherman* (New York: D. Appleton, 1875), 1:361–362.

the night of the 14th, reached Chattanooga the evening of the 15th, made the above-described inspection on the morning of the 16th, and started back the same evening to hurry up his command, fully appreciating the importance of time.

His march was conducted with as much expedition as the roads and season would admit of. By the 20th he was himself at Brown's Ferry with the head of column, but many of his troops were far behind, and one division (Ewing's[21]) was at Trenton, sent that way to create the impression that Lookout was to be taken from the south. Sherman received his orders at the ferry, and was asked if he could not be ready for the assault the following morning. News had been received that the battle had been commenced at Knoxville. Burnside had been cut off from telegraphic communications. The President, the Secretary of War, and General Halleck, were in an agony of suspense. My suspense was also great, but more endurable, because I was where I could soon do something to relieve the situation. It was impossible to get Sherman's troops up for the next day. I then asked him if they could not be got up to make the assault on the morning of the 22d, and ordered Thomas to move on that date.[22] But the elements were against us. It rained all the 20th and 21st. The river rose so rapidly that it was difficult to keep the pontoons in place.

General Orlando B. Willcox,[23] a division commander under Burnside, was at this time occupying a position farther up the valley than Knoxville—about Maynardville—and was still in telegraphic communication with the North.[24] A dispatch was received from him saying that he was threatened from the east. The following was sent in reply:

"If you can communicate with General Burnside, say to him that our attack on Bragg will commence in the morning. If successful, such a

---

[21] Hugh Boyle Ewing (1826–1905) was born in Ohio and was Sherman's brother-in-law. He commanded the 4th Div., 15th Corps, Army of the Tennessee, under Sherman. After the war, he was an attorney and was U.S. minister to Holland from 1886 to 1870. *CWHC,* 230.

[22] See USG's Nov. 20, 1863, letters to Sherman and Thomas, *PUSG,* 9:421, 423.

[23] Orlando B. Willcox (1823–1907) was born in Michigan and graduated from the USMA in 1847 and left the army to become an attorney in 1857. He became a colonel in the 1st Michigan Inf. in May 1861, was promoted to brigadier general in July that year, and retired from the U.S. Army in 1887. In 1895, Willcox received the Medal of Honor for his actions at the First Battle of Bull Run. *CWHC,* 570.

[24] On Nov. 20, 1863, Willcox was in the vicinity of Bean Station, Clinch Mountain, and Tazewell, TN. *OR,* I, 31(III), 205–207.

move will be made as I think will relieve East Tennessee, if he can hold out. Longstreet passing through our lines to Kentucky need not cause alarm. He would find the country so bare that he would lose his transportation and artillery before reaching Kentucky, and would meet such a force before he got through, that he could not return."[25]

Meantime, Sherman continued his crossing without intermission as fast as his troops could be got up. The crossing had to be effected in full view of the enemy on the top of Lookout Mountain. Once over, however, the troops soon disappeared behind the detached hills on the north side, and would not come to view again, either to watchmen on Lookout Mountain or Missionary Ridge, until they emerged between the hills to strike the bank of the river. But when Sherman's advance reached a point opposite the town of Chattanooga, Howard, who, it will be remembered, had been concealed behind the hills on the north side, took up his line of march to join the troops on the south side. His crossing was in full view both from Missionary Ridge and the top of Lookout, and the enemy of course supposed these troops to be Sherman's. This enabled Sherman to get to his assigned position without discovery.

[25] For telegrams between Willcox and USG, Nov. 20, 1863, see *PUSG,* 9:423–424, 424*n*–425*n*.

# 43

## Preparations for Battle—Thomas Carries the First Line of the Enemy—Sherman Carries Missionary Ridge—Battle of Lookout Mountain—General Hooker's Fight

O N THE 20TH, when so much was occurring to discourage—rains falling so heavily as to delay the passage of troops over the river at Brown's Ferry and threatening the entire breaking of the bridge; news coming of a battle raging at Knoxville; of Willcox being threatened by a force from the east—a letter was received from Bragg which contained these words: "As there may still be some non-combatants in Chattanooga, I deem it proper to notify you that prudence would dictate their early withdrawal."[1] Of course, I understood that this was a device intended to deceive; but I did not know what the intended deception was. On the 22d, however, a deserter[2] came in who informed me that Bragg was leaving our front, and on that day Buckner's division was sent to reinforce Longstreet at Knoxville, and another division started to follow but was recalled.[3] The object of Bragg's letter, no doubt, was in some way to detain me until Knoxville could be captured, and his troops there be returned to Chattanooga.

During the night of the 21st the rest of the pontoon boats, completed, one hundred and sixteen in all, were carried up to and placed in North Chickam-

---

[1] For Bragg's Nov. 20, 1863, letter to USG, see *PUSG*, 9:568n.

[2] According to USG's postbattle report, the unnamed deserter arrived on the morning of Nov. 23, 1863. Ibid., 9:560.

[3] On Nov. 22, 1863, Bragg designated the divisions of Maj. Gen. Patrick Cleburne and Brig. Gen. Simon B. Buckner to support Longstreet in East Tennessee. After U.S. troops began to advance on Nov. 23, Bragg recalled Cleburne's division and a brigade of Buckner's division before they had left the area. Ibid., 9:435n.

auga. The material for the roadway over these was deposited out of view of the enemy within a few hundred yards of the bank of the Tennessee, where the north end of the bridge was to rest.

Hearing nothing from Burnside, and hearing much of the distress in Washington on his account, I could no longer defer operations for his relief. I determined, therefore, to do on the 23d, with the Army of the Cumberland, what had been intended to be done on the 24th.

The position occupied by the Army of the Cumberland had been made very strong for defence during the months it had been besieged. The line was about a mile from the town, and extended from Citico Creek, a small stream running near the base of Missionary Ridge and emptying into the Tennessee about two miles below the mouth of the South Chickamauga, on the left, to Chattanooga Creek on the right. All commanding points on the line were well fortified and well equipped with artillery. The important elevations within the line had all been carefully fortified and supplied with a proper armament. Among the elevations so fortified was one to the east of the town, named Fort Wood.[4] It owed its importance chiefly to the fact that it lay between the town and Missionary Ridge, where most of the strength of the enemy was. Fort Wood had in it twenty-two pieces of artillery, most of which would reach the nearer points of the enemy's line. On the morning of the 23d Thomas, according to instructions, moved Granger's corps of two divisions, Sheridan and T. J. Wood commanding, to the foot of Fort Wood, and formed them into line as if going on parade, Sheridan on the right, Wood to the left, extending to or near Citico Creek. Palmer, commanding the 14th corps, held that part of our line facing south and south-west. He supported Sheridan with one division (Baird's[5]), while his other division under Johnson[6] remained in the trenches, under

---

[4] Fort Wood was renamed Fort Creighton on Dec. 1, 1863, in honor of Col. William R. Creighton of the 7th Ohio Inf., who had died at the Battle of Ringgold Gap, GA, on Nov. 27. In 1888, the fort's walls were demolished and houses were built on the site. Zella Armstrong, *The History of Hamilton County and Chattanooga, Tennessee* (1940; repr. Johnson City, TN: Overmountain Press, 1993), 2:48–49; *OR*, I, 31(III), 293.

[5] Absalom Baird (1824–1905) was born in Pennsylvania and graduated from the USMA in 1849. He was promoted to brigadier general in 1862 and commanded the 3rd Div., 14th Corps, Army of the Cumberland, at Chattanooga. He was brevetted major general in Sept. 1864. In 1896, he was awarded the Medal of Honor for his actions at Jonesboro, GA, in Sept. 1864. *CWHC*, 112.

[6] Richard W. Johnson (1827–1897) was born in Kentucky and graduated from the USMA in 1849. In Nov. 1863, he held the rank of brigadier general and commanded the 1st Div., 14th Corps, Army of the Cumberland. He was brevetted major general in Mar. 1865. Ibid., 321.

arms, ready to be moved to any point. Howard's corps was moved in rear of the centre. The picket lines were within a few hundred yards of each other. At two o'clock in the afternoon all were ready to advance. By this time the clouds had lifted so that the enemy could see from his elevated position all that was going on. The signal for advance was given by a booming of cannon from Fort Wood and other points on the line. The rebel pickets were soon driven back upon the main guards, which occupied minor and detached heights between the main ridge and our lines. These too were carried before halting, and before the enemy had time to reinforce their advance guards. But it was not without loss on both sides. This movement secured to us a line fully a mile in advance of the one we occupied in the morning, and the one which the enemy had occupied up to this time. The fortifications were rapidly turned to face the other way. During the following night they were made strong. We lost in this preliminary action about eleven hundred killed and wounded, while the enemy probably lost quite as heavily, including the prisoners that were captured.[7] With the exception of the firing of artillery, kept up from Missionary Ridge and Fort Wood until night closed in, this ended the fighting for the first day.

The advantage was greatly on our side now, and if I could only have been assured that Burnside could hold out ten days longer I should have rested more easily. But we were doing the best we could for him and the cause.

By the night of the 23d Sherman's command was in a position to move, though one division (Osterhaus's) had not yet crossed the river at Brown's Ferry. The continuous rise in the Tennessee had rendered it impossible to keep the bridge at that point in condition for troops to cross; but I was determined to move that night even without this division. Orders were sent to Osterhaus accordingly to report to Hooker, if he could not cross by eight o'clock on the morning of the 24th. Because of the break in the bridge, Hooker's orders were again changed, but this time only back to those first given to him.[8]

General W. F. Smith had been assigned to duty as Chief Engineer of the Military Division. To him were given the general direction of moving troops by the boats from North Chickamauga, laying the bridge after they reached their position, and generally all the duties pertaining to his office of chief engineer. During the night General Morgan L. Smith's[9] division was marched

[7] On Nov. 24, 1863, Thomas reported that he had lost about 111 men under his command and captured 169 Confederate soldiers. *OR,* I, 31(II), 90.

[8] For USG's Nov. 23 and Nov. 24, 1863, orders to Brig. Gen. Charles R. Woods (who was in command of Osterhaus's 1st Div. at the time) and to Hooker, see *PUSG,* 9:436n.

[9] Morgan L. Smith (1821–1874) was born in New York and eventually settled in Missouri. He served as an enlisted man in the U.S. Army from 1845 to 1850, reentered the military in 1861

to the point where the pontoons were, and the brigade of Giles A. Smith[10] was selected for the delicate duty of manning the boats and surprising the enemy's pickets on the south bank of the river. During this night also General J. M. Brannan,[11] chief of artillery, moved forty pieces of artillery, belonging to the Army of the Cumberland, and placed them on the north side of the river so as to command the ground opposite, to aid in protecting the approach to the point where the south end of the bridge was to rest. He had to use Sherman's artillery horses for this purpose, Thomas having none.

At two o'clock in the morning, November 24th, Giles A. Smith pushed out from the North Chickamauga with his one hundred and sixteen boats, each loaded with thirty brave and well-armed men. The boats with their precious freight dropped down quietly with the current to avoid attracting the attention of any one who could convey information to the enemy, until arriving near the mouth of South Chickamauga. Here a few boats were landed, the troops debarked, and a rush was made upon the picket guard known to be at that point. The guard were surprised, and twenty of their number captured. The remainder of the troops effected a landing at the point where the bridge was to start, with equally good results. The work of ferrying over Sherman's command from the north side of the Tennessee was at once commenced, using the pontoons for the purpose. A steamer was also brought up from the town to assist.[12] The rest of M. L. Smith's division came first, then the division of John E. Smith. The troops as they landed were put to work intrenching their

as a colonel in the 8th Missouri Inf., and was promoted to brigadier general in 1862. During the Chattanooga campaign, Smith commanded the 2nd Div., 15th Corps, Army of the Tennessee. His brother, Giles A. Smith, served as a brigade commander under him. Morgan L. Smith served as U.S. consul in Honolulu, HI, from 1866 to 1868. *CWHC*, 498.

[10] Giles A. Smith (1829–1876) was born in New York and entered the military as a captain in the 8th Missouri Inf. in 1861. In Aug. 1863, he attained the rank of brigadier general. During the Chattanooga campaign, he commanded the 1st Brigade, 2nd Div., 15th Corps, Army of the Tennessee. His brother, Morgan L. Smith, was his commanding officer. Pres. USG appointed Giles A. Smith second assistant postmaster in 1869. John T. Hubbell et al., eds., *Biographical Dictionary of the Union: Northern Leaders of the Civil War* (Westport, CT: Greenwood Press, 1995), 486–487; *CWHC*, 495; *OR*, I, 31(II), 86.

[11] John M. Brannan (1819–1892) was born in Washington, DC, and graduated from the USMA in 1841. He fought in the Mexican-American War and was promoted to brigadier general in 1861. He was brevetted general in Jan. 1865. *CWHC*, 142.

[12] The *Dunbar* was a Confederate steamer captured and repaired by U.S. forces. On Nov. 24, 1863, it was used to transport approximately 6,000 of Sherman's men across the Tennessee River. *OR*, I, 31(II), 77.

position. By daylight the two entire divisions were over, and well covered by the works they had built.

The work of laying the bridge, on which to cross the artillery and cavalry, was now begun. The ferrying over the infantry was continued with the steamer and the pontoons, taking the pontoons, however, as fast as they were wanted to put in their place in the bridge. By a little past noon the bridge was completed, as well as one over the South Chickamauga connecting the troops left on that side with their comrades below, and all the infantry and artillery were on the south bank of the Tennessee.

Sherman at once formed his troops for assault on Missionary Ridge. By one o'clock he started with M. L. Smith on his left, keeping nearly the course of Chickamauga River; J. E. Smith next to the right and a little to the rear; and Ewing still farther to the right and also a little to the rear of J. E. Smith's command, in column, ready to deploy to the right if an enemy should come from that direction. A good skirmish line preceded each of these columns. Soon the foot of the hill was reached; the skirmishers pushed directly up, followed closely by their supports. By half-past three Sherman was in possession of the height without having sustained much loss. A brigade from each division was now brought up, and artillery was dragged to the top of the hill by hand. The enemy did not seem to be aware of this movement until the top of the hill was gained.[13] There had been a drizzling rain during the day, and the clouds were so low that Lookout Mountain and the top of Missionary Ridge were obscured from the view of persons in the valley. But now the enemy opened fire upon their assailants, and made several attempts with their skirmishers to drive them away, but without avail. Later in the day a more determined attack was made, but this, too, failed, and Sherman was left to fortify what he had gained.[14]

Sherman's cavalry took up its line of march soon after the bridge was completed, and by half-past three the whole of it was over both bridges and on its

[13] At about 2 P.M. on Nov. 24, 1863, Confederate major general Patrick Cleburne was ordered to move his command to the right of Missionary Ridge. At the same time, Bragg informed him that the U.S. Army already had a division positioned opposite the line he was supposed to occupy. A brief skirmish ensued, with Sherman reporting no losses during this initial engagement. Ibid., I, 31(II), 573, 746.

[14] By day's end on Nov. 24, 1863, Sherman's forces were on Billy Goat Hill, about a mile away from Tunnel Hill, near the north end of Missionary Ridge. Bruce Catton, *Grant Takes Command,* (Boston: Little, Brown, 1969), 76–77; Wiley Sword, *Mountains Touched with Fire: Chattanooga Besieged, 1863* (New York: St. Martin's, 1995), 200.

way to strike the enemy's communications at Chickamauga Station. All of Sherman's command was now south of the Tennessee. During the afternoon General Giles A. Smith was severely wounded and carried from the field.[15]

Thomas having done on the 23d what was expected of him on the 24th, there was nothing for him to do this day except to strengthen his position. Howard, however, effected a crossing of Citico Creek and a junction with Sherman, and was directed to report to him. With two or three regiments of his command he moved in the morning along the banks of the Tennessee, and reached the point where the bridge was being laid. He went out on the bridge as far as it was completed from the south end, and saw Sherman superintending the work from the north side and moving himself south as fast as an additional boat was put in and the roadway put upon it. Howard reported to his new chief across the chasm between them, which was now narrow and in a few minutes closed.

While these operations were going on to the east of Chattanooga, Hooker was engaged on the west. He had three divisions: Osterhaus's, of the 15th corps, Army of the Tennessee; Geary's, 12th corps, Army of the Potomac; and Cruft's, 14th corps, Army of the Cumberland.[16] Geary was on the right at Wauhatchie, Cruft at the centre, and Osterhaus near Brown's Ferry. These troops were all west of Lookout Creek. The enemy had the east bank of the creek strongly picketed and intrenched, and three brigades of troops in the rear to reinforce them if attacked. These brigades occupied the summit of the mountain. General Carter L. Stevenson[17] was in command of the whole.[18] Why any troops, except artillery with a small infantry guard, were kept on the mountain-top, I do not see. A

---

[15] Smith was wounded in the chest and right arm during the assault. He was confined indoors for the rest of the winter in order to recover, however the chest wound caused hemorrhaging in his lungs which affected his health for the rest of his life. Jack D. Welsh, *Medical Histories of Union Generals* (Kent, OH: Kent State University Press, 1996), 308–309.

[16] Charles Cruft (1826–1883) was born in Indiana and entered the military as a colonel in the 31st Indiana Inf. at the start of the Civil War. He was promoted to brigadier general in 1862. During the Chattanooga campaign, Cruft commanded the 1st Div., 4th Corps, Army of the Cumberland. He was brevetted major general in Mar. 1865. *CWHC*, 193.

[17] Carter L. Stevenson (1817–1888) was born in Virginia and graduated from the USMA in 1838. In 1861, he left the U.S. Army and accepted a commission at the rank of major in the Confederate Army. In 1862, he was promoted to major general and on Nov. 23, 1863, he took charge of the defense of Lookout Mountain. Ibid., 510; *OR*, I, 31(II), 717–722.

[18] Brigades under the command of John C. Moore and Edward C. Walthall established pickets on the east side of Lookout Creek, while Stevenson designated Edmund W. Pettus's brigade as reinforcements. Troops commanded by John C. Brown remained on the summit.

hundred men could have held the summit—which is a palisade for more than thirty feet down—against the assault of any number of men from the position Hooker occupied.

The side of Lookout Mountain confronting Hooker's command was rugged, heavily timbered, and full of chasms, making it difficult to advance with troops, even in the absence of an opposing force. Farther up, the ground becomes more even and level, and was in cultivation. On the east side the slope is much more gradual, and a good wagon road, zigzagging up it, connects the town of Chattanooga with the summit.

Early on the morning of the 24th Hooker moved Geary's division, supported by a brigade of Cruft's, up Lookout Creek, to effect a crossing. The remainder of Cruft's division was to seize the bridge over the creek, near the crossing of the railroad. Osterhaus was to move up to the bridge and cross it. The bridge was seized by Gross's[19] brigade after a slight skirmish with the pickets guarding it. This attracted the enemy so that Geary's movement farther up was not observed. A heavy mist obscured him from the view of the troops on the top of the mountain. He crossed the creek almost unobserved, and captured the picket of over forty men on guard near by. He then commenced ascending the mountain directly in his front. By this time the enemy was seen coming down from their camps on the mountain slope, and filing into their rifle-pits to contest the crossing of the bridge. By eleven o'clock the bridge was complete. Osterhaus was up, and after some sharp skirmishing the enemy was driven away with considerable loss in killed and captured.

While the operations at the bridge were progressing, Geary was pushing up the hill over great obstacles, resisted by the enemy directly in his front, and in face of the guns on top of the mountain. The enemy, seeing their left flank and rear menaced, gave way, and were followed by Cruft and Osterhaus. Soon these were up abreast of Geary, and the whole command pushed up the hill, driving the enemy in advance. By noon Geary had gained the open ground on the north slope of the mountain, with his right close up to the base of the upper palisade, but there were strong fortifications in his front. The rest of

Peter Cozzens, *The Shipwreck of Their Hopes: The Battles for Chattanooga* (Urbana: University of Illinois Press, 1994), 163–165; *OR,* I, 31(II), 718–720.

[19] William Grose (1812–1900) was born in Ohio and later moved to Indiana. In 1861, he was commissioned as a colonel in the 36th Indiana Inf. He was wounded in the left shoulder and in the neck at the Battle of Chickamauga on Sept., 20, 1863. During the Battle of Lookout Mountain, Grose commanded the 3rd Brigade, 1st Div., 4th Corps, Army of the Cumberland. He was brevetted major general in Aug. 1865, served as a collector for the U.S. Internal Revenue Service from 1866 to 1874, and served in the Indiana legislature. *CWHC,* 270.

the command coming up, a line was formed from the base of the upper palisade to the mouth of Chattanooga Creek.

Thomas and I were on the top of Orchard Knob. Hooker's advance now made our line a continuous one. It was in full view, extending from the Tennessee River, where Sherman had crossed, up Chickamauga River to the base of Mission Ridge, over the top of the north end of the ridge to Chattanooga Valley, then along parallel to the ridge a mile or more, across the valley to the mouth of Chattanooga Creek, thence up the slope of Lookout Mountain to the foot of the upper palisade. The day was hazy, so that Hooker's operations were not visible to us except at moments when the clouds would rise. But the sound of his artillery and musketry was heard incessantly. The enemy on his front was partially fortified, but was soon driven out of his works. During the afternoon the clouds, which had so obscured the top of Lookout all day as to hide whatever was going on from the view of those below, settled down and made it so dark where Hooker was as to stop operations for the time. At four o'clock Hooker reported his position as impregnable.[20] By a little after five direct communication was established, and a brigade of troops was sent from Chattanooga to reinforce him. These troops had to cross Chattanooga Creek and met with some opposition, but soon overcame it, and by night the commander, General Carlin,[21] reported to Hooker and was assigned to his left. I now telegraphed to Washington: "The fight to-day progressed favorably. Sherman carried the end of Missionary Ridge, and his right is now at the tunnel, and his left at Chickamauga Creek. Troops from Lookout Valley carried the point of the mountain, and now hold the eastern slope and a point high up. Hooker reports two thousand prisoners taken, besides which a small number have fallen into our hands from Missionary Ridge." The next day the President replied: "Your dispatches as to fighting on Monday and Tuesday are here. Well done. Many thanks to all. Remember Burnside." And Halleck also telegraphed: "I congratulate you on the success thus far of your plans. I fear that Burnside is hard pushed, and that any further delay may prove fatal. I know you will do all in your power to relieve him."[22]

[20] For Hooker's Nov. 24, 1863, message to Reynolds, see OR, I, 31(II), 111.

[21] William P. Carlin (1829–1903) was born in Illinois and graduated from the USMA in 1850 and served in the U.S. Army. In Mar. 1861, he was promoted to captain and on Nov. 29, 1862, he was promoted to brigadier general. At Chattanooga, he commanded the 1st Brigade, 1st Div., 14th Corps, Army of the Cumberland. He was brevetted major general in Mar. 1865. CWHC, 163.

[22] For USG's Nov. 23–25, 1863, communications with Lincoln and Halleck, see PUSG, 9:439–440, 440n.

The division of Jefferson C. Davis, Army of the Cumberland, had been sent to the North Chickamauga to guard the pontoons as they were deposited in the river, and to prevent all ingress or egress of citizens. On the night of the 24th his division, having crossed with Sherman, occupied our extreme left from the upper bridge over the plain to the north base of Missionary Ridge. Firing continued to a late hour in the night, but it was not connected with an assault at any point.

# 44

Battle of Chattanooga—A Gallant Charge—Complete
Rout of the Enemy—Pursuit of the Confederates—
General Bragg—Remarks on Chattanooga

A T TWELVE O'CLOCK at night, when all was quiet, I began to give orders
for the next day, and sent a dispatch to Willcox to encourage Burnside. Sherman
was directed to attack at daylight. Hooker was ordered to move at the same
hour, and endeavor to intercept the enemy's retreat if he still remained; if he
had gone, then to move directly to Rossville and operate against the left and
rear of the force on Missionary Ridge.[1] Thomas was not to move until Hooker
had reached Missionary Ridge. As I was with him on Orchard Knob, he would
not move without further orders from me.

The morning of the 25th opened clear and bright, and the whole field was
in full view from the top of Orchard Knob. It remained so all day. Bragg's
headquarters were in full view, and officers—presumably staff officers—could
be seen coming and going constantly.[2]

The point of ground which Sherman had carried on the 24th was almost
disconnected from the main ridge occupied by the enemy. A low pass, over
which there is a wagon road crossing the hill, and near which there is a railroad tunnel, intervenes between the two hills. The problem now was to get to
the main ridge. The enemy was fortified on the point; and back farther,
where the ground was still higher, was a second fortification commanding the

---

[1] For USG's Nov. 24, 1863, letter to Sherman and Nov. 24 telegram to Willcox, see *PUSG*,
9:441*n*, 444. For USG's orders to Hooker issued by Maj. Gen. Joseph J. Reynolds, Thomas's
chief of staff, see *OR*, I, 31(II), 112, 113.

[2] Bragg's headquarters were in a small house along the top of Missionary Ridge. Zella Armstrong, *The History of Hamilton County and Chattanooga, Tennessee* (1940; repr. Johnson City,
TN: Overmountain Press, 1993), 2:45.

first.³ Sherman was out as soon as it was light enough to see, and by sunrise his command was in motion. Three brigades held the hill already gained. Morgan L. Smith moved along the east base of Missionary Ridge; Loomis⁴ along the west base, supported by two brigades of John E. Smith's division; and Corse⁵ with his brigade was between the two, moving directly towards the hill to be captured. The ridge is steep and heavily wooded on the east side, where M. L. Smith's troops were advancing, but cleared and with a more gentle slope on the west side. The troops advanced rapidly and carried the extreme end of the rebel works. Morgan L. Smith advanced to a point which cut the enemy off from the railroad bridge and the means of bringing up supplies by rail from Chickamauga Station, where the main depot was located. The enemy made brave and strenuous efforts to drive our troops from the position we had gained, but without success. The contest lasted for two hours. Corse, a brave and efficient commander, was badly wounded in this assault.⁶ Sherman now threatened both Bragg's flank and his stores, and made it necessary for him to weaken other points of his line to strengthen his right. From the position I occupied I could see column after column of Bragg's forces moving against Sherman. Every Confederate gun that could be brought to bear upon the Union forces was concentrated upon him.⁷ J. E. Smith, with two brigades, charged up the west side of the ridge to the support of Corse's command, over open ground and in the face of a heavy fire of both artillery

³ On Nov. 24, 1863, Sherman's troops ascended a rise known as Billy Goat Hill. The portion of the "main ridge" occupied by Confederate troops was called Tunnel Hill. Peter Cozzens, *The Shipwreck of Their Hopes: The Battles for Chattanooga* (Urbana: University of Illinois Press, 1994), 152; Wiley Sword, *Mountains Touched with Fire: Chattanooga Besieged, 1863* (New York: St. Martin's, 1995), 200.

⁴ John M. Loomis (1825–1900) was born in Connecticut and moved to Chicago in 1845. At the start of the Civil War, he was the colonel of the 26th Illinois Inf. During the Chattanooga campaign, he commanded the 1st Brigade, 4th Div., 15th Corps, Army of the Tennessee. Loomis resigned from the army in 1864 and went into the lumber business in Michigan. Elisha Loomis, *Descendants of Joseph Loomis in America* (Berea, OH: n.p., 1909), 316–319; OR, I, 31(II), 633.

⁵ John M. Corse (1835–1893) was born in Pennsylvania and moved to Iowa in 1842. He attended the USMA from 1853 to 1855 before resigning. In July 1861, he joined the U.S. Army as a major of the 6th Iowa Inf. Corse was promoted to brigadier general in 1863 and during the Chattanooga campaign commanded the 2nd Brigade, 4th Div., 15th Corps, Army of the Tennessee. *CWHC*, 185–186.

⁶ Corse was struck in the knee, but the injury was not serious. Cozzens, *Shipwreck of Their Hopes*, 214.

⁷ The Confederate forces confronting Sherman were reinforced by Brig. Gen. George Maney's brigade and Brig. Gen. Alfred Cumming's brigade. OR, I, 31(II), 751.

and musketry, and reached the very parapet of the enemy. He lay here for a time, but the enemy coming with a heavy force upon his right flank, he was compelled to fall back, followed by the foe. A few hundred yards brought Smith's troops into a wood, where they were speedily reformed, when they charged and drove the attacking party back to his intrenchments.

Seeing the advance, repulse, and second advance of J. E. Smith from the position I occupied, I directed Thomas to send a division to reinforce him.[8] Baird's division was accordingly sent from the right of Orchard Knob. It had to march a considerable distance directly under the eyes of the enemy to reach its position. Bragg at once commenced massing in the same direction. This was what I wanted. But it had now got to be late in the afternoon, and I had expected before this to see Hooker crossing the ridge in the neighborhood of Rossville and compelling Bragg to mass in that direction also.

The enemy had evacuated Lookout Mountain during the night, as I expected he would. In crossing the valley he burned the bridge over Chattanooga Creek, and did all he could to obstruct the roads behind him. Hooker was off bright and early, with no obstructions in his front but distance and the destruction above named. He was detained four hours crossing Chattanooga Creek, and thus was lost the immediate advantage I expected from his forces. His reaching Bragg's flank and extending across it was to be the signal for Thomas's assault of the ridge. But Sherman's condition was getting so critical that the assault for his relief could not be delayed any longer.

Sheridan's and Wood's divisions had been lying under arms from early morning, ready to move the instant the signal was given. I now directed Thomas to order the charge at once.* I watched eagerly to see the effect, and became impatient at last that there was no indication of any charge being made. The centre of the line which was to make the charge was near where Thomas and I stood, but concealed from view by an intervening forest. Turning to Thomas to inquire what caused the delay, I was surprised to see Thomas J. Wood, one of the division commanders who was to make the charge, standing talking to him. I spoke to General Wood, asking him why he did not charge as ordered an hour

*In this order authority was given for the troops to reform after taking the first line of rifle-pits preparatory to carrying the ridge.[9]

[8]The editors have not found a written order from USG to Thomas regarding reinforcements for Smith.

[9]The editors have not found a written order from USG to Thomas that matches this description.

before. He replied very promptly that this was the first he had heard of it, but that he had been ready all day to move at a moment's notice. I told him to make the charge at once. He was off in a moment, and in an incredibly short time loud cheering was heard, and he and Sheridan were driving the enemy's advance before them towards Missionary Ridge. The Confederates were strongly in-trenched on the crest of the ridge in front of us, and had a second line half-way down and another at the base. Our men drove the troops in front of the lower line of rifle-pits so rapidly, and followed them so closely, that rebel and Union troops went over the first line of works almost at the same time. Many rebels were captured and sent to the rear under the fire of their own friends higher up the hill. Those that were not captured retreated, and were pursued. The re-treating hordes being between friends and pursuers caused the enemy to fire high to avoid killing their own men. In fact, on that occasion the Union soldier nearest the enemy was in the safest position. Without awaiting further orders or stopping to reform, on our troops went to the second line of works; over that and on for the crest—thus effectually carrying out my orders of the 18th for the battle and of the 24th* for this charge.

I watched their progress with intense interest. The fire along the rebel line was terrific. Cannon and musket balls filled the air: but the damage

*CHATTANOOGA, *November* 24, 1863.

MAJOR-GENERAL GEO. H. THOMAS,
Chattanooga:

General Sherman carried Missionary Ridge as far as the tunnel with only slight skirmishing. His right now rests at the tunnel and on top of the hill, his left at Chickamauga Creek. I have instructed General Sherman to advance as soon as it is light in the morning, and your attack, which will be simulta-neous, will be in co-operation. Your command will either carry the rifle-pits and ridge directly in front of them, or move to the left, as the presence of the enemy may require. If Hooker's position on the mountain [cannot be maintained] with a small force, and it is found impracticable to carry the top from where he is, it would be advisable for him to move up the valley with all the force he can spare, and ascend by the first practicable road.

U. S. GRANT,
Major-General.[10]

[10] For USG's Nov. 18, 1863, orders to Thomas, see *PUSG*, 9:411–412. According to Meigs's journal entry regarding the battle, USG had originally intended for the troops to pause and reform lines of assault. However, upon seeing the advance progress up Missionary Ridge, he chose not to order a halt. Ibid., 9:447–448.

done was in small proportion to the ammunition expended. The pursuit continued until the crest was reached, and soon our men were seen climbing over the Confederate barriers at different points in front of both Sheridan's and Wood's divisions. The retreat of the enemy along most of his line was precipitate and the panic so great that Bragg and his officers lost all control over their men. Many were captured, and thousands threw away their arms in their flight.

Sheridan pushed forward until he reached the Chickamauga River at a point above where the enemy crossed. He met some resistance from troops occupying a second hill in rear of Missionary Ridge, probably to cover the retreat of the main body and of the artillery and trains. It was now getting dark, but Sheridan, without halting on that account pushed his men forward up this second hill slowly and without attracting the attention of the men placed to defend it, while he detached to the right and left to surround the position. The enemy discovered the movement before these dispositions were complete, and beat a hasty retrat, leaving artillery, wagon trains, and many prisoners in our hands. To Sheridan's prompt movement the Army of the Cumberland, and the nation, are indebted for the bulk of the capture of prisoners, artillery, and small-arms that day. Except for his prompt pursuit, so much in this way would not have been accomplished.[11]

While the advance up Mission Ridge was going forward, General Thomas with staff, General Gordon Granger, commander of the corps making the assault, and myself and staff occupied Orchard Knob, from which the entire field could be observed. The moment the troops were seen going over the last line of rebel defences, I ordered Granger to join his command, and mounting my horse I rode to the front. General Thomas left about the same time. Sheridan on the extreme right was already in pursuit of the enemy east of the ridge. Wood, who commanded the division to the left of Sheridan, accompanied his men on horseback in the charge, but did not join Sheridan in the pursuit. To the left, in Baird's front where Bragg's troops had massed against Sherman, the resistance was more stubborn and the contest lasted longer. I ordered Granger to follow the enemy with Wood's division, but he was so much excited, and kept up

---

[11] After reaching the summit of Missionary Ridge, Sheridan's forces pursued the retreating Confederates along Moore Road, which led to Chickamauga Station. They confronted the rear guard of the Confederate forces on a hill approximately one mile east of Missionary Ridge, and forced them to retreat from that point. In total, Sheridan's forces captured seventeen pieces of artillery and 1,762 prisoners. *OR,* I, 31(II), 191.

such a roar of musketry in the direction the enemy had taken, that by the time I could stop the firing the enemy had got well out of the way. The enemy confronting Sherman, now seeing everything to their left giving way, fled also. Sherman, however, was not aware of the extent of our success until after nightfall, when he received orders to pursue at daylight in the morning.

As soon as Sherman discovered that the enemy had left his front he directed his reserves, Davis's division of the Army of the Cumberland, to push over the pontoon-bridge at the mouth of the Chickamauga, and to move forward to Chickamauga Station. He ordered Howard to move up the stream some two miles to where there was an old bridge, repair it during the night, and follow Davis at four o'clock in the morning. Morgan L. Smith was ordered to reconnoitre the tunnel to see if that was still held. Nothing was found there but dead bodies of men of both armies. The rest of Sherman's command was directed to follow Howard at daylight in the morning to get on to the railroad towards Graysville.

Hooker, as stated, was detained at Chattanooga Creek by the destruction of the bridge at that point. He got his troops over, with the exception of the artillery, by fording the stream at a little after three o'clock. Leaving his artillery to follow when the bridge should be reconstructed, he pushed on with the remainder of his command. At Rossville he came upon the flank of a division of the enemy, which soon commenced a retreat along the ridge.[12] This threw them on Palmer. They could make but little resistance in the position they were caught in, and as many of them as could do so escaped. Many, however, were captured. Hooker's position during the night of the 25th was near Rossville, extending east of the ridge. Palmer was on his left, on the road to Graysville.

During the night I telegraphed to Willcox that Bragg had been defeated, and that immediate relief would be sent to Burnside if he could hold out;[13] to Halleck I sent an announcement of our victory, and informed him that forces would be sent up the valley to relieve Burnside.

---

[12] Hooker's troops encountered a portion of Alexander P. Stewart's division, which was under the command of John C. Breckinridge. Cozzens, *Shipwreck of Their Hopes*, 313–314; *OR*, I, 31(II), 318–319.

[13] On Nov. 25, 1863, USG sent Foster a telegram about the victory at Chattanooga. Asst. AG William P. Anderson forwarded the message to Willcox the next day. W. P. Anderson to O. B. Willcox, Nov. 26, 1863 (copy), Series 4, Box 9, Folder USG to J. G. Foster Nov. 25, 1863, U. S. Grant Presidential Collection, Mississippi State University Libraries (original in National Archives, Record Group 393); *PUSG*, 9:450.

Before the battle of Chattanooga opened I had taken measures for the relief of Burnside the moment the way should be clear. Thomas was directed to have the little steamer that had been built at Chattanooga loaded to its capacity with rations and ammunition.[14] Granger's corps was to move by the south bank of the Tennessee River to the mouth of the Holston, and up that to Knoxville, accompanied by the boat. In addition to the supplies transported by boat, the men were to carry forty rounds of ammunition in their cartridge-boxes, and four days' rations in haversacks.

In the battle of Chattanooga, troops from the Army of the Potomac, from the Army of the Tennessee, and from the Army of the Cumberland participated. In fact, the accidents growing out of the heavy rains and the sudden rise in the Tennessee River so mingled the troops that the organizations were not kept together, under their respective commanders, during the battle. Hooker, on the right, had Geary's division of the 12th corps, Army of the Potomac; Osterhaus's division of the 15th corps, Army of the Tennessee; and Cruft's division of the Army of the Cumberland. Sherman had three divisions of his own army, Howard's corps from the Army of the Potomac, and Jefferson C. Davis's division of the Army of the Cumberland. There was no jealousy—hardly rivalry. Indeed, I doubt whether officers or men took any note at the time of the fact of this intermingling of commands. All saw a defiant foe surrounding them, and took it for granted that every move was intended to dislodge him, and it made no difference where the troops came from so that the end was accomplished.

The victory at Chattanooga was won against great odds, considering the advantage the enemy had of position, and was accomplished more easily than was expected by reason of Bragg's making several grave mistakes: first, in sending away his ablest corps commander with over twenty thousand troops; second, in sending away a division of troops on the eve of battle; third, in placing so much of a force on the plain in front of his impregnable position.[15]

It was known that Mr. Jefferson Davis had visited Bragg on Missionary Ridge a short time before my reaching Chattanooga. It was reported and believed that

[14] For USG's Nov. 22, 1863, letter to Thomas regarding the steamer *Dunbar*, see *PUSG*, 9:432–433.

[15] On Nov. 3, 1863, Bragg had ordered Longstreet's force of 20,000 troops to move on East Tennessee in order to combat the U.S. Army forces near Knoxville, TN. On Nov. 22, Bragg had ordered Patrick Cleburne's and Buckner's divisions to join Longstreet, but Cleburne's division had not yet left the Chattanooga area and thus played a role in the Battle of Missionary Ridge. Bragg repeatedly refused to give up his positions along the line around Chattanooga, spreading his troops thinly across a large area. Cozzens, *Shipwreck of Their Hopes*, 32, 104, 116, 125, 137; *OR*, I, 31(I), 455.

he had come out to reconcile a serious difference between Bragg and Long-street, and finding this difficult to do, planned the campaign against Knox-ville, to be conducted by the latter general.[16] I had known both Bragg and Longstreet before the war, the latter very well. We had been three years at West Point together, and, after my graduation, for a time in the same regi-ment. Then we served together in the Mexican War. I had known Bragg in Mexico, and met him occasionally subsequently. I could well understand how there might be an irreconcilable difference between them.

Bragg was a remarkably intelligent and well-informed man, professionally and otherwise. He was also thoroughly upright. But he was possessed of an irascible temper, and was naturally disputatious. A man of the highest moral character and the most correct habits, yet in the old army he was in frequent trouble. As a subordinate he was always on the lookout to catch his com-manding officer infringing his prerogatives; as a post commander he was equally vigilant to detect the slightest neglect, even of the most trivial order.

I have heard in the old army an anecdote very characteristic of Bragg. On one occasion, when stationed at a post of several companies commanded by a field officer, he was himself commanding one of the companies and at the same time acting as post quartermaster and commissary. He was first lieutenant at the time, but his captain was detached on other duty. As commander of the company he made a requisition upon the quartermaster—himself—for something he wanted. As quartermaster he declined to fill the requisition, and endorsed on the back of it his reasons for so doing. As company commander he responded to this, urging that his requisition called for nothing but what he was entitled to, and that it was the duty of the quartermaster to fill it. As quartermaster he still persisted that he was right. In this condition of affairs Bragg referred the whole matter to the commanding officer of the post. The latter, when he saw the na-ture of the matter referred, exclaimed: "My God, Mr. Bragg, you have quarrelled with every officer in the army, and now you are quarrelling with yourself!"[17]

---

[16] On Oct. 4, 1863, twelve generals under Bragg's command (including Longstreet) peti-tioned Davis for Bragg's removal, prompting Davis's Oct. 9–12 visit to Chattanooga. During his meetings with Bragg, Davis suggested the plan of sending Longstreet to oust Burnside from Knoxville, which would position Longstreet and his troops to go from there to Virginia as rein-forcements for Robert E. Lee, who was urgently appealing to Davis for the return of Long-street's divisions to the Army of Northern Virginia. Cozzens, *Shipwreck of Their Hopes*, 23, 103; Jefferson Davis, *The Papers of Jefferson Davis*, vol. 10, ed. Lynda Laswell Crist, Kenneth H. Wil-liams, and Peggy L. Dillard (Baton Rouge: Louisiana State University Press, 1999), xlvii–xlviii.

[17] The editors have not found any published versions of this anecdote prior to the publica-tion of USG's *Memoirs*.

Longstreet was an entirely different man. He was brave, honest, intelligent, a very capable soldier, subordinate to his superiors, just and kind to his subordinates, but jealous of his own rights, which he had the courage to maintain. He was never on the lookout to detect a slight, but saw one as soon as anybody when intentionally given.

It may be that Longstreet was not sent to Knoxville for the reason stated, but because Mr. Davis had an exalted opinion of his own military genius, and thought he saw a chance of "killing two birds with one stone." On several occasions during the war he came to the relief of the Union army by means of his *superior military genius.*

I speak advisedly when I say Mr. Davis prided himself on his military capacity. He says so himself, virtually, in his answer to the notice of his nomination to the Confederate presidency. Some of his generals have said so in their writings since the downfall of the Confederacy.[18]

My recollection is that my first orders for the battle of Chattanooga were as fought. Sherman was to get on Missionary Ridge, as he did;[19] Hooker to cross the north end of Lookout Mountain, as he did, sweep across Chattanooga Valley and get across the south end of the ridge near Rossville. When Hooker had secured that position the Army of the Cumberland was to assault in the centre. Before Sherman arrived, however, the order was so changed as that Hooker was directed to come to Chattanooga by the north bank of the Tennessee River. The waters in the river, owing to heavy rains, rose so fast that the bridge at Brown's Ferry could not be maintained in a condition to be used in crossing troops upon it. For this reason Hooker's orders were changed by telegraph back to what they were originally.*

*NOTE.—From this point on this volume was written (with the exception of the campaign in the Wilderness, which had been previously written) by General Grant after his great illness in April, and the present arrangement of the subject-matter was made by him between the 10th and 18th of July, 1885.

[18] Davis stated that he was initially disappointed when he was elected as president of the Confederacy because he wanted to serve in a more direct military role. USG may have referred to comments like that of Beauregard, who wrote after the Civil War that "we needed for President either a military man of high order, or a politician of the first class without military pretensions." P. G. T. Beauregard, "The First Battle of Bull Run," in *Battles and Leaders of the Civil War,* vol. 1, ed. Robert Underwood Johnson and Clarence Clough Buel (New York: Century, 1887), 226; Jefferson Davis, *The Rise and Fall of the Confederate Government* (New York: D. Appleton, 1881), 230.

[19] USG's Nov. 18, 1863, orders indicate that he planned for Sherman's assault to be the main focus of the effort to take Missionary Ridge. However, the assault in the center by Thomas's troops accomplished that goal instead. Cozzens, *Shipwreck of Their Hopes,* 392; *PUSG,* 9:411–412.

# 45

## The Relief of Knoxville—Headquarters Moved to Nashville—Visiting Knoxville—Cipher Dispatches— Withholding Orders

CHATTANOOGA NOW BEING secure to the National troops beyond any doubt, I immediately turned my attention to relieving Knoxville, about the situation of which the President, in particular, was very anxious. Prior to the battles, I had made preparations for sending troops to the relief of Burnside at the very earliest moment after securing Chattanooga. We had there two little steamers which had been built and fitted up from the remains of old boats and put in condition to run. General Thomas was directed to have one of these boats loaded with rations and ammunition and move up the Tennessee River to the mouth of the Holston, keeping the boat all the time abreast of the troops.[1] General Granger, with the 4th corps reinforced to make twenty thousand men, was to start the moment Missionary Ridge was carried, and under no circumstances were the troops to return to their old camps.[2] With the provisions carried, and the little that could be got in the country, it was supposed he could hold out until Longstreet was driven away, after which event East Tennessee would furnish abundance of food for Burnside's army and his own also.

While following the enemy on the 26th, and again on the morning of the 27th, part of the time by the road to Ringgold, I directed Thomas, verbally, not to start Granger until he received further orders from me; advising him

---

[1] USG probably referred to *Dunbar* and *Chattanooga*. In a Nov. 22, 1863, letter to Thomas, USG ordered *Dunbar* to be supplied with dry wood and a crew under W. F. Smith. *Chattanooga* was loaded with rations and sent with soldiers under Granger to resupply and reinforce Burnside at Knoxville, TN. *PUSG*, 9:432–433, 451–452.

[2] According to USG's Nov. 27, 1863, orders to Thomas, Granger and his soldiers were to relieve Burnside only if Burnside remained besieged. If the siege was broken, Granger was to return to Chattanooga, TN. Ibid., 9:457, 458.

that I was going to the front to more fully see the situation. I was not right sure but that Bragg's troops might be over their stampede by the time they reached Dalton. In that case Bragg might think it well to take the road back to Cleveland, move thence towards Knoxville, and, uniting with Longstreet, make a sudden dash upon Burnside.

When I arrived at Ringgold, however, on the 27th, I saw that the retreat was most earnest. The enemy had been throwing away guns, caissons and small-arms, abandoning provisions, and, altogether, seemed to be moving like a disorganized mob, with the exception of Cleburne's[3] division, which was acting as rear-guard to cover the retreat.

When Hooker moved from Rossville toward Ringgold Palmer's division took the road to Graysville, and Sherman moved by the way of Chickamauga Station toward the same point. As soon as I saw the situation at Ringgold I sent a staff officer back to Chattanooga to advise Thomas of the condition of affairs, and direct him by my orders to start Granger at once.[4] Feeling now that the troops were already on the march for the relief of Burnside I was in no hurry to get back, but stayed at Ringgold through the day to prepare for the return of our troops.

Ringgold is in a valley in the mountains, situated between East Chickamauga Creek and Taylor's Ridge, and about twenty miles south-east from Chattanooga.[5] I arrived just as the artillery that Hooker had left behind at Chattanooga Creek got up. His men were attacking Cleburne's division, which had taken a strong position in the adjacent hills so as to cover the retreat of the Confederate army through a narrow gorge which presents itself at that point. Just beyond the gorge the valley is narrow, and the creek so tortuous that it has to be crossed a great many times in the course of the first mile. This attack was unfortunate, and cost us some men unnecessarily.[6] Hooker captured,

---

[3] Patrick R. Cleburne (1828–1864) was born in Ireland and moved to Louisiana in 1849 before eventually settling in Arkansas. He received a commission as a colonel in the 1st Arkansas Inf. in July 1861 and was promoted to major general in 1862. In 1864, Cleburne received the "Thanks of Congress" from the Confederate Congress for his actions at Ringgold, GA. He was killed at the Battle of Franklin on Nov. 30, 1864. *CWHC*, 176.

[4] The officer was probably Col. Clark B. Lagow. *PUSG*, 9:475*n*. For USG's Nov. 27, 1863, order to Thomas, see ibid., 9:457–458.

[5] USG was in Ringgold on Nov. 27, 1863, and had returned to Chattanooga by Nov. 28. Ibid., 9:458, 459*n*.

[6] Confederate forces killed or wounded 509 U.S. soldiers at Ringgold Gap. Peter Cozzens, *The Shipwreck of Their Hopes: The Battles for Chattanooga* (Urbana: University of Illinois Press, 1994), 384.

however, 3 pieces of artillery and 230 prisoners, and 130 rebel dead were left upon the field.

I directed General Hooker to collect the flour and wheat in the neighboring mills for the use of the troops, and then to destroy the mills and all other property that could be of use to the enemy, but not to make any wanton destruction.[7]

At this point Sherman came up, having reached Graysville with his troops, where he found Palmer had preceded him. Palmer had picked up many prisoners and much abandoned property on the route. I went back in the evening to Graysville with Sherman, remained there over night and did not return to Chattanooga until the following night, the 29th. I then found that Thomas had not yet started Granger, thus having lost a full day which I deemed of so much importance in determining the fate of Knoxville.[8] Thomas and Granger were aware that on the 23d of the month Burnside had telegraphed that his supplies would last for ten or twelve days and during that time he could hold out against Longstreet, but if not relieved within the time indicated he would be obliged to surrender or attempt to retreat.[9] To effect a retreat would have been an impossibility. He was already very low in ammunition, and with an army pursuing he would not have been able to gather supplies.

Finding that Granger had not only not started but was very reluctant to go, he having decided for himself that it was a very bad move to make, I sent word to General Sherman of the situation and directed him to march to the relief of Knoxville.[10] I also gave him the problem that we had to solve—that Burnside had now but four to six days supplies left, and that he must be relieved within that time.

---

[7] While Hooker was in Ringgold on Nov. 28, 1863, USG directed him to "destroy all materials that might be used in the support of an Army" if he were able to capture Dalton, GA. *PUSG,* 9:460.

[8] USG expected Granger's expedition to leave on the evening of Nov. 27, 1863, but it did not depart until the afternoon of Nov. 28. The expedition was delayed at least in part because the staff officer delivering the message (probably Lagow) was delayed six hours in traveling from Ringgold to Chattanooga to deliver USG's order. Ibid., 9:475*n*.

[9] For Burnside's Nov. 23, 1863, telegram to USG, see ibid., 9:449*n*–450*n*. Burnside did not mention the possibility of surrender or retreat in that telegram.

[10] In addition to the delay caused by the slow delivery of the orders, Granger delayed his departure in order to get clothing and other supplies for his men. Robert C. Conner, *General Gordon Granger: The Savior of Chickamauga and the Man behind "Juneteenth"* (Philadelphia: Casemate, 2013), 135. For USG's Nov. 29, 1863, instructions to Sherman, see *PUSG,* 9:473–474.

Sherman, fortunately, had not started on his return from Graysville, having sent out detachments on the railroad which runs from Dalton to Cleveland and Knoxville to thoroughly destroy that road, and these troops had not yet returned to camp. I was very loath to send Sherman, because his men needed rest after their long march from Memphis and hard fighting at Chattanooga. But I had become satisfied that Burnside would not be rescued if his relief depended upon General Granger's movements.

Sherman had left his camp on the north side of the Tennessee River, near Chattanooga, on the night of the 23d, the men having two days' cooked rations in their haversacks. Expecting to be back in their tents by that time and to be engaged in battle while out, they took with them neither overcoats nor blankets. The weather was already cold, and at night they must have suffered more or less. The two days' rations had already lasted them five days; and they were now to go through a country which had been run over so much by Confederate troops that there was but little probability of finding much food. They did, however, succeed in capturing some flour. They also found a good deal of bran in some of the mills, which the men made up into bread; and in this and other ways they eked out an existence until they could reach Knoxville.

I was so very anxious that Burnside should get news of the steps being taken for his relief, and thus induce him to hold out a little longer if it became necessary, that I determined to send a message to him. I therefore sent a member of my staff, Colonel J. H. Wilson, to get into Knoxville if he could, report to Burnside the situation fully, and give him all the encouragement possible. Mr. Charles A. Dana was at Chattanooga during the battle, and had been there even before I assumed command. Mr. Dana volunteered to accompany Colonel Wilson, and did accompany him. I put the information of what was being done for the relief of Knoxville into writing, and directed that in some way or other it must be secretly managed so as to have a copy of this fall into the hands of General Longstreet. They made the trip safely; General Longstreet did learn of Sherman's coming in advance of his reaching there, and Burnside was prepared to hold out even for a longer time if it had been necessary.[11]

Burnside had stretched a boom across the Holston River to catch scows and flats as they floated down. On these, by previous arrangements with the loyal people of East Tennessee, were placed flour and corn, with forage and provi-

[11] On Nov. 9, 1863, USG telegraphed Burnside that Wilson and Dana had left for Knoxville. They arrived on Nov. 12. Ibid., 9:359n, 360n. For USG's Nov. 29, 1863, letter to Burnside concerning efforts to relieve Knoxville, see ibid., 9:465.

sions generally, and were thus secured for the use of the Union troops.[12] They also drove cattle into Knoxville by the east side, which was not covered by the enemy; so that when relief arrived Burnside had more provisions on hand than when he had last reported.

Our total loss (not including Burnside's) in all these engagements amounted to 757 killed, 4,529 wounded and 330 missing. We captured 6,142 prisoners—about 50 per cent. more than the enemy reported for their total loss—40 pieces of artillery, 69 artillery carriages and caissons and over 7,000 stands of small-arms.[13] The enemy's loss in arms was probably much greater than here reported, because we picked up a great many that were found abandoned.

I had at Chattanooga, in round numbers, about 60,000 men. Bragg had about half this number, but his position was supposed to be impregnable. It was his own fault that he did not have more men present. He had sent Longstreet away with his corps swelled by reinforcements up to over twenty thousand men, thus reducing his own force more than one-third and depriving himself of the presence of the ablest general of his command. He did this, too, after our troops had opened a line of communication by way of Brown's and Kelly's ferries with Bridgeport, thus securing full rations and supplies of every kind; and also when he knew reinforcements were coming to me. Knoxville was of no earthly use to him while Chattanooga was in our hands. If he should capture Chattanooga, Knoxville with its garrison would have fallen into his hands without a struggle. I have never been able to see the wisdom of this move.

Then, too, after Sherman had arrived, and when Bragg knew that he was on the north side of the Tennessee River, he sent Buckner's division to reinforce Longstreet. He also started another division a day later, but our attack having commenced before it reached Knoxville Bragg ordered it back.[14] It

---

[12] USG referred to two separate events that Burnside described in his Nov. 13, 1865, report. Burnside reported being "deeply indebted to the loyal citizens for a large amount of grain and meat, sent down the French Broad River in flats." Later in the report Burnside stated that Confederates tried to destroy a pontoon bridge by floating rafts down the Holston River, but the construction of a boom prevented this from occurring. *OR*, I, 31(I), 276.

[13] These numbers come from the final version of USG's Dec. 23, 1863, report. The numbers in the *OR* differ slightly: 753 killed, 4,727 wounded, and 349 captured or missing. The Dec. 26 report of Confederate losses listed 361 killed, 2,180 wounded, and 4,146 missing. Ibid., I, 31(II), 36, 88, 684.

[14] On Nov. 22, 1863, Bragg ordered Cleburne's and Buckner's divisions to Knoxville to aid Longstreet. On Nov. 23, Cleburne received orders to cease sending troops to Longstreet and return from Chickamauga Station. At that point, all of Buckner's division had already left,

had got so far, however, that it could not return to Chattanooga in time to be of service there. It is possible this latter blunder may have been made by Bragg having become confused as to what was going on on our side. Sherman had, as already stated, crossed to the north side of the Tennessee River at Brown's Ferry, in full view of Bragg's troops from Lookout Mountain, a few days before the attack. They then disappeared behind foot hills, and did not come to the view of the troops on Missionary Ridge until they met their assault. Bragg knew it was Sherman's troops that had crossed, and, they being so long out of view, may have supposed that they had gone up the north bank of the Tennessee River to the relief of Knoxville and that Longstreet was therefore in danger. But the first great blunder, detaching Longstreet, cannot be accounted for in any way I know of.[15] If he had captured Chattanooga, East Tennessee would have fallen without a struggle. It would have been a victory for us to have got our army away from Chattanooga safely. It was a manifold greater victory to drive away the besieging army; a still greater one to defeat that army in his chosen ground and nearly annihilate it.

The probabilities are that our loss in killed was the heavier, as we were the attacking party. The enemy reported his loss in killed at 361: but as he reported his missing at 4,146, while we held over 6,000 of them as prisoners, and there must have been hundreds if not thousands who deserted, but little reliance can be placed on this report.[16] There was certainly great dissatisfaction with Bragg on the part of the soldiers for his harsh treatment of them, and a disposition to get away if they could. Then, too, Chattanooga, following in the same half year with Gettysburg in the East and Vicksburg in the West, there was much the same feeling in the South at this time that there had been in the North the fall and winter before. If the same license had been allowed the people and press in the South that was allowed in the North, Chattanooga would probably have been the last battle fought for the preservation of the Union.

with the exception of Alexander W. Reynolds's brigade, which returned with Cleburne's division to take part in the fighting. Ibid., I, 31(II), 745–746.

[15] While Bragg initially misjudged where Sherman's troops were headed and incorrectly believed that Sherman was on his way to Knoxville to reinforce Burnside, the decision to detach Longstreet was suggested by Jefferson Davis as a solution to conflict between Bragg and his staff and Robert E. Lee's request for additional reinforcements. Cozzens, *Shipwreck of Their Hopes*, 102, 103, 125.

[16] For Hardee's Dec. 26, 1863, casualty report for the engagements at Chattanooga and Ringgold, see *OR*, I, 31(II), 684.

General William F. Smith's services in these battles had been such that I thought him eminently entitled to promotion. I was aware that he had previously been named by the President for promotion to the grade of major-general, but that the Senate had rejected the nomination. I was not aware of the reasons for this course, and therefore strongly recommended him for a major-generalcy. My recommendation was heeded and the appointment made.[17]

Upon the raising of the siege of Knoxville I, of course, informed the authorities at Washington—the President and Secretary of War—of the fact, which caused great rejoicing there.[18] The President especially was rejoiced that Knoxville had been relieved* without further bloodshed. The safety of Burnside's army and the loyal people of East Tennessee had been the subject of much anxiety to the President for several months, during which time he was doing all he could to relieve the situation; sending a new commander† with a few thousand troops by the way of Cumberland Gap, and telegraphing me daily, almost hourly, to "remember Burnside," "do something for Burnside,"

*WASHINGTON, D. C.,
*December* 8, 1863, 10.2 A.M.

Maj.-General U. S. Grant:

Understanding that your lodgment at Knoxville and at Chattanooga is now secure, I wish to tender you, and all under your command, my more than thanks, my profoundest gratitude for the skill, courage, and perseverance with which you and they, over so great difficulties, have effected that important object. God bless you all.

A. LINCOLN,
President U. S.[19]

†General John G. Foster.

---

[17] Smith had been recommended for promotion to major general on July 4, 1862. Because of Smith's support of his close friend McClellan and his Dec. 1862 letter to Lincoln criticizing Burnside, the U.S. Senate allowed Smith's appointment as major general to expire in Mar. 1863. USG wrote to Stanton on Nov. 12 and to Lincoln on Nov. 30 recommending Smith's promotion. Smith was nominated major general on Mar. 9, 1864, and confirmed on Mar. 23. Stephen W. Sears, *Controversies and Commanders: Dispatches from the Army of the Potomac* (Boston: Houghton Mifflin, 1989), 140, 155–157; *CWHC,* 500–501; *PUSG,* 9:477 and *n*; John D. Wright, *The Routledge Encyclopedia of Civil War Era Biographies* (New York: Routledge, 2013), 553.

[18] For USG's Dec. 7, 1863, letter to Halleck about raising the siege of Knoxville, see *PUSG,* 9:500–501.

[19] See ibid., 9:503, for the entry containing Lincoln's telegram to USG.

and other appeals of like tenor.[20] He saw no escape for East Tennessee until after our victory at Chattanooga. Even then he was afraid that Burnside might be out of ammunition, in a starving condition, or overpowered: and his anxiety was still intense until he heard that Longstreet had been driven from the field.

Burnside followed Longstreet only to Strawberry Plains, some twenty miles or more east, and then stopped, believing that Longstreet would leave the State. The latter did not do so, however, but stopped only a short distance farther on and subsisted his army for the entire winter off East Tennessee. Foster now relieved Burnside. Sherman made disposition of his troops along the Tennessee River in accordance with instructions.[21] I left Thomas in command at Chattanooga, and, about the 20th of December, moved my headquarters to Nashville, Tennessee.[22]

Nashville was the most central point from which to communicate with my entire military division, and also with the authorities at Washington. While remaining at Chattanooga I was liable to have my telegraphic communications cut so as to throw me out of communication with both my command and Washington.

Nothing occurred at Nashville worthy of mention during the winter,* so I set myself to the task of having troops in positions from which they could move

*During this winter the citizens of Jo Davies County, Ill., subscribed for and had a diamond-hilted sword made for General Grant, which was always known as the Chattanooga sword. The scabbard was of gold, and was ornamented with a scroll running nearly its entire length, displaying in engraved letters the names of the battles in which General Grant had participated.[23]

Congress also gave him a vote of thanks for the victories at Chattanooga, and voted him a gold medal for Vicksburg and Chattanooga. All such things are now in the possession of the government at Washington.

[20] Foster had a force of about 5,000 men, consisting of approximately 3,000 infantry and 2,000 cavalry. *OR*, I, 31(III), 283, 311–312. For an example of Lincoln's communications to USG regarding Burnside, see Lincoln's Nov. 25, 1863, telegram to USG, *PUSG,* 9:440n.

[21] For USG's Dec. 8, 1863, instructions to Sherman, see ibid., 9:505.

[22] On Dec. 18, 1863, USG informed Halleck that he would leave for Nashville, TN, the following day. Ibid., 9:544.

[23] On Sept. 15, 1863, the Board of Supervisors of Jo Daviess County designated $1,000 to be used for purchasing a sword honoring USG. The final cost of the sword, created by Ames Manufacturing Works, was $1,400. The sword was presented to USG in Nashville on Mar. 18, 1864. *The History of Jo Daviess County Illinois: Containing a History of the County—Its Cities, Towns, Etc.* (Chicago: H. F. Kett, 1878), 417–418. For USG's speech accepting the sword, see *PUSG,* 10:214.

to advantage, and in collecting all necessary supplies so as to be ready to claim a due share of the enemy's attention upon the appearance of the first good weather in the spring. I expected to retain the command I then had, and prepared myself for the campaign against Atlanta. I also had great hopes of having a campaign made against Mobile from the Gulf. I expected after Atlanta fell to occupy that place permanently, and to cut off Lee's army from the West by way of the road running through Augusta to Atlanta and thence southwest. I was preparing to hold Atlanta with a small garrison, and it was my expectation to push through to Mobile if that city was in our possession: if not, to Savannah; and in this manner to get possession of the only east and west railroad that would then be left to the enemy. But the spring campaign against Mobile was not made.

The Army of the Ohio had been getting supplies over Cumberland Gap until their animals had nearly all starved. I now determined to go myself to see if there was any possible chance of using that route in the spring, and if not to abandon it. Accordingly I left Nashville in the latter part of December by rail for Chattanooga. From Chattanooga I took one of the little steamers previously spoken of as having been built there, and, putting my horses aboard, went up to the junction of the Clinch with the Tennessee.[24] From that point the railroad had been repaired up to Knoxville and out east to Strawberry Plains. I went by rail therefore to Knoxville, where I remained for several days.[25] General John G. Foster was then commanding the Department of the Ohio. It was an intensely cold winter, the thermometer being down as low as zero every morning for more than a week while I was at Knoxville and on my way from there on horseback to Lexington, Kentucky, the first point where I could reach rail to carry me back to my headquarters at Nashville.

The road over Cumberland Gap, and back of it, was strewn with *débris* of broken wagons and dead animals, much as I had found it on my first trip to Chattanooga over Waldron's Ridge. The road had been cut up to as great a depth as clay could be by mules and wagons, and in that condition frozen; so that the ride of six days from Strawberry Plains to Lexington over these holes and knobs in the road was a very cheerless one, and very disagreeable.

I found a great many people at home along that route, both in Tennessee and Kentucky, and, almost universally, intensely loyal. They would collect in

[24] USG issued the preparatory orders for the trip on Dec. 29, 1863, and arrived at Loudon, TN, on Dec. 30. He traveled from Chattanooga aboard the steamboat *Lookout.* Ibid., 9:577*n.*

[25] USG arrived at Knoxville on Dec. 31, 1863, and remained there until at least Jan. 2, 1864. Ibid., 9:577; 10:6–7.

little places where we would stop of evenings, to see me, generally hearing of my approach before we arrived. The people naturally expected to see the commanding general the oldest person in the party. I was then forty-one years of age, while my medical director was gray-haired and probably twelve or more years my senior.[26] The crowds would generally swarm around him, and thus give me an opportunity of quietly dismounting and getting into the house. It also gave me an opportunity of hearing passing remarks from one spectator to another about their general. Those remarks were apt to be more complimentary to the cause than to the appearance of the supposed general, owing to his being muffled up, and also owing to the travel-worn condition we were all in after a hard day's ride. I was back in Nashville by the 13th of January, 1864.

When I started on this trip it was necessary for me to have some person along who could turn dispatches into cipher, and who could also read the cipher dispatches which I was liable to receive daily and almost hourly. Under the rules of the War Department at that time, Mr. Stanton had taken entire control of the matter of regulating the telegraph and determining how it should be used, and of saying who, and who alone, should have the ciphers. The operators possessed of the ciphers, as well as the ciphers used, were practically independent of the commanders whom they were serving immediately under, and had to report to the War Department through General Stager[27] all the dispatches which they received or forwarded.

I was obliged to leave the telegraphic operator back at Nashville, because that was the point at which all dispatches to me would come, to be forwarded from there. As I have said, it was necessary for me also to have an operator during this inspection who had possession of this cipher to enable me to telegraph to my division and to the War Department without my dispatches being read by all the operators along the line of wires over which they were transmitted. Accordingly I ordered the cipher operator to turn over the key to

[26] Dr. Edward Kittoe (1814–1887) was born in Kent, England, and immigrated to the United States. He graduated from Pennsylvania Medical College in 1841 and worked as a doctor in Galena, IL, prior to the Civil War. He served on USG's personal staff until the spring of 1864. William B. Atkinson, *A Biographical Dictionary of Contemporary American Physicians and Surgeons* (Philadelphia: D. G. Brinton, 1880), 328.

[27] Anson Stager (1825–1885) was born in New York and served in the U.S. Military Telegraph Corps. He had devised a cipher system early in the war; as the system became more elaborate, only Stager, Stanton, and the telegraph operators had access to the codebooks. Stager was superintendent of the U.S. Military Telegraph from 1862 to 1866. He was brevetted brigadier general Mar. 13, 1865. David J. Eicher, *The Longest Night: A Military History of the Civil War* (New York: Simon and Schuster, 2001), 299–300; *CWHC*, 504.

Captain Cyrus B. Comstock, of the Corps of Engineers, whom I had selected as a wise and discreet man who certainly could be trusted with the cipher if the operator at my headquarters could.

The operator[28] refused point blank to turn over the key to Captain Comstock as directed by me, stating that his orders from the War Department were not to give it to anybody—the commanding general or any one else. I told him I would see whether he would or not. He said that if he did he would be punished. I told him if he did not he most certainly would be punished. Finally, seeing that punishment was certain if he refused longer to obey my order, and being somewhat remote (even if he was not protected altogether from the consequences of his disobedience to his orders) from the War Department, he yielded. When I returned from Knoxville I found quite a commotion. The operator had been reprimanded very severely and ordered to be relieved. I informed the Secretary of War, or his assistant secretary in charge of the telegraph, Stager, that the man could not be relieved, for he had only obeyed my orders.[29] It was absolutely necessary for me to have the cipher, and the man would most certainly have been punished if he had not delivered it; that they would have to punish me if they punished anybody, or words to that effect.[30]

This was about the only thing approaching a disagreeable difference between the Secretary of War and myself that occurred until the war was over, when we had another little spat. Owing to his natural disposition to assume all power and control in all matters that he had anything whatever to do with, he boldly took command of the armies, and, while issuing no orders on the subject, prohibited any order from me going out of the adjutant-general's office until he had approved it. This was done by directing the adjutant-general to hold any orders that came from me to be issued from the adjutant-general's office until

[28] Samuel H. Beckwith (1837–1916) was a telegraph operator from Madison, NY. In 1861, Beckwith enlisted in the 11th Illinois Inf. By Feb. 1863, Beckwith began working for USG as a civilian cipher and telegraph operator. After the assassination of Lincoln, Beckwith was integral in the capture of John Wilkes Booth. *PUSG*, 10:49*n*; John Y. Simon and David L. Wilson, eds., "Samuel H. Beckwith 'Grant's Shadow,'" in *Ulysses S. Grant: Essays and Documents,* ed. John Y. Simon and David L. Wilson (Carbondale and Edwardsville: Southern Illinois University Press, 1981), 78–79, 136–138. "Samuel H. Beckwith," *Lowville (NY) Journal and Republican,* Dec. 14, 1916.

[29] For USG's Jan. 20 and 21, 1864, telegrams to Halleck, see *PUSG*, 10:48–49, 49*n*.

[30] USG wrote to Halleck on Feb. 4, 1864, "Beckwith has been dismissed for obeying my order" and requesting that he be returned to his position. On Feb. 10, Halleck responded, "Mr. Beckwith has been restored." Ibid., 10:79–80, 82*n*.

he had examined them and given his approval. He never disturbed himself, either, in examining my orders until it was entirely convenient for him; so that orders which I had prepared would often lie there three or four days before he would sanction them. I remonstrated against this in writing, and the Secretary apologetically restored me to my rightful position of General-in-Chief of the Army. But he soon lapsed again and took control much as before.[31]

After the relief of Knoxville Sherman had proposed to Burnside that he should go with him to drive Longstreet out of Tennessee; but Burnside assured him that with the troops which had been brought by Granger, and which were to be left, he would be amply prepared to dispose of Longstreet without availing himself of this offer.[32] As before stated Sherman's command had left their camps north of the Tennessee, near Chattanooga, with two days' rations in their haversacks, without coats or blankets, and without many wagons, expecting to return to their camps by the end of that time. The weather was now cold and they were suffering, but still they were ready to make the further sacrifice, had it been required, for the good of the cause which had brought them into service. Sherman, having accomplished the object for which he was sent, marched back leisurely to his old camp on the Tennessee River.

[31] The editors found no documentary evidence of the conflict described here. However, in a Jan. 29, 1866, letter to Stanton, USG suggested that all orders should go through him as general-in-chief rather than going from the secretary of war to the AGO or to army commanders. At other times in his life, USG expressed admiration for Stanton. Ibid., 16:36; 20:77–78.

[32] For Sherman's Dec. 5, 1863, letter to Burnside, see *OR*, I, 31(I), 278.

# 46

## Operations in Mississippi—Longstreet in East Tennessee—Commissioned Lieutenant-General— Commanding the Armies of the United States— First Interview with President Lincoln

Soon after his return from Knoxville I ordered Sherman to distribute his forces from Stevenson to Decatur and thence north to Nashville; Sherman suggested that he be permitted to go back to Mississippi, to the limits of his own department and where most of his army still remained, for the purpose of clearing out what Confederates might still be left on the east bank of the Mississippi River to impede its navigation by our boats. He expected also to have the co-operation of Banks to do the same thing on the west shore. Of course I approved heartily.[1]

About the 10th of January Sherman was back in Memphis, where Hurlbut commanded, and got together his Memphis men, or ordered them collected and sent to Vicksburg. He then went to Vicksburg and out to where McPherson was in command, and had him organize his surplus troops so as to give him about 20,000 men in all.[2]

Sherman knew that General (Bishop) Polk was occupying Meridian with his headquarters, and had two divisions of infantry with a considerable force of cavalry scattered west of him. He determined, therefore, to move directly upon Meridian.

I had sent some 2,500 cavalry under General Sooy Smith to Sherman's department, and they had mostly arrived before Sherman got to Memphis. Hurlbut had 7,000 cavalry, and Sherman ordered him to reinforce Smith so

---

[1] For USG's Dec. 17, 1863, orders to Sherman, see *PUSG,* 9:535n. For Sherman's Dec. 19 telegram to USG suggesting an alternate distribution of forces, see ibid., 9:553n–554n.

[2] On Jan. 15, 1864, Sherman arrived at Vicksburg, MS. *OR,* I, 32(II), 113.

as to give the latter a force of about 7,000 with which to go against Forrest, who was then known to be south-east from Memphis. Smith was ordered to move about the 1st of February.[3]

While Sherman was waiting at Vicksburg for the arrival of Hurlbut with his surplus men, he sent out scouts to ascertain the position and strength of the enemy and to bring back all the information they could gather. When these scouts returned it was through them that he got the information of General Polk's being at Meridian, and of the strength and disposition of his command.[4]

Forrest had about 4,000 cavalry with him, composed of thoroughly well-disciplined men, who under so able a leader were very effective. Smith's command was nearly double that of Forrest, but not equal, man to man, for the lack of a successful experience such as Forrest's men had had.[5] The fact is, troops who have fought a few battles and won, and followed up their victories, improve upon what they were before to an extent that can hardly be counted by percentage. The difference in result is often decisive victory instead of inglorious defeat. This same difference, too, is often due to the way troops are officered, and for the particular kind of warfare which Forrest had carried on neither army could present a more effective officer than he was.

Sherman got off on the 3d of February and moved out on his expedition, meeting with no opposition whatever until he crossed the Big Black, and with no great deal of opposition after that until he reached Jackson, Mississippi. This latter place he reached on the 6th or 7th, Brandon on the 8th, and Morton on the 9th. Up to this time he moved in two columns to enable him to get a good supply of forage, etc., and expedite the march. Here, however, there were indications of the concentration of Confederate infantry, and he was obliged to keep his army close together. He had no serious engagement; but he met some of the enemy who destroyed a few of his wagons about Decatur, Mississippi, where, by the way, Sherman himself came near being picked up.[6]

He entered Meridian on the 14th of the month, the enemy having retreated toward Demopolis, Alabama. He spent several days in Meridian in thoroughly

[3] On Jan. 27, 1864, Sherman ordered Smith to move his force of approximately 7,000 men from Collierville, TN, to Okolona, MS, disable the Mobile and Ohio Railroad, and unite with him at Meridian, MS, by Feb. 10. Ibid., I, 32(I), 181.

[4] On Jan. 19, 1864, Sherman informed USG that Polk was at Meridian. *PUSG*, 10:20*n*.

[5] Smith had approximately 7,607 troops present for duty on Feb. 29, 1864, while Forrest's estimated strength on Feb. 1 was 4,000. *OR*, I, 32(I), 172, 174.

[6] According to Sherman's Mar. 7, 1864, report, his troops had reached Jackson, MS, on the evening of Feb. 5. On Feb. 12, Confederate cavalry troops attacked U.S. Army wagons passing through

destroying the railroad to the north and south, and also for the purpose of hearing from Sooy Smith, who he supposed had met Forrest before this time and he hoped had gained a decisive victory because of a superiority of numbers. Hearing nothing of him, however, he started on his return trip to Vicksburg.[7] There he learned that Smith, while waiting for a few of his men who had been ice-bound in the Ohio River, instead of getting off on the 1st as expected, had not left until the 11th. Smith did meet Forrest, but the result was decidedly in Forrest's favor.[8]

Sherman had written a letter to Banks, proposing a co-operative movement with him against Shreveport, subject to my approval.[9] I disapproved of Sherman's going himself, because I had other important work for him to do, but consented that he might send a few troops to the aid of Banks, though their time to remain absent must be limited. We must have them for the spring campaign. The trans-Mississippi movement proved abortive.

My eldest son, who had accompanied me on the Vicksburg campaign and siege, had while there contracted disease, which grew worse, until he had grown so dangerously ill that on the 24th of January I obtained permission to go to St. Louis, where he was staying at the time, to see him, hardly expecting to find him alive on my arrival.[10] While I was permitted to go, I was not permitted to turn over my command to any one else, but was directed to keep the headquarters with me and to communicate regularly with all parts of my division and with Washington, just as though I had remained at Nashville.

---

Decatur, MS. At the moment of the attack, Sherman was without an escort, but he was saved from capture by a regiment that had countermarched to Decatur. Ibid, I, 32(I), 175; William T. Sherman, *Memoirs of General William T. Sherman* (New York: D. Appleton, 1875), 1:391–392.

[7] On Feb. 20, 1864, Sherman began his trip back to Vicksburg. *OR*, I, 32(I), 176.

[8] In late Jan. 1864, Sherman instructed Smith to wait in Memphis, TN, for the cavalry to congregate, bringing their numbers to approximately 10,000. Sherman wanted Smith to quickly ride for Meridian by Feb. 10. Smith waited in Collierville for Col. George Waring and his cavalry brigade until Feb. 11. Once Forrest realized that Smith was moving to join Sherman in Meridian, he instigated a series of engagements in northwest Mississippi. On Feb. 21 and 22, Forrest's smaller force engaged Smith's troops. At dawn on Feb. 22, the fighting culminated in the Battle of Okolona, where Forrest repulsed Smith and his men, forcing them back to Tennessee. Michael B. Ballard, *The Civil War in Mississippi: Major Campaigns and Battles* (Oxford: University Press of Mississippi, 2011), 174–175, 187–193.

[9] For Sherman's Mar. 4, 1864, letter to Banks, see *OR*, I, 34(II), 494.

[10] On Jan. 17, 1864, USG telegraphed Halleck and requested permission to see FDG, who was ill with "typhoid pneumonia," in St. Louis, MO. On Jan. 27, USG wrote that the crisis of FDG's illness had passed. On Mar. 1, USG reported that his son had fully recovered. *PUSG*, 10:48*n*, 69, 183.

When I obtained this leave I was at Chattanooga, having gone there again to make preparations to have the troops of Thomas in the southern part of Tennessee co-operate with Sherman's movement in Mississippi. I directed Thomas, and Logan who was at Scottsboro, Alabama, to keep up a threatening movement to the south against J. E. Johnston, who had again relieved Bragg, for the purpose of making him keep as many troops as possible there.[11]

I learned through Confederate sources that Johnston had already sent two divisions in the direction of Mobile, presumably to operate against Sherman, and two more divisions to Longstreet in East Tennessee. Seeing that Johnston had depleted in this way, I directed Thomas to send at least ten thousand men, besides Stanley's[12] division which was already to the east, into East Tennessee, and notified Schofield, who was now in command in East Tennessee, of this movement of troops into his department and also of the reinforcements Longstreet had received.[13] My object was to drive Longstreet out of East Tennessee as a part of the preparations for my spring campaign.

About this time General Foster, who had been in command of the Department of the Ohio after Burnside until Schofield relieved him,* advised me that he thought it would be a good thing to keep Longstreet just where he was; that he was perfectly quiet in East Tennessee, and if he was forced to leave there,

*WASHINGTON, D. C.,
*December* 29, 1863.

MAJ.-GENERAL U. S. GRANT:

General Foster has asked to be relieved from his command on account of disability from old wounds. Should his request be granted, who would you like as his successor? It is possible that Schofield will be sent to your command.

H. W. HALLECK,
(*Official.*)                                    General-in-Chief.[14]

---

[11] On Jan. 24, 1864, USG ordered Logan and Thomas to continue their movement toward Rome, GA, with the goal of retaining a large enemy force in north Georgia. Ibid., 10:62–63.

[12] David S. Stanley (1828–1902) was born in Ohio and graduated from the USMA in 1852. His initial assignments were with the cavalry on the western frontier. In Dec. 1862, he was brevetted lieutenant colonel. In early 1864, he commanded the 1st Div., 4th Corps, Army of the Cumberland. He was awarded the Medal of Honor in 1893 for his actions at Franklin, TN, in Nov. 1864. *CWHC*, 504–505.

[13] USG wrote to Thomas about his plans on Feb. 6, 1864, and to Schofield on Feb. 11. *PUSG*, 10:86, 102.

[14] On Feb. 8, 1864, Schofield relieved Foster from command of the Dept. of the Ohio. Donald B. Connelly, *John M. Schofield and the Politics of Generalship* (Chapel Hill: University of North Carolina Press, 2006), 84. For Halleck's Dec. 29, 1863, telegram to USG, see *PUSG*, 9:573*n*.

his whole well-equipped army would be free to go to any place where it could effect the most for their cause. I thought the advice was good, and, adopting that view, countermanded the orders for pursuit of Longstreet.[15]

On the 12th of February I ordered Thomas to take Dalton and hold it, if possible; and I directed him to move without delay. Finding that he had not moved, on the 17th I urged him again to start, telling him how important it was, that the object of the movement was to co-operate with Sherman, who was moving eastward and might be in danger. Then again on the 21st, he not yet having started, I asked him if he could not start the next day. He finally got off on the 22d or 23d. The enemy fell back from his front without a battle, but took a new position quite as strong and farther to the rear. Thomas reported that he could not go any farther, because it was impossible with his poor teams, nearly starved, to keep up supplies until the railroads were repaired. He soon fell back.[16]

Schofield also had to return for the same reason. He could not carry supplies with him, and Longstreet was between him and the supplies still left in the country. Longstreet, in his retreat, would be moving towards his supplies, while our forces, following, would be receding from theirs.[17] On the 2d of March, however, I learned of Sherman's success, which eased my mind very much. The next day, the 3d, I was ordered to Washington.

The bill restoring the grade of lieutenant-general of the army had passed through Congress and became a law on the 26th of February. My nomination had been sent to the Senate on the 1st of March and confirmed the next day (the 2d). I was ordered to Washington on the 3d to receive my commission, and started the day following that.[18] The commission was handed to me on the 9th. It was delivered to me at the Executive Mansion by President Lincoln in the presence of his Cabinet, my eldest son, those of my staff who were with me and a few other visitors.[19]

[15] On Feb. 12, 1864, USG telegraphed Schofield about his decision not to pursue Longstreet and informed Thomas about his decision the next day. Ibid., 10:113*n*, 119.

[16] On Feb. 22, 1864, Thomas started to move his troops toward Dalton, GA. On Feb. 26, his troops were forced to end their movement toward Dalton when they faced substantial resistance from the Confederate forces at Buzzard Roost, GA. Ibid., 10:xxii.

[17] On Feb. 26, 1864, Schofield proposed to USG that he stop his pursuit of Longstreet because of a lack of rations and supplies. USG agreed to the proposal the same day. Ibid., 10:156–157, 157*n*.

[18] On Mar. 4, 1864, USG notified Schofield, Thomas, Logan, and Sherman of his departure for Washington, DC, the following morning. Ibid., 10:189*n*.

[19] Halleck was also present. Benjamin P. Thomas, *Abraham Lincoln* (New York: Knopf, 1952), 418.

The President in presenting my commission read from a paper—stating, however, as a preliminary, and prior to the delivery of it, that he had drawn that up on paper, knowing my disinclination to speak in public, and handed me a copy in advance so that I might prepare a few lines of reply. The President said:

"General Grant, the nation's appreciation of what you have done, and its reliance upon you for what remains to be done in the existing great struggle, are now presented, with this commission constituting you lieutenant-general in the Army of the United States. With this high honor, devolves upon you, also, a corresponding responsibility. As the country herein trusts you, so, under God, it will sustain you. I scarcely need to add, that, with what I here speak for the nation, goes my own hearty personal concurrence."

To this I replied: "Mr. President, I accept the commission, with gratitude for the high honor conferred. With the aid of the noble armies that have fought in so many fields for our common country, it will be my earnest endeavor not to disappoint your expectations. I feel the full weight of the responsibilities now devolving on me; and I know that if they are met, it will be due to those armies, and above all, to the favor of that Providence which leads both nations and men."

On the 10th I visited the headquarters of the Army of the Potomac at Brandy Station; then returned to Washington, and pushed west at once to make my arrangements for turning over the commands there and giving general directions for the preparations to be made for the spring campaign.[20]

It had been my intention before this to remain in the West, even if I was made lieutenant-general; but when I got to Washington and saw the situation it was plain that here was the point for the commanding general to be. No one else could, probably, resist the pressure that would be brought to bear upon him to desist from his own plans and pursue others. I determined, therefore, before I started back to have Sherman advanced to my late position, McPherson to Sherman's in command of the department, and Logan to the command of McPherson's corps. These changes were all made on my recommendation and without hesitation.[21] My commission as lieutenant-general was

[20] On Mar. 8, 1864, USG and FDG arrived in Washington, DC. On Mar. 9 USG received his commission as lieutenant general. After visiting Meade at the headquarters of the Army of the Potomac on Mar. 10, USG left Washington, DC, for Nashville, TN, the following day. *PUSG,* 10:xxii–xxiii.

[21] On Mar. 12, 1864, AGO Gen. Orders No. 98 made the changes sought by USG. Sherman was placed in command of the Military Div. of the Mississippi and McPherson was placed in command of the Dept. and Army of the Tennessee. Ibid., 10:195*n*–196*n*.

given to me on the 9th of March, 1864. On the following day, as already stated, I visited General Meade, commanding the Army of the Potomac, at his head-quarters at Brandy Station, north of the Rapidan. I had known General Meade slightly in the Mexican war, but had not met him since until this visit. I was a stranger to most of the Army of the Potomac, I might say to all except the officers of the regular army who had served in the Mexican war. There had been some changes ordered in the organization of that army before my promotion. One was the consolidation of five corps into three, thus throwing some officers of rank out of important commands.[22] Meade evidently thought that I might want to make still one more change not yet ordered. He said to me that I might want an officer who had served with me in the West, mentioning Sherman specially, to take his place. If so, he begged me not to hesitate about making the change. He urged that the work before us was of such vast importance to the whole nation that the feeling or wishes of no one person should stand in the way of selecting the right men for all positions. For himself, he would serve to the best of his ability wherever placed. I assured him that I had no thought of sub-stituting any one for him. As to Sherman, he could not be spared from the West.[23]

This incident gave me even a more favorable opinion of Meade than did his great victory at Gettysburg the July before. It is men who wait to be se-lected, and not those who seek, from whom we may always expect the most efficient service.

Meade's position afterwards proved embarrassing to me if not to him. He was commanding an army and, for nearly a year previous to my taking com-mand of all the armies, was in supreme command of the Army of the Potomac—except from the authorities at Washington. All other general officers occupying similar positions were independent in their commands so far as any one present with them was concerned. I tried to make General Meade's position as nearly as possible what it would have been if I had been in Washington or any other

[22] Although Meade had been planning the reorganization before USG's promotion, Gen. Orders No. 110, which enacted the plan, were not issued until Mar. 23, 1864. The plan abolished the 1st and 3rd Corps and restructured the 2nd, the 5th, and the 6th Corps. John J. Hennessy, " 'I Dread the Spring': The Army of the Potomac Prepares for the Overland Campaign," in *The Wilderness Campaign*, ed. Gary Gallagher (Chapel Hill: University of North Carolina Press, 1997), 81; *OR*, I, 33, 717–718.

[23] On Mar. 14, 1864, Meade wrote to his wife that this conversation with USG took place at a dinner in Washington, DC, on Mar. 12. George Gordon Meade, *The Life and Letters of George Gordon Meade* (New York: Charles Scribner's Sons, 1913), 2:178.

place away from his command. I therefore gave all orders for the movements of the Army of the Potomac to Meade to have them executed. To avoid the necessity of having to give orders direct, I established my headquarters near his, unless there were reasons for locating them elsewhere. This sometimes happened, and I had on occasions to give orders direct to the troops affected. On the 11th I returned to Washington and, on the day after, orders were published by the War Department placing me in command of all the armies. I had left Washington the night before to return to my old command in the West and to meet Sherman whom I had telegraphed to join me in Nashville.

Sherman assumed command of the military division of the Mississippi on the 18th of March, and we left Nashville together for Cincinnati. I had Sherman accompany me that far on my way back to Washington so that we could talk over the matters about which I wanted to see him, without losing any more time from my new command than was necessary. The first point which I wished to discuss was particularly about the co-operation of his command with mine when the spring campaign should commence. There were also other and minor points, minor as compared with the great importance of the question to be decided by sanguinary war—the restoration to duty of officers who had been relieved from important commands, namely McClellan, Burnside and Fremont in the East, and Buell, McCook, Negley[24] and Crittenden in the West.[25]

Some time in the winter of 1863–64 I had been invited by the general-in-chief to give my views of the campaign I thought advisable for the command under me—now Sherman's.[26] General J. E. Johnston was defending Atlanta and the interior of Georgia with an army, the largest part of which was stationed at Dalton, about 38 miles south of Chattanooga. Dalton is at the junction of the railroad from Cleveland with the one from Chattanooga to Atlanta.

[24] James S. Negley (1826–1901) was born in Pennsylvania. He fought as a private in the 1st Pennsylvania Inf. during the Mexican-American War. In Apr. 1861, he was promoted to brigadier general in the Pennsylvania Militia. In Nov. 1862, he was promoted to major general and commanded the 2nd Div., 14th Corps, Army of the Cumberland. Negley represented Pennsylvania in the U.S. House of Representatives from 1869 to 1875 and from 1885 to 1887. *CWHC*, 404.

[25] Burnside was assigned to the command of the 9th Corps in Apr. 1864. Crittenden was assigned to command of the 1st Div., 9th Corps, Army of the Potomac, in May. In July, McCook was placed in command of defenses of the Potomac River and Washington, DC, during Early's raid. None of the other officers mentioned (Buell, Frémont, McClellan, and Negley) was restored to command. Ibid., 156, 191, 374.

[26] On Jan. 8, 1864, Halleck asked for USG's opinion regarding the state of the war and future campaigns. *PUSG*, 10:17*n*–18*n*.

There could have been no difference of opinion as to the first duty of the armies of the military division of the Mississippi. Johnston's army was the first objective, and that important railroad centre, Atlanta, the second. At the time I wrote General Halleck giving my views of the approaching campaign,[27] and at the time I met General Sherman, it was expected that General Banks would be through with the campaign which he had been ordered upon before my appointment to the command of all the armies, and would be ready to co-operate with the armies east of the Mississippi, his part in the programme being to move upon Mobile by land while the navy would close the harbor and assist to the best of its ability.* The plan therefore was for Sherman to attack Johnston and destroy his army if possible, to capture Atlanta and hold it, and with his troops and those of Banks to hold a line through to Mobile, or at least to hold Atlanta and command the railroad running east and west, and the troops from one or other of the armies to hold important points on the southern road, the only east and west road that would be left in the possession of the enemy.[28] This would cut the Confederacy in two again, as our gaining possession of the Mississippi River had done before. Banks was not ready in time for the part assigned to him, and circumstances that could not be foreseen determined the campaign which was afterwards made, the success and grandeur of which has resounded throughout all lands.

In regard to restoring officers who had been relieved from important commands to duty again, I left Sherman to look after those who had been removed in the West while I looked out for the rest. I directed, however, that he should make no assignment until I could speak to the Secretary of War about the matter. I shortly after recommended to the Secretary the assignment of General Buell to duty. I received the assurance that duty would be offered to him; and afterwards the Secretary told me that he had offered Buell an assignment and that the latter had declined it, saying that it would be degradation to accept the assignment offered.[29] I understood afterwards that he refused to serve

*See letter to Banks, in General Grant's report, Appendix.[30]

[27] For USG's Jan. 15, 1864, letter to Halleck, see ibid., 10:14–17.

[28] The Georgia Central Railroad connected Savannah, GA, with Montgomery, AL. George B. Davis et al., *The Official Military Atlas of the Civil War* (New York: Fairfax Press, 1983), plates 144 and 148.

[29] On May 13, 1864, Stanton informed USG that Buell had declined the command. *PUSG*, 10:435*n.*

[30] For the text of USG's Mar. 15, 1864, letter to Banks, see ibid., 10:200–201.

under either Sherman or Canby[31] because he had ranked them both. Both graduated before him and ranked him in the old army. Sherman ranked him as a brigadier-general. All of them ranked me in the old army, and Sherman and Buell did as brigadiers. The worst excuse a soldier can make for declining service is that he once ranked the commander he is ordered to report to.

On the 23d of March I was back in Washington, and on the 26th took up my headquarters at Culpeper Court-House, a few miles south of the head-quarters of the Army of the Potomac.[32]

Although hailing from Illinois myself, the State of the President, I never met Mr. Lincoln until called to the capital to receive my commission as lieutenant-general. I knew him, however, very well and favorably from the accounts given by officers under me at the West who had known him all their lives. I had also read the remarkable series of debates between Lincoln and Douglas a few years before, when they were rival candidates for the United States Senate. I was then a resident of Missouri, and by no means a "Lincoln man" in that contest; but I recognized then his great ability.

In my first interview with Mr. Lincoln alone he stated to me that he had never professed to be a military man or to know how campaigns should be conducted, and never wanted to interfere in them: but that procrastination on the part of commanders, and the pressure from the people at the North and Congress, *which was always with him,* forced him into issuing his series of "Military Orders"—one, two, three, etc. He did not know but they were all wrong, and did know that some of them were. All he wanted or had ever wanted was some one who would take the responsibility and act, and call on him for all the assistance needed, pledging himself to use all the power of the government in rendering such assistance. Assuring him that I would do the best I could with the means at hand, and avoid as far as possible annoying him or the War Department, our first interview ended.

The Secretary of War I had met once before only, but felt that I knew him better.

While commanding in West Tennessee we had occasionally held conversations over the wires, at night, when they were not being otherwise used. He and

---

[31] Edward R. S. Canby (1817–1873) was born in Kentucky in 1817, graduated from the USMA in 1839, and served in the Mexican-American War. He was a major at the beginning of the Civil War and had reached the rank of major general by May 1864. *CWHC,* 161.

[32] On Mar. 24, 1864, USG established his headquarters at Culpeper Court House, VA, sixty miles southwest of Washington, DC, on the Orange and Alexandria Railroad. *PUSG,* 10:xxiii, 217*n.*

General Halleck both cautioned me against giving the President my plans of campaign, saying that he was so kind-hearted, so averse to refusing anything asked of him, that some friend would be sure to get from him all he knew. I should have said that in our interview the President told me he did not want to know what I proposed to do. But he submitted a plan of campaign of his own which he wanted me to hear and then do as I pleased about. He brought out a map of Virginia on which he had evidently marked every position occupied by the Federal and Confederate armies up to that time. He pointed out on the map two streams which empty into the Potomac, and suggested that the army might be moved on boats and landed between the mouths of these streams. We would then have the Potomac to bring our supplies, and the tributaries would protect our flanks while we moved out. I listened respectfully, but did not suggest that the same streams would protect Lee's flanks while he was shutting us up.[33]

I did not communicate my plans to the President, nor did I to the Secretary of War or to General Halleck.

March the 26th my headquarters were, as stated, at Culpeper, and the work of preparing for an early campaign commenced.

---

[33] No plan that matches this description has been found in Lincoln's papers. Donald Stoker, *The Grand Design: Strategy and the U.S. Civil War* (New York: Oxford University Press, 2010), 473*n.*

# 47

The Military Situation—Plans for the Campaign—
Sheridan Assigned to Command of the Cavalry—
Flank Movements—Forrest at Fort Pillow—
General Banks's Expedition—Colonel Mosby—
An Incident of the Wilderness Campaign

W HEN I ASSUMED command of all the armies the situation was about
this: the Mississippi River was guarded from St. Louis to its mouth; the line of
the Arkansas was held, thus giving us all the North-west north of that river. A few
points in Louisiana not remote from the river were held by the Federal troops, as
was also the mouth of the Rio Grande. East of the Mississippi we held substantially all north of the Memphis and Charleston Railroad as far east as Chattanooga, thence along the line of the Tennessee and Holston rivers, taking in nearly
all of the State of Tennessee. West Virginia was in our hands; and that part of old
Virginia north of the Rapidan and east of the Blue Ridge we also held. On the
sea-coast we had Fortress Monroe and Norfolk in Virginia; Plymouth, Washington and New Berne in North Carolina; Beaufort, Folly and Morris islands,
Hilton Head, Port Royal and Fort Pulaski in South Carolina and Georgia; Fer-
nandina, St. Augustine, Key West and Pensacola in Florida. The balance of the
Southern territory, an empire in extent, was still in the hands of the enemy.

Sherman, who had succeeded me in the command of the military division
of the Mississippi, commanded all the troops in the territory west of the Alleghanies and north of Natchez, with a large movable force about Chattanooga.
His command was subdivided into four departments, but the commanders
all reported to Sherman and were subject to his orders.[1] This arrangement,

[1] In Mar. 1864, the Military Div. of the Mississippi consisted of three departments: the Dept. of
the Ohio, commanded by John M. Schofield; the Dept. of the Tennessee, commanded by James B.
McPherson; and the Dept. of the Cumberland, commanded by George H. Thomas. *CWHC*, 833.

however, insured the better protection of all lines of communication through the acquired territory, for the reason that these different department commanders could act promptly in case of a sudden or unexpected raid within their respective jurisdictions without awaiting the orders of the division commander.

In the East the opposing forces stood in substantially the same relations towards each other as three years before, or when the war began; they were both between the Federal and Confederate capitals. It is true, footholds had been secured by us on the sea-coast, in Virginia and North Carolina, but, beyond that, no substantial advantage had been gained by either side. Battles had been fought of as great severity as had ever been known in war, over ground from the James River and Chickahominy, near Richmond, to Gettysburg and Chambersburg, in Pennsylvania, with indecisive results, sometimes favorable to the National army, sometimes to the Confederate army; but in every instance, I believe, claimed as victories for the South by the Southern press if not by the Southern generals. The Northern press, as a whole, did not discourage these claims; a portion of it always magnified rebel success and belittled ours, while another portion, most sincerely earnest in their desire for the preservation of the Union and the overwhelming success of the Federal armies, would nevertheless generally express dissatisfaction with whatever victories were gained because they were not more complete.

That portion of the Army of the Potomac not engaged in guarding lines of communication was on the northern bank of the Rapidan. The Army of Northern Virginia confronting it on the opposite bank of the same river, was strongly intrenched and commanded by the acknowledged ablest general in the Confederate army.[2] The country back to the James River is cut up with many streams, generally narrow, deep, and difficult to cross except where bridged. The region is heavily timbered, and the roads narrow, and very bad after the least rain. Such an enemy was not, of course, unprepared with adequate fortifications at convenient intervals all the way back to Richmond, so that when driven from one fortified position they would always have another farther to the rear to fall back into.

To provision an army, campaigning against so formidable a foe through such a country, from wagons alone seemed almost impossible. System and discipline were both essential to its accomplishment.

[2] Robert E. Lee commanded the Army of Northern Virginia from June 1862 to Apr. 1865. Ibid., 344.

The Union armies were now divided into nineteen departments, though four of them in the West had been concentrated into a single military division. The Army of the Potomac was a separate command and had no territorial limits. There were thus seventeen distinct commanders.[3] Before this time these various armies had acted separately and independently of each other, giving the enemy an opportunity often of depleting one command, not pressed, to reinforce another more actively engaged. I determined to stop this. To this end I regarded the Army of the Potomac as the centre, and all west to Memphis along the line described as our position at the time, and north of it, the right wing; the Army of the James, under General Butler,[4] as the left wing, and all the troops south, as a force in rear of the enemy. Some of these latter were occupying positions from which they could not render service proportionate to their numerical strength. All such were depleted to the minimum necessary to hold their positions as a guard against blockade runners; where they could not do this their positions were abandoned altogether. In this way ten thousand men were added to the Army of the James from South Carolina alone, with General Gillmore in command.[5] It was not contemplated that General Gillmore should leave his department; but as most of his troops were taken, presumably for active service, he asked to accompany them and was permitted to do so.[6] Officers and soldiers on furlough, of whom there were many thousands, were ordered to their proper commands; concentration was the order of the day, and to have it accomplished

[3] In Mar. 1864, the U.S. Army was divided into twenty departments and one military division: the Military Div. of the Mississippi. Ibid., 820–852.

[4] Benjamin F. Butler (1818–1893) was born in New Hampshire and moved to Massachusetts in 1838. In 1839, he was commissioned as a third lieutenant in the Massachusetts Militia. At the start of the Civil War, he was a brigadier general in the Massachusetts Militia and on May 16, 1861, was promoted to major general. Butler was commanding general, Army of the James, from May 1864 to Jan. 1865. Ibid., 156–157, 702.

[5] Quincy A. Gillmore (1825–1888) was born in Ohio and graduated from the USMA in 1849. At the start of the Civil War he was a captain in the U.S. Army but rose through the ranks to become a major general in July 1863. He commanded the Dept. of the South from June 1863 to April 1864. Ibid., 255.

[6] On Mar. 25, 1864, Gillmore wrote to Halleck requesting to be sent into the field in command of the 10th Army Corps. On Apr. 4, Halleck notified Gillmore that USG had approved his request. OR, I, 35(II), 28–29, 34.

in time to advance at the earliest moment the roads would permit was the problem.

As a reinforcement to the Army of the Potomac, or to act in support of it, the 9th army corps, over twenty thousand strong, under General Burnside, had been rendezvoused at Annapolis, Maryland.[7] This was an admirable position for such a reinforcement. The corps could be brought at the last moment as a reinforcement to the Army of the Potomac, or it could be thrown on the sea-coast, south of Norfolk, in Virginia or North Carolina, to operate against Richmond from that direction. In fact Burnside and the War Department both thought the 9th corps was intended for such an expedition up to the last moment.

My general plan now was to concentrate all the force possible against the Confederate armies in the field. There were but two such, as we have seen, east of the Mississippi River and facing north. The Army of Northern Virginia, General Robert E. Lee commanding, was on the south bank of the Rapidan, confronting the Army of the Potomac; the second, under General Joseph E. Johnston, was at Dalton, Georgia, opposed to Sherman who was still at Chattanooga. Beside these main armies the Confederates had to guard the Shenandoah Valley, a great storehouse to feed their armies from, and their line of communications from Richmond to Tennessee. Forrest, a brave and intrepid cavalry general, was in the West with a large force; making a larger command necessary to hold what we had gained in Middle and West Tennessee. We could not abandon any territory north of the line held by the enemy because it would lay the Northern States open to invasion. But as the Army of the Potomac was the principal garrison for the protection of Washington even while it was moving on Lee, so all the forces to the west, and the Army of the James, guarded their special trusts when advancing from them as well as when remaining at them. Better indeed, for they forced the enemy to guard his own lines and resources at a greater distance from ours, and with a greater force. Little expeditions could not so well be sent out to destroy a bridge or tear up a few miles of railroad track, burn a storehouse, or inflict other little annoyances. Accordingly I arranged for a simultaneous movement all along

---

[7] On Mar. 26, 1864, USG ordered members of the 9th Army Corps on furlough to assemble at Annapolis, MD. *PUSG,* 10:203*n*–204*n*.

the line. Sherman was to move from Chattanooga, Johnston's army and Atlanta being his objective points.*

Crook, commanding in West Virginia, was to move from the mouth of the Gauley River with a cavalry force and some artillery, the Virginia and Tennessee Railroad to be his objective. Either the enemy would have to keep a large force to protect their communications, or see them destroyed and a large amount of forage and provision, which they so much needed, fall into our hands. Sigel was in command in the Valley of Virginia. He was to advance up the valley, covering the North from an invasion through that channel as well

*[*Private and Confidential.*]
HEADQUARTERS ARMIES OF THE UNITED STATES,
WASHINGTON, D. C., *April* 4, 1864.

MAJOR-GENERAL W. T. SHERMAN,
Commanding Military Division of the Mississippi.

*General:*—It is my design, if the enemy keep quiet and allow me to take the initiative in the spring campaign, to work all parts of the army together, and somewhat towards a common centre. For your information I now write you my programme, as at present determined upon.

I have sent orders to Banks, by private messenger, to finish up his present expedition against Shreveport with all dispatch; to turn over the defence of Red River to General Steele and the navy, and to return your troops to you and his own to New Orleans; to abandon all of Texas, except the Rio Grande, and to hold that with not to exceed four thousand men; to reduce the number of troops on the Mississippi to the lowest number necessary to hold it, and to collect from his command not less than twenty-five thousand men.[8] To this I will add five thousand men from Missouri. With this force he is to commence operations against Mobile as soon as he can. It will be impossible for him to commence too early.

Gillmore joins Butler with ten thousand men, and the two operate against Richmond from the south side of the James River. This will give Butler thirty-three thousand men to operate with, W. F. Smith commanding the right wing of his forces and Gillmore the left wing. I will stay with the Army of the Potomac, increased by Burnside's corps of not less than twenty-five thousand effective men, and operate directly against Lee's army, wherever it may be found.

[8] For USG's Mar. 31, 1864, letter to Banks, see ibid., 10:242–243.

while advancing as by remaining near Harper's Ferry. Every mile he advanced also gave us possession of stores on which Lee relied. Butler was to advance by the James River, having Richmond and Petersburg as his objective.

Before the advance commenced I visited Butler at Fort Monroe. This was the first time I had ever met him. Before giving him any order as to the part he was

---

Sigel[9] collects all his available force in two columns, one, under Ord and Averell,[10] to start from Beverly, Virginia,[11] and the other, under Crook,[12] to start from Charleston on the Kanawha, to move against the Virginia and Tennessee Railroad.

Crook will have all cavalry, and will endeavor to get in about Saltville, and move east from there to join Ord. His force will be all cavalry, while Ord will have from ten to twelve thousand men of all arms.

You I propose to move against Johnston's army, to break it up and to get into the interior of the enemy's country as far as you can, inflicting all the damage you can against their war resources.

I do not propose to lay down for you a plan of campaign, but simply lay down the work it is desirable to have done and leave you free to execute it in your own way. Submit to me, however, as early as you can, your plan of operations.

[9] Franz Sigel (1824–1902) was born in Germany and graduated from the Karlsruhe Military Academy in 1843. He served as a lieutenant in the Baden Army from 1843 to 1847. In May 1852, he immigrated to New York. Two years later, he was appointed major in the 5th New York Militia. In May 1861, he was promoted to colonel of the 3rd Missouri Inf. and to brigadier general that same month. In Mar. 1862, he was promoted to major general. In Apr. 1864, Sigel commanded the Dept. of West Virginia. *CWHC,* 489.

[10] William W. Averell (1832–1900) was born in New York and graduated from the USMA in 1855. At the start of the Civil War, he was a first lieutenant in the U.S. Army. In July 1861, he became assistant adjutant general to Andrew Porter, but was transferred to the 3rd U.S. Cav. one month later. In Sept. 1862, he was promoted to brigadier general. In Apr. 1864, he commanded the 1st U.S. Cav. Div., Dept. of West Virginia. Ibid., 110.

[11] West Virginia had become a separate state in June 1863. By Apr. 1864, the town of Beverly was a part of West Virginia. George B. Davis et al., *The Official Military Atlas of the Civil War* (New York: Fairfax Press, 1983), plate 141; Otis K. Rice, *West Virginia: A History* (Lexington: University Press of Kentucky, 1985), 151.

[12] George Crook (1828–1890) was born in Ohio and graduated from the USMA in 1852. In May 1861, he was a captain in the U.S. Army. In Sept., he was promoted to colonel and commanded the 36th Ohio Inf. He was promoted to brigadier general in Sept. 1862. In early Apr. 1864, he commanded the U.S. 3rd Div., Dept. of West Virginia. *CWHC,* 191–192.

to play in the approaching campaign I invited his views. They were very much such as I intended to direct, and as I did direct,* in writing, before leaving.

General W. F. Smith, who had been promoted to the rank of major-general shortly after the battle of Chattanooga on my recommendation, had not yet been confirmed. I found a decided prejudice against his confirmation by a majority of the Senate, but I insisted that his services had been such that he should be rewarded. My wishes were now reluctantly complied with, and I assigned him to the command of one of the corps under General Butler. I was not long in finding out that the objections to Smith's promotion were well founded.[13]

In one of my early interviews with the President I expressed my dissatisfaction with the little that had been accomplished by the cavalry so far in the

---

As stated, Banks is ordered to commence operations as soon as he can. Gillmore is ordered to report at Fortress Monroe by the 18th inst., or as soon thereafter as practicable. Sigel is concentrating now. None will move from their places of rendezvous until I direct, except Banks. I want to be ready to move by the 25th inst., if possible. But all I can now direct is that you get ready as soon as possible. I know you will have difficulties to encounter in getting through the mountains to where supplies are abundant, but I believe you will accomplish it.

From the expedition from the Department of West Virginia I do not calculate on very great results; but it is the only way I can take troops from there. With the long line of railroad Sigel has to protect, he can spare no troops except to move directly to his front. In this way he must get through to inflict great damage on the enemy, or the enemy must detach from one of his armies a large force to prevent it. In other words, if Sigel can't skin himself he can hold a leg while some one else skins.

I am, general, very respectfully, your obedient servant,

U. S. GRANT,
Lieutenant-General.

*See instructions to Butler, in General Grant's report, Appendix.[14]

---

[13] On Jan. 13, 1864, USG recommended Smith for promotion. On the same day, Halleck indicated that the nomination must wait because, during the previous summer, Congress promoted more major generals than authorized by law. On Mar. 9, Smith was confirmed as major general. *CWHC*, 500; *PUSG*, 10:10*n*–11*n*.

[14] For USG's Apr. 2, 1864, instructions to Butler, see *PUSG*, 10:245–247.

war, and the belief that it was capable of accomplishing much more than it had done if under a thorough leader. I said I wanted the very best man in the army for that command. Halleck was present and spoke up, saying: "How would Sheridan do?" I replied: "The very man I want." The President said I could have anybody I wanted. Sheridan was telegraphed for that day, and on his arrival was assigned to the command of the cavalry corps with the Army of the Potomac.[15] This relieved General Alfred Pleasonton.[16] It was not a reflection on that officer, however, for I did not know but that he had been as efficient as any other cavalry commander.

Banks in the Department of the Gulf was ordered to assemble all the troops he had at New Orleans in time to join in the general move, Mobile to be his objective.

At this time I was not entirely decided as to whether I should move the Army of the Potomac by the right flank of the enemy, or by his left. Each plan presented advantages.*

If by his right—my left—the Potomac, Chesapeake Bay and tributaries would furnish us an easy line over which to bring all supplies to within hauling

> *IN FIELD, CULPEPER C. H., VA.,
> *April* 9, 1864.

MAJ.-GENERAL GEO. G. MEADE,
Com'd'g Army of the Potomac.

For information and as instruction to govern your preparations for the coming campaign, the following is communicated confidentially for your own perusal alone.

So far as practicable all the armies are to move together, and towards one common centre. Banks has been instructed to turn over the guarding of the Red River to General Steele and the navy, to abandon Texas with the exception of the Rio Grande, and to concentrate all the force he can, not less than 25,000 men, to move on Mobile. This he is to do without reference to other movements. From the scattered condition of his command, however, he cannot possibly get it together to leave New Orleans before the 1st of May,

---

[15] On Mar. 23, 1864, Halleck telegraphed Thomas the order for Sheridan to report to Washington, DC. On Apr. 4, at the direction of Lincoln, Sheridan was assigned to command of the Cav. Corps, Army of the Potomac. *PUSG*, 10:217n; *OR*, I, 33, 798.

[16] Alfred Pleasonton (1824–1897) was born in Washington, DC, and graduated from the USMA in 1844. In July 1862, he was promoted to brigadier general and to major general in June 1863. On Mar. 25, 1864, he was relieved of command of the Cav. Corps, Army of the Potomac. *CWHC*, 431; *OR*, I, 33, 732.

distance of every position the army could occupy from the Rapidan to the James River. But Lee could, if he chose, detach or move his whole army north on a line rather interior to the one I would have to take in following. A movement by his left—our right—would obviate this; but all that was done would have to be done with the supplies and ammunition we started with. All idea of adopting this latter plan was abandoned when the limited quantity of supplies possible to take with us was considered. The country over which we would

---

if so soon. Sherman will move at the same time you do, or two or three days in advance, Jo. Johnston's army being his objective point, and the heart of Georgia his ultimate aim. If successful he will secure the line from Chattanooga to Mobile with the aid of Banks.

Sigel cannot spare troops from his army to reinforce either of the great armies, but he can aid them by moving directly to his front. This he has been directed to do, and is now making preparations for it. Two columns of his command will make south at the same time with the general move; one from Beverly, from ten to twelve thousand strong, under Major-General Ord; the other from Charleston, Va.,[17] principally cavalry, under Brig.-General Crook. The former of these will endeavor to reach the Tennessee and Virginia Railroad, about south of Covington, and if found practicable will work eastward to Lynchburg and return to its base by way of the Shenandoah Valley, or join you. The other will strike at Saltville, Va., and come eastward to join Ord. The cavalry from Ord's command will try to force a passage southward, if they are successful in reaching the Virginia and Tennessee Railroad, to cut the main lines of the road connecting Richmond with all the South and South-west.

Gillmore will join Butler with about 10,000 men from South Carolina. Butler can reduce his garrison so as to take 23,000 men into the field directly to his front. The force will be commanded by Maj.-General W. F. Smith. With Smith and Gillmore, Butler will seize City Point, and operate against Richmond from the south side of the river. His movement will be simultaneous with yours.

Lee's army will be your objective point. Wherever Lee goes, there you will go also. The only point upon which I am now in doubt is, whether it will be better to cross the Rapidan above or below him. Each plan presents great advantages over the other with corresponding objections. By crossing above,

---

[17] By Apr. 1864, Charleston was located in the newly formed state of West Virginia. Davis et al., *Official Military Atlas of the Civil War,* plate 141.

have to pass was so exhausted of all food or forage that we would be obliged to carry everything with us.

While these preparations were going on the enemy was not entirely idle. In the West Forrest made a raid in West Tennessee up to the northern border, capturing the garrison of four or five hundred men at Union City, and followed it up by an attack on Paducah, Kentucky, on the banks of the Ohio. While he was able to enter the city he failed to capture the forts or any part

---

Lee is cut off from all chance of ignoring Richmond and going north on a raid. But if we take this route, all we do must be done whilst the rations we start with hold out. We separate from Butler so that he cannot be directed how to co-operate. By the other route Brandy Station can be used as a base of supplies until another is secured on the York or James rivers.

These advantages and objections I will talk over with you more fully than I can write them.

Burnside with a force of probably 25,000 men will reinforce you. Immediately upon his arrival, which will be shortly after the 20th inst., I will give him the defence of the road from Bull Run as far south as we wish to hold it. This will enable you to collect all your strength about Brandy Station and to the front.

There will be naval co-operation on the James River, and transports and ferries will be provided so that should Lee fall back into his intrenchments at Richmond, Butler's force and yours will be a unit, or at least can be made to act as such. What I would direct then, is that you commence at once reducing baggage to the very lowest possible standard. Two wagons to a regiment of five hundred men is the greatest number that should be allowed, for all baggage, exclusive of subsistence stores and ordnance stores. One wagon to brigade and one to division headquarters is sufficient and about two to corps headquarters.

Should by Lee's right flank be our route, you will want to make arrangements for having supplies of all sorts promptly forwarded to White House[18] on the Pamunkey. Your estimates for this contingency should be made at once. If not wanted there, there is every probability they will be wanted on the James River or elsewhere.

If Lee's left is turned, large provision will have to be made for ordnance stores. I would say not much short of five hundred rounds of infantry ammunition would do. By the other, half the amount would be sufficient.

U. S. GRANT,<br>Lieutenant-General.

---

[18] White House Landing was on the Pamunkey River in Virginia. Ibid., plate 137.

of the garrison. On the first intelligence of Forrest's raid I telegraphed Sherman to send all his cavalry against him, and not to let him get out of the trap he had put himself into. Sherman had anticipated me by sending troops against him before he got my order.[19]

Forrest, however, fell back rapidly, and attacked the troops at Fort Pillow, a station for the protection of the navigation of the Mississippi River. The garrison consisted of a regiment of colored troops, infantry, and a detachment of Tennessee cavalry. These troops fought bravely, but were overpowered.[20] I will leave Forrest in his dispatches to tell what he did with them.

"The river was dyed," he says, "with the blood of the slaughtered for two hundred yards. The approximate loss was upward of five hundred killed, but few of the officers escaping. My loss was about twenty killed. It is hoped that these facts will demonstrate to the Northern people that negro soldiers cannot cope with Southerners." Subsequently Forrest made a report in which he left out the part which shocks humanity to read.[21]

At the East, also, the rebels were busy. I had said to Halleck that Plymouth and Washington, North Carolina, were unnecessary to hold. It would be better to have the garrisons engaged there added to Butler's command. If success attended our arms both places, and others too, would fall into our hands naturally. These places had been occupied by Federal troops before I took command of the armies, and I knew that the Executive would be reluctant to

[19] On Mar. 24, 1864, a Confederate force of approximately 2,000 men captured the U.S. Army garrison in Union City, TN. The next day, the same Confederate force attacked Paducah, KY, which was defended by about 500 troops supported by two gunboats. The U.S. Army garrison successfully defended Paducah, but half of the city was burned. *OR,* I, 32(III), 153–154, 157, 159. For USG's Mar. 26, 1864, telegram to Sherman, see *PUSG,* 10:229.

[20] On Apr. 12, 1864, Fort Pillow was guarded by about 600 African American and white U.S. soldiers. The African American troops were from the 2nd U.S. Colored Light Art. and the 6th U.S. Colored Heavy Art. The white troops were from the 13th Tennessee Cav. Forrest and his men attacked the fort and killed 277–297 U.S. soldiers. Bruce Tap, *The Fort Pillow Massacre: North, South, and the Status of African-Americans in the Civil War Era* (New York: Routledge, 2014), 42, 63.

[21] USG quoted from Forrest's Apr. 15, 1864, report of the event; the subsequent report that USG referred to is the longer report that Forrest wrote on Apr. 26. The Joint Committee on the Conduct of the War investigated the incident and asserted that the Confederate troops killed more U.S. soldiers after they had surrendered than during the actual battle. Albert Castel, "The Fort Pillow Massacre: A Fresh Examination of the Evidence," *Civil War History* 4 (1958): 37–38; David J. Eicher, *The Longest Night: A Military History of the Civil War* (New York: Simon and Schuster, 2001), 656–657; *OR,* I, 32(I), 610, 613–617.

abandon them, and therefore explained my views; but before my views were carried out the rebels captured the garrison at Plymouth. I then ordered the abandonment of Washington, but directed the holding of New Berne at all hazards. This was essential because New Berne was a port into which blockade runners could enter.[22]

General Banks had gone on an expedition up the Red River long before my promotion to general command.[23] I had opposed the movement strenuously, but acquiesced because it was the order of my superior at the time. By direction of Halleck I had reinforced Banks with a corps of about ten thousand men from Sherman's command.[24] This reinforcement was wanted back badly before the forward movement commenced. But Banks had got so far that it seemed best that he should take Shreveport on the Red River, and turn over the line of that river to Steele, who commanded in Arkansas, to hold instead of the line of the Arkansas. Orders were given accordingly, and with the expectation that the campaign would be ended in time for Banks to return A. J. Smith's command to where it belonged and get back to New Orleans himself in time to execute his part in the general plan.[25] But the expedition was a failure. Banks did not get back in time to take part in the programme as laid down. Nor was Smith returned until long after the movements of May, 1864, had been begun. The services of forty thousand veteran troops, over and above the number required to hold all that was necessary in the Department of the Gulf, were thus paralyzed. It is but just to Banks, however, to say that his expedition was ordered from Washington and he was in no way responsible except for the conduct of it. I make no criticism on this point. He opposed the expedition.

By the 27th of April spring had so far advanced as to justify me in fixing a day for the great move. On that day Burnside left Annapolis to occupy Meade's

---

[22] On Apr. 20, 1864, Confederate forces captured Plymouth, NC. John G. Barrett, *The Civil War in North Carolina* (Chapel Hill: University of North Carolina Press, 1963), 213–220. For USG's Apr. 22 and 25 telegrams to Halleck, see *PUSG,* 10:337–338, 346*n*.

[23] Although the planning for the Red River campaign had begun in Jan. 1864, Banks did not set out on the expedition until Mar. 12, three days after USG signed his oath of office as lieutenant general. Ibid., 10:xxiii, 22*n*, 189*n*.

[24] On Jan. 8, 1864, Halleck wrote to USG explaining Lincoln's desire to have U.S. forces hold a portion of Texas because of French involvement in Mexico. He suggested that USG send a portion of Sherman's command to reinforce Banks in preparation for this expedition. Ibid., 10:17*n*–18*n*.

[25] For USG's Mar. 15, 1864, order to Banks to take Shreveport, LA, and his comments regarding A. J. Smith's forces, see ibid., 10:200–201. For USG's Mar. 31 order to turn over defense of the Red River to Steele, see ibid., 10:242–243.

position between Bull Run and the Rappahannock. Meade was notified and directed to bring his troops forward to his advance.[26] On the following day Butler was notified of my intended advance on the 4th of May, and he was directed to move the night of the same day and get as far up the James River as possible by daylight, and push on from there to accomplish the task given him. He was also notified that reinforcements were being collected in Washington City, which would be forwarded to him should the enemy fall back into the trenches at Richmond. The same day Sherman was directed to get his forces up ready to advance on the 5th. Sigel was in Winchester and was notified to move in conjunction with the others.[27]

The criticism has been made by writers on the campaign from the Rapidan to the James River that all the loss of life could have been obviated by moving the army there on transports.[28] Richmond was fortified and intrenched so perfectly that one man inside to defend was more than equal to five outside besieging or assaulting. To get possession of Lee's army was the first great object. With the capture of his army Richmond would necessarily follow. It was better to fight him outside of his stronghold than in it. If the Army of the Potomac had been moved bodily to the James River by water Lee could have moved a part of his forces back to Richmond, called Beauregard from the south to reinforce it, and with the balance moved on to Washington. Then, too, I ordered a move, simultaneous with that of the Army of the Potomac, up the James River by a formidable army already collected at the mouth of the river.

While my headquarters were at Culpeper, from the 26th of March to the 4th of May,[29] I generally visited Washington once a week to confer with the Secretary of War and President. On the last occasion, a few days before moving, a circumstance occurred which came near postponing my part in the campaign altogether. Colonel John S. Mosby[30] had for a long time been commanding a partisan corps, or regiment, which operated in the rear of the Army of the

[26] For USG's Apr. 27, 1864, telegram to Meade, see ibid., 10:344*n*.

[27] For USG's Apr. 28, 1864, telegram to Sherman, see ibid., 10:354*n*. On Apr. 27, USG had telegraphed Sigel about the expedition. Ibid., 10:314*n*.

[28] USG may have referred to Confederate general Jubal Early's criticism. Jubal Early, *A Memoir of the Last Year of the War for Independence in the Confederate States of America* (Lynchburg, VA: Charles W. Button, 1867), 33.

[29] On Mar. 24, 1864, USG established his headquarters in the field at Culpeper Court House, VA. *PUSG*, 10:xxiii.

[30] John S. Mosby (1833–1916) was born in Virginia and admitted to the bar in 1855. In 1861, he enlisted in the Confederate cavalry. On Jan. 2, 1863, he began independent operations as a ranger in Loudon County, VA. On Mar. 9, his forces captured U.S. Army general

Potomac. On my return to the field on this occasion, as the train approached Warrenton Junction, a heavy cloud of dust was seen to the east of the road as if made by a body of cavalry on a charge. Arriving at the junction the train was stopped and inquiries made as to the cause of the dust. There was but one man at the station, and he informed us that Mosby had crossed a few minutes before at full speed in pursuit of Federal cavalry. Had he seen our train coming, no doubt he would have let his prisoners escape to capture the train. I was on a special train, if I remember correctly, without any guard.[31]

Since the close of the war I have come to know Colonel Mosby personally, and somewhat intimately. He is a different man entirely from what I had supposed. He is slender, not tall, wiry, and looks as if he could endure any amount of physical exercise. He is able, and thoroughly honest and truthful. There were probably but few men in the South who could have commanded successfully a separate detachment in the rear of an opposing army, and so near the border of hostilities, as long as he did without losing his entire command.

On this same visit to Washington I had my last interview with the President before reaching the James River.[32] He had of course become acquainted with the fact that a general movement had been ordered all along the line, and seemed to think it a new feature in war. I explained to him that it was necessary to have a great number of troops to guard and hold the territory we had captured, and to prevent incursions into the Northern States. These troops could perform this service just as well by advancing as by remaining still; and by advancing they would compel the enemy to keep detachments to hold them back, or else lay his own territory open to invasion. His answer was: "Oh, yes! I see that. As we say out West, if a man can't skin he must hold a leg while somebody else does."

There was a certain incident connected with the Wilderness campaign of which it may not be out of place to speak; and to avoid a digression further on I will mention it here.

A few days before my departure from Culpeper the Honorable E. B. Washburne visited me there, and remained with my headquarters for some distance south, through the battle in the Wilderness and, I think, to Spott-

<hr />

Edwin H. Stoughton at Fairfax Court House, VA. In Dec. 1864, he was promoted to colonel. *Dictionary of American Biography,* 2nd ed., s.v. "Mosby, John Singleton."

[31] USG's near-encounter with Mosby at Bristoe Station, VA, occurred on Apr. 15, 1864. *PUSG,* 10:xxiv.

[32] USG visited Lincoln on Apr. 20, 1864. Ibid.

sylvania.[33] He was accompanied by a Mr. Swinton,[34] whom he presented as a literary gentleman who wished to accompany the army with a view of writing a history of the war when it was over. He assured me—and I have no doubt Swinton gave him the assurance—that he was not present as a correspondent of the press. I expressed an entire willingness to have him (Swinton) accompany the army, and would have allowed him to do so as a correspondent, restricted, however, in the character of the information he could give. We received Richmond papers with about as much regularity as if there had been no war, and knew that our papers were received with equal regularity by the Confederates. It was desirable, therefore, that correspondents should not be privileged spies of the enemy within our lines.

Probably Mr. Swinton expected to be an invited guest at my headquarters, and was disappointed that he was not asked to become so. At all events he was not invited, and soon I found that he was corresponding with some paper (I have now forgotten which one), thus violating his word either expressed or implied. He knew of the assurance Washburne had given as to the character of his mission. I never saw the man from the day of our introduction to the present that I recollect. He accompanied us, however, for a time at least.

The second night after crossing the Rapidan (the night of the 5th of May) Colonel W. R. Rowley, of my staff, was acting as night officer at my headquarters. A short time before midnight I gave him verbal instructions for the night. Three days later I read in a Richmond paper a verbatim report of these instructions.

A few nights still later (after the first, and possibly after the second, day's fighting in the Wilderness) General Meade came to my tent for consultation, bringing with him some of his staff officers. Both his staff and mine retired to the camp-fire some yards in front of the tent, thinking our conversation should be private. There was a stump a little to one side, and between the front of the tent and camp-fire. One of my staff, Colonel T. S. Bowers,[35] saw what he

[33] On May 3, 1864, Washburne arrived at USG's headquarters at Culpeper Court House. On May 11, he left Spotsylvania, VA, for Washington, DC. Gaillard Hunt, *Israel, Elihu and Cadwallader Washburn: A Chapter in American Biography* (New York: Macmillan, 1925), 207, 219.

[34] William Swinton (1833–1892) was born in Scotland and immigrated to Canada with his family in 1843. He entered Amherst College in 1852 but withdrew during his freshman year. He began writing for the *New York Times* in 1858 and was a special correspondent for the *Times* during the Civil War. *Dictionary of American Biography*, 2nd ed., s.v. "Swinton, William."

[35] Theodore S. Bowers (1832–1866) was born in Pennsylvania. In Oct. 1861, he enlisted as a private in the 48th Illinois Inf. He became USG's aide-de-camp in May 1862 and was assistant adjutant general by Mar. 1864. *CWHC*, 139.

took to be a man seated on the ground and leaning against the stump, listening to the conversation between Meade and myself. He called the attention of Colonel Rowley to it. The latter immediately took the man by the shoulder and asked him, in language more forcible than polite, what he was doing there. The man proved to be Swinton, the "historian," and his replies to the question were evasive and unsatisfactory, and he was warned against further eaves-dropping.

The next I heard of Mr. Swinton was at Cold Harbor. General Meade came to my headquarters saying that General Burnside had arrested Swinton, who at some previous time had given great offence, and had ordered him to be shot that afternoon. I promptly ordered the prisoner to be released, but that he must be expelled from the lines of the army not to return again on pain of punishment.[36]

---

[36] In early June 1864, after reading accounts critical of the 9th Corps, Burnside ordered Swinton to be arrested and threatened to have him executed for being a spy. On July 6, at USG's direction, Meade issued the order banning Swinton and *New York Tribune* correspondent William H. Kent from U.S. lines for inaccurate reporting. William Marvel, *Burnside* (Chapel Hill: University of North Carolina Press, 1991), 381; *OR*, I, 40(III), 40–41; *PUSG*, 11:158, 159*n*–161*n*.

# 48

## Commencement of the Grand Campaign—
## General Butler's Position—Sheridan's First Raid

T HE ARMIES WERE now all ready to move for the accomplishment of a single object. They were acting as a unit so far as such a thing was possible over such a vast field. Lee, with the capital of the Confederacy, was the main end to which all were working. Johnston, with Atlanta, was an important obstacle in the way of our accomplishing the result aimed at, and was therefore almost an independent objective. It was of less importance only because the capture of Johnston and his army would not produce so immediate and decisive a result in closing the rebellion as would the possession of Richmond, Lee and his army. All other troops were employed exclusively in support of these two movements. This was the plan; and I will now endeavor to give, as concisely as I can, the method of its execution, outlining first the operations of minor detached but co-operative columns.

As stated before, Banks failed to accomplish what he had been sent to do on the Red River, and eliminated the use of forty thousand veterans whose co-operation in the grand campaign had been expected—ten thousand with Sherman and thirty thousand against Mobile.[1]

Sigel's record is almost equally brief. He moved out, it is true, according to programme; but just when I was hoping to hear of good work being done in the valley I received instead the following announcement from Halleck: "Sigel is in full retreat on Strasburg. He will do nothing but run; never did anything else."[2] The enemy had intercepted him about New Market and handled him roughly, leaving him short six guns, and some nine hundred men out of his six thousand.[3]

---

[1] The returns from Mar. 31, 1864, show that Banks had 31,303 men present for duty. *OR,* I, 34(I), 167–168.

[2] For Halleck's May 17, 1864, telegram to USG, see *PUSG,* 10:460n.

[3] Sigel was defeated at New Market, VA, on May 15, 1864. Ibid., 10:xxv.

The plan had been for an advance of Sigel's forces in two columns. Though the one under his immediate command failed ingloriously the other proved more fortunate. Under Crook and Averell his western column advanced from the Gauley in West Virginia at the appointed time, and with more happy results. They reached the Virginia and Tennessee Railroad at Dublin and destroyed a depot of supplies, besides tearing up several miles of road and burning the bridge over New River. Having accomplished this they recrossed the Alleghanies to Meadow Bluffs and there awaited further orders.[4]

Butler embarked at Fort Monroe with all his command, except the cavalry and some artillery which moved up the south bank of the James River. His steamers moved first up Chesapeake Bay and York River as if threatening the rear of Lee's army. At midnight they turned back, and Butler by daylight was far up the James River. He seized City Point[5] and Bermuda Hundred early in the day, without loss and, no doubt, very much to the surprise of the enemy.[6]

This was the accomplishment of the first step contemplated in my instructions to Butler. He was to act from here, looking to Richmond as his objective point. I had given him to understand that I should aim to fight Lee between the Rapidan and Richmond if he would stand; but should Lee fall back into Richmond I would follow up and make a junction of the armies of the Potomac and the James on the James River. He was directed to secure a footing as far up the south side of the river as he could at as early a date as possible.[7]

Butler was in position by the 6th of May and had begun intrenching, and on the 7th he sent out his cavalry from Suffolk to cut the Weldon Railroad. He also sent out detachments to destroy the railroad between Petersburg and Richmond, but no great success attended these latter efforts. He made no great effort to establish himself on that road and neglected to attack Petersburg,

[4] On May 9, 1864, Crook attacked the Confederate forces at Dublin, VA. The next day, Crook destroyed the bridge across the New River. On May 19, he arrived at Meadow Bluff, WV. Stephen W. Brown and Otis K. Rice, *West Virginia: A History* (Lexington: University of Kentucky Press, 2010), 139; *OR,* I, 37(I), 12.

[5] City Point, VA, on the James River ten miles to the northeast of Petersburg, VA, became part of Hopewell, VA, in 1923. Ronald K. Bullis, *Hopewell and City Point* (Charleston, SC: Arcadia, 2011), 9; *PUSG,* 10:249n.

[6] On May 5, 1864, Butler telegraphed USG to report the successes at City Point and Bermuda Hundred, VA. *PUSG,* 10:411n.

[7] On Apr. 2, 1864, USG gave Butler preliminary orders to move up the James River and capture and fortify City Point. On Apr. 28, USG ordered Butler to begin his movement up the James River on May 4. Ibid., 10:246, 364.

which was almost defenceless. About the 11th he advanced slowly until he reached the works at Drury's Bluff, about half way between Bermuda Hundred and Richmond. In the mean time Beauregard had been gathering reinforcements. On the 16th he attacked Butler with great vigor, and with such success as to limit very materially the further usefulness of the Army of the James as a distinct factor in the campaign. I afterward ordered a portion of it to join the Army of the Potomac, leaving a sufficient force with Butler to man his works, hold securely the footing he had already gained and maintain a threatening front toward the rear of the Confederate capital.[8]

The position which General Butler had chosen between the two rivers, the James and Appomattox, was one of great natural strength, one where a large area of ground might be thoroughly inclosed by means of a single intrenched line, and that a very short one in comparison with the extent of territory which it thoroughly protected. His right was protected by the James River, his left by the Appomattox, and his rear by their junction—the two streams uniting near by. The bends of the two streams shortened the line that had been chosen for intrenchments, while it increased the area which the line inclosed.

Previous to ordering any troops from Butler I sent my chief engineer, General Barnard,[9] from the Army of the Potomac to that of the James to inspect Butler's position and ascertain whether I could again safely make an order for General Butler's movement in co-operation with mine, now that I was getting so near Richmond; or, if I could not, whether his position was strong enough to justify me in withdrawing some of his troops and having them brought round by water to White House to join me and reinforce the Army of the Potomac. General Barnard reported the position very strong for defensive purposes, and that I could do the latter with great security; but that General Butler could not move from where he was, in co-operation, to produce any effect. He said that the general occupied a place between the James and Appomattox rivers which was of great strength, and where with an inferior force he could hold it for an indefinite length of time against a superior; but that he could do nothing offensively. I then asked him why Butler could not move out from his lines and push across the Richmond and Petersburg Railroad to

---

[8] On May 16, 1864, Butler's attack on Richmond, VA, was thwarted by Confederate forces under the command of Beauregard at Fort Darling, Drewry's Bluff, VA. On May 26, Halleck communicated USG's order to Butler. *OR*, I, 36(III), 234; *PUSG*, 10:xxv.

[9] John G. Barnard (1815–1882) was born in Massachusetts and graduated from the USMA in 1833. He served as superintendent of the USMA from 1855 to 1856. On June 5, 1864, he was appointed chief engineer for the Army of the Potomac. *CWHC*, 116; *PUSG*, 11:31*n*.

the rear and on the south side of Richmond. He replied that it was impracticable, because the enemy had substantially the same line across the neck of land that General Butler had. He then took out his pencil and drew a sketch of the locality, remarking that the position was like a bottle and that Butler's line of intrenchments across the neck represented the cork; that the enemy had built an equally strong line immediately in front of him across the neck; and it was therefore as if Butler was in a bottle. He was perfectly safe against an attack; but, as Barnard expressed it, the enemy had corked the bottle and with a small force could hold the cork in its place. This struck me as being very expressive of his position, particularly when I saw the hasty sketch which General Barnard had drawn; and in making my subsequent report I used that expression without adding quotation marks, never thinking that anything had been said that would attract attention—as this did, very much to the annoyance, no doubt, of General Butler and, I know, very much to my own. I found afterwards that this was mentioned in the notes of General Badeau's book, which, when they were shown to me, I asked to have stricken out; yet it was retained there, though against my wishes.[10]

I make this statement here because, although I have often made it before, it has never been in my power until now to place it where it will correct history; and I desire to rectify all injustice that I may have done to individuals, particularly to officers who were gallantly serving their country during the trying period of the war for the preservation of the Union. General Butler certainly gave his very earnest support to the war; and he gave his own best efforts personally to the suppression of the rebellion.

The further operations of the Army of the James can best be treated of in connection with those of the Army of the Potomac, the two being so intimately associated and connected as to be substantially one body in which the individuality of the supporting wing is merged.

---

[10] In his July 22, 1865, report, USG described Butler's position with relation to Drewry's Bluff as "shut off from further operations directly against Richmond as if it had been in a bottle strongly corked." Adam Badeau later included this phrase in *Military History of Ulysses S. Grant* and attributed it to USG. Butler took the expression as an insult to his generalship. According to Butler's autobiography, the tension over the incident was resolved when he met with USG in Washington, DC, at some point after USG's inauguration as president. Adam Badeau, *Military History of Ulysses S. Grant, from April, 1861, to April, 1865* (New York: D. Appleton, 1881), 2:255 and *n*; Benjamin F. Butler, *Autobiography and Reminiscences of Major-General Benjamin F. Butler* (Boston: A. M. Thayer, 1892), 853–857; *OR*, I, 36(I), 20.

Before giving the reader a summary of Sherman's great Atlanta campaign, which must conclude my description of the various co-operative movements preparatory to proceeding with that of the operations of the centre, I will briefly mention Sheridan's first raid upon Lee's communications which, though an incident of the operations on the main line and not specifically marked out in the original plan, attained in its brilliant execution and results all the proportions of an independent campaign. By thus anticipating, in point of time, I will be able to more perfectly observe the continuity of events occurring in my immediate front when I shall have undertaken to describe our advance from the Rapidan.

On the 8th of May, just after the battle of the Wilderness and when we were moving on Spottsylvania I directed Sheridan verbally to cut loose from the Army of the Potomac, pass around the left of Lee's army and attack his cavalry: to cut the two roads—one running west through Gordonsville, Charlottesville and Lynchburg, the other to Richmond, and, when compelled to do so for want of forage and rations, to move on to the James River and draw these from Butler's supplies. This move took him past the entire rear of Lee's army. These orders were also given in writing through Meade.[11]

The object of this move was three-fold. First, if successfully executed, and it was, he would annoy the enemy by cutting his line of supplies and telegraphic communications, and destroy or get for his own use supplies in store in the rear and coming up. Second, he would draw the enemy's cavalry after him, and thus better protect our flanks, rear and trains than by remaining with the army. Third, his absence would save the trains drawing his forage and other supplies from Fredericksburg, which had now become our base. He started at daylight the next morning, and accomplished more than was expected. It was sixteen days before he got back to the Army of the Potomac.

The course Sheridan took was directly to Richmond. Before night Stuart,[12] commanding the Confederate cavalry, came on to the rear of his command.

[11] On May 8, 1864, Meade's chief of staff, Andrew A. Humphreys, sent Sheridan USG's order to move around Lee's army and head toward the James River for supplies if needed. *OR,* I, 36(II), 552.

[12] J. E. B. Stuart (1833–1864) was born in Virginia and graduated from the USMA in 1854. In Mar. 1861, he joined the Confederate Army, resigning from the U.S. Army in May. By Sept. that year he had been promoted to brigadier general, and in July 1862 he was promoted to major general. In May 1864, he commanded the Cav. Corps, Army of Northern Virginia. *CWHC,* 517–518.

But the advance kept on, crossed the North Anna, and at Beaver Dam, a station on the Virginia Central Railroad, recaptured four hundred Union prisoners on their way to Richmond, destroyed the road and used and destroyed a large amount of subsistence and medical stores.

Stuart, seeing that our cavalry was pushing towards Richmond, abandoned the pursuit on the morning of the 10th and, by a detour and an exhausting march, interposed between Sheridan and Richmond at Yellow Tavern, only about six miles north of the city. Sheridan destroyed the railroad and more supplies at Ashland, and on the 11th arrived in Stuart's front. A severe engagement ensued in which the losses were heavy on both sides, but the rebels were beaten, their leader mortally wounded, and some guns and many prisoners were captured.[13]

Sheridan passed through the outer defences of Richmond, and could, no doubt, have passed through the inner ones. But having no supports near he could not have remained. After caring for his wounded he struck for the James River below the city, to communicate with Butler and to rest his men and horses as well as to get food and forage for them.

He moved first between the Chickahominy and the James, but in the morning (the 12th) he was stopped by batteries at Mechanicsville. He then turned to cross to the north side of the Chickahominy by Meadow Bridge.[14] He found this barred, and the defeated Confederate cavalry, reorganized, occupying the opposite side. The panic created by his first entrance within the outer works of Richmond having subsided troops were sent out to attack his rear.

He was now in a perilous position, one from which but few generals could have extricated themselves. The defences of Richmond, manned, were to the right, the Chickahominy was to the left with no bridge remaining and the opposite bank guarded, to the rear was a force from Richmond. This force was attacked and beaten by Wilson's and Gregg's[15] divisions, while Sheridan

[13] On May 12, 1864, Stuart died after being shot in the abdomen the previous day. Maj. Gen. Wade Hampton assumed command of the Cav. Corps, Army of Northern Virginia. Ibid., 518; *PUSG*, 10:449n.

[14] Meadow Bridge crossed the Chickahominy River approximately two and one-half miles north of Richmond. Gordon C. Rhea, *To the North Anna River: Grant and Lee, May 13–25, 1864* (Baton Rouge: Louisiana State University Press, 2000), 43, 58 (map).

[15] David M. Gregg (1833–1916) was born in Pennsylvania and moved to Virginia in 1845. He returned to Pennsylvania in 1847 to attend the University of Lewisburg (now Bucknell University). He graduated from the USMA in July 1855. By May 1864, he was a brigadier general in the Cav. Corps, Army of the Potomac. *CWHC*, 267.

turned to the left with the remaining division and hastily built a bridge over the Chickahominy under the fire of the enemy, forced a crossing and soon dispersed the Confederates he found there. The enemy was held back from the stream by the fire of the troops not engaged in bridge building.

On the 13th Sheridan was at Bottom's Bridge,[16] over the Chickahominy. On the 14th he crossed this stream and on that day went into camp on the James River at Haxall's Landing.[17] He at once put himself into communication with General Butler, who directed all the supplies he wanted to be furnished.

Sheridan had left the Army of the Potomac at Spottsylvania, but did not know where either this or Lee's army was now. Great caution therefore had to be exercised in getting back. On the 17th, after resting his command for three days, he started on his return. He moved by the way of White House. The bridge over the Pamunkey had been burned by the enemy, but a new one was speedily improvised and the cavalry crossed over it. On the 22d he was at Aylett's on the Matapony,[18] where he learned the position of the two armies. On the 24th he joined us on the march from North Anna to Cold Harbor, in the vicinity of Chesterfield.[19]

Sheridan in this memorable raid passed entirely around Lee's army: encountered his cavalry in four engagements, and defeated them in all; recaptured four hundred Union prisoners and killed and captured many of the enemy; destroyed and used many supplies and munitions of war; destroyed miles of railroad and telegraph, and freed us from annoyance by the cavalry of the enemy for more than two weeks.

[16] Bottom's Bridge was approximately ten miles east of Richmond. Davis et al., *Official Military Atlas of the Civil War*, plate 137.

[17] Haxall's Landing, VA, was on the James River just below Turkey Island Bridge and opposite City Point. Brian K. Burton, *Extraordinary Circumstances: The Seven Days Battles* (Bloomington: Indiana University Press, 2010), 226; Davis et al., *Official Military Atlas of the Civil War*, plate 137.

[18] Aylett, VA, was situated along the Mattaponi River approximately twenty miles northeast of Richmond. P. H. Sheridan, *Personal Memoirs of P. H. Sheridan, General, United States Army* (New York: Charles L. Webster, 1888), 1:391.

[19] According to USG's July 22, 1865, report, Sheridan rejoined the Army of the Potomac on May 25, 1864. *OR*, I, 36(I), 19.

# 49

## Sherman's Campaign in Georgia—Siege of Atlanta—Death of General McPherson—Attempt to Capture Andersonville—Capture of Atlanta

AFTER SEPARATING FROM Sherman in Cincinnati I went on to Washington, as already stated, while he returned to Nashville to assume the duties of his new command.[1] His military division was now composed of four departments and embraced all the territory west of the Alleghany Mountains and east of the Mississippi River, together with the State of Arkansas in the trans-Mississippi. The most easterly of these was the Department of the Ohio, General Schofield commanding; the next was the Department of the Cumberland, General Thomas commanding; the third the Department of the Tennessee, General McPherson commanding; and General Steele still commanded the trans-Mississippi, or Department of Arkansas. The last-named department was so far away that Sherman could not communicate with it very readily after starting on his spring campaign, and it was therefore soon transferred from his military division to that of the Gulf, where General Canby, who had relieved General Banks, was in command.[2]

The movements of the armies, as I have stated in a former chapter, were to be simultaneous, I fixing the day to start when the season should be far enough advanced, it was hoped, for the roads to be in a condition for the troops to march.

---

[1] On Mar. 18, 1864, USG and Sherman met in Nashville, TN, where USG transferred command of the Military Div. of the Mississippi to Sherman. The two continued their discussion on the train to Cincinnati, OH. Grant arrived in Philadelphia, PA, on Mar. 22 and in Washington, DC, on the following day. *PUSG,* 10:xxii; William T. Sherman, *Memoirs of General William T. Sherman* (New York: D. Appleton, 1875), 2:5.

[2] On May 8, 1864, Halleck notified Sherman of Canby's appointment to the command of the Military Div. of West Mississippi (comprising the Dept. of the Gulf and the Dept. of Arkansas). *OR,* I, 38(IV), 70.

General Sherman at once set himself to work preparing for the task which was assigned him to accomplish in the spring campaign. McPherson lay at Huntsville with about twenty-four thousand men, guarding those points of Tennessee which were regarded as most worth holding; Thomas, with over sixty thousand men of the Army of the Cumberland, was at Chattanooga; and Schofield, with about fourteen thousand men, was at Knoxville.[3] With these three armies, numbering about one hundred thousand men in all, Sherman was to move on the day fixed for the general advance, with a view of destroying Johnston's army and capturing Atlanta. He visited each of these commands to inform himself as to their condition, and it was found to be, speaking generally, good.

One of the first matters to turn his attention to was that of getting, before the time arrived for starting, an accumulation of supplies forward to Chattanooga sufficiently large to warrant a movement. He found, when he got to that place, that the trains over the single-track railroad, which was frequently interrupted for a day or two at a time, were only sufficient to meet the daily wants of the troops without bringing forward any surplus of any kind. He found, however, that trains were being used to transport all the beef cattle, horses for the cavalry, and even teams that were being brought to the front. He at once changed all this, and required beef cattle, teams, cavalry horses, and everything that could travel, even the troops, to be marched, and used the road exclusively for transporting supplies.[4] In this way he was able to accumulate an abundance before the time finally fixed upon for the move, the 4th of May.

As I have said already, Johnston was at Dalton, which was nearly one-fourth of the way between Chattanooga and Atlanta. The country is mountainous all the way to Atlanta, abounding in mountain streams, some of them of considerable volume. Dalton is on ground where water drains towards Atlanta and into one of the main streams rising north-east from there and flowing south-west—this being the general direction which all the main streams of that section take, with smaller tributaries entering into them.[5] Johnston had been preparing himself for this campaign during the entire winter. The best

[3] Sherman reported on Sept. 15, 1864, that he had the following troops available on May 1: 24,465 men under McPherson; 60,773 under Thomas; and 13,559 under Schofield, for a total of 98,797 men. Ibid., I, 38(I), 62–63.

[4] For Sherman's orders regarding the use of the railroads, see Gen. Orders No. 6, Apr. 6, 1864. Ibid., I, 32(III), 279.

[5] USG may have referred to the Conasauga River, one of the main rivers near Dalton, GA. George B. Davis et al., *The Official Military Atlas of the Civil War* (New York: Fairfax Press, 1983), plate 97, map 1.

positions for defence had been selected all the way from Dalton back to Atlanta, and very strongly intrenched; so that, as he might be forced to fall back
from one position, he would have another to fall into in his rear. His position
at Dalton was so very strongly intrenched that no doubt he expected, or at least
hoped, to hold Sherman there and prevent him from getting any further. With
a less skilful general, and one disposed to take no risks, I have no doubt that he
would have succeeded.

Sherman's plan was to start Schofield, who was farthest back, a few days in
advance from Knoxville, having him move on the direct road to Dalton.
Thomas was to move out to Ringgold. It had been Sherman's intention to cross
McPherson over the Tennessee River at Huntsville or Decatur, and move him
south from there so as to have him come into the road running from Chattanooga to Atlanta a good distance to the rear of the point Johnston was occupying; but when that was contemplated it was hoped that McPherson alone
would have troops enough to cope with Johnston, if the latter should move
against him while unsupported by the balance of the army. In this he was disappointed. Two of McPherson's veteran divisions had re-enlisted on the express provision that they were to have a furlough. This furlough had not yet
expired, and they were not back.[6]

Then, again, Sherman had lent Banks two divisions under A. J. Smith, the
winter before, to co-operate with the trans-Mississippi forces, and this with the
express pledge that they should be back by a time specified, so as to be prepared
for this very campaign. It is hardly necessary to say they were not returned.
That department continued to absorb troops to no purpose to the end of the
war. This left McPherson so weak that the part of the plan above indicated had
to be changed. He was therefore brought up to Chattanooga and moved from
there on a road to the right of Thomas—the two coming together about
Dalton. The three armies were abreast, all ready to start promptly on time.[7]

Sherman soon found that Dalton was so strongly fortified that it was useless to make any attempt to carry it by assault; and even to carry it by regular
approaches was impracticable. There was a narrowing up in the mountain,
between the National and Confederate armies, through which a stream, a wagon
road and a railroad ran. Besides, the stream had been dammed so that the valley

---

[6] On Nov. 21, 1863, the War Dept. had issued Gen. Orders No. 376, awarding thirty-day
furloughs to soldiers who reenlisted before their terms of service expired. Sherman reported on
Apr. 27, 1864, that he intended to begin the campaign without McPherson's 20,000 men still
on furlough. *PUSG,* 10:27*n*, 354*n*.

[7] Sherman reported on June 8, 1864, that all the forces involved in the movement toward
Dalton were ready by May 6. *OR,* I, 38(I), 59.

was a lake.[8] Through this gorge the troops would have to pass. McPherson was therefore sent around by the right, to come out by the way of Snake Creek Gap into the rear of the enemy. This was a surprise to Johnston, and about the 13th he decided to abandon his position at Dalton.[9]

On the 15th there was very hard fighting about Resaca; but our cavalry having been sent around to the right got near the road in the enemy's rear. Again Johnston fell back, our army pursuing. The pursuit was continued to Kingston, which was reached on the 19th with very little fighting, except that Newton's[10] division overtook the rear of Johnston's army and engaged it. Sherman was now obliged to halt for the purpose of bringing up his railroad trains. He was depending upon the railroad for all of his supplies, and as of course the railroad was wholly destroyed as Johnston fell back, it had to be rebuilt. This work was pushed forward night and day, and caused much less delay than most persons would naturally expect in a mountainous country where there were so many bridges to be rebuilt.

The campaign to Atlanta was managed with the most consummate skill, the enemy being flanked out of one position after another all the way there. It is true this was not accomplished without a good deal of fighting—some of it very hard fighting, rising to the dignity of very important battles—neither were single positions gained in a day. On the contrary, weeks were spent at some; and about Atlanta more than a month was consumed.

---

[8] Mill Creek and the Western and Atlantic Railroad both ran through the area known as Mill Creek Gap or Buzzards Roost. In Mar. 1864, Confederate troops under the command of Maj. Gen. Alexander P. Stewart, a division commander in Buckner's Corps, had begun work to dam Mill Creek. Davis et al., *Official Military Atlas of the Civil War,* plate 55, map 6; plate 57, map 2; *OR,* I, 38(III), 816; Hiram Smith Williams, *This War So Horrible: The Civil War Diary of Hiram Smith Williams,* ed. Lewis N. Wynne and Robert A. Taylor (Tuscaloosa: University of Alabama Press, 1993), 34, 145.

[9] McPherson had successfully flanked Johnston at Snake Creek Gap to within one mile of Resaca, GA, but, worried about Johnston receiving reinforcements, he dug in and lost his advantage. Sherman, believing that Johnston's force could have been destroyed, was disappointed that McPherson was not more aggressive. In Johnston's Oct. 20, 1864, report, he stated that his artillery and infantry left for Resaca on the night of May 12, with the cavalry leaving on May 13. John F. Marszalek, *Sherman: A Soldier's Passion for Order* (New York: Free Press, 1993), 264–265; *OR,* I, 38(III), 615.

[10] John Newton (1822–1895) was born in Virginia and graduated from the USMA in 1842. He served in the Corps of Engineers and rose to the rank of captain by the start of the Civil War. Promoted to major general on Mar. 30, 1863, Newton commanded the 2nd Div., 4th Corps, Army of the Cumberland, during the Atlanta campaign. He retired as the chief of engineers of the U.S. Army in Aug. 1886. *CWHC,* 405–406.

It was the 23d of May before the road was finished up to the rear of Sherman's army and the pursuit renewed. This pursuit brought him up to the vicinity of Allatoona.[11] This place was very strongly intrenched, and naturally a very defensible position. An assault upon it was not thought of, but preparations were made to flank the enemy out of it. This was done by sending a large force around our right, by the way of Dallas, to reach the rear of the enemy. Before reaching there, however, they found the enemy fortified in their way, and there resulted hard fighting for about a week at a place called New Hope Church.[12] On the left our troops also were fortified, and as close up to the enemy as they could get. They kept working still farther around to the left toward the railroad. This was the case more particularly with the cavalry. By the 4th of June Johnston found that he was being hemmed in so rapidly that he drew off and Allatoona was left in our possession.

Allatoona, being an important place, was strongly intrenched for occupation by our troops before advancing farther, and made a secondary base of supplies. The railroad was finished up to that point, the intrenchments completed, store-houses provided for food, and the army got in readiness for a further advance. The rains, however, were falling in such torrents that it was impossible to move the army by the side roads which they would have to move upon in order to turn Johnston out of his new position.

While Sherman's army lay here, General F. P. Blair returned to it, bringing with him the two divisions of veterans who had been on furlough.[13]

Johnston had fallen back to Marietta and Kenesaw Mountain, where strong intrenchments awaited him. At this latter place our troops made an assault upon the enemy's lines after having got their own lines up close to him, and failed, sustaining considerable loss.[14] But during the progress of the battle Schofield was gaining ground to the left; and the cavalry on his left were gaining

[11] This area is now covered by Lake Allatoona, which was created by the damming of the Etowah River at a point approximately forty-eight miles upstream from Rome, GA. The project was completed in 1949. *Environmental Impact Statement: Allatoona Dam and Lake, Georgia, Flood Control and Power* (Mobile, AL: Mobile District Corps of Engineers, 1973), 1, 5.

[12] Confederate forces stopped Sherman's advance at New Hope Church, GA, on May 25, 1864. *PUSG,* 10:xxv.

[13] On June 8, 1864, Blair and the U.S. 17th Corps, Army of the Tennessee, joined McPherson's command near Acworth, GA. William E. Parrish, *Frank Blair: Lincoln's Conservative* (Columbia: University of Missouri Press, 1998), 196–197.

[14] U.S. losses were about 3,000, while the Confederate casualties numbered about 700. Albert Castel, *Decision in the West: The Atlanta Campaign* (Lawrence: University Press of Kansas, 1992), 319–320.

still more toward the enemy's rear. These operations were completed by the 3d of July, when it was found that Johnston had evacuated the place. He was pursued at once. Sherman had made every preparation to abandon the railroad, leaving a strong guard in his intrenchments. He had intended, moving out with twenty days' rations and plenty of ammunition, to come in on the railroad again at the Chattahoochee River. Johnston frustrated this plan by himself starting back as above stated. This time he fell back to the Chattahoochee.

About the 5th of July he was besieged again, Sherman getting easy possession of the Chattahoochee River both above and below him. The enemy was again flanked out of his position, or so frightened by flanking movements that on the night of the 9th he fell back across the river.

Here Johnston made a stand until the 17th, when Sherman's old tactics prevailed again and the final movement toward Atlanta began. Johnston was now relieved of the command, and Hood superseded him.[15]

Johnston's tactics in this campaign do not seem to have met with much favor, either in the eyes of the administration at Richmond, or of the people of that section of the South in which he was commanding. The very fact of a change of commanders being ordered under such circumstances was an indication of a change of policy, and that now they would become the aggressors—the very thing our troops wanted.

For my own part, I think that Johnston's tactics were right. Anything that could have prolonged the war a year beyond the time that it did finally close, would probably have exhausted the North to such an extent that they might then have abandoned the contest and agreed to a separation.

Atlanta was very strongly intrenched all the way around in a circle about a mile and a half outside of the city. In addition to this, there were advanced intrenchments which had to be taken before a close siege could be commenced.

Sure enough, as indicated by the change of commanders, the enemy was about to assume the offensive. On the 20th he came out and attacked the Army of the Cumberland most furiously. Hooker's corps, and Newton's and Johnson's

---

[15] Frustrated with Johnston's defensive strategy, Confederate president Jefferson Davis removed him from command on July 17, 1864. John Bell Hood (1831–1879) was born in Kentucky and graduated from the USMA in 1853. He served in the Mexican-American War and joined the Confederate Army in Mar. 1861, resigning from the U.S. Army in Apr. He was promoted to major general on Oct. 10, 1862, and was awarded temporary status as general on July 18, 1864. Thomas Lawrence Connelly, *Autumn of Glory: The Army of Tennessee, 1862–1865* (Baton Rouge: Louisiana State University Press, 1971), 433; *CWHC*, 302–303; Charles Royster, *The Destructive War: William Tecumseh Sherman, Stonewall Jackson, and the Americans* (New York: Alfred A. Knopf, 1991), 326–327.

divisions were the principal ones engaged in this contest, which lasted more than an hour; but the Confederates were then forced to fall back inside their main lines. The losses were quite heavy on both sides.[16] On this day General Gresham, since our Postmaster-General, was very badly wounded.[17] During the night Hood abandoned his outer lines, and our troops were advanced. The investment had not been relinquished for a moment during the day.

During the night of the 21st Hood moved out again, passing by our left flank, which was then in motion to get a position farther in rear of him, and a desperate battle ensued, which lasted most of the day of the 22d. At first the battle went very much in favor of the Confederates, our troops being somewhat surprised. While our troops were advancing they were struck in flank, and their flank was enveloped. But they had become too thorough veterans to be thrown into irreparable confusion by an unexpected attack when off their guard, and soon they were in order and engaging the enemy, with the advantage now of knowing where their antagonist was. The field of battle continued to expand until it embraced about seven miles of ground. Finally, however, and before night, the enemy was driven back into the city.*

*General John A. Logan, upon whom devolved the command of the Army of the Tennessee during this battle, in his report gave our total loss in killed, wounded and missing at 3,521; and estimated that of the enemy to be not less than 10,000:[18] and General G. M. Dodge, graphically describing to General Sherman the enemy's attack, the full weight of which fell first upon and was broken by his depleted command, remarks: "The disparity of forces can be seen from the fact that in the charge made by my two brigades under Fuller[19] and Mersy[20] they took 351 prisoners, representing

---

[16] Sherman's losses at the Battle of Peach Tree Creek were approximately 1,900 while Hood's were approximately 2,500. Castel, *Decision in the West,* 380–381.

[17] Walter Q. Gresham (1832–1895) was born in Indiana. Beginning the war as a private in the 38th Indiana Inf., Gresham was promoted to brigadier general on Aug. 11, 1863. He commanded the 4th Div., 17th Corps, Army of the Tennessee, before being wounded. He served as postmaster general from Apr. 3, 1883, to Sept. 25, 1884. *CWHC,* 268.

[18] For Logan's July 24, 1864, report, see *OR,* I, 38(III), 21.

[19] John W. Fuller (1827–1891) was born in Harston, England, and immigrated to the United States in 1833. He was a colonel in the 27th Ohio Inf. in 1861 and rose to brigadier general by Jan. 1864. Fuller was in temporary command of the 4th Div., 16th Corps, Army of the Tennessee, during the Battle of Atlanta. *CWHC,* 246.

[20] August Mersy (1821–1866) was born in Karlsruhe, Baden. He immigrated to Illinois in 1849. At the start of the Civil War, Mersy was captain of the 9th Illinois Inf. He was promoted

It was during this battle that McPherson, while passing from one column to another, was instantly killed. In his death the army lost one of its ablest, purest and best generals.[22]

Garrard[23] had been sent out with his cavalry to get upon the railroad east of Atlanta and to cut it in the direction of Augusta. He was successful in this, and returned about the time of the battle. Rousseau[24] had also come up from Tennessee with a small division of cavalry, having crossed the Tennessee River about Decatur and made a raid into Alabama. Finally, when hard pressed, he had come in, striking the railroad in rear of Sherman, and reported to him about this time.

The battle of the 22d is usually known as the Battle of Atlanta, although the city did not fall into our hands until the 2d of September. Preparations went on, as before, to flank the enemy out of his position. The work was tedious, and the lines that had to be maintained were very long. Our troops were gradually worked around to the east until they struck the road between Decatur and Atlanta. These lines were strongly fortified, as were those to the north and west of the city—all as close up to the enemy's lines as practicable—in order to hold them with the smallest possible number of men, the design being to detach an army to move by our right and try to get upon the railroad down south of Atlanta.

On the 27th the movement by the right flank commenced. On the 28th the enemy struck our right flank, General Logan commanding, with great vigor. Logan intrenched himself hastily, and by that means was enabled to resist all assaults and inflict a great deal of damage upon the enemy. These assaults

forty-nine different regiments, eight brigades and three divisions; and brought back eight battle flags from the enemy."[21]

---

to colonel on Sept. 5, 1861, and was temporarily in command of the 2nd Brigade, 2nd Div., 16th Corps, during the Atlanta campaign. Ibid., 388.

[21] For Dodge's Nov. 30, 1875, letter to Sherman containing this quotation, see Grenville M. Dodge, *Personal Recollections of President Abraham Lincoln, General Ulysses S. Grant, and General William T. Sherman* (Glendale, CA: Arthur H. Clark, 1914), 207–218.

[22] McPherson was killed on July 22, 1864. *PUSG*, 11:xxiv.

[23] Kenner Garrard (1827–1879) was born in Kentucky and graduated from the USMA in 1851. At the start of the Civil War, he was a captain in the U.S. 5th Cav. and was promoted to brigadier general on July 23, 1863. During the Atlanta campaign, he commanded the 2nd Div., U.S. Cav., Army of the Cumberland. *CWHC*, 250.

[24] Lovell H. Rousseau (1818–1869) was born in Kentucky. In 1861, he became a colonel in the 3rd Kentucky Inf. and was promoted to major general in 1862. In the summer of 1864, Rousseau commanded the District of Tennessee, Dept. of the Cumberland. Ibid., 463.

were continued to the middle of the afternoon, and resumed once or twice still later in the day. The enemy's losses in these unsuccessful assaults were fearful.[25]

During that evening the enemy in Logan's front withdrew into the town. This now left Sherman's army close up to the Confederate lines, extending from a point directly east of the city around by the north and west of it for a distance of fully ten miles; the whole of this line being intrenched, and made stronger every day they remained there.

In the latter part of July Sherman sent Stoneman[26] to destroy the railroads to the south, about Macon. He was then to go east and, if possible, release our prisoners about Andersonville.[27] There were painful stories current at the time about the great hardships these prisoners had to endure in the way of general bad treatment, in the way in which they were housed, and in the way in which they were fed. Great sympathy was felt for them; and it was thought that even if they could be turned loose upon the country it would be a great relief to them. But the attempt proved a failure. McCook,[28] who commanded a small brigade, was first reported to have been captured; but he got back, having inflicted a good deal of damage upon the enemy.[29] He had also taken some prisoners; but encountering afterwards a largely superior force of the

[25] In his official report, Sherman claimed that Logan's troops suffered 600 casualties, while Confederate losses exceeded 5,000. Modern estimates place U.S. losses at about 3,700 and Confederate losses at about 5,500. Castel, *Decision in the West*, 411–412; *OR*, I, 38(I), 78.

[26] George Stoneman Jr. (1822–1894) was born in New York and graduated from the USMA in 1842. He was a major in the U.S. 1st Cav. in May 1861 and was promoted to brigadier general in Aug. He was promoted to major general in 1862 and was in command of Cav. D, 23rd Corps, Army of the Ohio, in July 1864. In 1871 he retired from the military and moved to California, where he served as governor from 1883 to 1887. *CWHC*, 514.

[27] On July 25, 1864, Sherman ordered Stoneman's movement against the railroads. On July 26, Stoneman requested and received permission to attempt to free prisoners from the Andersonville area. *OR*, I, 38(V), 255, 264–265.

[28] Edward M. McCook (1833–1909) was born in Ohio. In 1849, he settled in the Kansas Territory where he became a lawyer and state legislator. He joined the U.S. Army as a cavalry lieutenant in 1861 and in July 1864 commanded the U.S. 1st Cav. Div., Dept. of the Cumberland. After the war he served as governor of the Colorado Territory from 1869 to 1873 and from 1874 to 1875. *CWHC*, 374.

[29] On Aug. 3, 1864, Sherman's aide-de-camp, L. M. Dayton, wrote to Schofield that a Confederate deserter claimed that McCook's brigade was destroyed or captured. In his Aug. 7 report, McCook described the destruction of more than five miles of railroad track and ten miles of telegraph lines, as well as "1,160 wagons burned; 2,000 mules killed or disabled; 1,000 bales cotton destroyed; 1,000 sacks of corn; 300 sacks of flour, and large quantities of bacon and tobacco." *OR*, I, 38(II), 762; I, 38(V), 348.

CHAPTER 49

507

enemy he was obliged to drop his prisoners and get back as best he could with what men he had left. He had lost several hundred men out of his small command. On the 4th of August Colonel Adams,[30] commanding a little brigade of about a thousand men, returned reporting Stoneman and all but himself as lost. I myself had heard around Richmond of the capture of Stoneman, and had sent Sherman word, which he received.[31] The rumor was confirmed there, also, from other sources. A few days after Colonel Adams's return Colonel Capron[32] also got in with a small detachment and confirmed the report of the capture of Stoneman with something less than a thousand men.

It seems that Stoneman, finding the escape of all his force was impossible, had made arrangements for the escape of two divisions. He covered the movement of these divisions to the rear with a force of about seven hundred men, and at length surrendered himself and this detachment to the commanding Confederate.[33] In this raid, however, much damage was inflicted upon the enemy by the destruction of cars, locomotives, army wagons, manufactories of military supplies, etc.

On the 4th and 5th Sherman endeavored to get upon the railroad to our right, where Schofield was in command, but these attempts failed utterly. General Palmer was charged with being the cause of this failure, to a great extent, by both General Sherman and General Schofield; but I am not prepared to say this, although a question seems to have arisen with Palmer as to whether Schofield had any right to command him. If he did raise this question while an action was going on, that act alone was exceedingly reprehensible.[34]

[30] Silas Adams (1839–1896) was born in Kentucky and served as colonel of the 1st Kentucky Cav. before leaving the army in Dec., 1864. He was a member of the Kentucky House of Representatives from 1889 to 1892. He served in the U.S. Congress from 1893 to 1895 but lost his bid for reelection in 1894. *A Biographical Congressional Directory, 1774 to 1903* (Washington, DC: Government Printing Office, 1903), s.v. "Adams, Silas."

[31] For USG's Aug. 3, 1864, telegram to Halleck, which Halleck then sent to Sherman on Aug. 4, see *PUSG,* 11:382n.

[32] Horace Capron (1804–1885) was born in Massachusetts. He entered the war as a lieutenant colonel in the 14th Illinois Cav. in Dec. 1862, and was promoted to colonel on Feb. 6, 1863. Capron commanded the 3rd Brigade, Cav. Div., 13th Corps, Army of the Ohio, during this raid. *CWHC,* 162.

[33] On July 31, 1864, Stoneman and about 500 of his men surrendered to Confederate forces commanded by Gen. Alfred Iverson Jr. *OR,* I, 38(V), 939.

[34] Palmer believed that he outranked Schofield, but Sherman concluded otherwise. On Aug. 4, 1864, Palmer asked to be relieved from command, but Sherman initially refused this request. Sherman granted the request on Sept. 6. Castel, *Decision in the West,* 454–458.

About the same time Wheeler got upon our railroad north of Resaca and destroyed it nearly up to Dalton. This cut Sherman off from communication with the North for several days. Sherman responded to this attack on his lines of communication by directing one upon theirs.[35]

Kilpatrick[36] started on the night of the 18th of August to reach the Macon road about Jonesboro. He succeeded in doing so, passed entirely around the Confederate lines of Atlanta, and was back again in his former position on our left by the 22d. These little affairs, however, contributed but very little to the grand result. They annoyed, it is true, but any damage thus done to a railroad by any cavalry expedition is soon repaired.

Sherman made preparations for a repetition of his tactics; that is, for a flank movement with as large a force as could be got together to some point in the enemy's rear. Sherman commenced this last movement on the 25th of August, and on the 1st of September was well up towards the railroad twenty miles south of Atlanta. Here he found Hardee intrenched, ready to meet him. A battle ensued, but he was unable to drive Hardee away before night set in. Under cover of the night, however, Hardee left of his own accord. That night Hood blew up his military works, such as he thought would be valuable in our hands, and decamped.

The next morning at daylight General H. W. Slocum, who was commanding north of the city, moved in and took possession of Atlanta, and notified Sherman. Sherman then moved deliberately back, taking three days to reach the city, and occupied a line extending from Decatur on the left to Atlanta in the centre, with his troops extending out of the city for some distance to the right.

The campaign had lasted about four months, and was one of the most memorable in history. There was but little if anything in the whole campaign, now that it is over, to criticise at all, and nothing to criticise severely. It was creditable alike to the general who commanded and the army which had executed it. Sherman had on this campaign some bright, wide-awake division and brigade commanders whose alertness added a host to the efficiency of his command.

---

[35] Wheeler's attack on the railroad began on Aug. 10, 1864, and disrupted communications from approximately Aug. 10 to 23. Sherman had planned a similar raid on Confederate forces and sent men under the command of H. Judson Kilpatrick out on Aug. 18. *OR*, I, 38(I), 79–80; I, 38(III), 957–961.

[36] H. Judson Kilpatrick (1836–1881) was born in New Jersey, graduated from the USMA in 1861, and became a second lieutenant in the U.S. 1st Art. Kilpatrick was promoted to brigadier general in 1863, commanding the 3rd Div., Cav. Corps, Army of the Cumberland, during the Atlanta campaign. *CWHC,* 332.

The troops now went to work to make themselves comfortable, and to enjoy a little rest after their arduous campaign. The city of Atlanta was turned into a military base. The citizens were all compelled to leave.[37] Sherman also very wisely prohibited the assembling of the army of sutlers and traders who always follow in the wake of an army in the field, if permitted to do so, from trading with the citizens and getting the money of the soldiers for articles of but little use to them, and for which they are made to pay most exorbitant prices. He limited the number of these traders to one for each of his three armies.

The news of Sherman's success reached the North instantaneously, and set the country all aglow. This was the first great political campaign for the Republicans in their canvass of 1864. It was followed later by Sheridan's campaign in the Shenandoah Valley; and these two campaigns probably had more effect in settling the election of the following November than all the speeches, all the bonfires, and all the parading with banners and bands of music in the North.

[37] For Sherman's Sept. 8, 1864, Special Field Orders No. 67, see *OR,* I, 38(V), 837.

# 50

## Grand Movement of the Army of the Potomac— Crossing the Rapidan—Entering the Wilderness— Battle of the Wilderness

Soon after midnight, May 3d–4th, the Army of the Potomac moved out from its position north of the Rapidan, to start upon that memorable campaign, destined to result in the capture of the Confederate capital and the army defending it. This was not to be accomplished, however, without as desperate fighting as the world has ever witnessed; not to be consummated in a day, a week, a month, or a single season. The losses inflicted, and endured, were destined to be severe; but the armies now confronting each other had already been in deadly conflict for a period of three years, with immense losses in killed, by death from sickness, captured and wounded; and neither had made any real progress toward accomplishing the final end. It is true the Confederates had, so far, held their capital, and they claimed this to be their sole object. But previously they had boldly proclaimed their intention to capture Philadelphia, New York, and the National Capital, and had made several attempts to do so, and once or twice had come fearfully near making their boast good—too near for complacent contemplation by the loyal North. They had also come near losing their own capital on at least one occasion. So here was a stand-off. The campaign now begun was destined to result in heavier losses, to both armies, in a given time, than any previously suffered; but the carnage was to be limited to a single year, and to accomplish all that had been anticipated or desired at the beginning in that time. We had to have hard fighting to achieve this. The two armies had been confronting each other so long, without any decisive result, that they hardly knew which could whip.

Ten days' rations, with a supply of forage and ammunition were taken in wagons. Beef cattle were driven with the trains, and butchered as wanted. Three days' rations in addition, in haversacks, and fifty rounds of cartridges, were carried on the person of each soldier.

The country over which the army had to operate, from the Rapidan to the crossing of the James River, is rather flat, and is cut by numerous streams which make their way to the Chesapeake Bay. The crossings of these streams by the army were generally made not far above tide-water, and where they formed a considerable obstacle to the rapid advance of troops even when the enemy did not appear in opposition. The country roads were narrow and poor. Most of the country is covered with a dense forest, in places, like the Wilderness and along the Chickahominy, almost impenetrable even for infantry except along the roads. All bridges were naturally destroyed before the National troops came to them.

The Army of the Potomac was composed of three infantry and one cavalry corps, commanded respectively by Generals W. S. Hancock,[1] G. K. Warren,[2] John Sedgwick[3] and P. H. Sheridan. The artillery was commanded by General Henry J. Hunt.[4] This arm was in such abundance that the fourth of it could not be used to advantage in such a country as we were destined to pass through. The surplus was much in the way, taking up as it did so much of the

[1] Winfield S. Hancock (1824–1886) was born in Pennsylvania and graduated from the USMA in 1844. Hancock served as the assistant quartermaster for the district of California from 1855 to 1861. In Sept. 1861 he was promoted to brigadier general and to major general in 1866. In the 1880 presidential election, Hancock, the Democratic candidate, was defeated by Republican James A. Garfield. *CWHC,* 277–278.

[2] Gouverneur K. Warren (1830–1882) was born in New York and graduated from the USMA in 1850. By the start of the Civil War, Warren had risen to captain and was promoted to major general on May 3, 1863. Ibid., 554.

[3] John Sedgwick (1813–1864) was born in Connecticut and graduated from the USMA in 1833. He fought in the Mexican-American War and was stationed at Fort Wise, Colorado Territory, when the Civil War began, rising to major general in July 1862. He was shot and killed at Spotsylvania Court House, VA, on May 9, 1864, by a Confederate sniper. He was one of the highest-ranking U.S. battle casualties of the war. Ibid., 477–478.

[4] Henry J. Hunt (1819–1889) was born in Michigan and graduated from the USMA in 1839, becoming a second lieutenant in the U.S. 2nd Art. Hunt fought in the Mexican-American War and was promoted to major of the U.S. 5th Art. in May 1861. He commanded the artillery of the Army of the Potomac from Sept. 1862 to May 1865. After the war, he became governor of the Soldiers' Home in Washington, DC, where he retired in 1883. Ibid., 310.

narrow and bad roads, and consuming so much of the forage and other stores brought up by the trains.*

The 5th corps, General Warren commanding, was in advance on the right, and marched directly for Germania Ford, preceded by one division of cavalry, under General J. H. Wilson.[5] General Sedgwick followed Warren with the 6th corps. Germania Ford was nine or ten miles below the right of Lee's line.[6] Hancock, with the 2d corps, moved by another road, farther east, directly upon Ely's Ford, six miles below Germania, preceded by Gregg's division of cavalry, and followed by the artillery. Torbert's[7] division of cavalry was left north of the Rap-

*UNION ARMY ON THE RAPIDAN, MAY 5, 1864.
[COMPILED.]
LIEUTENANT-GENERAL U. S. GRANT, Commander-in-Chief.

MAJOR-GENERAL GEORGE G. MEADE, Commanding Army of the Potomac.

| | | |
|---|---|---|
| **MAJ.-GEN. W. S. HANCOCK, commanding Second Army Corps** | First Division, Brig.-Gen. Francis C. Barlow | First Brigade, Col. Nelson A. Miles |
| | | Second Brigade, Col. Thomas A. Smyth |
| | | Third Brigade, Col. Paul Frank |
| | | Fourth Brigade, Col. John R. Brooke |
| | Second Division, Brig.-Gen. John Gibbon | First Brigade, Brig.-Gen. Alex. S. Webb |
| | | Second Brigade, Brig.-Gen. Joshua T. Owen |
| | | Third Brigade, Col. Samuel S. Carroll |
| | Third Division, Maj.-Gen. David B. Birney | First Brigade, Brig.-Gen. J. H. H. Ward |
| | | Second Brigade, Brig.-Gen. Alexander Hays |
| | Fourth Division, Brig.-Gen. Gershom Mott | First Brigade, Col. Robert McAllister |
| | | Second Brigade, Col. Wm. R. Brewster |
| | | Artillery Brigade, Col. John C. Tidball |

[5] Wilson led the 3rd Div., Cav. Corps, Army of the Potomac, during the Overland campaign. Ibid., 574.

[6] Germanna Ford was approximately fourteen miles from Chancellorsville, VA. *PUSG,* 10:412 (map).

[7] Alfred T. A. Torbert (1833–1880) was born in Delaware and graduated from the USMA in 1855. He began the war as a first lieutenant in the U.S. Army having refused a commission in the Confederate Army. Torbert was brevetted major general Sept. 9, 1864. During USG's presidency, Torbert served as U.S. consul in El Salvador in 1869; consul general in Havana, Cuba, in 1871; and consul general in Paris, France, in 1873. *CWHC,* 533.

idan, for the time, to picket the river and prevent the enemy from crossing and getting into our rear. The cavalry seized the two crossings before daylight, drove the enemy's pickets guarding them away, and by six o'clock A.M. had the pontoons laid ready for the crossing of the infantry and artillery. This was undoubtedly a surprise to Lee. The fact that the movement was unopposed proves this.

Burnside, with the 9th corps, was left back at Warrenton, guarding the railroad from Bull Run forward to preserve control of it in case our crossing the Rapidan should be long delayed. He was instructed, however, to advance at once on receiving notice that the army had crossed; and a dispatch was sent to him a little after one P.M. giving the information that our crossing had been successful.[8]

The country was heavily wooded at all the points of crossing, particularly on the south side of the river. The battle-field from the crossing of the Rapidan until the final movement from the Wilderness toward Spottsylvania was of the same character. There were some clearings and small farms within what might be termed the battle-field; but generally the country was covered with a dense forest. The roads were narrow and bad. All the conditions were favorable for defensive operations.

There are two roads, good for that part of Virginia, running from Orange Court House to the battle-field. The most southerly of these roads is known as

| | | |
|---|---|---|
| MAJ.-GEN. G. K. WARREN, commanding Fifth Army Corps | First Division, Brig.-Gen. Charles Griffin | First Brigade, Brig.-Gen. Romeyn B. Ayres |
| | | Second Brigade, Col. Jacob B. Sweitzer |
| | | Third Brigade, Brig.-Gen. J. J. Bartlett |
| | Second Division, Brig.-Gen. John C. Robinson | First Brigade, Col. Samuel H. Leonard |
| | | Second Brigade, Brig.-Gen. Henry Baxter |
| | | Third Brigade, Col. Andrew W. Denison |
| | Third Division, Brig.-Gen. Samuel W. Crawford | First Brigade, Col. Wm. McCandless |
| | | Third Brigade, Col. Joseph W. Fisher |
| | Fourth Division, Brig.-Gen. James S. Wadsworth | First Brigade, Brig.-Gen. Lysander Cutler |
| | | Second Brigade, Brig.-Gen. James C Rice |
| | | Third Brigade, Col. Roy Stone |
| | | Artillery Brigade, Col. C. S. Wainwright |

[8] For USG's May 4, 1864, telegrams to Burnside, see *PUSG*, 10:397n.

the Orange Court House Plank Road, the northern one as the Orange Turnpike. There are also roads from east of the battle-field running to Spottsylvania Court House, one from Chancellorsville, branching at Aldrich's;[9] the western branch going by Piney Branch Church, Alsop's,[10] thence by the Brock Road

| | | |
|---|---|---|
| **MAJ.-GEN. JOHN SEDGWICK,** commanding Sixth Army Corps | First Division, Brig.-Gen. H. G. Wright | First Brigade, Col. Henry W. Brown |
| | | Second Brigade, Col. Emory Upton |
| | | Third Brigade, Brig.-Gen. D. A. Russell |
| | | Fourth Brigade, Brig.-Gen. Alexander Shaler |
| | Second Division, Brig.-Gen. George W. Getty | First Brigade, Brig.-Gen. Frank Wheaton |
| | | Second Brigade, Col. Lewis A. Grant |
| | | Third Brigade, Brig.-Gen. Thos. H. Neill |
| | | Fourth Brigade, Brig.-Gen. Henry L. Eustis |
| | Third Division, Brig.-Gen. James B. Ricketts | First Brigade, Brig.-Gen. Wm. H. Morris |
| | | Second Brigade, Brig.-Gen. T. Seymour |
| | | Artillery Brigade, Col. C. H. Tompkins |
| **MAJ.-GEN. P. H. SHERIDAN,** commanding Cavalry Corps | First Division, Brig.-Gen. A. T. A. Torbert | First Brigade, Brig.-Gen. G. A. Custer |
| | | Second Brigade, Col. Thos. C. Devin |
| | | Reserve Brigade, Brig.-Gen. Wesley Merritt |
| | Second Division, Brig.-Gen. D. McM. Gregg | First Brigade, Brig.-Gen. Henry E. Davies, Jr. |
| | | Second Brigade, Col. J. Irvin Gregg |
| | Third Division, Brig.- Gen. J. H. Wilson | First Brigade, Col. T. M. Bryan, Jr. |
| | | Second Brigade, Col. Geo. H. Chapman |

[9]The Alrich farm was approximately two miles southeast of Chancellorsville. George B. Davis et al., *The Official Military Atlas of the Civil War* (New York: Fairfax Press, 1983), plate 39, map 3; Gordon C. Rhea, *The Battle of the Wilderness, May 5–6, 1864* (Baton Rouge: Louisiana State University Press, 1994), 378.

[10]The Alsop farm was about three miles from Todd's Tavern and approximately two miles from Spotsylvania Court House. Gordon C. Rhea, *The Battles for Spotsylvania Court House and the Road to Yellow Tavern, May 7–12, 1864* (Baton Rouge: Louisiana State University Press, 1997), 46 (map), 48.

to Spottsylvania; the east branch goes by Gates's,[11] thence to Spottsylvania. The Brock Road runs from Germania Ford through the battle-field and on to the Court House. As Spottsylvania is approached the country is cut up with numerous roads, some going to the town direct, and others crossing so as to connect the farms with roads going there.

Lee's headquarters were at Orange Court House.[12] From there to Fredericksburg he had the use of the two roads above described running nearly parallel to the Wilderness. This gave him unusual facilities, for that country, for

| | | |
|---|---|---|
| MAJ.-GEN. A. E. BURNSIDE, commanding Ninth Army Corps | First Division, Brig.-Gen. T. G. Stevenson | First Brigade, Col. Sumner Carruth |
| | | Second Brigade, Col. Daniel Leasure |
| | Second Division, Brig.-Gen. Robert B. Potter | First Brigade, Col. Zenas R. Bliss |
| | | Second Brigade, Col. Simon G. Griffin |
| | Third Division, Brig-Gen. Orlando B. Willcox | First Brigade, Col. John F. Hartranft |
| | | Second Brigade, Col. Benj. C. Christ |
| | Fourth Division, Brig.-Gen. Edward Ferrero | First Brigade, Col. Joshua K. Sigfried |
| | | Second Brigade, Col. Henry G. Thomas |
| | | Provisional Brigade, Col. Elisha G. Marshall |
| BRIG.-GEN. HENRY J. HUNT, commanding Artillery | Reserve, Col. H. S. Burton | First Brigade, Col. J. H. Kitching |
| | | Second Brigade, Maj. J. A. Tompkins |
| | | First Brig. Horse Art., Capt. J. M. Robertson |
| | | Second Brigade Horse Art., Capt. D. R. Ransom |
| | | Third Brigade, Maj. R. H. Fitzhugh |
| GENERAL HEADQUARTERS | | Provost Guard, Brig.-Gen. M. R. Patrick |
| | | Volunteer Engineers, Brig.-Gen. H. W. Benham |

[11] The "gate" was a landmark on the Fredericksburg Road about ten miles southeast of Chancellorsville. It was frequently confused with the Gayle house, which was approximately one and one-half miles to the northeast of Spotsylvania Court House. Rhea, *Battles for Spotsylvania Court House*, 102–103, 104, 368n; *PUSG*, 10:412 (map).

[12] Following the campaign season of 1863, Lee had established his winter headquarters at Orange Court House, VA. Emory M. Thomas, *Robert E. Lee: A Biography* (New York: W. W. Norton, 1995), 318.

concentrating his forces to his right. These roads strike the road from Germania Ford in the Wilderness.

As soon as the crossing of the infantry was assured, the cavalry pushed forward, Wilson's division by Wilderness Tavern[13] to Parker's store, on the Orange Plank Road;[14] Gregg to the left towards Chancellorsville. Warren followed Wilson and reached the Wilderness Tavern by noon, took position there and

---

### CONFEDERATE ARMY

Organization of the Army of Northern Virginia, Commanded by General Robert E. Lee, August 31st, 1864

#### First Army Corps: LIEUT.-GEN. R. H. ANDERSON, Commanding

MAJ.-GEN. GEO. E. PICKETT's Division
- Brig.-Gen. Seth M. Barton's Brigade (a)
-     "     M. D. Corse's    "
-     "     Eppa Hunton's    "
-     "     Wm. R. Terry's    "

MAJ.-GEN. C. W. FIELD's Division (b)
- Brig.-Gen. G. T. Anderson's Brigade
-     "     E. M. Law's (c)    "
-     "     John Bratton's    "

MAJ.-GEN. J. B. KERSHAW's Division (d)
- Brig.-Gen. W. T. Wofford's Brigade
-     "     B. G. Humphreys'    "
-     "     Kershaw's (Old)    "

#### Second Army Corps: MAJOR-GENERAL JUBAL A. EARLY, Commanding

MAJ.-GEN. JOHN B. GORDON's Division
- Brig.-Gen. H. T. Hays' Brigade (e)
-     "     John Pegram's    "  (f)
-     "     Gordon's    "  (g)
- Brig.-Gen. R. F. Hoke's  "[15]

---

[13] The Old Wilderness Tavern, at the intersection of the Orange Turnpike and Germanna Plank Road, was approximately six miles west of Chancellorsville. Davis et al., *Official Military Atlas of the Civil War*, plate 39, map 3; Rhea, *Battle of the Wilderness*, 54, 68.

[14] Parker's store, on Orange Plank Road, was approximately ten miles southwest of Chancellorsville. Davis et al., *Official Military Atlas of the Civil War*, plate 39, map 3; Rhea, *Battle of the Wilderness*, 72.

[15] In Apr. 1864, Hoke had been promoted to major general and commanded a division in the Dept. of North Carolina and Southern Virginia. *CWHC*, 300–301.

intrenched. Sedgwick followed Warren. He was across the river and in camp on the south bank, on the right of Warren, by sundown. Hancock, with the 2d corps, moved parallel with Warren and camped about six miles east of him. Before night all the troops, and by the evening of the 5th the trains of more than four thousand wagons, were safely on the south side of the river.

There never was a corps better organized than was the quartermaster's corps with the Army of the Potomac in 1864.[16] With a wagon-train that would have extended from the Rapidan to Richmond, stretched along in single file and separated as the teams necessarily would be when moving, we could still carry only three days' forage and about ten to twelve days' rations, besides a supply

| MAJ.-GEN. EDWARD JOHNSON's Division | Stonewall Brig. (Brig.-Gen. J. A. Walker). (h) |
| | Brig.-Gen. J. M. Jones' Brigade  "  (h) |
| | "      Geo. H. Stewart's  "  (h) |
| | "      L. A. Stafford's      "  (e) |

| MAJ.-GEN. R. E. RODES' Division | Brig.-Gen. J. Daniel's Brigade (i) |
| | "      Geo. Dole's      "  (k) |
| | "      S. D. Ramseur's Brigade |
| | "      C. A. Battle's      " |
| | "      R. D. Johnston's  "  (f) |

NOTE.

(a) Col. W. R. Aylett was in command Aug. 29th, and probably at above date.

(b) Inspection report of this division shows that it also contained Benning's and Gregg's Brigades.

(c) Commanded by Colonel P. D. Bowles.

(d) Only two brigadier-generals reported for duty; names not indicated.

(e) Constituting York's Brigade.

(f) In Ramseur's Division.

(g) Evan's Brigade, Colonel E. N. Atkinson commanding, and containing 12th Georgia Battalion.

(h) The Virginia regiments constituted Terry's Brigade, Gordon's Division.

(i) Grimes' Brigade.

(k) Cook's      "

Organization of the Army of the Valley District

[16] On Mar. 11, 1864, USG had complained to Sen. Henry Wilson, chairman of the Military Committee, about the lack of organization in the Quartermaster's Dept. *PUSG*, 10:197.

Third Army Corps : LIEUT.-GEN. A. P. Hill, Commanding

|  | Brig.-Gen. J. C. C. Sanders' Brigade |
|---|---|
| MAJ.-GEN. WM. MAHONE's Division. (*l*) | " Mahone's " |
|  | Brig.-Gen. N. H. Harris's " (*m*) |
|  | " A. R. Wright's " |
|  | " Joseph Finegan's " |

| MAJ.-GEN. C. M. WILCOX's Division | Brig.-Gen. E. L. Thomas's Brigade (*n*) |
|---|---|
|  | " James H. Lane's " |
|  | " Sam'l McGowan's " |
|  | " Alfred M. Scale's " |

| MAJ.-GEN. H. HETH's Division (*o*) | Brig.-Gen. J. R. Davis's Brigade |
|---|---|
|  | " John R. Cooke's " |
|  | " D. McRae's " |
|  | " J. J. Archer's " |
|  | " H. H. Walker's " |

*Unattached:* 5th Alabama Battalion

Cavalry Corps : LIEUTENANT-GENERAL WADE HAMPTON, Commanding (*p*)

| MAJ.-GEN. FITZHUGH LEE's Division | Brig.-Gen. W. C. Wickham's Brigade |
|---|---|
|  | " L. L. Lomax's " |

| MAJ.-GEN. M. C. BUTLER's Division | Brig.-Gen. John Dunovant's Brigade |
|---|---|
|  | " P. M. B. Young's " |
|  | " Thomas L. Rosser's " |

| MAJ.-GEN. W. H. F. LEE's Division | Brig.-Gen. Rufus Barringer's Brigade |
|---|---|
|  | " J. R. Chambliss's " |

(*l*) Returns report but one general officer present for duty; name not indicated.
(*m*) Colonel Joseph M. Jayne, commanding.
(*n*) Colonel Thomas J. Simmons, commanding.
(*o*) Four brigadier-generals reported present for duty; names not indicated.
(*p*) On face of returns appears to have consisted of Hampton's, Fitz-Lee's, and W. H. F. Lee's Division, and Dearing's Brigade.

of ammunition. To overcome all difficulties, the chief quartermaster, General Rufus Ingalls,[17] had marked on each wagon the corps badge with the division color and the number of the brigade. At a glance, the particular brigade to which any wagon belonged could be told. The wagons were also marked to note the contents: if ammunition, whether for artillery or infantry; if forage, whether grain or hay; if rations, whether bread, pork, beans, rice, sugar, coffee or whatever it might be. Empty wagons were never allowed to follow the army or stay in camp. As soon as a wagon was empty it would return to the base of supply for a load of precisely the same article that had been taken from it.

ARTILLERY RESERVE: BRIG.-GEN. W. N. PENDLETON, Commanding

BRIG.-GEN. E. P. ALEXANDER'S Division*

Cabell's Battalion
- Manly's Battery
- 1st Co. Richmond Howitzers
- Carleton's Battery
- Calloway's Battery

Haskell's Battalion
- Branch's Battery
- Nelson's "
- Garden's "
- Rowan "

Huger's Battalion
- Smith's Battery
- Moody "
- Woolfolk "
- Parker's "
- Taylor's "
- Fickling's "
- Martin's "

Gibb's Battalion
- Davidson's Battery
- Dickenson's "
- Otey's "

[17] Rufus Ingalls (1818–1893) was born in Maine and graduated from the USMA in 1843. He shared quarters with USG while they were stationed at Fort Vancouver in the 1850s. Ingalls was assistant quartermaster for the Dept. of Florida at the start of the Civil War. He served as the quartermaster for the Army of the Potomac from Apr. 1862 to June 1864 and was promoted to brigadier general in May 1863. In June 1864, he was made quartermaster of all the U.S. armies in Virginia. He was appointed quartermaster general in 1882. *CWHC*, 313; *PUSG*, 1:279, 281*n*.

Empty trains were obliged to leave the road free for loaded ones. Arriving near the army they would be parked in fields nearest to the brigades they belonged to. Issues, except of ammunition, were made at night in all cases. By this system the hauling of forage for the supply train was almost wholly dispensed with. They consumed theirs at the depots.

I left Culpeper Court House after all the troops had been put in motion, and passing rapidly to the front, crossed the Rapidan in advance of Sedgwick's corps; and established headquarters for the afternoon and night in a deserted house near the river.[18]

| | | |
|---|---|---|
| BRIG.-GEN. A. L. LONG'S Division | Braxton's Battalion | Lee Battery |
| | | 1st Md. Artillery |
| | | Stafford " |
| | | Alleghany " |
| | Cutshaw's Battalion | Charlotteville Artillery |
| | | Staunton " |
| | | Courtney " |
| | Carter's Battalion | Morris Artillery |
| | | Orange " |
| | | King William Artillery |
| | | Jeff Davis " |
| | Nelson's Battalion | Amherst Artillery |
| | | Milledge " |
| | | Fluvauna " |
| | Brown's Battalion | Powhatan Artillery |
| | | 2d Richmond Howitzers |
| | | 3d " " |
| | | Rockbridge Artillery |
| | | Salem Flying Artillery |

* But one general officer reported present for duty in the artillery, and Alexander's name not on the original.

[18] USG crossed the Rapidan at Germanna Ford May 4, 1864. Rhea, *Battle of the Wilderness*, 68.

Orders had been given, long before this movement began, to cut down the baggage of officers and men to the lowest point possible.[19] Notwithstanding this I saw scattered along the road from Culpeper to Germania Ford wagon-loads of new blankets and overcoats, thrown away by the troops to lighten their knapsacks; an improvidence I had never witnessed before.[20]

|  |  |  |
|---|---|---|
| COL. R. L. WALKER'S Division | Cutt's Battalion | Ross's Battery |
|  |  | Patterson's Battery |
|  |  | Irwin Artillery |
|  | Richardson's Battalion | Lewis Artillery |
|  |  | Donaldsonville Artillery |
|  |  | Norfolk Light " |
|  |  | Huger " |
|  | McIntosh's Battalion | Johnson's Battery |
|  |  | Hardaway Artillery |
|  |  | Danville " |
|  |  | 2d Rockbridge Artillery |
|  | Pegram's Battalion | Peedee Artillery |
|  |  | Fredericksburg Artillery |
|  |  | Letcher " |
|  |  | Purcell Battery |
|  |  | Crenshaw's Battery |
|  | Poague's Battalion | Madison Artillery |
|  |  | Albemarle " |
|  |  | Brooke " |
|  |  | Charlotte " |

[19] On Apr. 9, 1864, USG had directed Meade to reduce baggage and Burnside to do the same on Apr. 23. He also had Lt. Col. Cyrus B. Comstock reiterate those orders on May 5. *PUSG*, 10:275, 343, 398n.

[20] On May 4, 1864, Hancock's men became caught in a bottleneck as they crossed Ely's Ford. As men waited to cross, they began emptying contents from their knapsacks, which contained about fifty pounds of supplies. The men tore overcoats and blankets into pieces as they left them on the ground, thus preventing Confederates from using them. Rhea, *Battle of the Wilderness*, 68–69.

Lee, while his pickets and signal corps must have discovered at a very early hour on the morning of the 4th of May, that the Army of the Potomac was moving, evidently did not learn until about one o'clock in the afternoon by what route we would confront his army. This I judge from the fact that at 1.15 P.M., an hour and a quarter after Warren had reached Old Wilderness Tavern, our officers took off rebel signals which, when translated, were seen to be an order to his troops to occupy their intrenchments at Mine Run.[21]

Here at night dispatches were received announcing that Sherman, Butler and Crook had moved according to programme.[22]

On discovering the advance of the Army of the Potomac, Lee ordered Hill,[23] Ewell and Longstreet, each commanding corps, to move to the right to attack us, Hill on the Orange Plank Road, Longstreet to follow on the same road. Longstreet was at this time—middle of the afternoon—at Gordonsville, twenty or more miles away. Ewell was ordered by the Orange Pike. He was near by and arrived some four miles east of Mine Run before bivouacking for the night.

My orders were given through General Meade for an early advance on the morning of the 5th. Warren was to move to Parker's store, and Wilson's cavalry—then at Parker's store—to move on to Craig's meeting-house.[24] Sedgwick followed Warren, closing in on his right. The Army of the Potomac was facing to the west, though our advance was made to the south, except when facing the enemy. Hancock was to move south-westward to join on the left of Warren, his left to reach to Shady Grove Church.[25]

At six o'clock, before reaching Parker's store, Warren discovered the enemy. He sent word back to this effect, and was ordered to halt and prepare to meet

---

[21] By 11:00 A.M. on the morning of May 4, 1864, U.S. forces had observed Confederate signals that indicated a movement of troops toward Mine Run, a creek about eighteen miles west of Chancellorsville. *PUSG*, 10:412 (map); Rhea, *Battle of the Wilderness*, 70–71.

[22] No messages from May 4, 1864, with updates on Butler's, Crook's, and Sherman's progress have been found. USG may have referred to Stanton's May 10 message updating him on progress by Sherman and Butler. *OR*, I, 36(II), 595.

[23] Ambrose P. Hill Jr. (1825–1865) was born in Virginia and graduated from the USMA in 1847. He resigned from the U.S. Army in 1861 and subsequently joined the Confederate Army as a colonel. On May 24, 1863, he was promoted to lieutenant general. He was killed at Petersburg, VA, on Apr. 2, 1865. *CWHC*, 296.

[24] Craig's meeting house was on the Catharpin Road about six miles from Parker's store. Rhea, *Battle of the Wilderness*, 96 (map), 112.

[25] Shady Grove Church was approximately ten miles from Spotsylvania Court House. *PUSG*, 10:412 (map).

and attack him. Wright,[26] with his division of Sedgwick's corps, was ordered, by any road he could find, to join on to Warren's right, and Getty[27] with his division, also of Sedgwick's corps, was ordered to move rapidly by Warren's rear and get on his left. This was the speediest way to reinforce Warren who was confronting the enemy on both the Orange plank and turnpike roads.[28]

Burnside had moved promptly on the 4th, on receiving word that the Army of the Potomac had safely crossed the Rapidan. By making a night march, although some of his troops had to march forty miles to reach the river, he was crossing with the head of his column early on the morning of the 5th.

Meade moved his headquarters on to Old Wilderness Tavern, four miles south of the river, as soon as it was light enough to see the road. I remained to hasten Burnside's crossing and to put him in position. Burnside at this time was not under Meade's command, and was his senior in rank. Getting information of the proximity of the enemy, I informed Meade, and without waiting to see Burnside, at once moved forward my headquarters to where Meade was.

It was my plan then, as it was on all other occasions, to take the initiative whenever the enemy could be drawn from his intrenchments if we were not intrenched ourselves. Warren had not yet reached the point where he was to halt, when he discovered the enemy near by. Neither party had any advantage of position. Warren was, therefore, ordered to attack as soon as he could prepare for it. At nine o'clock Hancock was ordered to come up to the support of Getty. He himself arrived at Getty's front about noon, but his troops were yet far in the rear. Getty was directed to hold his position at all hazards until relieved. About this hour Warren was ready, and attacked with favorable though not decisive results. Getty was somewhat isolated from Warren and was in a precarious condition for a time. Wilson, with his division of cavalry, was farther south, and was cut off from the rest of the army. At two o'clock Hancock's troops began to arrive, and immediately he was ordered to join Getty

[26] Horatio G. Wright (1820–1899) was born in Connecticut and graduated from the USMA in 1841. He was captured at Gosport Navy Yard in Virginia at the outset of the Civil War but was exchanged within two months. He was promoted to major general July 18, 1862. Wright served as chief of engineers in the U.S. Army from 1879 to 1884. *CWHC,* 583.

[27] George W. Getty (1819–1901) was born in the Georgetown area of Washington, DC, and graduated from the USMA in 1840. Having fought in the Mexican-American War, Getty was transferred to the U.S. 5th Art. at the start of the Civil War and promoted to brigadier general in 1862. Ibid., 252.

[28] For USG's May 5, 1864, instructions to Warren regarding his advance and cooperation with Wright, see *PUSG,* 10:399n.

and attack the enemy. But the heavy timber and narrow roads prevented him from getting into position for attack as promptly as he generally did when receiving such orders. At four o'clock he again received his orders to attack, and General Getty received orders from Meade a few minutes later to attack whether Hancock was ready or not. He met the enemy under Heth[29] within a few hundred yards.

Hancock immediately sent two divisions, commanded by Birney[30] and Mott,[31] and later two brigades, Carroll's[32] and Owen's,[33] to the support of Getty. This was timely and saved Getty. During the battle Getty and Carroll were wounded, but remained on the field. One of Birney's most gallant brigade commanders—Alexander Hays—was killed.[34]

I had been at West Point with Hays for three years, and had served with him through the Mexican war, a portion of the time in the same regiment.

[29] Henry Heth (1825–1899) was born in Virginia and graduated from the USMA in 1847. He resigned from the U.S. Army Apr. 25, 1861, and entered the Confederate Army as a captain. In Jan. 1862, he was promoted to brigadier general. *CWHC*, 295.

[30] David B. Birney (1825–1864) was born in Alabama and moved to Ohio in 1838 and Pennsylvania in 1848. The son of abolitionist James G. Birney and the brother of William Birney, David Birney was a lieutenant colonel in the 23rd Pennsylvania Militia at the start of the war and promoted to brigadier general in 1862. He died of typhoid and dysentery in Oct. 1864. Ibid., 132.

[31] Gershom Mott (1822–1884) was born in New Jersey and served as a second lieutenant during the Mexican-American War until his discharge in 1848. Mott reentered the military in Aug. 1861, initially serving as a lieutenant colonel of the 5th New Jersey Inf. He was promoted to brigadier general Sept. 7, 1862. Wounded at Spotsylvania Court House, Mott was brevetted major general Aug. 1, 1864. Ibid., 400.

[32] Samuel S. Carroll (1832–1893) was born in Washington, DC, and graduated from the USMA in 1856. At the start of the Civil War, he was a first lieutenant in the U.S. Army. Promoted to brigadier general during the Overland campaign, Carroll retired as a major general in 1869. Ibid., 165.

[33] Joshua T. Owen (1821–1887) immigrated to Pennsylvania from Wales in 1830. A private in the Pennsylvania Militia at the start of the Civil War, he was named colonel of the 24th Pennsylvania Inf. on May 8, 1861, and a brigadier general at the start of the Overland campaign. He was arrested May 18, 1864, for disobedience during the battles of Cold Harbor and Spotsylvania. Lincoln ordered him discharged from the U.S. Army in July 1864. He later founded the New York *Daily Register.* Ibid., 412.

[34] Alexander Hays (1819–1864) was born in Pennsylvania and graduated from the USMA in 1844. He fought in the Mexican-American War, was named major of the 12th Pennsylvania Inf. in Apr. 1861, and rose to brigadier general. A personal friend of USG, Hays was killed on May 5, 1864, at the Battle of the Wilderness. Ibid., 290.

He was a most gallant officer, ready to lead his command wherever ordered. With him it was "Come, boys," not "Go."

Wadsworth's[35] division and Baxter's[36] brigade of the 2d division were sent to reinforce Hancock and Getty; but the density of the intervening forest was such that, there being no road to march upon, they did not get up with the head of column until night, and bivouacked where they were without getting into position.

During the afternoon Sheridan sent Gregg's division of cavalry to Todd's Tavern[37] in search of Wilson. This was fortunate. He found Wilson engaged with a superior force under General Rosser,[38] supported by infantry, and falling back before it. Together they were strong enough to turn the tables upon the enemy and themselves become aggressive. They soon drove the rebel cavalry back beyond Corbin's Bridge.[39]

Fighting between Hancock and Hill continued until night put a close to it. Neither side made any special progress.

After the close of the battle of the 5th of May my orders were given for the following morning. We knew Longstreet with 12,000 men was on his way to join Hill's right, near the Brock Road, and might arrive during the night. I was anxious that the rebels should not take the initiative in the morning, and therefore ordered Hancock to make an assault at 4.30 o'clock. Meade asked to have the hour changed to six. Deferring to his wishes as far as I was willing, the order was modified and five was fixed as the hour to move.[40]

[35] James S. Wadsworth (1807–1864) was born in New York and was a major general in the New York Militia in May 1861. He served as volunteer aide-de-camp to Brig. Gen. Irvin Mc-Dowell and was appointed brigadier general in Aug. 1861. Wadsworth was wounded at the Battle of the Wilderness on May 6, 1864, and died in a Confederate hospital on May 8, 1864. Ibid., 547.

[36] Henry Baxter (1821–1873) was born in New York, moved to Michigan in 1831, and to California in 1849. At the start of the Civil War, he was named captain of the 7th Michigan Inf. He was promoted to brigadier general Mar. 12, 1863. During USG's presidency, Baxter served as U.S. minister to Honduras from 1869 to1872. Ibid., 122.

[37] Todd's Tavern was approximately twenty miles west of Fredericksburg, VA. *PUSG*, 10:412 (map); *OR*, I, 36(I), 775.

[38] Thomas L. Rosser (1836–1910) was born in Virginia and moved to Texas in 1849. He joined the Confederate Art. as a first lieutenant in Mar. 1861 and was promoted to brigadier general in Sept. 1863. *CWHC*, 462–463.

[39] Corbin's Bridge was about five miles south of Catherine Furnace. *PUSG*, 10:412 (map).

[40] For USG's May 5, 1864, instructions to Meade, see Rowley's letter to Meade, ibid., 10:400n.

Hancock had now fully one-half of the Army of the Potomac. Wadsworth with his division, which had arrived the night before, lay in a line perpendicular to that held by Hill, and to the right of Hancock. He was directed to move at the same time, and to attack Hill's left.

Burnside, who was coming up with two divisions, was directed to get in between Warren and Wadsworth, and attack as soon as he could get in position to do so. Sedgwick and Warren were to make attacks in their front, to detain as many of the enemy as they could and to take advantage of any attempt to reinforce Hill from that quarter. Burnside was ordered if he should succeed in breaking the enemy's centre, to swing around to the left and envelop the right of Lee's army. Hancock was informed of all the movements ordered.

Burnside had three divisions, but one of them—a colored division—was sent to guard the wagon train, and he did not see it again until July.[41]

Lee was evidently very anxious that there should be no battle on his right until Longstreet got up. This is evident from the fact that notwithstanding the early hour at which I had ordered the assault, both for the purpose of being the attacking party and to strike before Longstreet got up, Lee was ahead in his assault on our right. His purpose was evident, but he failed.

Hancock was ready to advance by the hour named, but learning in time that Longstreet was moving a part of his corps by the Catharpin Road, thus threatening his left flank, sent a division of infantry, commanded by General Barlow,[42] with all his artillery, to cover the approaches by which Longstreet was expected. This disposition was made in time to attack as ordered. Hancock moved by the left of the Orange Plank Road, and Wadsworth by the right of it. The fighting was desperate for about an hour, when the enemy began to break up in great confusion.

I believed then, and see no reason to change that opinion now, that if the country had been such that Hancock and his command could have seen the confusion and panic in the lines of the enemy, it would have been taken ad-

[41]Two brigades of the 4th Div., 9th Corps, under Brig. Gen. Edward Ferrero were comprised of African American troops. Units of U.S. Colored Troops (USCT) were often relegated to support duty because white troops did not believe in the USCT's fighting ability until later in the war. Rhea, *Battle of the Wilderness,* 463; Noah Trudeau, *Like Men of War: Black Troops in the Civil War, 1862–1865* (Boston: Little, Brown, 1998), 206–209.

[42]Francis C. Barlow (1834–1896) was born in New York and moved to Massachusetts, graduating from Harvard University in 1855. He enlisted as a private in the New York Militia and rose to brigadier general by 1862. He was promoted to major general on May 25, 1865, resigning in Nov. to practice law and enter New York state politics. *CWHC,* 116.

vantage of so effectually that Lee would not have made another stand outside of his Richmond defences.

Gibbon[43] commanded Hancock's left, and was ordered to attack, but was not able to accomplish much.

On the morning of the 6th Sheridan was sent to connect with Hancock's left and attack the enemy's cavalry who were trying to get on our left and rear. He met them at the intersection of the Furnace and Brock roads and at Todd's Tavern, and defeated them at both places. Later he was attacked, and again the enemy was repulsed.

Hancock heard the firing between Sheridan and Stuart, and thinking the enemy coming by that road, still further reinforced his position guarding the entrance to the Brock Road. Another incident happened during the day to further induce Hancock to weaken his attacking column. Word reached him that troops were seen moving towards him from the direction of Todd's Tavern, and Brooke's[44] brigade was detached to meet this new enemy; but the troops approaching proved to be several hundred convalescents coming from Chancellorsville, by the road Hancock had advanced upon, to join their respective commands. At 6.50 o'clock A.M., Burnside, who had passed Wilderness Tavern at six o'clock, was ordered to send a division to the support of Hancock, but to continue with the remainder of his command in the execution of his previous order. The difficulty of making a way through the dense forests prevented Burnside from getting up in time to be of any service on the forenoon of the sixth.

Hancock followed Hill's retreating forces, in the morning, a mile or more. He maintained this position until, along in the afternoon, Longstreet came upon him. The retreating column of Hill meeting reinforcements that had not yet been engaged, became encouraged and returned with them. They were enabled, from the density of the forest, to approach within a few hundred yards of our advance before being discovered. Falling upon a brigade of Hancock's corps thrown to the advance, they swept it away almost instantly. The enemy followed up his advantage and soon came upon Mott's division, which fell back in great confusion. Hancock made dispositions to hold his advanced position,

---

[43] John Gibbon (1827–1896) was born in Pennsylvania and moved to North Carolina in 1838. He graduated from the USMA in 1847, entering the U.S. Army as a second lieutenant. By the start of the Civil War, he was a captain in the U.S. Army. On Aug. 1, 1864, during the Overland campaign, he was promoted to major general. Ibid., 253.

[44] John R. Brooke (1838–1926) was born in Pennsylvania and was a captain in the 3rd Pennsylvania Inf. in Apr. 1861. He was promoted to colonel in Nov. and became a brigadier general in 1864. He retired from the U.S. Army in 1902 as a major general. Ibid., 145.

but after holding it for a time, fell back into the position that he had held in the morning, which was strongly intrenched. In this engagement the intrepid Wadsworth while trying to rally his men was mortally wounded and fell into the hands of the enemy.[45] The enemy followed up, but made no immediate attack.

The Confederate General Jenkins was killed and Longstreet seriously wounded in this engagement.[46] Longstreet had to leave the field, not to resume command for many weeks. His loss was a severe one to Lee, and compensated in a great measure for the mishap, or misapprehensions, which had fallen to our lot during the day.

After Longstreet's removal from the field Lee took command of his right in person. He was not able, however, to rally his men to attack Hancock's position, and withdrew from our front for the purpose of reforming. Hancock sent a brigade to clear his front of all remnants that might be left of Longstreet's or Hill's commands. This brigade having been formed at right angles to the intrenchments held by Hancock's command, swept down the whole length of them from left to right. A brigade of the enemy was encountered in this move; but it broke and disappeared without a contest.

Firing was continued after this, but with less fury. Burnside had not yet been able to get up to render any assistance. But it was now only about nine in the morning, and he was getting into position on Hancock's right.

At 4.15 in the afternoon Lee attacked our left. His line moved up to within a hundred yards of ours and opened a heavy fire. This status was maintained for about half an hour. Then a part of Mott's division and Ward's[47] brigade of Birney's division gave way and retired in disorder. The enemy under R. H. Anderson took advantage of this and pushed through our line, planting their flags on a part of the intrenchments not on fire. But owing to the efforts of Hancock, their success was but temporary. Carroll, of Gibbon's division, moved at a double quick with his brigade and drove back the enemy, inflicting great

[45] Wadsworth died on May 8, 1864. Rhea, *Battle of the Wilderness,* 450.

[46] Micah Jenkins (1835–1864) was born in South Carolina and graduated from the South Carolina Military School in 1854. He entered the Confederate Army as a colonel, and was promoted to brigadier general in July 1862. On May 6, 1864, while riding at the head of a Confederate column on Orange Plank Road, Jenkins was shot in the head and Longstreet was wounded in the neck, both by friendly fire. *CWHC,* 318; Rhea, *Battle of the Wilderness,* 368–373.

[47] John H. H. Ward (1823–1903) was born in New York. He enlisted in the U.S. Army in 1842 and fought in the Mexican-American War. After being discharged, Ward was a leader in the New York Militia. He became a colonel in the 38th New York Inf. in June 1861. Ward was relieved of command on May 12, 1864, and on June 12 was arrested for drunkenness and abandoning his command. *CWHC,* 553.

loss. Fighting had continued from five in the morning sometimes along the whole line, at other times only in places. The ground fought over had varied in width, but averaged three-quarters of a mile. The killed, and many of the severely wounded, of both armies, lay within this belt where it was impossible to reach them. The woods were set on fire by the bursting shells, and the conflagration raged. The wounded who had not strength to move themselves were either suffocated or burned to death. Finally the fire communicated with our breastworks, in places. Being constructed of wood, they burned with great fury. But the battle still raged, our men firing through the flames until it became too hot to remain longer.

Lee was now in distress. His men were in confusion, and his personal efforts failed to restore order. These facts, however, were learned subsequently, or we would have taken advantage of his condition and no doubt gained a decisive success. His troops were withdrawn now, but I revoked the order, which I had given previously to this assault, for Hancock to attack, because his troops had exhausted their ammunition and did not have time to replenish from the train, which was at some distance.[48]

Burnside, Sedgwick, and Warren had all kept up an assault during all this time; but their efforts had no other effect than to prevent the enemy from reinforcing his right from the troops in their front.

I had, on the 5th, ordered all the bridges over the Rapidan to be taken up except one at Germania Ford.[49]

The troops on Sedgwick's right had been sent to reinforce our left. This left our right in danger of being turned, and us of being cut off from all present base of supplies. Sedgwick had refused his right and intrenched it for protection against attack. But late in the afternoon of the 6th Early[50] came out from

[48] For these orders, see Meade's May 6, 1864, instructions to Hancock. *OR*, I, 36(II), 444–445, 447.

[49] On May 2, 1864, Asst. AG S. Williams issued orders from Meade that called for the bridges at Germanna Ford and Ely's Ford to be left in place to facilitate Burnside's crossing, while the bridge at Culpeper Mine Ford was to be removed. On May 5, USG directed Burnside to "dispense with" the pontoon bridge at Ely's Ford once his crossing was complete. Ibid., I, 36(II), 334; *PUSG*, 10:398n.

[50] Jubal A. Early (1816–1894) was born in Virginia and graduated from the USMA in 1837. He worked as a lawyer and a politician prior to the Civil War. He entered the Confederate Army as a colonel in 1861 and was promoted to major general in 1863. He fled the country after the Civil War, returning in 1869. Early was president of the Southern Historical Society, which promoted pro-Confederate, Lost Cause perspectives on the Civil War. *CWHC*, 221; Jeffry D. Wert, "James Longstreet and the Lost Cause," in *The Myth of the Lost Cause and Civil War History*, ed. Gary W. Gallagher and Alan T. Nolan (Bloomington: Indiana University Press, 2000), 129–130.

his lines in considerable force and got in upon Sedgwick's right, notwith-standing the precautions taken, and created considerable confusion. Early captured several hundred prisoners, among them two general officers.[51] The defence, however, was vigorous; and night coming on, the enemy was thrown into as much confusion as our troops, engaged, were. Early says in his Mem-oirs that if we had discovered the confusion in his lines we might have brought fresh troops to his great discomfort.[52] Many officers, who had not been at-tacked by Early, continued coming to my headquarters even after Sedgwick had rectified his lines a little farther to the rear, with news of the disaster, fully impressed with the idea that the enemy was pushing on and would soon be upon me.

During the night all of Lee's army withdrew within their intrenchments. On the morning of the 7th General Custer[53] drove the enemy's cavalry from Catharpin Furnace[54] to Todd's Tavern. Pickets and skirmishers were sent along our entire front to find the position of the enemy. Some went as far as a mile and a half before finding him. But Lee showed no disposition to come out of his works. There was no battle during the day, and but little firing except in Warren's front; he being directed about noon to make a reconnoissance in force. This drew some sharp firing, but there was no attempt on the part of Lee to drive him back. This ended the Battle of the Wilderness.

---

[51] Truman Seymour and Alexander Shaler were both captured on May 6, 1864. Seymour (1824–1891) was born in Vermont and graduated from the USMA in 1846. He fought in the Mexican-American War, was at Fort Sumter at the beginning of the Civil War, and was promoted to brigadier general in Apr. 1862. Shaler (1827–1911) was born in Connecticut and moved to New York in 1834. He served as a captain in the New York Militia from 1845 to 1861. He joined the U.S. Army as a lieutenant colonel in June 1861, and was promoted to brigadier general by May 1863. Shaler was awarded the Medal of Honor in 1893 for his actions at Marye's Heights, VA, in May 1863. *CWHC,* 479–481; Rhea, *Battle of the Wilderness,* 419–420.

[52] See Jubal Early, *A Memoir of the Last Year of the War for Independence in the Confederate States of America* (Lynchburg, VA: Charles W. Button, 1867), 20.

[53] George A. Custer (1839–1876) was born in Ohio and graduated from the USMA in 1861. He was brevetted brigadier general Mar. 13, 1865, and was promoted to major general Apr. 15. He was killed in combat with the Lakota-Sioux at the Battle of Little Big Horn in June 1876. *CWHC,* 196.

[54] Other accounts from the time referred to this place as "Catherine Furnace," which was ap-proximately ten miles north of Spotsylvania Court House. Alfred Pleasonton, "The Successes and Failures of Chancellorsville," in *Battles and Leaders of the Civil War,* vol. 3, ed. Robert Under-wood Johnson and Clarence Clough Buel (New York: Century, 1888), 177; *PUSG,* 10:412 (map).

# 51

## After the Battle—Telegraph and Signal Service— Movement by the Left Flank

$M$ORE DESPERATE FIGHTING has not been witnessed on this continent than that of the 5th and 6th of May. Our victory consisted in having successfully crossed a formidable stream, almost in the face of an enemy, and in getting the army together as a unit. We gained an advantage on the morning of the 6th, which, if it had been followed up, must have proven very decisive. In the evening the enemy gained an advantage; but was speedily repulsed. As we stood at the close, the two armies were relatively in about the same condition to meet each other as when the river divided them. But the fact of having safely crossed was a victory.

Our losses in the Wilderness were very severe. Those of the Confederates must have been even more so; but I have no means of speaking with accuracy upon this point.[1] The Germania Ford bridge was transferred to Ely's Ford to facilitate the transportation of the wounded to Washington.

It may be as well here as elsewhere to state two things connected with all movements of the Army of the Potomac: first, in every change of position or halt for the night, whether confronting the enemy or not, the moment arms were stacked the men intrenched themselves. For this purpose they would build up piles of logs or rails if they could be found in their front, and dig a ditch, throwing the dirt forward on the timber. Thus the digging they did counted in making a depression to stand in, and increased the elevation in front of them. It was wonderful how quickly they could in this way construct

---

[1] Estimates of Confederate casualties in the Wilderness place the figure at about 11,000 (roughly 17 percent of Lee's approximately 65,000 men), while U.S. Army casualties stood at 17,666 (roughly 15 percent of USG's approximately 119,000 men). Gordon C. Rhea, *The Battle of the Wilderness, May 5–6, 1864* (Baton Rouge: Louisiana State University Press, 1994), 34, 435, 440.

defences of considerable strength. When a halt was made with the view of assaulting the enemy, or in his presence, these would be strengthened or their positions changed under the direction of engineer officers. The second was, the use made of the telegraph and signal corps. Nothing could be more complete than the organization and discipline of this body of brave and intelligent men. Insulated wires—insulated so that they would transmit messages in a storm, on the ground or under water—were wound upon reels, making about two hundred pounds weight of wire to each reel. Two men and one mule were detailed to each reel. The pack-saddle on which this was carried was provided with a rack like a sawbuck placed crosswise of the saddle, and raised above it so that the reel, with its wire, would revolve freely. There was a wagon, supplied with a telegraph operator, battery and telegraph instruments for each division, each corps, each army, and one for my headquarters. There were wagons also loaded with light poles, about the size and length of a wall tent pole, supplied with an iron spike in one end, used to hold the wires up when laid, so that wagons and artillery would not run over them. The mules thus loaded were assigned to brigades, and always kept with the command they were assigned to. The operators were also assigned to particular headquarters, and never changed except by special orders.

The moment the troops were put in position to go into camp all the men connected with this branch of service would proceed to put up their wires. A mule loaded with a coil of wire would be led to the rear of the nearest flank of the brigade he belonged to, and would be led in a line parallel thereto, while one man would hold an end of the wire and uncoil it as the mule was led off. When he had walked the length of the wire the whole of it would be on the ground. This would be done in rear of every brigade at the same time. The ends of all the wires would then be joined, making a continuous wire in the rear of the whole army. The men, attached to brigades or divisions, would all commence at once raising the wires with their telegraph poles. This was done by making a loop in the wire and putting it over the spike and raising the pole to a perpendicular position. At intervals the wire would be attached to trees, or some other permanent object, so that one pole was sufficient at a place. In the absence of such a support two poles would have to be used, at intervals, placed at an angle so as to hold the wire firm in its place. While this was being done the telegraph wagons would take their positions near where the headquarters they belonged to were to be established, and would connect with the wire. Thus, in a few minutes longer time than it took a mule to walk the length of its coil, telegraphic communication would be effected between all the headquarters of the army. No orders ever had to be given to establish the telegraph.

The signal service was used on the march. The men composing this corps were assigned to specified commands. When movements were made, they would go in advance, or on the flanks, and seize upon high points of ground giving a commanding view of the country, if cleared, or would climb tall trees on the highest points if not cleared, and would denote, by signals, the positions of different parts of our own army, and often the movements of the enemy. They would also take off the signals of the enemy and transmit them. It would sometimes take too long a time to make translations of intercepted dispatches for us to receive any benefit from them. But sometimes they gave useful information.

On the afternoon of the 7th I received news from Washington announcing that Sherman had probably attacked Johnston that day, and that Butler had reached City Point safely and taken it by surprise on the 5th.[2] I had given orders for a movement by the left flank, fearing that Lee might move rapidly to Richmond to crush Butler before I could get there.

My order for this movement was as follows:

> HEADQUARTERS ARMIES OF THE U. S.,
> *May* 7, 1864, 6.30 A.M.
>
> MAJOR-GENERAL MEADE,
> Commanding A. P.
>
> Make all preparations during the day for a night march to take position at Spottsylvania C. H. with one army corps, at Todd's Tavern with one, and another near the intersection of the Piney Branch and Spottsylvania road with the road from Alsop's to Old Court House. If this move is made the trains should be thrown forward early in the morning to the Ny River.
>
> I think it would be advisable in making the change to leave Hancock where he is until Warren passes him. He could then follow and become the right of the new line. Burnside will move to Piney Branch Church. Sedgwick can move along the pike to Chancellorsville and on to his destination. Burnside will move on the plank road to the intersection of it with the Orange and Fredericksburg plank road, then follow Sedgwick to his place of destination.
>
> All vehicles should be got out of hearing of the enemy before the troops move, and then move off quietly.

[2] Although the editors found no correspondence from May 7, 1864, matching USG's description, on May 10 Stanton wrote a letter to USG that detailed Sherman's and Butler's advances. *PUSG,* 10:415*n.*

It is more than probable that the enemy concentrate for a heavy attack on Hancock this afternoon. In case they do we must be prepared to resist them, and follow up any success we may gain, with our whole force. Such a result would necessarily modify these instructions.

All the hospitals should be moved to-day to Chancellorsville.

                                                            U. S. GRANT,
                                                            Lieut.-General.


During the 7th Sheridan had a fight with the rebel cavalry at Todd's Tavern, but routed them, thus opening the way for the troops that were to go by that route at night. Soon after dark Warren withdrew from the front of the enemy, and was soon followed by Sedgwick. Warren's march carried him immediately behind the works where Hancock's command lay on the Brock Road. With my staff and a small escort of cavalry I preceded the troops. Meade with his staff accompanied me. The greatest enthusiasm was manifested by Hancock's men as we passed by. No doubt it was inspired by the fact that the movement was south. It indicated to them that they had passed through the "beginning of the end" in the battle just fought. The cheering was so lusty that the enemy must have taken it for a night attack. At all events it drew from him a furious fusillade of artillery and musketry, plainly heard but not felt by us.

Meade and I rode in advance. We had passed but a little way beyond our left when the road forked. We looked to see, if we could, which road Sheridan had taken with his cavalry during the day. It seemed to be the right-hand one, and accordingly we took it. We had not gone far, however, when Colonel C. B. Comstock, of my staff, with the instinct of the engineer, suspecting that we were on a road that would lead us into the lines of the enemy, if he, too, should be moving, dashed by at a rapid gallop and all alone. In a few minutes he returned and reported that Lee was moving, and that the road we were on would bring us into his lines in a short distance. We returned to the forks of the road, left a man to indicate the right road to the head of Warren's column when it should come up, and continued our journey to Todd's Tavern, where we arrived after midnight.[3]

My object in moving to Spottsylvania was two-fold: first, I did not want Lee to get back to Richmond in time to attempt to crush Butler before I could

---

[3] Robert S. Robertson, who was then aide-de-camp to Col. Nelson A. Miles and on duty that evening, claimed that he (not Comstock) redirected USG's party to the correct road. Robert S. Robertson, *Personal Recollections of the War* (Milwaukee, WI: Swain and Tate, 1895), 94–95.

get there; second, I wanted to get between his army and Richmond if possible; and, if not, to draw him into the open field. But Lee, by accident, beat us to Spottsylvania. Our wagon trains had been ordered easterly of the roads the troops were to march upon before the movement commenced. Lee interpreted this as a semi-retreat of the Army of the Potomac to Fredericksburg, and so informed his government.[4] Accordingly he ordered Longstreet's corps—now commanded by Anderson—to move in the morning (the 8th) to Spottsylvania. But the woods being still on fire, Anderson could not go into bivouac, and marched directly on to his destination that night. By this accident Lee got possession of Spottsylvania. It is impossible to say now what would have been the result if Lee's orders had been obeyed as given; but it is certain that we would have been in Spottsylvania, and between him and his capital. My belief is that there would have been a race between the two armies to see which could reach Richmond first, and the Army of the Potomac would have had the shorter line. Thus, twice since crossing the Rapidan we came near closing the campaign, so far as battles were concerned, from the Rapidan to the James River or Richmond. The first failure was caused by our not following up the success gained over Hill's corps on the morning of the 6th, as before described: the second, when fires caused by that battle drove Anderson to make a march during the night of the 7th–8th which he was ordered to commence on the morning of the 8th. But accident often decides the fate of battle.

Sheridan's cavalry had had considerable fighting during the afternoon of the 7th, lasting at Todd's Tavern until after night, with the field his at the close. He issued the necessary orders for seizing Spottsylvania and holding the bridge over the Po River, which Lee's troops would have to cross to get to Spottsylvania. But Meade changed Sheridan's orders to Merritt[5]—who was holding the bridge—on his arrival at Todd's Tavern, and thereby left the road free for Anderson when he came up. Wilson, who was ordered to seize the town, did so, with his division of cavalry; but he could not hold it against the Confederate corps which had not been detained at the crossing of the Po, as it would

[4] On May 7, 1864, Asst. AG W. H. Taylor wrote to J. E. B. Stuart informing him about Lee's theories on why the U.S. Army was moving. Lee initially hypothesized that the U.S. Army supply trains were empty and needed to be refilled. *OR,* I, 36(II), 970.

[5] Wesley Merritt (1834–1910) was born in New York and graduated from the USMA in 1860. He was brevetted brigadier general in June 1863. He remained in the military after the war, serving as superintendent of the USMA from 1882 to 1887 and retiring as a major general in 1900. *CWHC,* 387.

have been but for the unfortunate change in Merritt's orders.[6] Had he been permitted to execute the orders Sheridan gave him, he would have been guarding with two brigades of cavalry the bridge over the Po River which Anderson had to cross, and must have detained him long enough to enable Warren to reinforce Wilson and hold the town.

Anderson soon intrenched himself—if indeed the intrenchments were not already made—immediately across Warren's front. Warren was not aware of his presence, but probably supposed it was the cavalry which Merritt had engaged earlier in the day. He assaulted at once, but was repulsed. He soon organized his men, as they were not pursued by the enemy, and made a second attack, this time with his whole corps. This time he succeeded in gaining a position immediately in the enemy's front, where he intrenched. His right and left divisions—the former Crawford's,[7] the latter Wadsworth's, now commanded by Cutler[8]—drove the enemy back some distance.

At this time my headquarters had been advanced to Piney Branch Church. I was anxious to crush Anderson before Lee could get a force to his support. To this end Sedgwick, who was at Piney Branch Church, was ordered to Warren's support. Hancock, who was at Todd's Tavern, was notified of Warren's engagement, and was directed to be in readiness to come up. Burnside, who was with the wagon trains at Aldrich's on our extreme left, received the same

[6] Meade arrived at Todd's Tavern about 1 A.M. and found David M. Gregg and Merritt without orders. He then ordered Gregg to move on Corbin's Bridge on the Po River and Merritt to move toward Spotsylvania Court House, VA, to prevent a Confederate advance from the west. At approximately the same time, Sheridan issued orders for Gregg to move beyond Corbin's Bridge and for Merritt to take another route to Spotsylvania Court House. Sheridan's orders arrived after Gregg's and Merritt's troops were in motion and were thus not implemented. In his May 13, 1866, report, Sheridan claimed that Meade had changed the orders he had already given Gregg and Merritt. *OR*, I, 36(I), 788–789; Gordon C. Rhea, *The Battles for Spotsylvania Court House and the Road to Yellow Tavern, May 7–12, 1864* (Baton Rouge: Louisiana State University Press, 1997), 40–42.

[7] Samuel W. Crawford (1829–1892) was born in Pennsylvania and was the surgeon at Fort Sumter, SC, from Dec. 24, 1860 to Apr. 14, 1861. During the bombardment, Crawford commanded an artillery detail. He became a major in the U.S. 13th Inf. in May, retiring in 1873 as a brigadier general. Samuel W. Crawford, *The Genesis of the Civil War: The Story of Sumter, 1860–1861* (New York: Charles L. Webster, 1887), 429–430; *CWHC*, 190.

[8] Lysander Cutler (1807–1866) was born in Massachusetts, moved to Maine in 1828, and settled in Wisconsin in 1857. He began the war as a colonel of the 6th Wisconsin Inf. and was promoted to brigadier general in Nov. 1862. Cutler was wounded in the face in Aug. 1864 and died from those wounds in 1866. *CWHC*, 196.

instructions.[9] Sedgwick was slow in getting up for some reason—probably un-avoidable, because he was never at fault when serious work was to be done—so that it was near night before the combined forces were ready to attack.[10] Even then all of Sedgwick's command did not get into the engagement. Warren led the last assault, one division at a time, and of course it failed.

Warren's difficulty was twofold: when he received an order to do anything, it would at once occur to his mind how all the balance of the army should be engaged so as properly to co-operate with him. His ideas were generally good, but he would forget that the person giving him orders had thought of others at the time he had of him. In like manner, when he did get ready to execute an order, after giving most intelligent instructions to division commanders, he would go in with one division, holding the others in reserve until he could superintend their movements in person also, forgetting that division com-manders could execute an order without his presence. His difficulty was con-stitutional and beyond his control. He was an officer of superior ability, quick perceptions, and personal courage to accomplish anything that could be done with a small command.

Lee had ordered Hill's corps—now commanded by Early—to move by the very road we had marched upon. This shows that even early in the morning of the 8th Lee had not yet become acquainted with my move, but still thought that the Army of the Potomac had gone to Fredericksburg. Indeed, he informed the authorities at Richmond that he had possession of Spottsylvania and was thus on my flank.[11] Anderson was in possession of Spottsylvania, through no foresight of Lee, however. Early only found that he had been following us when he ran against Hancock at Todd's Tavern. His coming detained Hancock from the battle-field of Spottsylvania for that day; but he, in like manner, kept Early back and forced him to move by another route.

Had I ordered the movement for the night of the 7th by my left flank, it would have put Hancock in the lead. It would also have given us an hour or

[9] For Meade's May 8, 1864, orders to Hancock, see *OR*, I, 36(II), 531. For USG's May 8 orders to Burnside, see *PUSG*, 10:413*n*.

[10] Part of the delay came from ambulances moving the wounded from the area of the Battle of the Wilderness. In addition, many of Sedgwick's troops, exhausted from marching and fighting during the previous days, were further worn down from the heat on May 8, 1864. Rhea, *Battles for Spotsylvania Court House*, 72.

[11] In a series of communications to Confederate secretary of war James Seddon on May 8, 1864, Lee wrote that he had taken Spotsylvania Court House and was on the U.S. Army's right flank. *OR*, I, 36(II), 974.

more earlier start. It took all that time for Warren to get the head of his column to the left of Hancock after he had got his troops out of their line confronting the enemy. This hour, and Hancock's capacity to use his whole force when necessary, would, no doubt, have enabled him to crush Anderson before he could be reinforced. But the movement made was tactical. It kept the troops in mass against a possible assault by the enemy. Our left occupied its intrenchments while the two corps to the right passed. If an attack had been made by the enemy he would have found the 2d corps in position, fortified, and, practically, the 5th and 6th corps in position as reserves, until his entire front was passed. By a left flank movement the army would have been scattered while still passing the front of the enemy, and before the extreme right had got by it would have been very much exposed. Then, too, I had not yet learned the special qualifications of the different corps commanders. At that time my judgment was that Warren was the man I would suggest to succeed Meade should anything happen to that gallant soldier to take him from the field. As I have before said, Warren was a gallant soldier, an able man; and he was beside thoroughly imbued with the solemnity and importance of the duty he had to perform.

# 52

## Battle of Spottsylvania—Hancock's Position—Assault of Warren's and Wright's Corps—Upton Promoted on the Field—Good News from Butler and Sheridan

THE MATTAPONY RIVER is formed by the junction of the Mat, the Ta, the Po and the Ny rivers, the last being the northernmost of the four. It takes its rise about a mile south and a little east of the Wilderness Tavern. The Po rises south-west of the same place, but farther away. Spottsylvania is on the ridge dividing these two streams, and where they are but a few miles apart. The Brock Road reaches Spottsylvania without crossing either of these streams. Lee's army coming up by the Catharpin Road, had to cross the Po at Wooden Bridge.[1] Warren and Hancock came by the Brock Road. Sedgwick crossed the Ny at Catharpin Furnace. Burnside coming by Aldrich's to Gates's house,[2] had to cross the Ny near the enemy. He found pickets at the bridge, but they were soon driven off by a brigade of Willcox's division, and the stream was crossed. This brigade was furiously attacked; but the remainder of the division coming up, they were enabled to hold their position, and soon fortified it.

About the time I received the news of this attack,[3] word came from Hancock that Early had left his front. He had been forced over to the Catharpin Road, crossing the Po at Corbin's and again at Wooden Bridge. These are the

---

[1] Based on USG's description, the "Wooden Bridge" he referred to was probably the Block House Bridge, which was approximately two miles from Spotsylvania Court House, VA. *OR*, I, 36(I), 333. Gordon C. Rhea, *The Battles for Spotsylvania Court House and the Road to Yellow Tavern, May 7–12, 1864* (Baton Rouge: Louisiana State University Press, 1997), 124 (map).

[2] "Gates's house" may have referred to the Gayle house, approximately one and one-half miles northeast of Spotsylvania Court House. The Gayle house was frequently confused with a nearby landmark on the Fredericksburg Road known as the "gate." Rhea, *Battles for Spotsylvania Court House*, 102–103, 104, 368*n*; *PUSG*, 10:412 (map).

[3] USG learned of the attack late on the morning of May 9, 1864. *PUSG*, 10:416*n*–17*n*.

bridges Sheridan had given orders to his cavalry to occupy on the 8th, while one division should occupy Spottsylvania.[4] These movements of the enemy gave me the idea that Lee was about to make the attempt to get to, or towards, Fredericksburg to cut off my supplies. I made arrangements to attack his right and get between him and Richmond if he should try to execute this design. If he had any such intention it was abandoned as soon as Burnside was established south of the Ny.[5]

The Po and the Ny are narrow little streams, but deep, with abrupt banks, and bordered by heavily wooded and marshy bottoms—at the time we were there—and difficult to cross except where bridged. The country about was generally heavily timbered, but with occasional clearings. It was a much better country to conduct a defensive campaign in than an offensive one.

By noon of the 9th the position of the two armies was as follows: Lee occupied a semicircle facing north, north-west and north-east, inclosing the town. Anderson was on his left extending to the Po, Ewell came next, then Early. Warren occupied our right, covering the Brock and other roads converging at Spottsylvania; Sedgwick was to his left and Burnside on our extreme left. Hancock was yet back at Todd's Tavern, but as soon as it was known that Early had left Hancock's front the latter was ordered up to Warren's right. He formed a line with three divisions on the hill overlooking the Po early in the afternoon, and was ordered to cross the Po and get on the enemy's flank. The fourth division of Hancock's corps, Mott commanding, was left at Todd's when the corps first came up; but in the afternoon it was brought up and placed to the left of Sedgwick's—now Wright's—6th corps. In the morning General Sedgwick had been killed near the right of his intrenchments by rebel sharpshooters. His loss was a severe one to the Army of the Potomac and to the Nation. General H. G. Wright succeeded him in the command of his corps.

Hancock was now, nine P.M. of the 9th of May, across the left flank of Lee's army, but separated from it, and also from the remainder of Meade's army, by the Po River. But for the lateness of the hour and the darkness of the night he would have attempted to cross the river again at Wooden Bridge, thus bringing himself on the same side with both friend and foe.

---

[4] Sheridan's May 8, 1864, orders indicated that his men should take up positions near Corbin's Bridge, Block House Bridge, and Snell's Bridge. *OR*, I, 36(II), 553; Rhea, *Battles for Spotsylvania Court House*, 15.

[5] On May 8, 1864, Lee indicated that he believed U.S. forces were moving toward Fredericksburg, VA, and began to prepare to defend against any such move by holding Spotsylvania Court House. Rhea, *Battles for Spotsylvania Court House*, 77.

The Po at the points where Hancock's corps crossed runs nearly due east. Just below his lower crossing—the troops crossed at three points—it turns due south, and after passing under Wooden Bridge soon resumes a more easterly direction. During the night this corps built three bridges over the Po; but these were in rear.

The position assumed by Hancock's corps forced Lee to reinforce his left during the night. Accordingly on the morning of the 10th, when Hancock renewed his effort to get over the Po to his front, he found himself confronted by some of Early's command, which had been brought from the extreme right of the enemy during the night.[6] He succeeded in effecting a crossing with one brigade, however, but finding the enemy intrenched in his front, no more were crossed.

Hancock reconnoitred his front on the morning of the 10th, with the view of forcing a crossing, if it was found that an advantage could be gained. The enemy was found strongly intrenched on the high ground overlooking the river, and commanding the Wooden Bridge with artillery. Anderson's left rested on the Po, where it turns south; therefore, for Hancock to cross over—although it would bring him to the same side of the stream with the rest of the army— would still farther isolate him from it. The stream would have to be crossed twice in the face of the enemy to unite with the main body. The idea of crossing was therefore abandoned.

Lee had weakened the other parts of his line to meet this movement of Hancock's, and I determined to take advantage of it. Accordingly in the morning, orders were issued for an attack in the afternoon on the centre by Warren's and Wright's corps, Hancock to command all the attacking force. Two of his divisions were brought to the north side of the Po. Gibbon was placed to the right of Warren, and Birney in his rear as a reserve. Barlow's division was left south of the stream, and Mott of the same corps was still to the left of Wright's corps. Burnside was ordered to reconnoitre his front in force, and, if an opportunity presented, to attack with vigor. The enemy seeing Barlow's division isolated from the rest of the army, came out and attacked with fury. Barlow repulsed the assault with great slaughter, and with considerable loss to himself. But the enemy reorganized and renewed the assault. Birney was now moved to the high ground overlooking the river crossings built by our troops, and covered the crossings. The second assault was repulsed, again with severe

[6]On the night of May 9, 1864, Brig. Gen. William Mahone, commanding Anderson's 3rd Corps, Army of Northern Virginia, and Heth, commanding a division in the 3rd Corps, reinforced Lee's left flank. *CWHC,* 361; Rhea, *Battles for Spotsylvania Court House,* 123.

loss to the enemy, and Barlow was withdrawn without further molestation.[7] General T. G. Stevenson was killed in this move.[8]

Between the lines, where Warren's assault was to take place, there was a ravine grown up with large trees and underbrush, making it almost impenetrable by man. The slopes on both sides were also covered with a heavy growth of timber. Warren, before noon, reconnoitred his front twice, the first time with one and the second with two divisions. He was repulsed on both occasions, but gained such information of the ground as to induce him to report recommending the assault.

Wright also reconnoitred his front and gained a considerably advanced position from the one he started from. He then organized a storming party, consisting of twelve regiments, and assigned Colonel Emory Upton,[9] of the 121st New York Volunteers, to the command of it. About four o'clock in the afternoon the assault was ordered, Warren's and Wright's corps, with Mott's division of Hancock's corps, to move simultaneously.[10] The movement was prompt, and in a few minutes the fiercest of struggles began. The battle-field was so densely covered with forest that but little could be seen, by any one person, as to the progress made. Meade and I occupied the best position we could get, in rear of Warren.

Warren was repulsed with heavy loss, General J. C. Rice being among the killed.[11] He was not followed, however, by the enemy, and was thereby enabled to reorganize his command as soon as covered from the guns of the enemy.

---

[7] Barlow's May 8–21, 1864, losses totaled 118 killed, 499 wounded, and 60 captured or missing, but the specific losses for May 10 are not given. *OR*, I, 36(I), 137.

[8] Thomas G. Stevenson (1836–1864) was born in Massachusetts, commissioned a colonel in the 24th Massachusetts Inf. in Dec. 1861, and promoted to brigadier general in Dec. 1862. Stevenson was killed in combat on May 10, 1864, at Spotsylvania Court House. *CWHC*, 511.

[9] Emory Upton (1839–1881) was born in New York and graduated from the USMA in 1861. He was commissioned a second lieutenant in the U.S. 4th Artillery in May 1861 and then promoted to colonel in Oct. 1862. Wounded at the Battle of Spotsylvania Court House, Upton recovered and served as commandant of the USMA from 1870 to 1875, becoming a renowned author of tactics. Ibid., 540. For a list of the regiments included in Upton's "storming party," see Rhea, *Battles for Spotsylvania Court House*, 163–164.

[10] Meade's chief of staff, Andrew A. Humphreys, issued the order at 3:30 P.M. on May 10, 1864. *OR*, I, 36(II), 600.

[11] James C. Rice (1829–1864) was born in Massachusetts and in 1855 moved to New York, where he worked as a journalist and a lawyer. He became a first lieutenant in the 39th New York Inf. in May 1861 and was promoted to brigadier general in Aug. 1863. On May 10, 1864, he was wounded in the leg at Spotsylvania Court House and died later that day. *CWHC*, 452.

To the left our success was decided, but the advantage was lost by the feeble action of Mott. Upton with his assaulting party pushed forward and crossed the enemy's intrenchments. Turning to the right and left he captured several guns and some hundreds of prisoners. Mott was ordered to his assistance but failed utterly. So much time was lost in trying to get up the troops which were in the right position to reinforce, that I ordered Upton to withdraw; but the officers and men of his command were so averse to giving up the advantage they had gained that I withdrew the order. To relieve them, I ordered a renewal of the assault. By this time Hancock, who had gone with Birney's division to relieve Barlow, had returned, bringing the division with him. His corps was now joined with Warren's and Wright's in this last assault. It was gallantly made, many men getting up to, and over, the works of the enemy; but they were not able to hold them. At night they were withdrawn.[12] Upton brought his prisoners with him, but the guns he had captured he was obliged to abandon. Upton had gained an important advantage, but a lack in others of the spirit and dash possessed by him lost it to us. Before leaving Washington I had been authorized to promote officers on the field for special acts of gallantry. By this authority I conferred the rank of brigadier-general upon Upton on the spot, and this act was confirmed by the President. Upton had been badly wounded in this fight.[13]

Burnside on the left had got up to within a few hundred yards of Spottsylvania Court House, completely turning Lee's right. He was not aware of the importance of the advantage he had gained, and I, being with the troops where the heavy fighting was, did not know of it at the time. He had gained his position with but little fighting, and almost without loss. Burnside's position now separated him widely from Wright's corps, the corps nearest to him. At night he

[12] There is no surviving documentary evidence that USG was directly involved in giving or rescinding earlier orders to Upton. According to Upton's postbattle report, he received permission for the withdrawal from Gen. David A. Russell on the evening of May 10, 1864. *OR*, I, 36(I), 668.

[13] According to Theodore Lyman, Meade's aide-de-camp, Upton's wound was only "a graze of the arm" and he continued to participate in the action. On May 13, 1864, Meade recommended Upton's promotion to USG, who included the recommendation in a letter to Stanton that same day. On May 15, Stanton informed USG that he had authority to provisionally promote officers in the field, and those promotions would be approved by Lincoln and forwarded to the U.S. Senate for final approval. David W. Lowe, ed., *Meade's Army: The Private Notebook of Lt. Col. Theodore Lyman* (Kent, OH: Kent State University Press, 2007), 150; *PUSG*, 10:434, 436n, 437n.

was ordered to join on to this. This brought him back about a mile, and lost to us an important advantage. I attach no blame to Burnside for this, but I do to myself for not having had a staff officer with him to report to me his position.[14]

The enemy had not dared to come out of his line at any point to follow up his advantage, except in the single instance of his attack on Barlow. Then he was twice repulsed with heavy loss, though he had an entire corps against two brigades. Barlow took up his bridges in the presence of this force.[15]

On the 11th there was no battle and but little firing; none except by Mott who made a reconnoissance to ascertain if there was a weak point in the enemy's line.

I wrote the following letter to General Halleck:

> NEAR SPOTTSYLVANIA C. H.,
> *May* 11, 1864—8.30 A.M.
>
> MAJOR-GENERAL HALLECK, Chief of Staff of the Army,
> Washington, D. C.
>
> We have now ended the 6th day of very hard fighting. The result up to this time is much in our favor. But our losses have been heavy as well as those of the enemy. We have lost to this time eleven general officers killed, wounded and missing, and probably twenty thousand men. I think the loss of the enemy must be greater—we having taken over four thousand prisoners in battle, whilst he has taken from us but few except a few stragglers. I am now sending back to Belle Plain[16] all my wagons for a fresh supply of provisions and ammunition, and purpose to fight it out on this line if it takes all summer.
>
> The arrival of reinforcements here will be very encouraging to the men, and I hope they will be sent as fast as possible, and in as great numbers. My object in having them sent to Belle Plain was to use

---

[14] On May 10, 1864, Horace Porter, USG's aide-de-camp, was with Burnside. Porter later claimed that he had sent two soldiers with messages to report on Burnside's positions, but neither reached USG. One messenger was presumed killed and the other arrived only after a significant delay. Horace Porter, *Campaigning with Grant* (New York: Century, 1897), 950.

[15] On May 10, 1864, Confederate brigades commanded by John R. Cooke, Joseph R. Davis, William W. Kirkland, William Mahone, and Henry H. Walker, and U.S. Army brigades commanded by John R. Brooke, Paul Frank, Nelson A. Miles, and Thomas A. Smyth were involved in the engagement. Rhea, *Battles for Spotsylvania Court House*, 133.

[16] Belle Plain, VA, was a landing on the south bank of Potomac Creek approximately ten miles east of Fredericksburg. *PUSG,* 10:378 (map).

them as an escort to our supply trains. If it is more convenient to send them out by train to march from the railroad to Belle Plain or Fredericksburg, send them so.

I am satisfied the enemy are very shaky, and are only kept up to the mark by the greatest exertions on the part of their officers, and by keeping them intrenched in every position they take.

Up to this time there is no indication of any portion of Lee's army being detached for the defence of Richmond.

U. S. GRANT,
Lieut.-General.

And also, I received information, through the War Department, from General Butler that his cavalry under Kautz had cut the railroad south of Petersburg, separating Beauregard from Richmond, and had whipped Hill,[17] killing, wounding and capturing many. Also that he was intrenched, and could maintain himself.[18] On this same day came news from Sheridan to the effect that he had destroyed ten miles of the railroad and telegraph between Lee and Richmond, one and a half million rations, and most of the medical stores for his army.[19]

On the 8th I had directed Sheridan verbally to cut loose from the Army of the Potomac and pass around the left of Lee's army and attack his cavalry and communications, which was successfully executed in the manner I have already described.

---

[17] Daniel H. Hill (1821–1889) was born in South Carolina and graduated from the USMA in 1842. He fought in the Mexican-American War, resigning from the army in 1849. In May 1861 he entered the Confederate Army as a colonel in the 1st North Carolina Inf. and was promoted to major general in 1862. He was president of the University of Arkansas from 1877 to 1884 and president of Middle Georgia College from 1886 to 1889. *CWHC*, 296–297.

[18] On May 9, 1864, Stanton sent USG information from other U.S. Army commanders. *PUSG*, 10:415n. For Butler's May 9, 1864, message to Stanton, see *OR*, I, 36(II), 10–11.

[19] For Sheridan's May 10, 1864, telegram to Meade, see *PUSG*, 10:426n.

# 53

## Hancock's Assault—Losses of the Confederates— Promotions Recommended—Discomfiture of the Enemy—Ewell's Attack—Reducing the Artillery

Iₙ ᴛʜᴇ ʀᴇᴄᴏɴɴᴏɪssᴀɴᴄᴇ made by Mott on the 11th, a salient was discovered at the right centre. I determined that an assault should be made at that point.*

Accordingly in the afternoon Hancock was ordered to move his command by the rear of Warren and Wright, under cover of night, to Wright's left, and there form it for an assault at four o'clock the next morning.[1] The night was dark, it rained heavily, and the road was difficult, so that it was midnight when

*HᴇᴀᴅQᴜᴀʀᴛᴇʀs Aʀᴍɪᴇs U. S.,
*May* 11, 1864.—3 ᴘ.ᴍ.

Mᴀᴊᴏʀ-Gᴇɴᴇʀᴀʟ Mᴇᴀᴅᴇ,
Commanding Army of the Potomac.

Move three divisions of the 2d corps by the rear of the 5th and 6th corps, under cover of night, so as to join the 9th corps in a vigorous assault on the enemy at four o'clock ᴀ.ᴍ. to-morrow. I will send one or two staff officers over to-night to stay with Burnside, and impress him with the importance of a prompt and vigorous attack. Warren and Wright should hold their corps as close to the enemy as possible, to take advantage of any diversion caused by this attack, and to push in if any opportunity presents itself. There is but little doubt in my mind that the assault last evening would have proved entirely successful if it had commenced one hour earlier and had been heartily entered into by Mott's division and the 9th corps.

U. S. GRANT,
Lieut.-General.

[1] On May 11, 1864, at 4 ᴘ.ᴍ., Meade sent Hancock the order to move at 4 ᴀ.ᴍ. the next day. *OR*, I, 36(II), 635.

he reached the point where he was to halt. It took most of the night to get the men in position for their advance in the morning. The men got but little rest. Burnside was ordered to attack* on the left of the salient at the same hour. I sent two of my staff officers to impress upon him the importance of pushing forward vigorously. Hancock was notified of this. Warren and Wright were ordered to hold themselves in readiness to join in the assault if circumstances made it advisable. I occupied a central position most convenient for receiving information from all points. Hancock put Barlow on his left, in double column, and Birney to his right. Mott followed Birney, and Gibbon was held in reserve.

*HEADQUARTERS ARMIES U. S.,
*May* 11, 1864.—4 P.M.

MAJOR-GENERAL A. E. BURNSIDE,
Commanding 9th Army Corps.

Major-General Hancock has been ordered to move his corps under cover of night to join you in a vigorous attack against the enemy at 4 o'clock A.M. to-morrow. You will move against the enemy with your entire force promptly and with all possible vigor at precisely 4 o'clock A.M. to-morrow the 12th inst. Let your preparations for this attack be conducted with the utmost secrecy and veiled entirely from the enemy.

I send two of my staff officers; Colonels Comstock and Babcock,[2] in whom I have great confidence and who are acquainted with the direction the attack is to be made from here, to remain with you and General Hancock with instructions to render you every assistance in their power. Generals Warren and Wright will hold their corps as close to the enemy as possible, to take advantage of any diversion caused by yours and Hancock's attack, and will push in their whole force if any opportunity presents itself.

U. S. GRANT,
Lieut.-General.

[2] Orville E. Babcock (1835–1884) was born in Vermont and graduated from the USMA in 1861. He was an engineer during the siege of Vicksburg and had risen to lieutenant colonel when he became aide-de-camp for USG in Mar. 1864. He served as private secretary for Pres. USG and visited the Dominican Republic (then known as Santo Domingo) as part of USG's effort to annex that nation. He was implicated in the Whisky Ring scandal in 1875 but was acquitted, USG having provided a deposition affirming his belief in Babcock's innocence. *Dictionary of American Biography,* 2nd ed., s.v. "Babcock, Orville E."; *CWHC,* III.

The morning of the 12th opened foggy, delaying the start more than half an hour.

The ground over which Hancock had to pass to reach the enemy, was ascending and heavily wooded to within two or three hundred yards of the enemy's intrenchments. In front of Birney there was also a marsh to cross. But, notwithstanding all these difficulties, the troops pushed on in quick time without firing a gun, and when within four or five hundred yards of the enemy's line broke out in loud cheers, and with a rush went up to and over the breastworks. Barlow and Birney entered almost simultaneously. Here a desperate hand-to-hand conflict took place. The men of the two sides were too close together to fire, but used their guns as clubs. The hand conflict was soon over. Hancock's corps captured some four thousand prisoners—among them a division and a brigade commander—twenty or more guns with their horses, caissons, and ammunition, several thousand stand of arms, and many colors.[3] Hancock, as soon as the hand-to-hand conflict was over, turned the guns of the enemy against him and advanced inside the rebel lines. About six o'clock I ordered Warren's corps to the support of Hancock's.[4] Burnside, on the left, had advanced up east of the salient to the very parapet of the enemy. Potter,[5] commanding one of his divisions, got over but was not able to remain

[3] On May 12, 1864, USG wrote Burnside that Hancock had captured "about 3000 prisoners" and "also about fifteen guns." *PUSG*, 10:430. The division commander captured was Edward Johnson and the brigade commander was George H. Steuart. Edward Johnson (1816–1873) was born in Virginia and moved to Kentucky. He graduated from the USMA in 1838 and fought in the Mexican-American War. He resigned from the U.S. Army in 1861 to accept a commission as colonel in the 12th Georgia Inf. in July 1861. He rose to major general in 1863. Johnson was captured at Spotsylvania Court House, VA, in May 1864 and exchanged in Aug., only to be recaptured at Nashville in Dec. *CWHC*, 320–321. George H. Steuart (1828–1903) was born in Maryland and graduated from the USMA in 1848. He resigned from the U.S. Army in Apr. 1861 and accepted a commission as a captain in the Confederate cavalry. He rose to brigadier general by 1862. Steuart was captured at Spotsylvania Court House on May 12, 1864, exchanged in Aug., and paroled at Appomattox Court House, VA, on Apr. 9, 1865. Ibid., 509.

[4] For the May 11, 1864, order from Meade's chief of staff Andrew A. Humphreys to Warren, see *OR*, I, 36(II), 637–638.

[5] Robert B. Potter (1829–1887) was born in New York and worked as a lawyer before the war. He was commissioned a major in the 51st New York Inf. in Oct. 1861 and rose to brigadier general by Mar. 1863. *CWHC*, 437.

there. However, he inflicted a heavy loss upon the enemy; but not without loss in return.[6]

This victory was important, and one that Lee could not afford to leave us in full possession of.[7] He made the most strenuous efforts to regain the position he had lost. Troops were brought up from his left and attacked Hancock furiously. Hancock was forced to fall back: but he did so slowly, with his face to the enemy, inflicting on him heavy loss, until behind the breastworks he had captured. These he turned, facing them the other way, and continued to hold. Wright was ordered up to reinforce Hancock, and arrived by six o'clock. He was wounded soon after coming up but did not relinquish the command of his corps, although the fighting lasted until one o'clock the next morning. At eight o'clock Warren was ordered up again, but was so slow in making his dispositions that his orders were frequently repeated, and with emphasis.[8] At eleven o'clock I gave Meade written orders to relieve Warren from his command if he failed to move promptly. Hancock placed batteries on high ground in his rear, which he used against the enemy, firing over the heads of his own troops.

Burnside accomplished but little on our left of a positive nature, but negatively a great deal. He kept Lee from reinforcing his centre from that quarter. If the 5th corps, or rather if Warren, had been as prompt as Wright was with the 6th corps, better results might have been obtained.[9]

Lee massed heavily from his left flank on the broken point of his line. Five times during the day he assaulted furiously, but without dislodging our troops from their new position. His losses must have been fearful. Sometimes the belligerents would be separated by but a few feet. In one place a tree, eighteen inches in diameter, was cut entirely down by musket balls. All the trees between

[6] During the May 12, 1864, assault, U.S. troops lost 6,020 killed and wounded and 800 missing. Confederate losses were estimated at 5,500 killed and wounded and 4,000 missing. Edward H. Bonekemper III, *A Victor, Not a Butcher: Ulysses S. Grant's Overlooked Military Genius* (Washington, DC: Regnery, 2004), 309.

[7] In this May 12, 1864, engagement the U.S. Army captured a salient known as the Mule Shoe. Gordon C. Rhea, *The Battles for Spotsylvania Court House and the Road to Yellow Tavern, May 7–12, 1864* (Baton Rouge: Louisiana State University Press, 1997), 234 (map), 241–242.

[8] For Meade's May 12, 1864, orders to Warren, see *OR*, I, 36(II), 662.

[9] Both Warren and Humphreys determined that assaults on Confederate defenses at Laurel Hill could not succeed and ordered a halt. Rhea, *Battles for Spotsylvania Court House*, 288.

the lines were very much cut to pieces by artillery and musketry. It was three o'clock next morning before the fighting ceased. Some of our troops had then been twenty hours under fire. In this engagement we did not lose a single organization, not even a company. The enemy lost one division with its commander, one brigade and one regiment, with heavy losses elsewhere.*

Our losses were heavy, but, as stated, no whole company was captured.[11] At night Lee took a position in rear of his former one, and by the following morning he was strongly intrenched in it.

Warren's corps was now temporarily broken up, Cutler's division sent to Wright, and Griffin's[12] to Hancock. Meade ordered his chief of staff, General Humphreys,[13] to remain with Warren and the remaining division, and authorized him to give it orders in his name.

> *HEADQUARTERS ARMIES U. S.,
> *May* 12, 1864, 6.30 P.M.
>
> MAJOR-GENERAL HALLECK,
> Washington, D. C.
>
> The eighth day of the battle closes, leaving between three and four thousand prisoners in our hands for the day's work, including two general officers, and over thirty pieces of artillery. The enemy are obstinate, and seem to have found the last ditch. We have lost no organizations, not even that of a company, whilst we have destroyed and captured one division (Johnson's), one brigade (Doles'),[10] and one regiment entire from the enemy.
>
> U. S. GRANT,
> Lieut.-General.

---

[10] George Doles (1830–1864) was born in Georgia and served as a captain in the Georgia Militia until receiving a commission as a captain in the 4th Georgia Inf. in May 1861. By 1862 he had been promoted to brigadier general. Doles fought in the Army of Northern Virginia until his death at the Battle of Bethesda Church, VA, on June 2, 1864. *CWHC,* 212.

[11] Estimated U.S. losses at what became known as the Bloody Angle place the total about 9,000; estimated Confederate losses were 8,000. Rhea, *Battles for Spotsylvania Court House,* 311–312.

[12] Charles Griffin (1825–1867) was born in Ohio and graduated from the USMA in 1847. He fought in the Mexican-American War and was a captain in the U.S. 5th Art. in May 1861. He was brevetted lieutenant colonel in May 1864 and was one of the surrender commissioners at Appomattox Court House. *CWHC,* 269.

[13] Andrew A. Humphreys (1810–1883) was born in Pennsylvania and graduated from the USMA in 1831. He served as aide-de-camp for McClellan from 1861 to 1862 and as chief of staff, Army of the Potomac, from July 1863 to Nov. 1864. He was involved in the founding of the National Academy of Sciences. Ibid., 309.

During the day I was passing along the line from wing to wing continuously. About the centre stood a house which proved to be occupied by an old lady and her daughter. She showed such unmistakable signs of being strongly Union that I stopped. She said she had not seen a Union flag for so long a time that it did her heart good to look upon it again. She said her husband and son, being Union men, had had to leave early in the war, and were now somewhere in the Union army, if alive. She was without food or nearly so, so I ordered rations issued to her, and promised to find out if I could where the husband and son were.[14]

There was no fighting on the 13th, further than a little skirmishing between Mott's division and the enemy. I was afraid that Lee might be moving out, and I did not want him to go without my knowing it. The indications were that he was moving, but it was found that he was only taking his new position back from the salient that had been captured. Our dead were buried this day. Mott's division was reduced to a brigade, and assigned to Birney's division.

During this day I wrote to Washington recommending Sherman and Meade* for promotion to the grade of Major-General in the regular army; Hancock for Brigadier-General; Wright, Gibbon and Humphreys to be Major-Generals of Volunteers; and Upton and Carroll to be Brigadiers. Upton had already

*Spottsylvania C. H., *May* 13, 1864.

Hon. E. M. Stanton, Secretary of War,
Washington, D. C.

I beg leave to recommend the following promotions be made for gallant and distinguished services in the last eight days' battles, to wit: Brigadier-General H. G. Wright and Brigadier-General John Gibbon to be Major-Generals; Colonel S. S. Carroll, 8th Ohio Volunteers; Colonel E. Upton, 121st New York Volunteers; Colonel William McCandless, 2d Pennsylvania Reserves, to be Brigadier-Generals. I would also recommend Major-General W. S. Hancock for Brigadier-General in the regular army. His services and qualifications are eminently deserving of this recognition. In making these recommendations I do not wish the claims of General G. M. Dodge for promotion forgotten, but recommend his name to be sent in at the same time. I would also ask to have General Wright assigned to the command of

[14] One of the women USG referred to may have been Katherine Couse, who lived in the area and was loyal to the Union. USG's aide Horace Porter wrote of this encounter and noted, "Her story was afterward found to be true in every particular." Horace Porter, *Campaigning with Grant* (New York: Century, 1897), 109–110; Rhea, *Battles for Spotsylvania Court House*, 35, 265.

been named as such, but the appointment had to be confirmed by the Senate on the nomination of the President.[15]

The night of the 13th Warren and Wright were moved by the rear to the left of Burnside. The night was very dark and it rained heavily, the roads were so bad that the troops had to cut trees and corduroy the road a part of the way, to get through. It was midnight before they got to the point where they were to halt, and daylight before the troops could be organized to advance to their position in line. They gained their position in line, however, without any fighting, except a little in Wright's front. Here Upton had to contend for an elevation which we wanted and which the enemy was not disposed to yield. Upton first drove the enemy, and was then repulsed in turn. Ayres[16] coming to his support with his brigade (of Griffin's division, Warren's corps), the position was secured and fortified. There was no more battle during the 14th. This brought our line east of the Court House and running north and south and facing west.

----

the Sixth Army Corps. I would further ask the confirmation of General Humphreys to the rank of Major-General.

General Meade has more than met my most sanguine expectations. He and Sherman are the fittest officers for large commands I have come in contact with. If their services can be rewarded by promotion to the rank of Major-Generals in the regular army the honor would be worthily bestowed, and I would feel personally gratified. I would not like to see one of these promotions at this time without seeing both.

U. S. GRANT,
Lieut.-General.

[15] On May 12, 1864, Upton and Carroll were promoted to brigadier generals of volunteers. On May 14, Wright was promoted to major general of volunteers, and Humphreys's prior promotion to major general of volunteers was confirmed, effective July 8, 1863. On June 7, 1864, Gibbon was promoted to major general of volunteers. On Aug. 12, Sherman was promoted to major general, and Hancock was promoted to brigadier general of the regular army. On Sept. 23, Meade was promoted to major general of the regular army. *CWHC,* 165, 253, 278, 309, 385, 485, 540, 583; Porter, *Campaigning with Grant,* 113–114; *OR,* I, 36(II), 746; *PUSG,* 10:437*n.*

[16] Romeyn B. Ayres (1825–1888) was born in New York and graduated from the USMA in 1847. He was a captain in the U.S. 5th Art. in 1861 and was promoted to brigadier general in 1862. *CWHC,* III.

During the night of the 14th–15th Lee moved to cover this new front. This left Hancock without an enemy confronting him.[17] He was brought to the rear of our new centre, ready to be moved in any direction he might be wanted.

On the 15th news came from Butler and Averill. The former reported the capture of the outer works at Drury's Bluff, on the James River, and that his cavalry had cut the railroad and telegraph south of Richmond on the Danville road: and the latter, the destruction of a depot of supplies at Dublin, West Virginia, and the breaking of New River Bridge on the Virginia and Tennessee Railroad.[18] The next day news came from Sherman and Sheridan. Sherman had forced Johnston out of Dalton, Georgia, and was following him south. The report from Sheridan embraced his operations up to his passing the outer defences of Richmond.[19] The prospect must now have been dismal in Richmond. The road and telegraph were cut between the capital and Lee. The roads and wires were cut in every direction from the rebel capital. Temporarily that city was cut off from all communication with the outside except by courier. This condition of affairs, however, was of but short duration.

I wrote Halleck:

NEAR SPOTTSYLVANIA C. H.,
*May* 16, 1864, 8 A.M.

MAJOR-GENERAL HALLECK,
Washington, D. C.:

We have had five days almost constant rain without any prospect yet of it clearing up. The roads have now become so impassable that ambulances with wounded men can no longer run between here and Fredericksburg. All offensive operations necessarily cease until we can have twenty-four hours of dry weather. The army is in the best of spirits, and feel the greatest confidence of ultimate success.

*       *       *       *       *       *       *

[17] The move was prompted because USG preferred that Hancock, rather than Warren, lead the upcoming attack. Gordon C. Rhea, *To the North Anna River: Grant and Lee, May 13–25, 1864* (Baton Rouge: Louisiana State University Press, 2000), 97–98.

[18] On May 14, 1864, Maj. Thomas T. Eckert, U.S. Military Telegraph, telegraphed news of Averill's operations to USG. The same day, Butler reported his success at Drewry's Bluff to Stanton. On May 15, Halleck informed USG that the expedition to cut the Danville Railroad had left on May 12. *OR,* I, 36(II), 771; *PUSG,* 10:447*n*, 455*n*.

[19] On May 13, 1864, Sheridan sent a report to Meade of his movement through Virginia. The next day, Halleck informed USG that Sherman had forced Johnston to evacuate Dalton, GA. *OR,* I, 36(I), 776–778; I, 36(II), 746.

You can assure the President and Secretary of War that the elements alone have suspended hostilities, and that it is in no manner due to weakness or exhaustion on our part.

U. S. Grant,
Lieut.-General.[20]

The condition of the roads was such that nothing was done on the 17th. But that night Hancock and Wright were to make a night march back to their old positions, and to make an assault at four o'clock in the morning. Lee got troops back in time to protect his old line, so the assault was unsuccessful. On this day (18th) the news was almost as discouraging to us as it had been two days before in the rebel capital. As stated above, Hancock's and Wright's corps had made an unsuccessful assault. News came that Sigel had been defeated at New Market, badly, and was retreating down the valley. Not two hours before, I had sent the inquiry to Halleck whether Sigel could not get to Staunton to stop supplies coming from there to Lee.[21] I asked at once that Sigel might be relieved, and some one else put in his place. Hunter's name was suggested, and I heartily approved.[22] Further news from Butler reported him driven from Drury's Bluff, but still in possession of the Petersburg road. Banks had been defeated in Louisiana, relieved, and Canby put in his place. This change of commander was not on my suggestion.[23] All this news was very discouraging. All of it must have been known by the enemy before it was by me. In fact, the good news (for the enemy) must have been known to him at the moment I thought he was in despair, and his anguish had been already relieved when we were enjoying his supposed discomfiture. But this was no time for repining. I immediately gave orders for a movement by the left flank, on towards Richmond, to commence on the night of the 19th. I also asked Halleck to secure the co-operation of the navy in changing our base of supplies from Fredericksburg to Port Royal, on the Rappahannock.[24]

[20] For the entire text of this telegram, see *PUSG,* 10:451–452.

[21] For USG's May 17, 1864, telegram to Halleck regarding Sigel's proposed move on Staunton, VA, see ibid., 10:459n–460n.

[22] Halleck first suggested replacing Sigel with Hunter in his May 17, 1864, response to USG regarding the proposed move on Staunton. He suggested it again on May 18, and USG approved the change on May 19. Ibid., 10:459n–460n, 470n.

[23] On May 16, 1864, USG suggested to Halleck that Banks be removed from his command. Ibid., 10:452.

[24] For USG's May 19, 1864, telegram to Halleck, see ibid., 10:465n.

Up to this time I had received no reinforcements, except six thousand raw troops under Brigadier-General Robert O. Tyler,[25] just arrived. They had not yet joined their command, Hancock's corps, but were on our right. This corps had been brought to the rear of the centre, ready to move in any direction. Lee, probably suspecting some move on my part, and seeing our right entirely abandoned, moved Ewell's corps about five o'clock in the afternoon, with Early's as a reserve, to attack us in that quarter. Tyler had come up from Fredericksburg, and had been halted on the road to the right of our line, near Kitching's[26] brigade of Warren's corps. Tyler received the attack with his raw troops, and they maintained their position, until reinforced, in a manner worthy of veterans.

Hancock was in a position to reinforce speedily, and was the soldier to do it without waiting to make dispositions. Birney was thrown to Tyler's right and Crawford to his left, with Gibbon as a reserve; and Ewell was whirled back speedily and with heavy loss.[27]

Warren had been ordered to get on Ewell's flank and in his rear, to cut him off from his intrenchments. But his efforts were so feeble that under the cover of night Ewell got back with only the loss of a few hundred prisoners, besides his killed and wounded. The army being engaged until after dark, I rescinded the order for the march by our left flank that night.

As soon as it was discovered that the enemy were coming out to attack, I naturally supposed they would detach a force to destroy our trains. The withdrawal of Hancock from the right uncovered one road from Spottsylvania to Fredericksburg over which trains drew our supplies. This was guarded by a division of colored troops, commanded by General Ferrero,[28] belonging to

[25] Robert O. Tyler (1831–1874) was born in New York and moved to Connecticut in 1839. He graduated from the USMA in 1853 and was a captain in the regular army and an assistant quartermaster at the start of the Civil War. He rose to brigadier general by 1862 and in May 1864 commanded the 4th Div., 2nd Corps, Army of the Potomac. *CWHC,* 539.

[26] John H. Kitching (1838–1865) was born in New York and enlisted in the 1st New York Cav. in 1861. He rose to colonel in 1863. In Jan. 1865, Kitching died of wounds received in the Battle of Cedar Creek. Ibid., 336.

[27] Ewell reported that approximately 900 of his men were killed, missing, or wounded in the May 19, 1864, Battle of Harris Farm. *OR,* I, 36(I), 1073; Rhea, *To the North Anna,* 185.

[28] Edward Ferrero (1831–1899) was born in Spain and moved to New York, where he served as dance instructor at the USMA. He was commissioned colonel of the 51st New York Inf. in Oct. 1861. Ferrero was promoted to brigadier general in 1863 but the commission was revoked after his involvement in the July 30, 1864, disaster at the Battle of the Crater at Petersburg, VA. *CWHC,* 233.

Burnside's corps. Ferrero was therefore promptly notified, and ordered to throw his cavalry pickets out to the south and be prepared to meet the enemy if he should come; if he had to retreat to do so towards Fredericksburg.[29] The enemy did detach as expected, and captured twenty-five or thirty wagons which, however, were soon retaken.

In consequence of the disasters that had befallen us in the past few days, Lee could be reinforced largely, and I had no doubt he would be. Beauregard had come up from the south with troops to guard the Confederate capital when it was in danger. Butler being driven back, most of the troops could be sent to Lee. Hoke[30] was no longer needed in North Carolina; and Sigel's troops having gone back to Cedar Creek, whipped, many troops could be spared from the valley.

The Wilderness and Spottsylvania battles convinced me that we had more artillery than could ever be brought into action at any one time. It occupied much of the road in marching, and taxed the trains in bringing up forage. Artillery is very useful when it can be brought into action, but it is a very burdensome luxury where it cannot be used. Before leaving Spottsylvania, therefore, I sent back to the defences of Washington over one hundred pieces of artillery, with the horses and caissons.[31] This relieved the roads over which we were to march of more than two hundred six-horse teams, and still left us more artillery than could be advantageously used. In fact, before reaching the James River I again reduced the artillery with the army largely.[32]

I believed that, if one corps of the army was exposed on the road to Richmond, and at a distance from the main army, Lee would endeavor to attack the exposed corps before reinforcements could come up; in which case the main army could follow Lee up and attack him before he had time to intrench. So I issued the following orders:

[29] For USG's May 19, 1864, orders to Ferrero, see *PUSG*, 10:467–468.

[30] Robert F. Hoke (1837–1912) was born in North Carolina and enlisted as a private in the 1st North Carolina Inf. in Apr. 1861. In May 1864, Hoke was a major general and commanded a division in the Dept. of North Carolina and Southern Virginia. *CWHC*, 300–301.

[31] On May 14, 1864, USG complained that the heavy rains had "made it almost impossible to move trains or Artillery." On May 16, Rawlins instructed Burnside and Meade to send reserve artillery back to Belle Plain, VA. *PUSG*, 10:445, 457*n*.

[32] On June 1, 1864, USG informed Brig. Gen. J. J. Abercrombie that forty pieces of artillery were being shipped to Washington, DC. Ibid., 11:4.

Near Spottsylvania C. H., Va.,⎫
*May* 18, 1864.⎭

Major-General Meade,
Commanding Army of the Potomac.

Before daylight to-morrow morning I propose to draw Hancock and Burnside from the position they now hold, and put Burnside to the left of Wright. Wright and Burnside should then force their way up as close to the enemy as they can get without a general engagement, or with a general engagement if the enemy will come out of their works to fight, and intrench. Hancock should march and take up a position as if in support of the two left corps. To-morrow night, at twelve or one o'clock, he will be moved south-east with all his force and as much cavalry as can be given to him, to get as far towards Richmond on the line of the Fredericksburg Railroad as he can make, fighting the enemy in whatever force he can find him. If the enemy make a general move to meet this, they will be followed by the other three corps of the army, and attacked, if possible, before time is given to intrench.

Suitable directions will at once be given for all trains and surplus artillery to conform to this movement.

U. S. GRANT.

On the 20th, Lee showing no signs of coming out of his lines, orders were renewed for a left-flank movement, to commence after night.

# 54

## Movement by the Left Flank—Battle of North Anna—An Incident of the March—Moving on Richmond—South of the Pamunkey— Position of the National Army

Wᴇ ᴡᴇʀᴇ ɴᴏᴡ to operate in a different country from any we had before seen in Virginia. The roads were wide and good, and the country well cultivated. No men were seen except those bearing arms, even the black man having been sent away. The country, however, was new to us, and we had neither guides nor maps to tell us where the roads were, or where they led to. Engineer and staff officers were put to the dangerous duty of supplying the place of both maps and guides. By reconnoitring they were enabled to locate the roads in the vicinity of each army corps. Our course was south, and we took all roads leading in that direction which would not separate the army too widely.

Hancock who had the lead had marched easterly to Guiney's Station,[1] on the Fredericksburg Railroad, thence southerly to Bowling Green and Milford. He was at Milford by the night of the 21st. Here he met a detachment of Pickett's[2] division coming from Richmond to reinforce Lee. They were speedily driven

---

[1] Now known as Guinea, VA, Guiney's Station was approximately ten miles south of Fredericksburg, VA. George B. Davis et al., *The Official Military Atlas of the Civil War* (New York: Fairfax Press, 1983), plate 74, map 1; Marshall Wingfield, *A History of Caroline County, Virginia* (Richmond: Trevvet Christian, 1924), 290.

[2] George E. Pickett (1825–1875) was born in Virginia, graduated from the USMA in 1846, and fought in the Mexican-American War. He resigned from the U.S. Army and joined the Confederate Army as a major in 1861, rose to major general by 1862, and became famous for his involvement in what became known as "Pickett's Charge" on July 3, 1863, at the Battle of Gettysburg. *CWHC,* 428–429; Carol Reardon, *Pickett's Charge in History and Memory* (Chapel Hill: University of North Carolina Press, 1997), 49, 62–63, 80–83.

away, and several hundred captured.[3] Warren followed on the morning of the 21st, and reached Guiney's Station that night without molestation. Burnside and Wright were retained at Spottsylvania to keep up the appearance of an intended assault, and to hold Lee, if possible, while Hancock and Warren should get start enough to interpose between him and Richmond.

Lee had now a superb opportunity to take the initiative either by attacking Wright and Burnside alone, or by following by the Telegraph Road and striking Hancock's and Warren's corps, or even Hancock's alone, before reinforcements could come up. But he did not avail himself of either opportunity. He seemed really to be misled as to my designs; but moved by his interior line—the Telegraph Road—to make sure of keeping between his capital and the Army of the Potomac. He never again had such an opportunity of dealing a heavy blow.

The evening of the 21st Burnside, 9th corps, moved out followed by Wright, 6th corps. Burnside was to take the Telegraph Road; but finding Stanard's Ford, over the Po,[4] fortified and guarded, he turned east to the road taken by Hancock and Warren without an attempt to dislodge the enemy. The night of the 21st I had my headquarters near the 6th corps, at Guiney's Station, and the enemy's cavalry was between us and Hancock. There was a slight attack on Burnside's and Wright's corps as they moved out of their lines; but it was easily repulsed.[5] The object probably was only to make sure that we were not leaving a force to follow upon the rear of the Confederates.

By the morning of the 22d Burnside and Wright were at Guiney's Station. Hancock's corps had now been marching and fighting continuously for several days, not having had rest even at night much of the time. They were, therefore, permitted to rest during the 22d. But Warren was pushed to Harris's Store, directly west of Milford, and connected with it by a good road, and Burnside was sent to New Bethel Church.[6] Wright's corps was still back at Guiney's Station.

---

[3] U.S. forces captured between sixty-six and seventy-five Confederates. Gordon C. Rhea, *To the North Anna River: Grant and Lee, May 13–25, 1864* (Baton Rouge: Louisiana State University Press, 2000), 227.

[4] Telegraph Road crossed the Po River at a place called Stanard's Mill, approximately four miles from the Richmond, Fredericksburg, and Potomac Railroad. Ibid., 108 (map), 124.

[5] Wright's men who were sent to investigate the sound of enemy gunfire emptied their repeating rifles into the woods, creating the impression of an attack. Ibid., 256.

[6] Harris's Store was about six miles from Milford, VA. New Bethel Church was just over a mile northwest of Milford. Ibid., 263 (map).

I issued the following order for the movement of the troops the next day:

NEW BETHEL, VA.,
*May* 22, 1864.

MAJOR-GENERAL MEADE,
Commanding Army of the Potomac.

Direct corps commanders to hold their troops in readiness to march at five A.M. to-morrow. At that hour each command will send out cavalry and infantry on all roads to their front leading south, and ascertain, if possible, where the enemy is. If beyond the South Anna, the 5th and 6th corps will march to the forks of the road, where one branch leads to Beaver Dam Station,[7] the other to Jericho Bridge,[8] then south by roads reaching the Anna, as near to and east of Hawkins Creek as they can be found.

The 2d corps will move to Chesterfield Ford.[9] The 9th corps will be directed to move at the same time to Jericho Bridge. The map only shows two roads for the four corps to march upon, but, no doubt, by the use of plantation roads, and pressing in guides, others can be found, to give one for each corps.

The troops will follow their respective reconnoitring parties. The trains will be moved at the same time to Milford Station.

Headquarters will follow the 9th corps.

U. S. GRANT,
Lieut.-General.

Warren's corps was moved from Harris's Store to Jericho Ford, Wright's following. Warren arrived at the ford early in the afternoon, and by five o'clock effected a crossing under the protection of sharpshooters. The men had to wade in water up to their waists. As soon as enough troops were over to guard the

[7] Beaver Dam Station was about six miles southwest of Chilesburg, VA, on the Virginia Central Railroad. *PUSG,* 10:378 (map).

[8] There was no Jericho Bridge, but, about three miles west of the Richmond, Fredericksburg and Potomac Railroad, there was a ford over the North Anna River at Jericho Mills. Rhea, *To the North Anna,* 263 (map), 283.

[9] Chesterfield Ford was listed on maps used by U.S. troops, but there was no such place. Chesterfield Bridge, which crossed the North Anna River approximately one-half a mile from the Richmond, Fredericksburg and Potomac Railroad, became the objective. Ibid., 283, 295 (map), 302.

ford, pontoons were laid and the artillery and the rest of the troops crossed. The line formed was almost perpendicular to the course of the river—Crawford on the left, next to the river, Griffin in the centre, and Cutler on the right. Lee was found intrenched along the front of their line. The whole of Hill's corps was sent against Warren's right before it had got in position. A brigade of Cutler's division was driven back, the enemy following, but assistance coming up the enemy was in turn driven back into his trenches with heavy loss in killed and wounded, with about five hundred prisoners left in our hands. By night Wright's corps was up ready to reinforce Warren.

On the 23d Hancock's corps was moved to the wooden bridge which spans the North Anna River just west of where the Fredericksburg Railroad crosses.[10] It was near night when the troops arrived. They found the bridge guarded, with troops intrenched, on the north side. Hancock sent two brigades, Egan's[11] and Pierce's,[12] to the right and left, and when properly disposed they charged simultaneously. The bridge was carried quickly, the enemy retreating over it so hastily that many were shoved into the river, and some of them were drowned. Several hundred prisoners were captured.[13] The hour was so late that Hancock did not cross until next morning.

Burnside's corps was moved by a middle road running between those described above, and which strikes the North Anna at Ox Ford,[14] midway between Telegraph Road and Jericho Ford. The hour of its arrival was too late to cross that night.

On the 24th Hancock's corps crossed to the south side of the river without opposition, and formed line facing nearly west. The railroad in rear was taken possession of and destroyed as far as possible. Wright's corps crossed at Jericho

[10] This was the Chesterfield Bridge. Ibid., 295, 302.

[11] Thomas W. Egan (1834–1887) was born in New York and rose from the rank of private in 1861 to colonel by 1862. At the engagement at Chesterfield Bridge, he commanded the 1st Brigade, 2nd Div., 2nd Corps. He was twice wounded in 1864 in battles around Petersburg, VA. After the war, he was deputy collector of the New York Customs House from 1866 to 1881. *CWHC,* 223–224.

[12] Byron R. Pierce (1829–1924) was born in New York and was a dentist before the war. He rose to colonel by Jan. 1863. He was wounded in his left hand and right arm at Chancellorsville, VA, and lost his left leg at Gettysburg. At the engagement at Chesterfield Bridge, he commanded the 2nd Brigade, 3rd Div., 2nd Corps. After the war, he was superintendent of the U.S. Soldiers' Home at Grand Rapids, MI. Ibid., 429.

[13] Estimates of Confederates captured ranged from 55 to 110. Rhea, *To the North Anna,* 303.

[14] Ox Ford was about two miles from the Richmond, Fredericksburg and Potomac Railroad. Ibid., 295 (map).

early the same day, and took position to the right of Warren's corps, extending south of the Virginia Central Railroad. This road was torn up for a considerable distance to the rear (west), the ties burned, and the rails bent and twisted by heating them over the burning ties. It was found, however, that Burnside's corps could not cross at Ox Ford. Lee had taken a position with his centre on the river at this point, with the two wings thrown back, his line making an acute angle where it overlooked the river.

Before the exact position of the whole of Lee's line was accurately known, I directed Hancock and Warren each to send a brigade to Ox Ford by the south side of the river.[15] They found the enemy too strong to justify a serious attack. A third ford was found between Ox Ford and Jericho.[16] Burnside was directed to cross a division over this ford, and to send one division to Hancock.[17] Crittenden was crossed by this newly-discovered ford, and formed up the river to connect with Crawford's left. Potter joined Hancock by way of the wooden bridge. Crittenden had a severe engagement with some of Hill's corps on his crossing the river, and lost heavily.[18] When joined to Warren's corps he was no further molested. Burnside still guarded Ox Ford from the north side.

Lee now had his entire army south of the North Anna. Our lines covered his front, with the six miles separating the two wings guarded by but a single division.[19] To get from one wing to the other the river would have to be crossed twice. Lee could reinforce any part of his line from all points of it in a very short march; or could concentrate the whole of it wherever he might choose to assault. We were, for the time, practically two armies besieging.

Lee had been reinforced, and was being reinforced, largely. About this time the very troops whose coming I had predicted, had arrived or were coming in. Pickett with a full division from Richmond was up; Hoke from North Carolina had come with a brigade; and Breckinridge was there: in all probably not less than fifteen thousand men. But he did not attempt to drive us from the field.

[15] For USG's May 23, 1864, instructions to Meade regarding Hancock and Warren, see *PUSG*, 10:482–483.

[16] The ford was at Quarles' Mill, just over three miles west of the Richmond, Fredericksburg and Potomac Railroad. Ibid., 10:485; Rhea, *To the North Anna*, 337, 357 (map).

[17] Potter's 2nd Div., 9th Corps, was temporarily assigned to Hancock's command. Rhea, *To the North Anna*, 353. For USG's May 24, 1864, correspondence with Burnside about the crossing, see *PUSG*, 10:484–485, 485n–487n.

[18] U.S. forces lost 450 men and 75 captured. Confederate losses were 75 men. Rhea, *To the North Anna*, 342.

[19] USG referred to Willcox's division. Ibid., 327 (map), 353.

On the 22d or 23d I received dispatches from Washington saying that Sherman had taken Kingston, crossed the Etowah River and was advancing into Georgia.[20]

I was seated at the time on the porch of a fine plantation house waiting for Burnside's corps to pass. Meade and his staff, besides my own staff, were with me. The lady of the house, a Mrs. Tyler, and an elderly lady, were present.[21] Burnside seeing us, came up on the porch, his big spurs and saber rattling as he walked. He touched his hat politely to the ladies, and remarked that he supposed they had never seen so many "live Yankees" before in their lives. The elderly lady spoke up promptly saying, "Oh yes, I have; many more." "Where?" said Burnside. "In Richmond." Prisoners, of course, was understood.

I read my dispatch aloud, when it was received. This threw the younger lady into tears. I found the information she had received (and I suppose it was the information generally in circulation through the South) was that Lee was driving us from the State in the most demoralized condition, and that in the South-west our troops were but little better than prisoners of war. Seeing our troops moving south was ocular proof that a part of her information was incorrect, and she asked me if my news from Sherman was true. I assured her that there was no doubt about it. I left a guard to protect the house from intrusion until the troops should have all passed, and assured her that if her husband was in hiding she could bring him in and he should be protected also. But I presume he was in the Confederate army.[22]

On the 25th I gave orders, through Halleck, to Hunter, who had relieved Sigel, to move up the Valley of Virginia, cross over the Blue Ridge to Charlottesville and go as far as Lynchburg if possible, living upon the country and cutting the railroads and canal as he went. After doing this he could find his way back to his base, or join me.

---

[20] On May 21, 1864, Sherman wrote Halleck from Kingston, GA, informing him that his troops were crossing the Etowah River. *OR*, I, 38(IV), 274.

[21] This home, known as Blenheim, was on the road to Downer's Bridge in Caroline County, VA. "Mrs. Tyler" was probably Julia Magruder Tyler (c.1837–c.1873). Rhea, *To the North Anna*, 277–278; "Tyler Family of Essex, Spotsylvania and Caroline Counties," *William and Mary Quarterly* 19 (1911): 285.

[22] George Tyler (c.1817–c.1889) owned Blenheim and served in the Virginia legislature during the Civil War. In Horace Porter's telling of the incident, Mrs. Tyler stated that her husband was a colonel in the Confederate Army serving under Joseph E. Johnston. Horace Porter, *Campaigning with Grant* (New York: Century, 1897), 137–138; Lyon G. Tyler, ed., *Men of Mark in Virginia*, vol. 1 (Washington, DC: Men of Mark Publishing, 1906), 66.

On the same day news was received that Lee was falling back on Richmond. This proved not to be true.[23] But we could do nothing where we were unless Lee would assume the offensive. I determined, therefore, to draw out of our present position and make one more effort to get between him and Richmond. I had no expectation now, however, of succeeding in this; but I did expect to hold him far enough west to enable me to reach the James River high up. Sheridan was now again with the Army of the Potomac.

On the 26th I informed the government at Washington of the position of the two armies; of the reinforcements the enemy had received; of the move I proposed to make;* and directed that our base of supplies should be shifted

*QUARLES' MILLS, VA., *May* 26, 1864.

MAJOR-GENERAL HALLECK,
Washington, D. C.

The relative position of the two armies is now as follows: Lee's right rests on a swamp east of the Richmond and Fredericksburg road and south of the North Anna, his centre on the river at Ox Ford, and his left at Little River with the crossings of Little River guarded as far up as we have gone. Hancock with his corps and one division of the 9th corps crossed at Chesterfield Ford and covers the right wing of Lee's army. One division of the 9th corps is on the north bank of the Anna at Ox Ford, with bridges above and below at points nearest to it where both banks are held by us, so that it could reinforce either wing of our army with equal facility. The 5th and 6th corps with one division of the 9th corps run from the south bank of the Anna from a short distance above Ox Ford to Little River, and parallel with and near to the enemy.

To make a direct attack from either wing would cause a slaughter of our men that even success would not justify. To turn the enemy by his right, between the two Annas, is impossible on account of the swamp upon which his right rests. To turn him by the left leaves Little River, New Found River and South Anna River, all of them streams presenting considerable obstacles to the movement of our army, to be crossed. I have determined therefore to turn the enemy's right by crossing at or near Hanover Town.[24] This crosses all three streams at once, and leaves us still where we can draw supplies.

[23] On May 24, 1864, USG wrote Halleck that African Americans who were crossing U.S. lines reported that Lee was falling back toward Richmond, VA. *PUSG*, 10:483.

[24] Hanovertown, VA, was approximately ten miles northeast of Mechanicsville, VA, on the Pamunkey River. Ibid., 10:379 (map).

to White House, on the Pamunkey. The wagon train and guards moved directly from Port Royal to White House. Supplies moved around by water, guarded by the navy. Orders had previously been sent, through Halleck, for Butler to send Smith's corps to White House.[25] This order was repeated on the 25th, with directions that they should be landed on the north side of the Pamunkey, and marched until they joined the Army of the Potomac.

---

During the last night the teams and artillery not in position, belonging to the right wing of our army, and one division of that wing were quietly withdrawn to the north bank of the river and moved down to the rear of the left. As soon as it is dark this division with most of the cavalry will commence a forced march for Hanover Town to seize and hold the crossings. The balance of the right wing will withdraw at the same hour, and follow as rapidly as possible. The left wing will also withdraw from the south bank of the river to-night and follow in rear of the right wing.

Lee's army is really whipped. The prisoners we now take show it, and the action of his army shows it unmistakably. A battle with them outside of intrenchments cannot be had. Our men feel that they have gained the *morale* over the enemy, and attack him with confidence. I may be mistaken, but I feel that our success over Lee's army is already assured. The promptness and rapidity with which you have forwarded reinforcements has contributed largely to the feeling of confidence inspired in our men, and to break down that of the enemy.

We are destroying all the rails we can on the Central and Fredericksburg roads. I want to leave a gap on the roads north of Richmond so big that to get a single track they will have to import rail from elsewhere.

Even if a crossing is not effected at Hanover Town it will probably be necessary for us to move on down the Pamunkey until a crossing is effected. I think it advisable therefore to change our base of supplies from Port Royal to the White House. I wish you would direct this change at once, and also direct Smith to put the railroad bridge there in condition for crossing troops and artillery and leave men to hold it.

U. S. GRANT,
Lieut.-General.

[25] For USG's May 25, 1864, orders regarding Butler, see ibid., 10:487.

It was a delicate move to get the right wing of the Army of the Potomac from its position south of the North Anna in the presence of the enemy. To accomplish it, I issued the following order:

QUARLES' MILLS, VA.,
*May 25, 1864.*

MAJOR-GENERAL MEADE,
Commanding A. P.

Direct Generals Warren and Wright to withdraw all their teams and artillery, not in position, to the north side of the river to-morrow. Send that belonging to General Wright's corps as far on the road to Hanover Town as it can go, without attracting attention to the fact. Send with it Wright's best division or division under his ablest commander. Have their places filled up in the line so if possible the enemy will not notice their withdrawal. Send the cavalry to-morrow afternoon, or as much of it as you may deem necessary, to watch and seize, if they can, Little-page's Bridge and Taylor's Ford,[26] and to remain on one or other side of the river at these points until the infantry and artillery all pass. As soon as it is dark to-morrow night start the division which you withdraw first from Wright's corps to make a forced march to Hanover Town, taking with them no teams to impede their march. At the same time this division starts commence withdrawing all of the 5th and 6th corps from the south side of the river, and march them for the same place. The two divisions of the 9th corps not now with Hancock, may be moved down the north bank of the river where they will be handy to support Hancock if necessary, or will be that much on their road to follow the 5th and 6th corps.[27] Hancock should hold his command in readiness to follow as soon as the way is clear for him. To-morrow it will leave nothing for him to do, but as

---

[26] Littlepage Bridge and Taylor's Ford were river crossings near Hanovertown on the Pamunkey River. Littlepage Bridge itself had been destroyed by U.S. troops in early July 1863, but the site remained an important river crossing. Gordon C. Rhea, *Cold Harbor: Grant and Lee, May 26–June 3, 1864* (Baton Rouge: Louisiana State University Press, 2002), 23, 32, 33 (map); *OR*, I, 27(II), 837–838.

[27] On May 24, 1864, Potter's 2nd Div. was temporarily under the command of Hancock. Crittenden's 1st Div. had been temporarily placed under the command of Warren, while Willcox's 3rd Div. continued to report to Burnside. Ferrero's 4th Div., which had been assigned to guard supply and communication lines, had been directed to report to Brig. Gen. John J. Abercrombie on May 20. *PUSG*, 10:474*n*; Rhea, *To the North Anna*, 353.

soon as he can he should get all his teams and spare artillery on the road or roads which he will have to take. As soon as the troops reach Hanover Town they should get possession of all the crossings they can in that neighborhood. I think it would be well to make a heavy cavalry demonstration on the enemy's left, to-morrow afternoon, also.

U. S. GRANT,

Lieut.-General.

Wilson's division of cavalry was brought up from the left and moved by our right south to Little River. Here he manœuvred to give the impression that we were going to attack the left flank of Lee's army.

Under cover of night our right wing was withdrawn to the north side of the river, Lee being completely deceived by Wilson's feint. On the afternoon of the 26th Sheridan moved, sending Gregg's and Torbert's cavalry to Taylor's and Littlepage's fords towards Hanover. As soon as it was dark both divisions moved quietly to Hanover Ferry, leaving small guards behind to keep up the impression that crossings were to be attempted in the morning. Sheridan was followed by a division of infantry under General Russell.[28] On the morning of the 27th the crossing was effected with but little loss, the enemy losing thirty or forty, taken prisoners.[29] Thus a position was secured south of the Pamunkey.

Russell stopped at the crossing while the cavalry pushed on to Hanover Town. Here Barringer's,[30] formerly Gordon's,[31] brigade of rebel cavalry was encountered, but it was speedily driven away.

---

[28] David A. Russell (1820–1864) was born in New York and graduated from the USMA in 1845. He fought in the Mexican-American War and was stationed in Oregon in 1861. He was brevetted brigadier general in May 1864. Russell was killed in action at Opequon, VA, in Sept. that year. *CWHC*, 466.

[29] On May 27, 1864, Sheridan reported that Torbert's troops had captured seventy-six Confederate cavalrymen near Hanover Court House, VA. *OR*, I, 36(I), 782.

[30] Rufus Barringer (1821–1895) was born in North Carolina and practiced law before receiving a commission as a first lieutenant in the 1st North Carolina Cav. in Apr. 1861. He was promoted to lieutenant colonel in 1863. He was captured on Apr. 3, 1865, and met Lincoln while being held as a prisoner of war at City Point, VA. *CWHC*, 118.

[31] John B. Gordon (1832–1904) was born in Georgia and worked as a coal mine operator before being commissioned a captain in the 6th Alabama Inf. in Apr. 1861. He rose through the ranks to become a brigadier general and division commander in the 2nd Corps, Army of Northern Virginia, in May 1864. After the war, Gordon served as a U.S. senator from Georgia from 1873 to 1880 and from 1891 to 1897 and was commander in chief of the United Confederate Veterans from 1890 to 1903. Ibid., 260.

Warren's and Wright's corps were moved by the rear of Burnside's and Hancock's corps. When out of the way these latter corps followed, leaving pickets confronting the enemy. Wilson's cavalry followed last, watching all the fords until everything had recrossed; then taking up the pontoons and destroying other bridges, became the rear-guard.

Two roads were traversed by the troops in this move. The one nearest to and north of the North Anna and Pamunkey was taken by Wright, followed by Hancock. Warren, followed by Burnside, moved by a road farther north, and longer.[32] The trains moved by a road still farther north, and had to travel a still greater distance. All the troops that had crossed the Pamunkey on the morning of the 27th remained quiet during the rest of the day, while the troops north of that stream marched to reach the crossing that had been secured for them.

Lee had evidently been deceived by our movement from North Anna; for on the morning of the 27th he telegraphed to Richmond: "Enemy crossed to north side, and cavalry and infantry crossed at Hanover Town."[33] The troops that had then crossed left his front the night of the 25th.

The country we were now in was a difficult one to move troops over. The streams were numerous, deep and sluggish, sometimes spreading out into swamps grown up with impenetrable growths of trees and underbrush. The banks were generally low and marshy, making the streams difficult to approach except where there were roads and bridges.

Hanover Town is about twenty miles from Richmond. There are two roads leading there; the most direct and shortest one crossing the Chickahominy at Meadow Bridge, near the Virginia Central Railroad, the second going by New and Old Cold Harbor.[34] A few miles out from Hanover Town there is a third

---

[32] Wright and Hancock traveled a part of the way along Ridge Road. Warren and Burnside traveled a route that utilized several different lanes across the countryside. Rhea, *Cold Harbor,* 40 (map).

[33] The text of Lee's May 27, 1864, telegram to Confederate secretary of war James Seddon that USG paraphrased read, "The enemy retired to the north side of the North Anna last night. A portion of his force is still visible on the north bank, but cavalry and infantry have crossed at Hanovertown." *OR,* I, 36(III), 836.

[34] New Cold Harbor was about five miles southeast of Mechanicsville. Old Cold Harbor was about one and one-half miles northeast of New Cold Harbor. The area was called Cool Arbor, Coal Harbor, and Cold Harbor by U.S. forces. The name Cool Arbor may derive from a summer retreat frequented by residents of Richmond. The name Cold Harbor may have come from an inn in the area owned by Isaac Burnett. Robert C. Eden, *The Sword and Gun: A History of the 37th Wisconsin Volunteer Infantry from Its First Organization to Its Final Muster Out* (Madison, WI: Atwood and Rublee, 1865), 15; Rhea, *Cold Harbor,* 206 (map); Mitchell Yockelson, *Grant: Savior of the Union* (Nashville, TN: Thomas Nelson, 2012), 135.

road by way of Mechanicsville to Richmond. New Cold Harbor was important to us because while there we both covered the roads back to White House
(where our supplies came from), and the roads south-east over which we would
have to pass to get to the James River below the Richmond defences.

On the morning of the 28th the army made an early start, and by noon all
had crossed except Burnside's corps. This was left on the north side temporarily
to guard the large wagon train. A line was at once formed extending south
from the river, Wright's corps on the right, Hancock's in the centre, and Warren's
on the left, ready to meet the enemy if he should come.

At the same time Sheridan was directed to reconnoitre towards Mechanicsville to find Lee's position. At Hawes' Shop, just where the middle road leaves
the direct road to Richmond, he encountered the Confederate cavalry dismounted and partially intrenched.[35] Gregg attacked with his division, but was
unable to move the enemy. In the evening Custer came up with a brigade. The
attack was now renewed, the cavalry dismounting and charging as infantry.
This time the assault was successful, both sides losing a considerable number of
men. But our troops had to bury the dead, and found that more Confederate
than Union soldiers had been killed.[36] The position was easily held, because
our infantry was near.

On the 29th a reconnoissance was made in force, to find the position of
Lee. Wright's corps pushed to Hanover Court House. Hancock's corps pushed
toward Totopotomoy Creek; Warren's corps to the left on the Shady Grove
Church Road, while Burnside was held in reserve. Our advance was pushed
forward three miles on the left with but little fighting. There was now an appearance of a movement past our left flank, and Sheridan was sent to meet it.

On the 30th Hancock moved to the Totopotomoy, where he found the
enemy strongly fortified. Wright was moved to the right of Hancock's corps,
and Burnside was brought forward and crossed, taking position to the left of
Hancock. Warren moved up near Huntley Corners on the Shady Grove Church
Road.[37] There was some skirmishing along the centre, and in the evening Early
attacked Warren with some vigor, driving him back at first, and threatening to
turn our left flank. As the best means of reinforcing the left, Hancock was

[35] Five roads met at the settlement of Haw's Shop, VA, which was about five and one-half
miles from the Virginia Central Railroad and three miles from the Pamunkey River. Two of
the five roads led to Richmond. Rhea, *Cold Harbor*, 40 (map), 43–44.

[36] Casualty estimates were 365 U.S. troops and 378 Confederate troops. Ibid., 87.

[37] Hundley's Corner was about three miles northeast of Mechanicsville on Shady Grove
Road. Ibid., 96 (map).

ordered to attack in his front. He carried and held the rifle-pits. While this was going on Warren got his men up, repulsed Early, and drove him more than a mile.

On this day I wrote to Halleck ordering all the pontoons in Washington to be sent to City Point. In the evening news was received of the arrival of Smith with his corps at White House. I notified Meade, in writing, as follows:

> NEAR HAWES' SHOP, VA.,
> 6.40 P.M., *May* 30, 1864.

MAJOR-GENERAL MEADE,
Commanding A. P.

General Smith will debark his force at the White House to-night and start up the south bank of the Pamunkey at an early hour, probably at 3 A.M. in the morning. It is not improbable that the enemy, being aware of Smith's movement, will be feeling to get on our left flank for the purpose of cutting him off, or by a dash to crush him and get back before we are aware of it. Sheridan ought to be notified to watch the enemy's movements well out towards Cold Harbor, and also on the Mechanicsville road. Wright should be got well massed on Hancock's right, so that, if it becomes necessary, he can take the place of the latter readily whilst troops are being thrown east of the Totopotomoy if necessary.

I want Sheridan to send a cavalry force of at least half a brigade, if not a whole brigade, at 5 A.M. in the morning, to communicate with Smith and to return with him. I will send orders for Smith by the messenger you send to Sheridan with his orders.

> U. S. GRANT.

I also notified Smith of his danger, and the precautions that would be taken to protect him.[38]

The night of the 30th Lee's position was substantially from Atlee's Station on the Virginia Central Railroad south and east to the vicinity of Cold Harbor. Ours was: The left of Warren's corps was on the Shady Grove Road, extending to the Mechanicsville Road and about three miles south of the Totopotomoy. Burnside to his right, then Hancock, and Wright on the extreme right, extending towards Hanover Court House, six miles south-east of it. Sheridan with two divisions of cavalry was watching our left front towards Cold Harbor.

---

[38] For USG's May 30, 1864, letter to Maj. Gen. William F. Smith, see *PUSG,* 10:498.

Wilson with his division on our right was sent to get on the Virginia Central Railroad and destroy it as far back as possible. He got possession of Hanover Court House the next day after a skirmish with Young's[39] cavalry brigade. The enemy attacked Sheridan's pickets, but reinforcements were sent up and the attack was speedily repulsed and the enemy followed some distance towards Cold Harbor.

---

[39] Pierce M. B. Young (1836–1896) was born in South Carolina and became a cadet at the Georgia Military Institute in 1857. He entered the Confederate Army as a second lieutenant in 1861 and rose to brigadier general by Sept. 1863. Young served as U.S. representative from South Carolina from 1868 to 1869 and from 1870 to 1875. He was U.S. consul general in St. Petersburg, Russia, from 1885 to 1887 and U.S. minister to Guatemala and Honduras from 1893 to 1896. *CWHC*, 585.

# 55

## Advance on Cold Harbor—An Anecdote of the War— Battle of Cold Harbor—Correspondence with Lee—Retrospective

O<small>N THE</small> 31ST Sheridan advanced to near Old Cold Harbor. He found it intrenched and occupied by cavalry and infantry. A hard fight ensued but the place was carried. The enemy well knew the importance of Cold Harbor to us, and seemed determined that we should not hold it. He returned with such a large force that Sheridan was about withdrawing without making any effort to hold it against such odds; but about the time he commenced the evacuation he received orders to hold the place at all hazards, until reinforcements could be sent to him. He speedily turned the rebel works to face against them and placed his men in position for defence. Night came on before the enemy was ready for assault.

Wright's corps was ordered early in the evening to march directly to Cold Harbor passing by the rear of the army. It was expected to arrive by daylight or before; but the night was dark and the distance great, so that it was nine o'clock the 1st of June before it reached its destination. Before the arrival of Wright the enemy had made two assaults on Sheridan, both of which were repulsed with heavy loss to the enemy.[1] Wright's corps coming up, there was no further assault on Cold Harbor.

Smith, who was coming up from White House, was also directed to march directly to Cold Harbor, and was expected early on the morning of the 1st of June; but by some blunder the order which reached Smith directed him to Newcastle instead of Cold Harbor. Through this blunder Smith did not reach his destination until three o'clock in the afternoon, and then with tired and

---

[1] Early on the morning of June 1, 1864, the 20th South Carolina Inf. attacked Sheridan's forces at Old Cold Harbor, losing eighty men during the assault. Gordon C. Rhea, *Cold Harbor: Grant and Lee, May 26–June 3, 1864* (Baton Rouge: Louisiana State University Press, 2002), 202.

worn-out men from their long and dusty march. He landed twelve thousand five hundred men from Butler's command, but a division was left at White House temporarily and many men had fallen out of ranks in their long march.[2]

Before the removal of Wright's corps from our right, after dark on the 31st, the two lines, Federal and Confederate, were so close together at that point that either side could detect directly any movement made by the other. Finding at daylight that Wright had left his front, Lee evidently divined that he had gone to our left. At all events, soon after light on the 1st of June Anderson, who commanded the corps on Lee's left, was seen moving along Warren's front. Warren was ordered to attack him vigorously in flank, while Wright was directed to move out and get on his front. Warren fired his artillery at the enemy; but lost so much time in making ready that the enemy got by, and at three o'clock he reported the enemy was strongly intrenched in his front, and besides his lines were so long that he had no mass of troops to move with. He seemed to have forgotten that lines in rear of an army hold themselves while their defenders are fighting in their front. Wright reconnoitred some distance to his front: but the enemy finding Old Cold Harbor already taken had halted and fortified some distance west.

By six o'clock in the afternoon Wright and Smith were ready to make an assault. In front of both the ground was clear for several hundred yards, and then became wooded. Both charged across this open space and into the wood, capturing and holding the first line of rifle-pits of the enemy, and also capturing seven or eight hundred prisoners.[3]

While this was going on, the enemy charged Warren three separate times with vigor, but were repulsed each time with loss. There was no officer more capable, nor one more prompt in acting, than Warren when the enemy forced him to it. There was also an attack upon Hancock's and Burnside's corps at the same time; but it was feeble and probably only intended to relieve Anderson who was being pressed by Wright and Smith.

During the night the enemy made frequent attacks with the view of dispossessing us of the important position we had gained, but without effecting their object.

---

[2] At 2:00 A.M. on June 1, 1864, Babcock sent W. F. Smith an order incorrectly stating that he should move his troops to New Castle Ferry. At 10:00 A.M., Dana wrote to Stanton and stated that Smith would connect with Wright "though a mistake in the terms of his order, in which the words New Castle were inserted instead of Cold Harbor, delayed his starting this morning." *OR*, I, 36(I), 84; *PUSG*, 10:499n.

[3] Confederate forces reported losses for their entire time at Cold Harbor and did not document losses specifically incurred on June 1, 1864. Rhea, *Cold Harbor*, 454n.

Hancock was moved from his place in line during the night and ordered to the left of Wright. I expected to take the offensive on the morning of the 2d, but the night was so dark, the heat and dust so excessive and the roads so intricate and hard to keep, that the head of column only reached Old Cold Harbor at six o'clock, but was in position at 7.30 A.M. Preparations were made for an attack in the afternoon, but did not take place until the next morning. Warren's corps was moved to the left to connect with Smith: Hancock's corps was got into position to the left of Wright's, and Burnside was moved to Bethesda Church in reserve. While Warren and Burnside were making these changes the enemy came out several times and attacked them, capturing several hundred prisoners.[4] The attacks were repulsed, but not followed up as they should have been. I was so annoyed at this that I directed Meade to instruct his corps commanders that they should seize all such opportunities when they occurred, and not wait for orders, all of our manœuvres being made for the very purpose of getting the enemy out of his cover.[5]

On this day Wilson returned from his raid upon the Virginia Central Railroad, having damaged it considerably. But, like ourselves, the rebels had become experts in repairing such damage. Sherman, in his memoirs, relates an anecdote of his campaign to Atlanta that well illustrates this point. The rebel cavalry lurking in his rear to burn bridges and obstruct his communications had become so disgusted at hearing trains go whistling by within a few hours after a bridge had been burned, that they proposed to try blowing up some of the tunnels. One of them said, "No use, boys, Old Sherman carries duplicate tunnels with him, and will replace them as fast as you can blow them up; better save your powder."[6]

Sheridan was engaged reconnoitring the banks of the Chickahominy, to find crossings and the condition of the roads. He reported favorably.[7]

During the night Lee moved his left up to make his line correspond to ours. His lines extended now from the Totopotomoy to New Cold Harbor. Mine from Bethesda Church by Old Cold Harbor to the Chickahominy, with a division of cavalry guarding our right. An assault was ordered for the 3d, to be made mainly by the corps of Hancock, Wright and Smith; but Warren and

[4] The Confederate Army reported capturing 500 troops on June 2, 1864, but U.S. Army reports put the number closer to 400. Ibid., 305.

[5] For USG's June 3, 1864, telegram to Meade, see *PUSG*, 11:14*n*.

[6] See William T. Sherman, *Memoirs of General William T. Sherman* (New York: D. Appleton, 1875), 2:151.

[7] For Sheridan's June 2, 1864, report, see *OR*, I, 36(III), 510.

Burnside were to support it by threatening Lee's left, and to attack with great earnestness if he should either reinforce more threatened points by drawing from that quarter or if a favorable opportunity should present itself.

The corps commanders were to select the points in their respective fronts where they would make their assaults. The move was to commence at half-past four in the morning. Hancock sent Barlow and Gibbon forward at the appointed hour, with Birney as a reserve. Barlow pushed forward with great vigor, under a heavy fire of both artillery and musketry, through thickets and swamps. Notwithstanding all the resistance of the enemy and the natural obstructions to overcome, he carried a position occupied by the enemy outside their main line where the road makes a deep cut through a bank affording as good a shelter for troops as if it had been made for that purpose. Three pieces of artillery had been captured here, and several hundred prisoners.[8] The guns were immediately turned against the men who had just been using them. No* assistance coming to him, he (Barlow) intrenched under fire and continued to hold his place. Gibbon was not so fortunate in his front. He found the ground over which he had to pass cut up with deep ravines, and a morass difficult to cross. But his men struggled on until some of them got up to the very parapet covering the enemy. Gibbon gained ground much nearer the enemy than that which he left, and here he intrenched and held fast.

Wright's corps moving in two lines captured the outer rifle-pits in their front, but accomplished nothing more. Smith's corps also gained the outer rifle-pits in its front. The ground over which this corps (18th) had to move was the most exposed of any over which charges were made. An open plain intervened between the contending forces at this point, which was exposed

*Near Cold Harbor, *June* 3, 1864, 7 a.m.

Major-General Meade,
Commanding A. P.

The moment it becomes certain that an assault cannot succeed, suspend the offensive; but when one does succeed, push it vigorously and if necessary pile in troops at the successful point from wherever they can be taken. I shall go to where you are in the course of an hour.

U. S. GRANT,
Lieut.-General.[9]

[8] Barlow reportedly captured 200 men during this assault on June 3, 1864. Ibid., I, 36(I), 369.

[9] For the broader context of this letter, see *PUSG,* 11:14n.

both to a direct and a cross fire. Smith, however, finding a ravine running towards his front, sufficiently deep to protect men in it from cross fire, and somewhat from a direct fire, put Martindale's[10] division in it, and with Brooks[11] supporting him on the left and Devens[12] on the right succeeded in gaining the outer—probably picket—rifle-pits.[13] Warren and Burnside also advanced and gained ground—which brought the whole army on one line.

This assault cost us heavily and probably without benefit to compensate:[14] but the enemy was not cheered by the occurrence sufficiently to induce him to take the offensive. In fact, nowhere after the battle of the Wilderness did Lee show any disposition to leave his defences far behind him.

Fighting was substantially over by half-past seven in the morning. At eleven o'clock I started to visit all the corps commanders to see for myself the different positions gained and to get their opinion of the practicability of doing anything more in their respective fronts.

Hancock gave the opinion that in his front the enemy was too strong to make any further assault promise success. Wright thought he could gain the lines of the enemy, but it would require the co-operation of Hancock's and Smith's corps. Smith thought a lodgment possible, but was not sanguine: Burnside thought something could be done in his front, but Warren differed. I concluded, therefore, to make no more assaults, and a little after twelve directed in the following letter that all offensive action should cease.

[10] John H. Martindale (1815–1881) was born in New York and graduated from the USMA in 1835. In Aug. 1861, he reentered the military as a brigadier general. During the Battle of Cold Harbor, he commanded the 2nd Div., 18th Corps, Army of the James. *CWHC,* 366–367.

[11] William T. H. Brooks (1821–1870) was born in Ohio and graduated from the USMA in 1841. He served in the Mexican-American War and in Sept. 1861 was promoted to brigadier general. During the Battle of Cold Harbor, he commanded the 1st Div., 18th Corps, Army of the James. Ibid., 145–146.

[12] Charles Devens (1820–1891) was born in Massachusetts and graduated from Harvard Law School in 1840. In 1861, he joined the Massachusetts Militia, in July was promoted to colonel of the 15th Massachusetts Inf., and in Apr. 1862 was promoted to brigadier general. During the Battle of Cold Harbor, he commanded the 3rd Div., 18th Corps, Army of the James. He served as U.S. attorney general from 1877 to 1881. Ibid., 208.

[13] On June 1, 1864, Devens captured the Confederate entrenchments of Wofford and Bryan at Cold Harbor. Rhea, *Cold Harbor,* 269.

[14] On June 3, 1864, 6,000 men from the Army of the Potomac were killed, missing, or wounded. In total, the Army of Northern Virginia lost 1,000–1,500 men. Ibid., 382.

COLD HARBOR, June 3, 1864.—12.30 P.M.

MAJOR-GENERAL MEADE,
Commanding A. P.

The opinion of corps commanders not being sanguine of success in case an assault is ordered, you may direct a suspension of farther advance for the present. Hold our most advanced positions and strengthen them. Whilst on the defensive our line may be contracted from the right if practicable. Reconnoissances should be made in front of every corps and advances made to advantageous positions by regular approaches. To aid the expedition under General Hunter it is necessary that we should detain all the army now with Lee until the former gets well on his way to Lynchburg. To do this effectually it will be better to keep the enemy out of the intrenchments of Richmond than to have them go back there.

Wright and Hancock should be ready to assault in case the enemy should break through General Smith's lines, and all should be ready to resist an assault.

U. S. GRANT,<br/>Lieutenant-General.

The remainder of the day was spent in strengthening the line we now held. By night we were as strong against Lee as he was against us.

During the night the enemy quitted our right front, abandoning some of their wounded, and without burying their dead. These we were able to care for. But there were many dead and wounded men between the lines of the contending forces, which were now close together, who could not be cared for without a cessation of hostilities.

So I wrote the following:

COLD HARBOR, VA., June 5, 1864.

GENERAL R. E. LEE,
Commanding Confederate Army.

It is reported to me that there are wounded men, probably of both armies, now lying exposed and suffering between the lines occupied respectively by the two armies. Humanity would dictate that some provision should be made to provide against such hardships. I would propose, therefore, that hereafter, when no battle is raging, either party be authorized to send to any point between the pickets or skirmish lines, unarmed men bearing litters to pick up their dead or wounded, without being fired upon by the other party. Any other method, equally fair to both parties, you may propose for meeting the end desired will be accepted by me.

U. S. GRANT,
Lieut.-General.

Lee replied that he feared such an arrangement would lead to misunderstanding, and proposed that in future, when either party wished to remove their dead and wounded, a flag of truce be sent.[15] I answered this immediately by saying:

COLD HARBOR, VA., *June* 6, 1864.

GENERAL R. E. LEE,
Commanding Army of N. Va.

Your communication of yesterday's date is received. I will send immediately, as you propose, to collect the dead and wounded between the lines of the two armies, and will also instruct that you be allowed to do the same. I propose that the time for doing this be between the hours of 12 M. and 3 P.M. to-day. I will direct all parties going out to bear a white flag, and not to attempt to go beyond where we have dead or wounded, and not beyond or on ground occupied by your troops.

U. S. GRANT,
Lieut.-General.

Lee's response was that he could not consent to the burial of the dead and removal of the wounded in the way I proposed, but when either party desired such permission it should be asked for by flag of truce; and he had directed that any parties I may have sent out, as mentioned in my letter, to be turned back.[16] I answered:

COLD HARBOR, VA., *June* 6, 1864.

GENERAL R. E. LEE.
Commanding Army, N. Va.

The knowledge that wounded men are now suffering from want of attention, between the two armies, compels me to ask a suspension of

---

[15] For Lee's June 5, 1864, reply, see *PUSG*, 11:17*n*.
[16] For Lee's June 6, 1864, reply, see ibid., 11:22*n*.

hostilities for sufficient time to collect them in, say two hours. Permit me to say that the hours you may fix upon for this will be agreeable to me, and the same privilege will be extended to such parties as you may wish to send out on the same duty without further application.

U. S. GRANT,
Lieut.-General.[17]

Lee acceded to this; but delays in transmitting the correspondence brought it to the 7th of June—forty-eight hours after it commenced—before parties were got out to collect the men left upon the field. In the meantime all but two of the wounded had died.[18] And I wrote to Lee:

COLD HARBOR, VA., *June* 7, 1864.
10.30 A.M.

GEN. R. E. LEE,
Commanding Army of N. Va.

I regret that your note of seven P.M. yesterday should have been received at the nearest corps headquarters, to where it was delivered, after the hour which had been given for the removal of the dead and wounded had expired; 10.45 P.M. was the hour at which it was received at corps headquarters, and between eleven and twelve it reached my headquarters. As a consequence, it was not understood by the troops of this army that there was a cessation of hostilities for the purpose of collecting the dead and wounded, and none were collected. Two officers and six men of the 8th and 25th North Carolina Regts., who were out in search of the bodies of officers of their respective regiments, were captured and brought into our lines, owing to this want of understanding.[19] I regret this, but will

[17] For USG's June 6, 1864, response to Lee, see ibid.

[18] Soldiers from the 19th Massachusetts Inf. reported finding a wounded man on June 7, 1864. Gen. C. H. Morgan, a staff officer in the 2nd Corps, also mentioned a wounded man who was recovered by the burial teams after the battle, but it is unclear if this was the same man found by the 19th Massachusetts Inf. or if there were others. John G. B. Adams, *Reminiscences of the Nineteenth Massachusetts Regiment* (Boston: Wright and Potter, 1899), 100–101; John C. Ropes, "The Battle of Cold Harbor," *Papers of the Military Historical Society of Massachusetts* 4 (1905): 361.

[19] On the night of June 6, 1864, Confederate lieutenant Harvey C. McAlister, Corporal Marion T. Martin, Private Handy Bass, a Lieutenant Hartman, a Corporal Kinlow, a Private Grey, and two unnamed privates were sent to look for Col. John R. Murchison's body. The group was captured by U.S. Army troops. *PUSG*, 11:27*n*.

state that as soon as I learned the fact, I directed that they should not be held as prisoners, but must be returned to their commands. These officers and men having been carelessly brought through our lines to the rear, I have not determined whether they will be sent back the way they came, or whether they will be sent by some other route.

Regretting that all my efforts for alleviating the sufferings of wounded men left upon the battle-field have been rendered nugatory, I remain, &c.,

U. S. GRANT,
Lieutenant-General.

I have always regretted that the last assault at Cold Harbor was ever made. I might say the same thing of the assault of the 22d of May, 1863, at Vicksburg. At Cold Harbor no advantage whatever was gained to compensate for the heavy loss we sustained. Indeed, the advantages other than those of relative losses, were on the Confederate side. Before that, the Army of Northern Virginia seemed to have acquired a wholesome regard for the courage, endurance, and soldierly qualities generally of the Army of the Potomac. They no longer wanted to fight them "one Confederate to five Yanks."[20] Indeed, they seemed to have given up any idea of gaining any advantage of their antagonist in the open field. They had come to much prefer breastworks in their front to the Army of the Potomac. This charge seemed to revive their hopes temporarily; but it was of short duration. The effect upon the Army of the Potomac was the reverse. When we reached the James River, however, all effects of the battle of Cold Harbor seemed to have disappeared.

There was more justification for the assault at Vicksburg. We were in a Southern climate, at the beginning of the hot season. The Army of the Tennessee had won five successive victories over the garrison of Vicksburg in the three preceding weeks. They had driven a portion of that army from Port Gibson with considerable loss, after having flanked them out of their stronghold at Grand Gulf.[21] They had attacked another portion of the same army at

[20] In Alfred C. Hills's *MacPherson: The Great Confederate Philosopher and Southern Blower* (New York: James Miller, 1864), which contains satirical letters written under the name of "James B. Macpherson," a Confederate sympathizer bets that the U.S. Army will not capture Vicksburg in 1863. He reasons that the city is "impregnable" and that "one Confederate is equal to five Yankees" (161).

[21] Although estimates vary, Confederate forces lost approximately 60 killed, 340 wounded, and 387 missing at the Battle of Port Gibson. *PUSG*, 8:139n.

Raymond, more than fifty miles farther in the interior of the State, and driven them back into Jackson with great loss in killed, wounded, captured and missing, besides loss of large and small arms:[22] they had captured the capital of the State of Mississippi, with a large amount of materials of war and manufactures. Only a few days before, they had beaten the enemy then penned up in the town first at Champion's Hill, next at Big Black River Bridge, inflicting upon him a loss of fifteen thousand or more men (including those cut off from returning) besides large losses in arms and ammunition.[23] The Army of the Tennessee had come to believe that they could beat their antagonist under any circumstances. There was no telling how long a regular siege might last. As I have stated, it was the beginning of the hot season in a Southern climate. There was no telling what the casualties might be among Northern troops working and living in trenches, drinking surface water filtered through rich vegetation, under a tropical sun.[24] If Vicksburg could have been carried in May, it would not only have saved the army the risk it ran of a greater danger than from the bullets of the enemy, but it would have given us a splendid army, well equipped and officered, to operate elsewhere with. These are reasons justifying the assault. The only benefit we gained—and it was a slight one for so great a sacrifice—was that the men worked cheerfully in the trenches after that, being satisfied with digging the enemy out. Had the assault not been made, I have no doubt that the majority of those engaged in the siege of Vicksburg would have believed that had we assaulted it would have proven successful, and would have saved life, health and comfort.

[22] Although the total loss is unclear, Confederate forces lost at least 73 killed, 252 wounded, and 190 missing at the Battle of Raymond. Timothy B. Smith, *Champion Hill: Decisive Battle for Vicksburg* (New York: Savas Beatie, 2006), 88.

[23] Confederate losses reported for the Battle of Champion Hill were 381 killed, 1,018 wounded, and 2,441 missing or captured. It is unclear how many Confederates were killed or wounded at the Battle of Big Black River Bridge, but there were 1,750 captured. Ibid., 372, 397.

[24] These conditions were believed in the nineteenth century to contribute to overall ill health and, in particular, malarial fevers. "Miasmatic Fevers," in *Military and Medical Surgical Essays,* ed. William A. Hammond (Philadelphia: Lippincott, 1864), 207–234.

# 56

## Left Flank Movement across the Chickahominy and James—General Lee—Visit to Butler—The Movement on Petersburg—The Investment of Petersburg

L EE'S POSITION WAS now so near Richmond, and the intervening swamps of the Chickahominy so great an obstacle to the movement of troops in the face of an enemy, that I determined to make my next left flank move carry the Army of the Potomac south of the James River.*

*Cold Harbor, *June* 5, 1864.

MAJOR-GENERAL HALLECK, Chief of Staff of the Army,
Washington, D. C.

A full survey of all the ground satisfies me that it would be impracticable to hold a line north-east of Richmond that would protect the Fredericksburg Railroad to enable us to use that road for supplying the army. To do so would give us a long vulnerable line of road to protect, exhausting much of our strength to guard it, and would leave open to the enemy all of his lines of communication on the south side of the James. My idea from the start has been to beat Lee's army if possible north of Richmond; then after destroying his lines of communication on the north side of the James River to transfer the army to the south side and besiege Lee in Richmond, or follow him south if he should retreat.

I now find, after over thirty days of trial, the enemy deems it of the first importance to run no risks with the armies they now have. They act purely on the defensive behind breastworks, or feebly on the offensive immediately in front of them, and where in case of repulse they can instantly retire behind them. Without a greater sacrifice of human life than I am willing to make all cannot be accomplished that I had designed outside of the city. I have therefore resolved upon the following plan:

I will continue to hold substantially the ground now occupied by the Army of the Potomac, taking advantage of any favorable circumstance that may

Preparations for this were promptly commenced. The move was a hazardous one to make: the Chickahominy River, with its marshy and heavily timbered approaches, had to be crossed; all the bridges over it east of Lee were destroyed; the enemy had a shorter line and better roads to travel on to confront me in crossing; more than fifty miles intervened between me and Butler, by the roads I should have to travel, with both the James and the Chickahominy unbridged to cross; and last, the Army of the Potomac had to be got out of a position but a few hundred yards from the enemy at the widest place. Lee, if he did not choose to follow me, might, with his shorter distance to travel and his bridges over the Chickahominy and the James, move rapidly on Butler and crush him before the army with me could come to his relief. Then too he might spare troops enough to send against Hunter who was approaching Lynchburg, living upon the country he passed through, and without ammunition further than what he carried with him.

But the move had to be made, and I relied upon Lee's not seeing my danger as I saw it. Besides we had armies on both sides of the James River and not far from the Confederate capital. I knew that its safety would be a matter of the first consideration with the executive, legislative and judicial branches of the

---

present itself until the cavalry can be sent west to destroy the Virginia Central Railroad from about Beaver Dam for some twenty-five or thirty miles west. When this is effected I will move the army to the south side of the James River, either by crossing the Chickahominy and marching near to City Point, or by going to the mouth of the Chickahominy on north side and crossing there. To provide for this last and most possible contingency, several ferry-boats of the largest class ought to be immediately provided.

Once on the south side of the James River, I can cut off all sources of supply to the enemy except what is furnished by the canal. If Hunter succeeds in reaching Lynchburg, that will be lost to him also. Should Hunter not succeed, I will still make the effort to destroy the canal by sending cavalry up the south side of the river with a pontoon train to cross wherever they can.

The feeling of the two armies now seems to be that the rebels can protect themselves only by strong intrenchments, whilst our army is not only confident of protecting itself without intrenchments, but that it can beat and drive the enemy wherever and whenever he can be found without this protection.

U. S. GRANT,
Lieutenant-General.

so-called Confederate government, if it was not with the military commanders. But I took all the precaution I knew of to guard against all dangers.

Sheridan was sent with two divisions, to communicate with Hunter and to break up the Virginia Central Railroad and the James River Canal, on the 7th of June, taking instructions to Hunter to come back with him.*

*COLD HARBOR, VA., *June 6, 1864.*

MAJOR-GENERAL D. HUNTER,
Commanding Dept. W. Va.

General Sheridan leaves here to-morrow morning, with instructions to proceed to Charlottesville, Va., and to commence there the destruction of the Va. Cen. R. R., destroying this way as much as possible. The complete destruction of this road and of the canal on James River is of great importance to us. According to the instructions I sent to General Halleck for your guidance, you were to proceed to Lynchburg and commence there.[1] It would be of great value to us to get possession of Lynchburg for a single day. But that point is of so much importance to the enemy, that in attempting to get it such resistance may be met as to defeat your getting onto the road or canal at all. I see, in looking over the letter to General Halleck on the subject of your instructions, that it rather indicates that your route should be from Staunton via Charlottesville. If you have so understood it, you will be doing just what I want. The direction I would now give is, that if this letter reaches you in the valley between Staunton and Lynchburg, you immediately turn east by the most practicable road until you strike the Lynchburg branch of the Va. Central road. From thence move eastward along the line of the road, destroying it completely and thoroughly, until you join General Sheridan. After the work laid out for General Sheridan and yourself is thoroughly done, proceed to join the Army of the Potomac by the route laid out in General Sheridan's instructions.

If any portion of your force, especially your cavalry, is needed back in your Department, you are authorized to send it back.

If on receipt of this you should be near to Lynchburg and deem it practicable to reach that point, you will exercise your judgment about going there.

If you should be on the railroad between Charlottesville and Lynchburg, it may be practicable to detach a cavalry force to destroy the canal. Lose no opportunity to destroy the canal.

U. S. GRANT,
Lieut.-General.

[1] For USG's May 25, 1864, telegram to Halleck, see *PUSG,* 10:487–488.

Hunter was also informed by way of Washington and the Valley that Sheridan was on the way to meet him. The canal and Central Road, and the regions penetrated by them, were of vast importance to the enemy, furnishing and carrying a large per cent. of all the supplies for the Army of Northern Virginia and the people of Richmond. Before Sheridan got off on the 7th news was received from Hunter reporting his advance to Staunton and successful engagement with the enemy near that place on the 5th, in which the Confederate commander, W. S. Jones, was killed.[2] On the 4th of June the enemy having withdrawn his left corps, Burnside on our right was moved up between Warren and Smith. On the 5th Birney returned to Hancock, which extended his left now to the Chickahominy, and Warren was withdrawn to Cold Harbor. Wright was directed to send two divisions to the left to extend down the banks of that stream to Bottom's Bridge.[3] The cavalry extended still farther east to Jones's Bridge.[4]

On the 7th Abercrombie—who was in command at White House, and who had been in command at our base of supplies in all the changes made from the start—was ordered to take up the iron from the York River Railroad and put it on boats, and to be in readiness to move by water to City Point.[5]

On the 8th Meade was directed to fortify a line down the bank overlooking the Chickahominy, under cover of which the army could move.

On the 9th Abercrombie was directed to send all organized troops arriving at White House, without debarking from their transports, to report to

[2] William E. Jones (1824–1864) was born in Virginia and graduated from the USMA in 1848. In May 1861, he joined the Confederate Army as a cavalry captain and in Sept. 1862 was promoted to brigadier general. In June 1864, he commanded a cavalry brigade in the Trans-Allegheny Dept. On June 5, 1864, Jones was killed near Piedmont, VA. *CWHC*, 326. For Hunter's June 8, 1864, letter reporting Jones's death, see *OR*, I, 37(I), 606.

[3] For Meade's June 5, 1864, orders to Warren and Hancock, see *OR*, I, 36(III), 603. The editors found no orders to Wright during that time that match USG's description, but on June 5, Hancock requested Wright's troops move to provide relief to Gibbon. Meade denied that request. Ibid., I, 36(III), 606–607.

[4] Jones's Bridge on the Chickahominy River was approximately twenty-five miles east of Richmond, VA. George B. Davis et al., *The Official Military Atlas of the Civil War* (New York: Fairfax Press, 1983), plate 137.

[5] John J. Abercrombie (1798–1877) was born in Maryland and graduated from the USMA in 1822. In Sept. 1846, he was promoted to colonel for his actions during the Mexican-American War. In Feb. 1861, he was colonel of the 7th U.S. Inf. and was promoted to brigadier general in Aug. On June 1, 1864, he took command of White House, VA. *CWHC*, 98. For USG's June 7, 1864, letter to Abercrombie, see *PUSG*, 11:28.

Butler. Halleck was at this time instructed to send all reinforcements to City Point.[6]

On the 11th I wrote:

COLD HARBOR, VA., *June 11, 1864.*

MAJOR-GEN. B. F. BUTLER,

Commanding Department of Va. and N. C.

The movement to transfer this army to the south side of the James River will commence after dark to-morrow night. Col. Comstock, of my staff, was sent specially to ascertain what was necessary to make your position secure in the interval during which the enemy might use most of his force against you, and also, to ascertain what point on the river we should reach to effect a crossing if it should not be practicable to reach this side of the river at Bermuda Hundred. Colonel Comstock has not yet returned, so that I cannot make instructions as definite as I would wish, but the time between this and Sunday night being so short in which to get word to you, I must do the best I can. Colonel Dent goes to make arrangements for gunboats and transportation to send up the Chicka-hominy to take to you the 18th corps. The corps will leave its position in the trenches as early in the evening, to-morrow, as possible, and make a forced march to Cole's Landing or Ferry,[7] where it should reach by ten A.M. the following morning. This corps numbers now 15,300 men. They take with them neither wagons nor artillery; these latter marching with the balance of the army to the James River. The remainder of the army will cross the Chickahominy at Long Bridge[8] and at Jones's, and strike the river at the most practicable crossing below City Point.

I directed several days ago that all reinforcements for the army should be sent to you. I am not advised of the number that may have gone, but suppose you have received from six to ten thousand.[9]

[6] On June 8, 1864, Rawlins ordered Abercrombie to send troops who arrived at White House to Butler at City Point, VA, or at Bermuda Hundred, VA. Ibid., 11:29*n*. For USG's June 9, 1864, telegram to Halleck, see ibid., 11:33*n*.

[7] Cole's Ferry on the Chickahominy River was approximately seven miles east of Charles City, VA. Davis et al., *Official Military Atlas of the Civil War,* plate 137.

[8] Long Bridge was upriver from Cole's Ferry on the Chickahominy approximately fifteen miles east of Richmond. Ibid.

[9] As of June 10, 1864, 4,552 reinforcements had been sent to Butler. *OR,* I, 36, III, 739.

General Smith will also reach you as soon as the enemy could, going by the way of Richmond.

The balance of the force will not be more than one day behind, unless detained by the whole of Lee's army, in which case you will be strong enough.

I wish you would direct the proper staff officers, your chief-engineer and your chief-quartermaster,[10] to commence at once the collection of all the means in their reach for crossing the army on its arrival. If there is a point below City Point where a pontoon bridge can be thrown, have it laid.

Expecting the arrival of the 18th corps by Monday night, if you deem it practicable from the force you have to seize and hold Petersburg, you may prepare to start, on the arrival of troops to hold your present lines. I do not want Petersburg visited, however, unless it is held, nor an attempt to take it, unless you feel a reasonable degree of confidence of success. If you should go there, I think troops should take nothing with them except what they can carry, depending upon supplies being sent after the place is secured. If Colonel Dent should not succeed in securing the requisite amount of transportation for the 18th corps before reaching you, please have the balance supplied.

U. S. GRANT,
Lieut.-General.

P. S.—On reflection I will send the 18th corps by way of White House. The distance which they will have to march will be enough shorter to enable them to reach you about the same time, and the uncertainty of navigation on the Chickahominy will be avoided.

U. S. GRANT.

[10] Godfrey Weitzel (1835–1884) was Butler's chief engineer in June 1864. He was born in Ohio and graduated from the USMA in 1855. In Oct. 1861, he was an engineer for the Defenses of Cincinnati, Dept. of the Ohio. In Aug. 1862, he was promoted to brigadier general. *CWHC,* 559. Lt. Col. Charles E. Fuller was Butler's chief quartermaster. In July 1864, Fuller was granted sick leave to return to his home in Boston, MA, and resigned from the military in Nov. "Army and Navy Personal," *Army and Navy Journal* 1 (1864): 807; *Official Army Register for 1865* (Washington, DC: n.p., 1865), 98; *OR,* I, 36(III), 770.

COLD HARBOR, VA., *June 11, 1864.*

MAJOR-GENERAL G. G. MEADE,
Commanding Army of the Potomac.

Colonel Comstock, who visited the James River for the purpose of ascertaining the best point below Bermuda Hundred to which to march the army has not yet returned. It is now getting so late, however, that all preparations may be made for the move to-morrow night without waiting longer.

The movement will be made as heretofore agreed upon, that is, the 18th corps make a rapid march with the infantry alone, their wagons and artillery accompanying the balance of the army to Cole's Landing or Ferry, and there embark for City Point, losing no time for rest until they reach the latter point.

The 5th corps will seize Long Bridge and move out on the Long Bridge Road to its junction with Quaker Road, or until stopped by the enemy.

The other three corps will follow in such order as you may direct, one of them crossing at Long Bridge, and two at Jones's Bridge. After the crossing is effected, the most practicable roads will be taken to reach about Fort Powhattan.[11] Of course, this is supposing the enemy makes no opposition to our advance. The 5th corps, after securing the passage of the balance of the army, will join or follow in rear of the corps which crosses the same bridge with themselves. The wagon trains should be kept well east of the troops, and if a crossing can be found, or made lower down than Jones's they should take it.

U. S. GRANT,
Lieut.-General.

P. S.—In view of the long march to reach Cole's Landing, and the uncertainty of being able to embark a large number of men there, the direction of the 18th corps may be changed to White House. They should be directed to load up transports, and start them as fast as loaded without waiting for the whole corps or even whole divisions to go together.

U. S. GRANT.

---

[11] Fort Powhatan was approximately thirty miles south of Richmond on the south bank of the James River. A. Wilson Greene, *Civil War Petersburg: Confederate City in the Crucible of War* (Charlottesville: University of Virginia Press, 2006), 280*n*.

About this time word was received (through the Richmond papers of the 11th) that Crook and Averell had united and were moving east. This, with the news of Hunter's successful engagement near Staunton, was no doubt known to Lee before it was to me.[12] Then Sheridan leaving with two divisions of cavalry, looked indeed threatening, both to Lee's communications and supplies. Much of his cavalry was sent after Sheridan, and Early with Ewell's entire corps was sent to the Valley. Supplies were growing scarce in Richmond, and the sources from which to draw them were in our hands. People from outside began to pour into Richmond to help eat up the little on hand. Consternation reigned there.

On the 12th Smith was ordered to move at night to White House, not to stop until he reached there, and to take boats at once for City Point, leaving his trains and artillery to move by land.[13]

Soon after dark some of the cavalry at Long Bridge effected a crossing by wading and floundering through the water and mud, leaving their horses behind, and drove away the cavalry pickets. A pontoon bridge was speedily thrown across, over which the remainder of the army soon passed and pushed out for a mile or two to watch and detain any advance that might be made from the other side. Warren followed the cavalry, and by the morning of the 13th had his whole corps over. Hancock followed Warren. Burnside took the road to Jones's Bridge, followed by Wright. Ferrero's division, with the wagon train, moved farther east, by Window Shades[14] and Cole's Ferry, our rear being covered by cavalry.

It was known that the enemy had some gunboats at Richmond. These might run down at night and inflict great damage upon us before they could be sunk or captured by our navy. General Butler had, in advance, loaded some vessels with stone ready to be sunk so as to obstruct the channel in an emergency. On the 13th I sent orders to have these sunk as high up the river as we could guard them, and prevent their removal by the enemy.[15]

As soon as Warren's corps was over the Chickahominy it marched out and joined the cavalry in holding the roads from Richmond while the army passed.

[12] USG may have read this news in the *Richmond Whig* or the *Richmond Examiner* and on June 11, 1864, reported the news to Halleck. Richard R. Duncan, *Lee's Endangered Left: The Civil War in Western Virginia, Spring of 1864* (Baton Rouge: Louisiana State University Press, 1998), 248; *PUSG*, 11:34.

[13] Rawlins gave W.F. Smith the order on June 13, 1864. Smith did not arrive at City Point until later that night. *PUSG*, 11:39 and *n*.

[14] Window Shades, or Windsor Shades, was approximately twenty-four miles below Cold Harbor, VA, on the Chickahominy River. Andrew A. Humphreys, *The Virginia Campaign of 1864 and 1865: The Army of the Potomac and the Army of the James* (New York: Charles Scribner's Sons, 1883), 199.

[15] For the orders regarding the boats, see Rawlins's June 13, 1864, letter to Butler. *PUSG*, 11:40*n*.

No attempt was made by the enemy to impede our march, however, but Warren and Wilson reported the enemy strongly fortified in their front. By the evening of the 13th Hancock's corps was at Charles City Court House on the James River. Burnside's and Wright's corps were on the Chickahominy, and crossed during the night, Warren's corps and the cavalry still covering the army. The material for a pontoon bridge was already at hand and the work of laying it was commenced immediately, under the superintendence of Brigadier-General Benham, commanding the engineer brigade.[16] On the evening of the 14th the crossing commenced, Hancock in advance, using both the bridge and boats.

When the Wilderness campaign commenced the Army of the Potomac, including Burnside's corps—which was a separate command until the 24th of May when it was incorporated with the main army—numbered about 116,000 men.[17] During the progress of the campaign about 40,000 reinforcements were received. At the crossing of the James River June 14th–15th the army numbered about 115,000. Besides the ordinary losses incident to a campaign of six weeks' nearly constant fighting or skirmishing, about one-half of the artillery was sent back to Washington, and many men were discharged by reason of the expiration of their term of service.*

*FROM A STATEMENT OF LOSSES COMPILED IN THE ADJUTANT-GENERAL'S OFFICE.[18]

| FIELD OF ACTION AND DATE. | KILLED. | WOUNDED. | MISSING. | AGGREGATE. |
|---|---|---|---|---|
| Wilderness, May 5th to 7th | 2,261 | 8,785 | 2,902 | 13,948 |
| Spottsylvania, May 8th to 21st | 2,271 | 9,360 | 1,970 | 13,601 |
| North Anna, May 23d to 27th | 186 | 792 | 165 | 1,143 |
| Totopotomoy, May 27th to 31st | 99 | 358 | 52 | 509 |
| Cold Harbor, May 31st to June 12th | 1,769 | 6,752 | 1,537 | 10,058 |
| Total | 6,586 | 26,047 | 6,626 | 39,259 |

---

[16] Henry W. Benham (1813–1884) was born in Connecticut and graduated from the USMA in 1837. Benham served in the Mexican-American War, was promoted to brigadier general in Aug. 1861, and was a member of the Engineer Corps until his retirement in 1882. *CWHC*, 127.

[17] On Apr. 30, 1864, USG's combined force (including the Army of the Potomac and the 9th Corps) was reportedly nearly 120,000 troops. Gordon C. Rhea, *The Battle of the Wilderness, May 5–6, 1864* (Baton Rouge: Louisiana State University Press, 1994), 34.

[18] This is a partial chart taken from Adam Badeau, *Military History of Ulysses S. Grant, from April, 1861, to April, 1865* (New York: D. Appleton, 1881), 3:713.

In estimating our strength every enlisted man and every commissioned officer present is included, no matter how employed; in bands, sick in field hospitals, hospital attendants, company cooks and all. Operating in an enemy's country, and being supplied always from a distant base, large detachments had at all times to be sent from the front, not only to guard the base of supplies and the roads to it, but all the roads leading to our flanks and rear. We were also operating in a country unknown to us, and without competent guides or maps showing the roads accurately.

The manner of estimating numbers in the two armies differs materially. In the Confederate army often only bayonets are taken into account, never, I believe, do they estimate more than are handling the guns of the artillery and armed with muskets or carbines. Generally the latter are far enough away to be excluded from the count in any one field. Officers and details of enlisted men are not included. In the Northern armies the estimate is most liberal, taking in all connected with the army and drawing pay.

Estimated in the same manner as ours, Lee had not less than 80,000 men at the start. His reinforcements were about equal to ours during the campaign, deducting the discharged men and those sent back.[19] He was on the defensive, and in a country in which every stream, every road, every obstacle to the movement of troops and every natural defence was familiar to him and his army. The citizens were all friendly to him and his cause, and could and did furnish him with accurate reports of our every move. Rear guards were not necessary for him, and having always a railroad at his back, large wagon trains were not required. All circumstances considered we did not have any advantage in numbers.

General Lee, who had led the Army of Northern Virginia in all these contests, was a very highly estimated man in the Confederate army and States, and filled also a very high place in the estimation of the people and press of the Northern States. His praise was sounded throughout the entire North after every action he was engaged in: the number of his forces was always lowered and that of the National forces exaggerated. He was a large, austere man, and I judge difficult of approach to his subordinates. To be extolled by the entire press of the South after every engagement, and by a portion of the press North with equal vehemence, was calculated to give him the entire confidence of his

[19] On Apr. 20, 1864, before the beginning of the Overland campaign, Lee's forces numbered over 54,000. The troops added during the campaign raised the number to over 65,000. Alfred C. Young III, *Lee's Army during the Overland Campaign: A Numerical Study* (Baton Rouge: Louisiana State University Press, 2013), 5–17, 227–231.

troops and to make him feared by his antagonists. It was not an uncommon thing for my staff-officers to hear from Eastern officers, "Well, Grant has never met Bobby Lee yet." There were good and true officers who believe now that the Army of Northern Virginia was superior to the Army of the Potomac man to man. I do not believe so, except as the advantages spoken of above made them so. Before the end I believe the difference was the other way. The Army of Northern Virginia became despondent and saw the end. It did not please them. The National army saw the same thing, and were encouraged by it.

The advance of the Army of the Potomac reached the James on the 14th of June. Preparations were at once commenced for laying the pontoon bridges and crossing the river. As already stated, I had previously ordered General Butler to have two vessels loaded with stone and carried up the river to a point above that occupied by our gunboats, where the channel was narrow, and sunk there so as to obstruct the passage and prevent Confederate gunboats from coming down the river. Butler had had these boats filled and put in position, but had not had them sunk before my arrival. I ordered this done, and also directed that he should turn over all material and boats not then in use in the river to be used in ferrying the troops across.[20]

I then, on the 14th, took a steamer and ran up to Bermuda Hundred to see General Butler for the purpose of directing a movement against Petersburg, while our troops of the Army of the Potomac were crossing.

I had sent General W. F. Smith back from Cold Harbor by the way of White House, thence on steamers to City Point for the purpose of giving General Butler more troops with which to accomplish this result. General Butler was ordered to send Smith with his troops reinforced, as far as that could be conveniently done, from other parts of the Army of the James.[21] He gave Smith about six thousand reinforcements, including some twenty-five hundred cavalry under Kautz, and about thirty-five hundred colored infantry under Hinks.[22]

The distance which Smith had to move to reach the enemy's lines was about six miles, and the Confederate advance line of works was but two miles out-

[20] On June 13, 1864, Butler reported that five vessels were sunk on the James River to obstruct the movement of Confederate gunboats. *PUSG*, 11:58*n*.

[21] See USG's June 11, 1864, letter to Butler included earlier in this chapter.

[22] Edward W. Hinks (1830–1894) was born in Maine and moved to Massachusetts in 1849. He was a second lieutenant in the U.S. 2nd Cav. at the start of the Civil War and in Nov. 1863 he was promoted to brigadier general. In June 1864, he commanded the 3rd Div., 18th Corps, Dept. of Virginia and North Carolina. On June 15, Hinks reinforced Smith at City Point with 3,747 troops. *CWHC*, 298; *OR*, I, 40(I), 721.

side of Petersburg. Smith was to move under cover of night, up close to the enemy's works, and assault as soon as he could after daylight. I believed then, and still believe, that Petersburg could have been easily captured at that time. It only had about 2,500 men in the defences besides some irregular troops, consisting of citizens and employees in the city who took up arms in case of emergency.[23] Smith started as proposed, but his advance encountered a rebel force intrenched between City Point and their lines outside of Petersburg. This position he carried, with some loss to the enemy;[24] but there was so much delay that it was daylight before his troops really got off from there. While there I informed General Butler that Hancock's corps would cross the river and move to Petersburg to support Smith in case the latter was successful, and that I could reinforce there more rapidly than Lee could reinforce from his position.[25]

I returned down the river to where the troops of the Army of the Potomac now were, communicated to General Meade, in writing, the directions I had given to General Butler and directed him (Meade) to cross Hancock's corps over under cover of night, and push them forward in the morning to Petersburg; halting them, however, at a designated point until they could hear from Smith.[26] I also informed General Meade that I had ordered rations from Bermuda Hundred for Hancock's corps, and desired him to issue them speedily, and to lose no more time than was absolutely necessary.[27] The rations did not reach him, however, and Hancock, while he got all his corps over during the night, remained until half-past ten in the hope of receiving them. He then moved without them, and on the road received a note from General W. F. Smith, asking him to come on. This seems to be the first information that General Hancock had received of the fact that he was to go to Petersburg, or that anything particular was expected of him. Otherwise he would have been there by four o'clock in the afternoon.[28]

[23] On June 15, 1864, Henry A. Wise had a total of 2,200 Confederate forces to defend Petersburg, VA. Edwin C. Bearss and Bryce A. Suderow, *The Petersburg Campaign: The Eastern Front Battles, June–August 1864* (El Dorado Hills, CA: Savas Beatie, 2012), 1:43n.

[24] No specific Confederate casualty numbers are available for this engagement. Thomas L. Livermore, *Numbers and Losses in the Civil War in America, 1861–65* (Boston: Houghton, Mifflin, 1900), 116.

[25] For USG's June 15, 1864, telegram to Butler, and their subsequent correspondence on the matter, see *PUSG*, 11:47 and *n*, 51, 51n–52n.

[26] For USG's June 15, 1864, order to Meade, see ibid., 11:54n.

[27] USG's June 14, 1864, letter about Hancock's supplies was directed to Butler. Ibid., 11:45–46.

[28] For Smith's June 15, 1864, order to Hancock, see *OR,* I, 40(II), 59.

Smith arrived in front of the enemy's lines early in the forenoon of the 15th, and spent the day until after seven o'clock in the evening in reconnoitering what appeared to be empty works. The enemy's line consisted of redans occupying commanding positions, with rifle-pits connecting them. To the east side of Petersburg, from the Appomattox back, there were thirteen of these redans extending a distance of several miles, probably three. If they had been properly manned they could have held out against any force that could have attacked them, at least until reinforcements could have got up from the north of Richmond.

Smith assaulted with the colored troops, and with success. By nine o'clock at night he was in possession of five of these redans and, of course, of the connecting lines of rifle-pits. All of them contained artillery, which fell into our hands. Hancock came up and proposed to take any part assigned to him; and Smith asked him to relieve his men who were in the trenches.[29]

Next morning, the 16th, Hancock himself was in command, and captured another redan. Meade came up in the afternoon and succeeded Hancock, who had to be relieved, temporarily, from the command of his corps on account of the breaking out afresh of the wound he had received at Gettysburg.[30] During the day Meade assaulted and carried one more redan to his right and two to his left. In all this we lost very heavily. The works were not strongly manned, but they all had guns in them which fell into our hands, together with the men who were handling them in the effort to repel these assaults.[31]

Up to this time Beauregard, who had commanded south of Richmond, had received no reinforcements, except Hoke's division from Drury's Bluff,* which

*City Point, Va., *June* 17, 1864.—11 A.M.

MAJOR-GEN. HALLECK,
Washington, D. C.

        *      *      *      *      *      *      *

The enemy in their endeavor to reinforce Petersburg abandoned their intrenchments in front of Bermuda Hundred. They no doubt expected troops from north of the James River to take their place before we discovered it.

[29] On June 15, 1864, Smith's assault was successful. According to his postbattle report, darkness and Confederate reinforcements coming in from Richmond prevented him from pushing further ahead. Ibid., I, 40(I), 705.

[30] At 2:00 P.M. on June 16, 1864, Meade arrived at Petersburg and took command. Ibid., I, 40(I), 168.

[31] On the morning of June 17, 1864, Meade reported that approximately 2,200 of his troops were killed, captured, or wounded during the June 16 assault. *PUSG*, 11:63n.

had arrived on the morning of the 16th; though he had urged the authorities very strongly to send them, believing, as he did, that Petersburg would be a valuable prize which we might seek.[33]

During the 17th the fighting was very severe and the losses heavy; and at night our troops occupied about the same position they had occupied in the morning, except that they held a redan which had been captured by Potter during the day.[34] During the night, however, Beauregard fell back to the line which had been already selected, and commenced fortifying it. Our troops advanced on the 18th to the line which he had abandoned, and found that the Confederate loss had been very severe, many of the enemy's dead still remaining in the ditches and in front of them.[35]

Colonel J. L. Chamberlain,[36] of the 20th Maine, was wounded on the 18th. He was gallantly leading his brigade at the time, as he had been in the habit of doing in all the engagements in which he had previously been engaged. He

---

General Butler took advantage of this and moved a force at once upon the railroad and plank road between Richmond and Petersburg, which I hope to retain possession of. Too much credit cannot be given to the troops and their commanders for the energy and fortitude displayed during the last five days. Day and night has been all the same, no delays being allowed on any account.

U. S. GRANT,
Lieut.-General.[32]

[32] For the entire telegram to Halleck, see ibid., 11:64–65.

[33] On June 14, 1864, in a dispatch to Bragg, Beauregard requested reinforcements to hold Petersburg. In response, Lee ordered Hoke's 6,000 troop division to reinforce Beauregard. Hoke's division began to arrive in Petersburg on the night of June 15. Bearss and Suderow, *Petersburg Campaign*, 1:44–45; Alfred Roman, *The Military Operations of General Beauregard in the War between the States, 1861 to 1865* (New York: Harper and Brothers, 1884), 2:578; *OR*, I, 40(II), 652, 654.

[34] The U.S. Army lost over 6,200 troops during the fighting on June 13–17, 1864. This total does not include losses for two volunteer regiments that failed to report their casualties. *OR*, I, 40(I), 307.

[35] No specific Confederate casualty numbers are available for the fighting on June 15–18, 1864. Livermore, *Numbers and Losses in the Civil War*, 116.

[36] Joshua L. Chamberlain (1828–1914) was born in Maine and graduated from Bowdoin College in 1852 and Bangor Theological Seminary in 1855. In Aug. 1862, he joined the 20th Maine Inf. as a lieutenant colonel. During the siege of Petersburg, he commanded the 1st Brigade, 1st Div., 5th Corps, Army of the Potomac. He served as governor of Maine from 1867 to 1871 and as president of Bowdoin College from 1871 to 1883. Chamberlain was awarded the Medal of Honor in 1893 for his actions at the Battle of Gettysburg. *CWHC*, 168.

had several times been recommended for a brigadier-generalcy for gallant and meritorious conduct. On this occasion, however, I promoted him on the spot, and forwarded a copy of my order to the War Department, asking that my act might be confirmed and Chamberlain's name sent to the Senate for confirmation without any delay. This was done, and at last a gallant and meritorious officer received partial justice at the hands of his government, which he had served so faithfully and so well.

If General Hancock's orders of the 15th had been communicated to him, that officer, with his usual promptness, would undoubtedly have been upon the ground around Petersburg as early as four o'clock in the afternoon of the 15th. The days were long and it would have given him considerable time before night. I do not think there is any doubt that Petersburg itself could have been carried without much loss; or, at least, if protected by inner detached works, that a line could have been established very much in rear of the one then occupied by the enemy. This would have given us control of both the Weldon and South Side railroads. This would also have saved an immense amount of hard fighting which had to be done from the 15th to the 18th, and would have given us greatly the advantage in the long siege which ensued.

I now ordered the troops to be put under cover and allowed some of the rest which they had so long needed.[37] They remained quiet, except that there was more or less firing every day, until the 22d, when General Meade ordered an advance towards the Weldon Railroad. We were very anxious to get to that road, and even round to the South Side Railroad if possible.[38]

Meade moved Hancock's corps, now commanded by Birney, to the left, with a view to at least force the enemy to stay within the limits of his own line. General Wright, with the 6th corps, was ordered by a road farther south, to march directly for the Weldon road. The enemy passed in between these two corps and attacked vigorously, and with very serious results to the National troops, who were then withdrawn from their advanced position.[39]

The Army of the Potomac was given the investment of Petersburg, while the Army of the James held Bermuda Hundred and all the ground we possessed north of the James River. The 9th corps, Burnside's, was placed upon the right at Petersburg; the 5th, Warren's, next; the 2d, Birney's, next; then the 6th, Wright's, broken off to the left and south. Thus began the siege of Petersburg.

[37] For USG's June 18, 1864, orders to Meade, see *PUSG,* 11:78.

[38] For Meade's June 21, 1864, orders to Birney, see *OR,* I, 40(II), 274.

[39] This incident was known as the Battle of Jerusalem Plank Road. On June 22–23, 1864, the U.S. Army lost 2,962 men, and the Confederates lost about 700 men. Bearss and Suderow, *Petersburg Campaign,* 1:199.

# 57

Raid on the Virginia Central Railroad—Raid on the
Weldon Railroad—Early's Movement upon
Washington—Mining the Works before Petersburg—
Explosion of the Mine before Petersburg—
Campaign in the Shenandoah Valley—
Capture of the Weldon Railroad

O<small>N THE</small> 7<small>TH</small> of June, while at Cold Harbor, I had as already indicated
sent Sheridan with two divisions of cavalry to destroy as much as he could of
the Virginia Central Railroad. General Hunter had been operating up the
Shenandoah Valley with some success, having fought a battle near Staunton
where he captured a great many prisoners, besides killing and wounding a good
many men.[1] After the battle he formed a junction at Staunton with Averell and
Crook, who had come up from the Kanawha, or Gauley River. It was supposed, therefore, that General Hunter would be about Charlottesville, Virginia,
by the time Sheridan could get there, doing on the way the damage that he was
sent to do.

I gave Sheridan instructions to have Hunter, in case he should meet him
about Charlottesville, join and return with him to the Army of the Potomac.
Lee, hearing of Hunter's success in the valley, started Breckinridge out for
its defence at once. Learning later of Sheridan's going with two divisions,

---

[1] On June 5, 1864, Hunter's forces captured over 1,000 Confederates and killed or
wounded approximately 600 Confederate troops near Staunton, VA. The next day, Hunter occupied Staunton without opposition and captured another 500 Confederates. The U.S. Army
suffered 500 casualties during this time. *OR*, I, 37(I), 94–96.

he also sent Hampton[2] with two divisions of cavalry, his own and Fitz-Hugh Lee's.[3]

Sheridan moved to the north side of the North Anna to get out west, and learned of the movement of these troops to the south side of the same stream almost as soon as they had started. He pushed on to get to Trevilian Station[4] to commence his destruction at that point. On the night of the 10th he bivouacked some six or seven miles east of Trevilian, while Fitz-Hugh Lee was the same night at Trevilian Station and Hampton but a few miles away.

During the night Hampton ordered an advance on Sheridan, hoping, no doubt, to surprise and very badly cripple him. Sheridan, however, by a counter move sent Custer on a rapid march to get between the two divisions of the enemy and into their rear. This he did successfully, so that at daylight, when the assault was made, the enemy found himself at the same time resisted in front and attacked in rear, and broke in some confusion. The losses were probably very light on both sides in killed and wounded, but Sheridan got away with some five hundred prisoners and sent them to City Point.

During that day, the 11th, Sheridan moved into Trevilian Station, and the following day proceeded to tear up the road east and west. There was considerable fighting during the whole of the day, but the work of destruction went on. In the meantime, at night, the enemy had taken possession of the crossing which Sheridan had proposed to take to go north when he left Trevilian. Sheridan learned, however, from some of the prisoners he had captured here, that

[2] Wade Hampton (1818–1902) was born in South Carolina and was a wealthy planter and legislator before the Civil War. He became a colonel in the Confederate Army in 1861 and rose to major general by 1863. He was governor of South Carolina from 1876 to 1879 and U.S. senator from South Carolina from 1879 to 1891. *CWHC*, 277.

[3] On June 7, 1864, Sheridan moved out from Cold Harbor, VA. On June 6, Lee had issued orders to Breckinridge about the defense of the Shenandoah Valley and on June 16 ordered Hampton to monitor Sheridan's movements. On June 26, Lee then ordered Fitzhugh Lee to follow Hampton. Fitzhugh Lee (1835–1905), the nephew of Robert E. Lee, was born in Virginia and graduated from the USMA in 1856. He resigned from the U.S. Army in 1861 and joined the Confederate artillery, rising to major general in the cavalry by 1863. He was governor of Virginia from 1886 to 1890 and consul-general in Cuba from 1896 to 1898. Ibid., 343; William C. Davis, *Breckinridge: Statesman, Soldier, Symbol* (Lexington: University of Kentucky Press, 2015), 438; *OR*, I, 36(III), 901, 903; *PUSG*, 11:xxi.

[4] Trevilian Station was approximately forty miles northwest of Richmond, VA, on the Virginia Central Railroad. Eric J. Wittenburg, *Glory Enough for All: Sheridan's Second Raid and the Battle of Trevilian Station* (Lincoln: University of Nebraska Press, 2001), 40 (map).

General Hunter was about Lynchburg, and therefore that there was no use of his going on to Charlottesville with a view to meet him.

Sheridan started back during the night of the 12th, and made his way north and farther east, coming around by the north side of White House, and arriving there on the 21st. Here he found an abundance of forage for his animals, food for his men, and security while resting. He had been obliged to leave about ninety of his own men in the field-hospital which he had established near Trevilian, and these necessarily fell into the hands of the enemy.[5]

White House up to this time had been a depot; but now that our troops were all on the James River, it was no longer wanted as a store of supplies. Sheridan was, therefore, directed to break it up;[6] which he did on the 22d of June, bringing the garrison and an immense wagon train with him. All these were over the James River by the 26th of the month, and Sheridan ready to follow.

In the meantime Meade had sent Wilson's division on a raid to destroy the Weldon and South Side roads.[7] Now that Sheridan was safe and Hampton free to return to Richmond with his cavalry, Wilson's position became precarious. Meade therefore, on the 27th, ordered Sheridan over the river to make a demonstration in favor of Wilson. Wilson got back, though not without severe loss, having struck both roads, but the damage done was soon repaired.[8]

After these events comparative quiet reigned about Petersburg until late in July. The time, however, was spent in strengthening the intrenchments and making our position generally more secure against a sudden attack. In the meantime I had to look after other portions of my command, where things had not been going on so favorably, always, as I could have wished.

General Hunter who had been appointed to succeed Sigel in the Shenandoah Valley immediately took up the offensive. He met the enemy on the 5th of June at Piedmont, and defeated him. On the 8th he formed a junction with Crook and Averell at Staunton, from which place he moved direct on Lynchburg, via Lexington, which he reached and invested on the 16th. Up to this time he was very successful; and but for the difficulty of taking with him sufficient ordnance stores over so long a march, through a hostile country, he would,

---

[5] U.S. casualties for the Battle of Trevilian Station were 1,007. *OR,* I, 36(I), 187.

[6] On June 19, 1864, USG ordered Sheridan to move on White House, VA, and await further orders. Ibid., I, 36(III), 779; *PUSG,* 11:84 and *n.*

[7] On June 20, 1864, Meade ordered Wilson to make a raid on the South Side and Danville Railroads. *PUSG,* 11:92–93, 93*n.*

[8] Wilson reported a loss of about 900 men killed, missing, or wounded during his late June 1864 raid on railroads around Petersburg, VA. *OR,* I, 40(I), 624.

no doubt, have captured Lynchburg. The destruction of the enemy's supplies and manufactories had been very great. To meet this movement under General Hunter, General Lee sent Early with his corps, a part of which reached Lynchburg before Hunter. After some skirmishing on the 17th and 18th, General Hunter, owing to a want of ammunition to give battle, retired from before the place. Unfortunately, this want of ammunition left him no choice of route for his return but by the way of the Gauley and Kanawha rivers, thence up the Ohio River, returning to Harper's Ferry by way of the Baltimore and Ohio Railroad. A long time was consumed in making this movement. Meantime the valley was left open to Early's troops, and others in that quarter; and Washington also was uncovered. Early took advantage of this condition of affairs and moved on Washington.[9]

In the absence of Hunter, General Lew Wallace, with headquarters at Baltimore, commanded the department in which the Shenandoah lay.[10] His surplus of troops with which to move against the enemy was small in number. Most of these were raw and, consequently, very much inferior to our veterans and to the veterans which Early had with him; but the situation of Washington was precarious, and Wallace moved with commendable promptitude to meet the enemy at the Monocacy. He could hardly have expected to defeat him badly, but he hoped to cripple and delay him until Washington could be put into a state of preparation for his reception. I had previously ordered General Meade to send a division to Baltimore for the purpose of adding to the defences of Washington, and he had sent Ricketts's[11] division of the 6th corps (Wright's), which arrived in Baltimore on the 8th of July.[12] Finding that Wal-

[9] On June 13, 1864, Early began his march toward Lynchburg, VA, to confront Hunter. He began his march toward Washington, DC, on the morning of June 19. Hunter arrived at Harper's Ferry, WV, on July 14. Ibid., I, 37(I), 94–103, 160; Jeffry D. Wert, *From Winchester to Cedar Creek: The Shenandoah Campaign of 1864* (New York: Simon and Schuster, 1987), 7.

[10] In Mar. 1864, Wallace took command of the Middle Dept., 8th Army Corps. Spencer Tucker, ed., *American Civil War: The Definitive Encyclopedia and Document Collection* (Santa Barbara, CA: ABC-CLIO, 2013), s.v. "Wallace, Lewis."

[11] James B. Ricketts (1817–1887), the nephew-in-law of Pres. Franklin Pierce, was born in New York and graduated from the USMA in 1839. He held the rank of captain in the U.S. Army at the outbreak of the Civil War and in July 1861, after being wounded and captured at the First Battle of Bull Run, he was promoted to brigadier general. He coauthored the *Supplemental Report of the Joint Committee on the Conduct of the War*, 2 vols. (Washington, DC: Government Printing Office, 1866). *CWHC*, 453.

[12] On July 6, 1864, Ricketts's troops were ordered to Baltimore, MD, and left City Point, VA, later that day. *OR*, I, 37(I), 204; I, 40(III), 36.

lace had gone to the front with his command, Ricketts immediately took the cars and followed him to the Monocacy with his entire division. They met the enemy and, as might have been expected, were defeated; but they succeeded in stopping him for the day on which the battle took place.[13] The next morning Early started on his march to the capital of the Nation, arriving before it on the 11th.

Learning of the gravity of the situation I had directed General Meade to also order Wright with the rest of his corps directly to Washington for the relief of that place, and the latter reached there the very day that Early arrived before it. The 19th corps, which had been stationed in Louisiana, having been ordered up to reinforce the armies about Richmond, had about this time arrived at Fortress Monroe, on their way to join us. I diverted them from that point to Washington, which place they reached, almost simultaneously with Wright, on the 11th. The 19th corps was commanded by Major-General Emory.[14]

Early made his reconnoissance with a view of attacking on the following morning, the 12th; but the next morning he found our intrenchments, which were very strong, fully manned. He at once commenced to retreat, Wright following. There is no telling how much this result was contributed to by General Lew Wallace's leading what might well be considered almost a forlorn hope. If Early had been but one day earlier he might have entered the capital before the arrival of the reinforcements I had sent. Whether the delay caused by the battle amounted to a day or not, General Wallace contributed on this occasion, by the defeat of the troops under him a greater benefit to the cause than often falls to the lot of a commander of an equal force to render by means of a victory.

Farther west also the troubles were threatening. Some time before, Forrest had met Sturgis[15] in command of some of our cavalry in Mississippi and handled him very roughly, gaining a very great victory over him.[16] This left

[13] The Battle of Monocacy occurred on July 9, 1864. *PUSG,* 11:xxiv.

[14] William H. Emory (1811–1887) was born in Maryland and graduated from the USMA in 1831. By Jan. 1861, he was promoted to lieutenant colonel and in Mar. 1862 to brigadier general. On July 9, 1864, USG ordered Emory's 19th Corps, and the remainder of Wright's 6th Corps, to Washington, DC, to defend against Early. *CWHC,* 226–227; *PUSG,* 11:xxiii.

[15] Samuel D. Sturgis (1822–1889) was born in Pennsylvania and graduated from the USMA in 1846. In May 1861, he was promoted to major in the U.S. Army and in Aug. to brigadier general. He commanded an expeditionary force in the District of West Tennessee June 1–13, 1864. *CWHC,* 518.

[16] Forrest defeated Sturgis at the Battle of Brice's Crossroads on June 10, 1864. Tucker, *American Civil War,* s.v. "Brice's Crossroads, Battle of."

Forrest free to go almost where he pleased, and to cut the roads in rear of Sherman who was then advancing. Sherman was abundantly able to look after the army that he was immediately with, and all of his military division so long as he could communicate with it; but it was my place to see that he had the means with which to hold his rear. Two divisions under A. J. Smith had been sent to Banks in Louisiana some months before. Sherman ordered these back, with directions to attack Forrest. Smith met and defeated him very badly. I then directed that Smith should hang to Forrest and not let him go; and to prevent by all means his getting upon the Memphis and Nashville Railroad. Sherman had anticipated me in this matter, and given the same orders in substance; but receiving my directions for this order to Smith, he repeated it.[17]

On the 25th of June General Burnside had commenced running a mine from about the centre of his front under the Confederate works confronting him. He was induced to do this by Colonel Pleasants, of the Pennsylvania Volunteers, whose regiment was mostly composed of miners, and who was himself a practical miner.[18] Burnside had submitted the scheme to Meade and myself, and we both approved of it, as a means of keeping the men occupied. His position was very favorable for carrying on this work, but not so favorable for the operations to follow its completion. The position of the two lines at that point were only about a hundred yards apart with a comparatively deep ravine intervening. In the bottom of this ravine the work commenced. The position was unfavorable in this particular: that the enemy's line at that point was re-entering, so that its front was commanded by their own lines both to the right and left. Then, too, the ground was sloping upward back of the Confederate line for a considerable distance, and it was presumable that the enemy had, at least, a detached work on this highest point. The work progressed, and on the

[17] On Mar. 6, 1864, Sherman had ordered Smith to reinforce Banks. On June 14, Sherman ordered him to move against Forrest, and Smith began his pursuit on July 5. Smith defeated Forrest at the Battle of Harrisburg (Tupelo) on July 14–15. *OR*, I, 34(II), 514–516; I, 39(I), 250–253. For USG and Sherman's July 19–20 correspondence regarding Smith's pursuit of Forrest, see *PUSG*, 11:282, 282n–283n.

[18] Henry Pleasants (1833–1880) was born in Buenos Aires, Argentina, and immigrated to Philadelphia, PA, when he was thirteen. In the 1850s, he worked as an assistant engineer of the Pittsburgh and Connellsville Railroad, participating in the construction of the Sand Patch Tunnel in the Allegheny Mountains. In Apr. 1861, he joined the 6th Pennsylvania Inf. as a second lieutenant and reached lieutenant colonel in Sept. 1862. In June 1864, he commanded the 1st Brigade, 2nd Div., 9th Corps, Army of the Potomac. *CWHC*, 431; John F. Schmutz, *The Battle of the Crater: A Complete History* (Jefferson, NC: McFarland, 2009), 51.

23d of July the mine was finished ready for charging; but I had this work of charging deferred until we were ready for it.

On the 17th of July several deserters came in and said that there was great consternation in Richmond, and that Lee was coming out to make an attack upon us—the object being to put us on the defensive so that he might detach troops to go to Georgia where the army Sherman was operating against was said to be in great trouble. I put the army commanders, Meade and Butler, on the lookout, but the attack was not made.

I concluded, then, a few days later, to do something in the way of offensive movement myself, having in view something of the same object that Lee had had. Wright's and Emory's corps were in Washington, and with this reduction of my force Lee might very readily have spared some troops from the defences to send West. I had other objects in view, however, besides keeping Lee where he was. The mine was constructed and ready to be exploded, and I wanted to take that occasion to carry Petersburg if I could. It was the object, therefore, to get as many of Lee's troops away from the south side of the James River as possible. Accordingly, on the 26th, we commenced a movement with Hancock's corps and Sheridan's cavalry to the north side by the way of Deep Bottom,[19] where Butler had a pontoon bridge laid. The plan, in the main, was to let the cavalry cut loose and, joining with Kautz's cavalry of the Army of the James, get by Lee's lines and destroy as much as they could of the Virginia Central Railroad, while, in the mean time, the infantry was to move out so as to protect their rear and cover their retreat back when they should have got through with their work. We were successful in drawing the enemy's troops to the north side of the James as I expected. The mine was ordered to be charged, and the morning of the 30th of July was the time fixed for its explosion. I gave Meade minute orders* on the 24th directing how I wanted the assault conducted,

*CITY POINT, VA., *July* 24, 1864.

MAJOR-GENERAL MEADE,
Commanding, etc.

The engineer officers who made a survey of the front from Bermuda Hundred report against the probability of success from an attack there.[20] The chances they think will be better on Burnside's front. If this is attempted it will be necessary to concentrate all the force possible at the point in the

[19] Deep Bottom, VA, was approximately fifteen miles south of Richmond along the James River. *PUSG,* 14:7 (map).

[20] For the July 10, 1864, report by Brig. Gen. Henry J. Hunt and Maj. James C. Duane, see *OR,* I, 40(III), 125–126.

which orders he amplified into general instructions for the guidance of the troops that were to be engaged.

Meade's instructions, which I, of course, approved most heartily, were all that I can see now was necessary. The only further precaution which he could have taken, and which he could not foresee, would have been to have different men to execute them.

---

enemy's line we expect to penetrate. All officers should be fully impressed with the absolute necessity of pushing entirely beyond the enemy's present line, if they should succeed in penetrating it, and of getting back to their present line promptly if they should not succeed in breaking through.

To the right and left of the point of assault all the artillery possible should be brought to play upon the enemy in front during the assault. Their lines would be sufficient for the support of the artillery, and all the reserves could be brought on the flanks of their commands nearest to the point of assault, ready to follow in if successful. The field artillery and infantry held in the lines during the first assault should be in readiness to move at a moment's notice either to their front or to follow the main assault, as they should receive orders. One thing, however, should be impressed on corps commanders. If they see the enemy giving away on their front or moving from it to reinforce a heavily assaulted portion of their line, they should take advantage of such knowledge and act promptly without waiting for orders from army commanders. General Ord can co-operate with his corps in this movement, and about five thousand troops from Bermuda Hundred can be sent to reinforce you or can be used to threaten an assault between the Appomattox and James rivers, as may be deemed best.

This should be done by Tuesday morning,[21] if done at all. If not attempted, we will then start at the date indicated to destroy the railroad as far as Hicksford[22] at least, and to Weldon if possible.

$$* \qquad * \qquad * \qquad * \qquad * \qquad * \qquad *$$

Whether we send an expedition on the road or assault at Petersburg, Burnside's mine will be blown up. . . .

U. S. GRANT,
Lieutenant-General.[23]

---

[21] July 26, 1864.

[22] Hicksford is now known as Emporia, VA. Lee A. Wallace Jr., "Coppens Louisiana Zouaves," *Civil War History* 8 (1962): 282.

[23] For the full text of this letter, see *PUSG,* 11:305–307.

The gallery to the mine was over five hundred feet long from where it entered the ground to the point where it was under the enemy's works, and with a cross gallery of something over eighty feet running under their lines.[24] Eight chambers had been left, requiring a ton of powder each to charge them. All was ready by the time I had prescribed; and on the 29th Hancock and Sheridan were brought back near the James River with their troops. Under cover of night they started to recross the bridge at Deep Bottom, and to march directly for that part of our lines in front of the mine.

Warren was to hold his line of intrenchments with a sufficient number of men and concentrate the balance on the right next to Burnside's corps, while Ord, now commanding the 18th corps, temporarily under Meade, was to form in the rear of Burnside to support him when he went in. All were to clear off the parapets and the *abatis* in their front so as to leave the space as open as possible, and be able to charge the moment the mine had been sprung and Burnside had taken possession. Burnside's corps was not to stop in the crater at all but push on to the top of the hill, supported on the right and left by Ord's and Warren's corps.

Warren and Ord fulfilled their instructions perfectly so far as making ready was concerned. Burnside seemed to have paid no attention whatever to the instructions, and left all the obstruction in his own front for his troops to get over in the best way they could. The four divisions of his corps were commanded by Generals Potter, Willcox, Ledlie[25] and Ferrero. The last was a colored division; and Burnside selected it to make the assault. Meade interfered with this. Burnside then took Ledlie's division—a worse selection than the first could have been.[26] In fact, Potter and Willcox were the only division

---

[24] The main shaft of the mine faced west, with shafts running north and south off the main shaft. This "cross gallery" (as USG called it) ran thirty-seven feet to the south and thirty-eight feet to the north. Edwin C. Bearss and Bryce A. Suderow, *The Petersburg Campaign: The Eastern Front Battles, June–August 1864* (El Dorado Hills, CA: Savas Beatie, 2012), 1:212.

[25] James H. Ledlie (1832–1882) was born in New York and graduated from Union College. He joined the 19th New York Inf. as a major in May 1861 and reached brigadier general in Oct. 1863. In June 1864, he commanded the 1st Div., 6th Corps, Army of the Potomac. *CWHC,* 342.

[26] On July 29, 1864, Meade ordered a column of white troops to make the lead assault on the crater instead of Ferrero's division of African American troops, who were trained specifically for the task. This change in battle formation was approved by USG. In his later testimony before the Committee on the Conduct of the War, Meade claimed that he changed the order because the white troops were more experienced, not because he lacked faith in the capabilities of the African American troops. James McPherson, *Battle Cry of Freedom* (Oxford: Oxford University Press, 2003), 759; *OR,* I, 40(III), 608; "Battle of Petersburg," *Report of the Joint Committee on the Conduct of the War* (Washington, DC: Government Printing Office, 1865), 5.

commanders Burnside had who were equal to the occasion. Ledlie besides being otherwise inefficient, proved also to possess disqualification less common among soldiers.

There was some delay about the explosion of the mine so that it did not go off until about five o'clock in the morning. When it did explode it was very successful, making a crater twenty feet deep and something like a hundred feet in length.[27] Instantly one hundred and ten cannon and fifty mortars, which had been placed in the most commanding positions covering the ground to the right and left of where the troops were to enter the enemy's lines, commenced playing. Ledlie's division marched into the crater immediately on the explosion, but most of the men stopped there in the absence of any one to give directions; their commander having found some safe retreat to get into before they started.[28] There was some delay on the left and right in advancing, but some of the troops did get in and turn to the right and left, carrying the rifle-pits as I expected they would do.

There had been great consternation in Petersburg, as we were well aware, about a rumored mine that we were going to explode. They knew we were mining, and they had failed to cut our mine off by countermining, though Beauregard had taken the precaution to run up a line of intrenchments to the rear of that part of their line fronting where they could see that our men were at work. We had learned through deserters who had come in that the people had very wild rumors about what was going on on our side. They said that we had undermined the whole of Petersburg; that they were resting upon a slumbering volcano and did not know at what moment they might expect an eruption. I somewhat based my calculations upon this state of feeling, and expected that when the mine was exploded the troops to the right and left would flee in all directions, and that our troops, if they moved promptly, could get in and strengthen themselves before the enemy had come to a realization of the true situation. It was just as I expected it would be. We could see the men running without any apparent object except to get away. It was half an hour before musketry firing, to amount to anything, was opened upon our men in the crater. It was an hour before the enemy got artillery up to play upon them; and it was

---

[27] The crater was approximately 30 feet deep, 170 feet long, and 60 feet wide. Bearss and Suderow, *Petersburg Campaign*, 1:219.

[28] Ledlie and Ferrero reportedly drank liquor behind earthworks while the charge took place. Ledlie was criticized for his performance, which effectively ended his military career. *CWHC*, 233, 342.

nine o'clock before Lee got up reinforcements from his right to join in expelling our troops.

The effort was a stupendous failure. It cost us about four thousand men, mostly, however, captured;[29] and all due to inefficiency on the part of the corps commander and the incompetency of the division commander who was sent to lead the assault.

After being fully assured of the failure of the mine, and finding that most of that part of Lee's army which had been drawn north of the James River were still there, I gave Meade directions to send a corps of infantry and the cavalry next morning, before Lee could get his forces back, to destroy fifteen or twenty miles of the Weldon Railroad. But misfortunes never come singly. I learned during that same afternoon that Wright's pursuit of Early was feeble because of the constant and contrary orders he had been receiving from Washington, while I was cut off from immediate communication by reason of our cable across Chesapeake Bay being broken.[30] Early, however, was not aware of the fact that Wright was not pursuing until he had reached Strasburg. Finding that he was not pursued he turned back to Winchester, where Crook was stationed with a small force, and drove him out.[31] He then pushed north until he had reached the Potomac, then he sent McCausland[32] across to Chambersburg, Pa., to destroy that town. Chambersburg was a purely defenceless town with no garrison whatever, and no fortifications; yet McCausland, under

[29] The U.S. Army lost 3,798 men during the Battle of the Crater, with 1,413 listed as missing or captured. Bearss and Suderow, *Petersburg Campaign*, 1:237; Schmutz, *Battle of the Crater*, 355.

[30] In a July 26, 1864, letter to Halleck, USG mentioned the delay in communications between his headquarters and the forces in Washington, DC. He requested that someone in Washington should give orders to the troops "within reach of the line of the Potomac." The next day, by order of the president, Halleck was given command of the forces in the Washington area. *PUSG*, 11:316–317; *OR*, I, 40(III), 501–502.

[31] On July 22, 1864, Early positioned some of his forces near Strasburg, VA. On July 24, he attacked U.S. Army forces under the command of Crook at Kernstown, VA, near Winchester, VA. Scott C. Patchan, *Shenandoah Summer: The 1864 Valley Campaign* (Lincoln: University of Nebraska Press, 2007), 158–159, 182–183.

[32] John McCausland (1836–1927) was born in Missouri and later moved to Virginia, where he graduated from the Virginia Military Institute in 1858. In 1861, he joined the Virginia Militia and then the 36th Virginia Inf. as a colonel. In May 1864, he was promoted to brigadier general and from June 27 to Aug. 10 commanded a cavalry brigade, Ransom's Div., Valley District, 2nd Corps, Army of Northern Virginia. *CWHC*, 371.

Early's orders, burned the place and left about three hundred families houseless. This occurred on the 30th of July. I rescinded my orders for the troops to go out to destroy the Weldon Railroad, and directed them to embark for Washington City. After burning Chambersburg McCausland retreated, pursued by our cavalry, towards Cumberland. They were met and defeated by General Kelley and driven into Virginia.[33]

The Shenandoah Valley was very important to the Confederates, because it was the principal storehouse they now had for feeding their armies about Richmond. It was well known that they would make a desperate struggle to maintain it. It had been the source of a great deal of trouble to us heretofore to guard that outlet to the north, partly because of the incompetency of some of the commanders, but chiefly because of interference from Washington. It seemed to be the policy of General Halleck and Secretary Stanton to keep any force sent there, in pursuit of the invading army, moving right and left so as to keep between the enemy and our capital; and, generally speaking, they pursued this policy until all knowledge of the whereabouts of the enemy was lost. They were left, therefore, free to supply themselves with horses, beef cattle, and such provisions as they could carry away from Western Maryland and Pennsylvania. I determined to put a stop to this. I started Sheridan at once for that field of operation, and on the following day sent another division of his cavalry.[34]

I had previously asked to have Sheridan assigned to that command, but Mr. Stanton objected, on the ground that he was too young for so important a command.[35] On the 1st of August when I sent reinforcements for the protection of Washington, I sent the following orders:

[33] Benjamin F. Kelley (1807–1891) was born in New Hampshire and moved to Virginia in 1826. In May 1861, he became a brigadier general in the Confederate Army. In Apr. 1864, he commanded troops stationed west of Sleepy Creek in the Dept. of West Virginia. On Aug. 1, Kelley's forces defeated McCausland at Cumberland, MD. McCausland's force crossed into Virginia on or before Aug. 3. Ibid., 328–329; *OR*, I, 37(II), 580, 590.

[34] On Aug. 1, 1864, USG ordered Sheridan to the Shenandoah Valley to take command of the forces in that area. *PUSG*, 11:xxv, 358.

[35] On Aug. 4, 1864, Sheridan met with Lincoln in Washington, DC. Lincoln informed him that Stanton had objected to his taking over Hunter's command. Although Lincoln agreed with Stanton, he ultimately gave Sheridan the command because of USG's confidence in him. P. H. Sheridan, *Personal Memoirs of P. H. Sheridan, General, United States Army* (New York: Charles L. Webster, 1888), 1:463.

CITY POINT, VA.,
*August 1, 1864, 11.30 A.M.*

MAJOR-GENERAL HALLECK,
Washington, D. C.

I am sending General Sheridan for temporary duty whilst the enemy is being expelled from the border. Unless General Hunter is in the field in person, I want Sheridan put in command of all the troops in the field, with instructions to put himself south of the enemy and follow him to the death. Wherever the enemy goes let our troops go also. Once started up the valley they ought to be followed until we get possession of the Virginia Central Railroad. If General Hunter is in the field, give Sheridan direct command of the 6th corps and cavalry division. All the cavalry, I presume, will reach Washington in the course of to-morrow.

U. S. GRANT,
Lieutenant-General.

The President in some way or other got to see this dispatch of mine directing certain instructions to be given to the commanders in the field, operating against Early, and sent me the following very characteristic dispatch:

OFFICE U.S. MILITARY TELEGRAPH,
WAR DEPARTMENT,
WASHINGTON, D.C., *August 3, 1864.*

Cypher. 6 P.M.,
LT.-GENERAL GRANT,
City Point, Va.

I have seen your despatch in which you say, "I want Sheridan put in command of all the troops in the field, with instructions to put himself south of the enemy, and follow him to the death. Wherever the enemy goes, let our troops go also." This, I think, is exactly right, as to how our forces should move. But please look over the despatches you may have received from here, even since you made that order, and discover, if you can, that there is any idea in the head of any one here, of "putting our army *south* of the enemy," or of "following him to the *death*" in any direction. I repeat to you it will neither be done nor attempted unless you watch it every day, and hour, and force it.

A. LINCOLN.[36]

[36] *PUSG*, 11:360n.

I replied to this that "I would start in two hours for Washington," and soon got off, going directly to the Monocacy without stopping at Washington on my way.[37] I found General Hunter's army encamped there, scattered over the fields along the banks of the Monocacy, with many hundreds of cars and locomotives, belonging to the Baltimore and Ohio Railroad, which he had taken the precaution to bring back and collect at that point. I asked the general where the enemy was. He replied that he did not know. He said the fact was, that he was so embarrassed with orders from Washington moving him first to the right and then to the left that he had lost all trace of the enemy.[38]

I then told the general that I would find out where the enemy was, and at once ordered steam got up and trains made up, giving directions to push for Halltown, some four miles above Harper's Ferry, in the Shenandoah Valley. The cavalry and the wagon trains were to march, but all the troops that could be transported by the cars were to go in that way. I knew that the valley was of such importance to the enemy that, no matter how much he was scattered at that time, he would in a very short time be found in front of our troops moving south.

I then wrote out General Hunter's instructions.* I told him that Sheridan was in Washington, and still another division was on its way; and suggested that he establish the headquarters of the department at any point that would suit him best, Cumberland, Baltimore, or elsewhere, and give Sheridan command of the troops in the field. The general replied to this, that he thought he had better be relieved entirely. He said that General Halleck seemed so much to distrust his fitness for the position he was in that he thought somebody else ought to be there. He did not want, in any way, to embarrass the cause; thus showing a patriotism that was none too common in the army. There were not many major-generals who would voluntarily have asked to have the command of a department taken from them on the supposition that for some particular reason, or for any reason, the service would be better performed. I told him, "very well then," and telegraphed at once for Sheridan to come to the Monocacy, and suggested that I would wait and meet him there.[39]

Sheridan came at once by special train, but reached there after the troops were all off. I went to the station and remained there until he arrived. Myself

*See letter, August 5th, Appendix.[40]

[37] For USG's full Aug. 4, 1864, telegram to Lincoln, see ibid.
[38] For Halleck's orders to Hunter, see *OR,* I, 37(II), 451, 467, 482, 576.
[39] For USG's Aug. 5, 1864, telegram to Halleck, see *PUSG,* 11:376n.
[40] For USG's Aug. 5, 1864, instructions to Hunter, see ibid., 11:377–378.

and one or two of my staff were about all the Union people, except General Hunter and his staff, who were left at the Monocacy when Sheridan arrived. I hastily told Sheridan what had been done and what I wanted him to do, giving him, at the same time, the written instructions which had been prepared for General Hunter and directed to that officer.[41]

Sheridan now had about 30,000 men to move with, 8,000 of them being cavalry. Early had about the same number, but the superior ability of the National commander over the Confederate commander was so great that all the latter's advantage of being on the defensive was more than counterbalanced by this circumstance.[42] As I had predicted, Early was soon found in front of Sheridan in the valley, and Pennsylvania and Maryland were speedily freed from the invaders. The importance of the valley was so great to the Confederates that Lee reinforced Early, but not to the extent that we thought and feared he would.[43]

To prevent as much as possible these reinforcements from being sent out from Richmond, I had to do something to compel Lee to retain his forces about his capital. I therefore gave orders for another move to the north side of the James River, to threaten Richmond. Hancock's corps, part of the 10th corps under Birney, and Gregg's division of cavalry were crossed to the north side of the James during the night of the 13th–14th of August. A threatening position was maintained for a number of days, with more or less skirmishing, and some tolerably hard fighting; although it was my object and my instructions that anything like a battle should be avoided, unless opportunities should present themselves which would insure great success. General Meade was left in command of the few troops around Petersburg, strongly intrenched; and was instructed to keep a close watch upon the enemy in that quarter, and himself to take advantage of any weakening that might occur through an effort on the part of the enemy to reinforce the north side. There was no particular victory gained on either side; but during that time no more reinforcements were sent to the valley.

[41] According to Sheridan, he met with USG on Aug. 6, 1864. Sheridan, *Memoirs*, 1:464.

[42] On Aug. 12, 1864, Sheridan reported having 21,500 troops as his "effective line of battle strength." In his memoirs, he stated that he had 26,000 men under his command. Early had an estimated 30,800 troops under his command. *OR*, I, 43(I), 42, 893; Sheridan, *Memoirs*, 1:471, 475.

[43] On Aug. 12, 1864, USG informed Sheridan that two infantry divisions from Hill's and Longstreet's corps were reinforcing Early. The next day, Sheridan reported that he was unable to get south of Early. *PUSG*, 11:402*n*, 403, 404*n*.

I informed Sheridan of what had been done to prevent reinforcements being sent from Richmond against him, and also that the efforts we had made had proven that one of the divisions which we supposed had gone to the valley was still at Richmond, because we had captured six or seven hundred prisoners from that division, each of its four brigades having contributed to our list of captures. I also informed him that but one division had gone, and it was possible that I should be able to prevent the going of any more.[44]

To add to my embarrassment at this time Sherman, who was now near Atlanta, wanted reinforcements. He was perfectly willing to take the raw troops then being raised in the North-west, saying that he could teach them more soldiering in one day among his troops than they would learn in a week in a camp of instruction. I therefore asked that all troops in camps of instruction in the North-west be sent to him.[45] Sherman also wanted to be assured that no Eastern troops were moving out against him. I informed him of what I had done and assured him that I would hold all the troops there that it was possible for me to hold, and that up to that time none had gone. I also informed him that his real danger was from Kirby Smith, who commanded the trans-Mississippi Department.[46] If Smith should escape Steele, and get across the Mississippi River, he might move against him. I had, therefore, asked to have an expedition ready to move from New Orleans against Mobile in case Kirby Smith should get across.[47] This would have a tendency to draw him to the defence of that place, instead of going against Sherman.

Right in the midst of all these embarrassments Halleck informed me that there was an organized scheme on foot in the North to resist the draft, and

[44] For USG's Aug. 14, 1864, telegram to Sheridan, see ibid., 11:420.

[45] For Sherman's willingness to accept raw recruits, see his Aug. 7, 1864, telegram to USG, ibid., 11:381*n*. On Aug. 9, USG instructed Halleck to send additional reinforcements to Sherman. Ibid., 11:385.

[46] On Aug. 13, 1864, Sherman expressed to Halleck his desire for reassurance that no Confederate reinforcements were arriving in Georgia. In Aug. 9 and 14 telegrams to Sherman, USG discussed the need to keep the enemy occupied. He also warned Sherman about Kirby Smith in the Aug. 14 telegram. *OR*, I, 38(V), 482; *PUSG*, 11:388–389, 421.

[47] Edmund Kirby Smith (1824–1893) was born in Florida and graduated from the USMA in 1845. He fought in the Mexican-American War and joined the 2nd U.S. Cav. in 1855. In Mar. 1861, he resigned from the U.S. Army and became a cavalry colonel in the Confederate Army, reaching major general in Oct. 1862. That same month, he took command of the Trans-Mississippi Dept. John C. Fredriksen, *Civil War Almanac* (New York: Facts on File, 2007), s.v. "Kirby-Smith, Edmund." For USG's Aug. 15, 1864, instructions to Halleck regarding Smith, see *PUSG*, 11:423–424.

suggested that it might become necessary to draw troops from the field to put it down. He also advised taking in sail, and not going too fast.[48]

The troops were withdrawn from the north side of the James River on the night of the 20th. Before they were withdrawn, however, and while most of Lee's force was on that side of the river, Warren had been sent with most of the 5th corps to capture the Weldon Railroad. He took up his line of march well back to the rear, south of the enemy, while the troops remaining in the trenches extended so as to cover that part of the line which he had vacated by moving out. From our left, near the old line, it was about three miles to the Weldon Railroad. A division was ordered from the right of the Petersburg line to reinforce Warren, while a division was brought back from the north side of the James River to take its place.[49]

This road was very important to the enemy. The limits from which his supplies had been drawn were already very much contracted, and I knew that he must fight desperately to protect it. Warren carried the road, though with heavy loss on both sides. He fortified his new position, and our trenches were then extended from the left of our main line to connect with his new one. Lee made repeated attempts to dislodge Warren's corps, but without success, and with heavy loss.

As soon as Warren was fortified and reinforcements reached him, troops were sent south to destroy the bridges on the Weldon Railroad; and with such success that the enemy had to draw in wagons, for a distance of about thirty miles, all the supplies they got thereafter from that source. It was on the 21st that Lee seemed to have given up the Weldon Railroad as having been lost to him; but along about the 24th or 25th he made renewed attempts to recapture it; again he failed and with very heavy losses to him as compared with ours.[50]

---

[48] In an Aug. 11, 1864, letter to USG, Halleck had warned USG of the potential resistance to the draft and concluded, "Are not the appearances such that we ought to take in sail and prepare the ship for a storm?" Ibid., 11:424n–425n.

[49] On Aug. 18, 1864, Warren's forces were sent to capture the Weldon Railroad. On the same day, Meade ordered Mott's division to move from Deep Bottom and relieve Parke, who would then send reinforcements to Warren. OR, I, 42(I), 428; I, 42(II), 276; PUSG, 12:33n.

[50] Warren reported a total loss of 1,417 men killed, missing, or wounded during the fight for the Weldon Railroad on Aug. 18–21, 1864. The Confederate losses were not reported, but it was estimated that approximately 1,600 Confederate soldiers were killed, missing, or wounded during the assault. Noah A. Trudeau, The Last Citadel: Petersburg, Virginia, June 1864–April 1865 (Baton Rouge: Louisiana State University Press, 1991), 174; OR, I, 42(I), 429–431.

On the night of the 20th our troops on the north side of the James were withdrawn, and Hancock and Gregg were sent south to destroy the Weldon Railroad. They were attacked on the 25th at Reams's Station, and after desperate fighting a part of our line gave way, losing five pieces of artillery.[51] But the Weldon Railroad never went out of our possession from the 18th of August to the close of the war.

[51] On Aug. 25, 1864, Confederates under the command of Hill attacked Hancock's men near Ream's Station, VA, approximately ten miles south of Petersburg on the Weldon Railroad. The U.S. Army suffered 2,372 losses (mostly prisoners) and the Confederate Army lost 720 men. David J. Eicher, *The Longest Night: A Military History of the Civil War* (New York: Simon and Schuster, 2001), 722 (map), 725.

# 58

## Sheridan's Advance—Visit to Sheridan—Sheridan's Victory in the Shenandoah—Sheridan's Ride to Winchester—Close of the Campaign for the Winter

W E HAD OUR troops on the Weldon Railroad contending against a large force that regarded this road of so much importance that they could afford to expend many lives in retaking it; Sherman just getting through to Atlanta with great losses of men from casualties, discharges and detachments left along as guards to occupy and hold the road in rear of him; Washington threatened but a short time before, and now Early being strengthened in the valley so as, probably, to renew that attempt. It kept me pretty active in looking after all these points.

On the 10th of August Sheridan had advanced on Early up the Shenandoah Valley, Early falling back to Strasburg. On the 12th I learned that Lee had sent twenty pieces of artillery, two divisions of infantry and a considerable cavalry force to strengthen Early. It was important that Sheridan should be informed of this, so I sent the information to Washington by telegraph, and directed a courier to be sent from there to get the message to Sheridan at all hazards, giving him the information.[1] The messenger, an officer of the army, pushed through with great energy and reached Sheridan just in time. The officer went through by way of Snicker's Gap, escorted by some cavalry. He found Sheridan just making his preparations to attack Early in his chosen position. Now, however, he was thrown back on the defensive.[2]

---

[1] For USG's Aug. 12, 1864, telegram for Sheridan, sent to Halleck, see *PUSG*, 11:403.

[2] Sheridan's response (though dated Aug. 13, 1864), did not reach USG's headquarters until Aug. 16. By that time, USG was already with Sheridan and discussed his Aug. 12 message, which had kept Sheridan from taking the offensive. P. H. Sheridan, *Personal Memoirs of P. H. Sheridan, General, United States Army* (New York: Charles L. Webster, 1888), 2:9. For Sheridan's Aug. 13 telegram to USG, see *PUSG*, 11:404n.

On the 15th of September I started to visit General Sheridan in the Shenandoah Valley. My purpose was to have him attack Early, or drive him out of the valley and destroy that source of supplies for Lee's army. I knew it was impossible for me to get orders through Washington to Sheridan to make a move, because they would be stopped there and such orders as Halleck's caution (and that of the Secretary of War) would suggest would be given instead, and would, no doubt, be contradictory to mine. I therefore, without stopping at Washington, went directly through to Charlestown, some ten miles above Harper's Ferry, and waited there to see General Sheridan, having sent a courier in advance to inform him where to meet me.

When Sheridan arrived I asked him if he had a map showing the positions of his army and that of the enemy. He at once drew one out of his side pocket, showing all roads and streams, and the camps of the two armies. He said that if he had permission he would move so and so (pointing out how) against the Confederates, and that he could "whip them." Before starting I had drawn up a plan of campaign for Sheridan, which I had brought with me; but, seeing that he was so clear and so positive in his views and so confident of success, I said nothing about this and did not take it out of my pocket.[3]

Sheridan's wagon trains were kept at Harper's Ferry, where all of his stores were. By keeping the teams at that place, their forage did not have to be hauled to them. As supplies of ammunition, provisions and rations for the men were wanted, trains would be made up to deliver the stores to the commissaries and quartermasters encamped at Winchester. Knowing that he, in making preparations to move at a given day, would have to bring up wagon trains from Harper's Ferry, I asked him if he could be ready to get off by the following Tuesday. This was on Friday. "O yes," he said, he "could be off before daylight on Monday."[4] I told him then to make the attack at that time and according to his own plan; and I immediately started to return to the army about Richmond. After visiting Baltimore and Burlington, New Jersey, I arrived at City Point on the 19th.[5]

---

[3] USG met with Sheridan at Charles Town, WV, on Sept. 16–17, 1864. Ibid., 12:xxii.

[4] USG referred to Friday, Sept. 16, 1864, Monday, Sept. 19, and Tuesday, Sept. 20.

[5] On Sept. 16, 1864, USG visited Baltimore, MD. During his visit to Burlington, NJ, USG made arrangements to send his children to school. He arrived there about midnight on Sept. 17, and departed about 10 P.M. on Sept. 18. *PUSG*, 12:xxii, 171*n*–72*n*.

On the way out to Harper's Ferry I had met Mr. Robert Garrett, President of the Baltimore and Ohio Railroad.[6] He seemed very anxious to know when workmen might be put upon the road again so as to make repairs and put it in shape for running. It was a large piece of property to have standing idle. I told him I could not answer then positively but would try and inform him before a great while. On my return Mr. Garrett met me again with the same question and I told him I thought that by the following Wednesday he might send his workmen out on his road. I gave him no further information however, and he had no suspicion of how I expected to have the road cleared for his workmen.

Sheridan moved at the time he had fixed upon. He met Early at the crossing of Opequon Creek, and won a most decisive victory—one which electrified the country. Early had invited this attack himself by his bad generalship and made the victory easy.[7] He had sent G. T. Anderson's[8] division east of the Blue Ridge before I went to Harper's Ferry; and about the time I arrived there he started with two other divisions (leaving but two in their camps) to march to Martinsburg for the purpose of destroying the Baltimore and Ohio Railroad at that point. Early here learned that I had been with Sheridan and, supposing there was some movement on foot, started back as soon as he got the information.[9] But his forces were separated and, as I have said, he was very badly defeated. He fell back to Fisher's Hill,[10] Sheridan following.

[6] Robert Garrett (1847–1896) became president of the Baltimore and Ohio Railroad in 1884. His father, John W. Garrett (1820–1884), was president of the Baltimore and Ohio Railroad during the Civil War. John was born in Maryland and was a successful businessman. In 1855, he became a board member for the railroad and was president from 1858 until his death. John F. Stover, *History of the Baltimore and Ohio Railroad* (West Lafayette, IN: Purdue University Press, 1995), 79–80, 164, 371.

[7] On Sept. 19, 1864, Sheridan defeated Early at the Third Battle of Winchester (also known as the Battle of Opequon). *PUSG,* 12:xxii.

[8] George T. Anderson (1824–1901) was born in Georgia and joined the U.S. 1st Cav. in 1855 but resigned in 1858. He was commissioned colonel of the 11th Georgia Inf. in July 1861 and promoted to brigadier general in 1862. *CWHC,* 104.

[9] Early was in the Martinsburg, WV, telegraph office on the morning of Sept. 18, 1864, when he learned that USG was visiting Sheridan. Sheridan, *Memoirs,* 2:10.

[10] Fisher's Hill was approximately three miles south of Strasburg, VA. George B. Davis et al., *The Official Military Atlas of the Civil War* (New York: Fairfax Press, 1983), plate 137.

The valley is narrow at that point, and Early made another stand there, behind works which extended across. But Sheridan turned both his flanks and again sent him speeding up the valley, following in hot pursuit. The pursuit was continued up the valley to Mount Jackson and New Market. Sheridan captured about eleven hundred prisoners and sixteen guns.[11] The houses which he passed all along the route were found to be filled with Early's wounded, and the country swarmed with his deserters. Finally, on the 25th, Early turned from the valley eastward, leaving Sheridan at Harrisonburg in undisputed possession.

Now one of the main objects of the expedition began to be accomplished. Sheridan went to work with his command, gathering in the crops, cattle, and everything in the upper part of the valley required by our troops; and especially taking what might be of use to the enemy. What he could not take away he destroyed, so that the enemy would not be invited to come back there. I congratulated Sheridan upon his recent great victory and had a salute of a hundred guns fired in honor of it, the guns being aimed at the enemy around Petersburg. I also notified the other commanders throughout the country, who also fired salutes in honor of his victory.[12]

I had reason to believe that the administration was a little afraid to have a decisive battle fought at that time, for fear it might go against us and have a bad effect on the November elections. The convention which had met and made its nomination of the Democratic candidate for the presidency had declared the war a failure.[13] Treason was talked as boldly in Chicago at that convention as ever it had been in Charleston. It was a question whether the government would then have had the power to make arrests and punish those who thus talked treason. But this decisive victory was the most effective campaign argument made in the canvass.

[11] On Sept. 22, 1864, Sheridan defeated Early at the Battle of Fisher's Hill. Sheridan lost 52 killed, 457 wounded, and 19 missing. Early reported 30 killed, 210 wounded, 995 missing, and 12 guns lost. *OR*, I, 43(I), 124, 556–557; *PUSG*, 12:xxiii.

[12] On Sept. 20, 1864, one day after Sheridan's victory at Opequon, USG ordered a salute to be fired. On Sept. 23, USG informed Sheridan that he had ordered another one-hundred-gun salute after Sheridan's victory at Fisher's Hill. That same day, USG ordered Butler and Meade to issue a salute along their lines. *PUSG*, 12:xxii, 193*n*.

[13] On Aug. 31, 1864, the Democratic National Convention had selected the former commanding general of the U.S. Army, George B. McClellan, as the Democratic nominee for president. Stan M. Haynes, *The First American Political Conventions: Transforming Presidential Nominations, 1832–1872* (Jefferson, NC: McFarland, 2012), 198–199.

Sheridan, in his pursuit, got beyond where they could hear from him in Washington, and the President became very much frightened about him. He was afraid that the hot pursuit had been a little like that of General Cass[14] was said to have been, in one of our Indian wars, when he was an officer of the army. Cass was pursuing the Indians so closely that the first thing he knew he found himself in their front, and the Indians pursuing him.[15] The President was afraid that Sheridan had got on the other side of Early and that Early was in behind him. He was afraid that Sheridan was getting so far away that reinforcements would be sent out from Richmond to enable Early to beat him. I replied to the President that I had taken steps to prevent Lee from sending reinforcements to Early, by attacking the former where he was.[16]

On the 28th of September, to retain Lee in his position, I sent Ord with the 18th corps and Birney with the 10th corps to make an advance on Richmond, to threaten it. Ord moved with the left wing up to Chaffin's Bluff;[17] Birney with the 10th corps took a road farther north;[18] while Kautz with the cavalry took the Darby road, still farther to the north. They got across the river by the next morning, and made an effort to surprise the enemy. In that, however, they were unsuccessful.

---

[14] Lewis Cass (1782–1866) was born in New Hampshire and studied law at Dartmouth College. He served as a brigadier general in the War of 1812, and was appointed governor of the Michigan Territory in 1813. In 1831, he was appointed secretary of war, where he implemented Pres. Andrew Jackson's Indian removal policy. He served as U.S. ambassador to France 1836–1842, senator from Michigan 1845–1848, and U.S. secretary of state 1857–1860. He ran for president in 1848 as the Democratic candidate, but lost to Zachary Taylor. Spencer Tucker, ed., *American Civil War: The Definitive Encyclopedia and Document Collection* (Santa Barbara, CA: ABC-CLIO, 2013), s.v. "Cass, Lewis."

[15] During the presidential election of 1848, Whig opponents, including Lincoln, frequently made jokes about Cass's military record. Willard Carl Klunder, *Lewis Cass and the Politics of Moderation* (Kent, OH: Kent State University Press, 1996), 205–206.

[16] For Lincoln's Sept. 29, 1864, telegram to USG expressing concern that the Confederate Army would attack Sheridan if Lee sent reinforcements to Early, see *PUSG*, 12:229n. For USG's Sept. 29 response, see ibid., 12:228–229.

[17] Chaffin's Bluff was approximately ten miles northwest of City Point, VA, on the north side of the James River. Davis et al., *Official Military Atlas of the Civil War*, plate 100, map 2.

[18] USG probably referred to New Market Road. Richard J. Sommers, *Richmond Redeemed: The Siege at Petersburg* (Garden City, NY: Doubleday, 1981), 105.

The enemy's lines were very strong and very intricate. Stannard's[19] division of the 18th corps with General Burnham's[20] brigade leading, tried an assault against Fort Harrison and captured it with sixteen guns and a good many prisoners. Burnham was killed in the assault. Colonel Stevens who succeeded him was badly wounded; and his successor also fell in the same way.[21] Some works to the right and left were also carried with the guns in them—six in number—and a few more prisoners. Birney's troops to the right captured the enemy's intrenched picket-lines, but were unsuccessful in their efforts upon the main line.

Our troops fortified their new position, bringing Fort Harrison into the new line and extending it to the river. This brought us pretty close to the enemy on the north side of the James, and the two opposing lines maintained their relative positions to the close of the siege.

In the afternoon a further attempt was made to advance, but it failed. Ord fell badly wounded, and had to be relieved; the command devolved upon General Heckman,[22] and later General Weitzel was assigned to the command of the 18th corps. During the night Lee reinforced his troops about Fort Gilmer, which was at the right of Fort Harrison, by transferring eight additional brigades from Petersburg, and attempted to retake the works which we had captured by concentrating ten brigades against them. All their efforts failed, their attacks being all repulsed with very heavy loss. In one of these assaults upon us General Stannard, a gallant officer, who was defending Fort Harrison, lost

[19] George J. Stannard (1820–1886) was born in Vermont and joined the 4th Vermont Militia as a colonel in 1860. In June 1861, he became a colonel of the 2nd Vermont Inf. and was promoted to brigadier general in Mar. 1863. On Sept. 29, 1864, at the Battle of Fort Harrison, he commanded the 1st Div., 18th Corps, Army of the James. *CWHC*, 505.

[20] Hiram Burnham (1814–1864) was born in Maine and was a lieutenant colonel in the 6th Maine Inf. at the start of the Civil War. In Dec. 1861, he was promoted to colonel and to brigadier general in Apr. 1864. On Sept. 29, he died after being shot in the abdomen at Fort Harrison. Ibid., 155.

[21] Burnham was succeeded by his second-in-command, Michael Donohoe (1838–1895), who was also wounded in the fighting. There is no indication that Aaron F. Stevens (1819–1887) replaced Burnham, although Stevens was wounded in the hip at Fort Harrison on Sept. 29, 1864. Ibid., 212, 509; *OR*, I, 42(I), 135.

[22] Charles A. Heckman (1822–1896) was born in Pennsylvania and graduated from the Minerva Seminary in 1837. In Apr. 1861, he joined the 1st Pennsylvania Inf. as a captain and was promoted to brigadier general in Nov. 1862. On Sept. 29, 1864, he took over Ord's command of the 18th Corps, Army of the James. *CWHC*, 292.

an arm. Our casualties during these operations amounted to 394 killed, 1,554 wounded and 324 missing.[23]

Whilst this was going on General Meade was instructed to keep up an appearance of moving troops to our extreme left. Parke and Warren were kept with two divisions, each under arms, ready to move, leaving their enclosed batteries manned, with a scattering line on the other intrenchments. The object of this was to prevent reinforcements from going to the north side of the river. Meade was instructed to watch the enemy closely and, if Lee weakened his lines, to make an attack.[24]

On the 30th these troops moved out, under Warren, and captured an advanced intrenched camp at Peeble's farm,[25] driving the enemy back to the main line. Our troops followed and made an attack in the hope of carrying the enemy's main line; but in this they were unsuccessful and lost a large number of men, mostly captured. The number of killed and wounded was not large.[26] The next day our troops advanced again and established themselves, intrenching a new line about a mile in front of the enemy. This advanced Warren's position on the Weldon Railroad very considerably.

Sheridan having driven the enemy out of the valley, and taken the productions of the valley so that instead of going there for supplies the enemy would have to bring his provisions with him if he again entered it, recommended a reduction of his own force, the surplus to be sent where it could be of more use. I approved of his suggestion, and ordered him to send Wright's corps back to the James River. I further directed him to repair the railroad up the Shenandoah Valley towards the advanced position which we would hold with a small force. The troops were to be sent to Washington by the way of Culpeper, in order to watch the east side of the Blue Ridge, and prevent the

[23] Combined U.S. casualties for the battles of New Market Heights, Chaffin's Farm, Laurel Hill, and Forts Harrison and Gilmer on Sept. 28–30, 1864, were 383 killed, 2,299 wounded, and 645 missing. Combined Confederate casualties were 250 killed, 1,250 wounded, and 500 missing. Edward H. Bonekemper III, *A Victor, Not a Butcher: Ulysses S. Grant's Overlooked Military Genius* (Washington, DC: Regnery, 2004), 317.

[24] For USG's Sept. 29, 1864, telegram to Meade regarding a potential assault, see *PUSG*, 12:237–238.

[25] Peeble's Farm was approximately four miles south of Petersburg, VA. Davis et al., *Official Military Atlas of the Civil War*, plate 77, map 2.

[26] Meade reported that approximately 2,500 troops under Parke and Warren were killed, captured, or missing. *OR*, I, 42(III), 36.

enemy from getting into the rear of Sheridan while he was still doing his work of destruction.[27]

The valley was so very important, however, to the Confederate army that, contrary to our expectations, they determined to make one more strike, and save it if possible before the supplies should be all destroyed. Reinforcements were sent therefore to Early, and this before any of our troops had been withdrawn.[28] Early prepared to strike Sheridan at Harrisonburg; but the latter had not remained there.

On the 6th of October Sheridan commenced retiring down the valley, taking or destroying all the food and forage and driving the cattle before him, Early following. At Fisher's Hill Sheridan turned his cavalry back on that of Early, which, under the lead of Rosser, was pursuing closely, and routed it most completely, capturing eleven guns and a large number of prisoners. Sheridan lost only about sixty men.[29] His cavalry pursued the enemy back some twenty-five miles. On the 10th of October the march down the valley was again resumed, Early again following.

I now ordered Sheridan to halt, and to improve the opportunity if afforded by the enemy's having been sufficiently weakened, to move back again and cut the James River Canal and Virginia Central Railroad. But this order had to go through Washington where it was intercepted; and when Sheridan received what purported to be a statement of what I wanted him to do it was something entirely different. Halleck informed Sheridan that it was my wish for him to hold a forward position as a base from which to act against Charlottesville and Gordonsville; that he should fortify this position and provision it.[30]

Sheridan objected to this most decidedly; and I was impelled to telegraph him, on the 14th, as follows:

[27] On Oct. 1, 1864, Sheridan informed USG that his forces could be reduced if needed. On Oct. 3, USG accepted Sheridan's offer. *PUSG*, 12:268, 269n.

[28] On Sept. 27, 1864, Lee informed Early that "all the reserves in the Valley have been ordered to you." Adam Badeau, *Military History of Ulysses S. Grant, from April, 1861, to April, 1865* (New York: D. Appleton, 1881), 3:85n.

[29] Confederate casualties at Fisher's Hill were 32 killed and 229 wounded. U.S. forces lost 52 killed, 457 wounded, and 19 missing. *OR* I, 43(I), 124, 557.

[30] On Oct. 11, 1864, USG sent Halleck his orders for Sheridan to cut off the Virginia Central Railroad. The next day, Halleck sent Sheridan the order to take a "position far enough south to serve as a base for future operations upon Gordonsville and Charlottesville." *PUSG*, 12:286; *OR*, I, 43(II), 345.

CITY POINT, VA.,
*October* 14, 1864.—12.30 P.M.

MAJOR-GENERAL SHERIDAN,
Cedar Creek, Va.

What I want is for you to threaten the Virginia Central Railroad
and canal in the manner your judgment tells you is best, holding
yourself ready to advance, if the enemy draw off their forces. If you
make the enemy hold a force equal to your own for the protection of
those thoroughfares, it will accomplish nearly as much as their destruction. If you cannot do this, then the next best thing to do is to send
here all the force you can. I deem a good cavalry force necessary for
your offensive, as well as defensive operations. You need not therefore
send here more than one division of cavalry.

U. S. GRANT,
Lieutenant-General.

Sheridan having been summoned to Washington City, started on the 15th
leaving Wright in command. His army was then at Cedar Creek, some twenty
miles south of Winchester. The next morning while at Front Royal, Sheridan
received a dispatch from Wright, saying that a dispatch from Longstreet to
Early had been intercepted. It directed the latter to be ready to move and to
crush Sheridan as soon as he, Longstreet, arrived.[31] On the receipt of this news
Sheridan ordered the cavalry up the valley to join Wright.

On the 18th of October Early was ready to move, and during the night succeeded in getting his troops in the rear of our left flank, which fled precipitately
and in great confusion down the valley, losing eighteen pieces of artillery and
a thousand or more prisoners.[32] The right under General Getty maintained
a firm and steady front, falling back to Middletown where it took a position
and made a stand. The cavalry went to the rear, seized the roads leading to
Winchester and held them for the use of our troops in falling back, General
Wright having ordered a retreat back to that place.

Sheridan having left Washington on the 18th, reached Winchester that night.
The following morning he started to join his command. He had scarcely got

---

[31] On Oct. 16, 1864, Wright sent Longstreet's dispatch on to Sheridan. The Confederate
message proved to be a diversion but it made Sheridan cautious about Early's real strength.
Sheridan, *Memoirs*, 2:63.

[32] The total number of U.S. soldiers captured or missing in the Cedar Creek campaign was
1,591. *OR*, I, 43(I), 137.

out of town, when he met his men returning in panic from the front and also heard heavy firing to the south. He immediately ordered the cavalry at Winchester to be deployed across the valley to stop the stragglers. Leaving members of his staff to take care of Winchester and the public property there, he set out with a small escort directly for the scene of battle. As he met the fugitives he ordered them to turn back, reminding them that they were going the wrong way. His presence soon restored confidence. Finding themselves worse frightened than hurt the men did halt and turn back. Many of those who had run ten miles got back in time to redeem their reputation as gallant soldiers before night.[33]

When Sheridan got to the front he found Getty and Custer still holding their ground firmly between the Confederates and our retreating troops. Everything in the rear was now ordered up. Sheridan at once proceeded to intrench his position; and he awaited an assault from the enemy. This was made with vigor, and was directed principally against Emory's corps, which had sustained the principal loss in the first attack. By one o'clock the attack was repulsed. Early was so badly damaged that he seemed disinclined to make another attack, but went to work to intrench himself with a view to holding the position he had already gained. He thought, no doubt, that Sheridan would be glad enough to leave him unmolested; but in this he was mistaken.

About the middle of the afternoon Sheridan advanced. He sent his cavalry by both flanks, and they penetrated to the enemy's rear. The contest was close for a time, but at length the left of the enemy broke, and disintegration along the whole line soon followed. Early tried to rally his men, but they were followed so closely that they had to give way very quickly every time they attempted to make a stand. Our cavalry, having pushed on and got in the rear of the Confederates, captured twenty-four pieces of artillery, besides retaking what had been lost in the morning. This victory pretty much closed the campaigning in the Valley of Virginia. All the Confederate troops were sent back to Richmond with the exception of one division of infantry and a little cavalry. Wright's corps was ordered back to the Army of the Potomac, and two other divisions were withdrawn from the valley. Early had lost more men in

---

[33] This engagement, known as the Battle of Cedar Creek, was the last major battle in the Shenandoah Valley. Sheridan's ride to Cedar Creek to rally his troops became one of the most well-known events of the war, inspiring the poem "Sheridan's Ride," which took liberties with the actual distance covered but captured the nation's imagination. Tucker, *American Civil War,* s.v. "Thomas Buchanan Read: Poem, 'Sheridan's Ride' (1864)"; Charles Bracelen Flood, *1864: Lincoln at the Gates of History* (New York: Simon and Schuster, 2009), 342; *PUSG,* 12:xxiv.

killed, wounded and captured in the valley than Sheridan had commanded from first to last.[34]

On more than one occasion in these engagements General R. B. Hayes, who succeeded me as President of the United States, bore a very honorable part.[35] His conduct on the field was marked by conspicuous gallantry as well as the display of qualities of a higher order than that of mere personal daring. This might well have been expected of one who could write at the time he is said to have done so: "Any officer fit for duty who at this crisis would abandon his post to electioneer for a seat in Congress, ought to be scalped."[36] Having entered the army as a Major of Volunteers at the beginning of the war, General Hayes attained by meritorious service the rank of Brevet Major-General before its close.

On the north side of the James River the enemy attacked Kautz's cavalry on the 7th of October, and drove it back with heavy loss in killed, wounded and prisoners, and the loss of all the artillery.[37] This was followed up by an attack on our intrenched infantry line, but was repulsed with severe slaughter. On the 13th a reconnoissance was sent out by General Butler, with a view to drive the enemy from some new works he was constructing, which resulted in heavy loss to us.[38]

On the 24th I ordered General Meade to attempt to get possession of the South Side Railroad, and for that purpose to advance on the 27th. The attempt proved a failure, however, the most advanced of our troops not getting

[34] The aggregate total of Sheridan's killed, wounded, and missing in his 1864 Shenandoah Valley campaign was approximately 17,000 men. The losses for Early are difficult to compute because Confederate records are incomplete. However, Confederate casualties for this time period were approximately 7,000. Thomas L. Livermore, *Numbers and Losses in the Civil War in America, 1861–65* (Boston: Houghton, Mifflin, 1900), 127–131; George E. Pond, *The Shenandoah Valley in 1864* (New York: Charles Scribner's Sons, 1886), 269.

[35] Rutherford B. Hayes (1822–1893) was born in Ohio and later graduated from Harvard Law School in 1845. In June 1861, he joined the 23rd Ohio Inf. as a major. In Oct. 1864, he was promoted to brigadier general. During the Battle of Cedar Creek, he commanded the 1st Brigade, 2nd Div., Dept. of West Virginia. On Mar. 12, 1865, he was made brevet major general. Hayes served as president of the United States from 1877 to 1881. *CWHC*, 290.

[36] Hayes made the statement in an Aug. 24, 1864, letter to William H. Smith. Charles Richard Williams, *The Life of Rutherford Birchard Hayes: Nineteenth President of the United States* (Boston: Houghton Mifflin, 1914), 1:234.

[37] Kautz reported that 218 of his men were killed, missing, or wounded. *OR*, I, 42(I), 823.

[38] The Oct. 13, 1864, Battle of Darbytown Road resulted in 437 U.S. losses and 513 Confederate losses. Ibid., I, 42(I), 128, 681–682.

nearer than within six miles of the point aimed for. Seeing the impossibility of its accomplishment I ordered the troops to withdraw, and they were all back in their former positions the next day.

Butler, by my directions, also made a demonstration on the north side of the James River in order to support this move, by detaining there the Confederate troops who were on that side.[39] He succeeded in this, but failed of further results by not marching past the enemy's left before turning in on the Darby road and by reason of simply coming up against their lines in place.

This closed active operations around Richmond for the winter. Of course there was frequent skirmishing between pickets, but no serious battle was fought near either Petersburg or Richmond. It would prolong this work to give a detailed account of all that took place from day to day around Petersburg and at other parts of my command, and it would not interest the general reader if given. All these details can be found by the military student in a series of books published by the Scribners, Badeau's history of my campaigns, and also in the publications of the War Department, including both the National and Confederate reports.[40]

In the latter part of November General Hancock was relieved from the command of the 2d corps by the Secretary of War and ordered to Washington, to organize and command a corps of veteran troops to be designated the 1st corps.[41] It was expected that this would give him a large command to co-operate with in the spring. It was my expectation, at the time, that in the final operations Hancock should move either up the valley, or else east of the Blue Ridge to Lynchburg; the idea being to make the spring campaign the close of the war. I expected, with Sherman coming up from the South, Meade south of Petersburg and around Richmond, and Thomas's command in Tennessee with depots of supplies established in the eastern part of that State, to move from the

[39] The copy of the order to Butler published in *PUSG* was dated Oct. 20, 1864, but the version of the letter in *OR*, I, 42(III), 331–332 is dated Oct. 24. According to the note in *PUSG*, the Oct. 20 date is probably incorrect since USG tended to discuss orders given to Butler with Meade first. USG conferred with Meade on Oct. 21 and provided directions to him on Oct. 24 for the proposed movement on Oct. 27. *PUSG*, 12:331–332, 332*n*.

[40] USG referred to *Campaigns of the Civil War* (New York: Scribner, 1883) series; Badeau's *Military History of Ulysses S. Grant*; and *OR*, the first volume of which was published in 1881.

[41] On Nov. 26, 1864, Hancock relinquished his command of the 2nd Corps. On Nov. 28, Stanton's General Orders No. 287 placed Hancock in command of the 1st Corps. *OR*, I, 42(III), 713, 728.

direction of Washington or the valley towards Lynchburg. We would then have Lee so surrounded that his supplies would be cut off entirely, making it impossible for him to support his army.

General Humphreys, chief-of-staff of the Army of the Potomac, was assigned to the command of the 2d corps, to succeed Hancock.[42]

---

[42] Because of a wound received during the Battle of Gettysburg, Hancock was unable to continue as a field commander. Humphreys officially took command on Nov. 25, 1864. *CWHC*, 277–278; Andrew A. Humphreys, *The Virginia Campaign of 1864 and 1865: The Army of the Potomac and the Army of the James* (New York: Charles Scribner's Sons, 1883), 312; *OR*, I, 42(III), 713.

# 59

## The Campaign in Georgia—Sherman's March to the Sea—War Anecdotes—The March on Savannah— Investment of Savannah—Capture of Savannah

L ET US NOW return to the operations in the military division of the Mississippi, and accompany Sherman in his march to the sea.

The possession of Atlanta by us narrowed the territory of the enemy very materially and cut off one of his two remaining lines of roads from east to west.[1]

A short time after the fall of Atlanta Mr. Davis visited Palmetto and Macon and made speeches at each place. He spoke at Palmetto on the 20th of September, and at Macon on the 22d.[2] Inasmuch as he had relieved Johnston and appointed Hood, and Hood had immediately taken the initiative, it is natural to suppose that Mr. Davis was disappointed with General Johnston's policy. My own judgment is that Johnston acted very wisely: he husbanded his men and saved as much of his territory as he could, without fighting decisive battles in which all might be lost. As Sherman advanced, as I have shown, his army became spread out, until, if this had been continued, it would have been easy to destroy it in detail. I know that both Sherman and I were rejoiced when we

[1] The capture of Atlanta, GA, gave U.S. forces control of the Western and Atlantic Railroad, as well as the Georgia Railroad, the Macon and Western Railroad, and the Atlanta and West Point Railroad. However, numerous other railroads north and south of Atlanta remained in Confederate control. Robert C. Black III, *The Railroads of the Confederacy* (Chapel Hill: University of North Carolina Press, 1952), enclosed map.

[2] Jefferson Davis spoke at Macon, GA, on Sept. 23, 1864, and at Palmetto, GA, on Sept. 25. William J. Cooper Jr., *Jefferson Davis, American* (New York: Knopf, 2000), 489; Jefferson Davis, *The Papers of Jefferson Davis,* vol. 11, ed. Lynda Laswell Crist, Barbara J. Rozek, and Kenneth H. Williams (Baton Rouge: Louisiana State University Press, 2003), xli. For the text of Davis's Macon speech, see ibid., 61–63.

heard of the change. Hood was unquestionably a brave, gallant soldier and not destitute of ability; but unfortunately his policy was to fight the enemy wherever he saw him, without thinking much of the consequences of defeat.

In his speeches Mr. Davis denounced Governor Brown, of Georgia,[3] and General Johnston in unmeasured terms, even insinuating that their loyalty to the Southern cause was doubtful. So far as General Johnston is concerned, I think Davis did him a great injustice in this particular. I had known the general before the war and strongly believed it would be impossible for him to accept a high commission for the purpose of betraying the cause he had espoused. Then, as I have said, I think that his policy was the best one that could have been pursued by the whole South—protract the war, which was all that was necessary to enable them to gain recognition in the end. The North was already growing weary, as the South evidently was also, but with this difference. In the North the people governed, and could stop hostilities whenever they chose to stop supplies. The South was a military camp, controlled absolutely by the government with soldiers to back it, and the war could have been protracted, no matter to what extent the discontent reached, up to the point of open mutiny of the soldiers themselves. Mr. Davis's speeches were frank appeals to the people of Georgia and that portion of the South to come to their relief. He tried to assure his frightened hearers that the Yankees were rapidly digging their own graves; that measures were already being taken to cut them off from supplies from the North; and that with a force in front, and cut off from the rear, they must soon starve in the midst of a hostile people. Papers containing reports of these speeches immediately reached the Northern States, and they were republished.[4] Of course, that caused no alarm so long as telegraphic communication was kept up with Sherman.

When Hood was forced to retreat from Atlanta he moved to the south-west and was followed by a portion of Sherman's army. He soon appeared upon the railroad in Sherman's rear, and with his whole army began destroying the road.[5] At the same time also the work was begun in Tennessee and Kentucky

[3] Joseph E. Brown (1821–1894) was born in South Carolina and moved to Georgia. He was elected state senator in 1849, circuit court judge in 1855, and governor in 1857. He served as a U.S. senator from Georgia from 1880 to 1891. *CWHC*, 147.

[4] The speech itself was printed in the Macon *Telegraph* on Sept. 24, 1864. Davis, *Papers*, 11:63.

[5] On Sept. 21, 1864, Hood established his army on the Montgomery and Selma Railroad near Palmetto Station, GA. John F. Marszalek, *Sherman: A Soldier's Passion for Order* (New York: Free Press, 1993), 290.

which Mr. Davis had assured his hearers at Palmetto and Macon would take place. He ordered Forrest (about the ablest cavalry general in the South) north for this purpose; and Forrest and Wheeler carried out their orders with more or less destruction, occasionally picking up a garrison. Forrest indeed performed the very remarkable feat of capturing, with cavalry, two gunboats and a number of transports, something the accomplishment of which is very hard to account for.[6] Hood's army had been weakened by Governor Brown's withdrawing the Georgia State troops for the purpose of gathering in the season's crops for the use of the people and for the use of the army.[7] This not only depleted Hood's forces but it served a most excellent purpose in gathering in supplies of food and forage for the use of our army in its subsequent march. Sherman was obliged to push on with his force and go himself with portions of it hither and thither, until it was clearly demonstrated to him that with the army he then had it would be impossible to hold the line from Atlanta back and leave him any force whatever with which to take the offensive. Had that plan been adhered to, very large reinforcements would have been necessary; and Mr. Davis's prediction of the destruction of the army would have been realized, or else Sherman would have been obliged to make a successful retreat, which Mr. Davis said in his speeches would prove more disastrous than Napoleon's retreat from Moscow.[8]

These speeches of Mr. Davis were not long in reaching Sherman.[9] He took advantage of the information they gave, and made all the preparation possible for him to make to meet what now became expected, attempts to break his communications. Something else had to be done: and to Sherman's sensible

---

[6] During the Nov. 4–5, 1864, Battle of Johnsonville, TN, Confederate troops captured and destroyed several gunboats. The battle allowed Forrest to commence a twenty-three-day raid that ultimately destroyed over $2 million worth of U.S. supplies and property. Earl J. Hess, *The Civil War in the West: Victory and Defeat from the Appalachians to the Mississippi* (Chapel Hill: University of North Carolina Press, 2012), 252–253.

[7] On Sept. 10, 1864, Brown issued the troops thirty-day furloughs to harvest crops. Joseph H. Parks, *Joseph E. Brown of Georgia and the Confederacy* (Baton Rouge: Louisiana State University Press, 1977), 294–295.

[8] Davis made this claim in his Sept. 23, 1864, speech in Macon. French emperor Napoleon I (1769–1821) invaded Russia in 1812 but overextended his supply lines and was forced to retreat with his decimated force. Paul Legassé, ed., *The Columbia Encyclopedia* (New York: Columbia University Press, 2000), s.v. "Napoleon I"; Davis, *Papers,* 11:61.

[9] Sherman learned of Davis's speeches on Sept. 26, 1864, when a spy reported the details. Marszalek, *Sherman,* 290; William T. Sherman, *Memoirs of General William T. Sherman* (New York: D. Appleton, 1875), 2:141.

and soldierly mind the idea was not long in dawning upon him, not only that something else had to be done, but what that something else should be.

On September 10th I telegraphed Sherman as follows:

CITY POINT, VA., *Sept.* 10, 1864.

MAJOR-GENERAL SHERMAN,
Atlanta, Georgia.

So soon as your men are sufficiently rested, and preparations can be made, it is desirable that another campaign should be commenced. We want to keep the enemy constantly pressed to the end of the war. If we give him no peace whilst the war lasts, the end cannot be distant. Now that we have all of Mobile Bay that is valuable, I do not know but it will be the best move to transfer Canby's troops to act upon Savannah, whilst you move on Augusta. I should like to hear from you, however, in this matter.

U. S. GRANT,
Lieutenant-General.

Sherman replied promptly:

"If I could be sure of finding provisions and ammunition at Augusta, or Columbus, Georgia, I can march to Milledgeville, and compel Hood to give up Augusta or Macon, and then turn on the other. * * * If you can manage to take the Savannah River as high up as Augusta, or the Chattahoochee as far up as Columbus, I can sweep the whole State of Georgia."[10]

On the 12th I sent a special messenger, one of my own staff, with a letter inviting Sherman's views about the next campaign.

CITY POINT, VA., *Sept.* 12, 1864.

MAJOR-GENERAL W. T. SHERMAN,
Commanding Mil. Division of the Mississippi.

I send Lieutenant-Colonel Porter,[11] of my staff, with this. Colonel Porter will explain to you the exact condition of affairs here better than I can do in the limits of a letter. Although I feel myself strong enough

---

[10] For Sherman's full Sept. 10, 1864, telegram, see *PUSG,* 12:144*n.*

[11] Horace Porter (1837–1921) was born in Pennsylvania and graduated from the USMA in 1860. He served as aide-de-camp to USG from Apr. 1864 to Mar. 1869 and as USG's secretary from 1869 to 1873. Porter was ambassador to France from 1897 to 1905 and was awarded the Medal of Honor in 1902. *CWHC,* 435–436.

for offensive operations, I am holding on quietly to get advantage of recruits and convalescents, who are coming forward very rapidly. My lines are necessarily very long, extending from Deep Bottom north of the James across the peninsula formed by the Appomattox and the James, and south of the Appomattox to the Weldon Road. This line is very strongly fortified, and can be held with comparatively few men, but from its great length takes many in the aggregate. I propose, when I do move, to extend my left so as to control what is known as the South Side, or Lynchburg and Petersburg Road, then if possible to keep the Danville Road cut. At the same time this move is made, I want to send a force of from six to ten thousand men against Wilmington.

The way I propose to do this is to land the men north of Fort Fisher, and hold that point. At the same time a large naval fleet will be assembled there, and the iron-clads will run the batteries as they did at Mobile. This will give us the same control of the harbor of Wilmington that we now have of the harbor of Mobile. What you are to do with the forces at your command, I do not see. The difficulties of supplying your army, except when you are constantly moving, beyond where you are, I plainly see. If it had not been for Price's movements Canby would have sent twelve thousand more men to Mobile. From your command on the Mississippi an equal number could have been taken. With these forces my idea would have been to divide them, sending one half to Mobile and the other half to Savannah. You could then move as proposed in your telegram, so as to threaten Macon and Augusta equally. Whichever was abandoned by the enemy you could take and open up a new base of supplies. My object now in sending a staff officer is not so much to suggest operations for you, as to get your views and have plans matured by the time everything can be got ready. It will probably be the 5th of October before any of the plans herein indicated will be executed.

If you have any promotions to recommend, send the names forward and I will approve them. * * *

U. S. GRANT,
Lieutenant-General.[12]

---

[12] For the full letter, see *PUSG,* 12:154–155.

This reached Sherman on September 20th.

On the 25th of September Sherman reported to Washington that Hood's troops were in his rear. He had provided against this by sending a division to Chattanooga and a division to Rome, Georgia, which was in the rear of Hood, supposing that Hood would fall back in the direction from which he had come to reach the railroad. At the same time Sherman and Hood kept up a correspondence relative to the exchange of prisoners, the treatment of citizens, and other matters suitable to be arranged between hostile commanders in the field. On the 27th of September I telegraphed Sherman as follows:

CITY POINT, VA.,
*September* 27, 1864.—10.30 A.M.

MAJOR-GENERAL SHERMAN:

I have directed all recruits and new troops from the Western States to be sent to Nashville, to receive their further orders from you. * * *

U. S. GRANT,
Lieutenant-General.[13]

On the 29th Sherman sent Thomas back to Chattanooga, and afterwards to Nashville, with another division (Morgan's)[14] of the advanced army. Sherman then suggested that, when he was prepared, his movements should take place against Milledgeville and then to Savannah. His expectation at that time was, to make this movement as soon as he could get up his supplies. Hood was moving in his own country, and was moving light so that he could make two miles to Sherman's one. He depended upon the country to gather his supplies, and so was not affected by delays.

As I have said, until this unexpected state of affairs happened, Mobile had been looked upon as the objective point of Sherman's army. It had been a favorite move of mine from 1862, when I first suggested to the then commander-in-chief that the troops in Louisiana, instead of frittering away their time in the trans-Mississippi, should move against Mobile. I recommended this from time to time until I came into command of the army, the last of March 1864.[15]

---

[13] For the full telegram, see ibid., 12:212*n*.

[14] James D. Morgan (1810–1896) was born in Massachusetts and moved to Illinois in 1839. He became a lieutenant colonel in the 10th Illinois Inf. in Apr. 1861 and rose to brigadier general in 1862. *CWHC,* 397.

[15] For USG's July 24 and Aug. 1, 1863, letters to Halleck about the proposed capture of Mobile, AL, see *PUSG,* 9:109, 137–138.

Having the power in my own hands, I now ordered the concentration of supplies, stores and troops, in the department of the Gulf about New Orleans, with a view to a move against Mobile, in support of, and in conjunction with, the other armies operating in the field.[16] Before I came into command, these troops had been scattered over the trans-Mississippi department in such a way that they could not be, or were not, gotten back in time to take any part in the original movement; hence the consideration, which had caused Mobile to be selected as the objective point for Sherman's army to find his next base of supplies after having cut loose from Atlanta, no longer existed.

General G. M. Dodge, an exceedingly efficient officer, having been badly wounded, had to leave the army about the first of October.[17] He was in command of two divisions of the 16th corps, consolidated into one. Sherman then divided his army into the right and left wings—the right commanded by General O. O. Howard and the left by General Slocum. General Dodge's two divisions were assigned, one to each of these wings. Howard's command embraced the 15th and 17th corps, and Slocum's the 14th and 20th corps, commanded by Generals Jeff. C. Davis and A. S. Williams.[18] Generals Logan and Blair commanded the two corps composing the right wing. About this time they left to take part in the presidential election, which took place that year, leaving their corps to Osterhaus and Ransom. I have no doubt that their leaving was at the earnest solicitation of the War Department. General Blair got back in time to resume his command and to proceed with it throughout the march to the sea and back to the grand review at Washington. General Logan did not return to his command until after it reached Savannah.[19]

[16] For USG's Mar. 31, 1864, orders to Banks regarding cooperation with other armies, see ibid., 10:242–243.

[17] On Aug. 19, 1864, Confederate sharpshooters near Atlanta hit Dodge in the head. Dodge was assigned to the Dept. of the Missouri from Dec. 1864 to July 1865 and resigned from the military in 1866. *CWHC*, 212; Stanley P. Hirshon, *Grenville M. Dodge* (Bloomington: Indiana University Press, 1967), 104–105.

[18] Alpheus S. Williams (1810–1878) was born in Connecticut and graduated from Yale University in 1831. He served in the Mexican-American War and in Apr. 1861 was a brigadier general in the Michigan Militia. Williams was U.S. minister to El Salvador from 1866 to 1869 and a U.S. representative from Michigan from 1875 to 1878. *CWHC*, 571.

[19] Both Blair and Logan were granted leave in Sept. 1864 to travel home for the fall political campaign. Blair returned to military service in late Oct., while Logan returned in Jan. 1865. James P. Jones, *Black Jack: John A. Logan and Southern Illinois in the Civil War Era* (Carbondale: Southern Illinois University Press, 1995), 233, 244; William E. Parrish, *Frank Blair: Lincoln's Conservative* (Columbia: University of Missouri Press, 1998), 201, 205.

Logan felt very much aggrieved at the transfer of General Howard from that portion of the Army of the Potomac which was then with the Western Army, to the command of the Army of the Tennessee, with which army General Logan had served from the battle of Belmont to the fall of Atlanta—having passed successively through all grades from colonel commanding a regiment to general commanding a brigade, division and army corps, until upon the death of McPherson the command of the entire Army of the Tennessee devolved upon him in the midst of a hotly contested battle. He conceived that he had done his full duty as commander in that engagement; and I can bear testimony, from personal observation, that he had proved himself fully equal to all the lower positions which he had occupied as a soldier. I will not pretend to question the motive which actuated Sherman in taking an officer from another army to supersede General Logan. I have no doubt, whatever, that he did this for what he considered would be to the good of the service, which was more important than that the personal feelings of any individual should not be aggrieved; though I doubt whether he had an officer with him who could have filled the place as Logan would have done. Differences of opinion must exist between the best of friends as to policies in war, and of judgment as to men's fitness. The officer who has the command, however, should be allowed to judge of the fitness of the officers under him, unless he is very manifestly wrong.

Sherman's army, after all the depletions, numbered about sixty thousand effective men.[20] All weak men had been left to hold the rear, and those remaining were not only well men, but strong and hardy, so that he had sixty thousand as good soldiers as ever trod the earth; better than any European soldiers, because they not only worked like a machine but the machine thought. European armies know very little what they are fighting for, and care less.[21] Included in these sixty thousand troops, there were two small divisions of cavalry, numbering altogether about four thousand men. Hood had about thirty-five to forty thousand men, independent of Forrest, whose forces were operating in Tennessee and Kentucky, as Mr. Davis had promised they should. This part of Mr. Davis's military plan was admirable, and promised the best

[20] Sherman left Atlanta with 62,000 men. John F. Marszalek, *Sherman's March to the Sea* (Abilene, TX: McWhiney Foundation Press, 2005), 33.

[21] USG expressed a misconception of European armies common in the United States from the time of the American Revolution. For further discussion of this perspective, see Don H. Hagist, *British Soldiers, American War: Voice of the American Revolution* (Yardley, PA: Westholme, 2014).

results of anything he could have done, according to my judgment. I say this because I have criticised his military judgment in the removal of Johnston, and also in the appointment of Hood. I am aware, however, that there was high feeling existing at that time between Davis and his subordinate, whom I regarded as one of his ablest lieutenants.

On the 5th of October the railroad back from Atlanta was again very badly broken, Hood having got on the track with his army. Sherman saw after night, from a high point, the road burning for miles. The defence of the railroad by our troops was very gallant, but they could not hold points between their intrenched positions against Hood's whole army; in fact they made no attempt to do so; but generally the intrenched positions were held, as well as important bridges, and stores located at them. Allatoona, for instance, was defended by a small force of men under the command of General Corse, one of the very able and efficient volunteer officers produced by the war. He, with a small force, was cut off from the remainder of the National army and was attacked with great vigor by many times his own number. Sherman from his high position could see the battle raging, with the Confederate troops between him and his subordinate. He sent men, of course, to raise the temporary siege, but the time that would be necessarily consumed in reaching Corse, would be so great that all occupying the intrenchments might be dead. Corse was a man who would never surrender. From a high position some of Sherman's signal corps discovered a signal flag waving from a hole in the block house at Allatoona. It was from Corse. He had been shot through the face, but he signalled to his chief a message which left no doubt of his determination to hold his post at all hazards.[22] It was at this point probably, that Sherman first realized that with the forces at his disposal, the keeping open of his line of communications with the North would be impossible if he expected to retain any force with which to operate offensively beyond Atlanta. He proposed, therefore, to destroy the roads back to Chattanooga, when all ready to move, and leave the latter place garrisoned.[23] Yet, before abandoning the railroad, it was necessary that he should repair damages already done, and hold the road until he could get forward such supplies, ordnance stores and small rations, as he wanted to

[22] The story developed that Sherman sent a message by flag to Corse: "Hold the Fort! for I am Coming" and thus inspired the Civil War song of the same name. In 1887, Sherman said this was not true, but he would let the story "stand uncontradicted." Marszalek, *Sherman*, 291–292.

[23] Sherman first began discussing this plan with USG in an Oct. 11, 1864, telegram and continued to share details of the proposed strategy with USG in Oct. 22 and Nov. 1 telegrams. *PUSG*, 12:290n, 318n–319n, 371n.

carry with him on his proposed march, and to return to the north his surplus artillery; his object being to move light and to have no more artillery than could be used to advantage on the field.

Sherman thought Hood would follow him, though he proposed to prepare for the contingency of the latter moving the other way while he was moving south, by making Thomas strong enough to hold Tennessee and Kentucky. I, myself, was thoroughly satisfied that Hood would go north, as he did. On the 2d of November I telegraphed Sherman authorizing him definitely to move according to the plan he had proposed: that is, cutting loose from his base, giving up Atlanta and the railroad back to Chattanooga. To strengthen Thomas he sent Stanley (4th corps) back, and also ordered Schofield, commanding the Army of the Ohio, twelve thousand strong, to report to him. In addition to this, A. J. Smith, who, with two divisions of Sherman's army, was in Missouri aiding Rosecrans in driving the enemy from that State, was under orders to return to Thomas and, under the most unfavorable circumstances, might be expected to arrive there long before Hood could reach Nashville.[24]

In addition to this, the new levies of troops that were being raised in the North-west went to Thomas as rapidly as enrolled and equipped.[25] Thomas, without any of these additions spoken of, had a garrison at Chattanooga— which had been strengthened by one division—and garrisons at Bridgeport, Stevenson, Decatur, Murfreesboro, and Florence. There were already with him in Nashville ten thousand soldiers in round numbers, and many thousands of employees in the quartermaster's and other departments who could be put in the intrenchments in front of Nashville, for its defence. Also, Wilson was there with ten thousand dismounted cavalrymen, who were being equipped for the field. Thomas had at this time about forty-five thousand men without any of the reinforcements here above enumerated. These reinforcements gave him altogether about seventy thousand men, without counting what might be added by the new levies already spoken of.

About this time Beauregard arrived upon the field, not to supersede Hood in command, but to take general charge over the entire district in which Hood and Sherman were, or might be, operating. He made the most frantic appeals to the citizens for assistance to be rendered in every way: by sending reinforcements,

[24] For USG's orders regarding A. J. Smith, see his Oct. 29, 1864, letter to Rawlins, ibid., 12:363.

[25] In mid-Mar. 1864, Lincoln extended the Feb. 1 draft of 500,000 by another 200,000 men. John F. Marszalek, *Lincoln and the Military* (Carbondale: Southern Illinois University Press, 2014), 74.

by destroying supplies on the line of march of the invaders, by destroying the bridges over which they would have to cross, and by, in every way, obstructing the roads to their front. But it was hard to convince the people of the propriety of destroying supplies which were so much needed by themselves, and each one hoped that his own possessions might escape.[26]

Hood soon started north, and went into camp near Decatur, Alabama, where he remained until the 29th of October, but without making an attack on the garrison of that place.

The Tennessee River was patrolled by gunboats, from Muscle Shoals east; and, also, below the second shoals out to the Ohio River. These, with the troops that might be concentrated from the garrisons along the river at any point where Hood might choose to attempt to cross, made it impossible for him to cross the Tennessee at any place where it was navigable. But Muscle Shoals is not navigable, and below them again is another shoal which also obstructs navigation.[27] Hood therefore moved down to a point nearly opposite Florence, Alabama, crossed over and remained there for some time, collecting supplies of food, forage and ammunition. All of these had to come from a considerable distance south, because the region in which he was then situated was mountainous, with small valleys which produced but little, and what they had produced had long since been exhausted. On the 1st of November I suggested to Sherman, and also asked his views thereon, the propriety of destroying Hood before he started on his campaign.

On the 2d of November, as stated, I approved definitely his making his proposed campaign through Georgia, leaving Hood behind to the tender mercy of Thomas and the troops in his command. Sherman fixed the 10th of November as the day of starting.

Sherman started on that day to get back to Atlanta, and on the 15th the real march to the sea commenced. The right wing, under Howard, and the cavalry went to Jonesboro, Milledgeville, then the capital of Georgia, being Sherman's objective or stopping place on the way to Savannah. The left wing moved to Stone Mountain, along roads much farther east than those taken by the right wing. Slocum was in command, and threatened Augusta as the point

[26] For Beauregard's Nov. 18, 1864, message to the "People of Georgia," see *OR*, I, 44, 867.

[27] In addition to the area around Muscle Shoals, AL, numerous shoals along the Tennessee River hindered navigation during the nineteenth century. It is unclear which other shoals USG referred to. J. Haden Alldredge et al., *A History of Navigation on the Tennessee River System* (Washington, DC: Government Printing Office, 1937), 101; George B. Davis et al., *The Official Military Atlas of the Civil War* (New York: Fairfax Press, 1983), plate 149.

to which he was moving, but he was to turn off and meet the right wing at Milledgeville.

Atlanta was destroyed so far as to render it worthless for military purposes before starting, Sherman himself remaining over a day to superintend the work, and see that it was well done. Sherman's orders for this campaign were perfect. Before starting, he had sent back all sick, disabled and weak men, retaining nothing but the hardy, well-inured soldiers to accompany him on his long march in prospect. His artillery was reduced to sixty-five guns. The ammunition carried with them was two hundred rounds for musket and gun. Small rations were taken in a small wagon train, which was loaded to its capacity for rapid movement. The army was expected to live on the country, and to always keep the wagons full of forage and provisions against a possible delay of a few days.

The troops, both of the right and left wings, made most of their advance along the line of railroads, which they destroyed. The method adopted to perform this work, was to burn and destroy all the bridges and culverts, and for a long distance, at places, to tear up the track and bend the rails. Soldiers to do this rapidly would form a line along one side of the road with crowbars and poles, place these under the rails and, hoisting all at once, turn over many rods of road at one time. The ties would then be placed in piles, and the rails, as they were loosened, would be carried and put across these log heaps. When a sufficient number of rails were placed upon a pile of ties it would be set on fire. This would heat the rails very much more in the middle, that being over the main part of the fire, than at the ends, so that they would naturally bend of their own weight; but the soldiers, to increase the damage, would take tongs and, one or two men at each end of the rail, carry it with force against the nearest tree and twist it around, thus leaving rails forming bands to ornament the forest trees of Georgia. All this work was going on at the same time, there being a sufficient number of men detailed for that purpose. Some piled the logs and built the fire; some put the rails upon the fire; while others would bend those that were sufficiently heated: so that, by the time the last bit of road was torn up, that it was designed to destroy at a certain place, the rails previously taken up were already destroyed.

The organization for supplying the army was very complete. Each brigade furnished a company to gather supplies of forage and provisions for the command to which they belonged. Strict injunctions were issued against pillaging, or otherwise unnecessarily annoying the people; but everything in shape of food for man and forage for beast was taken. The supplies were turned over to the brigade commissary and quartermaster, and were issued by them to their respective commands precisely the same as if they had been purchased. The captures consisted largely of cattle, sheep, poultry, some bacon, cornmeal, often molasses, and occasionally coffee or other small rations.

The skill of these men, called by themselves and the army "bummers," in collecting their loads and getting back to their respective commands, was marvellous. When they started out in the morning, they were always on foot; but scarcely one of them returned in the evening without being mounted on a horse or mule. These would be turned in for the general use of the army, and the next day these men would start out afoot and return again in the evening mounted.

Many of the exploits of these men would fall under the head of romance; indeed, I am afraid that in telling some of their experiences, the romance got the better of the truth upon which the story was founded, and that, in the way many of these anecdotes are told, very little of the foundation is left. I suspect that most of them consist chiefly of the fiction added to make the stories better. In one instance it was reported that a few men of Sherman's army passed a house where they discovered some chickens under the dwelling. They immediately proceeded to capture them, to add to the army's supplies. The lady of the house, who happened to be at home, made piteous appeals to have these spared, saying they were a few she had put away to save by permission of other parties who had preceded and who had taken all the others that she had. The soldiers seemed moved at her appeal; but looking at the chickens again they were tempted and one of them replied: "The rebellion must be suppressed if it takes the last chicken in the Confederacy," and proceeded to appropriate the last one.

Another anecdote characteristic of these times has been told. The South, prior to the rebellion, kept bloodhounds to pursue runaway slaves who took refuge in the neighboring swamps, and also to hunt convicts. Orders were issued to kill all these animals as they were met with.[28] On one occasion a soldier picked up a poodle, the favorite pet of its mistress, and was carrying it off to execution when the lady made a strong appeal to him to spare it. The soldier replied, "Madam, our orders are to kill every bloodhound." "But this is not a bloodhound," said the lady. "Well, madam, we cannot tell what it will grow into if we leave it behind," said the soldier as he went off with it.

[28] After hearing stories of dogs being used to track down escaped slaves or U.S. soldiers, the men under Sherman's command routinely killed all dogs they encountered, although no official orders to do so were ever given. Marszalek, *Sherman*, 305.

Notwithstanding these anecdotes, and the necessary hardship they would seem to imply, I do not believe there was much unwarrantable pillaging considering that we were in the enemy's territory and without any supplies except such as the country afforded.

On the 23d Sherman, with the left wing, reached Milledgeville. The right wing was not far off: but proceeded on its way towards Savannah destroying the road as it went. The troops at Milledgeville remained over a day to destroy factories, buildings used for military purposes, etc., before resuming its march.

The governor, who had been almost defying Mr. Davis before this, now fled precipitately, as did the legislature of the State and all the State officers. The governor, Sherman says, was careful to carry away even his garden vegetables, while he left the archives of the State to fall into our hands.[29] The only military force that was opposed to Sherman's forward march was the Georgia militia, a division under the command of General G. W. Smith, and a battalion under Harry Wayne.[30] Neither the quality of the forces nor their numbers was sufficient to even retard the progress of Sherman's army.[31]

The people at the South became so frantic at this time at the successful invasion of Georgia that they took the cadets from the military college and added them to the ranks of the militia. They even liberated the State convicts under promise from them that they would serve in the army. I have but little doubt that the worst acts that were attributed to Sherman's army were committed by these convicts, and by other Southern people who ought to have been under sentence—such people as could be found in every community, North and South—who took advantage of their country being invaded to commit crime. They were in but little danger of detection, or of arrest even if detected.

The Southern papers in commenting upon Sherman's movements pictured him as in the most deplorable condition: stating that his men were starving,

[29] Governor Brown fled on June 24, 1864, the afternoon after most citizens had fled the city. Parks, *Joseph E. Brown of Georgia,* 310. For Sherman's description of what was taken and what was left behind by Brown, see Sherman, *Memoirs,* 2:188.

[30] Henry C. Wayne (1815–1883) was born in Georgia and graduated from the USMA in 1838. He resigned from the U.S. Army and became a colonel in the Georgia Militia in Dec. 1860, was promoted to major general in 1861, and was commander in chief of the militia from 1862 to 1864. *CWHC,* 557.

[31] On Nov. 21, 1864, at Griswoldville, GA, seven miles northeast of Macon, U.S. forces defeated units of the Georgia Militia composed of old men and young boys. Marszalek, *Sherman's March to the Sea,* 57–59; Davis et al, *Official Military Atlas of the Civil War,* plate 144.

that they were demoralized and wandering about almost without object, aiming only to reach the sea coast and get under the protection of our navy. These papers got to the North and had more or less effect upon the minds of the people, causing much distress to all loyal persons—particularly to those who had husbands, sons or brothers with Sherman.[32] Mr. Lincoln seeing these accounts, had a letter written asking me if I could give him anything that he could say to the loyal people that would comfort them. I told him there was not the slightest occasion for alarm; that with 60,000 such men as Sherman had with him, such a commanding officer as he was could not be cut off in the open country. He might possibly be prevented from reaching the point he had started out to reach, but he would get through somewhere and would finally get to his chosen destination: and even if worst came to worst he could return North.[33] I heard afterwards of Mr. Lincoln's saying, to those who would inquire of him as to what he thought about the safety of Sherman's army, that Sherman was all right: "Grant says they are safe with such a general, and that if they cannot get out where they want to, they can crawl back by the hole they went in at."

While at Milledgeville the soldiers met at the State House, organized a legislature, and proceeded to business precisely as if they were the legislative body belonging to the State of Georgia. The debates were exciting, and were upon the subject of the situation the South was in at that time, particularly the State of Georgia. They went so far as to repeal, after a spirited and acrimonious debate, the ordinance of secession.[34]

The next day (24th) Sherman continued his march, going by the way of Waynesboro and Louisville, Millen being the next objective and where the two columns (the right and left wings) were to meet. The left wing moved to the left of the direct road, and the cavalry still farther off so as to make it look as though Augusta was the point they were aiming for. They moved on all the roads they could find leading in that direction. The cavalry was sent to make

[32] In the absence of reliable accounts of the progress of Sherman's advance, many Northern newspapers published speculative accounts with an optimistic tone. J. Cutler Andrews, *The North Reports the Civil War* (Pittsburgh, PA: University of Pittsburgh Press, 1983), 580; John F. Marszalek, *Sherman's Other War: The General and the Civil War Press* (Kent, OH: Kent State University Press, 1999), 188–189.

[33] Stanton telegraphed USG on Oct. 12, 1864, to express Lincoln's concern regarding Sherman's proposed march through Georgia. USG replied on Oct. 13. *PUSG,* 12:302–303, 303n.

[34] Sherman arrived in Milledgeville, GA, on Nov. 22, 1864. Marszalek, *Sherman's March to the Sea,* 62.

a rapid march in hope of surprising Millen before the Union prisoners could be carried away; but they failed in this.[35]

The distance from Milledgeville to Millen was about one hundred miles.[36] At this point Wheeler, who had been ordered from Tennessee, arrived and swelled the numbers and efficiency of the troops confronting Sherman.[37] Hardee, a native of Georgia, also came, but brought no troops with him. It was intended that he should raise as large an army as possible with which to intercept Sherman's march. He did succeed in raising some troops, and with these and those under the command of Wheeler and Wayne, had an army sufficient to cause some annoyance but no great detention.[38] Our cavalry and Wheeler's had a pretty severe engagement, in which Wheeler was driven towards Augusta, thus giving the idea that Sherman was probably making for that point.[39]

Millen was reached on the 3d of December, and the march was resumed the following day for Savannah, the final objective. Bragg had now been sent to Augusta with some troops. Wade Hampton was there also trying to raise cavalry sufficient to destroy Sherman's army. If he ever raised a force it was too late to do the work expected of it. Hardee's whole force probably numbered less than ten thousand men.[40]

From Millen to Savannah the country is sandy and poor, and affords but very little forage other than rice straw, which was then growing. This answered

[35] The prisoners were held at Camp Lawton, five miles outside Millen, GA, on the Georgia Central Railroad. The camp had ceased to house prisoners by Nov. 22, 1864. William Giles, ed., *Disease, Starvation, and Death: Personal Accounts of Camp Lawton* (n.p.: Lulu Press, 2005), 19; Marszalek, *Sherman's March to the Sea,* 88.

[36] The approximate distance from Milledgeville to Millen was seventy miles. Davis et al., *Official Military Atlas of the Civil War,* plate 101, map 21.

[37] Wheeler rejoined Hood's army on Oct. 8, 1864. John P. Dyer, *"Fighting Joe" Wheeler* (Baton Rouge: Louisiana State University Press, 1941), 200.

[38] Wheeler had about 4,500 troops. John E. Fisher, *They Rode with Forrest and Wheeler* (Jefferson, NC: McFarland, 1995), 122.

[39] The Battle of Waynesboro, GA, began on Nov. 28, 1864, ending several days later with Wheeler's defeat of Kilpatrick. Marszalek, *Sherman's March to the Sea,* 86.

[40] During the fall of 1864, Hampton's forces were operating in the area around Petersburg, VA. He arrived in South Carolina in late Jan. 1865 as part of the effort to defend the Carolinas against Sherman's impending campaign. Hardee had a little more than 12,000 soldiers in the entire Dept. of South Carolina, Georgia, and Florida. Rod Andrew Jr., *Wade Hampton: Confederate Warrior to Southern Redeemer* (Chapel Hill: University of North Carolina Press, 2008), 241, 255; Nathaniel Cheairs Hughes Jr., *General William J. Hardee: Old Reliable* (Baton Rouge: Louisiana State University Press, 1965), 251.

a very good purpose as forage, and the rice grain was an addition to the soldier's rations. No further resistance worthy of note was met with, until within a few miles of Savannah. This place was found to be intrenched and garrisoned. Sherman proceeded at once on his arrival to invest the place, and found that the enemy had placed torpedoes in the ground, which were to explode when stepped on by man or beast. One of these exploded under an officer's horse, blowing the animal to pieces and tearing one of the legs of the officer so badly that it had to be amputated. Sherman at once ordered his prisoners to the front, moving them in a compact body in advance, to either explode the torpedoes or dig them up. No further explosion took place.

On the 10th of December the siege of Savannah commenced. Sherman then, before proceeding any further with operations for the capture of the place, started with some troops to open communication with our fleet, which he expected to find in the lower harbor or as near by as the forts of the enemy would permit. In marching to the coast he encountered Fort McAllister, which it was necessary to reduce before the supplies he might find on shipboard could be made available. Fort McAllister was soon captured by an assault made by General Hazen's division.[41] Communication was then established with the fleet. The capture of Savannah then only occupied a few days, and involved no great loss of life.[42] The garrison, however, as we shall see, was enabled to escape by crossing the river and moving eastward.

When Sherman had opened communication with the fleet he found there a steamer, which I had forwarded to him, carrying the accumulated mails for his army, also supplies which I supposed he would be in need of. General J. G. Foster, who commanded all the troops south of North Carolina on the Atlantic sea-board, visited General Sherman before he had opened communication with the fleet, with the view of ascertaining what assistance he could be to him.[43] Foster returned immediately to his own headquarters at Hilton Head, for the purpose of sending Sherman siege guns, and also if he should find he had them to spare, supplies of clothing, hard bread, etc., thinking that these articles might not be found outside. The mail on the steamer which I sent down, had been collected by Colonel A. H. Markland of the Post Office

---

[41] Hazen's forces captured Fort McAllister on Dec. 13, 1864. *OR*, I, 44, 110.

[42] Sherman's losses during the entire march to the sea were 108 killed, 428 wounded, and 278 missing. U.S. forces captured 1,338 Confederate troops. Sherman, *Memoirs*, 2:221.

[43] Sherman met with Foster immediately after the fall of Fort McAllister on Dec. 13, 1864. Marszalek, *Sherman's March to the Sea*, 107.

Department,[44] who went in charge of it. On this same vessel I sent an officer of my staff (Lieutenant Dunn) with the following letter to General Sherman:

CITY POINT, VA., *Dec.* 3, 1864.

MAJOR-GENERAL W. T. SHERMAN,
Commanding Armies near Savannah, Ga.

The little information gleaned from the Southern press, indicating no great obstacle to your progress, I have directed your mails (which had been previously collected at Baltimore by Colonel Markland, Special Agent of the Post Office Department) to be sent as far as the blockading squadron off Savannah, to be forwarded to you as soon as heard from on the coast.

Not liking to rejoice before the victory is assured, I abstain from congratulating you and those under your command, until bottom has been struck. I have never had a fear, however, for the result.

Since you left Atlanta, no very great progress has been made here. The enemy has been closely watched though, and prevented from detaching against you. I think not one man has gone from here, except some twelve or fifteen hundred dismounted cavalry. Bragg has gone from Wilmington. I am trying to take advantage of his absence to get possession of that place. Owing to some preparations Admiral Porter and General Butler are making to blow up Fort Fisher (which, while hoping for the best, I do not believe a particle in), there is a delay in getting this expedition off. I hope they will be ready to start by the 7th, and that Bragg will not have started back by that time.

In this letter I do not intend to give you anything like directions for future action, but will state a general idea I have, and will get your views after you have established yourself on the sea-coast. With your veteran army I hope to get control of the only two through routes from east to west possessed by the enemy before the fall of Atlanta.[45] The

[44] Absalom H. Markland (1825–c.1888) was born in Kentucky and, like USG, attended the Maysville Academy of Richeson and Rand in Maysville, KY. He became a special agent of the U.S. Post Office Dept. in 1861 and was commissioned a colonel on USG's staff in Nov. 1863. Allen Thorndike Rice, ed., *Reminiscences of Abraham Lincoln by Distinguished Men of His Time* (New York: J. J. Little, 1885), 629–630.

[45] The two railroads USG referred to were probably the Central Railroad of Georgia, with its terminus at Savannah, GA, and the Georgia Railroad, which ran from Atlanta to Augusta, GA. Black, *Railroads of the Confederacy,* enclosed map.

condition will be filled by holding Savannah and Augusta, or by holding any other port to the east of Savannah and Branchville. If Wilmington falls, a force from there can co-operate with you.

Thomas has got back into the defences of Nashville, with Hood close upon him. Decatur has been abandoned, and so have all the roads except the main one leading to Chattanooga.[46] Part of this falling back was undoubtedly necessary, and all of it may have been. It did not look so, however, to me. In my opinion, Thomas far outnumbers Hood in infantry. In cavalry, Hood has the advantage in *morale* and numbers.[47] I hope yet that Hood will be badly crippled if not destroyed. The general news you will learn from the papers better than I could give it.

After all becomes quiet, and roads become so bad up here that there is likely to be a week or two when nothing can be done, I will run down the coast to see you. If you desire it, I will ask Mrs. Sherman[48] to go with me.

Yours truly,
U. S. GRANT,
Lieutenant-General.

I quote this letter because it gives the reader a full knowledge of the events of that period.

Sherman now (the 15th) returned to Savannah to complete its investment and insure the surrender of the garrison. The country about Savannah is low and marshy, and the city was well intrenched from the river above to the river below, and assaults could not be made except along a comparatively narrow causeway. For this reason assaults must have resulted in serious destruction of life to the Union troops, with the chance of failing altogether. Sherman therefore decided upon a complete investment of the place. When he believed this investment completed, he summoned the garrison to surrender. General

---

[46] USG referred to the Nashville and Chattanooga Railroad. Ibid., 5, enclosed map.

[47] At the Battle of Nashville, Thomas had over 55,000 soldiers to Hood's 30,000. Most of the Confederate cavalry was with Forrest near Murfreesboro, TN, and did not participate in the battle. James Lee McDonough, *Nashville: The Western Confederacy's Final Gamble* (Knoxville: University of Tennessee Press, 2004), 45, 141, 211.

[48] Ellen Ewing Sherman (1824–1888) was born in Ohio, the daughter of Whig politician Thomas Ewing. After his father's death in 1829, William T. Sherman was raised as a part of the Ewing family. William and Ellen married in 1850. Candice Shy Hooper, *Lincoln's Generals' Wives* (Kent, OH: Kent State University Press, 2016), 153–242.

Hardee, who was in command, replied in substance that the condition of affairs was not such as Sherman had described. He said he was in full communication with his department and was receiving supplies constantly.

Hardee, however, was cut off entirely from all communication with the west side of the river, and by the river itself to the north and south. On the South Carolina side the country was all rice fields, through which it would have been impossible to bring supplies—so that Hardee had no possible communication with the outside world except by a dilapidated plank road starting from the west bank of the river. Sherman, receiving this reply, proceeded in person to a point on the coast, where General Foster had troops stationed under General Hatch,[49] for the purpose of making arrangements with the latter officer to go through by one of the numerous channels running inland along that part of the coast of South Carolina, to the plank road which General Hardee still possessed, and thus to cut him off from the last means he had of getting supplies, if not of communication.

While arranging for this movement, and before the attempt to execute the plan had been commenced, Sherman received information through one of his staff officers that the enemy had evacuated Savannah the night before. This was the night of the 21st of December. Before evacuating the place Hardee had blown up the navy yard. Some iron-clads had been destroyed, as well as other property that might have been valuable to us; but he left an immense amount of stores untouched, consisting of cotton, railroad cars, workshops, numerous pieces of artillery, and several thousand stands of small arms.[50]

A little incident occurred, soon after the fall of Savannah, which Sherman relates in his Memoirs, and which is worthy of repetition. Savannah was one of the points where blockade runners entered. Shortly after the city fell into our possession, a blockade runner came sailing up serenely, not doubting but the Confederates were still in possession. It was not molested, and the captain did not find out his mistake until he had tied up and gone to the Custom House, where he found a new occupant of the building, and made a less profitable disposition of his vessel and cargo than he had expected.[51]

---

[49] John P. Hatch (1822–1901) was born in New York and graduated from the USMA in 1845. He fought in the Mexican-American War and had been promoted to captain by 1860. Hatch was promoted to brigadier general in 1861 and, for his actions at South Mountain, MD, in 1862, was awarded the Medal of Honor in 1893. *CWHC,* 287.

[50] On Dec. 22, 1864, Sherman wrote USG that he had captured approximately 800 prisoners, over 100 guns, 12,000 bales of cotton, 190 railroad cars, 13 locomotives, 3 steamboats, and "an immense supply of shells, shot, and all kinds of ammunition." *PUSG,* 13:170*n.*

[51] For a more detailed version of the story, see Sherman, *Memoirs,* 2:218–219.

As there was some discussion as to the authorship of Sherman's march to the sea, by critics of his book when it appeared before the public, I want to state here that no question upon that subject was ever raised between General Sherman and myself.[52] Circumstances made the plan on which Sherman expected to act impracticable, and as commander of the forces he necessarily had to devise a new one which would give more promise of success: consequently he recommended the destruction of the railroad back to Chattanooga, and that he should be authorized then to move, as he did, from Atlanta forward. His suggestions were finally approved, although they did not immediately find favor in Washington. Even when it came to the time of starting, the greatest apprehension, as to the propriety of the campaign he was about to commence, filled the mind of the President, induced no doubt by his advisers.[53] This went so far as to move the President to ask me to suspend Sherman's march for a day or two until I could think the matter over. My recollection is, though I find no record to show it, that out of deference to the President's wish I did send a dispatch to Sherman asking him to wait a day or two, or else the connections between us were already cut so that I could not do so.[54] However this may be, the question of who devised the plan of march from Atlanta to Savannah is easily answered: it was clearly Sherman, and to him also belongs the credit of its brilliant execution. It was hardly possible that any one else than those on the spot could have devised a new plan of campaign to supersede one that did not promise success.*

I was in favor of Sherman's plan from the time it was first submitted to me. My chief of staff, however, was very bitterly opposed to it and, as I learned subsequently, finding that he could not move me, he appealed to the authorities at Washington to stop it.[55]

*See Appendix, letters of Oct. 11th.[56]

---

[52] The 1875 publication of Sherman's *Memoirs* resulted in a torrent of criticism from northern generals and the southern press. USG quieted some of this criticism when he wrote Sherman on Jan. 29, 1876, praising the book. Marszalek, *Sherman*, 461–467; *PUSG*, 27:16–19.

[53] The editors found no record of Lincoln's advisers attempting to persuade him to oppose the proposed plan.

[54] The editors found no correspondence between USG and Sherman asking for a delay before the start of the campaign.

[55] Rawlins was so opposed to the plan that he spoke to Lincoln and Stanton without USG's knowledge. USG never realized this until after Rawlins's death. Adam Badeau, *Military History of Ulysses S. Grant, from April, 1861, to April, 1865* (New York: D. Appleton, 1881), 3:156–157.

[56] For the Oct. 11, 1864, letters between USG and Sherman, see *PUSG*, 12:289–290, 290n.

# 60

## The Battle of Franklin—The Battle of Nashville

A s we have seen, Hood succeeded in crossing the Tennessee River between Muscle Shoals and the lower shoals at the end of October, 1864. Thomas sent Schofield with the 4th and 23d corps, together with three brigades of Wilson's cavalry to Pulaski to watch him. On the 17th of November Hood started and moved in such a manner as to avoid Schofield, thereby turning his position. Hood had with him three infantry corps, commanded respectively by Stephen D. Lee,[1] Stewart[2] and Cheatham.[3] These, with his cavalry, numbered about forty-five thousand men. Schofield had, of all arms, about thirty thousand.[4] Thomas's orders were, therefore, for Schofield to watch the movements of the enemy, but

---

[1] Stephen D. Lee (1833–1908) was born in South Carolina and graduated from the USMA in 1854. In Feb. 1861, he resigned from the U.S. Army and in Mar. joined the Confederate Army as a captain in the South Carolina Militia. In Nov. 1862, he was promoted to brigadier general. He fought and was captured at Vicksburg, MS, in 1863 and reached major general in Aug. that year. In Nov. 1864, he commanded the 2nd Corps, Army of Tennessee. Lee was president of Mississippi A&M College (now Mississippi State University) from 1880 to 1889. *CWHC*, 345.

[2] Alexander P. Stewart (1821–1908) was born in Tennessee and graduated from the USMA in 1842. He taught at Cumberland University and joined the Confederacy in the fall of 1861, reaching major general in June 1863. In Nov. 1864, he commanded the 3rd Corps, Army of Tennessee. After the war, he moved to Mississippi and served as the chancellor of the University of Mississippi from 1874 to 1886. He was the commissioner of the Chickamauga and Chattanooga National Military Park from 1890 to 1908. Ibid., 511.

[3] Benjamin Franklin Cheatham (1820–1886) was born in Tennessee, fought in the Mexican-American War, and participated in the California Gold Rush. He entered the Confederate Army as a brigadier general in May 1861. In Mar. 1862, he reached major general. In Nov. 1864, he commanded the 1st Corps, Army of Tennessee. Ibid., 170–171.

[4] Hood had approximately 27,000 troops at the Battle of Franklin, and Schofield had about the same number. Thomas L. Livermore, *Numbers and Losses in the Civil War in America, 1861–65* (Boston: Houghton, Mifflin, 1900), 57.

not to fight a battle if he could avoid it; but to fall back in case of an advance on Nashville, and to fight the enemy, as he fell back, so as to retard the enemy's movements until he could be reinforced by Thomas himself. As soon as Schofield saw this movement of Hood's, he sent his trains to the rear, but did not fall back himself until the 21st, and then only to Columbia. At Columbia there was a slight skirmish but no battle. From this place Schofield then retreated to Franklin. He had sent his wagons in advance, and Stanley had gone with them with two divisions to protect them. Cheatham's corps of Hood's army pursued the wagon train and went into camp at Spring Hill, for the night of the 29th.

Schofield retreating from Columbia on the 29th, passed Spring Hill, where Cheatham was bivouacked, during the night without molestation, though within half a mile of where the Confederates were encamped. On the morning of the 30th he had arrived at Franklin.

Hood followed closely and reached Franklin in time to make an attack the same day. The fight was very desperate and sanguinary. The Confederate generals led their men in the repeated charges, and the loss among them was of unusual proportions.[5] This fighting continued with great severity until long after the night closed in, when the Confederates drew off. General Stanley, who commanded two divisions of the Union troops, and whose troops bore the brunt of the battle, was wounded in the fight, but maintained his position.

The enemy's loss at Franklin, according to Thomas's report, was 1,750 buried upon the field by our troops, 3,800 in the hospital, and 702 prisoners besides. Schofield's loss, as officially reported, was 189 killed, 1,033 wounded, and 1,104 captured and missing.[6]

Thomas made no effort to reinforce Schofield at Franklin, as it seemed to me at the time he should have done, and fight out the battle there. He simply ordered Schofield to continue his retreat to Nashville, which the latter did during that night and the next day.

[5] On Nov. 30, 1864, five Confederate officers were killed at the Battle of Franklin: Maj. Gen. Patrick Cleburne, Brig. Gens. States Rights Gist, John Adams, Otto Strahl, and Hiram B. Granbury. Another officer, Brig. Gen. John C. Carter, was mortally wounded and died on Dec. 10. *CWHC*, 166; *OR*, I, 45(I), 654.

[6] In his postbattle report, Thomas excluded the number of wounded Confederates who were not hospitalized. There were approximately 700 additional wounded Confederate troops. James L. McDonough and Thomas L. Connelly, *Five Tragic Hours: The Battle of Franklin* (Knoxville: University of Tennessee Press, 1983), 157.

Thomas, in the meantime, was making his preparations to receive Hood. The road to Chattanooga was still well guarded with strong garrisons at Murfreesboro, Stevenson, Bridgeport and Chattanooga. Thomas had previously given up Decatur and had been reinforced by A. J. Smith's two divisions just returned from Missouri. He also had Steedman's[7] division and R. S. Granger's,[8] which he had drawn from the front. His quartermaster's men, about ten thousand in number, had been organized and armed under the command of the chief quartermaster, General J. L. Donaldson,[9] and placed in the fortifications under the general supervision of General Z. B. Tower, of the United States Engineers.

Hood was allowed to move upon Nashville, and to invest that place almost without interference. Thomas was strongly fortified in his position, so that he would have been safe against the attack of Hood. He had troops enough even to annihilate him in the open field. To me his delay was unaccountable—sitting there and permitting himself to be invested, so that, in the end, to raise the siege he would have to fight the enemy strongly posted behind fortifications. It is true the weather was very bad. The rain was falling and freezing as it fell, so that the ground was covered with a sheet of ice, that made it very difficult to move. But I was afraid that the enemy would find means of moving, elude Thomas and manage to get north of the Cumberland River. If he did this, I apprehended most serious results from the campaign in the North, and was afraid we might even have to send troops from the East to head him off if he got there, General Thomas's movements being always so deliberate and so slow, though effective in defence.

[7] James B. Steedman (1817–1883) was born in Pennsylvania and moved to Ohio in 1835. In 1857, he joined the Ohio Militia as a major general. In Apr. 1861, he became a colonel in the 14th Ohio Inf. He was promoted to brigadier general in July 1863 and to major general in Apr. 1864. He later served as an Ohio legislator. *CWHC,* 507.

[8] Robert S. Granger (1816–1894) was born in Ohio and graduated from the USMA in 1838. He served in the Seminole War in Florida and as a professor at the USMA. At the start of the Civil War, he commanded Fort Lancaster in Texas. He was promoted to brigadier general in Oct. 1862 and was brevetted major general in Mar. 1865. Ibid., 263.

[9] James L. Donaldson (1814–1885) was born in Maryland and graduated from the USMA in 1836. He fought in both the Seminole War and the Mexican-American War. In May 1861, he was brevetted lieutenant colonel and served as a quartermaster throughout most of the war. In Sept. 1864, he was brevetted brigadier general for his actions at Atlanta, GA. Ibid., 212.

I consequently urged Thomas in frequent dispatches sent from City Point*
to make the attack at once. The country was alarmed, the administration was
alarmed, and I was alarmed lest the very thing would take place which I have just
described—that is, Hood would get north. It was all without avail further than to
elicit dispatches from Thomas saying that he was getting ready to move as soon as
he could, that he was making preparations, etc. At last I had to say to General
Thomas that I should be obliged to remove him unless he acted promptly. He
replied that he was very sorry, but he would move as soon as he could.[10]

*CITY POINT VA., *December* 2, 1864.

MAJOR-GENERAL THOMAS,
Nashville, Tenn.

If Hood is permitted to remain quietly about Nashville, you will lose all the
road back to Chattanooga and possibly have to abandon the line of the
Tennessee. Should he attack you it is all well, but if he does not you should
attack him before he fortifies. Arm and put in the trenches your quartermaster
employees, citizens, etc.

U. S. GRANT,
Lieutenant-General.

CITY POINT, VA., *December* 2, 1864.—1.30 P.M.

MAJOR-GENERAL THOMAS,
Nashville, Tenn.

With your citizen employees armed, you can move out of Nashville with all
your army and force the enemy to retire or fight upon ground of your own
choosing. After the repulse of Hood at Franklin, it looks to me that instead of
falling back to Nashville we should have taken the offensive against the enemy
where he was. At this distance, however, I may err as to the best method of
dealing with the enemy. You will now suffer incalculable injury upon your
railroads if Hood is not speedily disposed of. Put forth therefore every possible
exertion to attain this end. Should you get him to retreating give him no peace.

U. S. GRANT,
Lieutenant-General.

[10] USG wrote Thomas repeatedly on Dec. 5, 6, and 8, 1864, urging him to attack Hood.
Thomas responded each time on the same day, stating that he would move when he was completely organized to do so. On Dec. 9, USG told Halleck to relieve Thomas from command, but
then suspended the order later that same day to see if Thomas would take action. Ibid., 13:67
and *n*, 77 and *n*, 87–88, 88*n*, 90 and *n*, 90–91, 91*n*.

City Point, Va., *December 5, 1864.*

Major-General Thomas,
Nashville, Tenn.

Is there not danger of Forrest moving down the Cumberland to where he can cross it? It seems to me whilst you should be getting up your cavalry as rapidly as possible to look after Forrest, Hood should be attacked where he is. Time strengthens him in all possibility as much as it does you.

U. S. GRANT,
Lieutenant-General.

City Point, Va., *December 6, 1864.*—4 p.m.

Major-General Thomas,
Nashville, Tenn.

Attack Hood at once and wait no longer for a remnant of your cavalry. There is great danger of delay resulting in a campaign back to the Ohio River.

U. S. GRANT,
Lieutenant-General.

City Point, Va., *December 8, 1864.*—8.30 p.m.

Major-General Thomas,
Nashville, Tenn.

Your dispatch of yesterday received. It looks to me evident the enemy are trying to cross the Cumberland River, and are scattered. Why not attack at once? By all means avoid the contingency of a foot race to see which, you or Hood, can beat to the Ohio. If you think necessary call on the governors of States to send a force into Louisville to meet the enemy if he should cross the river. You clearly never should cross except in rear of the enemy. Now is one of the finest opportunities ever presented of destroying one of the three armies of the enemy. If destroyed he never can replace it. Use the means at your command, and you can do this and cause a rejoicing that will resound from one end of the land to the other.

U. S. GRANT,
Lieutenant-General.

General Logan happening to visit City Point about that time, and knowing him as a prompt, gallant and efficient officer, I gave him an order to proceed to Nashville to relieve Thomas. I directed him, however, not to deliver the order or publish it until he reached there, and if Thomas had moved, then

CITY POINT, VA., *December* 11, 1864.—4 P.M.

MAJOR-GENERAL THOMAS,
Nashville, Tenn.

If you delay attack longer the mortifying spectacle will be witnessed of a rebel army moving for the Ohio River, and you will be forced to act, accepting such weather as you find. Let there be no further delay. Hood cannot even stand a drawn battle so far from his supplies of ordnance stores. If he retreats and you follow, he must lose his material and much of his army. I am in hopes of receiving a dispatch from you to-day announcing that you have moved. Delay no longer for weather or reinforcements.

U. S. GRANT,
Lieutenant-General.

WASHINGTON, D. C., *December* 15, 1864.

MAJOR-GENERAL THOMAS,
Nashville, Tenn.

I was just on my way to Nashville, but receiving a dispatch from Van Duzer[11] detailing your splendid success of to-day, I shall go no further. Push the enemy now and give him no rest until he is entirely destroyed. Your army will cheerfully suffer many privations to break up Hood's army and render it useless for future operations. Do not stop for trains or supplies, but take them from the country as the enemy have done. Much is now expected.

U. S. GRANT,
Lieutenant-General.

[11] For Capt. John C. Van Duzer's Dec. 15, 1864, telegram to Maj. Thomas T. Eckert, see *PUSG*, 13:125*n*–126*n*. Van Duzer (1827–?) was born in New York and was a telegraph office manager in Missouri in 1861. For USG's Nov.–Dec. 1862 conflict with Van Duzer regarding telegraphic operations, see ibid., 6:377–381, 381*n*–385*n*.

not to deliver it at all, but communicate with me by telegraph.[12] After Logan
started, in thinking over the situation, I became restless, and concluded to go
myself. I went as far as Washington City, when a dispatch was received from
General Thomas announcing his readiness at last to move, and designating
the time of his movement. I concluded to wait until that time. He did move,
and was successful from the start. This was on the 15th of December.[13] General
Logan was at Louisville at the time this movement was made, and telegraphed
the fact to Washington, and proceeded no farther himself.[14]

The battle during the 15th was severe, but favorable to the Union troops,
and continued until night closed in upon the combat. The next day the battle
was renewed. After a successful assault upon Hood's men in their intrenchments the enemy fled in disorder, routed and broken, leaving their dead, their
artillery and small arms in great numbers on the field, besides the wounded
that were captured. Our cavalry had fought on foot as infantry, and had not
their horses with them; so that they were not ready to join in the pursuit the
moment the enemy retreated. They sent back, however, for their horses, and
endeavored to get to Franklin ahead of Hood's broken army by the Granny
White Road, but too much time was consumed in getting started. They had
got but a few miles beyond the scene of the battle when they found the enemy's
cavalry dismounted and behind intrenchments covering the road on which
they were advancing. Here another battle ensued, our men dismounting and
fighting on foot, in which the Confederates were again routed and driven in
great disorder.[15] Our cavalry then went into bivouac, and renewed the pursuit
on the following morning. They were too late. The enemy already had possession of Franklin, and was beyond them. It now became a chase in which the
Confederates had the lead.

[12] On Dec. 13, 1864, Bowers issued Special Orders No. 149: "Maj. Gen'l. John A. Logan, will
proceed immediately to Nashville Tenn., reporting by telegraph to the Lieutenant General Commanding, his arrival at Louisville Ky. and also his arival [sic] at Nashville, Tenn." Ibid., 13:128n.

[13] USG set out for Nashville on Dec. 15, 1864, going first to Washington, DC. Later that
day, USG received a telegram from Van Duzer announcing Thomas's movement. On
Dec. 17, USG telegraphed Logan and told him not to proceed any further because of Thomas's
success. Ibid., 13:124n, 125n, 127–128n.

[14] See Logan's Dec. 17, 1864, telegram to USG, ibid., 13:128n.

[15] The Battle of Nashville lasted two days, during which Thomas reportedly captured 4,462
Confederates. Approximately 2,300 Confederates were either killed or wounded. OR, I, 45(I),
40; Wiley Sword, Embrace an Angry Wind: The Confederacy's Last Hurrah: Spring Hill, Franklin,
and Nashville (New York: HarperCollins, 1992), 425.

Our troops continued the pursuit to within a few miles of Columbia, where they found the rebels had destroyed the railroad bridge as well as all other bridges over Duck River. The heavy rains of a few days before had swelled the stream into a mad torrent, impassable except on bridges. Unfortunately, either through a mistake in the wording of the order or otherwise, the pontoon bridge which was to have been sent by rail out to Franklin, to be taken thence with the pursuing column, had gone toward Chattanooga.[16] There was, consequently, a delay of some four days in building bridges out of the remains of the old railroad bridge. Of course Hood got such a start in this time that farther pursuit was useless, although it was continued for some distance, but without coming upon him again.

[16] In issuing his orders, Thomas had mistakenly sent the bridge in the wrong direction by the wrong road. It arrived five days later. Ibid., 400.

# 61

## Expedition against Fort Fisher—Attack on the Fort— Failure of the Expedition—Second Expedition against the Fort—Capture of Fort Fisher

U P TO JANUARY, 1865, the enemy occupied Fort Fisher, at the mouth of Cape Fear River and below the City of Wilmington. This port was of immense importance to the Confederates, because it formed their principal inlet for blockade runners by means of which they brought in from abroad such supplies and munitions of war as they could not produce at home. It was equally important to us to get possession of it, not only because it was desirable to cut off their supplies so as to insure a speedy termination of the war, but also because foreign governments, particularly the British Government, were constantly threatening that unless ours could maintain the blockade of that coast they should cease to recognize any blockade.[1] For these reasons I determined, with the concurrence of the Navy Department, in December, to send an expedition against Fort Fisher for the purpose of capturing it.[2]

To show the difficulty experienced in maintaining the blockade, I will mention a circumstance that took place at Fort Fisher after its fall. Two English blockade runners came in at night. Their commanders, not supposing the fort had fallen, worked their way through all our fleet and got into the river unobserved. They then signalled the fort, announcing their arrival. There was a colored man in the fort who had been there before and who understood these

---

[1] Early in the war, the legality of the blockades was often disputed and trade between European powers and the Confederate states continued virtually uninterrupted. Chris E. Fonvielle Jr., *The Wilmington Campaign: Last Rays of Departing Hope* (Mechanicsburg, PA: Stackpole Books, 2001), 6–7.

[2] For USG's Nov. 30, 1864, proposal to Porter regarding a move against Fort Fisher, see *PUSG,* 13:36.

signals. He informed General Terry[3] what reply he should make to have them come in, and Terry did as he advised. The vessels came in, their officers entirely unconscious that they were falling into the hands of the Union forces. Even after they were brought in to the fort they were entertained in conversation for some little time before suspecting that the Union troops were occupying the fort. They were finally informed that their vessels and cargoes were prizes.[4]

I selected General Weitzel, of the Army of the James, to go with the expedition, but gave instructions through General Butler.[5] He commanded the department within whose geographical limits Fort Fisher was situated, as well as Beaufort and other points on that coast held by our troops; he was, therefore, entitled to the right of fitting out the expedition against Fort Fisher.[6]

General Butler conceived the idea that if a steamer loaded heavily with powder could be run up to near the shore under the fort and exploded, it would create great havoc and make the capture an easy matter. Admiral Porter, who was to command the naval squadron, seemed to fall in with the idea, and it was not disapproved of in Washington; the navy was therefore given the task of preparing the steamer for this purpose. I had no confidence in the success of the scheme, and so expressed myself; but as no serious harm could come of the experiment, and the authorities at Washington seemed desirous to have it tried, I permitted it.[7] The steamer was sent to Beaufort, North Carolina, and was there loaded with powder and prepared for the part she was to play in the reduction of Fort Fisher.[8]

---

[3] Alfred H. Terry (1827–1890) was born in Connecticut and entered the military in 1861 as a colonel in the 2nd Connecticut Inf. He was brevetted major general in Aug. 1864 and received the Thanks of Congress in 1865 for the victory at Fort Fisher. He remained in the regular army and commanded the Dept. of Dakota, later assisting in the planning of the Little Bighorn Campaign. *CWHC,* 524; Thom Hatch, *The Last Days of George Armstrong Custer: The True Story of the Battle of the Little Bighorn* (New York: St. Martin's Press, 2015), 119.

[4] USG may have referred to the Jan. 20, 1865, capture of the Confederate steamer *Stag,* commanded by Lt. Richard H. Gayle of the Confederate Navy, and the British steamer *Charlotte,* captained by Thomas E. Cocker. Fonvielle, *Wilmington Campaign,* 315.

[5] For USG's Nov. 30, 1864, telegram and Dec. 6 letter to Butler, see *PUSG,* 13:37, 71.

[6] Butler commanded the Dept. of Virginia and North Carolina from Nov. 11, 1863, to Aug. 27, 1864; from Sept. 7, 1864, to Dec. 14, 1864; and from Dec. 24, 1864, to Jan. 8, 1865. *CWHC,* 157.

[7] Butler presented his idea to USG and Porter on Nov. 29, 1864, and USG expressed skepticism regarding its potential for success in a Dec. 3 letter to Sherman. Rod Gragg, *Confederate Goliath: The Battle of Fort Fisher* (New York: HarperCollins, 1991), 40–41; *PUSG,* 13:xxii, 56.

[8] The ship was the steamer *Louisiana.* Gragg, *Confederate Goliath,* 41.

General Butler chose to go in command of the expedition himself, and was all ready to sail by the 9th of December (1864). Very heavy storms prevailed, however, at that time along that part of the sea-coast, and prevented him from getting off until the 13th or 14th. His advance arrived off Fort Fisher on the 15th. The naval force had been already assembled, or was assembling, but they were obliged to run into Beaufort for munitions, coal, etc.; then, too, the powder-boat was not yet fully prepared. The fleet was ready to proceed on the 18th; but Butler, who had remained outside from the 15th up to that time, now found himself out of coal, fresh water, etc., and had to put into Beaufort to replenish. Another storm overtook him, and several days more were lost before the army and navy were both ready at the same time to co-operate.[9]

On the night of the 23d the powder-boat was towed in by a gunboat as near to the fort as it was safe to run.[10] She was then propelled by her own machinery to within about five hundred yards of the shore. There the clockwork, which was to explode her within a certain length of time, was set and she was abandoned. Everybody left, and even the vessels put out to sea to prevent the effect of the explosion upon them. At two o'clock in the morning the explosion took place—and produced no more effect on the fort, or anything else on land, than the bursting of a boiler anywhere on the Atlantic Ocean would have done. Indeed when the troops in Fort Fisher heard the explosion they supposed it was the bursting of a boiler in one of the Yankee gunboats.[11]

Fort Fisher was situated upon a low, flat peninsula north of Cape Fear River. The soil is sandy. Back a little the peninsula is very heavily wooded, and covered with fresh-water swamps. The fort ran across this peninsula, about five hundred yards in width, and extended along the sea coast about thirteen hundred yards. The fort had an armament of 21 guns and 3 mortars on the land side, and 24 guns on the sea front. At that time it was only garrisoned by four companies of infantry, one light battery and the gunners at the heavy guns less than seven hundred men with a reserve of less than a thousand men five miles

[9] Porter's fleet left on Dec. 13, 1864 and Butler's army transports followed on Dec. 14. Ibid., 44–45.

[10] The gunboat *Wilderness* towed the steamer *Louisiana* into position. Ibid., 50.

[11] Confederate troops at Fort Fisher initially identified the sound as an exploding shell, but then decided it was from a U.S. vessel that had run aground and caught fire, causing its magazine to explode. Ibid., 53; David W. Kummer, *U.S. Marines in Battle: Fort Fisher, December 1864–January 1865* (Washington, DC: United States Marine Corps History Division, 2012), 16.

up the peninsula.[12] General Whiting[13] of the Confederate army was in command, and General Bragg was in command of the force at Wilmington. Both commenced calling for reinforcements the moment they saw our troops landing. The Governor of North Carolina[14] called for everybody who could stand behind a parapet and shoot a gun, to join them. In this way they got two or three hundred additional men into Fort Fisher; and Hoke's division, five or six thousand strong, was sent down from Richmond.[15] A few of these troops arrived the very day that Butler was ready to advance.

On the 24th the fleet formed for an attack in arcs of concentric circles, their heavy iron-clads going in very close range, being nearest the shore, and leaving intervals or spaces so that the outer vessels could fire between them. Porter was thus enabled to throw one hundred and fifteen shells per minute. The damage done to the fort by these shells was very slight, only two or three cannon being disabled in the fort. But the firing silenced all the guns by making it too hot for the men to maintain their positions about them and compelling them to seek shelter in the bomb-proofs.

On the next day part of Butler's troops under General Adelbert Ames[16] effected a landing out of range of the fort without difficulty. This was accom-

---

[12] Other sources indicate that there were twenty-six guns and two mortars on the seaward side, with 928 men in the fort by Dec. 23, 1864. Fonvielle, *Wilmington Campaign,* 43; Kummer, *Fort Fisher,* 119, 507n.

[13] William H. C. Whiting (1824–1865) was born in Mississippi and graduated first in his class from the USMA in 1845. He resigned from the U.S. Army in 1861 to join the Confederate Army. In Feb. 1863, he was promoted to major general. From 1862 to 1864, he commanded the Military District of Wilmington (NC) and was severely wounded at Fort Fisher. He was sent to Governor's Island, NY, where he died in Mar. 1865. *CWHC,* 566.

[14] Zebulon B. Vance (1830–1894) was born in North Carolina and served in the Confederate Army from May 1861 to Aug. 1863. He served as Confederate governor of North Carolina from 1862 to 1865 and as governor from 1877 to 1879. Ibid., 541.

[15] Approximately 443 additional troops entered Fort Fisher to reinforce the 928 on hand. Hoke's division is estimated to have had about 6,500 troops. Fonvielle, *Wilmington Campaign,* 117; Gragg, *Confederate Goliath,* 60–61.

[16] Adelbert Ames (1835–1933) was born in Maine. He graduated from the USMA in May 1861 and ten weeks later was fighting at the First Battle of Bull Run, receiving the Medal of Honor in 1893 for his bravery. In May 1863, he was promoted to brigadier general. During the Battle of Fort Fisher, he commanded the 2nd Div., 24th Corps (Terry's Provisional Corps), Dept. of North Carolina. He was promoted to major general for his actions at Fort Fisher. After the war, he served as U.S. senator from Mississippi from 1870 to 1874 and as governor from 1874 to 1876. Mississippi Democrats, who opposed his Reconstruction policies, impeached him in

plished under the protection of gunboats sent for the purpose, and under cover of a renewed attack upon the fort by the fleet. They formed a line across the peninsula and advanced, part going north and part toward the fort, covering themselves as they did so. Curtis[17] pushed forward and came near to Fort Fisher, capturing the small garrison at what was called the Flag Pond Battery. Weitzel accompanied him to within a half a mile of the works. Here he saw that the fort had not been injured, and so reported to Butler, advising against an assault. Ames, who had gone north in his advance, captured 228 of the reserves. These prisoners reported to Butler that sixteen hundred of Hoke's division of six thousand from Richmond had already arrived and the rest would soon be in his rear.

Upon these reports Butler determined to withdraw his troops from the peninsula and return to the fleet. At that time there had not been a man on our side injured except by one of the shells from the fleet. Curtis had got within a few yards of the works. Some of his men had snatched a flag from the parapet of the fort, and others had taken a horse from the inside of the stockade. At night Butler informed Porter of his withdrawal, giving the reasons above stated, and announced his purpose as soon as his men could embark to start for Hampton Roads. Porter represented to him that he had sent to Beaufort for more ammunition. He could fire much faster than he had been doing, and would keep the enemy from showing himself until our men were within twenty yards of the fort, and he begged that Butler would leave some brave fellows like those who had snatched the flag from the parapet and taken the horse from the fort.

Butler was unchangeable. He got all his troops aboard, except Curtis's brigade, and started back. In doing this, Butler made a fearful mistake. My instructions to him, or to the officer who went in command of the expedition, were explicit in the statement that to effect a landing would be of itself a great victory, and if one should be effected, the foothold must not be relinquished; on the contrary, a regular siege of the fort must be commenced and, to guard against interference by reason of storms, supplies of provisions must be laid in as soon as they could be got on shore. But General Butler

1876, but Ames resigned in response. *CWHC*, 102–103; William S. McFeely, *Grant: A Biography* (New York: Norton, 1981), 425.

[17] Newton Martin Curtis (1835–1910) was born in New York and entered the U.S. Army in 1861 as a captain of the 16th New York Inf. In Oct. 1864, he was promoted to brigadier general. During the Battle of Fort Fisher, he commanded the 1st Brigade, 2nd Div., 24th Corps (Terry's Provisional Corps), Army of the James. He received the Medal of Honor in 1891 for his bravery there, having received four wounds and lost one eye. Curtis was a U.S. representative from New York from 1891 to 1897. *CWHC*, 195.

seems to have lost sight of this part of his instructions, and was back at Fort Monroe on the 28th.[18]

I telegraphed to the President as follows:

> CITY POINT, VA.,
> *Dec.* 28, 1864.—8.30 P.M.
>
> The Wilmington expedition has proven a gross and culpable failure. Many of the troops are back here. Delays and free talk of the object of the expedition enabled the enemy to move troops to Wilmington to defeat it. After the expedition sailed from Fort Monroe, three days of fine weather were squandered, during which the enemy was without a force to protect himself. Who is to blame will, I hope, be known.
>
> U. S. GRANT,
> Lieutenant-General.

Porter sent dispatches to the Navy Department in which he complained bitterly of having been abandoned by the army just when the fort was nearly in our possession, and begged that our troops might be sent back again to co-operate, but with a different commander. As soon as I heard this I sent a messenger to Porter with a letter asking him to hold on.[19] I assured him that I fully sympathized with him in his disappointment, and that I would send the same troops back with a different commander, with some reinforcements to offset those which the enemy had received. I told him it would take some little time to get transportation for the additional troops; but as soon as it could be had the men should be on their way to him, and there would be no delay on my part. I selected A. H. Terry to command.

It was the 6th of January before the transports could be got ready and the troops aboard. They sailed from Fortress Monroe on that day. The object and destination of the second expedition were at the time kept a secret to all except a few in the Navy Department and in the army to whom it was necessary to impart the information. General Terry had not the slightest idea of where he was going or what he was to do. He simply knew that he was going to sea and that he had his orders with him, which were to be opened when out at sea.

He was instructed to communicate freely with Porter and have entire harmony between army and navy, because the work before them would require

---

[18] For USG's Dec. 1864 instructions to Butler regarding the Fort Fisher expedition, see *PUSG*, 13:61, 71–72, 72*n*, 80–81, 119, 119*n*–120*n*.

[19] For USG's Dec. 30, 1864, letter to Porter, see ibid., 13:190–191.

the best efforts of both arms of the service.[20] They arrived off Beaufort on the 8th. A heavy storm, however, prevented a landing at Fort Fisher until the 13th. The navy prepared itself for attack about as before, and at the same time assisted the army in landing, this time five miles away. Only iron-clads fired at first; the object being to draw the fire of the enemy's guns so as to ascertain their positions. This object being accomplished, they then let in their shots thick and fast. Very soon the guns were all silenced, and the fort showed evident signs of being much injured.

Terry deployed his men across the peninsula as had been done before, and at two o'clock on the following morning was up within two miles of the fort with a respectable *abatis* in front of his line. His artillery was all landed on that day, the 14th. Again Curtis's brigade of Ames's division had the lead. By noon they had carried an unfinished work less than a half mile from the fort, and turned it so as to face the other way.

Terry now saw Porter and arranged for an assault on the following day. The two commanders arranged their signals so that they could communicate with each other from time to time as they might have occasion. At daylight the fleet commenced its firing. The time agreed upon for the assault was the middle of the afternoon, and Ames who commanded the assaulting column moved at 3.30. Porter landed a force of sailors and marines to move against the sea-front in co-operation with Ames's assault. They were under Commander Breese[21] of the navy. These sailors and marines had worked their way up to within a couple of hundred yards of the fort before the assault. The signal was given and the assault was made; but the poor sailors and marines were repulsed and very badly handled by the enemy, losing 280 killed and wounded out of their number.[22]

Curtis's brigade charged successfully though met by a heavy fire, some of the men having to wade through the swamp up to their waists to reach the

[20] For USG's Jan. 3, 1865, letter to Terry, see ibid., 13:219–220.

[21] Kidder Randolph Breese (1831–1881) was born in Pennsylvania and joined the U.S. Navy as a midshipman in 1846. He served under David Farragut during the Mexican-American War and in 1861 commanded the 3rd Div. of Porter's Mortar Flotilla. In July 1862, he was promoted to lieutenant commander and served as fleet captain at the Battle of Fort Fisher. After the war, he served as assistant to the superintendent of the U.S. Naval Academy. William H. Powell and Edward Shippen, *Officers of the Army and the Navy (Regular) Who Served in the Civil War* (Philadelphia: L. R. Hamersly, 1892), 50.

[22] Casualty estimates range from 284 to over 300 out of the approximately 1,600 U.S. sailors and marines involved in the attack. Fonvielle, *Wilmington Campaign*, 258; Gragg, *Confederate Goliath*, 167.

fort. Many were wounded, of course, and some killed;[23] but they soon reached the palisades. These they cut away, and pushed on through. The other troops then came up, Pennypacker's[24] following Curtis, and Bell,[25] who commanded the 3d brigade of Ames's division, following Pennypacker. But the fort was not yet captured though the parapet was gained.

The works were very extensive. The large parapet around the work would have been but very little protection to those inside except when they were close up under it. Traverses had, therefore, been run until really the work was a succession of small forts enclosed by a large one. The rebels made a desperate effort to hold the fort, and had to be driven from these traverses one by one. The fight continued till long after night. Our troops gained first one traverse and then another, and by 10 o'clock at night the place was carried. During this engagement the sailors, who had been repulsed in their assault on the bastion, rendered the best service they could by reinforcing Terry's northern line—thus enabling him to send a detachment to the assistance of Ames. The fleet kept up a continuous fire upon that part of the fort which was still occupied by the enemy. By means of signals they could be informed where to direct their shots.

During the succeeding nights the enemy blew up Fort Caswell[26] on the opposite side of Cape Fear River, and abandoned two extensive works on Smith's Island in the river.

---

[23] The 1st Brigade, 2nd Div., 24th Corps, under Curtis lost thirty-nine killed and 184 wounded. *OR,* I, 46(I), 405.

[24] Galusha Pennypacker (1844–1916) was born in Pennsylvania and enlisted in 1861 as a quartermaster sergeant, but soon gained a commission as a captain in the 97th Pennsylvania Inf. In Aug. 1864, he was promoted to colonel. During the Battle of Fort Fisher, he commanded the 2nd Brigade, 2nd Div., 24th Corps (Terry's Provisional Corps), Dept. of North Carolina. He was wounded at Fort Fisher and in 1891 was awarded the Medal of Honor. *CWHC,* 425.

[25] Louis Bell (1837–1865) was born in New Hampshire, entered the military as a lieutenant colonel in 1861, and was promoted to colonel in 1862. Bruce D. Heald, *New Hampshire in the Civil War* (Charleston, SC: Arcadia, 2001), 27.

[26] Fort Caswell is approximately thirty miles south of Wilmington at the mouth of the Cape Fear River. Most of the fort was destroyed during the battle, but it was later restored in 1896. It was used by the military during the Spanish-American War (1898), World War I (1914–1918), the U.S. occupation of Haiti (1915–1934), and World War II (1941–1945). It was purchased by the Baptist State Convention of North Carolina in 1949 and was used to house troops during the Persian Gulf War. Anita Price Davis, *North Carolina and World War II: A Documentary Portrait* (Jefferson, NC: McFarland, 2015), 101–102.

Our captures in all amounted to 169 guns, besides small-arms, with full supplies of ammunition, and 2,083 prisoners. In addition to these, there were about 700 dead and wounded left there. We had lost 110 killed and 536 wounded.[27]

In this assault on Fort Fisher, Bell, one of the brigade commanders, was killed,[28] and two, Curtis and Pennypacker, were badly wounded.

Secretary Stanton, who was on his way back from Savannah, arrived off Fort Fisher soon after it fell. When he heard the good news he promoted all the officers of any considerable rank for their conspicuous gallantry.[29] Terry had been nominated for major-general, but had not been confirmed. This confirmed him; and soon after I recommended him for a brigadier-generalcy in the regular army, and it was given to him for this victory.[30]

---

[27] Confederate dead and wounded from the fighting on Jan. 15, 1865, were estimated at approximately 500. U.S. losses were 119 killed and 540 wounded. *OR,* I, 46(I), 401, 434.

[28] Bell died on Jan. 16, 1865. Heald, *New Hampshire in the Civil War,* 27.

[29] Among those promoted were Comstock and Joseph C. Abbott, who were brevetted brigadier general; Ames, brevetted major general; Adrian Terry and Charles H. Graves, promoted to major; Pennypacker, promoted to brigadier general; and Newton Martin Curtis, promoted to brigadier general. Gragg, *Confederate Goliath,* 238.

[30] USG recommended Terry for brigadier general in the regular army on Jan. 17, 1865. He was later confirmed as brigadier general in the regular army and major general of volunteers, effective Jan. 15. *CWHC,* 524; *PUSG,* 13:271n.

# 62

## Sherman's March North—Sheridan Ordered to Lynchburg—Canby Ordered to Move against Mobile—Movements of Schofield and Thomas— Capture of Columbia, South Carolina— Sherman in the Carolinas

W HEN NEWS OF Sherman being in possession of Savannah reached the North, distinguished statesmen and visitors began to pour in to see him. Among others who went was the Secretary of War, who seemed much pleased at the result of his campaign.[1] Mr. Draper, the collector of customs of New York, who was with Mr. Stanton's party, was put in charge of the public property that had been abandoned and captured.[2] Savannah was then turned over to General Foster's command to hold, so that Sherman might have his own entire army free to operate as might be decided upon in the future. I sent the chief engineer of the Army of the Potomac (General Barnard) with letters to General Sherman. He remained some time with the general, and when he returned brought back letters, one of which contained suggestions from Sherman as to what ought to be done in co-operation with him, when he should have started upon his march northward.[3]

---

[1] Stanton met with Sherman for four days in Savannah, GA, in early Jan. 1865. *PUSG*, 13:272n.

[2] Simeon Draper (1804–1866) was born in Massachusetts and moved to New York City. In 1862, Lincoln appointed him as collector of the Port of New York. *American Annual Cyclopedia and Register of Important Events of the Year 1866,* vol. 6 (New York: D. Appleton, 1867), 275.

[3] On Jan. 2, 1865, Barnard delivered USG's letters to Sherman and on Jan. 21 delivered Sherman's response to USG. *PUSG*, 13:171n, 291. For Sherman's Jan. 16 letter to USG, see ibid., 13:293n.

I must not neglect to state here the fact that I had no idea originally of having Sherman march from Savannah to Richmond, or even to North Carolina. The season was bad, the roads impassable for anything except such an army as he had, and I should not have thought of ordering such a move. I had, therefore, made preparations to collect transports to carry Sherman and his army around to the James River by water, and so informed him. On receiving this letter he went to work immediately to prepare for the move, but seeing that it would require a long time to collect the transports, he suggested the idea then of marching up north through the Carolinas. I was only too happy to approve this; for if successful, it promised every advantage.[4] His march through Georgia had thoroughly destroyed all lines of transportation in that State, and had completely cut the enemy off from all sources of supply to the west of it. If North and South Carolina were rendered helpless so far as capacity for feeding Lee's army was concerned, the Confederate garrison at Richmond would be reduced in territory, from which to draw supplies, to very narrow limits in the State of Virginia; and, although that section of the country was fertile, it was already well exhausted of both forage and food. I approved Sherman's suggestion therefore at once.[5]

The work of preparation was tedious, because supplies, to load the wagons for the march, had to be brought from a long distance. Sherman would now have to march through a country furnishing fewer provisions than that he had previously been operating in during his march to the sea. Besides, he was confronting, or marching toward, a force of the enemy vastly superior to any his troops had encountered on their previous march; and the territory through which he had to pass had now become of such vast importance to the very existence of the Confederate army, that the most desperate efforts were to be expected in order to save it.

Sherman, therefore, while collecting the necessary supplies to start with, made arrangements with Admiral Dahlgren, who commanded that part of the navy on the South Carolina and Georgia coast,[6] and General Foster,

[4] USG instructed Sherman to come to Virginia in a Dec. 6, 1864, letter delivered by Lt. William Dunn. Sherman responded on Dec. 16, indicating that he would comply with USG's instructions but suggesting instead a march into South Carolina. Ibid., 13:72–73, 73n–76n.

[5] For USG's Dec. 27, 1864, letter to Sherman, see ibid., 13:168–170.

[6] John A. B. Dahlgren (1809–1870) was born in Pennsylvania and joined the U.S. Navy as a midshipman in 1826, reaching commander in 1855. He was stationed at the Washington Navy Yard from Apr. 1861 to July 1862. By Feb. 1863, he had reached rear admiral. In late 1864, he commanded the South Atlantic Blockading Squadron. *CWHC*, 197–198.

commanding the troops, to take positions, and hold a few points on the sea coast, which he (Sherman) designated, in the neighborhood of Charleston.

This provision was made to enable him to fall back upon the sea coast, in case he should encounter a force sufficient to stop his onward progress. He also wrote me a letter, making suggestions as to what he would like to have done in support of his movement farther north. This letter was brought to City Point by General Barnard at a time when I happened to be going to Washington City, where I arrived on the 21st of January.[7] I cannot tell the provision I had already made to co-operate with Sherman, in anticipation of his expected movement, better than by giving my reply to this letter.

HEADQUARTERS ARMIES OF THE UNITED STATES,
WASHINGTON, D. C., *Jan.* 21, 1865.

MAJOR-GENERAL W. T. SHERMAN,
Commanding Mil. Div. of the Mississippi.

GENERAL:—Your letters brought by General Barnard were received at City Point, and read with interest. Not having them with me, however, I cannot say that in this I will be able to satisfy you on all points of recommendation. As I arrived here at one P.M., and must leave at six P.M., having in the meantime spent over three hours with the Secretary and General Halleck, I must be brief. Before your last request to have Thomas make a campaign into the heart of Alabama, I had ordered Schofield to Annapolis, Md., with his corps.[8] The advance (six thousand) will reach the seaboard by the 23d, the remainder following as rapidly as railroad transportation can be procured from Cincinnati. The corps numbers over twenty-one thousand men. I was induced to do this because I did not believe Thomas could possibly be got off before spring. His pursuit of Hood indicated a sluggishness that satisfied me that he would never do to conduct one of your campaigns. The command of the advance of the pursuit was left to subordinates, whilst Thomas followed far behind. When Hood had crossed the Tennessee, and those in pursuit had reached it, Thomas had not much more than half crossed the State, from whence he returned to Nashville to take steamer for Eastport. He is possessed of excellent judgment,

---

[7] For Sherman's Jan. 16, 1865, letter to USG, see *PUSG,* 13:293*n*–294*n.*

[8] On Jan. 7, 1865, USG ordered Schofield's corps to Annapolis, MD. Sherman had requested that Thomas's forces, including those under Schofield, make a campaign through Alabama. Ibid., 13:245, 245*n*–246*n,* 293*n.*

great coolness and honesty, but he is not good on a pursuit. He also reported his troops fagged, and that it was necessary to equip up. This report and a determination to give the enemy no rest determined me to use his surplus troops elsewhere.

Thomas is still left with a sufficient force surplus to go to Selma under an energetic leader. He has been telegraphed to, to know whether he could go, and, if so, which of the several routes he would select. No reply is yet received. Canby has been ordered to act offensively from the sea-coast to the interior, towards Montgomery and Selma. Thomas's forces will move from the north at an early day, or some of his troops will be sent to Canby. Without further reinforcements Canby will have a moving column of twenty thousand men.[9]

Fort Fisher, you are aware, has been captured. We have a force there of eight thousand effective. At New Bern about half the number. It is rumored, through deserters, that Wilmington also has fallen. I am inclined to believe the rumor, because on the 17th we knew the enemy were blowing up their works about Fort Caswell, and that on the 18th Terry moved on Wilmington.[10]

If Wilmington is captured, Schofield will go there. If not, he will be sent to New Bern. In either event, all the surplus forces at the two points will move to the interior toward Goldsboro' in co-operation with your movements. From either point, railroad communications can be run out, there being here abundance of rolling-stock suited to the gauge of those roads.

There have been about sixteen thousand men sent from Lee's army south. Of these, you will have fourteen thousand against you, if Wilmington is not held by the enemy, casualties at Fort Fisher having overtaken about two thousand.

All these troops are subject to your orders as you come in communication with them. They will be so instructed. From about Richmond I will watch Lee closely, and if he detaches much more, or attempts to evacuate, will pitch in. In the meantime, should you be brought to a halt anywhere, I can send two corps of thirty thousand effective men to your support, from the troops about Richmond.

[9] On Jan. 18, 1865, USG instructed Halleck to see when Thomas could start a campaign through Alabama. USG also suggested that Halleck order Canby to make an independent campaign to capture Mobile, AL, Montgomery, AL, and Selma, AL. Ibid., 13:273.

[10] Wilmington, NC, was not captured until Feb. 22, 1865. Ibid., 14:xxi.

To resume: Canby is ordered to operate to the interior from the Gulf. A. J. Smith may go from the north, but I think it doubtful. A force of twenty-eight or thirty thousand will co-operate with you from New Bern or Wilmington, or both. You can call for reinforcements.

This will be handed you by Captain Hudson, of my staff,[11] who will return with any message you may have for me. If there is anything I can do for you in the way of having supplies on ship-board, at any point on the sea-coast, ready for you, let me know it.

Yours truly,
U. S. GRANT,
Lieut.-General.

I had written on the 18th of January to General Sherman, giving him the news of the battle of Nashville. He was much pleased at the result, although, like myself, he had been very much disappointed at Thomas for permitting Hood to cross the Tennessee River and nearly the whole State of Tennessee, and come to Nashville to be attacked there. He, however, as I had done, sent Thomas a warm congratulatory letter.[12]

On the 10th of January, 1865, the resolutions of thanks to Sherman and his army passed by Congress were approved.[13]

Sherman, after the capture, at once had the *débris* in Savannah cleared up, commencing the work by removing the piling and torpedoes from the river, and taking up all other obstructions. He had then intrenched the city, so that it could be held by a small garrison. By the middle of January all his work was done, except the accumulation of supplies to commence his movements with.

He proposed to move in two columns, one from Savannah, going along by the river of the same name, and the other by roads farther east, threatening Charleston. He commenced the advance by moving his right wing to Beau-

---

[11] Peter T. Hudson (?–1892), the nephew of USG's cousin Silas A. Hudson, was from Burlington, IA. He served as USG's aide-de-camp during the Civil War. Arthur H. Grant, *The Grant Family: A Genealogical History of the Descendants of Matthew Grant of Windsor, Conn., 1601–1898* (Poughkeepsie, NY: A. V. Haight, 1898), 142; *PUSG*, 6:319–320, 320*n*, 357 and *n*; 15:3.

[12] For Sherman's Dec. 25, 1864, congratulatory letter to Thomas, see Brooks D. Simpson and Jean V. Berlin, eds., *Sherman's Civil War: Selected Correspondence of William T. Sherman, 1860–1865* (Chapel Hill: University of North Carolina, 1999), 779–780.

[13] See *Acts and Resolutions of the Second Session of the Thirty-Eighth Congress, Begun on Monday, December 5, 1864, and Ended on Saturday, March 4, 1865* (Washington, DC: Government Printing Office, 1865), 166–167.

fort, South Carolina, then to Pocotaligo[14] by water. This column, in moving north, threatened Charleston, and, indeed, it was not determined at first that they would not have a force visit Charleston. South Carolina had done so much to prepare the public mind of the South for secession, and had been so active in precipitating the decision of the question before the South was fully prepared to meet it, that there was, at that time, a feeling throughout the North and also largely entertained by people of the South, that the State of South Carolina, and Charleston, the hot-bed of secession in particular, ought to have a heavy hand laid upon them. In fact, nothing but the decisive results that followed, deterred the radical portion of the people from condemning the movement, because Charleston had been left out. To pass into the interior would, however, be to insure the evacuation of the city, and its possession by the navy and Foster's troops. It is so situated between two formidable rivers[15] that a small garrison could have held it against all odds as long as their supplies would hold out. Sherman therefore passed it by.

By the first of February all preparations were completed for the final march, Columbia, South Carolina, being the first objective; Fayetteville, North Carolina, the second; and Goldsboro, or neighborhood, the final one, unless something further should be determined upon. The right wing went from Pocotaligo, and the left from about Hardeeville on the Savannah River, both columns taking a pretty direct route for Columbia. The cavalry, however, were to threaten Charleston on the right, and Augusta on the left.

On the 15th of January Fort Fisher had fallen, news of which Sherman had received before starting out on his march. We already had New Bern and had soon Wilmington, whose fall followed that of Fort Fisher; as did other points on the sea coast, where the National troops were now in readiness to co-operate with Sherman's advance when he had passed Fayetteville.

On the 18th of January I ordered Canby, in command at New Orleans, to move against Mobile, Montgomery and Selma, Alabama, for the purpose of destroying roads, machine shops, etc.[16] On the 8th of February I ordered Sheridan, who was in the Valley of Virginia, to push forward as soon as the weather would permit and strike the canal west of Richmond at or about Lynchburg;

[14] On Jan. 15, 1865, Sherman's forces captured Pocotaligo, SC, approximately sixty miles west of Charleston, SC. George B. Davis et al., *The Official Military Atlas of the Civil War* (New York: Fairfax Press, 1983), plate 143; *PUSG*, 13:350n.

[15] The Ashley and Cooper Rivers. Davis et al., *Official Military Atlas of the Civil War*, plate 143.

[16] USG wrote to Halleck on Jan. 18, 1865, and on Jan. 26 Halleck informed Canby of the plan and instructed him to begin preparations. *OR*, I, 49(I), 593; *PUSG*, 13:273.

and on the 20th I made the order to go to Lynchburg as soon as the roads would permit, saying: "As soon as it is possible to travel, I think you will have no difficulty about reaching Lynchburg with a cavalry force alone. From there you could destroy the railroad and canal in every direction, so as to be of no further use to the rebellion. * * * This additional raid, with one starting from East Tennessee under Stoneman, numbering about four or five thousand cavalry; one from Eastport, Mississippi, ten thousand cavalry; Canby, from Mobile Bay, with about eighteen thousand mixed troops—these three latter pushing for Tuscaloosa, Selma and Montgomery; and Sherman with a large army eating out the vitals of South Carolina—is all that will be wanted to leave nothing for the rebellion to stand upon. I would advise you to overcome great obstacles to accomplish this. Charleston was evacuated on Tuesday last."[17]

On the 27th of February, more than a month after Canby had received his orders, I again wrote to him, saying that I was extremely anxious to hear of his being in Alabama. I notified him, also, that I had sent Grierson to take command of his cavalry, he being a very efficient officer. I further suggested that Forrest was probably in Mississippi, and if he was there, he would find him an officer of great courage and capacity whom it would be difficult to get by. I still further informed him that Thomas had been ordered to start a cavalry force into Mississippi on the 20th of February, or as soon as possible thereafter. This force did not get off however.

All these movements were designed to be in support of Sherman's march, the object being to keep the Confederate troops in the West from leaving there. But neither Canby nor Thomas could be got off in time. I had some time before depleted Thomas's army to reinforce Canby, for the reason that Thomas had failed to start an expedition which he had been ordered to send out, and to have the troops where they might do something. Canby seemed to be equally deliberate in all of his movements. I ordered him to go in person; but he prepared to send a detachment under another officer. General Granger had got down to New Orleans, in some way or other, and I wrote Canby that he must not put him in command of troops. In spite of this he asked the War Department to assign Granger to the command of a corps.[18]

---

[17] For USG's full Feb. 20, 1865, telegram to Sheridan, see *PUSG*, 13:457–458.

[18] With support from Andrew Johnson, military governor of Tennessee, and Maj. Gen. James A. Garfield, an Ohio congressman, Granger secured a position under Canby in New Orleans, LA, in July 1864. On Jan. 18, 1865, USG wrote Halleck: "It will not do for Canby to rely on either Granger or Hurlbut as first in command of any important campaign." On Feb. 18,

Almost in despair of having adequate service rendered to the cause in that quarter, I said to Canby: "I am in receipt of a dispatch * * *[19] informing me that you have made requisitions for a construction corps and material to build seventy miles of railroad. I have directed that none be sent. Thomas's army has been depleted to send a force to you that they might be where they could act in winter, and at least detain the force the enemy had in the West. If there had been any idea of repairing railroads, it could have been done much better from the North, where we already had the troops. I expected your movements to be co-operative with Sherman's last. This has now entirely failed. I wrote to you long ago, urging you to push promptly and to live upon the country, and destroy railroads, machine shops, etc., not to build them. Take Mobile and hold it, and push your forces to the interior—to Montgomery and to Selma. Destroy railroads, rolling stock, and everything useful for carrying on war, and, when you have done this, take such positions as can be supplied by water. By this means alone you can occupy positions from which the enemy's roads in the interior can be kept broken."

Most of these expeditions got off finally, but too late to render any service in the direction for which they were designed.[20]

The enemy, ready to intercept his advance, consisted of Hardee's troops and Wheeler's cavalry, perhaps less than fifteen thousand men in all; but frantic efforts were being made in Richmond, as I was sure would be the case, to retard Sherman's movements. Everything possible was being done to raise troops in the South. Lee dispatched against Sherman the troops which had been sent to relieve Fort Fisher, which, including those of the other defences of the harbor and its neighborhood, amounted, after deducting the two thousand killed, wounded and captured, to fourteen thousand men. After Thomas's victory at Nashville what remained, of Hood's army were gathered together and forwarded as rapidly as possible to the east to co-operate with these forces; and, finally, General Joseph E. Johnston, one of the ablest commanders of the South

Canby placed Granger in charge of the U.S. 13th Corps. Robert C. Conner, *General Gordon Granger: The Savior of Chickamauga and the Man behind "Juneteenth"* (Philadelphia: Casemate, 2013), 150–151; *OR*, I, 48(I), 891; *PUSG*, 13:274n.

[19] The text omitted from USG's Mar. 9, 1865, telegram to Canby reads "from Gen. Meigs." *PUSG*, 14:124–125.

[20] On Feb. 27, 1865, Sheridan's expedition set out from Winchester, VA. On Mar. 5, Canby left New Orleans to start his expedition against Mobile. Under the direction of Thomas, both Wilson and Stoneman departed on their raids on Mar. 20. *OR*, I, 46(I), 474–475; *PUSG*, 14:125n, 196, 203.

though not in favor with the administration (or at least with Mr. Davis), was put in command of all the troops in North and South Carolina.[21]

Schofield arrived at Annapolis in the latter part of January, but before sending his troops to North Carolina I went with him down the coast to see the situation of affairs, as I could give fuller directions after being on the ground than I could very well have given without. We soon returned, and the troops were sent by sea to Cape Fear River.[22] Both New Bern and Wilmington are connected with Raleigh by railroads which unite at Goldsboro.[23] Schofield was to land troops at Smithville, near the mouth of the Cape Fear River on the west side, and move up to secure the Wilmington and Charlotteville Railroad.[24] This column took their pontoon bridges with them, to enable them to cross over to the island south of the city of Wilmington. A large body was sent by the north side to co-operate with them. They succeeded in taking the city on the 22d of February. I took the precaution to provide for Sherman's army, in case he should be forced to turn in toward the sea coast before reaching North Carolina, by forwarding supplies to every place where he was liable to have to make such a deflection from his projected march. I also sent railroad rolling stock, of which we had a great abundance, now that we were not operating the roads in Virginia. The gauge of the North Carolina railroads being the same as the Virginia railroads had been altered too; these cars and locomotives were ready for use there without any change.

On the 31st of January I countermanded the orders given to Thomas to move south to Alabama and Georgia. (I had previously reduced his force by sending a portion of it to Terry.)[25] I directed in lieu of this movement, that he should send Stoneman through East Tennessee, and push him well down toward Columbia, South Carolina, in support of Sherman. Thomas did not get Stoneman off in time, but, on the contrary, when I had supposed he was on his march in support of Sherman I heard of his being in Louisville, Kentucky. I

---

[21] Thomas defeated Hood's army at Nashville, TN, on Dec. 15–16, 1864. Johnston assumed command on Mar. 6, 1865. *PUSG,* 13:134; William T. Sherman, *Memoirs of General William T. Sherman* (New York: D. Appleton, 1875), 2:292.

[22] USG had ordered Schofield's troops to Annapolis but with Asst. Secretary of the Navy Gustavus V. Fox and Schofield, he visited Fort Fisher from Jan. 26 to 31, 1865. *PUSG,* 13:xxv, 291.

[23] The Wilmington and Weldon Railroad and the Atlanta and North Carolina Railroad met at Goldsboro, NC. Robert C. Black III, *The Railroads of the Confederacy* (Chapel Hill: University of North Carolina Press, 1952), enclosed map.

[24] This railroad was the Wilmington, Charlotte, and Rutherford. Ibid., 360 and enclosed map.

[25] For USG's Jan. 3, 1865, letter to Porter regarding troops sent to Terry, see *PUSG,* 13:218.

immediately changed the order, and directed Thomas to send him toward Lynchburg.[26] Finally, however, on the 12th of March, he did push down through the north-western end of South Carolina, creating some consternation. I also ordered Thomas to send the 4th corps (Stanley's) to Bull Gap and to destroy no more roads east of that. I also directed him to concentrate supplies at Knoxville, with a view to a probable movement of his army through that way toward Lynchburg.[27]

Goldsboro is four hundred and twenty-five miles from Savannah.[28] Sherman's march was without much incident until he entered Columbia, on the 17th of February. He was detained in his progress by having to repair and corduroy the roads, and rebuild the bridges. There was constant skirmishing and fighting between the cavalry of the two armies, but this did not retard the advance of the infantry. Four days, also, were lost in making complete the destruction of the most important railroads south of Columbia;[29] there was also some delay caused by the high water, and the destruction of the bridges on the line of the road. A formidable river[30] had to be crossed near Columbia, and that in the face of a small garrison under General Wade Hampton. There was but little delay, however, further than that caused by high water in the stream. Hampton left as Sherman approached, and the city was found to be on fire.

There has since been a great deal of acrimony displayed in discussions of the question as to who set Columbia on fire. Sherman denies it on the part of his troops, and Hampton denies it on the part of the Confederates. One thing is certain: as soon as our troops took possession, they at once proceeded to extinguish the flames to the best of their ability with the limited means at hand.[31]

[26] On Feb. 27, 1865, USG directed Thomas to send Stoneman toward Lynchburg, VA. Ibid., 14:64.

[27] For USG's Mar. 7, 1865, telegram to Thomas, see ibid., 14:112.

[28] The distance between Goldsboro and Savannah was approximately 300 miles. Davis et al., *Official Military Atlas of the Civil War,* plate 135-A.

[29] For Sherman's destruction of the major railroads below Columbia, SC (e.g., the South Carolina Railroad and the Greenville and Columbia Railroad), see Black, *Railroads of the Confederacy,* 272–273 and enclosed map.

[30] The Congaree River is formed in Columbia by the merging of the Saluda and Broad Rivers. Davis et al., *Official Military Atlas of the Civil War,* plate 135-A.

[31] Confederate lore has blamed Sherman for the destruction of Columbia, but modern scholarship indicates that Sherman's troops did not burn the city. For further analysis and discussion of the controversy, see Marion B. Lucas, *Sherman and the Burning of Columbia* (College Station: Texas A&M University Press, 1988).

In any case, the example set by the Confederates in burning the village of Chambersburg, Pa., a town which was not garrisoned, would seem to make a defence of the act of firing the seat of government of the State most responsible for the conflict then raging, not imperative.[32]

The Confederate troops having vacated the city, the mayor[33] took possession, and sallied forth to meet the commander of the National forces for the purpose of surrendering the town, making terms for the protection of property, etc. Sherman paid no attention at all to the overture, but pushed forward and took the town without making any conditions whatever with its citizens. He then, however, co-operated with the mayor in extinguishing the flames and providing for the people who were rendered destitute by this destruction of their homes. When he left there he even gave the mayor five hundred head of cattle to be distributed among the citizens, to tide them over until some arrangement could be made for their future supplies.[34] He remained in Columbia until the roads, public buildings, workshops and everything that could be useful to the enemy were destroyed. While at Columbia, Sherman learned for the first time that what remained of Hood's army was confronting him, under the command of General Beauregard.[35]

Charleston was evacuated on the 18th of February, and Foster garrisoned the place. Wilmington was captured on the 22d. Columbia and Cheraw farther north, were regarded as so secure from invasion that the wealthy people of Charleston and Augusta had sent much of their valuable property to these two points to be stored. Among the goods sent there were valuable carpets, tons of old Madeira, silverware, and furniture. I am afraid much of these goods

---

[32] On July 30, 1864, Early's troops burned Chambersburg, PA, after its citizens refused to pay a financial levy to reimburse Virginia for Hunter's destruction in the Shenandoah Valley. Edward Smith, "Chambersburg: Anatomy of a Confederate Reprisal," *American Historical Review* 96 (1991): 432–455.

[33] Thomas J. Goodwyn (c.1800–c.1877) was mayor of Columbia from 1863 to 1865. John Hammond Moore, *Columbia and Richland County: A South Carolina Community, 1740–1990* (Columbia: University of South Carolina Press, 1993), 466.

[34] By some accounts, Sherman also arranged for 1,200 bushels of grain and some salt for the people of Columbia. Charles Royster, *The Destructive War: William Tecumseh Sherman, Stonewall Jackson, and the Americans* (New York: Alfred A. Knopf, 1991), 31; Mary Elizabeth Massy, *Refugee Life in the Confederacy* (1964; repr. Baton Rouge: Louisiana State University Press, 2001), 300*n*.

[35] Around Oct. 17, 1864, Sherman had learned that Beauregard "had reached Hood's army at Gadsden [AL]; that, without assuming direct command of the army, he had authority from the Confederate government to direct all its movements." Sherman, *Memoirs*, 2:160.

fell into the hands of our troops. There was found at Columbia a large amount of powder, some artillery, small-arms and fixed ammunition.[36] These, of course, were among the articles destroyed. While here, Sherman also learned of Johnston's restoration to command.[37] The latter was given, as already stated, all troops in North and South Carolina. After the completion of the destruction of public property about Columbia, Sherman proceeded on his march and reached Cheraw without any special opposition and without incident to relate. The railroads, of course, were thoroughly destroyed on the way. Sherman remained a day or two at Cheraw; and, finally, on the 6th of March crossed his troops over the Pedee and advanced straight for Fayetteville. Hardee and Hampton were there, and barely escaped. Sherman reached Fayetteville on the 11th of March. He had dispatched scouts from Cheraw with letters to General Terry, at Wilmington, asking him to send a steamer with some supplies of bread, clothing and other articles which he enumerated.[38] The scouts got through successfully, and a boat was sent with the mail and such articles for which Sherman had asked as were in store at Wilmington; unfortunately, however, those stores did not contain clothing.

Four days later, on the 15th, Sherman left Fayetteville for Goldsboro. The march, now, had to be made with great caution, for he was approaching Lee's army and nearing the country that still remained open to the enemy. Besides, he was confronting all that he had had to confront in his previous march up to that point, reinforced by the garrisons along the road and by what remained of Hood's army. Frantic appeals were made to the people to come in voluntarily and swell the ranks of our foe. I presume, however, that Johnston did not have in all over 35,000 or 40,000 men.[39] The people had grown tired of the war, and desertions from the Confederate army were much more numerous than the voluntary accessions.

[36] The Confederate troops in Columbia failed to remove their ordnance and other supplies from the city, which consisted of "fifty boxes of machinery, five hundred boxes of valuable stores, and two hundred pigs of lead" along with "seventy carloads of equipment that had been shipped from the Charleston arsenal. Of the ninety carloads of government supplies, Confederate officials managed to evacuate [only] 105,000 of small ammunition." Lucas, *Sherman and the Burning of Columbia*, 60.

[37] Jefferson Davis restored Johnston to command in the West on Feb. 25, 1865, and Sherman learned this on Mar. 5 or 6. *CWHC*, 323; Sherman, *Memoirs*, 2:292.

[38] For Sherman's Mar. 12, 1865, message to Terry, see *OR*, I, 47(II), 803.

[39] A modern estimate of Johnston's troops puts the number closer to 25,000. John G. Barrett, *Sherman's March through the Carolinas* (Chapel Hill: University of North Carolina Press, 1956), 112–113.

There was some fighting at Averysboro on the 16th between Johnston's troops and Sherman's, with some loss; and at Bentonville on the 19th and 21st of March, but Johnston withdrew from the contest before the morning of the 22d. Sherman's loss in these last engagements in killed, wounded, and missing, was about sixteen hundred.[40] Sherman's troops at last reached Goldsboro on the 23d of the month and went into bivouac; and there his men were destined to have a long rest. Schofield was there to meet him with the troops which had been sent to Wilmington.

Sherman was no longer in danger. He had Johnston confronting him; but with an army much inferior to his own, both in numbers and morale.[41] He had Lee to the north of him with a force largely superior; but I was holding Lee with a still greater force, and had he made his escape and gotten down to reinforce Johnston, Sherman, with the reinforcements he now had from Schofield and Terry, would have been able to hold the Confederates at bay for an indefinite period. He was near the sea-shore with his back to it, and our navy occupied the harbors. He had a railroad to both Wilmington and New Bern, and his flanks were thoroughly protected by streams, which intersect that part of the country and deepen as they approach the sea.[42] Then, too, Sherman knew that if Lee should escape me I would be on his heels, and he and Johnston together would be crushed in one blow if they attempted to make a stand. With the loss of their capital, it is doubtful whether Lee's army would have amounted to much as an army when it reached North Carolina. Johnston's army was demoralized by constant defeat and would hardly have made an offensive movement, even if they could have been induced to remain on duty. The men of both Lee's and Johnston's armies were, like their brethren of the North, as brave as men can be; but no man is so brave that he may not meet such defeats and disasters as to discourage him and dampen his ardor for any cause, no matter how just he deems it.

[40] At Averasboro, NC, Confederate forces lost about 860 men, while U.S. Army losses were about 680. At Bentonville, NC, the losses were about 1,500 U.S. troops and about 2,600 Confederate troops. The battle took place on the east bank of the Cape Fear River, fifty miles south of Goldsboro. Ibid., 155–156, 184; Davis et al., *Official Military Atlas of the Civil War,* plate 135-A.

[41] Sherman had an army of approximately 60,000 men, while Johnston's force was approximately 22,000. Mark L. Bradley, *Last Stand in the Carolinas: The Battle of Bentonville* (Campbell, CA: Savas, 1995), 20, 22.

[42] It is unclear to which of the many streams in the area USG referred, but Stoney Creek and Little River are two of the most prominent ones. Davis et al., *Official Military Atlas of the Civil War,* plate 143.

# 63

Arrival of the Peace Commissioners—Lincoln and
the Peace Commissioners—An Anecdote of
Mr. Lincoln—The Winter before Petersburg—
Sheridan Destroys the Railroad—Gordon Carries
the Picket Line—Parke Recaptures the Line—
The Battle of White Oak Road

O<small>N THE LAST</small> of January, 1865, peace commissioners from the so-called
Confederate States presented themselves on our lines around Petersburg, and
were immediately conducted to my headquarters at City Point. They proved to
be Alexander H. Stephens, Vice-President of the Confederacy,[1] Judge Campbell,
Assistant-Secretary of War,[2] and R. M. T. Hunter, formerly United States
Senator and then a member of the Confederate Senate.[3]

[1] Alexander H. Stephens (1812–1883) was born in Georgia and served in the U.S. House of
Representatives from 1843 to 1859 and from 1873 to 1882. He was vice president of the Confederate States of America from 1861 to 1865. He was governor of Georgia from 1882 to 1883 and
authored numerous books. *CWHC,* 508–509.

[2] John A. Campbell (1811–1889) was born in Georgia and, after practicing law and serving in
the state legislature in Alabama, was appointed to the U.S. Supreme Court in 1853. In Apr. 1861,
he resigned from the Supreme Court and soon accepted the position of assistant secretary of war
for the Confederate government. Spencer Tucker, ed., *American Civil War: The Definitive Encyclopedia and Document Collection* (Santa Barbara, CA: ABC-CLIO, 2013), s.v. "Campbell, John
Archibald."

[3] R. M. T. Hunter (1809–1887) was born in Virginia and served in the U.S. House of Representatives from 1837 to 1843 and from 1845 to 1847 and in the U.S. Senate from 1847 to 1861.
He was the Confederate secretary of state from July 1861 to Feb. 1862 and president pro tem-
pore of the Confederate Senate from Feb. 1862 to Mar. 1865. *CWHC,* 311.

It was about dark when they reached my headquarters, and I at once conducted them to the steamer *Mary Martin,* a Hudson River boat which was very comfortably fitted up for the use of passengers. I at once communicated by telegraph with Washington and informed the Secretary of War and the President of the arrival of these commissioners and that their object was to negotiate terms of peace between the United States and, as they termed it, the Confederate Government. I was instructed to retain them at City Point, until the President, or some one whom he would designate, should come to meet them. They remained several days as guests on board the boat. I saw them quite frequently, though I have no recollection of having had any conversation whatever with them on the subject of their mission.[4] It was something I had nothing to do with, and I therefore did not wish to express any views on the subject. For my own part I never had admitted, and never was ready to admit, that they were the representatives of a *government.* There had been too great a waste of blood and treasure to concede anything of the kind. As long as they remained there, however, our relations were pleasant and I found them all very agreeable gentlemen. I directed the captain to furnish them with the best the boat afforded, and to administer to their comfort in every way possible. No guard was placed over them and no restriction was put upon their movements; nor was there any pledge asked that they would not abuse the privileges extended to them. They were permitted to leave the boat when they felt like it, and did so, coming up on the bank and visiting me at my headquarters.

I had never met either of these gentlemen before the war, but knew them well by reputation and through their public services, and I had been a particular admirer of Mr. Stephens. I had always supposed that he was a very small man, but when I saw him in the dusk of the evening I was very much surprised to find so large a man as he seemed to be. When he got down on to the boat I found that he was wearing a coarse gray woollen overcoat, a manufacture that had been introduced into the South during the rebellion. The cloth was thicker than anything of the kind I had ever seen, even in Canada. The overcoat extended nearly to his feet, and was so large that it gave him the appearance of being an average-sized man. He took this off when he reached the cabin of the boat, and I was struck with the apparent change in size, in the coat and out of it.[5]

[4] On Feb. 1, 1865, USG wrote Stanton that he was "convinced upon conversations with Messrs Stevens & Hunter that their intentions are good and their desire sincere to restore peace and Union." *PUSG,* 13:345–346.

[5] Stephens was five feet, seven inches tall and his weight usually stayed between seventy and eighty pounds. Thomas E. Schott, *Alexander Stephens of Georgia: A Biography* (Baton Rouge: Louisiana State University Press, 1988), 20–21.

After a few days, about the 2d of February, I received a dispatch from Washington, directing me to send the commissioners to Hampton Roads to meet the President and a member of the cabinet.[6] Mr. Lincoln met them there and had an interview of short duration. It was not a great while after they met that the President visited me at City Point.[7] He spoke of his having met the commissioners, and said he had told them that there would be no use in entering into any negotiations unless they would recognize, first: that the Union as a whole must be forever preserved, and second: that slavery must be abolished. If they were willing to concede these two points, then he was ready to enter into negotiations and was almost willing to hand them a blank sheet of paper with his signature attached for them to fill in the terms upon which they were willing to live with us in the Union and be one people. He always showed a generous and kindly spirit toward the Southern people, and I never heard him abuse an enemy. Some of the cruel things said about President Lincoln, particularly in the North, used to pierce him to the heart; but never in my presence did he evince a revengeful disposition—and I saw a great deal of him at City Point, for he seemed glad to get away from the cares and anxieties of the capital.

Right here I might relate an anecdote of Mr. Lincoln. It was on the occasion of his visit to me just after he had talked with the peace commissioners at Hampton Roads. After a little conversation, he asked me if I had seen that overcoat of Stephens's. I replied that I had. "Well," said he, "did you see him take it off?" I said yes. "Well," said he, "didn't you think it was the biggest shuck and the littlest ear that ever you did see?" Long afterwards I told this story to the Confederate General J. B. Gordon, at the time a member of the Senate. He repeated it to Stephens, and, as I heard afterwards, Stephens laughed immoderately at the simile of Mr. Lincoln.

The rest of the winter, after the departure of the peace commissioners,[8] passed off quietly and uneventfully, except for two or three little incidents. On one occasion during this period, while I was visiting Washington City for the purpose of conferring with the administration, the enemy's cavalry under

---

[6] Secretary of State William H. Seward was the cabinet member who attended the meeting. David Herbert Donald, *Lincoln* (New York: Simon and Schuster, 1995), 557. For Lincoln's Feb. 2, 1865, telegram to USG, see *PUSG,* 13:346n.

[7] Lincoln left the area on Feb. 3, 1865, soon after his meeting with the Confederate officials. He and Seward arrived in Washington, DC, by Feb. 4. David Herbert Donald and Harold Holzer, ed., *Lincoln in the Times: The Life of Abraham Lincoln as Originally Reported in The New York Times* (New York: St. Martin's, 2005), 218–219.

[8] The peace commissioners left the area on Feb. 3, 1865. Schott, *Alexander Stephens,* 447.

General Wade Hampton, passing our extreme left and then going to the south, got in east of us. Before their presence was known, they had driven off a large number of beef cattle that were grazing in that section. It was a fair capture, and they were sufficiently needed by the Confederates.[9] It was only retaliating for what we had done, sometimes for many weeks at a time, when out of supplies—taking what the Confederate army otherwise would have gotten. As appears in this book, on one single occasion we captured five thousand head of cattle which were crossing the Mississippi River near Port Hudson on their way from Texas to supply the Confederate army in the East.[10]

One of the most anxious periods of my experience during the rebellion was the last few weeks before Petersburg. I felt that the situation of the Confederate army was such that they would try to make an escape at the earliest practicable moment, and I was afraid, every morning, that I would awake from my sleep to hear that Lee had gone, and that nothing was left but a picket line. He had his railroad by the way of Danville south, and I was afraid that he was running off his men and all stores and ordnance except such as it would be necessary to carry with him for his immediate defence. I knew he could move much more lightly and more rapidly than I, and that, if he got the start, he would leave me behind so that we would have the same army to fight again farther south—and the war might be prolonged another year.

I was led to this fear by the fact that I could not see how it was possible for the Confederates to hold out much longer where they were. There is no doubt that Richmond would have been evacuated much sooner than it was, if it had not been that it was the capital of the so-called Confederacy, and the fact of evacuating the capital would, of course, have had a very demoralizing effect upon the Confederate army. When it was evacuated (as we shall see further on), the Confederacy at once began to crumble and fade away. Then, too, desertions were taking place, not only among those who were with General Lee in the neighborhood of their capital, but throughout the whole Confederacy. I remember that in a conversation with me on one occasion long prior to this, General Butler remarked that the Confederates would find great difficulty in getting more men for their army; possibly adding, though I am not certain as to this, "unless they should arm the slave."

The South, as we all knew, were conscripting every able-bodied man between the ages of eighteen and forty-five; and now they had passed a law for

[9]This so-called Beefsteak Raid took place in Sept. 1864 during the siege of Petersburg, VA. The U.S. Army lost 2,000 cattle. Robert Ackerman, *Wade Hampton* (Columbia: University of South Carolina Press, 2007), 67.

[10]USG described this incident in Chapter 39.

the further conscription of boys from fourteen to eighteen, calling them the junior reserves, and men from forty-five to sixty to be called the senior reserves.[11] The latter were to hold the necessary points not in immediate danger, and especially those in the rear. General Butler, in alluding to this conscription, remarked that they were thus "robbing both the cradle and the grave," an expression which I afterwards used in writing a letter to Mr. Washburn.[12]

It was my belief that while the enemy could get no more recruits they were losing at least a regiment a day, taking it throughout the entire army, by desertions alone. Then by casualties of war, sickness, and other natural causes, their losses were much heavier. It was a mere question of arithmetic to calculate how long they could hold out while that rate of depletion was going on. Of course long before their army would be thus reduced to nothing the army which we had in the field would have been able to capture theirs. Then too I knew from the great number of desertions, that the men who had fought so bravely, so gallantly and so long for the cause which they believed in—and as earnestly, I take it, as our men believed in the cause for which they were fighting—had lost hope and become despondent. Many of them were making application to be sent North where they might get employment until the war was over, when they could return to their Southern homes.

For these and other reasons I was naturally very impatient for the time to come when I could commence the spring campaign, which I thoroughly believed would close the war.

There were two considerations I had to observe, however, and which detained me. One was the fact that the winter had been one of heavy rains, and the roads were impassable for artillery and teams. It was necessary to wait until they had dried sufficiently to enable us to move the wagon trains and artillery necessary to the efficiency of an army operating in the enemy's country. The other consideration was that General Sheridan with the cavalry of the Army of the Potomac was operating on the north side of the James River, having

---

[11] In Apr. 1862, the Confederate government had passed the war's first draft with the First Conscription Act. That act required service from men eighteen to thirty-five. The Second Conscription Act, passed in Sept., raised the age of service to forty-five but was not implemented until July 1863. In Feb. 1864, conscription was expanded to include men from seventeen to fifty. Seventeen-year-olds formed junior reserve units, while men forty-five to fifty were incorporated into senior reserve units. David Carlson, "Conscription C.S.A.," in *Encyclopedia of the American Civil War,* ed. David S. Heidler and Jeanne T. Heidler (Santa Barbara, CA: ABC-CLIO, 2000), 486–487; Walter C. Hilderman III, *Theophilus Hunter Holmes: A North Carolina General in the Civil War* (Jefferson, NC: McFarland, 2014), 150.

[12] See USG to Elihu Washburne, Aug. 16, 1864, *PUSG,* 12:16.

come down from the Shenandoah. It was necessary that I should have his cavalry with me, and I was therefore obliged to wait until he could join me south of the James River.

Let us now take account of what he was doing.

On the 5th of March I had heard from Sheridan. He had met Early between Staunton and Charlottesville and defeated him, capturing nearly his entire command. Early and some of his officers escaped by finding refuge in the neighboring houses or in the woods.[13]

On the 12th I heard from him again.[14] He had turned east, to come to White House. He could not go to Lynchburg as ordered, because the rains had been so very heavy and the streams were so very much swollen. He had a pontoon train with him, but it would not reach half way across some of the streams, at their then stage of water, which he would have to get over in going south as first ordered.

I had supplies sent around to White House for him, and kept the depot there open until he arrived. We had intended to abandon it because the James River had now become our base of supplies.[15]

Sheridan had about ten thousand cavalry with him, divided into two divisions commanded respectively by Custer and Devin.[16] General Merritt was acting as chief of cavalry. Sheridan moved very light, carrying only four days' provisions with him, with a larger supply of coffee, salt and other small rations, and a very little else besides ammunition. They stopped at Charlottesville and commenced tearing up the railroad back toward Lynchburg. He also sent a division along the James River Canal to destroy locks, culverts, etc. All mills and factories along the lines of march of his troops were destroyed also.

Sheridan had in this way consumed so much time that his making a march to White House was now somewhat hazardous. He determined therefore to

[13] On Mar. 2, 1865, with two cavalry divisions totaling approximately 10,000 troops, Sheridan defeated Early's force of about 1,700 troops at the Battle of Waynesboro, VA. USG first heard reports of the victory on Mar. 5 from Confederate deserters. Sheridan's Mar. 2 report of the battle was not received by Halleck until Mar. 8. Tucker, *American Civil War,* s.v. "Waynesboro, Virginia, Battle of"; *OR,* I, 46(II), 792; *PUSG,* 14:102.

[14] For Sheridan's Mar. 10, 1865, letter to USG, see *PUSG,* 14:142*n*–143*n*.

[15] For USG's Mar. 12, 1865, instructions to Babcock regarding supplies for Sheridan, see ibid., 14:145.

[16] Thomas C. Devin (1822–1878) was born in New York and became a captain in the 1st New York Cav. in July 1861. He rose to brigadier general by 1864 and commanded the 1st Div., Cav. Corps, Army of the Shenandoah, in Mar. 1865. *CWHC,* 208.

fight his way along the railroad and canal till he was as near to Richmond as it was possible to get, or until attacked. He did this, destroying the canal as far as Goochland, and the railroad to a point as near Richmond as he could get. On the 10th he was at Columbia. Negroes had joined his column to the number of two thousand or more, and they assisted considerably in the work of destroying the railroads and the canal. His cavalry was in as fine a condition as when he started, because he had been able to find plenty of forage. He had captured most of Early's horses and picked up a good many others on the road. When he reached Ashland he was assailed by the enemy in force. He resisted their assault with part of his command, moved quickly across the South and North Anna, going north, and reached White House safely on the 19th.

The time for Sherman to move had to be fixed with reference to the time he could get away from Goldsboro where he then was. Supplies had to be got up to him which would last him through a long march, as there would probably not be much to be obtained in the country through which he would pass. I had to arrange, therefore, that he should start from where he was, in the neighborhood of Goldsboro, on the 18th of April, the earliest day at which he supposed he could be ready.

Sherman was anxious that I should wait where I was until he could come up, and make a sure thing of it; but I had determined to move as soon as the roads and weather would admit of my doing so. I had been tied down somewhat in the matter of fixing any time at my pleasure for starting, until Sheridan, who was on his way from the Shenandoah Valley to join me, should arrive, as both his presence and that of his cavalry were necessary to the execution of the plans which I had in mind. However, having arrived at White House on the 19th of March, I was enabled to make my plans.

Prompted by my anxiety lest Lee should get away some night before I was aware of it, and having the lead of me, push into North Carolina to join with Johnston in attempting to crush out Sherman, I had, as early as the 1st of the month of March, given instructions to the troops around Petersburg to keep a sharp lookout to see that such a movement should not escape their notice, and to be ready to strike at once if it was undertaken.[17]

It is now known that early in the month of March Mr. Davis and General Lee had a consultation about the situation of affairs in and about Richmond and Petersburg, and they both agreed that these places were no longer tenable

[17] On Mar. 1, 1865, after receiving a report about the possibility of Lee moving a part of his army away from Petersburg, USG ordered Meade to be prepared to make an assault. *PUSG*, 14:77–78, 78n–79n.

for them, and that they must get away as soon as possible.[18] They, too, were waiting for dry roads, or a condition of the roads which would make it possible to move.

General Lee, in aid of his plan of escape, and to secure a wider opening to enable them to reach the Danville Road with greater security than he would have in the way the two armies were situated, determined upon an assault upon the right of our lines around Petersburg. The night of the 24th of March was fixed upon for this assault, and General Gordon was assigned to the execution of the plan. The point between Fort Stedman and Battery No. 10, where our lines were closest together, was selected as the point of his attack.[19] The attack was to be made at night, and the troops were to get possession of the higher ground in the rear where they supposed we had intrenchments, then sweep to the right and left, create a panic in the lines of our army, and force me to contract my lines. Lee hoped this would detain me a few days longer and give him an opportunity of escape. The plan was well conceived and the execution of it very well done indeed, up to the point of carrying a portion of our line.

Gordon assembled his troops under the cover of night, at the point at which they were to make their charge, and got possession of our picket-line, entirely without the knowledge of the troops inside of our main line of intrenchments; this reduced the distance he would have to charge over to not much more than fifty yards. For some time before the deserters had been coming in with great frequency, often bringing their arms with them, and this the Confederate general knew. Taking advantage of this knowledge he sent his pickets, with their arms, creeping through to ours as if to desert. When they got to our lines they at once took possession and sent our pickets to the rear as prisoners. In the main line our men were sleeping serenely, as if in great security. This plan was to have been executed and much damage done before daylight; but the troops that were to reinforce Gordon had to be brought from the north side of the

---

[18] Lee met with Davis in Richmond, VA, during the first week of Mar. 1865, probably on Mar. 4, and then again on Mar. 18. Jefferson Davis, *The Papers of Jefferson Davis,* vol. 11, ed. Lynda Laswell Crist, Barbara J. Rozek, and Kenneth H. Williams (Baton Rouge: Louisiana State University Press, 2003), xlv; Emory M. Thomas, *Robert E. Lee: A Biography* (New York: W. W. Norton, 1995), 348.

[19] Only 200 yards separated U.S. and Confederate lines in the area around Fort Stedman. A. Wilson Greene, *The Final Battles of the Petersburg Campaign* (Knoxville: University of Tennessee Press, 2008), 157.

James River and, by some accident on the railroad on their way over, they were detained for a considerable time; so that it got to be nearly daylight before they were ready to make the charge.[20]

The charge, however, was successful and almost without loss, the enemy passing through our lines between Fort Stedman and Battery No. 10. Then turning to the right and left they captured the fort and the battery, with all the arms and troops in them. Continuing the charge, they also carried batteries Eleven and Twelve to our left, which they turned toward City Point.

Meade happened to be at City Point that night, and this break in his line cut him off from all communication with his headquarters. Parke, however, commanding the 9th corps when this breach took place, telegraphed the facts to Meade's headquarters, and learning that the general was away, assumed command himself and with commendable promptitude made all preparations to drive the enemy back. General Tidball[21] gathered a large number of pieces of artillery and planted them in rear of the captured works so as to sweep the narrow space of ground between the lines very thoroughly. Hartranft[22] was soon out with his division, as also was Willcox. Hartranft to the right of the breach headed the rebels off in that direction and rapidly drove them back into Fort Stedman. On the other side they were driven back into the intrenchments which they had captured, and batteries eleven and twelve were retaken by Willcox early in the morning.

Parke then threw a line around outside of the captured fort and batteries, and communication was once more established. The artillery fire was kept up so continuously that it was impossible for the Confederates to retreat, and equally impossible for reinforcements to join them. They all, therefore, fell captives into

[20] Pickett's division of the 1st Confederate Corps was under Lee's orders to move from its position north of the James River to aid Gordon's advance, but was unable to arrive in time because of transportation problems. Ibid.; John Horn, *The Petersburg Campaign: June 1864– April 1865* (Conshohocken, PA: Combined Books, 1993), 216.

[21] John C. Tidball (1825–1906) was born in Virginia and graduated from the USMA in 1848. He had reached captain by May 1861. After the Civil War, he served as aide-de-camp to Sherman from 1881 to 1884 and retired as a colonel in 1889. *CWHC,* 530–531.

[22] John F. Hartranft (1830–1889) was born in Pennsylvania and was a lieutenant colonel in the Pennsylvania Militia at the start of the Civil War. He was promoted to colonel in the 4th Pennsylvania Inf. in 1861. He served as governor of Pennsylvania from 1873 to 1879 and as the commander in chief of the Grand Army of the Republic from 1875 to 1876. In 1886, he was awarded the Medal of Honor for his actions at the Battle of First Bull Run. Ibid., 284.

our hands. This effort of Lee's cost him about four thousand men, and resulted in their killing, wounding and capturing about two thousand of ours.[23]

After the recapture of the batteries taken by the Confederates, our troops made a charge and carried the enemy's intrenched picket line, which they strengthened and held. This, in turn, gave us but a short distance to charge over when our attack came to be made a few days later.

The day that Gordon was making dispositions for this attack (24th of March) I issued my orders for the movement to commence on the 29th. Ord, with three divisions of infantry and Mackenzie's[24] cavalry, was to move in advance on the night of the 27th, from the north side of the James River and take his place on our extreme left, thirty miles away. He left Weitzel with the rest of the Army of the James to hold Bermuda Hundred and the north of the James River. The engineer brigade was to be left at City Point, and Parke's corps in the lines about Petersburg.*

Ord was at his place promptly. Humphreys and Warren were then on our extreme left with the 2d and 5th corps. They were directed on the arrival of Ord, and on his getting into position in their places, to cross Hatcher's Run and extend out west toward Five Forks, the object being to get into a position from which we could strike the South Side Railroad and ultimately the Danville Railroad. There was considerable fighting in taking up these new positions for the 2d and 5th corps, in which the Army of the James had also to participate somewhat, and the losses were quite severe.

This was what was known as the Battle of White Oak Road.[25]

*See orders to Major-Generals Meade, Ord, and Sheridan, March 24th, Appendix.[26]

---

[23] U.S. casualties were just over 1,000, while Confederate losses were approximately 4,000. Edward Bonekemper III, *A Victor Not a Butcher: Ulysses S. Grant's Overlooked Military Genius* (Washington, DC: Regnery, 2004), 319.

[24] Ranald S. Mackenzie (1840–1889) was born in New York and graduated first in his class at the USMA in 1862. He rose to brigadier general by 1864. Mackenzie commanded Cav. D, 18th Corps, Army of the James, in Mar. 1865. *CWHC*, 359.

[25] The Battle of White Oak Road took place on Mar. 31, 1865. Mark M. Boatner III, *The Civil War Dictionary* (New York: David McKay, 1988), 914.

[26] For USG's Mar. 24, 1865, orders to Meade, see *PUSG*, 14:211–214. Copies were sent to Ord and Sheridan. Ibid. 14:214*n*.

# 64

Interview with Sheridan—Grand Movement of the Army of the Potomac—Sheridan's Advance on Five Forks—Battle of Five Forks—Parke and Wright Storm the Enemy's Line—Battles before Petersburg

Sheridan reached City Point on the 26th day of March. His horses, of course, were jaded and many of them had lost their shoes. A few days of rest were necessary to recuperate the animals and also to have them shod and put in condition for moving. Immediately on General Sheridan's arrival at City Point I prepared his instructions for the move which I had decided upon. The movement was to commence on the 29th of the month.

After reading the instructions I had given him, Sheridan walked out of my tent, and I followed to have some conversation with him by himself—not in the presence of anybody else, even of a member of my staff. In preparing his instructions I contemplated just what took place; that is to say, capturing Five Forks, driving the enemy from Petersburg and Richmond and terminating the contest before separating from the enemy. But the Nation had already become restless and discouraged at the prolongation of the war, and many believed that it would never terminate except by compromise. Knowing that unless my plan proved an entire success it would be interpreted as a disastrous defeat, I provided in these instructions that in a certain event he was to cut loose from the Army of the Potomac and his base of supplies, and living upon the country proceed south by the way of the Danville Railroad,[1] or near it, across the Roanoke, get in the rear of Johnston, who was guarding that road, and co-operate with Sherman in destroying Johnston; then with these combined forces to help

---

[1] The Richmond and Danville Railroad. Robert C. Black III, *The Railroads of the Confederacy* (Chapel Hill: University of North Carolina Press, 1952), 283.

carry out the instructions which Sherman already had received, to act in co-operation with the armies around Petersburg and Richmond.

I saw that after Sheridan had read his instructions he seemed somewhat disappointed at the idea, possibly, of having to cut loose again from the Army of the Potomac, and place himself between the two main armies of the enemy. I said to him: "General, this portion of your instructions I have put in merely as a blind;" and gave him the reason for doing so, heretofore described. I told him that, as a matter of fact, I intended to close the war right here, with this movement, and that he should go no farther. His face at once brightened up, and slapping his hand on his leg he said: "I am glad to hear it, and we can do it."[2]

Sheridan was not however to make his movement against Five Forks until he got further instructions from me.

One day, after the movement I am about to describe had commenced, and when his cavalry was on our extreme left and far to the rear, south, Sheridan rode up to where my headquarters were then established, at Dabney's Mills.[3] He met some of my staff officers outside, and was highly jubilant over the prospects of success, giving reasons why he believed this would prove the final and successful effort. Although my chief-of-staff[4] had urged very strongly that we return to our position about City Point and in the lines around Petersburg, he asked Sheridan to come in to see me and say to me what he had been saying to them. Sheridan felt a little modest about giving his advice where it had not been asked; so one of my staff came in and told me that Sheridan had what they considered important news, and suggested that I send for him. I did so, and was glad to see the spirit of confidence with which he was imbued. Knowing as I did from experience, of what great value that feeling of confidence by a commander was, I determined to make a movement at once, although on account of the rains which had fallen after I had started out the roads were still very heavy. Orders were given accordingly.

Finally the 29th of March came, and fortunately there having been a few days free from rain, the surface of the ground was dry, giving indications that the time had come when we could move. On that date I moved out with all the army available after leaving sufficient force to hold the line about Petersburg. It soon set in raining again however, and in a very short time the roads

[2] For USG's Mar. 28, 1865, orders to Sheridan, see *PUSG*, 14:243–244, 244*n*.

[3] On Mar. 31, 1865, USG relocated his headquarters to Dabney's Mill, approximately eight miles southwest of Petersburg, VA. George B. Davis et al., *The Official Military Atlas of the Civil War* (New York: Fairfax Press, 1983), plate 77, map 2; *PUSG*, 14:xxiv.

[4] John A. Rawlins. *CWHC*, 447.

became practically impassable for teams, and almost so for cavalry. Sometimes a horse or mule would be standing apparently on firm ground, when all at once one foot would sink, and as he commenced scrambling to catch himself all his feet would sink and he would have to be drawn by hand out of the quicksands so common in that part of Virginia and other southern States. It became necessary therefore to build corduroy roads every foot of the way as we advanced, to move our artillery upon. The army had become so accustomed to this kind of work, and were so well prepared for it, that it was done very rapidly. The next day, March 30th, we had made sufficient progress to the south-west to warrant me in starting Sheridan with his cavalry over by Dinwiddie with instructions to then come up by the road leading north-west to Five Forks, thus menacing the right of Lee's line.

This movement was made for the purpose of extending our lines to the west as far as practicable towards the enemy's extreme right, or Five Forks. The column moving detached from the army still in the trenches was, excluding the cavalry, very small. The forces in the trenches were themselves extending to the left flank. Warren was on the extreme left when the extension began, but Humphreys was marched around later and thrown into line between him and Five Forks.

My hope was that Sheridan would be able to carry Five Forks, get on the enemy's right flank and rear, and force them to weaken their centre to protect their right so that an assault in the centre might be successfully made. General Wright's corps had been designated to make this assault, which I intended to order as soon as information reached me of Sheridan's success. He was to move under cover as close to the enemy as he could get.

It is natural to suppose that Lee would understand my design to be to get up to the South Side and ultimately to the Danville Railroad, as soon as he had heard of the movement commenced on the 29th. These roads were so important to his very existence while he remained in Richmond and Petersburg, and of such vital importance to him even in case of retreat, that naturally he would make most strenuous efforts to defend them. He did on the 30th send Pickett with five brigades to reinforce Five Forks.[5] He also sent around to the right of his army some two or three other divisions, besides directing that other troops

[5] On the night of Mar. 30, 1865, Pickett arrived at Five Forks, VA, with five brigades under the command of Brig. Gens. Montgomery Corse, William R. Terry, George H. Steuart, Matt Ransom, and William Henry Wallace. Andrew A. Humphreys, *The Virginia Campaign of 1864 and 1865: The Army of the Potomac and the Army of the James* (New York: Charles Scribner's Sons, 1883), 328.

be held in readiness on the north side of the James River to come over on call. He came over himself to superintend in person the defence of his right flank.

Sheridan moved back to Dinwiddie Court-House on the night of the 30th, and then took a road leading north-west to Five Forks. He had only his cavalry with him. Soon encountering the rebel cavalry he met with a very stout resistance. He gradually drove them back however until in the neighborhood of Five Forks. Here he had to encounter other troops besides those he had been contending with, and was forced to give way.[6]

In this condition of affairs he notified me of what had taken place and stated that he was falling back toward Dinwiddie gradually and slowly, and asked me to send Wright's corps to his assistance. I replied to him that it was impossible to send Wright's corps because that corps was already in line close up to the enemy, where we should want to assault when the proper time came, and was besides a long distance from him; but the 2d (Humphreys's) and 5th (Warren's) corps were on our extreme left and a little to the rear of it in a position to threaten the left flank of the enemy at Five Forks, and that I would send Warren.[7]

Accordingly orders were sent to Warren to move at once that night (the 31st) to Dinwiddie Court House and put himself in communication with Sheridan as soon as possible, and report to him. He was very slow in moving, some of his troops not starting until after 5 o'clock next morning. When he did move it was done very deliberately, and on arriving at Gravelly Run he found the stream swollen from the recent rains so that he regarded it as not fordable. Sheridan of course knew of his coming, and being impatient to get the troops up as soon as possible, sent orders to him to hasten. He was also hastened or at least ordered to move up rapidly by General Meade. He now felt that he could not cross that creek without bridges, and his orders were changed to move so as to strike the pursuing enemy in flank or get in their rear; but he was so late in getting up that Sheridan determined to move forward without him. However, Ayres's division of Warren's corps reached him in time to be in the fight all day, most of the time separated from the remainder of the 5th corps and fighting directly under Sheridan.

[6] On Mar. 30, 1865, Sheridan sent Merritt and one division of cavalry to capture Five Forks. They were repulsed the next day by Pickett's division and cavalry forces commanded by Rosser and William Henry Fitzhugh "Rooney" Lee. Ed Bearss and Chris Calkins, *The Battle of Five Forks* (Lynchburg, VA: H. E. Howard, 1985), 36–37; *PUSG,* 14:268*n.*

[7] For the Mar. 31, 1865, exchange between USG and Sheridan, see *PUSG,* 14:287–288, 288*n.*

Warren reported to Sheridan about 11 o'clock on the 1st, but the whole of his troops were not up so as to be much engaged until late in the afternoon. Griffin's division in backing to get out of the way of a severe cross fire of the enemy was found marching away from the fighting. This did not continue long, however; the division was brought back and with Ayres's division did most excellent service during the day. Crawford's division of the same corps had backed still farther off, and although orders were sent repeatedly to bring it up, it was late before it finally got to where it could be of material assistance. Once there it did very excellent service.

Sheridan succeeded by the middle of the afternoon or a little later, in advancing up to the point from which to make his designed assault upon Five Forks itself.[8] He was very impatient to make the assault and have it all over before night, because the ground he occupied would be untenable for him in bivouac during the night. Unless the assault was made and was successful, he would be obliged to return to Dinwiddie Court-House, or even further than that for the night.

It was at this junction of affairs that Sheridan wanted to get Crawford's division in hand, and he also wanted Warren. He sent staff officer after staff officer in search of Warren, directing that general to report to him, but they were unable to find him. At all events Sheridan was unable to get that officer to him. Finally he went himself. He issued an order relieving Warren and assigning Griffin to the command of the 5th corps. The troops were then brought up and the assault successfully made.[9]

I was so much dissatisfied with Warren's dilatory movements in the battle of White Oak Road and in his failure to reach Sheridan in time, that I was very much afraid that at the last moment he would fail Sheridan. He was a man of fine intelligence, great earnestness, quick perception, and could make his dispositions as quickly as any officer, under difficulties where he was forced to act. But I had before discovered a defect which was beyond his control, that was very prejudicial to his usefulness in emergencies like the one just before us. He could see every danger at a glance before he had encountered it. He would not only make preparations to meet the danger which might occur, but he would inform his commanding officer what others should do while he was executing his move.

[8] At 2:00 P.M. on Apr. 1, 1865, Sheridan's forces reached the White Oak Road and prepared to make an assault on Five Forks. *OR*, I, 46(I), 1104.

[9] At the end of fighting on Apr. 1, 1865, Sheridan replaced Warren with Griffin. David Coffey, *Sheridan's Lieutenants: Phil Sheridan, His Generals, and the Final Year of the Civil War* (Lanham, MD: Rowman and Littlefield, 2005), 117.

I had sent a staff officer[10] to General Sheridan to call his attention to these defects, and to say that as much as I liked General Warren, now was not a time when we could let our personal feelings for any one stand in the way of success; and if his removal was necessary to success, not to hesitate. It was upon that authorization that Sheridan removed Warren. I was very sorry that it had been done, and regretted still more that I had not long before taken occasion to assign him to another field of duty.[11]

It was dusk when our troops under Sheridan went over the parapets of the enemy. The two armies were mingled together there for a time in such manner that it was almost a question which one was going to demand the surrender of the other. Soon, however, the enemy broke and ran in every direction; some six thousand prisoners, besides artillery and small-arms in large quantities, falling into our hands.[12] The flying troops were pursued in different directions, the cavalry and 5th corps under Sheridan pursuing the larger body which moved north-west.

This pursuit continued until about nine o'clock at night, when Sheridan halted his troops, and knowing the importance to him of the part of the enemy's line which had been captured, returned, sending the 5th corps across Hatcher's Run[13] to just south-west of Petersburg, and facing them toward it. Merritt, with the cavalry, stopped and bivouacked west of Five Forks.

This was the condition which affairs were in on the night of the 1st of April. I then issued orders for an assault by Wright and Parke at four o'clock on the morning of the 2d. I also ordered the 2d corps, General Humphreys, and

[10] USG sent Babcock to Sheridan with this message on Apr. 1, 1865. P. H. Sheridan, *Personal Memoirs of P. H. Sheridan, General, United States Army* (New York: Charles L. Webster, 1888), 2:160.

[11] Warren was reassigned to the defenses of Petersburg, City Point, VA, and Bermuda Hundred, VA (along with other areas in the rear of the fighting). He requested an investigation into his actions, but these requests were initially refused by USG. In 1879, his request was approved and a court of inquiry found that his movements at Five Forks showed no "unnecessary delay" and that he had taken "the usual methods of a corps commander to prevent delay." These findings were not made public until after Warren's death in 1882. David M. Jordan, *"Happiness Is Not My Companion": The Life of General G. K. Warren* (Bloomington: Indiana University Press, 2001), 237, 239–240, 262, 310–312; *PUSG*, 15:21, 21n–22n.

[12] Sheridan stated in his May 16, 1865, report that between 5,000 and 6,000 Confederates were captured. *OR*, I, 46(I), 1105.

[13] Hatcher's Run is a creek southwest of Petersburg and north of the Five Forks area. *PUSG*, 14:304–305 (map).

General Ord with the Army of the James, on the left, to hold themselves in readiness to take any advantage that could be taken from weakening in their front.

I notified Mr. Lincoln at City Point of the success of the day; in fact I had reported to him during the day and evening as I got news, because he was so much interested in the movements taking place that I wanted to relieve his mind as much as I could.[14] I notified Weitzel on the north side of the James River, directing him, also, to keep close up to the enemy, and take advantage of the withdrawal of troops from there to promptly enter the city of Richmond.[15]

I was afraid that Lee would regard the possession of Five Forks as of so much importance that he would make a last desperate effort to retake it, risking everything upon the cast of a single die. It was for this reason that I had ordered the assault to take place at once, as soon as I had received the news of the capture of Five Forks. The corps commanders, however, reported that it was so dark that the men could not see to move, and it would be impossible to make the assault then. But we kept up a continuous artillery fire upon the enemy around the whole line including that north of the James River, until it was light enough to move, which was about a quarter to five in the morning.

At that hour Parke's and Wright's corps moved out as directed, brushed the *abatis* from their front as they advanced under a heavy fire of musketry and artillery, and went without flinching directly on till they mounted the parapets and threw themselves inside of the enemy's line. Parke, who was on the right, swept down to the right and captured a very considerable length of line in that direction, but at that point the outer was so near the inner line which closely enveloped the city of Petersburg that he could make no advance forward and, in fact, had a very serious task to turn the lines which he had captured to the defence of his own troops and to hold them; but he succeeded in this.

Wright swung around to his left and moved to Hatcher's Run, sweeping everything before him. The enemy had traverses in rear of his captured line, under cover of which he made something of a stand, from one to another, as Wright moved on; but the latter met no serious obstacle. As you proceed to the left the outer line becomes gradually much farther from the inner one, and along about Hatcher's Run they must be nearly two miles apart. Both Parke and Wright captured a considerable amount of artillery and some prisoners—Wright about three thousand of them.

---

[14] On Apr. 1, 1865, USG sent at least three separate updates to Lincoln. Ibid., 14:293–296.

[15] For USG's Apr. 1, 1865, orders to Weitzel, see ibid., 14:309.

In the meantime Ord and Humphreys, in obedience to the instructions they had received, had succeeded by daylight, or very early in the morning, in capturing the intrenched picket-lines in their front; and before Wright got up to that point, Ord had also succeeded in getting inside of the enemy's intrenchments. The second corps soon followed; and the outer works of Petersburg were in the hands of the National troops, never to be wrenched from them again. When Wright reached Hatcher's Run, he sent a regiment to destroy the South Side Railroad just outside of the city.

My headquarters were still at Dabney's saw-mills. As soon as I received the news of Wright's success, I sent dispatches announcing the fact to all points around the line, including the troops at Bermuda Hundred and those on the north side of the James, and to the President at City Point.[16] Further dispatches kept coming in, and as they did I sent the additional news to these points. Finding at length that they were all in, I mounted my horse to join the troops who were inside the works. When I arrived there I rode my horse over the parapet just as Wright's three thousand prisoners were coming out.[17] I was soon joined inside by General Meade and his staff.

Lee made frantic efforts to recover at least part of the lost ground. Parke on our right was repeatedly assaulted, but repulsed every effort. Before noon Longstreet was ordered up from the north side of the James River, thus bringing the bulk of Lee's army around to the support of his extreme right. As soon as I learned this I notified Weitzel and directed him to keep up close to the enemy and to have Hartsuff,[18] commanding the Bermuda Hundred front, to do the same thing, and if they found any break to go in; Hartsuff especially should do so, for this would separate Richmond and Petersburg.[19]

Sheridan, after he had returned to Five Forks, swept down to Petersburg, coming in on our left. This gave us a continuous line from the Appomattox

[16] In an Apr. 2, 1865, message to Stanton, Lincoln summarized USG's telegram from the same day regarding Wright's success. That morning, USG had informed Weitzel, then in command on the north side of the James River, of the news. The editors were unable to find an Apr. 2 direct communication that contained the news from USG to George L. Hartsuff or anyone else at Bermuda Hundred. *OR*, I, 46(III), 447; *PUSG*, 14:322.

[17] In an Apr. 2, 1865, telegram to Bowers, USG reported that Wright's 6th Corps had captured more than 3,000 prisoners. *PUSG*, 14:326.

[18] George L. Hartsuff (1830–1874) was born in New York and graduated from the USMA in 1852. He fought in the Seminole War and suffered a wound that troubled him for the rest of his life. He was brevetted major general on Mar. 13, 1865, and oversaw the defense of Bermuda Hundred from Mar. 19 to Apr. 16. *CWHC*, 284–285.

[19] See USG's Apr. 2, 1865, telegram to Weitzel, *PUSG*, 14:324.

River below the city to the same river above. At eleven o'clock, not having heard from Sheridan, I reinforced Parke with two brigades from City Point.[20] With this additional force he completed his captured works for better defence, and built back from his right, so as to protect his flank. He also carried in and made an *abatis* between himself and the enemy. Lee brought additional troops and artillery against Parke even after this was done, and made several assaults with very heavy losses.[21]

The enemy had in addition to their intrenched line close up to Petersburg, two enclosed works outside of it, Fort Gregg and Fort Whitworth. We thought it had now become necessary to carry them by assault. About one o'clock in the day, Fort Gregg was assaulted by Foster's division of the 24th corps (Gibbon's), supported by two brigades from Ord's command. The battle was desperate and the National troops were repulsed several times; but it was finally carried, and immediately the troops in Fort Whitworth evacuated the place. The guns of Fort Gregg were turned upon the retreating enemy, and the commanding officer[22] with some sixty of the men of Fort Whitworth surrendered.

I had ordered Miles[23] in the morning to report to Sheridan. In moving to execute this order he came upon the enemy at the intersection of the White Oak Road and the Claiborne Road. The enemy fell back to Sutherland Station on the South Side Road and were followed by Miles. This position, naturally a strong and defensible one, was also strongly intrenched. Sheridan now came up and Miles asked permission from him to make the assault, which Sheridan gave.

[20] On Apr. 2, 1865, brigades from City Point, commanded by Benham and Charles H. T. Collis, reinforced Parke, along with another brigade commanded by Joseph E. Hamblin. *OR,* I, 46(I), 1018.

[21] On Apr. 2, 1865, Parke reportedly lost a total of 1,719 troops during the skirmish along the main line of works around Petersburg: 253 killed, 1,305 wounded, and 161 missing. Confederate losses were not reported. Thomas L. Livermore, *Numbers and Losses in the Civil War in America, 1861–65* (Boston: Houghton, Mifflin, 1900), 139; *OR,* I, 46(I), 1020.

[22] Nathaniel H. Harris (1834–1900) commanded Fort Whitworth in Petersburg during the Petersburg campaign. He was born in Mississippi and graduated from the University of Louisiana. In June 1861, he joined the Confederate Army as a captain and rose to brigadier general in Jan. 1864. *CWHC,* 282; Earl J. Hess, *In the Trenches at Petersburg: Field Fortifications & Confederate Defeat* (Chapel Hill: University of North Carolina Press, 2009), 274.

[23] Nelson A. Miles (1839–1925), Sherman's nephew-in-law, was born in Massachusetts. He entered the military in 1861 as a first lieutenant in the 22nd Massachusetts Inf. and rose to brigadier general by 1864. In 1892, Miles was awarded the Medal of Honor for his actions at the Battle of Chancellorsville. *CWHC,* 389.

By this time Humphreys had got through the outer works in his front, and came up also and assumed command over Miles, who commanded a division in his corps. I had sent an order to Humphreys to turn to his right and move towards Petersburg. This order he now got, and started off, thus leaving Miles alone. The latter made two assaults, both of which failed, and he had to fall back a few hundred yards.

Hearing that Miles had been left in this position, I directed Humphreys to send a division back to his relief. He went himself.[24]

Sheridan before starting to sweep down to Petersburg had sent Merritt with his cavalry to the west to attack some Confederate cavalry that had assembled there. Merritt drove them north to the Appomattox River. Sheridan then took the enemy at Sutherland Station on the reverse side from where Miles was, and the two together captured the place, with a large number of prisoners and some pieces of artillery, and put the remainder, portions of three Confederate corps, to flight.[25] Sheridan followed, and drove them until night, when further pursuit was stopped. Miles bivouacked for the night on the ground which he with Sheridan had carried so handsomely by assault. I cannot explain the situation here better than by giving my dispatch to City Point that evening:

BOYDTON ROAD, NEAR PETERSBURG,
*April* 2, 1865.—4.40 P.M.

COLONEL T. S. BOWERS,
City Point.

We are now up and have a continuous line of troops, and in a few hours will be intrenched from the Appomattox below Petersburg to the river above. Heth's and Wilcox's divisions, such part of them as were not captured, were cut off from town, either designedly on their part or because they could not help it. Sheridan with the cavalry and 5th corps is above them. Miles's division, 2d corps, was sent from the White Oak Road to Sutherland Station on the South Side Railroad, where he met them, and at last accounts was engaged with them. Not knowing whether Sheridan would get up in time, General Humphreys was sent with another division from here. The whole captures since the

---

[24] In compliance with the orders given by Meade, Sheridan placed Humphreys in command of Miles's division when he arrived. *OR,* I, 46(I), 679, 1106. For USG's Apr. 1–2, 1865, instructions to Meade regarding Miles and Humphreys, see *PUSG,* 14:300–302, 302*n.*

[25] U.S. forces reported capturing 150 Confederate soldiers and two pieces of artillery. *OR,* I, 46(I), 725.

army started out gunning will amount to not less than twelve thousand men, and probably fifty pieces of artillery. I do not know the number of men and guns accurately however. * * *[26] I think the President might come out and pay us a visit tomorrow.

U. S. GRANT,
Lieutenant-General.

During the night of April 2d our line was intrenched from the river above to the river below. I ordered a bombardment to be commenced the next morning at five A.M., to be followed by an assault at six o'clock; but the enemy evacuated Petersburg early in the morning.[27]

---

[26] The section of this letter omitted from this text read as follows: "A portion of Gen. Foster's Div. 24th Corps made one of the most gallant charges and captured a very important fort from the enemy, with its entire garrison. All seems well with us and everything quiet just now." *PUSG*, 14:327.

[27] For USG's Apr. 2, 1865, order to Meade regarding a potential assault of Petersburg on the morning of Apr. 3, see ibid., 14:317–318.

# 65

## The Capture of Petersburg—Meeting President Lincoln in Petersburg—The Capture of Richmond— Pursuing the Enemy—Visit to Sheridan and Meade

GENERAL MEADE AND I entered Petersburg on the morning of the 3d and took a position under cover of a house which protected us from the enemy's musketry which was flying thick and fast there.[1] As we would occasionally look around the corner we could see the streets and the Appomattox bottom, presumably near the bridge, packed with the Confederate army. I did not have artillery brought up, because I was sure Lee was trying to make his escape, and I wanted to push immediately in pursuit. At all events I had not the heart to turn the artillery upon such a mass of defeated and fleeing men, and I hoped to capture them soon.

Soon after the enemy had entirely evacuated Petersburg, a man came in who represented himself to be an engineer of the Army of Northern Virginia. He said that Lee had for some time been at work preparing a strong enclosed intrenchment, into which he would throw himself when forced out of Petersburg, and fight his final battle there; that he was actually at that time drawing his troops from Richmond, and falling back into this prepared work. This statement was made to General Meade and myself when we were together.[2]

[1] This house was owned by Thomas Wallace, a lawyer. A. Wilson Greene, *Civil War Petersburg: Confederate City in the Crucible of War* (Charlottesville: University of Virginia Press, 2006), 259.

[2] On Apr. 4, 1865, USG wrote Sheridan that he had spoken with an engineer of the Southside Railroad, who reported that Jefferson Davis and his cabinet had passed south through Burkesville, VA, about 3:00 A.M. on Apr. 3. USG also stated that Lee was passing through Farmville, VA, on his way to Danville, VA. It is unclear whether this is the same incident USG described here. *PUSG*, 14:344.

I had already given orders for the movement up the south side of the Appomattox for the purpose of heading off Lee; but Meade was so much impressed
by this man's story that he thought we ought to cross the Appomattox there
at once and move against Lee in his new position. I knew that Lee was no fool,
as he would have been to have put himself and his army between two formidable streams like the James and Appomattox rivers, and between two such
armies as those of the Potomac and the James. Then these streams coming
together as they did to the east of him, it would be only necessary to close up
in the west to have him thoroughly cut off from all supplies or possibility of
reinforcement. It would only have been a question of days, and not many of
them, if he had taken the position assigned to him by the so-called engineer,
when he would have been obliged to surrender his army. Such is one of the
ruses resorted to in war to deceive your antagonist. My judgment was that
Lee would necessarily have to evacuate Richmond, and that the only course
for him to pursue would be to follow the Danville Road. Accordingly my object was to secure a point on that road south of Lee, and I told Meade this.
He suggested that if Lee was going that way we would follow him. My reply
was that we did not want to follow him; we wanted to get ahead of him and
cut him off, and if he would only stay in the position he (Meade) believed
him to be in at that time, I wanted nothing better; that when we got in possession of the Danville Railroad, at its crossing of the Appomattox River, if
we still found him between the two rivers, all we had to do was to move eastward and close him up. That we would then have all the advantage we could
possibly have by moving directly against him from Petersburg, even if he remained in the position assigned him by the engineer officer.

I had held most of the command aloof from the intrenchments, so as to
start them out on the Danville Road early in the morning, supposing that Lee
would be gone during the night. During the night I strengthened Sheridan
by sending him Humphreys's corps.[3]

Lee, as we now know, had advised the authorities at Richmond, during the
day, of the condition of affairs, and told them it would be impossible for him
to hold out longer than night, if he could hold out that long. Davis was at
church when he received Lee's dispatch.[4] The congregation was dismissed with
the notice that there would be no evening service. The rebel government left
Richmond about two o'clock in the afternoon of the 2d.

---

[3] For USG's Apr. 2, 1865, letter to Meade, see, ibid., 14:315.

[4] On Apr. 2, 1865, Davis attended St. Paul's Church in Richmond, VA. Jefferson Davis, *The
Rise and Fall of the Confederate Government* (New York: D. Appleton, 1881), 2:667.

At night Lee ordered his troops to assemble at Amelia Court House, his object being to get away, join Johnston if possible, and to try to crush Sherman before I could get there. As soon as I was sure of this I notified Sheridan and directed him to move out on the Danville Railroad to the south side of the Appomattox River as speedily as possible. He replied that he already had some of his command nine miles out.[5] I then ordered the rest of the Army of the Potomac under Meade to follow the same road in the morning. Parke's corps followed by the same road, and the Army of the James was directed to follow the road which ran alongside of the South Side Railroad to Burke's Station,[6] and to repair the railroad and telegraph as they proceeded. That road was a 5 feet gauge, while our rolling stock was all of the 4 feet 8½ inches gauge; consequently the rail on one side of the track had to be taken up throughout the whole length and relaid so as to conform to the gauge of our cars and locomotives.

Mr. Lincoln was at City Point at the time, and had been for some days.[7] I would have let him know what I contemplated doing, only while I felt a strong conviction that the move was going to be successful, yet it might not prove so; and then I would have only added another to the many disappointments he had been suffering for the past three years. But when we started out he saw that we were moving for a purpose, and bidding us Godspeed, remained there to hear the result.

The next morning after the capture of Petersburg, I telegraphed Mr. Lincoln asking him to ride out there and see me, while I would await his arrival. I had started all the troops out early in the morning, so that after the National army left Petersburg there was not a soul to be seen, not even an animal in the streets. There was absolutely no one there, except my staff officers and, possibly, a small escort of cavalry. We had selected the piazza of a deserted house, and occupied it until the President arrived.[8]

---

[5] For USG's Apr. 2, 1865, orders to Sheridan and his subsequent reply, see *PUSG* 14:321 and *n.*

[6] Burke's Station was approximately forty miles southwest of Richmond, near the intersection of the South Side Railroad and the Richmond and Danville Railroad. George B. Davis et al., *The Official Military Atlas of the Civil War* (New York: Fairfax Press, 1983), plate 137.

[7] On Mar. 24, 1865, Lincoln arrived at City Point, VA, and traveled around the area over the following two weeks. On Apr. 8, he left City Point and returned to Washington, DC. Harold Holzer and Sara Vaughn Gabbard, ed., *1865: America Makes War and Peace in Lincoln's Final Year* (Carbondale: Southern Illinois University Press, 2015), 166–169; *PUSG,* 14:xxiii.

[8] On Apr. 2, 1865, USG wrote Bowers to request a meeting with Lincoln in Petersburg, VA. USG met with Lincoln the next morning at the Wallace House on South Market Street. Greene, *Civil War Petersburg,* 259–260; *PUSG,* 14:327*n.*

About the first thing that Mr. Lincoln said to me, after warm congratulations for the victory, and thanks both to myself and to the army which had accomplished it, was: "Do you know, general, that I have had a sort of a sneaking idea for some days that you intended to do something like this." Our movements having been successful up to this point, I no longer had any object in concealing from the President all my movements, and the objects I had in view. He remained for some days near City Point, and I communicated with him frequently and fully by telegraph.

Mr. Lincoln knew that it had been arranged for Sherman to join me at a fixed time, to co-operate in the destruction of Lee's army. I told him that I had been very anxious to have the Eastern armies vanquish their old enemy who had so long resisted all their repeated and gallant attempts to subdue them or drive them from their capital. The Western armies had been in the main successful until they had conquered all the territory from the Mississippi River to the State of North Carolina, and were now almost ready to knock at the back door of Richmond, asking admittance. I said to him that if the Western armies should be even upon the field, operating against Richmond and Lee, the credit would be given to them for the capture, by politicians and non-combatants from the section of country which those troops hailed from. It might lead to disagreeable bickerings between members of Congress of the East and those of the West in some of their debates. Western members might be throwing it up to the members of the East that in the suppression of the rebellion they were not able to capture an army, or to accomplish much in the way of contributing toward that end, but had to wait until the Western armies had conquered all the territory south and west of them, and then come on to help them capture the only army they had been engaged with.

Mr. Lincoln said he saw that now, but had never thought of it before, because his anxiety was so great that he did not care where the aid came from so the work was done.

The Army of the Potomac has every reason to be proud of its four years' record in the suppression of the rebellion. The army it had to fight was the protection to the capital of a people which was attempting to found a nation upon the territory of the United States. Its loss would be the loss of the cause. Every energy, therefore, was put forth by the Confederacy to protect and maintain their capital. Everything else would go if it went. Lee's army had to be strengthened to enable it to maintain its position, no matter what territory was wrested from the South in another quarter.

I never expected any such bickering as I have indicated, between the soldiers of the two sections; and, fortunately, there has been none between the politicians. Possibly I am the only one who thought of the liability of such a state of things in advance.

When our conversation was at an end Mr. Lincoln mounted his horse and started on his return to City Point, while I and my staff started to join the army, now a good many miles in advance. Up to this time I had not received the report of the capture of Richmond.

Soon after I left President Lincoln I received a dispatch from General Weitzel which notified me that he had taken possession of Richmond at about 8.15 o'clock in the morning of that day, the 3d, and that he had found the city on fire in two places.[9] The city was in the most utter confusion. The authorities had taken the precaution to empty all the liquor into the gutter, and to throw out the provisions which the Confederate government had left, for the people to gather up. The city had been deserted by the authorities, civil and military, without any notice whatever that they were about to leave. In fact, up to the very hour of the evacuation the people had been led to believe that Lee had gained an important victory somewhere around Petersburg.[10]

Weitzel's command found evidence of great demoralization in Lee's army, there being still a great many men and even officers in the town. The city was on fire. Our troops were directed to extinguish the flames, which they finally succeeded in doing. The fire had been started by some one connected with the retreating army. All authorities deny that it was authorized, and I presume it was the work of excited men who were leaving what they regarded as their capital and may have felt that it was better to destroy it than have it fall into the hands of their enemy.[11] Be that as it may, the National troops found the city in flames, and used every effort to extinguish them.

The troops that had formed Lee's right, a great many of them, were cut off from getting back into Petersburg, and were pursued by our cavalry so hotly and closely that they threw away caissons, ammunition, clothing, and almost everything to lighten their loads, and pushed along up the Appomattox River until finally they took water and crossed over.

I left Mr. Lincoln and started, as I have already said, to join the command, which halted at Sutherland Station, about nine miles out. We had still time

---

[9] For Weitzel's Apr. 3, 1865, telegram, see *PUSG,* 14:340*n*–341*n.*

[10] At 4:00 P.M. on Apr. 2, 1865, Richmond mayor Joseph C. Mayo informed the city council of the impending departure of the Confederate government. Ernest B. Furgurson, *Ashes of Glory: Richmond at War* (New York: Knopf, 1997), 323.

[11] Confederate troops lit the fires that consumed the city as they were rushing to escape oncoming U.S. forces. Nelson D. Lankford, *Richmond Burning* (New York: Penguin, 2003), 136–137.

to march as much farther, and time was an object; but the roads were bad and the trains belonging to the advance corps had blocked up the road so that it was impossible to get on. Then, again, our cavalry had struck some of the enemy and were pursuing them; and the orders were that the roads should be given up to the cavalry whenever they appeared. This caused further delay.

General Wright, who was in command of one of the corps which were left back, thought to gain time by letting his men go into bivouac and trying to get up some rations for them, and clearing out the road, so that when they did start they would be uninterrupted.[12] Humphreys, who was far ahead, was also out of rations. They did not succeed in getting them up through the night; but the Army of the Potomac, officers and men, were so elated by the reflection that at last they were following up a victory to its end, that they preferred marching without rations to running a possible risk of letting the enemy elude them. So the march was resumed at three o'clock in the morning.

Merritt's cavalry had struck the enemy at Deep Creek, and driven them north to the Appomattox, where, I presume, most of them were forced to cross.[13]

On the morning of the 4th I learned that Lee had ordered rations up from Danville for his famishing army, and that they were to meet him at Farmville. This showed that Lee had already abandoned the idea of following the railroad down to Danville, but had determined to go farther west, by the way of Farmville. I notified Sheridan of this and directed him to get possession of the road before the supplies could reach Lee. He responded that he had already sent Crook's division to get upon the road between Burkesville and Jetersville, then to face north and march along the road upon the latter place; and he thought Crook must be there now. The bulk of the army moved directly for Jetersville by two roads.[14]

After I had received the dispatch from Sheridan saying that Crook was on the Danville Road, I immediately ordered Meade to make a forced march with the Army of the Potomac, and to send Parke's corps across from the road they were on to the South Side Railroad, to fall in the rear of the Army of the James and to protect the railroad which that army was repairing as it went along.

---

[12] In Apr. 1865, Wright commanded the 6th Corps, Army of the Potomac. *CWHC,* 583.

[13] On Apr. 3, 1865, Merritt's forces pushed the Confederate troops across Deep Creek and toward Amelia Court House, VA, approximately twenty miles west of Petersburg. *OR,* I, 46(I), 1119.

[14] It is unclear exactly which two roads USG referred to, but likely routes in the area include the Namozine, River, and Cox roads. Davis et al., *Official Military Atlas of the Civil War,* plate 76, map 5; plate 77, map 2.

Our troops took possession of Jetersville and in the telegraph office, they found a dispatch from Lee, ordering two hundred thousand rations from Danville. The dispatch had not been sent, but Sheridan sent a special messenger with it to Burkesville and had it forwarded from there.[15] In the meantime, however, dispatches from other sources had reached Danville, and they knew there that our army was on the line of the road; so that they sent no further supplies from that quarter.

At this time Merritt and Mackenzie, with the cavalry, were off between the road which the Army of the Potomac was marching on and the Appomattox River, and were attacking the enemy in flank. They picked up a great many prisoners and forced the abandonment of some property.[16]

Lee intrenched himself at Amelia Court House, and also his advance north of Jetersville, and sent his troops out to collect forage. The country was very poor and afforded but very little. His foragers scattered a great deal; many of them were picked up by our men, and many others never returned to the Army of Northern Virginia.

Griffin's corps was intrenched across the railroad south of Jetersville, and Sheridan notified me of the situation. I again ordered Meade up with all dispatch, Sheridan having but the one corps of infantry with a little cavalry confronting Lee's entire army. Meade, always prompt in obeying orders, now pushed forward with great energy, although he was himself sick and hardly able to be out of bed. Humphreys moved at two, and Wright at three o'clock in the morning, without rations, as I have said, the wagons being far in the rear.

I stayed that night at Wilson's Station[17] on the South Side Railroad. On the morning of the 5th I sent word to Sheridan of the progress Meade was making, and suggested that he might now attack Lee.[18] We had now no other objective than the Confederate armies, and I was anxious to close the thing up at once.

---

[15] Lt. William Dunn delivered an Apr. 5, 1865, letter from Sheridan at Jetersville, VA, reporting that Confederate forces were "out or nearly out of rations" but not specifically mentioning a captured dispatch from Lee. *PUSG,* 14:347 and *n.*

[16] On Apr. 6, 1865, Merritt reported capturing a large force of Confederate troops (including eight general officers). *OR,* I, 46(I), 1120.

[17] Wilson's Station was approximately twenty miles west of Petersburg. Davis et al., *Official Military Atlas of the Civil War,* plate 137.

[18] On Apr. 4, 1865, USG informed Sheridan of Ord's movements and told Sheridan to "try to intercept the enemy" at Farmville. The editors found no letter from Apr. 5 that matches the description given by USG here. *PUSG,* 14:344–345, 345*n.*

On the 5th I marched again with Ord's command until within about ten miles of Burkesville, where I stopped to let his army pass. I then received from Sheridan the following dispatch:

"The whole of Lee's army is at or near Amelia Court House, and on this side of it. General Davies,[19] whom I sent out to Painesville[20] on their right flank, has just captured six pieces of artillery and some wagons. We can capture the Army of Northern Virginia if force enough can be thrown to this point, and then advance upon it. My cavalry was at Burkesville yesterday, and six miles beyond, on the Danville Road, last night. General Lee is at Amelia Court House in person. They are out of rations, or nearly so. They were advancing up the railroad towards Burkesville yesterday, when we intercepted them at this point."[21]

It now became a life and death struggle with Lee to get south to his provisions.

Sheridan, thinking the enemy might turn off immediately towards Farmville, moved Davies's brigade of cavalry out to watch him. Davies found the movement had already commenced. He attacked and drove away their cavalry which was escorting wagons to the west, capturing and burning 180 wagons. He also captured five pieces of artillery. The Confederate infantry then moved against him and probably would have handled him very roughly, but Sheridan had sent two more brigades of cavalry to follow Davies, and they came to his relief in time. A sharp engagement took place between these three brigades of cavalry and the enemy's infantry, but the latter was repulsed.[22]

Meade himself reached Jetersville about two o'clock in the afternoon, but in advance of all his troops. The head of Humphreys's corps followed in about an hour afterwards. Sheridan stationed the troops as they came up, at Meade's request, the latter still being very sick. He extended two divisions of this corps off to the west of the road to the left of Griffin's corps, and one division to the right.[23]

---

[19] Henry E. Davies Jr. (1836–1894) was born in New York and became a captain in the 5th New York Inf. in May 1861. In Oct. 1864, he was brevetted major general. *CWHC*, 200.

[20] Painesville, VA, was approximately thirty miles southwest of Richmond and five miles north of the Richmond and Danville Railroad. Davis et al., *Official Military Atlas of the Civil War*, plate 137.

[21] On Apr. 5, 1865, Sheridan sent this letter while at Jetersville. *PUSG*, 14:347n.

[22] Sheridan reinforced Davies with troops from the 2nd Brigade and portions of the 3rd Brigade, 2nd Div., Army of the Potomac. *OR*, I, 46(I), 1145.

[23] When Humphreys's 2nd Corps reached Jetersville on Apr. 5, 1865, Sheridan placed its 1st and 2nd Divs. on the left of Griffin's 5th Corps and its 3rd Div. on Griffin's right. Ibid., I, 46(I), 681.

The cavalry by this time had also come up, and they were put still farther off to the left, Sheridan feeling certain that there lay the route by which the enemy intended to escape. He wanted to attack, feeling that if time was given, the enemy would get away; but Meade prevented this, preferring to wait till his troops were all up.

At this juncture Sheridan sent me a letter which had been handed to him by a colored man, with a note from himself saying that he wished I was there myself.[24] The letter was dated Amelia Court House, April 5th, and signed by Colonel Taylor. It was to his mother, and showed the demoralization of the Confederate army.[25] Sheridan's note also gave me the information as here related of the movements of that day. I received a second message from Sheridan on the 5th, in which he urged more emphatically the importance of my presence. This was brought to me by a scout in gray uniform. It was written on tissue paper, and wrapped up in tin-foil such as chewing tobacco is folded in. This was a precaution taken so that if the scout should be captured he could take this tin-foil out of his pocket and putting it into his mouth, chew it. It would cause no surprise at all to see a Confederate soldier chewing tobacco. It was nearly night when this letter was received.[26] I gave Ord directions to continue his march to Burkesville and there intrench himself for the night, and in the morning to move west to cut off all the roads between there and Farmville.

I then started with a few of my staff and a very small escort of cavalry, going directly through the woods, to join Meade's army. The distance was about sixteen miles; but the night being dark our progress was slow through the woods in the absence of direct roads. However, we got to the outposts about ten

[24] For Sheridan's Apr. 5, 1865, letter to USG, see *PUSG,* 14:348*n.*

[25] On Apr. 4, 1865, U.S. forces captured an African American man who carried a letter written by Confederate colonel William B. Taylor and addressed to his mother. The letter, dated Apr. 5, began, "Our army is ruined, I fear." Philip H. Sheridan, "Last Days of the Rebellion," in *Battles and Leaders of the Civil War,* vol. 6, ed. Peter Cozzens (Urbana: University of Illinois Press, 2004), 528.

[26] According to Horace Porter's account, the scout was a man named Campbell who was carrying the famous "I wish you were here yourself" message from Sheridan (which USG identified as an earlier message). This scout was probably James A. Campbell (1844–1904), who enlisted in the New York state militia in 1861 and joined the 2nd New York Cav. in 1862. He was awarded the Medal of Honor for his actions at Woodstock, VA, on Jan. 22, 1865. Horace Porter, *Campaigning with Grant* (New York: Century, 1897), 454–455; *The Union Army: A History of Military Affairs in the Loyal States 1861–65* . . . (1908; repr. Wilmington, NC: Broadfoot, 1998), 8:588–592. For Sheridan's Apr. 5, 1865, letters to USG, see *PUSG,* 14:347*n*–348*n.*

o'clock in the evening, and after some little parley convinced the sentinels of our identity and were conducted in to where Sheridan was bivouacked. We talked over the situation for some little time, Sheridan explaining to me what he thought Lee was trying to do, and that Meade's orders, if carried out, moving to the right flank, would give him the coveted opportunity of escaping us and putting us in rear of him.

We then together visited Meade, reaching his headquarters about midnight. I explained to Meade that we did not want to follow the enemy; we wanted to get ahead of him, and that his orders would allow the enemy to escape, and besides that, I had no doubt that Lee was moving right then. Meade changed his orders at once. They were now given for an advance on Amelia Court House, at an early hour in the morning, as the army then lay; that is, the infantry being across the railroad, most of it to the west of the road, with the cavalry swung out still farther to the left.

# 66

## Battle of Sailor's Creek—Engagement at Farmville—
## Correspondence with General Lee—
## Sheridan Intercepts the Enemy

THE APPOMATTOX, GOING westward, takes a long sweep to the south-west from the neighborhood of the Richmond and Danville Railroad bridge,[1] and then trends north-westerly. Sailor's Creek, an insignificant stream, running northward, empties into the Appomattox between the High Bridge[2] and Jeters-ville. Near the High Bridge the stage road from Petersburg to Lynchburg crosses the Appomattox River, also on a bridge. The railroad runs on the north side of the river to Farmville, a few miles west, and from there, recrossing, con-tinues on the south side of it. The roads coming up from the south-east to Farmville cross the Appomattox River there on a bridge and run on the north side, leaving the Lynchburg and Petersburg Railroad[3] well to the left.

Lee, in pushing out from Amelia Court House, availed himself of all the roads between the Danville Road and Appomattox River to move upon, and never permitted the head of his columns to stop because of any fighting that might be going on in his rear. In this way he came very near succeeding in getting to his provision trains and eluding us with at least part of his army.

As expected, Lee's troops had moved during the night before, and our army in moving upon Amelia Court House soon encountered them. There was a good deal of fighting before Sailor's Creek was reached. Our cavalry charged

[1] The Richmond and Danville Railroad crossed over the Appomattox River about twenty miles west of Richmond, VA. *PUSG*, 14:246–247 (map).

[2] The South Side Railroad crossed over the Appomattox River six miles from Farmville, VA, on the High Bridge. Ibid.

[3] The line connecting Lynchburg, VA, and Petersburg, VA, was the South Side Railroad. Ibid.

in upon a body of theirs which was escorting a wagon train in order to get it past our left. A severe engagement ensued, in which we captured many prisoners, and many men also were killed and wounded.[4] There was as much gallantry displayed by some of the Confederates in these little engagements as was displayed at any time during the war, notwithstanding the sad defeats of the past week.

The armies finally met on Sailor's Creek, when a heavy engagement took place, in which infantry, artillery and cavalry were all brought into action. Our men on the right, as they were brought in against the enemy, came in on higher ground, and upon his flank, giving us every advantage to be derived from the lay of the country. Our firing was also very much more rapid, because the enemy commenced his retreat westward and in firing as he retreated had to turn around every time he fired. The enemy's loss was very heavy, as well in killed and wounded as in captures. Some six general officers fell into our hands in this engagement, and seven thousand men were made prisoners.[5] This engagement was commenced in the middle of the afternoon of the 6th, and the retreat and pursuit were continued until nightfall, when the armies bivouacked upon the ground where the night had overtaken them.

When the move towards Amelia Court House had commenced that morning, I ordered Wright's corps, which was on the extreme right, to be moved to the left past the whole army, to take the place of Griffin's, and ordered the latter at the same time to move by and place itself on the right.[6] The object of this movement was to get the 6th corps, Wright's, next to the cavalry, with which they had formerly served so harmoniously and so efficiently in the valley of Virginia.

---

[4] On Apr. 5, 1865, the 1st Pennsylvania Cav. attacked a Confederate cavalry brigade commanded by Brig. Gen. Martin W. Gary near Painesville, VA. The U.S. force captured approximately 700 Confederates. Twenty U.S. soldiers were killed and ninety-six wounded. David J. Eicher, *The Longest Night: A Military History of the Civil War* (New York: Simon and Schuster, 2001), 815.

[5] At the Battle of Sailor's Creek on Apr. 6, 1865, Confederate losses totaled approximately 7,700 men. Nine Confederate generals were captured at the battle: Seth M. Barton (1829–1900); Meriwether Lewis Clark (1809–1881), son of explorer William Clark; Montgomery D. Corse (1816–1895); Dudley M. DuBose (1834–1883); Richard S. Ewell (1817–1872); Eppa Hunton II (1822–1908); Joseph B. Kershaw (1822–1894); George Washington Custis Lee (1832–1913), son of Robert E. Lee; and James P. Simms (1837–1887). Edwin C. Bearss and Bryce A. Suderow, *The Petersburg Campaign: The Eastern Front Battles, June–August 1864* (El Dorado Hills, CA: Savas Beatie, 2012), 2:553; *CWHC*, 120, 174–175, 186, 216, 229, 311, 330, 343, 489.

[6] On Apr. 6, 1865, Meade gave Wright and Griffin the orders related to these movements. *PUSG*, 14:354, 354*n*–355*n*.

The 6th corps now remained with the cavalry and under Sheridan's direct command until after the surrender.

Ord had been directed to take possession of all the roads southward between Burkesville and the High Bridge. On the morning of the 6th he sent Colonel Washburn[7] with two infantry regiments with instructions to destroy High Bridge and to return rapidly to Burkesville Station; and he prepared himself to resist the enemy there. Soon after Washburn had started Ord became a little alarmed as to his safety and sent Colonel Read,[8] of his staff, with about eighty cavalrymen, to overtake him and bring him back. Very shortly after this he heard that the head of Lee's column had got up to the road between him and where Washburn now was, and attempted to send reinforcements, but the reinforcements could not get through. Read, however, had got through ahead of the enemy. He rode on to Farmville and was on his way back again when he found his return cut off, and Washburn confronting apparently the advance of Lee's army. Read drew his men up into line of battle, his force now consisting of less than six hundred men, infantry and cavalry, and rode along their front, making a speech to his men to inspire them with the same enthusiasm that he himself felt.[9] He then gave the order to charge. This little band made several charges, of course unsuccessful ones, but inflicted a loss upon the enemy more than equal to their own entire number. Colonel Read fell mortally wounded, and then Washburn; and at the close of the conflict nearly every officer of the command and most of the rank and file had been either killed or wounded. The remainder then surrendered. The Confederates took this to be only the advance of a larger column which had headed them off, and so stopped to intrench; so that this gallant band of six hundred had checked the progress of a strong detachment of the Confederate army.

This stoppage of Lee's column no doubt saved to us the trains following. Lee himself pushed on and crossed the wagon road bridge near the High

[7] Francis Washburn (1838–1865) was born in Massachusetts and graduated from Harvard University. In Dec. 1861, he joined the 1st Massachusetts Cav. as a second lieutenant and was promoted to colonel in Feb. 1865. *CWHC,* 555.

[8] Theodore Read (1835–1865) was born in Ohio and later served as a clerk for the U.S. Dept. of the Interior. In Oct. 1861, he entered the military as a captain and served as an assistant adjutant general. He was brevetted brigadier general in 1864. By Apr. 1865, he was chief of staff and assistant adjutant general, Army of the James. Ibid., 447.

[9] Read's force numbered approximately 900. Spencer Tucker, ed., *American Civil War: The Definitive Encyclopedia and Document Collection* (Santa Barbara, CA: ABC-CLIO, 2013), s.v. "High Bridge, Battle of."

Bridge, and attempted to destroy it. He did set fire to it, but the flames had made but little headway when Humphreys came up with his corps and drove away the rear-guard which had been left to protect it while it was being burned up. Humphreys forced his way across with some loss, and followed Lee to the intersection of the road crossing at Farmville with the one from Petersburg. Here Lee held a position which was very strong, naturally, besides being intrenched. Humphreys was alone, confronting him all through the day, and in a very hazardous position. He put on a bold face, however, and assaulted with some loss, but was not assaulted in return.[10]

Our cavalry had gone farther south by the way of Prince Edward's Court House,[11] along with the 5th corps (Griffin's), Ord falling in between Griffin and the Appomattox. Crook's division of cavalry and Wright's corps pushed on west of Farmville. When the cavalry reached Farmville they found that some of the Confederates were in ahead of them, and had already got their trains of provisions back to that point; but our troops were in time to prevent them from securing anything to eat, although they succeeded in again running the trains off, so that we did not get them for some time. These troops retreated to the north side of the Appomattox to join Lee, and succeeded in destroying the bridge after them. Considerable fighting ensued there between Wright's corps and a portion of our cavalry and the Confederates, but finally the cavalry forded the stream and drove them away. Wright built a foot-bridge for his men to march over on and then marched out to the junction of the roads to relieve Humphreys, arriving there that night. I had stopped the night before at Burkesville Junction. Our troops were then pretty much all out of the place, but we had a field hospital there, and Ord's command was extended from that point towards Farmville.

Here I met Dr. Smith, a Virginian and an officer of the regular army,[12] who told me that in a conversation with General Ewell, one of the prisoners and a relative of his, Ewell had said that when we had got across the James River he knew their cause was lost, and it was the duty of their authorities to make the

[10] Humphreys reported total losses for the fighting on Apr. 7, 1865, as 572 troops killed, missing, or wounded. *OR*, I, 46(I), 685–686.

[11] Prince Edward's Court House, VA, was approximately fifty miles west of Petersburg and approximately five miles south of the Lynchburg and Petersburg Railroad. *PUSG*, 14:246–247 (map).

[12] The story about Dr. Smith is repeated in contemporary accounts and modern publications, but they provide no further identification of Dr. Smith. For example, see Donald C. Pfanz, *Richard S. Ewell: A Soldier's Life* (Chapel Hill: University of North Carolina Press, 2000), 443.

best terms they could while they still had a right to claim concessions. The authorities thought differently, however. Now the cause was lost and they had no right to claim anything. He said further, that for every man that was killed after this in the war somebody is responsible, and it would be but very little better than murder. He was not sure that Lee would consent to surrender his army without being able to consult with the President, but he hoped he would.

I rode in to Farmville on the 7th, arriving there early in the day. Sheridan and Ord were pushing through, away to the south. Meade was back towards the High Bridge, and Humphreys confronting Lee as before stated. After having gone into bivouac at Prince Edward's Court House, Sheridan learned that seven trains of provisions and forage were at Appomattox, and determined to start at once and capture them; and a forced march was necessary in order to get there before Lee's army could secure them. He wrote me a note telling me this.[13] This fact, together with the incident related the night before by Dr. Smith, gave me the idea of opening correspondence with General Lee on the subject of the surrender of his army. I therefore wrote to him on this day, as follows:

> HEADQUARTERS ARMIES OF THE U. S.,
> 5 P.M., *April* 7, 1865.
>
> GENERAL R. E. LEE,
> Commanding C. S. A.
>
> The results of the last week must convince you of the hopelessness of further resistance on the part of the Army of Northern Virginia in this struggle. I feel that it is so, and regard it as my duty to shift from myself the responsibility of any further effusion of blood, by asking of you the surrender of that portion of the Confederate States army known as the Army of Northern Virginia.
>
> U. S. GRANT,
> Lieut.-General.

Lee replied on the evening of the same day as follows:

> *April* 7, 1865.
>
> GENERAL:—I have received your note of this day. Though not entertaining the opinion you express on the hopelessness of further resistance

---

[13] Sheridan's Apr. 7, 1865, letter to USG mentioned eight trains at Appomattox Court House, VA. *PUSG,* 14:366n.

on the part of the Army of Northern Virginia, I reciprocate your desire to avoid useless effusion of blood, and therefore before considering your proposition, ask the terms you will offer on condition of its surrender.

R. E. LEE,
General.

LIEUT.-GENERAL U. S. GRANT,
Commanding Armies of the U. S.[14]

This was not satisfactory, but I regarded it as deserving another letter and wrote him as follows:

*April* 8, 1865.

GENERAL R. E. LEE,
Commanding C. S. A.

Your note of last evening in reply to mine of same date, asking the condition on which I will accept the surrender of the Army of Northern Virginia is just received. In reply I would say that, peace being my great desire, there is but one condition I would insist upon, namely: that the men and officers surrendered shall be disqualified for taking up arms again against the Government of the United States until properly exchanged. I will meet you, or will designate officers to meet any officers you may name for the same purpose, at any point agreeable to you, for the purpose of arranging definitely the terms upon which the surrender of the Army of Northern Virginia will be received.

U. S. GRANT,
Lieut.-General.

Lee's army was rapidly crumbling. Many of his soldiers had enlisted from that part of the State where they now were, and were continually dropping out of the ranks and going to their homes. I know that I occupied a hotel almost destitute of furniture at Farmville, which had probably been used as a Confederate hospital.[15] The next morning when I came out I found a Confederate

[14] See ibid., 14:361*n.*

[15] On Apr. 7, 1865, USG stayed at the Prince Edward Hotel in Farmville where Lee had slept the night before. Adam Badeau, *Military History of Ulysses S. Grant, from April, 1861, to April, 1865* (New York: D. Appleton, 1881), 3:588; William Marvel, *Lee's Last Retreat: The Flight to Appomattox* (Chapel Hill: University of North Carolina Press, 2002), 135.

colonel there, who reported to me and said that he was the proprietor of that house, and that he was a colonel of a regiment that had been raised in that neighborhood.[16] He said that when he came along past home, he found that he was the only man of the regiment remaining with Lee's army, so he just dropped out, and now wanted to surrender himself. I told him to stay there and he would not be molested. That was one regiment which had been eliminated from Lee's force by this crumbling process.

Although Sheridan had been marching all day, his troops moved with alacrity and without any straggling. They began to see the end of what they had been fighting four years for. Nothing seemed to fatigue them. They were ready to move without rations and travel without rest until the end. Straggling had entirely ceased, and every man was now a rival for the front. The infantry marched about as rapidly as the cavalry could.

Sheridan sent Custer with his division to move south of Appomattox Station, which is about five miles south-west of the Court House, to get west of the trains and destroy the roads to the rear. They got there the night of the 8th, and succeeded partially; but some of the train men had just discovered the movement of our troops and succeeded in running off three of the trains. The other four were held by Custer.

The head of Lee's column came marching up there on the morning of the 9th, not dreaming, I suppose, that there were any Union soldiers near. The Confederates were surprised to find our cavalry had possession of the trains. However, they were desperate and at once assaulted, hoping to recover them. In the melée that ensued they succeeded in burning one of the trains, but not in getting anything from it. Custer then ordered the other trains run back on the road towards Farmville, and the fight continued.

So far, only our cavalry and the advance of Lee's army were engaged. Soon, however, Lee's men were brought up from the rear, no doubt expecting they had nothing to meet but our cavalry. But our infantry had pushed forward so rapidly that by the time the enemy got up they found Griffin's corps and the Army of the James confronting them. A sharp engagement ensued, but Lee quickly set up a white flag.

---

[16] Richard A. Booker (1817–1904) was born in Virginia and was the hotel keeper prior to the Civil War. He was a Virginia legislator and, in Apr. 1861, joined the Confederate Army as captain of Co. F, 18th Virginia Inf. He was wounded at the Second Battle of Manassas and resigned in May 1863. He joined the Virginia Reserves in Apr. 1864 and was promoted to colonel in Sept. Bruce S. Allardice, *Confederate Colonels: A Biographical Register* (Columbia: University of Missouri Press, 2008), 65.

# 67

## Negotiations at Appomattox—Interview with Lee at McLean's House—The Terms of Surrender— Lee's Surrender—Interview with Lee after the Surrender

O N THE 8TH I had followed the Army of the Potomac in rear of Lee. I was suffering very severely with a sick headache, and stopped at a farmhouse on the road some distance in rear of the main body of the army.[1] I spent the night in bathing my feet in hot water and mustard, and putting mustard plasters on my wrists and the back part of my neck, hoping to be cured by morning.[2] During the night I received Lee's answer to my letter of the 8th, inviting an interview between the lines on the following morning.* But it was for a different purpose from that of surrendering his army, and I answered him as follows:

HEADQUARTERS ARMIES OF THE U. S.,
*April* 9, 1865.

GENERAL R. E. LEE,
Commanding C. S. A.
  Your note of yesterday is received. As I have no authority to treat on the subject of peace, the meeting proposed for ten A.M. to-day could

*See Appendix.[3]

[1] On Apr. 8, 1865, USG's headquarters were in a large, white farmhouse in Curdsville, VA, known as the Clifton House. Fitzhugh Lee, *General Lee* (New York: University Society, 1905), 389; Ishbel Ross, *The General's Wife: The Life of Mrs. Ulysses S. Grant* (New York: Dodd, Mead, 1959), 187.
  [2] Mustard plaster was a common nineteenth-century remedy for headaches. *The Family Physician: A Manual of Domestic Medicine, by Physicians and Surgeons of the Principal London Hospitals* (London: Cassell, 1886), 669.
  [3] For Lee's Apr. 8, 1865, letter to USG, calling for peace and not surrender, see *PUSG*, 14:367n.

lead to no good. I will state, however, General, that I am equally anxious for peace with yourself, and the whole North entertains the same feeling. The terms upon which peace can be had are well understood. By the South laying down their arms they will hasten that most desirable event, save thousands of human lives, and hundreds of millions of property not yet destroyed. Sincerely hoping that all our difficulties may be settled without the loss of another life, I subscribe myself, etc.,

U. S. GRANT,<br>
Lieutenant-General.

I proceeded at an early hour in the morning, still suffering with the headache, to get to the head of the column.[4] I was not more than two or three miles from Appomattox Court House at the time, but to go direct I would have to pass through Lee's army, or a portion of it. I had therefore to move south in order to get upon a road coming up from another direction.

When the white flag was put out by Lee, as already described, I was in this way moving towards Appomattox Court House, and consequently could not be communicated with immediately, and be informed of what Lee had done. Lee, therefore, sent a flag to the rear to advise Meade and one to the front to Sheridan, saying that he had sent a message to me for the purpose of having a meeting to consult about the surrender of his army, and asked for a suspension of hostilities until I could be communicated with. As they had heard nothing of this until the fighting had got to be severe and all going against Lee, both of these commanders hesitated very considerably about suspending hostilities at all. They were afraid it was not in good faith, and we had the Army of Northern Virginia where it could not escape except by some deception. They, however, finally consented to a suspension of hostilities for two hours to give an opportunity of communicating with me in that time, if possible. It was found that, from the route I had taken, they would probably not be able to communicate with me and get an answer back within the time fixed unless the messenger should pass through the rebel lines.

Lee, therefore, sent an escort with the officer bearing this message through his lines to me.[5]

---

[4] By 11:50 A.M. on Apr. 9, 1865, USG had begun to move toward the head of the column. Ibid., 14:372.

[5] Lee sent this Apr. 9, 1865, letter to USG in duplicate. Both Charles E. Pease and Frederic Newhall delivered a copy of the letter to USG. Pease (1838–1886) was born in New York and

*April 9, 1865.*

GENERAL:—I received your note of this morning on the picket-line whither I had come to meet you and ascertain definitely what terms were embraced in your proposal of yesterday with reference to the surrender of this army. I now request an interview in accordance with the offer contained in your letter of yesterday for that purpose.

R. E. LEE, General.
LIEUTENANT-GENERAL U. S. GRANT,
Commanding U. S. Armies.

When the officer reached me I was still suffering with the sick headache; but the instant I saw the contents of the note I was cured. I wrote the following note in reply and hastened on:

*April 9, 1865.*

GENERAL R. E. LEE,
Commanding C. S. Armies.

Your note of this date is but this moment (11.50 A.M.) received, in consequence of my having passed from the Richmond and Lynchburg road to the Farmville and Lynchburg road. I am at this writing about four miles west of Walker's Church⁶ and will push forward to the front for the purpose of meeting you. Notice sent to me on this road where you wish the interview to take place will meet me.

U. S. GRANT,
Lieutenant-General.

I was conducted at once to where Sheridan was located with his troops drawn up in line of battle facing the Confederate army near by. They were

---

graduated from Union College. In Sept. 1861, he joined the 44th New York Inf. as a first lieutenant in Co. G. In Aug. 1864, he was brevetted major. Newhall (1840–1898) was born in Pennsylvania and joined the 6th Pennsylvania Cav. at the start of the Civil War, rising to lieutenant colonel in 1865. Eugene A. Nash, *A History of the Forty-Fourth Regiment, New York Volunteer Infantry in the Civil War, 1861–1865* (Chicago: R. R. Donnelley and Sons, 1911), 296; Horace Porter, "The Surrender at Appomattox Court House," in *Battles and Leaders of the Civil War,* vol. 4, ed. Robert Underwood Johnson and Clarence Clough Buel (New York: Century, 1888), 733; Eric J. Wittenberg, editor's introduction to Frederick C. Newhall, *With Sheridan in the Final Campaign against Lee* (Baton Rouge: Louisiana State University Press, 2002), xx–xxvi.

⁶Walker's Church was approximately twelve miles east of Appomattox Court House, VA. Henry E. Tremain, *Sailor's Creek to Appomattox Court House* (New York: Charles H. Ludwig, 1885), xvi.

very much excited, and expressed their view that this was all a ruse employed to enable the Confederates to get away. They said they believed that Johnston was marching up from North Carolina now, and Lee was moving to join him; and they would whip the rebels where they now were in five minutes if I would only let them go in. But I had no doubt about the good faith of Lee, and pretty soon was conducted to where he was. I found him at the house of a Mr. McLean,[7] at Appomattox Court House, with Colonel Marshall,[8] one of his staff officers, awaiting my arrival. The head of his column was occupying a hill, on a portion of which was an apple orchard, beyond a little valley which separated it from that on the crest of which Sheridan's forces were drawn up in line of battle to the south.

Before stating what took place between General Lee and myself, I will give all there is of the story of the famous apple tree.

Wars produce many stories of fiction, some of which are told until they are believed to be true. The war of the rebellion was no exception to this rule, and the story of the apple tree is one of those fictions based on a slight foundation of fact. As I have said, there was an apple orchard on the side of the hill occupied by the Confederate forces. Running diagonally up the hill was a wagon road, which, at one point, ran very near one of the trees, so that the wheels of vehicles had, on that side, cut off the roots of this tree, leaving a little embankment. General Babcock, of my staff, reported to me that when he first met General Lee he was sitting upon this embankment with his feet in the road below and his back resting against the tree. The story had no other

---

[7] Wilmer McLean (1814–1882) was born in Virginia and served as a major in the state militia before the Civil War. He was too old to serve during the Civil War, but his farm was located near the site of the first major battle, the First Battle of Bull Run (Manassas). McLean moved to Appomattox Court House to get away from the war. Ironically, USG and Lee would use his house at Appomattox Court House to sign the terms of surrender, which effectively ended the war. John D. Wright, *The Routledge Encyclopedia of Civil War Era Biographies* (New York: Routledge, 2013), s.v. "McLean, Wilmer 1814–82"; Elizabeth R. Varon, *Appomattox: Victory, Defeat, and Freedom at the End of the Civil War* (New York: Oxford University Press, 2014), 53.

[8] Charles Marshall (1830–1902), a relative of U.S. Supreme Court chief justice John Marshall, was born in Virginia. At the start of the Civil War, he was practicing law in Baltimore, MD, and in Mar. 1862 joined the Confederacy as an aide-de-camp to Lee. He was Lee's military secretary and was promoted to lieutenant colonel in 1864. Clayton Colman Hall, ed., *Baltimore: Its History and Its People* (New York: Lewis Historical Publishing, 1912), 3:673; Charles Marshall, *Lee's Aide-de-Camp: Being the Papers of Colonel Charles Marshall, Assistant Adjutant General on the Staff of Robert E. Lee,* ed. Frederick Maurice (Boston: Little, Brown, 1927), xiii-xiv.

foundation than that. Like many other stories, it would be very good if it was only true.[9]

I had known General Lee in the old army, and had served with him in the Mexican War; but did not suppose, owing to the difference in our age and rank, that he would remember me; while I would more naturally remember him distinctly, because he was the chief of staff of General Scott in the Mexican War.[10]

When I had left camp that morning I had not expected so soon the result that was then taking place, and consequently was in rough garb. I was without a sword, as I usually was when on horseback on the field, and wore a soldier's blouse for a coat, with the shoulder straps of my rank to indicate to the army who I was. When I went into the house I found General Lee. We greeted each other, and after shaking hands took our seats. I had my staff with me, a good portion of whom were in the room during the whole of the interview.[11]

What General Lee's feelings were I do not know. As he was a man of much dignity, with an impassible face, it was impossible to say whether he felt inwardly glad that the end had finally come, or felt sad over the result, and was too manly to show it. Whatever his feelings, they were entirely concealed from my observation; but my own feelings, which had been quite jubilant on the receipt of his letter, were sad and depressed. I felt like anything rather than rejoicing at the downfall of a foe who had fought so long and valiantly, and had suffered so much for a cause, though that cause was, I believe, one of the

[9] On Apr. 9, 1965, Babcock and Lt. William McKee Dunn met with Lee underneath an apple tree to deliver a note from USG. Immediately after the war, a myth circulated that Lee had met USG under the tree to surrender. Sylvanus Cadwallader, a Northern war correspondent who accompanied USG during the final days of the war, confirmed that the story of Lee meeting USG under the tree was false. Sylvanus Cadwallader, *Three Years with Grant,* ed. Benjamin P. Thomas (Lincoln: University of Nebraska Press, 1996), 325.

[10] Lee was assigned as chief engineer of Scott's forces during the Mexican-American War and remained an important aide, though not chief of staff, to Scott throughout the war. John W. Jones, *Personal Reminiscences, Anecdotes, and Letters of Gen. Robert E. Lee* (New York: D. Appleton, 1875), 492.

[11] Although there is debate about who was in the room with USG and Lee, the following people were present for at least part of the time: Orville Babcock, Adam Badeau, John G. Barnard, Theodore S. Bowers, Sylvanus Cadwallader, Frederick T. Dent, Rufus Ingalls, Robert T. Lincoln, Michael R. Morgan, E. O. C. Ord, Ely S. Parker, Horace Porter, John A. Rawlins, George H. Sharpe, Philip H. Sheridan, and Confederate officer Charles Marshall. Varon, *Appomattox,* 54, 57.

worst for which a people ever fought, and one for which there was the least excuse. I do not question, however, the sincerity of the great mass of those who were opposed to us.

General Lee was dressed in a full uniform which was entirely new, and was wearing a sword of considerable value, very likely the sword which had been presented by the State of Virginia; at all events, it was an entirely different sword from the one that would ordinarily be worn in the field.[12] In my rough traveling suit, the uniform of a private with the straps of a lieutenant-general, I must have contrasted very strangely with a man so handsomely dressed, six feet high and of faultless form.[13] But this was not a matter that I thought of until afterwards.

We soon fell into a conversation about old army times. He remarked that he remembered me very well in the old army;[14] and I told him that as a matter of course I remembered him perfectly, but from the difference in our rank and years (there being about sixteen years' difference in our ages),[15] I had thought it very likely that I had not attracted his attention sufficiently to be remembered by him after such a long interval. Our conversation grew so pleasant that I almost forgot the object of our meeting. After the conversation had run on in this style for some time, General Lee called my attention to the object of our meeting, and said that he had asked for this interview for the purpose of getting from me the terms I proposed to give his army. I said that I meant merely that his army should lay down their arms, not to take them up again during the continuance of the war unless duly and properly exchanged. He said that he had so understood my letter.

Then we gradually fell off again into conversation about matters foreign to the subject which had brought us together. This continued for some little time, when General Lee again interrupted the course of the conversation by suggesting that the terms I proposed to give his army ought to be written out. I

[12] During the surrender at Appomattox Court House, Lee wore a ceremonial sword given to him by an unknown Marylander. Ibid., 54.

[13] USG was five feet, eight inches tall. Horace Porter, *Campaigning with Grant* (New York: Century, 1897), 14.

[14] According to Horace Porter's account of the meeting, Lee told USG "I know I met you on that occasion [during the Mexican-American War], and I have often thought of it, and tried to recollect how you looked, but I have never been able to recall a single feature." Ibid., 475.

[15] Lee was approximately fifteen years and three months older than USG. *CWHC,* 264, 344.

called to General Parker, secretary on my staff,[16] for writing materials, and commenced writing out the following terms:

Appomattox C. H., Va.,<br>
Ap l 9th, 1865.

Gen. R. E. Lee,
Comd'g C. S. A.

Gen: In accordance with the substance of my letter to you of the 8th inst., I propose to receive the surrender of the Army of N. Va. on the following terms, to wit: Rolls of all the officers and men to be made in duplicate. One copy to be given to an officer designated by me, the other to be retained by such officer or officers as you may designate. The officers to give their individual paroles not to take up arms against the Government of the United States until properly exchanged, and each company or regimental commander sign a like parole for the men of their commands. The arms, artillery and public property to be parked and stacked, and turned over to the officer appointed by me to receive them. This will not embrace the side-arms of the officers, nor their private horses or baggage. This done, each officer and man will be allowed to return to their homes, not to be disturbed by United States authority so long as they observe their paroles and the laws in force where they may reside.

Very respectfully,

U. S. GRANT,<br>
Lt. Gen.

When I put my pen to the paper I did not know the first word that I should make use of in writing the terms. I only knew what was in my mind, and I wished to express it clearly, so that there could be no mistaking it. As I wrote on, the thought occurred to me that the officers had their own private horses and

---

[16] Ely S. Parker (1828–1895) was born in New York and became chief of the Tonawanda Senecas and later Grand Sachem of the Six Indian Nations (Iroquois). He was initially refused entry into the U.S. Army because of his ethnicity, but in 1863 entered the military as a captain. In June 1864 he became an aide-de-camp to USG and in Aug. was promoted to lieutenant colonel and military secretary to USG. During USG's presidency, Parker was U.S. commissioner of Indian affairs from 1869 to 1871. Ibid., 416; Arthur C. Parker, *The Life of General Ely S. Parker* (Buffalo, NY: Buffalo Historical Society, 1919), 102–103.

effects, which were important to them, but of no value to us; also that it would be an unnecessary humiliation to call upon them to deliver their side arms.

No conversation, not one word, passed between General Lee and myself, either about private property, side arms, or kindred subjects. He appeared to have no objections to the terms first proposed; or if he had a point to make against them he wished to wait until they were in writing to make it. When he read over that part of the terms about side arms, horses and private property of the officers, he remarked, with some feeling, I thought, that this would have a happy effect upon his army.

Then, after a little further conversation, General Lee remarked to me again that their army was organized a little differently from the army of the United States (still maintaining by implication that we were two countries); that in their army the cavalrymen and artillerists owned their own horses; and he asked if he was to understand that the men who so owned their horses were to be permitted to retain them. I told him that as the terms were written they would not; that only the officers were permitted to take their private property. He then, after reading over the terms a second time, remarked that that was clear.

I then said to him that I thought this would be about the last battle of the war—I sincerely hoped so; and I said further I took it that most of the men in the ranks were small farmers. The whole country had been so raided by the two armies that it was doubtful whether they would be able to put in a crop to carry themselves and their families through the next winter without the aid of the horses they were then riding. The United States did not want them and I would, therefore, instruct the officers I left behind to receive the paroles of his troops to let every man of the Confederate army who claimed to own a horse or mule take the animal to his home. Lee remarked again that this would have a happy effect.

He then sat down and wrote out the following letter:

HEADQUARTERS ARMY OF NORTHERN VIRGINIA,
*April 9, 1865.*

GENERAL:—I received your letter of this date containing the terms of the surrender of the Army of Northern Virginia as proposed by you. As they are substantially the same as those expressed in your letter of the 8th inst., they are accepted. I will proceed to designate the proper officers to carry the stipulations into effect.

R. E. LEE, General.
LIEUT.-GENERAL U. S. GRANT.

While duplicates of the two letters were being made, the Union generals present were severally presented to General Lee.

The much talked of surrendering of Lee's sword and my handing it back, this and much more that has been said about it is the purest romance.[17] The word sword or side arms was not mentioned by either of us until I wrote it in the terms. There was no premeditation, and it did not occur to me until the moment I wrote it down. If I had happened to omit it, and General Lee had called my attention to it, I should have put it in the terms precisely as I acceded to the provision about the soldiers retaining their horses.

General Lee, after all was completed and before taking his leave, remarked that his army was in a very bad condition for want of food, and that they were without forage; that his men had been living for some days on parched corn exclusively, and that he would have to ask me for rations and forage. I told him "certainly," and asked for how many men he wanted rations. His answer was "about twenty-five thousand:" and I authorized him to send his own commissary and quartermaster to Appomattox Station, two or three miles away, where he could have, out of the trains we had stopped, all the provisions wanted.[18] As for forage, we had ourselves depended almost entirely upon the country for that.

Generals Gibbon, Griffin and Merritt were designated by me to carry into effect the paroling of Lee's troops before they should start for their homes— General Lee leaving Generals Longstreet, Gordon and Pendleton[19] for them to confer with in order to facilitate this work. Lee and I then separated as cordially as we had met, he returning to his own lines, and all went into bivouac for the night at Appomattox.

---

[17] Days after the surrender, some newspapers reported the sword myth as fact. The myth spread across the country, but it was later dismissed by people who witnessed the surrender, including Lee. "Capitulation of Lee's Army," *Anderson [SC] Intelligencer,* Apr. 27, 1865; Jones, *Personal Reminiscences,* 303–304.

[18] USG ordered Col. Michael R. Morgan to arrange and issue rations to the defeated Confederates. In Apr. 1865, Robert G. Cole (c.1828–1887) served as Lee's chief commissary. Jefferson Davis, *The Papers of Jefferson Davis, 1861,* vol. 8, ed. Lynda L. Crist and Mary S. Dix (Baton Rouge: Louisiana State University Press, 1995), 381; Porter, "Surrender at Appomattox Court House," 742.

[19] William N. Pendleton (1809–1883) was born in Virginia and graduated from the USMA in 1830. He accepted a commission as a captain in the Confederate Art. in Mar. 1861 and rose to brigadier general by Mar. 1862. *CWHC,* 424.

Soon after Lee's departure I telegraphed to Washington as follows:

> HEADQUARTERS APPOMATTOX C. H., VA.,
> *April* 9th, 1865, 4.30 P.M.
>
> HON. E. M. STANTON, Secretary of War,
> Washington.
>   General Lee surrendered the Army of Northern Virginia this afternoon on terms proposed by myself. The accompanying additional correspondence will show the conditions fully.
>
> U. S. GRANT,
> Lieut.-General.[20]

When news of the surrender first reached our lines our men commenced firing a salute of a hundred guns in honor of the victory. I at once sent word, however, to have it stopped. The Confederates were now our prisoners, and we did not want to exult over their downfall.

I determined to return to Washington at once, with a view to putting a stop to the purchase of supplies, and what I now deemed other useless outlay of money. Before leaving, however, I thought I* would like to see General Lee

*NOTE.—The fac-simile of the terms of Lee's surrender inserted at this place, was copied from the original document furnished the publishers through the courtesy of General Ely S. Parker, Military Secretary on General Grant's staff at the time of the surrender.[21]

Three pages of paper were prepared in General Grant's manifold order book on which he wrote the terms, and the interlineations and erasures were added by General Parker at the suggestion of General Grant. After such alteration it was handed to General Lee, who put on his glasses, read it, and handed it back to General Grant. The original was then transcribed by General Parker upon official headed paper and a copy furnished General Lee.

The fac-simile herewith shows the color of the paper of the original document and all interlineations and erasures.

There is a popular error to the effect that Generals Grant and Lee each signed the articles of surrender. The document in the form of a letter was signed only by General Grant, in the parlor of McLean's house while General Lee was sitting in the room, and General Lee immediately wrote a letter accepting the terms and handed it to General Grant. This letter is copied on page 494.[22]

PUBLISHERS.

[20] See *PUSG*, 14:375n.
[21] USG's Apr. 9, 1865, letter to Lee outlining the terms is not reproduced in this edition. For its transcription and contextual notes, see ibid., 14:373–374, 374n–376n.
[22] See Lee's Apr. 9, 1865, letter to USG reprinted earlier in this chapter.

again; so next morning I rode out beyond our lines towards his headquarters, preceded by a bugler and a staff-officer carrying a white flag.

Lee soon mounted his horse, seeing who it was, and met me. We had there between the lines, sitting on horseback, a very pleasant conversation of over half an hour, in the course of which Lee said to me that the South was a big country and that we might have to march over it three or four times before the war entirely ended, but that we would now be able to do it as they could no longer resist us. He expressed it as his earnest hope, however, that we would not be called upon to cause more loss and sacrifice of life; but he could not foretell the result. I then suggested to General Lee that there was not a man in the Confederacy whose influence with the soldiery and the whole people was as great as his, and that if he would now advise the surrender of all the armies I had no doubt his advice would be followed with alacrity. But Lee said, that he could not do that without consulting the President first. I knew there was no use to urge him to do anything against his ideas of what was right.

I was accompanied by my staff and other officers, some of whom seemed to have a great desire to go inside the Confederate lines. They finally asked permission of Lee to do so for the purpose of seeing some of their old army friends, and the permission was granted. They went over, had a very pleasant time with their old friends, and brought some of them back with them when they returned.[23]

When Lee and I separated he went back to his lines and I returned to the house of Mr. McLean. Here the officers of both armies came in great numbers, and seemed to enjoy the meeting as much as though they had been friends separated for a long time while fighting battles under the same flag. For the time being it looked very much as if all thought of the war had escaped their minds. After an hour pleasantly passed in this way I set out on horseback, accompanied by my staff and a small escort, for Burkesville Junction, up to which point the railroad had by this time been repaired.

---

[23] In addition to his staff, USG was accompanied by Sheridan, Ord, Griffin, and other officers. Sheridan, Ingalls, and Williams received permission to cross over Confederate lines to converse with their old friends. Adam Badeau, *Military History of Ulysses S. Grant, from April, 1861, to April, 1865* (New York: D. Appleton, 1881), 3:609, 611.

# 68

Morale of the Two Armies—Relative Conditions of
the North and South—President Lincoln Visits
Richmond—Arrival at Washington—President
Lincoln's Assassination—President Johnson's Policy

AFTER THE FALL of Petersburg, and when the armies of the Potomac and
the James were in motion to head off Lee's army, the *morale* of the National
troops had greatly improved. There was no more straggling, no more rear
guards. The men who in former times had been falling back, were now, as I
have already stated, striving to get to the front. For the first time in four weary
years they felt that they were now nearing the time when they could return to
their homes with their country saved. On the other hand, the Confederates
were more than correspondingly depressed. Their despondency increased
with each returning day, and especially after the battle of Sailor's Creek. They
threw away their arms in constantly increasing numbers, dropping out of the
ranks and betaking themselves to the woods in the hope of reaching their
homes. I have already instanced the case of the entire disintegration of a regiment whose colonel I met at Farmville. As a result of these and other influ-
ences, when Lee finally surrendered at Appomattox, there were only 28,356
officers and men left to be paroled, and many of these were without arms. It
was probably this latter fact which gave rise to the statement sometimes made,
North and South, that Lee surrendered a smaller number of men than what
the official figures show. As a matter of official record, and in addition to the
number paroled as given above, we captured between March 29th and the
date of surrender 19,132 Confederates, to say nothing of Lee's other losses, killed,
wounded and missing, during the series of desperate conflicts which marked
his headlong and determined flight. The same record shows the number of

cannon, including those at Appomattox, to have been 689 between the dates named.[1]

There has always been a great conflict of opinion as to the number of troops engaged in every battle, or all important battles, fought between the sections, the South magnifying the number of Union troops engaged and belittling their own. Northern writers have fallen, in many instances, into the same error. I have often heard gentlemen, who were thoroughly loyal to the Union, speak of what a splendid fight the South had made and successfully continued for four years before yielding, with their twelve million of people against our twenty, and of the twelve four being colored slaves, non-combatants. I will add to their argument. We had many regiments of brave and loyal men who volunteered under great difficulty from the twelve million belonging to the South.[2]

But the South had rebelled against the National government. It was not bound by any constitutional restrictions. The whole South was a military camp. The occupation of the colored people was to furnish supplies for the army. Conscription was resorted to early,[3] and embraced every male from the age of eighteen to forty-five, excluding only those physically unfit to serve in the field, and the necessary number of civil officers of State and intended National government. The old and physically disabled furnished a good portion of these. The slaves, the non-combatants, one-third of the whole, were required to work in the field without regard to sex, and almost without regard to age. Children from the age of eight years could and did handle the hoe; they were not much older when they began to hold the plough. The four million of colored non-combatants were equal to more than three times their number in the North, age for age and sex for sex, in supplying food from the soil to support

---

[1] According to an 1868 report by Asst. AG Samuel Breck, the U.S. Army captured 46,495 Confederate troops between Mar. 29 and Apr. 9, 1865, in addition to the 27,416 Confederate troops paroled at Appomattox Court House, VA. Adam Badeau, *Military History of Ulysses S. Grant, from April, 1861, to April, 1865* (New York: D. Appleton, 1881), 3:692.

[2] There were approximately 22 million people in the North and 9 million in the South, of whom some 3.5 million were slaves. Mary Ellen Snodgrass, *The Civil War and Reconstruction: An Encyclopedia of Social, Political, Cultural, and Economic History* (London: Routledge, 2015), 2:487.

[3] Passed on Apr. 16, 1862, the Confederate Conscription Act was the first such conscription in American history. Spencer Tucker, ed., *American Civil War: The Definitive Encyclopedia and Document Collection* (Santa Barbara, CA: ABC-CLIO, 2013), s.v. "Conscription Acts (April 16, 1862, and March 3, 1863)."

armies. Women did not work in the fields in the North, and children attended school.[4]

The arts of peace were carried on in the North. Towns and cities grew during the war. Inventions were made in all kinds of machinery to increase the products of a day's labor in the shop, and in the field. In the South no opposition was allowed to the government which had been set up and which would have become real and respected if the rebellion had been successful. No rear had to be protected. All the troops in service could be brought to the front to contest every inch of ground threatened with invasion. The press of the South, like the people who remained at home, were loyal to the Southern cause.

In the North, the country, the towns and the cities presented about the same appearance they do in time of peace. The furnace was in blast, the shops were filled with workmen, the fields were cultivated, not only to supply the population of the North and the troops invading the South, but to ship abroad to pay a part of the expense of the war. In the North the press was free up to the point of open treason. The citizen could entertain his views and express them. Troops were necessary in the Northern States to prevent prisoners from the Southern army being released by outside force, armed and set at large to destroy by fire our Northern cities. Plans were formed by Northern and Southern citizens to burn our cities, to poison the water supplying them, to spread infection by importing clothing from infected regions, to blow up our river and lake steamers—regardless of the destruction of innocent lives.[5] The copperhead disreputable portion of the press magnified rebel successes, and belittled those of the Union army. It was, with a large following, an auxiliary to the Confederate army. The North would have been much stronger with a hun-

---

[4] In his 1863 annual report, Commissioner of Agriculture Isaac Newton cited immigrants and "maturing youth" as the main source of field labor in the North. Mary Livingston, chair of the Chicago branch of the U.S. Sanitary Commission, indicated that she observed countless Northern women involved in planting, cultivating, and harvesting during the war. Judith Giesberg, *Army at Home: Women and the Civil War on the Northern Home Front* (Chapel Hill: University of North Carolina Press, 2009), 17–18.

[5] In Apr. 1865, rumors spread that Southerners led by Dr. Luke P. Blackburn plotted to spread yellow fever in New York City using infected clothing. Later that year he was tried and acquitted of any wrongdoing. In addition, rumors circulated that Confederates operating from Canada planned to poison New York City's Central Park Reservoir and blow up the Croton Dam. Nancy D. Baird, *Luke Pryor Blackburn: Physician, Governor, Reformer* (Lexington: University Press of Kentucky, 2015), 31; Edward K. Spann, *Gotham at War: New York City, 1860–1865* (Wilmington, DE: Scholarly Resources, 2002), 164.

dred thousand of these men in the Confederate ranks and the rest of their kind thoroughly subdued, as the Union sentiment was in the South, than we were as the battle was fought.

As I have said, the whole South was a military camp. The colored people, four million in number, were submissive, and worked in the field and took care of the families while the able-bodied white men were at the front fighting for a cause destined to defeat.[6] The cause was popular, and was enthusiastically supported by the young men. The conscription took all of them. Before the war was over, further conscriptions took those between fourteen and eighteen years of age as junior reserves, and those between forty-five and sixty as senior reserves. It would have been an offence, directly after the war, and perhaps it would be now, to ask any able-bodied man in the South, who was between the ages of fourteen and sixty at any time during the war, whether he had been in the Confederate army. He would assert that he had, or account for his absence from the ranks. Under such circumstances it is hard to conceive how the North showed such a superiority of force in every battle fought. I know they did not.[7]

During 1862 and '3, John H. Morgan, a partisan officer, of no military education, but possessed of courage and endurance, operated in the rear of the Army of the Ohio in Kentucky and Tennessee. He had no base of supplies to protect, but was at home wherever he went. The army operating against the South, on the contrary, had to protect its lines of communication with the North, from which all supplies had to come to the front. Every foot of road had to be guarded by troops stationed at convenient distances apart. These guards could not render assistance beyond the points where stationed. Morgan was foot-loose and could operate where his information—always correct—led him to believe he could do the greatest damage. During the time he was operating in this way he killed, wounded and captured several times the number he ever had under his command at any one time. He destroyed many millions of property in addition. Places he did not attack had to be guarded as if threatened by him.[8] Forrest, an abler soldier, operated farther west, and held

[6] For discussion of the types of active resistance to the Confederate war effort undertaken by enslaved people, see James M. McPherson, *The Negro's Civil War* (New York: Pantheon, 1965).

[7] Most battles involved either near-equal opposing forces or U.S. Army numerical superiority. For a convenient synopsis of statistical information on the Civil War, see Thomas L. Livermore, *Numbers and Losses in the Civil War in America, 1861–65* (Boston: Houghton, Mifflin, 1900).

[8] For a summary of Morgan's multiple raids throughout the Civil War, see Tucker, *American Civil War*, s.v. "Morgan, John Hunt."

from the National front quite as many men as could be spared for offensive operations. It is safe to say that more than half the National army was engaged in guarding lines of supplies, or were on leave, sick in hospital or on detail which prevented their bearing arms. Then, again, large forces were employed where no Confederate army confronted them. I deem it safe to say that there were no large engagements where the National numbers compensated for the advantage of position and intrenchment occupied by the enemy.

While I was in pursuit of General Lee, the President went to Richmond in company with Admiral Porter, and on board his flagship.[9] He found the people of that city in great consternation. The leading citizens among the people who had remained at home surrounded him, anxious that something should be done to relieve them from suspense. General Weitzel was not then in the city, having taken offices in one of the neighboring villages after his troops had succeeded in subduing the conflagration which they had found in progress on entering the Confederate capital. The President sent for him, and, on his arrival, a short interview was had on board the vessel, Admiral Porter and a leading citizen of Virginia being also present.[10] After this interview the President wrote an order in about these words, which I quote from memory: "General Weitzel is authorized to permit the body calling itself the Legislature of Virginia to meet for the purpose of recalling the Virginia troops from the Confederate armies."

Immediately some of the gentlemen composing that body wrote out a call for a meeting and had it published in their papers. This call, however, went very much further than Mr. Lincoln had contemplated, as he did not say the "Legislature of Virginia" but "the body which called itself the Legislature of Virginia." Mr. Stanton saw the call as published in the Northern papers the very next issue and took the liberty of countermanding the order authorizing any meeting of the Legislature, or any other body, and this notwithstanding the fact that the President was nearer the spot than he was.[11]

---

[9] On Apr. 4, 1865, Lincoln left City Point, VA, aboard *River Queen* and met Porter on *Malvern*. *Malvern* arrived in Richmond, VA, later that day. William C. Harris, *Lincoln's Last Months* (Cambridge, MA: Harvard University Press, 2004), 204.

[10] This "leading citizen of Virginia" was John A. Campbell, former U.S. Supreme Court associate justice and Confederate assistant secretary of war. During the Civil War, he acted as mediator between the United States and Confederate governments, meeting with Lincoln on Apr. 4, 1865, to discuss an end to hostilities. Ibid., 205–206.

[11] Lincoln's exact wording in that portion of the Apr. 6, 1865, orders to Weitzel was as follows: "It has been intimated to me that the gentlemen who have acted as the legislature of

This was characteristic of Mr. Stanton. He was a man who never questioned his own authority, and who always did in war time what he wanted to do. He was an able constitutional lawyer and jurist; but the Constitution was not an impediment to him while the war lasted. In this latter particular I entirely agree with the view he evidently held. The Constitution was not framed with a view to any such rebellion as that of 1861–5. While it did not authorize rebellion it made no provision against it. Yet the right to resist or suppress rebellion is as inherent as the right of self-defence, and as natural as the right of an individual to preserve his life when in jeopardy. The Constitution was therefore in abeyance for the time being, so far as it in any way affected the progress and termination of the war.

Those in rebellion against the government of the United States were not restricted by constitutional provisions, or any other, except the acts of their Congress, which was loyal and devoted to the cause for which the South was then fighting. It would be a hard case when one-third of a nation, united in rebellion against the national authority, is entirely untrammeled, that the other two-thirds, in their efforts to maintain the Union intact, should be restrained by a Constitution prepared by our ancestors for the express purpose of insuring the permanency of the confederation of the States.

After I left General Lee at Appomattox Station, I went with my staff and a few others directly to Burkesville Station on my way to Washington. The road from Burkesville back having been newly repaired and the ground being soft, the train got off the track frequently, and, as a result, it was after midnight of the second day when I reached City Point. As soon as possible I took a dispatch-boat thence to Washington City.[12]

While in Washington I was very busy for a time in preparing the necessary orders for the new state of affairs; communicating with my different

Virginia in support of the rebellion may now desire to assemble at Richmond and take measures to withdraw the Virginia troops and other support from resistance to the General Government." On Apr. 8, 1865, Stanton learned about the meeting via a message from his assistant, Dana. Stanton saw Lincoln's actions as allowing Virginia to effectively resume statehood, derailing Republican plans for reconstruction. The next day, Stanton ordered Weitzel to "hold no further conference with Mr. Campbell on any subject without specific authority, to be given by the President or this Department." William Marvel, *Lincoln's Autocrat: The Life of Edwin Stanton* (Chapel Hill: University of North Carolina Press, 2015), 366–367; *OR,* I, 46(III), 612, 678. For Lincoln's correspondence with USG relating to the matter, see *PUSG,* 14:355*n*–356*n*.

[12] On the evening of Apr. 10, 1865, USG left from Prospect Station on the South Side Railroad, arriving at Burke's Station the next day. On Apr. 12, he arrived at City Point and left for Washington, DC, that afternoon. Ibid., 14:xxv.

commanders of separate departments, bodies of troops, etc. But by the 14th I was pretty well through with this work, so as to be able to visit my children, who were then in Burlington, New Jersey, attending school.[13] Mrs. Grant was with me in Washington at the time, and we were invited by President and Mrs. Lincoln to accompany them to the theatre on the evening of that day. I replied to the President's verbal invitation to the effect, that if we were in the city we would take great pleasure in accompanying them; but that I was very anxious to get away and visit my children, and if I could get through my work during the day I should do so. I did get through and started by the evening train on the 14th, sending Mr. Lincoln word, of course, that I would not be at the theatre.[14]

At that time the railroad to New York entered Philadelphia on Broad Street; passengers were conveyed in ambulances to the Delaware River, and then ferried to Camden, at which point they took the cars again. When I reached the ferry, on the east side of the City of Philadelphia, I found people awaiting my arrival there; and also dispatches informing me of the assassination of the President and Mr. Seward, and of the probable assassination of the Vice-President, Mr. Johnson, and requesting my immediate return.[15]

It would be impossible for me to describe the feeling that overcame me at the news of these assassinations, more especially the assassination of the President. I knew his goodness of heart, his generosity, his yielding disposition, his

[13] Starting in Sept. 1864, USG's family stayed at 304 Wood Street in Burlington, NJ. USG's daughter, Nellie, attended school at St. Mary's Hall, while his sons FDG and Buck attended Burlington College. Michael W. Kauffman, *American Brutus: John Wilkes Booth and the Lincoln Conspiracies* (New York: Random House, 2004), 402*n*; Jack H. Newman, *St. Mary's Hall and Doane Academy* (Charleston, SC: Arcadia, 2012), 26.

[14] At 11:00 A.M. on Apr. 14, 1865, USG met with Lincoln in the White House. Lincoln invited USG and JDG to join him and his wife, Mary Todd Lincoln, at Ford's Theatre later that night. USG consulted with JDG, who sent a note to the White House declining the invitation because of her desire to see their children in Burlington. William S. McFeely, *Grant: A Biography* (New York: Norton, 1981), 223–224.

[15] At 12:20 A.M. on Apr. 15, 1865, Maj. Thomas T. Eckert sent a message to USG describing the murder of Lincoln and the attack on Seward and requesting USG's return to Washington, DC. Seward survived the attack. There were rumors and concerns that USG would be assassinated as well. Confederate sympathizer George Atzerodt intended to assassinate Vice President Andrew Johnson but did not follow through with his plans. Later that year, Atzerodt was convicted and hanged along with three other coconspirators in the plot to assassinate Lincoln. *CWHC,* 479; McFeely, *Grant,* 224–225; *PUSG,* 14:390*n*; Edward Steers Jr. and Harold Holzer, *The Lincoln Assassination Conspirators: Their Confinement and Execution, as Recorded in the Letterbook of John Frederick Hartranft* (Baton Rouge: Louisiana State University Press, 2009), 26, 48.

desire to have everybody happy, and above all his desire to see all the people of the United States enter again upon the full privileges of citizenship with equality among all. I knew also the feeling that Mr. Johnson had expressed in speeches and conversation against the Southern people, and I feared that his course towards them would be such as to repel, and make them unwilling citizens;[16] and if they became such they would remain so for a long while. I felt that reconstruction had been set back, no telling how far.

I immediately arranged for getting a train to take me back to Washington City; but Mrs. Grant was with me; it was after midnight and Burlington was but an hour away. Finding that I could accompany her to our house and return about as soon as they would be ready to take me from the Philadelphia station, I went up with her and returned immediately by the same special train. The joy that I had witnessed among the people in the street and in public places in Washington when I left there, had been turned to grief; the city was in reality a city of mourning. I have stated what I believed then the effect of this would be, and my judgment now is that I was right. I believe the South would have been saved from very much of the hardness of feeling that was engendered by Mr. Johnson's course towards them during the first few months of his administration. Be this as it may, Mr. Lincoln's assassination was particularly unfortunate for the entire nation.

Mr. Johnson's course towards the South did engender bitterness of feeling. His denunciations of treason and his ever-ready remark, "Treason is a crime and must be made odious,"[17] was repeated to all those men of the South who came to him to get some assurances of safety so that they might go to work at something with the feeling that what they obtained would be secure to them. He uttered his denunciations with great vehemence, and as they were accompanied with no assurances of safety, many Southerners were driven to a point almost beyond endurance.

The President of the United States is, in a large degree, or ought to be, a representative of the feeling, wishes and judgment of those over whom he presides; and the Southerners who read the denunciations of themselves and

[16] On Apr. 3, 1865, Johnson delivered a speech in Washington, DC, celebrating the fall of Richmond. In reference to those who fought in the Confederate Army, Johnson said: "I would arrest them. I would try them. I would convict them, and I would hang them." Andrew Johnson, *The Papers of Andrew Johnson*, vol. 7, ed. LeRoy P. Graf (Knoxville: University of Tennessee Press, 1986), 544.

[17] Johnson made this remark in an Apr. 21, 1865, public speech to a delegation from Indiana led by Gov. Oliver P. Morton. Johnson, *Papers*, 7:612, 615.

their people must have come to the conclusion that he uttered the sentiments of the Northern people; whereas, as a matter of fact, but for the assassination of Mr. Lincoln, I believe the great majority of the Northern people, and the soldiers unanimously, would have been in favor of a speedy reconstruction on terms that would be the least humiliating to the people who had rebelled against their government. They believed, I have no doubt, as I did, that besides being the mildest, it was also the wisest, policy. The people who had been in rebellion must necessarily come back into the Union, and be incorporated as an integral part of the nation. Naturally the nearer they were placed to an equality with the people who had not rebelled, the more reconciled they would feel with their old antagonists, and the better citizens they would be from the beginning. They surely would not make good citizens if they felt that they had a yoke around their necks.

I do not believe that the majority of the Northern people at that time were in favor of negro suffrage. They supposed that it would naturally follow the freedom of the negro, but that there would be a time of probation, in which the ex-slaves could prepare themselves for the privileges of citizenship before the full right would be conferred; but Mr. Johnson, after a complete revolution of sentiment, seemed to regard the South not only as an oppressed people, but as the people best entitled to consideration of any of our citizens. This was more than the people who had secured to us the perpetuation of the Union were prepared for, and they became more radical in their views. The Southerners had the most power in the executive branch, Mr. Johnson having gone to their side; and with a compact South, and such sympathy and support as they could get from the North, they felt that they would be able to control the nation at once, and already many of them acted as if they thought they were entitled to do so.

Thus Mr. Johnson, fighting Congress on the one hand, and receiving the support of the South on the other, drove Congress, which was overwhelmingly republican, to the passing of first one measure and then another to restrict his power.[18] There being a solid South on one side that was in accord with the political party in the North which had sympathized with the rebellion, it finally, in the judgment of Congress and of the majority of the legislatures of the States, became necessary to enfranchise the negro, in all his

[18] These acts included the Military Reconstruction Act, the Command of the Army Act, and the Tenure of Office Act. Ibid., 12:xii–xiii.

ignorance.[19] In this work, I shall not discuss the question of how far the policy of Congress in this particular proved a wise one. It became an absolute necessity, however, because of the foolhardiness of the President and the blindness of the Southern people to their own interest. As to myself, while strongly favoring the course that would be the least humiliating to the people who had been in rebellion, I gradually worked up to the point where, with the majority of the people, I favored immediate enfranchisement.

[19] In July 1868, the Fourteenth Amendment was ratified, guaranteeing citizenship to African Americans. In Feb. 1870, the Fifteenth Amendment was ratified, granting voting rights to men regardless of "race, color, or previous condition of servitude." John R. Vile, *Encyclopedia of Constitutional Amendments, Proposed Amendments, and Amending Issues, 1789–2002* (Santa Barbara, CA: ABC-CLIO, 2003), s.vv. "Fourteenth Amendment"; "Fifteenth Amendment."

# 69

## Sherman and Johnston—Johnston's Surrender to Sherman—Capture of Mobile—Wilson's Expedition—Capture of Jefferson Davis—General Thomas's Qualities—Estimate of General Canby

W HEN I LEFT Appomattox I ordered General Meade to proceed leisurely back to Burkesville Station with the Army of the Potomac and the Army of the James, and to go into camp there until further orders from me.[1] General Johnston, as has been stated before, was in North Carolina confronting General Sherman. It could not be known positively, of course, whether Johnston would surrender on the news of Lee's surrender, though I supposed he would; and if he did not, Burkesville Station was the natural point from which to move to attack him. The army which I could have sent against him was superior to his, and that with which Sherman confronted him was also superior; and between the two he would necessarily have been crushed, or driven away. With the loss of their capital and the Army of Northern Virginia it was doubtful whether Johnston's men would have the spirit to stand. My belief was that he would make no such attempt; but I adopted this course as a precaution against what might happen, however improbable.

Simultaneously with my starting from City Point, I sent a messenger to North Carolina by boat with dispatches to General Sherman, informing him of the surrender of Lee and his army;[2] also of the terms which I had given

---

[1] On Apr. 9, 1865, Parker sent Meade USG's order to return to Burkesville Station, VA. *PUSG*, 14:378*n*.

[2] On Apr. 9, 1865, Bowers, at Appomattox Court House, VA, telegraphed Sherman the terms of surrender between USG and Lee. Sherman stated that he received the message on Apr. 12. *OR*, I, 47(III), 140; *PUSG*, 14:375*n*; William T. Sherman, *Memoirs of General William T. Sherman* (New York: D. Appleton, 1875), 2:344.

him; and I authorized Sherman to give the same terms to Johnston if the latter chose to accept them. The country is familiar with the terms that Sherman agreed to *conditionally*, because they embraced a political question as well as a military one and he would therefore have to confer with the government before agreeing to them definitely.[3]

General Sherman had met Mr. Lincoln at City Point while visiting there to confer with me about our final movement,[4] and knew what Mr. Lincoln had said to the peace commissioners when he met them at Hampton Roads, viz.: that before he could enter into negotiations with them they would have to agree to two points: one being that the Union should be preserved, and the other that slavery should be abolished; and if they were ready to concede these two points he was almost ready to sign his name to a blank piece of paper and permit them to fill out the balance of the terms upon which we would live together. He had also seen notices in the newspapers of Mr. Lincoln's visit to Richmond, and had read in the same papers that while there he had authorized the convening of the Legislature of Virginia.

Sherman thought, no doubt, in adding to the terms that I had made with General Lee, that he was but carrying out the wishes of the President of the United States. But seeing that he was going beyond his authority, he made it a point that the terms were only conditional. They signed them with this understanding, and agreed to a truce until the terms could be sent to Washington for approval; if approved by the proper authorities there, they would then be final; if not approved, then he would give due notice, before resuming hostilities. As the world knows, Sherman, from being one of the most popular generals of the land (Congress having even gone so far as to propose a bill providing for a second lieutenant-general for the purpose of advancing him to that grade), was denounced by the President and Secretary of War in very bitter terms.[5] Some

---

[3] On Apr. 18, 1865, Sherman and Johnston signed a "memorandum or basis of agreement" that halted all hostilities between their two armies. It also included additional terms that related to political matters, such as the recognition, by the president, of state governments dependent upon their representatives signing an oath to the Constitution, the reestablishment of federal courts in the former Confederate states, and general amnesty. David J. Eicher, *The Longest Night: A Military History of the Civil War* (New York: Simon and Schuster, 2001), 835. For a copy of this memorandum, see Sherman, *Memoirs*, 2:356–357.

[4] Sherman, USG, and Porter met with Lincoln aboard *River Queen* at City Point, VA, on Mar. 27, 1865. Eicher, *Longest Night*, 804–806.

[5] On Apr. 21, 1865, Stanton informed USG that he and President Johnson disapproved of the terms proposed by Sherman. In relation to Sherman's promotion, USG wrote to Stanton on

people went so far as to denounce him as a traitor—a most preposterous term to apply to a man who had rendered so much service as he had, even supposing he had made a mistake in granting such terms as he did to Johnston and his army. If Sherman had taken authority to send Johnston with his army home, with their arms to be put in the arsenals of their own States, without submitting the question to the authorities at Washington, the suspicions against him might have some foundation. But the feeling against Sherman died out very rapidly, and it was not many weeks before he was restored to the fullest confidence of the American people.

When, some days after my return to Washington, President Johnson and the Secretary of War received the terms which General Sherman had forwarded for approval, a cabinet meeting was immediately called and I was sent for. There seemed to be the greatest consternation, lest Sherman would commit the government to terms which they were not willing to accede to and which he had no right to grant. A message went out directing the troops in the South not to obey General Sherman. I was ordered to proceed at once to North Carolina and take charge of matters there myself. Of course I started without delay, and reached there as soon as possible. I repaired to Raleigh, where Sherman was, as quietly as possible, hoping to see him without even his army learning of my presence.[6]

When I arrived I went to Sherman's headquarters, and we were at once closeted together. I showed him the instructions and orders under which I visited him.[7] I told him that I wanted him to notify General Johnston that the terms which they had conditionally agreed upon had not been approved in Washington, and that he was authorized to offer the same terms I had given General Lee. I sent Sherman to do this himself. I did not wish the knowledge of

July 25, 1866, suggesting that Sherman be promoted to lieutenant general. Three days later, Johnson told Rawlins that he had already called for Sherman to be promoted to the position. On Aug. 1, Sherman, accompanied by USG, received his commission as lieutenant general in Washington, DC. *PUSG,* 14:423*n*; 16:261, 262*n*–263*n*.

[6] A cabinet meeting was called on Apr. 21, 1865, to discuss the terms of surrender forwarded by Sherman. The terms were not approved and USG was sent to North Carolina to manage the situation. He left Washington, DC, that night and arrived in Raleigh, NC, on Apr. 24. Ibid., 14:xxvi. For Sherman's response to accusations against him by Halleck and Stanton, see John F. Marszalek, *Sherman: A Soldier's Passion for Order* (New York: Free Press, 1993), 349–353.

[7] When he arrived in Raleigh, USG gave Sherman his Apr. 21, 1865, written correspondence with Stanton outlining President Johnson's disapproval of the terms of surrender proposed by Sherman and Johnston. Sherman, *Memoirs,* 2:358–359, 362.

my presence to be known to the army generally; so I left it to Sherman to negotiate the terms of the surrender solely by himself, and without the enemy knowing that I was anywhere near the field. As soon as possible I started to get away, to leave Sherman quite free and untrammelled.

At Goldsboro', on my way back, I met a mail, containing the last newspapers, and I found in them indications of great excitement in the North over the terms Sherman had given Johnston; and harsh orders that had been promulgated by the President and Secretary of War. I knew that Sherman must see these papers, and I fully realized what great indignation they would cause him, though I do not think his feelings could have been more excited than were my own. But like the true and loyal soldier that he was, he carried out the instructions I had given him, obtained the surrender of Johnston's army, and settled down in his camp about Raleigh, to await final orders.[8]

There were still a few expeditions out in the South that could not be communicated with, and had to be left to act according to the judgment of their respective commanders. With these it was impossible to tell how the news of the surrender of Lee and Johnston, of which they must have heard, might affect their judgment as to what was best to do.

The three expeditions which I had tried so hard to get off from the commands of Thomas and Canby did finally get off: one under Canby himself, against Mobile, late in March;[9] that under Stoneman from East Tennessee on the 20th; and the one under Wilson, starting from Eastport, Mississippi, on the 22d of March. They were all eminently successful, but without any good result. Indeed much valuable property was destroyed and many lives lost at a time when we would have liked to spare them. The war was practically over before their victories were gained. They were so late in commencing operations, that they did not hold any troops away that otherwise would have been operating against the armies which were gradually forcing the Confederate armies to a surrender. The only possible good that we may have experienced from these raids was by Stoneman's getting near Lynchburg about the time the armies of the Potomac and the James were closing in on Lee at Appomattox.

[8] In an Apr. 28, 1865, letter to USG, Sherman acknowledged that he had read the Apr. 24 *New York Times,* containing Stanton's critical response to Sherman's initial terms of surrender. Later that night, Sherman met with his corps commanders in Raleigh and established their plans moving forward. Sherman, *Memoirs,* 2:365–368.

[9] On Mar. 5, 1865, Canby left New Orleans, LA, to start his expedition against Mobile, AL, but was delayed along the way. On Mar. 9 USG sent him a telegram urging him to hasten his movement against the city. *PUSG,* 14:124–125, 125*n.*

Stoneman entered North Carolina and then pushed north to strike the Virginia and Tennessee Railroad. He got upon that road, destroyed its bridges at different places and rendered the road useless to the enemy up to within a few miles of Lynchburg. His approach caused the evacuation of that city about the time we were at Appomattox, and was the cause of a commotion we heard of there.[10] He then pushed south, and was operating in the rear of Johnston's army about the time the negotiations were going on between Sherman and Johnston for the latter's surrender.[11] In this raid Stoneman captured and destroyed a large amount of stores, while fourteen guns and nearly two thousand prisoners were the trophies of his success.[12]

Canby appeared before Mobile on the 27th of March. The city of Mobile was protected by two forts, besides other intrenchments—Spanish Fort, on the east side of the bay, and Fort Blakely, north of the city. These forts were invested. On the night of the 8th of April, the National troops having carried the enemy's works at one point, Spanish Fort was evacuated; and on the 9th, the very day of Lee's surrender, Blakely was carried by assault, with a considerable loss to us.[13] On the 11th the city was evacuated.[14]

I had tried for more than two years to have an expedition sent against Mobile when its possession by us would have been of great advantage. It finally cost lives to take it when its possession was of no importance, and when, if left alone, it would within a few days have fallen into our hands without any bloodshed whatever.

Wilson moved out with full 12,000 men, well equipped and well armed. He was an energetic officer and accomplished his work rapidly. Forrest was in his front, but with neither his old-time army nor his old-time prestige. He

---

[10] On Apr. 7, 1865, Stoneman's cavalry destroyed a significant number of Confederate stores approximately ninety miles west of Lynchburg, VA. Charles E. Little, *Cyclopedia of Classified Dates with an Exhaustive Index* (New York: Funk and Wagnalls, 1900), 245.

[11] On Apr. 13, 1865, Stoneman's cavalry had made it to Salisbury, NC. The same day, Johnston, Davis, and his cabinet met approximately fifty miles to the north in Greensboro, NC. Chris J. Hartley, *Stoneman's Raid, 1865* (Winston-Salem, NC: John F. Blair, 2010), 265, 269; *PUSG*, 14:52–53 (map).

[12] Near the end of his expedition through North Carolina, Stoneman reported capturing 1,364 Confederates and fourteen pieces of artillery outside of Salisbury. *OR*, I, 49(I), 324.

[13] At the Battle of Fort Blakely, U.S. forces suffered 682 casualties and captured approximately 3,200 Confederate troops. The Confederate Army did not provide a report of their total casualties. Spencer Tucker, ed., *American Civil War: The Definitive Encyclopedia and Document Collection* (Santa Barbara, CA: ABC-CLIO, 2013), s.v. "Fort Blakely, Alabama, Siege of."

[14] The Confederate Army surrendered Mobile to U.S. forces on Apr. 12, 1865. *PUSG*, 14:xxv.

now had principally conscripts. His conscripts were generally old men and boys. He had a few thousand regular cavalry left, but not enough to even retard materially the progress of Wilson's cavalry. Selma fell on the 2d of April, with a large number of prisoners and a large quantity of war material, machine shops, etc., to be disposed of by the victors.[15] Tuscaloosa, Montgomery and West Point fell in quick succession.[16] These were all important points to the enemy by reason of their railroad connections, as depots of supplies, and because of their manufactories of war material. They were fortified or intrenched, and there was considerable fighting before they were captured. Macon surrendered on the 21st of April. Here news was received of the negotiations for the surrender of Johnston's army. Wilson belonged to the military division commanded by Sherman, and of course was bound by his terms. This stopped all fighting.

General Richard Taylor had now become the senior Confederate officer still at liberty east of the Mississippi River, and on the 4th of May he surrendered everything within the limits of this extensive command. General E. Kirby Smith surrendered the trans-Mississippi department on the 26th of May, leaving no other Confederate army at liberty to continue the war.

Wilson's raid resulted in the capture of the fugitive president of the defunct confederacy before he got out of the country. This occurred at Irwinsville, Georgia, on the 11th of May.[17] For myself, and I believe Mr. Lincoln shared the feeling, I would have been very glad to have seen Mr. Davis succeed in escaping, but for one reason: I feared that if not captured, he might get into the trans-Mississippi region and there set up a more contracted confederacy. The young men now out of homes and out of employment might have rallied under his standard and protracted the war yet another year. The Northern people were tired of the war, they were tired of piling up a debt which would be a further mortgage upon their homes.

Mr. Lincoln, I believe, wanted Mr. Davis to escape, because he did not wish to deal with the matter of his punishment. He knew there would be people clamoring for the punishment of the ex-Confederate president, for high

[15] When Selma, AL, fell on Apr. 2, 1865, the U.S. Army captured some 2,700 Confederates, thirty-two artillery pieces, and a large amount of military supplies. Spencer C. Tucker and Paul G. Pierpaoli Jr., eds., *American Civil War: A State-by-State Encyclopedia* (Santa Barbara, CA: ABC-CLIO, 2015), s.v. "Selma, Battle of (April 2, 1865)."

[16] On Apr. 4, 1865, the U.S. Army occupied Tuscaloosa, AL. Montgomery, AL, was captured on Apr. 12, and West Point, GA, Apr. 16. Eicher, *Longest Night*, 837; *OR*, I, 49(I), 340.

[17] Jefferson Davis was captured on May 10, 1865. *PUSG*, 15:29*n*.

treason. He thought blood enough had already been spilled to atone for our wickedness as a nation. At all events he did not wish to be the judge to decide whether more should be shed or not. But his own life was sacrificed at the hands of an assassin before the ex-president of the Confederacy was a prisoner in the hands of the government which he had lent all his talent and all his energies to destroy.[18]

All things are said to be wisely directed, and for the best interest of all concerned. This reflection does not, however, abate in the slightest our sense of bereavement in the untimely loss of so good and great a man as Abraham Lincoln.

He would have proven the best friend the South could have had, and saved much of the wrangling and bitterness of feeling brought out by reconstruction under a President who at first wished to revenge himself upon Southern men of better social standing than himself, but who still sought their recognition, and in a short time conceived the idea and advanced the proposition to become their Moses to lead them triumphantly out of all their difficulties.

The story of the legislation enacted during the reconstruction period to stay the hands of the President is too fresh in the minds of the people to be told now. Much of it, no doubt, was unconstitutional; but it was hoped that the laws enacted would serve their purpose before the question of constitutionality could be submitted to the judiciary and a decision obtained. These laws did serve their purpose, and now remain "a dead letter" upon the statute books of the United States, no one taking interest enough in them to give them a passing thought.[19]

Much was said at the time about the garb Mr. Davis was wearing when he was captured. I cannot settle this question from personal knowledge of the facts; but I have been under the belief, from information given to me by General Wilson shortly after the event, that when Mr. Davis learned that he was

---

[18] On Apr. 14, 1865, Lincoln was shot in the back of the head while attending a play at Ford's Theatre in Washington, DC, and died early the next morning. He was assassinated by Confederate sympathizer John Wilkes Booth (1838–1865), who was born in Maryland and became an actor. He joined a Richmond militia regiment but did not fight in the Civil War. Booth worked as a Confederate spy and smuggler. William L. Barney, *The Oxford Encyclopedia of the Civil War* (New York: Oxford University Press, 2011), s.v. "Booth, John Wilkes"; *PUSG*, 14:390n.

[19] Such laws as the Freedmen's Bureau Act, Tenure of Office Act, and the Congressional Reconstruction Act of 1867 were among the Reconstruction laws under debate. For further discussion, see Eric Foner, *Reconstruction: America's Unfinished Revolution* (New York: Harper-Perennial, 2014).

surrounded by our cavalry he was in his tent dressed in a gentleman's dressing gown.[20] Naturally enough, Mr. Davis wanted to escape, and would not reflect much how this should be accomplished provided it might be done successfully. If captured, he would be no ordinary prisoner. He represented all there was of that hostility to the government which had caused four years of the bloodiest war—and the most costly in other respects of which history makes any record. Every one supposed he would be tried for treason if captured, and that he would be executed. Had he succeeded in making his escape in any disguise it would have been adjudged a good thing afterwards by his admirers.

As my official letters on file in the War Department, as well as my remarks in this book, reflect upon General Thomas by dwelling somewhat upon his tardiness, it is due to myself, as well as to him, that I give my estimate of him as a soldier. The same remark will apply also in the case of General Canby. I had been at West Point with Thomas one year, and had known him later in the old army.[21] He was a man of commanding appearance, slow and deliberate in speech and action; sensible, honest and brave. He possessed valuable soldierly qualities in an eminent degree. He gained the confidence of all who served under him, and almost their love. This implies a very valuable quality. It is a quality which calls out the most efficient services of the troops serving under the commander possessing it.

Thomas's dispositions were deliberately made, and always good. He could not be driven from a point he was given to hold. He was not as good, however, in pursuit as he was in action. I do not believe that he could ever have conducted Sherman's army from Chattanooga to Atlanta against the defences and the commander guarding that line in 1864. On the other hand, if it had been given him to hold the line which Johnston tried to hold, neither that general nor Sherman, nor any other officer could have done it better.

Thomas was a valuable officer, who richly deserved, as he has received, the plaudits of his countrymen for the part he played in the great tragedy of 1861–5.

General Canby was an officer of great merit. He was naturally studious, and inclined to the law. There have been in the army but very few, if any, officers

---

[20] On May 10, 1865, U.S. cavalry forces captured Davis in Irwinville, GA. During his attempted escape, his wife Varina placed her shawl on his head. Northern newspapers published inaccurate reports that Davis was captured wearing female clothing. Michael B. Ballard, *The Long Shadow: Jefferson Davis and the Final Days of the Confederacy* (Athens: University of Georgia Press, 1997), 142, 155.

[21] Thomas attended the USMA from 1836 to 1840 and USG arrived in July 1839. *CWHC*, 264, 527.

who took as much interest in reading and digesting every act of Congress and every regulation for the government of the army as he. His knowledge gained in this way made him a most valuable staff officer, a capacity in which almost all his army services were rendered up to the time of his being assigned to the Military Division of the Gulf.[22] He was an exceedingly modest officer, though of great talent and learning. I presume his feelings when first called upon to command a large army against a fortified city, were somewhat like my own when marching a regiment against General Thomas Harris in Missouri in 1861. Neither of us would have felt the slightest trepidation in going into battle with some one else commanding. Had Canby been in other engagements afterwards, he would, I have no doubt, have advanced without any fear arising from a sense of the responsibility. He was afterwards killed in the lava beds of Southern Oregon, while in pursuit of the hostile Modoc Indians.[23] His character was as pure as his talent and learning were great. His services were valuable during the war, but principally as a bureau officer. I have no idea that it was from choice that his services were rendered in an office, but because of his superior efficiency there.

[22] Canby was assigned to the Army of the Gulf and the Dept. of the Gulf on June 3, 1865. Ibid., 161.

[23] Canby was killed by Modoc chief Captain Jack during peace talks on Apr. 11, 1873, in Siskiyou County, CA. Boyd Cothran, *Remembering the Modoc War: Redemptive Violence and the Making of American Innocence* (Chapel Hill: University of North Carolina Press, 2014), 48; *CWHC*, 161.

# 70

The End of the War—The March to
Washington—One of Lincoln's Anecdotes—
Grand Review at Washington—Characteristics of
Lincoln and Stanton—Estimate of the
Different Corps Commanders

THINGS BEGAN TO quiet down, and as the certainty that there would be no more armed resistance became clearer, the troops in North Carolina and Virginia were ordered to march immediately to the capital, and go into camp there until mustered out.[1] Suitable garrisons were left at the prominent places throughout the South to insure obedience to the laws that might be enacted for the government of the several States, and to insure security to the lives and property of all classes. I do not know how far this was necessary, but I deemed it necessary, at that time, that such a course should be pursued. I think now that these garrisons were continued after they ceased to be absolutely required; but it is not to be expected that such a rebellion as was fought between the sections from 1861 to 1865 could terminate without leaving many serious apprehensions in the mind of the people as to what should be done.

Sherman marched his troops from Goldsboro, up to Manchester, on the south side of the James River, opposite Richmond, and there put them in camp, while he went back to Savannah to see what the situation was there.[2]

---

[1] On Apr. 29, 1865, USG informed Halleck that on May 1 the army in North Carolina would march for Alexandria, VA. He requested that Halleck order the Army of the Potomac to march to Alexandria as well. *PUSG*, 14:435–436, 436n.

[2] On May 2, 1865, Sherman was in Savannah, GA, to move supplies to Augusta, GA, in preparation for occupying the city. Brooks D. Simpson and Jean V. Berlin, eds., *Sherman's Civil War: Selected Correspondence of William T. Sherman, 1860–1865* (Chapel Hill: University of North Carolina, 1999), 886.

It was during this trip that the last outrage was committed upon him. Halleck had been sent to Richmond to command Virginia, and had issued orders prohibiting even Sherman's own troops from obeying his, Sherman's, orders.[3] Sherman met the papers on his return, containing this order of Halleck, and very justly felt indignant at the outrage. On his arrival at Fortress Monroe returning from Savannah, Sherman received an invitation from Halleck to come to Richmond and be his guest. This he indignantly refused, and informed Halleck, furthermore, that he had seen his order.[4] He also stated that he was coming up to take command of his troops, and as he marched through it would probably be as well for Halleck not to show himself, because he (Sherman) would not be responsible for what some rash person might do through indignation for the treatment he had received. Very soon after that, Sherman received orders from me to proceed to Washington City, and to go into camp on the south side of the city pending the mustering-out of the troops.[5]

There was no incident worth noting in the march northward from Goldsboro, to Richmond, or in that from Richmond to Washington City. The army, however, commanded by Sherman, which had been engaged in all the battles of the West and had marched from the Mississippi through the Southern States to the sea, from there to Goldsboro, and thence to Washington City, had passed over many of the battle-fields of the Army of the Potomac, thus having seen, to a greater extent than any other body of troops, the entire theatre of the four years' war for the preservation of the Union.

The march of Sherman's army from Atlanta to the sea and north to Goldsboro, while it was not accompanied with the danger that was anticipated, yet was magnificent in its results, and equally magnificent in the way it was conducted. It had an important bearing, in various ways, upon the great object we had in view, that of closing the war. All the States east of the Mississippi River up to the State of Georgia, had felt the hardships of the war. Georgia, and South Carolina, and almost all of North Carolina, up to this time, had been exempt from invasion by the Northern armies, except upon their im-

[3] On Apr. 22, 1865, Halleck, in Richmond, VA, assumed command of the Military Div. of the James. On Apr. 25, he told Meade to "pay no attention whatever to any agreement made by Sherman" and instructed Meade to forward the order to Sheridan and Wright. *OR,* I, 46(III), 891, 941.

[4] The editors did not find any surviving copies of Halleck's invitation to Sherman. For Sherman's May 7, 1865, refusal to meet Halleck, see Simpson and Berlin, *Sherman's Civil War,* 892.

[5] In a May 10, 1865, telegram, USG directed Sherman to move his army to Alexandria. *PUSG,* 15:73*n*.

mediate sea coasts. Their newspapers had given such an account of Confederate success, that the people who remained at home had been convinced that the Yankees had been whipped from first to last, and driven from pillar to post, and that now they could hardly be holding out for any other purpose than to find a way out of the war with honor to themselves.

Even during this march of Sherman's the newspapers in his front were proclaiming daily that his army was nothing better than a mob of men who were frightened out of their wits and hastening, panic-stricken, to try to get under the cover of our navy for protection against the Southern people.[6] As the army was seen marching on triumphantly, however, the minds of the people became disabused and they saw the true state of affairs. In turn they became disheartened, and would have been glad to submit without compromise.

Another great advantage resulting from this march, and which was calculated to hasten the end, was the fact that the great storehouse of Georgia was entirely cut off from the Confederate armies. As the troops advanced north from Savannah, the destruction of the railroads in South Carolina and the southern part of North Carolina, further cut off their resources and left the armies still in Virginia and North Carolina dependent for supplies upon a very small area of country, already very much exhausted of food and forage.

In due time the two armies, one from Burkesville Junction and the other from the neighborhood of Raleigh, North Carolina, arrived and went into camp near the Capital, as directed.[7] The troops were hardy, being inured to fatigue, and they appeared in their respective camps as ready and fit for duty as they had ever been in their lives. I doubt whether an equal body of men of any nation, take them man for man, officer for officer, was ever gotten together that would have proved their equal in a great battle.

The armies of Europe are machines: the men are brave and the officers capable; but the majority of the soldiers in most of the nations of Europe are

[6] On Nov. 30, 1864, Henry L. Flash, editor of the *Macon Telegraph,* asserted in an editorial that Sherman's march would destroy and demoralize his own troops. He was one of multiple Southern newspaper editors who portrayed Sherman's march through Georgia as futile. David B. Sachsman et al., *The Civil War and the Press* (London: Transaction, 2000), 276, 281–284.

[7] On May 11, 1865, Meade's army arrived and camped opposite the Georgetown area of Washington, DC. On May 19, Sherman's army set up camp near Alexandria. George Gordon Meade, *The Life and Letters of George Gordon Meade* (New York: Charles Scribner's Sons, 1913), 2:279; William T. Sherman, *Memoirs of General William T. Sherman* (New York: D. Appleton, 1875), 2:375.

taken from a class of people who are not very intelligent and who have very little interest in the contest in which they are called upon to take part. Our armies were composed of men who were able to read, men who knew what they were fighting for, and could not be induced to serve as soldiers, except in an emergency when the safety of the nation was involved, and so necessarily must have been more than equal to men who fought merely because they were brave and because they were thoroughly drilled and inured to hardships.

There was nothing of particular importance occurred during the time these troops were in camp before starting North.

I remember one little incident which I will relate as an anecdote characteristic of Mr. Lincoln. It occurred a day after I reached Washington, and about the time General Meade reached Burkesville with the army.[8] Governor Smith of Virginia[9] had left Richmond with the Confederate States government, and had gone to Danville. Supposing I was necessarily with the army at Burkesville, he addressed a letter to me there informing me that, as governor of the Commonwealth of the State of Virginia, he had temporarily removed the State capital from Richmond to Danville, and asking if he would be permitted to perform the functions of his office there without molestation by the Federal authorities. I give this letter only in substance. He also inquired of me whether in case he was not allowed to perform the duties of his office, he with a few others might not be permitted to leave the country and go abroad without interference. General Meade being informed that a flag of truce was outside his pickets with a letter to me, at once sent out and had the letter brought in without informing the officer who brought it that I was not present. He read the letter and telegraphed me its contents.[10] Meeting Mr. Lincoln shortly after receiving this dispatch, I repeated its contents to him. Mr. Lincoln, supposing I was asking for instructions, said, in reply to that part of Governor Smith's letter which inquired whether he with a few friends would be permitted to leave the country unmolested, that his position was like that of a certain Irishman (giving the name) he knew in Springfield who was very popular with

[8] On Apr. 12, 1865, Meade's army began to arrive in Burkesville, VA. *PUSG,* 14:384 and *n,* 385*n.*

[9] William "Extra Billy" Smith (1797–1887) was born in Virginia and served as a U.S. representative from that state from 1841 to 1843 and from 1853 to 1861. He was promoted to major general in the Confederate Army in 1863 and was governor of Virginia from 1846 to 1849 and from 1864 to 1865. *CWHC,* 499.

[10] For Gov. Smith's Apr. 11, 1865, letter to USG and the Apr. 11–14 correspondence between USG and Meade, see *PUSG,* 14:389 and *n.*

the people, a man of considerable promise, and very much liked. Unfortunately he had acquired the habit of drinking, and his friends could see that the habit was growing on him. These friends determined to make an effort to save him, and to do this they drew up a pledge to abstain from all alcoholic drinks. They asked Pat to join them in signing the pledge, and he consented. He had been so long out of the habit of using plain water as a beverage that he resorted to soda-water as a substitute. After a few days this began to grow distasteful to him. So holding the glass behind him, he said: "Doctor, couldn't you drop a bit of brandy in that unbeknownst to myself."

I do not remember what the instructions were the President gave me, but I know that Governor Smith was not permitted to perform the duties of his office.[11] I also know that if Mr. Lincoln had been spared, there would have been no efforts made to prevent any one from leaving the country who desired to do so. He would have been equally willing to permit the return of the same expatriated citizens after they had time to repent of their choice.

On the 18th of May orders were issued by the adjutant-general for a grand review by the President and his cabinet of Sherman's and Meade's armies.[12] The review commenced on the 23d and lasted two days. Meade's army occupied over six hours of the first day in passing the grand stand which had been erected in front of the President's house. Sherman witnessed this review from the grand stand which was occupied by the President and his cabinet. Here he showed his resentment for the cruel and harsh treatment that had unnecessarily been inflicted upon him by the Secretary of War, by refusing to take his extended hand.[13]

Sherman's troops had been in camp on the south side of the Potomac. During the night of the 23d he crossed over and bivouacked not far from the Capitol. Promptly at ten o'clock on the morning of the 24th, his troops commenced to pass in review. Sherman's army made a different appearance from that of the Army of the Potomac. The latter had been operating where they received directly from the North full supplies of food and clothing regularly:

[11] USG's Apr. 14, 1865, response to Smith stated that he had "no reply to make to the questions propounded." On May 20, Smith appealed to Halleck, stating that he had reached out to USG but to no avail. *OR*, I, 46(III), 1179; *PUSG*, 14:389.

[12] On USG's orders, Asst. AG E. D. Townsend issued Special Orders No. 239 on May 18, 1865. *OR*, I, 47(III), 526.

[13] On the second day of the Grand March, after leading his troops in the parade and ascending the stands, Sherman snubbed Stanton. John F. Marszalek, *Sherman: A Soldier's Passion for Order* (New York: Free Press, 1993), 356–357.

the review of this army therefore was the review of a body of 65,000 well-drilled, well-disciplined and orderly soldiers inured to hardship and fit for any duty, but without the experience of gathering their own food and supplies in an enemy's country, and of being ever on the watch. Sherman's army was not so well-dressed as the Army of the Potomac, but their marching could not be excelled; they gave the appearance of men who had been thoroughly drilled to endure hardships, either by long and continuous marches or through exposure to any climate, without the ordinary shelter of a camp. They exhibited also some of the order of march through Georgia where the "sweet potatoes sprung up from the ground"[14] as Sherman's army went marching through. In the rear of a company there would be a captured horse or mule loaded with small cooking utensils, captured chickens and other food picked up for the use of the men. Negro families who had followed the army would sometimes come along in the rear of a company, with three or four children packed upon a single mule, and the mother leading it.

The sight was varied and grand: nearly all day for two successive days, from the Capitol to the Treasury Building, could be seen a mass of orderly soldiers marching in columns of companies. The National flag was flying from almost every house and store; the windows were filled with spectators; the door-steps and side-walks were crowded with colored people and poor whites who did not succeed in securing better quarters from which to get a view of the grand armies. The city was about as full of strangers who had come to see the sights as it usually is on inauguration day when a new President takes his seat.

It may not be out of place to again allude to President Lincoln and the Secretary of War, Mr. Stanton, who were the great conspicuous figures in the executive branch of the government. There is no great difference of opinion now, in the public mind, as to the characteristics of the President. With Mr. Stanton the case is different. They were the very opposite of each other in almost every particular, except that each possessed great ability. Mr. Lincoln gained influence over men by making them feel that it was a pleasure to serve him. He preferred yielding his own wish to gratify others, rather than to insist upon having his own way. It distressed him to disappoint others. In matters of public duty, however, he had what he wished, but in the least offensive way. Mr. Stanton never

---

[14] USG paraphrased a line from Henry Clay Work's 1865 song "Marching through Georgia," celebrating Sherman's march to the sea. The line in verse two reads: "How the sweet potatoes even started from the ground." Christian McWhirter, *Battle Hymns: The Power and Popularity of Music in the Civil War* (Chapel Hill: University of North Carolina Press, 2012), 146–149, 164, 169, 186–187.

questioned his own authority to command, unless resisted. He cared nothing for the feeling of others. In fact it seemed to be pleasanter to him to disappoint than to gratify. He felt no hesitation in assuming the functions of the executive, or in acting without advising with him. If his act was not sustained, he would change it—if he saw the matter would be followed up until he did so.

It was generally supposed that these two officials formed the complement of each other. The Secretary was required to prevent the President's being imposed upon. The President was required in the more responsible place of seeing that injustice was not done to others. I do not know that this view of these two men is still entertained by the majority of the people. It is not a correct view, however, in my estimation. Mr. Lincoln did not require a guardian to aid him in the fulfilment of a public trust.

Mr. Lincoln was not timid, and he was willing to trust his generals in making and executing their plans. The Secretary was very timid, and it was impossible for him to avoid interfering with the armies covering the capital when it was sought to defend it by an offensive movement against the army guarding the Confederate capital. He could see our weakness, but he could not see that the enemy was in danger. The enemy would not have been in danger if Mr. Stanton had been in the field. These characteristics of the two officials were clearly shown shortly after Early came so near getting into the capital.[15]

Among the army and corps commanders who served with me during the war between the States, and who attracted much public attention, but of whose ability as soldiers I have not yet given any estimate, are Meade, Hancock, Sedgwick, Burnside, Terry and Hooker. There were others of great merit, such as Griffin, Humphreys, Wright and Mackenzie. Of those first named, Burnside at one time had command of the Army of the Potomac, and later of the Army of the Ohio. Hooker also commanded the Army of the Potomac for a short time.

General Meade was an officer of great merit, with drawbacks to his usefulness that were beyond his control. He had been an officer of the engineer corps before the war, and consequently had never served with troops until he was over forty-six years of age. He never had, I believe, a command of less than a brigade. He saw clearly and distinctly the position of the enemy, and the topography of the country in front of his own position. His first idea was to

---

[15] On July 11–12, 1864, Early had made an unsuccessful attack on Fort Stevens in Washington, DC. Lincoln witnessed the attack in person. Leading up to the assault, Stanton had ordered inspections and weekly reports on the condition of Washington's defenses. Benjamin F. Cooling III, *The Day Lincoln Was Almost Shot: The Fort Stevens Story* (Lanham, MD: Scarecrow Press, 2013), 44, 161, 189.

take advantage of the lay of the ground, sometimes without reference to the direction we wanted to move afterwards. He was subordinate to his superiors in rank to the extent that he could execute an order which changed his own plans with the same zeal he would have displayed if the plan had been his own. He was brave and conscientious, and commanded the respect of all who knew him. He was unfortunately of a temper that would get beyond his control, at times, and make him speak to officers of high rank in the most offensive manner. No one saw this fault more plainly than he himself, and no one regretted it more. This made it unpleasant at times, even in battle, for those around him to approach him even with information. In spite of this defect he was a most valuable officer and deserves a high place in the annals of his country.

General Burnside was an officer who was generally liked and respected. He was not, however, fitted to command an army. No one knew this better than himself. He always admitted his blunders, and extenuated those of officers under him beyond what they were entitled to. It was hardly his fault that he was ever assigned to a separate command.

Of Hooker I saw but little during the war. I had known him very well before, however. Where I did see him, at Chattanooga, his achievement in bringing his command around the point of Lookout Mountain and into Chattanooga Valley was brilliant. I nevertheless regarded him as a dangerous man. He was not subordinate to his superiors. He was ambitious to the extent of caring nothing for the rights of others. His disposition was, when engaged in battle, to get detached from the main body of the army and exercise a separate command, gathering to his standard all he could of his juniors.

Hancock stands the most conspicuous figure of all the general officers who did not exercise a separate command. He commanded a corps longer than any other one, and his name was never mentioned as having committed in battle a blunder for which he was responsible. He was a man of very conspicuous personal appearance. Tall, well-formed and, at the time of which I now write, young and fresh-looking, he presented an appearance that would attract the attention of an army as he passed. His genial disposition made him friends, and his personal courage and his presence with his command in the thickest of the fight won for him the confidence of troops serving under him. No matter how hard the fight, the 2d corps always felt that their commander was looking after them.

Sedgwick was killed at Spottsylvania before I had an opportunity of forming an estimate of his qualifications as a soldier from personal observation.[16] I had

---

[16] On May 9, 1864, Sedgwick was killed at the Battle of Spotsylvania Court House while in command of the 6th Corps, Army of the Potomac. *CWHC*, 477–478.

known him in Mexico when both of us were lieutenants, and when our service gave no indication that either of us would ever be equal to the command of a brigade. He stood very high in the army, however, as an officer and a man. He was brave and conscientious. His ambition was not great, and he seemed to dread responsibility. He was willing to do any amount of battling, but always wanted some one else to direct. He declined the command of the Army of the Potomac once, if not oftener.[17]

General Alfred H. Terry came into the army as a volunteer without a military education. His way was won without political influence up to an important separate command—the expedition against Fort Fisher, in January, 1865.[18] His success there was most brilliant, and won for him the rank of brigadier-general in the regular army and of major-general of volunteers. He is a man who makes friends of those under him by his consideration of their wants and their dues. As a commander, he won their confidence by his coolness in action and by his clearness of perception in taking in the situation under which he was placed at any given time.

Griffin, Humphreys, and Mackenzie were good corps commanders, but came into that position so near to the close of the war as not to attract public attention. All three served as such, in the last campaign of the armies of the Potomac and the James, which culminated at Appomattox Court House, on the 9th of April, 1865. The sudden collapse of the rebellion monopolized attention to the exclusion of almost everything else. I regarded Mackenzie as the most promising young officer in the army. Graduating at West Point, as he did, during the second year of the war, he had won his way up to the command of a corps before its close. This he did upon his own merit and without influence.[19]

---

[17] After Hooker resigned the command of the Army of the Potomac in June 1863, Sedgwick was offered command and turned it down. Stephen R. Taaffe, *Commanding the Army of the Potomac* (Lawrence: University Press of Kansas, 2006), 106.

[18] On Jan. 16, 1865, Terry met with Stanton aboard the steamer *Spaulding,* anchored near Fort Fisher. Stanton then promoted Terry and all of his brigade and division commanders. On Jan. 24, Terry and the rest of his command received the "Thanks of Congress." *CWHC,* 524; William Marvel, *Lincoln's Autocrat: The Life of Edwin Stanton* (Chapel Hill: University of North Carolina Press, 2015), 361; *PUSG,* 13:232n–233n.

[19] After graduating first in his class from the USMA in 1862, Ranald S. Mackenzie was brevetted major general in Mar. 1865 and commanded the cavalry division of the Army of the James from Mar. to Apr. He never held a corps-level command during the Civil War. *CWHC,* 359.

# Conclusion

T HE CAUSE OF the great War of the Rebellion against the United States will have to be attributed to slavery. For some years before the war began it was a trite saying among some politicians that "A state half slave and half free cannot exist."[1] All must become slave or all free, or the state will go down. I took no part myself in any such view of the case at the time, but since the war is over, reviewing the whole question, I have come to the conclusion that the saying is quite true.

Slavery was an institution that required unusual guarantees for its security wherever it existed; and in a country like ours where the larger portion of it was free territory inhabited by an intelligent and well-to-do population, the people would naturally have but little sympathy with demands upon them for its protection. Hence the people of the South were dependent upon keeping control of the general government to secure the perpetuation of their favorite institution. They were enabled to maintain this control long after the States where slavery existed had ceased to have the controlling power, through the assistance they received from odd men here and there throughout the Northern States. They saw their power waning, and this led them to encroach upon the prerogatives and independence of the Northern States by enacting such laws as the Fugitive Slave Law.[2] By this law every Northern man was obliged, when properly summoned, to turn out and help apprehend the runaway slave of a Southern man. Northern marshals became slave-catchers, and Northern courts had to contribute to the support and protection of the institution.

[1] On June 16, 1858, Lincoln gave his "House Divided" speech in accepting the Republican nomination for U.S. senator from Illinois. It included the statement "I believe this government cannot endure, permanently half slave and half free." David Herbert Donald, *Lincoln* (New York: Simon and Schuster, 1995), 206.

[2] The Fugitive Slave Act, passed on Sept. 18, 1850, was a component of the Compromise of 1850. Spencer Tucker, ed., *American Civil War: The Definitive Encyclopedia and Document Collection* (Santa Barbara, CA: ABC-CLIO, 2013), s.v. "Fugitive Slave Act of 1850."

This was a degradation which the North would not permit any longer than until they could get the power to expunge such laws from the statute books. Prior to the time of these encroachments the great majority of the people of the North had no particular quarrel with slavery, so long as they were not forced to have it themselves. But they were not willing to play the rôle of police for the South in the protection of this particular institution.

In the early days of the country, before we had railroads, telegraphs and steamboats—in a word, rapid transit of any sort—the States were each almost a separate nationality. At that time the subject of slavery caused but little or no disturbance to the public mind. But the country grew, rapid transit was established, and trade and commerce between the States got to be so much greater than before, that the power of the National government became more felt and recognized and, therefore, had to be enlisted in the cause of this institution.

It is probably well that we had the war when we did. We are better off now than we would have been without it, and have made more rapid progress than we otherwise should have made. The civilized nations of Europe have been stimulated into unusual activity, so that commerce, trade, travel, and thorough acquaintance among people of different nationalities, has become common; whereas, before, it was but the few who had ever had the privilege of going beyond the limits of their own country or who knew anything about other people. Then, too, our republican institutions were regarded as experiments up to the breaking out of the rebellion, and monarchical Europe generally believed that our republic was a rope of sand that would part the moment the slightest strain was brought upon it. Now it has shown itself capable of dealing with one of the greatest wars that was ever made, and our people have proven themselves to be the most formidable in war of any nationality.

But this war was a fearful lesson, and should teach us the necessity of avoiding wars in the future.

The conduct of some of the European states during our troubles shows the lack of conscience of communities where the responsibility does not come upon a single individual. Seeing a nation that extended from ocean to ocean, embracing the better part of a continent, growing as we were growing in population, wealth and intelligence, the European nations thought it would be well to give us a check. We might, possibly, after a while threaten their peace, or, at least, the perpetuity of their institutions. Hence, England was constantly finding fault with the administration at Washington because we were not able to keep up an effective blockade. She also joined, at first, with France and Spain in setting up an Austrian prince upon the throne in Mexico, totally disregarding any rights or claims that Mexico had of being treated as an independent power.

It is true they trumped up grievances as a pretext, but they were only pretexts which can always be found when wanted.

Mexico, in her various revolutions, had been unable to give that protection to the subjects of foreign nations which she would have liked to give, and some of her revolutionary leaders had forced loans from them. Under pretence of protecting their citizens, these nations seized upon Mexico as a foothold for establishing a European monarchy upon our continent, thus threatening our peace at home.[3] I, myself, regarded this as a direct act of war against the United States by the powers engaged, and supposed as a matter of course that the United States would treat it as such when their hands were free to strike. I often spoke of the matter to Mr. Lincoln and the Secretary of War, but never heard any special views from them to enable me to judge what they thought or felt about it. I inferred that they felt a good deal as I did, but were unwilling to commit themselves while we had our own troubles upon our hands.

All of the powers except France very soon withdrew from the armed intervention for the establishment of an Austrian prince upon the throne of Mexico; but the governing people of these countries continued to the close of the war to throw obstacles in our way. After the surrender of Lee, therefore, entertaining the opinion here expressed, I sent Sheridan with a corps to the Rio Grande to have him where he might aid Juarez in expelling the French from Mexico.[4] These troops got off before they could be stopped; and went to the Rio Grande, where Sheridan distributed them up and down the river, much to the consternation of the troops in the quarter of Mexico bordering on that stream. This soon led to a request from France that we should withdraw our troops from the Rio Grande and to negotiations for the withdrawal of theirs. Finally Bazaine was withdrawn from Mexico by order of the French Government. From that day the empire began to totter. Mexico was then able to maintain her independence without aid from us.[5]

---

[3] Archduke Ferdinand Maximilian von Habsburg (1832–1867), younger brother of Austrian emperor Franz Joseph, was born near Vienna, Austria. He joined the Austrian Navy in 1850. In Dec. 1861, France, Britain, and Spain sent forces to Mexico to collect debts, but their main goal was to establish a monarchy. Chosen as the new emperor, Maximilian took power in May 1864. Ibid., s.v. "Maximilian von Habsburg, Ferdinand."

[4] On May 17, 1865, USG assigned Sheridan to command the Military Div. of the Southwest. His mission was to finalize the surrender of Confederate forces in the West and to place pressure on French forces near the Rio Grande River. *CWHC,* 484; *PUSG,* 15:xxi, 43–45, 45*n.*

[5] François-Achille Bazaine (1811–1888) was born in Versailles, France, and entered the French Army in 1831. In 1862, he went to Mexico to support Maximilian and was promoted to marshal

France is the traditional ally and friend of the United States. I did not blame France for her part in the scheme to erect a monarchy upon the ruins of the Mexican Republic. That was the scheme of one man, an imitator without genius or merit. He had succeeded in stealing the government of his country, and made a change in its form against the wishes and instincts of his people. He tried to play the part of the first Napoleon, without the ability to sustain that rôle. He sought by new conquests to add to his empire and his glory; but the signal failure of his scheme of conquest was the precursor of his own overthrow.[6]

Like our own war between the States, the Franco-Prussian war was an expensive one; but it was worth to France all it cost her people. It was the completion of the downfall of Napoleon III. The beginning was when he landed troops on this continent. Failing here, the prestige of his name—all the prestige he ever had—was gone. He must achieve a success or fall. He tried to strike down his neighbor, Prussia—and fell.[7]

I never admired the character of the first Napoleon; but I recognize his great genius. His work, too, has left its impress for good on the face of Europe. The third Napoleon could have no claim to having done a good or just act.

To maintain peace in the future it is necessary to be prepared for war. There can scarcely be a possible chance of a conflict, such as the last one, occurring among our own people again; but, growing as we are, in population, wealth and military power, we may become the envy of nations which led us in all these particulars only a few years ago; and unless we are prepared for it we may be in danger of a combined movement being some day made to crush us out. Now, scarcely twenty years after the war, we seem to have forgotten the lessons

in 1864. In Nov. 1866, he began to evacuate French troops from Mexico, with the last troops leaving in Feb. 1867. In June, forces under the command of former Mexican president Juarez captured and executed Maximilian. Tucker, *American Civil War*, s.v. "Maximilian von Habsburg, Ferdinand"; Mark Grossman, *World Military Leaders: A Biographical Dictionary* (New York: Facts on File, 2007), s.v. "Bazaine, François-Achille"; G. L. Lamborn, *Arms of Little Value: The Challenge of Insurgency and Global Instability in the Twenty-First Century* (Philadelphia: Casemate, 2012), 137 and *n*.

[6] Charles Louis Napoleon Bonaparte (1808–1873), son of Napoleon Bonaparte's youngest brother, was born in Paris, France, and raised in Switzerland. In Dec. 1851, after a bloodless coup, he was crowned emperor Napoleon III of France. Tucker, *American Civil War*, s.v. "Napoleon III."

[7] After the debacle in Mexico, France went to war with Prussia in July 1870. Napoleon III was forced to surrender his army and was taken prisoner, with the war ending in May 1871. After the defeat, Napoleon's government was overthrown and he was sent into exile in England. Ibid.; Carl C. Hodge, *Encyclopedia of the Age of Imperialism, 1800–1914* (Westport, CT: Greenwood Press, 2008), s.v. "Franco-Prussian War (1870–1871)."

it taught, and are going on as if in the greatest security, without the power to resist an invasion by the fleets of fourth-rate European powers for a time until we could prepare for them.

We should have a good navy, and our sea-coast defences should be put in the finest possible condition. Neither of these cost much when it is considered where the money goes, and what we get in return. Money expended in a fine navy, not only adds to our security and tends to prevent war in the future, but is very material aid to our commerce with foreign nations in the meantime. Money spent upon sea-coast defences is spent among our own people, and all goes back again among the people. The work accomplished, too, like that of the navy, gives us a feeling of security.

England's course towards the United States during the rebellion exasperated the people of this country very much against the mother country. I regretted it. England and the United States are natural allies, and should be the best of friends. They speak one language, and are related by blood and other ties. We together, or even either separately, are better qualified than any other people to establish commerce between all the nationalities of the world.

England governs her own colonies, and particularly those embracing the people of different races from her own, better than any other nation. She is just to the conquered, but rigid. She makes them self-supporting, but gives the benefit of labor to the laborer. She does not seem to look upon the colonies as outside possessions which she is at liberty to work for the support and aggrandizement of the home government.

The hostility of England to the United States during our rebellion was not so much real as it was apparent. It was the hostility of the leaders of one political party.[8] I am told that there was no time during the civil war when they were able to get up in England a demonstration in favor of secession, while these were constantly being gotten up in favor of the Union, or, as they called it, in favor of the North. Even in Manchester, which suffered so fearfully by having the cotton cut off from her mills, they had a monster demonstration in favor of the North at the very time when their workmen were almost famishing.[9]

It is possible that the question of a conflict between races may come up in the future, as did that between freedom and slavery before. The condition of

[8] The Liberal Party, under the leadership of Lord Palmerston, favored the Confederacy. H. C. G. Matthew and Brian Harrison, eds., *Oxford Dictionary of National Biography* (Oxford: Oxford University Press, 2004), s.v. "Temple, Henry John, Third Viscount Palmerston (1784–1865)."

[9] On Dec. 1, 1862, a massive, pro-Union demonstration occurred in the Manchester Free Trade Hall. Philip S. Foner, *British Labor and the American Civil War* (New York: Holmes and Meier, 1981), 43–44.

the colored man within our borders may become a source of anxiety, to say the least. But he was brought to our shores by compulsion, and he now should be considered as having as good a right to remain here as any other class of our citizens. It was looking to a settlement of this question that led me to urge the annexation of Santo Domingo during the time I was President of the United States.[10]

Santo Domingo was freely offered to us, not only by the administration, but by all the people, almost without price. The island is upon our shores, is very fertile, and is capable of supporting fifteen millions of people. The products of the soil are so valuable that labor in her fields would be so compensated as to enable those who wished to go there to quickly repay the cost of their passage. I took it that the colored people would go there in great numbers, so as to have independent states governed by their own race. They would still be States of the Union, and under the protection of the General Government; but the citizens would be almost wholly colored.

By the war with Mexico, we had acquired, as we have seen, territory almost equal in extent to that we already possessed. It was seen that the volunteers of the Mexican war largely composed the pioneers to settle up the Pacific coast country. Their numbers, however, were scarcely sufficient to be a nucleus for the population of the important points of the territory acquired by that war. After our rebellion, when so many young men were at liberty to return to their homes, they found they were not satisfied with the farm, the store, or the workshop of the villages, but wanted larger fields. The mines of the mountains first attracted them; but afterwards they found that rich valleys and productive grazing and farming lands were there. This territory, the geography of which was not known to us at the close of the rebellion, is now as well mapped as any portion of our country. Railroads traverse it in every direction, north, south, east, and west. The mines are worked. The high lands are used for grazing purposes, and rich agricultural lands are found in many of the valleys. This is the work of the volunteer. It is probable that the Indians would have had control of these lands for a century yet but for the war. We must conclude, therefore, that wars are not always evils unmixed with some good.

Prior to the rebellion the great mass of the people were satisfied to remain near the scenes of their birth. In fact an immense majority of the whole people did not feel secure against coming to want should they move among entire strangers. So much was the country divided into small communities that

[10] On Jan. 10, 1870, USG submitted the Santo Domingo annexation treaty to the Senate, which voted against the treaty on June 30. *PUSG,* 20:xix, xxi.

localized idioms had grown up, so that you could almost tell what section a person was from by hearing him speak. Before, new territories were settled by a "class"; people who shunned contact with others; people who, when the country began to settle up around them, would push out farther from civilization. Their guns furnished meat, and the cultivation of a very limited amount of the soil, their bread and vegetables. All the streams abounded with fish. Trapping would furnish pelts to be brought into the States once a year, to pay for necessary articles which they could not raise—powder, lead, whiskey, tobacco and some store goods. Occasionally some little articles of luxury would enter into these purchases—a quarter of a pound of tea, two or three pounds of coffee, more of sugar, some playing cards, and if anything was left over of the proceeds of the sale, more whiskey.

Little was known of the topography of the country beyond the settlements of these frontiersmen. This is all changed now. The war begot a spirit of independence and enterprise. The feeling now is, that a youth must cut loose from his old surroundings to enable him to get up in the world. There is now such a commingling of the people that particular idioms and pronunciation are no longer localized to any great extent; the country has filled up "from the centre all around to the sea"; railroads connect the two oceans and all parts of the interior; maps, nearly perfect, of every part of the country are now furnished the student of geography.

The war has made us a nation of great power and intelligence. We have but little to do to preserve peace, happiness and prosperity at home, and the respect of other nations. Our experience ought to teach us the necessity of the first; our power secures the latter.

I feel that we are on the eve of a new era, when there is to be great harmony between the Federal and Confederate. I cannot stay to be a living witness to the correctness of this prophecy; but I feel it within me that it is to be so. The universally kind feeling expressed for me at a time when it was supposed that each day would prove my last, seemed to me the beginning of the answer to "Let us have peace."[11]

The expressions of these kindly feelings were not restricted to a section of the country, nor to a division of the people. They came from individual citizens of all nationalities; from all denominations—the Protestant, the Cath-

[11] USG concluded his letter accepting the 1868 Republican nomination for president with this phrase, and it became a slogan regularly used during the ensuing campaign. Ibid., 18:263–264; Brooks D. Simpson, *Let Us Have Peace: Ulysses S. Grant and the Politics of War and Reconstruction, 1861–1868* (Chapel Hill: University of North Carolina Press, 1991), 246.

olic, and the Jew; and from the various societies of the land—scientific, educational, religious, or otherwise. Politics did not enter into the matter at all.

I am not egotist enough to suppose all this significance should be given because I was the object of it. But the war between the States was a very bloody and a very costly war. One side or the other had to yield principles they deemed dearer than life before it could be brought to an end. I commanded the whole of the mighty host engaged on the victorious side. I was, no matter whether deservedly so or not, a representative of that side of the controversy. It is a significant and gratifying fact that Confederates should have joined heartily in this spontaneous move. I hope the good feeling inaugurated may continue to the end.

# *Acknowledgments*

The creation of this new edition has been a lengthy and detailed process. Over several years, Associate Editor David S. Nolen and Assistant Editor Louie P. Gallo have put in countless hours and consulted literally thousands of books, articles, and online sources to discover information never before used in conjunction with this literary and historical masterpiece. Too often in such acknowledgments, an editor will insist that a book in question could never have been completed without an associate editor's and assistant editor's participation. This is indeed no exaggeration in this case. Without Nolen's and Gallo's enthusiastic and persistent efforts, Ulysses S. Grant Association (USGA) Executive Director John F. Marszalek could not have completed this important edition. The Grant world owes these two men thanks and appreciation for their mighty efforts.

The concept of producing a scholarly edition of the Grant *Memoirs* goes back to the origins of the USGA and the managing editorship of its first executive director, John Y. Simon. However, it was only in recent times that a digital edition became technologically possible. After USGA came to Mississippi State University (MSU) in 2008, the editorial team established digitization as a goal. First it had to bring to publication volume 31 of *The Papers of Ulysses S. Grant,* which John Y. Simon and his staff at Southern Illinois University, Carbondale (SIU), had nearly completed. Then, the new team at MSU published volume 32, the supplementary volume, containing material not available when the earlier volumes were published.

Over the years, as USGA editors completed the publication of the thirty-two volumes of *The Papers of Ulysses S. Grant* and now this first scholarly edition of the *The Personal Memoirs of U. S. Grant,* they have benefited from the financial support of the National Historical Publications and Records Commission, the National Endowment for the Humanities, SIU, and MSU. None of the USGA's work would have been possible without that support.

Many individuals played important roles in the completion of this hardcover edition. USGA president Frank J. Williams, chief justice (ret.) of the Rhode

Island Supreme Court, led the Board of Directors and the five-hundred-member USGA, not only in the move to MSU but also in all the tasks the association has accomplished since its arrival in Mississippi. It was in 2012 that the Ulysses S. Grant Presidential Library was born, the result of the cooperation between the leaders of MSU and USGA.

MSU president Mark Keenum began his term of office just a few weeks before he signed the agreement with Chief Justice Williams to formalize the relationship between MSU and USGA, a union that has benefited both institutions. Early on, President Keenum promised the association that he would work to provide a larger facility. In late 2017, the new fourth floor of the Mitchell Memorial Library will become the headquarters for a new state-of-the-art facility for the Ulysses S. Grant Presidential Library.

Frances Coleman, the dean of MSU Libraries, has played a major role in uniting MSU with USGA. At the beginning, she helped organize the cooperation between the Mitchell Memorial Library and the association, and she enthusiastically supported the construction of the presidential library. Her role has been and continues to be essential to the success of USGA at MSU.

Without the hard work of the presidential library staff, none of this success would have been possible. When longtime executive director and managing editor John Y. Simon died in 2008, President Williams and the USGA Board of Directors asked retired MSU historian John F. Marszalek to take his place. Quickly a team was established to carry on at MSU the good work of the previous forty-six years, primarily at SIU.

The new staff stepped up to the challenge, and not enough can be said about their outstanding work. These individuals have included the late Michael B. Ballard, Amanda Carlock, Elizabeth Coggins, Aaron Crawford, Louie P. Gallo, Kate Gregory, Meg Henderson, Rebecca Houston, Bob Karachuk, David Nolen, and Ryan P. Semmes.

In addition to this professional staff, the Grant Presidential Library has had the good fortune to have the services of outstanding graduate students and undergraduate student workers. The graduate students have included Hannah Berman, Dave Burford, Kevin Cook, Justin Dornbush, Doug Forrest, Matt Himel, Anthony Johnson, Cadra McDaniel, Larsen Plyler, Stephen Powell, Eddie Rangel, Jay Ratcliff, Karen Senaga, Kristen Theriot, Nancy Traylor-Heard, and Lucas Wilder. Undergraduates have included Mary Beth Cox, Kynia Crigler, Rachael Damms, Sarah Dauterive, Lacy Duplantis, Nicholas Fowler, Lauren Fulton, Ryan Lawrence, Ashley Lea, Jon Miller, Bailey Powell, David Sides, Kasey Trammell, and Blass Watson.

There have been others, too, who have made the editorial work on the *Memoirs* possible. Harriet Furst Simon, widow of the first USGA executive director, continued her decades of service by serving as an outside reader for this project. Mandy Gagel, of the Mark Twain Papers staff, also served as an outside reader. Jeanne A. Marszalek, wife of the present executive director, read and edited the executive director's work. Amelia Nolen, wife of the associate editor, contributed helpful comments and suggestions. The late Michael Ballard, Gary L. Dornhardt, Sam Elliott, Thomas Horrocks, Timothy B. Smith, Walter Starr, and Terrence Winschel have also provided research help, as have Gerald Chaudron, Chris Marszalek, and Ben Nagel. The many visiting scholars such as Charles Calhoun, Edwina Campbell, Ron Chernow, Joan Waugh, and Ron White, to name only a few, have provided insight while doing their own research at MSU.

In addition to all these, the support of the entire faculty, staff, and student workers of the MSU Libraries has been invaluable. The staff of the Access Services Department (and especially Interlibrary Loan) helped with the retrieval of many resources used for the research that went into this project. The student workers of the Congressional and Political Research Center also provided significant help in making sure this project came to fruition: Meagan Bray, Dalton Coleman, Zach Crain, Joe Davis, Kelsey LaSaicherre, Jessie Lewis, Haley McManus, Elizabeth Miskelly, Amanda Patterson, Tyler Powell, Zoe Schroder, Haley Semmes, Emily Smith, Ben Voytas, Linh Vuong, Calvin Waddy, and Tarishae Yarbor.

In the end, however, it is Ulysses S. Grant himself who remains the inspiration that keeps us pressing forward. He said in his *Memoirs:* "Everyone has his superstitions. One of mine is that in positions of great responsibility everyone should do his duty to the best of his ability." We have tried to do just that.

# Index